ANTITRUST ANALYSIS

ANTITRUST ANALYSIS
Problems, Text, Cases

Fifth Edition

PHILLIP AREEDA
Late Langdell Professor of Law
Harvard University

LOUIS KAPLOW
Professor of Law
Harvard University

Formerly published by
Little, Brown and Company

ASPEN LAW & BUSINESS
A Division of Aspen Publishers, Inc.

Permissions
Aspen Law & Business
1185 Avenue of the Americas
New York, NY 10036

Printed in the United States of America

Library of Congress Cataloging-in-Publication Data

Areeda, Phillip.
    Antitrust analysis : problems, text, cases / Phillip Areeda,
Louis Kaplow. — 5th ed.
        p.   cm.
    Includes index.
    ISBN 1-56706-566-X (casebound)
    1. Antitrust law — United States — Cases.   I. Kaplow,
Louis.   II. Title.
KF1648.A7   1997
343.73'0721 — dc21   97-27101
                                                                CIP

About Aspen Law & Business, Law School Division

In 1996, Aspen Law & Business welcomed the Law School Division of Little, Brown and Company into its growing business — already established as a leading provider of practical information to legal practitioners.

Acquiring much more than a prestigious collection of educational publications by the country's foremost authors, Aspen Law & Business inherited the long-standing Little, Brown tradition of excellence — born over 150 years ago. As one of America's oldest and most venerable publishing houses, Little, Brown and Company commenced in a world of change and challenge, innovation and growth. Sharing that same spirit, Aspen Law & Business has dedicated itself to continuing and strengthening the integrity begun so many years ago.

ASPEN LAW & BUSINESS
A Division of Aspen Publishers, Inc.
A Wolters Kluwer Company

Summary of Contents

Contents

Preface to the Fifth Edition

This edition is the first to appear since Phillip Areeda passed away in 1995. His presence will be missed by all in the field of Antitrust, but his life's work will continue to cast light upon the subject well into the future.

Although he was not actively involved in its preparation, this revision carries the imprint of its originator in many ways. A substantial amount of the material remains from prior editions, and much of what is new consists of court decisions and government policy statements that were issued previously, so that I was able to benefit from his input. Moreover, throughout the editing process, this author could not help but contemplate what Phil would have said about all matters, large and small.

New material in this edition consists primarily of recent Supreme Court cases and government policy statements. In addition, some problems have been added to focus attention on areas that have become increasingly important, such as health care and intellectual property. Finally, there has been substantial condensation of older material so that, in total, the current edition is about the same length as the prior one.

The prefaces to the first and fourth editions, which state what continue to be the pedagogical premises underlying this book, follow. I wish to thank both a large and energetic group of research assistants and my students for making this edition possible and to acknowledge Phil's and my debts to the many who have helped us in the past.

L.K.

April 1997

Preface to the Fourth Edition*

This fourth edition provides not only the occasion for updating the book but also for streamlining it. New cases and text have been added without increasing the size of the book. This has been done by changing some cases to abstracts, by eliminating some of the overlapping hypotheticals, by reducing the detail of less frequently taught portions of the patent and price-discrimination materials, and by reordering some of the materials.

This edition also brings a second author to the book. The addition of a different, although complementary, viewpoint coupled with a doctorate in economics contributes to what has always been the book's object: to expose students to the difficulties of the subject and to the full range of possible resolutions.

Much in debate today is the proper role and utility of economic analysis in applying the antitrust laws. This book neither denigrates nor elevates it. Although the authors have their own, and somewhat different, conclusions about the content of wise antitrust rules, the book's approach is agnostic and presents contrasting approaches to the problems at hand. But whatever the values one chooses to promote, one must understand both the precedents and the assumed, proved, or possible effects of the practices or situations addressed by antitrust law. To assess such effects, we need to know *both* what economic theory can tell and how actual markets work; the two are not always the same, because the economic models — like all social science models — are simplifications that may ignore important complexities in order to isolate important truths. Thus, the dispute among commentators turns out to involve not one conflict but several — not just whether the antitrust laws reflect some values different from or not reflected in what economic analysis can illuminate, but also whether particular forms of economic anlaysis illuminate the effects brightly enough to dictate that antitrust law should encourage, tolerate, or condemn a practice, either generally or in a particular case.

That economic perceptions are useful in antitrust analysis is not the least bit novel. Even many of the earliest cases reflect knowledge, assumptions, or intuitions about how markets work and how a challenged practice might lead to lower production, higher prices, and consumer exploitation — or the opposite. Modern cases and commentary tend to be more explicit about it and, sometimes, to

---

*This preface has been modified where appropriate.

show how an intuition may be erroneous. Not surprisingly, therefore, a good bit of economics must be put before the student —
more with every edition, it has turned out. As in previous editions,
great care has been taken to inform students of economic learning,
including some of its subtleties, in plain language with a minimum
of technical apparatus. Experience with prior editions suggests that
readers without training in economics will find the economics materials intelligible, although concise, and neither intimidating nor
obscure.

P.A. & L.K.

March 1988

Preface to the First Edition*

Although this book may have some usefulness elsewhere, it was prepared to meet the threefold needs of antitrust classes for problems, text, and cases. The cases have been edited and organized for maximum ease of comprehension. But an improved casebook was never the primary object. The distinguishing features of this book lie in its text and in its extensive questions and problems.

Text. I am convinced that a contemporary antitrust course requires a judicious use of text to meet several clear needs. The relevance of economics to antitrust law is unquestioned. Although students need study economic theory and behavior only as useful to the law, they must know about market power, justifications for cartelization, price behavior in markets with few firms, basing point pricing, the economic rationale of the patent system, manufacturer interests in resale prices, the objects of tying and exclusive dealing arrangements, the competitive significance of large firms and of mergers, and various aspects of price discrimination. These are all subjects of textual discussion in this book, and in addition there is a summary exposition of the competitive system in Chapter 1A. The utility of such material is quite clear. As one example, consider the economics of vertical restraints. The cases are hardly illuminating, and, in prior years, neither lecture nor class discussion produced anything beyond confusion for most students. By contrast, my class has understood the essentials presented in text. The greater efficiency and effectiveness of economics text is manifest in two respects. First, limited class time is not used for conveying information that is more easily grasped when read and studied. Second, discussion may give the appearance that some members of the class comprehend the economics at hand, but the instructor may be quite uncertain as to how many of the class have mastered the economic argument. To reap these advantages fully, the text is sometimes made more elaborate than would on first consideration seem necessary for law students in order to meet complications or confusions that in fact have developed in the classroom when a simpler treatment has been used.

A second variety of text is more "legal." Chapter 1 is entirely textual. In addition to the economics material already mentioned, and the historical background of the antitrust statutes, there is exposition of three matters that cannot receive full treatment in an

*There have been slight modifications where appropriate.

antitrust course of usual length. Chapter 1C discusses procedures for enforcing the antitrust laws, Chapter 1D notes the statutes' "jurisdiction" over interstate and foreign commerce and the major exemptions from the antitrust laws, with special attention to developing doctrines on state action and preemption, and Chapter 1E describes the premises and operation of the patent system. These sections attempt to steer a delicate course between undue generality and excessive detail. Text in other chapters has varying objectives. There is the brief exposition of noteworthy issues that can be efficiently developed in text and that do not warrant class time, the compact presentation of an issue analogous to one analyzed in detail through questions and problems, especially where the related issue lends itself to great compression, and a presentation of necessary technical details.

Third, there are occasional brief paragraphs of introduction, connection, or comment scattered through the book. Finally, there is material that is midway between text and question: Questions are sometimes put in a way that tends to suggest at least one possible line of answers. This device is used where authority is scant, issues are important but difficult, and conventional text might seem prematurely definitive.

Let me add that I fully appreciate the difficulties in preparing text that is clear, concise, accurate, and yet free of unnecessary detail. This book is, I hope, a useful step in that direction.

Questions and problems. The several hundred questions and problems — categories that I do not distinguish sharply — are the heart of this effort for my own classroom. They try to achieve the advantages and avoid the disadvantages of both case and problem approaches. Problems force students to manipulate and apply antitrust ideas to difficult issues extracted from complex facts with uncertain economic and legal implications. That process tests the usefulness of doctrine, often demonstrates its inadequacies, and helps students focus both on private planning and on "legislative" considerations.

Adequate problems, however, are sometimes overly complex for effective classroom use. The difficulties are several. Problem analysis and solution often demand prior mastery of numerous cases and concepts, but few students can or will attain that command of a topic at the outset of its consideration. When analysis and solution require so much preparation, many students will do little more than read the cases. More manageable questions will be more adequately prepared.

To discuss a complex problem, moreover, is necessarily to discuss the meaning and reasoning of the relevant cases. The appropriate questions can, of course, be posed orally in class, but I find several overwhelming advantages in providing questions in the coursebook. First, students can and do think about them before class. Second, printed questions eliminate some of the delay, confusion, or misunderstanding inevitable with oral questions. Third, the greater precision of a written question invites more precise responses. Fourth, the structure of questions approximates an outline of the class discussion and thus enhances student understanding and sometimes lessens the compulsion to take notes. The result is greater confidence and a more relaxed classroom attitude.

There is, of course, no single best way to treat an antitrust topic. The teacher must often choose among several historical and analytical avenues. And student confusion may result from opaque opinions, complex facts, elusive business context, and obscure economic implications. In striving for orderly development and maximum clarity, I have endeavored to present questions and problems that are highly structured. The questions and problems are designed to expose easier or basic ideas before complex ones. Where experience has shown that a complicating issue unduly obstructs progress toward "answering" a problem, the complicating factor has either been excluded from the problem or made the subject of a prior question that clears the way for a later inquiry. Although it is neither possible nor desirable to narrow questions and problems too finely, a conscious effort has been made to build from basic ideas to more elusive ones. Indeed, for this purpose, occasional elementary questions with clear-cut answers are scattered through the materials to emphasize fundamental points and remind students that some "answers" do exist. Other questions and problems vary in specificity, breadth, object, and student role. The statement of facts or of issues or both may be complete or require the student to supplement them. There may be subordinate questions to aid the analysis, or a complete fact statement may pose a variety of issues without further written guidance. The problem may call on the student to take the viewpoint of business manager, counselor, advocate, judge, or legislator, as well as to identify the legal issues, to use and distinguish cases after careful exegesis, to consider what data are available and how they can be used by either party or the judge, to understand the strengths and limits of the institutions that must decide, to explore the private and social interests at issue, and to resolve the issue within the limits imposed by the relevant institutions, doctrines, and interests.

Antitrust cases offer a particular challenge to orderly development. Some difficulties have already been noted. In addition, litigants have not arranged their affairs nor have judges written with the needs of the classroom in mind. Yet, in an institutional system in which judges and commissioners have such vital roles in develop-

ing and applying antitrust policy, cases provide an object of analysis
and discussion, show the tribunals struggling with our problems
and creating antitrust law, and, it is hoped, illuminate the subject
and the process. Before preparing these materials, I sometimes
asked students to read all the reproduced cases on, say, boycotts or
tying arrangements and then attempted to discuss the subject as a
unit. The results were far less successful than when students read
one case, pondered a few questions about it, read another case,
then considered questions about both cases, and so on. That is
often the pattern of these materials. The questions immediately
after a case will not necessarily exhaust its implications. It sometimes happens that the case that opens a section may not be fully
explored until the end of that section, or even later. The effort is to
open a theme and then, in orderly stages, to elaborate on it with
richness and variations of reality.

Spontaneity and flexibility. The virtues — if such they be — of this
structured approach raise two questions. First, will the orderly development and detailed questions reduce classroom spontaneity?
Experience has provided satisfactory answers. Detailed questions
have not reduced classroom spontaneity. The channeling of energies has increased the relevance of student observations or challenges without diminishing their originality, variety, or intensity.
For all their detail, moreover, many questions remain quite difficult. The questions seemed to aid all students to grasp the subject
and yet tax many to dig deeper. In my own classes there has been a
more rapid and more subtle response from more students when
using these materials.

The other question about structured materials is this: Will other
teachers find the structure congenial? The tested sequence of cases,
questions, and problems will be useful to those teachers who have
not had occasion to develop a different approach to antitrust peda-
gogy. Other teachers will, I hope, find at least some of the structure
suitable for their tastes. But few teachers will use all these materials
in the printed sequence. At least on occasion, other teachers will
use cases and text without using the questions or will use the questions or problems in a different order. A teacher who wishes to vary
the order of topics or their development will find that the book's
system of numbered paragraphs will greatly facilitate the task of
making up a syllabus or assignment list.

The questions and problems need not, of course, be used in their
entirety. Teachers who prefer to concentrate on problems in class
may wish to urge students to answer the nonproblem questions for
themselves. Teachers who emphasize case-analysis questions may
wish to encourage their students to solve the problems for themselves as an aid to study and review. Indeed, no course of conven-

tional length will have time to consider all the questions, problems, or topics in class. Some selection is therefore inevitable in the use of these materials, which are somewhat more extensive than I can cover in a semester-long course of four hours per week.

The organization of topics is by no means inevitable. To emphasize the unity of subject matter, I have used only a few chapter divisions. They need not be treated in the order printed. The content and development of each chapter is not, in the main, dependent on the order of topics. There are standard progressions. Price fixing must precede most of the other horizontal issues. Vertical restraints should precede vertical mergers. But most topics need not be pursued in any particular order. The answers to be expected and the development of the discussion will, of course, vary according to what has gone before, but most questions can be usefully discussed regardless of the order of topics.

The questions within each topic need not always be treated in the order in which they are printed, and some omissions can usually be made. A topic may include several distinct subtopics. But even where the questions are cumulative, a different progression is usually possible. At only a few points is the solution of a question totally dependent on what has directly preceded it. Most questions can be discussed out of the printed order when the instructor considers some other sequence preferable.

Editorial matters. All paragraphs other than statutes or principal cases are numbered to facilitate assignment, cross-reference, and general use of the book. Paragraphs of text or case abstracts are identified by boldfaced headings. Paragraphs without headings are questions or problems. Problems should be regarded as entirely hypothetical, although they are sometimes based on the case, if any, cited to the problem. A citation to a problem may simply identify a fact situation, or it may identify a discussion of some aspect of the problem. More elaborate footnotes to many questions and problems will provide considerable information about the relevant cases.

Some of the principal cases have been edited severely, but omissions are indicated in the conventional way with these exceptions: omitted without further notation are repetitive statutory or code citations to the antitrust laws, repetitive reporter references within an opinion, cross-references within an opinion, citations for a court's references to a lower court decision in the same case, and excessive citations by a court to a case already cited. Where a court refers to important cases presented elsewhere in the book or already considered in the opinion, a short-name for that case may be substituted for the full name and citation. Footnotes are frequently omitted from quoted material; reproduced footnotes retain their original numbers. Footnotes within a case are always those of the court unless a notation indicates otherwise. "Inc." has been omitted from case names. Finally, it should be noted that very occasional liberties have been taken with punctuation, capitalization, and paragraphing in the course of editing.

P.A.

January 1967

ANTITRUST ANALYSIS

Chapter 1

The Setting for Antitrust Analysis

100. Prologue. This book is intended for the study of antitrust law. Text, cases, and problems are integrated to make it a useful tool for learning. While questions and problems are usually placed after the cases to which they pertain, students may often find it useful to sample the questions and problems before reading the materials that precede them. This reverse order will sometimes permit a more perceptive reading. Indeed, it is the questions and problems that are the heart of the materials because they provide the major focus for analysis and an invitation to understanding. Analysis is at the heart of antitrust law because the broad principles cannot solve concrete cases without an analytical framework.

One important point about problemsolving deserves emphatic mention here. Students often ask whether questions and problems should be answered according to what "the law is" or according to what it ought to be. Although the latter often determines the former, when they diverge the student must consider both. Many antitrust opinions are, to say the least, confused. Accordingly, the contemporary vitality of a precedent is often affected less by what it says than by present perceptions of the problem. To be sure, some things are settled, some approaches are relatively fixed, and precedent and doctrine do have force. But the fixed stars are relatively few; once past them, antitrust analysis must often be a three-step process. (1) What is the underlying social problem? What interests are affected and how? What is the possible benefit to a party? The possible harm to society? The alternatives? (2) How should the particular problem be solved by a legislature that appreciates the limitations of judicial and other relevant institutions, the need for general solutions, and the desire for sound doctrinal development? (3) Is such a solution available to the court, agency, or private planner in light of relevant precedents?

Before encountering the problems, this chapter presents some background text. First are some general comments about antitrust study; second, some basic reminders of economics and competitive policy; third, a few historical notes; fourth, some essential procedural aspects of antitrust enforcement; fifth, some problems of antitrust coverage; and sixth, basic information about the patent system. At this point a special caveat is in order. The subject matter of this chapter is admittedly difficult to discuss without either exhausting the student or remaining quite general. This chapter purports to resolve very little; its purpose is merely to alert the student to some important broader issues.

101. Organization; caveat. The notes are not always organized along conventional textbook lines; they are arranged for maximum ease of student reception. Similarly, the management of topics reflects the authors' views of orderly development of antitrust ideas. The order of discussion within each topic is determined by pedagogical convenience; a text would proceed in quite different ways.

Antitrust law is itself a "seamless web" that we must enter at some point and pursue with some semblance of order. For that reason, we cannot exhaust the approaches and implications of a topic when we first consider it. Later topics will give added meaning and understanding to earlier ones. Thus, the problems, questions, and cases will often mean more on review than when initially considered. And the course itself has much built-in review, for later topics often invite or even require renewed attention to earlier ones. Thinking about antitrust problems should not be compartmentalized by these classifications of convenience.

102. Bibliographic note. Although antitrust writings are numerous, the references contained in this book will be highly selective, with an emphasis on analytical works and certain articles that, apart from their analytical quality, conveniently collect useful citations. Cited at this point are general works and a few research aids in the antitrust field.

The most comprehensive analysis is the treatise by Areeda and coauthors, of which ten volumes with supplementation have been published at this writing.[1]

Scherer and Ross's book deserves particular mention among the many good economics texts.[2] It is an excellent treatment of the economic issues bearing on antitrust law and policy; it also includes comprehensive references to relevant empirical work, together with commentary on current empirical and theoretical disputes among economists. And almost all of it is entirely comprehensible to the noneconomist.

1. Citations to relevant portions of this treatise appear throughout this book.
2. F.M. Scherer & D. Ross, Industrial Market Structure and Economic Performance (3d ed. 1990). See also W.K. Viscusi, J. Vernon & J. Harrington, Economics of Regulation and Antitrust (2d ed. 1995); D. Carlton & J. Perloff, Modern Industrial Organization (1990); R. Blair & D. Kaserman, Antitrust Economics (1985). For surveys of relevant economics literature, see R. Schmalensee & R. Willig, Handbook of Industrial Organization (2 vols., 1989).

Studies of particular industries can illuminate concretely the nature of economic power, variety of business practices actually employed, relationship between such practices and the structure of an industry, and relationship between such structure and the industry's economic performance. Such studies may tell us how the economy arrived at its present state and suggest how law and policy may be shaped to achieve better results in the future. There are several collections of industry studies[3] and noteworthy books on most major industries.[4] Among the many works specifically addressed to antitrust policy, a few are noted.[5]

The two loose-leaf reporters are useful sources for statutory references, case citations, and very current material.[6] And there are several periodicals concentrating on antitrust matters.[7]

Antitrust Study, Generally

103. Economic power. These materials are concerned with the control of private economic power through the antitrust laws. They focus on that area within which competition — in contrast to extensive regulation or government-owned enterprise — is the accepted technique of social control. Although these materials deal with the Sherman Act, Clayton Act, Robinson-Patman Act, and Federal Trade Commission Act, the student should realize that the protec-

3. F.M. Scherer, Industry Structure, Strategy, and Public Policy (1996); F.M. Scherer, A. Bechenstein, E. Kaufer & R. Murphy, The Economies of Multiplant Operation: An International Comparison Study (1975); L. Weiss, Economics and American Industry (1961); The Structure of American Industry (W. Adams ed., 9th ed. 1994); S. Whitney, Antitrust Policies (2 vols. 1958).

4. Industry studies (as well as other relevant economics publications) are indexed in the Journal of Economic Literature (available in printed form, on CD-ROM, and in DIALOG's ECONLIT database).

5. J. Blair, Economic Concentration: Structure, Behavior, and Public Policy (1972); R. Bork, The Antitrust Paradox: A Policy at War with Itself (rev. ed. 1993); M. Green et al., The Closed Enterprise System (1972); C. Kaysen & D. Turner, Antitrust Policy (1959); E. Mason, Economic Concentration and the Monopoly Problem (1964); R. Posner, Antitrust Law: An Economic Perspective (1976); J. McGee, In Defense of Industrial Concentration (1971); Perspectives on Antitrust Policy (A. Phillips ed. 1965).

6. Commerce Clearing House, Trade Regulation Reporter (5 vols.), with back material collected in more-or-less annual volumes of Trade Cases or simply in transfer binders; Bureau of National Affairs, Antitrust and Trade Regulation Reporter.

7. Antitrust Bulletin; Antitrust Law Journal; Antitrust Law and Economics Review; Journal of Reprints for Antitrust Law and Economics. Another useful reference is The Patent Trademark and Copyright Journal of Research and Education, which is now known as Idea, The Journal of the Patent Office Society.

tion of competition is also the object of other federal statutes, state statutes, and the common law, which, for example, touches false advertising and unfair competition. Federal antitrust law is but one of the legal forces directed to regulating economic behavior.

104. The antitrust laws. (a) *Nature of the statutes.* The federal antitrust laws are much simpler than commercial codes or tax statutes. The basic statute, the Sherman Act, simply condemns (1) contracts, combinations, and conspiracies in restraint of trade and (2) monopolization, combinations and conspiracies to monopolize, and attempts to monopolize. Although this is a statutory subject and we are concerned with statutory interpretation, the prohibition of trade restraints and monopolization in the Sherman Act is extremely vague and general. Indeed, the Act may be little more than a legislative command that the judiciary develop a common law of antitrust. Thus, while the judicial application of nearly every statute involves judicial lawmaking, such "judicial legislation" is particularly significant when the statute is as general as the Sherman Act. Although some later enactments, as we shall see, more specifically address particular practices, the proscriptions remain uncertain.

The antitrust laws intrude very deeply into U.S. business. The statutes apply to interstate commerce, and very little commerce falls outside the "interstate" definition of contemporary constitutional doctrine. The judicial notions of what constitutes a "restraint of trade" have become increasingly sophisticated. In short, the broad definition of conduct subject to antitrust scrutiny together with the broad reach of the federal commerce power have greatly expanded the coverage of the antitrust laws.

(b) *Legislative history; congressional role.* Antitrust study will occasion some close acquaintance with the use and abuse of legislative history. Committee reports are often no more precise than the statute itself. Comments made on the floor of the House or Senate may be even less useful: debates often resemble discussions of motherhood or sin — one is either for or against; there are no subtle gradations of opinion. Although such discussions may be useful to indicate congressional feeling or mood, condemning sin in the abstract and in gross gives little guidance with respect to conduct that is arguably not sinful at all.

When situation, statute, and legislative history are all unclear, should the courts avoid controversial innovations until Congress legislates with greater clarity? Unfortunately, clear standards are often difficult to formulate. Perhaps we cannot decide very precisely how, in general and for all cases, to balance our desire for efficient business, which sometimes may be large, with our Jeffersonian wish to preserve small businesses. And even if more definite standards are intellectually possible, Congress may nevertheless be incapable of enacting them. The balance of political forces will often prevent significant precision in legislation. Once a statute is enacted, change may be impracticable. In short, the wisdom, energy, and consensus necessary to produce legislation solving these problems are hard to come by.

105. Economic theory, uncertainty, and the judicial role. Since these far-reaching statutes are rooted in notions of "competition," antitrust study requires an appreciation of the structure of the U.S. economy and some acquaintance with economic theory. Fortunately, the economic background needed for understanding the heart of most antitrust issues seldom requires detailed mastery of technical refinements. While some of the economic materials may seem complex at the outset, experience amply demonstrates that students without prior exposure do successfully master the necessities. Students should not feel troubled or overwhelmed by occasional economics notes. The textual material may contain more detail than is absolutely necessary, but the detail may give color and content to the core. In particular, the dosage may seem heavy at the outset, but the essentials will soon be quite familiar.

Although economic theory is indispensable to our task, clear-cut answers are often impossible. The complexities of economic life may outrun theoretical tools and empirical knowledge. We often will remain uncertain about the economic results of the particular practice or market structure under examination. Nor can we always predict the consequences of prohibiting some particular behavior. Thus we shall time and again meet this question: How far must we search for economic truth in a particular case when the economic facts may be obscure at best, when the relevant economic understandings may be controversial or indefinite, and when the statute does not give us a clear-cut value choice?

1A. THE ROLE OF COMPETITION: ANALYTIC MODEL AND USEFUL TENDENCY

The Value of Perfect Competition[8]

106. Perfect competition defined. A market economy will be perfectly competitive if the following conditions hold:

8. This section owes much to F. Bator, The Question of Government Spending, ch. 6 (1960); F. Bator, The Simple Analytics of Welfare Maximization, 47 Am. Econ. Rev. 22 (1957).

(1) Sellers and buyers are so numerous that no one's actions can have a perceptible impact on the market price,[9] and there is no collusion among buyers or sellers.

(2) Consumers register their subjective preferences among various goods and services[10] through market transactions at fully known market prices.

(3) All relevant prices are known to each producer, who also knows of all input combinations technically capable of producing any specific combination of outputs and who makes input-output decisions solely to maximize profits.[11]

(4) Every producer has equal access to all input markets and there are no artificial barriers to the production of any product.

107. Competition and efficiency. In equilibrium,[12] the allocation of inputs and the production and distribution of outputs in a perfectly competitive economy will be *efficient* in the following, very specific sense: No rearrangement of inputs, outputs, and distribution is possible that would make someone better off without making someone else worse off — where well-being is measured in terms of consumers' own preferences. This formulation is called Pareto efficiency. It roughly corresponds to the condition that there be no waste of resources in the production of goods and services and that the mix of goods and services produced and their allocation among consumers be in accordance with individual preferences.[13] The efficiency concept is at once powerful and weak: powerful because

9. To satisfy this condition in each market, the products of each seller must be homogeneous. This means that each seller's product has perfect substitutes in the products of numerous other sellers. In addition, this condition would fail if substantial economies result from large-scale production or distribution. In that event, only a small number of firms could survive in equilibrium.

10. Factors of production owned by consumers, including their own labor, are treated similarly. For example, it is assumed that consumers reveal their preferences between labor and leisure by their sales of labor in the marketplace. It is also assumed that consumer satisfaction does not depend on the choices of other persons.

11. It is also assumed that inputs not purchased in the market do not affect production — that is, that there are no "externalities." See ¶110a.

12. Equilibrium is simply the state of economy that results from the adjustment process discussed in ¶108. An actual economy may never reach equilibrium in the sense that it is fully at rest. There is one equilibrium for every set of tastes, technologies, and distribution of ownership of scarce inputs. Changes in these underlying economic data force the system to adjust toward a new equilibrium. Since tastes, technologies, and scarcities are continually changing, the system is constantly being buffeted in new directions.

13. To illustrate the latter, an economy that produced many canoes and few bicycles (where each takes the same amount of resources) but where most consumers prefer bicycles to canoes would violate this condition. In addition, the condition requires that the bicycles be allocated to cyclists and canoes to those fond of canoe trips rather than vice versa.

it is arguably the minimum necessary condition of any ideal economic system's equilibrium, weak because it is only one of many values considered important by our society.

Competitive forces generate efficiency in two ways. Productive efficiency occurs as low cost producers undersell and thereby displace the less efficient. Allocative efficiency occurs as exchanges in the marketplace direct production away from goods and services that consumers value less and toward those they value more, as we now describe.

108. The dynamic adjustment process. In a perfectly competitive economy that is in equilibrium, profit rates (adjusted for differences in risk) in all productive activities are equal — which can be seen from the following description of how equilibrium is reached. Suppose that consumers' preferences change so that more is demanded of one product than is being produced at the prevailing price. Consumers would bid its price up and thus generate more profits for its producers. In the opposite situation of decreased demand, producer profits would decline with the fall in the price of goods in excess supply. At that point, production of the undersupplied product will exhibit a higher profit rate than production elsewhere in the economy. Production of the oversupplied products will exhibit a lower profit rate.

This differential in profit rates will induce a compensating flow of resources. Firms and individuals will devote more of their resources to the production of the undersupplied good. They will devote less to the production of the oversupplied goods. These resource flows will tend to depress the prices and profits of firms originally producing the undersupplied good (they face new competition) and elevate the prices and profits of firms still producing the oversupplied products (some of their former competition has withdrawn to produce the undersupplied good). The economy will eventually reach a new equilibrium in which profit rates in all activities will again be equal — because as long as profits are unequal, firms earning lower profits will be induced to shift to production of high-profit goods. This equal profit condition characterizes both the old equilibrium and the new. The difference is that production of the once undersupplied good will have been increased and production of the once oversupplied goods will have decreased.

The market system, even if imperfect, organizes a vast quantity of information about consumer desires.

> [It] is a social order, and one of unfathomable complexity, yet constructed and operated without social planning or direction, through selfish individual thought and motivation alone.... [I]n a fairly tolerable way, "it works," and grows and changes. We have an amaz-

ingly elaborate division of labor, yet each person finds his own place in the scheme; we use a highly involved technology with minute specialization of industrial equipment, but this too is created, placed and directed by individuals, for individual ends, with little thought of larger social relations or any general social objective. Innumerable conflicts of interest are constantly resolved, and the bulk of the working population kept generally occupied, each person ministering to the wants of an unknown multitude and having his own wants satisfied by another multitude equally vast and unknown — not perfectly indeed, but tolerable on the whole. . . .[14]

This is the so-called invisible hand of classical laissez-faire economics, and it is today the primary organizational instrument of our economy within, of course, a framework defined by an array of property rights and government institutions, including matters as simple as who owns particular objects and as complex as the government's macroeconomic and foreign policies.

109. Consumer decisions as the basis for market choice. (a) *Consumer preferences weighted by wealth.* Perfect competition efficiently caters to consumer tastes. But whose tastes count? The market counts preferences backed by dollars spent. The market thus weights preferences according to the amounts available for spending. The latter depends on the ownership of inputs. Individuals who own more or "better" inputs — surgeons, movie stars, large stockholders or landholders, and the like — receive more of the final outputs than do individuals who own less, and therefore they exercise a greater influence over market inputs and outputs. Initial input ownership is thus closely linked to the division of final output. For each initial distribution of input ownership there is a corresponding equilibrium set of inputs, outputs, and distribution in a perfectly competitive economy.

Legal rules defining ownership of "property" and specifying taxes and government expenditures determine an income distribution while leaving the market free to achieve an efficient equilibrium for the resulting set of consumer decisions then reflected in market demand. Because of the variety and flexibility of available policy instruments, significant discretion over the choice of income distribution is possible — at least in a society with the wealth of the United States — while still leaving many economic decisions to the marketplace.[15]

14. F. Knight, The Economic Organization 31-32 (1951). See also M. Friedman & R. Friedman, Free to Choose: A Personal Statement, ch. 1 (1980). The adjustment process is described graphically in note 29. For a qualification on the meaning of "profit," see note 48.
15. The difficulties are substantial. There is disagreement about the appropriate extent of income inequality. Moreover, taxes introduce some inefficiency into the system. They involve administrative costs. More importantly, they distort individu-

(b) Consumer choice "mistaken." The decisions of consumers reflect not only their income but also their preferences. Those who doubt the wisdom or propriety of consumer tastes will have reason to question and perhaps to alter the perfectly competitive result. They may seek to have government restrict or tax individual or business choices when existing consumers have "insufficient" regard for future generations or when the "wrong" kinds of commodities are purchased. They may want government to subsidize certain goods and services that they feel individuals and firms undervalue. Finally, they may ask government to affect consumer choice through education and persuasion.

In each instance, consumer tastes are the underlying problem. By efficiently catering to them, perfect competition only compounds the situation. But in some instances — to which we now turn — markets fail to implement unquestioned consumer tastes efficiently.

110. Competition unhelpful or limited. *(a) Externalities.* Externalities refer to costs that one economic actor imposes on another (or benefits that one receives from another) without paying in the market for doing so. A familiar example is the firm that discharges its wastes into the environment without paying the cost of the harm it causes. Because the market overlooks that genuine cost, neither the profit-maximizing firm nor its customers take it into account. Thus, more of the product will be produced and purchased than if its true costs (including the externality) were reflected in its price. Such uncompensated social costs spoil the efficiency of a competitive equilibrium, bringing about results that do not accord with true consumer preferences.[16]

A different sort of example is that real-world consumers may worry about "keeping up with the Joneses." These individuals pick jobs on the basis of their position relative to that of other individuals.[17] Thus, whether intentionally or not, the "Joneses" impose on

---

als' choices. For example, a tax on labor income causes an employee to place less value on an extra hour of work than the value of what is produced because a portion of wages must be shared with the government. Similar distortions attend the imposition of virtually any tax or transfer scheme. For evidence on the incentive effects of taxes, see How Taxes Affect Economic Behavior (H. Aaron & J. Pechman eds. 1981); I Handbook of Public Economics, chs. 4 & 5 (A. Auerbach & M. Feldstein eds. 1985). Other programs oriented toward income distribution, like agricultural price supports, typically create more serious distortions.

16. Efficiency also requires that producers be compensated for their beneficial externalities. The orchard farmer should pay the neighboring beekeeper for the assistance the bees provide in fertilizing the farmer's orchard. Similarly, all citizens should, and do, pay the public schools to educate children who are not their own. Presumably, everybody benefits from a more educated citizenry.

17. An interesting study of these and related issues is R. Frank, Choosing the Right Pond: Human Behavior and the Quest for Status (1985).

their imitators costs that do not pass through the marketplace. These interactions are assumed away by the perfectly competitive model that postulates that consumer preferences are independently rather than enviously determined.

(b) _Public goods._ For some goods and services, the efficient price is literally zero. There is no extra cost in use by an additional individual. Both national defense and knowledge have this quality — more for one person does not mean less for others. No private firm could afford to produce a pure public good at the efficient price. Production, if it is to occur, must be financed by the government. But private firms may be able to afford production of goods with a partially "public" character at the efficient price. For example, private colleges produce knowledge for the public as well as education for their tuition-paying students. The efficient price for the public part of their output may be difficult to determine. Consumers have strong incentives to misspecify their preferences for a public good. Once it has been produced, each consumer receives its benefit whether paying for it or not. Before it is produced, strategic considerations lead consumers to misstate their willingness to pay for its production.[18] As a result, private firms are not likely to produce the "right" amount of partially public goods. The "publicness" of goods, therefore, is another cause of the inefficiency of actual markets.

(c) _Economies of scale._ As we have seen, an otherwise perfectly competitive system will not always achieve an efficient result. In addition, competition itself may not be perfect. Most notable in the study of monopoly, perfect competition requires "very many" producers in every market. But production at least cost will sometimes be possible only at a scale of production where a few firms or even a single firm can satisfy the entire demand. In that event, competition will not be sustainable, price will probably exceed the competitive price,[19] and competitive efficiency will be lost.[20] Proper regulation could theoretically restore pricing efficiency. This is one explanation of government regulation of public utilities.[21]

18. Two examples: If the consumer is one among many favoring provision of a public good (such as knowledge produced at private universities) to be financed by individual contribution, the incentive is to understate one's willingness to pay, hoping the others have pledged enough to insure provision. If the good is to be financed by tax funds to which one contributes less than proportionately to one's relative use, the temptation is to overstate the value one attaches to the project.

19. See ¶112.

20. Note that the price charged by a low-cost monopolist might be lower than that charged by intensively competing but high-cost firms.

21. Where unit costs are constantly declining, the "efficient" price, which equals marginal (see ¶112) or incremental cost, is always below average unit costs. And there are other situations where the efficient price will not permit the supplier to

(d) Additional imperfections. In addition to the defects already mentioned, real-world markets depart from the perfectly competitive ideal in the fundamental conditions that define it; for example: (1) The number of firms is seldom very large and sellers may act collusively rather than independently. (2) Buyers have imperfect knowledge of the products available to them and sellers have imperfect knowledge of the input-output combinations available to them. (3) Inertia, ignorance, and artificial barriers restrict the mobility and reallocation of labor, capital, and other productive resources. (4) Producers do not single-mindedly pursue profit maximization and consumers may not always make rational decisions.

111.   The value of perfect competition and the role of antitrust policy. The perfect competition model has been used to perpetuate laissez-faire policies in the face of reform demands. Because everything worked out "for the best" in the model, it was asserted that government intervention, regardless of good intentions, would upset the economy's autonomous tendency toward a beneficial equilibrium. To accept abuse, injustice, and avoidable human misery for that reason was not only callous, it was also illogical on two grounds: (1) In practice, the economy fails to satisfy a number of critical assumptions of the perfect competition model. As a result, actual markets do not always cater efficiently to consumer tastes. (2) Even if the price system were efficient, the result would not reflect all important social and economic values. Laissez-faire in these circumstances represents neither a devotion to perfect competition nor an exercise of social wisdom, although it will sometimes be preferable to ill-conceived or poorly executed government correctives.

Wise government intervention through varied and mixed devices may be appropriate. The nature and extent of this intervention depend on the type of market failure to be remedied as well as the values to be promoted. Adjusting taxes and transfers may improve income distributions that are deemed to be unsatisfactory. Other market failures may demand regulation, complete control, or a combination of taxes and subsidies. Still other market failures are the domain of antitrust policy.

Antitrust law implicitly but clearly takes a particular stance toward the economic problems to which it applies. On one hand, its very

---

break even. Once a subway or bridge is built, for example, the social or resource cost of using it is simply the incremental or marginal cost of additional persons riding or crossing it. Fares or tolls at that level, however, would never finance the construction of the subway or bridge. Accordingly, society must either permit inefficient above-marginal-cost pricing (restricting use of the bridge unnecessarily but confining its financial support to those who use it) or subsidize construction of the facility out of general tax revenues.

enactment indicates that Congress rejected the belief that market forces are sufficiently strong, self-correcting, and well-directed to guarantee the results that perfect competition would bring. On the other hand, antitrust's domain is intrinsically limited. Antitrust is not the nationalization of industry, which would reflect a decision that only direct government operation can provide the desired result. Antitrust also is not direct, extensive regulation of industry, an alternative that has been enacted for some public utilities. Rather, antitrust supplements or, perhaps, defines the rules of the game by which competition takes place. It thus assumes that market forces — guided by the limitations imposed by antitrust law — will produce good results or at least better results than any of the alternatives that largely abandon reliance on market forces. Therefore, the perfect competition model can be viewed as a central target, the results of which antitrust seeks, but the conditions for which antitrust does not take for granted. Antitrust thus looks to perfect competition for guidance, but the analysis inevitably emphasizes the myriad and complex imperfections of actual markets.

The economic model of competition also provides antitrust with a major value: efficiency. Other values impinge, however, to strengthen or retard the force of the unqualified competitive criteria. The task of antitrust, accordingly, is much more complex than simply moving the economy toward more nearly perfect competition. Let us begin our analysis of this task with a brief look at the targets of antitrust — monopolists and oligopolists.

Perfect and Imperfect Competition Compared[22]

112. Price and output decisions. *(a) Monopoly.* A profit-maximizing monopolist will take account of two phenomena in deciding how much to produce. On the revenue side, it knows that consumers ordinarily will not purchase more of its product except at a lower price and that they will purchase less at a higher price.[23] To sell another unit, the monopolist must reduce the price not only for that unit but

---

22. The reader who finds the following discussion too concise should consult P. Samuelson & W. Nordhaus, Economics, chs. 9, 10, 18 (15th ed. 1995); E. Mansfield, Microeconomics, chs. 9-12 (8th ed. 1994); R. Dorfman, Prices and Markets, ch. 6 (3d ed. 1978), or any other basic microeconomics text.

23. Economists use the term elasticity to describe consumers' responsiveness to price changes. When small percentage changes in price produce great percentage changes in volume, demand is said to be very elastic. When large percentage changes in price produce little change in volume, demand is said to be very inelastic. The demand curve facing the imperfectly competitive firm is not completely elastic; price increases do not eliminate all sales. This is explored further in ¶¶336c, 338, 340c.

for all other units sold; ordinarily, a seller cannot effectively discriminate among buyers in order to lower the price only for the last unit sold.[24] This necessity of reducing price to all buyers in order to expand sales means that the monopolist receives less incremental revenue from each successive sale. Thus, the extra (or "marginal") revenue it receives from producing an additional unit falls as it produces and sells more.[25] A similar phenomenon governs every producer's cost calculations. It knows that it cannot squeeze more output from its existing scale of plant and equipment in the short run without eventually incurring increasing incremental costs. Thus, in the short run, the marginal cost of an extra unit of output will eventually increase as output is increased.[26] Short of that point, marginal costs may remain roughly constant over a considerable output range.

The monopolist is thus concerned with its costs and revenues "at the margin." It will increase output as long as the marginal revenue exceeds the marginal cost.[27] At some point, its marginal costs will

24. See ¶285a.

25. Eventually, the revenue lost by lowering price on all units will exceed the revenue gained from selling an additional unit — that is, marginal revenue would be negative. The monopolist obviously will stop somewhere short of this point.

26. Although this is a common case, the price setting mechanism about to be described also applies when marginal costs are constant or even falling.

27. The following example illustrates the cost and revenue constraints facing a monopolist (presented graphically in note 29).

Q	TC	AC	MC	P	TR	MR
1	10	10.0	10	20	20	20
2	15	7.5	5	19	38	18
3	18	6.0	3	18	54	16
4	20	5.0	2	17	68	14
5	21	4.2	1	16	80	12
6	22	3.7	1	15	90	10
7	23	3.3	1	14	98	8
8	24	3.0	1	13	104	6
9	26	2.9	2	12	108	4
10	30	3.0	4	11	110	2
11	36	3.3	6	10	110	0
12	44	3.7	8	9	108	-2
13	54	4.2	10	8	104	-4
14	66	4.7	12	7	98	-6
15	80	5.3	14	6	90	-8

Q: quantity produced and sold.
TC: total cost.
AC: average cost = TC/Q.
MC: marginal cost (change in TC resulting from an increase of 1 unit in Q).
P: price = TR/Q = average revenue.
TR: total revenue = P × Q.
MR: marginal revenue (change in TR resulting from an increase of 1 unit in Q).

just equal its falling marginal revenues, which is where it will stop.[28] Beyond this point, incremental output would add less to revenue than to costs and thus would be unprofitable. The monopolist therefore maximizes profits by selling that output at which its marginal revenue just matches its marginal cost. The monopolist, of course, is free to produce less than this and, accordingly, to charge higher prices, but doing so will forgo sales that would have yielded more revenue than the cost incurred and thus forgo extra profit.

(b) *Perfect competition compared.* Paragraph 106 indicated that perfect competition assumes that no one competitor's actions have a perceptible impact on the market price. The perfect competitor's output is so small relative to total demand that its output variations cannot affect market price; its marginal revenue from additional output, therefore, will simply equal the market price. Accordingly, it takes price as given in deciding how much to produce. It has no reason to charge less, and charging more will drive all its customers to competitors.

Because its marginal revenue is the market price, the perfect competitor adds to its profits by increasing its output until the marginal cost of producing the last unit just equals the market price at which it can sell all its output. Additional output would earn less than it cost and would therefore be unprofitable. Like a monopolist, the perfect competitor equates marginal cost with marginal revenue, but the practical results are quite different. Unlike a perfect competitor whose individual output is too small to affect price, a monopolist affects price and can sell more only by reducing price. Accordingly, the monopolist's marginal revenue is always less than price. It follows that any given level of marginal costs will bump against the profitable ceiling of marginal revenue sooner — that is, at smaller levels of output — for a monopolist than for perfect competitors.[29] (Of course, if the many small producers banded together

28. Of course, neither the monopolist nor the perfect competitor will produce at all, unless revenues cover all variable (out-of-pocket) costs. (Marginal costs will be lower than average variable costs when the latter are declining.) Variable costs are costs that vary with output, unlike the fixed costs that the firm bears whether it produces a lot, a little, or even nothing at all. Variable costs plus fixed costs equal total costs. (When total costs exceed total revenues, a firm would nevertheless minimize its losses by continuing to operate as long as it recovers its variable costs.)

29. The discussion to this point can be summarized graphically. In Figure 1, D is the monopolist's demand curve. For each quantity of output, it indicates the highest price at which it can sell all of its output. The monopolist's marginal revenue curve (MR) and its average (AC) and marginal cost (MC) curves are also shown. All the curves are based on the table in note 27. The monopolist will produce where $MC = MR$, at $Q_m = 9.5$. At this point, its price is indicated by the demand curve as $P_m = 11.5$. (Note: The revenue and cost curves are independent of each other. It is fortuitous that MR intersects MC close to the minimum point of the AC curve in this diagram.)

If the monopolist were broken up into 100 identical competing firms, this and made their output decisions collectively, the cartel would view marginal revenue in the same way as a monopolist.) This means that

demand curve would not change. Consumers are assumed to be indifferent to the number of producers of a given good. If there were no economies of scale in production, the industry cost curves would not change either. One hundred firms would produce Q_m at the same unit cost as the monopolist. Accordingly, the monopolist's demand curve is the competitive industry's demand curve, and the monopolist's marginal cost curve is the competitive industry's supply curve. The competitive industry will always produce where its demand curve crosses its marginal cost curve, here at $Q_c = 12.25$ and $P_c = 8.75$.

Each individual firm in the industry will take this competitive market price as given. Its demand curve will thus be completely elastic — a horizontal line at $P_c = 8.75$, represented by $D'D'$ in Figure 2. By our assumption of no economies of scale in production, each firm will incur the same costs as the monopolist at one hundredth the output level, hence the MC and AC curves of Figure 2. The individual competitive firm will produce where $P_c = MC$, at $Q'_c = 0.1225$.

Observe that P'_c is greater than AC at Q'_c. Suppose that AC here includes the profits this firm would earn in a competitive equilibrium. These profits represent the return necessary to induce investment in a competitive industry. Here, however, the firm earns an excess return. These surplus profits mean that the industry is not in a long-run competitive equilibrium. Producers have not completely adjusted to a shift in consumer tastes, for example. Further adjustment will occur as long as firms in the industry earn surplus profits. New firms will enter the industry, shifting the industry supply curve of Figure 1 (the monopolist's MC curve) to the right. The individual firm's *demand* curve, $D'D'$ of Figure 2, will also shift downward. The new entrants compete with the firms already in the industry to satisfy an unchanged consumer demand. Each firm's share of the total drops, and so its demand curve falls. Thus, the effect of firms entering an industry is to shift the industry supply curve to the right and to push each firm's demand curve downward. Both changes reduce the prevailing market price P_c and individual firm surplus profits, the excess of $P_c \times Q'_c$ over $AC \times Q'_c$. New entry will cease when individual firm surplus profits are driven to zero. When this equilibrium is reached, each firm's demand curve will cross its MC and AC curves at their point of intersection. If this process were to overshoot the equilibrium (or, alternatively, if one started in the opposite situation), firms would suffer losses, inducing exit until equilibrium was restored.

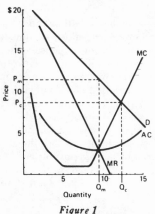

Figure 1

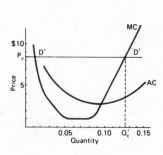

Figure 2

output will be less in the monopoly case, and that will command a correspondingly higher price.

For efficient allocation, the monopolist should produce more, until marginal cost equals price. The perfect competitor produces at this point of equality between marginal cost and price. It throws all of its resources into production until its incremental costs rise to meet the market price. The monopolist, in contrast, contrives a scarcity of its product. It "withholds" some output from consumers to raise its price and thereby maximize its personal gain at the expense of society. It thus affects both the distribution of income and the efficiency of the economy, as discussed in ¶¶113, 117a. Before that discussion, we preview Chapter 2C with a brief word about oligopoly.

(c) *Oligopoly.* The term "oligopoly" describes a market populated by a small number of producers. Behavior and performance in an oligopolistic industry fall between that of monopoly and perfect competition.[30] Some firms in an oligopolistic industry may be sufficiently large so that they can profitably restrict output and increase price on their own, much as a single-firm monopolist does.

Moreover, economic results may depend on firms' aggregate behavior. When the number of firms is small, each will be conscious of the others' actions and will take them into account in determining its own behavior. The strength of this "interdependence," rather than the exact size of each firm or the total number, is the critical determinant of such oligopolistic behavior. Each oligopolist is acutely aware that it may reap large gains if it can initiate a profitable move that its competitors cannot match, at least for a time. But every oligopolist also knows that most of its profitable moves will be matched quickly and that most of its disastrous projects will be completed without companionship. While a perfect competitor would expand output without concern about its impact on rivals, an oligopolist knows that it is large enough to affect market prices and

30. Economists use the term "competition" in a sense that differs in some respects from the usage of business competitors. Competition in the business world is a conscious striving for profits, typically at the expense of a limited number of readily identifiable rivals. This jockeying for mutually incompatible positions may take the form of lowering production costs. Very often it appears as changes in product design or advertising. Such rivalry is the dominant mode of behavior in oligopolies in consumer products. Firms in an industry populated by a few sellers accordingly will often describe their market conditions as wearingly competitive. The economist, however, would reserve the term for industries approaching the conditions described in ¶106, where firms pay little heed to their fellow producers. Their only goal is to produce as cheaply as possible and select the appropriate output, given price. This section and others like it later in the book speak of competition in the economist's sense, unless the context indicates otherwise.

that its output expansion and price reduction would probably invite imitation by its rivals. Thus, if price is somehow above the competitive level, it may remain there in an oligopoly. Similarly, an oligopolistic price leader among them may rise prices toward monopoly levels with the expectation that rivals will follow because they will know that the leader will retract an unfollowed price increase. By contrast, where there are many firms in the market, some of them are likely to defect from supracompetitive prices, hoping that rivals will not notice or react, or in any event hoping to profit from increased sales in the interim. Here, as with many other endeavors, cooperation and joint action are often more feasible when numbers are smaller.[31]

Oligopoly is a central antitrust problem. Many proscriptions are intended to prevent markets from becoming oligopolistic in the first place or to obstruct the ability of oligopolists to coordinate their behavior.

113. Allocative efficiency. If a perfectly competitive industry were monopolized, the amount produced would shrink and the price at which it was offered for sale would rise. Monopoly pricing might result, for example, from government grants of exclusive privilege or from a cartel agreement among competitors. Both situations have produced startling price increases. The oil-producing countries' cartel raised oil prices nearly 1000 percent from 1970 to 1981. An international quinine cartel formed in the early 1960s raised the price of quinine on the world market nearly six-fold.[32] Classic cartels and single-firm monopolies are rare; more numerous are industries dominated by oligopolists, who also tend to raise prices.[33]

These excessive prices upset the efficiency of the economy. When the price of a good exceeds its marginal cost, it will be denied to those consumers who are willing and able to pay only its real cost of production. For example, when production costs (including a competitive return on investment) are $100 per unit and the monopoly or cartel price $150, customers valuing the product at $125 would be dissuaded from purchasing the product, which would have been sold to them under perfect competition at $100. Instead they spend their funds elsewhere, and thus induce increased production of other commodities — commodities that such consumers would not

31. For a more complete description of informal coordination among oligopolists, see ¶¶228-230.
32. Neither a sudden spurt in demand nor a sudden shortage of quinine (uncontrived by the cartel) caused this price rise. See Antitrust and Monopoly Subcommittee, Senate Judiciary Committee, 90th Cong., 1st Sess., Report on Prices of Quinine and Quinidine 68-75 (1967).
33. See ¶232.

want under competitive pricing conditions. Imperfect competition thus diverts productive energies to less-valued undertakings, preventing the economy from efficiently catering to consumer tastes.[34] That existing consumer preferences may sometimes be "unwise" is, of course, no excuse for the varied resource misallocations that result from imperfect competition.

114.   Barriers to entry. The market power of imperfect competitors to restrict output, raise prices, and earn monopoly profits may not be permanent. Other firms may penetrate their markets, wrest sales away from them, and force more competitive performance. Whether encroaching firms can do this depends on the height of barriers to entry. Before considering particular barriers and their significance, a number of points concerning the concept should be noted.

First, barriers are not an all-or-nothing phenomena. Barriers that bar some firms may not bar others. Many barriers may be overcome if profits greatly exceed the competitive level but not if the monopoly overcharge is more modest. And barriers often slow entry rather than make it impossible. Even so, entry may be insufficient to prevent some degree of supracompetitive pricing for some period of time.

Second, the height of entry barriers depends not merely on objective factors but also on the anticipated reactions of incumbent firms. Thus, modest excess profits may induce entry where prospective entrants expect such profits to continue after entry, while larger profits would not do so where entrants expect intense price competition to result from their entry, thereby leaving insufficient profits to recover their investment.

Third, entry barriers may obstruct not only the entry of new firms but also the expansion of smaller incumbents. For example, regional soft drink producers may face barriers in challenging Coke and Pepsi similar to those facing a new entrant.[35]

Barriers to entry arise from four main sources:

(1) *Blocked access:* Established firms might control the supply of essential raw materials, necessary patents, distribution channels, or other strategic factors and thus make new entry either impossible or impractical because of a relative cost disadvantage. And in some industries, regulation limits entry.

---

34. It is difficult to assess quantitatively the importance of this inefficiency. Scherer and Ross, note 2, at 661-667, survey the literature and conclude that the welfare loss due to monopolistic resource misallocation is between 0.5 and 2 percent of gross national product. They also discuss, but do not quantify, other inefficiencies. See id. at 667-679.

35. R. Caves & M. Porter, From Entry Barriers to Mobility Barriers, 91 Q. J. Econ. 241 (1977).

(2) *Scale economies:* The minimum size of an efficient firm may be so large with respect to total consumer demand that entry at efficient scale would depress prices so severely as to be unprofitable.

(3) *Capital requirements:* Efficient entry might require the construction of so large a plant, the entry into so many related fields, the expense of such prolonged start-up costs, and the prospect of such slow acceptance by customers that a vast initial outlay of capital would be needed. Capital requirements would not necessarily impede entry whenever suppliers of capital share the entrepreneur's vision of the likelihood of success. But the likelihood of obtaining the needed capital at costs comparable to those of established producers may diminish with increases in the volume of capital necessary to support efficient entry.

(4) *Product differentiation:* Established producers of consumer goods will often enjoy the benefit of accumulated goodwill. The new entrant will often have to bear a higher promotional cost or suffer a lower selling price than do existing firms, in order to counteract their consumer loyalty. It has been suggested that such entrenched goodwill should not be considered an entry barrier any more than existing plants. In both cases, the newcomer must simply do for itself what the established firms have already done for themselves. Nevertheless, brand loyalty must be overcome, and the necessity of overcoming it makes entry more risky and costly — and thus less likely — than it would otherwise be.[36]

The possibility that product differentiation may be an important barrier to entry has been elaborated by Professor Sutton.[37] His argument begins with the intuition that advertising, by creating product differentiation and brand image, can effectively raise the price that consumers are willing to pay for a firm's product. He further observes that although per-customer advertising (e.g., door-to-door sales, in-store sales assistance) is usually analyzed as a variable cost, rising as firm output rises, advertising in the mass media may be analyzed as a separate fixed cost, substantially independent of output or sales. (For example, the cost of a television ad does not depend on sales, and there are also economies of scale in producing such ads in that the cost of creation need only be incurred once, regardless of how many times an ad is used.) Thus, larger industries and industries in which advertising is particularly influential should tend to be more concentrated. This may explain why specific industries in different countries often tend to have similar levels of con-

36. Product differentiation might sometimes facilitate entry by an established firm with a respected name that can be transferred to a new product or market.
37. J. Sutton, Sunk Costs and Market Structure: Price Competition, Advertising, and the Evolution of Concentration (1991).

centration. Moreover, industries characterized by such advertising-induced product differentiation may tend to remain concentrated even in the long run.

When barriers to entry are extremely low, established firms must set prices near competitive levels. In the absence of governmental obstacles, for example, the sole trucking firm operating between two points could probably not charge freight rates above competitive levels without leading shippers to seek service from other truck owners, who could quickly shift their extremely mobile resources to serve those shippers. Although entry is seldom this easy, there are many situations in which the barriers to entry are sufficiently modest to be of little practical significance. When barriers to entry are relatively high, but still surmountable, established firms have a choice. They might set a price that maximizes their short-run profits but induces entry and lower long-run profits. Or they might sacrifice immediate profits by setting a so-called limit price that is above competitive levels but low enough to discourage future entry. Their profit rate is less attractive and their own output at the limit price may occupy so much of the market as to leave little for new entry at an efficient scale.[38] In any case, high entry barriers protect the exercise of market power over time. Low entry barriers, in contrast, circumscribe the exercise of market power.

Professor Bain has suggested that product differentiation is a wide-spread and significant barrier to entry.[39] Product differentiation, then, may be the cause of many persistent oligopolies. New firms may simply be unwilling to pay the price of an expensive campaign to counteract carefully built-up consumer devotion to established firms. In some industries, like chemicals and electronics, the necessary productive resources are usually available, especially to established firms seeking diversification, but patents are important and may block entry. As discussed in ¶119, scale economies often pose a mild barrier to entry but, equally often, they raise no barrier at all.

Entry barriers are generally low in agriculture, forestry, fisheries, wholesale and retail distributive trades, construction, and most service industries — in short, where atomistic competition is the rule. Entry barriers in manufacturing are of varying heights. Of the 23

38. Scherer & Ross, note 2, at 353. The rationale of limit pricing may not be immediately apparent and does not hold in all contexts. For example, one might ask why a monopolist might not prefer to charge the monopoly price, waiting to lower its price until the new entrant actually appears. One theory is that a higher price and profit rate itself will attract entry. Another is that the current price is evidence of how incumbents will price in response to entry. If the price already allows only modest room for profit, entrants might speculate that there will be less profit after their arrival than if current prices were higher.

39. J. Bain, Barriers to New Competition (1956). See also Sutton, note 37.

industries Bain studied in detail, 6 were listed as having very high barriers to entry (as reflected by prices 10 percent or more above minimum average costs), 6 as having substantial barriers (prices 6 to 8 percent above average costs), and 11 as having moderate to low entry barriers (prices 1 to 4 percent above competitive levels). As expected, Bain and others have found that high barriers to entry are conducive to high concentration; that among highly concentrated industries, higher entry barriers produce higher profits; and that low concentration generally occurs with low barriers to entry and competitive rates of return on invested capital.

Potential competition, then, like actual competition, exerts a restraining effect on prices and profits. Its influence, controlled by the various barriers to entry, has made competition more workable than it would otherwise be and more than concentration ratios alone would suggest. But imperfect competition on an extensive scale obviously persists. Barriers to entry account for this staying power.

115. Cost minimization. The survival of the perfect competitor depends, in the long run, on its use of the lowest-cost production and distribution techniques. Otherwise, firms using these techniques will enter its market at a lower price, making its continued operation unprofitable. Monopolists or oligopolists also maximize profits by minimizing their costs at each output level; however limited their output, a dollar saved in costs is a dollar more in profit. But unlike the perfectly competitive firm, monopolists or oligopolists may be less quickly or fatally penalized when they fail to minimize costs because they have excessive profits to begin with. They may tolerate obsolescent equipment, swollen bureaucracy, and outworn production techniques. United States Steel, for example, was said to be lax in the 1930s. It was

> a big sprawling inert giant, whose production operations were improperly coordinated; suffering from a lack of a long-run planning agency; relying on an antiquated system of cost accounting; with an inadequate knowledge of the costs or of the relative profitability of the many thousands of items it sold; with production and cost standards generally below those considered everyday practice in other industries; with inadequate knowledge of its domestic markets and no clear appreciation of its opportunities in foreign markets; with less efficient production facilities than its rivals had; slow in introducing new processes and new products.[40]

40. Statement of G. Stocking, Monopoly Power Subcommittee, House Judiciary Committee, 81st Cong., 2d Sess., Hearings on Steel, ser. 14, pt. 4-A, at 967 (1950). These difficulties were not immediately eliminated. As of 1968, nearly one-quarter of the equipment used in the steel industry was regarded as obsolete. See McGraw-Hill Economics Dept., How Modern Is American Industry? (1968).

To the extent that freedom from competition has permitted many companies to pursue the quiet life, wasteful excesses have been the result. Moreover, bloated costs usually mean that price will be even higher and output even lower than with a cost-minimizing monopolist.[41]

116. Promotion and product differentiation. (a) *Product identification.* The perfectly competitive firm is an anonymous producer. Purchasers of its output have no incentive to trace the product to its source. By definition, the product is identical in price and grade to all of its numerous competitors, and consumers are fully informed of its qualities. In many actual markets, however, products are identified with particular producers. Strengthening this identification can be very important in the case of consumer goods, especially when there is a handful of sellers who avoid price competition. Such a seller prefers to persuade buyers that its product differs from rival products because then it may charge higher prices without losing all its customers to the competition. It will emphasize brand names, media advertising, elaborate packaging, and other consumer-directed marketing efforts. The amounts involved in these efforts are enormous. More than $148 billion went into advertising alone in 1994. More than half of this sum was spent on newspaper, television, or direct mail advertising.[42] Some of this type of advertising serves the necessary informational function of telling buyers which producers have which products for sale at what prices. Some portion of other advertising, even on television, serves the same purpose. But some part of it is false, misleading, or ethically questionable, and much is directed to appealing to powerful images rather than informing.

Beyond this, product identification efforts are art or entertainment to some. They create pleasurable image for others. They subsidize (although they also perhaps distort) the content of magazines, radio, and television. And, of course, promotional efforts enable consumers regularly and easily to associate the quality of goods they buy with particular producers. In some cases, consumers

---

41. No one knows the extent of such excess-cost operations, but economists have come to give it greater attention. For a recent survey, see Scherer and Ross, note 2, at 668-672. In addition to inefficient operation, firms with some market power may compete in services rather than price and thus drive costs up. See ¶230e. Beyond this, the effort to gain market power may itself induce higher costs for the actor, its rivals, and government institutions — such as the costs of lobbying, counterlobbying, patenting, and antitrust litigation. See R. Posner, The Social Costs of Monopoly and Regulation, 83 J. Pol. Econ. 807 (1975); F.M. Scherer, Book Review, 86 Yale L.J. 974, 978-979 (1977).

42. Statistical Abstract of the United States 584 (115th ed. 1995).

seem willing to pay for these advantages because many heavily promoted goods command a substantial price premium over unpromoted but physically identical products.

But by the very fact that advertising does persuade, this behavior does not represent desires wholly original to the consumer. Advertising also encourages "demonstration effects" — products are bought because peers have recently purchased similar items. The implications are not altogether clear because individual taste formation is inevitably a social process. Nevertheless, some part of product differentiation merely exploits consumer ignorance. Moreover, advertising may raise product differentiation barriers to entry. Finally, there is considerable theoretical and some empirical evidence that many oligopolists advertise more extensively than would be useful for the industry viewed collectively.[43] And their expenditures need not substantially affect the market share each would have obtained had none advertised. Much promotional expense is probably a waste of resources.

(b) *Product differentiation.* The oligopolist strengthens the consumer identification of its product by differentiating it slightly from that of its rivals. It may vary design, serviceability, terms of sale, or outlet location. By thus appealing to distinctive tastes, each seller attracts a more or less loyal band of buyers for its product. In effect, product differentiation enables a seller to decrease the elasticity of its demand curve and appropriate monopolistic gains for itself.[44]

One cost of product differentiation, then, is the bit of monopoly power it engenders. Because potential monopoly profits await successful product differentiation or those able to overcome the differentiation of competitors, additional costs are incurred. In addition, firms may be forced to produce at inefficiently small scales to satisfy their small but loyal clienteles. Thus, product changes are them-

---

43. There are plausible incentives for this collectively irrational behavior. If advertising is relevant to sales, the individual oligopolist gains a significant advantage by advertising heavily when its rivals do not. When its rivals are advertising heavily, it must do the same to protect its relative position. Thus, the individual oligopolist will find it advantageous to advertise regardless of what its rivals do. Barring collusion among them, each will do the same, even if abandonment of advertising by all would make them better off than continued advertising by all. Oligopolistic pricing presents a similar dilemma, but it is more easily resolved. See ¶230e.

44. The essence of perfect competition is that all sellers face perfectly elastic (flat) demand curves. Recall note 29. The standard economic measure of the market power of an imperfect competitor is the extent to which its demand curve departs from perfect elasticity. See ¶¶336c, 338a, 340c. The less elastic it is, the less a price increase will diminish sales, and the more monopoly profit it can appropriate. Of course, it has been argued that a willingness to pay the resulting price demonstrates consumer satisfaction with both the costs and the results of advertising; but willingness may also reflect ignorance that is exploited rather than remedied.

selves expensive,[45] and differentiation may be the source of substantial barriers to entry.[46]

But consumers genuinely enjoy a variety and diversity of products. Yet would not considerable variety remain, even in an economy more competitive than the present one? In general, markets may produce too much or too little product variety, depending on subtle characteristics of consumer demand.[47]

117.   Other values of competition. (a) *Income distribution.* In the long run, the perfect competitor will earn no profits above the return necessary to keep its productive resources employed. In the short run, it may temporarily earn profits in excess of that amount or it may earn less, but such differences will last only until existing firms expand or until new firms enter the market in response to high profits or contract and exit when profits are low.[48] The profit-maximizing monopolist will usually earn more profits than the perfect competitor. So may the oligopolists. These beneficiaries of imperfect competition, then, receive income unnecessary to induce their production. Their capital would have been invested without the promise of such large returns. The ultimate recipients of this surplus may be the firms' owners (stockholders,[49] including, perhaps, the wealthiest people in the population as well as pension funds, nonprofit organizations, and some small investors), input suppliers (including labor union members), and the tax collector.

45. The total cost of automobile style changes was estimated to be $3.3 billion a year between 1956 and 1960, or $584 per car sold. See F. Fisher, Z. Griliches & C. Kaysen, The Costs of Automobile Model Changes Since 1949, 70 J. Pol. Econ. 433 (1962).

46. See W. Comanor & T. Wilson, Advertising and Market Power (1974); Y. Brozen, Entry Barriers, Advertising and Product Differentiation, in Industrial Concentration: The New Learning (H. Goldschmid, H. Mann & J. Weston eds. 1974); H. Mann, Advertising, Concentration, and Profitability: The State of Knowledge and Directions for Public Policy, in id.; Scherer & Ross, note 2, ch. 16.

47. See, e.g., K. Lancaster, Socially Optimal Product Differentiation and Market Structure, 65 Am. Econ. Rev. 580 (1975); A.M. Spence, Product Differentiation and Welfare, 66 Am. Econ. Rev. 407 (May 1976); A.M. Spence, Product Selection, Fixed Costs, and Monopolistic Competition, 43 Rev. Econ. Stud. 217 (1976).

48. These temporary profits and losses are themselves valuable in the competitive system as incentives for resource shifts in response to changing tastes, technologies, and scarcities. See ¶108 and note 29. It should be realized, moreover, that economic profits are imperfectly measured by conventional accounting. Accordingly, statistical studies relating accounting or book profits to market structure, advertising, or other variables should always be approached with caution. See ¶¶232a, 337b.

49. Some stockholders would have sold their shares at prices reflecting the firm's extra return. The purchasers would realize no extraordinary return on their investment.

Even if one favored this distributive effect, one would ordinarily rely on governments, not on private monopolists or oligopolists, to do whatever transferring of income is necessary to achieve an equitable income distribution.

A separate question is whether the distributive effects of noncompetitive pricing should be credited as an additional reason for preserving competition.[50] One argument is that the distribution arising from competition is per se more equitable. The basis for such a view, however, is unclear because the competitive distribution will depend on innate skills, consumer preferences, technology, and luck, factors many would deem arbitrary as bases for determining distributive shares. Alternatively, because owners of firms tend on average to be wealthier than consumers, one may favor a competitive distribution as providing a more equitable allocation between the rich and the poor. But this dimension of distribution can be influenced directly through tax and transfer policies, and higher social welfare can generally be achieved by setting legal rules to promote efficiency, leaving distribution to the tax system.[51] A somewhat different ground for attempting to eliminate profits from supercompetitive pricing is that inefficient investments may be undertaken in the attempt to obtain or maintain such profits.[52] If firms were to undertake inefficient mergers, induced by the prospect of higher prices, or to expend resources to erect entry barriers, excess profits would be translated into social waste. On the other hand, the prospect of excess profits may induce desirable investment; indeed, this is the premise of the patent system.[53]

(b) *The distribution of opportunities.* Quite apart from the economic results associated with competition, there may be independent value in dispersing economic power and relying on impersonal market forces. Especially valued is free individual opportunity to carry on business and to prosper on one's merits as determined by a free market. That is, a free market may be seen as emphasizing competition as an aspect of human liberty. To favor competition for this reason relates to its assumed economic benefits but differs because it emphasizes the social rather than economic merits of competition and is broader because it emphasizes opportunity and choice for producers and consumers even where fewer opportuni-

50. Concretely, this question may be presented when there are economies of scale, as from a horizontal merger, but the savings will not be passed on to consumers. For example, if a merger reduces production costs by 5 percent but raises prices by 1 percent, there is a net efficiency gain, but consumers lose.

51. See L. Kaplow & S. Shavell, Why the Legal System Is Less Efficient Than the Income Tax in Redistributing Income, 23 J. Leg. Stud. 667 (1994).

52. See Posner, note 41.

53. See ¶¶179-181.

ties and choices might produce equally or more "efficient" economic results.

(c) The control of unchecked power. An additional benefit of compeitition is independent of the power to affect price and production in particular markets: It is the fear of concentrated power in its social and political aspects and a desire for the dispersal of power throughout society.[54] It is the fear of bigness. For example, a giant corporation that produced 5 percent of every product might not have substantial power in any market. Yet, its size and pervasiveness might give us pause. The symbols are those of Jeffersonian democracy, in which small, local, responsible, and individually owned enterprises are contrasted with large, politically irresponsible, absentee-owned, and possibly corrupt giants capable of crushing smaller businesses and of subverting democratic government.

The emotional and political force of these ideas should not be underestimated.[55] Ours is a pluralistic society that is wary of power aggregations unchecked by market or political forces. For example, some suggest that small, disorganized units have little weight in political decisionmaking, while larger units will more often invest in the political system and thus have a disproportionate influence. Such processes may be representative when all actors are small, but the fear is that they will be dominated by a few when some organizations are large. Of course, in some instances smaller firms manage to organize and to obtain their own special interest legislation at the expense of consumers.

(d) Fairness in economic behavior. Competition may promote fairness in the sense of prices close to cost and of alternatives for buyers and sellers. Fairness in other, more usual senses is more a supplement to competition than a product of it. Some kinds of unfair practices threaten to eliminate competition. Examples are false advertising, boycotts against competitors to influence their conduct, and temporary and excessively low prices designed to drive another out of business. The control or elimination of this kind of unfairness is an essential part of any policy that would preserve competition.

But fairness is a vagrant claim. It may call for forbearance from the use of market power — for "reasonable" rather than market

---

54. Chief Justice Warren was ready to sacrifice real cost savings in order to achieve dispersal of power in *Brown Shoe Co. v. United States*, 370 U.S. 294, 344 (1962):

> [W]e cannot fail to recognize Congress' desire to promote competition through the protection of viable, small, locally owned businesses. Congress appreciated that occasional higher costs and prices might result from the maintenance of fragmented industries and markets. It resolved these competing considerations in favor of decentralization. We must give effect to that decision.

55. The Nader report contains a vigorous indictment of big business on this count. Green, note 5, at 17-21.

prices. Unequal bargaining power is often called unfair. Competition itself is sometimes called unfair. As will be seen in Chapter 4A, so-called fair trade laws sought to reduce one dimension of competition, as did pro-cartel policies of the early 1930s. Sentiment against unfairness is reflected in the almost universal provision of regulatory statutes forbidding discrimination. It is also reflected in the Robinson-Patman Act, considered in Chapter 6.

(e) *Economic stabilization.* Economists have advanced countless theories attempting to explain the determinants of unemployment and inflation. Since the time of the Great Depression, some have suggested that monopolistic or oligopolistic market structures may play a role. One commonly advanced thesis is that such industries are less flexible in response to price changes, at least in the short run. In a depression, prices would not be reduced sufficiently (or at all), thus contributing to unemployment. The contrary result could occur during an expansionary period: Prices might not increase as rapidly as in competitive industries because monopolists may not quickly reflect cost changes completely in price and oligopolists always fear that price changes might destabilize their informal coordination.

Another common argument is that monopoly and oligopoly contribute to inflation because they price higher than would perfect competitors. This point simply misunderstands the definition of inflation, which refers to the *rate* at which prices increase rather than to absolute price levels. For example, if a monopolist begins with prices 50 percent above the competitive level and inflation is running at 10 percent, there is no obvious reason that the monopolist's prices would increase any more rapidly than 10 percent.

Additional arguments have been advanced as well, but existing evidence and theory do not provide any strong basis for preferring or condemning market concentration on macroeconomic grounds. The most plausible effects are not likely to be that significant in the long run, and other policies relating to unemployment and inflation — such as monetary and fiscal policy — are probably of far greater importance than antitrust policy in this realm.

Possible Grounds for Deemphasizing Competition

118. The example of public restraints. In some situations, atomistic competition has been explicitly qualified or completely abandoned.[56] We mention a few. (1) Monopoly is considered worth the price, at least for a limited period, as a reward for new inventions. Thus, the patent system confers a legally protected monopoly

56. See ¶¶109-110, 160-162, 179-181.

on inventors in order to stimulate invention. (2) In "natural monopoly" situations, best illustrated by some local public utilities, competition may not arise and cannot survive. Public regulation takes its place. (3) There are other industries that many believe are subject either to unwholesome monopoly or the vices of excessive competition. On these grounds, railroads, trucks, airlines, and shipping firms were once subjected to a regime of direct regulation in which competition was mainly but not entirely displaced, although the past decades have witnessed substantial deregulation of many facets of transportation. (4) For quite different reasons, the states are given precedence in the control of certain activities, such as the liquor and insurance businesses. (5) For yet other reasons, certain combinations prohibited in domestic commerce are permitted in the export trade. (6) National security interests are sometimes considered inconsistent with competition. Only the federal government, for example, can make certain nuclear substances and devices. In addition, it is sometimes suggested that industrial capacity must be preserved as part of the "mobilization base," or that exploration of domestic fuel and raw material sources must be stimulated so that the nation can adequately defend itself in time of war. (7) In several areas there is a widespread conviction that competition is too harsh, or at least that producers should have more than competition gives them. For example, the individual seller of labor or of wheat is thought to be unfairly disadvantaged in dealing with large and powerful buyers on the other side of the market. Collective bargaining and agricultural price supports have traditionally been justified on this ground. Another variation is weakness relative to the rest of society. This is the problem of "sick" or declining industries and communities in which displaced workers seem unable or unwilling to find alternative employment. When affirmative government assistance seems too expensive or too obvious to be politically feasible, these groups have sometimes been permitted by statute to organize in ways generally condemned by the antitrust laws.

Competition, then, is not universally regarded as worthwhile. Indeed, the fabric of restraint woven by government is so extensive that private restraints may seem trivial in comparison. But that fact can hardly justify private restraints.

119. Economies of scale. (a) *Efficiency and firm size.* Efficiency — here in the sense of production and distribution at minimum cost — is often said to require bigness in business. Specialization of labor and complicated production techniques can be exploited more fully when production runs are long. Large high-capacity machines are more profitable if their costs can be spread over a wide base of activity. And process industries like petroleum refining enjoy "natural" economies of scale.[57]

But bigness can breed its own higher costs. Its bureaucracy may become unwieldly, its communications fouled, and its management unrealistic. Although improved communications and computer technology may widen the span of effective management control, other new technological forces are pushing for operations on a smaller scale. Long-distance transmission of electricity and truck transportation allow decentralization. New materials and new processes require less heavy machinery than before. Multipurpose machines may reduce the need for the massive installations of yesterday. Personal computers permit very small businesses to perform complex tasks at negligible cost. Of course, technological change can also increase the size of the minimum efficient plant.

If larger size permits cost reductions and if some firms achieve such economies, their rivals must seek the same economies in order to survive. Thus, large-firm economies raise the specter of increasing concentration. But even if scale economies lead to monopoly pricing, the cost savings may be so substantial that a monopolist's profit-maximizing price and output would be more favorable, or no less favorable than if the market had a large number of less efficient firms. Even if the substitution of market power for competitive structures should lead to higher prices, there would still be a trade-off between the welfare loss from restricted output and the welfare gain from the savings in resources; and it has been demonstrated that in welfare terms a relatively modest cost reduction may offset a relatively large price increase.[58]

As noted in ¶502, however, concentration has not actually increased in this manner. One reason may be that economies of scale are a function of a firm's absolute size, which may be large although it occupies a small share of a large national market. But another reason may be that small plants can be efficient. Bear in mind, however, that the size of individual plants does not reflect the possible economies of the multiplant firm with respect to research, promotion, distribution, management, or risk diversification.

(b) *Data.* Efficiency statistics are both scanty and relatively crude. The pioneering data are those compiled by Professor Bain.[59] He

57. The cost of pipes and storage tanks, for example, increases as the surface area of this equipment increases, whereas their output increases as their volume increases. Hence, process industries can double their output without doubling their costs.

58. O. Williamson, Economies as an Antitrust Defense: The Welfare Tradeoffs, 58 Am. Econ. Rev. 18 (1968).

59. Bain, note 39, at 53-93; J. Bain, Economics of Scale, Concentration, and the Condition of Entry in Twenty Manufacturing Industries, 44 Am. Econ. Rev. 15 (1954).

gathered some engineering estimates of the smallest efficient plant size for 20 industries. This optimal plant would be the smallest one capable of enjoying the lowest possible unit costs of production. His statistics suggested that efficiency can usually be achieved at relatively low levels of national capacity. Note, of course, that small shares of national capacity can imply significant levels of concentration in narrower geographic or product submarkets.

Other statistical and accounting studies reach similar, although not identical, conclusions. The study by Professor Scherer and others of 12 industries showed that in only one would scale economies require a plant output in excess of 10 percent of national sales, and the figure in that industry was 14 percent.[60] Of course, such studies understate the impact of scale economies where the true market is regional rather than national. With respect to firm-size economies, the Scherer study showed that multiplant economies raised from one to two the number of industries in which four-firm national concentration ratios in excess of 50 percent might be required.

(c) *Implications.* One may conclude that seller concentration in many industries is either moderately higher or much higher than required for least-cost production. Firms with relatively small shares of large markets may be large enough in absolute size to achieve all possible economies of scale. As a technological matter, therefore, many large, multiplant firms with large market shares could be reorganized into firms the size of one optimal plant, with a substantial reduction in seller concentration but without sacrificing economies of scale. But any such conclusion must be qualified because of possible multiplant economies in research, promotion, distribution, management, and risk pooling. Another possibility is that some large firms might be more efficient because of unusually skilled management, which one might be unable to maintain if a firm were restructured into many separate entities. The evidence is very elusive.

In addition to the "technological" economies of scale considered in this Paragraph, many large firms enjoy "pecuniary" economies of scale to some degree, for example, higher discounts for volume advertising or lower rates for heavy utility use not related to resource savings. Unlike technological economies, these pecuniary economies do not represent long-run savings in the use of socially valued resources. And they may raise barriers to entry in some cases. Indeed, pecuniary economies may be a euphemism for the surplus profits made possible by monopoly on the buyer's side of the market. Monopsony, as buyer monopoly is called, spoils economic efficiency just as seller monopoly does. Consequently, restructuring of large firms can hardly be resisted on the ground that it would deprive them of pecuniary economies.

60. Scherer, et al., note 3; see also Scherer & Ross, note 2, at 97-141.

120.   Invention and innovation.[61] *(a) The argument.* In the long run, technological progress contributes far more to consumer welfare than does the elimination of the allocative inefficiencies discussed in ¶113.[62] The course of technological progress is largely controlled by the pace of innovative activity. According to an argument associated with Professor Schumpeter, that pace is quickened by firms with considerable market power.[63] Such power guarantees them a stable future conducive to planning and heavy investment in new technology. It protects them from imitators and thus allows them to reap for themselves all the gains of their innovative activity. It provides them with both the resources and incentives to finance risky research and development and to invest in the results.[64]

(b) Size. Market power is loosely related to size. But contrary to Schumpeter's contention, it has not been established that big firms produce most new ideas. Some authorities concluded that more than two-thirds of the "most important" inventions early in this century were made by independent researchers.[65] But because there is no satisfactory measure of invention, others have turned to relative inputs (research and development expenditures) and outputs (patents). Neither is satisfactory. Nevertheless, it appears that firms with more than 5000 employees spend 88 percent of private research and development (R&D) dollars but receive only 50 percent of the patents issued.[66] Furthermore, R&D expenditures are not proportional to size. The ratio of R&D outlays to sales increases as firm size increases only up to firms with 5000 employees. Above that size, smaller than a single automobile plant, the ratio of R&D outlays to sales falls slightly as firm size increases.

Big firms assume a larger role in the innovative translation of a new idea into a marketable product or process. Innovation can be very expensive. du Pont invested 12 years and $27 million before it marketed its first pound of nylon in 1940. Color television cost RCA $65 million to develop. And private investment in commercial jet-

---

61. Most of the data and illustrations in this Paragraph are taken from Scherer and Ross, note 2, ch. 17, which the reader is encouraged to consult.

62. Technological progress is an important determinant of the rate of growth of real income. If technological progress could be stimulated to raise real income growth from 3 to 4 percent a year, then imperfect competition's inefficiencies, grossly estimated at note 34 to be under 2 percent of real income, would be outdistanced within two years.

63. J. Schumpeter, Capitalism, Socialism, and Democracy, chs. 7-8 (1942).

64. Professor Schumpeter also argued that market power is rather quickly eroded over the long run by innovation, a process he called "creative destruction."

65. J. Jewkes, D. Sawers & R. Stillerman, The Sources of Invention 71-90 (1958).

66. A single invention may result in one or several dozen patents. Inventions differ widely in their import for consumer welfare. The connection is not strong, therefore, between the number of patents issued to a firm and the contribution of its inventions to the pace of progress.

liner development has sometimes exceeded $100 million. Most in-
novation, however, is not prohibitively expensive for small- and
medium-sized firms. One study concluded that the most frequently
occurring size of all development projects is approximately $1 mil-
lion in 1987 dollars, although that figure has been rising.[67]

(c) *Concentration.* The relationship between technological progress and market power is difficult to assess. Many studies seem to
show a positive correlation between industry concentration and
R&D expenditures per unit of sales.[68] It is possible that market-
dominating firms will have much to fear by rivals' innovations and
thus will invest heavily in their own innovation or in copying rivals.[69] Nonetheless, important inventions are often made by
others.[70] Also, oligopolists may find tacit coordination of R&D
rather difficult, allowing innovation to become an intensive form of
nonprice competition among them.[71] By contrast, firms in extremely competitive industries may not be able to obtain sufficient
profits or predictability to justify extensive research. Evidence suggests that industries where the largest four firms accounted for less
than 15 percent of sales do suffer from a major lack of innovation
incentives, but that these R&D incentives peak when the four-firm
concentration reaches 50 to 55 percent.[72]

(d) *Synthesis.* Although much research is financed directly by the
government or is performed in academic institutions and thus is
presumably immune from the effects of the market structure on
innovation, the overwhelming majority of consumer-oriented products derives from investments in R&D that put company funds directly at risk.[73] The influence of market power on innovative activity
is thus confined to only a portion of the nation's R&D budget.
Within this range, independent researchers, small business, and
new entrants of all types originate a disproportionate share of new
ideas. Perfecting and marketing these insights often, but not always,
require the efforts of somewhat larger firms. Moreover, these larger
firms are frequently knitted together into loose oligopolies and thus
find their innovative activity further stimulated as part of their
nonprice competition. Some concentration, therefore, may be con-

67. Scherer & Ross, note 2, at 619-620.

68. Id. at 646.

69. See ¶331.

70. See J. Baker, Fringe Firms and Incentives to Innovate, 63 Antitrust L.J. 621
(1995).

71. See ¶¶112c, 116, 230e; F.M. Scherer, Research and Development Resource
Allocation Under Rivalry, 81 Q.J. Econ. 359 (1967).

72. Scherer & Ross, note 2, at 646.

73. See id. at 615 (although a third of industrial R&D was financed by the government, most was for military and space projects).

ducive to innovation. Additional concentration probably has little effect, positive or negative.[74]

121. Adjustment pains. A competitive economy responding to changes in tastes, technologies, and scarcities inflicts losses on entrepreneurs, investors, workers, and communities. In today's affluent society, is the efficiency of this adjustment process worth these losses? We are, it is true, a rich society, and our wealth excuses many of our follies, or at least makes them tolerable. We can afford to cushion economic adjustment through government subsidies to dislocated individuals and communities, but affluence cannot make waste desirable or even tolerable on a regular, permanent, and cumulative basis. The longer necessary adjustment is delayed, the greater its cost, and the more difficult the ultimate reckoning may be.

122. Social responsibility. Most large, powerful firms attempt to maximize the return on their investments. Factors that push a firm toward profit maximization include: (1) stockholder rather than management control, (2) stock ownership by firm executives or the use of stock options and other profit-related bonuses for management, (3) use of profit centers to simulate competitive price-market conditions in divisions and subsidiaries, and (4) the prospect of a takeover by another firm.[75] We might well prefer generally to rely on profit maximization to guide production and leave social objectives to individuals and their social institutions, including government. Yet, perceived deficiencies in those institutions sometimes tempt us to welcome the existence of private market power that contributes toward "good" ends. But most private power will not be used for appropriate social objectives. To tolerate otherwise remediable excesses of power would be to pay a great price in distortion, waste, and other misbehavior in order to capture a relatively small benefit. Yet, there might be specific instances in which the claim of social virtue may redeem anticompetitive acts or at least mitigate the application of antitrust rules.[76]

74. This is the conclusion of Scherer and Ross, id. at 647-648. Only in industries where technological opportunities are small is increasing concentration noticeably associated with innovative activity. In all other industries, the association is slight, nonexistent, or negative.

75. Under one version of a profit center regime, firm headquarters will tell a division manager the prices at which inputs can be purchased from other divisions of the firm and the range of products to be produced. Headquarters will evaluate its divisions on the basis of profits produced, given the input prices and product choices specified centrally. See O. Williamson, Managerial Discretion, Organizational Form, and the Multi-Division Hypothesis, in The Corporate Economy (R. Marris & A. Wood eds. 1971).

76. The Supreme Court has taken a negative view of this notion in applying the antitrust laws. See *Engineers,* Ch. 2B. Such claims are sometimes advanced by non-

123.   Countervailing power. There are those who believe that power tends to beget opposing power, that economic power is checked by power on the opposite side of the market.[77] It is true that powerful buyers who can credibly threaten to integrate backward into self-supply may be able to obtain competitive prices even from concentrated suppliers. It may also be that oligopolistic sellers will compete in price in order to obtain the patronage of especially large buyers. But these circumstances are not themselves induced by concentration among sellers, and a benefit to the ultimate consumer depends on the existence of substantial competition among those powerful buyers in the markets in which they sell to consumers.

124.   The theory of second best. The problem of the second best, as economists refer to it, is that fixing something that is broken is desirable when everything else works perfectly but not necessarily when related systems also malfunction. That is, two wrongs may be right, or at least better than a single wrong. Fixing a bad bearing that drags a car in one direction would worsen the situation if there is another uncorrected (or uncorrectable) flaw dragging the car in the opposite direction. If the best solution of correcting both flaws is not available, the second best approach may be to leave the bad bearing uncorrected. That is, we cannot be sure that improving one flaw will actually make us better off as long as other imperfections remain.

The identified flaw might best be left undisturbed, for it may be offsetting some other undetected or uncorrectable problem and therefore should not really be considered a flaw at all. True enough, but few are so agnostic as to be totally immobilized in the public policy area or otherwise. In general, we deem it prudent to correct such flaws as we can, with careful attention to identifiable possibilities that the cure may be worse than the disease and, where feasible, with subsequent readjustment after observing the results of the cure.

In the antitrust context, the second best argument begins by noting that the effect of monopoly is to decrease output in the monopolized sector, inefficiently shifting resources to other sectors. If, by chance, every market except wheat were irremediably monopolized, too many resources would have been shifted to wheat production, and a wheat cartel might be just the right step to move resources out of wheat and thereby allocate resources efficiently

---

profit institutions. See *Brown University,* Ch. 2B, note 30; Ch. 5D, note 36 (non-profit hospitals).

77. Compare J.K. Galbraith, American Capitalism: The Concept of Countervailing Power (1952), with Scherer & Ross, note 2, at 527-536.

among the various sectors of the economy. To condemn such a wheat cartel could worsen consumer welfare. Although the example is extreme, it shows that the inevitably episodic use of antitrust law could hurt the economy.

To this argument for suspending the antitrust laws, there are several responses. In some situations, competitive pricing is optimal despite widespread monopoly elsewhere.[78] In addition, monopoly is not everywhere except for a few antitrust targets. Also, competitive policy might be supported by reference to goals other than efficiency. In any event, until repealed, the antitrust statutes mandate a policy in favor of competition.

Workable Competition[79]

125. The problem. Even the preceding summary presentation suggests that antitrust policy is inevitably a complex matter. The institutions of antitrust law are not capable of effecting atomistic competition in all markets, nor would that objective seem desirable for our society as it may interfere with productive efficiency or with innovation. Political and social concerns interact with these economic values. And the cost of restructuring would be immense. Not only would there be the disruption, idle resources, and increased uncertainty of reorganizing firms and markets, but collecting and evaluating the data necessary to make intelligent decisions would itself consume vast resources. Nor would we be sure, after all is done, that economic welfare would be improved sufficiently to compensate for the costs (including the mistakes) of doing so. In antitrust law, as elsewhere, the lack of solid evidence often means that analysis will remain at least somewhat speculative.

Nevertheless, it can be said that the antitrust laws are not demonstrably unwise in promoting competition and in challenging the impediments to it. Ensuring that there is at least some rivalry can tend toward the results of the competitive model, although less

---

78. See Scherer & Ross, note 2, at 33-38. In particular, they point out that total monopoly will not result in an efficient configuration of inputs, outputs, and distribution when "price elasticities of demand" at equilibrium are not equal in each market. The chances of such equality occurring naturally are negligible. It is possible to imagine a price control system that would force every seller to set its price at a uniform ratio to its marginal cost, but this could achieve efficiency only if workers increased their valuation of leisure in the same proportion. Furthermore, because many goods are sold to be used as intermediate products in producing other goods, equal monopoly in the production of each good would not be equal monopoly in the production of final products.

79. See, e.g., id., at 52-55.

precisely ~~or inevitably~~ so. Rivalry tends to keep costs and prices lower and quality higher than monopoly would. It provides a stimulus to more efficient production, to lower costs, and thus to lower prices. It also tends to induce resources to move out of areas of declining demand and into industries of increasing demand — with, to be sure, time lags and imperfections.

But, of course, the question is: How much rivalry? And how can it be tested? It is said that an imperfect market whose results are reasonably compatible with general economic welfare is workably competitive. Workable competition is not a precise concept, nor is it intended to be. It directs our attention to practical approximations rather than the hypothetical, rarely existing extreme of "perfect" competition.

126. Criteria. Behavioral criteria have long been the staple ingredient of laws designed to protect competition. For example, each firm should make its production and marketing decisions — especially on price and output — independently and without collusion with its competitors. Firms should not attempt to exclude or eliminate rivals from the market except through competition "on the merits." The chief difficulty with behavioral criteria is that it is often difficult to distinguish predatory behavior toward rivals from vigorous competition.

Another criterion for judging whether a market is workably competitive is its actual performance. The following appear to be general signs of nonworkable competition:[80] (1) profits persistently above usual investment returns, (2) "scale of many firms seriously outside the optimal range," (3) "considerable chronic excess capacity not justified by secular change or reasonable stand-by provision," (4) "excessive" selling costs, and (5) "persistent lag in adoption of cost-reducing technical changes or persistent suppression of product changes which would advantage buyers."

> A market could be considered a case of unworkable competition if it had an extremely bad rating in any direction or moderately bad or suspicious ratings in several. . . . For criteria of tolerable deviations, we have little more than the ad hoc judgments of the observer concerning what might be had and how serious the adverse impact of a given deviation is. In view of all this, any economist's assessment of the workability of competition is likely to have a highly provisional and even personal character and is likely to rest heavily on the ad hoc assessment of obvious alternatives in given situations.

80. The following list and quotations are from J. Bain, Workable Competition in Oligopoly: Theoretical Considerations and Some Empirical Evidence, 40 Am. Econ. Rev. 35, 37-38 (1950) (reproduced by permission of the American Economic Association).

In addition, the evidence itself will often be ambiguous. Consider profit rates. High returns might be attributable to rapidly growing demand for the industry's product or, for a particular firm, superior production resources or managerial skill. Perhaps, however, such competitive explanations become less likely as the period of high profits is more prolonged. Low profits are also ambiguous. They may indicate intense rivalry and close-to-cost prices or they may represent collusion with inflated costs or sluggish motivations. Nevertheless, such data may become more meaningful when considered together with (1) other performance indicators and (2) market structure and behavior.

The key structural variables bearing on workable competition are (1) the number and size distribution of sellers and (2) the conditions of entry by other firms into the market. Whatever the number of producers, competitive results are more likely when barriers to entry by new producers are relatively low.[81] And competitive results will be approached more closely as buyers and sellers are more numerous.[82] Each increase in the number of traders makes coordinated behavior more difficult because each trader may prefer a different mix of prices, products, promotion, and progressiveness. Moreover, once a collective decision is reached, whether tacitly or expressly, each additional firm makes enforcement of this decision more difficult. Problems of surveillance and communication may grow exponentially with the number of traders. Each increase in the number of firms also increases the probability of a "maverick," one who habitually refuses to follow collective decisions. Finally, because at least someone's market share is reduced, each increase in the number of traders tends to dampen everyone's sensitivity to their mutual interdependence. Each firm tends to feel less willing and able to take account of the effect of its actions on its rivals.

When other things are equal, therefore, more firms are better. But at what point is the fewness of rivals likely to threaten competition? Some have suggested that a market would ordinarily be workably competitive when there are five to ten "effective" rivals, where the largest firm does not exceed 20 to 33 percent of the market.[83] Others suggest that firms begin seriously to take each other into account when there are as few as eight firms with two-thirds or more of a market.[84]

---

81. See ¶114.

82. See ¶¶228-231.

83. Report of the Task Force on Productivity and Competition (1969), reprinted in 1 J. Reprints Antitr. L. & Econ. 829 (1969).

84. R. Caves, American Industry: Structure, Conduct, Performance 107 (5th ed. 1982).

Predictability and low-cost administration sometimes justify the use of simple decision rules focusing on firm numbers, market shares, or concentration. Nevertheless, the serious and inevitable deficiencies in the use of such rules should be appreciated. To preview Chapter 3B, a few points may be mentioned. Such numbers are only as meaningful as the market definition on which they are based. Even if the market were defined as precisely as possible, the characteristics of demand might allow relatively little power even to a single-firm monopolist to exploit buyers or distort resource allocation. Available substitutes might properly be excluded from the market definition and yet narrow significantly the capacity of the firms in that market to act anticompetitively. Entry might be relatively easy. Or effective oligopolistic coordination might be seriously impaired because transactions are secret, infrequent, or highly differentiated, because the firms, although few in number, differ greatly in costs or attitudes, because the industry is highly capital-intensive, or because there is a fringe of firms capable of expanding output significantly. On the other hand, when such factors are notably absent, the opposite inference — one suggesting greater than usual danger — is warranted. Such factors, together with the number and size of firms, determine how the structure of a market affects its economic performance and the likelihood of workably competitive results.

127. Summary. Real competition — as distinguished from the purely theoretical perfect competition — is a meaningful and desirable institution for much of the economy, although not absolutely or everywhere. Competitive policy is not a road to Utopia or a complete basis for public policy. We must not overemphasize its contribution to human welfare nor overlook the serious burdens of government-created cartels and inefficiencies. Yet, competitive policy can often prevent the defects of social organization from being made worse by deliberate adoption of restrictive policies designed to serve private interests. It is no panacea, but it does prove useful.

1B. ENACTING THE ANTITRUST LAWS

128. Common-law background.[1] Although the nineteenth-century background is not crucial in contemporary applications of the antitrust laws because the statutes have grown far beyond their

---

1. See generally H. Thorelli, The Federal Antitrust Policy 12-35 (1954); W. Letwin, The English Common Law Concerning Monopolies, 21 U. Chi. L. Rev. 355 (1954).

origins, knowing where we started helps illuminate the antitrust growth process.

(a) *Middleman offenses.* The common law had addressed itself to competition through five concepts of shifting content. Oldest were the middleman offenses. Indictable at common law and under statutes as early as 1266 were buying goods before they came to the general market (forestalling), buying in bulk and selling in smaller quantities (regrating), or buying crops in the field before they were harvested or at least before they were sent to the market (engrossing). These occasionally enforced prohibitions concerning foods reflected the belief that middlemen enhanced prices without performing any useful social function. It was customarily assumed that middlemen were attempting to corner the market, escape market-price regulation by trading outside it, or avoid paying fees to the monopolist holding the royal franchise for a town market. When local trading gave way to a more national economy needing middlemen, these prohibitions were ignored long before repeal of the statutory offenses in 1772 and abolition of the common-law crimes in 1844. The middleman offenses never achieved importance in the United States.

(b) *Monopoly.* English towns often restricted trading by strangers in order to protect entrenched local interests. Courts sometimes held that the municipal charter did not authorize such restrictions. This ultra vires notion was also used to control some of the excessively monopolistic practices of the guilds. In the famous *Case of Monopolies,*[2] Queen Elizabeth had granted the plaintiff the sole right to import playing cards into England. In a suit against defendant importer of playing cards, the court held the monopoly "utterly void because contrary to the common law." Monopoly was seen to harm actual and potential competitors, deprive others of the opportunity to practice a trade, and injure the public through inevitably higher prices and poorer quality. As for Queen Elizabeth, the court rationalized its position by saying that she had been deceived in her grant. In opposition to such Crown grants, Parliament enacted the Statute of Monopolies in 1623 to void "all" monopolies, but with significant exceptions for limited patents for inventors and new manufacturers, customary monopolies held by the towns and the guilds for the ordering of trade, and all Parliamentary grants.[3]

References to monopolies effected neither by quasi-public organizations nor by sovereign grant appear only in dicta. The English courts occasionally said that a private agreement having the effect of establishing a clear-cut, powerful, and absolute monopoly would

2. Darcy v. Allein, 11 Coke 84, 77 Eng. Rep. 1260 (K.B. 1603).
3. 21 Jac. 1, ch. 3 (1623).

be void. That degree of private power is very rare. And while the courts declared that a "pernicious monopoly" would be illegal even though not absolute, perniciousness was not elaborated, and there seems to be no English case applying the doctrine.

(c) *Restraints of trade. Mitchel v. Reynolds*[4] was an action of debt upon a bond enforcing a baker's covenant incident to the sale of his bakery to the plaintiff. Defendant had promised not to compete for five years in the immediate locality. Such promises ancillary to a lawful transaction had been held unenforceable in earlier cases — not because they might limit competition but from the fear that artisans deprived of their trade would become a burden on the public. Thus, it was not only for the good of their souls that the early courts believed that those with a trade should practice it. At a time when trade was tightly controlled by the guilds and towns, a promise not to practice one's trade locally meant that it could not be practiced anywhere. The earlier view was gradually relaxed, and the *Mitchel* case enforced the covenant with the proposition that trade restraints may be justified as reasonable if ancillary to some principle transaction and if limited in time and space. *Nordenfelt v. Maxim Nordenfelt Guns & Ammunition Co.*[5] stated the general rule that

> [1] All interference with individual liberty of action in trading, and all restraints of trade ... are contrary to public policy. ... [2] [but] may be justified ... if the restriction is reasonable — [a] reasonable, that is, in reference to the interests of the parties concerned and [b] reasonable in reference to the interests of the public, [and c] so framed and so guarded as to afford adequate protection to the [parties without injuring the public].

But the exceptions soon engulfed the rule. The parties themselves were held to be the best judges of what is reasonable between them. Reasonableness in terms of the public interest came to be presumed in the absence of contrary proof, which could not be established because the courts refused to admit evidence of the general economic conditions of the marketplace. The English courts came to uphold "naked" restraints not ancillary to otherwise lawful transactions. They even enforced price-fixing agreements. While the American courts were usually less hospitable to private restraints, the decisions varied from state to state.

(d) *Conspiracy.* Common-law conspiracy doctrines condemned otherwise lawful acts done by several persons with the intent to accomplish an unlawful objective (or unlawful means used to effect proper objectives). "Unlawful" in this context meant "contrary to

4. 1 P. Wms. 181, 24 Eng. Rep. 347 (K.B. 1711).
5. [1894] A.C. 535, 565.

public policy," but this doctrine had little application as English public policy came to tolerate even naked restraints. A combination to commit a tort remained an illegal conspiracy. Combinations of workers in labor unions were challenged as tortious or criminal conspiracies until Parliament began the modern reform of British labor law in the 1870-1875 period. Combining competitors injuring another were left within the common-law regime until the House of Lords effectively destroyed the action in 1891.[6] In the United States, conspiracy doctrines were briefly applied mostly to labor activities and had little impact on the regulation of commercial competition.

(e) *Limiting corporate powers.* A few state courts invalidated corporate combinations formed for the main purpose of eliminating or restricting competition. This was done on the grounds that the participating corporations had acted beyond their corporate powers. This ultra vires doctrine was seldom applied even in the few states that ventured to innovate in this area.

129. Political background. (a) *Reform sentiment.* The post-Civil War United States boomed tremendously. The population settled the open spaces of the West, crisscrossed the country with railroads, and expanded manufacturing; and their numbers, swelled by continuing immigration, sweated in the mills and filled the cities. The economic growth rate was enviable. But explosive economic growth is never easy, and in the second half of the nineteenth century, periodic depressions ruined many, and the excesses of industrial and financial buccaneers generated both scandal and oppression.

Agrarian discontent furnished strong and often persistent pressure toward reform. The farmers were numerous and they formed political organizations, such as the National Grange. They were distressed because they received low agricultural prices while paying high prices for farm equipment and other manufactures because of monopolies and import tariffs. Harried by high and discriminatory railroad and grain elevator charges, they were also oppressed by tight credit and high interest rates exacted by the eastern money magnates, whose opposition to easier money and silver coinage "crucified" the West "upon a cross of gold," in William Jennings

6. Mogul S.S. Co. v. McGregor Gow & Co., [1892] A.C. 25 (1891). Defendant shipping lines formed a cartel that fixed freight rates, divided cargoes, gave rebates to shippers dealing exclusively with the cartel, and preyed on nonmember competitors. The Lords held for the defendant on the ground that only malicious action is tortious. They defined maliciousness in terms only of disinterested malice, unrelated to the competitive interests of the actors. Thus, there would be no tort whenever the combining competitors seek to promote their own trading interests, as they usually do.

Bryan's immortal words. Dissatisfaction with manufacturers of farm machinery and other goods, railroads, and eastern financiers became a cry against monopoly, a cry that also came to voice the frustrations of urban dislocation. Long hours, child labor, crowded slums, and related conditions reinforced the pressure toward reform.

Business, especially big business, hardly behaved with today's decorum. Industrial expansion created many new firms, but the promoters and would-be monopolists absorbed many through mergers — some voluntary, but many coerced by tycoons of the day who could threaten "sell or be ruined" and who had both the power and the audacity to mean it. Predatory practices — secret rebates from the railroads for favorite customers (usually the monopolies), local price cutting to drive out a competitor, pressure against a competitor's customers, suppliers, or creditors — were thought to be both outrageously unfair and widely prevalent. Cartels fixed prices, controlled output, and thus exploited consumers. Many markets seemed to exhibit either "predatory, cutthroat competition" or none at all. And lending color to anticompetitive conduct were financial scandal and corruption on an elegant scale, worthless stock, unashamed market manipulation, and bribery of public officials. Each exposure shocked the public conscience and helped create the demand for some sort of action. It was not unnoticed that much of the scandal was tied to the trusts, monopolies, and railroads. Lord Bryce observed that many people in the United States had come to feel that private enterprise, which sometimes acted "in combination, has developed with unexpected strength in unexpected ways, overshadowing individuals and even communities, and showing that the very freedom of association . . . may, under the shelter of law, ripen into a new form of tyranny."[7]

(b) *Political manifestations.* The record proves neither the overwhelming public clamor often asserted nor the indifferent public attitudes asserted by a few. There is, for example, more evidence of populist and Granger agitation for inflation than for antitrust. But even if not overwhelming, some popular concern was evident, and that might well have been enough because an age of reform was beginning. Congress did not choose regulation or state enterprise, as some advocated, but trusted market competition if kept free of private restraints. Some regard this as entirely natural because the Congress generally, and the Senate particularly, reflected business attitudes. And, in any event, despite scandals and dissatisfaction, faith in the market and private enterprise was widespread. Perhaps that reflected the optimism of the frontier spirit or of the United States's manifest destiny to achieve affluence. On the other hand,

7. 2 J. Bryce, The American Commonwealth 540 (1895).

there are those who see the Sherman Act not as a testament to competition but as a modest measure of appeasement by powerful business interests of the day who purposely invoked the vague and seemingly innocuous language of the common law. That interpretation is a possible one, although it is not reflected in the language of congressional discussion, which was that of opposition to monopoly and concern with the freedom of economic opportunity. But whatever the reason, Congress created the Interstate Commerce Commission in 1887 to regulate railroad power and the Sherman Act in 1890 to condemn trade restraints and monopolies.

130.   Enactment of the Sherman Act: legislative history and contemporary political understanding. (a) *Relationship of Sherman Act and common law.* In condemning monopolies and contracts, combinations, and conspiracies in restraint of trade, the Sherman Act employs terms known to the common law. In the Senate, where the Act was drafted, most of those who spoke referred to the common law. Senator Sherman himself said that language similar to that ultimately enacted "does not announce a new principle of law, but applies old and well-recognized principles of the common law."[8] But Sherman's remarks contain some contradictions as to what the common law was and what the bill might do. Senator Hoar, who was closely involved in drafting the final version in the Committee, told the Senate that "We have affirmed the old doctrine of the common law" and later said " 'monopoly' is a technical term known to the common law."[9] Senator Edmunds, who was chairman of the Judiciary Committee, spoke to the same effect.[10]

It does not follow that Congress purported to enact the common law. Congress neither specifically adopted any particular English doctrines nor those of any state. Neither the statute nor its legislative history gives any concrete meaning to "restraint of trade," and the §2 reference to "monopolize" is even less clear because the monopoly known to the common law was that granted or held by public or quasi-public authority. Thus, the use of unelaborated common-law words and references seems simply to have invested the federal courts with a new jurisdiction. When Senator Hoar was asked why Congress should bother to denounce monopoly, if it were already prohibited at common law, he replied: "Because there is not any common law of the United States."[11]

8. 21 Cong. Rec. 2456 (1890). See also W. Letwin, Law and Economic Policy in America 96 (1965); Thorelli, note 1, at 181-184.
9. 21 Cong. Rec. 3146, 3152 (1890).
10. Id. at 3152.
11. Id.

Creation of a new federal jurisdiction inevitably required the courts to receive, apply, and develop the common law in the same way that a new jurisdiction customarily does. Perhaps the enactment of the Sherman Act itself could be taken as a legislative indication of the proper direction. As the following excerpts indicate, however, the legislative history lacked careful weighing and deliberate choices on many key issues where conflicts — perhaps then largely unforeseen — have subsequently arisen. Thus, the Sherman Act may be seen not as a prohibition of specific classes of conduct but as a general authority to do what common-law courts usually do: to use certain customary techniques of judicial reasoning, to consider the reasoning and results of other common-law courts, and to develop, refine, and innovate in the dynamic common-law tradition. But since the antitrust laws clearly constitute a departure from the substantive content of preexisting common law, one must ask where such development should begin and by what substantive values it should be guided. At this broader level, the legislative history does provide some information. Yet much ambiguity remains, and one must also consider the weight to be given to such history that inevitably reflects a different stage in the country's economic development and in the understanding of how the economy functions.

Lively dispute rages over identifying and implementing those legislative goals.[12] That debate may appear more acrimonious than informative because several distinct issues are often mixed together and the debate is often conducted at a sterile level of abstraction that has little bearing on how courts do or should decide actual cases. More sense can be made out of the immediately following material by constantly asking how a general value or purpose underlying the antitrust laws helps us to solve particular cases. Whatever the goals may be, the facts and theories necessary for their imple-

---

12. Representative samples include: I P. Areeda & D. Turner, Antitrust Law, ch. 1B (1978); R. Bork, The Antitrust Paradox: A Policy at War with Itself, ch. 2 (rev. ed. 1993); L. Kaplow, Antitrust, Law & Economics, and the Courts, 50 L. & Contemp. Probs. 181 (1987); C. Kaysen & D. Turner, Antitrust Policy, ch. 3 (1959); R. Lande, Wealth Transfers as the Original and Primary Concern of Antitrust: The Efficiency Interpretation Challenged, 34 Hastings L.J. 65 (1982); R. Pitofsky, The Political Content of Antitrust, 127 U. Pa. L. Rev. 1051 (1979); R. Posner, Antitrust Law: An Economic Perspective, ch. 2 (1976); F.M. Scherer, Book Review, 86 Yale L.J. 974 (1977); L. Sullivan, Handbook of the Law of Antitrust, ch. 1 (1977). Rather than include excerpts from these or the many other statements concerning the appropriate goals of antitrust, we present material that discusses more directly information concerning the relevant history, leaving it to the reader through the course of the book to develop answers to the question of appropriate objectives. We do, however, close this Paragraph with some suggestions indicating that the differences often aired may be of less practical significance than might appear.

mentation will often be incomplete, obscure, or conflicting. The resolution of actual cases will therefore often depend on prevailing (and changing) assumptions about how the economy works and the relative administrability of various approaches. The question of goals is most concretely addressed by trying to identify the criteria by which to assess the "reasonableness" of an agreement among competitors "restraining" trade: Efficiency in production or resource allocation? Consumer welfare viewed in terms of lower prices that pass on savings in production costs to consumers? A preference for preserving small firms — only when other things are equal or regardless of higher production costs or higher prices to consumers? Or fairness in some sense? The debate often contrasts economic with social and political values.

(b) Senator Sherman, 12 Cong. Rec. 2455ff (1890).

> The purpose of this bill is to enable the courts of the United States to apply the same remedies against combinations . . . that have been applied in the several States. . . . It aims at unlawful combinations. It does not in the least affect combinations in aid of production where there is free and fair competition.
>
> This bill does not seek to cripple combinations of capital and labor, the formation of partnerships or of corporations, but only to prevent and control combinations made with a view to prevent competition, or for the restraint of trade, or to increase the profits of the producer at the cost of the consumer. It is the unlawful combination, tested by the rules of common law and human experience, that is aimed at by this bill, and not the lawful and useful combination. . . . If their business is lawful they can combine in any way and enjoy the advantage of their united skill and capital, provided they do not combine to prevent competition. . . .
>
> But associated enterprise and capital are not satisfied with partnerships and corporations competing with each other, and have invented a new form of combination commonly called trusts, that seeks to avoid competition by combining the controlling corporation, partnerships, and individuals engaged in the same business, and placing the power and property of the combination under the government of a few individuals, and often under the control of a single man called a trustee, a chairman, or a president.
>
> The sole object of such a combination is to make competition impossible. . . . The law of selfishness, uncontrolled by competition, compels it to disregard the interest of the consumer. . . .
>
> If we would not submit to an emperor we should not submit to an autocrat of trade, with power to prevent competition and to fix the price of any commodity. . . .
>
> I admit that it is difficult to define in legal language the precise line between lawful and unlawful combinations. This must be left for the courts to determine in each particular case. All that we, as lawmakers, can do is to declare general principles, and we can be as-

sured that the courts will apply them so as to carry out the meaning of the law, as the courts of England and the United States have done for centuries. . . .

It is sometimes said of these combinations that they reduce prices to the consumer by better methods of production, but all experience shows that this saving of cost goes to the pockets of the producer. The price to the consumer depends upon the supply, which can be reduced at pleasure by the combination. . . .

(c) H. Thorelli, The Federal Antitrust Policy 226-227 (1954).[13]

There can be no doubt that Sherman's views were typical in the sense that the vast majority of congressmen were sincere proponents of a private enterprise system founded on the principle of "full and free competition." Most of the legislators sponsoring bills or participating in debates with speeches relating to the principal issues involved made vigorous statements to this effect. But, generally speaking, little need was felt to attempt penetrating analyses of the underlying economic theory or to support the prevalent belief by extended argument — the members of Congress proclaimed "the norm of a free competition too self-evident to be debated, too obvious to be asserted." The two or three odd attacks that were made on competition as the mainspring of American progress and prosperity were given no attention, and those who launched the attacks in the end voted for the passage of the Sherman Act.

Congress believed in competition. It believed, moreover, that competition was the normal way of life in business. Competition was the "life of trade" in spite of the challenging trust and combination movement. As a general rule, business operated best when left alone. The government's natural role in the system of free private enterprise was that of a patrolman policing the highways of commerce. It is the duty of the modern patrolman to keep the road open for all and everyone and to prevent highway robbery, speeding, the running of red lights and other violations that will endanger and hence, in the end, slow down the overall movement of the traffic. Translated into the terms of commerce this means that occupations were to be kept open to all who wished to try their luck, that the individual was to be protected in his "common right" to choose his calling and that hindrances to equal opportunity were to be eliminated. Government intervention should remove obstacles to the free flow of commerce, not itself become an additional obstacle.

There can be no doubt that the Congress felt that the ultimate beneficiary in this whole process was the consumer, enjoying a continuous increase in production and commodity quality at progressively lowered prices. The immediate beneficiary legislators had in mind, however, was in all probability the small business proprietor or tradesman whose opportunities were to be safeguarded from the dangers emanating from those recently-evolving elements of business that seemed so strange, gigantic, ruthless and awe-inspiring. This is one reason why it was natural to adopt the old doctrines of the common law, doctrines whose meaning had been established largely in cases brought by business or professional people dissatisfied with the behavior of competitors. Perhaps we are even justified in saying that the Sherman Act is not to be viewed exclusively as an expression of economic policy. In safeguarding rights of the "common man" in business "equal" to those of the evolving more "ruthless" and impersonal forms of enterprise the Sherman Act embodies what is to be characterized as an eminently "social" purpose. A moderate limitation of the freedom of contract was expected to yield a maximization of the freedom of enterprise. Sherman himself, furthermore, expressed the idea probably in the minds of many of his colleagues that the legislation contemplated constituted an important means of achieving freedom from corruption and maintaining freedom of independent thinking in political life, a treasured cornerstone of democratic government. . . .

What was the relationship between the ideology of Congress and the intent manifested in the Sherman Act? Most congressmen, indeed most Americans, would say in 1890 that antitrust legislation was but the projection of the philosophy of competition on the plane of policy. According to this line of thinking there was a direct and reversible relationship between competition on the one hand and monopoly on the other. If you removed the monopolistic elements in any industry full and free competition would ensue automatically, or even ex definitione. Not until the antitrust policy had been confronted with stark realities did it dawn upon the public mind that to legislate against monopolies and restraints of trade may not necessarily be the same as to enforce, or maintain, free competition.

(d) R. Hofstadter, What Happened to the Antitrust Movement?, in The Paranoid Style in American Politics and Other Essays 205-211 (1965).[14]

The political and social arguments against monopoly were pressed with greater clarity than the economic argument and with hardly less fervor. Antitrust must be understood as the political judgment of a nation whose leaders had always shown a keen awareness of the economic foundations of politics. In this respect, the Sherman Act was simply another manifestation of an enduring American suspicion of concentrated power. From the pre-Revolutionary tracts through the Declaration of Independence and The Federalist to the writings of the states' rights advocates, and beyond the Civil War into the era of the antimonopoly writers and the Populists, there had

---

14. Reprinted by permission. This excerpt is not strictly limited to the time of enactment but rather spans the period shortly before to a couple of decades after 1890.

been a perennial quest for a way of dividing, diffusing, and checking power and preventing its exercise by a single interest or by a consolidated group of interests at a single center. Hence, the political impulse behind the Sherman Act was clearer and more articulate than the economic theory. Men who used the vaguest language when they talked about "the trusts" and monopolies, who had not thought through the distinction between size itself and monopolistic practices, who had found no way of showing how much competition was necessary for efficiency, who could not in every case say what competitive acts they thought were fair or unfair, or who could not state a rational program that reconciled their acceptance of size with their desire for competition, were reasonably clear about what it was that they were trying to avoid: they wanted to keep concentrated private power from destroying democratic government. . . .

Where power *must* be exercised, it was agreed that it should be located in governmental and not in private hands. But the state governments were inadequate; in sheer mass, business enterprises already overshadowed them. Charles William Eliot pointed out as early as 1888 that the large corporations, considered as units of economic organization, had already begun to tower over the states. A Boston railroad company, for example, employed 18,000 persons and had gross receipts of about $40,000,000 a year, whereas the Commonwealth of Massachusetts employed only 6,000 and had receipts of only $7,000,000. Even individually, some corporations were big enough to dominate state governments, and if they should combine among themselves, they might come to dominate the federal government as well.

The existence of the industrial combinations and the threat that under one auspice or another — perhaps that of the investment bankers — there would come about some day a combination of the combinations that would be stronger than civil government itself, provided a fear that haunted the minds of the writers of the industrial era, including many whose social views were . . . conservative. . . .

The third objective of antitrust action, hardly less important than the others, was psychological and moral. It sprang from the conviction that competition has a disciplinary value for character, quite aside from its strictly economic uses. America was thought to have been made possible by the particular type of character that was forged by competitive individualism, a type that had flourished in the United States because competitive opportunities had been so widespread that alert men could hardly fail to see them, to grasp and use them, and hence, to be shaped by them. The American male character was believed to have been quickened and given discipline by the sight and pursuit of opportunity. For this process to take place it was important that business be carried on fairly — the sporting vocabulary was never far below the surface — and that newcomers be able to enter the game as entrepreneurs on reasonably open terms.

The significance of this faith that competition could be relied upon to form character can be fully grasped only if we bear in mind the Protestant background of our economic thinking. Economists themselves had not been in the habit of analyzing economic relationships in purely mechanical and secular terms, and what may be said of them on this count can be said with greater force about laymen, when they thought about economic issues. Behind the American way of thinking there lay a long Protestant tradition, which tended to identify economic forces with religious and moral forces and which regarded economic processes from the standpoint of their contribution to the discipline and development of character. The economic order was not merely an apparatus for the production of goods and services; it was a set of rules for forging good conduct. Everyone is familiar, I believe, with the proposition that some of the concepts of classical economics were shaped under the influence of a kind of prudential morality in which savings and abstinence were not merely instruments of economic analysis but moral sanctions. In our time we have heard conservatives frankly condemn government fiscal policy that deviates from the prudential rules suitable to a family budget by appealing to the Puritan tradition. Such critics are the legitimate heirs of the men of the nineteenth and the early twentieth century who saw the protection of competition and its incentives as a safeguard of national morale, as a means for mobilizing and rewarding the industrious and the prudent and for penalizing those whom William Graham Sumner called "the poor and the weak, the negligent, shiftless, inefficient, silly, and imprudent . . . the idle, intemperate, and vicious." . . .

The prospect that these "fine fires of enterprise" were about to be quenched suggested that the old kind of character would be destroyed, that the old America was about to die — a reason even more imperative than mere industrial efficiency for seeking out the possibilities of antitrust action.

(e) *Antitrust policy goals in light of legislative history.* In summary, we see that the possible goals of antitrust beyond economic efficiency include consumer interests in lower prices (perhaps at the expense of productive efficiency), the political and social values of dispersed control over economic resources, multiple choices for producers and consumers free of the arbitrary dictates of monopolies or cartels, equal opportunity, and "fairness" in economic dealings. As a general proposition, most find such goals to be attractive.

Of course, these very goals are widely served by effective competition. For example, productive and allocative efficiency are opposed to price-fixing cartels and are thereby congruent with most social and political values as well. There is an important exception to this universal claim: Supercompetitive prices may help protect small businesses that are not efficient enough to survive under competition. For example, the development of the supermarket has lowered the cost of food distribution to consumers. It has also entailed the exit of numerous small grocers, meaning that there are fewer owner-managers and fewer independent economic units in this industry than there would be without supermarket chains. Even supposing (as is unlikely) that judges could have stopped the supermarket revolution, they could only have done so at the expense of the average consumer's food budget. As the excerpts indicate, concerns for small business, still expressed today, were among the factors considered at the time the Sherman Act was passed. As we shall see, antitrust courts have rejected such preferences in condemning cartels but have in some time periods been more receptive to them in other contexts.

Consider another example. Producers fix prices and manage to engage in perfect price discrimination against final consumers. This means that the last unit produced will be sold at its marginal cost. Output will be at the perfectly competitive level. This cartel will be producing as much as the perfectly competitive market would, but, of course, it will be charging many buyers far more than the competitive price. Our hypothetical defendants, and some others, would argue that no harm is done because output is not reduced. Income is merely transferred from some consumers to some producers and their shareholders and employees, and the latter are not necessarily higher in the national income distribution than the exploited consumers. Even some critics of focusing exclusively on efficiency concede this. Still, the perfectly discriminating cartel is taking from some people and giving to other people more than competition would. In the minds of many, and one suspects this is true of the 1890 legislature, consumer welfare embraces what individual consumers are entitled to expect from a competitive economy.

Finally, imagine that 100 producers of widgets compete perfectly with each other, with both output and price at the competitive level. Suppose that they somehow gang up to prevent a 101st firm from entering their market. If output and even price are the only concerns of antitrust law, should it ignore this boycott? Three considerations point toward condemnation. First, the 100 firms would be acting against their economic self-interest to devote any resources to excluding the 101st firm from the market, unless they believed it helped their profits to do so. That is, they must be assuming that there would be a price-output effect. Given that certain proof of anything is both difficult and socially costly, it is both convenient and sensible to assume that business people are acting in their own self-interest and to assume that an unambiguously exclusionary purpose tends to indicate an anticompetitive effect. Second, as a general proposition, entry opportunities free of private restraint are critical to the achievement of economic efficiency. Third, when a challenged restraint is of a type that generally impairs competition and no offsetting redeeming values are offered, it is prudent for antitrust law to condemn it without burdening the legal system with proof of a detrimental power or effect. The strong fairness claims of allowing access to markets are often entirely consistent with economic efficiency, not opposed to it.

Although there is no substitute for disciplined inquiry into how challenged arrangements actually serve or impair competition, a

healthy skepticism toward absolute and abstract statements of antitrust goals is prudent. Bear in mind, moreover, that most discussions of antitrust objectives are based only on enactment of the
Sherman Act, our oldest and most central antitrust law. As we shall
see below and later in the book, subsequent enactments may reflect
different and possibly conflicting motivations. Finally, antitrust enactments and enforcement may be understood as reflecting political interest group power rather than public-spirited objectives.[15]

131. Sherman Act: procedure and early cases. (a) *Procedure.*
Whatever the substantive content of the original Sherman Act may
have been thought to be, its administrative innovations were visible
and important. It supplemented variant state rules with a uniform
federal law. Its positive prohibitions would be far more effective
than the common law's mere refusal to enforce offensive contracts:
Restraining trade and monopolizing were to be punished as crimes;
equity's broad powers were brought to the service of antitrust policy; and private enforcement was enlisted by awarding treble damages to persons injured by antitrust violations.

(b) *Early cases.* Many of the early Supreme Court Sherman Act cases
will be discussed later. Here we note only a few salient features. Early
enforcement under the Act was modest—with many cases being
directed against labor unions[16]—and one of the most important
initial decisions held that the Sugar Trust was not engaged in interstate commerce and was therefore beyond the jurisdictional reach of
the Act.[17] There were also important victories during its first two
decades. The courts read the Sherman Act to condemn price fixing
by combining railroads, the amalgamation of two great western railroads, and the three powerful trusts that controlled meat, oil, and
tobacco. The antitrust climax of the period was the famous and
cloudy opinion of Chief Justice White in *Standard Oil Co.*[18] Although
the oil trust could have been condemned on almost any theory of the
statute, the Court declared the "rule of reason": The statute, despite
its all-inclusive language, denounces only unreasonable conduct. (We
shall worry later about its content and meaning.) The result in the
immediate case, however, was the dissolution of Standard Oil and,
shortly thereafter, American Tobacco Co.

132. The 1914 legislation. There was unhappiness with the rule
of reason from opposing quarters. To some it was the portent of

15. See F. McChesney & W. Shughart, The Causes and Consequences of Antitrust: The Public-Choice Perspective (1995).
16. See ¶161.
17. See ¶166.
18. Standard Oil Co. v. United States, 221 U.S. 1 (1911).

undue judicial hospitality for anticompetitive conduct. Others feared a vagrant judicial discretion that might condemn great industries. In 1914, new legislation was enacted. The background is summarized by Robert Cushman:

> The Sherman Antitrust Act of 1890, unlike the Interstate Commerce Act, did not set up an administrative commission to aid its enforcement. It relied for that purpose on the Department of Justice and the courts. The actual enforcement of the act did not inspire public confidence either in the adequacy of the law or in the zeal of the Attorney General in prosecuting those who violated it. A conviction that new and clarifying antitrust legislation was necessary was reenforced by the Supreme Court's announcement of the "rule of reason" in the *Standard Oil* decision of 1911. If the Sherman Act did not prohibit all restraints of trade, but only those that were unreasonable, then some way ought to be devised to let the businessmen know in advance which was which. Antitrust laws should be enforced not merely by inflicting punishments but through the steady supervision of a permanent administrative agency.
>
> The movement for an "interstate trade commission" received support from three different sources. It came first from those who were hostile to big business in all its forms and who demanded the restoration by law of the competitive system. Antitrust laws should be more detailed and more drastic. A strong commission with powers to investigate unfair trade practices would assure vigorous enforcement of the law. It could aid the courts by expert advice in working out decrees of dissolution, a job believed to have been badly fumbled in the *Standard Oil* and *American Tobacco* cases. It could secure the publicity about business organizations necessary to keep them within the law, and could give to Congress its expert recommendations for further regulatory legislation. Second, people in the business world favored a commission for wholly different reasons. They believed that the point of recognizing business combinations, if not monopolies, had been reached as the inevitable outgrowth of the modern economic order. They should be tolerated and supervised. The businessman had no way of knowing which trade practices were lawful and which were not. He favored a commission or board that would, on his request, scrutinize the conduct of his business, and either point out his unlawful conduct or give him a clean bill of health. It should not have too wide powers of publicity or of regulation but should serve as a friendly adviser to American business. It should have authority to legalize numerous trade practices that might be technical restraints of trade but that were deemed necessary to wholesome business expansion. In the third place, a substantial body of opinion believed that large interstate commerce corporations should be either licensed or incorporated under Federal law, a plan calling for an administrative commission for its adequate enforcement.
>
> President Wilson threw his weight on the side of those who urged the retention and protection of free competition, and his influence was controlling. There was to be no underwriting of business combi-

nations but there was to be administrative supervision which, combined with the sharper definitions of unlawful practices in the Clayton Act, would help the businessman to know where he stood.

Issue was sharply joined on the question of whether the new Trade Commission was to deal with "unfair methods of competition" or whether the law should attempt to define those methods with some precision. The weight of opinion was against an elaborate enumeration of such unfair practices. The Commission, under judicial supervision, could work out the exact meaning of "unfair methods of competition" as concrete cases arose. It is clear, however, that Congress expected the Commission to build up its own administrative law of unfair trade practices and not be limited rigidly to what had already been held to be unfair trade practices at common law.[19]

Similar differences of opinion were reflected in the Clayton Act, passed in the same year. Some favored absolute prohibitions while others opposed certain provisions entirely. These differences were compromised in the ultimate enactment that proscribed price discrimination (§2), sales on condition that the buyer cease dealing with the seller's competitors (§3), and certain corporate mergers (§7) "where the effect . . . may be to substantially lessen competition" or "tend to create a monopoly in any line of commerce."[20] In addition, §8 prohibited certain interlocking corporate directorates; §10 concerned common carrier transactions; and the remaining sections affected procedures.

Together, the two enactments reflected a two-pronged response to *Standard Oil*: ensuring that particular practices thought to be anticompetitive would be addressed by the antitrust laws (avoiding potential ambiguity of the rule of reason) and providing an open-ended jurisdiction for a special commission to deal with the limitless creativity of those seeking anticompetitive objectives.

19. R. Cushman, The Problem of the Independent Regulatory Commissions, in Report of United States President's Committee on Administrative Management in the Federal Government 205, 211 (1937). These statements are elaborated in R. Cushman, The Independent Regulatory Commissions 177-213 (1941). The fullest statement is G. Henderson, The Federal Trade Commission, ch. 1 (1924). See also W. Letwin, note 8, at 265-278.

20. As first passed by the House, the Clayton Bill carried criminal sanctions, various qualifications to §§2 and 7, and no qualifications to §3. The Senate version eliminated §2 and most of §3 on the ground that those practices should be dealt with in a discretionary manner by the Federal Trade Commission under its flexible authority to prevent "unfair methods of competition." The Conference Committee compromised these differences by eliminating criminal penalties, restoring the prohibitions deleted by the Senate, and incorporating the quoted "effect" clause in §§2, 3, and 7. See W. Lockhart & H. Sacks, The Relevance of Economic Factors in Determining Whether Exclusive Arrangements Violate Section 3 of the Clayton Act, 65 Harv. L. Rev. 913, 934-935 (1952); M. Handler, Antitrust in Perspective 113-114 (1957).

133.   Later statutes. The full statutory texts reproduced in the Appendix note most amendments, including the three major ones: In 1936 the Robinson-Patman Act rewrote the price discrimination provisions of Clayton Act §2. The Miller-Tydings Act of 1937 exempted from Sherman Act §1 certain resale price agreements between a manufacturer and its dealers, but this exemption was repealed in 1975. The Celler-Kefauver Act of 1950 substantially tightened the antimerger provisions of Clayton Act §7. Finally, a number of procedural amendments have been enacted, as noted in the next section.

1C.   PROCEDURES FOR ENFORCING THE ANTITRUST LAWS

134.   Sanctions generally.[1] This section sketches the procedures used to enforce the antitrust laws and several important procedural problems that are especially relevant for understanding the substantive issues emphasized in this book. Its selective coverage will omit many procedural issues and give only passing mention to some others. For the most part, it will describe current procedures rather than analyze them in any detail.[2]

Criminal Punishment

135.   Which statutes? Violations of the Clayton Act and the Federal Trade Commission Act are not crimes.[3] Violations of §1 and §2 of the Sherman Act, however, are criminal and are punishable by imprisonment up to three years and fines up to $350,000 for an individual and up to $10 million for a corporation.[4] Imprisonment

1. See II P. Areeda & H. Hovenkamp, Antitrust Law, ch. 3 (1995); R. Posner, A Statistical Study of Antitrust Enforcement, 13 J.L. & Econ. 365 (1970).
2. One might, for example, consider both why criminal penalties are necessary or appropriate for antitrust offenses (or many others, for that matter) and why any sanctions should be applied to individuals within a corporation rather than being limited to the corporation itself. Such issues have recently begun to receive scrutiny, at a rather general and theoretical level. Among the most thoughtful works are R. Kraakman, Corporate Liability Strategies and the Costs of Legal Controls, 93 Yale L.J. 857 (1984); S. Shavell, Criminal Law and the Optimal Use of Nonmonetary Sanctions as a Deterrent, 85 Colum. L. Rev. 1232 (1985). Some of the relevant issues are examined in the antitrust context in R. Posner, Antitrust Law: An Economic Perspective, ch. 10 (1976).
3. The exception is Clayton Act §10, which concerns dealings between a common carrier and another firm with interlocking officers or directors.
4. In addition, an alternative fine of up to twice the defendant's pecuniary gain or twice victims' pecuniary losses may be imposed under 18 U.S.C. §3571(d).

up to one year and a fine up to $5000 or both are the maximum penalties for violations of the rarely invoked Robinson-Patman Act §3 price discrimination provisions, but the more important provisions of the Robinson-Patman Act are noncriminal.

136. Frequency; government practice. Criminal prosecutions are a major element of the Department of Justice's antitrust policy, representing over 80 percent of the Department's cases between 1980 and 1993.[5] The primary targets of criminal prosecutions are the "hard-core" per se violations such as price fixing, bid rigging, and schemes for market allocation.[6] Indeed, 98 percent of criminal cases allege horizontal per se violations, most involving smaller firms in regional markets.[7] Where the legal standards are more difficult to discern, civil actions are more likely to be initiated. Recently, it has also become more common (although still in a minority of cases) for individuals to be the only defendants in a case.

The actual application of criminal sanctions has been increasing. Only a few dozen prison sentences were imposed from 1890 through the mid-1970s, running from a low of four hours to a high of two years. Two-thirds of these sentences, and all until 1960, involved in some manner either a labor dispute or violence, while the most recent have been for price fixing (typically not involving violence).[8] In the decade between 1986 and 1995, the government filed 50 to 100 criminal cases annually, and it prevailed in most of them. Total corporate fines have been about $40 million annually in recent years, and the number of corporations fined has averaged more than 50. About 20 individuals were sentenced to actual jail time each year, with sentences averaging more than 6 months.[9] Although fines on individuals are used more frequently than jail sentences, their total dollar amount was typically very small in comparison to the sales figures involved in price-fixing conspiracies.

137. Fairness of criminal brand. Are criminal penalties appropriate for the enforcement of the Sherman Act when the statutory prohibitions are vague and general and the conduct is not so reprehensible that we would want to discourage businesses from even

---

See also 18 U.S.C.S. App. §2R1.1 (1996) (Sentencing Guidelines for the U.S. Courts).

  5. See J. Gallo et al., Criminal Penalties Under the Sherman Act: A Study in Law and Economics, 16 Res. L. & Econ. 25, 27 (1994).

  6. See D. Baker, To Indict or Not to Indict: Prosecutorial Discretion in Sherman Act Enforcement, 63 Corn. L. Rev. 412 (1978).

  7. Gallo et al., note 5, at 28.

  8. Posner, note 2, at 33.

  9. These data are from U.S. Department of Justice, Antitrust Division, Workload Statistics FY 1986-1995, in 70 Antitrust & Trade Reg. Rep. 299 (1996).

approaching the line of illegality? If criminal enforcement is often thought unfair in such circumstances, or if criminal sanctions are, for whatever reason, rarely imposed, will the moral force of criminal legislation generally be weakened? There are obviously no easy answers to these questions.

Suppose that a court were confronted with a Sherman Act §1 criminal prosecution involving a merger that would, in a civil case, be declared an unlawful combination because the court found the economic effects unreasonable, although it recognized that fair-minded people could reasonably conclude otherwise. Would the defendant be convicted of a crime even if acting in good faith?[10] Would the statute be read, in its criminal aspects, to require that the defendant be shown to have criminal intent to commit an act it knew or should have known to be unlawful? Since actual prosecutions are usually confined to flagrant cases, these questions may seem unimportant in practice. Moreover, with respect to corporate antitrust defendants, criminal punishment is not necessarily more severe than a civil penalty or treble damages.

138. Differentiating antitrust offenses according to remedy? We ask here whether the courts do or should define the antitrust offense somewhat differently, depending on the remedy sought. This will appear most obvious in contrasting criminal and equity cases. For example, we might enjoin certain conduct or restructure a monopoly in circumstances where we would not hold the defendant to be a criminal. And in some contexts, one might argue that punitive treble damages should be treated similarly to criminal sanctions. Although less obvious, it might be wise occasionally to distinguish equity suits brought by the government from those brought by private parties. For example, the best solution for some problems would be a stringent judicial rule if we could rely on the prosecutor to use discretion not to bring those suits that ought not to be brought even though they fall within such a rule.

(a) *Statutory language.* Sherman Act §1 and §2 and the relevant procedural provisions make no express distinction with respect to

---

10. See generally Nash v. United States, 229 U.S. 373, 376-377 (1913). It was agreed that defendants were to be convicted only if the jury found the conspiracy for which they were indicted unreasonable.

> And thereupon it is said that the crime thus defined by the statute contains in its definition an element of degree as to which estimates may differ, with the result that a man might find himself in prison because his honest judgment did not anticipate that of a jury of less competent men.

The Court rejected the claim on the ground that "the law is full of instances where a man's fate depends on his estimating rightly, that is, as the jury subsequently estimates it, some matter of degree."

the civil-criminal, the legal-equitable, or the public-private nature of the lawsuit that brings an antitrust question before the courts. The substantive Sherman Act offenses are stated in §1 and §2, which define the criminal offenses. The provisions authorizing other lawsuits speak simply of antitrust violations without further definition. Thus, the statutes seem to put the public and private plaintiffs on the same footing. A violation does not depend on the identity of the plaintiff, and it seems to trigger civil and criminal, legal and equitable, and private as well as public actions. The prerequisite for equitable relief in a government suit is a violation of §1 or §2. And if there is a sufficient violation to warrant equitable relief for the government, what prevents those same facts from warranting a criminal action, treble damages, or a private suit for equitable relief?

(b) *Criminal offense distinguished.* The Supreme Court has recognized the Sherman Act as "a charter of freedom" with "a generality and adaptability comparable to that found to be desirable in constitutional provisions."[11] That purpose and function could never have been achieved had the courts interpreted and applied the Sherman Act in the manner of a criminal statute. And the courts have not in fact done so. They have not hesitated to expand and extend the scope and reach of the Sherman Act, notwithstanding the fact that it is a criminal statute. They have rejected countless pleas since 1890 to construe the statute narrowly or to hold the criminal prohibition too vague to satisfy the Constitution. They have, for example, applied Sherman Act §1 to tying and exclusive dealing arrangements with the same zeal as under the noncriminal Clayton Act §3.[12] Section 2 has been applied to monopolists against whom criminal penalties would not likely be entertained.[13] Although the Sherman Act states expressly only a unitary standard for violations of §1 or §2, it is not surprising that the courts have interpreted and applied it in the manner of a noncriminal enactment. This is but one of many examples presented in this book where the courts have not interpreted antitrust legislation literally, in order to achieve best what they understood to be the underlying statutory purposes.

This history does not mean that the courts have been insensitive to the usual qualms about the creation of crimes by judges rather than by legislators.[14] Nor does this history demonstrate a judicial

11. Appalachian Coals v. United States, 288 U.S. 344, 359-360 (1933).

12. Northern Pac. Ry. Co. v. United States, 356 U.S. 1 (1958); United States v. Loew's, 371 U.S. 38 (1962); cf. FTC v. Motion Picture Adv. Serv. Co., 344 U.S. 392 (1953).

13. United States v. Aluminum Co. of Am., 148 F.2d 416 (2d Cir. 1945). See Ch. 3A.

14. While the interpretation and elaboration of any criminal statute involves the courts in crime creation, the Sherman Act does so to an unusual degree.

willingness to punish defendants who have committed no act identifiable as reprehensible or have acted reasonably with confidence that the Sherman Act did not prohibit their behavior. The fact is that novel interpretations or great departures have seldom, if ever, occurred in criminal cases, which prosecutors have usually reserved for defendants whose knowing behavior would generally be recognized as deserving of criminal sanctions.

Because they were usually dealing with civil proceedings, the courts have implicitly understood the Sherman Act as a mandate to develop a common law of antitrust — as indeed it would have to be in order to fulfill its purpose as a "charter of freedom." In the unlikely event that a prosecutor initiated criminal proceedings against one who engaged in no act that the law reprehends as such, it is probable that courts would not find a criminal violation even though they might find a civil violation.[15] Perhaps the courts would permit the defense of "mistake of law." And the courts do require a criminal intent and a higher standard of proof as a prerequisite to the conviction.

The courts harmonized these concerns by implicitly divorcing the Sherman Act's criminal sanctions from its civil sweep. The Supreme Court expressly did so in its 1978 *Gypsum* decision.[16] The *Gypsum* defendants had been convicted of price fixing, although not of the ordinary sort. Rival firms had exchanged presale price quotations, allegedly to enable them to satisfy a defense to otherwise unlawful price discrimination under the Robinson-Patman Act.[17] The Court rejected the defense in principle and then took the evidence to be sufficient to show a Sherman Act violation for the purpose of its noncriminal sanctions. Nevertheless, the Court reversed the criminal conviction, holding that criminality required a showing of mens rea.[18] The Court defined the requisite mental state as knowledge that the consequences of one's conduct would be anticompetitive or a specific intent to violate the law (regardless of whether an anticompetitive result actually occurred).[19] The last word has by no means been said on the content of the requisite intent, but the

15. The same might be true where the defendant committed an act that the law now proscribes but which the defendant could and did reasonably believe to be lawful at the time.

16. United States v. United States Gypsum Co., 438 U.S. 422 (1978).

17. See ¶617b.

18. Two Justices dissented. One believed that the actual instruction required the jury to pay sufficient attention to the defendants' state of mind. The other believed that the statutory standard of illegality was the same for a criminal violation as for a civil violation.

19. See, e.g., United States v. Foley, 598 F.2d 1323, 1336 (4th Cir. 1979), cert. denied, 444 U.S. 1043 (1980), which affirmed a conviction after a jury instruction that "defendants must have known that their agreement, if effectuated, would have an effect on prices; that they knowingly joined a conspiracy whose purpose was to fix prices; and that in joining they intended to further that purpose."

Court's explicit recognition that a civil violation is not necessarily a criminal offense was significant. It should be emphasized, however, that *Gypsum* offers no relief from criminal convictions for those who offend those clear standards of illegality that antitrust law sometimes provides.[20]

(c) *Behavioral prerequisite for damages.* If a criminal intent requirement would save the innocent monopolist or oligopolist subject to injunction from criminal sanctions, is there any analog that would save it from treble damages?[21] In fact, courts have not generally developed different, more stringent tests of liability for treble damage claims than for injunctions, although proof of damages poses an added hurdle not required of plaintiffs seeking only injunctive relief.[22]

A related issue is the propriety of treble damages where liability is expanded by overruling precedent. The Supreme Court hinted that a defendant might be protected where new decisions "constitute a sharp break in the line of earlier authority or an avulsive change which caused the current of the law thereafter to flow between new banks."[23] In *Simpson,* the Court purported to distinguish, but actually overruled, the case on which the defendant had relied; it suggested that its new decision might be given only prospective application.[24] The Court subsequently held, however, that the plaintiff must be awarded the fruits of its victory in order to encourage the bringing of such suits.[25] Although exacerbated by the trebling of

20. United States v. Gillen, 599 F.2d 541 (3d Cir.), cert. denied, 444 U.S. 866 (1979) (*Gypsum* requires no proof of intention for clear-cut violation not in the grey zone of illegality; result would be otherwise where challenged conduct could reasonably be thought not to violate the statute); United States v. Brighton Bldg. & Maintenance Co., 598 F.2d 1101 (7th Cir.), cert. denied, 444 U.S. 840 (1979) (same).

21. The basic similarity is that trebling is far more severe than requiring compensation, especially from defendants whose behavior was not obviously reprehensible or who "reasonably" supposed they had acted lawfully. Even so, treble damages do not carry the stigma of imprisonment or its deprivation of liberty; nor do they entail the costs of running the prison system. See Shavell, note 2.

22. Note, however, that in Consolidated Express v. New York Shipping Assn., 602 F.2d 494, 519 (3d Cir. 1979), remanded on other grounds, 444 U.S. 896 (1980), the court imposed a more restrictive test for the award of damages than it would have imposed for an injunction.

23. Hanover Shoe v. United Shoe Mach. Corp., 392 U.S. 481, 499 (1968).

24. Simpson v. Union Oil Co., 377 U.S. 13, 24-25 (1964): "We reserve the question whether, when all the facts are known, there may be any equities that would warrant only prospective application in damage suits of the rule ... which we announce today."

25. Simpson v. Union Oil Co., 396 U.S. 13, 14 (1969): "The question we reserved was not an invitation to deny the fruits of successful litigation to this petitioner. Congress has determined the causes of action that arise from antitrust violations; and there has been an adjudication that a cause of action against respondent has been established."

damages, the problem is not limited to antitrust but arises whenever rules are uncertain or subject to change. Of course, it must be acknowledged that most "new" developments are foreshadowed; few would surprise the antitrust expert. Whether this should alleviate concerns over treble damages, which are mandatory, cannot be pursued here.[26]

(d) *Denying some private equity actions.* The question here is not one of judicial power to entertain a private suit for equitable relief. The question is one of appropriateness — for either the specific case or a class of cases. Clayton Act §16 expressly subjects private injunctive relief to "the same conditions and principles" applied by courts of equity. And such courts have repeatedly declared that equitable remedies are discretionary and not automatically available to an injured person. The factors properly affecting the exercise of such discretion are numerous and diverse. A further question is whether principles of equitable discretion permit the denial of particular categories of private suits, where the availability of a private suit would militate against an otherwise sensible decision to expand some antitrust prohibition.

Equitable Relief

139. Proceeding in equity. Sherman Act §4 and Clayton Act §15 confer jurisdiction on the federal courts "to prevent and restrain violations of this act" and direct the government "to institute proceedings in equity to prevent and restrain [antitrust] violations." The Supreme Court has understood the power under this statute to embrace "such orders and decrees as are necessary or appropriate" to enforce the statute.[27] This means that the courts will forbid the continuation of illegal acts and may also force the defendant to surrender the fruits of its wrong and restore competitive conditions.[28] The purpose of the decree is deemed not to be punitive,

---

In a suit by a later plaintiff, however, "the fact of reliance should prevent the retroactive application of the overruling doctrine." Lyons v. Westinghouse Elec. Corp., 235 F. Supp. 526, 537 (S.D.N.Y. 1964).

26. See generally Areeda & Turner, note 1, ¶¶321-322; R. Fallon & D. Meltzer, New Law, Non-Retroactivity, and Constitutional Remedies, 104 Harv. L. Rev. 1731 (1991); L. Kaplow, An Economic Analysis of Legal Transitions, 99 Harv. L. Rev. 509 (1986).

27. Northern Sec. Co. v. United States, 193 U.S. 197, 344 (1904) (decree enjoined holding company from exercising any control over competing railroads and enjoined the railroads from paying any dividends to the holding company).

28. "[T]he problem of the District Court does not end with enjoining continuance of the unlawful restraints nor with dissolving the combination which launched the conspiracy. Its function includes undoing what the conspiracy

and it will not embody harsh measures when less severe ones will suffice.[29] But "[e]conomic hardship can influence choice only as among two or more effective remedies."[30] In fashioning effective relief, the courts have considerable discretion in their choice of remedy.[31] Antitrust decrees have, for example, ordered defendants to (1) dispose of subsidiary companies, (2) create a company with appropriate assets and personnel to compete effectively with defendant, (3) make patents, trademarks, trade secrets, or know-how available to competitors at reasonable royalties or even without any royalties, (4) provide goods and services to all who wish to buy, (5) revise the terms on which defendant buys or sells, and (6) cancel, shorten, or modify outstanding agreements with competitors, suppliers, or customers.[32] After final judgment, the court may be faced with difficult problems in supervising compliance.[33] The court usually retains jurisdiction to modify the decree, and it may require the defendant to submit certain reports and give the Justice Department certain visitorial rights into defendant's affairs.[34] Some decrees may result in long-term supervision by the government and courts of an individual company or an entire industry.[35] As we shall see, some remedial questions have fairly obvious answers, but many of the more elusive ones will appear in later chapters.

---

achieved." United States v. Paramount Pictures, 334 U.S. 131, 171 (1948). See ¶¶314-315.

29. Timken Roller Bearing Co. v. United States, 341 U.S. 593, 603 (1951) (concurring opinion).

30. United States v. du Pont, 366 U.S. 316, 327 (1961).

31. In general, the nature of the decree is left to the discretion of the district court. Maryland & Va. Milk Prod. Assn. v. United States, 362 U.S. 458, 473 (1960). But if the Supreme Court concludes that the district court's injunction is ineffective to remedy the violation, it may remand with instructions to alter the decree. See *du Pont,* note 30.

32. See Areeda & Turner, note 1, ¶346.

33. An example of the complications that may follow a divestiture order is Utah Pub. Ser. Commn. v. El Paso Natural Gas Co., 395 U.S. 464 (1969). For critiques of the effectiveness of injunctive relief against §7 violations, see K. Elzinga, The Antimerger Law: Pyrrhic Victories?, 12 J.L. & Econ. 43 (1969); M. Pfunder, D. Plaine & A. Whittemore, Compliance with Divestiture Orders Under Section 7 of the Clayton Act: An Analysis of the Relief Obtained, 17 Antitr. Bull. 19 (1972).

34. See United States v. Bausch & Lomb Optical Co., 321 U.S. 707, 725, 727-728 (1944); Ch. 3A, note 15. Observe that the court's power to modify a decree does not depend on an express reservation of power to do so. United States v. United Shoe Mach. Corp., 391 U.S. 244, 251-252 (1968).

35. See Note, An Experiment in Preventive Antitrust: Judicial Regulation of the Motion Picture Exhibition Market Under the Paramount Decrees, 74 Yale L.J. 1041 (1965).

In recognition of the possibly broad character of relief, Sherman Act §5 and Clayton Act §15 authorize the court to summon before it persons not named in the original suit as defendants.

In some cases, of course, the government will believe that relief cannot await the outcome of a lengthy trial and will seek a preliminary injunction. In deciding whether to grant it, the court will usually consider the probability of government victory on the merits, the hardship a preliminary injunction would impose on the defendant, and the possibility that final relief could undo any anticompetitive harm in the interim.[36]

140. Private suits in equity. Since 1914, Clayton Act §16 has permitted private persons to obtain injunctive relief against actual or threatened antitrust injuries. To have standing, the private litigant must demonstrate a significant threat of injury to itself. But where the anticompetitive effect or potential of the defendant's behavior would warrant an injunction in a government suit, the court may well proscribe the defendant's activity without close scrutiny of the harm claimed by the private plaintiff.[37]

Although the question remained unsettled for some time, the Supreme Court has held that private plaintiffs may seek divestiture to remedy an unlawful merger.[38] The Court noted, however, that divestiture would not always be an appropriate remedy in a private suit even if the federal government would have been entitled to such relief. Standing may bar relief, and "equitable defenses such as laches, or perhaps 'unclean hands' may protect consummated transactions from belated attacks by private parties when it would not be too late for the Government to vindicate the public interest."

The timing of relief is, of course, also a problem. Preliminary injunctions are available to a private plaintiff where they would be available to the government. In addition, a number of courts do not

36. E.g., United States v. Wilson Sporting Goods Co., 288 F. Supp. 543, 567-570 (N.D. Ill. 1968). Permanent injunction results are sometimes caused by preliminary injunctions that induce the defendants to abandon the challenged activities. For example, preliminary injunctions have led to the abandonment of many mergers between parties unwilling to bear the cost of litigation, the uncertainty about their futures at a time when important business decisions have to be made, or the difficulty of adjusting a stock-for-stock exchange for possible changes in the relative market values of their stocks at some future consummation date.

37. Zenith Radio Corp. v. Hazeltine Research, 395 U.S. 100, 130-131 (1969):

> [T]he purpose of giving private parties treble damage and injunctive remedies was not merely to provide private relief, but was to serve as well the high purpose of enforcing the antitrust laws. . . . Section 16 should be construed and applied with this purpose in mind, and with the knowledge that the remedy it affords, like other equitable remedies, is flexible and capable of "nice adjustment and reconciliation between the public interest and private needs as well as between competing private claims." . . . Its availability should be "conditioned by the necessities of the public interest which Congress has sought to protect."

See also ¶146c.

38. California v. American Stores, 495 U.S. 271 (1990).

require the private plaintiff to show a likelihood of success on the merits. In one standard formulation, "if the harm that may occur to the plaintiff is sufficiently serious, it is only necessary that there be a fair chance of success on the merits."[39]

141. Consent decrees. (a) *Nature and significance.* Most civil antitrust actions initiated by the Justice Department terminate in a settlement that is filed with the court and incorporated in a judicial order known as a "consent decree." This may occur at any time: soon after the complaint is filed, after discovery but before trial, after the trial begins, after an adjudication of liability, or even after an adjudication of nonliability.

Consent decree provisions do not necessarily reflect the state of the law. Defendants sometimes agree — either because of pressure or indifference — to consent decree provisions that might not be insisted on by a court. Nor does the decree necessarily go as far as a court might because rarely does the defendant agree to all of the provisions that might possibly result from a trial in which all liability and relief issues are adversely resolved. Given the enormous expense and great length of much antitrust litigation, consent settlement offers obvious advantages for both the defendant and the government. The Justice Department can spread its limited enforcement resources over more suits and thus achieve broader antitrust enforcement than would be possible if every suit had to be fully litigated. Settlement can also benefit the defendant who prefers to avoid the expense, publicity, and business disruption of discovery procedures and trial as well as the treble damage consequences of adjudicated liability.[40]

(b) *Modification.* Either the government or the defendant may petition the court for modification of a previously entered consent decree. But the modification will seldom be granted if the other party opposes it because the courts hesitate to deprive either party of the benefit of its agreement.[41] In *Swift,* the Supreme Court established modification criteria, placing a very high burden of proof on defendants who seek to alter the injunctive provisions of a

39. William Inglis & Sons Baking Co. v. ITT Continental Baking Co., 526 F.2d 86, 88 (9th Cir. 1975); Triebwasser & Katz v. AT&T, 535 F.2d 1356, 1359 (2d Cir. 1976).

40. See ¶¶141c, 158c.

41. Compare United States v. Swift & Co., 189 F. Supp. 885 (N.D. Ill. 1960), aff'd per curiam, 367 U.S. 909 (1961) (court denied defendant's petition for modification, reading the 1932 *Swift* case, note 42, as establishing a stringent test), with United States v. Swift & Co., 1971 Trade Cas. ¶73760 (N.D. Ill.) (court approved joint petition by government and defendant for modification of that same consent decree).

consent decree.[42] The *Swift* test is generally applied to government motions for modification as well, although some see a more relaxed standard when the government is the moving party.[43] In any event, a judge may modify a decree at the unilateral demand of one party only on the basis of evidence submitted at a hearing.[44]

(c) *Third-party interests.* Third parties may not maintain an action for damages,[45] or initiate contempt proceedings,[46] for a defendant's violation of a consent decree. And while Clayton Act §5(a) allows a litigated decree to be used as prima facie evidence of liability in subsequent private actions against the defendant, it explicitly prohibits such use of pretrial consent decrees.[47] Indeed, wherever liability has not been adjudicated, the consent decree almost invariably states that it is neither an adjudication on the merits nor an admission of liability on the part of defendant. In only a few cases has the government negotiated a nonlitigated consent decree in which defendant admitted liability such that the decree would serve as prima facie evidence in subsequent private suits.[48]

---

42. United States v. Swift & Co., 286 U.S. 106, 119 (1932): "Nothing less than a clear showing of grievous wrong evoked by new and unforeseen conditions should lead us to change what was decreed after years of litigation with the consent of all concerned."

43. Compare Chrysler Corp. v. United States, 316 U.S. 556 (1942) (over defendant's objection, court granted government request for one-year extension of time provision in consent decree designed to correlate with timing of government civil suit against General Motors), with Ford Motor Co. v. United States, 335 U.S. 303 (1948) (court denied government's sixth request for extension of a similar provision in *Ford* consent decree; earlier findings of lack of competitive disadvantage and of diligent government prosecution of *GM* case no longer applicable). See also *United Shoe,* Ch. 3A, note 15.

44. The court may not circumvent the hearing requirement by effectively modifying a consent decree under the guise of constructing its terms. Hughes v. United States, 342 U.S. 353 (1952); Liquid Carbonic Corp. v. United States, 350 U.S. 869 (1955) (per curiam), rev'g 123 F. Supp. 653 (E.D.N.Y. 1954).

45. E.g., Data Processing Fin. & Gen. Corp. v. IBM, 430 F.2d 1277 (8th Cir. 1970), aff'g Control Data Corp. v. IBM, 306 F. Supp. 839 (D. Minn. 1969). For a contrary argument, see C. Sullivan, Enforcement of Government Antitrust Decrees by Private Parties: Third Party Beneficiary Rights and Intervenor Status, 123 U. Pa. L. Rev. 822 (1975).

46. United States v. ASCAP, 341 F.2d 1003 (2d Cir.), cert. denied, 382 U.S. 877 (1965).

47. See ¶158c.

48. United States v. Allied Chem. Corp., 1961 Trade Cas. ¶69923 (D. Mass. 1960); United States v. Bituminous Concrete Assn., 1960 Trade Cas. ¶69878 (D. Mass.); United States v. The Lake Asphalt & Petro. Co., 1960 Trade Cas. ¶69835 (D. Mass.) (prima facie effect only as to suits by certain state and municipal plaintiffs). Compare United States v. Brunswick-Balke-Collender Co., 203 F. Supp. 657 (E.D. Wis. 1962) (judge entered consent decree over government objections, where terms proposed by defendant were "materially identical" to those proposed by government, and the government's insistence on inclusion of such a liability clause was deemed arbitrary and unwarranted).

Third parties have increasingly attempted to intervene in the consent settlement process with the aim of forcing the government to litigate, obtain an admission of guilt, or alter the terms of the settlement. In *El Paso*,[49] the Supreme Court reversed a denial of private intervention at the consent decree stage of a litigated antitrust suit. Since then, private parties have increasingly attempted to invoke Federal Rule of Civil Procedure 24(a)(2), which authorizes intervention of right when petitioner can show that (1) its ability to protect an interest in the property or transaction will "as a practical matter" be impaired by the disposition and (2) such interest is not adequately represented by existing parties. But these attempts have largely failed because (1) of the strong presumption of adequate representation by the government, (2) of the insufficient personal interest of would-be intervenors, and (3) most courts consider *El Paso* sui generis and have strictly confined it to its facts.[50]

Nevertheless, the consent settlement process cannot ignore third-party interests, especially after the 1974 enactment of Clayton Act §§5(b)-5(h) (the Tunney Act) establishing elaborate procedures governing consent decrees. Although settlement negotiations remain private, the proposed decree must be published 60 days before its effective date unless the court finds that a shorter period is required by "extraordinary circumstances" and is not adverse to the public interest. Publication must include "any other materials and documents which the United States considered determinative in formulating such proposal." The government is also obliged to publish a "competitive impact statement" (1) stating the alleged

---

49. Cascade Natural Gas Corp. v. El Paso Natural Gas Co., 386 U.S. 129 (1967). Earlier, United States v. El Paso Natural Gas Co., 376 U.S. 651 (1964), held that an El Paso acquisition violated Clayton Act §7. (For an even earlier stage of the litigation, see California v. FPC, 369 U.S. 482 (1962).) The Court remanded to the district court with directions to order divestiture "without delay." Three years later the consent decree entered by the trial court came before the Court in 386 U.S. 129, which reviewed the trial court's denial of intervention to the appellant. The Court's decision to permit intervention seems to have been motivated largely by what it felt to be the government's disregard of its earlier mandate. In Utah Pub. Serv. Commn. v. El Paso Natural Gas Co., 395 U.S. 464 (1969), the district court's decree was held not to comply with the Supreme Court's mandate, and the case was vacated and remanded. Finally, in California-Pacific Utils. Co. v. United States, 410 U.S. 962 (1973), the Supreme Court affirmed without opinion the district court judgment and selection of a purchaser of the new company.

50. E.g., United States v. Associated Milk Producers, 534 F.2d 113 (8th Cir.), cert. denied, 429 U.S. 940 (1976) (no intervention without showing government bad faith or malfeasance); United States v. NBC, 449 F. Supp. 1127 (C.D. Cal. 1978), aff'd mem., 603 F.2d 227 (9th Cir.), cert. denied, 444 U.S. 991 (1979) (presumption of adequacy unless strong showing that the government is not vigorously and faithfully representing the public interest). But see United States v. Simmonds Precision Prods., 319 F. Supp. 620 (S.D.N.Y. 1970) (union intervened to protect job security of members employed at subsidiary subject to piecemeal sale).

violation, (2) explaining the proposed consent decree and its anticipated effects on competition, (3) noting the private remedies that
might be available, (4) describing the procedure available for public comment and possible modification of the proposed decree, and
(5) evaluating the alternative decrees actually considered by the
government. Written comments from the public must be received
and considered by the government under specified procedures.

Whatever may be the participation of third parties, the critical
question concerns the judge's proper role in entering a consent
decree.

(d) *Judicial role.* Although a judicial order entered by consent is
more than a contract between the parties,[51] the judge's role is far
from clear. The proposed decree, of course, must be approved by
the court before it is formally entered, but such approval was traditionally perfunctory. Yet judges resist the notion that they are mere
clerks who must rubber stamp what the parties put before them.[52]
On occasion, courts — of their own motion or at the urging of
amici curiae or of a would-be intervenor — would require hearings[53] or would enter a consent decree only on condition that certain third-party interests be protected.[54] But even those courts exercising greater scrutiny stopped far short of attempting to assess the
competitive merits of one form of relief or another. Courts traditionally have refrained especially from any attempt to assess the
merits of the government's decision to settle because that decision,
like the decision to prosecute, was largely held to be outside the
scope of judicial review.[55]

51. *Swift,* note 42, at 115.
52. See Esco Corp. v. United States, 340 F.2d 1000, 1005 (9th Cir. 1965). A
consent decree may not, however, be entered by the court without government
consent. United States v. Ward Baking Co., 376 U.S. 327 (1964). Contra, *Brunswick,*
note 48.
There is an instance of the court forcing the parties to trial. United States v. Pan
Am. World Airways, 1959 Trade Cas. ¶69300 (S.D.N.Y.).
53. In United States v. Standard Oil Co. (Cal.), 1959 Trade Cas. ¶69399 (S.D.
Cal.), the court learned in pretrial hearings that the parties' disagreement over
one prayer of the government complaint had repeatedly blocked settlement efforts. The court ordered the parties to present extensive data — through counsel
and without prima facie evidence effect — in a special hearing designed to determine what relief would be appropriate under this prayer should defendant's antitrust liability be established at trial. The parties ultimately compromised and
agreed on a consent decree after the court ruled that a finding of liability would
not entitle the government to the disputed relief.
54. United States v. Ling-Temco-Vought, 315 F. Supp. 1301 (W.D. Pa. 1970)
(court approved consent decree on condition that integrity of subsidiary company's employee benefit and pension trust fund be assured).
55. United States v. Automobile Mfrs. Assn., 307 F. Supp. 617, 620 (C.D. Cal.
1969), aff'd mem. sub nom. City of New York v. United States, 397 U.S. 248 (1970)
(absent evidence of bad faith, the government was under no pre-1974 duty to
disclose its motives for settlement).

The 1974 legislation, mentioned earlier, contemplates a deeper judicial involvement than was customarily exercised. One court described the motivation for the enactment as follows:

> The legislative history shows that Congress was particularly concerned that the "excessive secrecy" of the consent decree process deprived the public of the opportunity to scrutinize and comment upon proposed decrees, thereby undermining confidence in the legal system. In addition, the legislators found that consent decrees often failed to provide appropriate relief, either because of miscalculations by the Justice Department or because of the "great influence and economic power" wielded by antitrust violators. The history, indeed, contains references to a number of antitrust settlements deemed "blatantly inequitable and improper" on these bases.[56]

The Tunney Act, however, does not offer much direction to guide the judge. It allows the court to review the public comments filed with the government, take testimony, and use special masters or consultants. The court is not to enter a consent judgment unless it determines that doing so "is in the public interest." In making that decision, the court may consider the impact of the judgment on "the public benefit, if any, to be derived from a determination of the issues at trial." The Act does not say how the judge is to make those judgments without trying the case and without forcing expenditure of the Justice Department's limited prosecutorial resources.[57]

A notable controversy arising under the Tunney Act concerned the disposition of the massive, 13-year-long *IBM* case in 1982.[58] The government had moved to dismiss the case outright and convinced the Second Circuit that the Act should be applied only according to

---

56. United States v. AT&T, 552 F. Supp. 131, 148 & n. 72 (D.D.C. 1982), aff'd, 460 U.S. 1001 (1983):

> References were made, among others, to Cascade Natural Gas Corp. v. El Paso Natural Gas Corp., 386 U.S. 129 (1967), where the Supreme Court found that the Department of Justice had consented to a decree which completely failed to alleviate the conditions found to violate the antitrust laws; to the 1956 decree in the *Western Electric* action . . . and to the questionable circumstances surrounding the consent decrees entered in 1971 in cases involving the International Telephone and Telegraph Corp. . . .

For further discussion of the *ITT* settlement, see ¶543c.

57. For an interesting opinion that grapples with these issues, see United States v. Gillette Co., 406 F. Supp. 713 (D. Mass. 1975).

58. On the same day, a settlement in the *AT&T* case pending before Judge Greene was also announced. Instead of triggering the Tunney Act procedures by filing a proposed consent decree in the current suit, the government proposed to dismiss it in return for AT&T's agreement to amend an outstanding 1956 consent decree in another district court. When Judge Greene refused to allow this, the parties complied with the Tunney Act (without conceding that they had to). *AT&T*, note 56, at 145. The settlement restructuring the telephone industry was then approved, with a few modifications. See ¶327.

its terms: to consent judgments. The court rested its decision on the legislative history and on its belief that restricting the prosecutor's freedom to dismiss raised constitutional issues relating to the separation of powers.[59]

Another controversy under the Tunney Act arose in the *Microsoft* litigation.[60] As is common practice, the government filed its complaint after settlement negotiations had produced an agreement on a consent decree. The allegations in the government's complaint closely matched the relief under the parties' proposed decree. The district court judge refused to accept the decree, in substantial part because it failed to address allegedly improper behavior not challenged by the government. The Court of Appeals reversed the lower court and remanded the case with instructions to reassign it to a different district court judge and for such judge to approve the consent decree. The court ruled, in essence, that a district judge may not require government prosecutors to bring a case that they have not chosen to pursue. The appellate courts' decisions in *IBM* and *Microsoft* indicate that the Tunney Act will play only a limited role in policing prosecutorial discretion. It is not clear, however, that Congress could vest courts with significantly greater power.[61]

142. Cease and desist orders. The Federal Trade Commission is empowered to issue cease and desist orders. These orders carry no criminal or civil penalties for past conduct, nor do they assess damages; rather, like a judicial injunction, they undo and prevent further unlawful action. There is no private right of action for violations of the FTC Act or Commission orders.[62]

(a) *FTC jurisdiction.* The Clayton Act commits its enforcement to the FTC as well as to the Justice Department and the courts.[63] The

59. In re IBM Corp., 687 F.2d 591, 600-603 (1982) (mandamus directing district judge to cease consideration of the case).

60. United States v. Microsoft, 159 F.R.D. 318 (D.D.C.), rev'd, 56 F.3d 1448 (D.C. Cir. 1995). For a discussion of the antitrust violations charged by the government, see ¶312.

61. Indeed, the dissent from the summary affirmance of *AT&T*, note 56, suggested that there were grounds for doubting the constitutionality of the Act as to whether it properly involves a judicial function where prosecutorial discretion is committed to a coordinate political department.

62. E.g., Holloway v. Bristol-Meyers Corp., 485 F.2d 986 (D.C. Cir. 1973); Carlson v. Coca-Cola Co., 483 F.2d 279 (9th Cir. 1973). Contra, Guernsey v. Rich Plan of Midwest, 408 F. Supp. 582 (N.D. Ind. 1976).

63. Section 11 provides for FTC enforcement of §2, §3, §7, and §8 of the Clayton Act: except that the Interstate Commerce Commission enforces the Act where applicable to regulated common carriers, the Federal Communications Commission to communications carriers, the Secretary of Transportation to air carriers, and the Federal Reserve Board to banks, banking associations, and trust companies. These administrative jurisdictions are concurrent with that of the Justice Department and the courts under §15, except as qualified by judicial doctrines loosely described as "primary jurisdiction." See ¶162.

Commission also has jurisdiction under FTC Act §5 to forbid "unfair methods of competition."[64] It is now quite clear that the Commission has discretion to condemn as "unfair" practices that seem harmful or potentially harmful to competition, whether or not they are false, fraudulent, or morally reprehensible. Thus, the Commission may enforce the Clayton Act directly, and under §5 it may condemn conduct that offends the Sherman Act,[65] violates "the spirit" of the Sherman or Clayton Acts,[66] or is otherwise "unfair."[67]

(b) *FTC proceedings.* The FTC has five members who are appointed by the President and confirmed by the Senate for seven-year terms. These commissioners supervise a large staff of economists and lawyers, whose many duties include the investigation and prosecution of offenses within the Commission's jurisdiction.

Most FTC proceedings are disposed of before reaching formal adjudication. Once an investigation has been completed, the FTC will generally afford a party the opportunity to settle under a consent order procedure roughly similar to that used by the Justice Department. The Commission notifies the party of the terms of a proposed complaint and submits a proposed cease and desist order. Without admitting any violation of law, the party may then agree to negotiate the terms of a cease and desist order that, when entered, will have the same force and effect as a regular FTC final order.[68]

Where the consent order procedure is not made available by the FTC, or where negotiations fail, formal adjudicatory proceedings are initiated by complaint and tried at a hearing by an administra-

---

64. Amendments enacted in 1938 extended the prohibition to "unfair or deceptive acts or practices." The FTC also has an extensive mandate to weed out unfair and false advertising and enforce statutes requiring accurate labeling of furs, textiles, and other goods.

65. FTC v. Motion Picture Advertising Serv. Co., 344 U.S. 392 (1953); FTC v. Cement Inst., 333 U.S. 683 (1948).

66. FTC v. Brown Shoe, 384 U.S. 316 (1966).

67. FTC v. Sperry & Hutchinson Co., 405 U.S. 233, 244-245 & n.5 (1972):

> [T]he Federal Trade Commission does not arrogate excessive power to itself if, in measuring a practice against the elusive, but congressionally mandated standard of fairness, it, like a court of equity, considers public values beyond simply those enshrined in the letter or encompassed in the spirit of the antitrust laws.

Continuing in a footnote, the Court cited, with apparent approval

> factors [the FTC] considers in determining whether a practice that is neither in violation of the antitrust laws nor deceptive is nonetheless unfair: "(1) whether the practice, without necessarily having been previously considered unlawful, offends public policy as it has been established by statutes, the common law, or otherwise — whether, in other words, it is within at least the penumbra of some common-law, statutory, or other established concept of unfairness; (2) whether it is immoral, unethical, oppressive, or unscrupulous; (3) whether it causes substantial injury to consumers (or competitors or other businessmen)."

68. The FTC, like the Justice Department, allows for a 60-day public comment period before the consent order can be entered. 16 C.F.R. §2.32.

tive law judge.[69] The administrative law judge's findings and orders are subject to review by the Commission sitting as a body. Commission orders are reviewable by the federal courts of appeals. Federal Trade Commission Act §5(b) also provides that the Commission may, "after notice and opportunity for hearing," modify or vacate its orders "whenever in the opinion of the Commission conditions of fact or law have so changed as to require such action or if the public interest shall so require."[70]

As originally enacted, violation of FTC orders carried no sanction, although the FTC could petition a court of appeals for enforcement. Subsequent amendments make FTC orders final unless the respondent seeks timely judicial review. Each violation of a final FTC order incurs a civil penalty of up to $5000; every day of continuing disobedience counts as a separate offense. The district courts have original jurisdiction over civil penalty proceedings.

(c) *FTC remedial powers.* The Federal Trade Commission

> is the expert body to determine what remedy is necessary to eliminate the unfair or deceptive trade practices which have been disclosed. It has wide latitude for judgment and the courts will not interfere except where the remedy selected has no reasonable relation to the unlawful practices found to exist.[71]

Commission orders often range far beyond a mere negative injunction against repetition of the challenged practice. The FTC, for

69. FTC rules provide respondent with post-complaint discovery procedures, although not on as broad a scale as those in the Federal Rules of Civil Procedure. 16 C.F.R. §§3.31-3.39. Commission rules also provide for third-party intervention. Indigent respondents will be supplied legal counsel. American Chinchilla Corp., 76 F.T.C. 1016 (1969).

70. Clayton Act §11(b) contains a similar provision. Compare ITT Continental Baking Co., 81 F.T.C. 1021 (1972) (FTC claimed authority unilaterally to modify consent order on a proper showing of need, relying on Clayton Act §11(b), although statute does not expressly speak to consent orders), with Nabisco v. FTC, 459 F.2d 1023 (5th Cir. 1972) (per curiam, invalidating unilateral modification of consent order by FTC).

71. Jacob Siegel Co. v. FTC, 327 U.S. 608, 612-613 (1946). The Commission may, for example, prohibit a wider range of activities than those specifically attacked in the FTC proceedings. See, e.g., FTC v. Henry Broch & Co., 368 U.S. 360, 364 (1962) ("We cannot say that the Commission exceeded its discretion in banning repetitions of [respondent's] violation in connection with transactions involving *any* seller and buyer, rather than simply forbidding recurrence of the transgression in sales between [seller and buyer involved in the instant case].").Accord, Atlantic Ref. Co. v. FTC, 381 U.S. 357 (1965).

The Supreme Court has recognized a very broad discretion in the Commission as to whether it should proceed against an individual firm or a whole industry. The Court has rejected claims that the Commission was acting arbitrarily in ordering a single firm to cease and desist from practices characteristic of the industry and thus subjecting it to a competitive disadvantage. FTC v. Universal-Rundle Corp., 387 U.S. 244 (1967); Moog Indus. v. FTC, 355 U.S. 411 (1958) (per curiam).

example, has ordered respondents to license patents on a reasonable royalty basis, seek FTC approval for future acquisitions, and dispose of an illegally acquired corporation.[72] And the Supreme Court has hinted that administrative cease and desist powers may be as extensive as necessary to implement the statutory purpose.[73]

The Commission cannot issue preliminary orders to preserve the status quo pending the completion of its own proceedings or any appeal from its orders; but a 1973 amendment of the FTC Act authorizes the district courts to grant temporary injunctions upon suit by the Commission at any time before its own order becomes final, and even before issuance of its own complaint.[74]

(d) *Judicial review.* The courts of appeals have jurisdiction to review and affirm, modify, or vacate FTC orders. The courts are supposed to uphold the Commission's orders where its findings are supported by substantial evidence, its rulings of law are consistent with the governing statutes, and the remedy imposed does not constitute an abuse of the Commission's discretion.[75] As might be expected, however, the scope of judicial review is not entirely uniform. When the Commission is enforcing Sherman and Clayton Act standards concurrently with the judiciary, there may be little room for divergent legal standards, and an appellate court might review Commission findings and orders in roughly the same way that it

---

72. See Areeda & Turner, note 1, at ¶305e.

The FTC clearly is empowered to order divestiture for a Clayton Act §7 violation. E.g., Seeburg Corp. v. FTC, 425 F.2d 124 (6th Cir. 1970). The Commission also has ordered divestiture under FTC Act §5 on a finding of monopolization. L.G. Balfour Co. v. FTC, 442 F.2d 1, 18, 23 (7th Cir. 1971) (divestiture of subsidiary ordered where defendant's secret acquisition and operation of a competitor company was found to constitute monopolization under §5; complaint did not charge a Clayton Act §7 violation). Observe that the power to order divestiture after a finding of improper behavior constituting an "unfair method of competition" does not imply the power to intervene in monopoly or oligopoly where there has been no improper behavior. As to judicial power under the Sherman Act to remedy anticompetitive market structures independently of improper behavior, see ¶320.

73. See Pan Am. World Airways v. United States, 371 U.S. 296, 312 (1963), concerning the Civil Aeronautics Board, whose statutory mandate exceeded the FTC's "merely" concurrent responsibility for the antitrust laws. The CAB was responsible for promoting the development of aviation, entry into that industry, and rates, routes, and service. It had broad regulatory, supervisory, and even managerial duties with respect to aviation. "Cease and desist" need not have had the same scope for the FTC and CAB.

74. The Commission need not establish a strong likelihood of ultimate success on the merits. E.g., FTC v. National Tea Co., 603 F.2d 694, 698 (8th Cir. 1979) (FTC must raise "questions going to the merits so serious, substantial, difficult and doubtful as to make them fair ground for thorough investigation, study, deliberation and determination").

75. E.g., FTC v. Curtis Publishing Co., 260 U.S. 568, 580 (1923); Lenox v. FTC, 417 F.2d 126 (2d Cir. 1969).

reviews trial courts. Yet, some reviewing courts approach Commission lawmaking (for example, what is the proper test for finding a conspiracy or assessing the reasonableness of a restraint?) as if the FTC had merely drawn an inference of simple fact (for example, did *A* discuss the matter with *B*?). And even when Commission lawmaking is acknowledged, the Supreme Court has affirmed without noticeable reasoning by either tribunal as to why §5 should be so interpreted.[76] But where the Commission order was not grounded in either the letter or spirit of the Sherman or Clayton Acts, the Court has both (1) accorded the agency considerable discretion in defining "unfairness" and (2) required it to explain in its formal opinion the reasoning which lay behind its ruling.[77]

(e) *Rulemaking.* To simplify its adjudicative process, and to allow all interested parties to participate in formulating a proposition affecting their welfare, the Commission has promulgated substantive rules, so-called Trade Regulation Rules, defining the scope of FTC Act §5 as it applies to specific industry practices. The Commission's authority to issue such substantive rules has been upheld.[78] Where a respondent's conduct is found to fall within the rule in question, the issue of a §5 violation is resolved, although the respondent may appeal by challenging the statutory authorization for the rule or its application. Rulemaking does have the virtue of informing affected persons in advance about the Commission's conclusions.[79]

The FTC Improvement Act of 1975[80] adds to the FTC Act a new §18, which provides that the Commission may prescribe interpretive rules with respect to unfair or deceptive acts or practices and may also define with specificity the acts or practices that are unfair or deceptive. A subordinate section provides that the new statute "shall not affect any authority of the Commission to prescribe rules (including

76. See *Brown Shoe,* note 66.

77. See, e.g., *Sperry,* note 67, at 247-250.

78. National Petro. Refiners Assn. v. FTC, 482 F.2d 672, 674 (D.C. Cir. 1973), cert. denied, 415 U.S. 951 (1974) (rule declared service station's failure to display octane ratings clearly on gas pump an "unfair method of competition and an unfair or deceptive act or practice").

79. Note that precedent established on a case-by-case basis has many of the same attributes. Although they had no role in influencing a prior decision, persons affected by it can adjust their conduct accordingly. And whether a precedent or formal rule is involved, the later respondent has the burden of persuading the Commission to change an adverse earlier conclusion. See D. Shapiro, The Choice of Rulemaking or Adjudication in The Development of Administrative Policy, 78 Harv. L. Rev. 921 (1965); B. Burrus & H. Teter, Antitrust: Rulemaking v. Adjudication in the FTC, 54 Geo. L.J. 1106 (1966).

80. Section 18 sets out detailed procedures for implementing the new rulemaking authority conferred on the Commission. (The former §18 of the FTC Act is redesignated as §21.)

interpretive rules), and general statements of policy, with respect to unfair methods of competition in or affecting commerce."

(f) *Intragovernmental coordination.* Because the Department of Justice and the FTC have concurrent jurisdiction, they try to avoid duplication of effort. Each informs the other of proposed investigations before actually proceeding and can thus adjust its planned activities if necessary. To some extent each agency seems to concentrate on different industries.

Private Actions

143. Treble damages. (a) *Generally.*[81] The treble damage remedy gives private persons[82] a powerful financial incentive to enforce the antitrust laws. Under both the Sherman Act and the Clayton Act,[83] any private person "injured in his business or property by reason of anything forbidden in the antitrust laws ... shall recover threefold the damages by him sustained, and the cost of suit, including a reasonable attorney's fee."[84] The result is that public enforcement, which is inevitably selective and least likely to concern itself with local, episodic, or less-than-flagrant violations, is supplemented by private enforcement. The additional remedy available through private actions increases the likelihood that a violator will be found out, greatly enlarges its penalties, and thereby helps discourage illegal conduct. Some antitrust violators have found the cost of violation to be very high, even though treble damages are usually a deductible business expense for federal income tax purposes.[85]

81. See W. Breit & K. Elzinga, Antitrust Enforcement and Economic Efficiency: The Uneasy Case for Treble Damages, 17 J.L. & Econ. 329 (1974); A.M. Polinsky, Detrebling versus Decoupling Antitrust Damages: Lessons from the Theory of Enforcement, 74 Geo. L.J. 1231 (1986).

82. Treble damages are also available to the federal government. Congress has limited foreign governments to single damages. 96 Stat. 1964 (1982), adding new Clayton Act §4(b).

83. Clayton Act §4, superseding the later-repealed equivalent sections of the Sherman Act. Clayton Act §1 defines "antitrust laws" as the Sherman Act, the Wilson Tariff Act, and the Clayton Act. This includes Robinson-Patman Act §2 but not §3. See Nashville Milk Co. v. Carnation Co., 355 U.S. 373, 378-379 (1958).

84. Amendments in 1976 to §16 made clear that attorney's fees are also to be awarded in equity actions. For illustrative problems in calculating reasonable attorney's fees, which may be less than the successful plaintiff actually agreed to pay, see Baughman v. Wilson Freight Forwarding Co., 583 F.2d 1208 (3d Cir. 1978); Detroit v. Grinnell Corp., 560 F.2d 1093 (2d Cir. 1977). The court might limit the plaintiff's lawyer's recovery when the agreed-on figure is deemed excessive. Farmington Dowel Prods. v. Forster Mfg. Co., 421 F.2d 61, 86-90 (1st Cir. 1970).

85. Internal Revenue Code §162(g) was amended in 1969 to prohibit any deduction for two-thirds of the amount paid by an antitrust defendant to an antitrust plaintiff (whether by way of judgment or settlement) when the defendant has previously been convicted or has pleaded guilty or nolo contendere in a related criminal action.

(b) *Proving damages.*[86] The plaintiff must establish the extent of its damages. Although the courts seem to require more proof of the fact of injury than of the quantum of injury,[87] it may be exceedingly difficult to show how the plaintiff's actual situation differs from what it would have been in the absence of the defendant's antitrust violation. The proof required depends on the nature of the alleged injury. For example, the plaintiff who paid the price fixed by the defendants' unlawful price-fixing conspiracy is deemed to be injured by the excess of the fixed price over the free market price that would otherwise have prevailed. This latter price must be estimated somehow — by assuming, for example, that the pre- or post-conspiracy price would otherwise have prevailed, but paying "appropriate" attention to the ways in which circumstances during the conspiracy period differed from those preceding or following it.[88]

Other kinds of antitrust violations may cause even more difficult problems of proof.[89] To establish lost profits, plaintiff's actual profits may be compared to its profits before and after defendant's violations or to the profits of competitors or firms in related businesses unaffected by the violation.[90] But there may be grave doubts as to the comparability of different time periods or of different firms.[91] The plaintiff may also seek to prove hypothetical profits through the testimony of experts knowledgeable about the industry; to be persuasive, the expert must explain the methods used and convince the court or jury that an estimate is based on facts.[92]

---

86. See generally Areeda & Turner, note 1, ¶365; E. Timberlake, Federal Treble Damage Antitrust Actions §21 (1965); Annot., 16 A.L.R. Fed. 14 (1986); A. Parker, Measuring Damages in Federal Treble Damage Actions, 17 Antitr. Bull. 497 (1972); J. Davidow, Proof of Purchases and Damages by Public Buyers of Price-Fixed Goods, 17 Antitr. Bull. 363 (1972).

87. Story Parchment Co. v. Paterson Parchment Paper Co., 282 U.S. 555, 562 (1931): "[T]here is a clear distinction between the measure of proof necessary to establish the fact that petitioner has sustained some damage and the measure of proof necessary to enable the jury to fix the amount."

88. See, e.g., Wall Prods. Co. v. National Gypsum, 357 F. Supp. 832 (N.D. Cal. 1973); Ohio Valley Elec. v. GE, 244 F. Supp. 914 (S.D.N.Y. 1965).

89. If the plaintiff is driven out of business altogether by defendant's violation, the court must attempt to determine the value of the business. This can be measured in terms of out-of-pocket investment or capitalized, reasonably anticipated, future net profits. But the court cannot award the plaintiff the going value of the business *and* anticipated future profits, which would amount to double-counting. Albrecht v. Herald Co., 452 F.2d 124 (8th Cir. 1971).

90. See Note, Private Treble Damage Antitrust Suits: Measure of Damages for Destruction of All or Part of a Business, 80 Harv. L. Rev. 1566 (1967).

91. See Theatre Inv. Co. v. RKO Radio Pictures, 72 F. Supp. 650, 656 (W.D. Wash. 1947).

92. *Farmington Dowel*, note 84, at 82; Sunkist Growers v. Winckler & Smith Citrus Prods. Co., 284 F.2d 1, 33 (9th Cir. 1960), rev'd on other grounds, 370 U.S. 19 (1962).

[E]ven where the defendant by his own wrong has prevented a more precise computation, the jury may not render a verdict based on speculation or guesswork. But the jury may make a just and reasonable estimate of the damage based on relevant data, and render its verdict accordingly. In such circumstances "juries are allowed to act upon probable and inferential, as well as direct and positive proof." ... The most elementary conceptions of justice and public policy require that the wrongdoer shall bear the risk of the uncertainty which its own wrong has created.[93]

(c) *Joint and several liability; contribution.* Defendants generally are jointly and severally liable for the damages resulting from their conspiracy. In *Texas Industries*,[94] the Supreme Court held that a party liable for damages for participating in a price-fixing conspiracy in violation of Sherman Act §1 may not obtain any contribution from fellow conspirators. The antitrust laws themselves make no provision for such contribution and the Justices concluded unanimously that the federal courts were not empowered to create a federal common-law rule of contribution among antitrust violators. The Supreme Court acknowledged the arguments in favor of contribution but believed that the policy issues should be resolved by Congress rather than by the courts. "Ascertaining what is 'fair' in this setting ... [and] whether contribution would strengthen or weaken enforcement ... or what form a right to contribution should take, cannot be resolved without going beyond the record of a single lawsuit."[95]

Allowing contribution would mean that each defendant would be liable only for the damage it caused (trebled). The wisdom of doing so has been much debated.[96] On one side, it is said to be both fair and fully consistent with deterrence. Without contribution, a minor conspirator could end up paying the entire judgment. Indeed, that danger may generate inexorable pressure to settle. To finance their lawsuit, plaintiffs may settle cheaply even with the major or most culpable defendants, eager to escape for less than their pro rata share of damages. Only the actual amount of the settlement — not the settling defendants' pro rata share of the judgment — will ultimately be deducted from any final judgment. Fearful then that they will be left holding the bag, minor or even innocent defen-

93. Bigelow v. RKO Radio Pictures, 327 U.S. 251, 264-265 (1946).
94. 451 U.S. 630 (1981).
95. Id. at 646-647.
96. E.g., ABA Antitrust Section, Monograph No. 11, Contribution and Claim Reduction in Antitrust Litigation (1986); F. Easterbrook, W. Landes & R. Posner, Contribution Among Antitrust Defendants: A Legal and Economic Analysis, 23 J.L. & Econ. 331 (1980); A.M. Polinsky & S. Shavell, Contribution and Claim Reduction Among Antitrust Defendants: An Economic Analysis, 33 Stan. L. Rev. 447 (1981).

dants may also feel forced to settle. Furthermore, proponents of contribution argue that pro rata damages suffice to deter most potential violators.

Opponents of contribution argue that potential liability for the damage caused by fellow conspirators increases the deterrence to antitrust violations and encourages settlements, thereby compensating plaintiffs regardless of the ultimate disposition of the case. If settling defendants also cooperate in disclosing the conspiracy, justice is further served.

144. Standing and related doctrines: an introduction.[97] Although Clayton Act §4 appears superficially clear in affording standing to "any" affected person, the courts have limited the universe of plaintiffs allowed to seek treble damages. The nature of these limitations as well as their grounding in statutory language, antitrust policy, or administrative necessity are noted below, after a brief suggestion of several possible impulses underlying them.

First, there is the fear of endlessly proliferating recoveries, subjecting the defendant to multiple payments for the same injury and requiring the courts to make increasingly speculative determinations about the amount and source of remote injuries. This danger may seem particularly grave once the defendant's liability has been litigated by the government, and therefore is prima facie established for treble damages purposes.[98] Thereafter, any number of private parties may seek to jump on the treble damage bandwagon.

Second, judges without discretion over the trebling of damages may hesitate to punish a defendant whose transgression was minor or undertaken in good faith. And they hesitate most when the suit is brought by a relative "stranger" whose interests are not at the core of antitrust concerns.

Third, judges may be reluctant to subject the defendants and themselves to the burdens of a lengthy trial on elusive issues at the instance of such strangers. Finally, many antitrust complaints may seem insubstantial and yet contain sufficient allegations, often in the form of legal conclusions, to survive dismissal. The wish to dispose of such cases on standing grounds is understandable, although the increasing availability of summary judgment[99] may ease that pressure.

---

97. See generally Areeda & Turner, note 1, ch. 3G; D. Berger & R. Bernstein, An Analytical Framework for Antitrust Standing, 86 Yale L.J. 809 (1977); D. Lytle & B. Purdue, Antitrust Target Area Under Section 4 of the Clayton Act: Determination of Standing in Light of the Alleged Antitrust Violation, 25 Am. U.L. Rev. 795 (1976).

98. See ¶158c.

99. See ¶152.

Of course, any limitation on private actions necessarily reduces the ability of private plaintiffs to challenge antitrust violations, and the Supreme Court has declared that the courts "should not add requirements to burden the private litigant beyond what is specifically set forth by Congress in those [antitrust] laws."[100] Yet the Court itself has occasionally limited standing and has noted various standing limits without disapproval.[101] More recently it has issued a number of opinions articulating more precisely the limits it will endorse. The cases may seem inconsistent and the opinions confusing because the usual formulations do not fully capture the range of considerations bearing on standing. The following Paragraphs describe doctrine in two major areas: (1) limitations concerning the directness of damages, noting in particular limitations on recoveries by consumers who do not purchase directly from price-fixing conspirators, provisions for states to sue in their "parens patriae" capacity, and contrasting requirements in suits seeking only equitable relief and (2) the evolving requirement that plaintiffs must allege "antitrust injury" as a requisite to bringing suit.

145. Standing and limitations concerning the directness of injury. (a) *Introduction.* Because satisfactory proof of damages is itself an essential element of the treble-damage suit, the court can and should terminate the suit whenever it appears that damages are unlikely to be proved, incapable of proof with reasonable judicial economy, or, if proved, would not flow from the doctrinal reasons for finding that the defendant's conduct violates the antitrust laws. Once it is realized that these judgments can often be made at the outset of the litigation, there may be little need for any separate doctrine of standing. Nevertheless, many courts seem hesitant to make express judgments about damages until after trial. Yet they appreciate the obvious social utility of avoiding unnecessary and burdensome inquiries into liability. Accordingly, the impulse toward early termination is often expressed in terms of standing. In addition, there are some areas where granting standing may permit suits by parties only remotely connected with the purposes of the antitrust proscription, where better-situated parties would be available. Moreover, suit in such instances may threaten multiple treble-damage recoveries for a single violation as well as complicate the measurement or tracing of damages.

(b) *Passing on and consumer recoveries.* One recurrent problem has involved the private plaintiff who may have shifted the injury to a

---

100. Radovich v. National Football League, 352 U.S. 445, 454 (1957).

101. Hawaii v. Standard Oil Co. (Cal.), 405 U.S. 251, 262 n.14 (1972), limited standing and cited various lower court decisions confining standing. *Brunswick*, 429 U.S. at 488 n.13, cited with apparent approval cases denying standing.

third party. In a typical case, the private plaintiff is a processor or distributor who purchased goods from defendant manufacturer at prices allegedly enhanced through a price-fixing conspiracy among manufacturers. According to the Supreme Court decision in *Hanover Shoe*, the defendant will not normally be allowed to prove that the plaintiff passed on the price increases to its customers and therefore suffered no injury.[102]

This doctrine has implications for the ultimate consumer. Consumers may recover treble damages for injuries caused by the antitrust violation of an immediate supplier.[103] But the Supreme Court held in *Illinois Brick*[104] that the consumer purchasing from an innocent middleman may not recover from the manufacturer who, for example, unlawfully agreed with rival manufacturers to raise prices. The Court held this conclusion to be a corollary of *Hanover Shoe*, which allowed the middlemen to recover the full amount of the manufacturer's illegal overcharge without any deduction for the

---

102. *Hanover Shoe*, note 23, at 489, 491-494: "At whatever price the buyer sells, the price he pays the seller remains illegally high, and his profits would be greater were his costs lower." This approach,

> United argues, should be subject to the defense that economic circumstances were such that the overcharged buyer could only charge his customers a higher price *because* the price to him was higher.... This situation might be present, it is said, where the overcharge is imposed equally on all of a buyer's competitors and where the demand for the buyer's product is so inelastic that the buyer and his competitors could all increase their prices by the amount of the cost increase without suffering a consequent decline in sales.

The Court refused to recognize such a qualification, even in principle, because a convincing demonstration of its applicability in actual cases would depend on "virtually unascertainable figures" such that "the task would normally prove insurmountable." Nevertheless, defendants would "frequently seek to establish its applicability" and thus prolong and complicate treble-damage proceedings. To allow a passing-on defense, moreover, might allow monopolists and price fixers to "retain the fruits of their illegality" because "ultimate consumers, in today's case the buyers of single pairs of shoes, would have only a tiny stake in a lawsuit and little interest in attempting a class action." Thus, no one would be available to sue and

> [t]reble-damage actions ... would be substantially reduced in effectiveness.
> We recognize that there might be situations — for instance, when an overcharged buyer has a pre-existing "cost-plus" contract [— calling for a different result.] We also recognize that where no differential can be proved between the price unlawfully charged and some price that the seller was required by law to charge, establishing damages might require a showing of loss of profits to the buyer.

Subsequent cases have focused on whether plaintiff's pricing policy was discretionary or involved automatic markups. Compare *Wall Prods.*, note 88, with Obron v. Union Camp Corp., 355 F. Supp. 902 (E.D. Mich. 1972), aff'd per curiam, 477 F.2d 542 (6th Cir. 1973). See E. Schaefer, Passing-On Theory in Antitrust Treble Damage Actions: An Economic and Legal Analysis, 16 Wm. & Mary L. Rev. 883 (1975); R. Harris & L. Sullivan, Passing On the Monopoly Overcharge: A Comprehensive Policy Analysis, 128 U. Pa. L. Rev. 269 (1979).

103. Reiter v. Sonotone Corp., 442 U.S. 330 (1979).

104. Illinois Brick Co. v. Illinois, 431 U.S. 720 (1977).

portion of that overcharge passed on to down-the-line purchasers.[105] *Illinois Brick* precluded the consumer from proving injury from a passed-on overcharge whenever the defendant is precluded from proving that its overcharge did not injure its immediate customer because it was passed on to consumers. The Court feared duplicate recoveries, even if passing on were allowed symmetrically, both offensively by consumers and defensively by suppliers against middlemen. It also thought that the difficulties of measuring, tracing, and apportioning damages would bring excessive uncertainties and complexity into damage actions, and thereby overburden the courts. Furthermore, to increase the cost of litigation and to diffuse its benefits among a larger group of plaintiffs would diminish the incentive to sue and thus reduce the effectiveness of the treble damage action as a deterrent to wrongdoers. This reasoning would not necessarily preclude indirect purchasers from equitable relief.[106]

(c) *Employees.* The statute authorizes recovery only for injury to "business or property." A loss of employment or reduction in wages is generally not considered to be an injury to business or property[107] unless the plaintiff's job is itself shown to be a commercial venture or enterprise.[108] The result is appropriate in some cases but not in others, and the stated "unless" clause does not serve to distinguish proper from improper standing. An employee injured because of an employer conspiracy fixing wages is within the class designed to be protected by a statute guaranteeing the benefits of competition to sellers of services as well as to buyers of goods.[109] But

---

105. Although *Illinois Brick* suggested that indirect purchasers might be allowed to sue where they bore the full upstream overcharge under a preexisting fixed-quantity cost-plus contract, a closely divided Supreme Court declined to make such an exception in a case in which indirect purchasers from a state-regulated utility did not have a fixed volume. Kansas v. Utilicorp, 497 U.S. 199 (1990). The Court indicated that there was uncertainty about whether the middleman utility bore some of the overcharge, and the Court saw little benefit for consumers in creating a complex exception to its general proscription of indirect purchaser suits because state regulators can force a public utility to share the fruits of its own antitrust suit with its customers.

106. E.g., Mid-West Paper Prods. Co. v. Continental Group, 596 F.2d 573, 590 (3d Cir. 1979). On analogies to cost-plus contracts, see Beef Indus. Antitr. Litigation, 600 F.2d 1148 (5th Cir. 1979), cert. denied, 449 U.S. 905 (1980).

107. E.g., Reibert v. Atlantic Richfield Co., 471 F.2d 727 (10th Cir.), cert. denied, 411 U.S. 938 (1973).

108. E.g., Dailey v. Quality School Plan, 380 F.2d 484 (5th Cir. 1967) (commissioned salesman with his own territory); Vandervelde v. Put & Call Brokers & Dealers Assn., 344 F. Supp. 118, 153-154 (S.D.N.Y. 1972) (sole owner whose salary was a cash draw that varied according to the financial situation of the firm).

109. E.g., *Radovich,* note 100; Wilson v. Ringsby Truck Lines, 320 F. Supp. 699 (D. Colo. 1970) (truck drivers suffering reduced wages because of employer's alleged market division were within class that Congress intended to protect).

a loss of employment following a merger that is deemed illegal because of its possible product market effects is only indirectly related to the reasons for condemning the merger.[110] This point may be expressed by saying that such an employee is not within the "target area" of the offense.[111] To be sure, it might be argued that any injury following upon an antitrust violation should be compensable, even if that injury is not at the core of the reason for condemning the conduct.[112] So broad a view, however, would not limit the universe of permitted plaintiffs at all and may be inconsistent with the *Brunswick* case discussed in ¶146(b).

(d) *Derived injuries.*[113] In a large number of cases, the plaintiff's injury results from an injury to a more immediate victim of the defendant's conduct. Some of these situations are easier to resolve than others.

Where the immediate victim is a city or a corporation, standing is usually denied to "indirectly" injured taxpayers,[114] shareholders,[115] or creditors.[116] Although such plaintiffs are once-removed, that alone is not determinative, as we shall see in a moment. Ordinarily,

110. E.g., *Reibert*, note 107; Bywater v. Matsushita Elec. Indus. Co., 1971 Trade Cas. ¶73759 (S.D.N.Y.) (workers not directly injured by competitive injury to their employer).

111. E.g., *Vandervelde*, note 108 (suspended dealer within foreseeable area of impact).

112. *Wilson*, note 109, at 702-703: "It may also be argued that the purpose and language of this [antitrust] legislation are so sweeping that any person injured by the proscribed conduct should be considered within the class which Congress intended to protect." Another potentially broad approach was taken by the Sixth Circuit's *Malamud* decision, which declared that direct injury or target area tests "really demand too much from plaintiffs at the pleading stage of the case." Malamud v. Sinclair Oil Corp., 521 F.2d 1142, 1149, 1151 (6th Cir. 1975). Instead, the court thought it sufficient that "the interest sought to be protected by the complainant is arguably within the zone of interests to be protected or regulated by the statute or constitutional guarantee in question." That language was drawn from Association of Data Processing Serv. Orgs. v. Camp, 397 U.S. 150, 153 (1970), which, however, was grounded in the different standing language of a statute involving judicial supervision of illegal governmental action rather than damages between private parties. Even so, *Malamud*'s adoption of "interests protected" is unexceptionable because that language can reflect the same judgments just stated in regard to employee standing.

113. For qualifications and comprehensive analyses, see Areeda & Turner, note 1, ¶¶373-376, 378.

114. Ragar v. J.T. Raney & Sons, 521 F.2d 795 (8th Cir. 1975), aff'g 388 F. Supp. 1184 (E.D. Ark. 1975).

115. E.g., Kreager v. GE, 497 F.2d 468 (2d Cir.), cert. denied, 419 U.S. 861 (1974). Courts are divided over whether a stockholder has standing under the antitrust laws to bring a shareholder's derivative action. Compare Ash v. IBM, 353 F.2d 491, 493 (3d Cir. 1965), cert. denied, 384 U.S. 927 (1966) (no derivative action), with Rogers v. American Can Co., 305 F.2d 297 (3d Cir. 1962).

116. Loeb v. Eastman Kodak Co., 183 F. 704 (3d Cir. 1910).

the interests of these plaintiffs are identical with those of the immediate victim, which is in a better position to sue on its own behalf. Permitting suit only from the immediate victim will both offer full protection for the more remote persons and eliminate expensive multiple suits with their complex dangers of duplicate recoveries or difficulties of apportionment.

Although the analysis is more complex, similar reasons ordinarily justify the denial of standing to licensors,[117] franchisors,[118] or percentage-lease landlords,[119] whose revenues have allegedly declined as a result of injuries to licensees, franchisees, or tenants. As an example, the percentage-lease landlord of a movie theater is usually said to be only indirectly injured or not within the target area of the defendant's violation — which is defined as the exhibition or distribution market rather than the property rental market.

Finer distinctions are required in a final group of cases, of which we pose one example. Suppose that plaintiff *A* complains that its sometime or potential dealer *D* has been the victim of a tying or exclusive dealing agreement imposed by *A*'s competitor, *B*. In a sense, *A*'s injury is indirect as compared with the immediate victim *D*. But the primary reason that antitrust law is concerned with the agreement in question is its impact on the market opportunities of *B*'s rivals.[120] Accordingly, *A* is usually granted standing as within the target area of the alleged violation.[121]

The "target area" language is used to express the result in the last illustration. But the metaphor can mislead. For example, some courts have thought that targeting has something to do with the defendant's intention. For them, the target area is the zone covering the intended or foreseeable effects of defendant's viola-

117. SCM Corp. v. RCA, 407 F.2d 166 (2d Cir.), cert. denied, 395 U.S. 943 (1969).
118. Billy Baxter v. Coca-Cola Co., 431 F.2d 183 (2d Cir. 1970), cert. denied, 401 U.S. 923 (1971).
119. Calderone Enter. Corp. v. United Artists Theatre Circuit, 454 F.2d 1292 (2d Cir. 1971), cert. denied, 406 U.S. 930 (1972).
120. See Chs. 4B, 4C.
121. E.g., Karseal Corp. v. Richfield Oil Corp., 221 F.2d 358 (9th Cir. 1955). Compare Sanitary Milk Producers v. Bergjans Farm Dairy, 368 F.2d 679, 688-689 (8th Cir. 1966); South Carolina Council of Milk Producers v. Newton, 360 F.2d 414 (4th Cir.), cert. denied, 385 U.S. 934 (1966). In *Billy Baxter,* note 118, at 187, the court said that the causal connection between violation and injury must "link a specific form of illegal act to a plaintiff engaged in the sort of legitimate activities which the prohibition of this type of violation was clearly intended to protect." Among the other cases denying standing to a supplier whose customer was injured are Volasco Prods. Co. v. Lloyd A. Fry Roofing Co., 308 F.2d 383, 394-395 (6th Cir. 1962), cert. denied, 372 U.S. 907 (1963); Minersville Coal Co. v. Anthracite Export Assn., 335 F. Supp. 360 (M.D. Pa. 1971).

tion.[122] Whether or not the absence of foreseeable injury might be grounds for limiting liability, the foreseeability of an impact on a percentage-lease landlord should not suffice to support standing that is otherwise inappropriate. In any event, traditional target area and direct injury formulations may be less in vogue after two more recent Supreme Court cases.[123]

The Supreme Court's decision in *McCready*[124] clarifies the standing of certain indirect victims. The Court faced a so-called boycott of psychologists by Blue Shield, which refused to reimburse subscribers for mental health care by clinical psychologists not arranged through physicians. (This limitation did not affect competing psychiatrists who are, of course, physicians.) A subscriber who independently had arranged for treatment by a psychologist was granted standing to sue the insurer for damages although the premium she (or her employer) had paid for her health insurance contract did not provide coverage for independent care by psychologists. She was granted standing on the grounds that her injury was not too remote and awarding her damages involved no difficult problems of apportionment or duplication because her psychologist had already been paid.[125] The Court emphasized that denying reimbursement to subscribers patronizing psychologists was the very means by which the insurer's illegal disruption of competition between psychologists and psychiatrists was effected. Moreover, the alleged boycott disrupted competition in health care and the price of insurance, and the plaintiff purchased both care and insurance.[126]

Shortly after *McCready,* the Court decided *Associated General Contractors,*[127] which insisted that the general language of §4 was implicitly qualified. The plaintiff labor union alleged a conspiracy among

122. E.g., Hoopes v. Union Oil, 374 F.2d 480 (9th Cir. 1967) (lessors of service station have standing to establish that gas supplier prevented them from operating or selling station).

123. Several lower courts have disowned them, Chelson v. Oregonian Publishing Co., 715 F.2d 1368, 1370 (9th Cir. 1983); Merican v. Caterpillar Tractor Co., 713 F.2d 958, 964 (3d Cir. 1983), cert. denied, 465 U.S. 1024 (1984), while others continue to use these tests, e.g., Construction Aggregate Transp. v. Florida Rock Indus., 710 F.2d 752, 762 n.23 (11th Cir. 1983); Parks v. Watson, 716 F.2d 646, 658-659 (9th Cir. 1983).

124. Blue Shield of Va. v. McCready, 457 U.S. 465 (1982).

125. Observe that her psychologist might still be injured because the insurer's illegal discrimination against psychologists would tend to depress the fees they could command in the marketplace. In addition, there would be other patients who would forgo the psychologist option as a result of the arrangement that would have used a psychologist if there were no discrimination in the insurance arrangement as to reimbursement.

126. See ¶146.

127. Associated Gen. Contractors v. California State Council of Carpenters, 459 U.S. 519 (1983).

nonunion builders to coerce their customers (property owners awarding building contracts) and other general contractors (like themselves) to give some, but not necessarily all, of their business to nonunionized firms. The alleged consequence was less business for unionized firms, less employment for union members, and less payment of dues to the plaintiff union.

In one sense, the union's standing claim seems stronger than that of Ms. McCready because the union alleged that it was the intended victim of defendants' alleged restraint. But the Court decided that such an intention to harm the plaintiff was in itself insufficient to create standing. Not only were the union's injuries in this case an indirect result of whatever harm may have been suffered by certain contractors, but the latter were fully capable of vindicating their own interests. "The existence of an identifiable class of persons whose self-interest would normally motivate them to vindicate the public interest in antitrust enforcement diminishes the justification for allowing a more remote party such as the Union to perform the office of a private attorney general."[128] The Court summed up by noting a variety of factors bearing on standing, all of which pointed toward denial in this case: the risk of duplicative recoveries, danger of complex apportionment, nature of the alleged injury, relationship between the alleged violation and alleged injury (here, tenuous and speculative), and existence of more direct victims of the alleged conspiracy — reasoning generally parallel to that invoked in *Illinois Brick* to deny standing to indirect consumers. The Court did not say how these factors should be balanced when they point in different directions.

(e) *Other business or property questions.* Predicating the otherwise proper denial of standing on the absence of business or property can create unnecessary problems. The difficulty of proving damages may be good reason for rejecting the suit of a plaintiff claiming illegal exclusion from a business it had not yet entered.[129] Perhaps for the same reason, standing is also denied to a state claiming damage to its general economy.[130] Such denials are grounded in the absence of business or property, which the Supreme Court

---

128. Id. at 542.

129. To determine whether such a plaintiff may sue, the courts usually look to background and experience in the prospective "business," financial ability, and depth of actual or potential financial or contractual obligation. E.g., Martin v. Phillips Petro. Co., 365 F.2d 629 (5th Cir.), cert. denied, 385 U.S. 991 (1966). Some courts bypass the ready-and-able question altogether and insist that the plaintiff have a current business or property interest. Duff v. Kansas City Star Co., 299 F.2d 320 (8th Cir. 1962).

130. *Hawaii*, note 101.

defined as a commercial interest.[131] But the courts have not followed the logic of such definitions and have properly granted standing to nonprofit or professional groups[132] and ultimate, direct-purchasing consumers.[133]

(f) *Clayton Act §7 violations.* Clayton Act §4 authorizes private actions for those injured by reason of a violation of the antitrust laws that are defined in §1 to include the Clayton Act itself. Clayton Act §7 forbids certain mergers that "may" substantially lessen competition or "tend" to a monopoly. As Chapter 5 will reveal, a merger may be held to violate §7 even though its harmful effects are quite remote. Because such possible effects may make a merger unlawful without harming any present person, some courts have denied the possibility of a private treble damage action for violation of §7.[134] This seems clearly erroneous; there is no reason to deny a private cause of action where the threat has ripened into injury.

(g) *Parens patriae.* Damage suits are available to states meeting the regular standing requirements. In the typical case, the state alleges that it was forced to pay higher prices because of defendants' price-fixing conspiracy.[135] In addition, a state may try to sue in its sovereign capacity as parens patriae without demonstrating injury to its proprietary business or property.[136] Such a suit is allowed insofar as it seeks injunctive relief.[137] In addition, Congress enacted Clayton Act §4C in 1976 to authorize the states to attack Sherman Act violations by recovering three times the damages suffered by natural persons residing in a state. Anyone who prefers to sue independently can choose to be excluded from the state suit. The award to the state must exclude damages obtained by or allocable to those

131. Id. at 264.

132. See ¶146; Friends of Animals v. American Veterinary Medical Assn., 310 F. Supp. 1016 (S.D.N.Y. 1970).

133. See *Reiter,* note 103.

134. E.g., Highland Supply Corp. v. Reynolds Metals Co., 327 F.2d 725, 728 n.3 (8th Cir. 1964). But see Gottesman v. General Motors Corp., 414 F.2d 956 (2d Cir. 1969), cert. denied, 403 U.S. 911 (1971).

135. E.g., Philadelphia v. American Oil Co., 53 F.R.D. 45 (D.N.J. 1971); Minnesota v. U.S. Steel, 44 F.R.D. 559 (D. Minn. 1968).

136. See generally M. Malina & M. Blechman, Parens Patriae Suits for Treble Damages Under the Antitrust Laws, 65 Nw. U.L. Rev. 193 (1970).

137. In Georgia v. Pennsylvania R.R., 324 U.S. 439 (1945), Georgia had standing to bring a suit, seeking injunctive relief, against defendant railroad companies that allegedly fixed freight rates that discriminated against the state. See also Burch v. Goodyear Tire & Rubber Co., 554 F.2d 633 (4th Cir. 1977). But in *Hawaii,* note 101, the Court denied Hawaii standing to bring a treble-damage suit for injury to its economy. The Court held that the state's economy was not business or property within the meaning of §4, and that in the absence of clear congressional intent, the state should not be permitted to sue because of the danger of double recovery by both state and individuals for the same injury.

who have already sued, those who opt out of the state suit, and all business entities. Section 4D allows damages in price-fixing cases to be proved in the aggregate by statistical, sampling, or other techniques, without the necessity for separate proof of each purchaser's own damages. The resulting award would be distributed or retained by the state, as the court may direct, as long as each injured party is given the opportunity to obtain an appropriate portion.

(h) *Equity suits compared.* Clayton Act §16 authorizing equitable relief can be distinguished from §4 in several respects. Its requirement is "threatened loss or damage" rather than actual injury, and it is not explicitly limited to business or property interests. Accordingly, equitable relief is frequently available when treble damages are not.[138] In contrast to the mandatory trebling provision of §4, moreover, §16 "is flexible and capable of nice 'adjustment and reconciliation between the public interest and private needs as well as between competing private claims.'"[139] And injunctive relief does not present the danger of several parties recovering for the same injury.[140]

146. Antitrust injury. (a) *Introduction; relationship of antitrust injury doctrine to standing.* Beginning with *Brunswick,* the Supreme Court has fashioned a requirement that a plaintiff's case demonstrate antitrust injury. The plaintiff seeking damages (or an injunction) must show that it (1) suffers injury (or threatened injury) that is both (2) actually caused by the defendant's illegal conduct and (3) of the kind that the antitrust laws were designed to prevent. Although the first two requirements had been expressly required long before the term "antitrust injury" was first used, that term is increasingly used to include all three requirements. We need not enter the debate about whether antitrust injury is an aspect of standing or something additional. Unlike standing, it does not usually involve such questions as remoteness, the availability of other more directly injured plaintiffs, tracing of damages, or the dangers of multiple recovery. Like standing, it asks whether the injury of which the plaintiff complains or the damages it has actually proved connect closely enough with the purposes of the antitrust laws[141] —

138. *Zenith,* note 37, at 130-131; Multidistrict Vehicle Air Pollution Litigation, 481 F.2d 122 (9th Cir.), cert. denied, 414 U.S. 1045, remanded and dismissed, 367 F. Supp. 1298 (C.D. Cal. 1973), aff'd, 538 F.2d 231 (9th Cir. 1976) (equitable remedies more widely available than damages, but only to promote antitrust goals).
139. *Zenith,* note 37, at 131.
140. *Hawaii,* note 101, at 261 ("the fact is that one injunction is as effective as 100, and, concomitantly, that 100 injunctions are no more effective than one").
141. Reconsider, for example, the employee standing problem in ¶145c.

as *Brunswick* itself well illustrates. Although many recent decisions about standing or antitrust injury mix language from both, one must not, for example, regard a holding that a plaintiff's damage is not too remote for standing as if it were a holding that such damages are a proper measure of antitrust injury.

(b) **Brunswick Corp. v. Pueblo Bowl-O-Mat,** 429 U.S. 477, 489 (1977). In *Brunswick,* the Supreme Court held that the treble damage plaintiff must "prove more than injury causally linked" to the defendant's illegal act. "Plaintiffs must prove *antitrust* injury, that is to say injury of the type that the antitrust laws were intended to prevent and that flows from that which makes the defendants' acts unlawful." The Court's meaning is made clear by the facts before it. The plaintiff operated bowling centers that competed with other centers acquired by the defendant. Absent the acquisition, the acquired centers allegedly would have gone out of business, with the result that the plaintiff would have had less competition and greater profits. The lower courts found the acquisitions unlawful because of possible future harms to the retail bowling market. Without disturbing that finding, the Supreme Court unanimously held that the plaintiff's injury resulted from lawful competition on the part of the acquired and preserved bowling centers and that it was not the purpose of the antitrust laws to prevent such competition or to compensate such injury.[142] Denying damages to the plaintiff diminishes its incentive to attack the unlawful acquisition, but the purpose of the damage remedy was held to be remedial.

(c) **Cargill v. Monfort,** 479 U.S. 104, 115-117 (1986). *Cargill* extended *Brunswick* to require that private plaintiffs show antitrust injury in equity suits as well as in damage actions. In this case, the plaintiff sought to enjoin the horizontal merger of two of its competitors. The lower courts found the merger unlawful on the usual ground that it would so increase concentration in the market as to increase the danger of express collusion or of tacit price coordination among oligopolists. Obviously, however, such a prospect would not have injured the plaintiff or its fellow competitors because they would have benefited from the higher prices or other reductions in competition. Accordingly, it seemed to the Court that the plaintiff must have been worrying that the merger would *increase* competition.[143]

142. For an analysis of this case in the lower courts and for other situations in which an antitrust violation need not result in damages, see P. Areeda, Antitrust Violations Without Damage Recoveries, 89 Harv. L. Rev. 1127 (1976).

143. For this reason, some writers would deny standing, or at least be very skeptical toward, any antitrust suit in which one firm complains of its rivals' merger or joint venture. Indeed, such a suit might be taken as presumptive evidence that the merger or joint venture increases competition, according to W. Baumol & J. Ordover, Use of Antitrust to Subvert Competition, 28 J.L. & Econ. 247 (1985).

At this point, the reader may wonder how a given merger could both confront the plaintiff with increased competition and yet be illegal. One reason, to preview

To hold that the antitrust laws protect competitors from the loss of profits due to such price competition would, in effect, render illegal any decision by a firm to cut prices in order to increase market share. . . . The logic of *Brunswick* compels the conclusion that the threat of loss of profits due to possible price competition following a merger does not constitute a threat of antitrust injury.

The Court did not wholly rule out the prospect of standing for a competitor because it suggested that an injunction might be available to a competitor if, for example, a merger of its rivals created a significant danger of predatory pricing.[144] Such predation would harm not only the plaintiff but also long-run competition.

(d) *Atlantic Richfield Co. v. USA Petroleum Co.*, 495 U.S. 328 (1990). In *ARCO*, a refiner and its dealers had allegedly agreed illegally that they would charge no more than specified resale prices. Facing competition from these dealers, other dealers selling rival brands complained that they could not charge as much as they liked. Attributing their lost profits to the refiner's illegal agreements, they sued the refiner. The Supreme Court ruled that such losses were not compensable "antitrust injury." Unless the ceiling on dealer resale prices was so low as to compel predatory pricing, the Court reasoned, any injury to competitors of the retailers subject to ceiling prices resulted from competition and thus was not the type of loss that antitrust law was designed to prevent. The protection of rival dealers was not within the rationale for condemning maximum resale price agreements, which are illegal primarily because they deprive the agreeing dealers of the freedom to choose the appropriate mix of prices and services, thereby depriving the consumers of the services they desire. Such

---

Chapter 5, is that the law so fears increased concentration that it prevents many mergers prophylactically without any assurance that competition will in fact be injured at some future time. Thus, a merger may be illegal even though it impairs no competition at all. Another reason is noted in the text.

144. In the Court's view, the plaintiff had not raised or proved any such claim, making erroneous the Court of Appeals' generous interpretation of plaintiff's allegations.

Corporations that are the targets of unfriendly takeover attempts by another corporation frequently seek to enjoin the takeover on the ground that the merger of the two corporations would violate the antitrust laws. But is the target company or its shareholders (as distinct from its management) threatened with any injury at all or any injury of the kind the antitrust laws are intended to prevent? If the merger is anticompetitive, it would presumably increase the profits of the merging firms. And the elimination of unnecessary management or labor as a result of the merger has not been regarded as sufficient for standing. Cases denying standing or antitrust injury include Central Natl. Bank v. Rainbolt, 720 F.2d 1183 (10th Cir. 1983); Anago v. Tecnol Medical Products, 976 F.2d 248 (5th Cir. 1992), cert. dismissed, 510 U.S. 985 (1993). More atypical are cases allowing the target to prove the illegality of the merger. See Grumman Corp. v. LTV Corp., 665 F.2d 10, 11 (2d Cir. 1981); Consolidated Gold Fields PLC v. Minorco, 871 F.2d 252 (2d Cir.), cert. dismissed, 492 U.S. 939 (1989).

deprivations would benefit, not harm, rival dealers. Antitrust injury to rival dealers, the Court held, would arise only from predatorily low prices that could destroy efficient dealers selling other brands and thereby impair long-run competition.[145]

147. Class actions.[146] When the government does not sue, a malefactor may greatly profit from its antitrust violation at the expense of numerous victims whose individual treble-damage recoveries would be too small to warrant suit. An individual plaintiff, however, might sue as a representative of a class of injured persons, and the prospect of an attorney's fee for a class recovery may induce a lawyer to undertake the case.

To bring a class action, the plaintiff must satisfy Federal Rule of Civil Procedure 23(a) and come within one of the subdivisions of Rule 23(b). The former authorizes one to sue as a representative of a class if

> (1) the class is so numerous that joinder of all members is impracticable, (2) there are questions of law or fact common to the class, (3) the claims or defenses of the representative parties are typical of the claims or defenses of the class, and (4) the representative parties will fairly and adequately protect the interests of the class.

Most antitrust class suits are filed under Rule 23(b)(3), which also requires "that the questions of law or fact common to the members of the class predominate over any questions affecting only individual members, and the class action is superior to other available methods for the fair and efficient adjudication of the controversy."

Class actions may seem well suited to antitrust violations, which often victimize many on the same basis and where individual suits would either be impractical or would burden the legal system far more than a single class action. In many antitrust cases the evidence establishing damages varies from class member to member, but this trait, common to many suits, does not usually threaten class certification.[147]

---

145. See also ¶407.

146. See generally 7A & 7B C. Wright, A. Miller & M. Kane, Federal Practice and Procedure, Civil §§1751-1804 (2d ed. 1995); 10 J. von Kalinowski, Antitrust Laws and Trade Regulation, ch. 108 (1996).

147. See, e.g., In re Workers' Compensation, 130 F.R.D. 99 (D. Minn. 1990) (fact that plaintiffs purchased their goods at varying prices did not prevent class certification, where the question of the existence of a conspiracy was sufficient to satisfy the predominance requirement); Bogosian v. Gulf Oil Corp., 561 F.2d 434 (3d Cir.), cert. denied, 434 U.S. 1086 (1977). Only when the issues of damages and liability blend to such a degree that bifurcation into class and individual trials is impossible can the individuality of damage claims bar class certification. See, e.g., Windham v. American Brands, 565 F.2d 59 (4th Cir.), cert. denied, 435 U.S. 968 (1977).

148. Plaintiff participation in defendant's antitrust violation. Where the plaintiff was itself a willing participant in the unlawful arrangement that it now challenges or was engaged in an independent antitrust violation that induced the defendant's violation, there is an understandable reluctance to reward it with treble damages, although the reward may induce the disclosure of, suit against, and termination of the defendant's antitrust violation. This reluctance was expressed in the in pari delicto doctrine denying treble-damage relief to plaintiffs who participated in some way in the defendant's unlawful activities or committed related antitrust violations.[148] Of course, the reluctance to grant a treble-damage windfall is not grounds for failing to enforce antitrust policy by declaring an illegal contract unenforceable for the future.[149] Naturally, many courts rejected the in pari delicto defense where the defendant had, realistically speaking, unilaterally imposed illegal terms in a contract through economic coercion; the inappropriateness of that defense was clear where the plaintiff, although a participant, was in reality a victim of the defendant's unlawful conduct.[150] In all events, the Supreme Court has disfavored the defense, and its *Perma Life* decision[151] has all but ruled it out as a bar to suit, except perhaps where the plaintiff is a co-initiator or "equal" participant in the defendant's illegality.[152] Nevertheless, it should be remembered that the plaintiff's participation in an antitrust violation will often mean that it has not suffered actual compensable injury.[153]

149. Unclean hands in nonantitrust suit. A related unclean-hands issue is presented in the nonantitrust suit that defendant resists on the ground that plaintiff is violating antitrust policy. Suppose, for example, that the plaintiff licenses defendant to use a

148. E.g., Kershaw v. Kershaw Mfg. Co., 209 F. Supp. 447, 454 (M.D. Ala. 1962), aff'd per curiam, 327 F.2d 1002 (5th Cir. 1964).

149. See Florists' Nationwide Tel. Delivery Network v. Florists' Tel. Delivery Assn., 371 F.2d 263 (7th Cir.), cert. denied, 387 U.S. 909 (1967).

150. Goldlawr v. Shubert, 268 F. Supp. 965 (E.D. Pa. 1967) (plaintiff participating in defendant booking office's illegal practices had no alternative source; not barred); Ring v. Spina, 148 F.2d 647, 652-653 (2d Cir. 1945).

151. Perma Life Mufflers v. International Parts Corp., 392 U.S. 134 (1968).

152. E.g., Sullivan v. Tagliabue, 34 F.3d 1091 (1st Cir. 1994) (holding that while plaintiff had been a major participant in formulating the rule that it presently challenged, other evidence suggested plaintiff was not fully informed about the substantive policy and believed his own team was exempt; this created a factual issue on defendant's assertion of an in pari delicto defense); Thi-Hawaii v. First Commercial Fin. Corp., 627 F.2d 991 (9th Cir. 1980); Javelin Corp. v. Uniroyal, 546 F.2d 276, 279 (9th Cir. 1976), cert. denied, 431 U.S. 938 (1977) (defense available only where plaintiff "participated in the formation" and when "illegal conspiracy would not have been formed but for the plaintiff's participation").

153. See Areeda & Turner, note 1, ¶365c3.

patented invention and that the license contract restrains defendant's conduct in some way. Suppose further that plaintiff sues to
recover contractual royalties due from defendant, compel its obedience to the contract's restriction, and enjoin a third person who is
infringing the patent. Plaintiff would prevail entirely if the contractual restraint on defendant were lawful. But if the restraint were
unlawful,[154] plaintiff might lose entirely. The court will not compel
obedience to the unlawful provision on the customary ground that
courts will not enforce unlawful promises. The court may also wash
its hands of the "whole unlawful enterprise" and refuse to make
defendant pay for using plaintiff's patent. And even the third-party
infringer may escape plaintiff's patent on the claim that plaintiff
lacks the clean hands necessary to petition a court of equity.[155]

Although the dirty-hands defense is "equitable" in historical deri-
vation, it will bar both legal and equitable claims.[156] But which
antitrust violations may successfully be asserted as defenses to which
nonantitrust suits? What must be the relationship of plaintiff's alleged antitrust violation to its nonantitrust cause of action? Misuse
of a patent, for example, is likely to bar its enforcement, at least
until the misuse ends and the evil consequences are purged, but it
probably will not bar plaintiff's enforcement of totally unrelated
patents.[157] At least where one party has delivered goods pursuant to
the illegal agreement, "[p]ast the point where the judgment of the
Court would itself be enforcing the precise conduct made unlawful
by the Act, the courts are to be guided by the overriding general
policy . . . 'of preventing people from getting other people's property for nothing when they purport to be buying it.'"[158]

The Supreme Court applied these ideas in *Kaiser*.[159] The defendant steel company, Kaiser, had promised the United Mine Workers

154. The courts often speak of patent misuse, which includes antitrust violations
but is not limited to proved antitrust offenses. Judicial refusal to protect the patent
monopoly from being misused in ways offensive to public policy developed as a
product of equity prior to and independently of the antitrust laws. As might be
expected, the courts have come to look to the antitrust laws generally as the embodiment of public policy protecting competition and controlling monopoly. See ¶186.

155. Morton Salt Co. v. G.S. Suppiger Co., 314 U.S. 488 (1942).

156. Associated Press v. Taft-Ingalls Corp., 340 F.2d 753 (6th Cir.), cert. denied,
382 U.S. 820 (1965); Preformed Line Prods. Co. v. Fanner Mfg. Co., 328 F.2d 265,
279 (6th Cir. 1964).

157. Aluminum Co. v. Sperry Prods., 285 F.2d 911, 925-927 (6th Cir. 1960), cert.
denied, 368 U.S. 890 (1961).

158. Kelly v. Kosuga, 358 U.S. 516, 520-521 (1959). Lewis v. Seanor Coal Co.,
382 F.2d 437, 441 (3d Cir. 1967), cert. denied, 390 U.S. 947 (1968), declared that
"It is now well established that the remedy for violation of the antitrust law is not
avoidance of payments due under a contract, but rather the redress which the
antitrust statute establishes, — a treble damage action." See Note, The Defense of
Antitrust Illegality in Contract Actions, 27 U. Chi. L. Rev. 758 (1960).

159. Kaiser Steel Corp. v. Mullins, 455 U.S. 72 (1982).

Union that it would contribute certain sums to UMW health and retirement trust funds based not only on the coal it produced and the hours worked by covered employees but also on coal it purchased from sources that had not contributed to the UMW funds. Kaiser had not made the payments with respect to its purchases from those represented by a different union (and whose wages and benefits equaled or surpassed UMW levels). When the UMW trust funds sued, Kaiser asserted that the purchased-coal clause violated federal antitrust and labor laws. The Supreme Court reversed the lower court's rejection of the defense:

> if Kaiser's agreement to contribute based on purchased coal is assumed to be illegal under either the Sherman Act or the [National Labor Relations Act], its promise to contribute could [not] be enforced without commanding unlawful conduct.... If the purchased-coal agreement is illegal, it is precisely because the promised contributions are linked to purchased coal and are a penalty for dealing with producers not under contract with the UMW.[160]

Preparing and Trying Antitrust Cases

150. Venue and jurisdiction. Clayton Act §12 permits any antitrust proceeding against a corporation to be brought "not only in the judicial district whereof it is an inhabitant, but also in any district where it may be found or transacts business."[161] The same section permits service of process throughout the country.

151. Investigations and discovery. The Justice Department and the Federal Trade Commission often pursue their investigations

---

160. Id. at 79-82. Three Justices dissented on the ground that a federal statute requires that promised payments to employee retirement funds must be made " 'to the extent not inconsistent with law.' " Id. at 91. The minority interpreted the quoted language to excuse contractual nonperformance

only when the payment at issue is *inherently* illegal — for example, when the payment is in the nature of a bribe [— that is,] only when the payment in question itself constitutes an illegal act, [as distinct from] payments that would "lead to" situations condemned by law, or that would allow a party to "reap the fruits" of illegal collective-bargaining provisions. [Id. at 92-93.]

161. The "transacts business" test is a broad test; it is not a technical concept but rather the "practical, everyday business or commercial concept of doing or carrying on business of 'any substantial character.' " United States v. Scophony Corp., 333 U.S. 795, 807 (1948). Compare Friends of Animals v. American Veterinary Medical Assn., 310 F. Supp. 620 (S.D.N.Y. 1970) (association that sent representatives into district three times annually does not transact business there), with ABC Great States v. Globe Ticket Co., 310 F. Supp. 739 (N.D. Ill. 1970) (venue established over firm that sold in district and sent officials there four times to attend meetings at which alleged conspiracy formed).

quite informally without subpoenas or other formal procedures. The Justice Department sometimes uses a grand jury because of its extensive investigatory powers to require the production of documents, summon witnesses, and compel testimony.[162] And since 1962 the Justice Department has been empowered to issue a "civil investigative demand,"[163] which resembles but is narrower than the subpoena issued by the Federal Trade Commission. In either case, if the addressee refuses to comply, the agency must seek the aid of a court. Once the government or a private party brings a suit, the usual discovery procedures are available to all parties and, in civil antitrust cases, extensive use of interrogatories and depositions is customary.

152. Pleadings; summary judgment. Private antitrust complaints alleging antitrust offenses in highly conclusionary terms might present a tempting target for summary judgment when the plaintiff fails to assert any facts or evidence supporting its general allegations. But, as in many other areas of the law, the courts tend to allow such unsupported complaints to stand long enough to permit the plaintiff access to discovery against the defendant, particularly where the relevant evidence is likely to be available only from the defendant.[164]

In 1962, the Supreme Court ruled that "summary procedures should be used sparingly in complex antitrust litigation where motive and intent play leading roles, the proof is largely in the hands of the alleged conspirators, and hostile witnesses thicken the plot."[165] Such language may imply, however, that courts were more restrictive in granting summary judgment than they actually had been.[166] Under

---

162. Until 1970, the grand jury could compel testimony that might tend to incriminate the witness because the Immunity Act of 1903 granted immunity from prosecution on evidence or testimony compelled in Sherman Act proceedings. 32 Stat. 904 (1903), 34 Stat. 798 (1906), 15 U.S.C. §§32-33 (1964). See United States v. Welden, 377 U.S. 95 (1964). Antitrust proceedings are now governed by the generally applicable immunity provisions of 84 Stat. 926 (1970), 18 U.S.C. §§6001-6005.

163. 76 Stat. 548, as amended, 15 U.S.C. §§1311-1314.

164. In Bogosian v. Gulf Oil Corp., 337 F. Supp. 1234, 1235 (E.D. Pa. 1972), plaintiff's motion to amend his complaint to add a conspiracy charge was resisted as not made in good faith where his deposition had established that he personally knew no fact implying a conspiracy. The court permitted the amendment: "Experience has shown that where a conspiracy is suspected, the proof of it most frequently emerges from discovery. . . ."

165. Poller v. Columbia Broadcasting System, 368 U.S. 464, 473 (1962). See also Norfolk Monument Co. v. Woodlawn Memorial Gardens, 394 U.S. 700 (1969).

166. See Areeda & Turner, note 1, ¶¶322-323. One study (predating the 1986 Supreme Court decisions noted in text) of antitrust litigation indicated that summary procedures (summary judgment and motions to dismiss for failure to state a claim) are not used less frequently in antitrust cases than in other cases. S. Calkins,

Rule 56 of the Federal Rules of Civil Procedure, summary judgment is appropriate where there is no "genuine issue as to any material fact." Before 1986, some courts ruled that the existence of any evidence tending to support the plaintiff's claims precluded summary judgment. In several 1986 decisions, however, the Supreme Court found a genuine issue to exist only when the whole summary judgment record supported a jury verdict in the plaintiff's favor.[167] Thus, if the summary judgment record were the evidence at trial and the defendant would be entitled to a directed verdict, it is entitled to summary judgment before trial. These decisions are likely to lead to more summary dispositions, although still only after lengthy discovery.[168]

153. Jury trial. Criminal defendants have a constitutional right to a jury trial, and either party in a treble-damage action may demand trial by jury. There is, of course, no right to a jury trial in equity proceedings. But even in private equity actions, a damage counterclaim having issues in common with plaintiff's equity claim has been held to require jury trial on the common issues.[169] The availability of jury trial does not mean that everyone demands it. Many litigants recognize the relative unsuitability of juries for determining the complex issues of an antitrust case. But a party with a weak case may feel that it has nothing to lose and perhaps something to gain from a confused jury. Or a small business suing or being sued by a corporate giant might see a tactical advantage in appealing to a jury's sympathies.

A significant problem in jury-trial cases is deciding which issues must be submitted to the jury.[170] That question cannot be pursued apart from the substantive content of the several antitrust offenses. The reader should be alerted here, however, to the apparent willingness of many counsel and judges to leave to the jury questions that require the application of an unelaborated legal standard. The

Summary Judgment, Motions to Dismiss, and Other Examples of Equilibrating Tendencies in the Antitrust System, 74 Geo. L.J. 1065, 1129-1131 (1986).

167. Matsushita Elec. Indus. Co. v. Zenith Radio Corp., 475 U.S. 574 (1986) (although "'the inferences to be drawn from the underlying facts ... must be viewed in the light most favorable to the party opposing the motion'" for summary judgment, "[w]here the record taken as a whole could not lead a rational trier of fact to find for the non-moving party, there is no 'genuine issue for trial'"); Anderson v. Liberty Lobby, 477 U.S. 242 (1986); Celotex Corp. v. Catrett, 477 U.S. 317 (1986) ("Summary judgment procedure is properly regarded not as a disfavored procedural shortcut, but rather as an integral part of the Federal Rules as a whole, which are designed to secure the just, speedy and inexpensive determination of every action...."). Only *Matsushita* was an antitrust case; it is discussed further in ¶238, and in *Brooke Group*, Ch. 3A.

168. See also *Brooke Group*, Ch. 3A; *Kodak*, Ch. 4B.

169. Beacon Theatres v. Westover, 359 U.S. 500 (1959).

170. See Areeda & Turner, note 1, ¶321.

legality of some contracts, for example, will depend on their "reasonableness." To be sure, juries do decide on the reasonableness of conduct in negligence cases without particular help from the court, but we leave that decision to the jury out of a willingness to rely on lay judgment for an ad hoc definition of the standard of conduct. In such contexts, it may be sensible to assume that ordinary experience has much to offer in determining an appropriate standard. It is difficult to argue, however, that lay judgment based on ordinary experience has much relevance to many of the issues that arise in antitrust disputes. Furthermore, reasoning about the legal standard should be openly articulated and consistently developed to the maximum possible extent from case to case. Leaving such matters to the jury without meaningful instructions is to invite confusion. Accordingly, several courts have declared that jury trial may be denied in cases too complex for jurors to handle.[171] Such results are generally premised on a belief that the right to a rational decision, guaranteed by the Fifth Amendment Due Process clause, holds greater importance than the Seventh Amendment right to "jury equity."[172]

154. The big case. The government's monopoly attack on IBM began in 1968 and trial did not near completion until 13 years later (the trial itself consumed 6 years).[173] "Prolonged proceedings and a massive record are almost inevitable ... for the rules of law that have been developed, with respect to both the offense and the proof which may be adduced, generally permit the entire history of a major company or industry to be placed in issue."[174] Federal

171. E.g., Japanese Elec. Prods. Antitrust Litigation, 631 F.2d 1069 (3d Cir. 1980). Contra, U.S. Financial Securities Litigation, 609 F.2d 411 (9th Cir. 1979), cert. denied, 446 U.S. 929 (1980).

172. *Japanese Elec. Prods.*, note 171, at 1085:

> The function of "jury equity" may be legitimate when the jury actually modifies the law to conform to community values. However, when the jury is unable to determine the normal application of the law to the facts of a case and reaches a verdict on the basis of nothing more than its own determination of community wisdom and values, its operation is indistinguishable from arbitrary and unprincipled decisionmaking.

173. The ultimate dismissal is noted in ¶141d.

174. B. McAllister, The Big Case: Procedural Problems in Antitrust Litigation, 64 Harv. L. Rev. 27 (1950); C. Kaysen, An Economist as the Judge's Law Clerk in Sherman Act Cases, 12 A.B.A. Antitr. Sect. Rep. 43 (1958).
See Judge Wyzanski's statement that

> This Court is mindful that in recent years antitrust litigation ... [has] involved an enormous, nearly cancerous, growth of exhibits, depositions, and ore tenus testimony. Few judges who have sat in such cases have attempted to digest the plethora of evidence, or indeed could do so and at the same time do justice to other litigation in their courts. [United States v. Grinnell Corp., 236 F. Supp. 244, 247 (D.R.I. 1964), aff'd except as to decree, 384 U.S. 563 (1966).]

Trade Commission proceedings present many of the same problems, although one might hope that an expert tribunal with greater ability to tailor its procedures to its specialized docket could deal with such complex litigation more expeditiously. Lest the reader assume that all antitrust cases are of such proportions, it should be noted that most are more modest, although the 17-month median total length, from complaint to termination, of private antitrust cases exceeds the 9-month median for federal litigation generally.[175] This should not be surprising because most antitrust cases, like other cases, are settled, often at an early stage. Moreover, many antitrust cases involve little more than ordinary contract disputes where an antitrust claim or counterclaim has been included in the pleadings. Still, antitrust cases are often more complex than average cases, and a number assume truly immense proportions.

155. Appeals. Appeals in criminal cases and in private civil cases are effected in the usual way. In government civil cases, the procedures established by the Expediting Act of 1903 were replaced by 1974 amendments.[176] Under the old procedure, an appeal from a district court decision in a government civil antitrust case would lie only to the Supreme Court. Under the new statute, appeals are ordinarily handled in the usual way by the courts of appeals.

Repose

156. Advisory opinions and clearances. One may, of course, assess the lawfulness of proposed conduct by considering precedent and general enforcement policy guidelines.[177] In addition, one may request specific comments from the antitrust enforcement agencies. The Justice Department has no formal general power to approve

175. S. Salop & L. White, Economic Analysis of Private Antitrust Litigation, 74 Geo. L.J. 1001, 1009 (1986).

176. 88 Stat. 1708 (1974), repealing 32 Stat. 823 (1903). The 1974 amendment eliminated the 1903 Act's provision for the trial by a three judge district court of cases certified by the Attorney General to be "of general public importance" — a procedure that does not appear to have been used for several decades. The new statute still authorizes such a certificate from the Attorney General, but its effect is only to require the relevant judge "to assign the case for hearing at the earliest practicable date ... and to cause the case to be in every way expedited."

177. Both the Justice Department and the FTC have, for example, published enforcement policy guidelines on acquisitions and mergers. See Ch. 5. Such guidelines are not binding on the agency or the courts. United States v. Atlantic Richfield Co., 297 F. Supp. 1061, 1073 (S.D.N.Y. 1969). But a court may choose to give them some weight. Allis-Chalmers Mfg. Co. v. White Consol. Indus., 414 F.2d 506, 524 (3d Cir. 1969), cert. denied, 396 U.S. 1009 (1970).

planned conduct and thereby make it legal, but the Department may approve a transaction by stating in a "business review letter" its present intention not to bring any suit.[178] Similarly, the Federal Trade Commission may issue an advisory opinion approving a proposed course of action within its jurisdiction.[179] These clearances and advisory opinions are not binding.[180] The agency giving them reserves a free hand for the future,[181] and neither agency purports to speak for the other. In practice, however, a recipient of such advice can reasonably assume that the government will not attack its actions.

But private plaintiffs are, of course, not restricted by government approval, and a court would presumably hesitate to give weight to the administrative clearance or advice for at least two reasons: As a formal matter, neither agency has statutory immunizing power; practically, the court will neither be convinced that everything relevant was known to the agency nor suppose that everything has remained unchanged.

157. Statutes of limitation. (a) *Private suits: generally.* Private treble-damage actions were governed by state statutes of limitation until the 1955 amendments to the Clayton Act added §4B, which provides for a uniform antitrust limitation of four years. The running of the statute of limitation is tolled either by the pendency of a government suit as provided in §5(i) or by defendant's fraudulent concealment of plaintiff's cause of action.[182]

Application of §4B raises the usual problems in pinpointing when plaintiff's cause of action accrues. As a general rule, the statute of

178. See 28 C.F.R. §50.6. See also Holly Farms Poultry Indus. v. Kleindienst, 1973 Trade Cas. ¶74535 (M.D.N.C.) (interpretation of Capper-Volstead Act given in the course of issuing a business review letter, in which the Justice Department declined to state its present enforcement intentions, held not to be a final agency act reviewable by action for declaratory judgment).

179. See 16 C.F.R. §§1.1-1.4.

180. United States v. New Orleans Chapter, Assoc. Gen. Contractors of Am., 238 F. Supp. 273 (E.D. La. 1965), held the government estopped to indict defendants for practices openly conducted for many years following a government investigation that did not lead to any complaint. The Supreme Court reversed per curiam, 382 U.S. 17 (1965).

181. One partial exception is that the FTC

will not proceed against the requesting party with respect to any action taken in good faith reliance upon the Commission's advice under this section, where all the relevant facts were fully, completely, and accurately presented to the Commission and where such action was promptly discontinued upon notification of rescission or revocation of the Commission's approval. [16 C.F.R. §1.3(b).]

182. E.g., Rutledge v. Boston Woven Hose & Rubber Co., 576 F.2d 248 (9th Cir. 1978); Akron Presform Mold Co. v. McNeil Corp., 496 F.2d 230 (6th Cir.), cert. denied, 419 U.S. 997 (1974).

limitation runs from the date on which defendant commits an act violative of the antitrust laws that injures plaintiff's business or property. "In the context of a continuing conspiracy, . . . each time a plaintiff is injured by an act of the defendants a cause of action accrues to him to recover the damages caused by that act and . . . as to those damages, the statute of limitations runs from the commission of the act."[183] A private plaintiff therefore may bring a treble-damage action long after the inception of an antitrust conspiracy as long as it can prove that its damages were proximately caused by an overt act occurring within the statutory period. The overt act could be a price-fixing conspirator's elevated price,[184] a seller's collection of rent for a tied product,[185] or an unlawful refusal to deal.[186] Similarly, where defendant's actions constitute a continuing violation of Sherman Act §2, and where plaintiff alleges defendant's exertion of that monopoly power to its detriment within the statutory period, suit will not be barred merely because plaintiff was first injured many years earlier.[187] Although there is little case law on point, one court has suggested that where a private plaintiff seeks damages for a violation of Clayton Act §7, the statute should not necessarily run from the date of the allegedly illegal merger but rather should begin to run from the date of the overt act that directly caused plaintiff's injury.[188] While in all of the above situa-

183. Zenith Radio Corp. v. Hazeltine Research, 401 U.S. 321, 338 (1971).

184. Cf. *Hanover,* note 23, at 502 n.15.

185. Compare Imperial Point Colonnades Condominiums v. Mangurian, 549 F.2d 1029 (5th Cir.), cert. denied, 434 U.S. 859 (1977), with El Paso v. Darbyshire Steel Co., 575 F.2d 521 (5th Cir. 1978), cert. denied, 439 U.S. 1121 (1979).

186. Compare Vehicle Air Pollution Litigation, 591 F.2d 68, 72 (9th Cir.), cert. denied, 444 U.S. 900 (1979) (period begins with unequivocal refusal to deal; not restarted by renewed refusals, at least where renewed requests "were forlorn inquiries by one all of whose reasonable hopes had previously been dashed"), with Braun v. Berenson, 432 F.2d 538, 543 (5th Cir. 1970) (separate cause of action accrues each time plaintiff was refused store space, which was not a continuously available commodity but was available "only periodically and under uniquely different circumstances").

187. *Hanover,* note 23, at 502 n.15 ("[W]e are dealing with conduct which constituted a continuing violation of the Sherman Act and which inflicted continuing and accumulating harm on Hanover. Although Hanover could have sued in 1912 for the injury then being inflicted, it was equally entitled to sue in 1955.").

188. Metropolitan Liquor Co. v. Heublein, 305 F. Supp. 946 (E.D. Wis. 1969) (where plaintiff claimed that defendant's alleged Clayton Act §7 violation caused it to lose an exclusive distributorship, statute of limitation did not begin to run until date when defendant appointed additional distributors; court noted that since plaintiff could not have sued until termination of exclusive dealership due to lack of injury to it, it would be inappropriate to have a hard and fast rule that cause of action accrues at the time of acquisition). See J. Stein, Section 7 of the Clayton Act as a Basis for the Treble Damage Action: When May the Private Litigant Bring His Suit?, 56 Cal. L. Rev. 968 (1968).

tions it would follow that damages may not be recovered for an act occurring prior to the four-year limitation period, the Supreme Court has allowed an exception to this rule where such damages would have been deemed speculative or incapable of proof, and thus unrecoverable, had suit been brought earlier.[189] There may also be special circumstances in which the usual limitation period will not be a bar.[190]

(b) *Government suit tolls statute of limitation.* Clayton Act §5(i) — §5(b) until 1974 — provides an alternative to the four-year statute of limitation on private treble-damage suits. It declares that where there is pending a civil or criminal proceeding by the United States, any private suit based on the same matters shall not be barred until one year after the conclusion of the government action.[191] Thus, the private plaintiff can use the §5(i) provision to tack additional

189. *Zenith,* note 37, at 339-340:

> In antitrust and treble-damage actions, refusal to award future profits as too speculative is equivalent to holding that no cause of action has yet accrued for any but those damages already suffered. In these instances, the cause of action for future damages, if they ever occur, will accrue only on the date they are suffered; thereafter the plaintiff may sue to recover them at any time within four years from the date they were inflicted.... Otherwise future damages that could not be proved within four years of the conduct from which they flowed would be forever incapable of recovery, contrary to the congressional purpose that private actions serve "as a bulwark of antitrust enforcement."

See M. Wheeler & R. Jones, The Statute of Limitations for Antitrust Damage Actions: Four Years or Forty?, 41 U. Chi. L. Rev. 72 (1973).

190. In Greyhound Corp. v. Mt. Hood Stages, 616 F.2d 394 (9th Cir.), cert. denied, 449 U.S. 831 (1980), the court found equitable reasons for tolling the statute of limitation: The defendant had behaved outrageously, plaintiff had promptly initiated ICC proceedings, which it reasonably thought to be its only remedy, and the Justice Department had intervened in those proceedings. This court had previously thought that such intervention triggered the §5(i) tolling provision, but the Supreme Court had held otherwise in Greyhound Corp. v. Mt. Hood Stages, 437 U.S. 322 (1978).

191. Michigan v. Morton Salt Co., 259 F. Supp. 35, 50 (D. Minn. 1966), aff'd sub nom. Hardy Salt Co. v. Illinois, 377 F.2d 768 (8th Cir.), cert. denied, 389 U.S. 912 (1967) ("government litigation continues to pend against each defendant until concluded as to all," therefore §5(i) tolls the statute of limitation against defendants who signed consent decrees until litigation against all other defendants is terminated). Accord, New Jersey v. Morton Salt Co., 387 F.2d 94 (3d Cir. 1967), cert. denied, 391 U.S. 967 (1968). Where tolling periods overlap, a district court has held that government criminal and civil proceedings may be tacked together to suspend the running of the statute of limitation until the last government action is terminated. Maricopa County v. American Pipe & Constr. Co., 303 F. Supp. 77 (D. Ariz. 1969), aff'd per curiam, 431 F.2d 1145 (9th Cir. 1970), cert. denied, 401 U.S. 937 (1971). And see Russ Togs v. Grinnell Corp., 426 F.2d 850, 857 (2d Cir.), cert. denied, 400 U.S. 878 (1970) (government suit does not cease to pend when liability is finally established but "continues until the expiration of the time to appeal from the final decree resolving all issues of liability and relief" because even when remand proceedings involve only issues of relief, they may generate evidence and legal rulings of benefit to private plaintiffs).

time onto the regular statutory period. Although §5(i) speaks of civil or criminal actions to enforce the "antitrust laws," the Supreme Court has held that FTC proceedings also trigger §5(i).[192] The government and private actions need not be identical to suspend the statute of limitation; it is enough if the private action is based in whole or in part on any matter complained of in such government proceedings.[193]

> Doubtlessly, care must be exercised to insure that reliance upon the government proceedings is not mere sham and that the matters complained of in the government suit bear a real relation to the private plaintiff's claim for relief. But the courts must not allow a legitimate concern that invocation of §5[(i)] be made in good faith to lead them into a niggardly construction of the statutory language here in question.[194]

(c) *Government suits.* Government suits under §4A for treble damages for injury to its business or property are subject to the same time limitation as private actions. Criminal prosecutions are governed by the general provisions of 18 U.S.C. §3282, which forbids prosecutions not instituted within five years after the commission of the offense.[195] Equitable actions by the government are subject to

192. Minnesota Mining & Mfg. Co. v. New Jersey Wood Finishing Co., 381 U.S. 311, 320-321 (1965). The Court did not distinguish, for §5(i) purposes, FTC proceedings brought under the Clayton Act from those brought under FTC Act §5. (*3M* itself involved a Clayton Act §7 violation.) Some courts have concluded that an FTC Act §5 proceeding triggers Clayton Act §5(i) if the proceeding is directed at "alleged conduct which involves either an existing or incipient violation" of the Sherman or Clayton Acts. E.g., Rader v. Balfour, 440 F.2d 469, 473 (7th Cir.), cert. denied, 404 U.S. 983 (1971). But see Laitram Corp. v. Deepsouth Packing Co., 279 F. Supp. 883 (E.D. La. 1968) (FTC Act §5 is not one of the "antitrust laws" and therefore does not toll the running of the statute of limitation).

193. E.g., *Zenith*, note 183 (statute of limitation tolled against all participants in conspiracy that is object of a government suit, whether or not they are named as defendants or conspirators therein).

194. Leh v. General Petro. Corp., 382 U.S. 54, 55-56, 59, 65 (1965):

> In general, consideration of the applicability of [§5(i)] must be limited to a comparison of the two complaints on their face. Obviously suspension of the running of the statute of limitations . . . may not be made to turn on whether the United States is successful in proving the allegations of its complaint.

Note that in *Leh* the private action was deemed to be "based in whole or in part" on the prior government suit although the two sets of defendants were not completely identical, the time periods of the alleged conspiracies did not completely overlap, and the relevant geographic areas were not coterminous.

195. But evidence of prior conduct may be admissible. See Kansas City Star Co. v. United States, 240 F.2d 643, 651 (8th Cir.), cert. denied, 354 U.S. 923 (1957):

> In order to show intent, it was entirely proper to receive evidence of a course of conduct engaged in by the appellants over a period of years leading up to the indictment period which might assist the jury in attempting to determine whether or not the appellants possessed that necessary intent during the time covered by the indictment. It would be illogical not to admit evidence as to a course of conduct over

no statute of limitation, and laches cannot ordinarily be asserted against the sovereign;[196] herein lie some nice problems that will be explored in the monopoly and merger chapters.

158.   Res judicata. (a) *Merger and bar.* Litigation has the same conclusive powers in antitrust as elsewhere. The usual principles of merger and bar and collateral estoppel apply. But courts will avoid too mechanical an application of these principles where the result would be to shelter defendant unduly from antitrust attack or undermine the statutory scheme that authorizes both private and government suits.

Private and government suits are not preclusive of each other. A private suit terminating in a consent decree or an outright victory for defendant does not bar a subsequent government suit.[197] Nor would defendant's victory in a government civil suit preclude a later private suit.[198]

Similarly, the Federal Trade Commission and the Justice Department may usually bring simultaneous or successive civil suits against the same defendant, even where basically the same misconduct is alleged in both suits.[199] Because the range of practices prohibited under Federal Trade Commission Act §5 is wider than that under the Sherman and Clayton Acts, defendant's victory in a Justice Department suit would not preclude an FTC proceeding to prevent the same conduct. And even where the FTC and the Justice Department proceed simultaneously against practices that probably could be reached apart from FTC Act §5, the Supreme Court has concluded that the congressional purpose "not to confine each of these proceedings within narrow, mutually exclusive limits" authorizes "the simultaneous use of both types of proceedings."[200]

---

many years which manifested an intent to monopolize.... The federal courts in antitrust cases have long admitted evidence of conduct prior to the statutory period.

196. There is likewise no statute of limitation on private suits seeking injunctive or other equitable relief. As to whether the doctrine of laches should apply, see ITT v. General Tel. & Elec. Corp., 518 F.2d 913, 928 (9th Cir. 1975) (four-year damage limitation is proper guideline for laches period).

197. United States v. Borden Co., 347 U.S. 514, 519 (1954) ("Congress did not intend that the efforts of a private litigant should supersede the duties of the Department of Justice in policing an industry").

198. See Sam Fox Publishing Co. v. United States, 366 U.S. 683 (1961) (denial of private intervention in government antitrust suit grounded on argument that private litigants are not bound by outcome of government suits and cannot be barred from bringing subsequent treble-damage action).

199. *Cement Institute,* note 65 (filing of Justice Department suit to restrain violations of Sherman Act does not require termination of pending FTC proceedings).

200. Id. at 694-695 (dictum). But where the FTC brings subsequent proceedings to enforce the Clayton Act as such and alleges the same misconduct, covering the

The Justice Department, of course, can bring both civil and criminal suits against the same defendant. Matters necessarily determined in a criminal conviction will operate as collateral estoppel in a later government civil suit. But defendant's acquittal in a criminal suit does not bar a subsequent government civil suit[201] because the burden of proof in the former proceeding is higher.

Issues of merger and bar become especially important when defendant's conduct gives rise to repeated civil suits by the government. Continuation of conduct attacked in a prior antitrust suit is generally held to give rise to a new cause of action.[202] Thus defendant's victory in a government suit does not preclude a later proceeding on the same theory for defendant's later repetition of the very conduct held lawful in the prior suit.[203] The later court may follow the earlier ruling, but that would illustrate stare decisis rather than merger and bar.[204] And even if there are antitrust cases where collateral estoppel would ordinarily apply, courts may refuse to follow an earlier validation of defendant's conduct when there has been a significant intervening change in the decisional law.[205] This judicial willingness to reexamine matters formerly litigated rests on the premise that defendant should not be able to use a former

same time period, as that adjudicated in a former Justice Department suit, the res judicata policy of repose should apply.

201. United States v. National Assn. of Real Est. Bds., 339 U.S. 485 (1950). Note, however, that res judicata, as well as the related doctrine of double jeopardy, may be invoked where the government brings successive criminal antitrust suits against the same defendant. See, e.g., United States v. American Honda Motor Co., 289 F. Supp. 277 (S.D. Ohio 1968) (dismissal of prior California and Illinois suits on grounds of double jeopardy provided res judicata defense in third criminal suit involving identical issue of single versus multiple conspiracies). See generally IB J. Moore, Federal Practice ¶0.418[2] (2d ed. 1984).

202. Lawlor v. National Screen Serv. Corp., 349 U.S. 322 (1955) (settlement of private suit by consent decree following allegation of Sherman Act §1 violations does not bar suit six years later for damages arising from continuation of conspiracy); FTC v. Raladam Co., 316 U.S. 149 (1942) (vacation of FTC cease and desist order on grounds of inadequate findings and proof does not bar later proceeding based on conduct subsequent to that order).

203. See *Raladam*, note 202.

204. See United States v. United Shoe Mach. Corp., 110 F. Supp. 295, 343 (D. Mass. 1953), aff'd per curiam, 347 U.S. 521 (1954), where the court felt limited by earlier decisions validating defendant's merger and the terms on which it leased its machines. The judge thought that the merged company enjoyed a "legal license." With respect to the earlier decision on leasing terms, however, the court spoke the language of stare decisis. Compare United States v. GE, 82 F. Supp. 753, 826 (D.N.J. 1949) (Supreme Court's validation of defendant's consignment agency system in 1926 held binding in later government suit where agency system remained essentially unchanged), with United States v. GE, 358 F. Supp. 731 (S.D.N.Y. 1973) (where subsequent Supreme Court decisions effectively overruled earlier cases validating defendant's agency system, defendant could not invoke res judicata to shield practices from later antitrust attack).

205. See generally Commissioner v. Sunnen, 333 U.S. 591, 599 (1948).

judgment as a means of gaining immunity from a change in the law or of assuring a permanent advantage over its competitors.[206]

While continuation of the same course of conduct will give rise to separate suits, notions of fairness and efficiency may call for consolidation of plaintiff's theories in one action. Suppose, for example, that the government seeks to enjoin certain practices, such as the use of tying restrictions, which could be attacked under either Sherman Act §1 or Clayton Act §3. Where the remedies are identical and the legal theories do not vary significantly, there seems to be no reason why the government should not be required to assert all relevant legal theories associated with a given set of facts in one suit.

A substantially different issue arises, however, when defendant has sufficient market power to make proceedings under Sherman Act §2, as well as under §1, possible. The government may prefer to limit anticompetitive practices under §1 and defer attack under §2 because injunctions under Sherman Act §1 might eliminate the monopoly power in question. An alternative, of course, would be to adjudicate both §1 and §2 allegations in one suit and then postpone relief under §2, pending the results of relief ordered under §1.[207] While this second approach may be more consistent with the res judicata policy of fostering economy of litigation, avoiding premature litigation of defendant's market power represents a strong countervailing consideration. Given the complex nature of a Sherman Act §2 suit, there seems to be no reason to make a proceeding under §1 preclusive of a later suit under §2.[208]

Like the government, private plaintiffs may bring successive suits where defendant continues a wrongful course of conduct following an earlier decree.[209] Where conduct within the same time period is at issue, however, courts generally require a treble-damage plaintiff to consolidate all of its theories in one action.[210]

206. See *GE* (1973), note 204; *Lawlor*, note 202.

207. The difficulties in fashioning appropriate §2 relief are illustrated in *United Shoe* (1953), note 204 (remedy of dissolution rejected by district court though parties were to be allowed to petition for modification of decree), and United States v. United Shoe Mach. Corp., 391 U.S. 244 (1968) (Supreme Court reversed district court's denial of government petition for modification of decree to provide for formation of two fully competing companies).

208. See, e.g., Aluminum Co. of Am. v. United States, 302 U.S. 230 (1937) (1912 consent decree enjoining certain restraints of trade does not bar government suit in 1937 for violation of Sherman Act §2). Cf. *Motion Picture Advertising*, note 65 (previous cease and desist order designed to end conspiracy between defendant and other distributors does not bar later FTC proceeding alleging that defendant's individual contracts restrain competition and tend to monopoly).

209. *Lawlor*, note 202.

210. E.g., Williamson v. Columbia Gas & Elec. Corp., 186 F.2d 464 (3d Cir. 1950), cert. denied, 341 U.S. 921 (1951) (where essentially same wrongful acts are alleged, private treble-damage plaintiff may not bring one suit alleging conspiracy

(b) *Collateral estoppel.* The traditional rule precludes the same parties from relitigating a factual issue that they had actually litigated in a prior lawsuit.[211] Thus, even if the cause of action is different, a previously determined issue may not be tried again.

The original parties and those in "privity" with them are bound by the result of their prior litigation. In addition, that result may also bind one of the original parties in subsequent litigation with a third party. Defensive use of the prior judgment has been upheld by the Supreme Court. In *Blonder-Tongue,*[212] a patentee whose patent was held invalid in a prior infringement suit was precluded from suing a different infringer. This defensive use of a prior judgment against a former plaintiff seems appropriate because it chose the former forum and defined the issues of the prior case. Even here, the estoppel is contingent on the plaintiff having had "'a fair opportunity procedurally, substantively and evidentially to pursue his claim the first time.'"[213] Subsequent decisions have not limited *Blonder-Tongue* to patent infringement cases.[214]

Although less compelling, offensive use of a prior judgment has also been approved by the Supreme Court. In *Parklane Hosiery,*[215] a corporation and certain of its officers and directors were held bound in a shareholder suit by the determination in a prior SEC suit against them that their proxy statement was false and misleading. *Parklane* may imply that an antitrust plaintiff may use as conclusive against a defendant a determination of fact against that defendant in a prior private or government suit. This might seem inconsistent with Clayton Act §5(a), as noted in ¶c, which gives the determination of a prior governmental suit only prima facie effect. But that 1914 statute, which afforded antitrust plaintiffs more generous treatment than prevailing 1914 doctrines of collateral estoppel, does not necessarily reflect a judgment that antitrust

---

in violation of Sherman Act and another suit alleging defendant's violation of Clayton Act §7).

211. E.g., Azalea Drive-In Theatre v. Hanft, 540 F.2d 713 (4th Cir. 1976), cert. denied, 430 U.S. 941 (1977) (collateral estoppel prevented plaintiff from litigating, in an antitrust suit, its charge that defendant had exerted duress and made threats, where those issues had been determined adversely to plaintiff in a state court suit between the same parties involving a promissory note).

212. Blonder-Tongue Laboratories v. University of Illinois Research Found., 402 U.S. 313 (1971).

213. Id. at 333 (quoting Eisel v. Columbia Packing Co., 181 F. Supp. 298, 301 (D. Mass. 1960)).

214. Poster Exch. v. National Screen Serv. Corp., 517 F.2d 117 (5th Cir. 1975). See Parklane Hosiery Co. v. Shore, 439 U.S. 322, 327-328 (1979); Note, Collateral Estoppel of Non-Parties, 87 Harv. L. Rev. 1485 (1974).

215. *Parklane,* note 214. See L. George, Sweet Uses of Adversity: Parklane Hosiery and the Collateral Class Action, 32 Stan. L. Rev. 655 (1980).

plaintiffs should receive less by way of collateral estoppel than plain-tiffs in nonantitrust suits. Congress made this clear by a 1980 amendment providing that §5(a) does not "impose any limitation on the application of collateral estoppel, except that ... [in any antitrust proceeding] collateral estoppel effect shall not be given to any finding made by the Federal Trade Commission. ..."

(c) *Government judgments and private suits.* Clayton Act §5(a) gives private plaintiffs the benefit of government antitrust suits resulting in "a final judgment or decree ... to the effect that a defendant has violated" the antitrust laws. That judgment "shall be prima facie evidence against such defendant" in private antitrust actions. Section 5(a) is triggered by the government's civil or criminal suits, perhaps by Federal Trade Commission orders,[216] but not by private judgments or by consent decrees.[217] Criminal judgments after a plea of nolo contendere are regarded as consent judgments,[218] but guilty pleas are regarded as all-purpose admissions and as prima facie evidence under §5. Because the nolo plea thus permits the defendant to escape the §5(a) consequences of an offense, judges sometimes reject the plea in flagrant cases.

216. *Minnesota,* note 192, at 317, 318, held that §5(i) was triggered by FTC proceedings. While many of the Supreme Court's reasons would apply to §5(a), the Court did say that §5(a) involved a more "delicate area in which a judgment secured in an action between two parties may be used by a third." The Court then "assumed arguendo that §5(a) is inapplicable to Commission proceedings — a question upon which we venture no opinion." Lower courts have subsequently ruled that an FTC proceeding is under the antitrust laws for the purpose of §5(a) when the FTC is directly enforcing the Sherman or Clayton Acts — Purex Corp. v. Procter & Gamble Co., 453 F.2d 288 (9th Cir. 1971), cert. denied, 405 U.S. 1065 (1972) (Clayton Act §7); *Farmington,* note 84 (Clayton Act §2(a)) — but not when it proceeds under the broader powers of FTC Act §5, which is not itself an "antitrust law" within the definition of Clayton Act §1. E.g., Y & Y Popcorn Supply Co. v. ABC Vending Corp., 263 F. Supp. 709 (E.D. Pa. 1967).

The 1980 amendments to §5(a), noted in ¶b, limiting the collateral estoppel effect of FTC decisions, do not appear to affect the prima facie effect, if any, of FTC findings. See H.R. Rep. No. 96-874, 96th Cong., 2d Sess. 4-5 (1980) (distinguishing prima facie effect from collateral estoppel).

217. An express proviso to §5(a) excludes "consent judgments or decrees entered before any testimony has been taken." As to whether a case tried on stipulated facts falls within the exclusionary proviso concerning consent decrees, compare Gurwitz v. Singer, 1963 Trade Cas. ¶70905 (S.D. Cal.) (prima facie effect of §5(a) still applies), with Ulrich v. Ethyl Gas. Corp., 2 F.R.D. 357 (W.D. Ky. 1942) (no prima facie effect).

218. Federal Rule of Criminal Procedure 11(b) permits nolo pleas subject to the consent of the court. See Burbank v. GE, 329 F.2d 825, 834-835 (9th Cir. 1964) ("unanimity of opinion [exists] with respect to the holding that nolo contendere pleas come within" the consent judgment proviso of §5(a)). And see Obron v. Union Camp Corp., 324 F. Supp. 390 (E.D. Mich. 1971) (admissions made by defendant at the time of, and in conjunction with, the entry of a plea of nolo contendere in a criminal antitrust prosecution are not admissible in a subsequent private treble-damage action).

To use §5(a), one must determine (1) what matters are prima facie established by the prior government judgment and (2) how those matters are relevant to the private plaintiff's case. Section 5 makes the government judgment prima facie evidence — but not conclusive — "as to all matters respecting which said judgment or decree would be an estoppel as between the parties thereto."[219] The problem is that a general verdict or judgment makes it extremely difficult to tell exactly what matters were distinctly put in issue and directly determined in the government suit. Such determinations are admissible under §5(a) to whatever extent they are relevant in establishing ultimate facts in issue in the subsequent suit.

(d) *Res judicata and state law.*[220] Troublesome problems have arisen when a federal suit under federal law follows a state court determination under state law, or vice versa. The problem arises because exclusive jurisdiction for federal antitrust claims lies in federal courts, and every state has antitrust and related laws of its own that may give rise to independent state claims. Because the two bodies of law are often so similar, courts generally hold that a judgment under one sovereign's law triggers res judicata or collateral estoppel in a suit under the other's law or in the other's court. For example, a federal court's dismissal of a federal antitrust claim has been held to bar a later state or federal suit under state law involving the same transaction, if it could have been brought in the first suit.[221] State court suits under state law may also bar later federal

---

219. *Michigan,* note 191, at 65:

[W]hen a Government decree is introduced in a subsequent private action it only means that, standing alone, that decree will be sufficient to sustain a judgment on the issues for which it is submitted. But once the defendant comes forward with countervailing evidence to rebut the prima facie effect of the decree, the case proceeds much the same as if it had never been introduced. The decree does not relieve the plaintiff of satisfying the burden of persuasion, but simply requires that defendant carry forward the burden of producing evidence.

See Franchon & Marco v. Paramount Pictures, 215 F.2d 167 (9th Cir. 1954), cert. denied, 348 U.S. 912 (1955) (evidence as a whole rebutted presumption that defendants' refusal to grant plaintiff a first-run film license was part of conspiracy found in prior government suits).

220. See generally Note, The Collateral Estoppel Effect of Prior State Court Findings in Cases with Exclusive Federal Jurisdiction, 91 Harv. L. Rev. 1281 (1978); Note, The Res Judicata Effect of Prior State Court Judgments in Sherman Act Suits: Exalting Substance Over Form, 51 Fordham L. Rev. 1374 (1983).

221. See Harper Plastics v. Amoco Chems. Corp., 657 F.2d 939 (7th Cir. 1981); Boccardo v. Safeway Stores, 134 Cal. App. 3d 1037, 184 Cal. Rptr. 903 (1982) (federal dismissal of indirect purchaser's Sherman Act suit barred subsequent state action where state law did not deny standing to indirect purchasers, when state claim could have been included as a pendent claim in the federal proceeding). A state claim can be included in the federal antitrust suit if there is diversity jurisdiction or if the facts supporting it are connected to those of the federal claim — making it a valid pendent claim — as they usually are. In addition, where a state claim is substantially identical to the federal claim, as is often the case, the federal

antitrust suits, although the analysis is more complex since the federal antitrust claim initially could not have been filed in state court. When the state's law is substantially the same as federal antitrust law, a subsequent federal suit will be barred if it is based on the same "cause of action,"[222] but preclusion is less likely when the two bodies of law have important substantive differences. In *Marrese,* the Supreme Court ruled that the preclusive effect of the initial state suit is governed in the first instance by state law of res judicata.[223] But even if the state would not give res judicata effect to claims that could not have been brought in state court, factual determinations in one suit are generally given collateral estoppel effect in a later suit in either court.[224]

1D.   THE REACH OF THE ANTITRUST LAWS[1]

159.   Introduction. Although the antitrust laws are of general application, covering all industries and virtually all economic activity, several "exemptions" have arisen over the years. We use the quoted term loosely to cover quite different limitations on the reach of the antitrust laws. There are literal exemptions by which statutes expressly allow certain conduct — for example, by agricultural cooperatives or by labor unions — that would otherwise violate the antitrust laws. Some federal statutes create regulatory bodies that are expressly authorized to grant antitrust immunity to firms within their jurisdiction. In other federally regulated industries, regulation is so pervasive that the courts infer that Congress must have intended the industry to be supervised by the regulators rather than by the antitrust laws. In yet other cases, the courts have attempted to harmonize the application of antitrust laws to nonexempt but regulated industries by fashioning special substantive rules or by deferring to the analysis and decisions of the regulators. In addition, the courts have assumed that Congress meant to respect principles of federalism by leaving "state action" outside the antitrust regime. Finally, the federal antitrust laws apply only where interstate and

---

judge may decide the former even after the federal claim has been dismissed. See Bright v. Bechtel Petro., 780 F.2d 766, 771 (9th Cir. 1986).

222. See Derish v. San Mateo-Burlingame Bd. of Realtors, 724 F.2d 1347 (9th Cir. 1983); Nash County Bd. of Educ. v. Biltmore Co., 640 F.2d 484 (4th Cir.), cert. denied, 454 U.S. 878 (1981) (consent decree under state antitrust law is res judicata as to subsequent federal proceeding on same "cause of action").

223. Marrese v. American Acad. of Orthopaedic Surgeons, 470 U.S. 373 (1985).

224. See Eichman v. Fotomat Corp., 759 F.2d 1434 (9th Cir. 1985).

1. See I P. Areeda & D. Turner, Antitrust Law, ch. 2 (1978; Supp. 1996).

foreign commerce are involved, although applying U.S. law to foreign activity creates special difficulty.

Before elaborating briefly on these matters, we note a few narrow express statutory exemptions. Certain private conduct may be exempted from the antitrust laws when approved by the President, using elaborate procedures, to further national defense objectives.[2] Also exempt are certain programs for cooperative research among small business firms, as approved by the Small Business Administration.[3] These powers have not proved to be important. In addition, particular statutes have been enacted from time to time to validate conduct that is thought to raise antitrust problems. For example, special statutes permit banks to merge under more generous standards than are generally applicable,[4] newspapers to eliminate competition by agreement when one of them is failing,[5] football leagues to merge,[6] or sports leagues to deal for all league members in selling television rights, provided that telecasting is not limited in any city other than "the home territory of a member club of the league on a day when such club is playing a game at home."[7]

Exemptions

160. Agricultural and fishermen's organizations. Since 1914, Clayton Act §6 has partially exempted agricultural organizations from the antitrust laws to allow farmers to form cooperative associations without the associations as such being held illegal.

> The Capper-Volstead Act of 1922[8] extended §6 of the Clayton Act exemption to capital stock agricultural cooperatives which had not previously been covered by that section.... This indicates a purpose to make it possible for farmer-producers to organize together, set association policy, fix prices at which their cooperative will sell their

2. Defense Production Act of 1950, 64 Stat. 798, 818, as amended, 50 U.S.C. App. §2158.

3. 72 Stat. 391 (1958), 15 U.S.C. §§638, 640.

4. See Ch. 5D, note 7.

5. See id., note 18.

6. 80 Stat. 1515 (1966), 15 U.S.C. §1291.

7. 75 Stat. 732 (1961), 15 U.S.C. §§1291-1295. It is interesting that this statutory permission does not apply to arrangements involving the telecast of professional football games on Friday evenings or on Saturday between mid-September and mid-December within 75 miles of the site of an intercollegiate football contest. Agreements against televising sold-out games were prohibited for two years by Pub. L. 93-107 (1973).

8. 42 Stat. 388 (1922), 7 U.S.C. §291.

produce, and otherwise carry on like a business corporation without thereby violating the antitrust laws.[9]

Similar in language and construction to the Capper-Volstead Act is the Fisheries Cooperative Marketing Act, applicable to "persons engaged in the fishery industry . . . collectively catching, producing, preparing for market, processing, handling, and marketing."[10]

The exemption covers only producers[11] and agreements among exempt organizations[12] but not processors, cooperatives including processors,[13] or those that merely contract out production to farmers.[14] An otherwise exempt organization may not lawfully engage in activities that coerce others to join the association or coerce competing producers, processors, or distributors to comply with the association's will.[15] Nor may the association combine with nonexempt organizations either through merger[16] or by agreement.[17] The Secretary of Agriculture (or the Secretary of the Interior in the case of fishery organizations), on finding that "such association monopolizes or restrains trade . . . to such an extent that the price of any agricultural product is unduly enhanced," may order the association "to cease and desist from monopolization or restraint of trade."[18] This provision does not give the Secretary primary or exclusive jurisdiction and does not preclude the initiation of ordinary antitrust suits against coercive practices, acquisitions, and the

9. Maryland & Va. Milk Producers Assn. v. United States, 362 U.S. 458, 466 (1960).

10. 48 Stat. 1213 (1934), 15 U.S.C. §521. The administrative duties of the Secretary of Agriculture in the case of agricultural cooperatives are here performed by the Secretary of the Interior.

11. A farmers' cooperative is exempt even though it does not grow, harvest, ship, sell, or negotiate for sale but only sets the price at which its members sell. E.g., Northern Cal. Supermarkets v. Central Cal. Lettuce Producers Coop., 580 F.2d 369 (9th Cir. 1978), cert. denied, 439 U.S. 1090 (1979).

12. Sunkist Growers v. Winckler & Smith Citrus Prods. Co., 370 U.S. 19 (1962) (agreement among several associations with overlapping farmer membership).

13. Case-Swayne Co. v. Sunkist Growers, 389 U.S. 384 (1967) (nongrower packinghouse members). Sunkist then reorganized and was held exempt, 355 F. Supp. 408 (C.D. Cal. 1971).

14. National Broiler Mktg. Assn. v. United States, 436 U.S. 816 (1978) (no exemption for chicken producers not owning flock, hatchery, or growing facilities; furnishing growers with chicks, feed, medical supplies, and services insufficient).

15. *Maryland,* note 9, at 464-466; North Tex. Producers Assn. v. Metzger Dairies, 348 F.2d 189 (5th Cir. 1965), cert. denied, 382 U.S. 977 (1966); Gulf Coast Shrimpers & Oystermans Assn. v. United States, 236 F.2d 658, 665 (5th Cir.), cert. denied, 352 U.S. 927 (1956) (Association exceeded exemption "when it undertook not simply to fix the prices demanded by its members, but to exclude from the market all persons not buying and selling in accordance with its fixed prices").

16. *Maryland,* note 9, at 464-467.

17. United States v. Borden Co., 308 U.S. 188, 203-205 (1939).

18. 42 Stat. 388 (1922), 7 U.S.C. §292; 48 Stat. 1213, 1214 (1934), 15 U.S.C. §522.

like.[19] But the Secretary's power may be the only limitation on a voluntary organization's power to charge monopoly prices.[20]

161. Labor unions. The exemption for organized labor raises two antitrust issues, one simple (at least in determining the applicable legal principles) and the other more complex. First, absent any statutory or implied exemption, many activities of organized labor would directly violate the antitrust laws. For example, a union's insistence on a particular wage would constitute cartel price fixing on the part of its members. In fact, many of the earliest applications of the antitrust laws, shortly after their enactment, were against activities of organized labor,[21] although the most plausible understanding of the legislative history of the Sherman Act is that it was not meant to apply to standard union activities.[22] Subsequent legislation, noted below, ultimately established a clear exemption for organized labor.

With an exemption, a new dilemma arose: Labor unions are legal combinations that serve worker interests and also possess substantial power to control the character of competition within an industry. Unions with power over industry wages may determine which firms, with which automation policies, survive; power over equipment may determine the use of efficient machinery which might reduce cost and prices; power over materials and methods may determine the potential for beneficial innovation; power over hours of work may determine when and where consumers may shop. Thus, labor organizations can bring about production and distribution decisions that antitrust policy reserves for market determination free of collective, industry-wide decisions. Yet antitrust policy obviously does not embody all national purposes. The labor policy of the United States favors collective determination of wages and other working conditions and has not objected to industry-wide labor organizations or even to joint industry-wide negotiations and discussions with all producers. Striking the balance between these sets of poli-

---

19. *Maryland,* note 9, at 462-463; *Borden,* note 17, at 206; Local 36, Intl. Fishermen v. United States, 177 F.2d 320, 334 (9th Cir. 1949), cert. denied, 339 U.S. 947 (1950).

20. A contrary view is taken by FTC Bureau of Competition, Staff Report on Agricultural Cooperatives 5-6, 52-83 (1975); Fairdale Farms v. Yankee Milk, 1980 Trade Cas. ¶63029 (D. Vt. 1979). See also Sunkist Growers v. FTC, 464 F. Supp. 302 (C.D. Cal. 1979) (refusing to enjoin FTC §5 proceedings against cooperatives because challenge is not to price enhancement but to entry-deterring prices).

21. See W. Letwin, Law and Economic Policy in America: The Evolution of the Sherman Antitrust Act 123-128, 155-161 (1965). One of the more prominent actions involved the government's attempts to end the Pullman strike.

22. See id. at 98; H. Thorelli, The Federal Antitrust Policy 572 (1954).

cies has continued to occupy the courts, long after the basic exemption was established.

As the law now stands, Clayton Act §6 immunizes labor organizations and their members lawfully carrying out their legitimate objectives. Clayton Act §20 specifically immunizes such employee activities as strikes and boycotts, in their own interest, in the course of disputes "concerning terms or conditions of employment." The later Norris-LaGuardia Act[23] prohibits injunctions in most labor disputes. The Supreme Court held that these several statutes combine to exempt the bulk of union activities and collective bargaining agreements from the antitrust laws.[24] Although these statutory provisions expressly address only unilateral acts of employees and their unions, the Supreme Court has held that a "non-statutory" labor exemption will also shield unilateral action by *employers* from antitrust liability, provided that the action is the result of a collective bargaining process encouraged by U.S. labor law.[25] It would indeed be foolish policy to immunize strikes for certain goals without also immunizing the collective bargaining peace treaty that achieves these goals.

The exemption, although uncertain in scope, does not apply unless the collaborators (on one side of the agreement) are employees and not entrepreneurs or independent contractors.[26] Nor may employers restrain other employers with whom the union had no collective bargaining relationship.[27]

Second, there is no exemption where the union agrees with one or more employers to deny competing employers access to the market. The electricians of a city, for example, may not agree with local

23. 47 Stat. 70 (1932), 29 U.S.C. §§101-115.

24. United States v. Hutcheson, 312 U.S. 219 (1941). The preceding course of decision is a long and bitter story summarized briefly in Justice Goldberg's dissenting and concurring opinions in *Pennington* and *Jewel Tea,* notes 29 and 31, 381 U.S. at 697-709 (1965).

25. See Brown v. Pro Football, 116 S. Ct. 2116 (1996) (exempting from the Sherman Act the National Football League's decision, after an impasse of the collective bargaining process, to implement its last good faith offer unilaterally). See also Connell Constr. Co. v. Plumbers & Steamfitters Local 100, 421 U.S. 616, 622 (1975). Observe that all labor exemptions are drawn from the labor and antitrust statutes and are therefore statutory; at the same time, they are largely judge made, for the statutes are not very specific as to what is exempt. The statutory-nonstatutory dichotomy might therefore mislead the unwary. It does remind us, however, that some labor exemptions are more clearly inferred from statutory language than are other labor exemptions.

26. Columbia River Packers Assn. v. Hinton, 315 U.S. 143 (1942) (union of fishermen not within labor exemption because they were selling fish, not their services).

27. California State Council of Carpenters v. Associated Gen. Contractors, 648 F.2d 527 (9th Cir. 1980), rev'd on other grounds, 459 U.S. 519 (1983).

manufacturers and contractors that they will refuse to install electrical equipment made elsewhere.[28] Nor, the Supreme Court has held, may a union agree with one group of employers that it will extract a certain wage from other employers where the agreement's purpose is to destroy the latter.[29] The formula is obviously troublesome.[30]

Third, the exemption may be denied certain collective bargaining agreements even though they are initiated by the union in its own self-interest. The Supreme Court has suggested that the antitrust laws condemn agreements that greatly affect the character of competition among employers but that are not closely enough related to the traditional union objectives of better wages and working conditions.[31] Although the Court split on the application of this proposition, all the Justices agreed that the antitrust laws would be offended by a collective bargaining agreement binding employers to charge a certain price for their goods.[32]

Other applications have been very much in dispute. A legitimate interest in protecting union wages, for example, was not sufficient to save an agreement between a local Dallas plumber union and a general contractor. The contractor hired no plumbers directly but agreed to subcontract certain work only to mechanical contractors who had bargaining contracts with this local union.[33] In the Supreme Court's view, the challenged arrangement eliminated competition from unionized mechanical contractors based outside Dallas and from all nonunion contractors paying wages equal to or even higher than the Dallas union scale. The restraint was held outside the labor exemption because it restricted product market competition among contractors more than was necessary to achieve

---

28. Allen-Bradley Co. v. Local 3 IBEW, 325 U.S. 797 (1945). See R. Winter, Collective Bargaining and Competition: The Application of Antitrust Standards to Union Activities, 73 Yale L.J. 14 (1963).

29. United Mine Workers v. Pennington, 381 U.S. 657 (1965).

30. This rule might be very far-reaching if it embraced implicit understandings because one employer's wage decisions are necessarily related to what he expects the union will demand and obtain from the others. The purposive element is also obscure. On remand in *Pennington*, the district court held that plaintiff failed to prove that the union agreements were made with predatory intent. Lewis v. Pennington, 257 F. Supp. 815 (E.D. Tenn. 1966), aff'd, 400 F.2d 806 (6th Cir.), cert. denied, 393 U.S. 983 (1968). Also decided in favor of the union but then remanded for reconsideration because the trial court had applied too stringent a standard of proof was Ramsey v. United Mine Workers, 401 U.S. 302 (1971). In another case, a jury verdict against the union was upheld. Tennessee Consol. Coal Co. v. United Mine Workers, 416 F.2d 1192 (6th Cir. 1969), cert. denied, 397 U.S. 964 (1970).

31. Amalgamated Meat Cutters v. Jewel Tea Co., 381 U.S. 676 (1965).

32. Id. Compare Intercontinental Container Transp. Corp. v. New York Shipping Assn., 426 F.2d 884 (2d Cir. 1970).

33. *Connell*, note 25.

the legitimate union goal of eliminating wage competition. Similarly, the Third Circuit held that a union interest in preserving work for its members — which is regarded as a legitimate labor interest — would not necessarily save an agreement between longshoremen and shipping companies forbidding the companies from receiving containers packed within 50 miles of the port by freight forwarders employing non-longshoremen.[34] On the other hand, work preservation goals were held to justify a baker's agreement with the Teamsters' Union forbidding anyone other than union members from picking up and delivering baked goods to retailers.[35]

162. Regulated industries.[36] (a) *Generally.* In our private enterprise economy, we turn to public regulation when dissatisfied with market results. If, for example, publicly subsidized activities, such as ocean shipping or local service airlines, are privately operated, public supervision may substitute for market constraints on the subsidized firm. Or when a necessary resource is naturally scarce, as in the broadcast spectrum, conscious public allocation may seem desirable; such a rationing system could be accompanied by further controls, but it need not be. The regulated industries vary greatly in the rationale, administration, and intensity of their regulation. Thus, the relation of the regulatory policies to the antitrust laws will vary from industry to industry; the tighter the regulatory control, the less room there is for antitrust policy.

(b) *Natural monopoly.* Competition cannot protect the public interest when only one producer is possible.[37] Nature might physically

34. Consolidated Express v. New York Shipping Assn., 602 F.2d 494 (3d Cir. 1979), remanded for reconsideration, 448 U.S. 902 (1980), on remand, 641 F.2d 90 (3d Cir. 1981). See also United States Steel v. Fraternal Assn. of Steel Haulers, 601 F.2d 1269 (3d Cir. 1979); Larry V. Muko v. Southwestern Pa. Bldg. & Constr. Trades Council, 609 F.2d 1368 (3d Cir. 1979).

35. Granddad Bread v. Continental Baking Co., 612 F.2d 1105, 1110 (9th Cir. 1979), cert. denied, 449 U.S. 1076 (1981) (whether agreement "is *primarily* for work preservation depends upon whether it was entered into, or applied, for the purpose of preserving work traditionally performed by the union members or for some secondary purpose to satisfy union objectives elsewhere").

36. For a more complete discussion, see Areeda & Turner, note 1, ch. 2C-1. A portion of this Paragraph first appeared in P. Areeda, Antitrust Laws and Public Utility Regulation, 3 Bell J. Econ. & Man. Sci. 42. Copyright © 1972, The American Telephone and Telegraph Company, 195 Broadway, New York, New York 10007. Reprinted with permission.

37. This general proposition has come to be disputed. To oversimplify, consider a city contemplating the grant of a single franchise to build and operate a local electric distribution utility. The city might invite competitive bids from numerous prospective franchisees. Competition among them will induce promises to serve at competitive rather than monopoly prices. H. Demsetz, Why Regulate Utilities?, 11 J.L. & Econ. 55 (1968). If the franchise is of limited duration, the process can be

permit only a single enterprise — for example, the Suez Canal. Or the limitation might be economic. In local water, gas, electric, or telephone service,[38] large capital costs relative to output may mean continuously declining costs per unit of output. Such service can be provided at lower costs by one firm than by several. If there were rivals in this situation, they would be likely to compete ruinously or not at all. Regulated monopoly is the usual answer, but it is exceedingly difficult to protect the public from exploitation and still leave the utility management with the freedom, incentive, and willingness to cut costs, improve service, and innovate. Where there is natural monopoly there is little room for antitrust policy except insofar as (1) the maintenance of the monopoly ceases to be inevitable or (2) power in the monopoly area radiates outward into areas where competition is both possible and desirable.[39]

(c) *Transportation and communication.* Regulation of transportation and communication began as the control of monopoly. Although not all nineteenth-century railroads had substantial power, some of them did, and all were transportation monopolies in some areas. Their practices generated sufficiently widespread dissatisfaction to cause the creation of the Interstate Commerce Commission, which came to control the maximum and minimum rates, quality of service, entry into and exit from railroading, agreements between railroads, mergers and consolidations among railroads, and much more. The Commission came to administer a similar regime for

---

repeated to accommodate changes in technology, demand, and the general economy. In this manner, the apparent monopoly of a single franchisee might in fact achieve competitive results. Obviously, many questions remain to be answered. For any complex service, is it possible to specify all relevant terms at the time the franchise is awarded? Will the uncertain duration of the franchise mean that bidders bear a greater risk, for which consumers will have to pay? When substantial fixed assets are involved, will the city actually displace the established firm? On what terms (and how will they be determined) will the fixed assets be transferred from old to new franchisees? For these and other problems, see O. Williamson, Franchise Bidding for Natural Monopolies — In General and with Respect to CATV, 7 Bell J. Econ. 73 (1976).

38. Telephone service may no longer be in this category. See the discussion of the Telecommunications Act of 1996 in ¶327.

39. In this connection, Keogh v. Chicago & N.W. Ry., 260 U.S. 156 (1922), forbids antitrust damage actions by shippers based on allegedly excessive carrier's rates because such an award would work a discriminatory preference in favor of the plaintiff relative to other shippers, which offends the statutory requirement of uniform rates for all shippers. *Keogh* was reaffirmed in Square D Co. v. Niagara Tariff Bureau, 476 U.S. 409 (1986), where the Court characterized the commission-approved rate, even without a hearing, as the "lawful rate." *Keogh,* however, has not prevented a damage award to a competitor complaining of predatory pricing. See City of Kirkwood v. Union Elec. Co., 671 F.2d 1173, 1177-1179 (8th Cir. 1982), cert. denied, 459 U.S. 1170 (1983); Clipper Exxpress v. Rocky Mtn. Motor Tariff, 690 F.2d 1240, 1266 (9th Cir. 1982), cert. denied, 459 U.S. 1227 (1983).

interstate trucking. The Civil Aeronautics Board had broadly similar powers over civil aviation, as does the Federal Communications Commission with respect to common carrier communications by wire or radio. The Federal Maritime Commission exercises somewhat similar powers over ocean shipping, except that it does not control entry or exit and its rate powers are less comprehensive.

Subsequently, comprehensive deregulation of civil aviation was enacted, and there has been partial deregulation of surface freight transportation, as well as in other areas.[40] Many of the cases and situations discussed in this Paragraph involve the pre-deregulation situation, which is relevant to principles concerning the application of the antitrust laws to regulation, where and to the extent it still exists.

These industries — unlike local electric utilities — exhibit both monopoly and competition. A railroad may be the sole carrier between two cities but share other routes with several other lines, although even on routes it has to itself it may face substantial competition from trucks or barges. Trucks and barges, in turn, probably have no monopoly routes (absent regulations limiting entry) because another firm can readily enter and begin shipping between any two points. Competition in domestic voice communication is growing, as it is in other communication services. These summary comments suggest the interplay between antitrust and regulatory policies. The regulator's power and the exercise of that power are never complete. Varying degrees of discretion are always left to the management of the regulated enterprise, and that management may act in ways that impair such competition as remains possible, notwithstanding the existence of regulation.

(d) *Competition in the public interest.* Many regulatory statutes instruct an administrative agency to regulate in the public interest. The Justice Department or a private party[41] will often complain that industry actions or proposals are in some respect anticompetitive and therefore contrary to the public interest. And the courts usually require the administrators to give appropriate weight to the national policy

40. E.g., 92 Stat. 1705 (1978) (aviation); 94 Stat. 1895 (1980) (railroads).

41. There are few limitations on the persons who may appear before an agency to make a claim that a regulated firm's acts or proposed acts will have an unreasonable anticompetitive effect. Governing statutes often grant any aggrieved person standing to raise questions before the agency and then to challenge the agency action in court. A competitive firm or industry or even a consumer as a private attorney general may be granted standing. Association of Data Processing Serv. Orgs. v. Camp, 397 U.S. 150 (1970); Hardin v. Kentucky Util. Co., 390 U.S. 1 (1968); FCC v. Sanders Bros. Radio Station, 309 U.S. 470 (1940); Pittsburgh v. FPC, 237 F.2d 741 (D.C. Cir. 1956); Associated Indus. v. Ickes, 134 F.2d 694 (2d Cir.), vacated for mootness, 320 U.S. 707 (1943). And not only is the range of persons broad, the issues they are permitted to raise sometimes seem limitless. Gulf States Util. Co. v. FPC, 411 U.S. 747 (1973), and *Pittsburgh.*

favoring competition as expressed in the antitrust laws, even though the agency has the express statutory power to grant an exemption from the antitrust laws. This proposition is illustrated by *McLean*,[42] where Interstate Commerce Commission approval — and consequent antitrust exemption — of a merger of truckers was challenged on the ground that the Commission had failed to apply the antitrust law standard. The Supreme Court rejected that challenge and upheld the Commission. But although the Commission decision is not precisely controlled by the standard of antitrust law, the Court made it clear that the Commission is obliged to consider the effect of the merger on competitors and on the general competitive situation in the light of the objectives of the regulatory statute.[43]

The general notion that the regulator ought to value competition to the extent consistent with regulatory goals will provide clear guidance where the regulatory premise is both clear and inapplicable to the challenged conduct. For example, the limited broadcast spectrum must be allocated somehow. But the necessity of preventing physical interference among freely entering broadcasters does not warrant limiting cable TV operations in order to protect broadcasters.[44] And even if telephone service were considered a natural monopoly, equipment manufacture is not. There is, therefore, little warrant for agency approval of a telephone company tariff preventing customer installation of auxiliary devices that do not impair the general system; there are less restrictive ways of requiring compliance with reasonable technical standards designed to ensure system integrity.[45]

The proper place for competitive standards is more difficult to locate when the legislative mandate is understood to include promotional or distributive objectives. Were airlines regulated in order to give the public the benefits of competition in the absence of perfectly competitive market structure? Or did regulation seek to hold up rates between major markets in order to provide sufficient carrier revenues to subsidize non-self-supporting service to and among lesser markets — possibly to further national cohesion or industrial and population dispersal?[46]

42. McLean Trucking Co. v. United States, 321 U.S. 67 (1944).

43. See also United States v. ICC, 396 U.S. 491 (1970), and *Gulf States,* note 41.

44. Although rationing is the raison d'être for FCC licensing, the Commission may believe that it has the duty to assure free over-the-air television and thus to protect at least some broadcasters from possible ruination at the hands of cable systems.

45. See Specialized Common Carriers, 29 F.C.C.2d 870 (1971), aff'd sub nom. Washington Utils. & Transp. Commn. v. FCC, 513 F.2d 1142 (9th Cir.), cert. denied, 423 U.S. 836 (1975) (so ruling).

46. Of course, passenger safety, a powerful justification for safety regulation, is supervised by the Federal Aviation Administration independently of the rate and entry controls once administered by the CAB.

In yet another class of cases, the regulatory and antitrust objectives
are similar: as much competition as is practicable, consistent with the
economic and technical imperatives of efficiency. This objective
guides both antitrust and administrative doctrines about mergers, but
the implementing approaches have developed differently. With respect to horizontal mergers, Chapter 5D will show that the antitrust
courts have come to adopt a rather simple prohibition of mergers
involving an undue market share. In contrast, the regulatory agencies
purport to consider every factor bearing on competition and efficiency. Yet it must be said that railroad merger decisions often involved cumbersome agency and judicial procedures that burdened
the parties and the government without illuminating the issues. In so
many of the decisions, the anticompetitive tendencies and the alleged offsetting cost savings were usually addressed at a level of vague
generality that was quite unpersuasive. There has been considerable
comment on the decisions of some Comptrollers of the Currency,
who approved bank mergers with no apparent justification beyond
the parties' desires. In many instances it may be that the critical
difference between courts and administrators is one of methodology,
as the different approaches toward mergers illustrate.

Often, however, the difference will be one of attitude. Usually,
the antitrust authorities will be more skeptical than the regulators
about firm or industry claims of social efficiency. An interesting
apparent reversal of outlook is illustrated by the Federal Maritime
Commission. Its predecessors approved shipping cartel practices injuring noncartel ships without inquiring into the necessity of such
coercive tactics to achieve the purposes of the statute. More recently, the Commission condemned a cartel ("conference") of Atlantic passenger carriers who boycotted travel agents booking any
passengers on noncartel ships. In the words of the Supreme Court,
the Commission disapproved of this practice on a

> principle that conference restraints which interfere with the policies
> of antitrust laws will be approved only if the conferences can "bring
> forth such facts as would demonstrate that the . . . rule was required
> by a serious transportation need, necessary to secure important pub-
> lic benefits or in furtherance of a valid regulatory purpose of the
> Shipping Act."[47]

The Supreme Court upheld the agency's refusal to grant antitrust
immunity to the cartel. The Court held "that the antitrust test
formulated by the Commission is an appropriate refinement of the
statutory 'public interest' standard."

47. Federal Maritime Commn. v. Swedish Am. Line, 390 U.S. 238, 243, 246
(1968).

As a practical matter, the court confronted with an antitrust claim concerning conduct by a regulated firm must face one or more of the following questions. (1) Does the very existence of the regulatory regime administered by the agency immunize the challenged conduct, or does the agency have the express or implied power by affirmative action to confer such immunity? (2) Has the agency already immunized it? (3) If not, should the agency now have the opportunity to do so? (4) Even if there is no immunity for future or past conduct, should the court require the parties to seek the agency's judgment on either the reasonableness of the challenged conduct or on any relevant fact?

(e) *Primary jurisdiction and pervasive regulation.* Cartel agreements specifically approved by the Federal Maritime Commission are expressly exempted from federal antitrust law. Failure to file such an agreement violates the Shipping Act, and such violations can be punished by penalties of $1000 per day and are also subject to cease and desist orders from the Maritime Commission. The *Far East* case[48] involved an unfiled cartel agreement that included a so-called dual rate provision for higher charges to shippers not agreeing to use cartel vessels exclusively. The Antitrust Division attacked the cartel in court and sought an injunction against continuation of the cartel agreement that was unfiled and therefore not exempted by any Commission action. Nevertheless, the Supreme Court dismissed the complaint.

In dealing with such an industry, perhaps one should hold that the existence of regulation supersedes antitrust law, such that the Commission would become the exclusive judge and enforcer of the competitive rules of the game. To hold that regulation would oust judicially enforced antitrust law has the virtue of unencumbered simplicity. But total displacement would also have several costs. Improper conduct could no longer be challenged directly by injured private persons. To be sure, they could complain to the Commission, but they would have no independent remedy. Second, the flexible arsenal of antitrust remedies would be lost. In place of injunction, private damages, and criminal sanctions, there would be only the administrative cease and desist order and civil fines. Third, the general and comprehensive proscription of unreasonable agreements and anticompetitive exercises of power would be lost. In their place would be a rather more specific catalog of permitted and prohibited acts. Fourth, in place of impartial, disinterested, skeptical courts, private plaintiffs, and the Justice Department, decisions would be made by administrators who sometimes grow too close to their regulated clients. Finally, total displacement would seem in-

48. Far East Conference v. United States, 342 U.S. 570, 574-575 (1952).

consistent with the statute. Its specific antitrust exemption for approved agreements would imply a congressional intention that unapproved conduct remain subject to the antitrust law.

If one rejects the view that regulation supersedes antitrust, should one take the rather obvious view that an unfiled, unapproved, and unexempted cartel agreement is to be tested by ordinary antitrust standards? Of course, the basic antitrust standard of reasonableness takes into account the particular circumstances of the industry. But the agency charged with regulating the particular industry is presumably more knowledgeable and more expert about that industry and thus better able to judge the reasonableness of competitive or anticompetitive behavior there.[49] We must consider whether the agency or the court is better able to make an intelligent judgment about market behavior.

It was this issue of relative competence that the Court emphasized in *Far East*:

> [C]ases raising issues of fact not within the conventional experience of judges or cases requiring the exercise of administrative discretion [should be decided first by the relevant administrative agency,] even though the facts after they have been appraised by specialized competence serve as a premise for legal consequences to be judicially defined. [And further,] [u]niformity and consistency in the regulation of business entrusted to a particular agency are secured, and the limited functions of review by the judiciary are more rationally exercised, by preliminary resort for ascertaining and interpreting the circumstances underlying legal issues to agencies that are better equipped than courts by specialization, by insight gained through experience, and by more flexible procedure.[50]

It should be observed that this formulation does not necessarily oust the antitrust laws. It merely says that the agency must be consulted first. And once the agency is consulted, the courts are available for antitrust remedies that the agency could not grant, such as criminal penalties or private treble damages. Such damages were allowed in a subsequent case after the Commission had in fact

49. To be sure, the defendants could have availed themselves of administrative expertise through the simple expedient of obeying the Shipping Act and filing their agreement. Their failure to file deprives them of our sympathy. But that is not really the issue.

50. It is ironic that, in a later episode, the Commission's approval of dual-rate cartel provisions was reviewed by the unspecialized courts and held inconsistent with the Shipping Act. Federal Maritime Bd. v. Isbrandtsen Co., 356 U.S. 481 (1958). Although Congress subsequently amended the statute to empower the Commission to approve dual-rate agreements, the statute imposed significant limitations on such cartels beyond anything the Commission had earlier done.

held that the defendant's price-fixing agreement was unfiled, un-approved, and unlawful.[51]

In *Pan American*,[52] the Justice Department mounted a Sherman Act attack, at the request of the Civil Aeronautics Board, against certain arrangements between Pan American, Grace, and their jointly owned subsidiary, Panagra, alleging the division of rates among carriers. The alleged behavior began long before enactment of the Federal Aviation Act that required filing of agreements among carriers and exempted those approved by the Board from the antitrust laws.[53] The Board was also authorized to prohibit "unfair or deceptive practices or unfair methods of competition."

The Supreme Court dismissed the antitrust complaint, noting that the Board can immunize conduct from the antitrust laws and can halt all unfair practices and unfair methods of competition, including those that started prior to the Act. The Court went on to declare that "[if] the courts were to intrude independently with their construction of the antitrust laws, two regimes might collide." Accordingly, the Court held that all questions of injunctive relief had to be left to the Board but also declared itself hesitant to hold that a regulatory scheme "was designed completely to displace the antitrust laws — absent an unequivocally declared Congressional purpose to do so." For example, "the whole criminal law enforce-ment problem remains unaffected by the Act."

Although the Court expressly left criminal antitrust remedies in-tact, and presumably private treble-damage actions as well, it did not illuminate the respective roles of Board, judge, and jury in the course of such an action. The Supreme Court did note the availabil-ity, at least in civil cases, of a procedure whereby "litigation is held by a court until the basic facts and findings are first determined by the administrative agency." But is the agency to collect evidence or find facts on the context in which the parties operated — that is, what they did, alternatives open to them, possibilities and costs of acting differently, and social consequences of various actions? It

---

51. Carnation Co. v. Pacific Westbound Conference, 383 U.S. 213 (1966).

52. Pan Am. World Airways v. United States, 371 U.S. 296, 305, 310, 313 n.19 (1963).

53. An interesting illustration is Hughes Tool Co. v. Trans World Airlines, 409 U.S. 363 (1973). TWA had sought treble damages from Hughes for the latter's "monopolization" of the TWA market in jet aircraft when Hughes controlled TWA. In effect, TWA objected to Hughes' "bad" management in deciding when and how to equip TWA with jets. The delay allegedly caused TWA to lose profits. After a default judgment of nearly $140 million plus some $7 million in lawyers' fees, the Supreme Court ruled that the complaint should have been dismissed because the CAB had approved Hughes' control of TWA by Hughes and had also approved the jet and financial dealings between the two companies. Accordingly, the Court declared that such dealings were immune from antitrust attack.

may very well be that the agency could do these things better than a court. But the Court did not explain whether the judges would remain the ultimate arbiters of the appropriate degree of competition for the regulated industry. For the future, the same standard must govern court decisions as that which governs agency decisions. And even as to the past, the court cannot adopt an independent standard if the regulatory scheme is to be administered as a coherent whole.

(f) *Where regulation is less pervasive.* The necessity and degree of deference by the antitrust court to the administrative agency is far from clear. In *El Paso,*[54] the Supreme Court held that although certain pipeline mergers required Federal Power Commission approval, such approval did not oust the antitrust laws. The Court then held, rather surprisingly, that the FPC must postpone its decision until the decision of the court, when the merger is also attacked by the Justice Department under the antitrust laws. The Court purported to fear that the administrative decision would influence the antitrust court in some improper way. Where advance administrative approval is not required by the regulatory statute, there seems to be less reason to defer to the agency.[55] Even there, however, the experience, resources, and assessments of the administrative agency might inform the antitrust court, which may be cut off by the regulatory statute from its usual premises concerning the role of competition.[56]

54. California v. FPC, 369 U.S. 482 (1962).

55. E.g., United States v. Borden Co., 308 U.S. 188 (1939). Although the Secretary of Agriculture's approval would immunize certain marketing agreements from the antitrust laws, the Supreme Court held that unapproved agreements would be judged by the Court on customary antitrust grounds. The Secretary did not have comprehensive jurisdiction over the producers, processors, and distributors involved in the case.

56. Compare Ricci v. Chicago Mercantile Exch., 409 U.S. 289 (1973). Plaintiff and defendant Siegal disputed the ownership of a seat on the Chicago Mercantile Exchange. When the Exchange, at Siegal's request, transferred that seat to another, plaintiff claimed an unlawful conspiracy in violation of Sherman Act §1 and the Commodity Exchange Act. The court of appeals reversed the dismissal of plaintiff's complaint but ordered a stay of antitrust proceedings pending administrative action before the Secretary of Agriculture or the Commodity Exchange Commission. The Supreme Court affirmed: (1) Application of the antitrust laws might be inconsistent with the regulatory scheme that provides no express antitrust exemption but that clearly contemplates a membership organization with rules about memberships and their transfer. The agency should decide whether there is a valid membership rule and whether this controversy was within it. (2) Some aspects of this dispute lie within administrative jurisdiction because plaintiff alleges a violation of the Exchange Act. (3) In all events, adjudication by the agency will materially aid the court in deciding factual questions and in resolving the first issue. (4) Thus, said the Court, this case is unlike *Silver* (note 57) where it was clear that the Securities Act did not require NYSE proceedings without a hearing and where the SEC had no authority to review specific applications of NYSE rules. The

(g) *"If necessary to make the [regulatory] Act work."* The New York Stock Exchange has provided a battleground for a confrontation between the SEC with its Act and the Justice Department with the Sherman Act. In *Silver,*[57] the NYSE's refusal to deal with Mr. Silver might have seemed presumptively unlawful in a different industry. But the NYSE acted pursuant to a rather clearly implied provision of its rules, and self-government by the NYSE was certainly assumed by Congress in enacting the Securities Exchange Act of 1934. Although Congress did not expressly prohibit or permit any particular NYSE rule, §19(b) of the Act authorized the SEC "to alter or supplement" NYSE rules "in respect of" 12 enumerated matters (such as safeguards of members' financial responsibility and the manner, method, and time of soliciting and trading) and "similar matters." The SEC had jurisdiction, which had not been exercised, to change the NYSE rule applied to the plaintiff.

The Act did not explicitly exempt NYSE rules from the antitrust laws, and

> [r]epeal [of the Sherman Act] is ... implied only if necessary to make the Securities Exchange Act work, and even then only to the minimum extent necessary. . . . The entire public policy of self-regulation, beginning with the idea that the Exchange may set up barriers to membership, contemplates that the Exchange will engage in restraints of trade which might well be unreasonable absent sanction by the Securities Exchange Act. [But] the statutory scheme of that Act is not sufficiently pervasive to create a total exemption from the antitrust laws. . . . [E]xchange self-regulation is to be regarded as justified in response to antitrust charges only to the extent necessary to protect the achievement of the aims of the [Act].

In the application of that standard, the views of the expert body charged with responsibility in this area would seem relevant. Instead of referring the question to the Commission, however, the Court purported to distinguish Commission jurisdiction to alter NYSE rules for the future from jurisdiction to review a particular application to the plaintiff. But there is not really a difference; the Court, in effect, ruled as to the future when it held that no statutory objective prevented the NYSE from "telling a protesting nonmember why a rule is being invoked so as to harm him and allowing him to reply in explanation of his position. . . . The requirement of such a hearing will ... [discourage] anticompetitive application of exchange rules."

---

dissent said the Secretary was not compelled to proceed, the plaintiff was not a party before the agency, the agency could not award damages, a conspiracy was not even arguably lawful, and the agency could not definitively resolve the first issue. See also Chicago Mercantile Exch. v. Deaktor, 414 U.S. 113 (1973).

57. Silver v. New York Stock Exch., 373 U.S. 341, 357-362 (1963).

The *Silver* Court thus seemed to insist on a rather clear legislative preclusion before subordinating antitrust policy to regulatory goals. Later in *Gordon,*[58] the Supreme Court seemed readier to find a regulatory sphere displacing antitrust law. In that case, investors challenged New York Stock Exchange rules by which stockbrokers fixed their commission charges. Under Securities Exchange Act §19(b)(9), the Securities and Exchange Commission could alter or supplement exchange rules relating to "the fixing of reasonable rates of commission." The Court held that this authority, coupled with the SEC's actual record of vigorous scrutiny over commissions, immunized the challenged behavior from the antitrust laws. In view of the SEC studies and orders that had led gradually to the elimination of fixed rates — a result subsequently codified by legislative amendments — it could hardly be said that fixed commissions were "necessary to make the Act work." Nevertheless, the Court believed that exclusive agency jurisdiction and antitrust immunity were necessary to make the Act work, lest antitrust courts impose on the Exchange a requirement different from that imposed by the SEC pursuant to its express statutory power to supervise and set brokerage rates. Although the *Gordon* Court emphasized both SEC power over commission rates and the exercise of that power, the Court's *NASD* decision[59] then held that, at least in some circumstances, an unexercised oversight power would imply an immunity.

Perhaps we can take some comfort in the fact that the federal judges ultimately interpret and apply both the regulatory and antitrust regimes and can therefore ensure harmonious coexistence between them.

State Law and State Action

163.   State law: primacy, invalidity, or accommodation. (a) *Generally.* The relationship of state and federal law is too complex for comprehensive treatment here. This Paragraph notes several situations in which federal law gives express primacy to state law and other situations in which state law is invalid because it is inconsistent with the federal Constitution or statutes. The next Paragraph focuses on the preemption of state laws by the federal antitrust laws in particular. Where state laws limiting competition are not preempted, the doctrine of Parker v. Brown accommodates them by immunizing some, but not all, conduct of governmental bodies and private persons acting under them.

58. Gordon v. New York Stock Exch., 422 U.S. 659, 662, 683 (1975).
59. United States v. National Assn. of Sec. Dealers, 422 U.S. 694 (1975).

(b) *Express primacy for state law.* In at least two areas, state law has special force. The Twenty-First Amendment to the Constitution confers particularly broad powers and a measure of precedence on the states with respect to trade in alcoholic beverages. But this does not allow a state to authorize or to require otherwise unlawful private price fixing that is not supervised by state officials.[60]

In the insurance area, a federal statute establishes an express immunity.[61] The Sherman Act, Clayton Act, and Federal Trade Commission Act are only "applicable to the business of insurance to the extent that such business is not regulated by State law."[62] What constitutes the business of insurance is not altogether clear, but it is held to focus on the underwriting relationship between insurer and insured.[63] The Supreme Court examined the business of insurance issue in *Pireno.*[64] Health insurers customarily undertake to reimburse only "reasonable" charges by doctors or other health providers. To help assess the reasonableness of a chiropractor's fee, an insurer consulted a panel of chiropractors. Such peer review was challenged by an unhappy chiropractor. If the antitrust laws had been violated — which is extremely doubtful — the Court held that peer review and other insurer arrangements with those who provide services to its subscribers are not "the business of insurance."

There are two qualifications on the exemption. The antitrust laws continue to apply to transactions so interstate in character as to be beyond full regulation by a single state.[65] According to an express statutory provision, moreover, the antitrust laws remain fully applicable to boycotts, which have been defined quite expansively for this purpose.[66]

60. California Retail Liquor Dealers Assn. v. Midcal Aluminum, 445 U.S. 97 (1980).

61. 59 Stat. 33 (1945), 61 Stat. 448 (1947), 15 U.S.C. §§1011, 1012. This statute was enacted after United States v. South-Eastern Underwriters Assn., 322 U.S. 533 (1944), held that insurance transactions were interstate commerce and thus subject to the antitrust laws. Repeal of the insurance exemption has recently been proposed.

62. This statutory immunity parallels the "state action" doctrine considered in ¶165, in that regulated conduct meeting the requirements specified there would be immune. In practice, the statutory exemption is broader because it encompasses state regulatory schemes that have jurisdiction over the challenged practice when the requisite supervision for *Parker* immunity is lacking. See P. Areeda & H. Hovenkamp, Antitrust Law ¶210.1b (Supp. 1996).

63. Group Life & Health Ins. Co. v. Royal Drug Co., 440 U.S. 205, 211-216 (1979).

64. Union Labor Life Ins. Co. v. Pireno, 458 U.S. 119 (1982).

65. Compare FTC v. Travelers Health Assn., 362 U.S. 293 (1960), with FTC v. National Cas. Co., 357 U.S. 560 (1958); see Maryland Cas. Co. v. American Gen. Ins. Co., 232 F. Supp. 620 (D.D.C. 1964).

66. St. Paul Fire & Marine Ins. Co. v. Barry, 438 U.S. 531 (1978); United States v. New Orleans Ins. Exch., 148 F. Supp. 915 (E.D. La.), aff'd per curiam, 355 U.S. 22 (1957).

(c) *Invalid state laws.* An anticompetitive state law may be invalid because it is inconsistent with (1) the Constitution's Commerce Clause in that it unduly burdens commerce, (2) the First Amendment, or (3) federal statutes, such as the FTC Act or patent laws. A few examples will have to suffice.

Commerce Clause. Even in the absence of federal legislation, the Commerce Clause, by its own force, has been held to constitute an inherent limitation on state interference with interstate commerce.[67] The various historical formulae with which the Supreme Court has stated these limitations rest on the assumption that the Constitution ordains a national economy. This is most obvious in the express constitutional prohibitions of state tariffs on goods entering or leaving a state.

There is no absolute rule against burdening the free flow of interstate commerce, as is clearly shown by the many cases allowing states to impose taxes affecting costs and thereby affecting the volume of interstate goods produced or consumed in that state. Similarly, a state is allowed wide latitude under the police power to protect the health and safety of its citizens, although this power is not absolute. In place of a per se test against such burdens, the Supreme Court has favored a balancing of state and federal interests. The general rule is that stated in *Pike.*[68]

> Where the statute regulates even-handedly to effectuate a legitimate local public interest, and its effects on interstate commerce are only incidental, it will be upheld unless the burden imposed on such commerce is clearly excessive in relation to the putative local benefits.... [T]he extent of the burden that will be tolerated will ... depend [inter alia] ... on whether it could be promoted as well with a lesser impact on interstate activities.

Under this formulation, the Commerce Clause would seem to invalidate some anticompetitive state laws.[69]

---

67. E.g., Cooley v. Board of Wardens, 53 U.S. (12 How.) 299 (1851).

68. Pike v. Bruce Church, 397 U.S. 137, 142 (1970). See also Brown-Forman Distillers Corp. v. New York State Liquor Auth., 476 U.S. 573 (1986) (invalidating statute requiring liquor distillers to post a monthly wholesale price that was no higher than the lowest price the distiller charged wholesalers anywhere in the country); Reeves v. Stake, 440 U.S. 429 (1980) (state-owned cement plant may confine sales to residents during period of shortage); Exxon Corp. v. Governor of Maryland, 437 U.S. 117 (1978) (upholding statute prohibiting producers or refiners of gasoline from operating intrastate retail service stations); Great A&P Tea Co. v. Cottrell, 424 U.S. 366, 371 (1976) (invalidating regulation providing that milk products from another state may be sold in Mississippi only if the other state reciprocally accepts milk products produced in Mississippi).

69. For a fuller statement, see Areeda & Turner, note 1, ¶220b.

First Amendment. In *Virginia Pharmacy,*[70] the Supreme Court affirmed an injunction against enforcement of a Virginia statute that effectively prohibited the advertisement of prescription drugs. The anticompetitive effects of such restraints on advertising — in keeping up prices and preventing efficient resource allocation — are clear. But *Virginia Pharmacy* was brought on First Amendment grounds, rather than as an antitrust challenge, and the Court struck down Virginia's statute for its incompatibility with the amendment. The key was the Court's decision that even purely commercial speech deserved constitutional protection. That decision was based in part on the Court's belief that commercial information is "indispensable to the proper allocation of resources in a free enterprise system."[71] In the following year, the Supreme Court's *Bates* decision[72] held that Arizona's blanket ban on lawyer advertising, including price advertising, was offensive to the First Amendment.

Federal Trade Commission Act. In 1975, the FTC issued proposed regulations purporting to preempt state laws forbidding the advertising of prescription drugs.[73] Although the proposed regulation was mooted by *Virginia Pharmacy,* the Commission believes it has the power to define an unfair method of competition by rule, which assumes the force of law and thereby preempts state law.[74] Although there are grounds for doubting that power,[75] the issue remains unresolved.

Preemption by federal statutes. State laws preventing competition in unpatented goods provide an important example of federal preemption of state limitations on competition. In *Stiffel,*[76] the Supreme Court held that Illinois was not permitted to use its common law of unfair competition to prevent Sears from copying Stiffel's unpatented and unpatentable lamp. Such action would interfere

70. Virginia State Bd. of Pharmacy v. Virginia Citizens Consumer Council, 425 U.S. 748 (1976).

71. Id. at 765.

72. Bates v. State Bar of Ariz., 433 U.S. 350 (1977). Compare Friedman v. Rogers, 440 U.S. 1 (1979) (upholding Texas statute forbidding use of trade names by optometrists); Consolidated Edison Co. v. Public Serv. Commn., 447 U.S. 530 (1980) (invalidating order prohibiting bill inserts on controversial public issues); Central Hudson Gas & Elec. Corp. v. Public Serv. Commn., 447 U.S. 557 (1980) (invalidating ban on promotional advertising).

73. Proposed 16 C.F.R. §447, 40 Fed. Reg. 24031, 24032 (1975), indefinitely postponed, 41 Fed. Reg. 27391 (1976).

74. See FTC, Staff Report on Prescription Drug Price Disclosures 493-538 (1975); Note, The State Action Exemption and Antitrust Enforcement Under the Federal Trade Commission Act, 89 Harv. L. Rev. 715 (1976).

75. See Areeda & Turner, note 1, ¶218.

76. Sears, Roebuck & Co. v. Stiffel Co., 376 U.S. 225 (1964). But see Goldstein v. California, 412 U.S. 546 (1973) (upholding California statute prohibiting commercial reproduction of recordings produced by others).

too much with the federal policy, expressed in the antitrust and patent laws, of favoring copying and competition that is not otherwise protected by the patent laws. Similarly, the Court ruled in *Lear*[77] that federal law preempted state contract law that prevented a licensee from challenging the validity of a licensed patent. Preemption by the federal antitrust laws is considered next.

164. Preemption by the antitrust laws. (a) *State antitrust laws.* Many states have enacted a "baby Sherman Act" or other antitrust legislation that forbids conduct already reached by the federal antitrust laws. It is generally assumed that federal antitrust laws are not intended to preempt the field in this respect. In addition, state law may condemn conduct that would be held lawful under the Sherman Act, which is also generally permissible. The fact that the Sherman Act tolerates certain conduct does not necessarily mean that there is an affirmative federal policy encouraging such conduct. *New Motor*[78] sustained a California statute requiring auto manufacturers to obtain the approval of a state board before opening or relocating a retail outlet in the marketing area of an existing outlet that protests. The Court also sustained, in *Exxon,*[79] a Maryland statute forbidding refiners from owning retail service stations. The Maryland statute also condemned certain price discriminations allowed by the Robinson-Patman Act.[80] In *ARC America,*[81] the Court permitted a California law to allow antitrust recovery by indirect purchasers in spite of the prohibition against such recoveries under the federal antitrust laws.[82] The Court commented that Congress intended the federal antitrust law to supplement rather than to displace antitrust remedies.

Of course, there might be situations in which Sherman Act legality does express an affirmative federal policy. Furthermore, state regulation remains subject to the usual imperative that it must not unduly burden interstate commerce.

(b) *State laws limiting competition.* A state statute authorizing private parties to engage in unsupervised price fixing is clearly invalid. A state may not grant anyone "authority to restrain interstate . . . commerce against the will of . . . Congress."[83] A state statute com-

---

77. Lear v. Adkins, 395 U.S. 653 (1969).
78. New Motor Vehicle Bd. v. Orrin W. Fox Co., 439 U.S. 96 (1978).
79. Exxon Corp. v. Governor of Md., 437 U.S. 117 (1978).
80. See also Shell Oil Co. v. Younger, 587 F.2d 34 (9th Cir. 1978), cert. denied, 440 U.S. 947 (1979).
81. California v. ARC America Corp., 490 U.S. 93 (1989).
82. See ¶145b.
83. Northern Sec. Co. v. United States, 193 U.S. 197, 346 (1904); Schwegmann Bros. v. Calvert Distillers Corp., 341 U.S. 384 (1951).

pelling such price fixing is equally invalid.[84] Determining the boundary between state laws that permissibly displace competition — and thus are both valid and result in *Parker* immunity, where applicable, for private parties — and those that permit or command action sufficiently in conflict with the antitrust laws to be preempted, has proved troublesome indeed. As will become clear, the standards governing preemption have tended to coalesce with those governing the state action immunity considered in ¶165.

In its *Rice* decision,[85] the Supreme Court considered the validity of a state statute that forbids liquor wholesalers from handling a brand without the approval of the distiller of that brand, thus giving the distiller control of the number and identity of wholesalers handling its brand. The Court declared that such a statute would be preempted only if it mandated or authorized conduct that would necessarily violate the antitrust laws in all cases or placed irresistible pressure on a private party to violate the antitrust laws. This statute was not preempted because the restrictions on distribution that it created were not necessarily unlawful under *Sylvania*, which we will examine in Chapter 4A.[86]

Rice should be contrasted with the earlier *Midcal* case.[87] There, a California statute required wine dealers to charge the resale prices specified by their supplier. No one was in violation of Sherman Act §1, which categorically forbids supplier-dealer *agreements* specifying resale prices,[88] because dealer prices were controlled not by agreement but by state law. Nevertheless, the state statute created the same effect as such an unlawful supplier-dealer agreement and did so without any state regulation of the resulting resale price. Accordingly, the Supreme Court held that the state law was preempted by federal law and affirmed an injunction prohibiting state officials from enforcing the California statute.

The *Midcal* Court made clear that even an agreement between a supplier and its dealer fixing resale prices — which is ordinarily per se unlawful — would be immunized by the *Parker* doctrine (¶165)

---

84. *Midcal,* note 60.

85. Rice v. Norman Williams Co., 458 U.S. 654 (1982).

86. There have been understandable difficulties in applying the *Rice* test. For example, the Second Circuit upheld a statute requiring manufacturers and wholesalers of alcoholic beverages to post their wholesale prices and, except for downward adjustments to meet competition, to adhere to these prices for 30 days. Battipaglia v. New York State Liquor Auth., 745 F.2d 166 (2d Cir. 1984), cert. denied, 470 U.S. 1027 (1985). The dissent found the agreement more akin to *Midcal* since the statute required not only posting of prices but also adherence, which has been held per se unlawful. 745 F.2d at 179. The dissent's approach was largely accepted (although without mentioning it) in Miller v. Hedlund, 803 F.2d 1007 (9th Cir. 1986).

87. *Midcal,* note 60.

88. See *Dr. Miles,* Ch. 4A.

from Sherman Act attack if (1) the restraint on competition was clearly articulated and affirmatively expressed as state policy with the purpose of displacing the antitrust laws and (2) the resulting private power was supervised by public authorities. The *Midcal* statute failed to displace the Sherman Act because California allowed suppliers to control dealer prices without state supervision of the resulting price level.

In *Fisher*,[89] the Supreme Court held that a city's rent control ordinance was not preempted by the Sherman Act. For this preemption purpose, a municipal ordinance stands on the same footing as a state statute.[90] The Court acknowledged that municipal rent control affects the housing market in much the same way as an agreement among landlords to stabilize rents at reasonable levels for the benefit of tenants and that such an agreement would be per se unlawful. But there can be no violation of Sherman Act §1 without a "contract, combination, or conspiracy," and no such concerted action is involved here, because the city acted unilaterally to impose its will on unwilling landlords. To be sure, the state statute in *Midcal* was preempted notwithstanding the absence of any agreement between the state and wine suppliers, between the state and the suppliers' dealers, or between suppliers and dealers. But the *Midcal* restraint on dealers' prices was characterized by the *Fisher* Court as hybrid rather than unilateral because it enforced the prices privately specified by the suppliers without state review or supervision. Thus, the difference was that the public supervision lacking in *Midcal* was present in *Fisher*.[91]

165. Antitrust immunity for state action.[92] (a) *Initial develop-*

89. Fisher v. City of Berkeley, 475 U.S. 260 (1986).

90. This is the principal respect in which the Court's preemption analysis differs from its *Parker* analysis, discussed in the next Paragraph.

91. The Court said in *Fisher* and *Rice* that it need not go on to consider the availability of an immunity under *Parker* because the ordinance or statute involved was not preempted. The implication that *Parker* immunity might be available after a state statute was preempted is curious indeed. What the Court apparently meant was that a state statute that fails the first-level preemption inquiry (inconsistency with federal antitrust policy) can nevertheless be saved from preemption if the restraint in question satisfies the *Parker* test of articulated state policy supplemented by the active supervision of public authorities. This reading is confirmed by 324 Liquor Corp. v. Duffy, 479 U.S. 335 (1987), which invalidated a state statute permitting wholesalers to control the minimum retail prices of retailers. The Court first determined that the state statute allowed conduct equivalent to a per se antitrust violation and thus was preempted unless saved by *Parker*; then it held that the supervision requirement was not satisfied.

92. For competing views concerning the appropriate scope of displacement of antitrust principles by state law, see Areeda & Turner, note 1, ch. 2B; F. Easterbrook, Antitrust and the Economics of Federalism, 26 J.L. & Econ. 23 (1983); M. Garland, Antitrust and State Action: Economic Efficiency and the Political

ment. It was declared in *Parker*[93] that the antitrust laws are addressed to action by private parties and not action by state legislatures or state administrative bodies. There, California's scheme for raising and fixing raisin prices had been challenged under the antitrust laws. To be sure, California itself set the price and marketing limitations, but it did so at the request and on the consent of a majority of the growers. The effects were clear. California produced half the world's supply of raisins and most of that consumed in the United States. When California controlled the production, price, or marketing of raisins, interstate commerce was clearly and substantially affected. Such state action could have been considered an obvious burden on interstate commerce, and the interstate effects clearly empowered Congress to override state legislation pursuant to the constitutional power of Congress over such commerce. But the Supreme Court did not consider whether the Sherman Act amounted to a preclusive exertion of federal power in favor of competition because it found the California regulation consistent with the national policy embodied in the Agricultural Adjustment Act, which authorized the Secretary of Agriculture to impose similar marketing restrictions and recognized the simultaneous coexistence of state regulation in its general instructions to the Secretary of Agriculture to harmonize state and federal regulation. Thus, said the Court, the state regulation coincided with federal congressional agricultural policy.

(b) *Adequate supervision and clearly articulated purpose to displace competition. Goldfarb*[94] involved the promulgation, by a county bar association, of a schedule of minimum fees for legal services. Lawyers charging less than the minimum were considered unethical and were subject to discipline by the state bar association, acting under general authority conferred by the state Supreme Court, which retained ultimate control over the disciplining of lawyers. The United States Supreme Court denied antitrust immunity and held the restraint subject to the Sherman Act. The state court had not specifically required minimum fee schedules. Thus, price fixing had not been "required by the state acting as a sovereign." Although clothed for some purposes in official state garb, the bar associations were made up of private persons dealing with their own economic interests.

In *Patrick,*[95] the Supreme Court ruled that medical peer review was not immune from the antitrust laws when not actively supervised by the state. The state health division had authority only over peer

---

Process, 96 Yale L.J. 486 (1987); H. Hovenkamp & J. MacKerron, Municipal Regulation and Federal Antitrust Policy, 32 U.C.L.A. L. Rev. 719 (1985); J. Wiley, A Capture Theory of Antitrust Federalism, 99 Harv. L. Rev. 713 (1986).

93. Parker v. Brown, 317 U.S. 341 (1943).

94. Goldfarb v. Virginia State Bar, 421 U.S. 773, 790 (1975).

95. Patrick v. Burget, 486 U.S. 94 (1988).

review procedures, not over actual decisions made by hospital committees. Claims that exemption of medical peer review is essential to the provision of quality medical care must be directed to Congress, which did provide some immunity in the Health Care Quality Improvement Act of 1986[96] (an act not retroactively applicable).

In *Ticor Title,*[97] the Supreme Court ruled that rate bureau activity involving the setting of fees that were filed with state insurance offices was not immune from the antitrust laws because state supervision was inadequate. The states employed a negative option rule, under which rates became effective unless the state agency rejected them within a given time period. The Court held that inaction could not constitute substantive approval when the Commission's findings indicated that the state agencies did not in fact actively review the rates. The mere potential for state supervision was not a sufficient substitute for an actual decision by the state.[98]

By contrast, a Sherman Act immunity was found in *Bates,*[99] which concerned a state Supreme Court rule forbidding lawyers from advertising prices. Although the state bar had a role in the enforcement of such rules, its role was completely defined by the state court. The state court itself had adopted the challenged rule. It had clearly articulated its policy and its rationale about the practice of law, which was a matter of great interest to the state. There was, moreover, active supervision and pointed reexamination of that policy by the state court in the course of its enforcement decisions.

It may be concluded that there can be no immunity under *Parker* without (1) adequate public supervision and (2) a clear state purpose to displace competition. More recently, these requirements were emphasized in *Midcal,* noted in ¶164b. These two requirements are often interrelated. The existence of state supervision over

---

96. 100 Stat. 3784 (1986), 42 U.S.C. §11111.

97. FTC v. Ticor Title Insurance Co., 504 U.S. 621 (1992).

98. In Cantor v. Detroit Edison Co., 428 U.S. 579 (1976), the Detroit Edison Company distributed "free" lightbulbs to residential consumers and recovered its overall costs through its charges for electricity. This practice, challenged as an unlawful tie-in of bulbs to electricity, was described in the utility's tariffs, which had been approved by the Michigan regulatory commission and was therefore binding on the utility until changed. Nevertheless, the challenged tie was not immune from the antitrust laws. The absence of a single majority opinion makes it difficult to summarize the grounds for the decision, but the following points seem central to the result. The state had no articulated policy about lightbulbs, which were subject to ordinary competition elsewhere in Michigan and in most other states and were not therefore an integral part of regulating the rates and services of monopolized generation and distribution of electricity. Thus, state approval seemed to reflect state toleration of Detroit Edison's decisions rather than state compulsion of the utility.

99. *Bates,* note 72.

anticompetitive behavior may indicate, for example, the requisite state intent as well. Similarly, inaction on the part of the state may both represent a failure of supervision and reflect an ambiguous state purpose. One recurring feature of this issue is examined next.

(c) *Compulsion.* Although compulsion by the state does not guarantee an immunity, compulsion may evidence both a state purpose to substitute regulation for competition and active state supervision. Furthermore, although the absence of compulsion was emphasized as grounds for denying *Parker* immunity in *Goldfarb* and *Cantor*, compulsion does not seem critical to immunity where the challenged behavior is an integral part of a valid state regulatory scheme. The Supreme Court ruled in *Southern Motor Carriers*[100] that compulsion was not required. Several states regulated motor carrier rates and authorized, but did not compel, the truckers to discuss and agree — in so-called rate bureaus — on the rates that they would file with the state regulatory agency. The expression of state policy favoring rate bureaus was found sufficient[101] and the lower court found, and the plaintiff conceded, that state agencies actively supervise the private agreements on rates to be filed.

The Court reasoned that requiring compulsion would improperly narrow the range of regulatory alternatives available to the states and could even lead to greater restraints if such a prerequisite induced states to require bureau cooperation. The absence of compulsion does not mean that the state lacks a sufficient interest in rate bureaus. Joint filings reduce the number of submissions and make the agency's task more manageable, and Congress itself followed the same permissive procedure for interstate rates. Compulsion is powerful evidence of state policy but is not essential "when other evidence conclusively shows that a state intends to adopt a permissive policy."

(d) *Immunity of government bodies.* With increasing frequency, subordinate government bodies — municipalities especially, but state agencies as well — have been challenged under the federal antitrust laws. Such bodies do not automatically enjoy the *Parker* immunity. In *Lafayette*,[102] the Supreme Court held that a municipality's alleg-

---

100. Southern Motor Carriers Rate Conference v. United States, 471 U.S. 48 (1985).

101. Statutes provided for rate bureaus in several of the states. The Mississippi statute did not so provide but it clearly chose regulation over competition and delegated details to a state agency, which then actively encouraged rate bureaus. The Court held that requiring more would diminish or destroy the utility of administrative agencies to develop state policy.

102. Lafayette v. Louisiana Power & Light Co., 435 U.S. 389 (1978). Eight Justices divided equally on whether political subdivisions are covered by the *Parker* exemption as such. The Chief Justice believed that this city was not exempt because the challenged conduct involved business activity.

edly anticompetitive behavior in operating its local electric distribution system was subject to the antitrust laws, unless "directed or authorized" by the state in connection with a state policy to substitute regulation or monopoly for competition. Of course, many challenged activities by governmental agencies would not ordinarily constitute an antitrust offense even if undertaken by a private party—such as a state highway authority's grant of an exclusive privilege to operate the restaurant concession on a turnpike.[103] But that question need not be faced if the challenged municipality or other agency is adequately authorized by the state to engage in the challenged conduct. In *Boulder*,[104] the Supreme Court held that a state constitution's or statute's home rule provision giving municipalities general authority to act as they choose was not sufficiently particularized to satisfy *Lafayette*'s requirement. Even apart from general home rule provisions, however, the relevant statutes will seldom be very explicit.

In *Hallie*,[105] the Supreme Court elaborated its "state authorization" requirement and also held that the *Midcal* active supervision requirement did not apply to authorized municipal action. In that case, the defendant city, with the only sewage treatment facility in the area, refused to supply sewage treatment to plaintiff towns. It did serve landowners in areas that had agreed to be annexed and use the city's sewage collection and transportation services. The plaintiff towns claimed that this amounted to unlawful tying and monopolization of sewage collection and transport.

A state statute authorized the city to provide sewage service and to delineate unincorporated areas it wished to serve. The statute allowed a state agency to require broader service but also allowed the city to decline if that area refused to be annexed. Although the statutes did not expressly address monopolization or tying, "[s]uch conduct is a foreseeable result of empowering the City to refuse to serve unannexed areas." The statute did not *require* the city to demand annexation, but this is not state neutrality in the same sense as home rule in *Boulder*. To demand greater explicitness in the statute or in its legislative history would rest on "an unrealistic view of how legislatures work and of how statutes are written." These statutes "contemplate" that cities will condition service on annexation and this satisfies the clear articulation test.

Furthermore, the *Hallie* Court held that whatever may be the prerequisites for the immunity of private parties, state compulsion is clearly not required in the case of municipalities, which are pre-

103. See ¶409.
104. Community Communications Co. v. City of Boulder, 455 U.S. 40 (1982).
105. Town of Hallie v. City of Eau Claire, 471 U.S. 34, 42-43, 45-46 (1985).

sumed, "absent a showing to the contrary," to act in the public interest.[106] Finally, the Court held that active state supervision is not required "in cases in which the actor is a municipality."[107] The only real danger to be feared in this context is that the municipality will serve its parochial interests at the expense of state goals, but this risk was said to be "minimal" given a clearly articulated state policy.[108]

In *Columbia*,[109] the Supreme Court rejected the possibility of a "conspiracy" exception to state action immunity under *Parker*. The plaintiff claimed that its competitor conspired with the municipality that enacted a zoning ordinance effectively prohibiting future competition. The Court stated that public officials often act at the behest of private citizens, so a conspiracy exception would virtually swallow the rule in *Parker*. The Court's opinion, see Chapter 2F, also rejected a conspiracy exception to *Noerr* immunity.

(e) *Local Government Antitrust Act of 1984*.[110] Following the *Lafayette* and *Boulder* decisions (but before *Hallie*) and the numerous private suits against subordinate governmental bodies, Congress responded to the fears of local governments that they would be burdened with enormous treble-damage liability. Although it did not alter the substantive antitrust rules imposing liability, new legislation eliminated all antitrust damage liability for any local government,[111] and for its officials or employees "acting in an official capacity." In addition, other persons were freed of damage liability on claims "based on any official action directed by a local government, or official or employee thereof acting in an official capacity."

(f) *Distinguishing private from governmental action*. Many cases involve a combination of private and public activity, and the courts continue to have difficulty in deciding which predominates. That question was at the heart of *Goldfarb* and *Cantor* and was faced again in the Supreme Court's 1984 *Hoover* decision.[112] The plaintiff was denied admission to the Arizona bar after failing the bar examination. His antitrust challenge alleged that the passing threshold was based on concern for limiting the number of passing scores and therefore the number of lawyers rather than on concern for compe-

106. Note that the Justices who dissented in *Southern Motor* did not dissent in *Hallie*.

107. The Court did not limit this holding, as had the Seventh Circuit in reaching the same result, to "traditional governmental functions." See 700 F.2d 376, 384 (7th Cir. 1983).

108. Although the Court expressly reserved the question, "it is likely" that supervision is also not required where the actor is a state agency.

109. City of Columbia v. Omni Outdoor Advertising, 499 U.S. 365 (1991).

110. 98 Stat. 2750 (1984), 15 U.S.C. §§34-36.

111. This includes cities, counties, villages, school districts, and other special function governmental units.

112. Hoover v. Ronwin, 466 U.S. 558 (1984).

tence. The defendants were the lawyers who set grading standards. They were appointed by the Arizona Supreme Court, which alone had the power to admit new lawyers or deny admission. As a formal matter, the state court completely controlled the defendants and completely controlled admissions. The United States Supreme Court held that private defendants were advisers to the state court that itself restrained trade (if anyone did). As the sovereign state in its realm, the state court enjoyed *Parker* immunity without the need for any other authorization.

The dissenters disagreed with the suggestion that the state court was the entity denying plaintiff's admission and thus believed that the relevant restrainers of trade were the private defendants who had not been clearly and expressly authorized to limit admissions on any basis other than competence. To force legislatures or courts to say expressly that they mean to limit competition would strongly discipline anticompetitive uses of governmental power. But if this case were not dismissed on state action grounds, all the Justices worried about the difficulty of recognizing an anticompetitive grading formula and the potential for a flood of suits by failed examinees. Apparently, the majority was not persuaded that summary judgment and other techniques of case management could deal with the flood.

Interstate Commerce

166. Sherman Act. The Sherman Act concerns restraints or monopolization of "trade or commerce among the several states." This language is interpreted as going "to the utmost extent of [Congress'] constitutional power."[113] But the extent of that power was understood very narrowly in the Supreme Court's first antitrust case. *Knight* held that mere manufacturing was not commerce and thus that a monopoly of sugar manufacture was not covered by the Act.[114] Subsequent cases avoided this doctrine by finding additional interstate incidents in a "flow of commerce,"[115] and the limiting doctrines have long since been put to rest.[116] In addition to the flow of commerce test, which continues to establish jurisdiction, the Court adopted an easier-to-satisfy "affecting commerce" test in *Mandeville*

113. *South-Eastern*, note 61, at 558.
114. United States v. E.C. Knight Co., 156 U.S. 1 (1895).
115. Addyston Pipe & Steel Co. v. United States, 175 U.S. 211 (1899); Northern Sec. Co. v. United States, 193 U.S. 197 (1904); Swift & Co. v. United States, 196 U.S. 375 (1905).
116. E.g., Wickard v. Filburn, 317 U.S. 111 (1942) (growing wheat for own on-farm consumption affected total wheat supply and disposition and was therefore within congressional commerce power).

Island Farms.[117] The Court held there that agreements to fix the price paid sugar beet growers in California violated the Sherman Act even though the beets were transformed into sugar before shipment to interstate markets. Pointing to the relationship of the price of beets to the price of sugar, the Court held that the agreement's consequences were projected substantially into the interstate distribution of the sugar: "[T]he vital thing is the effect on commerce, not the precise point at which the restraint occurs."[118] As the Court later put it, "If it is interstate commerce that feels the pinch, it does not matter how local the operation which applies the squeeze."[119]

Where effects need not be proved to establish the substantive offense — as in price fixing — some lower courts nevertheless insist on proof of interstate effects. These courts may not appreciate the rationale of those antitrust rules that do not require proof of effects. The Supreme Court has recognized this in *Burke* and *McLain.*[120] In *Burke,* the Court observed, "The wholesalers' territorial division here almost surely resulted in fewer sales to retailers — hence fewer purchases from out-of-state distillers — than would have occurred had free competition prevailed among the wholesalers. . . . Thus the state-wide wholesalers' market division inevitably affected interstate commerce."[121] The interstate effect was not obvious in *McLain,* which involved an alleged price-fixing conspiracy among local real estate brokers. The Court found it sufficient that "whatever stimulates or retards the volume of residential sales, or has an impact on the purchase price, affects the demand for financing and title insurance, those two commercial activities that on this record are shown to have occurred in interstate commerce."[122] Similarly, in *Hospital Building,*[123] the Court required a finding that a covered restraint "substantially and adversely affects interstate commerce" but held this test satisfied by allegations that the plaintiff purchased supplies from out-of-state sources, received revenues from out-of-state insurance firms, remitted management fees to its out-of-state parent corporation, and would borrow from out-of-state lenders to finance some of its planned expansion.

In *Summit Health,*[124] the Supreme Court ruled in a 5-4 decision that a single doctor's allegation that he was boycotted by rival

117. Mandeville Island Farms v. American Crystal Sugar Co., 334 U.S. 219 (1948).
118. Id. at 238.
119. United States v. Women's Sportswear Mfrs. Assn., 336 U.S. 460, 464 (1949).
120. Burke v. Ford, 389 U.S. 320 (1967); McLain v. Real Est. Bd., 444 U.S. 232 (1980).
121. 389 U.S. at 322.
122. 444 U.S. at 246.
123. Hospital Bldg. Co. v. Trustees of the Rex Hosp., 425 U.S. 738, 743 (1976), quoting Gulf Oil Corp. v. Copp Paving Co., 419 U.S. 186, 195 (1974).
124. Summit Health, Ltd. v. Pinhas, 500 U.S. 322 (1991).

doctors in the same city was sufficient to satisfy the Sherman Act's interstate commerce jurisdictional requirement. Although the Court's rationale was unclear, it alluded to four possible grounds for jurisdiction. First, the majority recalled, though only in a footnote, that Congress "left no area of its constitutional power [over commerce] unoccupied."[125] Second, the Court declared, "The restraint was accomplished by an alleged misuse of a congressionally regulated peer-review process. . . ."[126] Third, the hospital (and perhaps the defendant physicians) are engaged in interstate commerce. Without explaining its relevance, the majority said that a hypothetical conspiracy to prevent the hospital from expanding or to destroy the ophthalmological department involved here would affect interstate commerce. Fourth, the majority suggested that eliminating even a single surgeon from the market could have some interstate impact. The Court seemed to fear that failing to find jurisdiction would allow conspirators to destroy rivals one at a time such that the whole market would ultimately be affected in a way that would affect interstate commerce. That is, the Court hinted that jurisdiction could be found if the type of restraint alleged — hospitals and competing surgeons ganging up on disfavored surgeons — could ultimately affect interstate commerce. Of course, very few restraints would fail such a jurisdictional test.

167. Clayton Act; FTC Act. Unlike the Sherman Act's jurisdiction over matters affecting commerce, the Clayton Act and Robinson-Patman Act apply to persons and conduct "in commerce." There is no rationale for the differing jurisdictions of the several antitrust laws or for some differences within the later statutes. To be sure, the Clayton Act was enacted when the Commerce Clause was understood to confine federal regulation to conduct in the flow of interstate commerce. Congress may have been tracking these decisions in its jurisdictional enactments. As the federal commerce power expanded, however, the Sherman Act coverage of "commerce among the several states" was held to have grown and to embrace acts affecting interstate commerce. The question then arose whether or not the in commerce language of the other statutes had also been intended by Congress to extend to the full reach of its constitutional power. The Supreme Court has given a negative

125. Id. at 329 n.10, quoting United States v. Frankfort Distilleries, 324 U.S. 293, 298 (1945).
126. Id. at 332, referring to the Health Care Quality Improvement Act of 1986, 100 Stat. 3784, 42 U.S.C. §11101 et seq. The plaintiff alleged that the requirements of this statute had not been met, so the defendants could not claim its antitrust exemption.

answer with respect to the Robinson-Patman Act[127] and Clayton Act §7.[128] In 1980, however, Congress expanded Clayton Act §7 jurisdiction to reach mergers involving firms engaged "in any activity affecting commerce."

To some extent, violations of the Clayton Act or even of the Robinson-Patman Act will also violate the Sherman Act. In those situations, a failure of jurisdiction under the in commerce statutes will be irrelevant when the defendant's conduct affects commerce under the Sherman Act.

The Federal Trade Commission is expressly empowered to enforce Clayton Act §3 and §7 and the Robinson-Patman Act. But violations of those statutes are also unfair methods of competition under Federal Trade Commission Act §5. That Act only reached matters in commerce until amended in 1975 to embrace matters "in or affecting commerce." Thus, the Commission is no longer confined to in commerce jurisdiction even when it applies the substantive standards developed under the Clayton and Robinson-Patman Acts.

Foreign Commerce[129]

168. The problem. Sherman Act prohibitions extend to monopolizing or restraining "commerce ... with foreign nations."[130] These words have generated endless controversy centered on "extraterritoriality" and often confusing several distinct questions. (1) When are foreign actors subject to the personal jurisdiction of the U.S. antitrust court? (2) Does the Sherman Act purport to cover international transactions, and which ones? Is it constitutionally permissible to do so? (3) Should the United States attempt to regulate transactions within the legitimate concern of other coun-

---

127. Gulf Oil Corp. v. Copp Paving Co., 419 U.S. 186 (1974).

128. United States v. American Bldg. Maintenance Indus., 422 U.S. 271 (1975).

129. See U.S. Dept. of Justice & Federal Trade Commission, Antitrust Enforcement Guidelines for International Operations (1995); W. Fugate, Foreign Commerce and the Antitrust Laws (4th ed. 1991; Supp. 1994); Areeda & Turner, note 1, ch. 2E.

130. The quoted phrase is also included in the Clayton Act's definition of commerce, but the substantive provisions limit their foreign applications: §2(a) and §3 apply to sales "for use, consumption or resale within the United States." Section 7 concerns only those mergers with anticompetitive implications "in any section of the country." The reach of the Federal Trade Commission Act is expressly extended by Webb-Pomerene Export Act §4 to "unfair methods of competition used in export trade against competitors engaged in export trade, even though the acts constituting such unfair methods are done without the territorial jurisdiction of the United States."

tries?[131] (4) If so, are the antitrust laws an appropriate instrument for the purpose? Consider the (a) conflicting national interests that might seem to call for diplomacy rather than adjudication, (b) possible inappropriateness of judicial inquiry into the relations of foreign governments to firms operating in their countries, (c) immunity of foreign sovereigns who may share in the ownership of a defendant, (d) problem of subjecting a defendant acting in good faith to conflicting instructions from several sovereigns, (e) difficulties of controlling foreign situations through a domestic decree, and (f) peculiar difficulties in making sound judgments where the ordinarily elusive issues of antitrust are compounded by international markets, different mores, and vastly different economic circumstances. (5) If the antitrust laws are to be broadly applied to international conduct, which restraints should be considered significant enough to trigger the application?

169. Personal jurisdiction. A law suit would have little point without the presence of a natural person or assets to satisfy the judgment or coerce compliance with the decree.[132] The Supreme Court said in *International Shoe* that

> due process requires only that in order to subject a defendant to a judgment in personam, if he be not present within the territory of the forum, he have certain minimum contacts with it such that the maintenance of the suit does not offend "traditional notions of fair play and substantial justice."[133]

The immediate significance of *International Shoe* is qualified, of course, by the fact that the defendant in that case was a U.S. corporation acting in a federal system in which other U.S. states would be compelled to enforce the judgment.[134] The problem differs where foreign companies are charged under United States antitrust laws. (1) A U.S. forum may be greatly inconvenient to the foreign defen-

---

131. This question is increasingly being answered with a "yes" by the Justice Department, which has greatly increased international enforcement of the Sherman Act in the 1990s. See Fugate, note 129, at vii (Supp. 1994).

132. Presence within a second jurisdiction would suffice if its courts would assist the first jurisdiction. Whether a second court will enforce the judgment of another may depend on whether the second court believes that (1) the first court had proper jurisdiction, (2) the order is not "penal," (3) the first court's procedures were essentially fair, (4) the first court applied the proper national law to the transaction, and (5) enforcement is otherwise consistent with local public policy. There are additional problems where the second court is being asked to enforce the equity decree of another jurisdiction.

133. International Shoe Co. v. Washington, 326 U.S. 310, 316 (1945); World-Wide Volkswagen Corp. v. Woodson, 444 U.S. 286 (1980).

134. Milwaukee County v. M.E. White Co., 296 U.S. 268, 271, 275 (1935).

dant, who may also be surprised by U.S. substantive and procedural laws, although these considerations often would not be weighty for multinational defendants in international business. (2) Foreign courts and foreign governments may be or become involved, but this bears on sovereign immunity or on application of the statute's substantive terms. (3) Unlike most interstate controversies, there will be no alternative forum because there is little reason to expect foreign courts to entertain even private actions against their nationals for alleged violations of United States antitrust laws. The last consideration has had some influence on the courts.[135] The most frequent controversies have involved the validity of service of process on foreign parents or subsidiaries of U.S. corporations. To speak generally, the courts may be said to have become increasingly ready to regard the corporate family as a single entity without unduly fastidious regard for separate legal personalities.[136] One might have suspected that the Supreme Court's recent holding in *Copperweld* that a parent and a wholly owned subsidiary cannot be co-conspirators[137] would have accelerated this trend, but apparently it has not.[138]

170. In rem jurisdiction. Sherman Act §6 authorizes the forfeiture of goods owned "under any contract or by any combination or pursuant to any conspiracy" offensive to §1. There is a similar provision in the Wilson Tariff Act. These provisions would permit adjudication without personal jurisdiction over the foreign actors. Of course, any judgment would be limited to the particular goods seized. Such seizures might deprive foreign actors of their U.S. market and thus induce them to behave. If seizure were a serious threat, however, a foreign cartel could exact its monopoly price by selling abroad to American buyers.

135. United States v. Scophony Corp., 333 U.S. 795, 817 (1948); Scriptomatic v. Agfa-Gevaert, 1973 Trade Cas. ¶74594 (S.D.N.Y.) (personal jurisdiction over foreign corporation selling to two U.S. distributors and influencing their conduct toward the plaintiff).

136. E.g., Intermountain Ford Tractor Sales Co. v. Massey-Ferguson, 210 F. Supp. 930 (D. Utah 1962), aff'd, 325 F.2d 713 (10th Cir. 1963), cert. denied, 377 U.S. 931 (1964) (jurisdiction over Canadian parent of its U.S. subsidiary); Call Carl v. B.P. Oil Corp., 391 F. Supp. 367, 371 (D. Md. 1975) (jurisdiction over foreign parent able to control local subsidiary); United States v. Watchmakers of Switzerland Info. Ctr., 133 F. Supp. 40 (1955), 134 F. Supp. 710 (1955), 1963 Trade Cas. ¶70600, 1965 Trade Cas. ¶71352 (S.D.N.Y.). Compare Kramer Motors v. British Leyland, 628 F.2d 1175 (9th Cir.), cert. denied, 449 U.S. 1026 (1980) (no jurisdiction notwithstanding shared directors; no day-to-day control exercised).

137. This case appears in Ch. 2C.

138. E.g., Behr Automotive v. Mercedes-Benz of N. Am., 1986-2 Trade Cas. ¶67261 (E.D. Pa.).

171. Statutory reach. Suppose that European aluminum producers agreed to curtail their production and their exports to the
United States (perhaps in the hope that U.S. producers would
curtail their exports to Europe) and that such a "combination in
restraint of trade" would amount to output control that tends to fix
prices and would be clearly unlawful if all incidents were domestic.
Do the foreign aspects of this agreement remove it from Sherman
Act condemnation? A traditional starting point is the choice-of-law
problem in tort actions: The legality of an act was generally to be
judged by the law of the jurisdiction in which it occurs. In *American
Banana*,[139] the plaintiff complained of allegedly predatory acts in
Central America by defendant, with injury to the plaintiff, and
which thereby preserved defendant's domination of banana exports
to the United States, the home country of both corporations. The
Court said, through Justice Holmes, that "the general and almost
universal rule is that the character of an act as lawful or unlawful
must be determined wholly by the law of the country where the act
is done."[140] The courts subsequently retreated from *American Banana*— first by distinguishing it and emphasizing actions within the
United States,[141] even where the crucial conduct occurred
abroad,[142] and then by rejecting it and emphasizing effects upon
the United States. In *Alcoa*,[143] a Canadian corporation was held in
violation of Sherman Act §1 for its agreement with European aluminum producers to stay out of the United States market. Judge
Learned Hand there said that a "state may impose liabilities, even

139. American Banana Co. v. United Fruit Co., 213 U.S. 347 (1909). The complaint did not clearly allege any impact upon United States imports but the Court
did not remark about the absence.
140. Id. at 356.
141. United States v. Pacific & Arctic Ry. & Nav. Co., 228 U.S. 87 (1913) (combination formed in United States where transportation began and ended); Thomsen
v. Cayser, 243 U.S. 66 (1917) (combination put into effect in United States where
transportation affected by the combination began).
142. In United States v. Sisal Sales Corp., 274 U.S. 268 (1927), defendant secured
a monopoly of sisal in Mexico, which was the complained-about conduct. Any
conduct within the United States was merely incidental to the achievement of that
monopoly. Of course, it was the United States that felt the pinch.
143. United States v. Aluminum Co. of Am. (Alcoa), 148 F.2d 416, 440-445 (2d
Cir. 1945). (The famous domestic aspects of this case are reproduced in Ch. 3.)
Although the U.S. company, Alcoa, was not held to be a member of this agreement,
the foreign cartel's actions were presumably intended to induce Alcoa to stay out of
Europe. The evidence might have justified treating Alcoa and the Canadian company as a single entity for antitrust purposes, but the findings were otherwise and
the appellate court discussed the instant issue on the assumption that the Canadian
company was a separate entity not in the U.S. aluminum business, although unquestionably present in the United States for purposes of the court's in personam
jurisdiction. The final decree viewed the two companies as having an interrelation-
ship that had to be dissolved. 91 F. Supp. 333, 392-399 (S.D.N.Y. 1950).

upon persons not within its allegiance, for conduct outside its borders that has consequences within its borders which the state reprehends," at least where those effects were intended.[144] The Supreme Court has cited *Alcoa* with approval and has itself described the antitrust precedents as disowning *American Banana* when "the activities of the defendants had an impact within the United States and upon its foreign trade."[145]

172. Conflicting national interests. Domestic effects undoubtedly warrant domestic concern with foreign conduct causing those effects. Where there is a substantial international consensus as to the reprehensibility of the conduct involved — for example, counterfeiting — foreign governments would not object to the United States applying its laws, even though the conduct took place elsewhere. But application of U.S. antitrust laws to foreign conduct may be quite different. To be sure, recent years have seen the enactment and development of laws against trade restraints in many foreign countries and the European Union. But even where two jurisdictions would protect competition from private restraints or monopolies, they may differ greatly in their substantive provisions, procedures, and remedies. There remains, moreover, widespread disagreement over the basic principle of protecting competition. And conflict is likely to arise when there is no consensus and several countries plausibly assert an interest in a multinational transaction.

One might try to identify and compare the nature and rationale of each country's law in the manner of developing methodology in the conflict of laws.[146] There may be no real conflict at all. Although the European aluminum cartel was not then prohibited by European laws, nonprohibition is not necessarily affirmative ap-

144. 148 F.2d at 443. Judge Hand further held that an intent to cause effects within the United States shifted the (exceedingly difficult!) burden of proof to defendants to disprove effects within the United States.

145. Continental Ore Co. v. Union Carbide, 370 U.S. 690, 705 (1962). In Pacific Seafarers v. Pacific Far East Line, 404 F.2d 804 (D.C. Cir. 1968), cert. denied, 393 U.S. 1093 (1969), Sherman Act jurisdiction was found over an alleged conspiracy affecting shipping between Taiwan and South Vietnam of cement and fertilizer financed by the United States government and required by law to be carried by U.S.-flag ships. That law indicated congressional concern over the commerce involved. The court also emphasized that the plaintiff and many of the defendants were U.S. firms. For an extreme application of domestic law to foreign conduct, see Steele v. Bulova Watch Co., 344 U.S. 280 (1952), which held that a U.S. entity could be enjoined under the United States trademark statute from selling Bulova watches in Mexico under its Mexican trademark to U.S. tourists who brought the watches back to the United States. At the time of the Supreme Court decision, Mexico had canceled defendant's trademark, but the lower court had condemned defendant notwithstanding its then-outstanding Mexican mark.

146. See D. Trautman, The Role of Conflicts Thinking in Defining the International Reach of American Regulatory Legislation, 22 Ohio St. L.J. 586 (1961).

proval.[147] But the conflict may be unmistakable: Switzerland, for example, favored the activities of its watchmakers in controlling production, prices, and distribution arrangements — either because the cartel increased Switzerland's earnings at the expense of consumers in other countries or because it seemed intrinsically desirable. (As will be discussed in ¶174, the United States also is permissive toward export cartels.) As a country consuming Swiss watches, the opposing interest of the United States is clear. Neither country's interest is legally or morally superior because neither the cartel nor competition principle has an authoritative international mandate.[148] If most nations act more or less selfishly in matters of international trade, each must protect its own interests as best it can. And while diplomacy might seem preferable to adjudication, our courts do in fact apply the antitrust laws in these situations, emphasizing the presence and deep involvement of a U.S. firm, some domestic actions, substantial restraints on U.S. markets at the core of the restrictive arrangement, conduct highly reprehensible by antitrust standards, and usually minimal involvement by the foreign government, which may have permitted but certainly did not require the challenged conduct.

173. Remedial problems. Problems of remedy can be very great. In the Swiss watch case, for example, the decree did not attempt to compel the Swiss watchmakers to abandon their general output or price controls; the decree only affected Swiss agreements with U.S. distributors.[149] The usual decree, moreover, includes a general clause saving defendant from contempt for action or inaction compelled by another country. These provisions were relied on by an English court that enjoined Imperial Chemical Industries from complying with a U.S. antitrust decree.[150]

147. See *Hartford*, ¶175.

148. Chapter 5 of the International Trade Organization Charter of Havana (1948) spoke in terms of Sherman Act principles. But neither the Charter nor the later and weaker variations have obtained significant international support. The history is briefly surveyed in Report of the Attorney General's National Committee to Study the Antitrust Laws 98-108 (1955).

149. The decree dissolved agreements between U.S. and Swiss firms that (1) restricted or limited the importation of watches in the United States by United States firms, (2) limited either the volume or type of watches or parts that United States firms would be permitted to manufacture outside Switzerland, or (3) limited the sale or resale of watch parts within the United States. *Watchmakers*, note 136.

150. British Nylon Spinners v. Imperial Chem. Indus., [1955] 1 Ch. 37 (1954), [1953] 1 Ch. 19 (C.A. 1952); United States v. Imperial Chem. Indus., 100 F. Supp. 504 (S.D.N.Y. 1951) (liability), 105 F. Supp. 215 (S.D.N.Y. 1952) (remedies). du Pont transferred its British nylon patent to Imperial as part of an unlawful division of world markets. Before entry of the U.S. decree requiring Imperial to forgo enforcement of the patent, Imperial had contracted to convey an interest in the patent to British Nylon Spinners. The British court held that Spinners, which was

In *Imperial,* as in most international Sherman Act cases, U.S. firms were deeply involved. In the usual case, the conflict with other nations is minimized by emphasizing relief against the U.S. defendant. A U.S. firm might, of course, be held liable in a foreign court for its failure to perform the agreement enjoined by the antitrust court, but the foreign court would probably try to avoid so direct a conflict. The foreign aspects of some restrictive arrangements may be unalterable by a U.S. court without the affirmative aid of foreign authorities. Yet, appropriate sanctions can discourage U.S. firms from entering such arrangements. Where, however, all actors are foreign and without sufficient persons or assets here to coerce compliance, there may be no remedy. Indeed, there may be no antitrust case if necessary documents are located abroad and foreign law forbids their removal or disclosure even by a U.S. firm.[151]

174. Restraints affecting exports. This Paragraph considers whether restraints affecting exports alone are covered by the antitrust laws and notes the scope of statutory exemptions for export trade. It is sometimes argued that an agreement on export prices by two U.S. producers would not be "in restraint of trade or commerce . . . with foreign nations" because any resulting reduction in physical exports would be offset by increased export earnings. Thus, the dollar volume of exports would not be reduced and therefore trade would not be restrained. But, of course, increased revenues in interstate commerce would not justify interstate price fixing. The statutory restraint lies not in the increase or decrease of the commercial flow but in the interference with market forces. It might be thought that the Sherman Act cares exclusively for domestic consumers or producers, but perhaps the domestic consumers and producers are best served by unrestrained commerce. In any event, there is no doubt about Sherman Act coverage of restraints limiting the export opportunities of other U.S. firms.[152]

---

not a party in the U.S. suit, could not be deprived of its patent interest by the U.S. court. That the contract with Spinners was made after the antitrust suit had begun and that Imperial owned 50 percent of Spinners were not deemed pertinent by the British court.

151. See Note, Foreign Nondisclosure Laws and Domestic Discovery Orders in Antitrust Litigation, 88 Yale L.J. 612 (1979).

152. E.g., Hazeltine Research v. Zenith Radio Corp., 239 F. Supp. 51, 77 (N.D. Ill. 1965) (foreign patent pool preventing exports by U.S. plaintiff). This holding was not affected by the several subsequent decisions in the same case. See 388 F.2d 25 (7th Cir. 1967); 395 U.S. 100 (1969). One case found a violation by domestic manufacturers, accounting for four-fifths of an industry's exports, who agreed not to export to particular areas but to do their business there through jointly owned foreign factories. United States v. Minnesota Mining & Mfg. Co., 92 F. Supp. 947 (D. Mass. 1950).

In considering export restraints, one should distinguish adverse effects felt solely abroad from those partly felt at home. Beginning with the Webb-Pomerene Act, Congress exempted from the antitrust laws agreements or acts in the course of export trade by an association entered into for the sole purpose of engaging in such trade.[153] The statute does not exempt any "restraint of the export trade of any domestic competitor,"[154] or anything "which artificially or intentionally enhances or depresses prices within the United States ... or which substantially lessens competition within the United States or otherwise restrains trade therein." The statute is ostensibly intended to permit U.S. firms to compete on equal terms in a cartelized world, and indeed, there might be circumstances in which the export cartel seems necessary to achieve economics of scale or to resist threats of competing foreign cartels, or the pressures of foreign buying combinations. But quite apart from the persuasiveness of any such rationale, the antitrust exemption is not limited to instances where this reasoning would apply. The statutory qualifications only protect U.S. consumers or producers.

Alkasso held that an export association loses its exemption when it joins a foreign cartel or uses the export mechanism to regulate domestic supply and price.[155] The Alkasso Association exported the

153. 40 Stat. 516 (1918), as amended, 15 U.S.C. §§61-65. For an appraisal, see National Commission for the Review of Antitrust Laws 295 (1979). Does the existence of a narrow Webb-Pomerene Act exemption or the Export Trading Company Act imply that nonexempt export restraints are otherwise covered by the Sherman Act even if there is no impact within the United States? The possibility of an affirmative answer is noted in Pfizer v. India, 434 U.S. 308, 314 n.12 (1978). The contrary possibility is suggested in the dissenting opinion in the same case. 434 U.S. at 323 n.1. The question is more important in light of the Export Trading Company Act's failure to amend the Clayton Act, which can reach joint ventures. Given the apparent purpose of the new Act, it would seem difficult for a court to take jurisdiction under Clayton Act §7 over a venture explicitly immunized from Sherman Act coverage. This predicament might impel a court to read the new statute as a codification of the general jurisdictional standard for the antitrust laws, rather than as creating an exception for activity that otherwise would be covered.

154. What constitutes a prohibited "restraint of the export trade of any domestic competitor" is far from clear. See *Minnesota Mining*, note 152, at 964-966; Recommendations for Pacific Forest Indus., 40 F.T.C. 843 (1940); Export Screw Assn., 43 F.T.C. 980 (1947); Phosphate Export Assn., 42 F.T.C. 555 (1946).

155. United States v. United States Alkali Export Assn., 86 F. Supp. 59 (S.D.N.Y. 1949). For an unusual variation, see United States v. Concentrated Phosphate Export Assn., 393 U.S. 199, 208 (1968), which denied an antitrust exemption for price fixing on sales to foreign governments where the United States government's foreign aid agency "selected the commodity, determined the amount to be purchased, controlled the contracting process, and paid the bill." Because our government gives preference to domestic suppliers, this export cartel did not satisfy the Webb-Pomerene Act's purpose of (1) relying on world market competition (such as it may be) to determine export prices (2) while saving domestic interests (here, taxpayers) from injury.

"surplus" domestic supplies that could have depressed domestic prices. But every export association whose members account for a substantial share of domestic production can influence domestic supplies and prices through its export decisions. Nevertheless, the Webb-Pomerene Act exemption has been held available to combinations whose members account for the bulk of domestic production.[156]

United States firms have often complained that, despite the Webb-Pomerene Act, the antitrust laws impair their ability to expand exports through cooperation or aggressive competition. Congress responded in 1982 with the Export Trading Company Act,[157] which leaves little doubt that the concern of the antitrust laws is with U.S. consumers and exporters, not foreign consumers or producers. The Act contains a new §7 making the Sherman Act inapplicable to "conduct involving . . . commerce (other than import trade . . .) with foreign nations — unless such conduct has a direct, substantial, and reasonably foreseeable effect" on (1) domestic or import trade or (2) "on export . . . commerce . . . of a person . . . in the United States." In the latter event, only "injury to export business in the United States" is cognizable.

This statute also makes a similar amendment to Federal Trade Commission Act §5(a).[158] The statute also allows the Secretary of Commerce, with the concurrence of the Attorney General, to issue certificates that specified export trade or activities or methods of operation will not (1) lessen competition within the United States, (2) restrain any competitors' export trade, (3) unreasonably enhance, stabilize, or depress prices within the United States of goods of the class exported, (4) constitute unfair methods of competition against export competitors, or (5) "include any act that may reasonably be expected to result in the sale for consumption or resale within the United States of the goods . . . or services exported by the applicant."

Such a certificate saves the recipient from criminal or civil antitrust liability under state or federal laws, except that an injured person may obtain injunctive relief or single damages for violation of any of the first four enumerated standards. In such a suit, a "presumption [would exist] that conduct which is specified in and complies with a certificate . . . does comply with [those] standards."

---

156. *Minnesota Mining,* note 152. In order to qualify for the Webb-Pomerene Act exemption, certain documents must be filed with the Federal Trade Commission, which is empowered to investigate such associations and issue recommendations to them. If the association fails to comply with FTC recommendations, the Attorney General may sue in the district court to compel compliance. This procedure is not exclusive. A regular antitrust suit in the courts will lie notwithstanding the FTC procedure. United States v. United States Alkali Export Assn., 325 U.S. 196 (1945).

157. 96 Stat. 1233 (1982), codified in scattered sections of U.S.C. titles 12, 15, 30.

158. See note 153 with regard to the Clayton Act.

175.   Appraising restraints abroad: testing for significance. Aside
from U.S. exports, a wide range of activities in foreign commerce
may have domestic effects. As Judge Hand acknowledged in *Alcoa*,
"Almost any limitation of the supply of goods in Europe, for example, or in South America, may have repercussions in the United
States if there is trade between the two."[159] The 1982 legislation
noted in the last Paragraph seems unconcerned with restraints
abroad that do not have a "direct, substantial, and reasonably foreseeable effect" within the United States (or on the export opportunities of domestic firms). The Sherman Act is presumably not intended to run the commercial world, yet to say that only significant
effects on United States foreign commerce are covered does not
identify the threshold of significance.[160] Significance can be determined by the difficult factual assessment of effects on United States
commerce or, assuming jurisdiction, by the qualitative judgment of
the reasonableness of the restraint, or by balancing foreign and
domestic interests.

Most antitrust appraisals demand a sensitive appreciation of conduct's harm to the economy, redeeming benefits to the parties and
society, and alternative and less harmful means of accomplishing
legitimate ends. When these are unclear, that which is clearest or
most obviously important tends to be given most weight. A foreign
joint venture among competitors, for example, might be more
reasonable than a comparable domestic transaction in several respects: The actual or potential harms touching U.S. commerce may
be more remote, the parties' necessities may be greater in view of
foreign market circumstances, and the alternatives may be fewer,
more burdensome, or less helpful.

The so-called per se offenses — those condemned by domestic
antitrust policy without proof of particular effects — present some
very difficult questions. Suppose, for example, that a U.S. company
producing in many different countries agreed that its central Afri-
can plant will fix local prices with other local producers. Should
U.S. antitrust law apply generally?[161]

159. *Alcoa* (1945), note 143, at 443.
160. Most of the litigated cases have involved rather clear-cut offenses, substantial and obvious effects on competition within the United States, and often a long
history of restrictions. See United States v. National Lead Co., 63 F. Supp. 513
(S.D.N.Y. 1945), aff'd, 332 U.S. 319 (1947); United States v. General Elec., 80 F.
Supp. 989 (S.D.N.Y. 1948) (Carboloy); United States v. General Elec., 82 F. Supp.
753 (D.N.J. 1949) (lamps); 115 F. Supp. 835 (D.N.J. 1953) (lamp remedies).
161. See Metro Industries v. Sammi Corp., 82 F.3d 839 (9th Cir.), cert. denied,
117 S. Ct. 181 (1996) (even if per se rule applicable if market division had occurred
in a domestic context, per se rule inappropriate where conduct occurred in another country; moreover, conventional analysis may have to be modified because of
remoteness of effects on U.S. commerce or because of differing circumstances in
foreign markets).

The antitrust court may find sufficient effects for jurisdictional purposes and yet refuse to apply U.S. law. This was the Ninth Circuit's approach in *Timberlane*, where the plaintiff complained about a U.S. bank's activities in Honduras.[162] The court concluded that subject matter jurisdiction is established upon a showing of some actual or intended effect. Of course, additional effects might be necessary to establish the violation. Even then, the court insisted, it may refrain from asserting "extraterritorial authority" unless the magnitude of effects on United States commerce is sufficiently strong in light of (1) the several parties' nationality, allegiance, or principal locations, (2) the relative importance of domestic and foreign conduct in the alleged violation, (3) the relative effects on the several countries involved, (4) the clarity of foreseeability of a purpose to affect or harm U.S. commerce, (5) foreign law or policy and degree of conflict with our policy or law, and (6) compliance problems.[163] The *Timberlane* approach and criteria have been favorably received by other courts.[164]

A somewhat different approach is suggested by *Hartford*.[165] The Supreme Court held that the Sherman Act applies to alleged foreign conspiracies designed to produce and resulting in a substantial effect in the United States. While not deciding whether a court may decline to exercise Sherman Act jurisdiction over foreign conduct, the Court found that principles of international comity were not raised unless there was a "true conflict" between United States and foreign law. No such conflict was deemed to exist in the present case because British law did not require defendants to act in a manner prohibited by United States law.

176. Foreign government involved. (a) *Act of state*.[166] The antitrust court will ordinarily decline to scrutinize the public acts of a

162. Timberlane Lumber Co. v. Bank of Am., 549 F.2d 597, 608 (9th Cir. 1977).

163. The court ultimately dismissed the case, relying on the legitimacy of the defendant's conduct in Honduras and on the trivial effects on competition within the United States. Timberlane Lumber Co. v. Bank of Am., 749 F.2d 1378 (9th Cir. 1984), cert. denied, 472 U.S. 1032 (1985).

164. Mannington Mills v. Congoleum Corp., 595 F.2d 1287, 1297 (3d Cir. 1979) (listing 10 factors to be considered); Dominicus Americana Bohio v. Gulf & W. Indus., 473 F. Supp. 680, 687 (S.D.N.Y. 1979) ("the proper standard is a balancing test that weighs the impact of the foreign conduct on United States commerce against the potential international repercussions of asserting jurisdiction"). Federal government guidelines, note 129, list similar criteria as a basis for deciding whether to prosecute. In addition, the Restatement provides that jurisdiction can exist regulating foreign conduct provided that the conduct "has or is intended to have substantial effect within its territory" unless "the exercise of such jurisdiction is unreasonable," which is determined in part by factors paralleling those mentioned in *Timberlane*. Restatement (Third) of Foreign Relations Law §§402-403 (1987).

165. Hartford Fire Insurance Co. v. California, 509 U.S. 764 (1993).

166. Compare the view of causal attribution in the state action context (¶165) and in Ch. 2F (dealings with government).

foreign sovereign within its own territory. Thus, the private defendant escapes liability when the anticompetitive consequences at issue are attributable to a foreign "act of state." For example, the defendant may be the passive beneficiary of a monopoly created by a foreign government or may have joined a price-fixing cartel pursuant to the direct and formal orders of the foreign government.

In *Kirkpatrick,*[167] the Supreme Court held the act of state doctrine inapplicable to a suit in which the plaintiff claimed that the defendant obtained a contract from the Nigerian government by bribing Nigerian officials. This claim, the Justices explained, does not require a court to declare invalid the official act of a state. "The act of state doctrine is not some vague doctrine of abstention" but rather a principle of decision that arises only "when the outcome of the case turns upon . . . the effect of official action by a foreign sovereign." The issue is not raised merely because a factual finding may cast doubt on the validity of foreign sovereign acts. Any suggestion to the contrary in *American Banana*[168] was dictum and is overcome by the later holding in *Sisal.*[169] The act of state doctrine is not an exception to the obligation of United States courts to decide cases, but rather "merely requires that, in the process of deciding, the acts of foreign sovereigns taken in their own jurisdictions shall be deemed valid." Policies underlying the doctrine, such as international comity, may be relevant in deciding whether the doctrine should be invoked when it is technically applicable, but may not be used to expand "the act of state doctrine . . . into new and uncharted fields."

Finally, there is the unusual situation where the private defendant was the agent of a foreign government. Mere authorization by that government to commit the challenged act will be insufficient to create immunity, unless the challenged behavior reflects a clear affirmative policy of the foreign government to effect an anticompetitive result.[170]

(b) *Sovereign immunity.* Issues of sovereign immunity arise where the defendant is a foreign government or a corporation wholly or partially owned by that government. The United States has long followed the "restrictive theory of sovereign immunity," now embodied in the Foreign Sovereign Immunities Act,[171] which denies immunity with respect to "commercial activities." What is commer-

---

167. W.S. Kirkpatrick & Co. v. Environmental Tectonics Corp., Intl., 493 U.S. 400 (1990).

168. *American Banana,* note 139.

169. *Sisal,* note 142.

170. *Continental,* note 145. Compare ¶165.

171. 90 Stat. 2891 (1976), 28 U.S.C. §§1330, 1602-1611. For an examination of earlier practice, see T. Giuttari, The American Law of Sovereign Immunity: An Analysis of Legal Interpretation (1970).

cial is to be "determined by reference to the nature of the course of conduct or particular transaction or act, rather than by reference to its purpose." This language appears to endorse earlier decisions holding, for example, that mineral sales are commercial.[172] The statute appears inconsistent with an earlier case immunizing an oil company partly owned by the British government for the purpose of assuring fuel for its navy.[173] In any event, the dividing line seems very elusive. The *OPEC* case[174] immunized the member countries of the oil cartel who collectively decided on pricing targets and who implemented those decisions through national control of production. The court held these activities not to be commercial, defining that term narrowly to keep the court away from areas touching closely the sensitive nerves of foreign countries. "[I]t is clear that the nature of the activity engaged in by each of these OPEC member countries is the establishment by a sovereign state of terms and conditions for the removal of a prime natural resource . . . from its territory."[175]

177. Summary. A full examination of antitrust law's international aspects cannot be divorced from a careful appreciation of the substantive law. At this point, it should be emphasized that the locus of action is not determinative, impact on United States commerce is a critical factor, the subtleties of substantive antitrust analysis should be sensitively considered in this area, special problems of comity must be remembered, and remedial action may be particularly difficult.

1E. THE PATENT SYSTEM

178. Prologue. (a) *Relevance of patent laws to antitrust.* Antitrust law affects the acquisition and exploitation of patents just as it affects the acquisition and use of other powers over property. Thus, many patent-antitrust issues arise throughout this book. In understanding some of the special and often complex problems posed by the intersection of patent and antitrust law, it is useful to begin with a brief survey of the patent system's rationale and operation.

172. United States v. Deutsches Kalisyndikat Gesellschaft, 31 F.2d 199 (S.D.N.Y. 1929). See also Outboard Marine Corp. v. Pezetel, 461 F. Supp. 384 (D. Del. 1978) (golf carts); Grand Jury Investigation of the Shipping Indus., 186 F. Supp. 298, 318-319 (D.D.C. 1960).

173. Investigation of World Oil Arrangements, 13 F.R.D. 280 (D.D.C. 1952).

174. International Assn. of Machinists & Aerospace Workers v. OPEC, 477 F. Supp. 553 (C.D. Cal. 1979).

175. Id. at 567.

(b) *Introduction to patents.* The term "patent" originally embraced all government grants of exclusive or monopoly privileges. Now, however, the unqualified term refers only to patents of invention — which are defined by the Patent Code as a government grant for the term of 20 years of the right to exclude others from making, using, or selling the invention throughout the United States.[1] Such statutory grants are made within the federal Constitution's grant of legislative power "[t]o promote the progress of science and useful arts, by securing for limited times to authors and inventors the exclusive right to their respective writings and discoveries."[2] The resulting system will be discussed in this section, which considers the premises and operation of the patent system and the remedies when the antitrust laws are violated.

This section and the remainder of the book focus on patent-antitrust issues in large part because they have so heavily occupied the courts. But it should be clear that many of the concepts are applicable, at least in principle, with regard to other intellectual property, such as copyrights, trademarks, and trade secrets.[3]

Premises of the Patent System[4]

179. Costs of a patent system. Understanding the patent system requires some attention to its disadvantages. (1) The obvious and usual cost of monopoly is reduced output and higher prices. Absent the patent monopoly, knowledge of an invention could be used simultaneously by everyone without further cost to the economy.[5] A patented invention will thus be underutilized, and utilization may be limited further by restrictions attached to patent licenses.

(2) The cumbersome and costly incidents of operating the system include the costs and difficulties of bargaining and litigating about patents, both in the Patent and Trademark Office and in the courts.

(3) The system may impede the very thing it would encourage, technological progress. On the one hand, the patent monopoly may

1. 35 U.S.C. §154. The current codification is title 35 of the United States Code, enacted in 1952. In the remainder of this section, unless otherwise indicated, references to the current patent statute are to title 35.

2. U.S. Const. art. I, §8, cl. 8.

3. See, e.g., *BMI*, Ch. 2B.

4. See generally F.M. Scherer & D. Ross, Industrial Market Structure and Economic Performance, ch. 17 (3d ed. 1990); W.K. Viscusi, J. Vernon & J. Harrington, Economics of Regulation and Antitrust, ch. 24 (2d ed. 1995).

5. Once knowledge is achieved, the marginal cost of using it is zero. To charge for the use of knowledge, as the patentee does, necessarily means that it will be underutilized.

discourage further research. Most directly, other inventors may be deterred by the realization that any improvements could not be used without infringing the original patent. On the other hand, the system may induce "wasteful" research. Rivals of the patentee may have to invent around the patent. While useful discoveries sometimes result, inventing around does not always seek better technology and may only produce an equivalent or inferior alternative to overcome the roadblock posed by the initial patent.

(4) Significant patents may reinforce economic concentration. The patentee's monopoly may be perpetuated beyond 20 years, for example through the aggregation of patents resulting from inventions made within the company or by acquisition of patents from others. Even when held by several firms, moreover, a mass of patents makes it difficult for a newcomer to enter the industry without infringing some patent. And the interchange of patent rights has often been used as the vehicle for allocating markets among firms that would otherwise compete. The contrary also occurs. Possession of a patent monopoly may permit a small firm to enter a concentrated industry, survive, and thus strengthen competition in that industry. This occasional occurrence, however, may not offset the system's costs. The central justification for the patent monopoly is to be found elsewhere.

180. Rationale. Although not generally favored by our law, monopolies are granted to inventors on three related grounds. First is the incentive idea. The patent guarantees the inventor a monopoly of its invention, and the resulting prospect of monopoly profit stimulates both additional inventive efforts and the investments required to put such inventions rapidly into use. If others were permitted to copy the invention without consent or payment, the resulting competition may leave little profit to the inventor.[6]

Second is disclosure. To encourage the full and desirable propagation of knowledge, the government grants the patent monopoly in return for the inventor's disclosure of the invention,

---

6. If special incentives are needed for invention, a monetary reward to the inventor would in principle be preferable, as it could induce the invention without preventing its maximum social use. Such awards would be scaled to the social value of inventions, allowing further benefits given that patent rewards, as developed in this section, are often only loosely correlated with social benefit. The primary objection is that it would be exceedingly difficult to determine the appropriate amount of the award. The patent system's primary virtue is its reliance on decentralized market processes for valuation, the assumption being that its costs are justified because the approximation it provides in rewarding inventors is sufficiently better than what a government agency could accomplish. For a departure from the usual patent system, see the Atomic Energy Act, 68 Stat. 919, 943 (1954), as amended, 42 U.S.C. §§2181-2190.

which might otherwise be kept secret. Of course, no incentive is required when disclosure automatically results from selling the invented article, and where an invented manufacturing process could be kept secret, the inventor may choose to forgo the patent and avoid disclosure (unless, of course, it is feared that someone else may later discover and patent the invention, thereby blocking the original inventor from subsequent use).

Third is the natural property claim. Inventors may be thought entitled to a property right in their ideas. They are artisans whose work product is a design or concept rather than a tangible object. Like other artisans, it is said that they should possess the fruits of their labor. But unlike a chair or a share of a corporation's profits, an idea can be possessed and enjoyed by everyone simultaneously. And a patent is temporary. Moreover, the patent has the effect of precluding practice of the invention by someone who independently discovered it. Nevertheless, there remains the thought that inventors should be rewarded for their creations that, absent legal protection, will be used freely by others once they learn of them. But even this natural justice idea fails to explain why some valuable and new ideas are protected while others are not. It seems well established, for example, that the discovery of a basic law of nature cannot be patented. Nor are patents given for significant and important innovations in business methods, such as the idea and first embodiment of the large self-service supermarket.

181. Patents as incentives. (a) *Generally.* Society's need for patents to stimulate desirable invention is the critical question in assessing the system's net economic impact. The patent monopoly is most defensible, of course, when granted for inventions that would not have occurred without it. The monopoly reward is, however, a costly social gratuity when provided for inventions that would have occurred nearly as soon without it. We would therefore like to know whether any special incentives are needed to induce desirable inventions and whether the patent system provides such incentives in a reasonably efficient way. Does the patent system induce inventions that would not otherwise have occurred or induce them significantly earlier? If so, is the incremental inventive effort desirable? If so, is it worth the social cost of patents? Similar questions arise about the investment necessary to bring an invention into productive use. Does the patent system encourage such investments and is it desirable to encourage them? Only a few aspects of these issues can be examined here, but it may confidently be said that empirical studies permit few generalizations, and the arguments in principle are also inconclusive.

(b) *Need for protection.* Some research would produce profits and would therefore be undertaken with or without patents. Yet, it is certainly possible that the patent incentive, especially that flowing from a 20-year monopoly, would encourage more innovation than would otherwise occur where (1) an unprotected innovation would not pay for itself fairly promptly — before competition from imitators eroded profits — because there is a relatively low ratio of benefit to cost or (2) the market is both highly competitive and able to imitate the innovation rapidly. Beyond this, it is also possible that even large payoff innovations would not be pursued without the prospect of enormous gains to offset risk. Such enormous payoffs, even if only occasional, might stimulate considerable inventive activity.

To be more concrete, consider the expensive research and development that resulted in the production of nylon. If others could easily have discovered and copied the results, their competition would have forced the price toward production cost. The production cost of the copiers would not include the inventor's preproduction expenses; hence, the inventor would not recover development costs. When that is a significant risk, rational commercial inventors forgo inventive effort, notwithstanding its social utility. If the social value of research thus exceeds its private value to commercial firms, society profits from undertaking the research or encouraging it with subsidies to researchers, money awards to successful inventors, or patent grants. By thus raising the prospective rewards, the patent system tends to induce research whose private returns are otherwise insufficient. This disparity between private and social value is a classic rationale for government grants to business.

(c) *Nonpatent incentives.* The subsidy argument just considered will not always apply. The inventor will recover development costs in many common situations, and some important research is likely to be undertaken even if it does not promise to be profitable.

(1) The inventor's head start in exploiting an invention will often permit recoupment of development costs (and more) before others discover the secret, duplicate it and the accompanying know-how necessary to put it to use, enter into production, achieve equivalent productive experience and efficiency, and counteract the innovator's goodwill with buyers.[7] Indeed, there may be substantial nonpatent barriers impeding the development of rivalry to the innovator.

(2) Even if an invention is quickly imitated by firms without research expenses, competition will not always be so intense as to drive prices so low that earlier development costs cannot be recovered.

7. Such lags can be lengthy, even after an idea is disclosed in a published patent that fails to preempt alternative processes or products.

(3) Survival may require defensive research where rivals threaten innovations that would foreclose one from the field or that cannot be duplicated or offset without the experience or alternatives developed through one's own research.

(4) Research and invention will continue even if actual costs are not always recovered. Some inventors may optimistically suppose that they will profit. Others may invent from the instinct of contrivance or simply by accident, without much regard for actual rewards. In addition, some inventive activity is only loosely related to the actual financial result. An individual inventor may be engaged in a lottery that offers the vague hope of grandiose profits (although the possibility of patent protection may well contribute to that hope). Finally, and quite importantly, a large portion of all research is supported by universities, foundations, and government sponsors not moved by the prospect of commercial rewards.

(d) *Development incentives.* Whether or not the patent system increases invention, the patent monopoly may increase the readiness of investors to finance the utilization of an invention. The compulsive inventor or dedicated academic may invent regardless of reward, but no one will finance further development or construction in the face of significant risks that the innovator will be undersold by imitating firms that did not bear the preliminary development costs. Thus, post-invention activities may resemble initial research efforts — with many of the same qualifications. The innovator's head start, for example, may allow time to recover development expenses. In addition, some initial activities, such as building a plant, will be indispensable for the copiers as well. Nevertheless, some investment would doubtless not be undertaken without some temporary assurance against undue competition.

Our system of intellectual property protection is somewhat inconsistent with regard to such activity. After all, implementing any socially valuable innovation — a way of organizing production, a service, a mode of distribution, a nonpatentable product — may require substantial development and promotional expenditures that would not be incurred by imitators. We do not give monopoly protection to the exploitation of innovations generally, and preference for exploiting patented ideas does not automatically follow from the patent statute and the Constitution, which speak of invention and discovery and not of their subsequent commercial exploitation.

Yet (1) inventions will sometimes depend on the reward and will earn none unless exploited; (2) such exploitation will sometimes depend on protection from competition; and (3) therefore, protecting investment in patent exploitation will sometimes be necessary to bring any reward to the invention and thus to induce it.

(e) *Balanced resource allocation.* The incremental inventive effort possibly induced by the promise of a patent monopoly may not be significant and, if significant, is not necessarily desirable. (1) Patents might stimulate some invention and yet be a socially costly windfall in the preponderance of cases. (2) The incremental inventive effort itself might be at the expense of more fundamental and valuable nonprofit research. Because both commercial and nonprofit research compete for personnel and facilities, increasing the rewards of patentable research affects the distribution of resources among these alternative pursuits. (3) There is no necessary, direct identity between the reward provided by the patent monopoly and the social value of the invention. The creative invention made ahead of its time may earn nothing during the 20-year life of its patent.

But none of this is surprising. The patent grant is necessarily a gross device that cannot equate social value with reward or the need for additional inventive stimulus in particular cases. One critical observer has suggested that the available theory and data are so inconclusive as to make it impossible to justify either abandoning the patent system or, if it did not exist, adopting one.[8]

(f) *Implications.* Consider the implications of this conclusion in trying to assess the social utility of potentially anticompetitive practices by patentees. The only virtue in permitting such practices is that they increase the reward to patentees, which would be desirable on the theory that additional reward serves further to stimulate inventive activity, thereby serving the objectives of the patent statute. Yet one might hesitate to excuse an otherwise prohibited anticompetitive restriction on this account, for such marginal increases in patentees' prospective rewards would have little effect on the inventor's incentives at the time initial research decisions are made. But it would surely go too far — given the policy judgment represented by the enactment of the patent system — to limit all patent enforcement and exploitation on the ground that each action cannot be demonstrated to improve substantially the incentives for invention. Accordingly, one often hears courts and advocates looking for a touchstone "inherent in the patent." But such formulations often beg the question without illuminating the underlying tension, which will be pursued further in Chapter 2G.

8. F. Machlup, An Economic Review of the Patent System, Study No. 15 of the Subcomm. on Patents, Trademarks & Copyrights of the Sen. Comm. on the Judiciary, 85th Cong., 2d Sess., Committee Print, at 80 (1958). The text conclusion also bears on the wisdom of such possible patent law revisions as tightening the standard of patentability, shortening or lengthening the duration of the grant, or compelling the licensing of some or all patents upon the payment of "reasonable" royalties.

Operation of the Patent System

182. Patentability. Patent Code §101 provides: "Whoever invents or discovers any new and useful process, machine, manufacture, or composition of matter, or any new and useful improvement thereof, may obtain a patent therefor, subject to the conditions and requirements of this title."

(a) *Patentable subject matter.* A bare principle, sometimes called a law of nature, is not patentable. A discovery may be brilliant and useful and yet not patentable. "It may be the soul of an invention, but it cannot be the subject of the exclusive control of the patentee, or the patent law, until it inhabits a body. . . ."[9] Yet, the method or procedure for making an article or producing a result may be a patentable process, even though such processes obviously rest upon laws of nature. "Machine" and "manufacture" refer to products such as an operating device for shaping metals or a screwdriver in contrast to those occurring in nature. "Composition of matter" is a combination of substances, such as antiknock ethyl gasoline, whether effected by mechanical mixture or by chemical union. "Useful improvement" refers simply to an inventive change in an existing procedure, article, or composition; it does not have to be a qualitative change for the better. Of course, not all combinations, processes, products, or compositions are patentable.

(b) *Conditions of patentability.* Any patent system requires some criteria for determining what warrants the public grant of a monopoly. Section 101 focuses on the general requirements of utility, novelty, and invention.

Utility is seldom denied. Some cases hold that a device that could not be used lawfully or safely would lack utility. Usually, however, the utility requirement is invoked by the Patent and Trademark Office to refuse patents to devices that do not work to accomplish their intended results. An invention capable of producing a socially permissible result is usually "useful" in the statutory sense, although a patent has been denied on a chemical process producing

9. Morton v. New York Eye Infirmary, 17 Fed. Cas. 879, 882 (No. 9865) (S.D.N.Y. 1862); O'Reilly v. Morse, 56 U.S. (15 How.) 62, 112-114 (1853) (upholding Morse's patent on his telegraph device but not his broadest claim for the use of electricity and magnetism to transmit messages); LeRoy v. Tatham, 55 U.S. (14 How.) 156 (1852). See also Gottschalk v. Benson, 409 U.S. 631 (1972) (mathematical formula for controlling computer operation similar to law of nature; not patentable); Parker v. Flook, 437 U.S. 584 (1978) (similar, although the Court observed that an otherwise new and useful process may be patentable even though it contains either a mathematical algorithm or law of nature as one component). In Diamond v. Chakrabarty, 447 U.S. 303 (1980), the Supreme Court held that live, man-made microorganisms are patentable.

a product "which either has no known use or is useful only in the sense that it may be an object of scientific research."[10]

Novelty is a more complex question. To oversimplify, §102 provides that a patent shall not be granted for an invention previously known, used, patented, described in a printed publication, or invented by someone else who had not abandoned, suppressed, or concealed it.

Imbedded in the patent concept is the notion of invention. The public monopoly is conferred not on every development but only on those regarded as inventions or discoveries. Section 103 codifies this requirement, which forbids the grant of a patent when "the differences between the subject matter sought to be patented and the prior art are such that the subject matter as a whole would have been obvious at the time the invention was made to a person having ordinary skill in the art to which said subject matter pertains."[11]

183. Standard of invention. The application of §103 requires judgments on the scope and content of the prior art, the differences between the prior art and the claimed invention, and the level and significance of ordinary skill in the art. This test of nonobviousness is exceedingly difficult to use.

Inventiveness is not determined by reference to the rationale of the patent grant. A significant accidental discovery will certainly receive a patent. A subsequent step that would be "obvious" to one skilled in the art but that requires expensive development may not be patentable. Obviousness "to a person having ordinary skill in the art" cannot readily be determined by observation or expert judgment because the standard refers to a body of knowledge that no identifiable person may possess.

Before the event, very little is so easily seen as to be undeniably obvious. Consider *Hotchkiss*,[12] which originated the formulation now embodied in §103. The Supreme Court invalidated a patent for clay doorknobs whose only advance over prior wooden or metal knobs was the difference in material. If the patentee were the first ever to use clay and thereby produce a new and socially useful innovation, was it so obvious?

The Patent and Trademark Office often seems to resolve doubts about patentability in favor of issuance. Furthermore, the backlog of work in the Office may induce a bias toward making the grant in close cases because the grant disposes of a case while rejection may invite appeals or amendments to the application and thus further

10. Brenner v. Manson, 383 U.S. 519, 535 (1966).
11. Graham v. John Deere Co., 383 U.S. 1, 17 (1966).
12. Hotchkiss v. Greenwood, 52 U.S. 248, 264-267 (1850).

occupy an examiner. Thus, the Office grants many patents that would be held invalid if ever fully litigated. Judicial judgments on patent validity are not made by technically skilled persons. While the judges may react intelligibly to "simple" inventions, they may be quite confused in approaching more complex developments.

The many difficulties in assessing "invention" have generated interest in more readily ascertainable and nontechnical criteria. The existence of a long-felt commercial need that many have worked intensely to satisfy implies that the ultimate solution was not obvious, otherwise it would have been reached sooner with less effort. But even this inference may not be altogether persuasive when several researchers reach the solution more or less simultaneously. Commercial success is said to imply that the development filled a need that would have been fulfilled earlier if the development had been obvious. But any trivial improvement may be commercially successful. Should the clay doorknob be patentable if successful? Other nontechnical tests would include professional praise at the time the invention was made or acquiescence by industry members whose royalty payments indicate their belief in the presence of invention. The courts seldom rely very heavily on these nontechnical tests.[13]

Perhaps enough has been said to support Learned Hand's lament that the test of invention "is as fugitive, impalpable, wayward, and vague a phantom as exists in the whole paraphernalia of legal concepts."[14] The implications for patent-antitrust law will become clear in the course of this book. Note these facts: (1) A development may be patented and yet be quite insignificant both in technical and social terms. (2) Many existing patents are invalid and will be so declared by a court if ever fully litigated.[15] Yet, the existence of a patent is an anticompetitive fact because a mass of patents may discourage or impede new entry or competition by those who cannot afford to devote substantial effort and money to patent litigation. (3) In some instances, there may be wide room for bona fide dispute or doubt among competitors about the validity of their respective patents. And there is a powerful incentive for settlement. It is difficult to predict who will prevail in patent litigation, and all patentees will lose if all the patents are held invalid. Society's interests in such instances are considered in ¶288.

184. Obtaining a patent. The inventor files a patent application with the Patent and Trademark Office. The heart of the application

13. The Supreme Court has characterized these as "secondary considerations" that "may have relevancy." *Graham*, note 11, at 17-18.
14. Harries v. Air King Prods. Co., 183 F.2d 158, 162 (2d Cir. 1950).
15. See ¶185.

is the "specification," which describes the purposes and workings of the invention and "claims" the applicant's particular invention. The description, together with the drawings that usually accompany it, must be sufficiently detailed and complete to enable a person "skilled in the art" to make and use the invention, but the applicant will of course prefer to minimize the disclosure. And the lively trade in know-how that accompanies patent licensing may suggest that the patent does not in fact disclose all that is necessary for its effective practice. To assure the sufficiency of the application, both in the adequacy of its disclosure and in other respects, is the task of the patent examiner. In particular, the examiner must appraise the validity of the applicant's claim to inventiveness. That this will be difficult follows from what has already been said about the conditions of patentability and the standard of invention.

Whenever the examiner rejects some or all of applications' claims, applicants may revise their applications to meet the examiner's objections; this process may be repeated several times. Applicants may also seek administrative review in the Board of Patent Appeals and Interferences; thereafter they may obtain judicial review on the administrative record in the Court of Appeals for the Federal Circuit or bring an original action in the District Court for the District of Columbia.[16]

185. Patent validity. When the Patent and Trademark Office is satisfied that an application meets the statute, it issues a patent. According to §282, a patent "shall be presumed valid," and "[t]he burden of establishing invalidity of a patent . . . shall rest on the party asserting such invalidity." Nevertheless, issuance does not guarantee validity. Since the creation of the Court of Appeals for the Federal Circuit, the percentage of litigated patents found valid has risen to about two-thirds.[17] Establishing patent validity in one suit does not bind nonparties, but a judgment that a patent is invalid is determinative against the patentee in suits involving other persons.[18]

Validity may be put in issue when the patentee sues for infringement or when a possible infringer seeks a declaratory judgment that

16. Exclusive appellate jurisdiction for all patent decisions in federal District Courts lies in the Federal Circuit. See 35 U.S.C. §§134, 141, 145.

17. D. Dunner, The Court of Appeals for the Federal Circuit — Its First Three Years: Introduction, 13 A.I.P.L.A. 185, 186-189 (1985). See also R. Harman, Patents and the Federal Circuit 639 (2d ed. 1991) (findings of validity affirmed in 88 percent of appeals); R. Coolley, What the Federal Circuit Has Done and How Often: Statistical Study of the CAFC Patent Decisions — 1982-1988, 71 J. Pat. Off. Soc'y 385, 391 (1989) (findings of validity nearly always affirmed, but findings of invalidity equally likely to be reversed).

18. Blonder-Tongue Laboratories v. University of Ill. Research Found., 402 U.S. 313 (1971).

the patent is invalid. Licensees under a patent may challenge its validity notwithstanding state law estoppel doctrines.[19] A license clause barring the licensee from contesting the patent is unenforceable[20] and might itself constitute a "patent misuse."[21] The government may sue to cancel a patent procured by fraud on the Patent and Trademark Office.[22] Moreover, the government or private plaintiff in an antitrust suit may challenge the validity of any patent asserted by the defendant as a shield to a challenged practice that would be an antitrust violation in the absence of a valid patent.[23] Indeed, the government may contest the validity of a patent not relied on by the defendant as a shield but that was "involved" in the defendant's antitrust violation and that might affect the relief appropriate to defendant's violation.[24]

When sued as an infringer, a defendant often contests both the fact of infringement and the validity of the plaintiff's patent. To determine validity, the court applies the statutory standards of patentability to all the relevant facts proved in court, entirely independently of what was said or known at the Patent and Trademark Office. Although the patentee's candor or propriety in dealing with the Office — as distinct from the true facts known by the court — do not bear on validity, they are increasingly put in issue by the infringement defendant for three purposes. (1) As discussed in

19. Lear v. Adkins, 395 U.S. 653 (1969).

20. Panther Pumps & Equip. Co. v. Hydrocraft, 468 F.2d 225, 231 (7th Cir. 1972), cert. denied, 411 U.S. 965 (1973).

21. Bendix Corp. v. Balax, 421 F.2d 809, 819-821 (7th Cir.), cert. denied, 399 U.S. 911 (1970). See ¶186.

22. United States v. American Bell Tel. Co., 128 U.S. 315 (1888); United States v. Saf-T-Boom Corp., 164 U.S.P.Q. 283 (E.D. Ark.), aff'd per curiam, 431 F.2d 737 (8th Cir. 1970).

23. Walker Process Equip. v. Food Mach. & Chem. Corp., 382 U.S. 172 (1965). See United States v. United States Gypsum Co., 333 U.S. 364, 386-388 (1948):

> Appellees admit that in the absence of whatever protection is afforded by valid patents the licensing arrangements described would be in violation of the Sherman Act.... The trial court held that the Government was estopped to attack the validity of the patents in the present proceeding, on the ground that such attack would constitute a review of action by the Commissioner of Patents, which was not authorized by statute. The trial court thought that the issue was controlled by United States v. American Bell Telephone Co., 167 U.S. 224, in which the United States was held without standing to bring a suit in equity to cancel a patent on the ground of invalidity. While this issue need not be decided to dispose of this case, it seems inadvisable to leave the decision as a precedent.... We cannot agree with the conclusion of the trial court.... If the government were to succeed in showing that the patents were in fact invalid, such a finding would not in itself result in a judgment for cancellation of the patents. In an antitrust suit instituted by a licensee against his licensor we have repeatedly held that the licensee may attack the validity of the patent.... In a suit to vindicate the public interest by enjoining violations of the Sherman Act, the United States should have the same opportunity to show that the asserted shield of patentability does not exist.

24. United States v. Glaxo Group, 410 U.S. 52 (1973).

¶186, a patentee holding a valid patent but guilty of "misuse" may be denied any remedy against infringers. Misbehavior in dealing with the Patent and Trademark Office may constitute misuse even though not so bad or material as to constitute fraud.[25] (2) Patent invalidity does not usually entitle the successful infringement defendant to recover the costs of its defense. Patentee misbehavior, however, may constitute those "exceptional cases" that permit the court to award the successful defendant attorney's fees under §285. (3) Maintaining and attempting to enforce a fraudulently procured patent may itself violate the antitrust laws and therefore entitle an injured person to recover treble damages.[26] Such fraud is usually understood to consist of a knowingly willful and material misrepresentation or concealment. The clearest fraud would be an intentionally false statement about experimental facts that are both uniquely within the applicant's knowledge and indispensable to the Office's determinations of patentability.

The question of validity or scope may also arise in litigation between two patentees whose multiple and vague claims overlap. Two patents may seem to be competitive because they offer processes, objects, or compositions that are effective substitutes for each other. Both patents might be simultaneously valid or they might be conflicting in the sense that the two patents cover the same invention. Such conflicts may be litigated with the result that (1) one or both patents are narrowed in scope or (2) some or all claims of one or both patents may be invalidated for want of novelty or invention. Litigation also may arise when a patent is blocked by another patent. An improvement patent, for example, cannot be practiced without infringing the basic patent. A patent for frosting the inside of a patented light bulb, for example, could not be practiced without also making the patented bulb. The frosting patent is said to be subservient to the dominant bulb patent. And, of course, the holder of the dominant patent cannot practice the improvement without

25. du Pont v. Berkley & Co., 620 F.2d 1247, 1273-1274 (8th Cir. 1980) (inequitable conduct before Patent Office not antitrust violation although may be a defense to infringement); Kearney & Trecker Corp. v. Giddings & Lewis, 452 F.2d 579 (7th Cir. 1971), cert. denied, 405 U.S. 1066 (1972); SCM Corp. v. RCA, 318 F. Supp. 433 (S.D.N.Y. 1970) (absence of candor in disclosures to Patent Office may be sufficient to make patent unenforceable but not to be an antitrust violation, which requires willful misrepresentation).

26. See *Walker Process*, note 23; American Cyanamid Co. v. FTC, 363 F.2d 757 (6th Cir. 1966); III P. Areeda & D. Turner, Antitrust Law ¶707 (1978; Supp. 1996). The additional elements necessary to constitute an antitrust offense are considered in those materials. Note that such a violation can be committed not only by the fraudulent patentee but also by one who acquires and maintains a patent known to have been fraudulently procured. See Acme Precision Prods. v. American Alloys Corp., 422 F.2d 1395 (8th Cir. 1970).

infringing the subservient patent. In this situation, each patentee would be strongly motivated to practice the other's patent; they are likely either to cross-license or to litigate the validity of each other's patent.

Remedies

186.   Patent misuse doctrine. The courts will neither enjoin an infringement nor award damages for it when the patent has been "misused."[27] Misuse might also defeat enforcement of a trademark or copyright.[28] Traditionally, the rationale was that of equitable discretion. "It is a principle of general application that courts, and especially courts of equity, may appropriately withhold their aid where the plaintiff is using the right asserted contrary to the public interest."[29] And the disability continues until the patentee can show that it "has fully abandoned" the misuse and that its "consequences . . . have been fully dissipated."[30] What is sufficiently contrary to the public interest to constitute a misuse has not been precisely defined. It does seem clear, however, that conduct offensive to the antitrust laws is a misuse.[31] But the misuse notion has not always been limited to antitrust violations. For example, conduct offensive to Clayton Act §3 when certain effects are proved may constitute a misuse without proving such effects.[32] And there are other cases as well in which the Court has found a patent misuse where it has

27. Morton Salt Co. v. G.S. Suppiger Co., 314 U.S. 488 (1942).

28. Union Carbide Corp. v. Ever-Ready, 531 F.2d 366, 389 (7th Cir. 1976) ("burden of such proof [of misuse] is a heavy one on the proponent"; claim "much weaker than in patent cases which involve by their very nature a monopoly situation").

29. *Morton Salt,* note 27, 314 U.S. at 492.

30. B.B. Chem. Co. v. Ellis, 314 U.S. 495, 498 (1942); T. Arnold, Antitrust Misuse and Purgation, 42 Antitr. L.J. 675 (1973).

31. Finding a patent misuse may be relevant even though the patentee has clearly offended the antitrust laws. An unlawful provision in a patent license, for example, may not injure an unlicensed infringer. In that event, the infringer could not maintain a private antitrust action, see ¶¶144-146, but holding the unlawful provision to be a patent misuse will save the infringer from successful attack by the patentee.

32. Motion Picture Patents Co. v. Universal Film Mfg. Co., 243 U.S. 502 (1917); *Morton Salt,* note 27. In these cases the Court found misuse and declared it unnecessary to decide whether the patentee had offended the antitrust laws. Compare Berlenbach v. Anderson & Thompson Ski Co., 329 F.2d 782 (9th Cir.), cert. denied, 379 U.S. 830 (1964) (exclusive dealing arrangement, see Ch. 4C, held patent misuse without proving competitive effects ordinarily prerequisite to holding such arrangements offensive to antitrust laws), with Swofford v. B&W, 251 F. Supp. 811, 821-822 (S.D. Tex. 1966).

refused to find a violation of the antitrust laws.[33] Nevertheless, one may say generally that the misuse concept is grounded in the competitive considerations of antitrust analysis.[34]

Misuse may sometimes be defined more broadly than antitrust offenses, but no great divergence has appeared or is to be expected.[35] Divergence is even less likely on account of a 1988 enactment under which patent misuse may not be found for either (1) a refusal to license or use one's patent rights or (2) an attempt to tie a patent license to some other concession to the patentee — unless it is shown that the patentee holds market power in the relevant market for the patent or product on which the license or sale is conditioned.[36]

187. Antitrust remedies. The remedial powers of the antitrust court are considerable and may be directed to ending the violation, depriving the defendant of the fruits of its illegality, and facilitating competition in the market.[37] Agreements involving patents are subject to the same injunctions as nonpatent agreements, and patents may be controlled and divested in the same way as other forms of property. Certain remedies, however, are peculiar to patents. Among them is compulsory licensing at reasonable royalties. This is now a well-established antitrust remedy,[38] and it has occasionally been extended to require the licensing of patents not yet in existence but to be issued in the future to the defendant[39] or acquired

---

33. Laitram Corp. v. King Crab, 244 F. Supp. 9, modified, 245 F. Supp. 1019 (D. Alaska 1965). The court first held the patentee's conduct to be both a patent misuse and a violation of the Sherman Act but retracted its Sherman Act holding in a supplemental opinion. See Zenith Radio Corp. v. Hazeltine Research, 395 U.S. 100, 140 (1969), where the Court commented that "if there was such patent misuse, it does not necessarily follow that the misuse embodies the ingredients of a violation of either Section 1 or Section 2 of the Sherman Act."

34. See USM Corp. v. SPS Technologies, 694 F.2d 505 (7th Cir. 1982), cert. denied, 462 U.S. 1107 (1985).

35. The divergence, if any, seems to be this: More proof of anticompetitive effect may be required to establish the antitrust violation, while misuse may often be determined by the nature of the practice. See Ansul Co. v. Uniroyal, 448 F.2d 872 (2d Cir. 1971), cert. denied, 404 U.S. 1018 (1972); Waco-Porter Corp. v. Tubular Structures Corp., 220 F. Supp. 724, modified, 222 F. Supp. 332 (S.D. Cal. 1963); Ethyl Corp. v. Hercules Powder Co., 232 F. Supp. 453 (D. Del. 1963). More recent cases have found an increasing convergence between the requirements for misuse and for antitrust violations. E.g., *USM,* note 34.

36. 35 U.S.C. §271(d).

37. See ¶¶139, 314; M. Adelman, Property Rights Theory and Patent-Antitrust: The Role of Compulsory Licensing, 52 N.Y.U.L. Rev. 977 (1977).

38. Hartford-Empire Co. v. United States, 323 U.S. 386, 417 (1945); United States v. National Lead Co., 332 U.S. 319 (1947); *Glaxo,* note 24 (mandatory product sales and patent licensing on reasonable terms).

39. *Hartford-Empire,* note 38, at 413.

by it from persons other than its own employees.[40] The royalty level is not specified but is usually left to negotiation between the defendant and license applicants. If they cannot agree, the court decides.[41] The more drastic remedy is royalty-free compulsory licensing.[42] The Supreme Court has not favored this remedy, which it viewed as akin to confiscation.[43] The remedy is seldom used, perhaps because it is seldom truly necessary to restore competition,[44] but it has been used where the defendant was thought to have a patent stranglehold on the market.[45] It has been used more frequently in consent decrees.

40. United States v. United Shoe Mach. Corp., 110 F. Supp. 295, 354 (D. Mass. 1953), aff'd per curiam, 347 U.S. 521 (1954).

41. In one case, the decree provided for reasonable royalties determined by a group consisting of two persons selected by defendant and two determined by the government; in the event of disagreement, the judge would decide. United States v. Besser Mfg. Co., 96 F. Supp. 304 (E.D. Mich. 1951), aff'd, 343 U.S. 444 (1952).

42. Commentaries sometimes distinguish royalty-free licensing from a requirement that defendant "dedicate" its patent to the public and from an injunction against enforcement of a patent. The licensing route leaves room for subsequent modification and might be interpreted to permit the patentee to impose limitations other than royalties (for example, requiring licensee to make its patents available).

43. *Hartford-Empire*, note 38, at 414-417.

44. The Supreme Court so believed in *Hartford-Empire* and *National Lead*, note 38. In *National Lead*, at 349-351, the Court did not decide whether royalty-free licensing was permissible but held that relief was a matter within the sound discretion of the trial court that had decreed compulsory licensing at a reasonable royalty. Royalty-free licensing was held unnecessary in United States v. Glaxo Group, 328 F. Supp. 709 (D.D.C. 1971), rev'd on other grounds, 410 U.S. 52 (1973); United States v. Imperial Chem. Indus., 105 F. Supp. 215, 223-225 (S.D.N.Y. 1952); United States v. General Instrument Corp., 115 F. Supp. 582, 591 (D.N.J. 1953). In the latter case, the judge said that the appropriateness of royalty-free licensing was "left open" by *National Lead,* "which substantially diluted" *Hartford-Empire.*

45. United States v. General Elec. Co., 115 F. Supp. 835, 844-845 (D.N.J. 1953) (manufacturers of electric lamps were required to dedicate lamp patents to the public). Compare United States v. Vehicular Parking, 61 F. Supp. 656, 658 (D. Del. 1945) (rejecting compulsory royalty-free licensing but enjoining suits against infringement of specified patents until defendants "are able to show a course of conduct which will be free from past taints of illegality").

Chapter 2

Horizontal Restraints:
Collaboration Among Competitors

200. Prologue. *overview of chapter* The existing business firm — whether a single person or many persons joined together — is assumed to be the basic economic unit competing with other economic units.[1] The classic concern of antitrust law has been to preserve competition among such firms by preventing them from joining together to achieve for themselves the fruits of monopoly. This chapter begins by considering agreements that limit competition among a group of competitors. Chapter 2A traces the development of rules under Sherman Act §1, focusing on price fixing. Although the "per se" prohibition against price fixing has become settled law, it has long been understood that certain forms of collaborative activity should be permitted even though they limit price or other dimensions of competition among collaborators. Chapter 2B explores modern cases in which courts have attempted to distinguish reasonable restraints from those in the prohibited class.

Although most cases in the first two sections clearly involve an "agreement" within the meaning of Sherman Act §1, there are many problems in defining what constitutes an agreement and in proving that one exists. Once prohibitions are clear, cartels may conduct negotiations through secret channels to keep from creating incriminating paper trails. Chapter 2C addresses this problem of proving the existence of agreements, focusing on oligopolistic industries — those inhabited by relatively few firms. This issue is considered further in Chapter 2D, which analyzes a number of practices that sometimes are used to facilitate the formation or enforcement of a consensus among competitors. The cases examine such practices both as evidence of conspiracy and as potentially illegal actions in themselves.

The first four sections address group activity designed to eliminate competition among group members. Chapter 2E considers

---

1. The contours of any existing firm may be partly the result of historical circumstances having little bearing on the present issue; indeed, it might lawfully have been organized with a broader scope. And a firm may attempt to revise its structure by entering into a joint venture or merging with some other firm. See ¶222 (joint ventures) and Ch. 5, especially ¶500 (mergers).

collective refusals to deal, where the usual concern is with the adverse impact on competitors of those involved in a conspiracy. One particular form of such activity involves combinations designed to influence government to act in a manner that suppresses competition, a topic explored in Chapter 2F. Finally, Chapter 2G considers horizontal restraints involving patent licensing.[2]

2A.   DEVELOPMENT OF THE RULE OF REASON AND THE PER SE ILLEGALITY OF PRICE FIXING[3]

201.   Anticompetitive effect of cartels. (a) *The cartel problem.* In the absence of legal impediments, competitors would like to join together in the hope of eliminating competition among themselves, thereby restricting output and raising prices. A perfect scheme would permit them to realize the profits that could be earned if their market were occupied by a single-firm monopolist.[4] As a first approximation, the harm caused by such a cartel would equal that resulting from the hypothetical monopoly.

But cartels are often imperfect in a number of respects. Difficulties in reaching agreement, problems of enforcement against those who would cheat by undercutting the cartel price, and other impediments suggest that the monopoly result would not fully be achieved in most instances.[5] This is not, however, all to the good. Unlike the monopolist who will utilize only its most efficient, low-cost production facilities, the cartel must please its members in order to maintain their allegiance. Thus, neither the discipline of the competitive price nor the direction of central cartel management will organize production in a manner that minimizes industry costs. Furthermore, each member may augment its capacity in the hope of increasing its share of cartel sales, which can result in wasteful excess capacity for the industry as a whole. Finally, attempts to suppress

2. In the course of this chapter, the student will find it helpful to refer to Chs. 1A, 1B.

3. See generally R. Bork, The Rule of Reason and the Per Se Concept: Price Fixing and Market Division, 74 Yale L.J. 775 (1965), 75 Yale L.J. 373 (1966); J. Rahl, Price Competition and the Price Fixing Rule — Preface and Perspective, 57 Nw. U.L. Rev. 137 (1962); Note, The Per Se Illegality of Price-Fixing — Sans Power, Purpose, or Effect, 19 U. Chi. L. Rev. 837 (1952).

4. See ¶112 for the contrast between monopolistic and competitive price-output results.

5. See Ch. 2C for more about conflicts of interest among group members and about nonprice competition. Paragraph 229d compares cartels and lesser forms of collusion.

nonprice competition among cartel members, if successful, can reduce the variety of products or services available to consumers.

(b) *Cheating in cartels.* Recall that every firm finds it profitable to expand output and sales as long as the incremental revenue exceeds the incremental cost.[6] Thus, in the absence of sales quotas for each member, price fixing often carries the seeds of its own destruction because the effect of fixing a price well above costs is to induce each collaborator to try to win additional sales. If the cartel members are so numerous that each member's production is too small to affect market price, each will simply expand production with the result that the cartel price cannot be maintained. If each firm can see that its output will affect market price, it may still try to win additional sales by "cheating" on the cartel, secretly shading its price on selected transactions.[7] Once discovered, cheating may spread and the cartel could collapse.[8] Moreover, cartel members may engage in nonprice competition — for example, by offering additional services in the effort to win additional business. At various times, for example, international airlines fixed prices by agreement and also controlled some services such as seat space and free in-flight drinks and movies. The airlines continued to compete in other services and especially in offering frequent and convenient flights. Overscheduling resulted, with the consequence that many planes operated half full. The carriers thus failed to earn substantial profits although the consumers paid an artificially inflated price.[9] And even if cartel members do succeed in earning monopoly profits, new entry (with new capacity) may be drawn into those markets not protected by substantial entry barriers.[10] The instability of

6. See ¶112.

7. An examination of successful government cases between 1963 and 1972 against express horizontal price fixing is said to show that such price fixing "is most likely to occur and endure when numbers [of sellers] are small, concentration is high and the product is homogeneous." G. Hay & D. Kelley, An Empirical Survey of Price Fixing Conspiracies, 17 J.L. Econ. 13, 26-27 (1974). An explanation might be that such a conspiracy is most likely to be successful where "cheating" is most readily detected and thus least likely to occur. See ¶¶229d, 230.

8. Recent work in economics shows that occasional price wars can be a natural part of cartel behavior and may not be a sign of serious cartel breakdown. See J. Baker, Recent Developments in Economics That Challenge Chicago School Views, 58 Antitr. L.J. 645 (1989); G. Ellison, Theories of Cartel Stability and the Joint Executive Committee, 25 Rand J. Econ. 37 (1994).

9. A further illustration is the "battle of the sandwich." When economy-class service was introduced in the late 1950s, the cartel agreed that none would serve a hot meal but only sandwiches. A few carriers, however, began to serve elaborate meals on a thin token slice of bread. Upon complaint of rival carriers, the cartel devoted considerable resources to investigating the matter. It ultimately established six criteria for a "sandwich." The Economist, May 3, 1958, at 435. See ¶230e.

10. See ¶¶114, 231.

price-fixing cartels is not a sufficient argument to favor their legality, for most are dangerous while they last and some will survive. Rather, the purpose of this subparagraph is two-fold: (1) to suggest the nature and difficulties of express price agreements and (2) to set the stage for understanding the more elusive phenomenon of pricing coordination among oligopolists, which will be considered in Chapter 2C.[11]

(c) *Cartel justifications.*[12] The discussion to follow considers a number of the more common reasons collaborators have offered in attempts to justify their cartels. Paragraph d examines the argument that cartels prevent cutthroat competition, one of the most common claims and one that figured prominently in the line of cases considered in this section. This justification will be assessed by developing and applying three central criticisms of most proffered justifications for cartels: (1) that the allegedly baleful effect of competition is in fact a virtue, at least in most instances, (2) that price fixing is both almost certainly harmful despite its purported benefit and often only loosely connected to the problem needing cure, and (3) that it is bad policy to rely on the firms themselves to identify exceptional circumstances in which fixed prices might be socially desirable, given their self-interest — which leaves the difficult question of whether courts or other institutions should attempt to isolate exceptional cases for special treatment. The remainder of this Paragraph addresses more briefly a number of other arguments offered in defense of cartels and notes the applicability of the preceding criticisms. The cases that follow this introductory discussion explore the evolution of the courts' interpretation of Sherman Act §1 as it applies to price-fixing cartels and closely related practices.

(d) *Preventing cutthroat competition.* The most commonly proffered justification for price fixing is that it is necessary to avoid "cutthroat," "unfair," "predatory," "destructive," or "ruinous" competition. These impressive terms may mean only that the speaker prefers high profits and the quiet life to the rigors of competition. Losses imposed by competition serve the important social function of inducing shifts in resource allocation and inducing producers to perform more efficiently.

The strongest claim that competition can be "ruinous" arises in cases in which "fixed costs" are a large percentage of total production costs. Railroads are the classic example. The cost of building a

---

11. For a study of the behavior of cartels permitted by law, see D. Swann, D. O'Brien, M. Maunder & W. Howe, Competition in British Industry, ch. 4 (1974). Once express price fixing became unlawful in Great Britain, many firms substituted exchanges of information. See ¶246c.

12. This Paragraph does not attempt to be exhaustive. Many other rationales for cartels are subject to a similar analysis.

system of track is quite large and will be undertaken only if the firm anticipates that future operations will permit it to recover those costs as well as the variable costs of running the trains. But when there are many railroad systems in competition, prices tend to fall to the level of variable costs alone. As long as price exceeds that level, competitors have an incentive to undercut it modestly, thereby winning additional business from rivals at a price still in excess of variable cost, thus contributing more earnings to cover their own overhead. To the extent competition drives prices close to variable cost, the prospect of railroading over the long run would be unprofitable. This would be manifested by unwillingness to replace worn capital stock or an unwillingness to enter the industry in the first instance.

In general, however, such results will be desirable because the process just described arises only when capacity is excessive in relation to the demand for the industry's product or service. Competitors have an incentive to keep lowering their prices only if they have sufficient capacity to serve the additional customers. If total capacity were merely sufficient for demand at the price that covered all costs, rather than excessive, competition would not force prices lower. Thus, the process just described reflects competitive forces providing appropriate incentives for investment, replacement, and retirement of capacity.[13]

The railroad example is in some respects exceptional because one or two railroads may suffice to serve all of the demand. Even so, a cartel is hardly a good solution because it produces noncompetitive prices and performance nonetheless. By reducing market incentives to build or keep optimal capacity, we may face not only supracompetitive prices but also less efficient operation than would occur if there were monopoly. If in fact there is a situation of

13. It might be argued that this decrease in capacity may lessen the number of independent business units, in contravention of the Jeffersonian ideal (cf. ¶120), or reduce employment. At best, such an argument would be confined to one industry, viewed in isolation. Maintenance of unneeded or inefficient capacity cannot benefit society. Moreover, it would be surprising if the best way to preserve business or employment were to permit firms to form cartels, thereby collecting monopoly profits. Allowing unprofitable businesses to commit fraud or steal would accomplish similar ends but would not generally be supported on such grounds. In fact, allowing cartels can be counterproductive because higher prices are achievable only by reducing output, so employment would often be diminished unless the cartel's inefficiency were so high as to require more workers to produce the lower output than competition required for a greater output. Moreover, centralized cartel decisionmaking for an entire industry is hardly consistent with the notion of decentralized decisionmaking critical to the Jeffersonian ideal. There exist more direct and less destructive means available to the federal government to promote both goals.

"natural monopoly,"[14] some form of direct regulation may be appropriate and has been legislated for public utilities and railroads.[15] Thus, the United States has generally relied on market forces, turning in exceptional cases to government regulators rather than cartel members to set prices.[16]

(e) *Preserving needed capacity.* An industry's capacity might exceed immediate demand without exceeding normal requirements. Sales might decline sharply in the course of a temporary recession, and some plants may close. When the economy recovers, producers would then need to incur the added costs of reopening the plants, and, in the interim, valuable personnel may have left the industry. To avoid such expensive fluctuations in capacity, producers may assert that prices should be fixed in order to maintain capacity during a recession.[17]

The economic waste and unemployment resulting from such capacity losses may appear to present an appealing cartel justification, but the ¶c criticisms suggest some reservations. First, would capacity be lost during a recession if there was actually a serious prospect that it would become profitable shortly thereafter? Firms have an economic incentive to abandon only capacity that is excessive in the long run,[18] and it is one of the central purposes of a market system to encourage such capacity adjustments.[19] In addition, capacity temporarily abandoned in the short run often is not lost; rather it may merely lie idle or change its ownership (as when a firm is liquidated in bankruptcy). Second, the costs normally associated with price fixing are relevant in recessions as well as in normal times. Third, firms that have made unwise investments in excessive capacity or simply face bad luck will always seek protection, through legalized cartelization or otherwise, regardless of the social costs or benefits that result.

---

14. See ¶162b.

15. Federal railroad regulation began with the Interstate Commerce Act in 1887, shortly before the Sherman Act. As described in note 32, rate regulation did not commence until early in the twentieth century. More recently, there has been substantial railroad deregulation, due to the recognition that other modes of transportation provide significant competition to railroads.

16. See ¶111. The period of the New Deal, see *Appalachian Coals* and some of the discussion in *Socony*, was a partial exception. In addition, some regulation in practice may have had results akin to cartel pricing, as regulators gave to the regulated industry what it wanted.

17. Although holding prices up may reduce sales and output even more, increased profits might allow marginal producers to remain alive.

18. If firms did not perceive the future need for capacity, they would have no incentive to spend their cartel profits to preserve it in any event.

19. See ¶108.

One can find few, if any, historical examples in which national economic fluctuations were accompanied by wasteful alternation of scrapping and rebuilding of an industry's capacity. True enough, economic adjustment may entail unemployment and a decrease in the number of business units in affected industries, just as it tends to result in new entrepreneurial opportunities and employment growth in other areas.[20] Yet it is hardly suggested that existing businesses have an inalienable right to survive, protected from price competition. Moreover, even if fewer firms remain in a contracting industry — implying fewer independent decisionmaking units and greater prospects for collusion — a legal cartel involves centralized decisionmaking and probably even higher prices.[21]

(f) *Reducing uncertainty*. Price fixing, it is argued, can eliminate or at least smooth out price fluctuations without increasing the average price level for a product. Such price "stabilization" tends to make the future more predictable and permits businesses to plan investment and production with greater certainty over a longer time span. The closer long-run coordination of investment with demand conserves resources, and the reduction in risk lowers the return that must be paid to attract capital. But reduction of uncertainty in this manner is artificial and not generally desirable either for an individual firm or an industry as a whole.[22] It is artificial because the underlying causes of fluctuating prices are unaffected by merely pegging the price at some average level. Prices move in response to changes in cost and demand. If competitive forces call for a lower price, maintaining the "stable price" forgoes profitable, and presumptively desirable, sales. And if such forces indicate a higher price, maintaining the "stable price" requires additional output for which the cost of production exceeds the value to the consumer. Thus, such stability results in losses in both instances. This, of course, is why firms — even monopolists — do not maintain constant prices as conditions change.[23] Cartels are every bit as undesirable as usual in such circumstances, and the preceding analysis

20. See ¶121.

21. Higher prices also typically result in more, not less, unemployment. See note 13.

22. In some circumstances, competitors may add or subtract capacity too far in response to market signals, oscillating around the equilibrium rather than moving toward it. Coordinating their decisions through a cartel might then reduce resource waste. Of course, cartels themselves often perform this function poorly. It seems unlikely that gaining modest benefits from moderating such effects of uncertainty will be worth the sacrifice of all benefits from competition.

23. In both competition and monopoly, there is some tendency for stability in response to minor changes in conditions, simply to avoid the costs involved in changing one's listed prices. But such stability reflects cost savings rather than collective disobedience to market signals.

also suggests that cartels would have no incentive to be unresponsive to changing cost and demand conditions. If, for some reason, a price pattern differing from that emerging from competition were desirable, there is no reason to expect that self-interested firms would confine their cartelization to such cases or would choose the hypothetically preferable prices.

(g) *Financing desirable activities.* The increased profits resulting from price fixing may be put to socially desirable uses and defended on that account. Without price fixing, it may be argued, very intensive competition will force prices down to the minimum cost of production and thus leave no margin for research, development, modernization, or desirable services. For example, it may be that competition in selling popular books will leave bookstores with no margin to cover the cost of stocking slow-moving books. It has been argued that large-inventory, full-service bookstores are "desirable" entities that warrant subsidies from a surplus generated by cartel pricing of best sellers. The argument has an undeniable appeal to those of us who value the ready availability of a wide variety of books that are of limited interest to the general public. Once again, however, the general defect in market forces is unclear and the prospects of solution through cartelization are more dangerous than helpful. Services that are valuable generally will be provided by competition. Those not sufficiently cost-justified for a competitive firm will typically be unprofitable for a monopolist or cartel as well. True, monopolies and cartels make additional profits. But there is no reason to assume that they will be generous to their consumers rather than to their owners when additional funds are available. True, various complex and subtle market imperfections mean that competition will not necessarily produce all socially desirable research and development — even taking into account patent protection — or product variety and quality.[24] But monopoly or cartelization offers no general solution, and again there is little basis for assum-

___

24. For further discussion concerning research and development, see ¶120, Ch. 1E. As to product quality and durability, the fear has more often been that monopoly (and, by analogy, a perfect cartel) will be inferior to competition, although such fears have limited foundation. See F.M. Scherer & D. Ross, Industrial Market Structure and Economic Performance 608-610 (3d ed. 1990). The notion that competition will induce producers to cut corners on quality is subject to the previous arguments questioning why competitive provision of valued characteristics would be inadequate and suggesting that cartels would not generally have a stronger motive to improve quality. To the extent lack of consumer information is a problem, regulation may be warranted, but there is no general tendency for cartels or monopoly to provide better information or to resist making profits at the expense of ignorant consumers. Finally, product variety can be either too high or too low in competition, and monopoly is again an uncertain "solution." Id. at 600-607.

ing that firms would limit cartelization, their higher prices, or use of excess profits to cases in which consumers would benefit.[25]

(b) *Countervailing power.* Because workers were thought to be unfairly disadvantaged in dealing with more powerful employers, they formed labor unions.[26] Similarly, combinations of business firms are sometimes defended as necessary to offset the superior bargaining power of the collaborators' customers or suppliers. It is certainly true that numerous competitors facing a single customer (monopsonist) or a single supplier (monopolist) can be exploited. Suppose, for example, that *M*, the sole producer of an important drug *Z*, is the sole customer of numerous suppliers of ingredient *Y*, a chemical. *M* cannot, of course, push the *Y* price so low as to dissuade the *Y* firms from remaining in business. But, in general, *M* may be able to depress its buying price below the price that would exist were there competition on both levels. If the *Y* firms combine to behave like a monopolist, they can probably protect themselves from exploitation by *M*. From the standpoint of society as a whole, however, the overall effect is quite uncertain. One possible result is that output will be reduced further and the price of *Z* raised higher.[27] It would be better to control the initial monopoly through antitrust laws or by direct regulation. If such control is not available, then perhaps countervailing power would sometimes improve the situation. Even so, a number of questions remain. Permitting cartelization creates power, which will be exercised for the benefit of the cartel members, which may exceed that necessary to achieve a balance of power among market players, and which may have a net impact on price that results in a divergence from competitive conditions.

25. Sometimes it may be the case that joint action among firms may be necessary to achieve more efficient production capacity or to facilitate progress in research and development. It hardly follows that price fixing is a necessary accompaniment. These issues will be explored further in Ch. 2B's consideration of joint ventures and in Ch. 5, which addresses mergers.

26. Labor unions have been specifically exempted from the antitrust laws. See ¶161. See also ¶123 (countervailing power).

27. When a monopolist sells to a monopolist, the end result is indeterminate, but these general propositions may be stated: (1) Production will be lower and price higher than when both face competition. (2) The aggregate profits of the two combined can be maximized at that output and price that would be selected by a single integrated monopolist producing both *Y* and *Z*. (3) A *Y*-monopolist and a *Z*-monopolist can maximize their joint profits by behaving as the integrated monopolist would and then dividing the spoils in whatever manner they can. (4) If the *Y*-monopolist and the *Z*-monopolist each tries to maximize its own profits by setting its own selling price, output would be lower and price higher than would be the case with either an integrated monopolist or a single monopolist enjoying competition at the other level. See ¶¶210, 211 & note 51, 321c.

(i) *Assessment.* The preceding discussion outlined the dangers posed by cartels and suggested that most proffered justifications are unpersuasive in most contexts — often because they are misconceived in the first instance, fail to adequately justify a cartel in any event, can be used as excuses for cartelization even when inapplicable, and are often better addressed directly through other methods. To determine what is the appropriate antitrust rule for cartels, consider the following questions:

(1) Are there any social benefits to price fixing — i.e., benefits that cannot be achieved through competition — in any circumstances? Are they frequent? Are there no better mechanisms to address such problems?

(2) Are such benefits likely to be demonstrable in particular cases — i.e., will courts be able to determine in which cases the special justifications are plausible?

(3) To the extent there may be substantial cost in determining when exceptions are warranted or substantial uncertainty even after a full inquiry, what presumptions seem reasonable?

(4) To justify a cartel, there not only must exist a benefit not otherwise achievable, but it must be significant relative to the harms of price fixing, which are not generally negated by various purported justifications. Should courts be given discretion to permit cartels in the public interest? Serving any interest or only those within an enumerated class? How would the benefits be traded off against the harms from higher prices and lower output?

Preview. The courts faced these questions from the beginning in interpreting the Sherman Act, as the following cases demonstrate. Even after their apparent resolution for "price-fixing cartels" over the course of a half century of case law development, these issues continue to haunt the courts as they have confronted a baffling array of trade restraints, as we shall see throughout this chapter.

SHERMAN ACT §1

§1 { Every contract, combination in the form of trust or otherwise, or conspiracy, in restraint of trade or commerce among the several States, or with foreign nations, is hereby declared to be illegal. . . .

202. *United States v. Trans-Missouri Freight Assn.,* 166 U.S. 290, 312, 323, 329, 331-332, 340, 347 (1897). Eighteen railroads controlling rail traffic west of the Mississippi River created an association to set freight rates for all of the railroads. The government sued under the Sherman Act to dissolve the association and to enjoin any similar conduct in the future. The defendants argued that §1 prohibited only unreasonable restraints of trade, as was the case under the common law. The Court, through Justice Peckham, rejected this interpretation, holding that the statute's condemnation of *"every* contract . . . in restraint of trade" encompassed *all* contracts of that nature, not simply those invalid as unreasonable under the common law.[28] It was noted, however, that

> [a] contract which is the mere accompaniment of the sale of property, and thus entered into for the purpose of enhancing the price at which the vendor sells it, which in effect is collateral to such sale, and where the main purpose of the whole contract is accomplished by such sale, might not be included, within the letter or spirit of the statute in question.

The Court also rejected the argument that railroads, because of the impossibility of covering fixed costs when subject to unfettered competition,[29] were intended to be excluded from the statute. Responding more generally to the claim that rate agreements should be permissible as long as the rates themselves were reasonable, the Court stated:

> If only that kind of contract which is in unreasonable restraint of trade be within the meaning of the statute, and declared therein to be illegal, it is at once apparent that the subject of what is a reasonable rate is attended with great uncertainty. What is a proper standard by which to judge the fact of reasonable rates? Must the rate be so high as to enable the return for the whole business done to amount to a sum sufficient to afford the shareholder a fair and reasonable profit upon his investment? If so, what is a fair and reasonable profit? That depends sometimes upon the risk incurred, and the rate itself differs in different localities: which is the one to which reference is to be made as the standard? Or is the reasonableness of the profit to be limited to a fair return upon the capital that would have been sufficient to build and equip the road, if honestly expended? Or is still another standard to be created, and the reasonableness of the charges tried by the cost of the carriage of the article and a reasonable profit allowed on that? And in such case would contribution to a sinking fund to make repairs upon the roadbed and renewal of cars, etc., be assumed as a proper item? Or is the reasonableness of the charge to be tested by reference to the charges for the transportation of the same kind of property made by other roads similarly situated? If the latter, a combination among such

28. The Court also suggested that combinations might be undesirable not only when they raise prices but also when they reduce them. "Trade or commerce under those circumstances [of artificially low prices] may nevertheless be badly and unfortunately restrained by driving out of business the small dealers and worthy men whose lives have been spent therein, and who might be unable to readjust themselves to their altered surroundings."

29. See ¶201d.

roads as to rates would, of course, furnish no means of answering the question. It is quite apparent, therefore, that it is exceedingly difficult to formulate even the terms of the rule itself which should govern in the matter of determining what would be reasonable rates for transportation. While even after the standard should be determined there is such an infinite variety of facts entering into the question of what is a reasonable rate, no matter what standard is adopted, that any individual shipper would in most cases be apt to abandon the effort to show the unreasonable character of a charge, sooner than hazard the great expense in time and money necessary to prove the fact, and at the same time incur the ill-will of the road itself in all his future dealings with it. To say, therefore, that the act excludes agreements which are not in unreasonable restraint of trade ... is substantially to leave the question of reasonableness to the companies themselves.

Finally, the Court emphasized that the railroads' arguments were appropriately addressed to Congress; to accomplish the result desired by the railroads through statutory interpretation would amount to "judicial legislation."

Justice White, writing for four dissenting Justices, argued that the majority's interpretation suggested that Congress had departed from general principles of law, implying that Congress itself was unreasonable. The statute could be interpreted as the defendants suggested because, in the course of common law development, the words "restraint of trade" had come to encompass only those restraints that were unreasonable.

UNITED STATES v. ADDYSTON PIPE & STEEL CO.
85 F. 271 (6th Cir. 1898), aff'd, 175 U.S. 211 (1899)

TAFT, Circuit Judge. [Defendant manufacturers and vendors of cast-iron pipe entered into a combination to raise the price for pipe over some three-fourths of the United States. They accounted for about 65 percent of cast-iron producing capacity within the relevant area.]

From early times it was the policy of Englishmen to encourage trade in England, and to discourage those voluntary restraints which tradesmen were often induced to impose on themselves by contract. Courts recognized this public policy by refusing to enforce stipulations of this character. The objections to such restraints were mainly two. One was that by such contracts a man disabled himself from earning a livelihood with the risk of becoming a public charge, and deprived the community of the benefit of his labor. The other was that such restraints tended to give to the covenantee, the beneficiary of such restraints, a monopoly of the trade, from which he had thus excluded one competitor, and by the same means might exclude others. . . .

The inhibition against restraints of trade at common law seems at first to have had no exception. . . . After a time it became apparent to the people and the courts that it was in the interest of trade that . . . covenants in partial restraint of trade [be] generally upheld as valid when they are agreements (1) by the seller of property or business not to compete with the buyer in such a way as to derogate from the value of the property or business sold; (2) by a retiring partner not to compete with the firm; (3) by a partner pending the partnership not to do anything to interfere, by competition or otherwise, with the business of the firm; (4) by the buyer of property not to use the same in competition with the business retained by the seller; and (5) by an assistant, servant, or agent not to compete with his master or employer after the expiration of his time of service. Before such agreements are upheld, however, the court must find that the restraints attempted thereby are reasonably necessary (1, 2, and 3) to the enjoyment by the buyer of the property, good will, or interest in the partnership bought; or (4) to the legitimate ends of the existing partnership; or (5) to the prevention of possible injury to the business of the seller from use by the buyer of the thing sold; or (6) to protection from the danger of loss to the employer's business caused by the unjust use on the part of the employee of the confidential knowledge acquired in such business. . . .

It would be stating it too strongly to say that these five classes of covenants in restraint of trade include all of those upheld as valid at the common law; but it would certainly seem to follow from the tests laid down for determining the validity of such an agreement that no conventional restraint of trade can be enforced unless the covenant embodying it is merely ancillary to the main purpose of a lawful contract, and necessary to protect the covenantee in the enjoyment of the legitimate fruits of the contract, or to protect him from the dangers of an unjust use of those fruits by the other party. . . .

[To be lawful,] the contract must be one in which there is a main purpose, to which the covenant in restraint of trade is merely ancillary. The covenant is inserted only to protect one of the parties from the injury which, in the execution of the contract or enjoyment of its fruits, he may suffer from the unrestrained competition of the other. The main purpose of the contract suggests the measure of protection needed, and furnishes a sufficiently uniform standard by which the validity of such restraints may be judicially determined. In such a case, if the restraint exceeds the necessity presented by the main purpose of the contract, it is void for two reasons: First, because it oppresses the covenantor, without any corresponding benefit to the covenantee; and, second, because it tends to a monopoly. But where the sole object of both parties in making the contract as expressed therein is merely to restrain competition, and enhance or maintain prices, it would seem that there was nothing to justify or excuse the restraint, that it would necessarily have a tendency to monopoly, and therefore would be void. In such a case there is no measure of what is necessary to the protection of either party, except the vague and varying opinion of judges as to how much, on principles of political economy, men ought to be allowed to restrain competition. There is in such contracts no main lawful purpose, to subserve which partial restraint is permitted, and by which its reasonableness is measured, but the sole object is to restrain trade in order to avoid the competition which it has always been the policy of the common law to foster. . . .

It is true that there are some cases in which the courts, mistaking, as we conceive, the proper limits of the relaxation of the rules for determining the unreasonableness of restraints of trade, have set sail on a sea of doubt, and have assumed the power to say, in respect to contracts which have no other purpose and no other consideration on either side than the mutual restraint of the parties, how much restraint of competition is in the public interest, and how much is not.

The manifest danger in the administration of justice according to so shifting, vague, and indeterminate a standard would seem to be a strong reason against adopting it. . . .

Much evidence is adduced upon affidavit to prove that defendants had no power arbitrarily to fix prices, and that they were always obliged to meet competition. . . . The most cogent evidence that they had this power is the fact, everywhere apparent in the record, that they exercised it. . . . The defendants acquired this power by voluntarily agreeing to sell only at prices fixed by their committee, and by allowing the highest bidder at the secret "auction pool" to become the lowest bidder of them at the public letting. Now, the restraint thus imposed on themselves was only partial. It did not cover the United States. There was not a complete monopoly. It was tempered by the fear of competition, and it affected only a part of the price. But this certainly does not take the contract of association out of the annulling effect of the rule against monopolies. . . .

It has been earnestly pressed upon us that the prices at which the cast-iron pipe was sold . . . were reasonable. . . . We do not think the issue an important one, because, as already stated, we do not think that at common law there is any question of reasonableness open to the courts with reference to such a contract. Its tendency was certainly to give defendants the power to charge unreasonable prices, had they chosen to do so. But, if it were important, we should unhesitatingly find that the prices charged in the instances which were in evidence were unreasonable. . . .

[The court held that the agreement would be invalid at common law and was therefore condemned by §1 even apart from *Trans-Missouri*'s condemnation of "every" restraint.[30]]

203. *United States v. Joint Traffic Assn.*, 171 U.S. 505, 567-568 (1898). Shortly after *Trans-Missouri*, the Court again considered a case involving an association of railroads formed to fix rates. The defendants unsuccessfully urged the Court to reconsider its previous decision, with the Court splitting much as it had before. In reaffirming *Trans-Missouri*, Justice Peckham addressed the claim that the Court's construction of the act rendered illegal

> all organizations of mechanics engaged in the same business for the purpose of limiting the number of persons employed in the business, or of maintaining wages; the formation of a corporation to carry on any particular line of business by those already engaged therein; a contract of partnership or of employment between two persons previously engaged in the same line of business; the appointment by two producers of the same person to sell their goods on commission; the purchase by one wholesale merchant of the product of two producers; the lease or purchase by a farmer, manufacturer, or merchant of an additional farm, manufactory or shop; the withdrawal from business of any farmer, merchant, or manufacturer; a sale of the good will of a business with an agreement not to destroy its value by engaging in similar business; and a covenant in a deed restricting the use of real estate. It is added that the effect of most business contracts or combinations is to restrain trade in some degree.

He responded by stating that the formation of corporations and partnerships, appointments of joint sales agents, leases, withdrawals of business, and sales of goodwill accompanied by restrictive covenants (the latter example having been noted in *Trans-Missouri* as not within the Act) have never been understood to be restraints of trade, as that term is legally defined. He then referred to the Court's decision in the companion case of Hopkins v. United States, 171 U.S. 578 (1898), which held that the Sherman Act

---

30. The Supreme Court modified the decree slightly to make clear that purely intrastate matters were not covered. Several months after this decision, the defendants merged into a single firm and the government did not attack the merger. Is this result desirable? See Ch. 5, which addresses mergers, and the discussion of the 1904 *Northern Securities* case in ¶504a.

applies only to those contracts whose direct and immediate effect is a restraint upon interstate commerce....[31] An agreement entered into for the purpose of promoting the legitimate business of an individual or corporation, with no purpose to thereby affect or restrain interstate commerce, and which does not directly restrain such commerce, is not, as we think, covered by the act, although the agreement may indirectly and remotely affect that commerce.

The Court then quoted language from *Hopkins* to the effect that "the act of Congress must have a reasonable construction, or else there would scarcely be an agreement or contract among business men that could not be said to have, indirectly or remotely, some bearing upon interstate commerce, and possibly to restrain it." Finally, the Court again rejected the argument that the possibility of destructive competition among railroads justified excluding their arrangement from the Act's prohibition.[32]

204.   *Standard Oil Co. v. United States,* 221 U.S. 1, 60, 64-65, 68 (1911).[33] The decision was a victory for Justice White, who had become Chief Justice in 1910. Justice Harlan was the lone member in 1911 who had been both a member in 1897 and one of the majority Justices in *Trans-Missouri* and *Joint Traffic.* He was also the only dissenter to Justice White's announcement of the rule of reason. Although all agreed that Standard Oil's conduct was illegal, Chief Justice White took the occasion to establish his earlier dissenting views as the prevailing law.

The Chief Justice declared that the Act, "not specifying but indubitably contemplating and requiring a standard," must have "intended that the standard of reason which had been applied at the common law and in this country ... [remain] the measure" of illegality under the Sherman Act. Only after pronouncing this rule did he turn to the Court's prior decisions. He dismissed the contrary language in those opinions as being out of context, claiming

(handwritten margin note: rule of reason)

31. The Court developed the direct-indirect dichotomy in *Hopkins* in response to a claim that the activities at issue did not constitute interstate commerce within the meaning of the Sherman Act. In the late nineteenth century, the scope of the interstate commerce clause of the Constitution and, similarly, the scope of statutes enacted pursuant to that power were understood to be substantially narrower than is the case today. See ¶166. What do you think of relying on the constitutional or statutory test that defines the scope of interstate commerce as the primary means of determining which agreements should be allowed under Sherman Act §1?

32. Gray, Shiras, and White, JJ., dissented. McKenna, J., did not participate. Legislation in 1906 and 1910 empowered the Interstate Commerce Commission to regulate railroad rates, and Congress formally permitted railroad rate bureaus in 1948, after they had been held to violate the Sherman Act despite ICC regulation. Subsequently, however, railroads have been substantially deregulated. See ¶162.

33. For further discussion of *Standard Oil,* see ¶303a.

that in each instance the "contract or agreement ... was fully referred to and suggestions as to their unreasonableness pointed out in order to indicate that they were within the prohibitions of the statute." Just as he had argued in his *Trans-Missouri* dissent that any contrary interpretation of the statute would presume unreasonableness on the part of Congress, here he argued that any contrary interpretation of the earlier decisions would attribute unreasonableness to the Court. He also claimed that the direct-indirect test of *Joint Traffic*—a statement from which he also dissented—was ultimately the same as his rule of reason approach. He concluded by stating that his construction "does not in the slightest degree conflict with a single previous case ... every one [of which] applied the rule of reason for the purpose of determining whether the subject before the court was within the statute."[34]

This opinion provoked a sharp dissent from Justice Harlan, who quoted extensively from the prior opinions, emphasizing that the rule of reason, as expounded by Chief Justice White, had been explicitly rejected in each prior case. He also quoted from interim opinions by the Chief Justice that stated the prevailing rule in a manner flatly contrary to the rule of reason formulation now offered. Harlan repeatedly invoked the principle against "judicial legislation" in criticizing the majority, which, in light of the unanimous agreement that Standard Oil's acts were illegal, did not even have to decide this question of interpretation.

In the companion case, *American Tobacco* (1911), Chief Justice White described the rule of *Standard Oil* as embracing only

> acts or contracts or agreements or combinations which operated to the prejudice of the public interests by unduly restricting competition or unduly obstructing the due course of trade or which, either because of their inherent nature or effect or because of the evident purpose of the acts, etc., injuriously restrained trade....[35]

205. (a) Could Justice Peckham's original interpretation have survived? How could he say that the Act simultaneously prohibited

---

34. He reasoned that the earlier cases held only that

considering the contracts or agreements, their necessary effect and the character of the parties by whom they were made, they were clearly restraints of trade within the purview of the statute, they could not be taken out of that category by indulging in general reasoning as to the expediency or non-expediency of having made the contracts or the wisdom or want of wisdom of the statute which prohibited their being made.... [T]he nature and character of the contracts, creating ... a conclusive presumption which brought them within the statute ... was not to be disregarded by the substitution of a judicial appreciation of what the law ought to be for the plain judicial duty of enforcing the law as it was made.

35. United States v. American Tobacco Co., 221 U.S. 106, 179 (1911).

all restraints yet excluded the formation of corporations and partnerships, restrictive covenants related to the sale of a business, and other agreements? Is the direct-indirect test helpful in making these distinctions?

(b) What is the content of Judge Taft's ancillary restraint test? He says "ancillary to the main purpose of a lawful contract," but isn't the purpose of virtually all such contracts to make money, a purpose that would be furthered by virtually any anticompetitive restraint that a defendant would choose to adopt? Does his approach avoid the problems he identified with an inquiry into "how much competition is in the public interest, and how much is not"? Can his test be justified in light of the statutory language?

(c) Did Chief Justice White overrule *Trans-Missouri* and *Joint Traffic*, or is his rule of reason ultimately consistent with Justice Peckham's evolving approach? What is the content of the rule of reason? Does it create the problems Justice Peckham and Judge Taft associated with an open-ended approach?

(d) Does Chief Justice White's approach permit (require?) a court to determine the reasonableness of prices set by price fixers? If so, how would reasonableness be established in any particular case? Suppose, for example, that the collaborators in a price-fixing agreement showed negligible or even negative profits. Would such evidence demonstrate or suggest that defendants had fixed only reasonable prices?

(e) In what sense are each of these opinions "interpretations" of the statutory language?[36]

CHICAGO BOARD OF TRADE v. UNITED STATES
246 U.S. 231 (1918)

Justice BRANDEIS. . . . Chicago is the leading grain market in the world. Its Board of Trade is the commercial center through which most of the trading in grain is done. . . . The standard forms of trading are: (a) Spot sales; that is, sales of grain already in Chicago in railroad cars or elevators for immediate delivery by order on carrier or transfer of warehouse receipt. (b) Future sales; that is, agreements for delivery later in the current or in some future month. (c) Sales "to arrive"; that is, agreements to deliver on arrival grain which is already in transit to Chicago or is to be shipped there within a time specified. On every business day sessions of the Board are held at which all bids and sales are publicly made.

36. Congress's response is noted in ¶132.

Spot sales and future sales are made at the regular sessions of the Board from 9:30 A.M. to 1:15 P.M., except on Saturdays, when the session closes at 12 M. Special sessions, termed the "Call," are held immediately after the close of the regular session, at which sales "to arrive" are made. These sessions are not limited as to duration, but last usually about half an hour. At all these sessions transactions are between members only; but they may trade either for themselves or on behalf of others. Members may also trade privately with one another at any place, either during the sessions or after, and they may trade with non-members at any time except on the premises occupied by the Board.

Purchases of grain "to arrive" are made largely from country dealers and farmers throughout the whole territory tributary to Chicago, which includes besides Illinois and Iowa, Indiana, Ohio, Wisconsin, Minnesota, Missouri, Kansas, Nebraska, and even South and North Dakota. The purchases are sometimes the result of bids to individual country dealers made by telegraph or telephone either during the sessions or after; but most purchases are made by the sending out from Chicago by the afternoon mails to hundreds of country dealers offers to buy, at the prices named, any number of carloads, subject to acceptance before 9:30 A.M. on the next business day.

In 1906 the Board adopted what is known as the "Call" rule. By it members were prohibited from purchasing or offering to purchase, during the period between the close of the Call and the opening of the session on the next business day, any wheat, corn, oats or rye "to arrive" at a price other than the closing bid at the Call. The Call was over, with rare exceptions, by two o'clock. The change effected was this: Before the adoption of the rule, members fixed their bids throughout the day at such prices as they respectively saw fit; after the adoption of the rule, the bids had to be fixed at the day's closing bid on the Call until the opening of the next session.

In 1913 the United States filed ... this suit ... to enjoin the enforcement of the Call rule.... The defendants admitted the adoption and enforcement of the Call rule, and averred that its purpose was not to prevent competition or to control prices, but to promote the convenience of members by restricting their hours of business and to break up a monopoly in that branch of the grain trade acquired by four or five warehousemen in Chicago. On motion of the Government the allegations concerning the purpose of establishing the regulation were stricken from the record [and the Call rule was enjoined]....

The Government proved the existence of the rule and described its application and the change in business practice involved. It made no attempt to show that the rule was designed to or that it had the effect of limiting the amount of grain shipped to Chicago; or of retarding or accelerating shipment; or of raising or depressing prices; or of discriminating against any part of the public; or that it resulted in hardship to anyone. The case was rested upon the bald proposition, that a rule or agreement by which men occupying positions of strength in any branch of trade, fixed prices at which they would buy or sell during an important part of the business day, is an illegal restraint of trade under the Anti-Trust Law. But the legality of an agreement or regulation cannot be determined by so simple a test, as whether it restrains competition. Every agreement concerning trade, every regulation of trade, restrains. To bind, to restrain, is of their very essence. The true test of legality is whether the restraint imposed is such as merely regulates and perhaps thereby promotes competition or whether it is such as may suppress or even destroy competition. To determine that question the court must ordinarily consider the facts peculiar to the business to which the restraint is applied; its condition before and after the restraint was imposed; the nature of the restraint and its effect, actual or probable. The history of the restraint, the evil believed to exist, the reason for adopting the particular remedy, the purpose or end sought to be attained, are all relevant facts. This is not because a good intention will save an otherwise objectionable regulation or the reverse; but because knowledge of intent may help the court to interpret facts and to predict consequences. The District Court erred, therefore, in striking from the answer allegations concerning the history and purpose of the Call rule and in later excluding evidence on that subject. But the evidence admitted makes it clear that the rule was a reasonable regulation of business consistent with the provisions of the Anti-Trust Law.

First: The nature of the rule: ... [I]t required members who desired to buy grain "to arrive" to make up their minds before the close of the Call how much they were willing to pay during the interval before the next session of the Board. The rule made it to their interest to attend the Call; and if they did not fill their wants by purchases there, to make the final bid high enough to enable them to purchase from country dealers.

Second: The scope of the rule: It is restricted in operation to grain "to arrive." It applies only to a small part of the grain shipped from day to day to Chicago, and to an even smaller part of the day's sales: members were left free to purchase grain already in Chicago from anyone at any price throughout the day. It applies only during a small part of the business day; members were left free to purchase during the sessions of the Board grain "to arrive," at any price, from members anywhere and from non-members anywhere except on the premises of the Board. It applied only to grain shipped to

Chicago: members were left free to purchase at any price throughout the day from either members or non-members, grain "to
arrive" at any other market. Country dealers and farmers had available in practically every part of the territory called tributary to
Chicago some other market for grain "to arrive." ...

Third: The effects of the rule: As it applies to only a small part of
the grain shipped to Chicago and to that only during a part of the
business day and does not apply at all to grain shipped to other
markets, the rule had no appreciable effect on general market
prices; nor did it materially affect the total volume of grain coming
to Chicago. But within the narrow limits of its operation the rule
helped to improve market conditions thus:

(*a*) It created a public market for grain "to arrive." Before its
adoption, bids were made privately. Men had to buy and sell without adequate knowledge of actual market conditions. This was
disadvantageous to all concerned, but particularly so to country
dealers and farmers.

(*b*) It brought into the regular market hours of the Board sessions more of the trading in grain "to arrive."

(*c*) It brought buyers and sellers into more direct relations; because on the Call they gathered together for a free and open interchange of bids and offers.

(*d*) It distributed the business in grain "to arrive" among a far
larger number of Chicago receivers and commission merchants
than had been the case there before.

(*e*) It increased the number of country dealers engaging in this
branch of the business; supplied them more regularly with bids
from Chicago; and also increased the number of bids received by
them from competing markets.

(*f*) It eliminated risks necessarily incident to a private market,
and thus enabled country dealers to do business on a smaller margin. In that way the rule made it possible for them to pay more to
farmers without raising the price to consumers.

(*g*) It enabled country dealers to sell some grain "to arrive"
which they would otherwise have been obliged either to ship to
Chicago commission merchants or to sell for "future delivery."

(*h*) It enabled those grain merchants of Chicago who sell to
millers and exporters to trade on a smaller margin and, by paying
more for grain or selling it for less, to make the Chicago market
more attractive for both shippers and buyers of grain.

(*i*) Incidentally it facilitated trading "to arrive" by enabling those
engaged in these transactions to fulfil their contracts by tendering
grain arriving at Chicago on any railroad, whereas formerly shipments had to be made over the particular railroad designated by
the buyer.

The restraint imposed by the rule is less severe than that sustained in Anderson v. United States, 171 U.S. 604. Every board of trade and nearly every trade organization imposes some restraint upon the conduct of business by its members. Those relating to the hours in which business may be done are common; and they make a special appeal where, as here, they tend to shorten the working day or, at least, limit the period of most exacting activity. The decree of the District Court is reversed with directions to dismiss the bill.

Reversed.[37]

206.   (a) The Court states that the legality of a restraint depends on whether it promotes or suppresses competition. Where does this test come from? Is this what the "rule of reason" in *Standard Oil* meant? Does this test avoid the fears expressed by Justice Peckham and Judge Taft?

(b) What benefits or "legitimate purposes" are conceivable and not improbable in *Chicago Board of Trade*? What adverse effects? Consider: (1) "Promote the convenience of members by restricting their hours of business." (2) "Break up a monopoly in that branch of the grain trade acquired by four or five warehousemen in Chicago." (3) "Protect ignorant sellers of 'to arrive' grain from exploitation by those buying at night." (4) "Creation of a public market."

(c) Do the effects noted in ¶b amount to promoting competition on the exchange? Suppressing competition by nonmembers or members during off-hours? What is meant by "competition" in the Court's test?[38]

(d) Should the defendants' arrangement be held unlawful per se? After all, it is price fixing. Unlawful at all? What are the relevant differences between this case and the simple cartels in *Trans-Missouri*, *Addyston Pipe*, and *Joint Traffic*? Which elements of collaboration were necessary for the exchange to operate?

UNITED STATES v. TRENTON POTTERIES CO.
273 U.S. 392 (1927)

Justice STONE. . . . There is no contention here that the verdict was not supported by sufficient evidence that respondents, controlling some 82 per cent of the business of manufacturing and distributing in the United States vitreous pottery [for use in bathrooms

37. McReynolds, J., did not participate.
38. See generally P. Carstensen, The Context of the Hollow Core of Antitrust: The *Chicago Board of Trade* Case and the Meaning of the "Rule of Reason" in Restraint of Trade Analysis, Res. L. & Econ. 1 (1992).

and lavatories] combined to fix prices and to limit sales in interstate commerce. . . .

The question . . . to be considered here is whether the trial judge correctly withdrew from the jury the consideration of the reasonableness of the particular restraints charged. } *Issue*

That only those restraints upon interstate commerce which are unreasonable are prohibited by the Sherman Law was the rule laid down by the opinions of this Court in the *Standard Oil* and *Tobacco* cases. But it does not follow that agreements to fix or maintain prices are reasonable restraints and therefore permitted by the statute, merely because the prices themselves are reasonable. Reasonableness is not a concept of definite and unchanging content. Its meaning necessarily varies in the different fields of the law, because it is used as a convenient summary of the dominant considerations which control in the application of legal doctrines. Our view of what is a reasonable restraint of commerce is controlled by the recognized purpose of the Sherman Law itself. Whether this type of restraint is reasonable or not must be judged in part at least, in the light of its effect on competition, for whatever difference of opinion there may be among economists as to the social and economic desirability of an unrestrained competitive system, it cannot be doubted that the Sherman Law and the judicial decisions interpreting it are based upon the assumption that the public interest is best protected from the evils of monopoly and price control by the maintenance of competition. . . .

The aim and result of every price-fixing agreement, if effective, is the elimination of one form of competition. The power to fix prices, whether reasonably exercised or not, involves power to control the market and to fix arbitrary and unreasonable prices. The reasonable price fixed today may through economic and business changes become the unreasonable price of tomorrow. Once established, it may be maintained unchanged because of the absence of competition secured by the agreement for a price reasonable when fixed. Agreements which create such potential power may well be held to be in themselves unreasonable or unlawful restraints, without the necessity of minute inquiry whether a particular price is reasonable or unreasonable as fixed and without placing on the government in enforcing the Sherman Law the burden of ascertaining from day to day whether it has become unreasonable through the mere variation of economic conditions. Moreover, in the absence of express legislation requiring it, we should hesitate to adopt a construction making the difference between legal and illegal conduct in the field of business relations depend upon so uncertain a test as whether prices are reasonable — a determination which can be satisfactorily made only after a complete survey of our economic organization and a choice between rival philosophies. . . . Thus viewed, the Sherman Law is not only a prohibition against the infliction of a particular type of public injury. It "is a limitation of rights, . . . which may be pushed to evil consequences and therefore restrained." Standard Sanitary Mfg. Co. v. United States, 226 U.S. 20, 49.

That such was the view of this court in deciding the *Standard Oil* and *Tobacco* cases, and that such is the effect of its decisions both before and after those cases, does not seem fairly open to question. . . . [U]niform price-fixing by those controlling in any substantial manner a trade or business in interstate commerce is prohibited by the Sherman Law, despite the reasonableness of the particular prices agreed upon. . . .

Respondents rely upon *Chicago Board of Trade*, in which an agreement by members of the Chicago Board of Trade controlling prices during certain hours of the day in a special class of grain contracts and affecting only a small proportion of the commerce in question was upheld. The purpose and effect of the agreement there was to maintain for a part of each business day the price which had been that day determined by open competition on the floor of the Exchange. That decision, dealing as it did with a regulation of a board of trade, does not sanction a price agreement among competitors in an open market such as is presented here.

The charge of the trial court, viewed as a whole, fairly submitted to the jury the question whether a price-fixing agreement as described in the first count was entered into by the respondents. Whether the prices actually agreed upon were reasonable or unreasonable was immaterial. . . .

It follows that the judgment of the Circuit Court of Appeals must be reversed and the judgment of the District Court reinstated. . . .[39]

207. (a) What rule does the Court adopt? Is it consistent with the rule of reason? Is its view toward "every price-fixing agreement" consistent with that stated in *Chicago Board of Trade?*

(b) What concerns motivate the Court's formulation?

208. *Appalachian Coals v. United States,* 288 U.S. 344, 359-360, 364, 372-374, 376-377 (1933). Appalachian Coals (the "Company") was a combination of 137 producers in the Appalachian territory of Virginia, West Virginia, Kentucky, and Tennessee. They produced 74 percent of the bituminous coal mined in the Appalachian area, 54 percent of that in immediately surrounding areas,

---

39. Van Devanter, Sutherland, and Butler, JJ., dissented. Brandeis, J., did not participate.

and 12 percent of that mined east of the Mississippi River. Share ownership in the Company was in proportion to production. Each producer designated the Company as its exclusive sales agent, which would sell all the coal of its principals at the best prices obtainable and, if all could not be sold, would apportion orders among them. The agreement became effective upon securing membership of a minimum of 70 percent of the commercial tonnage in the territory. The lower court found that other selling agencies with similar control in their territories would be formed if the agreement in this case were deemed permissible. The Company had not yet begun operation at the time of suit.

The Court began by stating that

> The purpose of the Sherman Anti-Trust Act is to prevent undue restraints of interstate commerce, to maintain its appropriate freedom in the public interest, to afford protection from the subversive or coercive influences of monopolistic endeavor. As a charter of freedom, the Act has a generality and adaptability comparable to that found to be desirable in constitutional provisions. It does not go into detailed definitions which might either work injury to legitimate enterprise or through particularization defeat its purposes by providing loopholes for escape. The restrictions the Act imposes are not mechanical or artificial. Its general phrases, interpreted to attain its fundamental objects, set up the essential standard of reasonableness. They call for vigilance in the detection and frustration of all efforts unduly to restrain the free course of interstate commerce, but they do not seek to establish a mere delusive liberty either by making impossible the normal and fair expansion of that commerce or the adoption of reasonable measures to protect it from injurious and destructive practices and to promote competition upon a sound basis.

In applying the Act, the Court cited *Chicago Board of Trade* for the proposition that the elimination of competition among the parties is not in itself enough to condemn the arrangement. The Court then described the depressed condition of the industry as "deplorable," with capacity exceeding 700 million tons to meet a demand of less than 500 million tons. The District Court isolated several problems currently endemic in the industry. The first problem was presented by the presence of "distress coal." This expression described the excess supply of coal which inevitably results from a process of making coal in particular sizes. This manner of production yields a portion of the coal in unwanted sizes, the "distress coal," which nevertheless must be sold. A second problem arose when a producer authorized several agents to sell the same coal and thus led buyers to suppose that the quantity available exceeded the true supply. This practice was termed "pyramiding."

Finally, the court noted the presence of organized buyers and large consumers, which "constitute unfavorable forces." In the eyes of the Court, the Company secured a fair share of the market through more orderly operation. The Court did not view the Company's actions as involving any output limitation. "The interests of producers and consumers are interlinked. When industry is grievously hurt, when producing concerns fail, when unemployment mounts and communities dependent upon profitable production are prostrated, the wells of commerce go dry."

The Court focused its inquiry on the Company's effect on prices. Because ample coal reserves existed and the agreement did not contemplate and could not accomplish the "fixing of market price," but rather would only mitigate recognized evils by producing "fairer price levels" or "more reasonable prices," there was no inconsistency with the public interest. *Trenton Potteries* was distinguished on the ground that the present case did not involve the power or intent to fix prices. Although competition was eliminated among plan members, there were other producers that sold in the territory. In addition, the Court noted that there could be no valid objection under the Sherman Act "if the defendants had eliminated competition between themselves by a complete integration of their mining operations in a single ownership." Therefore, since mere size is not sufficient for condemnation,[40] it follows that "the mere number and extent of production of those engaged in a cooperative endeavor to remedy evils which may exist in an industry, and to improve competitive conditions, should not be regarded as producing illegality."[41]

Appalachian Coals is often regarded today as an aberration of the 1930s, when competition was often deemphasized. Direct government regulation replaced competition in some industries. And competition was widely abandoned during the brief life of the National Recovery Administration, which promulgated industry-formulated codes of "fair competition" that were often codes of noncompetition. There were few government antitrust prosecutions during this period, although by the end of the 1930s opinion had shifted significantly, leading to a surge in antitrust enforcement.[42] The *Socony* opinion, which follows, contains some further discussion of this decade. Although it has long been assumed that the holding of *Appalachian Coals* may have little contemporary relevance, more recent claims relating to fair competition and fair

40. See *United States Steel*, discussed in ¶303d.
41. McReynolds, J., dissented.
42. See R. Posner, A Statistical Study of Antitrust Enforcement, 13 J.L. & Econ. 365 (1970).

prices in the international trade and agricultural contexts invoke notions similar to those articulated in *Appalachian Coals*.[43]

It is also instructive to consider the nature of the agreement and the Court's analysis of it.

(a) Exactly what did defendants do? Would their plan eliminate price competition among themselves? Is the Court's statement that there was no limitation on production consistent with the fact that the Company was instructed to apportion orders of coal because not all production could be sold at the "best" prices?

(b) Would the plan be likely to reduce competition in the bituminous coal market? What would be the effect if producers in other regions formed similar organizations, as the Court suggested was likely in the event this scheme was upheld?

(c) What benefits might be expected to flow from the plan? Are there benefits other than the possible reduction of competition? Was the appointment of a single agent to set prices for all members necessary to achieve any other benefits?[44]

(d) What was defendants' purpose? Did they intend to reduce price competition? If you view the facts as the Court did, may you or must you read *Appalachian Coals* to tolerate price-increasing combinations designed to improve unsatisfactory, depressed prices? Can the Court's approach be reconciled with its decision in *Trenton Potteries*?

UNITED STATES v. SOCONY-VACUUM OIL CO.
310 U.S. 150 (1940)

Justice DOUGLAS. [The indicted defendants were major oil companies that owned, operated, or leased retail service stations in the Midwest, and all but one sold large quantities of gasoline to jobbers, who in turn distributed their purchases to service stations in the area. The bulk of the jobbers' purchases were from the defendants. The price in the sales contracts between the defendants and jobbers

43. In 1986, the Attorney General and Secretary of Commerce proposed legislation entitled The Promoting Competition in Distressed Industries Act, which would have authorized the President, upon a finding by the International Trade Commission that a domestic industry had been seriously injured by increased imports, to limit the application of the merger provisions of the antitrust laws for up to five years, in lieu of import restrictions. A more relaxed cartel policy also is advocated in J. Bower & E. Rhenman, Benevolent Cartels, 63 Harv. Bus. Rev. 124 (1985).

44. See Virginia Excelsior Mills v. FTC, 256 F.2d 538, 541 (4th Cir. 1958) (per se violation; court permits joint selling as long as "each producer reserves, and exercises, independence in pricing, acceptance of orders, production and other material matters").

was made a function of the spot market price, which substantially influenced retail prices in the area.

The evidence and respondents' offers of proof indicated that, beginning in 1926, large quantities of crude oil were produced, driving down the prices of oil and gasoline. State proration laws unsuccessfully attempted to restrict production. Oil unlawfully produced, known as "hot oil," and the "hot gasoline" made from it, sold substantially below the prices for legal oil and legal gasoline, respectively. Independent refiners relying on legal oil were in a precarious situation and had to sell their gasoline as fast as it was produced; this became known as "distress gasoline."

In June 1933, Congress passed the National Industrial Recovery Act, under which a Presidential executive order forbade illegal shipments and promulgated a "code of fair competition" for the petroleum industry. Prices rose sharply but fell again when the Court held the Act unconstitutional in January 1935. Immediately following that decision, there was a renewed influx of hot gasoline into the Midwest, and price wars broke out, affecting all markets.

Defendants first met in February 1935, at which time it was decided that certain major companies would purchase distress gasoline directly from the refiners producing it. A committee was to assemble lists of refiners each month, and the majors were to select "dancing partners" from whom they had responsibility to purchase distress supply. There was no formal contract; rather, they were governed by "an informal gentlemen's agreement or understanding whereby each undertook to perform his share of the joint undertaking." Purchases would be made at the "fair going market price."

The court charged the jury that it was a violation of the Sherman Act for a group to act together with the purpose of raising prices and the power to do so; it was immaterial whether the prices were reasonable or unreasonable or how significant the effect of the combination might be. However, the trial court allowed the jury criminally to convict only if it found beyond a reasonable doubt that the price rise and its continuation were caused by the combination and not exclusively by other factors. The Court of Appeals reversed, holding that the instructions improperly assumed that such a combination was illegal per se, and remanded for a new trial to determine whether the activities promoted rather than impaired fair competitive opportunities.]

In *Trenton Potteries*, this Court sustained a conviction under the Sherman Act where the jury was charged that an agreement on the part of the members of a combination, controlling a substantial part of an industry, upon the prices which the members are to charge for their commodity is in itself an unreasonable restraint of trade without regard to the reasonableness of the prices or the good intentions of the combining units. . . .

But respondents claim that other decisions of this Court afford them adequate defenses to the indictment. Among those on which they place reliance are *Appalachian Coals*; Sugar Institute, Inc. v. United States, 297 U.S. 553; *Maple Flooring*; *Cement Mfrs. Protective Assn.*; *Chicago Board of Trade*; and the *American Tobacco* and *Standard Oil* cases. But we do not think that line of cases is apposite. . . . *Appalachian Coals* is not in point. . . . [I]n reality the only essential thing in common between the instant case and the *Appalachian Coals* case is the presence in each of so-called demoralizing or injurious practices. The methods of dealing with them were quite divergent. In the instant case there were buying programs of distress gasoline which had as their direct purpose and aim the raising and maintenance of spot market prices and of prices to jobbers and consumers in the Mid-Western area, by the elimination of distress gasoline as a market factor. The increase in the spot market prices was to be accomplished by a well organized buying program on that market: regular ascertainment of the amounts of surplus gasoline; assignment of sellers among the buyers; regular purchases at prices which would place and keep a floor under the market. Unlike the plan in the instant case, the plan in the *Appalachian Coals* case was not designed to operate vis-à-vis the general consuming market and to fix the prices on that market. Furthermore, the effect, if any, of that plan on prices was not only wholly incidental but also highly conjectural. For the plan had not then been put into operation. Hence this Court expressly reserved jurisdiction in the District Court to take further proceedings if, inter alia, in "actual operation" the plan proved to be "an undue restraint upon interstate commerce." And as we have seen it would per se constitute such a restraint if price-fixing were involved. . . .

Nor can respondents find sanction in *Chicago Board of Trade* for the buying programs here under attack. That case involved a prohibition on the members of the Chicago Board of Trade from purchasing or offering to purchase between the closing of the session and its opening the next day grains (under a special class of contracts) at a price other than the closing bid. The rule was somewhat akin to rules of an exchange limiting the period of trading, for as stated by this Court the "restriction was upon the period of price-making." No attempt was made to show that the purpose or effect of the rule was to raise or depress prices. The rule affected only a small proportion of the commerce in question. And among its effects was the creation of a public market for grains under that special contract class, where prices were determined competitively and openly. Since it was not aimed at price manipulation or the control of the market prices and since it had "no appreciable effect on general market prices," the rule survived as a reasonable restraint of trade. . . .

Therefore the sole remaining question on this phase of the case is the applicability of the rule of the *Trenton Potteries* case to these facts. Respondents seek to distinguish the *Trenton Potteries* case from the instant one. They assert that in that case the parties substituted an agreed-on price for one determined by competition; that the defendants there had the power and purpose to suppress the play of competition in the determination of the market price; and therefore that the controlling factor in that decision was the destruction of market competition, not whether prices were higher or lower, reasonable or unreasonable. Respondents contend that in the instant case there was no elimination in the spot tank car market of competition which prevented the prices in that market from being made by the play of competition in sales between independent refiners and their jobber and consumer customers; that during the buying programs those prices were in fact determined by such competition; that the purchases under those programs were closely related to or dependent on the spot market prices; that there was no evidence that the purchases of distress gasoline under those programs had any effect on the competitive market price beyond that flowing from the removal of a competitive evil; and that if respondents had tried to do more than free competition from the effect of distress gasoline and to set an arbitrary non-competitive price through their purchases, they would have been without power to do so.

But we do not deem those distinctions material. In the first place, there was abundant evidence that the combination had the purpose to raise prices. And likewise, there was ample evidence that the buying programs at least contributed to the price rise and the stability of the spot markets, and to increases in the price of gasoline sold in the Mid-Western area during the indictment period. That other factors also may have contributed to that rise and stability of the markets is immaterial. . . . So far as cause and effect are concerned it is sufficient in this type of case if the buying programs of the combination resulted in a price rise and market stability which but for them would not have happened. For this reason the charge to the jury that the buying programs must have "caused" the price rise and its continuance was more favorable to respondents than they could have required. Proof that there was a conspiracy, that its purpose was to raise prices, and that it caused or contributed to a price rise is proof of the actual consummation or execution of a conspiracy under §1 of the Sherman Act.

Secondly, the fact that sales on the spot markets were still governed by some competition is of no consequence. For it is indisputable that that competition was restricted through the removal by respondents of a part of the supply which but for the buying programs would have been a factor in determining the going prices on those markets. But the vice of the conspiracy was not merely the restriction of supply of gasoline by removal of a surplus. As we have said, this was a well organized program. The timing and strategic placement of the buying orders for distress gasoline played an important and significant role. Buying orders were carefully placed so as to remove the distress gasoline from weak hands. Purchases were timed. Sellers were assigned to the buyers so that regular outlets for distress gasoline would be available. The whole scheme was carefully planned and executed to the end that distress gasoline would not overhang the markets and depress them at any time. And as a result of the payment of fair going market prices a floor was placed and kept under the spot markets. Prices rose and jobbers and consumers in the Mid-Western area paid more for their gasoline than they would have paid but for the conspiracy. Competition was not eliminated from the markets; but it was clearly curtailed, since restriction of the supply of gasoline, the timing and placement of the purchases under the buying programs and the placing of a floor under the spot markets obviously reduced the play of the forces of supply and demand.

The elimination of so-called competitive evils is no legal justification for such buying programs. The elimination of such conditions was sought primarily for its effect on the price structures. Fairer competitive prices, it is claimed, resulted when distress gasoline was removed from the market. But such defense is typical of the protestations usually made in price-fixing cases. Ruinous competition, financial disaster, evils of price cutting and the like appear throughout our history as ostensible justifications for price-fixing. If the so-called competitive abuses were to be appraised here, the reasonableness of prices would necessarily become an issue in every price-fixing case. In that event the Sherman Act would soon be emasculated; its philosophy would be supplanted by one which is wholly alien to a system of free competition; it would not be the charter of freedom which its framers intended.

The reasonableness of prices has no constancy due to the dynamic quality of the business facts underlying price structures. Those who fixed reasonable prices today would perpetuate unreasonable prices tomorrow, since those prices would not be subject to continuous administrative supervision and readjustment in light of changed conditions. Those who controlled the prices would control or effectively dominate the market. And those who were in that strategic position would have it in their power to destroy or drastically impair the competitive system. But the thrust of the rule is deeper and reaches more than monopoly power. Any combination which tampers with price structures is engaged in an unlawful activity. Even though the members of the price-fixing group were in no position to control the market, to the extent that they raised, lowered, or stabilized prices they would be directly interfering with the free play of market forces. The Act places all such schemes beyond the pale and protects that vital part of our economy against any degree of interference. Congress has not left us the determination of whether or not particular price-fixing schemes are wise or unwise, healthy or destructive. It has not permitted the age-old cry of ruinous competition and competitive evils to be a defense to price-fixing conspiracies. It has no more allowed genuine or fancied competitive abuses as a legal justification for such schemes than it has the good intentions of the members of the combination. If such a shift is to be made, it must be done by the Congress. Certainly Congress has not left us with any such choice. Nor has the Act created or authorized the creation of any special exception in favor of the oil industry. Whatever may be its peculiar problems and characteristics, the Sherman Act, so far as price-fixing agreements are concerned, establishes one uniform rule applicable to all industries alike. There was accordingly no error in the refusal to charge that in order to convict the jury must find that the resultant prices were raised and maintained at "high, arbitrary and non-competitive levels." The charge in the indictment to that effect was surplusage.

Nor is it important that the prices paid by the combination were not fixed in the sense that they were uniform and inflexible. Price-fixing as used in the *Trenton Potteries* case has no such limited meaning. An agreement to pay or charge rigid, uniform prices would be an illegal agreement under the Sherman Act. But so would agreements to raise or lower prices whatever machinery for price-fixing was used.... Hence, prices are fixed within the meaning of the *Trenton Potteries* case if the range within which purchases or sales will be made is agreed upon, if the prices paid or charged are to be at a certain level or on ascending or descending scales, if they are to be uniform, or if by various formulae they are related to the market prices. They are fixed because they are agreed upon. And the fact that, as here, they are fixed at the fair going market price is immaterial. For purchases at or under the market are one species of price-fixing. In this case, the result was to place a floor under the market—a floor which served the function of increasing the stability and firmness of market prices. That was repeatedly characterized in this case as stabilization. But in terms of market operations stabilization is but one form of manipulation. And market manipulation in its various manifestations is implicitly an artificial stimulus applied to (or at times a brake on) market prices, a force which distorts those prices, a factor which prevents the determination of those prices by free competition alone. . . .

Under the Sherman Act a combination formed for the purpose and with the effect of raising, depressing, fixing, pegging, or stabilizing the price of a commodity in interstate or foreign commerce is illegal per se. *rule*

Where the machinery for price-fixing is an agreement on the prices to be charged or paid for the commodity in the interstate or foreign channels of trade, the power to fix prices exists if the combination has control of a substantial part of the commerce in that commodity. Where the means for price-fixing are purchases or sales of the commodity in a market operation or, as here, purchases of a part of the supply of the commodity for the purpose of keeping it from having a depressive effect on the markets, such power may be found to exist though the combination does not control a substantial part of the commodity. In such a case that power may be established if as a result of market conditions, the resources available to the combinations, the timing and the strategic placement of orders and the like, effective means are at hand to accomplish the desired objective. But there may be effective influence over the market though the group in question does not control it. Price-fixing agreements may have utility to members of the group though the power possessed or exerted falls far short of domination and control. Monopoly power . . . is not the only power which the Act strikes down, as we have said. Proof that a combination was formed for the purpose of fixing prices and that it caused them to be fixed or contributed to that result is proof of the completion of a price-fixing conspiracy under §1 of the Act.[59] The

---

59. Under this indictment proof that prices in the Mid-Western area were raised as a result of the activities of the combination was essential, since sales of gasoline by respondents at the increased prices in that area were necessary in order to establish jurisdiction in the Western District of Wisconsin. Hence we have necessarily treated the case as one where exertion of the power to fix prices (i.e., the actual fixing of prices) was an ingredient of the offense. But that does not mean that both a purpose and a power to fix prices are necessary for the establishment of a conspiracy under §1 of the Sherman Act. That would be true if power or ability to commit an offense was necessary in order to convict a person of conspiring to commit it. But it is well established that a person "may be guilty of conspiring, although incapable of committing the objective offense." United States v. Rabinowich, 238 U.S. 78, 86. And it is likewise well settled that conspiracies under the Sherman Act are not dependent on any overt act other than the act of conspiring. Nash v. United States, 229 U.S. 373, 378. It is the "contract, combination . . . or conspiracy, in restraint of trade or commerce" which §1 of the Act strikes down, whether the concerted activity be wholly nascent or abortive on the one hand, or successful on the other. See *Trenton Potteries*. Cf. Retail Lumber Dealers' Assn. v. State, 95 Miss. 337. And the amount of interstate or foreign trade involved is not material (Montague & Co. v. Lowry, 193 U.S. 38), since §1 of the Act brands as illegal the character of the restraint not the amount of commerce affected. Steers

indictment in this case charged that this combination had that purpose and effect. And there was abundant evidence to support it. Hence the existence of power on the part of members of the combination to fix prices was but a conclusion from the finding that the buying programs caused or contributed to the rise and stability of prices.

As to knowledge or acquiescence of officers of the Federal government little need be said. The fact that Congress through utilization of the precise methods here employed could seek to reach the same objectives sought by respondents does not mean that respondents or any other group may do so without specific Congressional authority. Admittedly no approval of the buying programs was obtained under the National Industrial Recovery Act prior to its termi-

---

v. United States, 192 F. 1, 5; Patterson v. United States, 222 F. 599, 618, 619. In view of these considerations a conspiracy to fix prices violates §1 of the Act though no overt act is shown, though it is not established that the conspirators had the means available for accomplishment of their objective, and though the conspiracy embraced but a part of the interstate or foreign commerce in the commodity. Whatever may have been the status of price-fixing agreements at common law (Allen, Criminal Conspiracies in Restraint of Trade at Common Law, 23 Harv. L. Rev. 531) the Sherman Act has a broader application to them than the common law prohibitions or sanctions. See *Trans-Missouri.* Price-fixing agreements may or may not be aimed at complete elimination of price competition. The group making those agreements may or may not have power to control the market. But the fact that the group cannot control the market prices does not necessarily mean that the agreement as to prices has no utility to the members of the combination. The effectiveness of price-fixing agreements is dependent on many factors, such as competitive tactics, position in the industry, the formula underlying price policies. Whatever economic justification particular price-fixing agreements may be thought to have, the law does not permit an inquiry into their reasonableness. They are all banned because of their actual or potential threat to the central nervous system of the economy. See Handler, Federal Anti-Trust Laws — A Symposium (1931), pp. 91 et seq.

The existence or exertion of power to accomplish the desired objective (*United States Steel*; United States v. International Harvester Co., 274 U.S. 693, 708, 709) becomes important only in cases where the offense charged is the actual monopolizing of any part of trade or commerce in violation of §2 of the Act. An intent and a power to produce the result which the law condemns are then necessary. As stated in Swift & Co. v. United States, 196 U.S. 375, 396, ". . . when that intent and the consequent dangerous probability exists, this statute, like many others, and like the common law in some cases, directs itself against dangerous probability as well as against the completed result." But the crime under §1 is legally distinct from that under §2 (United States v. MacAndrews & Forbes Co., 149 F. 836; United States v. Buchalter, 88 F.2d 625) though the two sections overlap in the sense that a monopoly under §2 is a species of restraint of trade under §1. *Standard Oil*; Patterson v. United States, [222 F. at] 620. Only a confusion between the nature of the offenses under those two sections (see United States v. Nelson, 52 F. 646; United States v. Patterson, 55 F. 605; Chesapeake & O. Fuel Co. v. United States, 115 F. 610) would lead to the conclusion that power to fix prices was necessary for proof of a price-fixing conspiracy under §1. Cf. State v. Eastern Coal Co., 29 R.I. 254; State v. Scollard, 126 Wash. 335.

nation on June 16, 1935, (§2(c)) which would give immunity to respondents from prosecution under the Sherman Act. Though employees of the government may have known of those programs and winked at them or tacitly approved them, no immunity would have thereby been obtained. . . . Accordingly we conclude that the Circuit Court of Appeals erred in reversing the judgments on this ground. . . . [45]

209. (a) What is *Socony*'s rule?

(b) Does its famous footnote 59 indicate that power over price is presumed to exist or that it is irrelevant?[46] To assess the latter question, consider the situation in which all local producers agree to sell at a fixed price but the market is national and the local producers are but a modest fraction of the market. Illegal under *Socony*? Must effects be demonstrated? Would power be a sufficient basis to presume effects? What do you suppose is the purpose or intent of these producers? Should the law presume power or effect from intent?

(c) Is the arrangement in this case a more direct instance of price fixing than that in *Appalachian Coals*?[47] Than that in *Chicago Board*? Does the Court effectively distinguish those cases?[48]

(d) Compare the vision of the economy and market forces expressed in this case with that expressed in *Appalachian Coals*.

210. At a recent class reunion, the managing partner in the law firm of Billings & Prophet was complaining to classmates about the outrageously high salaries paid to associates these days and the inevitable increases to follow in the upcoming year. Alan Alum, a big partner in another leading firm in the same city, suggested that they all simply agree not to increase associates' salaries for the next few years. These conversations continued with partners at the other

45. Roberts and McReynolds, JJ., dissented. Hughes, C.J., and Murphy, J., did not participate.

46. Some economists have argued that the buying programs in *Socony* could not have fixed the price of gasoline. See D. Johnson, Property Rights to Cartel Rents: The Socony-Vacuum Story, 34 J.L. & Econ. 177 (1991).

47. Is the agreement in this case definite enough to be a contract in the usual sense? For purposes of Sherman Act §1? These issues are explored further in Ch. 2C.

48. Only Justice Stone was in the majority in both *Appalachian Coals* and *Socony*. Of the other two Justices involved in both, Justice Roberts went from the majority in the first to the dissenting group in *Socony*, and, interestingly enough, Justice McReynolds — the only dissenter in *Appalachian Coals* — also dissented in *Socony*. Two of the Justices in *Trenton*, including Justice Stone, who wrote that opinion, were also in the majority in *Appalachian Coals*, while only one remaining Justice from the *Trenton* majority dissented in the latter case. Overall, there is little evidence from these alignments to suggest that, during this time period, either the positions of Justices who were on the Court were unchanged or that many Justices necessarily thought the cases distinguishable.

large firms in their city over the next few weeks, resulting in an agreement to cap associates' salaries, passing some of the savings on to clients through lower billing rates.

(a) Illegal under *Socony*? Is it a defense that prices are lower and thus necessarily more reasonable?[49]

(b) Suppose instead that the firms reach an agreement on billings alone, such that each will charge no more than $75 per hour for a first-year associate. Is this price maximum legal? What do you suppose might be their motive in entering into such an arrangement?[50]

211. There is one local smelter of a rare metal that is made in small quantities from huge amounts of ore mined by a large number of local companies. The smelter faces competition in the national market from smelters located elsewhere, but it is too costly for local mines to ship their ore to any firm but the local smelter. The local smelter takes advantage of the situation by offering lower than competitive prices for ore. In response to this exploitation, the local mines form a joint sales agency so that they can bargain with the smelter as a unified group.

(a) Is this combination desirable?[51]

49. This is the case of monopsony, which is the mirror image of monopoly: A single buyer depresses price and purchases a smaller quantity than is the case with competition on the buyers' side of the market. This is developed further in a more complex context in note 51. See Reid Bros. Logging Co. v. Ketchikan Pulp Co., 1981 Trade Cas. ¶64228 (W.D. Wash.), aff'd, 692 F.2d 1292 (9th Cir.), cert. denied, 464 U.S. 916 (1983) (violation where defendants artificially depressed prices by agreeing not to compete against each other in bidding to purchase timber and logs). Compare Ch. 2B, note 22 (cases upholding arrangements where an insurance company acts as a single buyer on behalf of insureds). For further analysis of monopsony, see R. Blair & J. Harrison, Public Policy: Cooperative Buying, Monopsony Power, and Antitrust Policy, 86 Nw. U.L. Rev. 331 (1992); J. Jacobson & G. Dorman, Joint Purchasing, Monopsony and Antitrust, 36 Antitr. Bull. 1 (1991).

50. Maximum price fixing is addressed in *Maricopa*, Ch. 2B, which also contains a discussion of the earlier Supreme Court case on the subject, *Kiefer-Stewart.*

51. Some of the economic implications of this situation are portrayed in the following diagram.

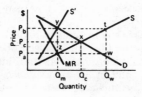

Curve *D* represents the smelter's demand for ore (and is, of course, a function of the demand for the product it sells in a highly competitive market). It slopes downward to indicate the usual fact that smelters will want more of the product at lower prices. Curve *MR* describes the miners' marginal revenue and indicates how

(b) Is it lawful?

(c) If the local smelter were instead a cartel of local smelters or an illegally created monopoly, should "self-defense" be recognized?

212. Per se rules. (a) *Rationale*. You have already seen that price fixing among competitors has been declared to be unlawful per se. The rationale for so hostile a legal approach has also been developed. To review it, reconsider the sorts of questions raised in ¶201i.

---

their aggregate revenue responds to increasing sales to the smelters. See ¶112, note 29. Curve S is the supply curve for ore, indicating the amount of ore that competitive miners would find it profitable to supply at each price. It slopes upward to indicate the usual fact that higher prices are needed to induce a larger supply. The S curve is the summation of the several miners' marginal cost curves. Viewing the suppliers collectively, it is the local mining marginal cost curve. Curve S' is derived from it and indicates the incremental sums that the smelter will have to pay for ore as it increases its demand for ore; it is the marginal ore cost to the smelter (as compared with S which represents the marginal cost to the miners of devoting additional resources to the production of ore). To reduce clutter in the diagram, the curves have been drawn such that Q_m describes both the S'-D and the S-MR intersections. These intersections need not occur at a single quantity, however, because the D (and MR) curves are entirely independent of the S (and S') curves.

(1) When both smelters and miners are acting competitively, the D-S intersection at point x governs and indicates output Q_c and price P_c.

(2) When miners are competitive but there is only one buyer or a buying cartel, production will occur where the buyer's marginal cost (indicated by S') equals the value of the ore (indicated by D). This is referred to as the monopsony result. See note 49. The S'-D intersection at point y indicates quantity Q_m, which competing miners are willing to supply at price P_a (indicated by the S-Q_m intersection at point z). Note that buyers acting individually would demand the larger quantity of ore Q_w when the ore price is P_a (indicated by the D-P_a intersection at point w). But that supply would not be forthcoming at the monopsony price P_a.

(3) When the buying side of the market is competitive but miners sell through a price-fixing cartel, the miners will produce up to the point where incremental revenue just equals incremental cost. This happens to occur at output Q_m (indicated by the S-MR intersection at point z). Competing buyers would pay price P_b for that quantity (indicated by the D-Q_m intersection at point y). At that price, miners acting individually would want to supply Q_w (indicated by the S-P_b intersection at point t). To maintain the cartel selling price, the miners must apportion sales quotas among themselves. This is the standard cartel case.

(4) Where both a miners' selling cartel and a producer's monopsony or buying cartel lack alternative outlets or sources, the buyer and seller groups will bargain with each other. They will find it in their mutual interest to agree upon the quantity of ore that maximizes their joint profits, which is quantity Q_c. Their disagreement would focus on the division of the bargaining surplus. Of course, if bargaining is imperfect (due, say, to each party's uncertainty about the marginal value of ore to the other party), the result may not be as desirable.

(5) It may be the case that a countervailing power cartel would reduce competition in other markets. For example, the cartel of mining companies might create monopsony power in the local labor market or, in other instances, a buying cartel may create monopoly power in the market in which the buyers sell. See ¶201h and note 27.

(1) Is price fixing ever beneficial? (2) Are some pernicious effects likely to be found in all or most manifestations of price fixing? (3) If price fixing is permitted in at least some cases, is any follow-up regulation required? Are the available institutions enforcing antitrust laws suitable for that purpose? (4) Are those enforcement agencies likely to be able to make reliable judgments in particular cases about the benefits of price fixing, the degree of harm, or the continuing adjustments necessary if ill effects are not to get out of hand? (5) Is an absolute prohibition particularly useful here to dissuade potential price fixers, either by the clarity of the prohibition or by the severe sanctions that accompany a categorical prohibition?

(b) *Meaning: scope of inquiry.* What does it mean to say that a particular practice, such as price fixing, is unlawful per se? Does it mean that illegality does not depend on the proof of anticompetitive effects in the particular case or proof of power to bring about such effects or proof of an intent to do so? Does it rather mean — or does it also mean — that no exculpatory justification will ever be considered?

(c) *Meaning: coverage of category.* Whenever X is declared to be unlawful per se in any of the senses just noted, one must often determine whether conduct challenged in a particular case falls within the X category. Difficulties are at least three. First, the initial definition of X may be uncertain, vague, or potentially all-embracing. Second, although apparently clear, at least at its core, the definition of any X may be difficult to apply to the particular conduct before the tribunal. Third, the conduct challenged in some instances will appear to fit within the X per se pigeonhole, which implies that the conduct is unlawful. The court will hesitate to reach this result, however, with respect to activities that have not yet been analyzed by any court and determined to be harmful in the generality of cases. This is particularly true when it is apparent, at least prima facie, that there may be some good reason to permit the practice. In such a situation, the court will feel a strong impulse (1) to believe that the particular conduct before it is not really X at all or (2) to create an exception if the legal classification seems ordained by linguistic analysis.

The issues raised in the latter two subparagraphs have in fact provided the impetus for much of the post-*Socony* development of many branches of antitrust law. The material in the following section — as well as that in Chapter 2E on concerted refusals to deal — will address these issues further in the context of Sherman Act §1.[52]

---

52. Per se rules will also be addressed in other contexts, most notably tying. See Ch. 4B.

2B. MODERN APPLICATIONS: DETERMINING WHICH RESTRAINTS ARE REASONABLE

213. Introduction. After the broad pronouncement in *Socony*, one might have thought that any agreement among competitors having any effect on price would be prohibited. Yet it was clear from the earliest Sherman Act cases examined in Chapter 2A that some restraints having such an effect — for example, agreements not to compete among partners or by one selling a business — were permitted. Neither *Trenton Potteries* nor *Socony* purported to reverse *Standard Oil*'s rule of reason. Many of the cases in the remainder of this chapter and elsewhere in the book focus on whether a particular set of practices is to be prohibited per se or governed under a more open-ended, case-by-case rule of reason approach and what such an approach should entail. This section explores more recent "price-fixing" cases in which the desirability of per se prohibition in a particular situation was called into question, but in a manner not necessarily inconsistent with a general prohibition of pure cartel behavior.

In reading the following cases, bear in mind three kinds of questions. First, should the challenged conduct be condemned out of hand and without further inquiry because it fixes prices? Is there a reasonable likelihood that conduct of this kind can benefit the economy? Are pernicious effects likely to accompany most concrete manifestations of this kind of conduct? If not, is it likely that any harm that does occur will be significant? If significant, can its concrete manifestations be detected fairly readily? If pernicious effects are likely to be frequent, an absolute prohibition might be justifiable whenever benefits are infrequent or benefits likely to occur most frequently are relatively small. If any significant benefits that do occur are readily detectable, they might be considered as a limited exception to a general prohibition. Are the dangers attending this kind of conduct so great and the temptations to engage in it so strong that the public must be protected by an absolute rule discouraging this conduct both by the clarity of its prohibition and by the severe sanctions with which we comfortably enforce clear rules? Does toleration of the conduct imply a burden of continuing supervision? Is there any agency readily available to carry that burden?

Second, if further inquiry is to be made in the particular case, who should bear the burdens of proof and persuasion? (1) When harm is unknown, conceivable but speculative, not improbable, probable but small, or very likely to occur and be serious? (2) When benefits are not claimed, are claimed but speculative and small, or are probable and significant? (3) When socially desirable objectives might conceivably be achieved by means substantially less danger-ous to competition but where those less restrictive alternatives are not mentioned or explored in the record, might be substantially more burdensome to the parties, or are proved to be much more burdensome? Moreover, if the general rule is a per se prohibition, justified in significant part by the desire to avoid complex, costly, and time-consuming inquiry, what showing should be required be-fore a court should feel compelled to consider further information?

Third, how should we decide the actual case, having regard both to the general characteristics of the type of behavior involved and also to its immediate manifestation? And how should the rule be formulated for future cases?

214. Cartel variations. As already illustrated by cases such as *Socony*, agreements limiting competition among members do not always involve the direct fixing of a group price. Because doubts concerning an across-the-board prohibition have often arisen in cases involving other sorts of restrictions, a few of the most impor-tant variations — many the subject of the cases to follow — will be explored briefly at the outset.

(a) *Allocating markets.* Simple price fixing allows each competitor to sell at the monopoly price without the fear that others will undercut that price, thereby taking away one's customers. Territo-rial agreements and other forms of specialization sometimes permit the same result. If landscaping companies divide a region into ex-clusive territories, each would face no competition as to the cus-tomers it served and thus would be free to charge the monopoly price.

In some instances, a division of product or geographic markets among competitors might permit more efficient production or marketing. Competitors may agree to abandon some products or areas and concentrate on others in order to achieve economies of scale and specialization. Greater efficiency through the more ratio-nal organization of production is a favorite argument in defense of cartels. But an agreement typically would be unnecessary to achieve such efficiencies; profitable specialization, for example, will usually be pursued by each firm without agreeing with its rivals.[1] Speaking generally, the courts have usually subjected horizontal market divi-sion agreements to the same rules as price-fixing agreements.[2]

(b) *Other limits on price competition.* As we have seen, competitors might agree on minimum or maximum prices, buying or selling

1. Cf. ¶¶201d-h.
2. Related problems will be addressed in Ch. 4A.

prices, limitation of their own output, or removal from the market of "excess" supply in the hands of others. Competitors also have been known to avoid competitive bidding[3] or to agree on formulae for the allocation of business or the determination of price. They might agree to rotate bids (where they take turns submitting low bids); circulate price lists;[4] charge published prices[5] or at least begin bargaining from list prices;[6] fix trade-in allowances,[7] discounts,[8] or mark-ups; or set the price spread between premium and lesser products. And although there are important differences, price-fixing effects may be implicit in the use of joint buying or selling agents[9] and other forms of joint ventures considered later in this section.

UNITED STATES v. TOPCO ASSOCIATES
405 U.S. 596 (1972)

Justice MARSHALL. [The United States sued to enjoin Topco Associates, Inc. (Topco) from violating §1 of the Sherman Act. Topco is a cooperative association of approximately 25 small to medium sized regional supermarket chains that operate in 33 states. It was founded in the 1940s by a group of small, local chains, which desired to cooperate to obtain high quality merchandise under private labels in order to compete more effectively with larger national and regional chains.[10] By 1967, sales of Topco members exceeded $2.3 billion; only A & P, Safeway, and Kroger boasted larger figures. In their respective areas, member chains had market shares ranging

3. Illustrations include *Engineers*, later in this section, and *Reid Bros. Logging Co.*, Ch. 2A, note 49.
4. Goldfarb v. Virginia St. Bar, 421 U.S. 773 (1975) (county bar association fixed prices unlawfully by suggesting fees with intimation that undercutting would be grounds for discipline).
5. United States v. American Linseed Oil Co., 262 U.S. 371 (1923).
6. Plymouth Dealers Assn. v. United States, 279 F.2d 128 (9th Cir. 1960).
7. Id.
8. Catalano v. Target Sales, 446 U.S. 643, 648 (1980) (reversing, per curiam, decision failing to find that an agreement to eliminate short-term trade credit was per se illegal price fixing; "interest-free credit for a period of time is equivalent to giving a discount" on price).
9. Recall *Appalachian Coals*, ¶208.
10. The founding members thought that part of their difficulty was attributable to the ability of large chains to develop private label programs. Private label products, unlike standard brand name products, are generally identified by and sold only in particular stores. Using private label products, it was thought that large chains achieved cost economies in purchasing, transportation, warehousing, promotion, and advertising as well as enabling them to bargain more favorably with national brand manufacturers. — eds.

from 1.5 to 16 percent, with 6 percent being average. Although relevant figures for the national chains were unavailable, Topco members were frequently in as strong a competitive position. This strength was due, in some measure, to the success of Topco brand products.

The agreement among member chains limited each to selling Topco products in a designated territory. Most licenses were exclusive, and even those allowing some overlap generally resulted in de facto exclusivity. The district court concluded that, even though this agreement prevented competition in Topco brand products, the increased ability of Topco members to compete with others outweighed any anticompetitive effect.]

III . . .

It is only after considerable experience with certain business relationships that courts classify them as per se violations of the Sherman Act. . . . One of the classic examples of a per se violation of §1 is an agreement between competitors at the same level of the market structure to allocate territories in order to minimize competition. Such concerted action is usually termed a "horizontal" restraint, in contradistinction to combinations of persons at different levels of the market structure, e.g., manufacturers and distributors, which are termed "vertical" restraints. This Court has reiterated time and time again that "[h]orizontal territorial limitations . . . are naked restraints of trade with no purpose except stifling of competition." White Motor Co. v. United States, 372 U.S. 253, 263 (1963). Such limitations are per se violations of the Sherman Act. See *Addyston Pipe*; United States v. National Lead Co., 332 U.S. 319 (1947); Timken Roller Bearing Co. v. United States, 341 U.S. 593 (1951); *Northern Pacific*; Citizen Publishing v. United States, 394 U.S. 131 (1969); United States v. Sealy, Inc., 388 U.S. 350 (1967); United States v. Arnold, Schwinn & Co., 388 U.S. 365, 390 (1967) (Stewart, J., concurring in part and dissenting in part); Serta Associates Inc. v. United States, 393 U.S. 534 (1969), aff'g, 296 F. Supp. 1121, 1128 (N.D. Ill. 1968).

We think that it is clear that the restraint in this case is a horizontal one, and, therefore, a per se violation of §1. . . .

If a decision is to be made to sacrifice competition in one portion of the economy for greater competition in another portion, this too is a decision which must be made by Congress and not by private forces or by the courts. Private forces are too keenly aware of their own interests in making such decisions and courts are ill-equipped and ill-situated for such decision-making. To analyze, interpret, and evaluate the myriad of competing interests and the endless data which would surely be brought to bear on such decisions, and to make the delicate judgment on the relative values to society of competitive areas of the economy, the judgment of the elected representatives of the people is required. . . .

[Justice Blackmun, concurring in the result, expressed dissatisfaction with the likely consequences of the Court's decision but felt that the per se rule was "so firmly established by the Court that, at this late date, I could not oppose it. Relief, if any is to be forthcoming, apparently must be by way of legislation."

Chief Justice Burger, in dissent, rejected the notion that the per se rule was so entrenched, primarily because this case did not involve price fixing as part of the allegations. In contrast, many prior horizontal market division cases typically involved pricing fixing as well, and restraints were designed solely to suppress competition rather than being ancillary, as here, to the creation of the new private label product line that aided Topco members in competing with large grocery chains. Given his view that the Court was "establishing a new per se rule," he thought it necessary to consider the situation in the case. The restraints should be permitted because "the invalidation of the restraints here at issue 'would not increase competition in Topco private label brands.' Indeed, the District Court seemed to believe that it would, on the contrary, lead to the likely demise of those brands in time." He referred to the fact that "[t]here was no such thing as a Topco line of products until this cooperative was formed" and that the endeavor was necessary to make economically feasible quality control, purchasing large quantities at bulk prices, and the like.][11]

215. (a) How is competition threatened by the exclusive territorial arrangement? Was the Court bound to apply the per se prohibition to the arrangement in *Topco*? Regardless of prior cases involving territorial restrictions, does *Socony* command such a result?[12]

(b) If the *Topco* restrictions were to be tested by a rule of reason, what should be the result in the case?[13] Consider which of the proffered justifications applied to the exclusive territories and

---

11. On remand, the district court entered a decree permitting Topco to designate areas of prime responsibility for each member, designate the locations for which trademark licenses are issued, determine the warehouse locations to which Topco will ship, and make arrangements for reasonable compensation for the goodwill developed by one member when another member sells Topco products in its area. The government objected. United States v. Topco Assoc., 319 F. Supp. 103 (N.D. Ill.), aff'd mem., 414 U.S. 801 (1973).

12. After reading Ch. 2E, consider the relevance of *Associated Press*, which was not cited in any opinion in *Topco*.

13. Reconsider the answer to this question after studying the *Sylvania* decision in Ch. 4A. See W. Baxter & D. Kessler, Toward a Consistent Theory of the Welfare Analysis of Agreements, 47 Stan. L. Rev. 615 (1995).

which to the mere existence of Topco. Did the defendants limit any significant competition that would otherwise have existed?[14] Why might the defendants have created their joint venture even if territorial limitations had been prohibited? Can you imagine other means of accomplishing their purposes that do not require territorial restrictions?[15] What seems probable on the evidence before you?

(c) Can one permit territorial agreements under exceptional circumstances without destroying the meaning and usefulness of a per se rule concerning territorial division? Would it be meaningful to state "Territorial agreements are generally unlawful per se"? Is "generally" consistent with "per se"? See ¶212.[16]

(d) Several members of the *Topco* Court invited new legislation to deal with the immediate problem. Sketch a draft of such legislation. How would it differ from the general provisions of Sherman Act §1?

(e) The primary function of the Federal Communications Act was to eliminate interference on the airwaves. To prevent chaos before such federal regulation, suppose that numerous radio stations had agreed among themselves on the frequencies (and power of each broadcaster) to be allocated to particular territories. Would such a division of territory have been unlawful under *Topco*?

(f) One of the reasons Topco was formed was to achieve the advantages of large-scale buying. The Court did not explicitly assess the joint buying agency aspect of Topco's activities. Is that arrange-

---

14. The government argued that limiting the ability of a Topco member to sell Topco brands in adjoining areas prevented any expansion into another member's territory. The district court believed that Topco did not have an appreciable influence on such expansion decisions. Can this be true, as the defendants argued, if the possession of a private brand is crucial to effective competition in the supermarket business?

15. In an earlier, similar case, United States v. Sealy, 388 U.S. 350 (1967), the Court found per se illegal the use of price fixing and exclusive territories in Sealy's licenses of mattress manufacturers to make and sell under its name and trademarks. Sealy, like Topco, was entirely owned by its licensees, who in turn carried out the production. See W. Mueller & F. Geithman, An Empirical Test of the Free Rider and Market Power Hypotheses, 73 Rev. Econ. & Stat. 301 (1991) (finding that Sealy territorial restraints decreased output and increased prices).

16. Union Processing Corp. v. Atkin, 465 U.S. 1038 (1984) (three Justices dissent from denial of certiorari, stating that the agreement between two firms to establish only one facility in a region on the ground that there was insufficient business in the area to support two operations was a per se illegal horizontal division of markets under *Topco*; irrelevant that parties still compete in other respects); General Leaseways v. National Truck Leasing Assn., 744 F.2d 588 (7th Cir. 1984) (truck renters association forbids members from doing business at other than specified locations — except under a different name — and forbids affiliation with other operations; per se illegal notwithstanding efficiency claims because horizontal market division is not ancillary to provision of services).

ment unlawful? Should it be? Would it be unlawful price fixing for Topco members to realize further savings by engaging in joint advertising of weekend specials, which would require that each store agree to adhere to the advertised prices during the period of the sale?

216. ***Palmer v. BRG of Georgia,*** 498 U.S. 46 (1990). In 1976, Harcourt Brace Jovanovich Legal and Professional Publications (HBJ) began offering a Georgia bar review course in direct competition with BRG, the only main provider of bar review courses in Georgia. In 1980, HBJ gave BRG an exclusive license to market HBJ's material in Georgia, and they agreed that HBJ would not compete with BRG in Georgia and that BRG would not compete with HBJ outside of Georgia. The agreement gave HBJ a share of BRG's revenues. Immediately after the agreement, the price of BRG's course rose from $150 to over $400. The Court, in a per curiam opinion, held the arrangement to be a per se illegal allocation of markets, quoting *Topco.*

(a) How might the territorial agreement in *Palmer* have been anticompetitive?

(b) Suppose instead that HBJ had never entered Georgia and instead had simply produced materials and licensed them to BRG, under the same terms as in *Palmer* (that is, including the territorial restriction). Would this license have been per se illegal? Illegal at all?

BROADCAST MUSIC v. COLUMBIA BROADCASTING SYSTEM
441 U.S. 1 (1979)

Justice WHITE. . . . This case involves an action under the antitrust and copyright laws brought by respondent Columbia Broadcasting System, Inc. (CBS), against petitioners, American Society of Composers, Authors and Publishers (ASCAP) and Broadcast Music, Inc. (BMI), and their members and affiliates. The basic question presented is whether the issuance by ASCAP and BMI to CBS of blanket licenses to copyrighted musical compositions at fees negotiated by them is price fixing per se unlawful under the antitrust laws. *— Issue*

I

CBS operates one of three national commercial television networks, supplying programs to approximately 200 affiliated stations and telecasting approximately 7,500 network programs per year. Many, but not all, of these programs make use of copyrighted music recorded on the soundtrack. CBS also owns television and radio stations in various cities. . . .

Since 1897 the copyright laws have vested in the owner of a copyrighted musical composition the exclusive right to perform the work publicly for profit, but the legal right is not self-enforcing. In 1914 Victor Herbert and a handful of other composers organized ASCAP because those who performed copyrighted music for profit were so numerous and widespread, and most performances so fleeting, that as a practical matter it was impossible for the many individual copyright owners to negotiate with and license the users and to detect unauthorized uses. "ASCAP was organized as a 'clearinghouse' for copyright owners and users to solve these problems" associated with the licensing of music. As ASCAP operates today, its 22,000 members grant it nonexclusive rights to license nondramatic performances of their works, and ASCAP issues licenses and distributes royalties to copyright owners in accordance with a schedule reflecting the nature and amount of the use of their music and other factors.

BMI, a nonprofit corporation owned by members of the broadcasting industry, was organized in 1939, is affiliated with or represents some 10,000 publishing companies and 20,000 authors and composers, and operates in much the same manner as ASCAP. Almost every domestic copyrighted composition is in the repertory either of ASCAP, with a total of three million compositions, or of BMI, with one million.

Both organizations operate primarily through blanket licenses, which give the licensees the right to perform any and all of the compositions owned by the members or affiliates as often as the licensees desire for a stated term. Fees for blanket licenses are ordinarily a percentage of total revenues or a flat dollar amount, and do not directly depend on the amount or type of music used. Radio and television broadcasters are the largest users of music, and almost all of them hold blanket licenses from both ASCAP and BMI. Until this litigation, CBS held blanket licenses from both organizations for its television network on a continuous basis since the late 1940's and had never attempted to secure any other form of license from either ASCAP[5] or any of its members.

The complaint filed by CBS charged various violations of the Sherman Act and the copyright laws. CBS argued that ASCAP and BMI are unlawful monopolies and that the blanket license is illegal price fixing, an unlawful tying arrangement, a concerted refusal to

---

5. Unless the context indicates otherwise, references to ASCAP alone in this opinion usually apply to BMI as well.

deal, and a misuse of copyrights. The District Court, though denying summary judgment to certain defendants, ruled that the practice did not fall within the per se rule. After an eight-week trial, limited to the issue of liability, the court dismissed the complaint, rejecting again the claim that the blanket license was price fixing and a per se violation of §1 of the Sherman Act, and holding that since direct negotiation with individual copyright owners is available and feasible there is no undue restraint of trade, illegal tying, misuse of copyrights, or monopolization.

Though agreeing with the District Court's factfinding and not disturbing its legal conclusions on the other antitrust theories of liability,[8] the Court of Appeals held that the blanket license issued to television networks was a form of price fixing illegal per se under the Sherman Act. This conclusion, without more, settled the issue of liability under the Sherman Act, established copyright misuse, and required reversal of the District Court's judgment, as well as a remand to consider the appropriate remedy.[10] ...

Because we disagree with the Court of Appeals' conclusions with respect to the per se illegality of the blanket license, we reverse its judgment and remand the cause for further appropriate proceedings.

II

In construing and applying the Sherman Act's ban against contracts, conspiracies, and combinations in restraint of trade, the

8. The Court of Appeals affirmed the District Court's rejection of CBS's monopolization and tying contentions but did not rule on the District Court's conclusion that the blanket license was not an unreasonable restraint of trade.

10. The Court of Appeals went on to suggest some guidelines as to remedy, indicating that despite its conclusion on liability the blanket license was not totally forbidden. The Court of Appeals said:

> Normally, after a finding of price-fixing, the remedy is an injunction against the price-fixing — in this case, the blanket license. We think, however, that if on remand a remedy can be fashioned which will ensure that the blanket license will not affect the price or negotiations for direct licenses, the blanket license need not be prohibited in all circumstances. The blanket license is not simply a "naked restraint" ineluctably doomed to extinction. There is not enough evidence in the present record to compel a finding that the blanket license does not serve a market need for those who wish full protection against infringement suits or who, for some other business reason, deem the blanket license desirable. The blanket license includes a practical covenant not to sue for infringement of any ASCAP copyright as well as an indemnification against suits by others.
>
> Our objection to the blanket license is that it reduces price competition among the members and provides a disinclination to compete. We think that these objections may be removed if ASCAP itself is required to provide some form of per use licensing which will ensure competition among the individual members with respect to those networks which wish to engage in per use licensing.

Court has held that certain agreements or practices are so "plainly anticompetitive" . . . and so often "lack . . . any redeeming virtue" . . . that they are conclusively presumed illegal without further examination under the rule of reason generally applied in Sherman Act cases. This per se rule is a valid and useful tool of antitrust policy and enforcement. And agreements among competitors to fix prices on their individual goods or services are among those concerted activities that the Court has held to be within the per se category. But easy labels do not always supply ready answers.

A

To the Court of Appeals and CBS, the blanket license involves "price fixing" in the literal sense: the composers and publishing houses have joined together into an organization that sets its price for the blanket license it sells.[13] But this is not a question simply of determining whether two or more potential competitors have literally "fixed" a "price." As generally used in the antitrust field, "price fixing" is a shorthand way of describing certain categories of business behavior to which the per se rule has been held applicable. The Court of Appeals' literal approach does not alone establish that this particular practice is one of those types or that it is "plainly anticompetitive" and very likely without "redeeming virtue." Literalness is overly simplistic and often overbroad. When two partners set the price of their goods or services they are literally "price fixing," but they are not per se in violation of the Sherman Act. . . . Thus, it is necessary to characterize the challenged conduct as falling within or without that category of behavior to which we apply the label "per se price fixing." That will often, but not always, be a simple matter.

Consequently, as we recognized in *Topco*, "[i]t is only after considerable experience with certain business relationships that courts

13. CBS also complains that it pays a flat fee regardless of the amount of use it makes of ASCAP compositions and even though many of its programs contain little or no music. We are unable to see how that alone could make out an antitrust violation or misuse of copyrights:

> Sound business judgment could indicate that such payment represents the most convenient method of fixing the business value of the privileges granted by the licensing agreement. . . . Petitioner cannot complain because it must pay royalties whether it uses Hazeltine patents or not. What it acquired by the agreement into which it entered was the privilege to use any or all of the patents and developments as it desired to use them.

Automatic Radio Manufacturing Co. v. Hazeltine Research, Inc., 339 U.S. 827, 834 (1950). See also Zenith Radio Corp. v. Hazeltine Research, Inc., 395 U.S. 100 (1969).

classify them as per se violations. . . ." . . . We have never examined a practice like this one before; indeed, the Court of Appeals recognized that "[i]n dealing with performing rights in the music industry we confront conditions both in copyright law and in antitrust law which are sui generis." And though there has been rather intensive antitrust scrutiny of ASCAP and its blanket licenses, that experience hardly counsels that we should outlaw the blanket license as a per se restraint of trade.

B . . .

[Government suits against ASCAP were settled through a consent decree, which was modified in 1950.] Under the amended decree, which still substantially controls the activities of ASCAP, members may grant ASCAP only nonexclusive rights to license their works for public performance. Members, therefore, retain the rights individually to license public performances, along with the rights to license the use of their compositions for other purposes. ASCAP itself is forbidden to grant any license to perform one or more specified compositions in the ASCAP repertory unless both the user and the owner have requested it in writing to do so. ASCAP is required to grant to any user making written application a nonexclusive license to perform all ASCAP compositions, either for a period of time or on a per-program basis. ASCAP may not insist on the blanket license, and the fee for the per-program license, which is to be based on the revenues for the program on which ASCAP music is played, must offer the applicant a genuine economic choice between the per program license and the more common blanket license. If ASCAP and a putative licensee are unable to agree on a fee within 60 days, the applicant may apply to the District Court for a determination of a reasonable fee, with ASCAP having the burden of proving reasonableness.

The 1950 decree, as amended from time to time, continues in effect, and the blanket license continues to be the primary instrument through which ASCAP conducts its business under the decree. The courts have twice construed the decree not to require ASCAP to issue licenses for selected portions of its repertory. It also remains true that the decree guarantees the legal availability of direct licensing of performance rights by ASCAP members; and the District Court found, and in this respect the Court of Appeals agreed, that there are no practical impediments preventing direct dealing by the television networks if they so desire. Historically, they have not done so. Since 1946, CBS and other television networks have taken blanket licenses from ASCAP and BMI. It was not until this suit arose that the CBS network demanded any other kind of license.

Of course, a consent judgment, even one entered at the behest of the Antitrust Division, does not immunize the defendant from liability for actions, including those contemplated by the decree, that violate the rights of nonparties.... But it cannot be ignored that the Federal Executive and Judiciary have carefully scrutinized ASCAP and the challenged conduct, have imposed restrictions on various of ASCAP's practices, and, by the terms of the decree, stand ready to provide further consideration, supervision, and perhaps invalidation of asserted anticompetitive practices. In these circumstances, we have a unique indicator that the challenged practice may have redeeming competitive virtues and that the search for those values is not almost sure to be in vain.... That fact alone might not remove a naked price-fixing scheme from the ambit of the per se rule, but, as discussed infra, Part III, here we are uncertain whether the practice on its face has the effect, or could have been spurred by the purpose, of restraining competition among the individual composers....

Finally, we note that Congress itself, in the new [1976] Copyright Act, has chosen to employ the blanket license and similar practices. Congress created a compulsory blanket license for secondary transmissions by cable television systems and provided that

> [n]otwithstanding any provisions of the antitrust laws, ... any claimants may agree among themselves as to the proportionate division of compulsory licensing fees among them, may lump their claims together and file them jointly or as a single claim, or may designate a common agent to receive payment on their behalf.

17 U.S.C. App. §111(d)(5)(A). And the newly created compulsory license for the use of copyrighted compositions in jukeboxes is also a blanket license, which is payable to the performing rights societies such as ASCAP unless an individual copyright holder can prove his entitlement to a share. §116(c)(4). Moreover, in requiring noncommercial broadcasters to pay for their use of copyrighted music, Congress again provided that "[n]otwithstanding any provision of the antitrust laws" copyright owners "may designate common agents to negotiate, agree to, pay, or receive payments." §118(b). Though these provisions are not directly controlling, they do reflect an opinion that the blanket license, and ASCAP, are economically beneficial in at least some circumstances....

III ...

A

As a preliminary matter, we are mindful that the Court of Appeals' holding would appear to be quite difficult to contain. If, as the court held, there is a per se antitrust violation whenever ASCAP issues a blanket license to a television network for a single fee, why would it not also be automatically illegal for ASCAP to negotiate and issue blanket licenses to individual radio or television stations or to other users who perform copyrighted music for profit? Likewise, if the present network licenses issued through ASCAP on behalf of its members are per se violations, why would it not be equally illegal for the members to authorize ASCAP to issue licenses establishing various categories of uses that a network might have for copyrighted music and setting a standard fee for each described use?

Although the Court of Appeals apparently thought the blanket license could be saved in some or even many applications, it seems to us that the per se rule does not accommodate itself to such flexibility and that the observations of the Court of Appeals with respect to remedy tend to impeach the per se basis for the holding of liability.[27]

CBS would prefer that ASCAP be authorized, indeed directed, to make all its compositions available at standard per-use rates within negotiated categories of use. But if this in itself or in conjunction with blanket licensing constitutes illegal price fixing by copyright owners, CBS urges that an injunction issue forbidding ASCAP to issue any blanket license or to negotiate any fee except on behalf of an individual member for the use of his own copyrighted work or works.[29] Thus, we are called upon to determine that blanket licensing is unlawful across the board. We are quite sure, however, that the per se rule does not require any such holding.

27. See n.10, supra. The Court of Appeals would apparently not outlaw the blanket license across the board but would permit it in various circumstances where it is deemed necessary or sufficiently desirable. It did not even enjoin blanket licensing with the television networks, the relief it realized would normally follow a finding of per se illegality of the license in that context. Instead, as requested by CBS, it remanded to the District Court to require ASCAP to offer in addition to blanket licensing some competitive form of per-use licensing. But per-use licensing by ASCAP, as recognized in the consent decrees, might be even more susceptible to the per se rule than blanket licensing.

The rationale for this unusual relief in a per se case was that "[t]he blanket license is not simply a 'naked restraint' ineluctably doomed for extinction." To the contrary, the Court of Appeals found that the blanket license might well "serve a market need" for some. This, it seems to us, is not the per se approach which does not yield so readily to circumstances, but in effect is a rather bobtailed application of the rule of reason, bobtailed in the sense that it is unaccompanied by the necessary analysis demonstrating why the particular licensing system is an undue competitive restraint.

29. In its complaint, CBS alleged that it would be "wholly impracticable" for it to obtain individual licenses directly from the composers and publishing houses, but it now says that it would be willing to do exactly that if ASCAP were enjoined from granting blanket licenses to CBS or its competitors in the network television business.

B . . .

Although the copyright law confers no rights on copyright owners to fix prices among themselves or otherwise to violate the antitrust laws, we would not expect that any market arrangements
reasonably necessary to effectuate the rights that are granted would
be deemed a per se violation of the Sherman Act. Otherwise, the
commerce anticipated by the Copyright Act and protected against
restraint by the Sherman Act would not exist at all or would exist
only as a pale reminder of what Congress envisioned.[32]

C – *effect + purpose?*

More generally, in characterizing this conduct under the per se
rule,[33] our inquiry must focus on whether the effect and, here
because it tends to show effect . . . the purpose of the practice is to
threaten the proper operation of our predominantly free-market
economy — that is, whether the practice facially appears to be one
that would always or almost always tend to restrict competition and
decrease output, and in what portion of the market, or instead one
designed to "increase economic efficiency and render markets
more rather than less competitive." . . .

The blanket license, as we see it, is not a "naked restrain[t]
of trade with no purpose except stifling of competition," . . . but
rather accompanies the integration of sales, monitoring, and enforcement against unauthorized copyright use. . . . Most users want
unplanned, rapid, and indemnified access to any and all of the
repertory of compositions, and the owners want a reliable method
of collecting for the use of their copyrights. Individual sales transactions in this industry are quite expensive, as would be individual
monitoring and enforcement, especially in light of the resources of
single composers. Indeed, as both the Court of Appeals and CBS
recognize, the costs are prohibitive for licenses with individual radio stations, nightclubs, and restaurants and it was in that milieu
that the blanket license arose.

32. . . . Because a musical composition can be "consumed" by many different
people at the same time and without the creator's knowledge, the "owner" has no
real way to demand reimbursement for the use of his property except through the
copyright laws *and* an effective way to enforce those legal rights. . . . It takes an
organization of rather large size to monitor most or all uses and to deal with users
on behalf of the composers. Moreover, it is inefficient to have too many such
organizations duplicating each other's monitoring of use.

33. The scrutiny occasionally required must not merely subsume the burdensome analysis required under the rule of reason, see *Engineers,* or else we should
apply the rule of reason from the start. That is why the per se rule is not employed
until after considerable experience with the type of challenged restraint.

A middleman with a blanket license was an obvious necessity if the thousands of individual negotiations, a virtual impossibility, were to be avoided. Also, individual fees for the use of individual compositions would presuppose an intricate schedule of fees and uses, as well as a difficult and expensive reporting problem for the user and policing task for the copyright owner. Historically, the market for public performance rights organized itself largely around the single-fee blanket license, which gave unlimited access to the repertory and reliable protection against infringement. When ASCAP's major and user-created competitor, BMI, came on the scene, it also turned to the blanket license.

With the advent of radio and television networks, market conditions changed, and the necessity for and advantages of a blanket license for those users may be far less obvious than is the case when the potential users are individual television or radio stations, or the thousands of other individuals and organizations performing copyrighted compositions in public. But even for television network licenses, ASCAP reduces costs absolutely by creating a blanket license that is sold only a few, instead of thousands,[35] of times, and that obviates the need for closely monitoring the networks to see that they do not use more than they pay for.[36] ASCAP also provides the necessary resources for blanket sales and enforcement, resources unavailable to the vast majority of composers and publishing houses. Moreover, a bulk license of some type is a necessary consequence of the integration necessary to achieve these efficiencies, and a necessary consequence of an aggregate license is that its price must be established.

D

This substantial lowering of costs, which is of course potentially beneficial to both sellers and buyers, differentiates the blanket license from individual use licenses. The blanket license is composed of the individual compositions plus the aggregating service. Here, the whole is truly greater than the sum of its parts; it is, to some extent, a different product. The blanket license has certain unique characteristics: It allows the licensee immediate use of covered compositions, without the delay of prior individual negotiations, and great flexibility in the choice of musical material. Many consumers clearly prefer the characteristics and cost advantages of this market-

---

35. The District Court found that CBS would require between 4,000 and 8,000 individual license transactions per year.

36. To operate its system for distributing the license revenues to its members, ASCAP relies primarily on the networks' records of which compositions are used.

able package, and even small performing-rights societies that have occasionally arisen to compete with ASCAP and BMI have offered blanket licenses. Thus, to the extent the blanket license is a different product, ASCAP is not really a joint sales agency offering the individual goods of many sellers, but is a separate seller offering its blanket license, of which the individual compositions are raw material.[40] ASCAP, in short, made a market in which individual composers are inherently unable to compete fully effectively.

E

Finally, we have some doubt — enough to counsel against application of the per se rule — about the extent to which this practice threatens the "central nervous system of the economy," . . . that is, competitive pricing as the free market's means of allocating resources. Not all arrangements among actual or potential competitors that have an impact on price are per se violations of the Sherman Act or even unreasonable restraints. Mergers among competitors eliminate competition, including price competition, but they are not per se illegal, and many of them withstand attack under any existing antitrust standard. Joint ventures and other cooperative arrangements are also not usually unlawful, at least not as price-fixing schemes, where the agreement on price is necessary to market the product at all.

Here, the blanket license fee is not set by competition among individual copyright owners, and it is a fee for the use of any of the compositions covered by the license. But the blanket license cannot be wholly equated with a simple horizontal arrangement among competitors. ASCAP does set the price for its blanket license, but that license is quite different from anything any individual owner could issue. The individual composers and authors have neither agreed not to sell individually in any other market nor use the blanket license to mask price fixing in such other markets. Moreover, the substantial restraints placed on ASCAP and its members by the consent decree must not be ignored. The District Court found that there was no legal, practical, or conspiratorial impediment to CBS obtaining individual licenses; CBS, in short, had a real choice.

---

40. Moreover, because of the nature of the product — a composition can be simultaneously "consumed" by many users — composers have numerous markets and numerous incentives to produce, so the blanket license is unlikely to cause decreased output, one of the normal undesirable effects of a cartel. And since popular songs get an increased share of ASCAP's revenue distributions, composers compete even within the blanket license in terms of productivity and consumer satisfaction.

With this background in mind, which plainly enough indicates that over the years, and in the face of available alternatives, the blanket license has provided an acceptable mechanism for at least a large part of the market for the performing rights to copyrighted musical compositions, we cannot agree that it should automatically be declared illegal in all of its many manifestations. Rather, when attacked, it should be subjected to a more discriminating examination under the rule of reason. It may not ultimately survive that attack, but that is not the issue before us today.

IV

As we have noted, the enigmatic remarks of the Court of Appeals with respect to remedy appear to have departed from the court's strict, per se approach and to have invited a more careful analysis. But this left the general import of its judgment that the licensing practices of ASCAP and BMI under the consent decree are per se violations of the Sherman Act. We reverse that judgment, and the copyright misuse judgment dependent upon it, and remand for further proceedings to consider any unresolved issues that CBS may have properly brought to the Court of Appeals.[43] . . .

[Justice Stevens dissented. Although he agreed that ASCAP's blanket license was not categorically forbidden price fixing, he concluded, based on the following reasoning, that it constituted an unreasonable restraint of trade: (1) To condition a desired license for one composition on taking a license for other compositions constitutes an unlawful tie. (2) This rule does not automatically condemn ASCAP's refusal to license anything less than its entire repertoire because ASCAP lacks exclusive control; a user can bypass ASCAP by licensing a particular composition directly from its composer or publisher. (3) Nevertheless, blanket licensing with fees based on a percentage of the broadcaster's advertising receipts reflects price discrimination. ASCAP charges broadcasters in accordance with their ability to pay rather than in accordance with factors normally affecting price in a competitive market, such as cost, quality, or quantity of the product. As a result of this price discrimina-

---

43. It is argued that the judgment of the Court of Appeals should nevertheless be affirmed on the ground that the blanket license is a tying arrangement in violation of §1 of the Sherman Act or on the ground that ASCAP and BMI have monopolized the relevant market contrary to §2. The District Court and the Court of Appeals rejected both submissions, and we do not disturb the latter's judgment in these respects, particularly since CBS did not file its own petition for certiorari challenging the Court of Appeals' failure to sustain its tying and monopolization claims.

tion, a user has no incentive to economize in the use of music or to play less popular compositions. These distortionary effects make it more difficult for new songwriters to enter the market by offering their songs at unusually low prices. Such barriers to entry are symptomatic of a cartelized market. (4) These noncompetitive results are not inevitable because a competitive market in licensing individual compositions has emerged where the ASCAP blanket license does not govern (for example, in the right to make or exhibit motion picture films with copyrighted music on the soundtrack). (5) Although CBS has the legal alternative of dealing directly with composers and publishers, the lower court did not find that such direct dealing was without risk or expense, least of all for buyers less powerful than CBS.][17]

217. (a) Does *Broadcast Music (BMI)* involve price fixing by competitors? Who sets the prices at which most buy? Is there price competition among artists for such uses? How would you state the Court's rule? Is the Court's statement that "[n]ot all arrangements among actual or potential competitors that have an impact on price are per se violations ... or even unreasonable restraints" consistent with *Socony*? With *Topco*?[18] See ¶212.

(b) Suppose that there are several alternative patented processes for making widgets, that each patent is undoubtedly valid and capable of being practiced independently without infringing another, that the several patent owners form the Widget Patent Holding Corporation and convey their patents to it, and that the Corporation licenses those patents (one or more, as desired by licensees) at prices set by the Corporation. Would this constitute price fixing?

17. On remand, the original district court decision was affirmed. CBS v. ASCAP, 620 F.2d 930 (2d Cir. 1980), cert. denied, 450 U.S. 970 (1981). See also Buffalo Broadcasting Co. v. ASCAP, 744 F.2d 917 (2d Cir. 1984), cert. denied, 469 U.S. 1211 (1985) (rejecting challenge to blanket license for local non-network owned television stations for non-network programming).

18. *Topco* is not cited in *BMI* except for the proposition that the application of per se rules requires experience with the practice before the court. Judge Bork has argued that

> there is in *BMI* reasoning of more general application which indicates that *Topco* does not state the modern rule as to horizontal restraints. There is, first, the Court's favorable citation of *Addyston Pipe & Steel*'s example of partners who eliminate price competition between themselves. If *Topco* meant, as it seemed to, that the existence of a joint venture could not justify an agreement eliminating competition between the joint venturers, the *BMI* Court must be read as overruling *Topco* to that extent. . . . In *BMI, NCAA,* and *Pacific Stationary,* the Supreme Court returned the law to the formulation of *Addyston Pipe & Steel* and thus effectively overruled *Topco* and *Sealy* as to the per se illegality of all horizontal restraints.

Rothery Storage & Van Co. v. Atlas Van Lines, 792 F.2d 210, 227, 229 (D.C. Cir. 1986), cert. denied, 479 U.S. 1033 (1987). But see *Palmer.*

Would it be unlawful per se after *BMI*? Is this case different from *BMI*?[19]

(c) In what ways, if any, does the behavior challenged in *BMI* restrain trade? What is the justification for the *BMI* defendants' behavior? Does the justification redeem some or all of that behavior? In *BMI*, does the Supreme Court hold that the defendants do not restrain trade or that any restraint is reasonable and therefore legal? Is the result in the Supreme Court fundamentally different from that reached by the Court of Appeals? Under the relief requested by CBS, would the alleged price fixing no longer exist?

(d) Does the existence of blanket licenses in *BMI* prevent those who desire to license fewer compositions from doing so? How? What is the Court of Appeals' answer? Does the Supreme Court disagree?

(e) Should the courts compel BMI and ASCAP to license individual compositions? At the rate they pay individual copyright holders from the revenues received on blanket license fees? At a price set by the licensing organization? Would this be competitively preferable to existing arrangements?

(f) How is the reasonableness of the *BMI* behavior affected by the number of licensing organizations — now apparently only BMI and ASCAP? Would the challenged arrangements be easier to justify if there were a dozen similar organizations, each with a separate repertory of musical compositions? Should *BMI* have been decided in such a way as to bring about that result?

ARIZONA v. MARICOPA COUNTY
MEDICAL SOCIETY
457 U.S. 332 (1982)

Justice STEVENS. . . . The question presented is whether §1 of the Sherman Act has been violated by an agreement among competing physicians setting, by majority vote, the maximum fees that they may claim in full payment for health services provided to policyholders of specified insurance plans. The United States Court of Appeals for the Ninth Circuit held that the question could not be answered without evaluating the actual purpose and effect of the agreement at a full trial. Because the undisputed facts disclose a violation of the statute, we . . . reverse. . . .

19. When studying Ch. 2G on the application of antitrust law to patent licensing, consider the Court's argument in *BMI* that the restraint facilitates "commerce anticipated by the Copyright Act."

II . . .

Approximately 1,750 doctors, representing about 70 percent of the practitioners in Maricopa County, are members [of the Maricopa Foundation. It] performs three primary activities. It establishes the schedule of maximum fees that participating doctors agree to accept as payment in full for services performed for patients insured under plans approved by the foundation. It reviews the medical necessity and appropriateness of treatment provided by its members to such insured persons. It is authorized to draw checks on insurance company accounts to pay doctors for services performed for covered patients. In performing these functions, the foundation is considered an "insurance administrator" by the Director of the Arizona Department of Insurance. Its participating doctors, however, have no financial interest in the operation of the foundation.

The Pima Foundation for Medical Care, which includes about 400 member doctors, performs similar functions. . . . No challenge is made to their peer review or claim administration functions. Nor do the foundations allege that these two activities make it necessary for them to engage in the practice of establishing maximum-fee schedules.

At the time this lawsuit was filed, each foundation made use of "relative values" and "conversion factors" in compiling its fee schedule. The conversion factor is the dollar amount used to determine fees for a particular medical specialty. Thus, for example, the conversion factors for "medicine" and "laboratory" were $8.00 and $5.50, respectively, in 1972, and $10.00 and $6.50 in 1974. The relative value schedule provides a numerical weight for each different medical service — thus, an office consultation has a lesser value than a home visit. The relative value was multiplied by the conversion factor to determine the maximum fee. The fee schedule has been revised periodically. The foundation board of trustees would solicit advice from various medical societies about the need for change in either relative values or conversion factors in their respective specialties. The board would then formulate the new fee schedule and submit it to the vote of the entire membership.[10]

The fee schedules limit the amount that the member doctors may recover for services performed for patients insured under plans approved by the foundations. To obtain this approval the insurers — including self-insured employers as well as insurance companies — agree to pay the doctors' charges up to the scheduled

10. The parties disagree over whether the increases in the fee schedules are the cause or the result of the increases in the prevailing rate for medical services in the relevant markets. There appears to be agreement, however, that 85-95 percent of physicians in Maricopa County bill at or above the maximum reimbursement levels set by the Maricopa foundation.

amounts, and in exchange the doctors agree to accept those amounts as payment in full for their services. The doctors are free to charge higher fees to uninsured patients, and they also may charge any patient less than the scheduled maxima. . . .

The impact of the foundation fee schedules on medical fees and on insurance premiums is a matter of dispute. The State of Arizona contends that the periodic upward revisions of the maximum-fee schedules have the effect of stabilizing and enhancing the level of actual charges by physicians, and that the increasing level of their fees in turn increases insurance premiums. The foundations, on the other hand, argue that the schedules impose a meaningful limit on physicians' charges, and that the advance agreement by the doctors to accept the maxima enables the insurance carriers to limit and to calculate more efficiently the risks they underwrite and therefore serves as an effective cost-containment mechanism that has saved patients and insurers millions of dollars. Although the Attorneys General of 40 different States, as well as the Solicitor General of the United States and certain organizations representing consumers of medical services, have filed amicus curiae briefs supporting the State of Arizona's position on the merits, we must assume that the respondents' view of the genuine issues of fact is correct. . . .

III

The respondents recognize that our decisions establish that price-fixing agreements are unlawful on their face. But they argue that the per se rule does not govern this case because the agreements at issue are horizontal and fix maximum prices, are among members of a profession, are in an industry with which the judiciary has little antitrust experience, and are alleged to have procompetitive justifications. . . .

A . . .

[W]e have analyzed most restraints under the so-called "rule of reason." As its name suggests, the rule of reason requires the fact-finder to decide whether under all the circumstances of the case the restrictive practice imposes an unreasonable restraint on competition.

The elaborate inquiry into the reasonableness of a challenged business practice entails significant costs. Litigation of the effect or purpose of a practice often is extensive and complex. . . . Judges often lack the expert understanding of industrial market structures and behavior to determine with any confidence a practice's effect on competition. . . . And the result of the process in any given case may provide little certainty or guidance about the legality of a practice in another context. . . .

The costs of judging business practices under the rule of reason, however, have been reduced by the recognition of per se rules. Once experience with a particular kind of restraint enables the Court to predict with confidence that the rule of reason will condemn it, it has applied a conclusive presumption that the restraint is unreasonable. As in every rule of general application, the match between the presumed and the actual is imperfect. For the sake of business certainty and litigation efficiency, we have tolerated the invalidation of some agreements that a full-blown inquiry might have proved to be reasonable. . . .

The application of the per se rule to maximum price-fixing agreements in Kiefer-Stewart Co. v. Joseph E. Seagram & Sons, 340 U.S. 211 (1951), followed ineluctably from *Socony-Vacuum*:

> For such agreements, no less than those to fix minimum prices, cripple the freedom of traders and thereby restrain their ability to sell in accordance with their own judgment. . . . "Under the Sherman Act a combination formed for the purpose and with the effect of raising, depressing, fixing, pegging, or stabilizing the price of a commodity in interstate or foreign commerce is illegal per se."

Over the objection that maximum price-fixing agreements were not the "economic equivalent" of minimum price-fixing agreements, *Kiefer-Stewart* was reaffirmed in *Albrecht*. . . .

We have not wavered in our enforcement of the per se rule against price fixing. Indeed, in our most recent price-fixing case we summarily reversed the decision of another Ninth Circuit panel that a horizontal agreement among competitors to fix credit terms does not necessarily contravene the antitrust laws. Catalano, Inc. v. Target Sales, Inc., 446 U.S. 643 (1980).

B

Our decisions foreclose the argument that the agreements at issue escape per se condemnation because they are horizontal and fix maximum prices. *Kiefer-Stewart* and *Albrecht* place horizontal agreements to fix maximum prices on the same legal — even if not economic — footing as agreements to fix minimum or uniform prices.[18] The per se rule "is grounded on faith in price competition

---

18. It is true that in *Kiefer-Stewart* as in *Albrecht* the agreement involved a vertical arrangement in which maximum resale prices were fixed. But the case also involved an agreement among competitors to impose the resale price restraint. In any event, horizontal restraints are generally less defensible than vertical restraints. See *Sylvania*. . . .

as a market force [and not] on a policy of low selling prices at the price of eliminating competition." Rahl, Price Competition and the Price Fixing Rule — Preface and Perspective, 57 Nw. U.L. Rev. 137, 142 (1962). In this case the rule is violated by a price restraint that tends to provide the same economic rewards to all practitioners regardless of their skill, their experience, their training, or their willingness to employ innovative and difficult procedures in individual cases. Such a restraint also may discourage entry into the market and may deter experimentation and new developments by individual entrepreneurs. It may be a masquerade for an agreement to fix uniform prices or it may in the future take on that character.

Nor does the fact that doctors — rather than nonprofessionals — are the parties to the price-fixing agreements support the respondents' position. In Goldfarb v. Virginia State Bar, 421 U.S. 773, 788, n.17 (1975), we stated that the "public service aspect, and other features of the professions, may require that a particular practice, which could properly be viewed as a violation of the Sherman Act in another context, be treated differently." ... The price-fixing agreements in this case, however, are not premised on public service or ethical norms....

We are equally unpersuaded by the argument that we should not apply the per se rule in this case because the judiciary has little antitrust experience in the health care industry. The argument quite obviously is inconsistent with *Socony-Vacuum*. ... [Y]et the Court of Appeals refused to apply the per se rule in this case in part because the health care industry was so far removed from the competitive model. Consistent with our prediction in *Socony-Vacuum*, the result of this reasoning was the adoption by the Court of Appeals of a legal standard based on the reasonableness of the fixed prices, an inquiry we have so often condemned. Finally, the argument that the per se rule must be rejustified for every industry that has not been subject to significant antitrust litigation ignores the rationale for per se rules....

The respondents' principal argument is that the per se rule is inapplicable because their agreements are alleged to have procompetitive justifications. The argument indicates a misunderstanding of the per se concept. The anticompetitive potential inherent in all price-fixing agreements justifies their facial invalidation even if procompetitive justifications are offered for some. Those claims of enhanced competition are so unlikely to prove significant in any particular case that we adhere to the rule of law that is justified in its general application. Even when the respondents are given every benefit of the doubt, the limited record in this case is not inconsistent with the presumption that the respondents' agreements will not significantly enhance competition....

It is true that a binding assurance of complete insurance coverage — as well as most of the respondents' potential for lower insurance premiums[25] — can be obtained only if the insurer and the doctor agree in advance on the maximum fee that the doctor will accept as full payment for a particular service. Even if a fee schedule is therefore desirable, it is not necessary that the doctors do the price fixing. The record indicates that the Arizona Comprehensive Medical/Dental Program for Foster Children is administered by the Maricopa Foundation pursuant to a contract under which the maximum fee schedule is prescribed by a state agency rather than by the doctors. . . . [I]nsurers are capable not only of fixing maximum reimbursable prices but also of obtaining binding agreements with providers guaranteeing the insured full reimbursement of a participating provider's fee. In light of these examples, it is not surprising that nothing in the record even arguably supports the conclusion that this type of insurance program could not function if the fee schedules were set in a different way.

The most that can be said for having doctors fix the maximum prices is that doctors may be able to do it more efficiently than insurers. The validity of that assumption is far from obvious, but in any event there is no reason to believe that any savings that might accrue from this arrangement would be sufficiently great to affect the competitiveness of these kinds of insurance plans. It is entirely possible that the potential or actual power of the foundations to dictate the terms of such insurance plans may more than offset the theoretical efficiencies upon which the respondents' defense ultimately rests.[29]

C — *Better for Congress to solve*

Our adherence to the per se rule is grounded not only on economic prediction, judicial convenience, and business certainty, but

25. We do not perceive the respondents' claim of procompetitive justification for their fee schedules to rest on the premise that the fee schedules actually reduce medical fees and accordingly reduce insurance premiums, thereby enhancing competition in the health insurance industry. Such an argument would merely restate the long rejected position that fixed prices are reasonable if they are lower than free competition would yield. It is arguable, however, that the existence of a fee schedule, whether fixed by the doctors or by the insurers, makes it easier — and to that extent less expensive — for insurers to calculate the risks that they underwrite and to arrive at the appropriate reimbursement on insured claims.

29. In this case it appears that the fees are set by a group with substantial power in the market for medical services, and that there is competition among insurance companies in the sale of medical insurance. Under these circumstances, the insurance companies are not likely to have significantly greater bargaining power against a monopoly of doctors than would individual consumers of medical services.

also on a recognition of the respective roles of the Judiciary and the Congress in regulating the economy. . . . By articulating the rules of law with some clarity and by adhering to rules that are justified in their general application, however, we enhance the legislative prerogative to amend the law. The respondents' arguments against application of the per se rule in this case therefore are better directed to the legislature. Congress may consider the exception that we are not free to read into the statute.

IV

Having declined the respondents' invitation to cut back on the per se rule against price fixing, we are left with the respondents' argument that their fee schedules involve price fixing in only a literal sense. For this argument, the respondents rely upon *Broadcast Music*.

In *Broadcast Music* we were confronted with an antitrust challenge to the marketing of the right to use copyrighted compositions derived from the entire membership of ASCAP. The so-called "blanket license" was entirely different from the product that any one composer was able to sell by himself. Although there was little competition among individual composers for their separate compositions, the blanket license arrangement did not place any restraint on the right of any individual copyright owner to sell his own compositions separately to any buyer at any price. But a "necessary consequence" of the creation of the blanket license was that its price had to be established. We held that the delegation by the composers to ASCAP of the power to fix the price for the blanket license was not a species of the price fixing agreements categorically forbidden by the Sherman Act. The record disclosed price fixing only in a "literal sense."

This case is fundamentally different. Each of the foundations is composed of individual practitioners who compete with one another for patients. Neither the foundations nor the doctors sell insurance, and they derive no profits from the sale of health insurance policies. The members of the foundations sell medical services. Their combination in the form of the foundation does not permit them to sell any different product. Their combination has merely permitted them to sell their services to certain customers at fixed prices and arguably to affect the prevailing market price of medical care. . . . If a clinic offered complete medical coverage for a flat fee, the cooperating doctors would have the type of partnership arrangement in which a price-fixing agreement among the doctors would be perfectly proper. But the fee agreements disclosed by the record in this case are among independent competing entrepreneurs. They fit squarely into the horizontal price-fixing mold.

The judgment of the Court of Appeals is reversed.

[Justice Powell, joined by Chief Justice Burger and Justice Rehnquist, dissented, arguing that since the case reaches the court on plaintiff's motion for summary judgment, it must be assumed that the effects are as respondents suggest — i.e., that the arrangement serves as effective cost containment, benefiting consumers. The Court's per se categorization is rejected as formalistic, particularly since the agreement in this case is novel, calling for an inquiry into the relevant facts. The literal fixing of prices is deemed insufficient, as suggested by *BMI*. Thus, a full record should have been developed to resolve the issues of fact.][20]

218.   (a) Why should the antitrust laws be concerned with maximum price fixing?[21]

(b) What will be the effect of the maximum prices in *Maricopa?* Do you suspect many (any) member doctors will charge less when serving patients covered under the plan?

(c) Could the health insurance companies have accomplished their purpose of establishing price schedules without leaving the decision to an association of doctors?[22] If so, why might they have gone along with the arrangement?

(d) Consider the Court's application of the per se rule. How many of its arguments could have been advanced in *BMI?* Are the two cases consistent on this score?

(e) The *Maricopa* opinion described the setting of fees for particular services as the product of two steps: establishing a relative value schedule that provides weights for each different medical service and assigning a dollar amount as the conversion factor. Price equaled the conversion factor multiplied by the weight. If a group of doctors simply promulgated a relative value schedule, without

20. Blackmun and O'Connor, JJ., did not participate.

21. See ¶210. Be sure to consider both the maximum set by a group of purchasers as well as that set by sellers.

22. Courts have generally denied §1 challenges to insurance arrangements that limit the amounts participating providers may charge when serving those insured under the program, reasoning that the insurance company is a single buyer and therefore is free to negotiate terms it finds favorable with individual sellers. E.g., Brillhart v. Mutual Med. Ins., 768 F.2d 196 (7th Cir. 1985); Kartell v. Blue Shield, 749 F.2d 922 (1st Cir. 1984), cert. denied, 471 U.S. 1029 (1985); Quality Auto Body v. Allstate Ins., 660 F.2d 1195 (7th Cir. 1981). Query: Does the fact that some of these insurance companies account for a substantial portion of all business in the region suggest that a buying cartel with a very large market share would similarly be legal? See ¶¶210, 224.

specifying the dollar amounts, would there be a Sherman Act violation?[23] After studying Chapters 2C, and 2D, consider whether you would answer this question in the same way for a trade association of steel producers that promulgated a similar relative value schedule for all of the grades of steel and varieties of steel products.

(f) What result in ¶e if an industry group also publishes a suggested dollar amount as the conversion factor?[24]

NATIONAL SOCIETY OF PROFESSIONAL ENGINEERS v. UNITED STATES
435 U.S. 679 (1978)

Justice STEVENS.... This is a civil antitrust case brought by the United States to nullify an association's canon of ethics prohibiting competitive bidding by its members. The question is whether the canon may be justified under the Sherman Act, because it was adopted by members of a learned profession for the purpose of minimizing the risk that competition would produce inferior engineering work endangering the public safety. The District Court rejected this justification without making any findings on the likelihood that competition would produce the dire consequences foreseen by the association. The Court of Appeals affirmed. We granted certiorari to decide whether the District Court should have considered the factual basis for the proferred justification before rejecting it. Because we are satisfied that the asserted defense rests on a fundamental misunderstanding of the Rule of Reason frequently applied in antitrust litigation, we affirm.

P.H.

I

Engineering is an important and learned profession. There are over 750,000 graduate engineers in the United States, of whom about 325,000 are registered as professional engineers.... About half of

23. See ¶¶ 230d, 250c; United States v. American Socy. of Anesthesiologists, 473 F. Supp. 147, 159 (S.D.N.Y. 1979) (relative value guides not unlawful per se because no agreement on price; although they "tend to affect price formation," practice is reasonable; anesthesiologists not really in competition where patients do not select them; no harm vis-à-vis insurers, no evidence of fee stabilization or increase); In re American College of Obstetricians & Gynecologists, 88 F.T.C. 955 (1976) (one of many consent orders prohibiting medical societies from taking any part in developing or circulating relative value scales).

24. Goldfarb v. Virginia St. Bar, 421 U.S. 773, 783 (1975) (in condemning a bar association's fee schedule enforced by the threat of disciplining "unethical" lawyers charging less, Court suggested that purely advisory fee schedule might be lawful).

those who are registered engage in consulting engineering on a fee basis. They perform services in connection with the study, design, and construction of all types of improvements to real property — bridges, office buildings, airports and factories are examples. . . .

The National Society of Professional Engineers (Society) was organized in 1935 to deal with the nontechnical aspects of engineering practice, including the promotion of the professional, social, and economic interests of its members. Its present membership of 69,000 resides throughout the United States and in some foreign countries. Approximately 12,000 members are consulting engineers who offer their services to governmental, industrial, and private clients. . . .

The charges of a consulting engineer may be computed in different ways. He may charge the client a percentage cost of the project, may set his fee at his actual cost plus overhead plus a reasonable profit, may charge fixed rates per hour for different types of work, may perform an assignment for a specific sum, or he may combine one or more of these approaches. Suggested fee schedules for particular types of services in certain areas have been promulgated from time to time by various local societies. This case does not, however, involve any claim that the National Society has tried to fix specific fees, or even a specific method of calculating fees. It involves a charge that the members of the Society have unlawfully agreed to refuse to negotiate or even to discuss the question of fees until after a prospective client has selected the engineer for a particular project. Evidence of this agreement is found in §11(c) of the Society's Code of Ethics, adopted in July 1964.[3] . . . Under the traditional method, the client initially selects an engineer on the basis of background and reputation, not price.[6] . . .

allegation

---

3. That section, which remained in effect at the time of trial, provided:

> Section 11 — The Engineer will not compete unfairly with another engineer by attempting to obtain employment or advancement or professional engagements by competitive bidding. . . .
> c. He shall not solicit or submit engineering proposals on the basis of competitive bidding. Competitive bidding for professional engineering services is defined as the formal or informal submission, or receipt, of verbal or written estimates of cost or proposals in terms of dollars, man days of work required, percentage of construction cost, or any other measure of compensation whereby the prospective client may compare engineering services on a price basis prior to the time that one engineer, or one engineering organization, has been selected for negotiations. The disclosure of recommended fee schedules prepared by various engineering societies is not considered to constitute competitive bidding. An Engineer requested to submit a fee proposal or bid prior to the selection of an engineer or firm subject to the negotiation of a satisfactory contract, shall attempt to have the procedure changed to conform to ethical practices, but if not successful he shall withdraw from consideration for the proposed work. These principles shall be applied by the Engineer in obtaining the services of other professions.

6. Having been selected, the engineer may then, in accordance with the Society's canons of ethics, negotiate a satisfactory fee arrangement with the client. If

In its answer the Society admitted the essential facts alleged by
the Government and pleaded a series of affirmative defenses, only
one of which remains in issue. In that defense, the Society averred
that the standard set out in the Code of Ethics was reasonable
because competition among professional engineers was contrary to
the public interest. It was averred that it would be cheaper and
easier for an engineer "to design and specify inefficient and unnecessarily expensive structures and methods of construction." Accordingly, competitive pressure to offer engineering services at the
lowest possible price would adversely affect the quality of engineering. Moreover, the practice of awarding engineering contracts to
the lowest bidder, regardless of quality, would be dangerous to the
public health, safety, and welfare. . . .

The District Court did not . . . make any finding on the question
whether, or to what extent, competition had led to inferior engineering work which, in turn, had adversely affected the public
health, safety, or welfare. That inquiry was considered unnecessary
because the court was convinced that the ethical prohibition against
competitive bidding was "on its face a tampering with the price
structure of engineering fees in violation of §1 of the Sherman
Act."

Although it modified the injunction entered by the District
Court, the Court of Appeals affirmed its conclusion that the agreement was unlawful on its face and therefore "illegal without regard
to claimed or possible benefits."

II

In Goldfarb v. Virginia State Bar, 421 U.S. 773, the Court held that
a bar association's rule prescribing minimum fees for legal services
violated §1 of the Sherman Act. In that opinion the Court noted
that certain practices by members of a learned profession might
survive scrutiny under the Rule of Reason even though they would
be viewed as a violation of the Sherman Act in another context. . . .

A. THE RULE OF REASON

One problem presented by the language of §1 of the Sherman
Act is that it cannot mean what it says. The statute says that "every"
contract that restrains trade is unlawful. But, as Justice Brandeis
perceptively noted, restraint is the very essence of every contract;
read literally, §1 would outlaw the entire body of private contract
law. Yet it is that body of law that establishes the enforceability of

---

the negotiations are unsuccessful, then the client may withdraw his selection and
approach a new engineer.

commercial agreements and enables competitive markets — indeed, a competitive economy — to function effectively.

Congress, however, did not intend the text of the Sherman Act to delineate the full meaning of the statute or its application in concrete situations. The legislative history makes it perfectly clear that it expected the courts to give shape to the statute's broad mandate by drawing on common-law tradition. The Rule of Reason, with its origins in common-law precedents long antedating the Sherman Act, has served that purpose. It has been used to give the Act both flexibility and definition, and its central principle of antitrust analysis has remained constant. Contrary to its name, the Rule does not open the field of antitrust inquiry to any argument in favor of a challenged restraint that may fall within the realm of reason. Instead, it focuses directly on the challenged restraint's impact on competitive conditions.

This principle is apparent in even the earliest of cases applying the Rule of Reason, Mitchel v. Reynolds [1 P. Wms. 181, 24 Eng. Rep. 347 (1711)]. *Mitchel* involved the enforceability of a promise by the seller of a bakery that he would not compete with the purchaser of his business. The covenant was for a limited time and applied only to the area in which the baker had operated. It was therefore upheld as reasonable, even though it deprived the public of the benefit of potential competition. The long-run benefit of enhancing the marketability of the business itself — and thereby providing incentives to develop such an enterprise — outweighed the temporary and limited loss of competition.

The Rule of Reason suggested by *Mitchel* has been regarded as a standard for testing the enforceability of covenants in restraint of trade which are ancillary to a legitimate transaction, such as an employment contract or the sale of a going business. Judge (later Chief Justice) Taft so interpreted the Rule in his classic rejection of the argument that competitors may lawfully agree to sell their goods at the same price as long as the agreed upon price is reasonable. *Addyston Pipe.* That case, and subsequent decisions by this Court, unequivocally foreclose an interpretation of the Rule as permitting an inquiry into the reasonableness of the prices set by private agreement.

The early cases also foreclose the argument that because of the special characteristics of a particular industry, monopolistic arrangements will better promote trade and commerce than competition. *Trans-Missouri; Joint Traffic.* That kind of argument is properly addressed to Congress and may justify an exemption from the statute for specific industries, but it is not permitted by the Rule of Reason. As the Court observed in *Standard Oil*, "restraints of trade within the purview of the statute ... [can] not be taken out of that category by indulging in general reasoning as to the expediency or nonexpediency of having made the contracts or the wisdom or want of wisdom of the statute which prohibited their being made."

The test prescribed in *Standard Oil* is whether the challenged contracts or acts "were unreasonably restrictive of competitive conditions." Unreasonableness under that test could be based either (1) on the nature or character of the contracts, or (2) on surrounding circumstances giving rise to the inference or presumption that they were intended to restrain trade and enhance prices. Under either branch of the test, the inquiry is confined to a consideration of impact on competitive conditions. . . .

[T]he inquiry mandated by the Rule of Reason is whether the challenged agreement is one that promotes competition or one that suppresses competition. "The true test of legality is whether the restraint imposed is such as merely regulates and perhaps thereby promotes competition or whether it is such as may suppress or even destroy competition." [*Chicago Board of Trade.*]

There are, thus, two complementary categories of antitrust analysis. In the first category are agreements whose nature and necessary effect are so plainly anticompetitive that no elaborate study of the industry is needed to establish their illegality — they are "illegal per se." In the second category are agreements whose competitive effect can only be evaluated by analyzing the facts peculiar to the business, the history of the restraint, and the reasons why it was imposed. In either event, the purpose of the analysis is to form a judgment about the competitive significance of the restraint; it is not to decide whether a policy favoring competition is in the public interest, or in the interest of the members of an industry. Subject to exceptions defined by statute, that policy decision has been made by the Congress.

B. THE BAN ON COMPETITIVE BIDDING . . .

In this case we are presented with an agreement among competitors to refuse to discuss prices with potential customers until after negotiations have resulted in the initial selection of an engineer. While this is not price fixing as such, no elaborate industry analysis is required to demonstrate the anticompetitive character of such an agreement. . . .

The Society's affirmative defense confirms rather than refutes the anticompetitive purpose and effect of its agreement. The Society argues that the restraint is justified because bidding on engineering services is inherently imprecise, would lead to deceptively low bids, and would thereby tempt individual engineers to do inferior work with consequent risk to public safety and health.[19] The logic of this argument rests on the assumption that the agreement will tend to maintain the price level; if it had no such effect, it would not serve its intended purpose. The Society nonetheless invokes the Rule of Reason, arguing that its restraint on price competition ultimately inures to the public benefit by preventing the production of inferior work and by insuring ethical behavior. As the preceding discussion of the Rule of Reason reveals, this Court has never accepted such an argument. . . .

[A] purchaser might conclude that his interest in quality — which may embrace the safety of the end product — outweighs the advantages of achieving cost savings by pitting one competitor against another. Or an individual vendor might independently refrain from price negotiation until he has satisfied himself that he fully understands the scope of his customers' needs. . . . [But the Society's] ban on competitive bidding prevents all customers from making price comparisons in the initial selection of an engineer, and imposes the Society's views of the costs and benefits of competition on the entire marketplace. It is this restraint that must be justified under the Rule of Reason, and petitioner's attempt to do so on the basis of the potential threat that competition poses to the public safety and the ethics of its profession is nothing less than a frontal assault on the basic policy of the Sherman Act.

The Sherman Act reflects a legislative judgment that ultimately competition will not only produce lower prices, but also better goods and services. "The heart of our national economic policy long has been faith in the value of competition." . . . The assumption that competition is the best method of allocating resources in a free market recognizes that all elements of a bargain — quality, service, safety, and durability — and not just the immediate cost, are favorably affected by the free opportunity to select among alternative offers. Even assuming occasional exceptions to the presumed consequences of competition, the statutory policy precludes inquiry into the question whether competition is good or bad. . . .

19. The Society also points out that competition, in the form of bargaining between the engineer and customer, is allowed under its canon of ethics once an engineer has been initially selected. . . . It then contends that its prohibition of competitive bidding regulates only the *timing* of competition, thus making this case analogous to *Chicago Board of Trade*. . . . We find this reliance on *Chicago Board of Trade* misplaced for two reasons. First, petitioner's claim mistakenly treats negotiation between a single seller and a single buyer as the equivalent of competition between two or more potential sellers. Second . . . *Chicago Board of Trade* . . . considered the exchange's regulation of price information as having a positive effect on competition. . . .

National Society of Professional Engineers

We adhere to the view expressed in *Goldfarb* that, by their nature, professional services may differ significantly from other business services, and, accordingly, the nature of the competition in such services may vary. Ethical norms may serve to regulate and promote this competition, and thus fall within the Rule of Reason.[22] But the Society's argument in this case is a far cry from such a position. We are faced with a contention that a total ban on competitive bidding is necessary because otherwise engineers will be tempted to submit deceptively low bids. Certainly, the problem of professional deception is a proper subject of an ethical canon. But, once again, the equation of competition with deception, like the similar equation with safety hazards, is simply too broad; we may assume that competition is not entirely conducive to ethical behavior, but that is not a reason, cognizable under the Sherman Act, for doing away with competition. . . .

III

The judgment entered by the District Court, as modified by the Court of Appeals, prohibits the Society from adopting any official opinion, policy statement, or guideline stating or implying that competitive bidding is unethical. Petitioner argues that this judgment abridges its First Amendment rights. We find no merit in this contention. . . .

Affirmed.

[Chief Justice Burger concurred in finding a violation but believed that the First Amendment protected the defendant's right to publish its view that competitive bidding is unethical. Justices Blackmun and Rehnquist concurred in part and in the judgment. They did not share the Court's apparent suggestion that the Sherman Act forbids any professional society's ethical rules that have an anticompetitive effect. They could imagine ethical rules — such as a medical association's prescription of standards of minimum competence — that would be proper, yet have anticompetitive effects. The present case could be more simply resolved because the Society's rule was overbroad in forbidding a client's solicitation of simultaneous bids from several engineers and thus of gaining competitive price information before engaging a single engineer, regardless

22. Courts have, for instance, upheld marketing restraints related to the safety of a product, provided that they have no anticompetitive effect and that they are reasonably ancillary to the seller's main purpose of protecting the public from harm or itself from product liability. See, e.g., Tripoli Co. v. Wella Corp., 425 F.2d 932 (3d Cir. 1970) (en banc). Cf. *Sylvania*.

of the sophistication of the purchaser or the complexity of the project.]²⁵

219. (a) Does the *Engineers* result reflect a per se or a rule of reason approach? What is the Court's rule as to admissible justifications? Does *Socony* allow even this much of a defense if the case involves price fixing? Is this a price-fixing case, as defined by *Socony*? Does the Court adequately distinguish the safety justification discussed in its footnote 22?

(b) Is the Court accurate in stating that it "has never accepted such an argument" concerning the need to maintain a price level? How about *Chicago Board of Trade*, which the Court quotes for its formulation of the rule of reason? Is the Court's two-branched test consistent with either *Socony* or *Standard Oil*?

(c) What does the Court mean by "competition" in its rule of reason test? Does *Engineers* condemn as unreasonable every restraint on competition?

(d) Why is the justification offered by the Society excluded but that offered in *BMI* admitted? If the difficulty of individual transactions and monitoring justify the restraint in *BMI*, why is the difficulty of quality monitoring irrelevant in *Engineers*?²⁶ Does *BMI* adhere to the Court's statement that "early cases also foreclose the argument that because of special characteristics of a particular industry, monopolistic arrangements will better promote trade and commerce than competition"?

220. Consider the following arrangements:

(a) Twenty firms account for 85 percent of the nation's production of canvas-topped, rubber-bottomed shoes, known by such names as tennis or gym shoes or sneakers. Imperfect shoes not of sufficiently high quality for distribution under their own names have been sold unbranded as "rejects" to merchandisers who sell them at reduced prices. Fearful that some consumers unknowingly buy imperfect shoes, and solicitous of the feet of our nation's youth, these 20 firms agree that they will no longer sell their rejects domestically. Is the agreement lawful? probably not

(b) Suppose that the three television networks agreed that each would set aside two prime-time hours each week for quality cultural programming and also established a procedure for noncompetitive scheduling of such programs so that willing viewers would have an opportunity to watch all of the quality programs. Is there any harm to competition? Is there a legitimate justification? Should the government prosecute?[27]

(c) Would it be legitimate for lawyers or physicians to agree not to advertise prices on the ground that such advertising was inherently deceptive?[28]

(d) A few years ago, an area's leading grocery chain began distributing trading stamps to its customers. For every grocery purchase, the customer received stamps that could be redeemed, when a sufficient number were collected, for "free gifts." The stamps and their "free gifts" attracted so much patronage that competing grocers adopted them in self-defense. One large chain resisted for six months, but it was unable to stem the loss of business by truthfully advertising that the use of trading stamps increased grocery costs by more than the value of the "gifts." Now that all grocers use stamps, they bring little advantage to any one of

27. United States v. National Assn. of Broadcasters, 536 F. Supp. 149, 156 (D.D.C. 1982) (challenge to NAB restrictions limiting commercial time and number of commercial interruptions per hour and forbidding advertising of more than one product in a 30 second advertisement; last restriction held per se unlawful, others to be tested by rule of reason because industry has "attributes which in a fundamental way contradict the assumed link between supply and price that underlies the per se treatment of supply restrictions"), 553 F. Supp. 621 (1982) (approving consent decree removing NAB advertising limits including those limiting advertising directed at children; removal contrary to public interest, but required by *Engineers*). Congress passed the "Television Program Improvement Act of 1990," 47 U.S.C. §303c. This Act granted a temporary antitrust exemption, covering only the three years following December 1, 1990, to "persons in the television industry" who engaged in "joint discussion, consideration, review, action, or agreement . . . for the purpose of, and limited to, developing and disseminating voluntary guidelines designed to alleviate the negative impact of violence in telecast material."

28. Bates v. State Bar of Ariz., 433 U.S. 350 (1977) (condemning state restrictions on price advertising by lawyers as unconstitutional violation of the First Amendment; state action immunity for Sherman Act claim); American Med. Assn. v. FTC, 638 F.2d 443 (2d Cir. 1980), aff'd by an equally divided court, 455 U.S. 676 (1982) (affirming FTC order forbidding AMA restrictions on price and other advertising while permitting reasonable guidelines governing false or deceptive advertising and regulating in-person solicitation of patients when peculiarly vulnerable to undue influence). For more on the impact that advertising may have on price, see L. Benham, The Effect of Advertising on the Price of Eyeglasses, 15 J.L. & Econ. 337 (1972) (empirical study demonstrating that prices were significantly lower in markets where advertising was allowed). See also Wilk v. American Med. Assn., 895 F.2d 352 (7th Cir.), cert. denied, 496 U.S. 927 (1990) (holding the ethical rule "prohibiting medical physicians from associating professionally with unscientific practitioners" to violate §1 of the Sherman Act under a rule of reason analysis).

them. Could they lawfully agree to abandon the use of trading stamps?[29] No

(e) Fifteen elite universities decide that in order to preserve a need-blind admissions policy, no school should be able to attract qualified, but non-needy students through merit scholarships or other forms of financial aid. The schools agree that they will compare the financial award packages individually determined for any student admitted to more than one of the participating schools. When the packages differ, they agree to arrive at a "compromise" award, so that no such student can use price as a basis of selection. The schools defend their agreement on the grounds that it serves the social goal of providing a better education to a broader group of students. Does the agreement violate the Sherman Act?[30]

NATIONAL COLLEGIATE ATHLETIC ASSOCIATION v. BOARD OF REGENTS OF THE UNIVERSITY OF OKLAHOMA
468 U.S. 85 (1984)

Justice STEVENS. . . . [This case involves a challenge to the NCAA's plan for televising college football games.] The plan adopted in 1981 for the 1982-85 seasons . . . like each of its predecessors, recites that it is intended to reduce, insofar as possible, the adverse effects of live television upon football game attendance. It provides that "all forms of television of the football games of NCAA member institutions during the Plan control periods shall be in accordance with this Plan." . . .

In separate agreements with each of the carrying networks, ABC and [CBS], the NCAA granted each the right to telecast the 14 live "exposures" described in the plan, in accordance with the "ground

29. United States v. Gasoline Retailers Assn., 285 F.2d 688 (7th Cir. 1961) (condemning retailers' agreement not to give trading stamps and not to advertise prices with curbside signs). See also *Catalano*, note 8.

30. This hypothetical is based on the facts surrounding the "Overlap" agreement, encompassing the Ivy League and MIT, among other prestigious schools. See United States v. Brown University, 5 F.3d 658 (3d Cir. 1993) (reversing the "quick look" rule of reason treatment accorded the agreement by the District Court and remanding for a full rule of reason analysis, in light of MIT's procompetitive justifications). After this decision, MIT joined the consent decree already binding on the Ivy League schools. See D. Carlton, G. Bamberger & R. Epstein, Antitrust and Higher Education: Was There a Conspiracy to Restrict Financial Aid?, 26 Rand J. Econ. 131 (1995); F. Espisito & L. Espisito, Monopolization, Social Welfare and Overlap, 40 Antitr. Bull. 433 (1995); M. Rothschild & L. White, The Analytics of the Pricing of Higher Education and Other Services in Which the Customers Are Inputs, 103 J. Pol. Econ. 573 (1995).

rules" set forth therein. Each of the networks agreed to pay a specified "minimum aggregate compensation to the participating NCAA
member institutions" during the 4-year period in an amount that
totaled $131,750,000. In essence the agreement authorized each
network to negotiate directly with member schools for the right to
televise their games. . . . Except for differences in payment between
national and regional telecasts, and with respect to Division II and
Division III games, the amount that any team receives does not
change with the size of the viewing audience, the number of markets in which the game is telecast, or the particular characteristic of
the game or the participating teams. Instead, the "ground rules"
provide that the carrying networks make alternate selections of
those games they wish to televise, and thereby obtain the exclusive
right to submit a bid at an essentially fixed price to the institutions
involved.

summary of agreement

The plan also contains "appearance requirements" and "appearance limitations" which pertain to each of the 2-year periods
that the plan is in effect. The basic requirement imposed on each of
the two networks is that it must schedule appearances for at least 82
different member institutions during each 2-year period. Under the
appearance limitations no member institution is eligible to appear
on television more than a total of six times and more than four
times nationally, with the appearances to be divided equally between the two carrying networks. The number of exposures specified in the contracts also sets an absolute maximum on the number
of games that can be broadcast. . . .

BACKGROUND OF THIS CONTROVERSY

Beginning in 1979 CFA [College Football Association, consisting
of major football-playing institutions] members began to advocate
that colleges with major football programs should have a greater
voice in the formulation of football television policy than they had
in the NCAA. CFA . . . obtained a contract offer from the National
Broadcasting Co. (NBC). This contract, which it signed in August
1981, would have allowed a more liberal number of appearances for
each institution, and would have increased the overall revenues
realized by CFA members.

Facts

In response the NCAA publicly announced that it would take
disciplinary action against any CFA member that complied with the
CFA-NBC contract. The NCAA made it clear that sanctions would
not be limited to the football programs of CFA members, but would
apply to other sports as well. On September 8, 1981, respondents
commenced this action. . . .

II . . .

By participating in an association which prevents member institutions from competing against each other on the basis of price or kind of television rights that can be offered to broadcasters, the NCAA member institutions have created a horizontal restraint — an agreement among competitors on the way in which they will compete with one another. A restraint of this type has often been held to be unreasonable as a matter of law. Because it places a ceiling on the number of games member institutions may televise, the horizontal agreement places an artificial limit on the quantity of televised football that is available to broadcasters and consumers. By restraining the quantity of television rights available for sale, the challenged practices create a limitation on output; our cases have held that such limitations are unreasonable restraints of trade. Moreover, the District Court found that the minimum aggregate price in fact operates to preclude any price negotiation between broadcasters and institutions, thereby constituting horizontal price fixing, perhaps the paradigm of an unreasonable restraint of trade.

Horizontal price fixing and output limitation are ordinarily condemned as a matter of law under an "illegal per se" approach because the probability that these practices are anticompetitive is so high; a per se rule is applied when "the practice facially appears to be one that would always or almost always tend to restrict competition and decrease output." *Broadcast Music.* In such circumstances a restraint is presumed unreasonable without inquiry into the particular market context in which it is found. Nevertheless, we have decided that it would be inappropriate to apply a per se rule to this case. This decision is not based on a lack of judicial experience with this type of arrangement,[21] on the fact that the NCAA is organized as a nonprofit entity,[22] or on our respect for the NCAA's historic

---

21. While judicial inexperience with a particular arrangement counsels against extending the reach of per se rules, see *Broadcast Music*; *Topco*; White Motor Co. v. United States, 372 U.S. 253, 263 (1963), the likelihood that horizontal price and output restrictions are anticompetitive is generally sufficient to justify application of the per se rule without inquiry into the special characteristics of a particular industry. See *Maricopa*; *Engineers*.

22. There is no doubt that the sweeping language of §1 applies to nonprofit entities, Goldfarb v. Virginia State Bar, 421 U.S. 773, 786-787 (1975), and in the past we have imposed antitrust liability on nonprofit entities which have engaged in anticompetitive conduct, American Society of Mechanical Engineers, Inc. v. Hydrolevel Corp., 456 U.S. 556, 576 (1982). Moreover, the economic significance of the NCAA's nonprofit character is questionable at best. Since the District Court found that the NCAA and its member institutions are in fact organized to maximize revenues, it is unclear why petitioner is less likely to restrict output in order to raise revenues above those that could be realized in a competitive market than

role in the preservation and encouragement of intercollegiate amateur athletics.[23] Rather, what is critical is that this case involves an
industry in which horizontal restraints on competition are essential
if the product is to be available at all. . . .

What the NCAA and its member institutions market in this case is
competition itself — contests between competing institutions. Of
course, this would be completely ineffective if there were no rules
on which the competitors agreed to create and define the competition to be marketed. A myriad of rules affecting such matters as the
size of the field, the number of players on a team, and the extent to
which physical violence is to be encouraged or proscribed, all must
be agreed upon, and all restrain the manner in which institutions
compete. Moreover, the NCAA seeks to market a particular brand
of football — college football. The identification of this "product"
with an academic tradition differentiates college football from and
makes it more popular than professional sports to which it might
otherwise be comparable, such as, for example, minor league baseball. In order to preserve the character and quality of the
"product," athletes must not be paid, must be required to attend
class, and the like. And the integrity of the "product" cannot be
preserved except by mutual agreement; if an institution adopted
such restrictions unilaterally, its effectiveness as a competitor on the
playing field might soon be destroyed. Thus, the NCAA plays a vital
role in enabling college football to preserve its character, and as a
result enables a product to be marketed which might otherwise be
unavailable. In performing this role, its actions widen consumer
choice — not only the choices available to sport fans but also those
available to athletes — and hence can be viewed as procompetitive.

Broadcast Music squarely holds that a joint selling arrangement
may be so efficient that it will increase sellers' aggregate output and
thus be procompetitive. Similarly, as we indicated in *Sylvania*, a
restraint in a limited aspect of a market may actually enhance
marketwide competition. Respondents concede that the great
majority of the NCAA's regulations enhance competition among
member institutions. Thus, despite the fact that this case involves
restraints on the ability of member institutions to compete in terms
of price and output, a fair evaluation of their competitive character
requires consideration of the NCAA's justifications for the restraints.

would be a for-profit entity. Petitioner does not rely on its nonprofit character as a
basis for reversal.

23. While as the guardian of an important American tradition, the NCAA's
motives must be accorded a respectful presumption of validity, it is nevertheless
well-settled that good motives will not validate an otherwise anticompetitive
practice. . . .

Our analysis of this case under the Rule of Reason, of course, does not change the ultimate focus of our inquiry. Both per se rules and the Rule of Reason are employed "to form a judgment about the competitive significance of the restraint." *Engineers*. . . .[26]

III

Because it restrains price and output, the NCAA's television plan has a significant potential for anticompetitive effects. The findings of the District Court indicate that this potential has been realized. The District Court found that if member institutions were free to sell television rights, many more games would be shown on television, and that the NCAA's output restriction has the effect of raising the price the networks pay for television rights. Moreover, the court found that by fixing a price for television rights to all games, the NCAA creates a price structure that is unresponsive to viewer demand and unrelated to the prices that would prevail in a competitive market. And, of course, since as a practical matter all member institutions need NCAA approval, members have no real choice but to adhere to the NCAA's television controls. . . .

Restrictions on price and output are the paradigmatic examples of restraints of trade that the Sherman Act was intended to prohibit. At the same time, the television plan eliminates competitors from the market, since only those broadcasters able to bid on television rights covering the entire NCAA can compete. Thus, as the District Court found, many telecasts that would occur in a competitive market are foreclosed by the NCAA's plan.

Petitioner argues, however, that its television plan can have no significant anticompetitive effect since the record indicates that it has no market power — no ability to alter the interaction of supply and demand in the market. We must reject this argument for two reasons, one legal, one factual.

As a matter of law, the absence of proof of market power does not justify a naked restriction on price or output. To the contrary, when there is an agreement not to compete in terms of price or output, "no elaborate industry analysis is required to demonstrate the anticompetitive character of such an agreement." *Engineers*.[39] Peti-

---

26. Indeed there is often no bright line separating per se from Rule of Reason analysis. Per se rules may require considerable inquiry into market conditions before the evidence justifies a presumption of anticompetitive conduct. For example, while the Court has spoken of a "per se" rule against tying arrangements, it has also recognized that tying may have procompetitive justifications that make it inappropriate to condemn without considerable market analysis.

39.

> The fact that a practice is not categorically unlawful in all or most of its manifestations certainly does not mean that it is universally lawful. For example, joint buying or

tioner does not quarrel with the District Court's finding that price and output are not responsive to demand. Thus the plan is inconsistent with the Sherman Act's command that price and supply be responsive to consumer preference. We have never required proof of market power in such a case. This naked restraint on price and output requires some competitive justification even in the absence of a detailed market analysis.

As a factual matter, it is evident that petitioner does possess market power. The District Court ... found that intercollegiate football telecasts generate an audience uniquely attractive to advertisers and that competitors are unable to offer programming that can attract a similar audience. These findings amply support its conclusion that the NCAA possesses market power. Indeed, the District Court's subsidiary finding that advertisers will pay a premium price per viewer to reach audiences watching college football because of their demographic characteristics is vivid evidence of the uniqueness of this product. Moreover, the District Court's market analysis is firmly supported by our decision in International Boxing Club v. United States, 358 U.S. 242 (1958), that championship boxing events are uniquely attractive to fans and hence constitute a market separate from that for nonchampionship events. . . .

IV

Relying on *Broadcast Music*, petitioner argues that its television plan constitutes a cooperative "joint venture" which assists in the marketing of broadcast rights and hence is procompetitive. While joint ventures have no immunity from the antitrust laws, ... a joint selling arrangement may "mak[e] possible a new product by reaping otherwise unattainable efficiencies." The essential contribution made by the NCAA's arrangement is to define the number of games that may be televised, to establish the price for each exposure, and to define the basic terms of each contract between the network and a home team. The NCAA does not, however, act as a selling agent for any school or for any conference of schools. . . . Unlike *Broadcast*

---

selling arrangements are not unlawful per se, but a court would not hesitate in enjoining a domestic selling arrangement by which, say, Ford and General Motors distributed their automobiles nationally through a single selling agent. Even without a trial, the judge will know that these two large firms are major factors in the automobile market, that such joint selling would eliminate important price competition between them, that they are quite substantial enough to distribute their products independently, and that one can hardly imagine a pro-competitive justification actually probable in fact or strong enough in principle to make this particular joint selling arrangement "reasonable" under Sherman Act §1. The essential point is that the rule of reason can sometimes be applied in the twinkling of an eye.

P. Areeda, The "Rule of Reason" in Antitrust Analysis: General Issues 37-38 (Federal Judicial Center, June 1981) (parenthetical omitted).

Music's blanket license covering broadcast rights to a large number of individual compositions, here the same rights are still sold on an individual basis, only in a noncompetitive market.

The District Court did not find that the NCAA's television plan produced any procompetitive efficiencies which enhanced the competitiveness of college football television rights; to the contrary it concluded that NCAA football could be marketed just as effectively without the television plan. . . . There is therefore no predicate in the findings for petitioner's efficiency justification. Indeed, petitioner's argument is refuted by the District Court's finding concerning price and output. If the NCAA's television plan produced procompetitive efficiencies, the plan would increase output and reduce the price of televised games. The District Court's contrary findings accordingly undermine petitioner's position. . . .

Neither is the NCAA's television plan necessary to enable the NCAA to penetrate the market through an attractive package sale. Since broadcasting rights to college football constitute a unique product for which there is no ready substitute, there is no need for collective action in order to enable the product to compete against its nonexistent competitors.[55] This is borne out by the District Court's finding that the NCAA's television plan *reduces* the volume of television rights sold.

V

Throughout the history of its regulation of intercollegiate football telecasts, the NCAA has indicated its concern with protecting live attendance. . . . [However] the television plan has evolved in a manner inconsistent with its original design to protect gate attendance. Under the current plan, games are shown on television during all hours that college football games are played. The plan simply does not protect live attendance by ensuring that games will not be shown on television at the same time as live events.

There is, however, a more fundamental reason for rejecting this defense. The NCAA's argument that its television plan is necessary to protect live attendance is not based on a desire to maintain the integrity of college football as a distinct and attractive product, but rather on a fear that the product will not prove sufficiently attractive to draw live attendance when faced with competition from televised games. At bottom the NCAA's position is that ticket sales

55. If the NCAA faced "interbrand" competition from available substitutes, then certain forms of collective action might be appropriate in order to enhance its ability to compete. See *Sylvania*. Our conclusion concerning the availability of substitutes forecloses such a justification in this case, however.

for most college games are unable to compete in a free market.[60]
The television plan protects ticket sales by limiting output — just as
any monopolist increases revenues by reducing output. By seeking
to insulate live ticket sales from the full spectrum of competition
because of its assumption that the product itself is insufficiently
attractive to consumers, petitioner forwards a justification that is
inconsistent with the basic policy of the Sherman Act. "[T]he Rule
of Reason does not support a defense based on the assumption that
competition itself is unreasonable." *Engineers.*

VI . . .

Our decision not to apply a per se rule to this case rests in large part
on our recognition that a certain degree of cooperation is necessary
if the type of competition that petitioner and its member institutions seek to market is to be preserved. . . . The specific restraints on
football telecasts that are challenged in this case do not, however,
fit into the same mold as do rules defining the conditions of the
contest, the eligibility of participants, or the manner in which members of a joint enterprise shall share the responsibilities and the
benefits of the total venture.

The NCAA does not claim that its television plan has equalized or
is intended to equalize competition within any one league. . . . The
television plan is not even arguably tailored to serve such an interest.
It does not regulate the amount of money that any college may
spend on its football program, nor the way in which the colleges may
use the revenues that are generated by their football programs,
whether derived from the sale of television rights, the sale of tickets,
or the sale of concessions or program advertising. The plan simply
imposes a restriction on one source of revenue that is more important to some colleges than to others. There is no evidence that this
restriction produces any greater measure of equality throughout the
NCAA than would a restriction on alumni donations, tuition rates, or
any other revenue-producing activity. At the same time, as the District Court found, the NCAA imposes a variety of other restrictions
designed to preserve amateurism which are much better tailored to
the goal of competitive balance than is the television plan, and which
are "clearly sufficient" to preserve competitive balance to the extent
it is within the NCAA's power to do so. . . .

60. Ironically, to the extent that the NCAA's position has merit, it rests on the
assumption that football telecasts are a unique product. If, as the NCAA argues, all
television programming is essentially fungible, it would not be possible to protect
attendance without banning all television during the hours at which intercollegiate
football games are held.

VII

The NCAA plays a critical role in the maintenance of a revered tradition of amateurism in college sports. There can be no question but that it needs ample latitude to play that role, or that the preservation of the student-athlete in higher education adds richness and diversity to intercollegiate athletics and is entirely consistent with the goals of the Sherman Act. But consistent with the Sherman Act, the role of the NCAA must be to *preserve* a tradition that might otherwise die; rules that restrict output are hardly consistent with this role. . . .

[Justices White and Rehnquist dissented. Their primary disagreement was that the case presented important noncommercial dimensions, and therefore should be judged differently. The NCAA's limitations were justified by their need to maintain competition in an amateur context. *Engineers* does not require educational institutions pursuing noneconomic values to justify their actions without regard to noneconomic values like the promotion of amateurism. In addition, the dissenters believed that output, as measured by total viewers, rather than by games telecast, could increase. Maximizing viewers would maximize what advertisers would be willing to pay the networks and thus maximize what networks would be willing to pay the NCAA. This would be the objective of the NCAA as a rational profit maximizer. In any event, reductions in output are not decisive since the NCAA markets a different product — exclusive television rights — that could not be sold by the schools individually. The dissent also disagreed that the NCAA had market power when competing against other forms of entertainment.]

221. (a) What was the NCAA's motive for enforcing the exclusive television arrangement? Who benefited from it?[31]

(b) Would the CFA members have sued if they were allowed more telecasts and dealt a bigger cut? Might the NCAA make such an offer in reaction to losing this case? If all members were satisfied, would the arrangement be legal? If not, who would have standing to challenge it?[32]

(c) If the plan were more stringent, and thus did more to protect live attendance, or really were necessary to prevent the few dozen best teams from becoming all the more dominant, would the Court have permitted the scheme? Would permission under such circum-

---

31. See A. Fleisher, B. Goff & R. Tollison, The National Collegiate Athletic Association: A Study in Cartel Behavior (1992).
32. See ¶¶144-146.

stances be consistent with *Engineers*? If not, what is the point of the rule of reason inquiry in this case?[33]

(d) How would you articulate a rule defining the nature of restrictions that should be permitted as ancillary to the creation of sports competition?[34]

(e) If unrestrained television exposure and revenue led colleges to "professionalize" sports or to deemphasize academic pursuits, would the NCAA's restraint lawfully preserve amateurism or scholarship?   *I agree here*

(f) Consider the College Football Bowl selection process. Numerous bowl games offer large sums of money to attract the best teams. Each year bowl invitations are made earlier and earlier, as each bowl attempts to secure the best teams possible. The early negotiations create inefficiencies because the best teams in the middle of the season may not be the best at season's end. Thus, better teams are excluded and some of the games match unequal teams. The College Football Association steps in and imposes a specified day for the first bowl offers, namely the day after the last regular-season football game is played. Legal under *Engineers* and *NCAA*? If not, should it be?[35]   *yes I think*

222.   Joint ventures — introduction.[36] Joint venture is an expansive notion without definite meaning or antitrust consequence.[37] The term commonly describes a combined undertaking requiring some degree of integration — as in *Chicago Board of Trade, Topco, BMI,* and *NCAA* — beyond concerted decisions that each party can implement separately (as in a product standardization agreement).

33. See Chicago Professional Sports Limited Partnership v. NBA, 961 F.2d 667 (7th Cir.), cert. denied, 506 U.S. 954 (1992) (condemning under the "quick look" rule of reason the league's limitation on the number of times league members could appear on television "superstations"; alleged free riding on network advertising could have been prevented by levying a charge).

34. See also *Molinas* and cases cited in note 10, Ch. 2E. In connection with that discussion, note the mechanism by which the NCAA was going to enforce its scheme against recalcitrant members.

35. A. Roth & X. Xing, Jumping the Gun: Imperfections and Institutions Related to the Timing of Market Transactions, 84 Am. Econ. Rev. 992 (1994).

36. See J. Brodley, Joint Ventures and Antitrust Policy, 95 Harv. L. Rev. 1523 (1982); R. Pitofsky, A Framework for Antitrust Analysis of Joint Ventures, 74 Geo. L.J. 1605 (1986); T. Piriano, Beyond Per Se, Rule of Reason or Merger Analysis: A New Antitrust Standard for Joint Ventures, 76 Minn. L. Rev. 1 (1991).

37. One of the most famous statements is in Timken Roller Bearing Co. v. United States, 341 U.S. 593, 598 (1951):

> Nor do we find any support in reason or authority for the proposition that agreements between legally separate persons and companies to suppress competition among themselves and others can be justified by labeling the project a "joint venture." Perhaps every agreement and combination to restrain trade could be so labeled.

Short of complete merger,[38] the venturers act as a single productive unit for purposes of the venture but retain their independent existence for other purposes.

A joint venture can appear in a variety of forms, including the simple agreement, formation of a partnership or association, merger of subsidiaries, or formation by two parents of a single, jointly owned subsidiary. Although the venture's form is generally irrelevant, the venturers' preexisting relationship often bears on the competitive significance of their collaboration. Before their joint undertaking, for example, the parent businesses might have been nonexistent, unrelated (automaker and book publisher), vertically complementary (iron-ore mine and steel maker), horizontally complementary (Atlantic and Pacific oil refiners or makers of different shoe machines), or actually competitive.[39] Competitive significance may also depend on the venture's relationship to its parents. A joint subsidiary's business, for example, may be unrelated, complementary, or competitive to the business of either or both parents.

As already indicated, joint ventures are addressed throughout this chapter, as well as at other points in the book. The Paragraphs that follow involve areas of the economy in which joint venture activity is significant and thought to be particularly important. In each case, the federal government has responded with policy guidance or legislation concerning the potential antitrust liability of the parties involved.

223.   Government health care enforcement policy statements.[40] In 1996, the Department of Justice and Federal Trade Commission jointly announced guidelines concerning enforcement policy in the health care industry.[41] Seven of the nine statements describe an "antitrust safety zone," characterizing circumstances in which no challenge would be made "absent extraordinary circumstances," and outline the agencies' "rule of reason" analysis for cases outside the safety zone.

Most of the statements concern joint ventures. Joint purchasing arrangements are in the safety zone if "(1) the purchases account for less than 35 percent of the total sales of the purchased products and services in the relevant market; and (2) the cost of the products

38. The fact that joint ventures are, in many respects, partial mergers suggests the applicability of the analysis in Ch. 5. See ¶532c.

39. Merging firms exhibit this same variety of relationships.

40. 4 Trade Reg. Rep. ¶13153 (1996).

41. These statements of enforcement policy supersede similar statements issued previously; the first version appeared in 1993.

and services purchased jointly accounts for less than 20 percent of the total revenues" of the competing participants. Hospital joint ventures involving high technology or other expensive equipment (involving new purchases or existing equipment) will be permitted when the venture "includes only the number of hospitals whose participation is needed to support the equipment" or that includes additional hospitals that could not otherwise support such equipment. Exclusive physician network joint ventures are in a safety zone if their members share substantial financial risk and the network includes no more than 20 percent of the physicians in each specialty in the relevant geographic market. Nonexclusive networks are in a safety zone if they include no more than 30 percent of such physicians. (When there are fewer than five physicians in a specialty, an exclusive venture may include one, but only on a nonexclusive basis; when there are fewer than four, a nonexclusive venture may include one.) Additional statements allow health care providers to provide information to buyers of health care services and to exchange price and cost information under certain circumstances. Exchange of fee-related information from health care providers to purchasers is also allowed under certain conditions that are designed to ensure that "an exchange of price or cost data is not used by competing providers for discussion or coordination of provider prices or costs."[42]

224. The management of Healthy Hospital is disappointed with its purchasing department, which seems to spend substantial staff resources in selecting supplies and yet has difficulty assessing quality and finding the best prices. It decides to combine with three other hospitals to form Super Supplier, which will be their joint purchasing agent. It will choose products and bargain for the best prices on behalf of the member hospitals as a whole; each hospital will no longer make independent selections and each will face the same prices. It is believed that a single joint agent will be better able to select quality supplies and intelligently bargain for good prices.

(a) Is this arrangement per se unlawful under *Socony?* Does Super Supplier "fix" the prices at which the members buy?[43] Should this arrangement be condemned? Even if the only alternative involves substantial duplication of effort and decreased quality in purchas-

---

42. A safety zone also is provided for hospital mergers in which one hospital has fewer than 100 licensed beds and an average occupancy of fewer than 40 patients. See ¶528.

43. Recall that *Socony* covers arrangements that lower prices. See ¶¶210, 211; *Maricopa.*

ing decisions?[44] Of what impact are the Statements of Antitrust Enforcement Policy in Health Care, summarized in ¶223?

(b) Should it matter whether the member hospitals constitute only a small portion of purchasers in their metropolitan area? What if all hospitals in the region joined Super Supplier? What if three national chains of hospitals and HMO's entered into such an arrangement? How do your answers square with footnote 59 in *Socony*?

225. National Cooperative Research and Production Act of 1993.[45] This legislation affects the application of the antitrust laws to research and development joint ventures and production joint ventures in the following manner. First, such joint ventures are to be judged under the rule of reason, "taking into account all relevant facts affecting competition, including, but not limited to, effects on competition in properly defined, relevant research, development, product, process, and service markets." This seems declaratory of preexisting law. Second, if such ventures are held unlawful, only actual damages, rather than treble damages, are to be awarded for any resulting injuries if the joint venturers have filed with the Justice Department and the Federal Trade Commission prompt notification of the nature and objectives of the venture and the identities of the parties. Furthermore, these provisions are to govern state law as well.

226. In evaluating the 1993 Act, consider the following problem. Twenty relatively small firms comprise the domestic industry that produces devices and materials required for civilian and military uses of nuclear energy. Although the cost of manufacture includes expensive automatic components and costly quality-control procedures, nearly half of the industry's aggregate expenditures are for research and development. To eliminate costly duplication and

---

44. Langston Corp. v. Standard Register Corp., 553 F. Supp. 632 (N.D. Ga. 1982) (denying preliminary injunction, because of no likelihood of success on the merits, sought by plaintiff terminated as supplier by hospital group purchasing organization; group purchasing not unlawful per se, and plaintiff does not suggest any anticompetitive effects). Cf. cases cited note 22 (insurance companies may act as single buyers on behalf of insureds).

45. 15 U.S.C. §§4301-4306. As originally enacted in 1984, this legislation applied only to research and development joint ventures. For economic analysis of the types of joint ventures governed by this legislation, see J. Ordover & R. Willig, Antitrust for High Technology Industries: Assessing Research Joint Ventures and Mergers, 28 J.L. & Econ. 311 (1985); M. Kamien, E. Muller & I. Zang, Research Joint Ventures and R&D Cartels, 82 Am. Econ. Rev. 1293 (1992); C. Shapiro & R. Willig, On the Treatment of Production Joint Ventures, 4 J. Econ. Persp. 113 (Summer 1990).

to conserve scarce research talent, these firms agree to establish a joint research laboratory whose work would be available to all firms contributing to its operations. Each member agrees to contribute 20 percent of its annual gross receipts toward the cost of operating the joint facility.

(a) What are the competitive dangers of this arrangement and how serious are they likely to be? How is your answer affected if the venture patents its results and makes them freely available to all members? What if members wishing to use the patents are charged royalties, which are then distributed among members in proportion to their annual contributions to operating costs?[46]

(b) Suppose that the arrangement has been in effect for five years. You are counsel for the firms. You recognize that you cannot conclusively demonstrate the absence of competitive harm, but you want to make as strong a factual showing as is possible. What facts might be both available and helpful to you?

(c) Are there any less dangerous ways in which most of the benefits of the joint research operation could be achieved?

(d) Would you hold the arrangement lawful under Sherman Act §1? How is your answer affected by the existence of the 1993 Act?

2C. WHEN DOES AN AGREEMENT EXIST?

227. Introduction. Sherman Act §1 is not addressed to individual conduct, no matter how anticompetitive or otherwise reprehensible. Rather, it applies only when several persons act with sufficient concert to form a "contract, combination, . . . or conspiracy." In the cases considered until now, the existence of an explicit agreement has generally been quite clear. But once it becomes known that such activity is prohibited, firms contemplating a conspiracy will conceal their tracks or attempt to achieve their goals more indirectly. As a result, proving a conspiracy in restraint of trade often involves the usual difficulties of inferring the existence of an agreement from defendants' behavior. But the cases in this section also involve a conspiracy issue that is peculiar to antitrust. As discussed next, oligopolists sometimes can achieve cartel-like results without any *express* agreement. We will then turn to cases deciding whether and under what circumstances firms acting in parallel fashion, with knowledge of each other's parallelism and with the realization that rivals will behave cooperatively, have entered into a

---

46. Review the second alternative after examining price-restricted patent licensing in Ch. 2G.

contract, combination, or conspiracy. This section closes by considering whether persons within a single economic unit are legally capable of conspiracy. Additional problems of conspiracy are treated in Chapter 4A.[1]

Oligopoly Theory[2]

228. The oligopoly or shared monopoly problem. There are markets where no single firm possesses sufficient power to be considered a monopoly but where the behavior of several firms results in economic performance that falls significantly short of a competitive result. Of course, the firms of every market necessarily account, when taken together, for 100 percent of that market. If they are numerous, however, such firms cannot achieve monopoly profits unless they form a cartel for express collusion. And if such firms, whether many or few, agree to restrict output and fix prices, they would offend the Sherman Act §1 proscription of agreements in unreasonable restraint of trade as well as the Sherman Act §2 condemnation of those who "conspire to monopolize."[3] In so-called oligopoly, however, where relatively few firms control the market, they may recognize their *interdependence*, with the result that each may restrict its output in order to charge a near-monopoly price.

The Paragraphs immediately following will examine the basic features of oligopoly behavior, pursue some of the complexities of oligopoly behavior that affect the likelihood of successful coordination, and discuss the evidence concerning the relationship between fewness and economic performance.[4] The reader should be aware that these topics are also relevant to the reasonableness of certain express agreements considered elsewhere in this chapter, to certain monopoly issues considered in Chapter 3, and to horizontal mergers, considered in Chapter 5D.

1. See generally VI P. Areeda, Antitrust Law, ch. 14 (1986; Supp. 1996); D. Turner, The Definition of Agreement Under the Sherman Act: Conscious Parallelism and Refusals to Deal, 75 Harv. L. Rev. 655 (1962); R. Posner, Oligopoly and the Antitrust Laws: A Suggested Approach, 21 Stan. L. Rev. 1562 (1969); J. Rahl, Conspiracy and the Antitrust Laws, 44 Ill. L. Rev. 743 (1950); W. Kovacic, The Identification and Proof of Horizontal Agreement Under the Antitrust Laws, 38 Antitr. Bull. 5 (1993).

2. See F.M. Scherer & D. Ross, Industrial Market Structure and Economic Performance, chs. 6-8 (3d ed. 1990); W.K. Viscusi, J. Vernon & J. Harrington, Economics of Regulation and Antitrust, ch. 5 (2d ed. 1995).

3. See Ch. 3A.

4. There is a limited degree of repetition here of material in Ch. 1A. Nevertheless, the reader should review ¶¶112, 114, 116.

229. Oligopoly — basic model and theory. (a) *Simple case.* When there exists a simple monopoly or a perfectly functioning cartel involving all firms in the industry, the result will be the price and output associated with monopoly. At the other extreme, if there are many firms, each competing with the others, there will be a competitive outcome, at which price equals marginal cost. No firm will charge more, because it would lose all its customers to competitors, and no firm would charge less, because losses would result.[5]

Now consider a simple oligopoly in which three identical firms together constitute the entire industry. First, if they were so lucky as to be charging the monopoly price, would any firm have an incentive to lower its price slightly? Each would be eager to do so in order to greatly expand sales at the expense of its competitors — all sales still being at a substantial profit. But each knows that the other firms would notice their own loss of sales, identify the cause, and probably react immediately by reducing their prices as well. At that point, the price-cutting firm has its previous share of the market, but at a price below the monopoly price, which is, by definition, that which maximizes profits for the industry and (because each is identical and is assumed to maintain the same share) for each firm. This contrasts with the competitive case. For example, in a market inhabited by 1000 small firms but in which the market price was somehow above the competitive level, a single firm would improve its profits by expanding output and sales and would do so, knowing that it is too small to have any significant impact on the market price or on its rivals. When there are numerous firms, many of them will reason similarly and expand output, the process continuing until the competitive price, equal to marginal cost, is reached. When the numbers are few, each will recognize their interdependence, knowing that each is too large to go unnoticed or be ignored by its rivals.[6]

Second, how do the firms get to the monopoly price in the first place and maintain it as conditions (and therefore the profit-maximizing price level) change over time? Suppose the price were below the monopoly price. With competition, any firm raising its price would face substantial lost sales and thus be deterred from any increase. But in oligopoly, a firm contemplating raising the price to the monopoly level will reason that each of the others will understand their common interest in following the price increase. The other firms will understand that if they do not follow quickly, the lead firm will lower its price to the previous level; if they follow, all will enjoy the benefits of the monopoly price. Moreover, the lead

5. See Ch. 1A.
6. Cf. ¶201b.

firm might be able to insulate itself from any risk by announcing such a price increase in advance, with the intention of rescinding it before the effective date if the others have not followed. Thus, even without direct communication, such firms may be able to reach and maintain the monopoly price through mutual coordination. They need only observe each other in the marketplace and act consistently with the group interest. Such action is fully consistent with the self-interest of each oligopolist, which obviously benefits by taking account of rivals' reactions to its behavior. But this self-interest is obviously different from that of the perfectly competitive firm that makes its decisions without regard to its impact on rivals.

(b) *Elements of successful oligopoly.* This simple illustration makes many assumptions favorable to successful oligopoly pricing that are not always present. The following Paragraphs, and other sections of the book, explore four key factors:

(1) The firms must be able to reach a consensus on the price. To the extent they differ in their costs, marketing strategies, information, or in other respects, they may prefer different market prices. (Although such disagreements may be resolved in a manner more favorable to some firms than others, the resulting price may still exceed the competitive level even if it does not attain the monopoly level.)

(2) The firms must be able to observe and compare each others' prices. If products differ in quality, there must be some understood relationship between them so that consensus is possible on appropriate price differentials between different products. If most sales involve unique, custom-made items, there must be a commonly understood method for determining when firms are undercutting the consensus price.

(3) "Cheating" must be detectable and punishable. If sales are large and infrequent, or price cuts can be made secretly, it may be difficult to know when a firm has defected. Moreover, the longer cheating can be kept secret, the greater the profit from defection and thus the greater the incentive to cheat.

(4) Producers of a given product may coordinate their behavior, but they must collectively enjoy market power if they are to succeed in moving prices above the competitive level. Such power would be absent if enough rival producers of the product refused to cooperate or if buyers can readily turn to substitute producers (including new entrants) or products.

(c) *Cartels compared.* To a large extent, the factors necessary for successful oligopoly pricing are the same as those necessary for a successful cartel. Cartel members must reach agreement, be able to compare members' prices and detect and punish defectors, and have sufficient power to gain from collaborating. The primary difference between the two cases involves communication and related problems of coordination. Disagreements, decisions to change prices in response to market conditions, and appropriate levels of punishment for defectors can be the subject of negotiation when there are meetings and written agreements. When firms rely on interdependent behavior, they often must signal their views indirectly, so there is additional room for misunderstanding, which can lead to competitive pricing.

(d) *Relevance of number of firms.* The degree of industry concentration is generally thought to be one of the most important factors affecting interdependent behavior. The illustration above was quite plausible with three firms, but would have been less plausible with 10, and rather implausible with 30 or more.[7] The number of firms affects all four factors. Larger numbers increase the likelihood of disagreements, the variety of differentiated products, the difficulty of detecting cheating by an individual firm and of enforcing a coordinated response, and the temptation to pursue an independent profit-maximizing course. Express cartels also face these problems, but their meetings and discussions may help them resolve some of them in a way not available to those relying on recognized interdependence.[8] But when numbers are small, costs similar, products relatively homogeneous, and transactions frequent and transparent, an express agreement may add little to the strength of tacit coordination. Indeed, those who can successfully coordinate their prices tacitly are likely to do so rather than form an express agreement, which is more likely to be detected and punished.

(e) *Oligopoly pricing in the absence of cooperative behavior.* Because the present subject concerns the application of the Sherman Act to agreements, the preceding discussion addresses cooperative behavior among firms in an oligopoly. It should be noted, however, that a lack of cooperation does not guarantee competitive results. Thus, a firm with a significant (even if far-from-dominant) market share might benefit from raising prices somewhat, if it anticipates losing only some of its sales to competitors. (Sales losses would be limited if competitors could not immediately expand their capacity or if products were differentiated.) Reduced sales at a supercompetitive price may be more profitable than greater sales at a competitive price. Moreover, if other firms also have significant market shares, they may act similarly. The possibility that increased concentration

7. T. Bresnahan & P. Reiss, Entry and Competition in Concentrated Markets, 99 J. Pol. Econ. 977 (1991) (empirical work showing that competition changes significantly with each new entrant until the market reaches three to five competitors; thereafter each new entrant has little impact).
8. See Ch. 2A, note 7.

may produce higher prices even in the absence of cooperation is an important concern of horizontal merger policy, as will be seen in Chapter 5D.

230.   Factors affecting likelihood of oligopolistic coordination.
(a) *Introduction.* The following factors affect the ability of a group of firms to achieve and maintain the most monopoly-like price. Many of these factors are largely beyond the firms' control, unlike the facilitating practices considered in Chapter 2D.

These factors will appear in a limitless array of combinations and in industries with varying numbers of firms. In addition, because the process of bargaining is often influenced by subtle factors — especially when communication is indirect and understandings are tacit — the history of interactions and the personalities of key individual decisionmakers may be influential. As a result, even the most careful and comprehensive analysis of a particular market often yields no certainties but only tendencies and probabilities. This is a common phenomenon in antitrust analysis.

(b) *Divergent interests.* A monopolist or a cartel does not seek high prices as such. Firms seek to maximize profits, which depend not only on price but also on sales volume and production cost. To maximize profits, one seeks the largest possible difference between aggregate revenues and aggregate costs. This is a relatively easy calculation for a monopolist.[9] But firms with different interests will tend to prefer different industry prices. For example, a lower price will be preferred by those with lower unit production costs, lower quality products, lower estimates of consumer demand, or greater fear that fringe competitors or new entrants will produce significant quantities at a given price. This preference will also vary if they suppose that different prices will alter the distribution of sales among firms. Such disagreement will often limit the ability of an oligopoly to price at the level that maximizes industry profits. Nor is there any ready mechanism (short of direct payments, which are more likely to be detectable and are clearly illegal) by which a firm preferring higher prices can transfer some of its profits to a firm preferring lower prices in exchange for an agreement to go along with the higher price.[10] At the same time, such differences do not

9. See ¶112a.
10. In principle, when there is an extensive cartel agreement, such sharing may be possible, allowing the cartel to achieve the same profit level as a monopolist that owned the same facilities as the cartel members. Such a cartel (1) may close down some plants entirely, (2) would operate industry facilities in the way that minimizes aggregate costs, (3) would set industry output at the level that yields the maximum excess of industry revenues over industry costs, and (4) would divide resulting industry profits among the members — in proportion, for example, to precartel

necessarily lead to a competitive price. If the three firms in the simple ¶229a example had varying price preferences, the one preferring the lowest price may prevail simply by refusing to charge more. But that price could still be substantially above the competitive level. In addition, a particular firm may have been acknowledged over the years as the industry leader. A sustained high price, although not optimal for each, may be preferred to the breakdown of cooperative pricing that could result when each firm insists on the price it prefers.

(c) *Available channels of verbal and nonverbal communication.* Conventional negotiation and agreement may be the most effective route for arriving at a mutually acceptable price. Implicit verbal negotiation and agreement may also be possible when each firm holds press conferences to state its views about (1) demand, cost, or recent or forthcoming changes in them, (2) the characteristics, adequacy, or desirability of past, present, or prospective prices, (3) industry profit, revenue, or price, or (4) its expectations or intentions with respect to output or price. The more detailed the statements about future price intentions, the closer they approach traditional negotiations. And if each speaks seriatim, in as many rounds as necessary, until they reach an identical price conclusion, the process would approximate conventional verbal negotiation and agreement. Observe that the process does not depend on any letters, meetings, or one-to-one communication. Seriatim public speeches or interviews with the press could be just as effective.[11]

Verbal channels facilitate coordination but are not always necessary. If there are few firms, the need for price changes is infrequent, and the necessary coordination is not complex, observed behavior may be sufficient. For example, one firm might simply begin selling at a higher price. Rivals would understand that such behavior was an invitation that could not long be kept open without a favorable response. Similarly, price cuts would be seen as defections or as demands to lower the industry price and could be matched almost immediately. Imagine an isolated town having two gas stations across the street from each other, each with posted gasoline prices. It would hardly take long for each to notice the other's price changes and to react accordingly. The inability of each gas station to keep secret its price cuts to consumers may well be sufficient to facilitate oligopoly pricing.

---

market shares. Most actual price fixers, however, even those with elaborate express agreements, do not pool facilities and profits. The ease of detection is one explanation. Another is that a firm closing an inefficient plant will weaken its future bargaining position in the cartel or ability to operate if the cartel breaks apart.

11. See ¶248.

Even if prices are not observable, a significant loss of one's customers may signal a seller's defection, although it may not identify the guilty party. As a result, it will be easier to maintain coordinated pricing when sales are frequent. In such instances, a large percentage loss in sales (absent alternative explanations) will be highly informative. In contrast, if only a few large units are sold each year, each rival has a greater incentive to secure a particular sale by offering a lower price, and each bears a greater risk that others may defect. If winning bids are published, the prospect of detection by rivals may still be enough to deter cheating. Without publication, the losing bidders may not know whether a successful rival bid less (or how much less) or was selected on some other basis.[12]

(d) *Price comparability of products.* When products are standardized, a lower price constitutes either a defection or a suggestion that changed conditions have rendered the industry price too high; either invites imitation by rivals. But when firms sell goods of varying qualities, a wide product line, or made-to-order products, the problem of coordination is more complex.[13] Put simply, more terms need to be coordinated. Oligopolists may solve this problem with standard formulas, by which one can determine the price of many varieties from one or a few base prices.[14] Such mechanisms will be considered further in Chapter 2D.

(e) *Nonprice competition.* Rivalry occurs not only in price but also in product quality and in sales promotion. Some products, like sulphuric acid, are not susceptible to much product variation or sales promotion. But the characteristics of a computer, automobile, or shirt can be varied and promoted in a variety of ways. As a result, decisions concerning quality and sales promotion may be more complex than pricing decisions. In principle, oligopolists could agree on these factors as well and behave in every respect as would a

---

12. See G. Stigler, A Theory of Oligopoly, 72 J. Pol. Econ 44 (1964).

13. Scherer & Ross, note 2, at 281:

Tires are fairly simple products and the industry is quite concentrated.... Yet the price structure in tires has been described as "chaotic"; tire manufacturers have been subjected to "an almost uninterrupted series of price buffetings"; and profits have been lower on the average than those of other industries with comparable market structures. One apparent reason is the great variety of manufacturers' and private-label grades, complicated by the welter of conflicting sales claims, labels, guarantees, and prices.

14. This fact accounts for some industry attempts to adopt delivered pricing so as to standardize transportation costs, reduce product variety, or adopt some common denominator for disparate goods. If, for example, the price of each of hundreds of steel products is determined by a specified standard addition or subtraction from the price of a specified base steel product, each transaction in any steel product would reflect a particular base price which would thus serve as a common and observable element in otherwise disparate transactions.

monopolist. In practice, such coordination will often be impossible, both in cartels and among firms coordinating tacitly. To hold price above competitive levels creates a powerful incentive for each oligopolist to win increased business by any means that does not threaten the price structure. And unlike a price cut that can be exactly and quickly duplicated by rivals, effective advertising or product alteration might be beyond imitation, or at least might force rivals to expend considerable time and energy before achieving parity. In addition, it is difficult to define what sorts of promotion or product design strategies constitute defections in the first place, making the process of detection and retaliation all the more difficult. Given this difficulty, a particular firm may be tempted to try to increase its market share by this route. And because there is always the possibility that a rival might make such a move, each oligopolist may feel compelled to continue planning for new advertising campaigns or style changes in order to be able to respond quickly when necessary. In any event, coordination appears more difficult on these matters than on price, even though the parties may recognize that their product and promotional decisions are interdependent.

Thus, firms may be sufficiently few in number to coordinate prices at noncompetitive levels through interdependence and yet may compete vigorously in other matters. The latter may include not only advertising and minor product variations but also research, development, and significant innovations. When nonprice competition occurs, it might drive costs up to a point where the oligopolists cannot earn high profits, notwithstanding the fact that the price exceeds the competitive level. This seems to have been the situation of the airline industry before deregulation: Rate regulation, enforced by federal law (and thus stronger than a cartel agreement), effectively maintained supracompetitive prices, but excessive and partially wasteful competition on service (frequent but half-filled flights, movies, meals) eroded most of the profits, leaving the industry as a whole with merely a competitive rate of return.[15] Although consumers enjoyed the services, given the price, many would have preferred fewer frills and much lower prices.

231. Factors affecting the potential gains from successful coordination, express or tacit. The fourth element noted in ¶229b concerns the ability of even a fully cooperative group of firms to price significantly above competitive levels. This issue will be examined in depth in Chapter 3B on monopoly power and revisited throughout the book. This Paragraph briefly notes two primary considerations.

15. See ¶201b and note 9.

(a) *Fringe expansion.*

As a very crude general rule, if evenly matched firms supply homogeneous products in a well-defined market, they are likely to begin ignoring their influence on price when their number exceeds ten or twelve. It is more difficult to generalize when the size distribution of sellers is highly skewed. Then pricing discipline depends critically upon ... the rate at which smaller firms can expand their sales through price cutting.[16]

If the smaller "fringe" firms can expand, they may act competitively and increase output as long as the market price exceeds their costs. If they find it profitable to expand their capacity at the price settled on by the dominant firms, they will do so and come to occupy an increasingly important place in the industry. The larger firms may thus be compelled to choose monopoly profits with declining market shares or to sacrifice such profits by setting their price at a level that is not profitable enough to encourage significant expansion by fringe firms. Whether such a price would earn any monopoly profit for the dominant firms depends on how the costs of the larger firms compare to those of the fringe firms.

(b) *Substitute products or new entry.* The availability of substitute products may so increase the number of players as to make coordination impossible. Or the closeness of substitutes or the ease of entry for new producers may so limit the opportunities for monopoly profits that efforts toward price coordination would not be worthwhile. Stated simply: When the collective market power of the coordinating oligopolists is relatively low, their price coordination will cause relatively little harm to the economy. As will be seen in Chapter 3B, the market power of even the sole producer of a product might be great or small.

232. Evidence on oligopoly pricing in the economy. Because the factors discussed in the preceding Paragraphs vary so widely among industries, we should not expect a close association in all industries between their profits and the degree of concentration. Moreover, any dividing line between concentrated and unconcentrated industries — for example, whether the four largest members of an industry account for one-half or more of its sales — is inevitably arbitrary. Measurements of profits will also be crude. Nevertheless, efforts have been made to assess the extent of oligopolistic pricing in the economy by asking whether concentrated industries generally earn larger profits than unconcentrated industries. (Of course, if they did, it might sometimes be attributable to express

16. Scherer & Ross, note 2, at 277.

cartel agreements rather than less explicit oligopolistic coordination.)

(a) *Measuring economic performance and concentration.* The benchmark is the performance of perfectly competitive firms in equilibrium. They will not charge more than marginal costs and cannot earn more than the cost of capital. Accordingly, noncompetitive performance could be indicated by prices greater than marginal cost or by profits greater than the cost of capital. Unfortunately, the relevant data is often both elusive and ambiguous.[17]

Marginal cost is not easy to find, and profit measurement problems are notorious. High accounting profits will overstate true economic profits to the extent that they exclude equity capital as a cost, base depreciation on historical cost rather than higher replacement cost (or otherwise undervalue assets), use liberal accounting conventions for the treatment of intangibles, include too few joint costs from the firm's operations in other markets, or fail to distinguish economic rents. Similarly, low accounting profits will understate economic profits to the extent that the firm bases depreciation on assets whose profit potential was previously capitalized,[18] pays out profit in the form of salaries or management perquisites, uses conservative accounting rules, or includes too many costs properly allocable to the firm's other operations.[19]

Once measured, moreover, the absence of excess profits may indicate inefficient excess capacity, high product differentiation costs, or temporary adjustments rather than competitive performance. Similarly, excess profits may reflect temporary excess demand, superior efficiency, or recent innovations rather than noncompetitive performance. Over a relatively long time period, however, some of these effects could disappear so that economic profits would indicate the presence or absence of competitive performance. Yet there

---

17. A recent study found prices well above marginal costs in several industries widely perceived to be competitive. See R. Hall, The Relationship Between Price and Marginal Cost in U.S. Industry, 96 Pol. Econ. 921 (1988). However, these results have been criticized on the grounds that measurement problems tainted the data used. See R. Waldmann, Implausible Results or Implausible Data? Anomalies in the Construction of Value-Added Data and Implications for Estimates of Price-Cost Markups, 99 J. Pol. Econ. 1315 (1991).

18. Some assets in limited supply may earn rents so that the purchase price of such an asset would be based on the discounted value of the future stream of earnings it is expected to generate, which would differ from the cost of creation. In that event, a monopoly return (rent) will be hidden in what appears to be merely normal profits earned by the firm using that asset.

19. See F. Fisher & J. McGowan, On the Misuse of Accounting Rates of Return to Infer Monopoly Profits, 73 Am. Econ. Rev. 82 (1983); comments and a rejoinder appear in 74 Am. Econ. Rev. 492-517 (1984), 75 Am. Econ. Rev. 495-504 (1985).

will be cases where continued high[20] or low[21] profits over a period of time could be misleading.

Once we are satisfied that a particular market is noncompetitive, measurement of that market's degree of concentration would offer no additional benefit to antitrust inquiry. But if we wanted to prove or disprove a general relationship between concentration and non-competitiveness, we could examine a number of markets to see if noncompetitiveness is associated with high concentration and competitiveness with low concentration. Unfortunately, all of the difficulties of the preceding Paragraphs recur, together with inconsistent measurements of each firm's profits, arbitrary measures of concentration, arbitrary dividing lines between concentrated and unconcentrated markets, and several other problems.

Concentration data are often based on national census classifications that do not necessarily reflect true geographic or product markets. A market may be erroneously classified as unconcentrated because the census classification is broader than the true market. A market may be erroneously classified as concentrated (or the leading firms' share overstated) because census data include a firm's sales of other products and exports, ignore relevant output of firms principally engaged elsewhere, and ignore substitute products and imports.

In short, one may be appropriately skeptical of the broad statistical correlations. In particular, with so many measurement problems, one might expect that it would be difficult to detect a significant relationship even if one existed.

(b) The empirical evidence on concentration and oligopoly pricing. For what they are worth, many such studies, beginning with Professor Bain's, show that profits are higher in markets in which the eight leading firms have accounted for at least 70 percent of sales than in less concentrated markets.[22] Some studies have reached more subtle conclusions. One suggests that performance of highly concen-

20. Even if one believes that the text statement would be true for most firms over the long run, a particular firm may continue to be exceptionally efficient and exceptionally innovative over a very long period. In that event, its great profits would be the competitive reward for superior performance and not an indicator of noncompetitiveness.

21. See ¶230e.

22. J. Bain, Relation of Profit Rate to Industry Concentration, American Manufacturing, 1936-1940, 65 Q.J. Econ. 293 (1951). For surveys, see R. Schmalensee, Inter-Industry Studies of Structure and Performance, in 2 Handbook of Industrial Organization (R. Schmalensee & R. Willig eds., 1989); M. Salinger, The Concentration-Margins Relationship Reconsidered, Brookings Papers on Economic Activity: Microeconomics 287 (1990); Scherer & Ross, note 2, at 426-447; L. Weiss, The Concentration-Profits Relationship and Antitrust, in Industrial Concentration: The New Learning 184 (H. Goldschmid, H. Mann & J. Weston eds. 1974).

trated industries is far better when there are three large firms than when there are only two.[23]

Other studies assert that the correlation is weak or nonexistent.[24] Professor Demsetz finds higher profits not for all of the firms in a concentrated market but only for those with the largest market shares.[25] He argues that if concentrated markets as such were less competitive, one would expect to find high profits for all of the participants; the fact that only the larger firms in concentrated markets earn high profits implies that they are simply earning the reward of high efficiency. Of course, it may also be true that the smaller firms are competitive and expanding their market share over time or are really operating in a quite different market or that product differentiation insulates the larger firms from their competition.[26]

The sharpest evidence is provided by studies of a particular industry in several different geographic markets. In commercial banking, for example, higher concentration is clearly associated with higher interest rates on loans as well as higher charges on other banking services.[27] Numerous such studies in a wide range of industries find consistently higher prices in more concentrated markets.[28] These studies are in many respects more reliable because, by comparing sales in the same industry, and often by the same firms, in different geographic markets, they avoid most of the problems associated with profit measurement. Yet the totality of evidence involves many

23. J. Kwoka, The Effect of Market Share Distribution on Industry Performance, 61 Rev. Econ. & Stats. 101 (1979). For a critical rejoinder that also finds that the fourth firm can be as important as the third, see W. Mueller & D. Greer, The Effect of Market Share Distribution on Industry Performance Reexamined, 66 Rev. Econ. & Stats. 353 (1984). See also Bresnahan & Reiss, note 7.

24. See H. Demsetz, Two Systems of Belief about Monopoly, in Industrial Concentration, note 22, at 164.

25. Id.

26. D. Mueller, Profits in the Long Run 229 (1986) (typical firms earning persistently high profits have large shares selling differentiated products; prices are higher than their competitors'; if they are more efficient than competition, it is not in lowering cost but in product development and marketing, maintaining the product's image as superior); R. Caves & M. Porter, From Entry Barriers to Mobility Barriers, 91 Q.J. Econ. 241 (1977).

27. Scherer & Ross, note 2, at 440.

28. Id. at 439-440; L. Weiss, ed., Concentration and Price (1989) (positive relationship between concentration and price in majority of comparisons); T. Bresnahan, Empirical Studies of Industries with Market Power, in 2 Handbook of Industrial Organization (R. Schmalensee & R. Willig eds. 1989) (significant market power in some concentrated industries); W. Mueller, A New Attack on Antitrust: The Chicago School, 18 Antitr. L. & Econ. Rev. 29, 45 (1986) (reporting studies on life insurance, newspaper and television advertising, gasoline retailing, prescription drugs, and microfilm).

conflicts, not all adequately explained, making it difficult to have great confidence concerning the relationship (particularly its magnitude) between oligopoly and higher prices.[29]

Tacit and Inferred Express Agreements

233. What constitutes an agreement? Sherman Act §1 requires a "contract, combination, ... or conspiracy,"[30] which is often spoken of as an agreement. The cases that follow indicate the circumstances in which an agreement will be inferred. In considering this issue, keep in mind the distinction — often obscured in courts' opinions — among three categories of behavior. First are express agreements, which are undoubtedly covered by Sherman Act §1.[31]

29. See generally R. Harris & L. Sullivan, Horizontal Merger Policy: Promoting Competition and American Competitiveness, 31 Antitr. Bull. 871, 907-923 (1986) (reviewing literature). Those who doubt the prevalence of oligopoly pricing ask why the higher profits allegedly associated with concentration do not lead to entry by new firms or expansion by existing smaller firms. Of course, this may occur, and the large oligopolists trying to hold prices up may suffer diminishing market shares. Indeed, as a general proposition, one would expect oligopoly power to disappear over time when entry or expansion is unobstructed. Thus, persistent excess profits would not be expected in an apparently concentrated market unless there were also significant barriers to the expansion of existing firms and the entry of new firms. See ¶114.

30. Unlike "contract" or "conspiracy," which have legal meaning apart from antitrust law, "combination" has little historical content. The statutory context — "combination in the form of trust or otherwise" — suggests a legislative intent to embrace trusts and other forms of pooling. And it was so used in 1904 to reach a holding company consolidating two railroads. Northern Sec. Co. v. United States, 193 U.S. 197 (1904). See Bogosian v. Gulf Oil Corp., 561 F.2d 434, 445-446 (3d Cir. 1977), cert. denied, 434 U.S. 1086 (1978) (combination and conspiracy interchangeable). That is, the substitution of unitary control for separate competing firms does not nullify the applicability of §1 to the amalgamation. Some cases, such as *Albrecht,* in ¶419, apparently give that term a broader meaning. Precisely because the concept has so little historical significance, some see it as a vehicle for reaching conduct that does not seem, for some reason, to be a conspiracy. The critical inquiry, however, must always be whether the challenged two-party conduct ought to be reached by §1 in order to fulfill the statutory purpose. The availability of the word "combination" invites this inquiry but should not be a substitute for it.

31. As a corollary, any party's unexpressed subjective intent to "cheat" would not negate the existence of an agreement for antitrust purposes any more than it would defeat the existence of an ordinary contract. It seems equally clear that the express agreement concept of §1 would apply to an arrangement that did not rise to the dignity of a contract because, for example, of indefiniteness or of an express intention not to be legally bound. As an illustration, recall the rather vague gentlemen's understanding in *Socony* studied earlier in this chapter. At some point, however, competitors' conversations may fail to suggest any consummated assurances of a common course of action (although the mere agreement to have a conversation might invoke §1). A proposal for common action that is not taken up

And much judicial discussion of the agreement issue amounts simply to the familiar holding that express agreements can be inferred from circumstantial evidence. The difficulty lies, of course, in deciding how much of what kind of evidence suffices to imply that an express agreement exists although it has not been established by direct evidence. When we speak of express agreements here, we include both those that are evidenced by the signed contract and those looser understandings traditionally considered agreements outside the antitrust world.

The other two categories are behavior that is *interdependent* (even if independently arrived at in the sense of there being no express agreement) and behavior that is *entirely independent* in the sense that decisions are made without regard to rivals' reactions. Firms may well act in parallel fashion in both cases. In a perfectly competitive market, prices tend toward perfect uniformity and tend to change in parallel with changes in costs or demand. One would expect orange prices in different stores in the New York produce market to rise together in response to reduced output in Florida. Such parallel behavior is completely consistent with entirely independent decisionmaking by each seller, which does not take into account that its decisions will affect the behavior of its rivals and therefore does not expect that the profitability of its decisions will be affected by any rival's reactions.

By contrast, recall the oligopoly behavior described in ¶229a: (1) no firm reduces price even though it could expand profits if it did so, provided that rivals did not imitate the reduction or (2) a firm follows a price leader upward even though it could expand profits by refusing to do so, provided that the price leader did not then retract its price increase. The firm's decisionmaker sitting on a desert island and receiving objective reports about plant costs, rivals' prices, and other market information may not take these steps because it expects that rivals will imitate a reduction or retract an increase. Each such firm decides what to do independently in the sense of not consulting with its rivals, but its decision is interdependent in the sense that the perceived profitability of its choices depends entirely on its estimate of how rivals will respond to any step it takes.

Perfectly competitive firms take market prices as given and adjust their output to it. Firms behaving that way will give us perfectly competitive results even if they are few in number. But, of course,

---

by any addressee would not create an agreement, United States v. Amax, 1977 Trade Cas. ¶61467 (N.D. Ill.), although an addressee who behaves in accordance with the proposal may have difficulty persuading a court that it acted unilaterally and without regard to the proposal.

when they are few in number, they tend to recognize their interdependence, and interdependent pricing, as we have seen, can have the same adverse consequences as an express agreement. Accordingly, we need to consider whether such tacit group action should be deemed to be a "contract, combination . . . or conspiracy" under Sherman Act §1. If so, it would be necessary to identify interdependent behavior (as contrasted with independent parallel behavior) and devise appropriate remedies.[32] If §1 is confined to express agreements, including those inferred from conduct, it is necessary to distinguish them from "mere" interdependent behavior,[33] although the only evidence before the court — for example, parallel price increases accompanied by very high levels of profit — may be consistent with each.

In reading the cases that follow, try to decipher (1) whether a court that allows an inference of agreement from parallel behavior has held that an express agreement may be inferred from circumstantial evidence or that interdependent behavior may (must?) be deemed to be an agreement or (2) whether a court insisting that no agreement can be found where the evidence is consistent with independent behavior intends to protect only entirely independent behavior or interdependent behavior short of express agreement as well.

Finally, the procedural posture of each case is important. Because reviewing courts often defer to the trial judge or jury, consistent appellate formulas may accompany inconsistent factual determinations. Moreover, try to sort out whether a court emphasizing certain facts has held that those facts compel the inference that an agreement exists, merely support such an inference drawn by a jury, create a sufficient dispute to prevent summary judgment in favor of the defendant before trial, or merely are relevant in some undefined way. Before a trial court sends the issue to the jury, it must first formulate intelligible instructions that state what the plaintiff must establish to meet §1's conspiracy requirement. We will return to these problems in ¶235 and ¶237.

234.   *Eastern States Retail Lumber Dealers' Assn. v. United States*, 234 U.S. 600, 609, 612 (1914). The Supreme Court upheld the trial

---

32. Remember that two gas stations on opposite corners may be interdependent but yet have only modest market power even if they formed an express cartel. If they expressly agreed on prices, they would be condemned without proof of market power. But in dealing with tacit coordination, we shall see a variety of complications that could make it necessary to determine whether interdependent firms possess significant market power.

33. Indeed, both may simultaneously be present. Parties might agree expressly to adopt a pricing formula and then, without any verbal communication, follow the leader on actual price.

court's finding that retail lumber dealers had agreed that they would not buy from wholesalers who had sold directly to consumers in competition with the retailers.[34] The conspiracy was inferred from the dealers' circulation among their members of lists of offending wholesalers. This activity "was intended to have the natural effect of causing such retailers to withhold their patronage from the concern listed," and that was often the result of the reports.

> It is elementary ... that conspiracies are seldom capable of proof by direct testimony and may be inferred from the things actually done, and when in this case by concerted action the names of wholesalers who were reported as having made sales to consumers were periodically reported to the other members of the associations, the conspiracy to accomplish that which was the natural consequence of such action may be readily inferred.

INTERSTATE CIRCUIT v. UNITED STATES
306 U.S. 208 (1939)

Justice STONE. . . . The case is now before us on findings of the District Court specifically stating that appellants did in fact agree with each other to enter into and carry out the contracts, which the court found to result in unreasonable and therefore unlawful restraints of interstate commerce. . . .

The distributor appellants are engaged in the business of distributing in interstate commerce motion picture films, copyrights on which they own or control, for exhibition in theatres throughout the United States. They distribute about 75 per cent of all first-class feature films exhibited in the United States. They solicit from motion picture theatre owners and managers in Texas and other states applications for licenses to exhibit films, and forward the applications, when received from such exhibitors, to their respective New York offices, where they are accepted or rejected. . . .

[Appellants] Interstate Circuit, Inc., and Texas Consolidated Theatres, Inc. . . . are affiliated with each other. . . . Interstate operates forty-three first-run and second-run motion picture theatres, located in six Texas cities. It has a complete monopoly of first-run theatres in these cities, except for one in Houston operated by one distributor's Texas agent. In most of these theatres the admission price for adults for the better seats at night is 40 cents or more. Interstate also operates several subsequent-run theatres in each of these cities, twenty-two in all, but in all but Galveston there are

---

34. For other aspects of this case, see ¶256a.

other subsequent-run theatres which compete with both its first- and subsequent-run theatres in those cities.

Texas Consolidated operates sixty-six theatres, some first- and some subsequent-run houses, in various cities and towns in the Rio Grande Valley and elsewhere in Texas and in New Mexico. In some of these cities there are no competing theatres, and in six leading cities there are no competing first-run theatres. It has no theatres in the six Texas cities in which Interstate operates. That Interstate and Texas Consolidated dominate the motion picture business in the cities where their theatres are located is indicated by the fact that at the time of the contracts in question Interstate and Consolidated each contributed more than 74 per cent of all the license fees paid by the motion picture theatres in their respective territories to the distributor appellants.

On July 11, 1934, following a previous communication on the subject to the eight branch managers of the distributor appellants, O'Donnell, the manager of Interstate and Consolidated, sent to each of them a letter on the letterhead of Interstate, each letter naming all of them as addressees, in which he asked compliance with two demands as a condition of Interstate's continued exhibition of the distributors' films in its 'A' or first-run theatres at a night admission of 40 cents or more. One demand was that the distributors "agree that in selling their product to subsequent runs, that this 'A' product will never be exhibited at any time or in any theatre at a smaller admission price than 25¢ for adults in the evening." The other was that "on 'A' pictures which are exhibited at a night admission of 40¢ or more — they shall never be exhibited in conjunction with another feature picture under the so-called policy of double features." The letter added that with respect to the "Rio Grande Valley situation," with which Consolidated alone was concerned, "We must insist that all pictures exhibited in our 'A' theatres at a maximum night admission price of 35¢ must also be restricted to subsequent runs in the Valley at 25¢."

The admission price customarily charged for preferred seats at night in independently operated subsequent-run theatres in Texas at the time of these letters was less than 25 cents. . . . In most of them the admission was 15 cents or less. It was also the general practice in those theatres to provide double bills either on certain days of the week or with any feature picture which was weak in drawing power. The distributor appellants had generally provided in their license contracts for a minimum admission price of 10 or 15 cents, and three of them had included provisions restricting double-billing. But none was at any time previously subject to contractual compulsion to continue the restrictions. The trial court found that the proposed restrictions constituted an important departure from prior practice.

The local representatives of the distributors, having no authority to enter into the proposed agreements, communicated the proposal to their home offices. Conferences followed between Hoblitzelle and O'Donnell, acting for Interstate and Consolidated, and the representatives of the various distributors. In these conferences each distributor was represented by its local branch manager and by one or more superior officials from outside the state of Texas. In the course of them each distributor agreed with Interstate for the 1934-35 season to impose both the demanded restrictions upon their subsequent-run licensees in the six Texas cities served by Interstate, except Austin and Galveston. While only two of the distributors incorporated the agreement to impose the restrictions in their license contracts with Interstate, the evidence establishes, and it is not denied, that all joined in the agreement, four of them after some delay in negotiating terms other than the restrictions and not now material. These agreements for the restrictions . . . were carried into effect by each of the distributors' imposing them on their subsequent-run licensees in the four Texas cities during the 1934-35 season. . . . [A]ll were in force when the present suit was begun.

None of the distributors yielded to the demand that subsequent runs in towns in the Rio Grande Valley served by Consolidated should be restricted. One distributor, Paramount, which was affiliated with Consolidated, agreed to impose the restrictions in certain other Texas and New Mexico cities. . . .

Although the films were copyrighted, appellants do not deny that the conspiracy charge is established if the distributors agreed among themselves to impose the restrictions upon subsequent-run exhibitors. . . . As is usual in cases of alleged unlawful agreements to restrain commerce, the Government is without the aid of direct testimony that the distributors entered into any agreement with each other to impose the restrictions upon subsequent-run exhibitors. In order to establish agreement it is compelled to rely on inferences drawn from the course of conduct of the alleged conspirators.

The trial court drew the inference of agreement from the nature of the proposals made on behalf of Interstate and Consolidated; from the manner in which they were made; from the substantial unanimity of action taken upon them by the distributors; and from the fact that appellants did not call as witnesses any of the superior officials who negotiated the contracts with Interstate or any official who, in the normal course of business, would have had knowledge of the existence or non-existence of such an agreement among the distributors. This conclusion is challenged by appellants [who claim that it is] not supported by subsidiary findings or by the evidence. We think this inference of the trial court was rightly drawn from the evidence. . . .

The O'Donnell letter named on its face as addressees the eight local representatives of the distributors, and so from the beginning each of the distributors knew that the proposals were under consideration by the others. Each was aware that all were in active competition and that without substantially unanimous action with respect to the restrictions for any given territory there was risk of a substantial loss of the business and good will of the subsequent-run and independent exhibitors, but that with it there was the prospect of increased profits. There was, therefore, strong motive for concerted action, full advantage of which was taken by Interstate and Consolidated in presenting their demands to all in a single document.

There was risk, too, that without agreement diversity of action would follow. Compliance with the proposals involved a radical departure from the previous business practices of the industry and a drastic increase in admission prices of most of the subsequent-run theatres. Acceptance of the proposals was discouraged by at least three of the distributors' local managers. Independent exhibitors met and organized a futile protest which they presented to the representatives of Interstate and Consolidated. While as a result of independent negotiations either of the two restrictions without the other could have been put into effect by any one or more of the distributors and in any one or more of the Texas cities served by Interstate, the negotiations which ensued and which in fact did result in modifications of the proposals resulted in substantially unanimous action of the distributors, both as to the terms of the restrictions and in the selection of the four cities where they were to operate.

One distributor, it is true, did not agree to impose the restrictions in Houston, but this was evidently because it did not grant licenses to any subsequent-run exhibitor in that city, where its own affiliate operated a first-run theatre. The proposal was unanimously rejected as to Galveston and Austin, as was the request that the restrictions should be extended to the cities of the Rio Grande Valley served by Consolidated. We may infer that Galveston was omitted because in that city there were no subsequent-run theatres in competition with Interstate. But we are unable to find in the record any persuasive explanation, other than agreed concert of action, of the singular unanimity of action on the part of the distributors by which the proposals were carried into effect as written in four Texas cities but not in a fifth or in the Rio Grande Valley. Numerous variations in the form of the provisions in the distributors' license agreements and the fact that in later years two of them extended the restrictions into all six cities, do not weaken the significance or force of the nature of the response to the proposals made by all the distributor appellants. It taxes credulity to believe that the several distributors would, in the circumstances, have accepted and put into operation with substantial unanimity such far-reaching changes in their business methods without some understanding that all were to join, and we reject as beyond the range of probability that it was the result of mere chance. . . .

[The inference of an agreement among the distributors] was supported and strengthened when the distributors, with like unanimity, failed to tender the testimony, at their command, of any officer or agent of a distributor who knew, or was in a position to know, whether in fact an agreement had been reached among them for concerted action. When the proof supported, as we think it did, the inference of such concert, the burden rested on appellants of going forward with the evidence to explain away or contradict it. They undertook to carry that burden by calling upon local managers of the distributors to testify that they had acted independently of the other distributors, and that they did not have conferences with or reach agreements with the other distributors or their representatives. The failure under the circumstances to call as witnesses those officers who did have authority to act for the distributors and who were in a position to know whether they had acted in pursuance of agreement is itself persuasive that their testimony, if given, would have been unfavorable to appellants. The production of weak evidence when strong is available can lead only to the conclusion that the strong would have been adverse. . . .

While the District Court's finding of an agreement of the distributors among themselves is supported by the evidence, we think that in the circumstances of this case such agreement for the imposition of the restrictions upon subsequent-run exhibitors was not a prerequisite to an unlawful conspiracy. It was enough that, knowing that concerted action was contemplated and invited, the distributors gave their adherence to the scheme and participated in it. Each distributor was advised that the others were asked to participate; each knew that cooperation was essential to successful operation of the plan. They knew that the plan, if carried out, would result in a restraint of commerce, which, we will presently point out, was unreasonable within the meaning of the Sherman Act, and knowing it, all participated in the plan. The evidence is persuasive that each distributor early became aware that the others had joined. With that knowledge they renewed the arrangement and carried it into effect for the two successive years.

It is elementary that an unlawful conspiracy may be and often is formed without simultaneous action or agreement on the part of the conspirators. . . . Acceptance by competitors, without previous agreement, of an invitation to participate in a plan, the necessary consequence of which, if carried out, is restraint of interstate commerce, is sufficient to establish an unlawful conspiracy under the Sherman Act. . . .[35]

Affirmed.[36]

THEATRE ENTERPRISES v. PARAMOUNT
FILM DISTRIBUTING CORP.
346 U.S. 537 (1954)

Justice CLARK. . . . Petitioner brought this suit for treble damages and an injunction under §§4 and 16 of the Clayton Act, alleging that respondent motion picture producers and distributors had violated the antitrust laws by conspiring to restrict "first-run" pictures to downtown Baltimore theatres, thus confining its suburban theatre to subsequent runs and unreasonable "clearances."[5] After hearing the evidence a jury returned a general verdict for respondents. The Court of Appeals for the Fourth Circuit affirmed. . . .

Petitioner now urges, as it did in the Court of Appeals, that the trial judge should have directed a verdict in its favor and submitted to the jury only the question of the amount of damages. Alternatively, petitioner claims that the trial judge erred by inadequately instructing the jury as to the scope and effect of the decrees in United States v. Paramount Pictures, Inc., the Government's prior equity suit against respondents. We think both contentions are untenable.

The opinion of the Court of Appeals contains a complete summary of the evidence presented to the jury. . . . It is sufficient to note that petitioner owns and operates the Crest Theatre, located in a neighborhood shopping district some six miles from the downtown shopping center in Baltimore, Maryland. The Crest, possessing the most modern improvements and appointments, opened on February 26, 1949. Before and after the opening, petitioner, through its president, repeatedly sought to obtain first-run features for the theatre. Petitioner approached each respondent separately, initially requesting exclusive first-runs, later asking for first-runs [simulta-

35. The Court's discussion of the individual vertical contracts between Interstate and each distributor is omitted. The Court held that the fact that each film was copyrighted property did not validate the varied restrictions on the other exhibitors, especially when such restrictions were imposed not for the benefit of the copyright holder but for the benefit of Interstate. — eds.

36. Roberts, McReynolds, and Butler, JJ., dissented; Frankfurter, J., did not participate.

5. "A clearance is the period of time, usually stipulated in license contracts, which must elapse between runs of the same feature within a particular area or in specified theatres." . . .

neously with a downtown theater]. But respondents uniformly rebuffed petitioner's efforts and adhered to an established policy of restricting first-runs in Baltimore to the eight downtown theatres. Admittedly there is no direct evidence of illegal agreement between the respondents and no conspiracy is charged as to the independent exhibitors in Baltimore, who account for 63% of first-run exhibitions. The various respondents advanced much the same reasons for denying petitioner's offers. Among other reasons they asserted that [simultaneous] first-runs are normally granted only to noncompeting theatres. Since the Crest is in "substantial competition" with the downtown theatres, a [simultaneous] arrangement would be economically unfeasible. And even if respondents wished to grant petitioner such a license, no downtown exhibitor would waive his clearance rights over the Crest and agree to a simultaneous showing. As a result, if petitioner were to receive first-runs, the license would have to be an exclusive one. However, an exclusive license would be economically unsound because the Crest is a suburban theatre, located in a small shopping center, and served by limited public transportation facilities; and, with a drawing area of less than one-tenth that of a downtown theatre, it cannot compare with those easily accessible theatres in the power to draw patrons. Hence the downtown theatres offer far greater opportunities for the widespread advertisement and exploitation of newly released features, which is thought necessary to maximize the overall return from subsequent runs as well as first-runs. The respondents, in the light of these conditions, attacked the guaranteed offers of petitioner, one of which occurred during the trial, as not being made in good faith. Respondents Loew's and Warner refused petitioner an exclusive license because they owned the three downtown theatres receiving their first-run product.

The crucial question is whether respondents' conduct toward petitioner stemmed from independent decision or from an agreement, tacit or express. To be sure, business behavior is admissible circumstantial evidence from which the fact finder may infer agreement.... But this Court has never held that proof of parallel business behavior conclusively establishes agreement or, phrased differently, that such behavior itself constitutes a Sherman Act offense. Circumstantial evidence of consciously parallel behavior may have made heavy inroads into the traditional judicial attitude toward conspiracy; but "conscious parallelism" has not yet read conspiracy out of the Sherman Act entirely. Realizing this, petitioner attempts to bolster its argument for a directed verdict by urging that the conscious unanimity of action by respondents should be "measured against the background and findings in the *Paramount* case." In other words, since the same respondents had conspired in the

Paramount case to impose a uniform system of runs and clearances without adequate explanation to sustain them as reasonable restraints of trade, use of the same device in the present case should be legally equated to conspiracy. But the *Paramount* decrees, even if admissible, were only prima facie evidence of a conspiracy covering the area and existing during the period there involved. Alone or in conjunction with the other proof of the petitioner, they would form no basis for a directed verdict. Here each of the respondents had denied the existence of any collaboration and in addition had introduced evidence of the local conditions surrounding the Crest operation which, they contended, precluded it from being a successful first-run house. They also attacked the good faith of the guaranteed offers of the petitioner for first-run pictures and attributed uniform action to individual business judgment motivated by the desire for maximum revenue. This evidence, together with other testimony of an explanatory nature, raised fact issues requiring the trial judge to submit the issue of conspiracy to the jury. . . .

Affirmed.[37]

AMERICAN TOBACCO CO. v. UNITED STATES
328 U.S. 781 (1946)

Justice BURTON. . . . The petitioners are The American Tobacco Company, Liggett & Myers Tobacco Company, R.J. Reynolds Tobacco Company, . . . and certain officials of the respective companies who were convicted by a jury . . . of violating §§1 and 2 of the Sherman Anti-Trust Act. . . .

The verdicts show . . . that the jury found that the petitioners conspired to fix prices and to exclude undesired competition in the distribution and sale of their principal products. The petitioners sold and distributed their products to jobbers and to selected dealers who bought at list prices, less discounts. . . . The list prices charged and the discounts allowed by petitioners have been practically identical since 1923 and absolutely identical since 1928. Since the latter date, only seven changes have been made by the three companies and those have been identical in amount. The increases were first announced by Reynolds. American and Liggett thereupon increased their prices in identical amounts.

The following record of price changes is circumstantial evidence of the existence of a conspiracy and of a power and intent to exclude competition coming from cheaper grade cigarettes. During

37. Black, J., dissented from the Court's approval of the trial court's instruction to the jury concerning Clayton Act §5 (see ¶158c). Douglas, J., did not participate.

the two years preceding June, 1931, the petitioners produced 90% of the total cigarette production in the United States. In that month tobacco farmers were receiving the lowest prices for their crops since 1905. The costs to the petitioners for tobacco leaf, therefore, were lower than usual during the past 25 years, and their manufacturing costs had been declining. It was one of the worst years of financial and economic depression in the history of the country. On June 23, 1931, Reynolds, without previous notification or warning to the trade or public, raised the list price of Camel cigarettes, constituting its leading cigarette brand, from $6.40 to $6.85 a thousand. The same day, American increased the list price for Lucky Strike cigarettes, its leading brand, and Liggett the price for Chesterfield cigarettes, its leading brand, to the identical price of $6.85 a thousand. No economic justification for this raise was demonstrated. The president of Reynolds stated that it was "to express our own courage for the future and our own confidence in our industry." The president of American gave as his reason for the increase, "the opportunity of making some money." He further claimed that because Reynolds had raised its list price, Reynolds would therefore have additional funds for advertising and American had raised its price in order to have a similar amount for advertising. The official of Liggett claimed that they thought the increase was a mistake as there did not seem to be any reason for making a price advance but they contended that unless they also raised their list price for Chesterfields, the other companies would have greater resources to spend in advertising and thus would put Chesterfield cigarettes at a competitive disadvantage. This general price increase soon resulted in higher retail prices and in a loss in volume of sales. Yet in 1932, in the midst of the national depression with the sales of the petitioners' cigarettes falling off greatly in number, the petitioners still were making tremendous profits as a result of the price increase. Their net profits in that year amounted to more than $100,000,000. This was one of the three biggest years in their history. . . .

There was evidence that when dealers received an announcement of the price increase from one of the petitioners and attempted to purchase some of the leading brands of cigarettes from the other petitioners at their unchanged prices before announcement of a similar change, the latter refused to fill such orders until their prices were also raised, thus bringing about the same result as if the changes had been precisely simultaneous. . . .

It is not the form of the combination or the particular means used but the result to be achieved that the statute condemns. It is not of importance whether the means used to accomplish the unlawful objective are in themselves lawful or unlawful. Acts done to give effect to the conspiracy may be in themselves wholly innocent acts. Yet, if they are part of the sum of the acts which are relied upon to effectuate the conspiracy which the statute forbids, they come within its prohibition. No formal agreement is necessary to constitute an unlawful conspiracy. Often crimes are a matter of inference deduced from the acts of the person accused and done in pursuance of a criminal purpose. Where the conspiracy is proved, as here, from the evidence of the action taken in concert by the parties to it, it is all the more convincing proof of an intent to exercise the power of exclusion acquired through that conspiracy. The essential combination or conspiracy in violation of the Sherman Act may be found in a course of dealing or other circumstances as well as in an exchange of words. . . . Where the circumstances are such as to warrant a jury in finding that the conspirators had a unity of purpose or a common design and understanding, or a meeting of minds in an unlawful arrangement, the conclusion that a conspiracy is established is justified. Neither proof of exertion of the power to exclude nor proof of actual exclusion of existing or potential competitors is essential to sustain a charge of monopolization under the Sherman Act. . . .[38]

235. (a) Did the *Interstate Circuit* distributors agree on how they would respond to Interstate Circuit's letter? What facts cited by the Court bear on this question? What does each such fact tend to prove? Do you believe there was an express agreement, interdependent behavior, entirely independent behavior, or something best captured by some other category? Which categories constitute a conspiracy under the Court's formulation?[39] Consider the same questions for *Eastern States*.[40]

(b) What evidence did the plaintiff in *Theatre Enterprises* offer indicating that defendants' actions were other than entirely independent behavior? In denying that " 'conscious parallelism' has . . . read conspiracy out of the Sherman Act entirely," what does the Court require beyond parallel behavior to prove conspiracy? Is it relevant that the jury decided in favor of the defendants?

38. Reed and Jackson, JJ., did not participate. Frankfurter and Rutledge, JJ., each offered additional remarks not relevant to the issues addressed in the excerpt.

As is suggested by some of the language in this final paragraph, the Court is discussing the application of Sherman Act §2 (see Ch. 3), which contains language on conspiracy similar to that of §1: "Every person who shall monopolize . . . or combine or conspire with any other person or persons, to monopolize. . . ."

39. Why was it not sufficient that there were express contracts between each distributor and the exhibitors? See Ch. 4A.

40. When examining the data dissemination cases in Ch. 2D, consider whether you would support the result in *Eastern States* if the only conspiracy that can be inferred is the agreement to exchange information.

(c) Do you suppose there was an express agreement in *American Tobacco*? Does the Court require such an agreement?[41]

236. Thirty firms make an important class of electrical transformer. The four largest firms have, on average, accounted for 80 percent of annual industry output over the last decade; the next largest four, 14 percent; and 22 small firms, the remaining 6 percent. Each of the many transformer types carries a different price, but one standard transformer is sold by each firm and accounts for 60 percent of industry revenues. Every firm publishes a price list. Almost every change in those lists over the past 35 years was initiated by Theta Corporation, the industry's largest firm, and followed within a few days by nearly all of the other firms. Nearly all firms do, on occasion, depart from their announced prices; the smaller firms depart from their quoted prices rather more frequently. Price lists have not changed very often. On at least three occasions since 1945, sales declined sharply but quoted prices were not reduced; in fact, they were raised after wage increases in the course of two of those

---

41. See United States v. Paramount Pictures, 334 U.S. 131, 142 (1948) ("it is enough that a concert of action is contemplated and that the defendants conformed to the arrangement").

In Norfolk Monument Co. v. Woodlawn Mem. Gardens, 394 U.S. 700, 701, 704 (1969), five defendant cemetery operators had adopted various restrictive practices that made it difficult, if not impossible, for the plaintiff retailer to sell and install his bronze grave markers. These restrictions had been suggested by the defendant manufacturer of bronze grave markers that also had pointed out to the cemeteries' the profitability of doing their own retailing and installing of markers. Four of the five cemeteries were customers of the defendant manufacturer. The plaintiff claimed that the defendants acted jointly and violated Sherman Act §1 and §2 but admitted that it had "no letters, agreements, correspondence, or any other testimonials to a conspiracy among the several defendants." Summary judgment in defendants' favor was reversed per curiam. A jury could

> have found that the respondents had conspired to exclude the petitioner from and monopolize the market for bronze grave markers.... We express no opinion, of course, on the strength or weakness of the petitioner's case, but hold only that the alleged conspiracy had not been conclusively disproved by pretrial discovery and that there remained material issues of fact which could only be resolved by the jury after a plenary trial.

The Court's short opinion did not consider why the cemeteries' acting in their respective interests would find it useful to have either a horizontal agreement with each other or a vertical agreement with the manufacturer.

See also Viking Theatre Corp. v. Paramount Film Dist. Corp., 320 F.2d 285, 299 (3d Cir. 1963) ("proof of a conspiracy may not rest on similarity of conduct in the absence of evidence that the alleged wrongdoers were mutually aware of such conduct and that the mutual awareness entered into their decisional processes"); Milgram v. Loew's, 192 F.2d 579, 583 (3d Cir. 1951), cert. denied, 343 U.S. 929 (1952) (each distributor, refusing to license first-run movies to a drive-in theater even where higher rental was offered, "acted in apparent contradiction to its own self-interest," and this "strengthens considerably the inference of conspiracy").

industry recessions. The average after-tax return on investment over the last decade for the eight largest firms (arranged in order of sales volume) was 11 percent, 7 percent, 11 percent, 15 percent, 12 percent, 6 percent, 12 percent, and 9 percent. Apart from meetings and consultations under government auspices from 1933 to 1935, there is no evidence that these firms have written or spoken to each other. The government has brought suit against the 30 firms, alleging price fixing in violation of Sherman Act §1. Can the government succeed? Should it?

(a) Can you infer an agreement — and, if so, of what kind — (1) from the fact that for more than 50 years all defendants quickly followed every price reduction made by Theta? (2) From the fact that defendants usually followed Theta's price increases? (3) Do you find it easier or more difficult to answer these questions for the smaller firms considered separately?[42]

(b) How would your ¶a answers differ when (1) departures from quoted prices are fewer? (2) Defendants follow Theta more regularly and more rapidly? (3) Price changes are fewer? (4) Profits are higher? (5) Defendants were convicted in 1939 for agreeing expressly to fix prices?

(c) Would an express price-fixing agreement in this industry be any worse for society than the situation described? Much worse? To the extent that the evils of interdependent behavior resemble those of express price fixing, should we insist on finding an express agreement before taking corrective action under §1?

(d) At a jury trial, all of the above facts are shown. What questions should be submitted to the jury? With what instructions? How do *Interstate Circuit, Theatre Enterprises,* and *American Tobacco* bear on this issue?

(e) If tacit price coordination were held to be a price-fixing agreement violative of Sherman Act §1, what is the appropriate remedy? If treble damages or criminal sanctions applied when such behavior could be demonstrated, how would such firms behave? What should an injunction provide?[43]

---

42. United States v. GM, 1974 Trade Cas. ¶75253 (E.D. Mich.):

Neither a pricing move by a competitor, nor a requested pricing change by a customer, can be regarded as an invitation to conspire which precludes a business from acting in its best economic interest by changing its prices when desirable.... The public announcement of a pricing decision cannot be twisted into an invitation or signal to conspire; it is instead an economic reality to which all other competitors must react....

43. See R. Posner & F. Easterbrook, Antitrust 333 (2d ed. 1981):

Oligopolistic interdependence is not an unconscious state. If tacit collusion can be detected at all in an industry, and can be proved at trial, there should be no special difficulty in proving that the same practices have continued despite an injunction

(f) If tacit collusion is not deemed to be enough, but express collusion is generally to be proved by circumstantial evidence, how is a court or jury to distinguish the two?[44]

237. The object of courts' inquiry. (a) *What issue?* The devoted reader of parallelism cases will often wonder what question the courts are asking. Is mere parallelism enough? If not, what more is required? Will tacit coordination suffice or must an express agreement be demonstrated?

The courts approach unanimity in saying that mere parallelism does not establish the contract, combination, or conspiracy required by Sherman Act §1. Sometimes the formula is that conscious parallelism does not itself establish a violation of §1 but is a factor "to be weighed, and generally to be weighed heavily."[45] Usually, they say that parallelism accompanied by some other fact supports a jury verdict or that parallelism is insufficient to get to the jury unless some other fact is established.[46] An occasional court will suggest that parallelism is sufficient to take the case to the jury,[47] at least in the absence of a satisfactory independent explanation of the uniformity.[48]

The other facts that serve to transform parallelism into conspiracy (or that allow a jury to do so) are often characterized as "plus factors." Although the courts have not defined the concept very clearly, there seem to be a number of identifiable types of plus factors. In order to test the relevance of a given plus factor, one must relate it to some underlying conception of a §1 agreement. We will see that these plus factors implicate several different con-

---

against them. The defendants can alter their behavior even if the behavior was once in their interest. Sanctions for disobedience change the incentives. The question is: Can tacit collusion be proved in the first place?

44. See ¶248; J. Baker, Two Sherman Act Section 1 Dilemmas: Parallel Pricing, the Oligopoly Problem, and Contemporary Economic Theory, 38 Antitr. Bull. 143 (1993).

45. United States v. Morton Salt Co., 235 F.2d 573, 577 (10th Cir. 1956).

46. One court described prior cases as

utilizing the theory of conscious parallelism to find conspiracy [where] at least two of the following three circumstances are present: "plus" factors such as those emphasized in the simple refusal to deal cases . . . ; parallelism of a much more elaborate and complex nature; a web of circumstantial evidence pointing very convincingly to the ultimate fact of agreement.

Delaware Valley Marine Supply Co. v. American Tobacco Co., 297 F.2d 199, 205 n.19 (3d Cir. 1961), cert. denied, 369 U.S. 839 (1962).

47. Does *Norfolk Monument*, note 41, amount to this?

48. E.g., Ambook Enterprises v. Time, 612 F.2d 604 (2d Cir. 1979); City of Long Beach v. Standard Oil Co., 872 F.2d 1401 (9th Cir. 1989), cert. denied, 493 U.S. 1076 (1990).

ceptions of an agreement and that the courts are frequently ambiguous as to which they have in mind.

(b) *Indications of express collusion.* The plus factor easiest to describe and to rationalize is evidence implying that the alleged conspirators expressly formulated a joint plan with each other. An example would be identical sealed bids on a complex, made-to-order product. Apart from extremely improbable coincidence, such uniformity could not occur without express collusion.[49]

One might reach a similar conclusion when an otherwise unexplained period of clearly noncompetitive behavior occurred in a market otherwise characterized by intense competition or in a market in which the ¶230 factors made tacit coordination implausible.[50] Even when the standard is relaxed to include lesser degrees of likelihood of express collusion,[51] the object of this inquiry is

49. Ball v. Paramount Pictures, 169 F.2d 317, 319 (3d Cir. 1948) (may infer conspiracy "when the concert of action 'could not possibly be sheer coincidence'"). Identical bids absent express collusion are possible with some unique products if the product can be defined in terms of a simple combination of components, each of which has a known, going price common to all firms. Even then, however, one might expect some firms to lower prices slightly in order to win the contract or if there were economies associated with billing and shipping the whole product rather than separate pieces. The strongest disincentive to such price cutting is where winning bids are made public, which notifies rivals of defection. For a discussion on how to detect bid rigging, see C. LaCasse, 26 Rand J. Econ. 398 (1995); R. Porter & J. Zona, Detection of Bid Rigging in Procurement Auctions, 101 J. Pol. Econ. 518 (1993).

50. Paradoxically, if courts would require proof of express agreement to satisfy §1's conspiracy requirement, plaintiffs might then reinforce their case by showing that conditions were *not* conducive to oligopoly behavior — suggesting that only express rather than tacit coordination was possible — while defendants would claim that conditions rendered oligopolistic coordination simple. Compare *du Pont*, ¶254.

51. Cackling Acres v. Olson Farms, 541 F.2d 242 (10th Cir. 1976), cert. denied, 429 U.S. 1122 (1977) (upholding jury verdict against defendants whose parallelism was accompanied by numerous meetings, telephone calls, and internal communications suggesting that combined action was occurring); United States v. Finis P. Ernest, 509 F.2d 1256 (7th Cir.), cert. denied, 423 U.S. 893 (1975) (after one defendant's sole bid rejected because thought high, city reopened bidding; other defendant bid higher on a few items and the same on the remainder, which had many uncertain elements, without inspecting the work site, usual preparation, and the funds to cover the security deposit that would have been required if successful; conspiracy inferred); Beatrice Foods Co. v. United States, 312 F.2d 29 (8th Cir.), cert. denied, 373 U.S. 904 (1963) (conviction for otherwise unexplained noncompetitive bidding where vigorous price competition had both preceded and followed it); Trist v. First Fed. Sav. & Loan Assn. of Chester, 466 F. Supp. 578 (E.D. Pa. 1979) (jury may consider plaintiffs' claims that local banks conspiratorially adopted a method for charging interest between the settlement date of a mortgage and the first regular monthly payment where that method is allegedly so idiosyncratic that it is improbable that the 20 defendants without conspiracy could have independently come to such a computation method).

clear: Is it proper to infer that the defendants got together and adopted a common course of action even though no meetings, conversations, or exchanged documents have been shown?

(c) *Motivation and acts against self-interest.* Some courts suggest that proof of a motivation for common action supports an inference of conspiracy from parallel behavior.[52] This is certainly true in the negative sense. To say that there is no motive for common action is to say that the defendants have nothing to gain from it. In that event, it is unlikely that they would risk the liability of forming an express agreement or even bother to coordinate their conduct tacitly, so parallelism does not imply agreement in any sense of that term. Accordingly, the presence of a benefit from, and thus a motive for, common action is a prerequisite to the inference of an agreement, although it does not itself demonstrate that the parties have, in fact, formed an agreement.

Another expression of the same thought is the frequent suggestion that parallelism loses any conspiratorial connotations when each firm's action is independently explained. For example, rival firms may each refuse to supply a would-be customer because supply is inadequate to satisfy existing customers or because existing distribution channels seem preferable to each firm without regard to what its rivals do. In fact, a competitor might prefer that its rivals make the mistake of using the unfit distributor because, in the long run, their competitive strength might suffer as a result.

For action to be conspiratorial in any sense, rather than entirely independent, there generally must exist both a motive to act in concert and some reason why such action might not occur absent sufficient coordination among rivals. As to the latter component, it is often said that an act contrary to the self-interest of the actor is evidence of conspiracy.[53]

test
under
this
factor

A few cases, without stating exactly why, have thought it relevant to the existence of a present conspiracy that the defendants have been found to have conspired in the past. E.g., C-O-Two Fire Equip. Co. v. United States, 197 F.2d 489, 497 (9th Cir.), cert. denied, 344 U.S. 892 (1952); *Milgram*, note 41.

52. *Ambook*, note 48; Reading Indus. v. Kennecott Copper Corp., 477 F. Supp. 1150, 1157 (S.D.N.Y. 1979), aff'd, 1980 Trade Cas. ¶63559 (2d Cir.) (complaint dismissed for lack of standing, although district court willing to infer conspiracy when concentration is high, and there is a common motive for such parallel behavior); United States v. FMC Corp., 306 F. Supp. 1106 (E.D. Pa. 1969) (inelastic demand implies strong collective interest in maintaining prices in face of excess supply).

53. E.g., Venzie Corp. v. U.S. Mineral Prods. Co., 521 F.2d 1309, 1314 (3d Cir. 1975); *Ambook*, note 48. Cf. du Pont v. FTC, 729 F.2d 128, 139-140 (2d Cir. 1984), discussed in ¶254 ("If, for instance, a seller's conduct, even absent identical behavior on the part of its competitors, is contrary to its independent self-interest, that circumstance would indicate that the business practice is unfair within the meaning of §5.").

But self-interest comes in a variety of forms. One is the self-interest that is unrelated to rivals' behavior. For example, a firm that refuses to lend to a bankrupt borrower serves its self-interest without regard to what its rivals have done or might do. But if each of numerous firms refuses, without explanation, to sell at the going market price to a large buyer, the conduct seems contrary to this first notion of self-interest and thus needs some other explanation, such as conspiracy among the sellers.

Another form is the self-interest that depends on rivals' behavior. An oligopolist who refuses to lower prices below the monopoly level — when that would increase its profits if rivals did not follow — serves its self-interest when it assumes that rivals will follow. Thus, acts that are contrary to self-interest *unless* rivals behave accordingly rule out an inference of entirely independent behavior, but the self-interest formula does not answer the critical question posed by the second case: Should interdependent behavior be deemed to be an agreement for Sherman Act purposes?

Finally, consider the situation in which interdependent decisions can probably not be coordinated without express agreements. Put yourself in the position of any one distributor defendant in *Interstate Circuit* and try to decide whether you would alter your contractual relations with exhibitors in the manner requested by Interstate Circuit. Assume that doing so would increase your profits if rivals did the same but that the exhibitors would largely cease to patronize you if rivals made no similar alterations. That choice is the same one that faces any oligopolistic price leader, but price increases can usually be quickly reversed without significant loss of profit or goodwill. If your altered distribution contracts cannot be quickly reversed without significant loss and you are not reasonably confident that your rivals will act in parallel with you, you will hesitate to initiate the alteration. At some point, that confidence would be so low and the danger of loss from unfollowed action so high that no rational firm would take the first step without securing the assent of rivals in advance. In that situation, parallel action would be evidence of explicit conspiracy.

Whether or not such a situation can be identified in actual practice, it is important to specify the object of the inquiry: evidence of express agreement, tacit coordination, or something else? Although rivals might profit more in the short run by leaving the initial actor to suffer the adverse consequences of unfollowed nonreversible action, they might follow in order not to dissuade each other from initiating moves that would increase industry profits when all do follow.[54]

---

54. Consider a pair of sellers located in adjacent areas; each is fully capable of selling in the other's area but declines to do so. In the absence of any other

(d) *Poor economic performance.* It is sometimes suggested that poor economic performance in an industry — as reflected in excessive prices, persistent excess profits, or increased prices when demand declines — bears on the existence of a conspiracy.[55] In relating such evidence to the existence of conspiracy, three issues must be kept in mind. First, some conspiracies are unsuccessful, so the absence of evidence of poor performance does not rule out conspiracy. Second, performance diverging from that expected from perfect competition could result from other forces or reflect inexact measurement. Third, like the motivation factor discussed above, evidence of poor performance may suggest interdependent behavior but does not directly distinguish between express agreement and less explicit forms of coordination. Some courts have been reluctant to admit profit data,[56] but without clearly articulating how economic performance bears on conspiracy or which definition of conspiracy is implicitly being invoked.

(e) *Summary.* The courts have often discussed conspiracy and the evidence bearing on it but usually[57] without clearly addressing the

---

explanation, it is reasonable to assume either that (a) the two sellers have expressly divided territories or (b) each refrains from selling in the other's territory, understanding that the other will refrain from selling in its — as it has thus far — and with the realization that selling across the boundary by one would almost surely invite a reciprocal invasion by the other. It may be difficult to determine from circumstantial evidence which explanation is true. Compare J & J Furniture & Sleep Shop v. Sealy Southeast, 1981 Trade Cas. ¶64166 (S.D. Tex.) (denying summary judgment for two manufacturers that allegedly divided markets and terminated dealers selling in the other's territory; no other explanation for the termination of an admittedly profitable arrangement with dealers).

55. E.g., *American Tobacco* (1946), at 805.

56. Estate of LeBaron v. Rohm & Haas Co., 506 F.2d 1261 (9th Cir. 1974) (affirming trial judge's discretion to exclude profit data because probative value outweighed by complexity and confusion; profits not high enough to be probative); United States v. Chas. Pfizer & Co., 426 F.2d 32, 39, modified, 437 F.2d 1257 (2d Cir. 1970), aff'd per curiam by an equally divided Court, 404 U.S. 548 (1972) (undue emphasis in jury trial on profits was prejudicial), on remand, 367 F. Supp. 91, 101 n.14 (S.D.N.Y. 1973) (guilt or innocence not demonstrated by excess or by nominal profits).

57. A potentially important recent exception is *Brooke Group*, Ch. 3A. The case concerned alleged predatory pricing for the purpose of inducing the plaintiff to raise its prices, restoring oligopoly profits to the industry. Before embarking on its analysis, the Court described tacit collusion and referred to it as a process "not in itself unlawful." It did not cite any precedent or discuss any of the cases or issues addressed here. Perhaps relevant to the Court's approach to the problem is the fact that both parties denied that any illegal collusion was involved in the case. (Because the plaintiff was also a member of what the Court described as the historic oligopoly in the industry and would have been involved in the collusion, it is not surprising that the plaintiff may not have pressed the view that its activity should be deemed illegal.)

distinction between express and tacit coordination.[58] Whether the latter should be deemed a "contract, combination ... or conspiracy" is partly a matter of the history and structure of the statute and partly a function of two questions highlighted here. (1) Can interdependent behavior producing cartel-like prices be deterred or properly cured by the antitrust remedies available? If an affirmative answer is appropriate in only some situations, can those situations be identified by the courts? (2) If "mere" interdependent behavior is not deemed a conspiracy for antitrust purposes, will the evidence usually available allow antitrust courts to distinguish and thereby catch express but hidden agreements? If all uncertain cases are deemed to be conspiracies, then some irremediable tacit coordination will be punished; if not, some express but hidden agreements will go unpunished.

Finally, we shall soon examine a variety of practices that facilitate tacit coordination such as meetings, information exchanges, or formulas that make it easier for oligopolists to predict the likely behavior of their rivals. Meetings obviously involve a collective decision to meet. But information may simply be volunteered unilaterally by several oligopolists to the others. Or one firm may initiate a basing point pricing system with the hope or expectation that rivals will do the same. That is, the facilitating device may itself arise through

---

58. One of the most well-known is *Bogosian*, note 30, at 446:

> The law is settled that proof of consciously parallel business behavior is circumstantial evidence from which an agreement, *tacit or express*, can be inferred but that such evidence, without more, is insufficient unless the circumstances under which it occurred make the inference of rational, *independent* choice less attractive than that of *concerted* action. [Emphasis added.]

None of the emphasized terms is defined.

In Levitch v. CBS, 495 F. Supp. 649, 673-675 (S.D.N.Y. 1980), aff'd, 697 F.2d 495 (2d Cir. 1983) (affirming dismissal of second amended complaint), the district court considered a case where plaintiffs alleged, "without further elaboration, that through a course of 'interdependent consciously parallel action,'" the defendants conspired in violation of §1. It stated that "conscious parallelism, without more, will not state a claim under §1. It must be demonstrated that the parallel decisions were interdependent in order to raise the inference of a tacit agreement." The question presented was whether the plaintiff may withstand a motion to dismiss merely by having "inserted the word 'interdependent' before the term 'conscious parallelism.'" The court concluded

> that in order to raise an inference of tacit agreement to boycott, facts or circumstances are required to show that a series of *apparently unilateral decisions were indeed interdependent....* [A] plaintiff must, at a minimum, allege *how these decisions are interdependent* by at least suggesting that there is some reason to believe that the defendants were committed to a common end. [Emphasis added.]

The plaintiff is only required to put the defendant on notice by stating the theory by which the action is alleged to constitute "interdependent conscious parallelism."

independently arrived at but interdependent decisions. We will get to these questions in Chapter 2D.

238. *Matsushita Electric Industrial Co. v. Zenith Radio Corp.*, 475 U.S. 574 (1986). The plaintiffs, U.S. television manufacturers, alleged that their Japanese rivals had conspired to charge unduly low prices in the United States in order to ruin the plaintiffs. After some 10 years of discovery, the district court granted summary judgment for the defendants.[59] The Third Circuit reversed, largely on the grounds that the defendants had an incentive to destroy their U.S. competitors and that their behavior was consistent with the existence of an agreement to do so. In a 5-4 decision, the Supreme Court reversed. The majority thought that the posited predation scheme was implausible[60] and thus that the defendants lacked the motive to conspire. But the Court also said, "We do not imply that, if petitioners had had a plausible reason to conspire, ambiguous conduct could suffice to create a triable issue of conspiracy. . . . [C]onduct that is as consistent with permissible competition as with illegal conspiracy does not, without more, support even an inference of conspiracy."[61] The Court also quoted *Monsanto*[62] for the proposition that the plaintiff "must present evidence 'that tends to exclude the possibility' that the alleged conspirators acted independently. [Plaintiffs] . . . must show that the inference of conspiracy is reasonable in light of the competing inferences of independent action or collusive action that could not have harmed respondents."

As *Matsushita* illustrates, the concrete question often litigated is whether there is sufficient evidence of an agreement to be submitted to a jury or to sustain a jury finding. Some litigants and courts seem to think that they can answer that question without first defining the nature of the agreement that amounts to a statutory contract, combination, or conspiracy. Obviously, one must specify how the evidence submitted bears on the existence of a conspiracy, as distinguished from entirely independent behavior and, if the legal definition of conspiracy does not embrace it, from interdependent behavior short of express agreement. Then, one should consider the reasoning process by which a factfinder could infer the

59. See ¶152 on summary judgment.
60. The Court's analysis of predatory pricing is discussed in *Brooke Group*, in Ch. 3A.
61. The Court indicated that much of the evidence pointed more clearly to a conspiracy to maintain higher prices than to one to maintain artificially low prices, a conspiracy under which plaintiffs would not have suffered antitrust injury — in fact they would have benefitted if their rivals charged higher prices. See ¶146.
62. See Ch. 4A.

existence of an agreement from given facts. The mere submission to the jury may reveal an implicit legal rule that the posited facts constitute an agreement, unless a jury chooses to be merciful or unless the defendant can establish some exculpatory fact.

Intraenterprise Conspiracy

239. Introduction. Concerted action by persons within a single business enterprise is not deemed a "contract, combination . . . or conspiracy" within the meaning of §1. Similarly, acts involving a corporation and its officers or employees are not viewed as conspiracies. In contrast, joint action by commonly owned corporations ("intraenterprise conspiracies") and by single entities in conjunction with agents have been examined under §1. The Supreme Court, in its *Copperweld* decision, reviewed the Court's previous rulings and reexamined the rationale for the intraenterprise conspiracy doctrine before charting a new course in the area.[63]

COPPERWELD CORP. v.
INDEPENDENCE TUBE CORP.
467 U.S. 752 (1984)

Chief Justice BURGER. . . .[64] Review of this case calls directly into question whether the coordinated acts of a parent and its wholly owned subsidiary can, in the legal sense contemplated by §1 of the Sherman Act, constitute a combination or conspiracy. The so-called "intra-enterprise conspiracy" doctrine provides that §1 liability is not foreclosed merely because a parent and its subsidiary are subject to common ownership. The doctrine derives from declarations in several of this Court's opinions.

In no case has the Court considered the merits of the intra-enterprise conspiracy doctrine in depth. Indeed, the concept arose from a far narrower rule. Although the Court has pressed approval of the doctrine on a number of occasions, a finding of intra-enterprise conspiracy was in all but perhaps one instance unnecessary to the result.

The problem began with United States v. Yellow Cab Co., 332 U.S. 218 (1947). The controlling shareholder of the Checker Cab

63. Intraenterprise conspiracy and related issues are extensively analyzed in VII P. Areeda, Antitrust Law, ch. 14E (1986; Supp. 1996).

64. Because the facts are not considered in most of the Court's discussion, and are sufficiently noted when they are, they are omitted from this excerpt. — eds.

Manufacturing Corp., Morris Markin, also controlled numerous companies operating taxicabs in four cities. With few exceptions, the operating companies had once been independent and had come under Markin's control by acquisition or merger. The complaint alleged conspiracies under §§1 and 2 of the Sherman Act among Markin, Checker, and five corporations in the operating system. The Court stated that even restraints in a vertically integrated enterprise were not "necessarily" outside of the Sherman Act, observing that an unreasonable restraint

> *may result as readily from a conspiracy among those who are affiliated or integrated under common ownership as from a conspiracy among those who are otherwise independent.* Similarly, any affiliation or integration flowing from an illegal conspiracy cannot insulate the conspirators from the sanctions which Congress has imposed. *The corporate interrelationships of the conspirators, in other words, are not determinative of the applicability of the Sherman Act. That statute is aimed at substance rather than form.* See *Appalachian Coals.*
>
> *And so in this case, the common ownership and control of the various corporate appellees are impotent to liberate the alleged combination and conspiracy from the impact of the Act.* The complaint charges that the restraint of interstate trade was not only effected by the combination of the appellees but was the primary object of the combination. The theory of the complaint . . . is that "dominating power" over the cab operating companies "was not obtained by normal expansion . . . but by deliberate, calculated purchase for control."

It is the underscored language that later breathed life into the intra-enterprise conspiracy doctrine. The passage as a whole, however, more accurately stands for a quite different proposition. It has long been clear that a pattern of acquisitions may itself create a combination illegal under §1, especially when an original anticompetitive purpose is evident from the affiliated corporations' subsequent conduct.[4] The *Yellow Cab* passage is most fairly read in light of this settled rule. In *Yellow Cab*, the affiliation of the defendants was irrelevant because the original acquisitions were *themselves* illegal. . . .

---

4. Under the arrangements condemned in Northern Sec. Co. v. United States, 193 U.S. 197, 354 (1904) (plurality opinion), "all the stock [a railroad holding company] held or acquired in the constituent companies was acquired and held to be used in suppressing competition between those companies. It came into existence only for that purpose." In *Standard Oil* and *American Tobacco* (1911), the trust or holding company device brought together previously independent firms to lessen competition and achieve monopoly power. Although the Court in the latter case suggested that the contracts between affiliated companies, and not merely the original combination, could be viewed as the conspiracy, the Court left no doubt that "the combination in and of itself" was a restraint of trade and a monopolization.

The ambiguity of the *Yellow Cab* holding yielded the one case giving support to the intra-enterprise conspiracy doctrine. In Kiefer-Stewart Co. v. Joseph E. Seagram & Sons, Inc., 340 U.S. 211 (1951), the Court held that two wholly owned subsidiaries of a liquor distiller were guilty under §1 of the Sherman Act for jointly refusing to supply a wholesaler who declined to abide by a maximum resale pricing scheme. The Court offhandedly dismissed the defendants' argument that "their status as 'mere instrumentalities of a single manufacturing-merchandizing unit' makes it impossible for them to have conspired in a manner forbidden by the Sherman Act." With only a citation to *Yellow Cab* and no further analysis, the Court stated that the "suggestion runs counter to our past decisions that common ownership and control does not liberate corporations from the impact of the antitrust laws" and stated that this rule was "especially applicable" when defendants "hold themselves out as competitors."

Unlike the *Yellow Cab* passage, this language does not pertain to corporations whose initial affiliation was itself unlawful. In straying beyond *Yellow Cab*, the *Kiefer-Stewart* Court failed to confront the anomalies an intra-enterprise doctrine entails. It is relevant nonetheless that, were the case decided today, the same result probably could be justified on the ground that the subsidiaries conspired with wholesalers other than the plaintiff. An intra-enterprise conspiracy doctrine thus would no longer be necessary to a finding of liability on the facts of *Kiefer-Stewart*.

Later cases invoking the intra-enterprise conspiracy doctrine do little more than cite *Yellow Cab* or *Kiefer-Stewart*, and in none of the cases was the doctrine necessary to the result reached. . . .

III

Petitioners, joined by the United States as amicus curiae, urge us to repudiate the intra-enterprise conspiracy doctrine. The central criticism is that the doctrine gives undue significance to the fact that a subsidiary is separately incorporated and thereby treats as the concerted activity of two entities what is really unilateral behavior flowing from decisions of a single enterprise.

We limit our inquiry to the narrow issue squarely presented: whether a parent and its wholly owned subsidiary are capable of conspiring in violation of §1 of the Sherman Act. We do not consider under what circumstances, if any, a parent may be liable for conspiring with an affiliated corporation it does not completely own.

A

The Sherman Act contains a "basic distinction between concerted and independent action." The conduct of a single firm is governed by §2 alone and is unlawful only when it threatens actual monopolization. It is not enough that a single firm appears to "restrain trade" unreasonably, for even a vigorous competitor may leave that impression. . . . In part because it is sometimes difficult to distinguish robust competition from conduct with long-run anti-competitive effects, Congress authorized Sherman Act scrutiny of single firms only when they pose a danger of monopolization. Judging unilateral conduct in this manner reduces the risk that the antitrust laws will dampen the competitive zeal of a single aggressive entrepreneur.

Section 1 of the Sherman Act, in contrast, reaches unreasonable restraints of trade effected by a "contract, combination . . . or conspiracy" between *separate* entities. It does not reach conduct that is "wholly unilateral." Concerted activity subject to §1 is judged more sternly than unilateral activity under §2. Certain agreements, such as horizontal price fixing and market allocation, are thought so inherently anticompetitive that each is illegal per se without inquiry into the harm it has actually caused. Other combinations, such as mergers, joint ventures, and various vertical agreements, hold the promise of increasing a firm's efficiency and enabling it to compete more effectively. Accordingly, such combinations are judged under a rule of reason, an inquiry into market power and market structure designed to assess the combination's actual effect. Whatever form the inquiry takes, however, it is not necessary to prove that concerted activity threatens monopolization.

The reason Congress treated concerted behavior more strictly than unilateral behavior is readily appreciated. Concerted activity inherently is fraught with anticompetitive risk. It deprives the marketplace of the independent centers of decision making that competition assumes and demands. In any conspiracy, two or more entities that previously pursued their own interests separately are combining to act as one for their common benefit. This not only reduces the diverse directions in which economic power is aimed but suddenly increases the economic power moving in one particular direction. Of course, such mergings of resources may well lead to efficiencies that benefit consumers, but their anticompetitive potential is sufficient to warrant scrutiny even in the absence of incipient monopoly.

B

The distinction between unilateral and concerted conduct is necessary for a proper understanding of the terms "contract, combination . . . or conspiracy" in §1. Nothing in the literal meaning of those terms excludes coordinated conduct among officers or employees of the *same* company. But it is perfectly plain that an internal "agreement" to implement a single, unitary firm's policies does not raise the antitrust dangers that §1 was designed to police. The officers of a single firm are not separate economic actors pursuing separate economic interests, so agreements among them do not suddenly bring together economic power that was previously pursuing divergent goals. Coordination within a firm is as likely to result from an effort to compete as from an effort to stifle competition. In the marketplace, such coordination may be necessary if a business enterprise is to compete effectively. For these reasons, officers or employees of the same firm do not provide the plurality of actors imperative for a §1 conspiracy.

There is also general agreement that §1 is not violated by the internally coordinated conduct of a corporation and one of its unincorporated divisions. Although this Court has not previously addressed the question, there can be little doubt that the operations of a corporate enterprise organized into divisions must be judged as the conduct of a single actor. The existence of an unincorporated division reflects no more than a firm's decision to adopt an organizational division of labor. A division within a corporate structure pursues the common interests of the whole rather than interests separate from those of the corporation itself; a business enterprise establishes divisions to further its own interests in the most efficient manner. Because coordination between a corporation and its division does not represent a sudden joining of two independent sources of economic power previously pursuing separate interests, it is not an activity that warrants §1 scrutiny.

Indeed, a rule that punished coordinated conduct simply because a corporation delegated certain responsibilities to autonomous units might well discourage corporations from creating divisions with their presumed benefits. This would serve no useful antitrust purpose but could well deprive consumers of the efficiencies that decentralized management may bring.

C

For similar reasons, the coordinated activity of a parent and its wholly owned subsidiary must be viewed as that of a single enterprise for purposes of §1 of the Sherman Act. A parent and its wholly owned subsidiary have a complete unity of interest. Their objectives are common, not disparate; their general corporate actions are guided or determined not by two separate corporate consciousnesses, but one. They are not unlike a multiple team of horses drawing a vehicle under the control of a single driver. With or without a formal "agreement," the subsidiary acts for the benefit of the parent, its sole shareholder. If a parent and a wholly owned subsidiary do "agree" to a course of action, there is no sudden joining of economic resources that had previously served different interests, and there is no justification for §1 scrutiny.

Indeed, the very notion of an "agreement" in Sherman Act terms between a parent and a wholly owned subsidiary lacks meaning. A §1 agreement may be found when "the conspirators had a unity of purpose or a common design and understanding, or a meeting of minds in an unlawful arrangement." *American Tobacco*. But in reality a parent and a wholly owned subsidiary *always* have a "unity of purpose or a common design." They share a common purpose whether or not the parent keeps a tight rein over the subsidiary; the parent may assert full control at any moment if the subsidiary fails to act in the parent's best interests.

The intra-enterprise conspiracy doctrine looks to the form of an enterprise's structure and ignores the reality. Antitrust liability should not depend on whether a corporate subunit is organized as an unincorporated division or a wholly owned subsidiary. A corporation has complete power to maintain a wholly owned subsidiary in either form. The economic, legal, or other considerations that lead corporate management to choose one structure over the other are not relevant to whether the enterprise's conduct seriously threatens competition. Rather, a corporation may adopt the subsidiary form of organization for valid management and related purposes. Separate incorporation may improve management, avoid special tax problems arising from multistate operations, or serve other legitimate interests. Especially in view of the increasing complexity of corporate operations, a business enterprise should be free to structure itself in ways that serve efficiency of control, economy of operations, and other factors dictated by business judgment without increasing its exposure to antitrust liability. Because there is nothing inherently anticompetitive about a corporation's decision to create a subsidiary, the intra-enterprise conspiracy doctrine "impose[s] grave legal consequences upon organizational distinctions that are of de minimis meaning and effect." Sunkist Growers, Inc. v. Winckler & Smith Citrus Products Co., 370 U.S. 19, 29 (1962).

If antitrust liability turned on the garb in which a corporate subunit was clothed, parent corporations would be encouraged to convert subsidiaries into unincorporated divisions. Indeed, this is precisely what the Seagram company did after this Court's decision in *Kiefer-Stewart*. Such an incentive serves no valid antitrust goals but merely deprives consumers and producers of the benefits that the subsidiary form may yield.

The error of treating a corporate division differently from a wholly owned subsidiary is readily seen from the facts of this case. Regal was operated as an unincorporated division of Lear Siegler for four years before it became a wholly owned subsidiary of Copperweld. Nothing in this record indicates any meaningful difference between Regal's operations as a division and its later operations as a separate corporation. Certainly nothing suggests that Regal was a greater threat to competition as a subsidiary of Copperweld than as a division of Lear Siegler. Under either arrangement, Regal might have acted to bar a new competitor from entering the market. In one case it could have relied on economic power from other quarters of the Lear Siegler corporation; instead it drew on the strength of its separately incorporated parent, Copperweld. From the standpoint of the antitrust laws, there is no reason to treat one more harshly than the other. As Chief Justice Hughes cautioned, "[r]ealities must dominate the judgment." *Appalachian Coals.*

D

Any reading of the Sherman Act that remains true to the Act's distinction between unilateral and concerted conduct will necessarily disappoint those who find that distinction arbitrary. It cannot be denied that §1's focus on concerted behavior leaves a "gap" in the Act's proscription against unreasonable restraints of trade. An unreasonable restraint of trade may be effected not only by two independent firms acting in concert; a single firm may restrain trade to precisely the same extent if it alone possesses the combined market power of those same two firms. Because the Sherman Act does not prohibit unreasonable restraints of trade as such—but only restraints effected by a contract, combination, or conspiracy—it leaves untouched a single firm's anticompetitive conduct (short of threatened monopolization) that may be indistinguishable in economic effect from the conduct of two firms subject to §1 liability.

We have already noted that Congress left this "gap" for eminently sound reasons. Subjecting a single firm's every action to judicial scrutiny for reasonableness would threaten to discourage the competitive enthusiasm that the antitrust laws seek to promote. Moreover, whatever the wisdom of the distinction, the Act's plain language leaves no doubt that Congress made a purposeful choice to accord different treatment to unilateral and concerted conduct. Had Congress intended to outlaw unreasonable restraints of trade as such, §1's requirement of a contract, combination, or conspiracy would be superfluous, as would the entirety of §2. Indeed, this Court has recognized that §1 is limited to concerted conduct at least since the days of *Colgate.*

The appropriate inquiry in this case, therefore, is not whether the coordinated conduct of a parent and its wholly owned subsidiary may ever have anticompetitive effects, as the dissent suggests.

Nor is it whether the term "conspiracy" will bear a literal construction that includes parent corporations and their wholly owned subsidiaries. For if these were the proper inquiries, a single firm's conduct would be subject to §1 scrutiny whenever the coordination of two employees was involved. Such a rule would obliterate the Act's distinction between unilateral and concerted conduct, contrary to the clear intent of Congress as interpreted by the weight of judicial authority. Rather, the appropriate inquiry requires us to explain the logic underlying Congress' decision to exempt unilateral conduct from §1 scrutiny, and to assess whether that logic similarly excludes the conduct of a parent and its wholly owned subsidiary. Unless we second-guess the judgment of Congress to limit §1 to concerted conduct, we can only conclude that the coordinated behavior of a parent and its wholly owned subsidiary falls outside the reach of that provision.

Although we recognize that any "gap" the Sherman Act leaves is the sensible result of a purposeful policy decision by Congress, we also note that the size of any such gap is open to serious question. Any anticompetitive activities of corporations and their wholly owned subsidiaries meriting antitrust remedies may be policed adequately without resort to an intra-enterprise conspiracy doctrine. A corporation's initial acquisition of control will always be subject to scrutiny under §1 of the Sherman Act and §7 of the Clayton Act. Thereafter, the enterprise is fully subject to §2 of the Sherman Act and §5 of the Federal Trade Commission Act. That these statutes are adequate to control dangerous anticompetitive conduct is suggested by the fact that not a single holding of antitrust liability by this Court would today be different in the absence of an intra-enterprise conspiracy doctrine. It is further suggested by the fact that the Federal Government, in its administration of the antitrust laws, no longer accepts the concept that a corporation and its wholly owned subsidiaries can "combine" or "conspire" under §1. Elimination of the intra-enterprise conspiracy doctrine with respect to corporations and their wholly owned subsidiaries will therefore not cripple antitrust enforcement. It will simply eliminate treble damages from private state tort suits masquerading as antitrust actions.

IV

We hold that Copperweld and its wholly owned subsidiary Regal are incapable of conspiring with each other for purposes of §1 of the Sherman Act. To the extent that prior decisions of this Court are to the contrary, they are disapproved and overruled....

[Justice Stevens, joined by Justices Brennan and Marshall, dissented. Their opinion emphasized three points. (1) "The majority's observation that in [the prior cases] there were alternative grounds that could have been used to reach the same result, disguises neither the fact that the holding that actually appears in these opinions rests on conspiracy between affiliated entities, nor that today's holding is inconsistent with what was actually held in those cases." (2) The language of §1 readily includes intraenterprise conspiracy. The rule of reason was developed in response to the fact that §1 similarly includes all "contracts" in restraint of trade. "Instead of redefining the word 'conspiracy,' the Court would be better advised to continue to rely on the Rule of Reason." Normal actions of integrated enterprises are not prohibited by the intraenterprise conspiracy doctrine because such actions are reasonable. In this case, because the jury found the challenged conduct to be anticompetitive, legal sanction is appropriate. (3) "Unilateral conduct by a firm with market power has no less anticompetitive potential than conduct by a plurality of actors which generates or exploits the same power, and probably more, since the unilateral actor avoids the policing problems faced by cartels." The intraenterprise conspiracy doctrine has the economic justification of filling a gap in antitrust enforcement: Where there is no agreement with a third party and when power is insufficient for §2 condemnation, it is the only way to bring such anticompetitive action under the antitrust laws. Thus, the question should not be the one asked by the Court — whether "a wholly owned subsidiary should be treated differently from a corporate division" — but rather "why two corporations that engage in a predatory course of conduct which produces a marketwide restraint on competition and which, as separate legal entities, can be easily fit within the language of §1, should be immunized from liability because they are controlled by the same godfather."][65]

240. (a) Is the majority's reading of prior cases persuasive in light of the dissent's challenge? Its reading of the statutory language? How does this opinion compare with the pronouncement of the rule of reason in *Standard Oil*?

(b) Why is the rule of reason insufficient to address the majority's concerns for efficient corporate operation?

(c) At one point, the dissent states that "[a] single firm, no matter what its corporate structure may be, is not expected to compete with itself." Does this suggest that, under its rule of reason approach, the dissent would permit coordinated pricing among separately incorporated subsidiaries? But what of the per se rule against price fixing? If it is not expected to compete with itself, why

65. White, J., did not participate.

would the dissenters appraise its coordinated decisionmaking under Sherman Act §1?

(d) *Kiefer-Stewart* had stated that the rule against intracorporate conspiracy was "especially applicable where, as here, respondents hold themselves out as competitors."[66] In other contexts, it has been argued that many of the significant benefits achieved by separate incorporation of subsidiaries — like some tax breaks and the benefits of limited liability — are often illegitimate but cannot directly be regulated because of the difficulty in determining when separately incorporated entities are truly separate. Thus, the law allows the presumption of separate existence to be overridden only upon strong contrary evidence. Might one argue from this that the intraenterprise conspiracy doctrine is consistent with this overall approach, whereas its rejection essentially permits corporations to benefit from the application of inconsistent presumptions in different contexts? Should corporations be forced to choose so that if they wish single entity treatment under the antitrust laws they cannot simultaneously insist that they are separate for tax or limited-liability purposes? Would that insistence reflect antitrust policy? If not, must it be rejected?[67]

(e) The *Copperweld* dissenters would retain the intraenterprise conspiracy doctrine in order to fill the gap between unilateral conduct by actual or prospective monopolists reached under Sherman Act §2 and multiparty conduct reached under §1. Is it necessary or wise to use Sherman Act §1 to reach potentially anticompetitive conduct by a single enterprise that lacks the actual or prospective monopoly power required for liability under §2 but that happens to include several separately incorporated units? Is it the purpose of the statute to do so?

241. Additional intraenterprise conspiracy issues.[68] *Copperweld* settles the question of conspiratorial capacity between a parent corporation and its wholly owned subsidiary, and the Court was careful

---

66. 340 U.S. at 215.

67. In thinking about intraenterprise conspiracy, consider the continuum of possible relationships among individuals interacting in a marketplace: spot-market exchanges (generally lawful), contracting (§1, Clayton Act §3), joint ventures (see ¶222), mergers (Clayton Act §7), and activity within a single firm (generally lawful, subject to Sherman Act §2). Recent work in economics compares contracting and spot-market trading through the market with implicit contractual arrangements within the firm and finds that they have much in common. See O.E. Williamson, Markets and Hierarchies: Analysis and Antitrust Implications (1975); S. Grossman & O. Hart, The Costs and Benefits of Ownership: A Theory of Vertical and Lateral Integration, 94 J. Pol. Econ. 691 (1986).

68. See S. Calkins, *Copperweld* in the Courts: The Road to *Caribe*, 63 Antitr. L.J. 345 (1995).

to say that it decided nothing else. Does its reasoning suggest that two corporations owned wholly in common by a single parent cannot conspire with each other?[69]

Can a parent conspire with a corporation that it does not wholly own? Would de facto control or majority ownership create a single unit for antitrust purposes?[70] Or should more evidence of integration — such as common officers, consolidated books, or day-to-day operating direction — be required? The pre-*Copperweld* decisions of the lower courts are suggestive. Most found a single economic unit, or allowed juries to do so, when common ownership was supplemented by varying degrees of actual integration. Even when affiliated corporations were held legally capable of conspiring, many courts refused to infer the existence of a conspiracy in fact from evidence that would probably have sufficed to find a conspiracy among unrelated firms. And even when a conspiracy was found among affiliated companies, its legality was tested by more lenient standards than those applied to unrelated conspirators.

Copperweld repeated the standard rule that operating divisions and employees comprise a single entity within the single corporation of which they are a part. But the employee might simultaneously serve a second master that can conspire with the first corporation or simultaneously occupy an independent role in the marketplace. Independent agents — such as lawyers, accountants, brokers, or distributors — might also be considered part of their principal's enterprise for some antitrust purposes and yet be capable of conspiring with the firm engaging them. We shall see more of this in Chapter 4A dealing with distribution intermediaries.

A final vexing issue, which we can only note here, is posed by trade associations, sports leagues, and other joint ventures.[71] In some important business and legal senses, the organization is a separate entity that is meant to function independently of its members. Yet, the members are not completely integrated and continue to be separate and competing forces in the market. As we shall see in the next two sections, the lawful formation of a trade association or sports league has not prevented the courts from finding subsequent illegal conspiracies among the members.

69. See Advanced Health-Care Serv. v. Radford, 738 F.2d 1473 (9th Cir. 1984) (*Copperweld* precludes liability for conspiracy between two wholly owned subsidiaries of the same parent corporation); H.R.M. v. Tele-Comm., 653 F. Supp. 645 (D. Colo. 1987) (two sister corporations wholly owned by a single parent incapable of conspiring to monopolize).

70. See Novatel Comm. v. Cellular Tel. Supply, 1986 Trade Cas. ¶67412 (N.D. Ga.) (51 percent ownership sufficient for full control, thereby making entities incapable of conspiracy under *Copperweld*).

71. Areeda, note 63, ¶¶1475-1478.

2D. FACILITATING PRACTICES

242. Introduction. As suggested in ¶¶229-230, supracompetitive pricing is far from automatic even in concentrated markets. Coordinating actions and effectively detecting and responding to defections are possible only when market conditions are congenial to such behavior or when unfavorable conditions can be overcome through appropriately devised strategies. Antitrust enforcers and courts have frequently confronted actions that may have the effect of facilitating oligopolistic collaboration.[1] Such actions might include meetings, the exchange of presale price quotations, and other practices relating to price or other dimensions of competition.

Such behavior can be analyzed on two levels. First, it may be evidence of a direct conspiracy to fix prices. As an example, the *Esco* court[2] posed a hypothetical in which five competitors met to discuss their problems; each of them said in turn, "I won't fix prices with any of you, but ... I am going to [set my price] at *X* dollars." The court observed,

> We do not say the foregoing illustration *compels* an inference in this case that the competitors' conduct constituted a price-fixing conspiracy, ... but neither can we say, as a matter of law, that an inference of no agreement is compelled. As in so many other instances, it remains a question for the trier of fact to consider and determine what inference appeals to it (the jury) as most logical and persuasive, after it has heard all the evidence as to what these competitors had done before such meeting, and what actions they took thereafter, or what actions they did not take.[3]

The hypothetical *Esco* meeting can be approached on a second level: The joint decision to have a meeting or to proceed in a

---

1. The government's horizontal merger guidelines, in Ch. 5D, take into account activities that facilitate collusion.

2. Esco Corp. v. United States, 340 F.2d 1000 (9th Cir. 1965).

3. Id. at 1007. See also United States v. Foley, 598 F.2d 1323, 1332 (4th Cir. 1979), cert. denied, 444 U.S. 1043 (1980) (announcement by dinner host that he would raise prices a specified amount coupled with evidence from which the jury could find that others at the dinner expressed or implied intent to adopt a similar change); United States v. Champion Intl. Corp., 1975 Trade Cas. ¶60453 (D. Or.), aff'd, 557 F.2d 1270 (9th Cir.), cert. denied, 434 U.S. 938 (1977) (intense price competition in bidding for the rights to harvest government timber suddenly stopped; thereafter the defendant most interested in a particular parcel turned out to be the only bidder for it; this may have begun innocently but the defendants then began meetings at which each participant told the others of which upcoming sale or sales interested his company; "[n]o one really committed himself not to bid but in sale after sale over a four year period, the one who had expressed the highest interest in the sale was the one who took the sale without opposition").

certain way at the meeting is itself a contract, combination, or conspiracy that violates Sherman Act §1 if it can be considered an unreasonable restraint of trade. As we have seen earlier in this chapter, joint action may be held to be an unreasonable restraint of trade if it significantly impairs or tends to impair competition without adequate justification. Does there, for example, exist any social justification for competitors getting together in the manner posed by the *Esco* court? Would such conversations make it easier for oligopolists to coordinate their pricing behavior? Even if the legal system reluctantly tolerates interdependent pricing behavior as such and hesitates to infer a conspiracy from parallel behavior and other "plus" factors, it still might condemn those concerted ancillary practices that unjustifiably facilitate interdependent pricing and which can be readily identified and enjoined. Under such an approach, the trier of fact need not find that the parties agreed to control prices but only that they agreed to undertake a practice that the court deems unreasonable. In considering the cases to follow, be sure to ask which of these approaches the court seems to be following.

This section considers a number of areas where facilitating practices have occupied the courts. The first concerns formal arrangements, often through trade associations, to exchange information among competitors. Then we examine basing point pricing, by which geographically dispersed competitors charge identical prices to customers at different locations, despite differences in transportation costs. Finally, *du Pont* involves a challenge under Federal Trade Commission Act §5 to a variety of practices employed in a concentrated, declining industry. This case also addresses the extent to which that statute goes beyond Sherman Act §1 in regulating facilitating practices. We begin with a few simple illustrations.

243. For each of the following practices, indicate (1) how they might facilitate oligopolistic pricing, (2) whether an agreement to adopt the practice should be forbidden, (3) whether parallel behavior adopting the practice is strong evidence of an agreement (as to adopting the practice or as to pricing itself), and (4) whether independent adoption should be forbidden even in the absence of a tacit or express agreement.

(a) General Electric and Westinghouse, the two leading producers of heavy electrical equipment, had price books from which one could calculate prices on complicated, made-to-order items. Such books were available to outsiders and inevitably to each other.[4]

4. See ¶230d. A consent decree prohibited the two producers from such activity, as well as from publicly announcing price changes (except to a customer on a

(b) Suppose that the airlines' trade association promulgates detailed standards for coach and first-class travel, including content of meals, availability of movies, leg-room, reservation services, and the like.

(c) Rivals who win competitive bids or gain customers agree to offer partial compensation to less fortunate competitors.[5]

244. Data dissemination. Competitors sometimes exchange information about their prices, output, inventories, investment, or other aspects of their business. This is often done through a trade association that is, of course, a statutory "combination" of its members and therefore subject to §1 examination. A fortiori, an agreement to exchange information is itself a "contract, combination . . . or conspiracy" that is subject to §1 scrutiny for any tendency unreasonably to restrain trade. In addition, an agreement to exchange price information, for example, may imply an agreement to raise or maintain prices. On the other hand, trade associations, in addition to the federal government, make available a wide array of information that can be useful to producers and consumers. The following cases consider when informational activities pose a sufficient danger to competition to justify prohibition.

AMERICAN COLUMN & LUMBER CO.
v. UNITED STATES
257 U.S. 377 (1921)

Justice CLARKE. . . . The unincorporated "American Hardwood Manufacturers' Association" was formed in December, 1918, by the consolidation of two similar associations, from one of which it took over a department of activity designated the "Open Competition Plan," and hereinafter referred to as the "Plan."

Participation in the "Plan" was optional with the members of the Association, but, at the time this suit was commenced, of its 400 members, 365, operating 465 mills, were members of the "Plan."

---

previous quotation) or from granting retroactive price cuts on previously concluded transactions. United States v. GE, 1977 Trade Cas. ¶61660 (E.D. Pa.) (consent decree); United States v. Westinghouse, 1977 Trade Cas. ¶61661 (E.D. Pa.) (consent decree).

5. United States v. Lake County Contractors Assn., 1977 Trade Cas. ¶61663 (N.D. Ill.) (consent decree forbidding rivals from requiring successful bidder to pay any fee except for bona fide services or from making any payments to unsuccessful bidders); United States v. Los Angeles Solid Waste Mgmt. Assn., 1974 Trade Cas. ¶74994 (C.D. Cal.) (consent decree forbidding rivals from requiring compensation from those who solicit each other's customers).

The importance and strength of the Association are shown by the admission in the joint answer that while the defendants operated only five per cent of the number of mills engaged in hardwood manufacture in the country, they produced one-third of the total production of the United States. . . .

[The objects and purposes of the Open Competition Plan, sometimes called the New Competition, were explained by the Association] in an appeal to members to join it, in which it is said:

> *Knowledge regarding prices actually made is all that is necessary to keep prices at reasonably stable and normal levels.*
>
> The Open Competition Plan is a central clearing house for information on prices, trade statistics and practices. By keeping all members fully and quickly informed of what the others have done, the work of the Plan results in *a certain uniformity of trade practice.* There is no agreement to follow the practice of others, *although members do naturally follow their most intelligent competitors,* if they know what these competitors have been actually doing. . . .

[The plan required each member to submit to the Association's secretary a (1) daily sales and shipping report identifying purchasers and all details of the sale with exact copies of orders and invoices, (2) monthly report of production and stocks for each variety of the product, and (3) price list at the beginning of each month with later filing of new lists whenever prices were changed. In addition, the Association was to inspect members' stocks and grading practices.] The declared purpose of the inspection service is not to change any member's grading except with his consent, but to furnish each member a basis on which he can compare his prices with those of other members, thereby making all members' reports more intelligible and accurate.

All of these reports by members are subject to complete audit by representatives of the Association. Any member who fails to report *shall not receive the reports* of the secretary, and failure to report for twelve days in six months shall cause the member failing to be dropped from membership.

Plainly it would be very difficult to devise a more minute disclosure of everything connected with one's business than is here provided for by this "Plan" and very certainly only the most attractive prospect could induce any man to make it to his rivals and competitors. . . .

[The Association's Manager of Statistics was to provide members with a (1) monthly summary of each member's production of each product grade, (2) weekly report of sales and shipments identifying each sale, price, and buyer, (3) monthly inventory of each member's stock, (4) monthly summary of each member's price list supplemented by immediate reports of changes in such lists, and (5) monthly market report letter.] This extensive interchange of reports, supplemented as it was by monthly meetings at which an opportunity was afforded for discussion "of all subjects of interest to the members," very certainly constituted an organization through which agreements, actual or implied, could readily be arrived at and maintained, if the members desired to make them. . . .

[In actual practice, meetings were held nearly every week in some areas. Before the meetings, each member was asked to state not only his past production but also to estimate his production and market conditions for the next two months. These estimates were reflected in the monthly report letter and the weekly sales report. Individual estimates] and a coordination of them by an expert analyst could readily evolve an attractive basis for cooperative, even if unexpressed, "harmony" with respect to future prices. . . .

This elaborate plan for the interchange of reports does not simply supply to each member the amount of stock held, the sales made and the prices received, by every other member of the group, thereby furnishing the data for judging the market, on the basis of supply and demand and current prices. It goes much farther. . . . [T]he only element lacking in this scheme to make it a familiar type of the competition suppressing organization is a definite agreement as to production and prices. But this is supplied: by the disposition of men "to follow their most intelligent competitors," especially when powerful; by the inherent disposition to make all the money possible, joined with the steady cultivation of the value of "harmony" of action; and by the system of reports, which makes the discovery of price reductions inevitable and immediate. The sanctions of the plan obviously are, financial interest, intimate personal contact, and business honor, all operating under the restraint of exposure of what would be deemed bad faith and of trade punishment by powerful rivals. . . .

Obviously the organization of the defendants constitutes a combination and confessedly they are engaged in a large way in the transportation and sale of lumber in interstate commerce so that there remains for decision only the question whether the system of doing business adopted resulted in that direct and undue restraint of interstate commerce which is condemned by this Antitrust statute. . . .

[T]he problem was to maintain the war prices then prevailing rather than to advance them, and although the minutes of the various meetings were kept in barest outline, we find that beginning within a month of the consolidation of the two associations, the members of the "Plan" began actively to cooperate, through the meetings, to suppress competition by restricting production. This is very clearly shown by the excerpts following from the minutes of meetings and from the market letters and sales reports distributed at them.

Thus, at the meeting held at Cincinnati, on January 21, 1919, in the discussion of business conditions, the chairman said: "If there is *no increase in production,* particularly in oak, there is going to be good business.... *No man is safe in increasing his production.* If he does, he will be in bad shape, as the demand won't come.". . .

Men in general are so easily persuaded to do that which will obviously prove profitable that this reiterated opinion from the analyst of their association, with all obtainable data before him, that higher prices were justified and could easily be obtained, must inevitably have resulted, as it did result, in concert of action in demanding them.

But not only does the record thus show a persistent purpose to encourage members to unite in pressing for higher and higher prices, without regard to cost, but there are many admissions by members, not only that this was the purpose of the "Plan," but that it was fully realized. . . .

As to the price conditions during the year. Without going into detail the record shows that the prices of the grades of hardwood in most general use were increased to an unprecedented extent during the year. Thus, the increases in prices of varieties of oak, range from 33.3% to 296% during the year; of gum, 60% to 343%; and of ash, from 55% to 181%. While it is true that 1919 was a year of high and increasing prices generally and that wet weather may have restricted production to some extent, we cannot but agree with the members of the "Plan" themselves, as we have quoted them, and with the District Court in the conclusion that the united action of this large and influential membership of dealers contributed greatly to this extraordinary price increase. . . .

Genuine competitors do not make daily, weekly, and monthly reports of the minutest details of their business to their rivals, as the defendants did; they do not contract, as was done here, to submit their books to the discretionary audit and their stocks to the discretionary inspection of their rivals for the purpose of successfully competing with them; and they do not submit the details of their business to the analysis of an expert, jointly employed, and obtain from him a "harmonized" estimate of the market as it is, and as, in his specially and confidentially informed judgment, it promises to be. This is not the conduct of competitors but is so clearly that of men united in an agreement, express or implied, to act together and pursue a common purpose under a common guide that, if it did not stand confessed a combination to restrict production and increase prices in interstate commerce and as, therefore, a direct restraint upon that commerce, as we have seen that it is, that conclusion must inevitably have been inferred from the facts which were proved. To pronounce such abnormal conduct on the part of 365 natural competitors, controlling one-third of the trade of the country in an article of prime necessity, a "new form of competition" and not an old form of combination in restraint of trade, as it so plainly is, would be for this court to confess itself blinded by words and forms to realities which men in general very plainly see and understand and condemn, as an old evil in a new dress and with a new name.

The "Plan" is, essentially, simply an expansion of the gentlemen's agreement of former days, skillfully devised to evade the law. To call it open competition because the meetings were nominally open to the public, or because some voluminous reports were transmitted to the Department of Justice, or because no specific agreement to restrict trade or fix prices is proved, cannot conceal the fact that the fundamental purpose of the "Plan" was to procure "harmonious" individual action among a large number of naturally competing dealers with respect to the volume of production and prices, without having any specific agreement with respect to them, and to rely for maintenance of concerted action in both respects, not upon fines and forfeitures as in earlier days, but upon what experience has shown to be the more potent and dependable restraints, of business honor and social penalties — cautiously reinforced by many and elaborate reports, which would promptly expose to his associates any disposition in any member to deviate from the tacit understanding that all were to act together under the subtle direction of a single interpreter of their common purposes, as evidenced in the minute reports of what they had done and in their expressed purposes as to what they intended to do.

In the presence of this record it is futile to argue that the purpose of the "Plan" was simply to furnish those engaged in this industry, with widely scattered units, the equivalent of such information as is contained in the newspaper and government publications with respect to the market for commodities sold on boards of trade or stock exchanges. One distinguishing and sufficient difference is that the published reports go to both seller and buyer, but these reports go to the seller only; and another is that there is no skilled interpreter of the published reports, such as we have in this case, to insistently recommend harmony of action likely to prove profitable in proportion as it is unitedly pursued. . . .

Affirmed.

Justice HOLMES, dissenting. . . . I should have supposed that the Sherman Act did not set itself against knowledge — did not aim at a transitory cheapness unprofitable to the community as a whole because not corresponding to the actual conditions of the country. I should have thought that the ideal of commerce was an intelligent interchange made with full knowledge of the facts as a basis for a forecast of the future on both sides. . . . A combination in unreasonable restraint of trade imports an attempt to override normal market conditions. An attempt to conform to them seems to me the most reasonable thing in the world. . . .

Justice BRANDEIS, dissenting, with whom Justice MCKENNA concurs. . . . The hardwood lumber mills are widely scattered. . . . No official, or other public means have been established for collecting from these mills and from dealers data as to current production, stocks on hand and market prices. Concerning grain, cotton, coal and oil, the Government collects and publishes regularly, at frequent intervals, current information on production, consumption and stocks on hand, and boards of trade furnish freely to the public details of current market prices of those commodities, the volume of sales, and even individual sales, as recorded in daily transactions. Persons interested in such commodities are enabled through this information to deal with one another on an equal footing. The absence of such information in the hardwood lumber trade enables dealers in the large centres more readily to secure advantage over the isolated producer. And the large concerns, which are able to establish their own bureaus of statistics, secure an advantage over smaller concerns. Surely it is not against the public interest to distribute knowledge of trade facts, however detailed. Nor are the other features of the Plan — the market letters and the regional conferences — an unreasonable interference with freedom in trade. Intelligent conduct of business implies not only knowledge of trade facts, but an understanding of them. To this understanding editorial comment and free discussion by those engaged in the business and by others interested are aids. . . .

MAPLE FLOORING MANUFACTURERS ASSN.
v. UNITED STATES
268 U.S. 563 (1925)

Justice STONE. . . . The defendants are the Maple Flooring Manufacturers Association, an unincorporated "trade association"; twenty-two corporate defendants, members of the Association, engaged in the business of selling and shipping maple, beech and birch flooring in interstate commerce, all but two of them having their principal places of business in Michigan, Minnesota or Wisconsin. .... [I]n the year of 1922 the defendants produced 70% of the total production of these types of flooring. ...

The defendants have engaged in many activities to which no exception is taken by the Government and which are admittedly beneficial to the industry and to consumers; such as co-operative advertising and the standardization and improvement of the product. The activities, however, of the present Association of which the Government complains may be summarized as follows:[6]

(1) The computation and distribution among the members of the association of the average cost to association members of all dimensions and grades of flooring.

(2) The computation and distribution among members of a booklet showing freight rates on flooring from Cadillac, Michigan, to between five and six thousand points of shipment in the United States.

(3) The gathering of statistics which at frequent intervals are supplied by each member of the Association to the Secretary of the Association giving complete information as to the quantity and kind of flooring sold and prices received by the reporting members, and the amount of stock on hand, which information is summarized by the Secretary and transmitted to members without, however, revealing the identity of the members in connection with any specific information thus transmitted.

(4) Meetings at which the representatives of members congregate and discuss the industry and exchange views as to its problems. ...

Although the bill alleges that the activities of the defendants hereinbefore referred to resulted in the maintenance of practical uniformity of net delivered prices as between the several corporate defendants, the evidence fails to establish such uniformity and it was not seriously urged before this Court that any substantial uniformity in price had in fact resulted from the activities of the Association, although it was conceded by defendants that the dissemination of information as to cost of the product and as to production and prices would tend to bring about uniformity in prices through the operation of economic law. Nor was there any direct proof that the activities of the Association had affected prices adversely to consumers. ...

[D]ata as to the average cost of flooring circulated among the members of the Association when combined with a calculated freight rate ... plus an arbitrary percentage of profit, could be made the basis for fixing prices or for an agreement for price

6. The Court noted that the Association in 1913 had adopted rules providing percentage allotments of shipments among plan members and in 1916 had adopted a minimum price plan. These were abolished in 1920 and 1921, respectively, and were not the subject of this case. — eds.

maintenance.... But ... the record is barren of evidence that the published list of costs and the freight-rate book have been so used by the present Association....

All reports of sales and prices dealt exclusively with past and closed transactions. The statistics gathered by the defendant Association are given wide publicity. They are published in trade journals which are read by from 90 to 95% of the persons who purchase the products of Association members. They are sent to the Department of Commerce which publishes a monthly survey of current business. They are forwarded to the Federal Reserve and other banks and are available to anyone at any time desiring to use them. It is to be noted that the statistics gathered and disseminated do not include current price quotations; information as to employment conditions; geographical distribution of shipments; the names of customers or distribution by classes of purchasers; the details with respect to new orders booked, such as names of customers, geographical origin of orders; or details with respect to unfilled orders, such as names of customers, their geographical location; the names of members having surplus stocks on hand; the amount of rough lumber on hand; or information as to cancellation of orders. Nor do they differ in any essential respect from trade or business statistics which are freely gathered and publicly disseminated in numerous branches of industry producing a standardized product such as grain, cotton, coal oil, and involving interstate commerce, whose statistics disclose volume and material elements affecting costs of production, sales price and stock on hand....

[M]eetings appear to have been held monthly.... There was no occasion to discuss past prices, as those were fully detailed in the statistical reports, and the Association was advised by counsel that future prices were not a proper subject of discussion. It was admitted by several witnesses, however, that upon occasion the trend of prices and future prices became the subject of discussion outside the meeting among individual representatives of the defendants attending the meeting. The Government, however, does not charge, nor is it contended, that there was any understanding or agreement, either express or implied, at the meetings or elsewhere, with respect to prices.

Upon this state of the record, the District Court, from whose decision this appeal was taken, held that the plan or system operated by the defendants had a direct and necessary tendency to destroy competition....

In urging that such is the necessary effect, the Government relies mainly upon the decisions of this Court in *Eastern States*; *American Column & Lumber*; and United States v. American Linseed Oil Company....

In *American Column & Lumber*, . . . [t]he record disclosed a systematic effort, participated in by the members of the Association and led and directed by the secretary of the Association, to cut down production and increase prices. The court not only held that this concerted effort was in itself unlawful, but that it resulted in an actual excessive increase of price to which the court found the "united action of this large and influential membership of dealers contributed greatly." The opinion of the court in that case rests squarely on the ground that there was a combination on the part of the members to secure concerted action in curtailment of production and increase of price, which actually resulted in a restraint of commerce, producing increase of price. . . .

It is not, we think, open to question that the dissemination of pertinent information concerning any trade or business tends to stabilize that trade or business and to produce uniformity of price and trade practice. Exchange of price quotations of market commodities tends to produce uniformity of prices in the markets of the world. Knowledge of the supplies of available merchandise tends to prevent over-production and to avoid the economic disturbances produced by business crises resulting from over-production. But the natural effect of the acquisition of wider and more scientific knowledge of business conditions, on the minds of the individuals engaged in commerce, and its consequent effect in stabilizing production and price, can hardly be deemed a restraint of commerce, or if so it cannot, we think, be said to be an unreasonable restraint, or in any respect unlawful. . . .

Persons who unite in gathering and disseminating information in trade journals and statistical reports on industry, who gather and publish statistics as to the amount of production of commodities in interstate commerce, and who report market prices, are not engaged in unlawful conspiracies in restraint of trade merely because the ultimate result of their efforts may be to stabilize prices or limit production through a better understanding of economic laws and a more general ability to conform to them, for the simple reason that the Sherman Law neither repeals economic laws nor prohibits the gathering and dissemination of information. . . .

We decide only that trade associations or combinations of persons or corporations which openly and fairly gather and disseminate information as to the cost of their product, the volume of production, the actual price which the product has brought in past transactions, stocks of merchandise on hand, approximate cost of transportation from the principal point of shipment to the points of consumption, as did these defendants, and who, as they did, meet and discuss such information and statistics without however reaching or attempting to reach any agreement or any concerted action

with respect to prices or production or restraining competition, do not thereby engage in unlawful restraint of commerce. . . .
[R]eversed.[7]

245. (a) Does *American Column & Lumber* hold that the information exchange was itself illegal, or that there was a conspiracy as to price? Did *Maple Flooring* find for the defendants because the information exchange posed no risk or because there was no proof of conspiracy concerning price or production?

(b) Consider how the information involved in each case might facilitate oligopolistic pricing. Of what relevance was the specificity of information, use of invoices, accounting inspections, and price notification in *American Column & Lumber*? Was the information involved in *Maple Flooring* of a sort that might facilitate collusion? (Consider what "average cost" means and the ways it might be calculated.)

(c) Is *Maple Flooring* consistent with *American Column & Lumber*?[8] Given the inevitable effect on pricing noted in *Maple Flooring*, does the decision survive *Socony*?

(d) What topics are permissible to discuss at trade association meetings in light of these two cases? Suppose a trade association held monthly meetings at which scholarly economists analyzed the firms' price and production decisions during the preceding month. Nothing was ever said about future output or prices. Some of the economists did expound the phenomenon of oligopoly pricing with respect to other industries. Are these meetings socially desirable? Are they lawful?

(e) In light of the number of competitors involved in each case, is it plausible that supracompetitive prices could be maintained? How does the *American Column & Lumber* Court suggest that this is accomplished?

(f) What harm might follow from prohibiting such exchanges of information? What of the *American Column & Lumber* dissent's argument that the information exchange might eliminate the competitive advantage of larger firms against the small?

(g) How about an information exchange agreement that made detailed information available to buyers as well, justified on the ground that it facilitates comparative shopping, reinforcing competition and producing lower prices? Does availability to buyers improve or worsen welfare? Should such availability be required? How,

---

7. Taft, C.J., and Sanford and McReynolds, JJ., dissented.

8. It is interesting to note that of the five Justices participating in both decisions, only Justice Van Devanter was in the majority in both cases. The dissenters in each instance were either in the majority in the other case or not on the Court.

if at all, does your answer depend on whether there are many sellers or few?

246. Historical notes on information exchange. (a) A number of other trade association cases involving information exchange reached the Court during this period. Two of the most prominent were *American Linseed Oil*[9] and *Sugar Institute*.[10] Each of these cases, in addition to the sorts of practices explored here, involved explicit agreements to adhere to listed prices.

(b) The concept of the New Competition in *American Column & Lumber* was not of the Association's own creation. In 1912, there appeared the first edition of Arthur Jerome Eddy's The New Competition, which advocated price information exchange as a way to limit price cutting. Shortly after Eddy began spreading this gospel, which included exhortations favoring cooperation over competition, hundreds of open price associations emerged.

(c) Further insight into systematic price exchanges can be gleaned from the British experience. Within a few years after the British Practices Court first decided that overt price fixing was prohibited, more than 150 price exchange agreements had been put into effect.[11]

UNITED STATES v. CONTAINER CORP. OF AMERICA
393 U.S. 333 (1969)

Justice DOUGLAS. . . . This is a civil antitrust action charging a price-fixing agreement in violation of §1 of the Sherman Act. The District Court dismissed the complaint. . . .[12]

The case as proved is unlike any other price decisions we have rendered. There was here an exchange of price information but no agreement to adhere to a price schedule as in Sugar Institute v. United States or *Socony*. There was here an exchange of information concerning specific sales to identified customers, not a statistical

9. United States v. American Linseed Oil Co., 262 U.S. 371 (1923).

10. Sugar Institute v. United States, 297 U.S. 553 (1936).

11. J. Heath, Some Economic Consequences, 70 Econ. J. 474, 475 (1960). After those agreements were terminated under British law, firms responded in different ways: substitutes for the prior agreements, mergers, or even competition. See D. Swann, D. O'Brien, M. Maunder & W. Howe, Competition in British Industry 181-195 (1974) (evaluating these responses in terms of resource allocation, cost minimization, and innovation).

12. The "dismissal" was after a full bench trial, with the judge making extensive findings of fact. 273 F. Supp. 18, 21. — eds.

report on the average cost to all members, without identifying the parties to specific transactions, as in *Maple Flooring*. While there was present here, as in *Cement Mfrs. Protective Assn.*, an exchange of prices to specific customers, there was absent the controlling circumstance, viz., that cement manufacturers, to protect themselves from delivering to contractors more cement than was needed for a specific job and thus receiving a lower price, exchanged price information as a means of protecting their legal rights from fraudulent inducements to deliver more cement than needed for a specific job.

Here all that was done was a request by each defendant from its competitor for information as to the most recent price charged or quoted, whenever it needed such information and whenever it was not available from another source. Each defendant on receiving that request usually furnished the data with the expectation that it would be furnished reciprocal information when it wanted it. That concerted action is of course sufficient to establish the combination or conspiracy, the initial ingredient of a violation of §1 of the Sherman Act.

There was of course freedom to withdraw from the agreement. But the fact remains that when a defendant requested and received price information, it was affirming its willingness to furnish such information in return.

There was to be sure an infrequency and irregularity of price exchanges between the defendants; and often the data was available from the records of the defendants or from the customers themselves. Yet the essence of the agreement was to furnish price information whenever requested.

Moreover, although the most recent price charged or quoted was sometimes fragmentary, each defendant had the manuals with which it could compute the price charged by a competitor on a specific order to a specific customer.

Further, the price quoted was the current price which a customer would need to pay in order to obtain products from the defendant furnishing the data.

The defendants account for about 90% of the shipment of corrugated containers from plants in the Southeastern United States. While containers vary as to dimensions, weight, color, and so on, they are substantially identical, no matter who produces them, when made to particular specifications. The prices paid depend on price alternatives. Suppliers when seeking new or additional business or keeping old customers, do not exceed a competitor's price. It is common for purchasers to buy from two or more suppliers concurrently. A defendant supplying a customer with containers would usually quote the same price on additional orders, unless costs had changed. Yet where a competitor was charging a particular price, a defendant would normally quote the same price or even a lower price.

The exchange of price information seemed to have the effect of keeping prices within a fairly narrow ambit. Capacity has exceeded the demand from 1955 to 1963, the period covered by the complaint, and the trend of corrugated container prices has been downward. Yet despite this excess capacity and the downward trend of prices, the industry has expanded in the Southeast from 30 manufacturers with 49 plants to 51 manufacturers with 98 plants. An abundance of raw materials and machinery makes entry into the industry easy with an investment of $50,000 to $75,000.

The result of this reciprocal exchange of prices was to stabilize prices though at a downward level. Knowledge of a competitor's price usually meant matching that price. The continuation of some price competition is not fatal to the Government's case. The limitation or reduction of price competition brings the case within the ban, for as we held in *Socony*, interference with the setting of price by free market forces is unlawful per se. Price information exchanged in some markets may have no effect on a truly competitive price. But the corrugated container industry is dominated by relatively few sellers. The product is fungible and the competition for sales is price. The demand is inelastic, as buyers place orders only for immediate, short-run needs. The exchange of price data tends toward price uniformity. For a lower price does not mean a larger share of the available business but a sharing of the existing business at a lower return. Stabilizing prices as well as raising them is within the ban of §1 of the Sherman Act. As we said in *Socony*, "in terms of market operations, stabilization is but one form of manipulation." The inferences are irresistible that the exchange of price information has had an anticompetitive effect in the industry, chilling the vigor of price competition. The agreement in the present case, though somewhat casual, is analogous to *American Column & Lumber*; United States v. American Linseed Oil Co.

Price is too critical, too sensitive a control to allow it to be used even in an informal manner to restrain competition.

Reversed.

Justice FORTAS, concurring. . . . I do not understand the Court's opinion to hold that the exchange of specific information among sellers as to price charged to individual customers, pursuant to mutual arrangement, is a per se violation of the Sherman Act.

Absent per se violation, proof is essential that the practice resulted in an unreasonable restraint of trade. There is no single test to determine when the record adequately shows an "unreasonable restraint of trade"; but a practice such as that here involved, which is adopted for the purpose of arriving at a determination of prices to be quoted to individual customers, inevitably suggests the probability that it so materially interfered with the operation of the price mechanism of the marketplace as to bring it within the condemnation of this Court's decisions. Cf. *Sugar Institute*; *American Column & Lumber*.

Theoretical probability, however, is not enough unless we are to regard mere exchange of current price information as so akin to price fixing by combination or conspiracy as to deserve the per se classification. I am not prepared to do this, nor is it necessary here. In this case, the probability that the exchange of specific price information led to an unlawful effect upon prices is adequately buttressed by evidence in the record. This evidence, although not overwhelming, is sufficient in the special circumstances of this case to show an actual effect on pricing and to compel us to hold that the court below erred in dismissing the Government's complaint.

In summary, the record shows that the defendants sought and obtained from competitors who were part of the arrangement information about the competitors' prices to specific customers. "[I]n the majority of instances," the District Court found, once a defendant had this information he quoted substantially the same price as the competitor, although a higher or lower price would "occasionally" be quoted. Thus the exchange of prices made it possible for individual defendants confidently to name a price equal to that which their competitors were asking. The obvious effect was to "stabilize" prices by joint arrangement — at least to limit any price cuts to the minimum necessary to meet competition. In addition, there was evidence that, in some instances, during periods when various defendants ceased exchanging prices exceptionally sharp and vigorous price reductions resulted.

On this record, taking into account the specially sensitive function of the price term in the antitrust equation, I cannot see that we would be justified in reaching any conclusion other than that defendants' tacit agreement to exchange information about current prices to specific customers did in fact substantially limit the amount of price competition in the industry. That being so, there is no need to consider the possibility of a per se violation.

Justice MARSHALL, with whom Justice HARLAN and Justice STEWART join, dissenting.... I do not believe that the agreement in the present case is so devoid of potential benefit or so inherently harmful that we are justified in condemning it without proof that it was entered into for the purpose of restraining price competition or that it actually had that effect....

Complete market knowledge is certainly not an evil in perfectly competitive markets. This is not, however, such a market, and there is admittedly some danger that price information will be used for anticompetitive purposes, particularly the maintenance of prices at a high level. If the danger that price information will be so used is particularly high in a given situation, then perhaps exchange of information should be condemned.

I do not think the danger is sufficiently high in the present case. Defendants are only 18 of the 51 producers of corrugated containers in the Southeastern United States. Together, they do make up 90% of the market and the six largest defendants do control 60% of the market. But entry is easy; an investment of $50,000 to $75,000 is ordinarily all that is necessary. In fact, the number of sellers has increased from 30 to the present 51 in the eight year period covered by the complaint. The size of the market has almost doubled because of increased demand for corrugated containers. Nevertheless, some excess capacity is present. The products produced by defendants are undifferentiated. Industry demand is inelastic, so that price changes will not, up to a certain point, affect the total amount purchased. The only effect of price changes will be to reallocate market shares among sellers.

In a competitive situation, each seller will cut his price in order to increase his share of the market, and prices will ultimately stabilize at a competitive level — i.e., price will equal cost, including a reasonable return on capital. Obviously, it would be to a seller's benefit to avoid such price competition and maintain prices at a higher level, with a corresponding increase in profit. In a market with very few sellers, and detailed knowledge of each other's price, such action is possible. However, I do not think it can be concluded that this particular market is sufficiently oligopolistic, especially in light of the ease of entry, to justify the inference that price information will necessarily be used to stabilize prices. . . .

In this market, we have a few sellers presently controlling a substantial share of the market. We have a large number competing for the remainder of the market, also quite substantial. And total demand is increasing. In such a case, I think it just as logical to assume that the sellers, especially the smaller and new ones,[1] will desire to capture a larger market share by cutting prices as it is that they will acquiesce in oligopolistic behavior. The likelihood that prices will be cut and that those lower prices will have to be met acts as a deterrent to setting prices at an artificially high level in the first place. Given the uncertainty about the probable effect of an ex-

---

1. The record does not indicate whether all manufacturers engaged in exchange of price information, or whether the practice was limited to defendants. There is no indication that other manufacturers would not have been given price information had they requested it.

change of price information in this context, I would require that the Government prove that the exchange was entered into for the purpose of or, that it had the effect of, restraining price competition. . . .

247.   (a) How might the information exchange in *Container* facilitate oligopolistic pricing? Do you suspect that sellers calling to verify rivals' prices tended to undercut them? Why do you think those receiving such calls were willing to answer? Why couldn't sellers rely on buyers to indicate what prices sellers' rivals had quoted?

(b) What did the Court hold in *Container?* Did the Court find an agreement to fix prices as well as an agreement to exchange information? Was the latter agreement express? If not, from what evidence was it inferred?

(c) Does the *Container* result depend on proof that the defendants' conduct affected market prices in some measurable way or only that there might be such effect?[13] What should one infer about industry performance from the simultaneous existence of new entry and excess capacity?

(d) Was adequate attention given to the possible "redeeming virtues" of defendants' conduct? What virtues might there be?[14]

(e) Does *Container* signal a retreat from *Maple Flooring* or a narrowing of it? (1) For all data exchanges? (2) For certain exchanges among numerous firms inhabiting a relatively competitive market? (3) For some or all exchanges among the relatively few firms inhabiting an oligopolistic market? (4) For exchange of price quotations with respect to specific, pending sales? If *Container* implies that more information may lawfully be exchanged in competitive markets than in oligopolistic markets, what criteria will serve to distinguish one situation from the other?

248.   Gypsum wallboard is a standardized product; in almost all instances buyers pick their source of supply solely on the basis of

13. Greenhaw v. Lubbock County Beverage Assn., 721 F.2d 1019, 1030 (5th Cir. 1983) ("'competitors exchange [of] price information . . . is sufficient to establish the existence of an agreement or conspiracy'"; such a conspiracy is unlawful "if the effect of such an exchange of prices among competitors is to fix, raise, maintain or stabilize those prices"); United States v. Citizens & Southern Natl. Bank, 422 U.S. 86, 113 (1975) ("dissemination of price information is not itself a per se violation"). For a critique of the *Container* decision, see R. Posner, Information and Antitrust: Reflections on the Gypsum and Engineers Decisions, 67 Geo. L.J. 1187 (1979).

14. For the Court's response to an argument that the exchange of presale price quotations may be necessary in order to avoid liability under the Robinson-Patman Act, see *Gypsum,* ¶617b.

price. In 1969, the industry had 14 sellers, the four leading sellers accounting for roughly 70 percent of nationwide sales. U.S. Gypsum had about 33 percent of sales; National, Kaiser, and Flintkote were the next largest firms with a total of roughly 37 percent of sales. The market for gypsum wallboard increased rapidly from 1945 to 1960. Despite a tripling of capacity during that period, prices and profits were highly favorable. After 1960, however, there was substantial excess capacity and considerable downward pressure on prices because expected further increases in demand failed to materialize.

(a) Would an unlawful agreement to exchange information on pending transactions be found on the basis of the following facts? (1) Defendants usually quoted their posted prices but (except as indicated in ¶b below) would go below those prices where necessary to meet a lower quotation to a particular buyer. Not infrequently, defendants discovered after the event that the buyers' statements — that they had received a lower quote from a competing seller — were false. (2) Early in 1964, defendants informally agreed to the following arrangement: Where a buyer stated to one seller that it had received a specified lower quotation from a named competitor, the seller would first attempt to obtain verification from the buyer; if the buyer refused to supply satisfactory proof, the seller would call the competitor, convey the report, and ask simply whether the report was "true" or "false"; the competitor would then investigate and report back accordingly. (3) Defendants attempted to get the smaller sellers to agree to this arrangement. Two did; the rest did not. Because of this procedure, because buyers frequently would not name the alleged low bidder, and because defendants' procedure only disclosed that a particular price quote alleged by the buyer was true or false, proof of actual effects on prices is inconclusive.

(b) Would an unlawful agreement to adhere to posted list prices be found on the basis of the following facts? (1) On November 15, 1968, U.S.G. publicly announced that after December 1 it would adhere strictly to its published list prices and credit terms (2 percent discount for cash within 30 days). Similar announcements were made by National, Kaiser, and Flintkote on November 17, November 25, and November 30, respectively. Flintkote specified December 15 as the date beyond which it would make no concessions off list prices. (2) Internal instructions issued to U.S.G. sales personnel on November 12, in addition to notifying them of the impending announcement, stated the following: "Despite our public position, we may make concessions to match any off-list quotations from Kaiser, National, or Flintkote. However, all such cases shall be referred to Mr. Jones, who has sole authority to make any concessions off list." (3) Internal instructions issued to National sales personnel on November 17 paralleled those of U.S.G. A Kaiser memorandum, dated November 20, simply stated that a named officer would have sole authority to make concessions. A Flintkote memorandum, also dated November 20, was like Kaiser's. (4) A memorandum to the U.S.G. Board of Directors recommending the above action stated in part as follows: "Severe price competition and poor profits require drastic action to endeavor to stabilize the situation. We anticipate that at least our major competitors will see it the same way, and that our lead will be followed." (5) From December 1968 until August 1969, the four defendants departed from list prices only rarely, and then only to meet lower prices known to be quoted by smaller competitors. During that period, the market shares of all four declined, and the collective share of the smaller producers rose by 15 percent. In August, first U.S.G. and then the other three defendants announced they would thereafter make concessions wherever necessary to meet competition.[15] How do these facts differ from typical patterns of price announcements in many industries?

(c) With the facts in ¶b, compare the following: Representatives of all four companies meet in a smoke-filled room. U.S.G.'s representative says "after December 1, we will adhere strictly to our published list prices and credit terms." After a brief silence, National (making no explicit reference to the preceding remark) states precisely the same words. Kaiser and Flintkote follow (with the exception that the latter gives the December 15 date). Similar internal memos to those in ¶b are discovered. Any doubt that this is an express price-fixing conspiracy? Is it saved by their lack of explicit reference to the others in the room or use of the language of deal-making? If it is a conspiracy, would it be saved if TV cameras were admitted to the meeting? Do the facts in ¶b differ materially?[16]

249. *General Motors Corp.*, 103 F.T.C. 374, 384, 387-388, 393 (1984). GM and Toyota formed a joint venture to manufacture 200,000 to 250,000 subcompact automobiles annually — based on

15. In somewhat altered form, this problem is drawn from Wall Prods. Co. v. National Gypsum Co., 326 F. Supp. 295 (N.D. Cal. 1971), where the court found an unlawful agreement to adhere to posted prices.

16. In the early 1990's, it was alleged that airlines used a computerized fare reservation system to signal pricing intentions. Private litigation was settled, In re Domestic Air Transportation Antitrust Litigation, 148 F.R.D. 297 (N.D. Ga. 1993), and a Justice Department investigation resulted in a consent decree. United States v. Airline Tariff Publishing Co., 1994-2 Trade Cas. ¶70687 (D.D.C.). See J. Baker, Identifying Horizontal Price Fixing in the Electronic Marketplace, 65 Antitr. L.J. 41 (1996).

Toyota's Sprinter, then sold only in Japan — at a then-idle GM plant in California. The output was to be sold to GM[17] at a price initially to be agreed to by the venturers and thereafter to be adjusted according to a specified index (in which the price of Toyota's Corolla figured prominently) but subject to adjustment by agreement. The two parents were to hold equal equity in the venture and to appoint an equal number of directors. Toyota was to appoint the chief management personnel.

In 1984, the Federal Trade Commission investigated the venture and, with two dissents, decided not to initiate formal proceedings when the venturers consented to an order (1) prohibiting any other joint venture between them; (2) limiting the duration of the venture to 12 years; (3) confining Toyota's sales to GM to 250,000 units annually; (4) prohibiting the parents from exchanging or discussing with each other or with the venture any nonpublic information relating to current or future (a) prices of the parents' new autos or components "except pursuant to a supplier-customer relationship entered into in the ordinary course of business," (b) costs of the parents' products, (c) sale or production forecasts or plans for any product other than the joint venture product or marketing plans for any product; (5) forbidding any exchange or discussion of nonpublic information relating to current or future model changes or designs of the venture's product, its sales or production forecasts, or costs of products supplied by the parents to the venture except as necessary solely to accomplish "the legitimate purposes or functioning" of the joint venture; and (6) requiring certain records and reports.[18]

With these limitations, the Commission majority concluded that the venture would not violate the antitrust laws. There was said to be a substantial likelihood that the venture would produce three

> significant procompetitive benefits to the American public: First, the ... venture would likely increase the total number of small cars available in America, thus allowing American consumers greater choice

17. Nothing prohibited the venture from manufacturing for and selling to Toyota.

18. Courts have had little trouble accepting less threatening joint ventures. E.g., National Bancard Corp. v. Visa, U.S.A., 596 F. Supp. 1231 (S.D. Fla. 1984), aff'd, 779 F.2d 592 (11th Cir. 1986) (no violation involved in fee arrangements covering interbank transactions; some arrangement necessary to offer the VISA card, and fees were within the range of reasonable business judgment); Association of Retail Travel Agents v. Air Transport Assn., 623 F. Supp. 893 (D.D.C. 1985) (per se rule inapplicable to joint venture of Air Transport Assn. that coordinated dealings between airlines and travel agencies; venture established financial stability requirements and made weekly collection of funds from ticket sales; individual airlines negotiated their own commission structures with travel agents).

at lower prices despite present restrictions on Japanese imports. Second, the joint venture car will cost less to produce than if GM were forced to rely immediately on some other production source. Finally, the joint venture offers a valuable opportunity for GM to complete its learning of more efficient Japanese manufacturing and management techniques.

GM would be able to gain the benefits of in-depth, daily accumulation of knowledge regarding seemingly minor details. A more efficient, more competitive U.S. automobile industry would result to the extent that the venture can demonstrate successfully that the Japanese system can work in America.

The dissenters believed that GM already knew about efficient Japanese methods and feared that the venture would reduce GM's uncertainty about technical advances in Japan and thereby reduce its incentive to innovate in product design. They also feared adverse price effects: Toyota could raise the price of the Corolla, knowing that this will drive up the index controlling the venture's price and lead GM to raise the price of its other products in order to maintain their usual premium over subcompacts; such prices would then be matched by other Japanese and U.S. producers in this concentrated market.

(In 1993, the FTC set aside the original order, citing "fundamental changes" in the market.[19] All restrictions regarding duration and output were thus ended, and, in order to allow GM and Toyota "to engage in communications ancillary to and reasonably necessary for the operation of the joint venture," the Com-

---

19. See Dkt. No. C-3132 (Dec. 10, 1993), 58 Fed. Reg. 64950. By 1992, 12 Japanese and 2 European transplant car assembly plants operated in North America (including Mexico), adding more than 2.5 million units of production of capacity, and Honda/Acura had surpassed Toyota as the largest foreign seller of automobiles. Ford was also involved in a joint venture with Mazda (in which it held a 25 percent stake) and with Nissan, and Chrysler had another arrangement with Mitsubishi. GM also had other arrangements with Suzuki, with which it produced the Geo line of cars. The Commission concluded that

> The changes in the industry that are described above are changed circumstances that eliminate the need for the order's limitations on the output and the duration of the joint venture. Entry and expansion in the automobile market in North America, although costly and time-consuming, have occurred on a significant scale. In the face of such entry and expansion, the joint venture is unlikely to create or facilitate the exercise of market power. In addition, the development by GM of the Saturn line of cars is a significant change that eliminates the concern that the establishment of NUMMI [the joint venture] would deter independent development and production of small cars in North America by GM. GM's substantial investment in Saturn, the increasing presence of transplant operations and the substantial increase in small car models available to consumers since 1984 all suggest that the basis for the concern reflected in the complaint and order about diminished competition in the small car market has been eliminated.

mission decided that restricting the flow of information was not practical.)

(a) Are the justifications accepted by the Commission in 1984 consistent with the preceding court decisions in this Chapter? If the venture were disallowed, might Toyota have built the plant itself?[20] Would this have been preferable? If a primary effect of the plan is to enhance GM's abilities, why is Toyota, GM's then-leading foreign competitor, so anxious to help?

(b) Consider items (4) and (5) in the FTC's original order, regarding information exchange. Was it realistic to expect that such information would not flow in the course of the joint venture's decisionmaking concerning design, production, or pricing?

(c) Were the dissent's fears concerning spillover effects on the pricing of other cars by the two companies well founded? Are there better ways the price charged by the venture to GM could be determined?

250. Basing point pricing.[21] (a) *Description.* When buyers or sellers are geographically dispersed, location becomes another important element of competition because the cost of transporting goods must be taken into account. When transportation costs are extremely low relative to the value of the product, or when a large producer has many plants throughout its selling area, all buyers may pay the same "delivered" price, which includes transportation. But when transportation costs are high — as is often the case for bulky intermediate goods such as steel and cement — a seller that

---

20. Note that, but for then-existing import restrictions, Toyota would have been able to increase its United States sales directly.

Also, after reading Chs. 5D and 5E, consider whether a merger between GM and Toyota would have been permitted. If not, how should that bear on the permissibility of the joint venture? In United States v. Penn-Olin Chem. Co., 378 U.S. 158 (1964), discussed in ¶532c, the Supreme Court required that a joint venture be evaluated under Clayton Act §7 to determine the effect of the venture on eliminating potential competition. On remand, 246 F. Supp. 917 (D. Del. 1965), aff'd by an equally divided Court, 389 U.S. 308 (1967), the venture was held lawful. See Yamaha Motor Co. v. FTC, 657 F.2d 971 (8th Cir. 1981) (court affirms FTC finding of §7 violation by venture between second largest United States seller of outboard motors and major foreign producer; collateral restraints on competition were also impermissible); Union Carbide & Carbon Corp. v. Nisley, 300 F.2d 561 (10th Cir. 1961), cert. dismissed, 371 U.S. 801 (1962) (upholding jury finding against two firms that cooperated to build and later to enlarge a plant on the property of one of them and that later agreed that one would allow the other to mine and mill its ore; parties chose to be partners rather than competitors).

21. See F.M. Scherer & D. Ross, Industrial Market Structure and Economic Performance 502-508 (3d ed. 1990); T. Gilligan, Imperfect Competition and Basing-Point Pricing: Evidence from the Softwood Plywood Industry, 82 Am. Econ. Rev. 1106 (1992).

charged uniform delivered prices would bear significantly different costs depending on where the buyer was located. One common response is an f.o.b. price for the goods at the seller's plant; the buyer then pays for transportation, even if it is arranged by the seller. When sellers are dispersed, a seller might charge a delivered price that is less than the sum of its f.o.b. price plus transportation costs in order to match the delivered price of a seller who is nearer to those buyers. Near the seller's own plant, it will charge as high a price as the market will bear. If there are many sellers at most locations, competitive prices will prevail throughout, and it will not generally be profitable to absorb transportation costs to sell in distant territories where other sellers have the locational advantage.

An important variant, which is the subject of the cases to follow, involves an industry-wide system of basing point pricing. The most famous instance involved the steel industry, earlier in this century. The "basing point" was Pittsburgh, and prices were referred to as "Pittsburgh-plus": In essence, all steel companies charged the same price to buyers in Pittsburgh; buyers located elsewhere paid this Pittsburgh price plus freight costs *from Pittsburgh*. For example, if the Pittsburgh price had been $100 per ton, and rail freight to Chicago had been $10 per ton, a Chicago buyer would pay $110 per ton for steel, regardless of where the producer was located. Thus, a Chicago producer would charge $110 locally (collecting "phantom freight" of $10) and $100 in Pittsburgh (absorbing freight costs of $10).[22]

A more complicated version of such systems involves the use of multiple basing points. Both Chicago and Pittsburgh might be basing points. Indiana buyers would pay Chicago-plus and New York buyers would pay Pittsburgh-plus; the base prices in Chicago and Pittsburgh need not be identical. Within the region covered by any particular basing point, however, the analysis is much the same as in the case where there is only one basing point.

(b) *Economic effects.* The most obvious effect is that buyers have no incentive to minimize transportation costs by purchasing from the nearest sellers. Those purchasing nearby receive no discount for the savings on freight; those buying from producers more distant than the basing point do not pay for the extra freight. Wasteful cross-hauling occurs as some Chicago buyers purchase from Pittsburgh producers and vice versa. Locational decisions will thus be distorted as well. Buyers will build their plants nearer to Pittsburgh,

---

22. Of course, if Chicago production was insufficient to satisfy local demand, which would be necessary for Chicago competitors to be able to charge the phantom freight, they would have no occasion to absorb freight charges by offering to sell in Pittsburgh, where they would earn $20 less per ton.

even though they otherwise prefer being near producers located elsewhere. Similarly, producers have less incentive to locate new plants near remote, expanding markets because the basing point system prevents them from fully exploiting any freight advantage. If they do build near those buyers distant from the basing point and serve only them, they charge phantom freight. Either result seems possible, although many commentators have conjectured that excessive concentration of production near the basing point is the more likely consequence.

(c) *Collusion or competition?* Two explanations are most often advanced to explain the appearance of basing point pricing. In the competitive story, one begins with a product made by a handful of firms at the same location, say, Seattle. Simple competition will produce "Seattle-plus" prices in New Orleans: Competition will tend to force identical Seattle prices, and distant buyers who request delivered price quotes will tend to be charged the common base price plus freight charges. As demand grows in New Orleans, a new entrant locates its plant there and sells its entire output locally at the preexisting Seattle-plus price, collecting phantom freight. Other producers may locate in New Orleans or other areas closer than Seattle, but as long as their capacity is less than local demand, they have no reason to sell at less than Seattle-plus prices. And they cannot charge more. Similarly, Seattle sellers cannot lower their New Orleans price to retain their former sales there because, by assumption, their original price was competitive and thus reflected their costs; a lower price would be unprofitable even if the new entrants did not meet or undercut it. But as New Orleans capacity expands to the point where it can satisfy local demand, competition among New Orleans producers should drive their local price down toward their costs, which, of course, do not include freight from Seattle.

But if New Orleans prices do not fall over time or if capacity does not expand notwithstanding ample profit potential, we might suspect an oligopoly story. Recall that where all buyers and sellers are in the same location, the sellers need only to agree on and police adherence to a single price. But where buyers and sellers are geographically dispersed, the sellers must somehow coordinate many prices. Each seller must also interpret its rivals' prices: Does a cut reflect a transportation cost saving, a response to local demand conditions, an invitation to change the base price, or "cheating" on the oligopoly price? One solution for the sellers is to meet periodically to set the myriad prices, taking all conditions into account and compromising disputes over the bargaining table rather than in the marketplace. But that would be hard to do without detection, and the need to haggle over so many items, where sellers with different plant locations will have differing interests, is an invitation to bargaining breakdown.

Basing point pricing offers an imperfect but far simpler means of coordination. Regardless of the number of locations, coordination will be possible after a consensus on only three things: a single base price, a basing point, and a single *set* of transportation charges — for example, $100, Pittsburgh, and prevailing rail freight rates filed with the Interstate Commerce Commission.[23] The first item is no different than for any oligopoly model. The second and third are rather simple additions that settle thousands of prices in one stroke, and with little ambiguity or dispute.[24] To raise or lower industry prices, only the base price need be modified, and any price other than an announced general change in the base price could be regarded as cheating. This strategy is less profitable than the successful express cartel because it generates wasteful cross-hauling at the expense of some oligopoly profits and its rigidity may prevent otherwise profitable geographic pricing that differs from that dictated by the basing point formula. But the basing point system, whether it involves one or more basing points, is a far simpler system that facilitates oligopolistic coordination and, once it comes into existence, maintains itself without any continuing consultation or other indicia of express agreements.

In comparing the competitive and oligopolistic scenarios just outlined, observe whether the producers offer an f.o.b. price or *only* a delivered price. In the competitive scenario, the New Orleans firms could just as readily sell at an f.o.b. base price equal to the delivered price of the Seattle firms.[25] With such a base price, to be sure, they would have to absorb freight in selling to the West (that is, at locations at which Seattle-plus would be less than freight added to the higher New Orleans base rate). But in the competitive scenario, the local New Orleans price equaling Seattle-plus indicates that New Orleans capacity is less than local demand, so New Orleans firms would have no desire to absorb freight in order to sell elsewhere, where sales would thus be less profitable. In the oligopoly scenario, producers do not offer any f.o.b. option; if they did, consumers would make f.o.b. purchases at plants nearer to them

23. Recall from *Maple Flooring* that the information circulated included an average cost figure (which could be used to determine a base price) and a booklet showing freight rates from Cadillac, Michigan, to thousands of points of shipment.

24. In fact, transportation rate schedules may have some ambiguity, which might be why firms or trade associations sometimes distribute freight rate books, as in note 23. Cf. ¶243a.

25. Similarly, the Seattle firms could sell at an f.o.b. price equal to their local price.

than the basing point.[26] Sellers hungry for sales would feel compelled to lower the base prices; the resulting price cutting and uncertainty among sellers could then fatally disrupt anything that remained of their efforts at oligopolistic coordination.

(d) *Legal issues.* An express agreement among sellers to use a basing point pricing system, like any agreement to adopt a pricing system, would be illegal. Suppose we find basing point pricing in circumstances in which the competitive scenario is no longer plausible. May we find an agreement to use that pricing system? Would an inference of agreement be stronger when the competitive scenario had never fit the defendants' industry? Could the practice have been implemented and maintained without an express agreement; or could it have come about through tacit coordination in which one firm announced a delivered pricing system and its rivals followed? Should basing point pricing be condemned under Sherman Act §1 or FTC Act §5?[27]

FEDERAL TRADE COMMISSION
v. CEMENT INSTITUTE
333 U.S. 683 (1948)

Justice BLACK. [The] respondents are: The Cement Institute, an unincorporated trade association composed of 74 corporations which manufacture, sell and distribute cement; the 74 corporate members of the Institute; and 21 individuals who are associated with the Institute. . . . The [complaint] charged that certain alleged conduct set out at length constituted an unfair method of competition in violation of §5 of the Federal Trade Commission Act.[28] The core of the charge was that the respondents had restrained and hindered competition in the sale and distribution of cement by means of a combination among themselves made effective through mutual understanding or agreement to employ a multiple basing point system of pricing.

[The Court first discussed challenges to the FTC's jurisdiction.] The Commission has jurisdiction to declare that conduct tending to

26. A related difference is that, under the competitive scenario, cross-hauling would not occur: Buyers would purchase at a distant plant only if its f.o.b. price were sufficiently below that of local plants, in which case other buyers near the lower-priced plant would not purchase from the higher-priced plant more distant from them.

27. See ¶609 for a discussion of how delivered prices may bring about price discrimination among buyers in violation of the Robinson-Patman Act.

28. A second count charged unlawful price discriminations in violation of Clayton Act §2. See ¶619a. — eds.

restrain trade is an unfair method of competition even though the selfsame conduct may also violate the Sherman Act. [In addition, the Court found nothing in the Attorney General's subsequent civil action under Sherman Act §1 against the same defendants to bar the Commission's action in the present case, since a violation of §5 does not necessarily imply a violation of §1 and the legislation independently authorizes remedies under both Acts.

The Commission here specifically alleges a combination to use the basing point system to secure price uniformity and that the FTC Act explicitly gave the Commission power] to restrain practices as "unfair" which, although not yet having grown into Sherman Act dimensions, would most likely do so if left unrestrained. The Commission and the courts were to determine what conduct, even though it might then be short of a Sherman Act violation, was an "unfair method of competition." This general language was deliberately left to the "Commission and the courts" for definition because it was thought that "There is no limit to human inventiveness in this field"; that consequently, a definition that fitted practices known to lead towards an unlawful restraint of trade today would not fit tomorrow's new inventions in the field; and that for Congress to try to keep its precise definitions abreast of this course of conduct would be an "endless task." ...

FINDINGS AND EVIDENCE ...

Although there is much more evidence to which reference could be made, we think that the following facts shown by evidence in the record, some of which are in dispute, are sufficient to warrant the Commission's finding of concerted action.

When the Commission rendered its decision there were about 80 cement manufacturing companies in the United States operating about 150 mills. Ten companies controlled more than half of the mills and there were substantial corporate affiliations among many of the others. This concentration of productive capacity made concerted action far less difficult than it would otherwise have been. The belief is prevalent in the industry that because of the standardized nature of cement, among other reasons, price competition is wholly unsuited to it. That belief is historic. It has resulted in concerted activities to devise means and measures to do away with competition in the industry. Out of those activities came the multiple basing point delivered price system. Evidence shows it to be a handy instrument to bring about elimination of any kind of price competition. The use of the multiple basing point delivered price system by the cement producers has been coincident with a situation whereby for many years, with rare exceptions, cement has been offered for sale in every given locality at identical prices and terms by all producers. Thousands of secret sealed bids have been received by public agencies which corresponded in prices of cement down to a fractional part of a penny.[15]

Occasionally foreign cement has been imported, and cement dealers have sold it below the delivered price of the domestic product. Dealers who persisted in selling foreign cement were boycotted by the domestic producers. Officers of the Institute took the lead in securing pledges by producers not to permit sales f.o.b. mill to purchasers who furnished their own trucks, a practice regarded as seriously disruptive of the entire delivered price structure of the industry.

During the depression in the 1930's, slow business prompted some producers to deviate from the prices fixed by the delivered price system. Meetings were held by other producers; an effective plan was devised to punish the recalcitrants and bring them into line. The plan was simple but successful. Other producers made the recalcitrant's plant an involuntary base point. The base price was driven down with relatively insignificant losses to the producers who imposed the punitive basing point, but with heavy losses to the recalcitrant who had to make all its sales on this basis. In one instance, where a producer had made a low public bid, a punitive base point price was put on its plant and cement was reduced 10¢ per barrel; further reductions quickly followed until the base price at which this recalcitrant had to sell its cement dropped to 75¢ per barrel, scarcely one-half of its former base price of $1.45. Within six weeks after the base price hit 75¢ capitulation occurred and the recalcitrant joined a Portland cement association. Cement in that locality then bounced back to $1.15, later to $1.35, and finally to $1.75.

---

15. The following is one among many of the Commission's findings as to the identity of sealed bids:

An abstract of the bids for 6,000 barrels of cement to the United States Engineer Office at Tucumcari, New Mexico, opened April 23, 1936, shows the following:

Name of Bidder	Price per Bbl.	Name of Bidder	Price per Bbl.
Monarch	$3.286854	Consolidated	$3.286854
Ash Grove	3.286854	Trinity	3.286854
Lehigh	3.286854	Lone Star	3.286854
Southwestern	3.286854	Universal	3.286854
U.S. Portland Cement Co.	3.286854	Colorado	3.286854
Oklahoma	3.286854		

All bids subject to 10¢ per barrel discount for payment in 15 days.

The foregoing are but illustrations of the practices shown to have been utilized to maintain the basing point price system. Respondents offered testimony that cement is a standardized product, that "cement is cement," that no differences existed in quality or usefulness, and that purchasers demanded delivered price quotations because of the high cost of transportation from mill to dealer. There was evidence, however, that the Institute and its members had, in the interest of eliminating competition, suppressed information as to the variations in quality that sometimes exist in different cements. Respondents introduced the testimony of economists to the effect that competition alone could lead to the evolution of a multiple basing point system of uniform delivered prices and terms of sale for an industry with a standardized product and with relatively high freight costs. These economists testified that for the above reasons no inferences of collusion, agreement, or understanding could be drawn from the admitted fact that cement prices of all United States producers had for many years almost invariably been the same in every given locality in the country. There was also considerable testimony by other economic experts that the multiple basing point system of delivered prices as employed by respondents contravened accepted economic principles and could only have been maintained through collusion.

The Commission did not adopt the views of the economists produced by the respondents. It decided that even though competition might tend to drive the price of standardized products to a uniform level, such a tendency alone could not account for the almost perfect identity in prices, discounts, and cement containers which had prevailed for so long a time in the cement industry. The Commission held that the uniformity and absence of competition in the industry were the results of understandings or agreements entered into or carried out by concert of the Institute and the other respondents. It may possibly be true, as respondents' economists testified, that cement producers will, without agreement express or implied and without understanding explicit or tacit, always and at all times (for such has been substantially the case here) charge for their cement precisely, to the fractional part of a penny, the price their competitors charge. Certainly it runs counter to what many people have believed, namely, that without agreement, prices will vary — that the desire to sell will sometimes be so strong that a seller will be willing to lower his prices and take his chances. We therefore hold that the Commission was not compelled to accept the views of respondents' economist-witnesses that active competition was bound to produce uniform cement prices. The Commission was authorized to find understanding, express or implied, from evidence that the industry's Institute actively worked, in cooperation with various of its members, to maintain the multiple basing point delivered price system; that this pricing system is calculated to produce, and has produced, uniform prices and terms of sale throughout the country; and that all of the respondents have sold their cement substantially in accord with the pattern required by the multiple basing point system.[17] . . .

We cannot say that the Commission is wrong in concluding that the delivered price system as here used provides an effective instrument which, if left free for use of the respondents, would result in complete destruction of competition and the establishment of monopoly in the cement industry. . . . We uphold the Commission's conclusion that the basing point delivered price system employed by respondents is an unfair trade practice which the Trade Commission may suppress.[19] . . .[29]

251. (a) Why would a firm able to undersell its rivals "within its own backyard" suffer rivals to sell there? Is there any explanation other than an agreement for the firm's surrendering its own geographical advantage? Once a basing point system appears, which party should bear the burden of proving or disproving an "unfair method of competition" under FTC Act §5 or an unreasonable "contract, combination . . . or conspiracy" under Sherman Act §1? And how could such a burden be met?

(b) What is the significance of the Institute "securing pledges by producers not to permit sales f.o.b. mill to purchasers who furnished their own trucks"? Why would the Institute have found it desirable to suppress information as to variations in the quality of cement? Why would a producer whose quality was slightly above average have gone along with this?[30]

(c) Does the effective implementation of basing point pricing require explicit or tacit coordination (if so, which?) or can it arise from completely independent decisionmaking? Did the Commission find an agreement? If so, which kind? Did the Court agree?

---

17. It is enough to warrant a finding of a "combination" within the meaning of the Sherman Act, if there is evidence that persons, with knowledge that concerted action was contemplated and invited, give adherence to and then participate in a scheme. *Interstate Circuit. . . .*

19. While we hold that the Commission's findings of combination were supported by evidence, that does not mean that existence of a "combination" is an indispensable ingredient of an "unfair method of competition" under the Trade Commission Act. See Federal Trade Commission v. Beech-Nut Packing Co., 257 U.S. 441, 455.

29. Burton, J., dissented. Douglas and Jackson, JJ., did not participate.

30. See ¶¶230d, 230e.

(d) If you were reluctant to condemn tacit coordination short of an express agreement, are you more or less reluctant to apply §1 or §5 to basing point pricing? Is it consistent to condemn under Sherman Act §1 basing point pricing absent proof of express agreement while requiring express agreement in other cases?

252. Observe that *Cement Institute* arises under Federal Trade Commission Act §5.

(a) To what extent do the Court's holding and opinion bear on the application of Sherman Act §1 as well?

(b) Can an action violate both statutes simultaneously? Are the statutes coterminous? See ¶¶132, 142. If an act offends both statutes, may the actor be pursued under both statutes simultaneously? Would a decision under one statute have any res judicata or collateral estoppel effects in an action under the other statute? See ¶158.

(c) What are the justifications for having a lower burden of proof for Commission actions under §5?[31]

(d) For a discussion of subsequent basing point pricing cases and FTC practice, as it applies to the Commission's power under §5, see footnote 34 in ¶254's discussion of the *du Pont* case.

253. Remedies for basing point pricing. In *Cement Institute*, the Court upheld the Commission's order that the defendants cease and desist from "entering into, continuing, cooperating in, or carrying out any planned common course of action, understanding, agreement, combination, or conspiracy, between and among any two or more of said respondents" or with others to, inter alia, quote or sell cement

> pursuant to or in accordance with any other plan or system which results in identical price quotations or prices for cement at points of quotation or sale or to particular purchasers by respondents using such plan or system, or which prevents purchasers from finding any advantage in price in dealing with one or more of the respondents against any of the other respondents.

In Federal Trade Commission v. National Lead Co.,[32] the Court approved the FTC decree directing each respondent to cease and desist from "quoting ... prices calculated ... in accordance with a zone delivered price system for the purpose or with the effect of systematically matching the delivered ... prices of other sellers."

(a) What exactly did these decrees enjoin? Individual use of basing points? Agreements to use basing points? Something else?

---

31. Reconsider this issue when examining *du Pont*, ¶254.
32. 352 U.S. 419, 423 (1957).

Does the *Cement Institute* order differ significantly from that in *National Lead*?

(b) A producer fears that it would be punished if found still a party to a basing point pricing arrangement. What must it do to prove that it is not part of any such arrangement?

254. *du Pont v. Federal Trade Commission,* 729 F.2d 128, 132, 134, 136-137, 139-140 (2d Cir. 1984). In the market for lead-based antiknock compounds, the respondents' 1974 market shares were: du Pont 38.4 percent, Ethyl 33.5 percent, PPG 16.2 percent, and Nalco 11.8 percent. No other firm has ever made or sold this product in the United States. The FTC found that the respondents had engaged in unfair methods of competition in violation of FTC Act §5(a)(1) by their unilateral adoption of some or all of the following practices: (1) sale of products only at delivered prices, (2) giving by du Pont and Ethyl of additional notice of price increases beyond the 30 days provided in their contracts, and (3) use by du Pont and Ethyl of a "most favored nation" clause, binding them to charge each customer no more than it charged its most favored customers.

The court noted that there were no normal entry barriers, although entry was unlikely in light of the substantial market decline (60 percent in four years, with a further decline in excess of 75 percent expected in a decade) due to government regulations limiting the use of leaded gasoline. PPG — subsequent to the period, 1974-1979, covered by the complaint — has recently ceased production. The court noted that the high concentration, small likelihood of entry, inelastic demand, and homogeneity of product "led to a natural oligopoly with a high degree of pricing interdependence." Profit targets were high, and generally met, leading to profits above the benchmark for the chemical industry. Despite such profits, evidence of competition was found because Nalco was making 80 percent of its sales at discounts from list price and PPG was making more than one-third of its sales at discounts. In addition, Ethyl and du Pont engaged in substantial nonprice competition, such as offering late billing and free services.

Each of the challenged practices was first initiated by Ethyl prior to 1948, at which time it was still the sole producer in the industry. Each of the three later entrants followed such practices upon its entry into the market. The court thought that delivered pricing had insignificant effects because transportation costs were under 2 percent of list price. The FTC order would have required respondents to offer consumers the option of purchasing at a point of origin price. The court cited testimony indicating that other firms could have determined equivalent delivered prices and matched them on a case-by-case basis. The court also thought that delivered prices were convenient for consumers.

As to the "most favored nation" clause, the court noted that the effect was to guarantee that no customers would be at a competitive disadvantage. "Even though such clauses arguably reduce price discounting, they comport with the requirements of the Robinson-Patman Act, which prohibits price discrimination between customers." The additional notice on price announcements was deemed insignificant in light of the contractual provision for 30 days notice to begin with and the fact that competitors usually heard about price changes within hours.

The FTC had found that the industry was susceptible to unilateral but interdependent conduct that lessened competition and that there was evidence of noncompetitive performance, which justified prohibiting the practices that facilitated the adverse result.[33] The Second Circuit majority interpreted the FTC's authority more narrowly.

> Although the Commission may under §5 enforce the antitrust laws, including the Sherman and Clayton Acts, ... it is not confined to their letter. It may bar incipient violations of those statutes ... and conduct which, although not a violation of the letter of the antitrust laws, is close to a violation or is contrary to their spirit.... As the Commission moves away from attacking conduct that is either a violation of the antitrust laws or collusive, coercive, predatory, restrictive or deceitful, and seeks to break new ground by enjoining otherwise legitimate practices, the closer must be our scrutiny upon judicial review. A test based solely upon restraint of competition, even if qualified by the requirement that the conduct be "analogous" to an antitrust violation, is so vague as to permit arbitrary or undue government interference with the reasonable freedom of action that has marked our country's competitive system.[34] ... [T]he FTC's rulings

33. The Commission opinion, 101 F.T.C. 425, 598, 601, 606 (1983), stated that §5 "prohibits conduct by individual firms which is shown to result in substantial harm to competition by promoting price uniformity at supracompetitive prices." It felt empowered to condemn behavior "where the effects on competition are clearly discernible and where no mitigating circumstances exist sufficient to offset the harmful effects of the practices." On the other hand, it did not feel that §5 prohibited "oligopolistic pricing *alone*, even supracompetitive parallel prices, in the absence of specific conduct which promotes such a result."

34. In addressing the Commission's authority, the court discussed two basing point pricing cases subsequent to *Cement Institute.*

Two decisions heavily relied on by the Commission, Triangle Conduit & Cable Co. v. FTC, 168 F.2d 175 (7th Cir. 1948), aff'd by an equally divided court sub nom., Clayton Mark & Co. v. FTC, 336 U.S. 956 (1949), and Boise Cascade Corp. v. FTC, 637 F.2d 573 (9th Cir. 1980), are not of assistance in resolving the issue before us. In *Triangle Conduit* the FTC had found that the use of a mathematical formula by members of a trade association to compute delivered price amounted to both a conspiracy to fix

and order appear to represent uncertain guesswork rather than workable rules of law. In our view, before business conduct in an oligopolistic industry may be labelled "unfair" within the meaning of §5 a minimum standard demands that, absent a tacit agreement, at least some indicia of oppressiveness must exist such as (1) evidence of anticompetitive intent or purpose on the part of the producer charged, or (2) the absence of an independent legitimate business reason for its conduct.[35]

---

prices and an unfair method of competition in violation of §5. Upon appeal the Seventh Circuit held that the conspiracy had been proved by circumstantial evidence. 168 F.2d at 180. Although it went on to state in reliance on *Cement Institute* that it could not "say the Commission was wrong in concluding that the individual use of the basing point method ... does constitute an unfair method of competition," the finding of a conspiracy sheds doubt on the significance of the latter statement. Indeed, a majority of the Commission took the view that *Cement Institute* and *Triangle Conduit* apply only to "conspiracy situations." Interim Report on the Study of the Federal Trade Commission Pricing Policies, S. Doc. No. 27, 81st Cong., 1st Sess. 62-63 (1949). The Commission's failure thereafter for over 30 years to seek to apply §5 to consciously parallel behavior not involving collusion, coercion or restrictive conduct indicates that it believed it has no power to curb otherwise legitimate behavior allegedly facilitating conscious price parallelism. See BankAmerica Corp. v. United States, 462 U.S. 122 (1983).

Boise Cascade Corp. is at best ambiguous. There the FTC alleged that plywood manufacturers, acting individually, had adopted a freight pricing scheme that lessened competition in the industry. The pricing scheme, use of a West Coast freight factor for determining freight prices from southern shipping points, was alleged to have resulted in an "artificial" method of calculating freight prices, contributing to pricing uniformity of southern plywood. The FTC argued that even though there was no agreement, there was liability because of the anticompetitive effect. The Ninth Circuit set aside the FTC order, finding no anticompetitive effect. The FTC in the instant case relies upon the following statement by the court: "We thus hold that in the absence of evidence of overt agreement to utilize a pricing system to avoid price competition, the Commission must demonstrate that the challenged pricing system has actually had the effect of fixing or stabilizing prices. Without such effect, a mere showing of parallel action will not establish a section 5 violation." Standing alone, the statement tends to support the Commission's position here, particularly since a finding of price conspiracy would obviate the necessity of proving that it had the effect of fixing or stabilizing prices. But earlier in the same paragraph the court stated: "It is important to stress that the weight of the case law and the Commission's own policy statement make it clear that we are looking for at least tacit agreement to use a formula which has the effect of fixing prices. Indeed, none of the delivered pricing cases supports a finding of a section 5 violation for the bare existence of an industry-wide artificial freight factor. In each case, the system had been utilized, tacitly or overtly, to match prices and avoid price competition." In view of this statement we cannot place much reliance on *Boise Cascade* as support for the Commission's position here.

35. Lumbard, J., concurring and dissenting, agreed that the record did not support the FTC's finding of anticompetitive effect but thought the majority construed §5 too narrowly. First, he emphasized that the court's opinion does not appear to rule out the possibility that §5 might cover noncollusive practices that facilitate oligopolistic pricing. Much of the vagueness the court attributed to the FTC's approach was stated to be inherent in all balancing tests, including decisions under the rule of reason and other applications of the antitrust laws. Finally, he noted that the rules for determining the existence of an agreement were so broad

In addition, the court indicated that the FTC failed to show sufficient anticompetitive impact, even if its broader formulation of §5 were accepted. The court suggested that the Commission's inability to state when the practices became unlawful demonstrated the weakness of its approach. "It is difficult to believe that a practice deemed lawful when competitive forces were producing changes in the market became 'unfair' when market conditions stabilized." It noted that prices were not always uniform and that the FTC's evidence did not directly prove the causal connection between the prohibited practices and behavior in the industry. To the extent that the result was anticompetitive, it plausibly arose from the tight oligopolistic nature of the industry, not from the challenged actions.

(a) For each of the three challenged practices in *du Pont* (1) make the strongest argument indicating that it might have had an anticompetitive facilitating effect, (2) assess the persuasiveness of the argument and the court's analysis based on the facts of this case, and (3) indicate what remedy would be appropriate for each, if you were persuaded that there had been a violation.[36]

(b) How could the Commission have directly proved the anticompetitive effect of such facilitating practices? Does the court's suggestion that any anticompetitive results might best be explained by the oligopolistic nature of the industry imply that facilitating practices are more insulated from attack as an industry becomes more concentrated, and thus more prone to successful supracompetitive pricing?[37]

(c) Should §5 of the FTC Act, in principle, cover such allegations? Of what relevance are the facts that actions can only be brought by the Commission and relief will be in the form of injunctions against future behavior, rather than criminal penalties or treble damages?

2E. CONCERTED REFUSALS TO DEAL

255. Introduction. Courts have often said that the concerted refusal to deal — or its evil-sounding equivalent, boycott — is unlawful

---

and ill-defined that it would be difficult to argue that a broader reading of §5 would substantially expand the FTC's enforcement power.

36. You should reconsider the "most favored nation clause" when studying price discrimination in Ch. 6. With regard to facilitating effects, see J. Baker, Vertical Restraints with Horizontal Consequences: Competitive Effects of "Most-Favored-Customer" Clauses, 64 Antitr. L.J. 517 (1996).

37. See ¶229d.

per se. Yet decisions in other cases have recognized that there may be restraints with some boycott characteristics that are not or should not be automatically unlawful. If that be accepted, either the initial proposition must be abandoned or boycott must be defined so as to exclude the possibly permissible situations. (Could the same be said of price fixing, especially after *BMI*?) A review of the preceding sections will find boycott issues in many earlier problems. Indeed, one might say that any agreement affecting competitive behavior is necessarily an agreement that the collaborators will not buy or sell on any other terms; and there is no sharp logical distinction between refusing to sell at all and refusing to sell except on condition. Thus, one should be particularly alert to look for the distinguishing features of the boycott and beware of categories.

There is, however, one common feature that distinguishes many boycott cases from the price-fixing and related cases considered thus far. A price-fixing conspiracy involves an agreement to refrain from competition within the group in order to exploit but not to destroy or weaken customers or suppliers, while boycotts often involve collective action among a group of competitors that may inhibit the competitive vitality of rivals.[1] Even in this respect, however, we shall see that boycotts are not a unitary phenomenon.

256. Early cases. (a) *Eastern States Retail Lumber Dealers' Assn. v. United States*, 234 U.S. 600 (1914).[2] Defendant associations, composed largely of retail lumber dealers, were found to have conspired to boycott wholesalers who had sold directly to consumers and thus competed directly with member dealers.

> Here are wholesale dealers in large number engaged in interstate trade upon whom it is proposed to impose as a condition of carrying on that trade that they shall not sell in such manner that a local retail dealer may regard such sale as an infringement of his exclusive right to trade, upon pain of being reported as an unfair dealer to a large number of other retail dealers associated with the offended dealer, the purpose being to keep the wholesaler from dealing not only with the particular dealer who reports him but with all others of the class who may be informed of his delinquency. . . . A retail dealer has the unquestioned right to stop dealing with a wholesaler for reasons sufficient to himself, and may do so because he thinks such dealer is acting unfairly in trying to undermine his trade. "But . . . when the [defendants] combine and agree that no one of them will trade with any producer or wholesaler who shall sell to a consumer within the

---

1. Boycotts are often similar to the monopolist's exclusionary practices, which are considered in Ch. 3, and sometimes involve vertical relationships as where a supplier agrees with one dealer not to supply another, considered in Ch. 4.
2. See ¶234 for a discussion of the question of conspiracy in this case.

trade range of any of them, quite another case is presented. An act harmless when done by one may become a public wrong when done by many acting in concert, for it then takes on the form of a conspiracy, and may be prohibited or punished, if the result be hurtful to the public or to the individual against whom the concerted action is directed." When the retailer goes beyond his personal right, and, conspiring and combining with others of like purpose, seeks to obstruct the free course of interstate trade and commerce and to unduly suppress competition by placing obnoxious wholesale dealers under the coercive influence of a condemnatory report circulated among others, actual or possible customers of the offenders, he exceeds his lawful rights. . . .[3]

(b) *Cement Manufacturers Protective Assn. v. United States*, 268 U.S. 588 (1925). Defendant cement manufacturers, through their trade association, exchange information on the credit of buyers and on "specific job contracts." "That a combination existed for the purposes of gathering and distributing these two classes of information is not denied."

The credit information indicated which customers were more than two months overdue and other information related to their delinquent payments, including the customer's explanations or disputes over sums due. The Court found no

> understanding on the basis of which credit was to be extended to customers or that any co-operation resulted from the distribution of this information, or that there were any consequences from it other than such as would naturally ensue from the exercise of the individual judgment of manufacturers in determining, on the basis of available information, whether to extend credit or to require cash or security from any given customer.

Specific job contracts are customary arrangements in the industry under which the cement manufacturer promises future delivery at a specified price of all the cement that a building contractor requires for a specified job; the contractor undertakes no obligation to accept delivery. This free option arrangement allows contractors to submit bids for construction work with confidence that a subsequent rise in cement prices would not affect its profit on the specified job. Unfortunately, some contractors arranged multiple

3. See also Oregon Restaurant & Beverage Assn. v. United States, 429 F.2d 516 (9th Cir. 1970) (affirming conviction of tavern operators collectively refusing to purchase beer from wholesalers making direct sales to consumers in amounts greater than five gallons as permitted by state law as well as in amounts less than five gallons prohibited by state law); Rowe Furniture Corp. v. Serta, 1982-1983 Trade Cas. ¶64993 (N.D. Ill. 1982) (preliminary injunction against resolution prohibiting licensees from selling mattresses to nonlicensees for resale in sleep sofas).

contracts and, if the market price rose, illegitimately demanded delivery on all such contracts. Thus taking more cement than required for the specific job was contrary to the purpose of the free option. The Court recognized that

> a consequence of the gathering and dissemination of information with respect to the specific job contracts was to afford, to manufacturers of cement, opportunity and grounds for refusing deliveries of cement which the contractors were not entitled to call for, an opportunity of which manufacturers were prompt to avail themselves, is also not open to dispute. We do not see, however, in the activity of the defendants with respect to specific job contracts any basis for the contention that they constitute an unlawful restraint of commerce. The Government does not rely on any agreement or understanding among members of the Association that members would either make use of the specific job contract, or that they would refuse to deliver excess cement under specific job contracts.... [D]emand for ... such deliveries by the contractor would be a fraud on the manufacturer, and, in our view, the gathering and dissemination of information which will enable sellers to prevent the perpetration of fraud upon them, which information they are free to act upon or not as they choose, cannot be held to be an unlawful restraint upon commerce, even though in the ordinary course of business most sellers would act on the information and refuse to make deliveries for which they were not legally bound.

(c) *Motion picture cases. Paramount*[4] and *First National Pictures*[5] both involved agreements among film distributors (and, in the former case, producers as well) that specified certain terms on which distributors would contract with exhibitors. In the first case, the conspirators required all distributors to arbitrate disputes, and in the second, they required purchasers of exhibitors to abide by outstanding contracts and to post a cash deposit assessed by their joint local credit committee. All distributors agreed not to deal with any exhibitor that violated such contractual provisions with any distributor. In both cases, the Supreme Court found violations of Sherman Act §1 because the agreement restricted the freedom of members, thus undermining the public interest in preserving competition. The intentions of the parties and even possibly good results were deemed irrelevant to the inquiry.

(d) *McCann v. New York Stock Exchange*, 107 F.2d 908 (2d Cir. 1939). The case involved a private treble-damage action against the New York Better Business Bureau, the New York Stock Exchange and its members, and others. Defendants allegedly conspired to drive the plaintiff out of business in order to rid themselves of his

4. Paramount Famous Lasky Corp. v. United States, 282 U.S. 30 (1930).
5. United States v. First National Pictures, 282 U.S. 44 (1930).

competition by spreading the information that plaintiff was a person unreliable morally and financially, with a record of criminal convictions. The court upheld a jury verdict for the defendant, reasoning that the question of the truth of the rumors was properly left to the jury and that the "end avowed — ridding the business of unscrupulous persons — was not only lawful but commendable, and while the defendants may have had other motives, they had to be proved and could not be assumed."

FASHION ORIGINATORS' GUILD OF AMERICA v. FEDERAL TRADE COMMISSION
312 U.S. 457 (1941)

Justice BLACK. . . . Some of the members of the combination design, manufacture, sell and distribute women's garments — chiefly dresses. Others are manufacturers, converters or dyers of textiles from which these garments are made. Fashion Originators' Guild of America (FOGA), an organization controlled by these groups, is the instrument through which petitioners work to accomplish the purposes condemned by the Commission. The garment manufacturers claim to be creators of original and distinctive designs of fashionable clothes for women, and the textile manufacturers claim to be creators of similar original fabric designs. After these designs enter the channels of trade, other manufacturers systematically make and sell copies of them, the copies usually selling at prices lower than the garments copied. Petitioners call this practice of copying unethical and immoral, and give it the name of "style piracy." And although they admit that their "original creations" are neither copyrighted nor patented, and indeed assert that existing legislation affords them no protection against copyists, they nevertheless urge that sale of copied designs constitutes an unfair trade practice and a tortious invasion of their rights. Because of these alleged wrongs, petitioners, while continuing to compete with one another in many respects, combined among themselves to combat and, if possible, destroy all competition from the sale of garments which are copies of their "original creations." They admit that to destroy such competition they have in combination purposely boycotted and declined to sell their products to retailers who follow a policy of selling garments copied by other manufacturers from designs put out by Guild members. As a result of their efforts, approximately 12,000 retailers throughout the country have signed agreements to "cooperate" with the Guild's boycott program, but more than half of these signed the agreements only because constrained by threats that Guild members would not sell to retailers who failed to yield to their demands — threats that have been carried out by the Guild practice of placing on red cards the names of noncooperators (to whom no sales are to be made), placing on white cards the names of cooperators (to whom sales are to be made), and then distributing both sets of cards to the manufacturers. . . .

In 1936, [Guild members] sold in the United States more than 38% of all women's garments wholesaling at $6.75 and up, and more than 60% of those at $10.75 and above. . . . And the power of the combination is made even greater by reason of the affiliation of some members of the National Federation of Textiles, Inc. . . .

The Guild employs "shoppers" to visit the stores of both cooperating and non-cooperating retailers, "for the purpose of examining their stocks, to determine and report as to whether they contain . . . copies of registered designs. . . ." [T]he Guild audits its members' books. And if violations of Guild requirements are discovered, as, for example, sales to red-carded retailers, the violators are subject to heavy fines.

In addition to the elements of the agreement set out above, all of which relate more or less closely to competition by so-called style copyists, the Guild has undertaken to do many things apparently independent of and distinct from the fight against copying. Among them are the following: the combination prohibits its members from participating in retail advertising; regulates the discount they may allow; prohibits their selling at retail; cooperates with local guilds in regulating days upon which special sales shall be held; prohibits its members from selling women's garments to persons who conduct businesses in residences, residential quarters, hotels or apartment houses; and denies the benefits of membership to retailers who participate with dress manufacturers in promoting fashion shows unless the merchandise used is actually purchased and delivered.

If the purpose and practice of the combination of garment manufacturers and their affiliates runs counter to the public policy declared in the Sherman and Clayton Acts, the Federal Trade Commission has the power to suppress it as an unfair method of competition. From its findings the Commission concluded that the petitioners, "pursuant to understandings, arrangements, agreements, combinations and conspiracies entered into jointly and severally," had prevented sales in interstate commerce, had "substantially lessened, hindered and suppressed" competition, and had tended "to create in themselves a monopoly." And paragraph 3 of the Clayton Act declares

It shall be unlawful for any person engaged in commerce . . . to . . . make a sale or contract for sale of goods . . . on the condition, agreement or understanding that the . . . purchaser thereof shall not use or deal in the goods . . . of a competitor or competitors of the seller, where the effect of such . . . sale, or contract for sale . . . may be to substantially lessen competition or tend to create a monopoly in any line of commerce. . . .

Not only does the plan in the respects above discussed thus conflict with the principles of the Clayton Act, the findings of the Commission bring petitioners' combination in its entirety well within the inhibition of the policies declared by the Sherman Act itself. . . . And among the many respects in which the Guild's plan runs contrary to the policy of the Sherman Act are these: it narrows the outlets to which garment and textile manufacturers can sell and the sources from which retailers can buy; . . . subjects all retailers and manufacturers who decline to comply with the Guild's program to an organized boycott; . . . takes away the freedom of action of members by requiring each to reveal to the Guild the intimate details of their individual affairs; . . . and has both as its necessary tendency and as its purpose and effect the direct suppression of competition from the sale of unregistered textiles and copied designs. . . . In addition to all this, the combination is in reality an extra-governmental agency, which prescribes rules for the regulation and restraint of interstate commerce, and provides extra-judicial tribunals for determination and punishment of violations, and thus "trenches upon the power of the national legislature and violates the statute." . . .

Nor is it determinative in considering the policy of the Sherman Act that petitioners may not yet have achieved a complete monopoly. For "it is sufficient if it really tends to that end, and to deprive the public of the advantages which flow from free competition." . . . It was, in fact, one of the hopes of those who sponsored the Federal Trade Commission Act that its effect might be prophylactic and that through it attempts to bring about complete monopolization of an industry might be stopped in their incipiency.

Petitioners, however, argue that the combination cannot be contrary to the policy of the Sherman and Clayton Acts, since the Federal Trade Commission did not find that the combination fixed or regulated prices, parcelled out or limited production, or brought about a deterioration in quality. But action falling into these three categories does not exhaust the types of conduct banned by the Sherman and Clayton Acts. And as previously pointed out, it was the object of the Federal Trade Commission Act to reach not merely in their fruition but also in their incipiency combinations which could lead to these and other trade restraints and practices deemed undesirable. In this case, the Commission found that the combination exercised sufficient control and power in the women's garments and textile businesses "to exclude from the industry those manufacturers and distributors who do not conform to the rules and regulations of said respondents, and thus tend to create in themselves a monopoly in the said industries." While a conspiracy to fix prices is illegal, an intent to increase prices is not an ever-present essential of conduct amounting to a violation of the policy of the Sherman and Clayton Acts; a monopoly contrary to their policies can exist even though a combination may temporarily or even permanently reduce the price of the articles manufactured or sold. For as this Court has said, "Trade or commerce under those circumstances may nevertheless be badly and unfortunately restrained by driving out of business the small dealers and worthy men whose lives have been spent therein, and who might be unable to readjust themselves to their altered surroundings. Mere reduction in the price of the commodity dealt in might be dearly paid for by the ruin of such a class and the absorption of control over one commodity by an all-powerful combination of capital."[7]

[margin note: rising price can be bad too]

But petitioners further argue that their boycott and restraint of interstate trade is not within the ban of the policies of the Sherman and Clayton Acts because "the practices of FOGA were reasonable and necessary to protect the manufacturer, laborer, retailer and consumer against the devastating evils growing from the pirating of original designs and had in fact benefited all four." The Commission declined to hear much of the evidence that petitioners desired to offer on this subject. As we have pointed out, however, the aim of petitioners' combination was the intentional destruction of one type of manufacture and sale which competed with Guild members. The purpose and object of this combination, its potential power, its tendency to monopoly, the coercion it could and did practice upon a rival method of competition, all brought it within the policy of the prohibition declared by the Sherman and Clayton Acts. . . . Under these circumstances it was not error to refuse to hear the evidence offered, for the reasonableness of the methods pursued by the combination to accomplish its unlawful object is no more material than would be the reasonableness of the prices fixed by the combination. . . . Nor can the unlawful combination be justified upon the argument that systematic copying of dress designs is itself tortious, or should now be declared so by us. In the first place, whether or not given conduct is tortious is a question of state law. . . . [E]ven if copying were an acknowledged tort under the law of every state, that situation would not justify petitioners in combining together to

[margin note: Δ argument]

7. *Trans-Missouri.*

regulate and restrain interstate commerce in violation of federal law. And for these same reasons, the principles declared in International News Service v. Associated Press, 248 U.S. 215, cannot serve to legalize petitioners' unlawful combination. . . .

Affirmed.

257. (a) In what ways, if any, is the *FOGA* collaboration more offensive than that in *Chicago Board of Trade, Cement Manufacturers,* or *BMI?*

(b) If the purposes of the *FOGA* collaboration were somehow consistent with the antitrust laws, would the collaboration be harmless or would it still present some anticompetitive dangers?

(c) On the assumption that one sentence in *FOGA* expresses, better than any other, the essence of judicial concern with concerted refusals to deal, which sentence would you select?

(d) In *FOGA,* did the Court hold that the Sherman Act made the collaborators' purpose illegitimate, irrelevant, or neither? Consider the extent to which the Court appeared to be concerned with (1) proof of the collaborators' purposes, (2) its morality or legality apart from the Sherman Act, or (3) its legitimacy under the antitrust laws.

(e) Why did the Court go to such lengths to note other provisions of the antitrust laws and the Commission's broad power under the FTC Act when there was clearly a conspiracy within the meaning of Sherman Act §1? Is it relevant to §1 that the case may not have involved price fixing? Did Guild members intend to affect price within the meaning of *Socony?*

(f) Suppose the Guild merely circulated to retailers the names of design pirates and circulated to its members the names of retailers selling pirated copies. Would they violate Sherman Act §1? Would such activity be more like *Eastern States* or like *Cement Manufacturers* and *McCann?* Are these cases consistent?[6]

258. Are the following banks violating Sherman Act §1? Would your answer differ in each case if fewer banks in each city were involved?

(a) The presidents of all the banks of metropolitan Langdell meet weekly to discuss all their applications for loans larger than $10,000. They compare notes, exchange information and insights,

6. Recall the discussion of the conspiracy aspect of *Eastern States* in ¶234, and contrast it with the discussion in *Cement.* In this regard, it is interesting to note that *Cement* did not cite *Eastern States.* In addition, *FOGA* cited *Eastern States* but not *Cement.* The reader should also consider the information exchange aspects of some of these cases in light of the data dissemination cases from Ch. 2D.

and vote on whether each loan should be made. The banks have agreed informally that no loans will be made unless they are approved by a majority of the banks. Does this agreement among the Langdell banks offend §1 of the Sherman Act?

(b) The banks of Austin City, a relatively small community, have established a Lending Center to take over the work and personnel of the several banks' credit investigators and loan officers; some of the banks' employees who used to work in those fields have now been transferred to other work. All borrowers are referred to the Lending Center, which investigates, decides, and arranges the loan for the account of whichever bank the borrower prefers. Is this arrangement lawful under §1 of the Sherman Act? Is this decision controlled by the decision of ¶a or are there significant distinctions?

(c) Suppose that the Langdell banks of ¶a agree merely to circulate information concerning the credit and character of persons seeking loans from any of the banks. Each bank makes its own credit decision, but the fact is that persons refused a loan by one bank are nearly always refused loans by all the banks. Has the Sherman Act been violated?[7]

(d) Although very little rental housing is available in Amesville, there is substantial turnover in home ownership. The Amesville banks have always provided all the mortgage financing for these home transfers. To help preserve their community as it is, the Amesville banks have agreed that they will not lend to blacks. Have the Amesville banks violated §1? Suppose instead that they refuse to lend to those who use racially restrictive covenants.

(e) Suppose that the Amesville banks of ¶d merely circulate information about loan applicants and that the data sheet includes blanks for race, religion, and color. There is no provable agreement on how this information would be used by each bank in making its independent decisions. Is this arrangement offensive to the Sherman Act?

(f) Suppose that the *Paramount Famous Lasky* defendants had collaborated in drafting a standard form exhibition contract but had not bound themselves to use it.[8] (1) Would such cooperative

---

7. See *Cement Manufacturers*, ¶256b; Michelman v. Clark-Schwebel Fiber Glass Corp., 534 F.2d 1036 (2d Cir.), cert. denied, 429 U.S. 885 (1976) (directed verdicts for defendants who were exchanging phone calls concerning plaintiff's creditworthiness; no tacit invitation for a conspiracy where no incentive for joint action; firms differ on willingness to grant credit and on terms).

8. Hayes v. National Football League, 469 F. Supp. 247, 252 (C.D. Cal. 1979) (permitting use of League's standard player contract where "no rule or understanding . . . among the member clubs . . . which in any way prohibited . . . [plaintiff] from negotiating modifications"; no injury to plaintiff who never sought better terms). Compare United States v. Utah Pharm. Assn., 201 F. Supp. 29 (D.

drafting be held lawful in a suit brought before the standard form contract is actually utilized? (2) What would be the result if the standard contract is actually used in about 95 percent of the transactions?

KLOR'S v. BROADWAY-HALE STORES
359 U.S. 207 (1959)

Justice BLACK. . . . Klor's, Inc., operates a retail store on Mission Street, San Francisco, California; Broadway-Hale Stores, Inc., a chain of department stores, operates one of its stores next door. The two stores compete in the sale of radios, television sets, refrigerators and other household appliances. [Klor's claimed] that Broadway-Hale and 10 national manufacturers and their distributors have conspired to restrain and monopolize commerce in violation of §§1 and 2 of the Sherman Act [by agreeing among themselves, induced by Broadway-Hale's "monopolistic" buying power, that the manufacturers and distributors would either not sell to Klor's or sell to it only at discriminatory prices and highly unfavorable terms.]

The defendants did not dispute these allegations, but sought summary judgment and dismissal of the complaint for failure to state a cause of action. They submitted unchallenged affidavits which showed that there were hundreds of other household appliance retailers, some within a few blocks of Klor's, who sold many competing brands of appliances, including those the defendants refused to sell to Klor's. From the allegations of the complaint, and from the affidavits supporting the motion for summary judgment, the District Court concluded that the controversy was a "purely private quarrel" between Klor's and Broadway-Hale, which did not amount to a "public wrong proscribed by the [Sherman] Act" [and granted summary judgment for the defendant. The Ninth Circuit affirmed, holding that public injury was required for a Sherman Act violation and]. . . was missing since "there was no charge or proof that by any act of defendants the price, quantity, or quality offered the public was affected, nor that there was any intent or purpose to effect a change in, or an influence on, prices, quantity, or quality. . . ." The holding, if correct, means that unless the opportunities for customers to buy in a competitive market are reduced, a group of powerful businessmen may act in concert to deprive a single merchant, like Klor, of the goods he needs to compete effectively. . . .

Utah), aff'd per curiam, 371 U.S. 24 (1962) (promulgation of pricing schedule with intent to promote uniformity illegal per se).

We think Klor's allegations clearly show one type of trade restraint and public harm the Sherman Act forbids, and that defendants' affidavits provide no defense to the charges.... [In *Standard Oil*, this Court stated that the effect of §1 and §2] was to adopt the common-law proscription of all "contracts or acts which it was considered had a monopolistic tendency" and which interfered with the "natural flow" of an appreciable amount of interstate commerce.... The Court recognized that there were some agreements whose validity depended on the surrounding circumstances. It emphasized, however, that there were classes of restraints which from their "nature or character" were unduly restrictive, and hence forbidden by both the common law and the statute. As to these classes of restraints, the Court noted, Congress has determined its own criteria of public harm and it was not for the courts to decide whether in an individual case injury had actually occurred. Group boycotts, or concerted refusals by traders to deal with other traders, have long been held to be in the forbidden category. They have not been saved by allegations that they were reasonable in the specific circumstances, nor by a failure to show that they "fixed or regulated prices, parcelled out or limited production, or brought about a deterioration in quality." *FOGA*. Cf. *Trenton Potteries*. Even when they operated to lower prices or temporarily to stimulate competition they were banned. For ... "such agreements, no less than those to fix minimum prices, cripple the freedom of traders and thereby restrain their ability to sell in accordance with their own judgment." ...

Plainly the allegations of this complaint disclose such a boycott. This is not a case of a single trader refusing to deal with another, nor even of a manufacturer and a dealer agreeing to an exclusive distributorship. Alleged in this complaint is a wide combination consisting of manufacturers, distributors and a retailer. This combination takes from Klor's its freedom to buy appliances in an open competitive market and drives it out of business as a dealer in the defendants' products. It deprives the manufacturers and distributors of their freedom to sell to Klor's at the same prices and conditions made available to Broadway-Hale and in some instances forbids them from selling to it on any terms whatsoever. It interferes with the natural flow of interstate commerce. It clearly has, by its "nature" and "character," a "monopolistic tendency." As such it is not to be tolerated merely because the victim is just one merchant whose business is so small that his destruction makes little difference to the economy. Monopoly can as surely thrive by the elimination of such small businessmen, one at a time, as it can by driving them out in large groups. In recognition of this fact the Sherman

Act has consistently been read to forbid all contracts and combinations "which 'tend to create a monopoly,'" whether "the tendency is a creeping one" or "one that proceeds at full gallop." *International Salt.* . . .

259. (a) Does the *Klor's* Court object to an agreement between defendant and a single manufacturer or distributor that the latter will not sell to plaintiff? Why or why not?

(b) What kind of injury was proved or alleged in *Klor's*? Does the Court hold that defendants' conduct may be judged without reference to its economic effects on anyone? If so, why? If not, what did the Court hold on this point?

(c) Does the Court hold or imply that concerted refusals to deal are "unlawful per se"? Without regard to redeeming purpose? What possibly redeeming purposes were proved or asserted in *Klor's*?

(d) Was there a serious monopolistic tendency or possibility? Why do you suppose Broadway-Hale engaged in its actions?

260. (a) *American Medical Assn. v. United States*, 130 F.2d 233, 248-249 (D.C. Cir. 1942), aff'd, 317 U.S. 519 (1943). The American Medical Association and its local societies adopted rules of ethics against salaried practice and prepaid medical care. It expelled or threatened to expel from membership the salaried doctors and those who consulted with them, making it difficult or impossible for such physicians to consult with other doctors or to use local hospitals, which generally deny their facilities to those disapproved by the Association. The Association was held to have violated the Sherman Act:

[A]ppellants were permitted to organize, to establish standards of professional conduct, to effect agreements for *self-discipline and control*. There is a very real difference between the use of such self-disciplines and an effort upon the part of such associations to destroy competing professional or business groups or organizations. . . . [A]ppellants have open to them always the safer and more kindly weapons of legitimate persuasion and reasoned argument, as a means of preserving professional esprit de corps, winning public sentiment to their point of view or securing legislation. . . . Neither the fact that the conspiracy may be intended to promote the public welfare, or that of the industry, nor the fact that it is designed to eliminate unfair, fraudulent and unlawful practices, is sufficient to avoid the penalties of the Sherman Act. Appellants are not law enforcement agencies. . . . [A]nd although persons who reason superficially concerning such matters may find justification for extra-legal action to secure what seems to them desirable ends, this is not the American way of life.[9]

(b) *Molinas v. National Basketball Assn.*, 190 F. Supp. 241, 244 (S.D.N.Y. 1961). Plaintiff was suspended from his team and the league after he admitted that he had placed bets on his team in violation of his contract and league rules. The league has refused to lift the suspension and thus prevented plaintiff's employment by any member team. Plaintiff's antitrust suit was dismissed.

Surely, every disciplinary rule which a league may invoke, although by its nature it may involve some sort of restraint, does not run afoul of the antitrust laws. And, a disciplinary rule invoked against gambling seems about as reasonable a rule as could be imagined. Furthermore, the application of the rule to the plaintiff's conduct is also eminently reasonable.[10]

9. See also Feminist Women's Health Center v. Mohammad, 586 F.2d 530, 546-547 (5th Cir. 1978), cert. denied, 444 U.S. 924 (1979) (reversing summary judgment for defendant physicians refusing to assist local abortion clinic and advising other doctors to do the same on the ground of inadequate aftercare facilities; trial required on contention "that the defendants not only sought to enforce a certain standard for aftercare, but conspired to assure that the clinic would be unable to meet that standard"; furthermore, "fact issues remain as to the genuineness of the defendants' justification, the reasonableness of the standards themselves, and the manner of their enforcement"); American Med. Assn., 1979 Trade Reg. Rep. ¶21652 (FTC) (restrictions on partnerships between doctors and nondoctors found to violate FTC Act §5).

10. The enforcement of ethical standards and collective decisionmaking in professional sports have generated a considerable volume of litigation. We note here a few cases of (1) enforcing ethical behavior, (2) limiting player eligibility, (3) limiting competition for player services among league members, and (4) a variety of disputes among actual or would-be entrepreneurs. See generally T. Rosenbaum, Antitrust Implications of Professional Sports Leagues Revisited: Emerging Trends in the Modern Era, 41 U. Miami L. Rev. 729 (1987).

Ethical standards. In Blalock v. Ladies Professional Golf Assn., 359 F. Supp. 1260, 1265 (N.D. Ga. 1973), the suspension of the plaintiff for alleged cheating was declared unlawful per se because players excluded a rival from the market and thus effected "a naked restraint of trade" through defendants' "completely unfettered, subjective discretion." Can you reconcile this with *Molinas?* See also Manok v. Southeast Dist. Bowling Assn., 306 F. Supp. 1215 (C.D. Cal. 1969) (summary judgment for defendant association that suspended plaintiff, after hearing, for fraudulent activities intended to manipulate handicaps).

Eligibility. Neeld v. National Hockey League, 594 F.2d 1297 (9th Cir. 1979) (summary judgment for league preventing one-eyed players from participation; danger to players on plaintiff's blind side; no anticompetitive motivation or effect); Bowman v. National Football League, 402 F. Supp. 754 (D. Minn. 1975) (preliminarily enjoining enforcement of league rule preventing "disruptive" mid-season hiring of defunct World Football League players).

Competition for player services. Mackey v. National Football League, 543 F.2d 606, 619, 621-622 (8th Cir. 1976), cert. dismissed, 434 U.S. 801 (1977) (under rule of

(c) Proposition: The *Molinas* result could be reached only by "persons who reason superficially concerning such matters" (as the *American Medical* court put it) and who fail to read *FOGA* and *Klor's*. Do you agree? If the Supreme Court were to review a case like *Molinas*, what result would it reach? Sketch the majority and dissenting opinions.

261. Last Christmas, the president of an important toy manufacturer observed his small grandchildren chewing on their tin soldiers and other toys. Believing that toy materials and paints regularly "eaten" by children are not adequately regulated, he immediately conferred with his three leading competitors who lived in the neighborhood. Without consulting their antitrust lawyers, they agreed to establish an industry safety committee to review the materials used in and on toys. Each agreed not to use any materials not approved by the committee. They were aware, however, that some marginal toymakers might continue to use cheap or attractive materials judged unsafe by the committee. In that event, they agreed to ask the government to name a distinguished scientific panel to examine the offending material. If that panel condemned the material as unsafe, the collaborators would stop dealing with any wholesaler who continued handling toys made with the condemned materials. The whole industry subscribed to the plan. Is it lawful under the Sherman Act when federal and state regulations are absent?[11]

---

reason, condemning requirement that teams hiring players compensate former teams).

Entrepreneurial disputes. Chicago Professional Sports, Ch. 2B note 33; Mid-South Grizzlies v. National Football League, 720 F.2d 772 (3d Cir. 1983) (summary judgment for NFL refusing to admit former World Football League team; NFL monopoly conferred by Congress; exclusion aids competition by creating possibility of rival league; plaintiff did not show how competition would be promoted by allowing it to share in the NFL's monopoly); Los Angeles Mem. Coliseum Comm. v. National Football League, 726 F.2d 1381 (9th Cir.), cert. denied, 469 U.S. 980 (1984) (although professional football was a unique business to which per se rule of Sherman Act §1 does not apply, court upheld jury verdict finding that rule requiring three-fourths of existing members to approve admission of new member or transfer of playing site was an unreasonable division of territories).

11. American Fedn. of TV & Radio Artists v. National Assn. of Broadcasters, 407 F. Supp. 900 (S.D.N.Y. 1976) (approving defendant's rule forbidding hosts of TV children's programs from also delivering commercials on or adjacent to those programs; no purpose to benefit one class of performers relative to another even if practice was adopted to forestall government regulation and without compelling evidence that buyer practice harmed children); American Brands v. National Assn. of Broadcasters, 308 F. Supp. 1166 (D.D.C. 1969) (denying preliminary injunction to cigarette manufacturers challenging broadcasters' guidelines for limiting cigarette advertising).

ASSOCIATED PRESS v. UNITED STATES
326 U.S. 1 (1945)

Justice BLACK. . . . [AP is a cooperative, incorporated, nonprofit association with 1200 newspaper members. AP distributes to its members the news gathered by its own employees, member newspapers, and foreign news agencies. The government complains of the following practices: (1) a member may effectively block membership by competing newspapers and thereby remain the exclusive outlet for AP news in its locality, (2) members are obligated to supply AP exclusively with the news they generate, and (3) the Canadian Press has contracted to supply Canadian news to AP exclusively in the United States in return for a reciprocal undertaking by AP.

The government's motion for summary judgment was granted by the district court which enjoined the first practice; the second and third arrangements were enjoined pending the abandonment of the membership restriction. Defendants appealed and the government also appealed from the denial of its request that the latter two practices be held to violate the Sherman Act apart from the membership restrictions. The government also asked for a broader decree assuring full access by all newspapers to AP services.]

The District Court found that the By-Laws in and of themselves were contracts in restraint of commerce in that they contained provisions designed to stifle competition in the newspaper publishing field. The court also found that AP's restrictive By-Laws had hindered and impeded the growth of competing newspapers. This latter finding, as to the *past* effect of the restrictions, is challenged. We are inclined to think that it is supported by undisputed evidence, but we do not stop to labor the point. For the court below found, and we think correctly, that the By-Laws on their face, and without regard to their past effect, constitute restraints of trade. Combinations are no less unlawful because they have not as yet resulted in restraint. An agreement or combination to follow a course of conduct which will necessarily restrain or monopolize a part of trade or commerce may violate the Sherman Act, whether it be "wholly nascent or abortive on the one hand or successful on the other." [*Socony.*] For these reasons the argument, repeated here in various forms, that AP had not yet achieved a complete monopoly, is wholly irrelevant. Undisputed evidence did show, however, that its By-Laws had tied the hands of all of its numerous publishers, to the extent that they could not and did not sell any part of their news so that it could reach any of their non-member competitors. In this respect the Court did find, and that finding cannot possibly be challenged, that AP's By-Laws had hindered and restrained the sale of interstate news to non-members who competed with members.

Inability to buy news from the largest news agency, or any one of its multitude of members, can have most serious effects on the publication of competitive newspapers, both those presently published and those which but for these restrictions, might be published in the future. This is illustrated by the District Court's finding that in 26 cities of the United States, existing newspapers already have contracts for AP news and the same newspapers have contracts with United Press and International News Service under which new newspapers would be required to pay the contract holders large sums to enter the field. The net effect is seriously to limit the opportunity of any new paper to enter these cities. Trade restraints of this character, aimed at the destruction of competition, tend to block the initiative which brings newcomers into a field of business and to frustrate the free enterprise system which it was the purpose of the Sherman Act to protect. . . .

Nor can we treat this case as though it merely involved a reporter's contract to deliver his news reports exclusively to a single newspaper, or an exclusive agreement as to news between two newspapers in different cities. . . . But however innocent such agreements might be, standing alone, they would assume quite a different aspect if utilized as essential features of a program to hamper or destroy competition. It is in this light that we must view this case.

It has been argued that the restrictive By-Laws should be treated as beyond the prohibitions of the Sherman Act, since the owner of the property can choose his associates and can, as to that which he has produced by his own enterprise and sagacity, efforts or ingenuity, decide for himself whether and to whom to sell or not to sell. While it is true in a very general sense that one can dispose of his property as he pleases, he cannot "go beyond the exercise of this right, and by contracts or combinations, express or implied, unduly hinder or obstruct the free and natural flow of commerce in the channels of interstate trade." . . . The Sherman Act was specifically intended to prohibit independent businesses from becoming "associates" in a common plan which is bound to reduce their competitor's opportunity to buy or sell the things in which the groups compete. Victory of a member of such a combination over its business rivals achieved by such collective means cannot consistently with the Sherman Act or with practical, everyday knowledge be attributed to *individual* "enterprise and sagacity"; such hampering of business rivals can only be attributed to that which really makes it possible — the collective power of an unlawful combination. That the object of sale is the creation or product of a man's ingenuity does not alter this principle.... It is obviously fallacious to view the By-Laws here in issue as instituting a program to encourage and permit full freedom of sale and disposal of property by its owners. Rather, these publishers have, by concerted arrangements, pooled their power to acquire, to purchase, and to dispose of news reports through the channels of commerce. They have also pooled their economic and news control power and, in exerting that power, have entered into agreements which the District Court found to be "plainly designed in the interest of preventing competition." [15]

It is further contended that since there are other news agencies which sell news, it is not a violation of the Act for an overwhelming majority of American publishers to combine to decline to sell their news to the minority. But the fact that an agreement to restrain trade does not inhibit competition in all of the objects of that trade cannot save it from the condemnation of the Sherman Act. It is apparent that the exclusive right to publish news in a given field, furnished by AP and all of its members, gives many newspapers a competitive advantage over their rivals. Conversely, a newspaper without AP service is more than likely to be at a competitive disadvantage. The District Court stated that it was to secure this advantage over rivals that the By-Laws existed. It is true that the record shows that some competing papers have gotten along without AP news, but morning newspapers, which control 96% of the total circulation in the United States, have AP news service. And the District Court's unchallenged finding was that "AP is a vast, intricately reticulated organization, the largest of its kind, gathering news from all over the world, the chief single source of news for the American press, universally agreed to be of great consequence."

Nevertheless, we are asked to reverse these judgments on the ground that the evidence failed to show that AP reports, which might be attributable to their own "enterprise and sagacity," are clothed "in the robes of indispensability." The absence of "indispensability" is said to have been established under the following chain of reasoning: AP has made its news generally available to the people by supplying it to a limited and select group of publishers in the various cities; therefore, it is said, AP and its member publishers have not deprived the reading public of AP news; all local readers have an "adequate access" to AP news, since all they need do in any city to get it is to buy, on whatever terms they can in a protected market, the particular newspaper selected for the public by AP and its members. We reject these contentions. The proposed "indispensability" test would fly in the face of the language

---

15. Even if additional purposes were involved, it would not justify the combination, since the Sherman Act cannot "be evaded by good motives." ...

of the Sherman Act and all of our previous interpretations of it. Moreover, it would make that law a dead letter in all fields of business, a law which Congress has consistently maintained to be an essential safeguard to the kind of private competitive business economy this country has sought to maintain. . . .

Here as in the *Fashion Originator's Guild* case, "the combination is in reality an extra-governmental agency, which prescribes rules for the regulation and restraint of interstate commerce, and provides extra-judicial tribunals for determination and punishment of violations, and thus 'trenches upon the power of the national legislature and violates the statute.'" . . . By the restrictive By-Laws each of the publishers in the combination has, in effect, "surrendered himself completely to the control of the association" . . . in respect to the disposition of news in interstate commerce. Therefore this contractual restraint of interstate trade, "designed in the interest of preventing competition," cannot be one of the "normal and usual agreements in aid of trade and commerce which may be found not to be within the [Sherman] Act. . . ." *Eastern States.* It is further said that we reach our conclusion by application of the "public utility" concept to the newspaper business. This is not correct. We merely hold that arrangements or combinations designed to stifle competition cannot be immunized by adopting a membership device accomplishing that purpose. . . .

Affirmed.

Justice DOUGLAS, concurring. . . . Every exclusive arrangement in the business or commercial field may produce a restraint of trade.

A manufacturer who has only one retail outlet for his product may be said to restrain trade in the sense that other retailers are prevented from dealing in the commodity. And to a degree, the same kind of restraint may be found wherever a reporter is gathering news exclusively for one newspaper. . . . I assume it would not be a violation of the Sherman Act if a newspaper in Seattle and one in New York made an agency agreement whereby each was to furnish exclusively to the other news reports from his locality. . . .

[But the exclusive arrangement] we have here might result in the growth of a monopoly in the furnishing of news, in the access to news, or in the gathering or distribution of news. . . . The District Court found that in its present stage of development the Associated Press had no monopoly of that character. Those findings are challenged here in the appeal taken by the United States. They are not reached in the present decision for the reason, discussed in the opinion of the Court, that they cannot be tried out on a motion for a summary judgment. The decree which we approve does not direct Associated Press to serve all applicants. It goes no further than to put a ban on Associated Press' practice of discriminating against competitors of its members in the same field or territory. That entails not only a discontinuance of the practice for the future but an undoing of the wrong which has been done. If Associated Press, after the effects of that discrimination have been eliminated, freezes its membership at a given level, quite different problems would be presented. Whether that would result in a monopoly in violation of §1 of the Act is distinct from the issue in this case.

Only if a monopoly were shown to exist would we be faced with the public utility theory which has been much discussed in connection with this case and adopted by Justice Frankfurter. The decrees under the Sherman Act directed at monopolies have customarily been designed to break them up or dissolve them. . . . There have been some exceptions. Thus in United States v. Terminal Railroad Assn., 224 U.S. 383, an action was brought under the Sherman Act to dissolve a combination among certain railroads serving St. Louis. The combination had acquired control of all available facilities for connecting railroads on the east bank of the Mississippi with those on the west bank. The Court held that as an alternative to dissolution a plan should be submitted which provided for equality of treatment of all railroads. . . . Whether that procedure would be appropriate in this type of case or should await further legislative action . . . is a considerable question, the discussion of which should not cloud the present decision. What we do today has no bearing whatsoever on it.[12]

262. (a) In the *Terminal R.R.* case mentioned in Justice Douglas's concurring opinion, is there any doubt that defendants' combination was unlawful? On what grounds?

(b) Suppose that George and Edward form a corporation to invent a better mousetrap; they succeed and earn enormous profits as existing producers expire. Existing producers cite *Terminal R.R.* and demand that they be allowed to participate in the ownership of the G & E corporation or at least to make the device. What result? Why?

(c) Does or should *Terminal R.R.* dictate the result in *AP*? How does the AP situation differ from that in *Terminal R.R.*? From that in ¶b?[13]

---

12. Frankfurter, J., concurred. Stone, C.J., and Roberts and Murphy, JJ., dissented. Jackson, J., did not participate.

13. Compare *Aspen*, Ch. 3A, a case involving action by a single firm. The reader should also compare *Topco* and the discussion of joint ventures from Ch. 2B; interestingly, *AP* was not cited in *Topco*.

(d) What is the Court's rationale in *AP* and does it make sense? Did the Association need exclusivity to function? If admissions of newspapers competing with members were required, what would be the impact on the utility of AP to its members? What long-run results might be anticipated from each possible outcome or remedy in this case?

(e) Would it be relevant if either diseconomies of scale relating to coordination or physical limits on transmission facilities made it more costly or impossible to admit all comers?

(f) Does the *AP* Court apply a per se rule?

263. Recall ¶226's 20 firms whose individual research and development expenditures were very high. If 19 of them form a joint research laboratory, could a 20th firm successfully maintain an antitrust suit to force its way into the joint operation?

(a) Who has the burden of proving what? What should be the result if: (1) the record shows only the foregoing? (2) defendants assert that plaintiff's contribution of personnel and ideas to the joint undertaking would not be as valuable as the contributions of the 19 collaborators? (3) defendants lack confidence in plaintiff's capacity to preserve industry research secrets? (4) plaintiff is generally supposed to be a price-cutter?

(b) How does your analysis differ, if at all, when the joint research facility is established only by 5 of the industry's 20 firms? Is plaintiff's claim to admission stronger or weaker? Significantly so?

(c) How do your answers to the preceding questions differ, if at all, when the joint laboratory makes a revolutionary invention whose exploitation will have the effect of destroying those producers without access to the new development?

NORTHWEST WHOLESALE STATIONERS v.
PACIFIC STATIONERY & PRINTING CO.
472 U.S. 284 (1985)

BRENNAN, J. . . . Because the District Court ruled on cross-motions for summary judgment after only limited discovery, this case comes to us on a sparse record. Certain background facts are undisputed. Petitioner Northwest Wholesale Stationers is a purchasing cooperative made up of approximately 100 office supply retailers in the Pacific Northwest States. The cooperative acts as the primary wholesaler for the retailers. Retailers that are not members of the cooperative can purchase wholesale supplies from Northwest at the same price as members. At the end of each year, however, Northwest distributes its profits to members in the form of a percentage rebate on purchases. Members therefore effectively purchase supplies at a price significantly lower than do nonmembers.[2] Northwest also provides certain warehousing facilities. The cooperative arrangement thus permits the participating retailers to achieve economies of scale in purchasing and warehousing that would otherwise be unavailable to them. In fiscal 1978 Northwest had $5.8 million in sales.

Respondent Pacific Stationery, Inc., sells office supplies at both the retail and wholesale levels. Its total sales in fiscal 1978 were approximately $7.6 million; the record does not indicate what percentage of revenue is attributable to retail and what percentage is attributable to wholesale. Pacific became a member of Northwest in 1958. In 1974 Northwest amended its bylaws to prohibit members from engaging in both retail and wholesale operations. A grandfather clause preserved Pacific's membership rights. In 1977 ownership of a controlling share of the stock of Pacific changed hands, and the new owners did not officially bring this change to the attention of the directors of Northwest. This failure to notify apparently violated another of Northwest's bylaws.... In 1978 the membership of Northwest voted to expel Pacific. Most factual matters relevant to the expulsion are in dispute. No explanation for the expulsion was advanced at the time and Pacific was given neither notice, a hearing, nor any other opportunity to challenge the decision. Pacific argues that the expulsion resulted from Pacific's decision to maintain a wholesale operation. Northwest contends that the expulsion resulted from Pacific's failure to notify the cooperative members of the change in stock ownership. The minutes of the meeting of Northwest's directors do not definitively indicate the motive for the expulsion. It is undisputed that Pacific received approximately $10,000 in rebates from Northwest in 1978, Pacific's last year of membership. Beyond a possible inference of loss from this fact, however, the record is devoid of allegations indicating the nature and extent of competitive injury the expulsion caused Pacific to suffer.

Pacific brought suit in 1980.... The gravamen of the action was that Northwest's expulsion of Pacific from the cooperative without procedural protections was a group boycott that limited Pacific's ability to compete and should be considered per se violative of §1. On cross-motions for summary judgment the District Court rejected application of the per se rule and held instead that rule-of-reason analysis should govern the case. Finding no anticompetitive effect on the basis of the record as presented, the court granted summary judgment for Northwest.

The Court of Appeals for the Ninth Circuit reversed.... The court reasoned that the cooperative's expulsion of Pacific was an

---

2. Although this patronage rebate policy is a form of price discrimination, §4 of the Robinson-Patman Act specifically sanctions such activity by cooperatives....

anticompetitive concerted refusal to deal with Pacific on equal footing, which would be a per se violation of §1 in the absence of any
specific legislative mandate for self-regulation sanctioning the expulsion. The court noted that §4 of the Robinson-Patman Act
specifically approves the price discrimination occasioned by such
expulsion and concluded that §4 therefore provided a mandate for
self-regulation. Such a legislative mandate, according to the court,
would ordinarily result in evaluation of the challenged practice under the rule of reason. But, drawing on Silver v. New York Stock
Exchange, 373 U.S. 341, 348-349 (1963), the court decided that
rule-of-reason analysis was appropriate only on the condition that
the cooperative had provided procedural safeguards sufficient to
prevent arbitrary expulsion and to furnish a basis for judicial review. Because Northwest had not provided any procedural safeguards, the court held that the expulsion of Pacific was not shielded
by Robinson-Patman immunity and therefore constituted a per se
group boycott in violation of §1 of the Sherman Act.
  We ... reverse.

II

The decision of the cooperative members to expel Pacific was
certainly a restraint of trade in the sense that every commercial
agreement restrains trade.... Whether this action violates §1 of the
Sherman Act depends on whether it is adjudged an unreasonable
restraint. Rule-of-reason analysis guides the inquiry ... unless the
challenged action falls into the category of "agreements or practices which because of their pernicious effect on competition and
lack of any redeeming virtue are conclusively presumed to be unreasonable and therefore illegal without elaborate inquiry as to the
precise harm they have caused or the business excuse for their
use." *Northern Pacific.*
  This per se approach permits categorical judgments with respect
to certain business practices that have proved to be predominantly
anticompetitive.... The decision to apply the per se rule turns on
"whether the practice facially appears to be one that would always
or almost always tend to restrict competition and decrease output
... or instead one designed to 'increase economic efficiency and
render markets more, rather than less, competitive.'" *Broadcast Music.* See also *NCAA* ("Per se rules are invoked when surrounding
circumstances make the likelihood of anticompetitive conduct so
great as to render unjustified further examination of the challenged conduct").
  This Court has long held that certain concerted refusals to deal
or group boycotts are so likely to restrict competition without any
offsetting efficiency gains that they should be condemned as per se

violations of §1 of the Sherman Act. See *Klor's*; United States v. General Motors Corp., 384 U.S. 127 (1966); Radiant Burners, Inc. v. Peoples Gas Light & Coke Co., 364 U.S. 656 (1961); *AP*; *Fashion Originators' Guild*; *Eastern States*. The question presented in this case is whether Northwest's decision to expel Pacific should fall within this category of activity that is conclusively presumed to be anticompetitive. The Court of Appeals held that the exclusion of Pacific from the cooperative should conclusively be presumed unreasonable on the ground that Northwest provided no procedural protections to Pacific. Even if the lack of procedural protections does not justify a conclusive presumption of predominantly anticompetitive effect, the mere act of expulsion of a competitor from a wholesale cooperative might be argued to be sufficiently likely to have such effects under the present circumstances and therefore to justify application of the per se rule. These possibilities will be analyzed separately.

A

The Court of Appeals drew from *Silver* a broad rule that the conduct of a cooperative venture — including a concerted refusal to deal — undertaken pursuant to a legislative mandate for self-regulation is immune from per se scrutiny and subject to rule-of-reason analysis only if adequate procedural safeguards accompany self-regulation. We disagree and conclude that the approach of the Court in *Silver* has no proper application to the present controversy.

The Court in *Silver* framed the issue as follows:

[W]hether the New York Stock Exchange is to be held liable to a nonmember broker-dealer under the antitrust laws or regarded as impliedly immune therefrom when, pursuant to rules the Exchange has adopted under the Securities Exchange Act of 1934, it orders a number of its members to remove private direct telephone wire connections previously in operation between their offices and those of the nonmember, without giving the nonmember notice, assigning him any reason for the action, or affording him an opportunity to be heard.

Because the New York Stock Exchange [in that case] occupied such a dominant position in the securities trading markets that the boycott would devastate the nonmember, the Court concluded that the refusal to deal with the nonmember would amount to a per se violation of §1 unless the Securities Exchange Act provided an immunity. The question for the Court thus was whether effectuation of the policies of the Securities Exchange Act required partial repeal of the Sherman Act insofar as it proscribed this aspect of exchange self-regulation.

Finding exchange self-regulation — including the power to expel members and limit dealings with nonmembers — to be an essential policy of the Securities Exchange Act, the Court held that the Sherman Act should be construed as having been partially repealed to permit the type of exchange activity at issue. But the interpretive maxim disfavoring repeals by implication led the Court to narrow permissible self-policing to situations in which adequate procedural safeguards had been provided.... Thus it was the specific need to accommodate the important national policy of promoting effective exchange self-regulation, tempered by the principle that the Sherman Act should be narrowed only to the extent necessary to effectuate that policy, that dictated the result in *Silver*.

Section 4 of the Robinson-Patman Act is not comparable to the self-policing provisions of the Securities Exchange Act. That section is no more than a narrow immunity from the price discrimination prohibitions of the Robinson-Patman Act itself.... In light of this circumscribed congressional intent, there can be no argument that §4 of the Robinson-Patman Act should be viewed as a broad mandate for industry self-regulation. No need exists, therefore, to narrow the Sherman Act in order to accommodate any competing congressional policy requiring discretionary self-policing.... In any event, the absence of procedural safeguards can in no sense determine the antitrust analysis. If the challenged concerted activity of Northwest's members would amount to a per se violation of §1 of the Sherman Act, no amount of procedural protection would save it. If the challenged action would not amount to a violation of §1, no lack of procedural protections would convert it into a per se violation because the antitrust laws do not themselves impose on joint ventures a requirement of process.

B

This case therefore turns not on the lack of procedural protections but on whether the decision to expel Pacific is properly viewed as a group boycott or concerted refusal to deal mandating per se invalidation. "Group boycotts" are often listed among the classes of economic activity that merit per se invalidation under §1.... Exactly what types of activity fall within the forbidden category is, however, far from certain.... Some care is therefore necessary in defining the category of concerted refusals to deal that mandate per se condemnation....

Cases to which this Court has applied the per se approach have generally involved joint efforts by a firm or firms to disadvantage competitors by "either directly denying or persuading or coercing suppliers or customers to deny relationships the competitors need in the competitive struggle." L. Sullivan, Law of Antitrust, 261-262 (1977). See, e.g., *Silver* (denial of necessary access to exchange members); *Radiant Burners* (denial of necessary certification of product); *Associated Press* (denial of important sources of news); *Klor's* (denial of wholesale supplies). In these cases, the boycott often cut off access to a supply, facility, or market necessary to enable the boycotted firm to compete, *Silver, Radiant Burners,* and frequently the boycotting firms possessed a dominant position in the relevant market. E.g., *Silver, Associated Press, Fashion Originators' Guild.* See generally Brodley, Joint Ventures and Antitrust Policy, 95 Harv. L. Rev. 1523, 1533, 1563-1565 (1982). In addition, the practices were generally not justified by plausible arguments that they were intended to enhance overall efficiency and make markets more competitive. Under such circumstances the likelihood of anticompetitive effects is clear and the possibility of countervailing procompetitive effects is remote.

Although a concerted refusal to deal need not necessarily possess all of these traits to merit per se treatment, not every cooperative activity involving a restraint or exclusion will share with the per se forbidden boycotts the likelihood of predominantly anticompetitive consequences. For example, we recognized last Term in *NCAA* that per se treatment of the NCAA's restrictions on the marketing of televised college football was inappropriate — despite the obvious restraint on output — because the "case involves an industry in which horizontal restraints on competition are essential if the product is to be available at all."

Wholesale purchasing cooperatives such as Northwest are not a form of concerted activity characteristically likely to result in predominantly anticompetitive effects. Rather, such cooperative arrangements would seem to be "designated to increase economic efficiency and render markets more, rather than less, competitive." *Broadcast Music.* The arrangement permits the participating retailers to achieve economies of scale in both the purchase and warehousing of wholesale supplies, and also ensures ready access to a stock of goods that might otherwise be unavailable on short notice. The cost savings and order-filling guarantees enable smaller retailers to reduce prices and maintain their retail stock so as to compete more effectively with larger retailers.

Pacific, of course, does not object to the existence of the cooperative arrangement, but rather raises an antitrust challenge to Northwest's decision to bar Pacific from continued membership.[6] It is

6. Because Pacific has not been wholly excluded from access to Northwest's wholesale operations, there is perhaps some question whether the challenged activity is properly characterized a concerted refusal to deal. To be precise, Northwest's activity is a concerted refusal to deal with Pacific on substantially equal

therefore the action of expulsion that must be evaluated to determine whether per se treatment is appropriate. The act of expulsion from a wholesale cooperative does not necessarily imply anticompetitive animus and thereby raise a probability of anticompetitive effect.... Wholesale purchasing cooperatives must establish and enforce reasonable rules in order to function effectively. Disclosure rules, such as the one on which Northwest relies, may well provide the cooperative with a needed means for monitoring the creditworthiness of its members.[7] Nor would the expulsion characteristically be likely to result in predominantly anticompetitive effects, at least in the type of situation this case presents. Unless the cooperative possesses market power or exclusive access to an element essential to effective competition, the conclusion that expulsion is virtually always likely to have an anticompetitive effect is not warranted. ...Absent such a showing with respect to a cooperative buying arrangement, courts should apply a rule-of-reason analysis. At no time has Pacific made a threshold showing that these structural characteristics are present in this case.

The District Court appears to have followed the correct path of analysis — recognizing that not all concerted refusals to deal should be accorded per se treatment and deciding this one should not. The foregoing discussion suggests, however, that a satisfactory threshold determination whether anticompetitive effects would be likely might require a more detailed factual picture of market structure than the District Court had before it. Nonetheless, in our judgment the District Court's rejection of per se analysis in this case was correct. A plaintiff seeking application of the per se rule must present a threshold case that the challenged activity falls into a category likely to have predominantly anticompetitive effects. The mere allegation of a concerted refusal to deal does not suffice because not all concerted refusals to deal are predominantly anticompetitive. When the plaintiff challenges expulsion from a joint buying cooperative, some showing must be made that the coopera-

---

terms. Such activity might justify per se invalidation if it placed a competing firm at a severe competitive disadvantage. See generally Brodley, Joint Ventures and Antitrust Policy, 95 Harv. L. Rev. 1521, 1532 (1982) ("Even if the joint venture does deal with outside firms, it may place them at a severe competitive disadvantage by treating them less favorably that it treats the [participants in the joint venture.]").

7. Pacific argues, however, that this justification for expulsion was a pretext because the members of Northwest were fully aware of the change in ownership despite lack of formal notice. According to Pacific, Northwest's motive in the expulsion was to place Pacific at a competitive disadvantage to retaliate for Pacific's decision to engage in an independent wholesale operation. Such a motive might be more troubling. If Northwest's action were not substantially related to the efficiency-enhancing or procompetitive purposes that otherwise justify the cooperative's practices, an inference of anticompetitive animus might be appropriate. But such an argument is appropriately evaluated under the rule of reason analysis.

tive possesses market power or unique access to a business element necessary for effective competition. Focusing on the argument that the lack of procedural safeguards required per se liability, Pacific did not allege any such facts. Because the Court of Appeals applied an erroneous per se analysis in this case, the court never evaluated the District Court's rule-of-reason analysis rejecting Pacific's claim. A remand is therefore appropriate for the limited purpose of permitting appellate review of that determination....[14]

264. (a) Does *Northwest* overturn the rule that boycotts are per se illegal? If not, what remains of the per se rule? Compare *BMI*. Is *Northwest* consistent with *Klor's*?

(b) What sort of market power does the Court require? That the plaintiff needs membership in order to compete effectively in the marketplace? That the market would be notably less competitive without the plaintiff?[15]

(c) What is the implication of this opinion for a small firm seeking initial admission to Northwest?[16]

(d) Could Pacific recover its higher costs of buying elsewhere if it can prove that the cooperative expelled it maliciously for the purpose of injuring it?

(e) If Northwest's purpose in expelling Pacific or refusing to admit a new applicant matters, was the Ninth Circuit wise to require due process within the defendant organization, as *Silver* had required for the New York Stock Exchange?

265. The Amesville Used Car Dealers Association has adopted bylaws forbidding members from using bait advertising (unlawful advertising of fictitious cars at very low prices to lure prospective buyers), turning back odometers to make cars seem newer than they are, and offering buyers oral assurances about the quality of a car. The bylaws also require members to make all guarantees in writing and to provide all prospective buyers with a complete checklist (appropriate to the age and type of car being considered) for judging quality. Because the Association is very highly regarded in Amesville, the Association tries to maintain consumer confidence by promptly expelling dealers who fail to live up to the bylaws. There is evidence that the fear of expulsion has induced many dealers to make prompt adjustments with those dissatisfied cus-

14. Marshall and Powell, JJ., did not participate.
15. See SCFC ILC v. Visa USA, 36 F.3d 958 (10th Cir. 1994), cert. denied, 115 S. Ct. 2600 (1995) (Visa system not required to admit Sears, which issued competing Discover Card; issuer market unconcentrated and no showing that Sears's new credit card could not succeed without Visa).
16. Cf. *AP*. Note that Pacific alone had more sales than the 100-firm cooperative from which it was expelled.

tomers who complained to the Association. An expelled member sues for damages and reinstatement under Sherman Act §1. What result? Would it matter if the remaining members, all competing locally, numbered 50?

FEDERAL TRADE COMMISSION v. INDIANA
FEDERATION OF DENTISTS
476 U.S. 447 (1986)

Justice WHITE.... Since the 1970's, dental health insurers ... have attempted to contain the cost of dental treatment.... In order to [evaluate care,] insurers frequently request dentists to submit, along with insurance claim forms requesting payment of benefits, any dental x rays that have been used by the dentist in examining the patient as well as other information concerning their diagnoses and treatment recommendations. Typically, claim forms and accompanying x rays are reviewed by lay claims examiners, who either approve payment of claims or, if the materials submitted raise a question whether the recommended course of treatment is in fact necessary, refer claims to dental consultants, who are licensed dentists, for further review....

Such review of diagnostic and treatment decisions has been viewed by some dentists as a threat to their professional independence and economic well-being. In the early 1970's, the Indiana Dental Association, a professional organization comprising some 85% of practicing dentists in the State of Indiana, initiated an aggressive effort to hinder insurers' efforts to implement alternative benefits plans by enlisting member dentists to pledge not to submit x rays in conjunction with claim forms.[1] The Association's efforts met considerable success: large numbers of dentists signed the pledge, and insurers operating in Indiana found it difficult to obtain compliance with their request for x rays and accordingly had to choose either to employ more expensive means of making alternative benefits determinations (for example, visiting the office of the

1. A presentation made in 1974 by D. David McClure, an Association official and later one of the founders of respondent Indiana Federation of Dentists, is revealing as to the motives underlying the dentists' resistance to the provision of x rays for use by insurers in making alternative benefits determinations: ...

> The name of the game is money. The government and labor are determined to reduce the cost of the dental health dollar at the expense of the dentist. There is no way a dental service can be rendered cheaper when the third party has to have its share of the dollar.
>
> Already we are locked into a fee freeze that could completely control the quality of dental care, if left on long enough.

treating dentist or conducting an independent oral examination) or to abandon such efforts altogether. . . .

In 1979, the Association and a number of its constituent societies consented to a Federal Trade Commission order requiring them to cease and desist from further efforts to prevent member dentists from submitting x rays. Not all Indiana dentists were content to leave the matter of submitting x rays to the individual dentist. In 1976, a group of such dentists formed the Indiana Federation of Dentists, respondent in this case, in order to continue to pursue the Association's policy of resisting insurers' requests for x rays. . . . Although the Federation's membership was small, numbering less than 100, its members were highly concentrated in and around three Indiana communities: Anderson, Lafayette, and Fort Wayne. The Federation succeeded in enlisting nearly 100% of the dental specialists in the Anderson area, and approximately 67% of the dentists in and around Lafayette. In the areas of its strength, the Federation was successful in continuing to enforce the Association's prior policy of refusal to submit x rays to dental insurers. . . .

[T]he Federal Trade Commission . . . ruled that the Federation's policy constituted a violation of §5. . . . [The] Court of Appeals for the Seventh Circuit . . . vacated the order on the ground that it was not supported by substantial evidence. . . . We now reverse.

III . . .

[The] Commission's finding that "[i]n the absence of . . . concerted behavior, individual dentists would have been subject to market forces of competition, creating incentives for them to . . . comply with the requests of patients' third-party insurers" finds support not only in common sense and economic theory, upon both of which the FTC may reasonably rely, but also in record documents, including newsletters circulated among Indiana dentists, revealing that Indiana dentists themselves perceived that unrestrained competition tended to lead their colleagues to comply with insurers' requests for x rays. Moreover, there was evidence that outside of Indiana, in States where dentists had not collectively refused to submit x rays, insurance companies found little difficulty in obtaining compliance by dentists with their requests. . . .

The Federation's collective activities resulted in the denial of the information the customers requested in the form that they requested it, and forced them to choose between acquiring that information in a more costly manner or forgoing it altogether. To this extent, at least, competition among dentists with respect to cooperation with the requests of insurers was restrained.

IV

The question remains whether these findings are legally sufficient to establish a violation of §1 of the Sherman Act — that is, whether the Federation's collective refusal to cooperate with insurers' requests for x rays constitutes an "unreasonable" restraint of trade. . . .

The policy of the Federation with respect to its members' dealing with third-party insurers resembles practices that have been labeled "group boycotts": the policy constitutes a concerted refusal to deal on particular terms with patients covered by group dental insurance. . . . Although this Court has in the past stated that group boycotts are unlawful per se, . . . we decline to resolve this case by forcing the Federation's policy into the "boycott" pigeonhole and invoking the per se rule. As we observed last Term in *Northwest Wholesale*, the category of restraints classed as group boycotts is not to be expanded indiscriminately, and the per se approach has generally been limited to cases in which firms with market power boycott suppliers or customers in order to discourage them from doing business with a competitor — a situation obviously not present here. Moreover, we have been slow to condemn rules adopted by professional associations as unreasonable per se, see *Engineers*, and, in general, to extend per se analysis to restraints imposed in the context of business relationships where the economic impact of certain practices is not immediately obvious, see *Broadcast Music*. Thus, as did the FTC, we evaluate the restraint at issue in this case under the Rule of Reason rather than a rule of per se illegality.

Application of the Rule of Reason to these facts is not a matter of any great difficulty. The Federation's policy takes the form of horizontal agreement among the participating dentists to withhold from their customers a particular service that they desire — the forwarding of x rays to insurance companies along with claim forms. . . . A refusal to compete with respect to the package of services offered to customers, no less than a refusal to compete with respect to the price term of an agreement, impairs the ability of the market to advance social welfare by ensuring the provision of desired goods and services to consumers at a price approximating the marginal cost of providing them. Absent some countervailing procompetitive virtue — such as, for example, the creation of efficiencies in the operation of a market or the provision of goods and services . . . — such an agreement limiting consumer choice by impeding the "ordinary give and take of the market place," *Engineers*, cannot be sustained under the Rule of Reason. No credible argument has been advanced for the proposition that making it more costly for the insurers and patients who are dentists' customers to obtain information needed for evaluating the dentists' diagnoses has any such procompetitive effect.

The Federation advances three principal arguments for the proposition that, notwithstanding its lack of competitive virtue, the Federation's policy of withholding x rays should not be deemed an unreasonable restraint of trade. First, as did the Court of Appeals, the Federation suggests that in the absence of specific findings by the Commission concerning the definition of the market in which the Federation allegedly restrained trade and the power of the Federation's members in that market, the conclusion that the Federation unreasonably restrained trade is erroneous as a matter of law, regardless of whether the challenged practices might be impermissibly anticompetitive if engaged in by persons who together possessed power in a specifically defined market. This contention, however, runs counter to the Court's holding in *NCAA* that "[a]s a matter of law, the absence of proof of market power does not justify a naked restriction on price or output," and that such a restriction "requires some competitive justification even in the absence of a detailed market analysis." Moreover, even if the restriction imposed by the Federation is not sufficiently "naked" to call this principle into play, the Commission's failure to engage in detailed market analysis is not fatal to its finding of violation of the Rule of Reason. The Commission found that in two localities in the State of Indiana (the Anderson and Lafayette areas), Federation dentists constituted heavy majorities of the practicing dentists and that as a result of the efforts of the Federation, insurers in those areas were, over a period of years, actually unable to obtain compliance with their requests for submission of x rays. Since the purpose of the inquiries into market definition and market power is to determine whether an arrangement has the potential for genuine adverse effects on competition, "proof of actual detrimental effects, such as a reduction of output" can obviate the need for an inquiry into market power, which is but a "surrogate for detrimental effects." 7 P. Areeda, Antitrust Law ¶1511, p. 429 (1986). . . .

Second, the Federation, again following the lead of the Court of Appeals, argues that a holding that its policy of withholding x rays constituted an unreasonable restraint of trade is precluded by the Commission's failure to make any finding that the policy resulted in the provision of dental services that were more costly than those that the patients and their insurers would have chosen were they able to evaluate x rays in conjunction with claim forms. This argument, too, is unpersuasive. Although it is true that the goal of the insurers in seeking submission of x rays for use in their review of benefits claims was to minimize costs by choosing the least expensive adequate course of dental treatment, a showing that this goal was actually achieved through the means chosen is not an essential step in establishing that the dentists' attempt to thwart its achievement by collectively refusing to supply the requested information was an unreasonable restraint of trade. A concerted and effective effort to withhold (or make more costly) information desired by consumers for the purpose of determining whether a particular purchase is cost-justified is likely enough to disrupt the proper functioning of the price-setting mechanism of the market that it may be condemned even absent proof that it resulted in higher prices or, as here, the purchase of higher-priced services, than would occur in its absence. *Engineers.* Moreover, even if the desired information were in fact completely useless to the insurers and their patients in making an informed choice regarding the least costly adequate course of treatment — or, to put it another way, if the costs of evaluating the information were far greater than the cost savings resulting from its use — the Federation would still not be justified in deciding on behalf of its members' customers that they did not need the information: presumably, if that were the case, the discipline of the market would itself soon result in the insurers' abandoning their requests for x rays. The Federation is not entitled to pre-empt the working of the market by deciding for itself that its customers do not need that which they demand.

Third, the Federation complains that the Commission erred in failing to consider, as relevant to its Rule of Reason analysis, noncompetitive "quality of care" justifications for the prohibition on provision of x rays to insurers in conjunction with claim forms. . . . The gist of the claim is that x rays, standing alone, are not adequate bases for diagnosis of dental problems or for the formulation of an acceptable course of treatment. Accordingly, . . . there is a danger that [insurance companies] will erroneously decline to pay for treatment that is in fact in the interest of the patient, and that the patient will as a result be deprived of fully adequate care.

The Federation's argument is flawed both legally and factually. The premise of the argument is that, far from having no effect on the cost of dental services chosen by patients and their insurers, the provision of x rays will have too great an impact: it will lead to the reduction of costs through the selection of inadequate treatment. Precisely such a justification for withholding information from customers was rejected as illegitimate in the *Engineers* case. The argument is, in essence, that an unrestrained market in which customers are given access to the information they believe to be relevant to their choices will lead them to make unwise and even dangerous choices. Such an argument amounts to "nothing less than a frontal assault on the basic policy of the Sherman Act." *Engineers.* Moreover, there is no particular reason to believe that the provision of information will be more harmful to consumers in the market for dental services than in other markets. Insurers deciding what level of care to pay for are not themselves the recipients of those services, but it is by no means clear that they lack incentives to consider the welfare of the patient as well as the minimization of costs. They are themselves in competition for the patronage of the patients — or, in most cases, the unions or businesses that contract on their behalf for group insurance coverage — and must satisfy their potential customers not only that they will provide coverage at a reasonable cost, but also that that coverage will be adequate to meet their customers' dental needs. There is thus no more reason to expect dental insurance companies to sacrifice quality in return for cost savings than to believe this of consumers in, say, the market for engineering services. Accordingly, if noncompetitive quality-of-service justifications are inadmissible to justify the denial of information to consumers in the latter market, there is little reason to credit such justifications here.

In any event, the Commission did not, as the Federation suggests, refuse even to consider the quality of care justification for the withholding of x rays. ... The Commission was amply justified in concluding on the basis of [the] conflicting evidence [before it] that even if concern for the quality of patient care could under some circumstances serve as a justification for a restraint of the sort imposed here, the evidence did not support a finding that the careful use of x rays as a basis for evaluating insurance claims is in fact destructive of proper standards of dental care.... [R]eversed.

266. (a) Does the *Indiana Dentists* Court apply a per se rule? If not, are there any cases where a per se rule would be applied against boycotts?

(b) Are there any redeeming virtues to the dentists' boycott? Ones that the antitrust laws should consider?

(c) Had there been no proof of power or effects, would the Commission have been vindicated? Could the entire opinion have read: "The Court of Appeals is reversed. See *Engineers*."? If the answers to the last two questions are in the affirmative, of what consequence was the application of the rule of reason?

(d) What are the practical differences between applying a per se rule in *Indiana Dentists* and applying the rule of reason as the Court did?

267. Additional varieties of concerted refusals to deal. Boycott challenges are frequently raised when a plaintiff supplier or buyer finds that it can no longer supply or buy from several past or possible customers or suppliers who have made some collective decision concerning their purchases or sales. *Northwest* illustrates concerted action by a large group that lacked dominant or essential position, unlike that in *Associated Press* or perhaps in *Indiana Dentists.* More common is group action on an even smaller scale. For example, in *Hawaiian Oke,*[17] the defendant replaced the plaintiff as its exclusive outlet in a certain area. Because the new outlet would require other brands to operate efficiently, the defendant allegedly discussed the matter with a rival supplier who also shifted from the plaintiff to the new outlet. The Ninth Circuit rejected the district court's charge to the jury that an agreement among two suppliers to shift their dealership from the plaintiff to another was unlawful per se. The boycott characterization was rejected on the ground that the defendants were seeking to create efficient distribution and were not acting for the purpose of excluding the plaintiff from the market or for any other anticompetitive purpose.[18]

To further illustrate the variety of possible exclusionary action by groups of competitors, consider the following cases where collaborators set rules governing their undertaking or standards relating to the subject of their activities.[19] (1) Two banks establish an electronic fund transfer system, placing computer terminals in the stores of subscribing merchants. The terminal is not connected to rival banks or rival suppliers of such systems; although a switching center could be devised for that purpose, merchants with one computer terminal are unlikely to have another.[20] (2) An insurance company reimburses only those suppliers of services that bill in a specified manner — for example, a health insurance company only pays doctors charging no more than specified prices.[21] (3) Real estate brokers exchange listings with each other and admit any broker having a sound credit rating and a favorable business reputation, subscribing $1,000 to the multiple-listing service working capital, engaging actively in the real estate business, and maintaining an

---

17. Joseph E. Seagram & Sons v. Hawaiian Oke & Liquors, 416 F.2d 71 (9th Cir. 1969), cert. denied, 396 U.S. 1062 (1970).

18. Note that here, as in many other displaced dealer cases considered in Ch. 4A, competition is not reduced when one exclusive outlet is replaced with another.

19. The reader should also recall the restrictions in the many professional sports cases in note 10 and in *Chicago Board of Trade.*

20. J. Murray, EFTS and Antitrust: Some Reflections on the Possibilities, 37 U. Pitt. L. Rev. 673 (1976); F. Ubell, Electronics Funds Transfer and Antitrust Laws, 93 Banking L.J. 43 (1976).

21. See cases in Ch. 2B, note 22, upholding such practices. The group alleged to be involved in a boycott is either the insureds (covered by a single company) or the insurance company and participating providers.

office open during normal business hours.[22] (4) A hospital peer review committee denies staff privileges to doctors found to be incompetent.[23] (5) An organization operating a tournament determines who may participate where it is impossible to accommodate all who would like to appear.[24] (6) The American Bar Association establishes guidelines and procedures for approving and accrediting paralegal schools and programs.[25]

268. Summary. Boycotts raise many of the issues considered elsewhere in antitrust. Why should we be so concerned with concerted action when the individual refusal to deal by a powerful firm may have much more serious consequences? Is the Sherman Act concerned with noneconomic objectives, and if so, are the courts able to determine which objectives are socially desirable and which are not? Even if confined to narrow economic objectives, are courts able to determine which restraints are appropriate accompaniments to joint activity? Is there any way to escape the necessity of making those judgments? Does a rule of reason approach implicitly

22. United States v. Realty Multi-List, 629 F.2d 1351 (5th Cir. 1980) (restrictions unreasonably broad); Brown v. Indianapolis Bd. of Realtors, 1977 Trade Cas. ¶61435 (S.D. Ind.) (membership criteria and procedures reasonable); Comment, Exclusion from Real Estate Multiple Listing Services as Antitrust Violations, 14 Cal. West. L. Rev. 298 (1978).

23. E.g., Marrese v. Interqual, 748 F.2d 373 (7th Cir. 1984), cert. denied, 472 U.S. 1027 (1985) (staff privileges were revoked upon findings by an outside medical audit organization and recommendation by medical staff committee; state action immunity where state statute not only authorizes but requires hospitals to engage in peer review; statute expressly provides that the participants in peer review and the hospitals are immune from all civil liability for actions taken in good faith; court concerned by the explosion of federal antitrust challenges to these hospital decisions, flowing from the expansive test of interstate commerce).

In 1986, Congress enacted legislation exempting physicians' professional review bodies (including individuals serving on them and staff) from damage actions under all federal and state law when taking action based on the competence or professional conduct of an individual physician. 100 Stat. 3784 (1986), 42 U.S.C. §11111. Excepted were civil rights laws and suits by the United States or state attorneys general under the antitrust laws.

24. Deesen v. Professional Golfers' Assn., 358 F.2d 165 (9th Cir.), cert. denied, 385 U.S. 846 (1966) (reasonable to exclude from professional competition plaintiff with insufficient playing ability who had failed to compete in the requisite number of tournaments; purpose not to destroy competition but to maintain high quality of game).

25. Paralegal Inst. v. American Bar Assn., 475 F. Supp. 1123 (E.D.N.Y. 1979) (no concerted refusal to deal; restraint, if any, is reasonable; absence of certification does not bar operation; ABA approval is apparently just a factor used in school advertising).

involve antitrust courts in regulation of myriad activities throughout the economy?

Are concerted refusals to deal illegal only when competition is substantially restrained? Need there be any effect? Are they illegal per se? The cases in this section, like those in Chapter 2B, demonstrate that the per se label can be misleading. There are cases where one can weigh harms, benefits, and alternatives and conclude almost instantaneously that conduct is unlawful; one decides the particular case so rapidly that the result may be expressed in per se language. On the other hand, the rule of reason formulation often admits standard presumptions and excludes certain justifications, as *Indiana Dentists* amply illustrates.

Can any single simple definition or rule of per se illegality do justice to the variety of circumstances in which there might be said to be a concerted refusal to deal or activities leading to it? If not, can more specific rules or presumptions be tailored to fit particular categories of such cases?

2F. INFLUENCING GOVERNMENT ACTION

269. Introduction. Individual firms or groups of competitors may seek to achieve anticompetitive ends through government decisions, including legislation, regulatory actions, the exercise of executive discretion, and court orders. There are two antitrust doctrines concerning government action. First is the state action exemption, under which there is no antitrust liability for activity that is attributable to state (and local) government action, as long as the state has clearly articulated a purpose to displace competition and the anticompetitive activity is adequately supervised. (See ¶165 for an extensive background discussion.) This immunity is often understood as an aspect of federalism, under which states remain free to regulate their economies as they wish. The immunity may also be interpreted as reflecting a notion of causation: To the extent anticompetitive activity is pursuant to a government mandate, any anticompetitive consequences might properly be attributed to the government rather than to private actors.

The second doctrine — the subject of the present section — immunizes activity designed to influence government action. This second immunity is closely related to the state action exemption, as it permits private actors to induce their government to adopt policies that would displace competition.

Both immunities apply to individual and joint action. Yet many of the relevant cases have involved horizontal agreements, so it is convenient to consider these subjects here. This section begins with the *Noerr* decision, with which the immunity for influencing government action is most identified. This is followed by a number of developments that refine or qualify the immunity.[1]

EASTERN RAILROAD PRESIDENTS CONFERENCE
v. NOERR MOTOR FREIGHT
365 U.S. 127 (1961)

Justice BLACK. [Pennsylvania truck operators filed a complaint against 24 eastern railroads and their public relations firm, alleging violations of §§1 and 2 of the Sherman Act. The truckers alleged that the railroads had conspired to eliminate their trucker competitors by conducting a public relations campaign designed to win support for laws harmful to the trucking business, to "create an atmosphere of distaste for the truckers among the general public," and to interfere in the truckers' relationships with their customers. The truckers' complaint described the campaign as "vicious, corrupt, and fraudulent," in part because the campaign was disguised as a spontaneous, independent effort. The complaint specifically alleged that the campaign had persuaded the governor to veto a bill which would have permitted truckers to carry heavier loads on Pennsylvania highways. The district court entered a judgment for the truckers, finding the campaign misleading, although not false in any particular claim, and also finding that the railroads' only purpose was to harm their competitors. A divided Court of Appeals affirmed.]

We accept, as the starting point for our consideration of the case, the same basic construction of the Sherman Act adopted by the courts below — that no violation of the Act can be predicated upon mere attempts to influence the passage or enforcement of laws.... [W]here a restraint upon trade or monopolization is the result of valid governmental action, as opposed to private action, no violation of the Act can be made out. These decisions rest upon the fact that under our form of government the question whether a law of that kind should pass, or if passed be enforced, is the responsibility of the appropriate legislative or executive branch of government so long as the law itself does not violate some provision of the Constitution.

1. See I P. Areeda & D. Turner, Antitrust Law, ch. 2A (1978; Supp. 1996); E. Elhauge, Making Sense of Antitrust Petitioning Immunity, 80 Cal. L. Rev. 1177 (1992); D. Fischel, Antitrust Liability for Attempts to Influence Government Action: The Basis and Limits of the Noerr-Pennington Doctrine, 45 U. Chi. L. Rev. 80 (1977).

We think it equally clear that the Sherman Act does not prohibit two or more persons from associating together in an attempt to persuade the legislature or the executive to take particular action with respect to a law that would produce a restraint or a monopoly. Although such associations could perhaps, through a process of expansive construction, be brought within the general proscription of "combination[s] . . . in restraint of trade," they bear very little if any resemblance to the combinations normally held violative of the Sherman Act. . . .

[Furthermore,] a holding that the Sherman Act forbids associations for the purpose of influencing the passage or enforcement of laws . . . would substantially impair the power of government to take actions through its legislature and executive that operate to restrain trade. In a representative democracy such as this, these branches of government act on behalf of the people and, to a very large extent, the whole concept of representation depends upon the ability of the people to make their wishes known to their representatives. To hold that the government retains the power to act in this representative capacity and yet hold, at the same time, that the people cannot freely inform the government of their wishes would impute to the Sherman Act a purpose to regulate, not business activity, but political activity, a purpose which would have no basis whatever in the legislative history of that Act. Secondly, and of at least equal significance, such a construction of the Sherman Act would raise important constitutional questions. The right of petition is one of the freedoms protected by the Bill of Rights, and we cannot, of course, lightly impute to Congress an intent to invade these freedoms. Indeed, such an imputation would be particularly unjustified in this case in view of all the countervailing considerations enumerated above. For these reasons, we think it clear that the Sherman Act does not apply to the activities of the railroads at least insofar as those activities comprised mere solicitation of governmental action with respect to the passage and enforcement of laws. We are thus called upon to consider whether the courts below were correct in holding that, notwithstanding this principle, the Act was violated here because of the presence in the railroads' publicity campaign of additional factors sufficient to take the case out of the area in which the principle is controlling.

The first such factor relied upon was the fact, established by the finding of the District Court, that the railroads' sole purpose in seeking to influence the passage and enforcement of laws was to destroy the truckers as competitors for the long-distance freight business. But we do not see how this fact, even if adequately supported in the record, could transform conduct otherwise lawful into a violation of the Sherman Act. . . . The right of the people to inform their representatives in government of their desires with respect to the passage or enforcement of laws cannot properly be made to depend upon their intent in doing so. It is neither unusual nor illegal for people to seek action on laws in the hope that they may bring about an advantage to themselves and a disadvantage to their competitors. . . . A construction of the Sherman Act that would disqualify people from taking a public position on matters in which they are financially interested would thus deprive the government of a valuable source of information and, at the same time, deprive the people of their right to petition in the very instances in which that right may be of the most importance to them. . . .

The second factor relied upon by the courts below to justify the application of the Sherman Act to the railroads' publicity campaign was the use in the campaign of the so-called third-party technique. The theory under which this factor was related to the proscriptions of the Sherman Act, though not entirely clear from any of the opinions below, was apparently that it involved unethical business conduct on the part of the railroads. As pointed out above, the third-party technique, which was aptly characterized by the District Court as involving "deception of the public, manufacture of bogus sources of reference, [and] distortion of public sources of information," depends upon giving propaganda actually circulated by a party in interest the appearance of being spontaneous declarations of independent groups. We can certainly agree with the courts below that this technique, though in widespread use among practitioners of the art of public relations, is one which falls short of the ethical standards generally approved in this country. It does not follow, however, that the use of the technique in a publicity campaign designed to influence governmental action constitutes a violation of the Sherman Act. Insofar as that Act sets up a code of ethics at all, it is a code that condemns trade restraints, not political activity, and, as we have already pointed out, a publicity campaign to influence governmental action falls clearly into the category of political activity. The proscriptions of the Act, tailored as they are for the business world, are not at all appropriate for application in the political arena. Congress has traditionally exercised extreme caution in legislating with respect to problems relating to the conduct of political activities, a caution which has been reflected in the decisions of this Court interpreting such legislation. All of this caution would go for naught if we permitted an extension of the Sherman Act to regulate activities of that nature simply because those activities have a commercial impact and involve conduct that can be termed unethical. . . .

In addition to the foregoing factors, both of which relate to the intent and methods of the railroads in seeking governmental action, the courts below rested their holding that the Sherman Act had been violated upon a finding that the purpose of the railroads was "more than merely an attempt to obtain legislation. *It was the purpose and intent . . . to hurt the truckers in every way possible even though they secured no legislation.*" (Emphasis in original.) Specifically, the District Court found that the purpose of the railroads was to destroy the goodwill of the truckers among the public generally and among the truckers' customers particularly, in the hope that by doing so the over-all competitive position of the truckers would be weakened, and that the railroads were successful in these efforts to the extent that such injury was actually inflicted. The apparent effect of these findings is to take this case out of the category of those that involve restraints through governmental action and thus render inapplicable the principles announced above. But this effect is only apparent and cannot stand under close scrutiny. There are no specific findings that the railroads attempted directly to persuade anyone not to deal with the truckers. Moreover, all of the evidence in the record, both oral and documentary, deals with the railroads' efforts to influence the passage and enforcement of laws. Circulars, speeches, newspaper articles, editorials, magazine articles, memoranda and all other documents discuss in one way or another the railroads' charges that heavy trucks injure the roads, violate the laws and create traffic hazards, and urge that truckers should be forced to pay a fair share of the costs of rebuilding the roads, that they should be compelled to obey the laws, and that limits should be placed upon the weight of the loads they are permitted to carry. In the light of this, the findings of the District Court that the railroads' campaign was intended to and did in fact injure the truckers in their relationships with the public and with their customers can mean no more than that the truckers sustained some direct injury as an incidental effect of the railroads' campaign to influence governmental action and that the railroads were hopeful that this might happen. Thus, the issue presented by the lower court's conclusion of a violation of the Sherman Act on the basis of this injury is no different than the issue presented by the factors already discussed. It is inevitable, whenever an attempt is made to influence legislation by a campaign of publicity, that an incidental effect of that campaign may be the infliction of some direct injury upon the interests of the party against whom the campaign is directed. And it seems equally inevitable that those conducting the campaign would be aware of, and possibly even pleased by, the prospect of such injury. To hold that the knowing infliction of such injury renders the campaign itself illegal would thus be tantamount to outlawing all such campaigns. We have already discussed the reasons which have led us to the conclusion that this has not been done by anything in the Sherman Act.

There may be situations in which a publicity campaign, ostensibly directed toward influencing governmental action, is a mere sham to cover what is actually nothing more than an attempt to interfere directly with the business relationships of a competitor and the application of the Sherman Act would be justified. But this certainly is not the case here. No one denies that the railroads were making a genuine effort to influence legislation and law enforcement practices. Indeed, if the version of the facts set forth in the truckers' complaint is fully credited, as it was by the courts below, that effort was not only genuine but also highly successful. Under these circumstances, we conclude that no attempt to interfere with business relationships in a manner proscribed by the Sherman Act is involved in this case.

In rejecting each of the grounds relied upon by the courts below to justify application of the Sherman Act to the campaign of the railroads, we have rejected the very grounds upon which those courts relied to distinguish the campaign conducted by the truckers. In doing so, we have restored what appears to be the true nature of the case — a "no-holds-barred fight" between two industries both of which are seeking control of a profitable source of income. Inherent in such fights, which are commonplace in the halls of legislative bodies, is the possibility, and in many instances even the probability, that one group or the other will get hurt by the arguments that are made. In this particular instance, each group appears to have utilized all the political powers it could muster in an attempt to bring about the passage of laws that would help it or injure the other. But the contest itself appears to have been conducted along lines normally accepted in our political system except to the extent that each group has deliberately deceived the public and public officials. And that deception, reprehensible as it is, can be of no consequence so far as the Sherman Act is concerned. . . .[2]

270. With respect to *Noerr*:
(a) Would a contrary holding impair one's "right to petition"? Could not each railroad still petition individually? Would that be a superior solution? Would a contrary holding impair the government's ability to obtain necessary information?

2. In United Mine Workers v. Pennington, 381 U.S. 657, 670 (1965), the Court said, "Joint efforts to influence public officials do not violate the antitrust laws even though intended to eliminate competition. Such conduct is not illegal, either standing alone or as part of a broader scheme itself violative of the Sherman Act." The combination had attempted to influence a minimum wage determination by the Secretary of Labor and the buying practices of the Tennessee Valley Authority. — eds.

(b) Is the Court interpreting the Sherman Act?[3] The Constitution? Both? (Reconsider this issue after reading *SCTLA*.)

(c) Could it ever be appropriate to impose antitrust or other sanctions on an individual or combination lobbying by fair and lawful means to obtain valid state or federal legislation? Would your answer depend on whether you approve of the resulting legislation? On whether the legislation wisely or unwisely created competition or monopoly? Whether the legislation is later held unconstitutional? Whether the proponents were public spirited or selfish? On whether they clearly declared a purpose to achieve monopoly, prevent rivalry, and destroy actual or potential rivals through legislation?

(d) How does the Court meet the plaintiff's claim that society has no interest in protecting defendants' deceptive behavior? How does the Court deal with the plaintiff's claim that the defendants' behavior not only induced legislation but also directly influenced the willingness of shippers to use trucks rather than railroads?

(e) In the *Noerr* situation, suppose it had been proved that the defendants bribed certain legislators in violation of Pennsylvania criminal law. Would the *Noerr* Court find a Sherman Act violation? If so, how should the Court treat false, biased, or selective testimony to a legislative committee, government official, or administrative agency? A large political contribution?

(f) Suppose that the *Noerr* Court had found a violation of the Sherman Act and that plaintiff was injured by legislation enacted as a result of defendants' activities. Would plaintiff's injury be attributable to defendants' behavior or to Pennsylvania's sovereign decisions through its legislature and governor? Could a federal antitrust court invalidate such legislation (relying on the supremacy clause)? If not, would it be proper to hold that the passage or implementation of otherwise valid Pennsylvania laws could be a source of compensable injury to the plaintiff?

(g) May behavior immunized from liability by *Noerr* be admitted as evidence of an exclusionary intention contaminating some nonpetitioning activity by the defendants? For example, does a defendant cooperative's intent in lobbying for regulations harmful to

3. With regard to the legislative history of the Sherman Act, consider the following statements by one commentator who has investigated the subject.

[I]t was less often argued that monopolists would abolish representative government and more often they would use their wealth to make it serve their own interests.... Trusts, it was said, threatened liberty, because they corrupted civil servants and bribed legislators; they enjoyed privileges such as protection by tariffs; they drove out competitors, ... victimized consumers, ... and somehow or other abused everyone. [W. Letwin, Law and Economic Policy in America (1965).]

plaintiff bear on its intent in barring plaintiff from membership in the cooperative?[4]

CALIFORNIA MOTOR TRANSPORT CO. v. TRUCKING UNLIMITED
404 U.S. 508 (1972)

Justice DOUGLAS. [Highway carriers operating in California alleged that a rival company instituted state and federal proceedings to resist applications for operating rights.] The District Court dismissed the complaint for failure to state a cause of action. The Court of Appeals reversed. . . .

The present case is akin to *Noerr.* . . . The same philosophy governs the approach of citizens or groups of them to administrative agencies (which are both creatures of the legislature, and arms of the executive) and to courts, the third branch of Government. . . . We conclude that it would be destructive of rights of association and of petition to hold that groups with common interests may not, without violating the antitrust laws, use the channels and procedures of state and federal agencies and courts to advocate their causes and points of view respecting resolution of their business and economic interests vis-à-vis their competitors.

We said, however, in *Noerr* that there may be instances where the alleged conspiracy "is a mere sham to cover what is actually nothing more than an attempt to interfere directly with the business relationships of a competitor and the application of the Sherman Act would be justified." In that connection the complaint in the present case alleged [among other things] that the power, strategy, and resources of the petitioners were used to harass and deter respondents in their use of administrative and judicial proceedings so as to deny them "free and unlimited access" to those tribunals. . . .

Petitioners rely on our statement in *Pennington* that "*Noerr* shields from the Sherman Act a concerted effort to influence public officials regardless of intent or purpose." In the present case, however,

4. Guarded affirmative replies are suggested in Alexander v. National Farmers Org., 687 F.2d 1173 (8th Cir. 1983); Feminist Women's Health Center v. Mohammad, 586 F.2d 530 (5th Cir. 1978), cert. denied, 444 U.S. 924 (1979) (relevant but, in this case, excluded because possible prejudice outweighed low probative value); MCI Communications v. AT&T, 708 F.2d 1081 (7th Cir.), cert. denied, 464 U.S. 891 (1983) (quoting *Feminist* approvingly). Cf. United States Football League v. National Football League, 634 F. Supp. 1155, 1181 (S.D.N.Y. 1986) (request for admission of evidence of protected activities should be scrutinized closely for prejudicial effect; "evidence by which its very nature chills the exercise of First Amendment rights . . . is properly viewed as presumptively prejudicial").

the allegations are not that the conspirators sought "to influence public officials," but that they sought to bar their competitors from meaningful access to adjudicatory tribunals and so to usurp that decision-making process. It is alleged that petitioners "instituted the proceedings and actions ... with or without probable cause, and regardless of the merits of the cases." The nature of the views pressed does not, of course, determine whether First Amendment rights may be invoked; but they may bear upon a purpose to deprive the competitors of meaningful access to the agencies and courts. As stated in the opinion concurring in the result, such a purpose or intent, if shown, would be "to discourage and ultimately to prevent the respondents from invoking" the processes of the administrative agencies and courts and thus fall within the exception to *Noerr.* . . .

[U]nethical conduct in the setting of the adjudicatory process often results in sanctions. Perjury of witnesses is one example. Use of a patent obtained by fraud to exclude a competitor from the market may involve a violation of the antitrust laws, as we held in Walker Process Equipment v. Food Machinery & Chemical Corp., 382 U.S. 172, 175-177. Conspiracy with a licensing authority to eliminate a competitor may also result in an antitrust transgression. Continental Ore Co. v. Union Carbide & Carbon Corp., 370 U.S. 690, 707; Harman v. Valley National Bank, 339 F.2d 564 (CA9 1964). Similarly, bribery of a public purchasing agent may constitute a violation of §2(c) of the Clayton Act, as amended by the Robinson-Patman Act. Rangen, Inc. v. Sterling Nelson & Sons, 351 F.2d 851 (CA9 1965).

There are many other forms of illegal and reprehensible practice which may corrupt the administrative or judicial processes and which may result in antitrust violations. Misrepresentations, condoned in the political arena, are not immunized when used in the adjudicatory process. Opponents before agencies or courts often think poorly of the other's tactics, motions, or defenses and may readily call them baseless. One claim, which a court or agency may think baseless, may go unnoticed; but a pattern of baseless, repetitive claims may emerge which leads the factfinder to conclude that the administrative and judicial processes have been abused. That may be a difficult line to discern and draw. But once it is drawn, the case is established that abuse of those processes produced an illegal result, viz., effectively barring respondents from access to the agencies and courts. Insofar as the administrative or judicial processes are involved, action of that kind cannot acquire immunity by seeking refuge under the umbrella of "political expression." . . .

A combination of entrepreneurs to harass and deter their competitors from having "free and unlimited access" to the agencies and courts, to defeat that right by massive, concerted, and purposeful activities of the group are ways of building up one empire and destroying another. As stated in the opinion concurring in the result, that is the essence of those parts of the complaint to which we refer. If these facts are proved, a violation of the antitrust laws has been established. If the end result is unlawful, it matters not that the means used in violation may be lawful.

What the proof will show is not known, for the District Court granted the motion to dismiss the complaint. We must, of course, take the allegations of the complaint at face value for the purposes of that motion. . . . On their face the above-quoted allegations come within the "sham" exception in the *Noerr* case, as adapted to the adjudicatory process.

Accordingly we affirm the Court of Appeals and remand the case for trial.[5]

271.   With respect to *California Motor*:

(a) In what respects, exactly, did defendants exceed the *Noerr* immunity? Were they condemned because of their subjective purpose? Their objective intention (that is, their behavior)? Was the plaintiff's injury primarily attributable to the government's regulatory decisions and procedures? Can you reconcile the result in *California Motor* with *Noerr*'s refusal to condemn action having adverse effects on political opponents (aside from the effects of the government action itself)?

(b) Suppose that a state or federal licensing agency grants licenses to new entrants into a certain industry without a hearing unless someone objects, the delay and cost of a hearing would itself discourage entry, and contested new licenses are denied unless the applicant shows that its entry is needed by consumers and would not unduly impair the economic health of existing licensees. Suppose further that existing licensees (including recent ones) believe that any new entry would unduly impair their economic health, organize an association to represent their views before the licensing agency, and always object to each new license application in the hope of preventing new competition. Suppose finally that the licensing agency usually rejects their claim but occasionally accepts it and accordingly rejects the new license application. Have existing licensees violated the Sherman Act? Would your answer differ if existing licensees had objected only to 90 percent rather than to all license applications? Is this case different from *California Motor*?

---

5. Stewart and Brennan, JJ., concurred in the result. Powell and Rehnquist, JJ., did not participate.

What will the *California Motor* plaintiff have to prove at trial in order to prevail?

(c) Under what circumstances would it be ethical for a lawyer to file or assist in actions under the circumstances described in *California Motor* or ¶b? What must be the chances of winning? How much investigation of the facts or claims of the client is necessary? Suppose the lawyer concludes that the chance of winning does not itself justify the cost of suing but that suit serves the client's anti-competitive interest in weakening or destroying a rival.[6]

PROFESSIONAL REAL ESTATE INVESTORS v. COLUMBIA PICTURES INDUSTRIES
508 U.S. 49 (1993)

Justice THOMAS. . . . This case requires us to define the "sham" exception to the doctrine of antitrust immunity first identified in *Noerr*, as that doctrine applies in the litigation context. Under the sham exception, activity "ostensibly directed toward influencing governmental action" does not quality for *Noerr* immunity if it "is a mere sham to cover . . . an attempt to interfere directly with the business relationships of a competitor." We hold that litigation cannot be deprived of immunity as a sham unless the litigation is objectively baseless. . . .

[Petitioners Professional Real Estate Investors (PRE) owned a resort hotel. PRE assembled a library of videodisc movies that it rented to guests for in-room viewing, and it sought to market video-disc players to other hotels for the same purpose. Respondents Columbia and other motion picture studios held copyrights to the movies and licensed a cable system operator to offer movies to hotel guests on a pay-per-view basis. Columbia sued PRE for copyright infringement. PRE counterclaimed, alleging that Columbia's copy-

---

6. Consider the following guidelines:

[A]n attorney [presenting a pleading] is certifying that to the best of the person's knowledge, information, and belief formed after an inquiry reasonable under the circumstances [that] it is not being presented or maintained for any improper purpose, such as to harass or to cause unnecessary delay or needless increase in the cost of litigation. [Federal Rules of Civil Procedure 11.]

A lawyer shall not bring or defend a proceeding, or assert or controvert an issue therein, unless there is a basis for doing so that is not frivolous, which includes a good faith argument for an extension, modification or reversal of existing law. [Model Rules of Professional Conduct 3.1.]

In his representation of a client, a lawyer shall not: (1) File a suit, assert a position, conduct a defense, delay a trial, or take other action on behalf of his client when he knows or it is obvious that such action would serve merely to harass or maliciously injure another. [Model Code of Professional Responsibility, DR 7-102(A)(1).]

right action was not legitimate litigation protected by *Noerr* but a mere sham designed to exclude a competitor. The district court ruled that PRE's videodisc rentals did not infringe Columbia's exclusive right to perform its copyrighted works publicly, and the Court of Appeals affirmed. On remand, the district court dismissed PRE's antitrust counterclaim, ruling that Columbia's original claim was "not a sham" and that "there was probable cause for bringing the action" to resolve the legal issue. The court denied PRE's request for further discovery on Columbia's intent in bringing the copyright action. The Court of Appeals affirmed, and the Supreme Court granted certiorari to address "inconsistent and contradictory" circuit court approaches to *Noerr*'s "sham" exception.]

II

PRE contends that "the Ninth Circuit erred in holding that an antitrust plaintiff must, as a threshold prerequisite ..., establish that a sham lawsuit is baseless as a matter of law." It invites us to adopt an approach under which either "indifference to ... outcome," or failure to prove that a petition for redress of grievances "would ... have been brought but for [a] predatory motive," would expose a defendant to antitrust liability under the sham exception. We decline PRE's invitation. ...

Noerr ... withheld immunity from "sham" activities because "application of the Sherman Act would be justified" when petitioning activity, "ostensibly directed toward influencing governmental action, is a mere sham to cover ... an attempt to interfere directly with the business relationships of a competitor." ... In *California Motor*, ... we held that the complaint showed a sham not entitled to immunity when it contained allegations that one group of highway carriers "sought to bar ... competitors from meaningful access to adjudicatory tribunals and so to usurp that decisionmaking process" by "institut[ing] ... proceedings and actions ... with or without probable cause, and regardless of the merits of the cases." We left unresolved the question presented by this case — whether litigation may be sham merely because a subjective expectation of success does not motivate the litigant. We now answer this question in the negative and hold that an objectively reasonable effort to litigate cannot be sham regardless of subjective intent.

Our original formulation of antitrust petitioning immunity required that unprotected activity lack objective reasonableness. *Noerr* rejected the contention that an attempt "to influence the passage and enforcement of laws" might lose immunity merely because the lobbyists' "sole purpose ... was to destroy [their] competitors." ... In short, "*Noerr* shields from the Sherman Act a concerted effort to influence public officials regardless of intent or purpose." *Pennington.*

Nothing in *California Motor* retreated from these principles.... Our recognition of a sham in that case signifies that the institution of legal proceedings "without probable cause" will give rise to a sham if such activity effectively "bar[s] ... competitors from meaningful access to adjudicatory tribunals and so ... usurp[s] th[e] decisionmaking process."

Since *California Motor,* we have consistently assumed that the sham exception contains an indispensable objective component. We have described a sham as "evidenced by repetitive lawsuits carrying the hallmark of insubstantial claims." *Otter Tail.* We regard as sham "private action that is not genuinely aimed at procuring favorable government action," as opposed to "a valid effort to influence government action." *Indian Head.* And we have explicitly observed that a successful "effort to influence governmental action ... certainly cannot be characterized as a sham." ... Whether applying *Noerr* as an antitrust doctrine or invoking it in other contexts, we have repeatedly reaffirmed that evidence of anticompetitive intent or purpose alone cannot transform otherwise legitimate activity into a sham. See, e.g., *SCTLA*; NAACP v. Claiborne Hardware Co., 458 U.S. 886, 913-914 (1982).... Our decisions therefore establish that the legality of objectively reasonable petitioning "directed toward obtaining governmental action" is "not at all affected by any anticompetitive purpose [the actor] may have had." *Noerr.*

Our most recent applications of *Noerr* immunity further demonstrate that neither *Noerr* immunity nor its sham exception turns on subjective intent alone. In *Indian Head* and *SCTLA*, we refused to let antitrust defendants immunize otherwise unlawful restraints of trade by pleading a subjective intent to seek favorable legislation or to influence governmental action.... In *Omni*, we similarly held that challenges to allegedly sham petitioning activity must be resolved according to objective criteria. We dispelled the notion that an antitrust plaintiff could prove a sham merely by showing that its competitor's "purposes were to delay [the plaintiff's] entry into the market and even to deny it a meaningful access to the appropriate ... administrative and legislative fora." We reasoned that such inimical intent "may render the manner of lobbying improper or even unlawful, but does not necessarily render it a 'sham.'" ...

In sum, fidelity to precedent compels us to reject a purely subjective definition of "sham." The sham exception so construed would undermine, if not vitiate, *Noerr.* And despite whatever "superficial certainty" it might provide, a subjective standard would utterly fail to supply "real 'intelligible guidance.'" *Indian Head.*

III

We now outline a two-part definition of "sham" litigation. First, the lawsuit must be objectively baseless in the sense that no reasonable litigant could realistically expect success on the merits. If an objective litigant could conclude that the suit is reasonably calculated to elicit a favorable outcome, the suit is immunized under *Noerr*, and an antitrust claim premised on the sham exception must fail.[5] Only if challenged litigation is objectively meritless may a court examine the litigant's subjective motivation. Under this second part of our definition of sham, the court should focus on whether the baseless lawsuit conceals "an attempt to interfere directly with the business relationships of a competitor," *Noerr*, through the "use [of] the governmental process as opposed to the outcome of that process as an anticompetitive weapon," *Omni*. This two-tiered process requires the plaintiff to disprove the challenged lawsuit's *legal* viability before the court will entertain evidence of the suit's *economic* viability. Of course, even a plaintiff who defeats the defendant's claim to *Noerr* immunity by demonstrating both the objective and the subjective components of a sham must still prove a substantive antitrust violation. Proof of a sham merely deprives the defendant of immunity; it does not relieve the plaintiff of the obligation to establish all other elements of his claim. . . .

IV

We conclude that the Court of Appeals properly affirmed summary judgment for Columbia on PRE's antitrust counterclaim. Under the objective prong of the sham exception, the Court of Appeals correctly held that sham litigation must constitute the pursuit of claims so baseless that no reasonable litigant could realistically expect to secure favorable relief.

The existence of probable cause to institute legal proceedings precludes a finding that an antitrust defendant has engaged in sham litigation. The notion of probable cause, as understood and applied in the common law tort of wrongful civil proceedings, requires the plaintiff to prove that the defendant lacked probable

---

5. A winning lawsuit is by definition a reasonable effort at petitioning for redress and therefore not a sham. On the other hand, when the antitrust defendant has lost the underlying litigation, a court must "resist the understandable temptation to engage in post hoc reasoning by concluding" that an ultimately unsuccessful "action must have been unreasonable or without foundation." . . . The court must remember that "[e]ven when the law or the facts appear questionable or unfavorable at the outset, a party may have an entirely reasonable ground for bringing suit." . . .

cause to institute an unsuccessful civil lawsuit and that the defendant pressed the action for an improper, malicious purpose.... Probable cause to institute civil proceedings requires no more than a "reasonabl[e] belie[f] that there is a chance that [a] claim may be held valid upon adjudication." ... Because the absence of probable cause is an essential element of the tort, the existence of probable cause is an absolute defense.... Just as evidence of anticompetitive intent cannot affect the objective prong of *Noerr*'s sham exception, a showing of malice alone will neither entitle the wrongful civil proceedings plaintiff to prevail nor permit the factfinder to infer the absence of probable cause. When a court has found that an antitrust defendant claiming *Noerr* immunity had probable cause to sue, that finding compels the conclusion that a reasonable litigant in the defendant's position could realistically expect success on the merits of the challenged lawsuit. Under our decision today, therefore, a proper probable cause determination irrefutably demonstrates that an antitrust plaintiff has not proved the objective prong of the sham exception and that the defendant is accordingly entitled to *Noerr* immunity.

The District Court and the Court of Appeals correctly found that Columbia had probable cause to sue PRE for copyright infringement.... When the District Court entered summary judgment for PRE on Columbia's copyright claim in 1986, it was by no means clear whether PRE's videodisc rental activities intruded on Columbia's copyrights. At that time, the Third Circuit and a District Court within the Third Circuit had held that the rental of video cassettes for viewing in on-site, private screening rooms infringed on the copyright owner's right of public performance.... Although the District Court and the Ninth Circuit distinguished these decisions by reasoning that hotel rooms offered a degree of privacy more akin to the home than to a video rental store, copyright scholars criticized both the reasoning and the outcome of the Ninth Circuit's decision. The Seventh Circuit expressly "decline[d] to follow" the Ninth Circuit and adopted instead the Third Circuit's definition of a "public place." ... In light of the unsettled condition of the law, Columbia plainly had probable cause to sue.

Any reasonable copyright owner in Columbia's position could have believed that it had some chance of winning an infringement suit against PRE. Even though it did not survive PRE's motion for summary judgment, Columbia's copyright action was arguably "warranted by existing law" or at the very least was based on an objectively "good faith argument for the extension, modification, or reversal of existing law." Fed. Rule Civ. Proc. 11. By the time the Ninth Circuit had reviewed all claims in this litigation, it became apparent that Columbia might have won its copyright suit in either the Third or the Seventh Circuit. Even in the absence of supporting authority, Columbia would have been entitled to press a novel copyright claim as long as a similarly situated reasonable litigant could have perceived some likelihood of success. A court could reasonably conclude that Columbia's infringement action was an objectively plausible effort to enforce rights. Accordingly, we conclude that PRE failed to establish the objective prong of *Noerr*'s sham exception.

Finally, the Court of Appeals properly refused PRE's request for further discovery on the economic circumstances of the underlying copyright litigation. As we have held, PRE could not pierce Columbia's *Noerr* immunity without proof that Columbia's infringement action was objectively baseless or frivolous. Thus, the District Court had no occasion to inquire whether Columbia was indifferent to the outcome on the merits of the copyright suit, whether any damages for infringement would be too low to justify Columbia's investment in the suit, or whether Columbia had decided to sue primarily for the benefit of collateral injuries inflicted through the use of legal process.... Such matters concern Columbia's economic motivations in bringing suit, which were rendered irrelevant by the objective legal reasonableness of the litigation....

We affirm.

[Justice Souter, concurring, expressed a preference that the test be phrased in the Court's own terms, so that other courts would not misinterpret the test as incorporating every detail of the test of wrongful civil procedures or Rule 11. Justice Stevens, joined by Justice O'Connor, concurred in the judgment. They indicated that a lawsuit could be objectively unreasonable even if a "reasonable litigant could realistically expect success on the merits," because the success might be insignificant.]

272. (a) *Professional Real Estate* holds that a lawsuit must be objectively baseless for it to constitute sham litigation. What does this test require? Will any possibility of success, no matter how remote, suffice?

(b) What is the Court's basis for imposing this requirement? Does it adequately protect against anticompetitive uses of litigation?[7] If not, is there some other test that would be better? Why not adopt the alternative of inquiring into whether a suit would have been

7. For an empirical analysis of cases involving antitrust claims alleging sham litigation, see C. Klein, Predation in the Courts: Legal versus Economic Analysis in Sham Litigation Cases, 10 Intl. Rev. L. & Econ. 29 (1990).

brought but for the anticompetitive effects caused by the litigation process? Is this test objective? Workable?

(c) Why not simply eliminate the *Noerr* exception for sham litigation, leaving injured parties to pursue other remedies (such as sanctions under Rule 11)?

CITY OF COLUMBIA v.
OMNI OUTDOOR ADVERTISING
499 U.S. 365 (1991)

Justice SCALIA. [Petitioner Columbia Outdoor Advertising (COA), a billboard company, controlled 95 percent of the relevant market. COA's owners had close relations with the city's political leaders, occasionally donating funds or billboard space for their political campaigns. In 1981, respondent Omni Outdoor Advertising began erecting billboards in the area. COA met with city officials, urging zoning restrictions on new billboards; concerned citizens urged similar action in editorials in local newspapers. After a series of public hearings and meetings, city officials enacted zoning ordinances limiting billboard construction. Omni filed suit against COA, alleging violations of Sherman Act §§1 and 2 and state claims. Omni alleged an anticompetitive conspiracy between city officials and COA that stripped them of any antitrust immunity. The jury found for Omni, awarding damages of $1 million (before trebling); the jury also answered special interrogatories, finding that the city and COA conspired to restrain trade and to monopolize the billboard market. The district court granted COA judgment notwithstanding the verdict, and the Court of Appeals reversed, reinstating the verdict.]

II

In the landmark case of *Parker v. Brown*, we rejected the contention that a program restricting the marketing of privately produced raisins, adopted pursuant to California's Agricultural Prorate Act, violated the Sherman Act. Relying on principles of federalism and state sovereignty, we held that the Sherman Act did not apply to anticompetitive restraints imposed by the States "as an act of government."

Since *Parker* emphasized the role of sovereign *States* in a federal system, it was initially unclear whether the governmental actions of political subdivisions enjoyed similar protection. In recent years, we have held that *Parker* immunity does not apply directly to local governments.... We have recognized, however, that a municipality's restriction of competition may sometimes be an authorized implementation of state policy, and have accorded *Parker* immunity where that is the case.

The South Carolina statutes under which the city acted in the present case authorize municipalities to regulate the use of land and the construction of buildings and other structures within their boundaries. It is undisputed that, as a matter of state law, these statutes authorize the city to regulate the size, location, and spacing of billboards. It could be argued, however, that a municipality acts beyond its delegated authority, for *Parker* purposes, whenever the nature of its regulation is substantively or even procedurally defective. On such an analysis it could be contended, for example, that the city's regulation in the present case was not "authorized" by S.C. Code §5-23-10 (1976), if it was not, as that statute requires, adopted "for the purpose of promoting health, safety, morals or the general welfare of the community." As scholarly commentary has noted, such an expansive interpretation of the *Parker*-defense authorization requirement would have unacceptable consequences. . . .

We agree with that assessment, and believe that in order to prevent *Parker* from undermining the very interests of federalism it is designed to protect, it is necessary to adopt a concept of authority broader than what is applied to determine the legality of the municipality's action under state law. . . . It suffices for the present to conclude that here no more is needed to establish, for *Parker* purposes, the city's authority to regulate than its unquestioned zoning power over the size, location, and spacing of billboards.

Besides authority to regulate, however, the *Parker* defense also requires authority to suppress competition — more specifically, "clear articulation of a state policy to authorize anticompetitive conduct" by the municipality in connection with its regulation. *Hallie*, 471 U.S., at 40 (internal quotation omitted). We have rejected the contention that this requirement can be met only if the delegating statute explicitly permits the displacement of competition, see id., at 41-42. It is enough, we have held, if suppression of competition is the "foreseeable result" of what the statute authorizes, id., at 42. That condition is amply met here. The very purpose of zoning regulation is to displace unfettered business freedom in a manner that regularly has the effect of preventing normal acts of competition, particularly on the part of new entrants. A municipal ordinance restricting the size, location, and spacing of billboards (surely a common form of zoning) necessarily protects existing billboards against some competition from newcomers.

The Court of Appeals was therefore correct in its conclusion that the city's restriction of billboard construction was prima facie entitled to *Parker* immunity. The Court of Appeals upheld the jury verdict, however, by invoking a "conspiracy" exception to *Parker* that has been recognized by several Courts of Appeals. That exception is thought to be supported by two of our statements in *Parker*: "[W]e have no question of the state or its municipality becoming a *participant in a private agreement* or combination by others for restraint of trade.... The state in adopting and enforcing the prorate program made no contract or agreement *and entered into no conspiracy in restraint of trade or to establish monopoly* but, as sovereign, imposed the restraint as an act of government which the Sherman Act did not undertake to prohibit." *Parker* does not apply, according to the Fourth Circuit, "where politicians or political entities are involved as conspirators" with private actors in the restraint of trade.

There is no such conspiracy exception. The rationale of *Parker* was that, in light of our national commitment to federalism, the general language of the Sherman Act should not be interpreted to prohibit anticompetitive actions by the States in their governmental capacities as sovereign regulators. The sentences from the opinion quoted above simply clarify that this immunity does not necessarily obtain where the State acts not in a regulatory capacity but as a commercial participant in a given market.... These sentences should not be read to suggest the general proposition that even governmental *regulatory* action may be deemed private — and therefore subject to antitrust liability — when it is taken pursuant to a conspiracy with private parties. The impracticality of such a principle is evident if, for purposes of the exception, "conspiracy" means nothing more than an agreement to impose the regulation in question. Since it is both inevitable and desirable that public officials often agree to do what one or another group of private citizens urges upon them, such an exception would virtually swallow up the *Parker* rule: All anticompetitive regulation would be vulnerable to a "conspiracy" charge....[5]

5. The dissent is confident that a jury composed of citizens of the vicinage will be able to tell the difference between "independent municipal action and action taken for the sole purpose of carrying out an anticompetitive agreement for the private party." No doubt. But those are merely the polar extremes, which like the geographic poles will rarely be seen by jurors of the vicinage. Ordinarily the allegation will merely be (and the dissent says this is enough) that the municipal action was not prompted "*exclusively* by a concern for the general public interest." Thus, the real question is whether a jury can tell the difference — whether *Solomon* can tell the difference — between municipal-action-not-entirely-independent-because-based-partly-on-agreement-with-private-parties that is *lawful* and municipal-action-not-entirely-independent-because-based-partly-on-agreement-with-private-parties that is *unlawful*. The dissent does not tell us how to put this question coherently, much less how to answer it intelligently. "*Independent* municipal action" is unobjectionable, "action taken for the *sole* purpose of carrying out an anticompetitive agreement for the private party" is unlawful, and everything else (this is, the known world between the two poles) is unaddressed....

Omni suggests, however, that "conspiracy" might be limited to instances of governmental "corruption," defined variously as "abandonment of public responsibilities to private interests," "corrupt or bad faith decisions," and "selfish or corrupt motives." Ultimately, Omni asks us not to define "corruption" at all, but simply to leave that task to the jury: "at bottom, however, it was within the jury's province to determine what constituted corruption of the governmental process in their community." Omni's amicus eschews this emphasis on "corruption," instead urging us to define the conspiracy exception as encompassing any governmental act "not in the public interest."

A conspiracy exception narrowed along such vague lines is similarly impractical. Few governmental actions are immune from the charge that they are "not in the public interest" or in some sense "corrupt." The California marketing scheme at issue in *Parker* itself, for example, can readily be viewed as the result of a "conspiracy" to put the "private" interest of the State's raisin growers above the "public" interest of the State's consumers. The fact is that virtually all regulation benefits some segments of the society and harms others; and that it is not universally considered contrary to the public good if the net economic loss to the losers exceeds the net economic gain to the winners. *Parker* was not written in ignorance of the reality that determination of "the public interest" in the manifold areas of government regulation entails not merely economic and mathematical analysis but value judgment, and it was not meant to shift that judgment from elected officials to judges and juries. If the city of Columbia's decision to regulate what one local newspaper called "billboard jungles" is made subject to ex post facto judicial assessment of "the public interest," with personal liability of city officials a possible consequence, we will have gone far to "compromise the States' ability to regulate their domestic commerce," Southern Motor Carriers Rate Conference, Inc. v. United States, 471 U.S. 48, 56 (1985). This situation would not be better, but arguably even worse, if the courts were to apply a subjective test: not whether the action was in the public interest, but whether the officials involved thought it to be so. This would require the sort of deconstruction of the governmental process and probing of the official "intent" that we have consistently sought to avoid. . . .

The foregoing approach to establishing a "conspiracy" exception at least seeks (however impractically) to draw the line of impermissible action in a manner relevant to the purpose of the Sherman Act and of *Parker*: prohibiting the restriction of competition for private gain but permitting the restriction of competition in the public interest. Another approach is possible, which has the virtue of practicality but the vice of being unrelated to those purposes. That is the approach which would consider *Parker* inapplicable only if, in connection with the governmental action in question, bribery or some other violation of state or federal law has been established. Such unlawful activity has no necessary relationship to whether the governmental action is in the public interest. A mayor is guilty of accepting a bribe even if he would and should have taken, in the public interest, the same action for which the bribe was paid. . . . To use unlawful political influence as the test of legality of state regulation undoubtedly vindicates (in a rather blunt way) principles of good government. But the statute we are construing is not directed to that end. Congress has passed other laws aimed at combatting corruption in state and local governments. See, e.g., 18 U.S.C. 1951 (Hobbs Act). "Insofar as [the Sherman Act] sets up a code of ethics at all, it is a code that condemns trade restraints, not political activity." *Noerr.*

For these reasons, we reaffirm our rejection of any interpretation of the Sherman Act that would allow plaintiffs to look behind the actions of state sovereigns to base their claims on "perceived conspiracies to restrain trade," *Hoover.* We reiterate that, with the possible market participant exception, any action that qualifies as state action is "ipso facto . . . exempt from the operation of the antitrust laws," id. This does not mean, of course, that the States may exempt *private* action from the scope of the Sherman Act; we in no way qualify the well-established principle that "a state does not give immunity to those who violate the Sherman Act by authorizing them to violate it, or by declaring that their action is lawful." *Parker.* . . .

III

While *Parker* recognized the States' freedom to engage in anticompetitive regulation, it did not purport to immunize from antitrust liability the private parties who urge them to engage in anticompetitive regulation. However, it is obviously peculiar in a democracy, and perhaps in derogation of the constitutional right "to petition the Government for a redress of grievances," U.S. Const., Amdt. 1, to establish a category of lawful state action that citizens are not permitted to urge. Thus, beginning with *Noerr*, we have developed a corollary to *Parker*: the federal antitrust laws also do not regulate the conduct of private individuals in seeking anticompetitive action from the government. This doctrine, like *Parker*, rests ultimately upon a recognition that the antitrust laws, "tailored as they are for the business world, are not at all appropriate for application in the political arena." *Noerr.* That a private party's political motives are selfish is irrelevant: "*Noerr* shields from the Sherman Act a concerted effort to influence public officials regardless of intent or purpose." United Mine Workers of America v. Pennington, 381 U.S. 657, 670 (1965).

Noerr recognized, however, what has come to be known as the "sham" exception to its rule: . . . The Court of Appeals concluded that the jury in this case could have found that COA's activities on behalf of the restrictive billboard ordinances fell within this exception. In our view that was error.

The "sham" exception to *Noerr* encompasses situations in which persons use the governmental *process* — as opposed to the *outcome* of that process — as an anticompetitive weapon. A classic example is the filing of frivolous objections to the license application of a competitor, with no expectation of achieving denial of the license but simply in order to impose expense and delay. See *California Motor.* A "sham" situation involves a defendant whose activities are "not genuinely aimed at procuring favorable government action" at all, *Indian Head,* not one "who 'genuinely seeks to achieve his governmental result, but does so *through improper means.'* "

Neither of the Court of Appeals' theories for application of the "sham" exception to the facts of the present case is sound. The court reasoned, first, that the jury could have concluded that COA's interaction with city officials "was 'actually nothing more than an attempt to interfere directly with the business relations [*sic*] of a competitor.'" (quoting *Noerr*). This analysis relies upon language from *Noerr,* but ignores the import of the critical word "directly." Although COA indisputably set out to disrupt Omni's business relationships, it sought to do so not through the very process of lobbying, or of causing the city council to consider zoning measures, but rather through the ultimate *product* of that lobbying and consideration, viz., the zoning ordinances. The Court of Appeals' second theory was that the jury could have found "that COA's purposes were to delay Omni's entry into the market and even to deny it a meaningful access to the appropriate city administrative and legislative fora." But the purpose of delaying a competitor's entry into the market does not render lobbying activity a "sham," unless (as no evidence suggested was true here) the delay is sought to be achieved only by the lobbying process itself, and not by the governmental action that the lobbying seeks. . . . Any lobbyist or applicant, in addition to getting himself heard, seeks by procedural and other means to get his opponent ignored. Policing the legitimate boundaries of such defensive strategies, when they are conducted in the context of a genuine attempt to influence governmental action, is not the role of the Sherman Act. In the present case, of course, any denial to Omni of "meaningful access to the appropriate city administrative and legislative fora" was achieved by COA in the course of an attempt to influence governmental action that, far from being a "sham," was if anything more in earnest than it should have been. If the denial was wrongful there may be other remedies, but as for the Sherman Act, the *Noerr* exemption applies.

Omni urges that if, as we have concluded, the "sham" exception is inapplicable, we should use this case to recognize another exception to *Noerr* immunity — a "conspiracy" exception, which would apply when government officials conspire with a private party to employ government action as a means of stifling competition. We have left open the possibility of such an exception, see, e.g., *Indian Head*. . . .

Giving full consideration to this matter for the first time, we conclude that a "conspiracy" exception to *Noerr* must be rejected. We need not describe our reasons at length, since they are largely the same as those set forth in Part II above for rejecting a "conspiracy" exception to *Parker*. As we have described, *Parker* and *Noerr* are complementary expressions of the principle that the antitrust laws regulate business, not politics; the former decision protects the States' acts of governing, and the latter the citizens' participation in government. Insofar as the identification of an immunity-destroying "conspiracy" is concerned, *Parker* and *Noerr* generally present two faces of the same coin. The *Noerr*-invalidating conspiracy alleged here is just the *Parker*-invalidating conspiracy viewed from the standpoint of the private-sector participants rather than the governmental participants. The same factors which, as we have described above, make it impracticable or beyond the purpose of the antitrust laws to identify and invalidate lawmaking that has been infected by selfishly motivated agreement with private interests likewise make it impracticable or beyond that scope to identify and invalidate lobbying that has produced selfishly motivated agreement with public officials. "It would be unlikely that effort to influence legislative action could succeed unless one or more members of the legislative body became . . . 'coconspirators'" in *some* sense with the private party urging such action, Metro Cable Co. v. CATV of Rockford, Inc., 516 F.2d 220, 230 (CA7 1975). And if the invalidating "conspiracy" is limited to one that involves some element of unlawfulness (beyond mere anticompetitive motivation), the invalidation would have nothing to do with the policies of the antitrust laws. In *Noerr* itself, where the private party "deliberately deceived the public and public officials" in its successful lobbying campaign, we said that "deception, reprehensible as it is, can be of no consequence so far as the Sherman Act is concerned."

[Justices Stevens, White, and Marshall dissented. The dissent emphasized the jury's finding that the city officials entered an agreement, motivated in part by favors and friendship, and not exclusively by a concern for the public interest. The majority's opinion was seen to rest on a distrust for the judicial system, conceding that anticompetitive results of this and similar agreements will accordingly be tolerated. Much of the dissent addressed the portion of the Court's opinion indicating that the state, in authorizing local regulation of billboards, had articulated a policy that competition may be displaced. The dissent, referring to *Lafayette, Boulder,* and other decisions on the immunity of municipalities (see ¶165d), argued that statutes adopted to promote health and safety do not authorize municipalities to act for the purpose of protecting favored citizens from competition. Although applying this distinction requires scrutiny of city officials' motivation, "the problems inherent in determining whether the actions of municipal officials are the product of an illegal agreement are substantially the same as those arising in cases in which the actions of business executives are subjected to antitrust scrutiny." Finally, the dissent concluded that, although the sham exception was inapplicable, the conspiracy found by the jury removed *Noerr* immunity.]

273. (a) Why does *OMNI* hold that there is no conspiracy exception to *Noerr* immunity? If there were an exception, what would the jury have to conclude to find a conspiracy?

(b) As discussed in the opinion (and in ¶165d), anticompetitive municipal action must be authorized by the state. What is the difference between the majority's and dissent's view with regard to the authorization requirement in this context? Can one be sure that the municipality's action is authorized without reviewing the motives for the action or whether the action serves the public interest?

ALLIED TUBE & CONDUIT CORP. v. INDIAN HEAD
486 U.S. 492 (1988)

Justice BRENNAN.... Petitioner contends that its efforts to affect the product standard-setting process of a private association are immune from antitrust liability under the *Noerr* doctrine primarily because the association's standards are widely adopted into law by state and local governments. The United States Court of Appeals for the Second Circuit held that *Noerr* immunity did not apply. We affirm.

[The National Fire Protection Association is a private, voluntary organization with members representing industry, labor, academia, insurers, health care professionals, firefighters, and government. The organization publishes standards to ensure that products do not present a fire hazard. One set of standards is the National Electric Code, which is extremely influential and often routinely adopted without significant change into law by states and localities. In addition, many private certification laboratories, insurers, inspectors, contractors, and distributors will not certify, insure, approve, use, or sell products outside the Code.

Respondent made "polyvinyl chloride conduits," a hollow tubing which carries electrical wires through buildings. Respondent's tubing was approved by an Association professional panel as an alternative to traditional steel conduit. Steel interests combined to defeat respondent's proposal to include its tubing as an approved electrical conduit at the Association's general meeting. Steel interests recruited 230 persons solely to vote against respondent's proposal, paid over $100,000 for these persons' expenses in attending the meeting, and used hand signals and walkie-talkies to instruct them how to vote. Few of these voters had the technical information to follow the meeting, and none of them spoke. The proposal was rejected by a vote of 394 to 390. Respondent appealed the decision to the board of directors, which affirmed the vote on the grounds that the steel interests had circumvented, but not violated, the rules of the Association.

Respondent filed suit in federal district court, alleging an unreasonable restraint of trade in violation of §1 of the Sherman Act. Instructed under the rule of reason, the jury found by special interrogatory that the steel interests had not violated the Association's rules, but did "subvert" the process, and that petitioner's actions had an adverse effect on competition and were not the least restrictive means of opposing the new conduit. The jury awarded respondent damages of $3.8 million (before trebling) for profits lost due to the effect of excluding their conduit due to the Code's force in the marketplace; no damages were awarded for injuries stemming from government entities' adoption of the Code. The district court granted petitioner judgment notwithstanding the verdict, reasoning that *Noerr* immunity applied because the standard-setting process was "akin to a legislature" and because the efforts were designed to influence the state and local bodies that adopt the Code. The Court of Appeals reversed.]

II

Concerted efforts to restrain or monopolize trade by petitioning government officials are protected from antitrust liability under the doctrine established by *Noerr*; Mine Workers v. Pennington, 381 U.S. 657, 669-672 (1965); and *California Motor.* The scope of this protection depends, however, on the source, context, and nature of the anticompetitive restraint at issue. "[W]here a restraint upon trade or monopolization is the result of valid governmental action, as opposed to private action," those urging the governmental action enjoy absolute immunity from antitrust liability for the anticompetitive restraint. *Noerr*; see also *Pennington*. In addition, where, independent of any government action, the anticompetitive restraint results directly from private action, the restraint cannot form the basis for antitrust liability if it is "incidental" to a valid effort to influence governmental action. *Noerr*. The validity of such efforts, and thus the applicability of *Noerr* immunity, varies with the context and nature of the activity. A publicity campaign directed at the general public, seeking legislation or executive action, enjoys antitrust immunity even when the campaign employs unethical and deceptive methods. *Noerr*. But in less political arenas, unethical and deceptive practices can constitute abuses of administrative or judicial processes that may result in antitrust violations. *California Motor*.

In this case, the restraint of trade on which liability was predicated was the Association's exclusion of respondent's product from the Code, and no damages were imposed for the incorporation of that Code by any government. The relevant context is thus the standard-setting process of a private association. Typically, private standard-setting associations, like the Association in this case, include members having horizontal and vertical business relations. See generally 7 P. Areeda, Antitrust Law ¶1477, p. 343 (1986) (trade and standard-setting associations routinely treated as continuing conspiracies of their members). There is no doubt that the members of such associations often have economic incentives to restrain competition and that the product standards set by such associations have a serious potential for anticompetitive harm. See American Society of Mechanical Engineers v. Hydrolevel Corp., 456 U.S. 556, 571 (1982). Agreement on a product standard is, after all, implicitly an agreement not to manufacture, distribute, or purchase certain types of products. Accordingly, private standard-setting associations have traditionally been objects of antitrust scrutiny. See, e.g., ibid.; Radiant Burners v. Peoples Gas Light & Coke Co., 364 U.S. 656 (1961). See also *Indiana Dentists*. When, however, private associations promulgate safety standards based on the merits of objective expert judgments and through procedures that prevent the standard-setting process from being biased by members with economic interests in stifling product competition, compare *Hydrolevel* (noting absence of "meaningful safeguards"), those private standards can have significant procompetitive advantages. It is this potential for procompetitive benefits that has led most lower courts to apply rule of reason analysis to product standard-setting by private associations.[6]

Given this context, petitioner does not enjoy the immunity accorded those who merely urge the government to restrain trade. We agree with the Court of Appeals that the Association cannot be treated as a "quasi-legislative" body simply because legislatures routinely adopt the Code the Association publishes. Whatever de facto authority the Association enjoys, no official authority has been conferred on it by any government, and the decisionmaking body of the Association is composed, at least in part, of persons with economic incentives to restrain trade. . . . "We may presume, absent a showing to the contrary, that [a government] acts in the public interest. A private party, on the other hand, may be presumed to be acting primarily on his or its own behalf." Hallie v. Eau Claire, 471 U.S. 34, 45 (1985). The dividing line between restraints resulting from governmental action and those resulting from private action may not always be obvious. But where, as here, the restraint is imposed by persons unaccountable to the public and without official authority, many of whom have personal financial interests in restraining competition, we have no difficulty concluding that the restraint has resulted from private action.

Noerr immunity might still apply, however, if, as petitioner argues, the exclusion of polyvinyl chloride conduit from the Code, and the effect that exclusion had of its own force in the marketplace, were incidental to a valid effort to influence governmental action. Petitioner notes that the lion's share of the anticompetitive effect in this case came from the predictable adoption of the Code into law by a large number of state and local governments. Indeed, petitioner argues that, because state and local governments rely so heavily on the Code and lack the resources or technical expertise to second-guess it, efforts to influence the Association's standard-setting process are the most effective means of influencing legislation regulating electrical conduit. This claim to *Noerr* immunity has some force. The effort to influence governmental action in this case certainly cannot be characterized as a sham given the actual adoption of the 1981 Code into a number of statutes and local ordinances. Nor can we quarrel with petitioner's contention that, given the widespread adoption of the Code into law, any effect the 1981 Code had in the marketplace of its own force was, in the main, incidental to petitioner's genuine effort to influence governmental action. And, as petitioner persuasively argues, the claim of *Noerr*

6. . . . Concerted efforts to *enforce* (rather than just agree upon) private product standards face more rigorous antitrust scrutiny. See *Radiant Burners*. See also *FOGA*.

immunity cannot be dismissed on the ground that the conduct at issue involved no "direct" petitioning of government officials, for *Noerr* itself immunized a form of "indirect" petitioning. . . .

Nonetheless, the validity of petitioner's actions remains an issue. We cannot agree with petitioner's absolutist position that the *Noerr* doctrine immunizes every concerted effort that is genuinely intended to influence governmental action. If all such conduct were immunized then, for example, competitors would be free to enter into horizontal price agreements as long as they wished to propose that price as an appropriate level for governmental ratemaking or price supports. But see Georgia v. Pennsylvania R. Co., 324 U.S. 439, 456-463 (1945). Horizontal conspiracies or boycotts designed to exact higher prices or other economic advantages from the government would be immunized on the ground that they are genuinely intended to influence the government to agree to the conspirators' terms. But see Georgia v. Evans, 316 U.S. 159 (1942). Firms could claim immunity for boycotts or horizontal output restrictions on the ground that they are intended to dramatize the plight of their industry and spur legislative action. Immunity might even be claimed for anticompetitive mergers on the theory that they give the merging corporations added political clout. Nor is it necessarily dispositive that packing the Association's meeting may have been the most effective means of securing government action, for one could imagine situations where the most effective means of influencing government officials is bribery, and we have never suggested that that kind of attempt to influence the government merits protection. We thus conclude that the *Noerr* immunity of anticompetitive activity intended to influence the government depends not only on its impact, but also on the context and nature of the activity.

Here petitioner's actions took place within the context of the standard-setting process of a private association. . . . That rounding up supporters is an acceptable and constitutionally protected method of influencing elections does not mean that rounding up economically interested persons to set private standards must also be protected. Nor do we agree with petitioner's contention that, regardless of the Association's nonlegislative status, the effort to influence the Code should receive the same wide latitude given ethically dubious efforts to influence legislative action in the political arena, see *Noerr*, simply because the ultimate aim of the effort to influence the private standard-setting process was (principally) legislative action. The ultimate aim is not dispositive. A misrepresentation to a court would not necessarily be entitled to the same antitrust immunity allowed deceptive practices in the political arena simply because the odds were very good that the court's decision would be codified — nor for that matter would misrepresentations made under oath at a legislative committee hearing in the hopes of spurring legislative action.

What distinguishes this case from *Noerr* and its progeny is that the context and nature of petitioner's activity make it the type of commercial activity that has traditionally had its validity determined by the antitrust laws themselves. True, in *Noerr* we immunized conduct that could be characterized as a conspiracy among railroads to destroy business relations between truckers and their customers. *Noerr*. But [*Noerr* involved] a classic "attempt ... to influence legislation by a campaign of publicity," an "inevitable" and "incidental" effect of which was "the infliction of some direct injury upon the interests of the party against whom the campaign is directed." The essential character of such a publicity campaign was, we concluded, political, and could not be segregated from the activity's impact on business. . . .

Here the context and nature of the activity do not counsel against inquiry into its validity. Unlike the publicity campaign in *Noerr*, the activity at issue here did not take place in the open political arena, where partisanship is the hallmark of decisionmaking, but within the confines of a private standard-setting process. The validity of conduct within that process has long been defined and circumscribed by the antitrust laws without regard to whether the private standards are likely to be adopted into law. Indeed, because private standard-setting by associations comprising firms with horizontal and vertical business relations is permitted at all under the antitrust laws only on the understanding that it will be conducted in a nonpartisan manner offering procompetitive benefits, the standards of conduct in this context are, at least in some respects, more rigorous than the standards of conduct prevailing in the partisan political arena or in the adversarial process of adjudication. The activity at issue here thus cannot, as in *Noerr*, be characterized as an activity that has traditionally been regulated with extreme caution, or as an activity that "bear[s] little if any resemblance to the combinations normally held violative of the Sherman Act." And petitioner did not confine itself to efforts to persuade an independent decisionmaker . . . ; rather, it organized and orchestrated the actual exercise of the Association's decisionmaking authority in setting a standard. Nor can the setting of the Association's Code be characterized as merely an exercise of the power of persuasion, for it in part involves the exercise of market power. The Association's members, after all, include consumers, distributors, and manufacturers of electrical conduit, and any agreement to exclude polyvinyl chloride conduit from the Code is in part an implicit agreement not to trade in that type of electrical conduit. Compare *Noerr*. Although one could reason backwards from the legislative impact of the Code to the conclusion that the conduct at issue here is "political," we think that, given the context and nature of the conduct, it can more aptly be characterized as commercial activity with a political impact. Just as the antitrust laws should not regulate political activities "simply because those activities have a commercial impact," *Noerr*, so the antitrust laws should not necessarily immunize what are in essence commercial activities simply because they have a political impact.[10] . . .

Thus in this case the context and nature of petitioner's efforts to influence the Code persuade us that the validity of those efforts must, despite their political impact, be evaluated under the standards of conduct set forth by the antitrust laws that govern the private standard-setting process. The antitrust validity of these efforts is not established, without more, by petitioner's literal compliance with the rules of the Association, for the hope of procompetitive benefits depends upon the existence of safeguards sufficient to prevent the standard-setting process from being biased by members with economic interests in restraining competition. An association cannot validate the anticompetitive activities of its members simply by adopting rules that fail to provide such safeguards. The issue of immunity in this case thus collapses into the issue of antitrust liability. Although we do not here set forth the rules of antitrust liability governing the private standard-setting process, we hold that at least where, as here, an economically interested party exercises decisionmaking authority in formulating a product standard for a private association that comprises market participants, that party enjoys no *Noerr* immunity from any antitrust liability flowing from the effect the standard has of its own force in the marketplace.

10. It is admittedly difficult to draw the precise lines separating anticompetitive political activity that is immunized despite its commercial impact from anticompetitive commercial activity that is unprotected despite its political impact, and this is itself a case close to the line. For that reason we caution that our decision today depends on the context and nature of the activity. Although criticizing the uncertainty of such a particularized inquiry, the dissent does not dispute that the types of activity we describe could not be immune under *Noerr* and fails to offer an intelligible alternative for distinguishing those non-immune activities from the activity at issue in this case. Rather, the dissent states without elaboration that the sham exception "is enough to guard against flagrant abuse." . . . Such a use of the word "sham" distorts its meaning and bears little relation to the sham exception *Noerr* described to cover activity that was not genuinely intended to influence governmental action. More importantly, [this] approach renders "sham" no more than a label courts could apply to activity they deem unworthy of antitrust immunity (probably based on unarticulated consideration of the nature and context of the activity), thus providing a certain superficial certainty but no real "intelligible guidance" to courts or litigants. . . .

This conclusion does not deprive state and local governments of input and information from interested individuals or organizations or leave petitioner without ample means to petition those governments. Cf. *Noerr.* See also *California Motor.* Petitioner, and others concerned about the safety or competitive threat of polyvinyl chloride conduit, can, with full antitrust immunity, engage in concerted efforts to influence those governments through direct lobbying, publicity campaigns, and other traditional avenues of political expression. To the extent state and local governments are more difficult to persuade through these other avenues, that no doubt reflects their preference for and confidence in the nonpartisan consensus process that petitioner has undermined. Petitioner remains free to take advantage of the forum provided by the standard-setting process by presenting and vigorously arguing accurate scientific evidence before a nonpartisan private standard-setting body. And petitioner can avoid the strictures of the private standard-setting process by attempting to influence legislatures through other forums. What petitioner may not do (without exposing itself to possible antitrust liability for direct injuries) is bias the process by, as in this case, stacking the private standard-setting body with decisionmakers sharing their economic interest in restraining competition.

The judgment of the Court of Appeals is affirmed.

[Justices White and O'Connor dissented. They feared that subjecting private standard-setting organizations to undue antitrust scrutiny would deter participation and the exchange of information allowing such entities to perform their important public functions. Like the majority, they would grant *Noerr* protection to petitioning of private bodies as a means of influencing governments. However, the dissenters objected that the majority's repeated vague references to the "context and nature" of the activity provided no workable boundary to that protection. Nevertheless, the dissenters would also remove *Noerr* protection when the defendants' activities exceeded the bounds of propriety. They put such an excess in the "sham" category that loses *Noerr* immunity.]

274. (a) Why did the Court find *Noerr* inapplicable in *Indian Head*? What if an industry packs a legislative hearing? What if an industry secretly arranges for (and pays) a group of respected, independent experts to testify before a legislative committee? How, if at all, is *Indian Head* different?

(b) The Court states that "[t]he issue of immunity in this case thus collapses into the issue of antitrust liability." What, then, is the legal test for standard-setting organizations? Does there remain any independent *Noerr* immunity?

(c) What relief? Can a court amend the National Electrical Code? A local building code? May a victim recover profits lost due to government actions?

275. *Missouri v. National Organization for Women,* 620 F.2d 1301 (8th Cir.), cert. denied, 449 U.S. 842 (1980). The National Organization for Women (NOW) organized a convention boycott against states that had not ratified the Equal Rights Amendment (ERA). In addition to the symbolic effect of the boycott, NOW intended the resulting adverse economic impact on local industry in the belief that injured persons might influence their legislators to support the ERA. The district court found that the boycott was "'non-economic' as it was not undertaken to advance the economic self-interest of the participants." The Court of Appeals affirmed the district court's conclusion that *Noerr* immunized the boycott from antitrust challenge: "[U]sing a boycott in a non-competitive political arena for the purpose of influencing legislation is not proscribed by the Sherman Act."[8]

(a) In what ways does *NOW* differ from *Noerr*?

(b) If the majority is correct that political motivation of the sort present in *NOW* immunizes otherwise illegal conduct, could NOW members have assaulted or threatened legislators or citizens of Missouri?

(c) Suppose that NOW only intended the boycott to have a symbolic, educational impact and that any adverse economic impacts were viewed by NOW as unhelpful or counterproductive to their cause, but unavoidable. Would this be an easier case for *Noerr* immunity?

(d) Suppose that Missouri had rejected the ERA, the state constitution prohibited reconsideration for 10 years, and a NOW boycott was intended solely to "punish" Missouri. An antitrust violation?

(e) Consider the dissent's suggestion that NOW and other organizations could "individually resolv[e] to boycott states that have not passed the ERA and then publiciz[e] their resolution." Would this permission be exceeded if supporters or individual members made statements to the effect that "No real supporter of equality can in good conscience hold a convention in such a state"? If other organizations or individuals not yet boycotting such states responded by saying "Right on!"? How does this scenario differ from that in *NOW*?

---

8. A dissenting judge believed that *Noerr* was inapplicable to an economic boycott that directly restrained trade. In addition, due to the presumption against implied exclusions to the antitrust laws, it was necessary for the court to decide whether the boycott was protected under the First Amendment.

(f) Is the court required to decide the First Amendment issue as the dissent suggested (see note 8)? Did the Supreme Court in *Noerr*?[9]

(g) If the dissent is correct, would all the well-known political boycotts throughout U.S. history have been illegal if challenged under the antitrust laws?[10] Consider past boycotts against some companies with ties to South Africa. Is concerted activity through the marketplace an important or necessary channel of political expression in some contexts?

FEDERAL TRADE COMMISSION v. SUPERIOR COURT TRIAL LAWYERS ASSOCIATION
493 U.S. 411 (1990)

Justice STEVENS. . . . Pursuant to a well-publicized plan, a group of lawyers agreed not to represent indigent criminal defendants in the District of Columbia Superior Court until the District of Columbia government increased the lawyers' compensation. The questions presented are whether the lawyers' concerted conduct violated §5 of the Federal Trade Commission Act and if so, whether it was nevertheless protected by the First Amendment to the Constitution.

[In the District of Columbia, 85 percent of indigent criminal defendants are represented by private attorneys appointed through the Criminal Justice Act (CJA). (The full-time Public Defender System represents defendants in the most serious cases.) After 1970, payment to CJA lawyers was capped by statute at $30 per hour for court time and $20 per hour for out-of-court time. Most appointments went to the approximately 100 lawyers known as "CJA regu-

9. Reconsider these questions after reading *SCTLA*.

10. Adolph Coors v. Wallace, 1984 Trade Cas. ¶65931 (N.D. Cal.) (defendants labor and consumer groups persuaded a local public broadcasting station to cancel its Coors Day; seeking public support for a boycott among its members and others in the community is constitutionally privileged by the First Amendment and plaintiff's damage is speculative and not the type of loss that the prohibition of group boycotts was intended to protect; also, labor union exemption); Allied Intl. v. International Longshoremen's Assn., 640 F.2d 1368 (1st Cir. 1981) (union boycotted goods from or to Soviet Union; no labor exemption because political dispute with Soviet Union does not relate to a legitimate union interest; antitrust claim dismissed because defendant has no economic or commercial objective and is not seeking to drive the plaintiff from business; but boycott did violate National Labor Relations Act prohibition of secondary boycotts), aff'd, 456 U.S. 212 (1982) (only NLRA question addressed), cert. denied, 458 U.S. 1120 (1982); Barr v. National Right to Life Comm., 1981 Trade Cas. ¶64315 (M.D. Fla.) (plaintiff denied staff privileges at three area hospitals following active pressure by anti-abortion groups; these noncommercial activities lie outside the Sherman Act: no anticompetitive purpose and First Amendment protection).

lars." Concerned by the low fees, the Superior Court Trial Lawyers Association (SCTLA) and other bar groups lobbied the District unsuccessfully for an increase. Subsequently, SCTLA organized a boycott of CJA appointments among the CJA regulars with a goal of increasing pay to $55 per hour for court time and $45 for out-of-court time. The CJA regulars commenced the boycott on September 6, 1983, and simultaneously organized events to attract publicity and win public support. Within 10 days, the District's criminal justice system's key figures believed the boycott had put the system on the brink of collapse. The District promised an immediate increase to $35 an hour for all time, and promised eventually to increase pay to match the SCTLA's demands. This response ended the boycott. The FTC commenced enforcement proceedings to enjoin further work stoppages as unlawful restraints of trade.]

III

Reasonable lawyers may differ about the wisdom of this enforcement proceeding. The dissent from the decision to file the complaint so demonstrates. So, too, do the creative conclusions of the ALJ and the Court of Appeals. Respondents' boycott may well have served a cause that was worthwhile and unpopular. We may assume that the preboycott rates were unreasonably low, and that the increase has produced better legal representation for indigent defendants. Moreover, given that neither indigent criminal defendants nor the lawyers who represent them command any special appeal with the electorate, we may also assume that without the boycott there would have been no increase in District CJA fees at least until the Congress amended the federal statute. These assumptions do not control the case for it is not our task to pass upon the social utility or political wisdom of price-fixing agreements.

As the ALJ, the FTC, and the Court of Appeals all agreed, respondents' boycott "constituted a classic restraint of trade within the meaning of Section 1 of the Sherman Act." As such, it also violated the prohibition against unfair methods of competition in §5 of the FTC Act. See *Cement Institute.* Prior to the boycott CJA lawyers were in competition with one another, each deciding independently whether and how often to offer to provide services to the District at CJA rates.[9]

9. The FTC found:

[T]he city's purchase of CJA legal services for indigents is based on competition. The price offered by the city is based on competition because the city must attract a sufficient number of individual lawyers to meet its needs at that price. The city competes with other purchasers of legal services to obtain an adequate supply of lawyers, and the city's offering price is an element of that competition. Indeed, an

The agreement among the CJA lawyers was designed to obtain higher prices for their services and was implemented by a concerted refusal to serve an important customer in the market for legal services and, indeed, the only customer in the market for the particular services that CJA regulars offered. "This constriction of supply is the essence of 'price-fixing,' whether it be accomplished by agreeing upon a price, which will decrease the quantity demanded, or by agreeing upon an output, which will increase the price offered." The horizontal arrangement among these competitors was unquestionably a "naked restraint" on price and output. See *NCAA*.

It is of course true that the city purchases respondents' services because it has a constitutional duty to provide representation to indigent defendants. It is likewise true that the quality of representation may improve when rates are increased. Yet neither of these facts is an acceptable justification for an otherwise unlawful restraint of trade. As we have remarked before, the "Sherman Act reflects a legislative judgment that ultimately competition will produce not only lower prices, but also better goods and services." *Engineers*. This judgment "recognizes that all elements of a bargain — quality, service, safety, and durability — and not just the immediate cost, are favorably affected by the free opportunity to select among alternative offers." That is equally so when the quality of legal advocacy, rather than engineering design, is at issue.

The social justifications proffered for respondents' restraint of trade thus do not make it any less unlawful. The statutory policy underlying the Sherman Act "precludes inquiry into the question whether competition is good or bad." Respondents' argument, like that made by the petitioners in *Engineers*, ultimately asks us to find that their boycott is permissible because the price it seeks to set is reasonable. But it was settled shortly after the Sherman Act was passed that it "is no excuse that the prices fixed are themselves

---

acknowledgement of this element of competition is implicit in the respondents' argument that an increase in the CJA fee was "necessary to attract, and retain, competent lawyers." If the offering price had not attracted a sufficient supply of qualified lawyers willing to accept CJA assignments for the city to fulfill its constitutional obligation, then presumably the city would have increased its offering price or otherwise sought to make its offer more attractive. In fact, however, the city's offering price before the boycott apparently was sufficient to obtain the amount and quality of legal services that it needed.

The Court of Appeals agreed with this analysis [and added:]

Nor should any significance be assigned to the origin of the demand for CJA services; here the District may be compelled by the Sixth Amendment to purchase legal services; there it may be compelled by the voters to purchase street paving services. The reason for the government's demand for a service is simply irrelevant to the issue of whether the suppliers of it have restrained trade by collectively refusing to satisfy it except upon their own terms....

reasonable. See, e.g., *Trenton Potteries*; *Trans-Missouri*." Catalano v. Target Sales, 446 U.S. 643, 647 (1980). Respondents' agreement is not outside the coverage of the Sherman Act simply because its objective was the enactment of favorable legislation.

Our decision in *Noerr* in no way detracts from this conclusion. [In] the *Noerr* case the alleged restraint of trade was the intended *consequence* of public action; in this case the boycott was the *means* by which respondents sought to obtain favorable legislation. The restraint of trade that was implemented while the boycott lasted would have had precisely the same anticompetitive consequences during that period even if no legislation had been enacted. In *Noerr*, the desired legislation would have created the restraint on the truckers' competition; in this case the emergency legislative response to the boycott put an end to the restraint.

Indeed, respondents' theory of *Noerr* was largely disposed of by our opinion in *Indian Head*. We held that the *Noerr* doctrine does not extend to "every concerted effort that is genuinely intended to influence governmental action." We explained:

> If all such conduct was immunized then, for example, competitors would be free to enter into horizontal price agreements as long as they wished to propose that price as an appropriate level for governmental ratemaking or price supports.... Horizontal conspiracies or boycotts designed to exact higher prices or other economic advantages from the government would be immunized on the ground that they are genuinely intended to influence the government to agree to the conspirators' terms.... Firms could claim immunity for boycotts or horizontal output restrictions on the ground that they are intended to dramatize the plight of their industry and spur legislative action.

IV

The lawyers' association argues that if its conduct would otherwise be prohibited by the Sherman Act and the Federal Trade Act, it is nonetheless protected by the First Amendment rights recognized in *Claiborne Hardware*. That case arose after black citizens boycotted white merchants in Claiborne County, Miss. The white merchants sued under state law to recover losses from the boycott. We found that the "right of the States to regulate economic activity could not justify a complete prohibition against a nonviolent, politically motivated boycott designed to force governmental and economic change and to effectuate rights guaranteed by the Constitution itself." We accordingly held that "the nonviolent elements of petitioners' activities are entitled to the protection of the First Amendment."

The lawyers' association contends that because it, like the boycotters in *Claiborne Hardware*, sought to vindicate constitutional rights, it should enjoy a similar First Amendment protection. It is, of course, clear that the association's efforts to publicize the boycott, to explain the merits of its cause, and to lobby District officials to enact favorable legislation — like similar activities in *Claiborne Hardware* — were activities that were fully protected by the First Amendment. But nothing in the FTC's order would curtail such activities, and nothing in the FTC's reasoning condemned any of those activities.

The activity that the FTC order prohibits is a concerted refusal by CJA lawyers to accept any further assignments until they receive an increase in their compensation; the undenied objective of their boycott was an economic advantage for those who agreed to participate. It is true that the *Claiborne Hardware* case also involved a boycott. That boycott, however, differs in a decisive respect. Those who joined the *Claiborne Hardware* boycott sought no special advantage for themselves. They were black citizens in Port Gibson, Mississippi, who had been the victims of political, social, and economic discrimination for many years. They sought only the equal respect and equal treatment to which they were constitutionally entitled. They struggled "to change a social order that had consistently treated them as second class citizens." As we observed, the campaign was not intended "to destroy legitimate competition." Equality and freedom are preconditions of the free market, and not commodities to be haggled over within it.

The same cannot be said of attorney's fees. As we recently pointed out, our reasoning in *Claiborne Hardware* is not applicable to a boycott conducted by business competitors who "stand to profit financially from a lessening of competition in the boycotted market." *Indian Head*. No matter how altruistic the motives of respondents may have been, it is undisputed that their immediate objective was to increase the price that they would be paid for their services. Such an economic boycott is well within the category that was expressly distinguished in the *Claiborne Hardware* opinion itself.

Only after recognizing the well-settled validity of prohibitions against various economic boycotts did we conclude in *Claiborne Hardware* that "peaceful, political activity such as found in the [Mississippi] boycott" [is] entitled to constitutional protection. We reaffirmed the government's "power to regulate [such] economic activity." This conclusion applies with special force when a clear objective of the boycott is to economically advantage the participants.

V . . .

The Court of Appeals . . . crafted a new exception to the per se rule, and it is this exception which provoked the FTC's petition to this

Court. The Court of Appeals derived its exception from United States v. O'Brien, 391 U.S. 367 (1968). In that case O'Brien had burned his Selective Service registration certificate on the steps of the South Boston Courthouse. He did so before a sizable crowd and with the purpose of advocating his antiwar beliefs. We affirmed his conviction. We held that the governmental interest in regulating the "nonspeech element" of his conduct adequately justified the incidental restriction on First Amendment freedoms. Specifically, we concluded that the statute's incidental restriction on O'Brien's freedom of expression was no greater than necessary to further the Government's interest in requiring registrants to have valid certificates continually available.

However, the Court of Appeals held that, in light of *O'Brien*, the expressive component of respondents' boycott compelled courts to apply the antitrust laws "prudently and with sensitivity," with a "special solicitude for the First Amendment rights" of respondents. The Court of Appeals concluded that the governmental interest in prohibiting boycotts is not sufficient to justify a restriction on the communicative element of the boycott unless the FTC can prove, and not merely presume, that the boycotters have market power. Because the Court of Appeals imposed this special requirement upon the Government, it ruled that per se antitrust analysis was inapplicable to boycotts having an expressive component.

There are at least two critical flaws in the Court of Appeals' antitrust analysis: it exaggerates the significance of the expressive component in respondents' boycott and it denigrates the importance of the rule of law that respondents violated. Implicit in the conclusion of the Court of Appeals are unstated assumptions that most economic boycotts do not have an expressive component, and that the categorical prohibitions against price fixing and boycotts are merely rules of "administrative convenience" that do not serve any substantial governmental interest unless the price-fixing competitors actually possess market power.

It would not much matter to the outcome of this case if these flawed assumptions were sound. *O'Brien* would offer respondents no protection even if their boycott were uniquely expressive and even if the purpose of the per se rules were purely that of administrative efficiency. We have recognized that the Government's interest in adhering to a uniform rule may sometimes satisfy the *O'Brien* test even if making an exception to the rule in a particular case might cause no serious damage. United States v. Albertini, 472 U.S. 675, 688 (1985) ("The First Amendment does not bar application of a neutral regulation that incidentally burdens speech merely because a party contends that allowing an exception in the particular case will not threaten important government interests"). The administrative efficiency interests in antitrust regulation are unusually compelling. The per se rules avoid "the necessity for an incredibly complicated and prolonged economic investigation into the entire history of the industry involved, as well as related industries, in an effort to determine at large whether a particular restraint has been reasonable." *Northern Pacific*. If small parties "were allowed to prove lack of market power, all parties would have the right, thus introducing the enormous complexities of market definition into every price-fixing case." R. Bork, The Antitrust Paradox 269 (1978). For these reasons, it is at least possible that the *Claiborne Hardware* doctrine, which itself rests in part upon *O'Brien*, exhausts *O'Brien*'s application to the antitrust statutes.

In any event, however, we cannot accept the Court of Appeals' characterization of this boycott or the antitrust laws. Every concerted refusal to do business with a potential customer or supplier has an expressive component. At one level, the competitors must exchange their views about their objectives and the means of obtaining them. The most blatant, naked price-fixing agreement is a product of communication, but that is surely not a reason for viewing it with special solicitude. At another level, after the terms of the boycotters' demands have been agreed upon, they must be communicated to its target: "we will not do business until you do what we ask." That expressive component of the boycott conducted by these respondents is surely not unique. On the contrary, it is the hallmark of every effective boycott.

At a third level, the boycotters may communicate with third parties to enlist public support for their objectives; to the extent that the boycott is newsworthy, it will facilitate the expression of the boycotters' ideas. But this level of expression is not an element of the boycott. Publicity may be generated by any other activity that is sufficiently newsworthy. Some activities, including the boycott here, may be newsworthy precisely for the reasons that they are prohibited: the harms they produce are matters of public concern. Certainly that is no reason for removing the prohibition.

In sum, there is thus nothing unique about the "expressive component" of respondents' boycott. A rule that requires courts to apply the antitrust laws "prudently and with sensitivity" whenever an economic boycott has an "expressive component" would create a gaping hole in the fabric of those laws. Respondents' boycott thus has no special characteristics meriting an exemption from the per se rules of antitrust law.

Equally important is the second error implicit in respondents' claim to immunity from the per se rules. In its opinion, the Court of Appeals assumed that the antitrust laws permit, but do not require, the condemnation of price fixing and boycotts without proof of market power. The opinion further assumed that the per se rule prohibiting such activity "is only a rule of 'administrative convenience and efficiency,' not a statutory command." This statement contains two errors. The per se rules are, of course, the product of judicial interpretations of the Sherman Act, but the rules nevertheless have the same force and effect as any other statutory commands. Moreover, while the per se rule against price fixing and boycotts is indeed justified in part by "administrative convenience," the Court of Appeals erred in describing the prohibition as justified only by such concerns. The per se rules also reflect a long-standing judgment that the prohibited practices by their nature have "a substantial potential for impact on competition." *Jefferson Parish.*

As we explained in *Engineers,* the rule of reason in antitrust law generates

> two complementary categories of antitrust analysis. In the first category are agreements whose nature and necessary effect are so plainly anticompetitive that no elaborate study of the industry is needed to establish their illegality — they are "illegal per se." In the second category are agreements whose competitive effect can only be evaluated by analyzing the facts peculiar to the business, the history of the restraint, and the reasons why it was imposed.

"Once experience with a particular kind of restraint enables the Court to predict with confidence that the rule of reason will condemn it, it has applied a conclusive presumption that the restraint is unreasonable." *Maricopa.*

The per se rules in antitrust law serve purposes analogous to per se restrictions upon, for example, stunt flying in congested areas or speeding. Laws prohibiting stunt flying or setting speed limits are justified by the State's interest in protecting human life and property. Perhaps most violations of such rules actually cause no harm. No doubt many experienced drivers and pilots can operate much more safely, even at prohibited speeds, than the average citizen.

If the especially skilled drivers and pilots were to paint messages on their cars, or attach streamers to their planes, their conduct would have an expressive component. High speeds and unusual maneuvers would help to draw attention to their messages. Yet the laws may nonetheless be enforced against these skilled persons without proof that their conduct was actually harmful or dangerous.

In part, the justification for these per se rules is rooted in administrative convenience. They are also supported, however, by the observation that every speeder and every stunt pilot poses some threat to the community. . . . So it is with boycotts and price fixing. Every such horizontal arrangement among competitors poses some threat to the free market. A small participant in the market is, obviously, less likely to cause persistent damage than a large participant. Other participants in the market may act quickly and effectively to take the small participant's place. For reasons including market inertia and information failures, however, a small conspirator may be able to impede competition over some period of time. Given an appropriate set of circumstances and some luck, the period can be long enough to inflict real injury upon particular consumers or competitors. . . .

Of course, some boycotts and some price-fixing agreements are more pernicious than others; some are only partly successful, and some may only succeed when they are buttressed by other causative factors, such as political influence. But an assumption that, absent proof of market power, the boycott disclosed by this record was totally harmless — when overwhelming testimony demonstrated that it almost produced a crisis in the administration of criminal justice in the District and when it achieved its economic goal — is flatly inconsistent with the clear course of our antitrust jurisprudence. Conspirators need not achieve the dimensions of a monopoly, or even a degree of market power any greater than that already disclosed by this record, to warrant condemnation under the antitrust laws.

VI

The judgment of the Court of Appeals is accordingly reversed insofar as that court held the per se rules inapplicable to the lawyers' boycott. . . .[19]

Justice BRENNAN, with whom Justice MARSHALL joins, dissenting in part. . . . In any particular case, it may be difficult to [determine] whether political or economic power was brought to bear on the government. The Court of Appeals thoughtfully analyzed this prob-

---

19. In response to the dissent, and particularly to its observation that some concerted arrangements that might be characterized as "group boycotts" may not merit per se condemnation, we emphasize that this case involves not only a boycott but also a horizontal price-fixing arrangement — a type of conspiracy that has been consistently analyzed as a per se violation for many decades. All of the "group boycott" cases cited in the dissent's footnote involved nonprice restraints. There was likewise no price-fixing component in any of the boycotts listed [elsewhere in] the dissenting opinion. Indeed, the text of the dissent virtually ignores the price-fixing component of respondent's concerted action.

lem and concluded, I believe correctly, that there could be no antitrust violation absent a showing that the boycotters possessed some degree of market power — that is, the ability to raise prices profitably through economic means or, more generally, the capacity to act other than as would an actor in a perfectly competitive market. The court reasoned that "[w]hen the government seeks to regulate an economic boycott with an expressive component . . . its condemnation without proof that the boycott could in fact be anticompetitive ignores the command of *O'Brien* that restrictions on activity protected by the First Amendment be *'no greater than is essential'* to preserve competition from the sclerotic effects of combination." The concurring judge added that if the participants wielded no market power, "the boycott must have succeeded out of persuasion and been a political activity." This approach is quite sensible, and I would affirm the Court of Appeals' decision to remand the case to the FTC for a showing of market power. . . .

Two well-established premises lead to the ineluctable conclusion that when applying the antitrust laws to a particular expressive boycott, the government may not presume an antitrust violation under the per se rule, but must instead apply the more searching, case-specific rule of reason. First, the per se rule is a *presumption* of illegality. . . . We have freely admitted that conduct condemned under the per se rule sometimes would be permissible if subjected merely to rule-of-reason analysis. See *Maricopa; Sylvania; Topco.* Second, the government may not in a First Amendment case apply a broad presumption that certain categories of speech are harmful without engaging in a more particularized examination. . . .

The Court's approach today is all the more inappropriate because the success of the Trial Lawyers' boycott could have been attributable to the persuasiveness of its message rather than any coercive economic force. When a boycott seeks to generate public support for the passage of legislation, it may operate on a *political* rather than *economic* level, especially when the Government is the target. . . .

As the Court appears to recognize, pre-boycott rates were unreasonably low. . . . The Court of Appeals concluded that "Mayor Barry and other important city officials were sympathetic to the boycotters' goals and may even have been supportive of the boycott itself," and that certain statements by the Mayor could be interpreted "as encouraging the [Trial Lawyers] to stage a demonstration of their political muscle so that a rate increase could more easily be justified to the public."

Taken together, these facts strongly suggest that the Trial Lawyers' campaign persuaded the city to increase CJA compensation levels by creating a favorable climate in which supportive District officials could vote for a raise without public opposition, even though the lawyers lacked the ability to exert economic pressure. As the court below expressly found, the facts at the very least do not exclude the possibility that the SCTLA succeeded due to political rather than economic power. The majority today permits the FTC to find an expressive boycott to violate the antitrust laws, without even requiring a showing that the participants possessed market power or that their conduct triggered any anticompetitive effects. I believe that the First Amendment forecloses such an approach. . . .

It is beyond peradventure that *sometimes* no exception need be made to a neutral rule of general applicability not aimed at the content of speech; "the arrest of a newscaster for a traffic violation," for example, does not offend the First Amendment. . . . Although *sometimes* such content-neutral regulations with incidental effects on speech leave open sufficient room for effective communication, application of the per se rule to expressive boycotts does not. The role of boycotts in political speech is too central, and the effective alternative avenues open to the Trial Lawyers were too few, to permit the FTC to invoke the per se rule in this case.

Expressive boycotts have been a principal means of political communication since the birth of the Republic. As the Court of Appeals recognized, "boycotts have historically been used as a dramatic means of communicating anger or disapproval and of mobilizing sympathy for the boycotters' cause." From the colonists' protest of the Stamp and Townsend Acts to the Montgomery bus boycott and the National Organization for Women's campaign to encourage ratification of the Equal Rights Amendment, boycotts have played a central role in our Nation's political discourse. In recent years there have been boycotts of supermarkets, meat, grapes, iced tea in cans, soft drinks, lettuce, chocolate, tuna, plastic wrap, textiles, slacks, animal skins and furs, and products of Mexico, Japan, South Africa, and the Soviet Union. See *NOW.* . . . Like soapbox oratory in the streets and parks, political boycotts are a traditional means of "communicating thoughts between citizens" and "discussing public questions." . . . Any restrictions on such boycotts must be scrutinized with special care in light of their historic importance as a mode of expression. . . .

The Court observes that all boycotts have "an expressive component" in the sense that participants must communicate their plans among themselves and to their target. The Court reasons that this expressive feature alone does not render boycotts immune from scrutiny under the per se rule. Otherwise, the rule could never be applied to any boycotts or to most price-fixing schemes. On this point I concur with the majority. But while some boycotts may not present First Amendment concerns, when a particular boycott appears to operate on a political rather than economic level, I believe that it cannot be condemned under the per se rule.[7] ...

[W]e have already recognized that an expressive boycott necessarily involves "constitutionally protected activity." *Claiborne Hardware*.... The Court contends that the SCTLA's motivation differed from that of the boycotters in *Claiborne Hardware*, because the former sought to supplement its members' own salaries rather than to remedy racial injustice. Even if true, the different *purposes* of the speech can hardly render the Trial Lawyers' boycott any less *expressive*.

Next, although the Court is correct that the media coverage of the boycott was substantial, this does not support the majority's argument that the boycott itself was not expressive.... The refusal of the Trial Lawyers to accept appointments by itself communicated a powerful idea: CJA compensation rates had deteriorated so much, relatively speaking, that the lawyers were willing to forgo their livelihoods rather than return to work....

Another reason why expressive boycotts are irreplaceable as a means of communication is that they are essential to the "poorly financed causes of little people." Martin v. Struthers, 319 U.S. 141, 146 (1943). It is no accident that boycotts have been used by the American colonists to throw off the British yoke and by the oppressed to assert their civil rights. See *Claiborne Hardware*. Such groups cannot use established organizational techniques to advance their political interests, and boycotts are often the only effective route available to them....

Furthermore, as the Court of Appeals noted, there may be significant differences between boycotts aimed at the government and those aimed at private parties. The government has options open to it that private parties do not; in this case, for example, the boycott was aimed at a legislative body with the power to terminate it at any time by requiring all members of the District Bar to represent defendants pro bono. If a boycott against the government achieves its goal, it likely owes its success to political rather than market power.

---

7. If a boycott uses economic power in an unlawful way to send a message, it cannot claim First Amendment protection from the antitrust laws, any more than a terrorist could use an act of violence to express his political views and then assert immunity from criminal prosecution. Thus, if a cartel in a regulated industry inflicts economic injury on consumers by raising prices in order to communicate with the government, it still would be subject to the per se rule. The instant case is different: there is a genuine question whether the SCTLA boycott involved *any* economic coercion at all. That is why a showing of market power is necessary before the boycott can be condemned as an unfair method of competition.

The Court's concern for the vitality of the per se rule, moreover, is misplaced, in light of the fact that we have been willing to apply rule-of-reason analysis in a growing number of group-boycott cases. See, e.g., *Indiana Dentists; Northwest Wholesale; NCAA; Broadcast Music* (criticizing application of per se rules because "[l]iteralness is overly simplistic and often overbroad").

We have recognized that "there is often no bright line separating per se from rule of reason analysis. Per se rules may require considerable inquiry into market conditions before the evidence justifies a presumption of anticompetitive conduct." *NCAA.*

In short, the conclusion that per se analysis is inappropriate in this boycott case would not preclude its application in many others, nor would it create insurmountable difficulties for antitrust enforcement. The plainly expressive nature of the Trial Lawyers' campaign distinguishes it from boycotts that are intended subjects of the antitrust laws.

I respectfully dissent.

[Justice Blackmun concurred in Parts I-IV of the Court's opinion and with the reasoning of Justice Brennan's dissent. He doubted that a remand was necessary because the lawyers had no real economic power, as the government bodies could have terminated the boycott by requiring members of the bar to represent indigent defendants pro bono.]

276.   (a) Assuming that there is no *Noerr*, First Amendment, or other special immunity,[11] what were the antitrust violations in *SCTLA*? Are any of the lawyers' defenses acceptable under *Engineers*?

(b) How does *SCTLA* differ from *Noerr*? From *NOW* and *Claiborne Hardware*? What is the First Amendment problem, if any? If the nonboycott alternatives are adequate in *SCTLA*, why were they inadequate in these other cases?

(c) Is substituting a rule of reason inquiry a useful compromise? How would a rule of reason have been applied to the defendants' conduct? Would market power be required? Was market power present?

(d) What remedy?

---

11. Observe that the labor exemption, see ¶161, is inapplicable because the CJA regulars were not employees of the District (in contrast to employees of the Public Defender System).

2G. PATENT LICENSING AND SETTLEMENTS[1]

Price-Restricted Licenses and the Patent-Antitrust Tension Generally

UNITED STATES v. GENERAL ELECTRIC CO.
272 U.S. 476 (1926)

Chief Justice TAFT.... [General Electric licensed Westinghouse to make, use, and sell lamps under GE's patents. Westinghouse agreed to pay a royalty and to follow the prices and other terms of sale fixed from time to time by GE on the sale of its own lamps.[2]]

Conveying less than title to the patent, or part of it, the patentee may grant a license to make, use and vend articles under the specification of his patent for any royalty or upon any condition the performance of which is reasonably within the reward which the patentee by the grant of the patent is entitled to secure. It is well settled ... that where a patentee makes the patented article and sells it, he can exercise no future control over what the purchaser may wish to do with the article after his purchase. It has passed beyond the scope of the patentee's rights.... But the question is a different one which arises when we consider what a patentee who grants a license to one to make and vend the patented article may do in limiting the licensee in the exercise of the right to sell. The patentee may make and grant a license to another to make and use the patented articles, but withhold his right to sell them. The licensee in such a case acquires an interest in the articles made. He owns the material of them and may use them. But if he sells them, he infringes the right of the patentee, and may be held for damages and enjoined. If the patentee goes further, and licenses the selling

---

1. This section constitutes the first and most extensive treatment of patent-antitrust issues in this book. Additional issues considered include patent accumulation (¶¶331-334), tying (¶424), and package licenses and royalty arrangements (¶¶434-435). Background material can be found in Ch. 1E. The reader is reminded that the analysis of patents is applicable more generally to intellectual property, particularly copyrights and trade secrets.

2. The Court did not mention these facts. Westinghouse output was also controlled by the agreement with GE. Originally, Westinghouse was licensed to manufacture and sell up to 15 percent of the combined net sales of patented lamps made by GE and Westinghouse at a royalty of 2 percent of the sales price; the royalty charge was 10 percent, however, on sales in excess of the quota. These figures were adjusted from time to time. Numerous other producers were licensed by GE under so-called B licenses that did not cover prices but that did restrict output. All the B licensees together were permitted to supply about 8 percent of the market. See A. Bright, The Electric Lamp Industry, ch. 9 (1949).

of the articles, may he limit the selling by limiting the method of sale and the price? We think he may do so, provided the conditions of sale are normally and reasonably adapted to secure pecuniary reward for the patentee's monopoly. One of the valuable elements of the exclusive right of a patentee is to acquire profit by the price at which the article sold. The higher the price, the greater the profit, unless it is prohibitory. When the patentee licenses another to make and vend, and retains the right to continue to make and vend on his own account, the price at which his licensee will sell will necessarily affect the price at which he can sell his own patented goods. It would seem entirely reasonable that he should say to the licensee, "Yes, you may make and sell articles under my patent, but not so as to destroy the profit I wish to obtain by making them and selling them myself." He does not thereby sell outright to the licensee the articles the latter may make and sell, or vest absolute ownership in them. He restricts the property and interest the licensee has in the goods he makes and proposes to sell.

This question was considered by this court in the case of Bement v. National Harrow Co., 186 U.S. 70. A combination of manufacturers owning a patent to make float spring tool harrows licensed others to make and sell the products under the patent, on condition that they would not during the continuance of the license sell the products at a less price, or on more favorable terms of payment and delivery to purchasers, than were set forth in a schedule made part of the license. That was held to be a valid use of the patent rights of the owners of the patent. It was objected that this made for a monopoly. The court, speaking by Justice Peckham, said:

> The very object of these laws is monopoly, and the rule is, with few exceptions, that any conditions which are not in their very nature illegal with regard to this kind of property, imposed by the patentee and agreed to by the licensee for the right to manufacture or use or sell the article, will be upheld by the courts. The fact that the conditions in the contracts keep up the monopoly or fix prices does not render them illegal....

It is argued, however, that *Bement* has been in effect overruled. The claim is based on the fact that one of the cases cited by Justice Peckham in that case was Heaton-Peninsular Button-Fastener Co. v. Eureka Specialty Co., 77 Fed. 288. [That case (like the later Supreme Court decision in Henry v. Dick Co., 224 U.S. 1) permitted the patentee to condition the use of a patented button-fastening (or mimeograph) machine on the user's purchasing its requirements of unpatented fasteners (or ink) from the patentee.]

The overruling of the *Dick* Case and the disapproval of the *Button-Fastener* Case by the *Motion Picture* Case did not carry with it the overruling of *Bement*. . . . The price at which a patented article sells is certainly a circumstance having a more direct relation, and is more germane to the rights of the patentee, than the unpatented material with which the patented article may be used. Indeed, as already said, price fixing is usually the essence of that which secures proper reward to the patentee.

Nor do we think that the decisions of this court holding restrictions as to price of patented articles invalid apply to a contract of license like the one in this case. . . . [Such decisions] really are only instances of the application of the principle of Adams v. Burke, 17 Wall. 453, 456, . . . that a patentee may not attach to the article made by him, or with his consent, a condition running with the article in the hands of purchasers, limiting the price at which one who becomes its owner for full consideration shall part with it. They do not consider or condemn a restriction put by a patentee upon his licensee as to the prices at which the latter shall sell articles which he makes and only can make legally under the license. The authority of *Bement* has not been shaken by the cases we have reviewed.

For the reasons given, we sustain the validity of the license granted by the Electric Company to the Westinghouse Company. . . .

277. The patent-antitrust conflict.[3] (a) *Is there a conflict?* The first step in dissecting the interaction of the patent and antitrust laws is to understand the nature of the conflict in their goals. The core purpose of the antitrust laws is to promote competition, which entails preventing acts of monopolization. By contrast, the patent system attempts to stimulate inventive activity by creating a government-protected monopoly and specifically by empowering patentees to enforce their monopolies against unwanted competition; preventing such competition is the very purpose of the legislative grant. Allowing patentees thus to limit competition conflicts directly with the antitrust law's promotion of competition.

In another sense, however, the two regimes are in substantial harmony. Both ultimately seek to benefit the public — one through technological progress and the other through competition. Moreover, both recognize that individual or group conduct in the decentralized marketplace they favor sometimes conflicts with the public

3. For a more complete exposition, with applications, see U.S. Department of Justice and Federal Trade Commission, Antitrust Guidelines for the Licensing of Intellectual Property (1995), reprinted in 4 Trade Reg. Rep. ¶13132 (1995); L. Kaplow, The Patent-Antitrust Intersection: A Reappraisal, 97 Harv. L. Rev. 1813 (1984).

interest and therefore requires some supervision and control. Accordingly, the challenge is to determine which acts of patent exploitation best promote patent policy with the least damage to competition policy.

(b) *Formalistic resolutions. General Electric* is hardly unique in purporting to resolve patent-antitrust conflicts through formalistic pronouncements. The Court suggests that patentees may impose "any condition the performance of which is reasonably within the reward which the patentee by the grant of the patent is entitled to secure."[4] Because neither the patent grant nor statute say anything about the appropriate reward for a patentee, apart from conferring the right to exclude infringements, one must find the reward concept or amount in the premises or purposes of the patent system. Although the Court seemed to regard the absence of price competition on the patented product as somehow inherent in the patent system, one can tease a limitation out of its opinion. It suggested that it would approve "any conditions which are not in their very nature illegal." But, of course, price fixing among competitors is illegal — a felony, in fact — and antitrust law has centuries-old roots in the common law's refusal to enforce contracts that unreasonably restrain trade. By nevertheless upholding price-fixing conditions, the Court must have had some sense of intrinsic illegality going beyond statutory felonies and long-established common-law principles. But what might that be?

A related argument approves the restricted license because it is less restrictive than a simple refusal to license, which clearly would be lawful.[5] But this argument compares the restricted license only to total exclusion. In fact, forbidding the restraint may lead the patentee not to withhold all licenses but to grant unrestricted licenses.[6] Moreover, some restricted licenses will harm competition more than a total refusal to license, as we shall consider shortly. Finally, many branches of the law reject the axiom that the power to

---

4. To similar effect is the Court's later statement that patentees may act "provided the conditions of sale are normally and reasonably adapted to secure pecuniary reward for the patentee's monopoly."

5. See ¶280 for the legality of refusals to license at all. The text argument is expressed by Justice Burton's dissent in United States v. Line Material Co., 333 U.S. 287, 343-344 (1948):

> Just as an unlimited license is a partial, but lawful, relaxation of the lawful restraint of trade imposed by patent, so a limited license is but a correspondingly less relaxation of that same restraint.... [T]he restraint of trade imposed by the patent itself is lawful. Therefore, as long as the license agreement has only the effect of reducing the lawful restraint imposed by the patent, such agreement merely converts the original lawful restraint into a lesser restraint, equally lawful.

6. See ¶278 on the patentee's incentives to license.

exclude logically entails the power to admit on any condition.[7] Even the *GE* Court noted that a patentee's power to refrain from licensing a patented machine did not validate as a lesser included right the power to condition the license on the licensee's use of a specified unpatented product with the machine.[8]

Another formula would reject the *GE* restraint *without any further analysis* on the ground that it involves price fixing, which is unlawful per se. To do so would apply the antitrust laws to the practice of patents without regard to the purposes of the patent statute and its policy of promoting invention through the restriction of competition.

(c) *Resolving the conflict.* In light of the objectives of the patent and antitrust statutes and the underlying harmony described at the outset, we must begin by comparing the likely results of permitting or forbidding such practices as the restricted license, either generally or in the particular case. The relevant question, admittedly difficult to answer, is whether the challenged practice contributes more to inventive activity than it costs in terms of lost competition. Unfortunately, the level of inventive activity is connected only uncertainly to the patent system itself; even more uncertain is its connection to any particular patent practice. Should we then condemn all restrictions in patent licenses because the competitive loss is clear while the benefits are uncertain? Or should we allow those restrictions that seem mainly to increase the patentee's return with minimum limitations on competition that is otherwise possible, while condemning those that seem excessively costly in terms of lost competition relative to the reward they provide the patentee?

As a simple illustration, imagine that all members of an industry accept, with trivial royalties and a price-fixing provision, a license to make a patented product that is not significantly different from nonpatented products previously made but no longer made after this licensing. This licensing organizes a cartel for the purpose of bringing all of its members monopoly returns. Here, the patentee's reward flows partly from its patent and partly from the elimination

7. For example, Congress's plenary power to exclude aliens from admittance to the United States clearly does not embrace the power to admit only those who undertake to speak or worship in a specified manner.

8. The Court noted its ruling in Motion Picture Patents Co. v. Universal Film Mfg. Co., 243 U.S. 502 (1917). The dissent in that case argued that the patentee

may keep his device wholly out of use.... So much being undisputed, I cannot understand why he may not keep it out of use unless the licensee, or, for the matter of that, the buyer, will use some unpatented thing in connection with it. Generally speaking the measure of a condition is the consequence of a breach, and if that consequence is one that the owner may impose unconditionally, he may impose it conditionally upon a certain event. [Id. at 519.]

of otherwise feasible rivalry of nonpatented products. The latter is not related to the social value of the invention and clearly is not the object of the patent laws; nor are the monopoly profits obtained by the other cartel members. One might say that such a cartel imposes too great a cost on society relative to the benefit it confers on the patentee.

But, the illustration ceases to be simple when we change the facts. Imagine industry-wide price-fixed licenses where the patented product is so superior to any alternative that no firm lacking access to it could survive. Was that the *GE* case? Would forbidding the price-fixing condition have dissuaded General Electric from licensing at all? Does it matter? To answer these questions, we need to consider why patentees license their patents and why they might want to restrict licensees' competition.

278. Use, assignment, or licensing. Inventors may choose to practice their patents. But those who are exclusively researchers or who lack the facilities for utilizing the patent may wish to transfer their patents to others.[9] Or they may retain formal title to the patent but grant others exclusive rights or grant licenses to many.

Even a patent holder engaged in a business that uses the patent may find it desirable to license others as well. Prompt industry-wide usage might increase consumer acceptance of the new product or the production of ancillary products. For example, when IBM introduced its personal computers, it disclosed sufficient information about its workings to allow independents to develop software for it; the extensive software that became available then made the IBM product more attractive to consumers. Another reason would be to share risk. If the success of a new product is uncertain, a single firm may not wish to invest the resources necessary to produce a sufficient amount for the entire market,[10] whereas many firms might each be willing to assume a small portion of the risk. In addition, there is also the potential risk to purchasers. Additional sources of production reduce the risk of supply interruptions and thus may help attract industrial patronage.

9. 35 U.S.C. §261 provides that "Applications for ... patents, or any interest therein, shall be assignable in law. ... The applicant, patentee, or his assigns or legal representatives may in like manner grant and convey an exclusive right under his application for patent, or patents, to the whole or any specified part of the United States."

10. Were the patentee to invest enough to satisfy the whole market, it might not be able to recover that investment if the patent were later held invalid or rivals invented an alternative or superior product or method.

Licensing can also utilize rather than waste capital in place.[11] For example, many patents involve modest, although important, modifications of existing production processes or products. There may be many firms in addition to the patentee with substantial production facilities in place that are specialized for producing the product in question. Licensing would benefit all. The patentee achieves industry-wide exploitation without the delay and expense of building enough new capacity to supply the whole market, while the others continue to profit by using capacity that would otherwise be wasted.

These benefits to the patentee and licensees are also benefits to society. In addition, licensing allows other firms to gain experience with the technology, expand its uses, improve it, and compete freely when the patent expires, becomes obsolete, or is invalidated. The latter benefits obviously do not motivate licensing because the patentee does not welcome competition in the post-patent period. In fact such prospects tend to discourage licensing or lead patentees to charge higher royalties.

Royalties can involve an initial lump sum payment, a constant sum per unit of use, a percentage of profits, or some combination.[12] The rates may be identical for all licensees and uses or there may be discriminatory charges. The amount of the royalty is not usually an antitrust issue.[13] The base on which the royalty is computed does not ordinarily, but can, create an antitrust problem.[14] And it is clear that royalties based on production, sales, or profits must be limited to the life of the patent.[15]

---

11. Existing capital should be understood broadly. For example, a firm with a good reputation for product quality has an intangible capital asset (goodwill) in place that will be valuable in marketing a new product and facilitating consumer acceptance.

12. The variations are endless. The constant sum may be set at different levels for different ranges of output. Percentages of the sale price may be used instead of a constant sum or percentage of profits. Rates may vary with the use of the patent.

13. W.L. Gore & Assoc. v. Carlisle Corp., 529 F.2d 614, 622-623 (3d Cir. 1976) (rejecting claim that unreasonably high royalty is patent misuse); Brulotte v. Thys Co., 379 U.S. 29, 33 (1964) (dictum: patentee has right "to exact royalties as high as he can negotiate within the leverage of that [patent] monopoly").

14. See ¶435.

15. *Brulotte*, note 13, and ¶435. Query: May royalties be charged for disclosing the contents of a secret patent application before the patent is issued? In Kewanee Oil Co. v. Bicron Corp., 416 U.S. 470 (1974), the Supreme Court held that the states are free to regulate trade secrets and other intellectual property in any manner not inconsistent with federal patent law, whose purposes were stated as (1) fostering and rewarding invention, (2) promoting disclosure of inventions to stimulate further invention and post-expiration dissemination of patented ideas, and (3) assuring free use of ideas in the public domain. The enforcement of contractual promises to pay for secret but nonpatentable ideas was held consistent

The royalty will, of course, be related to and reflected in the price of the product. For example, if a competitive price in the absence of royalties were $100 and royalties were $10, the price would be $110. If the patent is truly valuable, the result will presumably be better than if the invention had never been made. Suppose that the perfectly competitive price resulting when producers use existing, unpatented technology is $110 and that an invention allows production costs to be reduced by $10. The patentee would charge (just under) $10 per unit royalty, but no more; at a higher royalty, no producer would find it profitable to use the invention.[16]

In addition to or instead of the benefits described above, patent licensing may have other purposes or effects. Whether involving just two firms or nearly everyone in an industry, licensing arrangements can incorporate virtually any of the potentially anticompetitive restrictions examined in this book, either explicitly or as the indirect consequence of royalty payment terms. The restraint may be sought for its own sake through the masquerade of licensing an unimportant patent. And anticompetitive results may flow even from the licensing of important patents. Thus, we confront the usual problem: Patent licensing can serve the public interest, but care must be taken to avoid excessively anticompetitive results.

279. Price and related restrictions in patent licenses.[17] (a) *Reasons for refusing to license without a price restriction.* Might a patentee

---

with these purposes of the patent system. In Aronson v. Quick Point Pencil Co., 440 U.S. 257, 263 (1979), the Court enforced a promise to pay 5 percent royalties for disclosure of the idea in a patent application and to pay 2.5 percent in perpetuity if no patent issued within five years. "Enforcement of the agreement does not withdraw any idea from the public domain. . . . [E]nforcement of this agreement does not discourage anyone from seeking a patent."

16. With a product improvement, the resulting price could be higher than the pre-invention price, but presumably only if consumers value the improvement by more than the amount of any royalty. For example, if the pre-invention price were $110, and consumers valued an improvement by $10, firms would not be willing to pay more than $10 in royalties because, if they did, they would have to sell at more than $120, whereas firms producing the old product and selling at $110 would get all the business.

17. See generally Antitrust Guidelines, note 3; W. Bowman, Patent and Antitrust Law: A Legal and Economic Appraisal (1973); W. Baxter, Legal Restrictions on Exploitation of the Patent Monopoly: An Economic Analysis, 76 Yale L.J. 267 (1966); G. Gibbons, Domestic Territorial Restrictions in Patent Transactions and the Antitrust Laws, 34 Geo. Wash. L. Rev. 893 (1966); G. Gibbons, Field Restrictions in Patent Transactions: Economic Discrimination and Restraint of Competition, 66 Colum. L. Rev. 423 (1966); G. Gibbons, Patent License Price Fixing and the Antitrust Laws, 51 Va. L. Rev. 273 (1965); P. Hoff, Inventions in the Marketplace: Patent Licensing and the U.S. Antitrust Laws (1986); Kaplow, note 3; G. Priest, Cartels and Patent License Arrangements, 20 J.L. & Econ. 309 (1977).

hesitate to license if it could not restrict the price at which licensees sell the product controlled by the patent? Where the product is to be sold exclusively by one or a very few licensees, the patentee might fear that licensees would exploit their monopoly position and charge too high a price for the product.[18] The resulting loss of sales volume would depress royalties based on the number of units sold.[19] Thus, it is often in the patentee's interest to license many firms to ensure competition among them, just as it is often in a manufacturer's interest to ensure competition among its retailers. Were such competition impossible, a patentee might wish to limit the *maximum* price its licensees could charge.

Minimum price restrictions are different. A patentee practicing its own patent need not hesitate to license competition out of the fear that licensees would undercut its monopoly price for the product. The royalties paid by licensees protect its profits, and then some.[20] For example, suppose that the patentee sells the patented product at the monopoly price of $100, the production cost is $90 for all firms, and licensees must pay a royalty of $10 per unit. The patentee thus earns $10 per unit both on its own sales and on those of its licensees. If licensees undercut the patentee's price of $100 — presumably because their production costs had fallen — the patentee could lose sales but actually earns more; it still earns the $10 per unit through the royalty, and the licensees' price cut will increase total industry sales.

Thus, we can see that the patentee ought not to fear price competition from its licensees in many instances. But perhaps some less efficient patentees might nevertheless be reluctant to go out of business and leave the market to their licensees.[21] Also, the knowledge assumed in our simple illustration — present and future costs

---

18. Compare ¶402.

19. The patentee collecting a percentage of the licensee's profits wants the licensee to maximize its profits, but such a patentee then shares a portion of the value of the patent with the licensee. Such percentage-of-profit royalties need not involve any sharing of the patent's value with the licensee who pays an appropriate fixed sum in addition to royalties.

20. If per-unit royalties are infeasible due to difficulties in monitoring licensees, the analysis is more complex and the results may change. See M. Katz & C. Shapiro, On the Licensing of Innovations, 16 Rand J. Econ. 504 (1985).

21. A less efficient firm that believes it can lower its costs in the long run by virtue of increased experience — the learning curve effect — should regard its present high costs as a necessary investment in learning, which may justify continued production at the lower price charged by its licensees. See A.M. Spence, The Learning Curve and Competition, 12 Bell J. Econ. 49 (1981) (lower future costs achieved through experience of current operations should be understood as entailing a lower current marginal cost, justifying production at a lower price).

of the patentee and its licensees, technological developments, market demand, and optimum industry price — may not exist.[22]

Of course, if one believed that patentees can ordinarily maximize their profits without price-fixing conditions, then one might regard such restrictions as ordinarily explained by such ulterior motives as cartelization. Even so, room might be left for a particular patentee to explain how its price-fixed licensees actually aided the most effective exploitation of its patent.

(b) *Output limitations.* Higher prices are only possible with (and result from) reduced output; lower prices correspond to higher output. Thus, a ceiling on the output of licensees serves much the same function as a floor under their prices[23] and may be more closely tailored to such patentee reasons for licensing as the desire to avoid the risks in occupying the whole market or to assure customers of a second source. Again, however, we should question why the appropriate royalty would not adequately protect the patentee.

Whether licenses may lawfully contain output limitations is far from clear, although scant authority seems to permit it. One court failed to see any objection to limiting the licensee's output of a patented product.[24] Where the output limited was not that of a patented product but of an unpatented product made with the aid of a patented process or machine, no patent misuse was found in one case[25] and the restriction was enforced in another,[26] but not in a third.[27] It cannot be said, however, that the question has been carefully analyzed. Nor shall we do so here except to point out that many of the considerations appearing in this section also bear on the analysis of output limitations.

---

22. Although setting a price also depends upon such knowledge, a price restriction requiring licensees to match the patentee's price changes is more flexible than a royalty fixed at the outset. Even so, it cannot be said with confidence that such flexibility is often necessary or sufficient to solve the problems caused by uncertainty.

23. See ¶208.

24. United States v. du Pont, 118 F. Supp. 41, 226 (D. Del. 1953), aff'd on other grounds, 351 U.S. 377 (1956) (arising under Sherman Act §2).

25. Q-Tips v. Johnson & Johnson, 109 F. Supp. 657 (D.N.J. 1951), aff'd, 207 F.2d 509 (3d Cir. 1953), cert. denied, 347 U.S. 935 (1954).

26. Ethyl Corp. v. Hercules Powder Co., 232 F. Supp. 453, 457-459 (D. Del. 1963).

27. E.g., American Equip. Co. v. Tuthill Bldg. Material Co., 69 F.2d 406, 409 (7th Cir. 1934). American leased its patented brick-handling machinery to producers of 90 percent of the brick made in Chicago but imposed on each licensee a limitation on the number of bricks it could make with the machinery. The court found a conspiracy among all the participants to use the machinery patent to restrict competition in unpatented brick.

(c) *Territorial limitations.* Territorial restrictions can be used to keep licensees out of the patentee's home territory or, by assigning different territories to each licensee, to eliminate competition among them.[28] Unlike price restrictions, territorial limitations may have a longer-run impact because after the patent expires (or is invalidated or becomes obsolete), the licensees will need to create new distribution arrangements or, if transportation costs are important, build new plants before they can compete outside their assigned territories.

Several courts have declared such restrictions permissible,[29] relying on Patent Code §261 which declares that the patentee may convey an exclusive right under its patent "to the whole or any specified part of the United States." Several respected commentators have concluded that Congress did not intend to validate such restrictions.[30] In any event, it is well established that the patentee cannot prevent a consumer[31] or dealer[32] who purchases from a restricted licensee from using or reselling the product anywhere it chooses. It is usually said that the first sale of the product exhausts the patentee's legitimate interest. The early cases establishing the first sale rule were grounded not in competitive considerations but in the common law's traditional hostility to encumbrances attached to chattels that had passed into commerce.[33]

(d) *Exclusive licenses.*[34] Within a prescribed territory or field of use, or generally, the patentee might wish to have either a single licensee or many competing licensees. Ordinarily, its profits would be maximized by setting appropriate royalties, granting numerous

28. Both purposes may be served by limiting the products that may be made with a patent. Such use restrictions are explored in the following subsection.

29. Pfotzer v. Aqua Sys., 162 F.2d 779 (2d Cir. 1947); United States v. Crown Zellerbach Corp., 141 F. Supp. 118 (N.D. Ill. 1956). See Gibbons (Territorial Restrictions), note 17. Cf. Edwin K. Williams & Co. v. Edwin K. Williams & Co.-East, 542 F.2d 1053, 1061 (9th Cir. 1976), cert. denied, 433 U.S. 908 (1977) (territorial restrictions on offering certain business seminars reasonably ancillary to trademark and copyright license).

30. See note 17 articles, especially Baxter at 349-352 and Gibbons (Territorial Restrictions) at 895-900. For a differing view, see M. Wheeler, A Reexamination of Antitrust Law and Exclusive Territorial Grants by Patentees, 119 U. Pa. L. Rev. 642, 643-650 (1971).

31. Adams v. Burke, 84 U.S. 453 (1873). Security Mat. Co. v. Mixermobile Co., 72 F. Supp. 450, 455 (S.D. Cal. 1947), enforced an implied territorial restriction on a machine knowingly used by its purchaser in the territory of another purchaser granted local exclusivity.

32. Keeler v. Standard Folding Bed Co., 157 U.S. 659 (1895); American Industrial Fastener Corp. v. Flushing Enter., 362 F. Supp. 32 (N.D. Ohio 1973).

33. See Ch. 4A.

34. For a nonmanufacturing patentee, an assignment may serve the same purpose as an exclusive license.

licenses, and assuring maximum competition among the licensees.[35] There are a number of reasons to grant an exclusive license instead. First, exclusivity might be necessary to induce investments by licensees. For example, an initial licensee might be reluctant to undertake significant investments developing and producing the product and creating a market for it without some assurance that it will reap the profit from such investment.[36] Absent exclusive rights, the licensee might fear that after years of investment the patentee will license others who can take advantage of its expensive pioneering efforts and sell the product with little up-front cost.[37]

Second, if the value of a patent is difficult to calculate, a patentee not wishing to practice the patent itself may simply transfer its monopoly to an exclusive licensee in exchange for a share of the profits. Of course, there are other ways of coping with uncertainty, but some form of exclusive license is a common arrangement, especially by individual inventors.

Third, an exclusive license may be a masquerade for dividing markets. For example, two competitors may cross-license each other under their respective patents but specify that each may practice those patents only in a different territory or with respect to a different product. This is the concern inspiring recommendations that the patentee be compelled to license all qualified applicants if it licenses any one, although it would remain free to license no one.[38] It may often be difficult to distinguish this third case from the others.[39]

Exclusive licenses are treated in a variety of ways. One court characterized an exclusive license as unlawfully made with an intent to

35. Compare ¶402.

36. Compare ¶181d.

37. This explanation parallels the free rider argument developed in Ch. 4A with respect to dealers, particularly in ¶403*l*.

38. See note 17 articles, especially Baxter at 347-352 and Gibbons (Territorial Restrictions) at 894-904. See also White House Task Force on Antitrust Policy (1968), which recommended new legislation for this purpose.

39. The Task Force, note 38, would not apply its licensing requirement where the patentee proves to the FTC before it grants any license that exclusivity "is necessary to obtain commercial exploitation of the patent and will not tend substantially to lessen competition." Wheeler, note 30, at 665, recommends a compromise:

> A patentee should be allowed to grant one exclusive territorial license, the size and composition of the territory and the length of the exclusive period to be determined by the bargaining process.... [E]xclusive territorial licensing is rarely needed except to encourage entrepreneurial investment of risk capital for development purposes, and a patentee should rarely need to grant more than one exclusive license to promote development of a risky invention.... [C]ollusive cartels effectuated by a network of regional monopolies will be avoided....

confer a monopoly.[40] That court did not seem to perceive that such an intent could be found wherever a significant patent is assigned or exclusively licensed; it was reversed, with the suggestion that a rule of reason should govern.[41] In the main, an exclusive license is viewed benignly as "neither unusual nor sinister."[42] Although certainly not viewed as automatically unlawful, it can amount to an unreasonable restraint of trade.[43] Particularly troublesome to the courts have been license agreements that condition the patentee's power to grant other licenses on the consent of existing licensees[44] or licenses that are terminated after complaint from other licensees.[45] Such problems with the one-way license can be magnified in the case of reciprocal licenses of different patents, usually characterized as a cross-license. In *Honeywell*,[46] each of two computer firms licensed its patent to the other. Although not expressly exclusive in form, the licenses were found exclusive in fact and unreasonable because the defendants reaped an unfair advantage over unlicensed rivals. Perhaps reciprocal exclusive licenses could

---

40. United States v. Studiengesellschaft Kohle, 1978 Trade Cas. ¶62291 (D.D.C. 1981).

41. 670 F.2d 1122, 1128 (D.C. Cir. 1981).

42. Cataphote Corp. v. DeSoto Chem. Coatings, 450 F.2d 769, 774 (9th Cir. 1971), cert. denied, 408 U.S. 929 (1972).

43. Moraine Prods. v. ICI Am., 538 F.2d 134 (7th Cir.), cert. denied, 429 U.S. 941 (1976) (what might constitute unreasonableness was not spelled out; agreement permitted no additional license without permission of licensee who was exclusive except for licensor and another licensee).

44. E.g., United States v. Krasnov, 143 F. Supp. 184 (E.D. Pa. 1956), aff'd per curiam, 355 U.S. 5 (1957); United States v. Besser Mfg. Co., 96 F. Supp. 304 (E.D. Mich. 1951), aff'd, 343 U.S. 444 (1952); *Crown Zellerbach*, note 29.

45. In Mannington Mills v. Congoleum Corp., 610 F.2d 1059, 1073 (3d Cir. 1979), the court declared that

> a patentee's termination of a licensee, in concert with competing licensees, is not entitled to an antitrust exemption. Where ... restrictions are imposed vertically upon the licensee, in pursuit of the patentee's own marketing strategy ... [they seem] directed toward the legitimate exploitation of the patent monopoly ... [and] significant to the patentee's initial decision whether to license.... Where the patentee's anticompetitive conduct is undertaken after a number of non-exclusive licenses have been granted and in concert with competing licensees, however, there is a greater risk that the restriction is designed not to reward the patent monopoly, but to increase the licensee's reward ... [and perhaps] to assist in the policing of a horizontal agreement among licensees.

Although a conspiracy had not been shown, summary judgment was held inappropriate because the plaintiff had received an inadequate opportunity for discovery. The court affirmed judgment against the plaintiff's claim that the defendant had refused to grant it the know-how license granted to other producers. The court doubted that such a unilateral refusal to deal was actionable at all. Compare *Monsanto*, Ch. 4A.

46. Honeywell v. Sperry Rand Corp., 1974 Trade Cas. ¶74874 (D. Minn. 1973).

be seen as a concerted refusal to deal, but one must then analyze which circumstances, if any, should make the arrangement unreasonable and unlawful.

(e) *Patent licenses and vertical restraints.* As noted at a number of points, patent licensing can involve both horizontal competition and vertical restraints, the latter explored in Chapter 4. The relationship is in part vertical because the patentee supplies an input — technology — to licensees, and the patentee's profits (through royalties) depend on the licensee's sales, much as a manufacturer's profits depend on resales by its wholesalers and retailers.[47] Nevertheless, horizontal complications are often central, because either the patentee competes with its licensees or a nonproducing patentee might stand to share some of the monopoly profits if it assists in cartelizing an industry through its patents. This section emphasizes the horizontal elements, but, as the discussion in this Paragraph suggests, a full understanding of these issues is facilitated by incorporating the analysis later in this book.[48]

280. Suppression; compulsory licensing. (a) *Nonuse explained.* One significant way of exercising a patent is to suppress it — that is, neither to use nor to license it. Perhaps the primary reason for nonuse is that a patent lacks commercial value because its object is not marketable, its process unduly costly, or its substitutes superior.[49] If a patent has value in the marketplace, the rational

47. In addition to the restrictions already noted in text, a patentee may restrict licensees' dealing in rival products. Because a patentee's royalties often depend on the licensee's sales, the patentee will often want assurances that the licensee, especially an exclusive licensee, will devote substantial efforts to making and selling the product controlled by the licensed patent. Accordingly, the agreement might preclude the licensee from making or selling rival products. Such restrictions have sometimes been held unenforceable as a patent misuse. Columbus Auto. Corp. v. Oldberg Mfg. Co., 387 F.2d 643 (10th Cir. 1968), aff'g 264 F. Supp. 779 (D. Colo. 1967); Berlenbach v. Anderson & Thompson Ski Co., 329 F.2d 782 (9th Cir.), cert. denied, 379 U.S. 830 (1964). An agreement by the patentee that it will not produce or sell unpatented equipment competing with that produced and sold by its licensee has also been held to be an unreasonable restraint of trade. Compton v. Metal Prods., 453 F.2d 38 (4th Cir. 1971), cert. denied, 406 U.S. 968 (1972). Such results may seem sensible when the restriction is sufficiently anticompetitive to violate the antitrust laws, as explored in Ch. 4C. But why should the patent be unenforceable in the absence of such an impact? See ¶186.

48. Most of the analysis in Bowman, note 17, suggests that price restrictions should be analyzed as vertical restraints, much akin to resale price maintenance. The characterization issue is explored further in Kaplow, note 3, at 1862-1867.

49. See F. Machlup, An Economic Review of the Patent System 12 (Study No. 15 of the Subcommittee on Patents, Trademarks, and Copyrights of the Senate Committee on the Judiciary, 85th Cong., 2d Sess., Committee Print, 1958): "It has been estimated that between 80 and 90 percent of all patents may be in this category" of valueless patents.

patentee will generally make direct use of the patent, license it, or both.

It is often suggested that nonuse may be a more profitable yet socially detrimental alternative. First, a patentee may not find it profitable to scrap existing machinery in order to adopt a new production process or eliminate a product line that would be superseded by the new product. If the patent does not in fact produce sufficient cost savings or other benefits in the short run to merit its use, no social loss is entailed. In addition, the patentee could earn more by licensing than by suppressing the new technology even if sales based on the old technology declined. For example, if the royalty equaled or exceeded its unit profit under the old technology, it loses no profit by losing sales to licensees, and it would benefit from any increased volume resulting from the licensees' better product or lower price.[50] Of course, a patentee might refrain from licensing in expanding or technologically oriented markets for fear that its present and future image may be seriously impaired by offering old products while rivals offer better products. In such circumstances, it might accelerate its use of the new technology, despite its in-place capital.

It has also been supposed that a patentee practicing a better technology suppresses competition by refusing to license older patents that would allow competitors to make a higher-cost or inferior product. Here again, the patentee's profits would be greater by licensing the new technology while charging more for it. Still, it might hesitate if such licensing would put rivals in a position to leap ahead to still further advances.[51]

There is yet another reason for a patentee to keep its patents to itself. Although licensees must pay royalties as long as the patent remains valid and important, they will be immediately ready for unrestrained competition when the patent expires or is invalidated. When such competition becomes possible, it might take a long time for it to arise if there had been no licensees in the meantime.[52]

(b) *Precedent.* In any event, the courts have not yet held nonworking of a patent to be either an antitrust offense or a misuse that will bar the patentee from obtaining the aid of a court of equity to enforce its patent; nor have they entirely eliminated that threat. In

---

50. Compare ¶279a.

51. Perhaps the patentee could nevertheless be induced to license by contracting for a grant-back of at least nonexclusive rights under any new inventions made by licensees.

52. For the same long-run reason, licensees might be willing to pay higher royalties during the interval, but their potential future profits in a competitive market would typically be less than the patentee would lose in the shift from monopoly to competition. Compare ¶331.

Paper Bag,[53] an infringer argued that the Court should refuse to protect a patented invention "which has long and always and unreasonably been held in non-use."[54] One Justice agreed, but the Court questioned whether nonuse had affected the public and quoted approvingly from an earlier Court's statement that "[t]he inventor is one who has discovered something of value. It is his absolute property. He may withhold a knowledge of it from the public, and he may insist upon all the advantages and benefits which the statute promises to him who discloses to the public his invention."[55] The Court relied on the fact that Congress, although aware of foreign compulsory licensing statutes, had never provided for nonuse. The Court concluded that exclusion of competitors is "the very essence of the right conferred by the patent, as it is the privilege of any owner of property to use or not to use it, without question of motive."[56] Yet, the Court did indicate that it was not deciding whether there might be a case "where, regarding the situation of the parties in view of the public interest, a court of equity might be justified in withholding relief by injunction."[57]

Although the Supreme Court refused to overrule or limit *Paper Bag* in the subsequent *Special Equipment* case, the majority did not view the case as presenting a suppression issue,[58] notwithstanding an impassioned dissent.[59]

(c) *De facto compulsory licensing.* There are a very few cases limiting the patentee's discretion to prevent unwanted practice of its invention. One court declared that the partial refusal to license a health-giving invention was a patent misuse.[60] Several others have found an infringement and awarded damages to the patentee but refused to enjoin the infringement.[61] To confine the patentee to damages is similar in effect to compulsory licensing at a royalty amount equal to the damages awarded.

---

53. Continental Paper Bag Co. v. Eastern Paper Bag Co., 210 U.S. 405 (1908).
54. Id. at 422.
55. Id. at 424.
56. Id. at 429.
57. Id. at 430.
58. Special Equip. Co. v. Coe, 324 U.S. 370 (1945).
59. Id. at 382-383.
60. Vitamin Tech. v. Wisconsin Alumni Res. Found., 146 F.2d 941 (9th Cir.), cert. denied, 325 U.S. 876 (1945).
61. Milwaukee v. Activated Sludge, 69 F.2d 577 (7th Cir.), cert. denied, 293 U.S. 576 (1934) (enjoining infringing sewage treatment plant would force lake pollution); Bliss v. Brooklyn, 3 F. Cas. 706 (No. 1544) (E.D.N.Y. 1871); cf. Southwestern Brush Elec. Lt. & Power Co. v. Louisiana Elec. Lt. Co., 45 F. 893 (E.D. La. 1891) (preliminary injunction denied); Nerney v. New York, N.H. & H.R.R., 83 F.2d 409 (2d Cir. 1936) (supplementary injunction denied).

(d) *Compulsory licensing.*[62] Compulsory licensing is often required abroad,[63] frequently recommended at home, occasionally legislated,[64] and usually ignored, perhaps because the theoretical and practical problems seem so formidable. It has appeared most frequently as a remedy in patent misuse and antitrust cases, as noted in ¶190.

Compulsory licensing appears to be an attractive option because it can reduce some of the patent system's social costs. Arguably, it would reduce wasteful duplicating research by rivals seeking access to existing but patented technology, encourage development of improvement patents by outsiders who would fear that they would not have access to the underlying patents, and facilitate the spread of technology, enhancing competition when patents expired. These are the usual advantages of licensing. One must consider, however, why the patentee would not voluntarily have chosen to license its invention, and how the courts would set royalties for the compulsory license — two questions that prove to be related.

Advocates of general compulsory licensing usually speak of "reasonable" royalties for the license. But if we do not mean either zero royalties or royalties at less than commercial value, we must reconsider the purpose of compulsion. Consider the oversimplified case of a patented machine that costs $1000 to produce (including a competitive return on investment) and, over its useful life, saves its user $100,000 in production costs compared with the next best alternative. Were there no patent and a fully competitive machine market, such a machine would sell for $1000. The patentee with a legal monopoly would sell the machine for $100,000 (or a trifle less) or, equivalently, sell the machine for $1000 and charge royalties that, over the life of the machine, yielded the additional $99,000. If this commercial value is the reasonable royalty, which would be available even under compulsory licensing, why is compulsion needed? That is, why did the patentee refrain from licensing at

---

62. See F.M. Scherer, The Economic Effects of Compulsory Licensing (1977).

63. Observe, however, that the rationale of many of these provisions is mercantilistic, that is, to reserve power to force domestic manufacture rather than importation.

64. The Atomic Energy Act, 42 U.S.C. §§2183-2184, empowers the Atomic Energy Commission — now the Energy Department — to compel licensing of certain patents. See also Ch. 1E, note 6. The Clean Air Act, 84 Stat. 1708 (1970), 42 U.S.C. §7608, provides that the court may, upon certification by the Attorney General, order compulsory licensing on reasonable terms and conditions of any patent (1) whose use is necessary, and not otherwise reasonably available, to comply with government antipollution orders where (2) "the unavailability of such right may result in a substantial lessening of competition or tendency to create a monopoly...." See J. Gerber & P. Kitson, Compulsory Licensing of Patents Under the Clean Air Act of 1970, 4 Pat. L. Rev. 147 (1972).

that rate in the first place? Perhaps because the measurement above does not include the value to the patentee of maintaining its monopoly after the patent expires and before new firms could get started and established — a value that might be thought unworthy of respect. Perhaps because prospective licensees have not offered to pay the proper commercial value of the patent and seek to get a compulsory license for less.

In any event, the problems of calculation are formidable. Few actual situations will be as simple as the illustration used above. For that reason, other measures of reasonable royalty have been suggested other than the patent's commercial value — such as a royalty that would allow the patentee to recover the cost of making and developing the invention plus some arbitrary profit. But which costs are to be included? How is overhead to be allocated? And how do we adjust for the risk that the research and development would be a failure or less successful than it was?

In judging the attractiveness of compulsory licensing, we must remember that the patent system we have is based on something of a lottery principle, forcing inventors to bear their own losses from failure but holding out the prospect of monopoly in the event of success. Compulsory licensing assumes that judges can determine just what the right reward should be. But if that were possible, would it not be better to entrust the measurement to more expert hands and to provide the reward directly to inventors as a public bounty? Such a substitute for the patent system would fully compensate inventors without incurring monopolistic reductions in output, reductions that still occur with compulsory licensing at a "reasonable royalty."[65]

281. Consider the price-restricted license employed in *GE*.

(a) Why, generally, would a patentee license its patent rather than retain the full monopoly for itself? Why, in particular, would the General Electric Company license its patents rather than monopolize the production and sale of electric lamps as its patents apparently permit it to do?

(b) Would a patentee otherwise willing to license hesitate to do so if not permitted to control its licensee's price? Consider: (1) Why would the patentee want to restrict its licensee's price? (2) Does it need a price restriction or can it satisfy its concerns in some other way? (3) Will power to control a licensee's price often determine whether the patentee will license or not? Will it ever do so?

65. See Ch. 1E, note 6.

(c) What, generally, are the social advantages of more extensive licensing?

(d) Apart from price restrictions, are there any social disadvantages in more extensive licensing?

282. The New Wrinkle Company possesses certain patents covering the manufacture of wrinkle-finish enamels, varnishes, and paints. (The following facts are numbered for easy reference.) (1) New Wrinkle manufactures finishes under these patents and has undertaken to license other industry members with a minimum price provision (2) that was not to become operative until 12 of the largest producers of wrinkle finishes had subscribed to the price-restricted licenses. (3) New Wrinkle advised prospective licensees of the prices, terms, and conditions of sale in the license agreement and assured them that like advice was being given to other manufacturers (4) "in order to establish minimum prices throughout the industry." (5) Within a few months, 12 leading manufacturers had signed up. Ultimately, more than 200, or substantially all, manufacturers of wrinkle finishes in the United States held nearly identical 10-year extendable licenses from New Wrinkle. Minimum prices and other terms and conditions of sale were specified. (6) The minimum prices on various grades and quantities ranged from $2.45 per gallon to $4.00 per gallon. The royalty was set at 5¢ per gallon. (7) Each agreement provided that each licensee was bound by the minimum price provision only if it was imposed on all other licensees and (8) that each licensee would have the benefit of any lower royalty rate in any subsequent license.[66]

(a) Is there anything suspiciously anticompetitive about provisions 7 and 8?

(b) What was the purpose of provision 2? Would a prospective licensee in the *GE* situation care whether other firms took a license from the General Electric Company? Would it have preferred to see the largest possible number of lamp licensees? If not, how do you account for the presence of provision 2?

(c) On what grounds might you hold that New Wrinkle's 200 licensees have conspired among themselves to fix prices?

(d) Would your ¶c answer apply in the absence of provision 2?

(e) How would the following additional or altered facts help you to appraise the purpose, effect, and desirability of the arrangement?

66. These are the facts of United States v. New Wrinkle, 342 U.S. 371 (1952), with this exception: The actual New Wrinkle was a patent holding company formed by two members of the industry who had been engaged in patent litigation in which each had claimed that its patent was dominant and the other's subservient. For an apparently lawful most-favored-licensee clause, see Prestole Corp. v. Tinneman Prods., 271 F.2d 146 (6th Cir. 1959), cert. denied, 361 U.S. 964 (1960).

(1) The royalty charge is a fraction of a cent per gallon. (2) Before everyone took a license from New Wrinkle, industry members had produced a variety of unpatented wrinkle finishes, they no longer do so, and the general price level has increased.[67] (3) Disinterested experts testify that the licensed patent makes little difference to the product's quality or production cost.

(f) Would you be prepared to hold that industry-wide licensing itself is more dangerous to competition than a single price-restricted license? (1) Why might you be prepared to do so? (2) Would the ruling be appropriate where competitors cannot survive without access to the patent? (3) Would such a holding be consistent with *GE*?

(g) Are these collateral dangers of price-restricted licenses absent when there is a single license?

283. Post-*GE* developments. (a) *Does GE survive?* The continuing strength of the *GE* doctrine is in serious doubt; many believe it to be moribund. Four Supreme Court Justices would have overruled it in the 1948 *Line Material* case and perhaps again in 1965,[68] and, as suggested by many other opinions, its application has been limited. It has not, however, been expressly overruled.

(b) *Unpatented product or nonmanufacturing patentee.* The lower courts have tended to confine *GE* to its facts. Because General Electric was a manufacturer protecting the price of its own production, price-fixing permission has been denied to non-manufacturing patentees.[69] Because the price-fixed article in *GE* was itself the subject of the licensed patent, patentees have not been allowed to fix the price of an unpatented product made with a patented component, machine, or process.[70]

---

67. Compare National Lockwasher Co. v. George K. Garrett Co., 137 F.2d 355 (3d Cir. 1943) (nonexclusive licensees agree not to manufacture items not embraced within the patent); McCullough v. Kammerer Corp., 166 F.2d 759 (9th Cir.), cert. denied, 355 U.S. 813 (1948) (patentee and licensees agree not to make unpatented articles); *Crown Zellerbach*, note 29, at 127. These cases did not involve price fixing.

68. United States v. Huck Mfg. Co., 227 F. Supp. 791 (E.D. Mich. 1964), aff'd by an equally divided Court, 382 U.S. 197 (1965).

69. United States v. American Linen Supply Co., 141 F. Supp. 105 (N.D. Ill. 1956); United States v. Vehicular Parking, 54 F. Supp. 828 (D. Del. 1944). But see Royal Indus. v. St. Regis Paper Co., 420 F.2d 449 (9th Cir. 1969).

70. Cummer-Graham Co. v. Straight Side Basket Corp., 142 F.2d 646 (5th Cir.), cert. denied, 323 U.S. 726 (1944); Barber-Colman Co. v. National Tool Co., 136 F.2d 339 (6th Cir. 1943); United States v. GE, 80 F. Supp. 989, 1004-1005 (S.D.N.Y. 1948) (carboloy). Cf. Robintech v. Chemidus Wavin, 628 F.2d 142 (D.C. Cir. 1980) (patent misuse to restrict exports of unpatented article made with licensed patented process and apparatus).

(c) *Multiple patents.* Suppose that each of two manufacturing patentees has an equally valid and equally effective patent for making widgets. These may be called competing patents because each can be practiced independently of the other and licensees may choose among them to accomplish their purposes. One patentee licensing the other (or the patentees engaging in reciprocal licensing) with a price condition would probably be a masquerade for naked horizontal price fixing.[71] Of course, if one patent is clearly superior to the other or if they cannot be practiced independently, different purposes and effects might be imagined.

In *Line Material*,[72] Southern had a patent covering a mechanical circuit breaker. Line Material invented and patented a more efficient and less expensive device. Line's patent was a subservient or improvement patent in the sense that it could not be practiced without infringing Southern's more basic or dominant patent. They cross-licensed each other, enabling both to make the better product, and Line was permitted to license other firms under both patents. All the licenses granted by Line fixed the price of the improved product made under both patents.[73]

The eight Justices hearing the case split evenly on whether *GE* should be overruled, but one of those favoring upholding *GE*, Justice Reed, distinguished it and thus made a majority for invalidating Line's restraint. He reasoned:

> Where two or more patentees with competitive, non-infringing patents combine them and fix prices on all devices produced under any of the patents, competition is impeded to a greater degree than where a single patentee fixes prices for his licensees. The struggle for profit is less acute. Even when, as here, the devices are not commercially competitive because the subservient patent cannot be practiced without consent of the dominant, the statement holds good. The stimulus to seek competitive inventions is reduced by the mutually

71. After examining Ch. 5, consider the applicability of the Sherman Act and Clayton Act §7 to the merger of two such companies. If the merger would be illegal, should the licensing arrangement necessarily be illegal as well?

In evaluating judicial hostility to price restrictions when multiple patents and cross-licenses are involved, consider the statement in F.M. Scherer, Industrial Market Structure and Economic Performance 452 (2d ed. 1980):

> Some of the most egregious price-fixing schemes in American economic history were erected on a foundation of agreements to cross-license complementary and competing patents. . . . Typically, such arrangements have been implemented by adding to the patent exchange agreement provisions specifying prices, market quotas, membership in the industry, and other aspects of conduct and structure.

72. United States v. Line Material Co., 333 U.S. 287 (1948).

73. The price limitation was opposed by many licensees, including GE, the largest producer of patented appliances. And a number tried energetically to find substitutes for the patented product.

advantageous price-fixing arrangement.... The merging of the benefits of price fixing under the patents restrains trade in violation of
the Sherman Act in the same way as would the fixing of prices
between producers of nonpatentable goods.

If the objection is made that a price agreement between a patentee and a licensee equally restrains trade, the answer is not that there
is no restraint in such an arrangement but, when the validity of the
General Electric case is assumed, that reasonable restraint accords with
the patent monopoly granted by the patent law....

We think that ... when patentees join in an agreement as here to
maintain prices on their several products, that agreement, however
advantageous it may be to stimulate the broader use of patents, is
unlawful per se under the Sherman Act. It is more than an exploitation of patents. There is the vice that patentees have combined to fix
prices on patented products.

Does Justice Reed successfully distinguish *GE*? In any event, the
death knell for price-restricted licenses under combined patents
was sounded by *Line Material*. And *New Wrinkle*, ¶282, held simply
that "[p]rice control through cross-licensing was barred as beyond
the patent monopoly."[74]

(d) *Multiple licenses.* Even where a single patent is involved, several
cases have not hesitated to view the price-restricted patent license as
the industry's convenient cover vehicle for organizing a cartel and
suppressing competition that would otherwise be present.[75] Where
the lay observer would sense that the patent is being used in this
manner, the courts may condemn the arrangement notwithstanding the absence of compelling proof that the patent licenses were a
subterfuge for regimenting an industry.[76] It is the risk of such regi-

74. *New Wrinkle*, note 66, at 379.
75. United States v. United States Gypsum Co., 340 U.S. 76 (1950); United States
v. United States Gypsum Co., 333 U.S. 364, 400-401 (1948):

> *[GE]* gives no support for a patentee, acting in concert with all members of an
> industry, to issue substantially identical licenses to all members of the industry under
> the terms of which the industry is completely regimented, the production of competi-
> tive unpatented products suppressed, a class of distributors squeezed out, and prices
> on unpatented products stabilized.... [I]t would be sufficient to show that the defen-
> dants, constituting all former competitors in an entire industry, had acted in concert
> to restrain commerce in an entire industry under patent licenses in order to organize
> the industry and stabilize prices.

76. See United States v. Masonite Corp., 316 U.S. 265, 269, 275. The Court did
not upset the district court's finding that each licensee acted independently,
"desired the agreement regardless of the action that might be taken by any of the
others, [and] did not require as a condition of its acceptance that Masonite make
such an agreement with any of the others." Yet, the Court applied the *Interstate
Circuit* doctrine because Masonite informed each party of the terms of the agreements made with the others, and, therefore, it was "clear that, as the arrangement
continued, each became familiar with its purpose and scope."

mentation, perhaps, that has led at least one court to hold that a price-restricted license exceeds the bounds of the *GE* permission when it covers a plurality of an industry, admitting that "[t]he explanation probably lies more in history than in logic for history is an untidy housekeeper."[77]

Use Restrictions

284. Introduction. A use restriction[78] is a provision in a patent license stating that the licensee may employ the patent for some purposes and not for others. Although these restrictions are not uncommon, the case law is not well developed. Precedents are few and scattered, and there has been little judicial analysis of the antitrust questions involved.

The discussion begins with an analysis of price discrimination and its applicability to use restrictions. This is followed by a brief summary of leading cases, which will not readily permit the student to state the law of use restrictions but will illustrate how they are employed and how much thinking remains to be done. Finally, some questions explore further the anticompetitive potential of such arrangements.[79]

285. Price discrimination, patent exploitation, and use restrictions. Many practices scrutinized under the antitrust laws have price discrimination as one of their possible purposes. In addition, the Robinson-Patman Act (Clayton Act §2), explored in Chapter 6,

77. Newburgh Moire Co. v. Superior Moire Co., 237 F.2d 283, 293 (3d Cir. 1956). The court relied on *Line Material* and *New Wrinkle* without acknowledging that those cases rested on a combination of patents and, in *New Wrinkle*, a finding of conspiracy among the licensees. The court's rationale, however, is suggested by its statement that "[w]ere it not for the *GE* decision one could argue persuasively that a line could be drawn between the patent laws and the antitrust laws. The division would permit an inventor" to get such royalties as it could but prohibit it from controlling its licensee's price or output.

A lower court interpreted *Newburgh* to permit only a single price-restricted license. Tinnerman Prods. v. George K. Garrett Co., 185 F. Supp. 151, 158 (E.D. Pa. 1960), aff'd on other grounds, 292 F.2d 137 (3d Cir.), cert. denied, 368 U.S. 833 (1961). See also *Prestole*, note 66 (permitting single price-fixed license). Contrary to *Newburgh* is Westinghouse Elec. Corp. v. Bulldog Elec. Prods. Co., 179 F.2d 139, 142-143 (4th Cir. 1950).

78. Although the focus is use restrictions, emphasizing their unique aspects, much of the analysis from the preceding subsection is applicable and other restrictions may raise the issues explored here. The topics are separated to present clearly the primary and often differing problems raised by the different licensing arrangements.

79. See generally the note 17 articles.

directly addresses certain price discriminations. Because patent royalties and license restrictions, particularly use restrictions, are often motivated by the desire to charge discriminatory prices, this is a convenient point to explore the phenomenon briefly.

(a) *Discrimination's nature and prerequisites.* "Price discrimination" describes the practice of charging different customers different prices for essentially identical products.[80] Notwithstanding the term's derogatory flavor, price discrimination may be socially beneficial, harmful, or unimportant. Consider, for example, a fine pen for which some would pay $15. More people would, if necessary, pay $7. There are still more who would pay no more than $2. If the long-run average cost of producing the pen (regardless of volume and including a normal return on investment) is $1, vigorous competition would drive the price down to $1. But a monopolist of these pens might find advantage in producing only enough to sell to $15 customers. Or consumers might be so responsive to lower prices that it would earn more by increasing output even though it would surrender the extraordinary profit it could earn from those who most crave its pen.

Better than either choice for the monopolist would be price discrimination. The pen manufacturer would like to get $15 from those who would pay it and less from everyone else. Such price discrimination is possible only if the seller can (1) identify high-value customers and (2) prevent those buying at lower prices from reselling to high-value customers. Although no buyer will invite higher prices by candidly stating the highest price it is willing to pay, the seller may suppose that a polishing machine would be more valuable to diamond cutters than to brass makers. Even so, few sales will be made at high prices to the former if the latter can buy more than they need at lower prices and resell the excess to the diamond firms. If the product is a service, such resale will be impossible.

To eliminate resales and to identify high-value users, the seller[81] might vary the price according to the intensity of use. Lessors of copying machines or franchisors of a trade name (like McDonald's) understand that high-volume copier lessees or franchisees would pay more for using the machine or name. Charging lessees 1¢ per page or franchisees 5 percent of revenues extracts higher prices

80. The product is, of course, the whole bundle of goods and services received by the buyer from the seller. Thus, for example, identical prices for a single physical product would be discriminatory in the economic sense if the seller delivered the product to one buyer's distant plant but not to the other's. What constitutes a price discrimination for purposes of the Robinson-Patman Act will be considered in Ch. 6. The immediate discussion focuses on undoubted discrimination.

81. Observe that seller here includes lessor, licensor, and franchisor.

from those who obtain higher value from the machine or franchise, while those who pay less have nothing to resell. Another way to segregate high-value customers and to limit resales is to differentiate the product. Buyers of alcoholic beverages will pay more than buyers of alcoholic cleaning fluids; adding a poison to the latter prevents it from being resold as a beverage. Less perfectly, some of those who value the pen highly will identify themselves by purchasing the $15 version when plated in gold, packaged in velvet, and sold through fancy jewelry stores (although the incremental production and marketing costs relative to the $1 pen are modest). But this will work crudely because it entails additional expense and fails to identify all those willing to pay the higher price.[82]

Such price discrimination is an exercise of market or monopoly power, which is the ability to behave other than as a perfectly competitive firm would or, in other words, to charge more than marginal cost. The lower of the two prices would not be under marginal cost, otherwise it would be unprofitable; therefore, the higher of the two prices must exceed marginal cost. The higher price could not be maintained were there intense competition.

(b) *Discrimination's consequences.* Given the existence of market power, price discrimination by a patentee or other monopolist will sometimes be socially beneficial. This can be most clearly illustrated by beginning with a case in which the highest discriminatory price does not exceed the uniform price that would prevail if discrimination were impossible or impermissible. In setting a uniform price, for example, our hypothetical pen monopolist might choose either $15 or $2.

Uniform price high. If a single price of $15 maximized profit, output would be relatively low, and those willing to pay $2 would not enjoy the product at all. But if discrimination were possible, the pen manufacturer would also sell to the $2 customers without sacrificing its high returns from the $15 customers. Such price discrimination always serves the social interest by increasing output and thus providing the product to persons willing to pay its cost of production.

Uniform price low and perfect discrimination. Where a discriminatory price exceeds the uniform price that would otherwise have prevailed, the output effect depends upon the seller's perfection in

---

82. In another common instance, a seller charges less to those who enjoy access to alternative suppliers. For example, a local bank may charge competitive interest rates to a large borrower who can turn to capital sources throughout the country while charging monopoly rates to a small borrower without such access. If the two borrowers make and sell the same product in the same places, the smaller will suffer a competitive disadvantage. To simplify the present discussion, we assume that those paying different royalties or other prices do not compete with each other. For situations in which they do, see Ch. 6B.

categorizing customers. If a nondiscriminating pen monopolist would have maximized profits at a uniform price of $2, discrimination could not generate additional sales. And as long as the $15 price is demanded only from those customers willing to pay it, the discrimination will not reduce output below that which occurs at a uniform price of $2.[83] So far, in our simple example, we have seen that discrimination cannot lead to reduced output but only to expansion (last paragraph) or, at worst (this paragraph), to expropriation of so-called consumer surplus by the monopolistic seller. And this is always true of discrimination that does not deny the product to any customer willing to pay the uniform price that would prevail in the absence of discrimination.

Uniform price lower than highest imperfectly discriminatory price. In most instances, however, a seller can do no better than to catego-

---

83. The point may be illustrated in the following table.

	$15	$7	$2
Situation I:			
A. Without discrimination,			
1. Total number of buyers at each price	100,000	200,000	500,000
2. Total net revenue at each price (unit price less $1 average cost times number of buyers) (in millions of dollars)	1.4	1.2	0.5
B. With discrimination,			
1. Number of buyers at each price who would *not* pay a higher price	100,000	100,000	300,000
2. Total net revenue at each price if there is price discrimination **Total net revenue: $2.3 million**	1.4	0.6	0.3
Situation II (with much greater low-price demand than in situation I):			
A. Without discrimination,			
1. Total number of buyers at each price	100,000	200,000	2,000,000
2. Total net revenue at each price	1.4	1.2	2.0
B. With discrimination,			
1. Number of buyers at each price who would not pay a higher price	100,000	100,000	1,800,000
2. Total net revenue at each price if there is price discrimination **Total net revenue: $3.8 million**	1.4	0.6	1.8

In situation I, the manufacturer's best course in the absence of price discrimination is to sell 100,000 units at $15. Price discrimination increases its revenue (net of costs) from $1.4 million to $2.3 million and its sales (and output) from 100,000 to 500,000. In situation II, the manufacturer's best course in the absence of price discrimination is to sell 2,000,000 at $2. Permitting it to discriminate would increase its net revenues from $2 million to $3.8 million but would not increase its sales (or output).

rize customers crudely according to product version or use. Suppose, for example, that an aluminum monopolist has uniform costs for the versions of its product suitable for pipe or cable and would maximize profits at a uniform price of $50 or, with discrimination, at prices of $60 to pipe fabricators and $40 to cable manufacturers.[84] Such discrimination will obviously increase aluminum output used for cable and decrease output used for pipe. There is no general answer to the question whether such discrimination would raise or lower overall aluminum output or economic welfare.[85]

(c) *Discrimination and patent exploitation.* Antitrust courts seldom address price discrimination directly or consistently. We shall see in Chapter 3A that an otherwise lawful monopolist is allowed to charge what the traffic will bear, whether discriminatory or not. On the other hand, we shall see in Chapter 4B that the courts have been concerned by so-called tie-ins, which may be used to effect price discrimination. For example, instead of charging a fee for each copy, the seller of a copying machine might insist on supplying copiers with copy paper as well (at a premium price). Instead (or in addition), the seller might use the tie to enhance its position anticompetitively in the paper market.[86] Accordingly, we would need to determine (1) whether a particular tie-in is being used for such enhancement or merely for price discrimination and (2) if for both, whether the possible benefits of discrimination outweigh the other effect, either generally or in the particular case. The answer obviously depends on whether price discrimination is generally desirable or harmful or whether particular instances of desirable or harmful use can be identified. Moreover, if discrimination were generally harmful but only in small degree, the law might tolerate it standing alone but not when achieved through practices involving additional dangers to competition.

Let us now apply these thoughts to the patent context. If price discrimination were generally desirable, so would patent practices facilitating it. If not, antitrust law might still be more hospitable to it in the context of patents, whose very purpose is to confer a monopoly and to permit its exploitation. After all, excess returns for patentees may seem more worthy of regard than for other holders of market power. If, for example, discrimination reduced output mod-

84. This is sometimes called third degree discrimination, which is distinguished from second degree (imperfect discrimination arising from haggling between seller and individual buyers) and first degree (perfect) discrimination.

85. See F.M. Scherer & D. Ross, Industrial Market Structure and Economic Performance 494-496 (3d ed. 1990).

86. If such copying were the only use for paper, the copy machine monopolist would thereby obtain a monopoly over paper as well. See ¶423.

estly while increasing the patentee's profit greatly, it might seem a more cost-effective vehicle for rewarding patentees than other methods of exploiting the patent, which might then be outlawed.

Where a patent practice facilitating price discrimination could also have other effects that are anticompetitive, we need to consider the same two questions we asked a moment ago about tying. But the answers need not be the same because a patentee's reward, enhanced by discrimination, may be deemed a favored object of the patent system. Let us now turn to the connection between price discrimination and use-restricted patent licenses.[87]

(d) *Use restrictions and discriminatory royalties.* A patentee making a chemical that can be used both as a lifesaving drug and as a furniture spray can effect price discrimination simply by charging more for the former than for the latter. But licensing the patent to make that chemical may be profitable or even indispensable, as ¶278 explained. Obviously, the patentee cannot continue charging high prices for the drug if licensees sell it for less. To prevent such interference, the patentee might charge licensees differential royalties — say, $10 per unit sold as a drug and 10¢ per unit sold as spray. Naturally, licensees will have to charge higher prices for the drug than for the spray.[88]

The patentee might go further and limit a licensee's use of the patent to one product or other — perhaps simply to help collect discriminatory royalties. Fearing that licensees might misrepresent their relative drug and spray sales in order to pay the lower royalty on the former, the patentee who is unable to monitor their relative sales closely might limit each licensee to one field; then even a single sale in the forbidden field would demonstrate a violation of the agreement.

Or a patentee fully able to exploit the drug field itself may prefer to retain that use exclusively while licensing spray producers for the other use. Or a patentee might license only specified uses now, awaiting future developments and better estimates of optimum royalty levels before licensing other uses. Or one use of the patent might require extensive development or marketing efforts by a licensee who reasonably insists upon exclusive use of the patent in that field for a period of years. Finally, use-restricted licenses might disguise an anticompetitive market division, as we shall explore with the ¶287 problem.

87. For a more complete analysis of how antitrust law should be applied in the patent context, exploring further patent practices designed to facilitate price discrimination, see Kaplow, note 3.

88. For the ways in which the patent royalty is connected to the product price and the patentee's interests, see ¶279a.

286. The legality of use restrictions. (a) *General Talking Pictures v. Western Electric Co.*, 304 U.S. 175, reaff'd on rehearing, 305 U.S. 124 (1938). AT&T licensed electronics patents to American Transformer Company with the restriction that they be used only for home amplification devices (such as radio receivers), reserving the commercial field for its Western Electric subsidiary. Transformer produced amplifiers suitable for home or commercial use, though labeled for home use only, and sold them to General Talking Pictures, which used them in movie theaters. The Supreme Court upheld Western's claim of infringement, declaring that the knowing sale by Transformer in violation of restrictions on its license infringed the patents and General Talking Pictures knew of the restriction and contributed to the infringement. The Court held that the restriction on Transformer and its knowing vendee was not within the general rule condemning restrictions on the use or alienation of chattels that had passed into commerce in the ordinary course of business. The Court's holding necessarily implies that the restriction on the licensee was valid, and the case is often cited for the proposition that use restrictions are lawful. But neither the parties' briefs nor the Court explicitly considered the validity of the underlying restriction. The Court in *Hazeltine*[89] declined to reaffirm its earlier holding, however, and avoided the issue with the observation that the patentee had abandoned the use restriction. However, the lower courts often permit restrictions on what a manufacturer may do with a patented product made under license.[90]

(b) *Limiting use of purchased patented product.* Restrictions on subsequent use by a purchaser of a patented product were declared illegal in two lower court cases, *Consolidated* and *Baldwin*.[91] Consolidated manufactured and sold a patented metal alloy useful in making dental plates and other items under the restriction that

89. Automatic Radio Mfg. Co. v. Hazeltine Research, 339 U.S. 827 (1950).

90. E.g., Westinghouse Elec. Corp. v. Bulldog Elec. Prods. Co., 106 F. Supp. 819 (N.D. W. Va. 1952), aff'd, 206 F.2d 574 (4th Cir.), cert. denied, 346 U.S. 909 (1953) (upholding license of circuit breaker patent that restricted the licensees to the manufacture of specified types of electrical equipment); Turner Glass Corp. v. Hartford-Empire Co., 173 F.2d 49 (7th Cir.), cert. denied, 338 U.S. 830 (1949) (defendant entitled to lease its patented glassware manufacturing machinery on condition that the lessees use it only to manufacture certain types of glassware); Extractol Process v. Hiram Walker & Sons, 153 F.2d 264 (7th Cir. 1946) (dictum: license to use but not sell patented machine enforceable); United States v. Studiengesellschaft Kohle, 670 F.2d 1122 (D.C. Cir. 1981) (license of patented process may control or forbid use or sale of result of that process).

91. United States v. Consolidated Car-Heating Co., 1950 Trade Cas. ¶62655 (S.D.N.Y.); Baldwin-Lima-Hamilton Corp. v. Tatnall Measuring Sys. Co., 169 F. Supp. 1 (E.D. Pa. 1958), aff'd per curiam, 268 F.2d 395 (3d Cir.), cert. denied, 361 U.S. 894 (1959).

purchasers could use it for making dental plates only. The court found this restriction an unlawful restraint of trade, holding that the patentee had received all the reward to which it was entitled by getting the price it demanded for the alloy. Baldwin owned the patent on an instrument called a strain gauge, which could be used either as a part of a larger apparatus for testing the strain on metals or as a disposable element in certain other test procedures. Baldwin sold both the larger apparatus and the individual gauges but required purchasers of individual gauges to promise to use them only in procedures consuming them. Tatnall successfully defended an infringement action on the ground that Baldwin's attempt to restrict use of the product in the hands of purchasers constituted misuse of the patent and was a ground for denying relief.[92]

Query: Can *Consolidated* and *Baldwin* be persuasively distinguished from *General Talking Pictures?*

287. Dryday Company owns the patent on a synthetic fiber called xlon. It manufactures the fiber and weaves it into various fabrics that it sells to manufacturers of raincoats. Since xlon is less expensive to produce and more water-resistant than comparable materials, Dryday enjoys a substantial competitive advantage over other weavers of rainwear fabric. Xlon would also have a competitive advantage in other product lines. Dryday intends to license two manufacturers, Cloth and Weaver, to practice its patent. For each of the following licensing arrangements: (1) consider Dryday's reasons for licensing as compared with self-manufacture of each xlon product and for restricting uses as compared with differential royalties or no restriction, (2) consider the licensees' motivations for accepting the arrangements, (3) predict Dryday's likely action if the restriction were forbidden, (4) indicate a court's likely determination, and (5) assess the social benefits of permitting the arrangement.

(a) Dryday restricts Weaver and Cloth from making fabrics suitable for rainwear.

(b) Dryday limits Weaver to using the xlon patent to make shirt fabric and Cloth to stocking fabric.

(c) Dryday limits each licensee to particular uses and must seek their approval when granting licenses for future uses.

92. Compare United States v. American Linen Supply Co., 141 F. Supp. 105, 112-114 (N.D. Ill. 1956) (use restrictions on leased or sold product invalid if unrelated to patentee's reward but designed to limit competition among licensees for their benefit), with Sperry Prods. v. Aluminum Co. of Am., 171 F. Supp. 901, 930 (N.D. Ohio 1959), aff'd in part on other grounds and rev'd in part, 285 F.2d 911, 927 (6th Cir. 1960), cert. denied, 368 U.S. 980 (1961) (approving restriction preventing use of leased device in area in which lessor was itself working).

(d) Dryday, Cloth, and Weaver assign their patents to DCW Co., which they create, sharing ownership equally. DCW then licenses all the patents to the three companies, limiting Dryday to using them for rainwear, Weaver to shirt fabric, and Cloth to stocking fabric.

(e) How would your answers differ if you were told any or all of the following additional facts: (1) before the patent, all three companies produce all the relevant products, with little competition; (2) the patent is of modest value; and (3) prices were lower before the licensing agreement was created.

Patent Settlements

288. The problem. (a) *Private benefits of patent settlement.* Uncertainty as to the validity and coverage of many patents[93] makes dispute inevitable. Litigation is costly and may result in a judgment that one's patent is invalid. Indeed, the contestants as a group may emerge worse off after a patent battle if, for example, all their competing patents are declared invalid. Even if a large number of competing patents are upheld, there may be no winner from the parties' point of view, as each patentee's monopoly is of little value when effective substitutes are available. One cannot charge a significant premium for one's product or obtain substantial royalties when potential purchasers or licensees have many alternatives. Of course, each litigant can hope to emerge victorious — with its patent upheld and those of all its competitors declared invalid. But settlement will often be more profitable, especially if it eliminates competition among the litigants or limits access to the patents either by denying them to outsiders or by agreeing on high royalties for licensing the disputed set of patents.

(b) *Social benefits of settlement.* Settlement is generally thought socially desirable because it reduces conflict and the expenditure of resources on litigation. When settlement simply involves an agreement upon a sum to be transferred from one party to another, society's interest may be modest, or, if large, the direct conflict of interest between the parties as to the amount of the settlement limits the parties' ability to conspire in their own interest at society's expense.[94]

But the very reasons that make patent settlements beneficial to the parties may make them dangerous to the public. Many patents

---

93. See ¶¶182-185.
94. Even this modest claim in favor of settlement goes too far. See S. Shavell, The Social Versus the Private Incentive to Bring Suit in a Costly Legal System, 11 J. Leg. Stud. 333 (1982).

are issued that would have been denied if full information had been available to the Patent and Trademark Office. Thus, litigation about patent validity plays a vital role in the process by which only truly worthy inventions are rewarded with publicly protected monopolies. Moreover, the patent system does not purport to reward separate patents that are capable of competing in the marketplace by permitting several patentees to combine them monopolistically.[95] It does not follow that all patent settlements should be disapproved, but we must think carefully about the competitive values that might be sacrificed by a settlement and how best to preserve them.

289. The legality of patent settlements. The most well-known case on settlements is the *Cracking* case[96] — a decision that is often mentioned, sometimes relied on, but seldom analyzed. Conflict had developed among four leading oil companies concerning the validity of their patents on cracking processes — which allowed additional gasoline to be made from any given amount of crude oil.[97] To settle their disputes, the first patentee agreed with each of the others: Each could use the patents of all and license outsiders under all patents, outsiders would be charged a specified royalty — set at approximately the amount that the first inventor had charged when it had the only patent — and each would pay the others specified portions of the royalties it received from licensing all the patents to outsiders. The Court stated that

> [w]here there are legitimately conflicting claims or threatened interferences, a settlement by agreement, rather than litigation, is not precluded. . . . An interchange of patent rights and a division of royalties according to the value attributed by the parties to their respective patent claims is frequently necessary if technical advancement is not to be blocked by threatened litigation.

The Court stopped short of blanket permission.

> Where domination exists, a pooling of competing process patents, or an exchange of licenses for the purpose of curtailing the manufacture and supply of an unpatented product, is beyond the privileges

95. Settlements joining competing patents resemble some cross-licenses with price-restrictions. See ¶331's discussion of patent acquisitions. All may be analogized to horizontal mergers, the subject of Ch. 5D. See Antitrust Guidelines, note 3; Kaplow, note 3, at 1867-1873.

96. Standard Oil Co. (Indiana) v. United States, 283 U.S. 163, 171, 174-175 (1931).

97. The district court had found that the claims of the several patents "should be interpreted narrowly, and that the respective inventions might be practiced without infringement of adversely owned patents. But it confirmed the finding of presumptive validity and did not question the finding of good faith" by the settling parties. 283 U.S. at 181.

conferred by the patents and constitutes a violation of the Sherman Act. . . . But an agreement for cross-licensing and division of royalties violates the Act only when used to effect a monopoly, or to fix prices, or to impose otherwise an unreasonable restraint upon interstate commerce.

The Court found that the defendants lacked the requisite market dominance since they controlled only 55 percent of total cracking capacity and cracked gasoline was only about 26 percent of total gasoline production.[98]

Subsequently, the Court found a violation in United States v. Singer Manufacturing Co., 374 U.S. 174, 199-200 (1963), where a settlement was seen as designed to obtain protection against competition from Japanese sewing machines. Most notable is Justice White's statement in his concurring opinion:

> the settlement of an interference in which the only interests at stake are those of the adversaries, as in the case of a dispute over relative priority only and where possible invalidity, because of known prior art, is not involved, may well be consistent with the general policy favoring settlement of litigation. But the present case involved a less innocuous setting. Singer and Gegauf agreed to settle an interference, at least in part, to prevent an open fight over validity. There is a public interest here which the parties have subordinated to their private ends — the public interest in granting patent monopolies only when the progress of the useful arts and of science will be furthered because as the consideration for its grant the public is given a novel and useful invention. . . . Whatever may be the duty of a single party to draw the prior art to the [Patent] Office's attention . . . clearly collusion among applicants to prevent prior art from coming to or being drawn to the Office's attention is an inequitable imposition on the Office and on the public. . . . In my view, such collusion to secure a monopoly grant runs afoul of the Sherman Act's prohibitions against conspiracies in restraint of trade — if not bad per se, then such agreements are at least presumptively bad.

290. Firms *A, B, C,* and *D* — known in the trade as the Inventive Four — have each patented a different process for producing the industry's product (*Z*) in a manner that eliminates a known problem, thereby enhancing the *Z*'s value by 5 percent. Most other producers license and use one of these patents. Firm *A*, which has the oldest patent, has instituted suit for patent infringement against *B, C,* and *D*. Each defendant asserts the validity of its own patent and challenges the validity of *A*'s patent. Each defendant cross-claims, charging firm *A* with infringement. The pretrial motions

98. See J. McGee, Patent Exploitation: Some Economic and Legal Problems, 9 J.L. & Econ. 135, 150-160 (1966).

and discovery are intricate and costly. Eventually, firms *A, B, C,* and *D* agree on the following terms of settlement: (1) The parties release each other and their respective licensees from any liability for past infringement. (2) The *H* Holding Company is to be created to receive the parties' patents relating to *Z* production. Each of the four is to receive a quarter of the stock in *H.* (3) The parties will each receive licenses for all patents held by *H.* (4) *H,* as owner of the patents, will have the discretion to license other responsible firms at suitable royalties judged by *H* to be appropriate for each license.

The Antitrust Division of the Department of Justice asks you to analyze the proposed settlement and recommend appropriate action for the government to take. In particular, the Division wishes answers to the following questions:

(a) As a preliminary question, suppose that the disputants had simply cross-licensed each other on a royalty-free basis to settle their dispute. Lawful?[99]

(b) Turning now to the more elaborate arrangement described above, is it an illegal price-fixing agreement or is it otherwise unlawful under §1 of the Sherman Act?[100]

(c) If the agreement instead provides only for licenses to each of the four litigants, but prohibits licensing their rivals, is there an illegal boycott?[101] Does *AP* require that competitors be licensed?

(d) What royalty rate would you expect to be charged by the holding company? What royalty rate would each firm have charged had each patent been upheld? What industry prices would result from each alternative? What prices if all patents had been declared invalid? If all but one had been declared invalid? All but two?

(e) If the agreement is illegal, how might the parties have acted to avoid illegality? What is the effect of such alternatives on competition?

(f) On the assumption that the above arrangements might be held to violate the Sherman Act, what civil remedies might be available upon suit by the government? Would such remedies tend to increase competition in this industry?

(g) What rule concerning patent settlements seems appropriate in light of your analysis in ¶¶a-f?

99. See *Honeywell,* discussed in ¶279d.

100. After examining later chapters, consider whether the formation of *H* holding company offends Sherman Act §2 or Clayton Act §7.

101. See Zenith Radio Corp. v. Hazeltine Research, 395 U.S. 100 (1969) (foreign patent pools among foreign and domestic firms illegally exclude plaintiff's domestically manufactured goods from certain markets); *Honeywell,* note 46 (patent cross-license held to be an unreasonable restraint of trade because it conferred competitive advantage on collaborators and was de facto exclusive).

Chapter 3

Monopoly

300. Prologue. The first two sections of this chapter explore the elements of the Sherman Act §2 offense of monopolization. (1) Is anything more than the possession of monopoly power necessary to constitute the offense of monopolization? (2) How much market power is necessary to constitute "monopoly power" and how can it be detected? It is convenient and customary to discuss the two elements of monopolization separately, but they are closely related because the proper test for the existence of monopoly power may depend on the consequences of finding it. The final section of this chapter treats separately the notion of attempt to monopolize.

SHERMAN ACT §2

Every person who shall monopolize, or attempt to monopolize, or combine or conspire with any other person or persons, to monopolize any part of the trade or commerce among the several States, or with foreign nations, shall be deemed guilty of a felony. . . .

301. Useful definitions. Debate over §2 often contrasts power with conduct, structure with behavior. The following conventional definitions and approximations will be useful. They will be refined as the chapter proceeds.

Performance is the economist's appraisal in terms of competitive ideals of firm or industry prices, profits, productive and distributive efficiency, and progressiveness.

Conduct or behavior will be used to describe a firm's acts. Conduct, of course, does determine performance, but it will be useful to distinguish acts from the economic appraisal of the industry's success or failure.

The *market* is the arena within which the strength of competitive forces is measured. The power of the sole producer of aluminum, for example, may depend on supply and demand circumstances for aluminum and related metals but not on the production and consumption of corn. *Market definition* is the process of excluding corn from the area of inquiry and including those firms and products that are most relevant to appraising defendant's power.

Market structure concerns the breadth and character of the market, the number and size distribution of buyers and sellers, the capacity of firms to enter or expand, and other factors.

Market power is the capacity to act other than as would a perfectly competitive firm. In particular, most discussion of market power will concern the extent to which a firm's most profitable price exceeds competitive price levels. The existence of such power may sometimes be inferred from structure, conduct, performance, or some combination of the three.

Monopoly power is often defined in the cases as the power to control price or to exclude competition. It can be understood as a significant degree of market power.

3A.   MONOPOLIZATION[1]

Offense of Monopolization

302.   The basic issue. This section considers the relationship of power and conduct. The existence of monopoly power will be assumed here and issues of market definition and power deferred until Chapter 3B. The question here is whether mere monopoly is unlawful or whether illegality depends on reprehensible conduct in attaining or keeping monopoly power. If the latter, one then must consider what sorts of conduct constitute monopolization. These issues are also reflected in the judicial approach to remedies in monopoly cases and in legislative proposals to deconcentrate industry.

303.   Early landmarks. The following cases set the stage for much of the subsequent development of monopolization doctrine and, for that matter, much of antitrust law. Although the continuing legal importance of these cases lies in the language used to characterize the purposes of Section 2 and the tests to be applied, *Standard Oil* and *American Tobacco* are also notable for the relief they provided — substantial divestiture of two of America's leading mo-

1. For an extensive analysis of the principal monopolization cases, the rationale of the governing doctrines, and the nature and definition of monopolizing behavior, see III P. Areeda & D. Turner, Antitrust Law, chs. 6-7 (1978; Supp. 1996). Two interesting articles focusing on the historical development of monopoly law and its relationship to other antitrust issues are E. Levi, The Antitrust Laws and Monopoly, 14 U. Chi. L. Rev. 153 (1947); E. Rostow, Monopoly Under the Sherman Act, 43 Ill. L. Rev. 745 (1949).

nopolies. Standard Oil Company of New Jersey was dissolved into 33 geographically dispersed companies that have developed, over time, into the oil companies familiar today. The American Tobacco Company was split into 16 pieces, the most notable today being R.J. Reynolds and the successor American Tobacco Company.

(a) *Standard Oil Co. v. United States*, 221 U.S. 1, 55, 61-62, 75 (1911).[2] The Oil Company was held to be an illegal monopoly. Defendant had achieved undoubted dominance of domestic oil production and distribution through numerous mergers, some of which were coerced, and oppressive tactics against competitors, including the coercion of competitors' suppliers and customers. Chief Justice White went beyond these clear facts and offered a lengthy statutory explication remarkable for announcing the rule of reason[3] and for its cloudy prolixity. The Court addressed Sherman Act §2 as follows:

> Undoubtedly, the words "to monopolize" and "monopolize" as used in the section reach every act bringing about the prohibited results. The ambiguity, if any, is involved in determining what is intended by monopolize. But this ambiguity is readily dispelled in the light of the previous history of the law of restraint of trade ... and the ... practical evolution by which monopoly and the acts which produce the same result as monopoly ... all came to be spoken of as ... restraint of trade. In other words, having by the first section forbidden all means of monopolizing trade, that is, unduly restraining it by means of every contract, combination, etc., the second section seeks, if possible, to make the prohibitions of the act all the more complete and perfect by embracing all attempts to reach the end prohibited by the first section, that is, restraints of trade, by any attempt to monopolize, or monopolization thereof, even although the acts by which such results are attempted to be brought about or are brought about be not embraced within the general enumeration of the first section.... And it is worthy of observation, as we have previously remarked concerning the common law,[4] that although the statute by

---

2. See E. Granitz & B. Klein, Monopolization by "Raising Rivals' Costs": The Standard Oil Case, 39 J.L. & Econ. 1 (1996).

3. See ¶204.

4. Earlier in the opinion, the Court stated:

> It is remarkable that nowhere at common law can there be found a prohibition against the creation of monopoly by an individual. This would seem to manifest, either consciously or intuitively, a profound conception as to the inevitable operation of economic forces and the equipoise or balance in favor of the protection of the rights of individuals which resulted. That is to say ... it was deemed that monopoly in the concrete could only arise from an act of sovereign power, and, such sovereign power [was] restrained[. Therefore,] prohibitions as to individuals were directed, not against the creation of monopoly, but were only applied to such acts in relation to particular subjects as to which it was deemed, if not restrained, some of the consequences of monopoly might result.

the comprehensiveness of the enumerations embodied in both the first and second sections makes it certain that its purpose was to prevent undue restraints of every kind or nature, nevertheless by the omission of any direct prohibition against monopoly in the concrete it indicates a consciousness that the freedom of the individual right to contract when not unduly or improperly exercised was the most efficient means for the prevention of monopoly, since the operation of the centrifugal and centripetal forces resulting from the right to freely contract was the means by which monopoly would be inevitably prevented if no extraneous or sovereign power imposed it and no right to make unlawful contracts having a monopolistic tendency were permitted. . . .

[Defendant's many acquisitions and mergers give rise] in the absence of countervailing circumstances ... to the prima facie presumption of intent and purpose to maintain the dominancy over the oil industry, not as a result of normal methods of industrial development, but by new means of combination ... with the purpose of excluding others from the trade and thus centralizing in the combination a perpetual control of the movements of petroleum and its products in the channels of interstate commerce. . . .

[This] prima facie presumption of intent to restrain trade, to monopolize and to bring about monopolization ... is made conclusive by considering, *1*, the conduct of the persons or corporations who were mainly instrumental in bringing about the extension of power in the New Jersey corporation before the consummation of that result and prior to the formation of the trust agreements of 1879 and 1882; *2*, by considering the proof as to what was done under those agreements and the acts which immediately preceded the vesting of power in the New Jersey corporation as well as by weighing the modes in which the power vested in that corporation has been exerted and the results which have arisen from it.

(b) *United States v. American Tobacco Co.*, 221 U.S. 106, 182-183 (1911). The Court's decision in *Standard Oil* was followed almost immediately by a similar finding of monopolization in the tobacco industry. Among the facts emphasized by the Court in finding a "wrongful purpose and illegal combination" were the following:

a. . . . [T]he very first organization or combination was impelled by a previously existing fierce trade war, evidently inspired by one or more of the minds which brought about and became parties to that combination. *b.* . . . [T]he acts which ensued justify the inference that the intention existed to use the power of the combination as a vantage ground to further monopolize the trade in tobacco by means of trade conflicts designed to injure others, either by driving competitors out of the business or compelling them to become parties to a combination — a purpose whose execution was illustrated by the plug war which ensued and its results, by the snuff war which followed and its results, and by the conflict which immediately followed the entry of the combination in England and the division of the world's business by the two foreign contracts which ensued. . . . *d*. [The combination gradually absorbed] control over all the elements essential to the successful manufacture of tobacco products, and placing such control in the hands of seemingly independent corporations serving as perpetual barriers to the entry of others into the tobacco trade. . . . *e*. [It persisted in the] expenditure of millions upon millions of dollars in buying out plants, not for the purpose of utilizing them, but in order to close them up and render them useless for the purposes of trade. *f*. [It entered] constantly recurring stipulations, whose legality, isolatedly viewed, we are not considering, by which numbers of persons, whether manufacturers, stockholders, or employees, were required to bind themselves, generally for long periods, not to compete in the future.

(c) *United States v. American Can Co.*, 230 F. 859, 901-902 (D. Md. 1916), appeal dismissed, 256 U.S. 706 (1921).

One who sells only one-half of the cans that are sold does not, of course, possess a monopoly in the same sense as he would if he sold all or nearly all of them. Yet he may have more power over the industry than it is well for any one concern to possess. No one can say with any certainty that anybody would be better off if defendant had never, in any way, restrained or controlled absolutely free competition in cans. All that can be argued is that, in view of the declared policy of Congress, the legal presumption must be that which was done was against the public weal.

If it be true that size and power, apart from the way in which they were acquired, or the purpose with which they are used, do not offend against the law, it is equally true that one of the designs of the framers of the Anti-Trust Act was to prevent the concentration in a few hands of control over great industries. They preferred a social and industrial state in which there should be many independent producers. Size and power are themselves facts some of whose consequences do not depend upon the way in which they were created or in which they are used. It is easy to conceive that they might be acquired honestly and used as fairly as men who are in business for the legitimate purpose of making money for themselves and their associates could be expected to use them, human nature being what it is, and for all that constitute a public danger, or at all events give rise to difficult social, industrial and political problems.

The law wishes that industrial and trading corporations shall operate under the checks and balances imposed by free and unrestrained competition. Doubtless, no one is blind to the evil which such competition itself brings with it, precisely as no thoughtful man can close his eyes to the difficulties which some of our constitutional checks and balances put in the way of securing an ideally efficient government. Congress wished to preserve competition because, among other reasons, it did not know what to substitute for the restraints competition imposes. It has not accepted the suggestions of some influential men that the control of a certain percentage of industry should be penalized. It has not yet been willing to go far in the way of regulating and controlling corporations merely because they are large and powerful, perhaps because many people have always felt that government control is in itself an evil, and to be avoided whenever it is not absolutely required for the prevention of greater wrong.

The problem presented by size and power is one of such far-reaching difficulty that Congress has said, while it does not see how to deal with them when acquired in the legitimate expansion of a lawful business, it will prevent their illegitimate and unnatural acquirement by any attempt to restrain trade or monopolize industry. Perhaps the framers of the Anti-Trust Act believed that, if such illegitimate attempts were effectively prevented, the occasions on which it would become necessary to deal with size and power otherwise brought about would be so few and so long postponed that it might never be necessary to deal with them at all.

(d) *United States v. United States Steel Corp.*, 251 U.S. 417, 440-441, 451 (1920). The defendant company was organized in 1901 as the vehicle by which 180 independent firms were brought under unified control with the hope (found by two of four trial court judges) of attaining monopoly power. Immediately after its formation, it controlled 80 to 95 percent of domestic production of some lines, but its overall share of iron and steel products had declined to 50 percent by the time of the suit. That the defendant had attempted to induce other firms to cooperate in setting price indicated to the Court that it did not have power to impose its prices on the rest of the industry. In addition, the Court agreed with the findings below that defendant had "resorted to none of the brutalities or tyrannies that the cases illustrate of other combinations." Defendant had not obtained preferential freight rebates or engaged in predatory price cutting or other unfair tactics. As to the large size of the corporation, the Court stated that "the law does not make mere size an offense or the existence of unexerted power an offense. It, we repeat, requires overt acts, and trusts to its prohibition of them and its power to repress or punish them. It does not compel competition nor require all that is possible."[5] Defendant persuaded four of the seven sitting Justices that it did not have monopoly power and had abandoned any monopolistic intention. The dissent would have found the initial formation illegal, as well as the subsequent

5. See also United States v. International Harvester Co., 274 U.S. 693, 708 (1927).

practice of inducing competitors to follow the corporation's prices.[6]

304. (a) How did Chief Justice White view the relationship of §1 and §2? Did he understand §2 to condemn mere "monopoly in the concrete"? Was his answer to the last question consistent with his view of statutory purpose?

(b) (1) How was defendant's intention relevant in the *Standard Oil* and *Tobacco* excerpts? (2) Did the Court refer to defendant's subjective state of mind? (3) What is the content or object of the wrongful intent? (4) How does such a wrongful intent differ from a lawful intention?

(c) If the steel company had been attacked immediately after its formation, would the result have been different?[7]

UNITED STATES v. ALUMINUM CO. OF AMERICA (ALCOA)
148 F.2d 416 (2d Cir. 1945)

Before L. HAND, SWAN, and A. HAND, Circuit Judges.[8]

L. HAND, Circuit Judge.... The action was brought under §4 of [title 15], praying the district court to adjudge that the defendant, Aluminum Company of America, was monopolizing interstate and foreign commerce, particularly in the manufacture and sale of "virgin" aluminum ingot, and that it be dissolved....

[A] ...

The extraction of aluminum from alumina requires a very large amount of electrical energy, which is ordinarily, though not always, most cheaply obtained from water power. Beginning at least as early as 1895, "Alcoa" secured such power from several companies by contracts, containing in at least three instances, covenants binding

---

6. See generally W. Comanor & F.M. Scherer, Rewriting History: The Early Sherman Act Monopolization Cases, 2 Int'l J. Econ. & Bus. 263 (1995). For evidence indicating that the dissolution of U.S. Steel would have reduced prices and increased output, see G. Mullin, J. Mullin & W. Mullin, The Competitive Effects of Mergers: Stock Market Evidence from the U.S. Steel Dissolution Suit, 26 Rand J. Econ. 314 (1995).

7. See *Northern Securities*, ¶504a.

8. As then required, the government appealed the district court decision directly to the Supreme Court. Because four Justices disqualified themselves, thereby depriving the Court of a quorum, the case was heard by the Court of Appeals. — eds.

the power companies not to sell or let power to anyone else for the manufacture of aluminum. "Alcoa" — either itself or by a subsidiary — also entered into four successive "cartels" with foreign manufacturers of aluminum by which, in exchange for certain limitations upon its import into foreign countries, it secured covenants from the foreign producers, either not to import into the United States at all, or to do so under restrictions, which in some cases involved the fixing of prices. These "cartels" and restrictive covenants and certain other practices were the subject of a suit filed by the United States against "Alcoa" on May 16, 1912, in which a decree was entered by consent on June 7, 1912, declaring several of these covenants unlawful and enjoining their performance; and also declaring invalid other restrictive covenants obtained before 1903 relating to the sale of alumina. ("Alcoa" failed at this time to inform the United States of several restrictive covenants in water-power contracts; its justification — which the judge accepted — being that they had been forgotten.) "Alcoa" did not begin to manufacture alumina on its own behalf until the expiration of a dominant patent in 1903. In that year it built a very large alumina plant at East St. Louis, where all of its alumina was made until 1939, when it opened another plant in Mobile, Alabama.

None of the foregoing facts are in dispute, and the most important question in the case is whether the monopoly in "Alcoa's" production of "virgin" ingot, secured by the two patents until 1909, and in part perpetuated between 1909 and 1912 by the unlawful practices, forbidden by the decree of 1912, continued for the ensuing twenty-eight years; and whether, if it did, it was unlawful under §2 of the Sherman Act. It is undisputed that throughout this period "Alcoa" continued to be the single producer of "virgin" ingot in the United States; and the plaintiff argues that this without more was enough to make it an unlawful monopoly. It also takes an alternative position: that in any event during this period "Alcoa" consistently pursued unlawful exclusionary practices, which made its dominant position certainly unlawful, even though it would not have been, had it been retained only by "natural growth." Finally, it asserts that many of these practices were of themselves unlawful, as contracts in restraint of trade under §1 of the Act. "Alcoa's" position is that the fact that it alone continued to make "virgin" ingot in the country did not, and does not, give it a monopoly of the market; that it was always subject to the competition of imported "virgin" ingot, and of what is called "secondary" ingot; and that even if it had not been, its monopoly would not have been retained by unlawful means, but would have been the result of a growth which the Act does not forbid, even when it results in a monopoly. We shall first consider the amount and character of this competition; next, how far it established a monopoly; and finally, if it did, whether that monopoly was unlawful under §2 of the Act.

[B]

[This section, in which the court addressed Alcoa's market power, is reproduced in Chapter 3B, which considers that issue. The court concluded its discussion by noting that Alcoa's profits "could hardly be considered extortionate."]

[C]

[There are, however, two answers to the suggestion that moderate profits excused Alcoa's behavior]; and the first is that the profit on ingot was not necessarily the same as the profit of the business as a whole, and that we have no means of allocating its proper share to ingot. It is true that the mill cost appears; but obviously it would be unfair to "Alcoa" to take, as the measure of its profit on ingot, the difference between selling price and mill cost; and yet we have nothing else. It may be retorted that it was for the plaintiff to prove what was the profit upon ingot in accordance with the general burden of proof. We think not. Having proved that "Alcoa" had a monopoly of the domestic ingot market, the plaintiff had gone far enough; if it was an excuse, that "Alcoa" had not abused its power, it lay upon "Alcoa" to prove that it had not. But the whole issue is irrelevant anyway, for it is no excuse for "monopolizing" a market that the monopoly has not been used to extract from the consumer more than a "fair" profit. The Act has wider purposes. Indeed, even though we disregarded all but economic considerations, it would by no means follow that such concentration of producing power is to be desired, when it has not been used extortionately. Many people believe that possession of unchallenged economic power deadens initiative, discourages thrift and depresses energy; that immunity from competition is a narcotic, and rivalry is a stimulant, to industrial progress; that the spur of constant stress is necessary to counteract an inevitable disposition to let well enough alone. Such people believe that competitors, versed in the craft as no consumer can be, will be quick to detect opportunities for saving and new shifts in production, and be eager to profit by them. In any event the mere fact that a producer, having command of the domestic market, has not been able to make more than a "fair" profit, is no evidence that a "fair" profit could not have been made at lower prices.... True, it might have been thought adequate to condemn only those monopolies which could not show that they had exercised the highest possible ingenuity, had adopted every possible economy, had anticipated every conceivable improvement, stimulated every possible demand. No doubt, that would be one way of dealing with the matter, although it would imply constant scrutiny and constant supervision, such as courts are unable to provide. Be that as it may, that was not the way that Congress chose; it did not condone "good trusts" and condemn "bad" ones; it forbad all. Moreover, in so doing it was not necessarily actuated by economic motive alone. It is possible, because of its indirect social or moral effect, to prefer a system of small producers, each dependent for his success upon his own skill and character, to one in which the great mass of those engaged must accept the direction of a few. These considerations, which we have suggested only as possible purposes of the Act, we think the decisions prove to have been in fact its purposes.

It is settled, at least as to §1, that there are some contracts restricting competition which are unlawful, no matter how beneficent they may be; no industrial exigency will justify them; they are absolutely forbidden.... Starting ... with the authoritative premise that all contracts fixing prices are unconditionally prohibited, the only possible difference between them and a monopoly is that while a monopoly necessarily involves an equal, or even greater, power to fix prices, its mere existence might be thought not to constitute an exercise of that power. That distinction is nevertheless purely formal; it would be valid only so long as the monopoly remained wholly inert; it would disappear as soon as the monopoly began to operate; for, when it did — that is, as soon as it began to sell at all — it must sell at some price and the only price at which it could sell is a price which it itself fixed. Thereafter the power and its exercise must needs coalesce. Indeed it would be absurd to condemn such contracts unconditionally, and not to extend the condemnation to monopolies; for the contracts are only steps toward that entire control which monopoly confers: they are really partial monopolies....

Perhaps, it has been idle to labor the point at length; there can be no doubt that the vice of restrictive contracts and of monopoly is really one: it is the denial to commerce of the supposed protection of competition. To repeat, if the earlier stages are proscribed, when they are parts of a plan, the mere projecting of which condemns them unconditionally, the realization of the plan itself must also be proscribed.

We have been speaking only of the economic reasons which forbid monopoly; but, as we have already implied, there are others, based upon the belief that great industrial consolidations are inherently undesirable, regardless of their economic results. In the debates in Congress Senator Sherman himself in the passage quoted in the margin showed that among the purposes of Congress in 1890 was a desire to put an end to great aggregations of capital because of the helplessness of the individual before them.... Throughout the history of these statutes it has been constantly assumed that one of their purposes was to perpetuate and preserve, for its own sake and in spite of possible cost, an organization of industry in small units which can effectively compete with each other. We hold that "Alcoa's" monopoly of ingot was of the kind covered by §2.

[D]

It does not follow because "Alcoa" had such a monopoly, that it "monopolized" the ingot market: it may not have achieved monopoly; monopoly may have been thrust upon it. If it had been a combination of existing smelters which united the whole industry and controlled the production of all aluminum ingot, it would certainly have "monopolized" the market.... We may start therefore with the premise that to have combined ninety per cent of the producers of ingot would have been to "monopolize" the ingot market; and, so far as concerns the public interest, it can make no difference whether an existing competition is put an end to, or whether prospective competition is prevented.... Nevertheless, it is unquestionably true that from the very outset the courts have at least kept in reserve the possibility that the origin of a monopoly may be critical in determining its legality; and for this they had warrant in some of the congressional debates which accompanied the passage of the Act.... This notion has usually been expressed by saying that size does not determine guilt; that there must be some "exclusion" of competitors; that the growth must be something else than "natural" or "normal"; that there must be a "wrongful intent," or some other specific intent; or that some "unduly" coercive means must be used. At times there has been emphasis upon the use of the active verb, "monopolize," as the judge noted in the case at bar.... What engendered these compunctions is reasonably plain; persons may unwittingly find themselves in possession of a monopoly, automatically so to say: that is, without having intended either to put an end to existing competition, or to prevent competition from arising when none had existed; they may become monopolists by force of accident. Since the Act makes "monopolizing" a crime, as well as a civil wrong, it would be not only unfair, but presumably contrary to the intent of Congress, to include such instances. A market may, for example, be so limited that it is impossible to produce at all and meet the cost of production except by a plant large enough to supply the whole demand. Or there may be changes in taste or in cost which drive out all but one purveyor. A single producer may be the survivor out of a group of active competitors, merely by virtue of his superior skill, foresight and industry. In such cases a strong argument can be made that, although the result may expose the public to the evils of monopoly, the Act does not mean to condemn the resultant of those very forces which it is its prime object to foster: finis opus coronat. The successful competitor, having been urged to compete, must not be turned upon when he wins. The most extreme expression of this view is in *United States Steel,* from which we quote in the margin,[9] and which Sanford, J., in part repeated in United States v. International Harvester Corporation, 274 U.S. 693. It so chances that in both instances the corporation had less than two-thirds of the production in its hands, and the language quoted was not necessary to the decision; so that even if it had not later been modified, it has not the authority of an actual decision. But, whatever authority it does have was modified by the gloss of Cardozo, J., in United States v. Swift & Co., 286 U.S. 106, 116, when he said, "Mere size ... is not an offense against the Sherman Act unless magnified to the point at which it amounts to a monopoly ... but size carries with it an opportunity for abuse that is not to be ignored when the opportunity is proved to have been utilized in the past." "Alcoa's" size was "magnified" to make it a "monopoly"; indeed, it has never been anything else; and its size, not only offered it an "opportunity for abuse," but it "utilized" its size for "abuse," as can easily be shown.

It would completely misconstrue "Alcoa's" position in 1940 to hold that it was the passive beneficiary of a monopoly, following upon an involuntary elimination of competitors by automatically operative economic forces. Already in 1909, when its last lawful monopoly ended, it sought to strengthen its position by unlawful practices, and these concededly continued until 1912. In that year it had two plants in New York, at which it produced less than 42 million pounds of ingot; in 1934 it had five plants (the original two, enlarged; one in Tennessee; one in North Carolina; one in Washington), and its production had risen to about 327 million pounds, an increase of almost eight-fold. Meanwhile not a pound of ingot had been produced by anyone else in the United States. This increase and this continued and undisturbed control did not fall undesigned into "Alcoa's" lap; obviously it could not have done so. It could only have resulted, as it did result, from a persistent determination to maintain the control, with which it found itself vested in 1912. There were at least one or two abortive attempts to enter the industry, but "Alcoa" effectively anticipated and forestalled all competition, and succeeded in holding the field alone. True, it stimulated demand and opened new uses

9. The most relevant passage is quoted in ¶303d. — eds.

for the metal, but not without making sure that it could supply what it had evoked. There is no dispute as to this; "Alcoa" avows it as evidence of the skill, energy and initiative with which it has always conducted its business: as a reason why, having won its way by fair means, it should be commended, and not dismembered. We need charge it with no moral derelictions after 1912; we may assume that all it claims for itself is true. The only question is whether it falls within the exception established in favor of those who do not seek, but cannot avoid, the control of a market. It seems to us that that question scarcely survives its statement. It was not inevitable that it should always anticipate increases in the demand for ingot and be prepared to supply them. Nothing compelled it to keep doubling and redoubling its capacity before others entered the field. It insists that it never excluded competitors; but we can think of no more effective exclusion than progressively to embrace each new opportunity as it opened, and to face every newcomer with new capacity already geared into a great organization, having the advantage of experience, trade connections and the elite of personnel. Only in case we interpret "exclusion" as limited to manoeuvers not honestly industrial, but actuated solely by a desire to prevent competition, can such a course, indefatigably pursued, be deemed not "exclusionary." So to limit it would in our judgment emasculate the Act; would permit just such consolidations as it was designed to prevent.

"Alcoa" answers that it positively assisted competitors, instead of discouraging them. That may be true as to fabricators of ingot; but what of that? They were its market for ingot, and it is charged only with a monopoly of ingot. We can find no instance of its helping prospective ingot manufacturers. . . .

We disregard any question of "intent." Relatively early in the history of the Act — 1905 — Holmes, J., in Swift & Co. v. United States, 196 U.S. 375, 396, explained this aspect of the Act in a passage often quoted. Although the primary evil was monopoly, the Act also covered preliminary steps, which, if continued, would lead to it. These may do no harm of themselves; but, if they are initial moves in a plan or scheme which, carried out, will result in monopoly, they are dangerous and the law will nip them in the bud. For this reason conduct falling short of monopoly, is not illegal unless it is part of a plan to monopolize, or to gain such other control of a market as is equally forbidden. To make it so, the plaintiff must prove what in the criminal law is known as a "specific intent"; an intent which goes beyond the mere intent to do the act. By far the greatest part of the fabulous record piled up in the case at bar, was concerned with proving such an intent. The plaintiff was seeking to show that many transactions, neutral on their face, were not in fact necessary to the development of "Alcoa's" business, and had no motive except to exclude others and perpetuate its hold upon the ingot market. Upon that effort success depended in case the plaintiff failed to satisfy the court that it was unnecessary under §2 to convict "Alcoa" of practices unlawful of themselves. The plaintiff has so satisfied us, and the issue of intent ceases to have any importance; no intent is relevant except that which is relevant to any liability, criminal or civil: i.e. an intent to bring about the forbidden act. Note 59 of *Socony,* on which "Alcoa" appears so much to rely, is in no sense to the contrary. Douglas, J., was answering the defendants' argument that, assuming that a combination had attempted to fix prices, it had never had the power to do so, for there was too much competing oil. His answer was that the plan was unlawful, even if the parties did not have the power to fix prices, provided that they intended to do so; and it was to drive home this that he contrasted the case then before the court with monopoly, where power was a necessary element. In so doing he said: "An intent and a power ... are then necessary," which he at once followed by quoting the passage we have just mentioned from *Swift.* In order to fall within §2, the monopolist must have both the power to monopolize, and the intent to monopolize. To read the passage as demanding any "specific" intent, makes nonsense of it, for no monopolist monopolizes unconscious of what he is doing. So here, "Alcoa" meant to keep, and did keep, that complete and exclusive hold upon the ingot market with which it started. That was to "monopolize" that market, however innocently it otherwise proceeded. So far as the judgment held that it was not within §2, it must be reversed.

[The court then discussed Alcoa's allegedly unlawful practices which, the court expressly noted, were not essential to its holding that Alcoa monopolized. (1) The government claimed that Alcoa acquired bauxite deposits and electric power sources in excess of its needs in order to preempt possible competitors. The district judge held that the government did not satisfy its burden of proof, and this finding did not seem clearly erroneous to Judge Hand in view of the extraordinary expansion of production that did in fact occur. (2) The two courts similarly disposed of the government's claim that Alcoa acquired shares in certain other companies and properties in order to head off threatening rival developments. (3) Alcoa's investments in aluminum fabrications were not independently unlawful. As to other fabricated product issues, the court rather bypassed several allegations that Alcoa misused certain of its patents. The so-called price squeeze in sheet was proved and served as an example of the unlawful exercise of Alcoa's power. The portion of the opinion dealing with Aluminum Ltd. and the European aluminum cartel is summarily described in ¶171. Remedies were, in the main, deferred to further proceedings noted in ¶314.]

305. (a) If there were several producers of aluminum, §1 would condemn a price-fixing agreement among them. The sole producer of aluminum must necessarily affect price at least as much. Defend the proposition that the Sherman Act should permit the monopolist to do what would be prohibited if undertaken through a price-fixing agreement among competitors.

(b) Defend the proposition that only those who abuse their monopoly power should be held to violate §2. And the view that monopolists who earn only a fair profit should be tolerated.[10] Rebut your defenses. Where do you come out? Where did Judge Hand come out on this issue? Does he persuade you?

(c) Would a combination of 90 percent of aluminum capacity offend §2? If so, why? Did Judge Hand say that internal expansion achieving that degree of market control would be illegal monopolization under §2? What should one make of the quoted language from *Swift* indicating that "[m]ere size . . . is not an offense against the Sherman Act unless magnified to the point at which it amounts to a monopoly"? Does that mean that *huge* size *is* an offense?

(d) Consider the reasons offered in *Alcoa* and in *American Can*, ¶303c, for condemning monopolization. (Also review the material in ¶130 on the passage of the Sherman Act and the goals of the antitrust laws.) Are all these grounds consistent with the refusal to condemn monopoly absent its achievement or maintenance by abusive practices? What did the *Standard Oil* and *American Can* courts think to be the prospect of monopoly in the absence of improper acts?

306. (a) Did Judge Hand find that Alcoa lacked skill, foresight, and industry?

(b) Did he find that Alcoa utilized its size for abuse?

(c) Could Alcoa have escaped liability by refusing to expand production? Had Alcoa failed to expand production, what might have happened in the aluminum market? Would any such consequences have been preferable to what did happen?

(d) Was there anything reprehensible about Alcoa's behavior?

(e) What is the minimum holding of *Alcoa*? How would you state the reading most hostile to monopoly?

307. *American Tobacco Co. v. United States*, 328 U.S. 781, 811-814 (1946). The Court affirmed the conviction of the three leading cigarette manufacturers for monopolization and conspiracy to monopolize as well as for attempted monopolization and conspiracy to

---

10. Compare the Court's statements with regard to reasonable prices in *Trans-Missouri* and *Trenton Potteries*.

restrain trade. The jury found conspiracies to exclude rivals by impairing their ability to buy raw materials economically and to fix selling prices through price leadership.[11] The Supreme Court declared certain *Alcoa* ideas "especially appropriate" and "welcome[d]" the "opportunity to endorse them." The Supreme Court then quoted Judge Hand's language to the following effect: (1) Rivalry is a stimulant to industrial progress while unchallenged power deadens initiative. (2) Price fixing by competitors is like price setting by monopolists. (3) Monopoly is not monopolization because it may have been thrust upon the defendant. To achieve monopoly or control by combination would offend §2. (4) Progressive embracing of each new opportunity is exclusionary. (5) A violation of §2 requires power and intent but not specific intent because no monopolist monopolizes unconscious of what it is doing.

UNITED STATES v. GRIFFITH
334 U.S. 100 (1948)

Justice DOUGLAS. . . . The appellees are four affiliated corporations [that] operate (or own stock in corporations which operate) moving picture theatres in Oklahoma, Texas, and New Mexico. . . . In April, 1939, when the complaint was filed, the corporate appellees had interests in theatres in 85 towns. In 32 of those towns there were competing theatres. Fifty-three of the towns (62 per cent) were closed towns, i.e. towns in which there were no competing theatres. Five years earlier the corporate appellees had theatres in approximately 37 towns, 18 of which were competitive and 19 of which (51 per cent) were closed. It was during that five-year period that the acts and practices occurred which, according to the allegations of the complaint, constitute violations of §§1 and 2 of the Sherman Act.

[The appellees employed common agents to negotiate master agreements with distributors for entire circuits. These agreements generally secured first-run exhibitions of all the distributor's films for all of appellees' theatres, including those in towns with competing theatres.] The complaint charged that certain exclusive privileges which these agreements granted the appellee exhibitors over their competitors unreasonably restrained competition by preventing their competitors from obtaining enough first- or second-run films from the distributors to operate successfully. . . .

In United States v. Crescent Amusement Co., 323 U.S. 173, a group of affiliated exhibitors, such as we have in the present case,

---

11. The Court's discussion of the latter issue appears in Ch. 2C.

were found to have violated §§1 and 2 of the Sherman Act by the pooling of their buying power and the negotiation of master agreements similar to those we have here. A difference between that case and the present one, which the District Court deemed to be vital, was that in the former the buying power was used for the avowed purpose of eliminating competition and of acquiring a monopoly of theatres in the several towns, while no such purpose was found to exist here. To be more specific, the defendants in the former case through the pooling of their buying power increased their leverage over their competitive situations by insisting that they be given monopoly rights in towns where they had competition, else they would give a distributor no business in their closed towns.

It is, however, not always necessary to find a specific intent to restrain trade or to build a monopoly in order to find that the antitrust laws have been violated. . . . As stated in *Alcoa*, "no monopolist monopolizes unconscious of what he is doing." Specific intent in the sense in which the common law used the term is necessary only where the acts fall short of the results condemned by the Act. . . . And so, even if we accept the District Court's findings that appellees had no intent or purpose unreasonably to restrain trade or to monopolize, we are left with the question whether a necessary and direct result of the master agreements was the restraining or monopolizing of trade within the meaning of the Sherman Act.

Anyone who owns and operates the single theatre in a town, or who acquires the exclusive right to exhibit a film, has a monopoly in the popular sense. But he usually does not violate §2 of the Sherman Act unless he has acquired or maintained his strategic position, or sought to expand his monopoly, or expanded it by means of those restraints of trade which are cognizable under §1. For those things which are condemned by §2 are in large measure merely the end products of conduct which violates §1. . . . But that is not always true. Section 1 covers contracts, combinations, or conspiracies in restraint of trade. Section 2 is not restricted to conspiracies or combinations to monopolize but also makes it a crime for any person to monopolize or to attempt to monopolize any part of interstate or foreign trade or commerce. So it is that monopoly power, whether lawfully or unlawfully acquired, may itself constitute an evil and stand condemned under §2 even though it remains unexercised. For §2 of the Act is aimed, inter alia, at the acquisition or retention of effective market control. See *Alcoa*. Hence the existence of power "to exclude competition when it is desired to do so" is itself a violation of §2, provided it is coupled with the purpose or intent to exercise that power. *American Tobacco* [1946]. It is indeed "unreasonable, per se, to foreclose competitors from any substantial market." *International Salt*. The antitrust laws are as much violated by the prevention of competition as by its destruction. *Alcoa.* It follows a fortiori that the use of monopoly power, however lawfully acquired, to foreclose competition, to gain a competitive advantage, or to destroy a competitor, is unlawful.

A man with a monopoly of theatres in any one town commands the entrance for all films into that area. If he uses that strategic position to acquire exclusive privileges in a city where he has competitors, he is employing his monopoly power as a trade weapon against his competitors. It may be a feeble, ineffective weapon where he has only one closed or monopoly town. But as those towns increase in number throughout a region, his monopoly power in them may be used with crushing effect on competitors in other places. He need not be as crass as the exhibitors in United States v. Crescent Amusement Co., in order to make his monopoly power effective in his competitive situations. Though he makes no threat to withhold the business of his closed or monopoly towns unless the distributors give him the exclusive film rights in the towns where he has competitors, the effect is likely to be the same where the two are joined. When the buying power of the entire circuit is used to negotiate films for his competitive as well as his closed towns, he is using monopoly power to expand his empire. And even if we assume that a specific intent to accomplish that result is absent, he is chargeable in legal contemplation with that purpose since the end result is the necessary and direct consequence of what he did. . . .

What effect these practices actually had on the competitors of appellee exhibitors or on the growth of the Griffith circuit we do not know. . . . On the record as we read it, it cannot be doubted that the monopoly power of appellees had some effect on their competitors and on the growth of the Griffith circuit. Its extent must be determined on a remand of the cause. We remit to the District Court not only that problem but also the fashioning of a decree which will undo as near as may be the wrongs that were done and prevent their recurrence in the future. . . .

Reversed.[12]

308. (a)(1) Precisely what did Griffith do to violate §2? Did the challenged behavior achieve, maintain, or enhance Griffith's power in those towns in which it had a monopoly? In the other towns?[13] (2) In the short run, could Griffith have increased the profits it might have made negotiating for the monopoly and competitive towns separately by combining them? If so, how? (3) Why would

12. Frankfurter, J., dissented.
13. Was there an attempt to monopolize in the latter towns? See Ch. 3C.

each distributor agree to contracts in the competitive towns that increased the likelihood that it would have to bargain with monopolies in such towns in the future?[14]

(b) How can Griffith avoid liability in the future? What remedy could the district court impose to avoid the problem the Court cited?

(c) The Court said that monopoly power violates §2 when "coupled with the purpose or intent to exercise that power." What does the quoted phrase mean? Does a monopolist necessarily have a "purpose or intent" to exercise its power when, for example, it determines its prices or otherwise "breathes"?

UNITED STATES v. UNITED SHOE MACHINERY CORP.
110 F. Supp. 295 (D. Mass. 1953), aff'd per curiam,
347 U.S. 521 (1954)

WYZANSKI, District Judge. [United is the largest supplier of shoe machinery to approximately 1460 shoe manufacturers, themselves highly competitive in many respects. There are at least 10 other domestic and some foreign machinery concerns, making possible a complete shoe factory organized without a United machine. Nonetheless, United supplies over 75%, and probably 85%, of current demand. It is the only manufacturer that produces a full line of machine types and covers every major process. Machines are often complex and take great effort to design and produce; copying existing machines is possible, but not easy. United has 3915 patents. Although it is possible to "invent around" them, the aggregation of patents to some extent blocks potential competition.]

In supplying its complicated machines to shoe manufacturers, United, like its more important American competitors, has followed the practice of never selling, but only leasing. Leasing has been traditional in the shoe machinery field since the Civil War. So far as this record indicates, there is virtually no expressed dissatisfaction from consumers respecting that system; and Compo, United's principal competitor, endorses and uses it. Under the system, entry into shoe manufacture has been easy. The rates charged for all customers have been uniform. The machines supplied have performed excellently. United has, without separate charge, promptly and efficiently supplied repair service and many kinds of other service useful to shoe manufacturers. These services have been particularly

---

14. Compare vertical integration, ¶321, and the questions on *Lorain Journal*, ¶354.

important, because in the shoe manufacturing industry a whole line of production can be adversely affected, and valuable time lost, if some of the important machines go out of function, and because machine breakdowns have serious labor and consumer repercussions. The cost to the average shoe manufacturer of its own machines and services supplied to him has been less than 2% of the wholesale price of his shoes.

However, United's leases, in the context of the present shoe machinery market, have created barriers to the entry by competitors into the shoe machinery field.

First, the complex of obligations and rights accruing under United's leasing system in operation deter a shoe manufacturer from disposing of a United machine and acquiring a competitor's machine. He is deterred more than if he owned that same United machine, or if he held it on a short lease carrying simple rental provisions and a reasonable charge for cancellation before the end of the term. The lessee is now held closely to United by the combined effect of the 10 year term, the requirement that if he has work available he must use the machine to full capacity, and by the return charge which can in practice, through the right of deduction fund, be reduced to insignificance if he keeps this and other United machines to the end of the periods for which he leased them.

Second, when a lessee desires to replace a United machine, United gives him more favorable terms if the replacement is by another United machine than if it is by a competitive machine.

Third, United's practice of offering to repair, without separate charges, its leased machines, has had the effect that there are no independent service organizations to repair complicated machines. In turn, this has had the effect that the manufacturer of a complicated machine must either offer repair service with his machine, or must face the obstacle of marketing his machine to customers who know that repair service will be difficult to provide. . . .

Although maintaining the same nominal terms for each customer, United has followed, as between machine types, a discriminatory pricing policy. . . . United's own internal documents reveal that these sharp and relatively durable differentials are traceable, at least in large part, to United's policy of fixing a higher rate of return where competition is of minor significance, and a lower rate of return where competition is of major significance. Defendant has not borne the burden of showing that these variations in rates of return were motivated by, or correspond with, variations in the strength of the patent protection applicable to different machine types. Hence there is on this record no room for the argument that defendant's discriminatory pricing policy is entirely traceable to, and justified by, the patent laws of the United States.

On the foregoing facts, the issue of law is whether defendant in its shoe machinery business has violated ... §2 of the Sherman Act. ...

[In] recent authorities there are discernible at least three different, but cognate, approaches.

The approach which has the least sweeping implications really antedates the decision in *Alcoa.* But it deserves restatement. An enterprise has monopolized in violation of §2 of the Sherman Act if it has acquired or maintained a power to exclude others as a result of using an unreasonable "restraint of trade" in violation of §1 of the Sherman Act. ...

A more inclusive approach was adopted by Justice Douglas in *Griffith.* He ... concluded that an enterprise has monopolized in violation of §2 if it (a) has the power to exclude competition, and (b) has exercised it, or has the purpose to exercise it. The least that this conclusion means is that it is a violation of §2 for one having effective control of the market to use, or plan to use, any exclusionary practice, even though it is not a technical restraint of trade. But the conclusion may go further.

Indeed the way in which Justice Douglas used the terms "monopoly power" and "effective market control" and cited *Alcoa* suggests that he endorses a third and broader approach, which originated with Judge Hand. It will be recalled that Judge Hand said that one who has acquired an overwhelming share of the market "monopolizes" whenever he does business, apparently even if there is no showing that his business involves any exclusionary practice. But, it will also be recalled that this doctrine is softened by Judge Hand's suggestion that the defendant may escape statutory liability if it bears the burden of proving that it owes its monopoly solely to superior skill, superior products, natural advantages, (including accessibility to raw materials or markets), economic or technological efficiency, (including scientific research), low margins of profit maintained permanently and without discrimination, or licenses conferred by, and used within, the limits of law (including patents on one's own inventions, or franchises granted directly to the enterprise by a public authority).

In the case at bar, the Government contends that the evidence satisfies each of the three approaches to §2 of the Sherman Act, so that it does not matter which one is taken.

If the matter were res integra, this Court would adopt the first approach, and, as a preliminary step to ruling upon §2, would hold that it is a restraint of trade under §1 for a company having an overwhelming share of the market, to distribute its more important products only by leases which have provisions that go beyond assuring prompt, periodic payments of rentals, which are not terminable cheaply, which involve discrimination against competition, and which combine in one contract the right to use the product and to have it serviced. But this inferior court feels precluded from so deciding because of the overhanging shadows of United States v. United Shoe Machinery Co. of N.J., 247 U.S. 32, and United Shoe Machinery Corp. v. United States, 258 U.S. 451, the Sherman and Clayton Act cases involving this company's predecessor and itself. Though these cases may ultimately be overruled by the Supreme Court, they have not yet lost all authority. . . .

This Court finds it unnecessary to choose between the second and third approaches. For, taken as a whole, the evidence satisfies the tests laid down in both *Griffith* and *Alcoa*. The facts show that (1) defendant has, and exercises, such overwhelming strength in the shoe machinery market that it controls that market, (2) this strength excludes some potential, and limits some actual, competition, and (3) this strength is not attributable solely to defendant's ability, economies of scale, research, natural advantages, and adaptation to inevitable economic laws.

In estimating defendant's strength, this Court gives some weight to the 75 plus percentage of the shoe machinery market which United serves.[1] But the Court considers other factors as well. In the relatively static shoe machinery market where there are no sudden changes in the style of machines or in the volume of demand, United has a network of long-term, complicated leases with over 90% of the shoe factories. These leases assure closer and more frequent contacts between United and its customers than would exist if United were a seller and its customers were buyers. Beyond this general quality, these leases are so drawn and so applied as to strengthen United's power to exclude competitors. Moreover, United offers a long line of machine types, while no competitor offers more than a short line. Since in some parts of its line United faces no important competition, United has the power to discrimi-

---

1. . . . This Court does not consider whether this high percentage, by itself, would warrant (but not compel) an inference that United has such overwhelming strength that it could exclude competition. Nor does this Court consider whether . . . a bold, original court, mindful of what legal history teaches about the usual, if not invariable, relationship between overwhelming percentage of the market and control of the market, and desirous of enabling trial judges to escape the morass of economic data in which they are now plunged, might, on the basis of considerations of experience and judicial convenience, announce that an enterprise having an overwhelming percentage of the market was presumed to have monopoly power, that a plaintiff bore its burden of proof under §2 of the Sherman Act if it satisfied the trier of fact that defendant had the prohibited percentage, and that defendant, to escape liability, must bear the burden of proving that its share of the market was attributable to its ability, natural advantage, legal license, or, perhaps, to others' lack of interest in entering the market.

nate, by wide differentials and over long periods of time, in the rate of return it procures from different machine types. Furthermore, being by far the largest company in the field, with by far the largest resources in dollars, in patents, in facilities, and in knowledge, United has a marked capacity to attract offers of inventions, inventors' services, and shoe machinery businesses. And finally, there is no substantial substitute competition from a vigorous secondhand market in shoe machinery.

To combat United's market control, a competitor must be prepared with knowledge of shoemaking, engineering skill, capacity to invent around patents, and financial resources sufficient to bear the expense of long developmental and experimental processes. The competitor must be prepared for consumers' resistance founded on their long-term, satisfactory relations with United, and on the cost to them of surrendering United's leases. Also, the competitor must be prepared to give, or point to the source of, repair and other services, and to the source of supplies for machine parts, expendable parts, and the like. Indeed, perhaps a competitor who aims at any large scale success must also be prepared to lease his machines. These considerations would all affect *potential* competition, and have not been without their effect on *actual* competition.

Not only does the evidence show United has control of the market, but also the evidence does not show that the control is due entirely to excusable causes. The three principal sources of United's power have been the original constitution of the company, the superiority of United's products and services, and the leasing system. The first two of these are plainly beyond reproach. The original constitution of United in 1899 was judicially approved in United States v. United Shoe Machinery Company of New Jersey, 247 U.S. 32. It is no longer open to question, and must be regarded as protected by the doctrine of res judicata, which is the equivalent of a legal license. Likewise beyond criticism is the high quality of United's products, its understanding of the techniques of shoe making and the needs of shoe manufacturers, its efficient design and improvement of machines, and its prompt and knowledgeable service. These have illustrated in manifold ways that "superior skill, foresight and industry" of which Judge Hand spoke in *Alcoa*.

But United's control does not rest solely on its original constitution, its ability, its research, or its economies of scale. There are other barriers to competition, and these barriers were erected by United's own business policies. Much of United's market power is traceable to the magnetic ties inherent in its system of leasing, and not selling, its more important machines. The lease-only system of distributing complicated machines has many "partnership" aspects, and it has exclusionary features such as the 10-year term, the full capacity clause, the return charges, and the failure to segregate service charges from machine charges. Moreover, the leasing system has aided United in maintaining a pricing system which discriminates between machine types.

In addition to the foregoing three principal sources of United's power, brief reference may be made to the fact that United has been somewhat aided in retaining control of the shoe machinery industry by its purchases in the secondhand market, by its acquisitions of patents, and, to a lesser extent, by its activities in selling to shoe factories supplies which United and others manufacture.

In one sense, the leasing system and the miscellaneous activities just referred to (except United's purchases in the secondhand market) were natural and normal, for they were, in Judge Hand's words, "honestly industrial." They are the sort of activities which would be engaged in by other honorable firms. And, to a large extent, the leasing practices conform to long-standing traditions in the shoe machinery business. Yet, they are not practices which can be properly described as the inevitable consequences of ability, natural forces, or law. They represent something more than the use of accessible resources, the process of invention and innovation, and the employment of those techniques of employment, financing, production, and distribution, which a competitive society must foster. They are contracts, arrangements, and policies which, instead of encouraging competition based on pure merit, further the dominance of a particular firm. In this sense, they are unnatural barriers; they unnecessarily exclude actual and potential competition; they restrict a free market. While the law allows many enterprises to use such practices, the Sherman Act is now construed by superior courts to forbid the continuance of effective market control based in part upon such practices. Those courts hold that market control is inherently evil and constitutes a violation of §2 unless economically inevitable, or specifically authorized and regulated by law.

It is only fair to add that the more than 14,000 page record, and the more than 5,000 exhibits, representing the diligent seven year search made by Government counsel aided by this Court's orders giving them full access to United's files during the last 40 years, show that United's power does not rest on predatory practices. Probably few monopolies could produce a record so free from any taint of that kind of wrongdoing. The violation with which United is now charged depends not on moral considerations, but on solely economic considerations. United is denied the right to exercise effective control of the market by business policies that are not the inevitable consequences of its capacities or its natural advantages. That those policies are not immoral is irrelevant.

Defendant seems to suggest that even if its control of the market is not attributable exclusively to its superior performance, its research, and its economies of scale, nonetheless, United's market control should not be held unlawful, because only through the existence of some monopoly power can the thin shoe machinery market support fundamental research of the first order, and achieve maximum economies of production and distribution.

△ argument

To this defense the shortest answer is that the law does not allow an enterprise that maintains control of a market through practices not economically inevitable, to justify that control because of its supposed social advantage. Cf. *Fashion Originators' Guild.* It is for Congress, not for private interests, to determine whether a monopoly, not compelled by circumstances, is advantageous. And it is for Congress to decide on what conditions, and subject to what regulations, such a monopoly shall conduct its business.

Moreover, if the defense were available, United has not proved that monopoly is economically compelled by the thinness of the shoe machinery market. It has not shown that no company could undertake to develop, manufacture, and distribute certain types of machines, unless it alone met the total demand for those types of machines.

Nor has United affirmatively proved that it has achieved spectacular results at amazing rates of speed, nor has it proved that comparable research results and comparable economies of production, distribution, and service could not be achieved as well by, say, three important shoe machinery firms, as by one. Compo with a much smaller organization indicates how much research can be done on a smaller scale. Yet since Compo is limited to the simpler cement process machines, too much reliance should not be placed on this comparison. Nonetheless, one point is worth recalling. Compo's inventors first found practical ways to introduce the cement process which United had considered and rejected. This experience illustrates the familiar truth that one of the dangers of extraordinary experience is that those who have it may fall into grooves created by their own expertness. They refuse to believe that hurdles which they have learned from experience are insurmountable, can in fact be overcome by fresh, independent minds.

So far, nothing in this opinion has been said of defendant's *intent* in regard to its power and practices in the shoe machinery market. This point can be readily disposed of by reference once more to *Alcoa.* Defendant intended to engage in the leasing practices and pricing policies which maintained its market power. That is all the intent which the law requires when both the complaint and the judgment rest on a charge of "monopolizing," not merely "attempting to monopolize." Defendant having willed the means, has willed the end. . . .

Opinion on Remedy

Where a defendant has monopolized commerce in violation of §2, the principal objects of the decrees are to extirpate practices that have caused or may hereafter cause monopolization, and to restore workable competition in the market. . . .

Judges in prescribing remedies have known their own limitations. They do not ex officio have economic or political training. Their prophecies as to the economic future are not guided by unusually subtle judgment. They are not so representative as other branches of the government. The recommendations they receive from government prosecutors do not always reflect the over-all approach of even the executive branch of the government, sometimes not indeed the seasoned and fairly informed judgment of the head of the Department of Justice. Hearings in court do not usually give the remote judge as sound a feeling for the realities of a situation as other procedures do. Judicial decrees must be fitted into the framework of what a busy, and none too expert, court can supervise. Above all, no matter with what authority he is invested, with what facts and opinion he is supplied, a trial judge is only one man, and should move with caution and humility. . . .

In the light of these general considerations, it is now meet to consider four of the principal problems respecting a proposed decree: first, dissolution, second, treatment of the leases, third, divestiture of supply activities, and fourth, patents.

The Government's proposal that the Court dissolve United into three separate manufacturing companies is unrealistic. United conducts all machine manufacture at one plant in Beverly, with one set of jigs and tools, one foundry, one laboratory for machinery problems, one managerial staff, and one labor force. It takes no Solomon to see that this organism cannot be cut into three equal and viable parts. . . .

Although leasing should not now be abolished by judicial decree, the Court agrees with the Government that the leases should be purged of their restrictive features. In the decree filed herewith, the term of the lease is shortened, the full capacity clause is eliminated, the discriminatory commutative charges are removed, and United is required to segregate its charges for machines from its charges for repair service. For the most part, the decree speaks plainly enough upon these points. Yet, on two matters, a further word is in order.

The decree does not prohibit United from rendering service, because, in the Court's view, the rendition of service, if separately charged for, has no exclusionary effects. Moreover, the rendition of service by United will keep its research and manufacturing divisions abreast of technological problems in the shoe manufacturing industry; and this will be an economic advantage of the type fostered by the Sherman Act.

Nor does the decree attempt to deal with that feature of United's pricing policy which discriminates between machine types. To try to extirpate such discrimination would require either an order directing a uniform rate of markup, or an order subjecting each price term and each price change to judicial supervision. Neither course would be sound. Some price discrimination, if not too rigid, is inevitable. Some may be justified as resting on patent monopolies. Some price discrimination is economically desirable, if it promotes competition in a market where several multi-product firms compete. And while price discrimination has been an evidence of United's monopoly power, a buttress to it, and a cause of its perpetuation, its eradication cannot be accomplished without turning United into a public utility, and the Court into a public utility commission, or requiring United to observe a general injunction of non-discrimination between different products — an injunction which would be contrary to sound theory, which would require the use of practices not followed in any business known to the Court, and which could not be enforced.

The Court also agrees with the Government that if United chooses to continue to lease any machine type, it must offer that type of machine also for sale. . . . Insofar as United's machines are sold rather than leased, they will ultimately, in many cases, reach a second-hand market. From that market, United will face a type of substitute competition which will gradually weaken the prohibited market power which it now exercises. Moreover, from that market, or from United itself, a competitor of United can acquire a United machine in order to study it, to copy its unpatented features, and to experiment with improvements in, or alterations of, the machine. Thus, in another and more direct way, United's market power will be diminished. . . .

[I]t seems to the Court sufficient to direct defendant, if it offers any machine type for lease, to set such terms for leasing that machine as do not make it substantially more advantageous for a shoe factory to lease rather than to buy a machine. Admittedly, there is in this direction some flexibility. But defendant is forewarned by the decree itself that if it abuses this flexibility, the Court after the entry of this decree may modify it. . . . [15]

15. In 1966, the government petitioned for further relief. Judge Wyzanski refused. The Supreme Court reversed, United States v. United Shoe Mach. Corp., 391 U.S. 244, 251, 252 (1968): Relief is not necessarily limited to that decreed at the time of suit. If the government shows that a "decree [has] not achieved the adequate relief to which the government is entitled in a §2 case, it would [be] the duty of the court to modify the decree so as to assure the complete extirpation of

309.   *United States v. Grinnell Corp.*, 384 U.S. 563, 570-571, 576-580 (1966). The Supreme Court stated generally that]

> [t]he offense of monopoly . . . has two elements: (1) the possession of monopoly power in the relevant market and (2) the willful acquisition or maintenance of that power as distinguished from growth or development as a consequence of a superior product, business acumen, or historical accident. . . . Since the record clearly shows that [defendants'] monopoly power was consciously acquired, we have no reason to reach the further position of the District Court that once monopoly power is shown to exist, the burden is on the defendant to show that its eminence is due to skill, acumen, and the like.

310.   (a) Which of United's practices did the court find to be acts of monopolization? How might each adversely affect competition?[16] How does one explain the notion that such practices might constitute a violation of §2 when they are also employed by competitors and often by small companies in other industries as well?[17]

(b) The opinion noted that United was in a unique position "to attract offers of inventions, inventors' services, and shoe machinery businesses." Does this pose a danger to competition? One with which the antitrust laws should be concerned? See ¶331.

311.   (a) Consider the classic test of monopolization. Pre-*Alcoa* doctrine was thought to require a restraint of trade or tactics not honestly industrial as a prerequisite to unlawful monopolization. Does this accord with Judge Wyzanski's view of the classic test? How would Judge Wyzanski have applied the classic test to United's behavior? If United's behavior would satisfy this test, is there any need to look further?

(b) (1) Of the several tests for monopolization discussed by Judge Wyzanski, how would you describe the scope and source of the test

the illegal monopoly." The parties then entered a consent decree requiring divestiture of assets generating some $8.5 million in lease and sale revenues and reducing United's market share to 33 percent.

To aid him in the 1953 decision, Judge Wyzanski engaged Professor Kaysen, an economist, as his "law clerk." For the resulting economic analysis, see C. Kaysen, United States v. United Shoe Machinery Corp. (1956).

16. See J. Wiley, Jr., E. Rasmussen & J. Ramseyer, The Leasing Monopolist, 37 U.C.L.A. L. Rev. 693 (1990); S. Masten & E. Snyder, United States Versus United Shoe Machinery Corporation: On the Merits, 36 J.L. & Econ. 33 (1993).

17. For discussions of possible effects of contract provisions, see K. Spier & M. Whinston, On the Efficiency of Privately Stipulated Damages for Breach of Contract: Entry Barriers, Reliance, and Renegotiation, 26 Rand J. Econ. 180 (1995); T. Chung, On Strategic Commitment: Contracting Versus Investment, 85 Am. Econ. Assn. Papers & Proceedings 437 (1995); J. Brodley & C. Ma, Contract Penalties, Monopolizing Strategies, and Antitrust Policy, 45 Stan. L. Rev. 1161 (1993).

most hostile to monopoly? (2) What result would it call for in *United Shoe* if the government had failed to prove that United had engaged in any restrictive or exclusionary behavior? (3) Does United assert that its market position is unavoidable, compelled by economies of scale, or attributable to superior skill? (4) What is United's argument on the relationship of research and monopoly? What is the relevance of the argument? (5) Does Judge Wyzanski adopt this test?

(c) If Judge Wyzanski does not rest his holding on either the classic test or on the test most hostile to monopoly, on what does United's guilt rest? What is the *Grinnell* test, and how would it be applied to *United Shoe*? In what ways were United's intentions relevant to its offense?

(d) Once sufficient monopolizing behavior has been found to warrant holding the defendant guilty of monopolization, do the "defenses" discussed by Judges Hand and Wyzanski have any relevance? That is, if the defendant has actually behaved unlawfully, can he escape liability by proving one or more of the defenses? Suppose, for example, that United's leases were held to be monopolizing behavior. Would United be permitted to show that its dominant position is mainly attributable to its superior skill, foresight, and industry?

312. In 1993, Microsoft owned the right to MS-DOS, the dominant operating system for personal computers (PCs), with a market share above 70 percent. Over 80 percent of its sales were through the inclusion of MS-DOS on newly bought computers. Entering the operating system market is difficult because consumers do not want to buy computers with a new operating system that does not have much software written for it yet and because independent software venders (ISVs) do not want to make software for an operating system that does not have a large consumer base. The Department of Justice considered Microsoft's dominant position to be legally acquired — a result of IBM's previously having chosen MS-DOS for its PCs, which allowed Microsoft to obtain an installed base on millions of PCs. However, as time passed, Microsoft's business strategies came under increased scrutiny, and the following practices engaged in by Microsoft became the subject of antitrust litigation.[18] Assess whether either of the following practices constitutes monopolization.

(a) Microsoft used a "per-processor" license when licensing MS-DOS to computer manufacturers. A "per-processor" license

18. The facts of the Microsoft case are from United States v. Microsoft, 159 F.R.D. 318 (D.D.C.), and 56 F.3d 1448 (D.C. Cir. 1995).

means that the manufacturer pays Microsoft a royalty based on the number of computers sold, irrespective of how many of them contained Microsoft software. This, in effect, can result in computer manufacturers paying twice every time they sell a computer with a non-Microsoft operating system — once to the owner of the operating system and once to Microsoft. The Department of Justice charged that the per-processor licenses either discouraged manufacturers from licensing competing operating systems or forced manufacturers to raise the price of computers sold without Microsoft software, in order to recoup the fee paid to Microsoft.[19]

(b) Microsoft entered into a variety of nondisclosure agreements (NDAs) with ISVs during the development of new operating systems — specifically, Windows 95. ISVs work with Microsoft during the development and testing of a new operating system, so that they can create new applications to run on it and release their applications around the time the operating system is released. This cooperation benefits Microsoft by permitting it to receive input from the ISVs on how to improve the operating system. It also makes the operating system more marketable because there will already be new applications ready to use on it. To protect confidential information about its new software from potential competitors, Microsoft requires ISVs to sign NDAs regarding the product information. The Department of Justice maintained that these NDAs were overly restrictive: In addition to providing legitimate protection against the disclosure of confidential information to competing developers of operating systems, the agreements also made it more difficult for the ISVs to develop their own competing operating systems or to create applications for competing operating systems.

(c) The Department of Justice filed a proposed consent decree with its Microsoft complaint, which was the result of negotiation between it and Microsoft, under which these practices were to be discontinued. Is such a decree appropriate and adequate?[20]

---

19. One may also analyze these agreements as effectively exclusive dealing or requirements contracts. See Ch. 4C; Daniel J. Gifford, Microsoft Corporation, The Justice Department, and Antitrust Theory, 25 Sw. U. L. Rev. 621, 634-636. One way that Microsoft defended these licenses was to say that since operating systems software can be effortlessly copied by computer manufacturers, it is extremely difficult to monitor the number of Microsoft systems sold by a particular manufacturer selling machines with a variety of operating systems.

20. The appropriateness of this consent decree was initially challenged by the District Court Judge, who was later criticized by the Court of Appeals for refusing to approve it. See the discussion on the Tunney Act in ¶141. For discussion of the argument that the efficiencies gained by computer users from having one standard operating system, so that all computers are compatible, make attacks on Microsoft's monopoly unwise, see Gifford, note 19, at 638-643. Is this possibility relevant in light of *Engineers*, Ch. 2B?

313. (a) The Alpha Company invented, patented, and manufactured a unique and important article. It has monopoly power. On the several occasions when other firms began experimental production of competing articles, Alpha instituted immediate suit for infringement of its patent before its officials examined the allegedly infringing articles. Has Alpha violated §2?[21]

(b) Beta Company produces equipment for drilling oil wells. Its patented cutting tool ("bit") is the only one used for drilling deep wells in hard formations. Beta is considered to have monopoly power. Beta sells its bits to oil and drilling companies under a contract requiring buyers to return used bits to Beta for retipping, if practicable, or disposal. Beta maintains a large laboratory that examines all used and worn-out bits to discover defects that can be corrected by technical improvements in the composition, setting, or housing of the bit. Do these contracts offend §2?[22]

(c) Gamma Company is the sole producer of an important, unique, and much-demanded article purchased by consumers. Gamma has been earning profits at the rate of 100 percent on its investment. It spends about 10 percent of its revenues on advertising, notwithstanding the facts that its name is a household word, its sales increase only at the rate of national population growth, and it has no present competitors. The Justice Department is aware that several potential entrants into this market considered the ordinary risk of entry tolerable but decided that it would be too costly to overcome consumer preferences so intensely and artfully developed by Gamma. Have Gamma's advertising policies violated §2?

Remedies in Monopolization Cases

314. *United States v. Aluminum Co. of America*, 91 F. Supp. 333, 342-344, 399 (S.D.N.Y. 1950). *Alcoa* was more or less finally disposed of in 1950. Remember that Judge Hand's opinion concerned the prewar situation. During World War II, substantial aluminum capacity was constructed by the government and later sold mainly to Reynolds Metals and to Kaiser Aluminum, which thus became fully integrated competitors to Alcoa. By 1948, Alcoa accounted for 47 percent of the domestic supply of virgin-plus-secondary aluminum (the wartime supply of which had been greatly expanded

21. Compare *Professional Real Estate*, in Ch. 2F.
22. Cole v. Hughes Tool Co., 215 F.2d 924 (10th Cir. 1954), cert. denied, 348 U.S. 927 (1955); Williams v. Hughes Tool Co., 186 F.2d 278, 285 (10th Cir. 1950), cert. denied, 341 U.S. 903 (1951) (reasonable practice notwithstanding effect on retipping business or on secondhand market).

without Alcoa's control). And the Reynolds and Kaiser shares were growing. Although Alcoa's physical, financial, and patent resources exceeded those of Kaiser and Reynolds, that superiority, to Judge Knox, did not seem to bar effective competition. He was troubled, however, by the possible future superiority that might result from Alcoa's research and development activities. Of similar concern were provisions in certain patent licenses requiring the licensee to grant a royalty-free, nonexclusive license to Alcoa on any improvements it might make on Alcoa's patents. The grant-backs were enjoined. Also, the Judge was particularly worried by "control which may be exercised over [the Canadian company] Aluminum, Ltd. by the controlling stockholders of Alcoa." The two companies might act together to restrain the growth potential of Reynolds and Kaiser. In addition, the Canadian company, if fully independent, might be competitively significant in the U.S. market. Accordingly, the court directed the shareholders of Alcoa to dispose of their stock interests in either Aluminum or Alcoa. Alcoa itself was not dissolved. In the course of his opinion, Judge Knox reviewed some of the key decisions on remedies:

> The opinion of Judge Learned Hand in the case of United States v. Corn Products Refining Co., D.C.S.D.N.Y. 1916, 234 F. 964, clearly indicated that if the mere existence of monopoly power were the prime factor for inquiry, such criterion would necessarily affect the choice of remedy to be applied.... "If, on the other hand, the exercise of the power is what the statute touches, then the question arises What is practically necessary to prevent the repetition of those unfair means?" ...
>
> The latest remedy cases indicate two modifications of earlier judicial pronouncements, one practical, the other theoretical. On the practical side they show the courts are less likely than formerly to be impressed by evidence which tends to establish that defendants who have violated the Sherman Act in the past will not do so in the future. On the theoretical side, a rule has been formulated which, when applied, will serve to deprive defendants of the fruits of their wrongdoing. This, no doubt, is an outgrowth of an awareness that strong measures are required to restrain a tendency to recidivism....
>
> The opinion in United States v. Crescent Amusement Co., 1944, 323 U.S. 173, further emphasized the need of a practical approach towards the possibility of the return to improper conduct on the part of a monopolist. It also enunciated the "fruits" doctrine. Defendant having been found in that case to have conspired to restrain and monopolize trade in the exhibition of motion pictures, was prohibited from acquiring additional theatres without a showing that competition would not thereby be unreasonably restrained, and was ordered to divest itself of the stock of certain affiliated corporations. The Court said: "The pattern of past conduct is not easily forsaken.

Where the proclivity for unlawful activity has been as manifest as here, the decree should operate as an effective deterrent to a repetition of the unlawful conduct and yet not stand as a barrier to healthy growth on a competitive basis. Those who violate the Act may not reap the benefits of their violations and avoid an undoing of their unlawful project on the plea of hardship or inconvenience. That principle is adequate here to justify divestiture of all interest in some of the affiliates *since there acquisition was part of the fruits of the conspiracy.*" (Emphasis added.) . . .

In the following year . . . , the Supreme Court made a clear declaration as to the purpose to be served by an anti-trust remedy. In Schine Theatres v. United States, 1948, 334 U.S. 110, after finding that defendants had conspired to restrain and monopolize trade in the exhibition of motion pictures, the Court held that an injunction against future violations was an insufficient remedy. Without divestiture the defendants "could *retain the full dividends* of their monopolistic practices and profit from the unlawful restraints of trade which they had inflicted on competitors." (Emphasis added.) . . .

In United States v. Paramount Pictures, 1948, 334 U.S. 131, the Court indicated that divestiture is warranted where the acquisitions were the fruits of monopolistic practices or restraints of trade, or if lawfully acquired, they were utilized as part of a conspiracy to eliminate or suppress competition in furtherance of the ends of the conspiracy. The propriety of divestiture, it seems, is to be determined by the relationship of the unreasonable restraints of trade to the position of the defendant in the market.

That a new principle has been injected into the interpretation of Section 4 of the Sherman Act is amply demonstrated by the following comparison. The purpose of the remedy in an anti-trust suit was initially defined in *Standard Oil.* "1st. To forbid the doing in the future of acts like those which we have found to have been done in the past which would be violative of the statute. 2d. The exertion of such measure of relief as will effectually dissolve the combination found to exist in violation of the statute, and thus neutralize the extension and continually operating force which the possession of the power unlawfully obtained has brought and will continue to bring about."

The same thoughts were expressed in the *Schine* case, but the "fruits" theory was added. Divestiture or dissolution, it was said, serves several functions: "(1) It puts an end to the combination or conspiracy when that is itself the violation. (2) *It deprives the anti-trust defendants of the benefits of their conspiracy.* (3) It is designed to break up or render impotent the monopoly power which violates the Act."

315. (a) What should be the relationship of remedy to violation? In *United Shoe,* for example, defendant's monopolizing behavior centered around its leasing practices. Should the remedy be confined to enjoining that behavior? Should the remedy in *Griffith* be confined to correcting defendant's behavior or may dissolution be considered?

(b) Should the purpose of §2 remedies be solely to ensure future competition or also to deter violations? If the violator will be enjoined from further violations but keeps the fruits produced in the interim, is there any deterrence? If all gains are disgorged, but no further penalties are imposed, will prospective monopolizers have sufficient disincentive to engage in violations? (Consider the prospect that some violations will go undetected or unprosecuted.) In considering deterrence, of what relevance is the coexistence of injunctive relief with criminal penalties and private treble damage actions?

(c) In light of the purposes of antitrust remedies, was the final decree in *Alcoa* appropriate? What should have been the remedy if World War II had not intervened? Note that in both *Standard Oil* and *American Tobacco*, see ¶¶303a-303b, the remedy was to divest the combinations into a number of separate companies.[23] Up until 1989, structural reorganization had been ordered in only 34 §2 cases, all but 9 of those before 1950.[24]

(d) You are a lawyer asked for antitrust advice concerning a company's proposed strategy for beating its competition. After reviewing the new plans, you conclude that portions of the scheme are undoubtedly illegal under §2, but that prosecution may not occur and the likely remedy would enjoin future action but not impose any serious penalty on the violation. You also know that criminal sanctions are never applied in this context and a treble damage suit is unlikely and sufficiently costly that it could probably be settled for very little relative to the company's profits. May you (1) flatly advise violation on the ground that it is profitable? (2) Advise going forward, holding back your knowledge that it is illegal, since it is in the company's economic interest to proceed? (3) Write a memo with a boilerplate sentence advising against it on grounds of illegality but spending dozens of pages laying out how profitable it is likely to be in any event? (4) Simply describe both the legality and the penalties, leaving it for the company to decide? How much do these alternatives differ in practice? If the company goes forward against your advice (whether sincere or not), do you

23. For an economic analysis of divestiture as an antitrust remedy, see Comanor & Scherer, note 6.

24. See R. Posner, A Statistical Study of Antitrust Enforcement, 13 J.L. & Econ. 365, 406 (1970) (Table 29 indicates 32 reorganizations up until 1970); see also W. Kovacic, Failed Expectations: The Troubled Past and Uncertain Future of the Sherman Act as a Tool for Deconcentration, 74 Iowa L. Rev. 1105, 1111 (1989) (adding the *AT&T* and *Sunkist* cases to Posner's total).

have any obligation to inform others or to attempt to prevent the violation?[25]

316. (a) Do you find Judge Wyzanski's *United Shoe* opinion on remedy too timid? (1) Does he fairly characterize the law's general hostility to monopoly power? If so, is he not obliged to take every feasible step to set this industry on a more competitive course? Is a court an appropriate institution for that purpose? Whether or not a court is the best possible agency for this function, is it free to doubt its capacity to do what the statute entrusts to its care? Or would it be unrealistic for a court to ignore its limitations and the limits of economic science? Does Judge Wyzanski overstate those limitations? (2) To the extent a court's remedial powers are limited, how, if at all, should this bear on determining when it is appropriate to find a violation of §2?

(b) Do you agree with *United Shoe*'s disposition of the leasing question?[26] (1) Would you have forced United to cease leasing its machines and to substitute a sales-only policy? What would be the advantages? Disadvantages? How would a sales-only policy affect

25. It is no doubt of some interest to readers that being a lawyer does not insulate one from criminal law liability—for example, as an accomplice or conspirator. E.g., United States v. Clovis Retail Liquor Dealers Trade Assn., 540 F.2d 1389 (10th Cir. 1976) (conviction of lawyer for participation in criminal price-fixing conspiracy). The narrower question concerns which actions by lawyers cross the line of legality. More broadly, one should consider provisions of ethics codes. See Model Code of Professional Responsibility DR 7-102(A)(7) ("A lawyer shall not intentionally ... [c]ounsel or assist his client in conduct that the lawyer knows to be illegal or fraudulent."); Model Rules of Professional Conduct 1.2(d) ("A lawyer shall not counsel a client to engage, or assist a client, in conduct that the lawyer knows is criminal or fraudulent, but a lawyer may discuss the legal consequences of any proposed course of conduct with a client and may counsel or assist a client to make a good faith effort to determine the validity, scope, meaning or application of the law."). The comment to Model Rule 1.2 indicates that "[t]here is a critical distinction between presenting an analysis of legal aspects of questionable conduct and recommending the means by which a crime or fraud might be committed with impunity.... [T]he lawyer is required to avoid furthering the [wrongful] purpose, for example, by suggesting how it might be concealed." Where the client is an organization, Model Rule 1.13 describes additional measures available to the lawyer, including referring the matter to higher authority within the organization. All these requirements are discussed in C. Wolfram, Modern Legal Ethics §13.3.2 (1986). For a theoretical analysis, see S. Shavell, Legal Advice About Contemplated Acts: The Decision to Obtain Advice, Its Social Desirability, and Protection of Confidentiality, 17 J. Leg. Stud. 123 (1988).

26. Equipment Distributors' Coalition v. FCC, 824 F.2d 1197 (D.C. Cir. 1987) (no violation for use of optional leases—sales also available—with early termination charges by AT&T where the charges were waived if new equipment was bought or leased from AT&T).

United, its competitors, and customers? (2) Will the requirement
that United Shoe state service charges separately suffice, or must
the pricing be regulated?[27]

(c) What is the justification for *United Shoe*'s decree with respect
to defendant's patents? (1) Were United's patent practices involved
in its monopolizing behavior? Is this question relevant to the wisdom or propriety of the decree? (2) Proposition: Patents are gov-
ernment-granted monopolies designed to reward invention and
thus to encourage it; the *United Shoe* decree on present and future
patents conflicts with the purposes and premises of the patent system. In what respects do you agree or disagree with this proposition? (3) Could the court have required United to grant royalty-free
licenses? Should it have done so? (4) Who determines whether a
royalty is "reasonable"? How is this to be determined?[28] (5) If the
court can regulate royalties on United's patents, why should it not
also regulate profit margins on United's machines for which there
is little or no competition?

(d) If dissolution in *United Shoe* were more practicable, what
would be its advantages? (1) If, for example, United had three
plants and each plant manufactured all varieties of United machinery, would dissolution be appropriate? Would it be fair to the
stockholders? (2) Would the resultant three companies have to
duplicate management and research personnel? Would this be desirable? (3) If the supposed three plants each produced different
varieties of United machinery, would dissolution be more or less
appropriate?

Legislative Deconcentration

317. Deconcentration: no-fault monopoly and oligopoly. *Alcoa*
raised the possibility of condemning monopoly in the absence of
identifiable, exclusionary acts other than those ordinarily associated
with a firm's operation. The reasoning supporting no-fault monopoly is simple: To the extent monopoly produces evil results, even
when the monopoly has been "thrust upon" the actor, society suffers. Similarly, observing that many industries in the United States
are highly concentrated, even if well short of control by a single,
dominant firm, and fearing the prospects for express collusion or
tacit coordination[29] that might go undetected or unpunished under Sherman Act §1, industrial deconcentration legislation has

27. Cf. ¶¶430b, 431, 432.
28. See ¶280d.
29. See Ch. 2C.

been proposed from time to time. Paragraph 318 notes two such proposals and the rationales offered to support or oppose them. Paragraph 319 compares oligopoly and monopoly in terms of the potential evils associated with each, and ¶320 comments briefly on whether the existing Sherman Act can be construed to reach the results of the proposed legislation.

318. Legislative proposals. Two statutory proposals addressed to the problem of industrial concentration are briefly noted here for three purposes: (1) to indicate that some observers regard new legislation as necessary, (2) to examine the topics that might have to be covered, and (3) to provide a basis for comparing possible judicial approaches in extending and applying existing antitrust laws. Observe how each proposal addresses the four topics that must at a minimum be faced by deconcentration legislation: criteria, defenses, remedies, and procedures.

(a) *S. 2614.*[30] (1) Criteria: The tribunal must decree appropriate remedies once the specified structural criteria are met — namely, a stable four-firm concentration ratio of 70 percent within a $500 million market.[31] This particular bill does not make economic performance relevant. (2) Defenses: The bill would ignore performance or the derivation of firm or industry power. It does take minimum efficient scale into account by prohibiting restructuring proved by the defendant to cause a substantial loss of scale economies. (3) Remedies: The Department of Justice would decide which oligopolies to challenge, presumably on the basis of an appraisal of economic performance and the prospective gains from restructuring. There would be no criminal or private remedies. (4) Tribunal: Provision is made for a new tribunal that is to be selected from among the regular federal judges. The trial court would be authorized to appoint its own economic expert witnesses to examine data in the hands of any party and to offer their conclusions about the data. The Supreme Court would hear appeals.

---

30. 92d Cong., 1st Sess. (Sept. 30, 1971), incorporating the "Concentrated Industries Act" recommended by the White House Task Force Report on Antitrust Policy (1968).

31. More particularly, the bill deals only with markets in which aggregate annual sales exceed $500 million. Such markets fall within the bill when four firms aggregate 70 percent of the market during seven of the last ten or four of the last five years. To fall within the bill, moreover, the average aggregate share during the latest five years of the four leading firms must not be less than 80 percent of their average aggregate share during the five preceding years. The latter requirement would exclude industries in which there have been substantial changes in the identity of the four largest firms.

(b) *S. 1167.*[32] (1) Criteria: The bill establishes a rebuttable presumption that monopoly power is possessed by any firm with after-tax earnings regularly exceeding 15 percent of net worth, by firms that have not engaged in "substantial price competition" over three consecutive years, or by four or fewer firms accounting for 50 percent or more of any market. Monopoly power may also be proved by a new Commission in other unspecified ways. (2) Defenses: Monopoly power need not be divested by a defendant that can prove that its power is due solely to valid and lawfully used patents or that divestiture would result in the loss of substantial economies. (3) Remedies: The standard remedy would be dissolution of the offending firms and any other steps helpful to creating competition. No criminal or private remedies are provided. (4) Tribunal: The Supreme Court would hear appeals from a new court that would act upon suit of a new independent Industrial Reorganization Commission, which would also be charged with making industry studies and formulating plans to reorganize industries possessing unlawful monopoly power.[33]

(c) *Rationale.* The first bill outlined above is based on a recommendation of a group of lawyers and economists.[34] They justified their recommendation as follows:

> In general it may be said that the smaller the number of firms in an industry — at least where that number is very small or where a very small number is responsible for the overwhelming share of the industry's output — the greater the likelihood that the behavior of the industry will depart from the competitive norm. These propositions have found general acceptance in economic literature in the past 25 or 30 years. . . .
>
> Interpretation of the Sherman Act itself, however, has lagged behind these developments. . . . While Judge Hand had intimated that a share as low as 65% might suffice, no subsequent case has tested that proposition or explored the limits of the *Alcoa* doctrine.
>
> Nor has any case yet provided a basis for treating as illegal the shared monopoly power of several firms that together possess a predominant share of the market, absent proof of conspiracy among them. . . .

32. 93d Cong., 1st Sess. (Mar. 12, 1973); reintroduced as S. 1959, 94th Cong., 1st Sess. (June 17, 1975) (deleting rebuttable presumption based on profits).

33. The bill would direct studies of the following named industries: chemicals and drugs, electrical machinery and equipment, electronic computing and communication equipment, energy, iron and steel, motor vehicles, and nonferrous metals.

34. White House Task Force Report on Antitrust Policy (1968) (sometimes known as the Neal report), reprinted in 2 Antitr. L. & Econ. Rev. 11 (Winter 1968). For additional concentration data, see ¶502.

Thus a gap in the law remains.... This gap is of major significance. Highly concentrated industries account for a large share of manufacturing activity in the United States.... There is little evidence that economies of scale require firms the size of the dominant firms in most industries that are highly concentrated.... The success of very large firms may, of course, be explained on the basis of efficiencies other than economies of scale, such as superior management talent or other unique resources. To the extent that such efficiencies exist, however, they may ordinarily be transferred and thus would not necessarily be lost by reorganization of the industry into a larger number of smaller units. The same is true of advantages that inhere in legal monopolies, such as an accumulation of patents.

A dissent was offered by then-Professor Robert Bork:

The dissolution of such firms would be a disservice to consumers and to national strength. When firms grow to sizes that create concentration or when such a structure is created by merger and persists for many years, there is a very strong prima facie case that the firms' sizes are related to efficiency. By efficiency I mean "competitive effectiveness" within the bounds of the law, and competitive effectiveness means service to consumers. If the leading firms in a concentrated industry are restricting their output in order to obtain prices above the competitive level, their efficiencies must be sufficiently superior to that of all actual and potential rivals to offset that behavior. Were this not so, rivals would be enabled to expand their market shares because of the abnormally high prices and would thus deconcentrate the industry. Market rivalry thus automatically weighs the respective influences of efficiency and output restriction and arrives at the firm sizes and industry structures that serve consumers best....

319. Oligopoly and single-firm monopoly compared. The issue of whether oligopoly is or should be unlawful may be illuminated by comparing its performance or threat with monopoly. Monopoly generally appears to be the more harmful of the two industry structures because firms in oligopolistic industries are not always able to achieve the results of a monopoly. Accordingly, the argument for restructuring would be strongest for monopoly. Correspondingly, to the extent one would not interpret current antitrust law or enact new legislation to condemn a monopolist that has done nothing more than charge supracompetitive prices, one would not do so for an oligopoly either. The remainder of this Paragraph indicates the many respects in which this generalization concerning monopoly and oligopoly tends to be true and notes along the way some qualifications and exceptions.

First, and perhaps most important, oligopolies vary greatly in the degree to which they approach monopoly results. Interdependence may be weak. Coordination may be seriously impaired by some of the factors discussed in Chapter 2C. Performance may be workably competitive. On the other hand, in some cases the price-output results may be even worse than those of single-firm monopoly, which makes some effort to produce industry output at minimum costs. Oligopolistic pricing can also be more rigid and thus impede the ¶108 dynamic adjustment process even more than monopoly. Yet, oligopolistic price coordination can break down and offer us at least occasional price competition.

Second, suppliers or customers may have no real alternative to dealing with the single-firm monopoly, whereas there is at least some range of choice, even if not with respect to price, in the case of oligopoly. Similarly, there may be differences with respect to rivalry in quality and innovation. In oligopoly, the several firms may engage in considerable rivalry — especially nonprice rivalry which, to be sure, is not always a blessing. Advertising, for example, may serve merely to shift demand among the rivals and thus increase the costs of each without increasing aggregate demand. Complex product variations offer real choices to consumers, and thus real benefits, but, as explored in ¶230e, such rivalry can also be excessive, raising costs more than product enhancements are worth to consumers. Significant innovations are generally a social benefit. In this respect, oligopoly may be more progressive than single-firm monopoly and thus exhibit superior economic performance, although this result is by no means certain. Whether the social virtue of these latter possibilities offsets the social waste of some increased promotion and product variation cannot be known generally or a priori.

Third, in considering the prospects for improvements through restructuring, it should be noted that, since each oligopolist will be smaller than a single-firm monopoly would be, the oligopolist will exceed the minimum efficient scale for that industry by a smaller margin, if any, than a larger single-firm monopolist would. But this fact would relieve our concern for oligopoly altogether only if all or most oligopolies were in fact necessary to realize minimum efficient scale in production or distribution. Such evidence that does exist, however, suggests that the leading firms in many oligopolistic markets exceed the minimum efficient scale by several multiples.[35] Such studies, of course, do not dispose of any particular case where the question of fact must be faced and answered. In sum, the concern for unjustified oligopoly remains, although we must recognize that efficiency justifications will be plausible more frequently than in single-firm monopoly cases.

35. See ¶119.

Finally, because each oligopolist has only a fraction, albeit a substantial one, of the market, there may be less reason to suppose that it attained its position by improper means. Indeed, it is not improbable that one oligopolist attained and maintained its position by superior skill, foresight, and industry. But commendable activity in prior decades is not necessarily reason to tolerate an oligopoly (or monopoly) today.

Is it necessary to grant oligopoly a greater immunity than single-firm monopoly in order to preserve competitive incentives? The monopolist or the oligopolist might be deterred from business-expanding moves if corrective government action is feared. Even if condemned, however, the firm will not be expropriated but will only lose future monopoly profits. It will retain the excess profits earned before reaching the oligopoly state, before that state is detected, and during the inevitable delays before that state is attacked and remedied. Yet, it is possible that even such remedies would be feared, particularly if corrective action might mistakenly deprive firms of the very efficiencies that produced their success. Moreover, to the extent prohibition is triggered by a target market share or profit rate, firms approaching the liability threshold may have incentives to hold back by forgoing opportunities that allow them to achieve further advantage from their abilities.

However the comparison between the case for restructuring oligopoly and monopoly is resolved, it is apparent that remedies ought not to be attempted where unnecessary because the market works tolerably well (more plausible with oligopoly) or where futile because no efficient restructuring is possible. Quite apart from statutory limitations, therefore, one would consider restructuring only where it is likely to improve net economic performance or serve other objectives substantially; and we say "substantially" to take account of the costs of the process, particularly including the risk of erroneous judgment. Thus, we must ultimately ask three questions about any market that might be a candidate for restructuring. First, is significant restructuring feasible without losing important economies of scale or experience? Second, how workably competitive and progressive is the present market relative to the probable performance of a feasibly restructured market? Third, is the market in question significant enough to warrant the effort?

320. Sherman Act §2 coverage. Developments in monopolization law since *Alcoa* have not borne out its most expansive reading to forbid blameless monopoly. Courts do generally insist on some identifiable, exclusionary conduct. Similarly, oligopoly or shared monopoly has not, as such, been held covered by the §2 monopolization provision.[36] For oligopoly, one must also ask whether the condemnation of "every person who shall monopolize" embraces those who exert monopoly power together with others (but without "agreement"). Or may they be said to "combine" to monopolize?[37] Is it determinative that the Congress that enacted the Sherman Act did not know about the oligopoly problem? (Has the Sherman Act been confined to applications contemplated by the 1890 Congress?) How much weight may properly be given to Chief Justice Hughes's notion that "[a]s a charter of freedom, the Act has a generality and adaptability comparable to that found to be desirable in constitutional provisions"?[38] One can consider whether the differences between monopoly and oligopoly outlined in ¶319 justify the differences in legal treatment. If one finds that difference unjustified, one must still ask whether the courts should hesitate to declare novel rules of great significance without the legitimacy and perhaps the additional machinery that would flow from new legislation. Or should the courts overcome such compunctions and continue to develop antitrust "common law"[39] with the comforting assurance that Congress can, after all, undo any judicial steps it thinks mistaken? Can the courts either adopt or find substitutes for the arbitrary but perhaps necessary line-drawing of the typical legislative proposals discussed in ¶318? When dealing with such shared monopolies, are criminal, treble damage, or any private actions appropriate?[40] If not, can the courts condemn the monopoly or oligopoly in a government suit under Sherman Act §2 while denying or restricting criminal or private suits against the offenders?[41]

36. But query: What was the meaning of the 1946 *American Tobacco* case noted in ¶307? In addition, under Federal Trade Commission Act §5, the FTC had challenged the leading makers of ready-to-eat cereals with the collective possession of monopoly power and with exclusionary acts. Kellogg, 81 F.T.C. 1031 (1972). Ultimately, the FTC dismissed the case. 3 Trade Reg. Rep. ¶21899 (1982).

37. See Ch. 2C and *Albrecht*, ¶419.

38. *Appalachian Coals*, 288 U.S. at 359-360.

39. See ¶130.

40. Note that the judges may be somewhat more comfortable with arbitrary and stringent rules to the extent that they can rely on the prosecutor to weigh all relevant factors in the public interest and to challenge only those oligopolies that most require antitrust intervention and correction. Private suits may seek treble damages and do not reflect a disinterested public judgment that restructuring is warranted or the relative priority with which judicial resources should be expended.

41. See ¶138.

Vertical Integration and Dealing with Competitors[42]

321. Vertical integration in brief. (a) *Overview.* A firm may be said to be vertically integrated to the extent that it does for itself what otherwise could be done by independent firms in the marketplace. Thus vertically integrated are (1) a steel company mining iron ore that it uses, (2) a steel maker rolling steel ingot into fabrications rather than (or in addition to) selling steel ingot to independent rolling mills, (3) an auto manufacturer making carburetors or seat belts or processing accounts receivable on an internal computer, (4) a patentee practicing the invention itself rather than licensing others to do so, or (5) a manufacturer of athletic equipment owning its own sporting goods stores rather than selling to independent retailers.

The firm choosing to process accounts internally instead of buying such computer processing services on the market probably believes that outside work is more costly in terms of resources used or transaction costs or that the market price is monopolistic. Ordinarily, as in this illustration, vertical integration has no anticompetitive implications and is thus of no antitrust concern. In fact, as the initial series of illustrations suggests, most highly competitive industries exhibit at least some degree of vertical integration. For example, it is difficult to imagine an antitrust objection to those farmers who sell some or all of their produce at roadside stands.

(b) *A second monopoly?* A monopolist's vertical integration can sometimes "create monopoly at a different level." Suppose, for example, that Alcoa is the sole manufacturer of aluminum ingot and that it uses all its ingot output for self-manufacture of various aluminum fabrications (for example, sheet for airplanes and cans). Alcoa would then have a monopoly not only of ingot but also of aluminum fabrications.

Such a second monopoly at the fabrication level, however, does not tend to result in the usual detriment of higher prices and reduced output. The power already possessed by the ingot monopolist to control the price and output of ingot effectively controls the price and output of independent fabricators.[43] For example, sup-

---

42. See Areeda & Turner, note 1, ¶¶723-729, 736. For economic analysis, see F.M. Scherer & D. Ross, Industrial Market Structure and Economic Performance, ch. 15 (3d ed. 1990); W.K. Viscusi, J. Vernon & J. Harrington, Economics of Regulation and Antitrust, ch. 8 (2d ed. 1995). For more advanced treatments, see the additional references in Ch. 4, note 1.

43. R. Bork, Vertical Integration and the Sherman Act: The Legal History of an Economic Misconception, 22 U. Chi. L. Rev. 157, 197 (1954). Bork properly excepts the case in which vertical integration is necessary to facilitate price discrimination.

pose that an integrated aluminum ingot monopolist would maximize profit by selling aluminum pipe for $100 per unit and that the unit cost[44] of fabricating ingot into pipe were $10. It will charge $100 for pipe. If, instead, it sells ingot to perfectly competitive pipe fabricators, it will charge them $90 for ingot, and competition will not allow them to charge more than their costs ($90 + $10) for pipe. In either case, the price of pipe, and thus the output of ingot and pipe, will be identical. Integration thus has absolutely no short-run effect on price and output where fabrication is otherwise competitive, ingot is used in fixed proportion with other inputs into pipe fabrication, and buyers with different demands cannot be segregated.

(c) *Avoiding successive monopoly or inefficient input substitution.* There are two situations in which vertical integration could increase output and reduce prices. Suppose, first, that an ingot monopolist sold to a pipe monopolist or that pipe fabricators formed a selling cartel (or achieved similar results through oligopolistic price coordination). In that event, the pipe firm(s) would take the ingot price ($90 in the last example) as given and then add a monopolistic markup (exceeding their costs of $10). The resulting price thus exceeds that in ¶b ($100) — which corresponded to the maximum profits for the combined activities of ingot and pipe production — and thereby reduces output below that which the integrated monopolist would charge.[45] To avoid this result, the ingot monopolist might integrate into pipe fabrication and thereby prevent other fabricators from charging more than $100.[46]

Vertical integration might also avoid inefficient input substitution. Suppose, for example, that independent fabricators of pots and pans would use equal amounts of aluminum and copper if both were priced at their production costs of $60 and $80, respectively. That "efficient" allocation of resources will not occur, however,

44. Throughout this discussion, as throughout this book, cost refers not to accounting costs but to economic costs, which include a competitive return on investment.

45. This illustrates the general proposition that successive monopolies generate worse results than a single integrated monopoly — unless the two monopolies agree to maximize industry profits with the downstream price of $100 and then bargain to allocate the resulting profits between them in some manner. See Ch. 2A, note 51.

46. When the integrated firm charges $90 for ingot and $100 for pipe, the resulting price squeeze denies excess profits to the independent fabricators. This may seem unfair to them, but eliminating excess profits from the second level of monopoly is efficient even if undesirable monopoly profit continues at the ingot level. R. Blair & D. Kaserman, Law and Economics of Vertical Integration and Control 29-36 (1983); F. Warren-Boulton, Vertical Control of Markets: Business and Labor Practices 51-64 (1978).

when aluminum ingot is priced at the $90 monopoly level: The pot fabricators will use too little aluminum and too much copper. To avoid that inefficient result the monopolist could stop selling aluminum to the pot fabricators, make the pots itself, and thereby achieve a more efficient mix of inputs. Whether the final price for pots will be higher or lower depends on whether the more efficient input mix offsets the effect of the new monopoly in pots.[47]

(d) *Price discrimination.* Vertical integration might facilitate price discrimination, which can lead to higher or lower output, as explored in ¶285. As that discussion explained, market power is necessary to effectuate price discrimination; otherwise, the prices charged to high-value purchasers would be undercut. Suppose that ingot can be used for making both pots and pipe, where the latter use is more valuable. If the ingot monopolist charged more to pipe fabricators, they would buy ingot indirectly, through pot manufacturers who purchase more than their requirements, thus defeating the discrimination. But if the ingot monopolist takes over all production of aluminum pots, it need sell ingot only to pipe fabricators and, thus, can successfully charge the high price for that use.

(e) *Long-run effects on market structure and performance.* Even if vertical integration did not reduce output or raise price in the short run, adverse long-run effects are possible. First, substituting a single producer for many at the second level could lessen the competitive stimulus for cost reduction and innovation at that level. Second, a new entrant challenging the ingot monopoly would have to enter the second level as well if there were no independent fabricators to buy its ingot. The incremental expense, risk, and difficulties of two-level entry might reduce the likelihood of independent entry. As a related matter, if the ingot monopolist had less than a 100 percent market share, it might make life more difficult for its ingot rivals if it came to control a large share of fabrication, even if that share was no larger than its prior share of the ingot market.[48]

(f) *Summary.* The legal dilemma can be briefly put. Due to the pervasiveness of various degrees of vertical integration, it cannot generally be prevented, even in the case of monopolists, without losing the various efficiencies it makes possible. Nor can we hope to measure the magnitude of efficiencies involved in each instance of vertical integration. But once vertical integration as such is generally accepted, there are formidable difficulties in compelling an

47. See ¶423b.
48. Compare the questions on *Griffith*, ¶308, and *Lorain Journal*, ¶354. This issue is explored further in Ch. 4B's examination of tying. See T. Krattenmaker & S. Salop, Anticompetitive Exclusion: Raising Rivals' Costs to Achieve Power over Price, 96 Yale L.J. 209 (1986); M. Coate & A. Kleit, Exclusion, Collusion, or Confusion?: The Underpinnings of Raising Rivals' Costs, 16 Res. L. & Econ. 73 (1994).

integrated firm also to deal with independent suppliers, dealers, or processors. In particular, antitrust tribunals would not often find it congenial to supervise the price and other terms on which the integrated firm deals with outsiders.

Vertical integration takes many forms, is motivated for a variety of reasons, and raises many issues, only a few of which will be explored in the following paragraphs.[49]

322. *Otter Tail Power Co. v. United States*, 410 U.S. 366 (1973). The Supreme Court affirmed a lower court finding that Otter Tail had attempted to prevent communities in which its retail electric power distribution franchise had expired from replacing its franchise with a municipal distribution system. Otter Tail had refused to sell wholesale power to proposed municipal systems or to allow power produced by others to flow through its transmission system to reach such municipal systems. (It controlled the only transmission lines that would reach such localities.) These combined refusals were held (4-3) to violate Sherman Act §2. The dissent was based largely on the fact that there was heavy federal regulation through the Federal Power Commission, suggesting that any duties to deal should be imposed by Congress and regulatory authorities, not the courts through use of the antitrust laws. It also noted that, in this case, local monopoly was unavoidable, regardless of defendant's actions.[50]

323. *Berkey Photo v. Eastman Kodak Co.*, 603 F.2d 263, 276, 281 (2d Cir. 1979), cert. denied, 444 U.S. 1093 (1980). In 1972, Kodak introduced its new, pocket-sized 110 instamatic camera. At the same time, it introduced a new color film, which made it possible to produce quality photos with a film size small enough to fit its new cameras. This film was not initially made available in sizes that would fit other cameras, and it could not be processed using the equipment and chemicals used to process the old film. Berkey, a competitor, alleged violations of §2 arising from Kodak's failure to predisclose the nature of the new film, permitting it time to adapt to the new requirements. The Court of Appeals reversed a jury

49. See also Ch. 4, which examines vertical contractual arrangements that often have much in common with integration, and Ch. 5C, which examines vertical mergers.

50. Compare Union Leader Corp. v. Newspapers of New England, 180 F. Supp. 125 (D. Mass. 1959), aff'd in part and rev'd in part, 284 F.2d 582 (1st Cir. 1960), cert. denied, 365 U.S. 833 (1961); Fishman v. Estate of Wirtz, 807 F.2d 520, 536 (7th Cir. 1986) (competition to acquire a local monopoly basketball franchise protected by Sherman Act; emphasizing that "antitrust laws are concerned with the competitive *process*").

verdict and damage award (which, including trebling and attorney's fees, totaled $87 million) for Berkey.

The court indicated that

> the use of monopoly power attained in one market to gain a competitive advantage in another is a violation of §2, even if there has not been an attempt to monopolize in the second market.[51] . . . But . . . an integrated business [does not] offend the Sherman Act whenever one of its departments benefits from association with a division possessing a monopoly in its own market.

The court found it to be "an ordinary and acceptable business practice to keep one's new developments a secret," so it was erroneous to instruct the jury that Kodak had any duty to predisclose information regarding its new system. To hold otherwise would diminish its incentives to engage in research and development. Although its ability to introduce the new film without predisclosure was a benefit available to it only because it was integrated into film processing, that did not make Kodak's actions illegal because it was a benefit resulting from integration rather than from monopoly.

ASPEN SKIING CO. v. ASPEN HIGHLANDS SKIING CORP.
472 U.S. 585 (1985)

Justice STEVENS. . . . [T]he jury found that petitioner Aspen Skiing Company (Ski Co.) had monopolized the market for downhill skiing services in Aspen, Colorado. The question presented is whether that finding is erroneous as a matter of law because it rests on an assumption that a firm with monopoly power has a duty to cooperate with its smaller rivals in a marketing arrangement in order to avoid violating §2 of the Sherman Act.

I

[Ski Co. owned and operated facilities on three mountains in Aspen; Highlands had the fourth. Over the years, various arrange-

---

51. Compare Alaska Airlines v. United Airlines, 948 F.2d 536 (9th Cir. 1991), cert. denied, 503 U.S. 977. Plaintiff airlines claimed that United and American Airlines had failed to give them "reasonable access" to their powerful computer reservation systems. The Ninth Circuit specifically rejected *Berkey*'s claim that the Sherman Act prohibited the use of monopoly power (over computer reservations) merely to obtain a "competitive advantage" in another market (in selling flights), and required for liability proof that the defendants used their monopoly power in one market to gain, or attempt to gain, a monopoly in another market.

ments existed wherein a week-long pass, usable at any of the four mountains, was sold, usually at a discount from the price of daily tickets.] Highlands' share of the revenues from the ticket [based on usage] was 17.5% in 1973-1974, 18.5% in 1974-1975, 16.8% in 1975-1976, and 13.2% in 1976-1977. . . .[9] By 1977, multi-area tickets accounted for nearly 35% of the total market. . . .

Between 1962 and 1977, Ski Co. and Highlands had independently offered various mixes of 1-day, 3-day and 6-day passes at their own mountains. In every season except one, however, they had also offered some form of all-Aspen, 6-day ticket, and divided the revenues from those sales on the basis of usage. Nevertheless, for the 1977-1978 season, Ski Co. offered to continue the all-Aspen ticket only if Highlands would accept a 13.2% fixed share of the ticket's revenues.

Although that had been Highlands' share of the ticket revenues in 1976-1977, Highlands contended that that season was an inaccurate measure of its market performance since it had been marked by unfavorable weather and an unusually low number of visiting skiers. . . . Highlands eventually accepted a fixed percentage of 15% for the 1977-1978 season. No survey was made during that season of actual usage in the 4-area ticket at the two competitors' mountains. . . .

In March 1978, the Ski Co. . . . decided to offer Highlands a 4-area ticket provided that Highlands would agree to receive a 12.5% fixed percentage of the revenue — considerably below Highlands' historical average based on usage. Later in the 1978-1979 season, a member of Ski Co.'s Board of Directors candidly informed a Highlands' official that he had advocated making Highlands "an offer that [it] could not accept." . . .

Ski Co. took additional actions that made it extremely difficult for Highlands to market its own multiarea package to replace the joint offering. Ski Co. discontinued the 3-day, 3-area pass for the 1978-1979 season,[13] and also refused to sell Highlands any lift

9. In 1975, the Colorado Attorney General filed a complaint against Ski Co. and Highlands alleging, in part, that the negotiations over the 4-area ticket had provided them with a forum for price-fixing in violation of §1 of the Sherman Act and that they had attempted to monopolize the market for downhill skiing services in Aspen in violation of §2. In 1977, the case was settled by a consent decree that permitted the parties to continue to offer the 4-area ticket provided that they set their own ticket prices unilaterally before negotiating its terms.

13. Highlands' owner explained that there was a key difference between the 3-day, 3-area ticket and the 6-day, 3-area ticket: "with the three-day ticket, a person could ski on the . . . Aspen Skiing Corporation mountains for three days and then there would be three days in which he could ski on our mountain; but with the six-day ticket, we are absolutely locked out of those people." As a result of

tickets, either at the tour operator's discount or at retail. Highlands finally developed an alternative product, the "Adventure Pack," which consisted of a 3-day pass at Highlands and three vouchers, each equal to the price of a daily lift ticket at a Ski Co. mountain. The vouchers were guaranteed by funds on deposit in an Aspen bank, and were redeemed by Aspen merchants at full value. Ski Co., however, refused to accept them.

Later, Highlands redesigned the Adventure Pack to contain American Express Traveler's Checks or money orders instead of vouchers. Ski Co. eventually accepted these negotiable instruments in exchange for daily lift tickets.[15] Despite some strengths of the product, the Adventure Pack met considerable resistance from tour operators and consumers who had grown accustomed to the convenience and flexibility provided by the all-Aspen ticket.

Without a convenient all-Aspen ticket, Highlands basically "becomes a day ski area in a destination resort." Highlands' share of the market for downhill skiing services in Aspen declined steadily after the 4-area ticket based on usage was abolished in 1977: from 20.5% in 1976-1977, to 15.7% in 1977-1978, to 13.1% in 1978-1979, to 12.5% in 1979-1980, to 11% in 1980-1981. Highlands' revenues from associated skiing services like the ski school, ski rentals, amateur racing events, and restaurant facilities declined sharply as well.

II . . .

The case was tried to a jury which rendered a verdict finding Ski Co. guilty . . . and calculating Highlands' actual damages at $2.5 million.

In her instructions to the jury, the District Judge explained that the offense of monopolization under §2 of the Sherman Act has two elements: (1) the possession of monopoly power in a relevant market, and (2) the willful acquisition, maintenance, or use of that power by anticompetitive or exclusionary means or for anticompetitive or exclusionary purposes. Although the first element was vigorously disputed at the trial and in the Court of Appeals, in this Court Ski Co. does not challenge the jury's special verdict finding that it possessed monopoly power. Nor does Ski Co. criticize the trial court's instructions to the jury concerning the second element of the §2 offense.

"tremendous consumer demand" for a 3-day ticket, Ski Co. reinstated it late in the 1978-1979 season but without publicity or a discount off the daily rate.

15. . . . For the 1981-1982 season, Ski Co. set its single ticket price at $22 and discounted the 3-area, 6-day ticket to $114. According to Highlands, this price structure made the Adventure Pack unprofitable.

On this element, the jury was instructed that it had to consider whether "Aspen Skiing Corporation willfully acquired, maintained, or used that power by anti-competitive or exclusionary means or for anti-competitive or exclusionary purposes." The instructions elaborated:

> In considering whether the means or purposes were anti-competitive or exclusionary, you must draw a distinction here between practices which tend to exclude or restrict competition on the one hand and the success of a business which reflects only a superior product, a well-run business, or luck, on the other. . . .
>
> For example, a firm that has lawfully acquired a monopoly position is not barred from taking advantage of scale economies by constructing a large and efficient factory. These benefits are a consequence of size and not an exercise of monopoly power. Nor is a corporation which possesses monopoly power under a duty to cooperate with its business rivals. Also a company which possesses monopoly power and which refuses to enter into a joint operating agreement with a competitor or otherwise refuses to deal with a competitor in some manner does not violate Section 2 if valid business reasons exist for that refusal. . . .
>
> We are concerned with conduct which unnecessarily excludes or handicaps competitors. This is conduct which does not benefit consumers by making a better product or service available — or in other ways — and instead has the effect of impairing competition.
>
> To sum up, you must determine whether Aspen Skiing Corporation gained, maintained, or used monopoly power in a relevant market by arrangements and policies which rather than being a consequence of a superior product, superior business sense, or historic element, were designed primarily to further any domination of the relevant market or sub-market.

The jury answered a specific interrogatory finding the second element of the offense as defined in these instructions. . . .[22] . . .[23]

---

22. Counsel also appears to have argued that [Ski Co.] was under a legal obligation to refuse to participate in any joint marketing agreement with Highlands: "Aspen Skiing Corporation is required to compete. It is required to make independent decisions. It is required to price its own product. It is required to make its own determination of the ticket that it chooses to offer and the tickets that it chooses not to offer." In this Court, Ski Co. does not question the validity of the joint marketing arrangement under §1 of the Sherman Act. Thus, we have no occasion to consider the circumstances that might permit such combinations in the skiing industry. See generally, *NCAA*; *Broadcast Music*; *Sylvania.*

23. The District Court also entered an injunction requiring the parties to offer jointly a 4-area, 6-out-of-7 day coupon booklet substantially identical to the "Ski the Summit" booklet accepted by Ski Co. at its Breckenridge resort in Summit County, Colorado. The injunction was initially for a 3-year period, but was later extended through the 1984-1985 season by stipulation of the parties. Highlands represents that "it will not seek an extension of the injunction." No question is raised concerning the character of the injunctive relief ordered by the District Court.

The Court of Appeals affirmed in all respects. The court advanced two reasons. . . . First, relying on United States v. Terminal Railroad Assn. of St. Louis, 224 U.S. 383 (1912), the Court of Appeals held that the multiday, multiarea ticket could be characterized as an "essential facility" that Ski Co. had a duty to market jointly with Highlands. Second, it held that there was sufficient evidence to support a finding that Ski Co.'s intent in refusing to market the 4-area ticket, "considered together with its other conduct," was to create or maintain a monopoly. . . .

III

In this Court, Ski Co. contends that even a firm with monopoly power has no duty to engage in joint marketing with a competitor, that a violation of §2 cannot be established without evidence of substantial exclusionary conduct, and that none of its activities can be characterized as exclusionary. . . . [It] is surely correct in submitting that even a firm with monopoly power has no general duty to engage in a joint marketing program with a competitor. Ski Co. is quite wrong, however, in suggesting that the judgment in this case rests on any such proposition of law. For the trial court unambiguously instructed the jury that a firm possessing monopoly power has no duty to cooperate with its business rivals.

The absence of an unqualified duty to cooperate does not mean that every time a firm declines to participate in a particular cooperative venture, that decision may not have evidentiary significance, or that it may not give rise to liability in certain circumstances. The absence of a duty to transact business with another firm is, in some respects, merely the counterpart of the independent businessman's cherished right to select his customers and his associates. The high value that we have placed on the right to refuse to deal with other firms does not mean that the right is unqualified. In *Lorain Journal*,[52] we squarely held that the right was not unqualified. . . .

In *Lorain Journal*, the violation of §2 was an "attempt to monopolize," rather than monopolization, but the question of intent is relevant to both offenses. In the former case it is necessary to prove a "specific intent" to accomplish the forbidden objective — as Judge Hand explained, "an intent which goes beyond the mere intent to do the act." *Aloca*. In the latter case evidence of intent is merely relevant to the question whether the challenged conduct is fairly characterized as "exclusionary" or "anticompetitive" — to use the words in the trial court's instructions — or "predatory," to use a word that scholars seem to favor. Whichever label is used,

---

52. This case appears in Ch. 3C. — eds.

there is agreement on the proposition that "no monopolist monopolizes unconscious of what he is doing." As Judge Bork stated more recently: "Improper exclusion (exclusion not the result of superior efficiency) is always deliberately intended."[29]

The qualification on the right of a monopolist to deal with whom he pleases is not so narrow that it encompasses no more than the circumstances of *Lorain Journal.* In the actual case that we must decide, the monopolist did not merely reject a novel offer to participate in a cooperative venture that had been proposed by a competitor. Rather, the monopolist elected to make an important change in a pattern of distribution that had originated in a competitive market and had persisted for several years. The all-Aspen, 6-day ticket with revenues allocated on the basis of usage was first developed when three independent companies operated three different ski mountains in the Aspen area. It continued to provide a desirable option for skiers when the market was enlarged to include four mountains, and when the character of the market was changed by Ski Co.'s acquisition of monopoly power. Moreover, since the record discloses that interchangeable tickets are used in other multimountain areas which apparently are competitive, it seems appropriate to infer that such tickets satisfy consumer demand in free competitive markets.

Ski Co.'s decision to terminate the all-Aspen ticket was thus a decision by a monopolist to make an important change in the character of the market. Such a decision is not necessarily anticompetitive, and Ski Co. contends that neither its decision, nor the conduct in which it engaged to implement that decision, can fairly be characterized as exclusionary in this case. It recognizes, however, that as the case is presented to us, we must interpret the entire record in the light most favorable to Highlands and give to it the benefit of all inferences which the evidence fairly supports, even though contrary inferences might reasonably be drawn. . . .

Moreover, we must assume that the jury followed the court's instructions. The jury must, therefore, have drawn a distinction "between practices which tend to exclude or restrict competition on the one hand, and the success of a business which reflects only a superior product, a well-run business, or luck, on the other." Since the jury was unambiguously instructed that Ski Co.'s refusal to deal with Highlands "does not violate §2 if valid business reasons exist for that refusal," we must assume that the jury concluded that there were no valid reasons for the refusal. The question then is whether that conclusion finds support in the record.

---

29. R. Bork, The Antitrust Paradox 160 (1978) (hereinafter Bork).

IV

The question whether Ski Co.'s conduct may properly be character-ized as exclusionary cannot be answered by simply considering its effect on Highlands. In addition, it is relevant to consider its impact on consumers and whether it has impaired competition in an un-necessarily restrictive way. If a firm has been "attempting to exclude rivals on some basis other than efficiency," it is fair to characterize its behavior as predatory. It is, accordingly, appropriate to examine the effect of the challenged pattern of conduct on consumers, on Ski Co.'s smaller rival, and on Ski Co. itself.

SUPERIOR QUALITY OF THE ALL-ASPEN TICKET . . .

Over the years, [skiers] developed a strong demand for the 6-day, all-Aspen ticket in its various refinements. Most experienced skiers quite logically prefer to purchase their tickets at once for the whole period that they will spend at the resort; they can then spend more time on the slopes and enjoying après-ski amenities and less time standing in ticket lines. The 4-area attribute of the ticket allowed the skier to purchase his 6-day ticket in advance while reserving the right to decide in his own time and for his own reasons which mountain he would ski on each day. It provided convenience and flexibility, and expanded the vistas and the number of challenging runs available to him during the week's vacation.

While the 3-area, 6-day ticket offered by Ski Co. possessed some of these attributes, the evidence supports a conclusion that con-sumers were adversely affected by the elimination of the 4-area ticket. In the first place, the actual record of competition between a 3-area ticket and the all-Aspen ticket in the years after 1967 indi-cated that skiers demonstrably preferred four mountains to three. . . . A consumer survey undertaken in the 1979-1980 season indicated that 53.7% of the respondents wanted to ski Highlands, but would not; 39.9% said that they would not be skiing at the mountain of their choice because their ticket would not permit it. . . .

A major wholesale tour operator asserted that he would not even consider marketing a 3-area ticket if a 4-area ticket were available. During the 1977-1978 and 1978-1979 seasons, people with Ski Co.'s 3-area ticket came to Highlands "on a very regular basis" and at-tempted to board the lifts or join the ski school. Highlands officials were left to explain to angry skiers that they could only ski at High-lands or join its ski school by paying for a 1-day lift ticket. Even for the affluent, this was an irritating situation because it left the skier the option of either wasting one day of the 6-day, 3-area pass or obtaining a refund which could take all morning and entailed the forfeit of the 6-day discount. An active officer in the Atlanta Ski Club testified that the elimination of the 4-area pass "infuriated" him.

HIGHLAND'S ABILITY TO COMPETE

The adverse impact of Ski Co.'s pattern of conduct on Highlands is not disputed in this Court.... Highlands' share of the relevant market steadily declined after the 4-area ticket was terminated. The size of the damages award also confirms the substantial character of the effect of Ski Co.'s conduct upon Highlands.

SKI CO.'S BUSINESS JUSTIFICATION

Perhaps most significant, however, is the evidence relating to Ski Co. itself, for Ski Co. did not persuade the jury that its conduct was justified by any normal business purpose. Ski Co. was apparently willing to forgo daily ticket sales both to the skiers who sought to exchange the coupons contained in Highlands' Adventure Pack, and to those who would have purchased Ski Co. daily lift tickets from Highlands if Highlands had been permitted to purchase them in bulk. The jury may well have concluded that Ski Co. elected to forgo these short-run benefits because it was more interested in reducing competition in the Aspen market over the long run by harming its smaller competitor.

That conclusion is strongly supported by Ski Co.'s failure to offer any efficiency justification whatever for its pattern of conduct. In defending the decision to terminate the jointly offered ticket, Ski Co. claimed that usage could not be properly monitored. The evidence, however, established that Ski Co. itself monitored the use of the 3-area passes based on a count taken by lift operators, and distributed the revenues among its mountains on that basis. Ski Co. contended that coupons were administratively cumbersome, and that the survey takers had been disruptive and their work inaccurate. Coupons, however, were no more burdensome than the credit cards accepted at Ski Co. ticket windows. Moreover, in other markets Ski Co. itself participated in interchangeable lift tickets using coupons. As for the survey, its own manager testified that the problems were much overemphasized by Ski Co. officials, and were mostly resolved as they arose. Ski Co.'s explanation for the rejection of Highlands' offer to hire — at its own expense — a reputable national accounting firm to audit usage of the 4-area tickets at Highlands' mountain, was that there was no way to "control" the audit.

In the end, Ski Co. was pressed to justify its pattern of conduct on a desire to disassociate itself from — what it considered — the inferior skiing services offered at Highlands. The all-Aspen ticket based on usage, however, allowed consumers to make their own choice on these matters of quality. Ski Co.'s purported concern for the relative quality of Highlands' product was supported in the record by little more than vague insinuations, and was sharply contested by numerous witnesses. Moreover, Ski. Co. admitted that it was willing to associate with what it considered to be inferior products in other markets. . . . Thus the evidence supports an inference that Ski Co. was not motivated by efficiency concerns and that it was willing to sacrifice short-run benefits and consumer good will in exchange for a perceived long-run impact on its smaller rival.

Because we are satisfied that the evidence in the record,[44] construed most favorably in support of Highlands' position, is adequate to support the verdict under the instructions given by the trial court, the judgment of the Court of Appeals is affirmed.[53]

324. (a) What was the *Aspen* Court's test of monopolization? How does it relate to that pronounced in the earlier cases in this section?

(b) What rule emerges concerning exclusionary practices? Who has the burden of proof concerning legitimate business justifications?

(c) In footnote 44, the Court disclaims that this was an "essential facilities" case. Some commentators believe that *Aspen* and *Otter Tail*, along with *Associated Press* and *Terminal Railroad*, represent an implicit "essential facilities" doctrine, which acts to preclude the dominant firm in an industry from refusing to grant competitors access to its essential facilities. Support for this idea comes from its intuitive appeal as a method of explaining a variety of Supreme Court cases.[54] One court's version would require the plaintiff to show "(1) control of the essential facility by a monopolist; (2) a competitor's inability practically or reasonably to duplicate the es-

---

44. Given our conclusion that the evidence amply supports the verdict under the instructions as given by the trial court, we find it unnecessary to consider the possible relevance of the "essential facilities" doctrine, or the somewhat hypothetical question whether nonexclusionary conduct could ever constitute an abuse of monopoly power if motivated by an anticompetitive purpose. If, as we have assumed, no monopolist monopolizes unconscious of what he is doing, that case is unlikely to arise.

53. White, J., did not participate.

54. See P. Areeda & H. Hovenkamp, Antitrust Law, ¶736.1 (Supp. 1996); D. Reiffen & A. Kleit, Terminal Railroad Revisited: Foreclosure of an Essential Facility or Simple Horizontal Monopoly?, 33 J.L. & Econ. 419 (1990).

sential facility; (3) the denial of the use of the facility to a competitor; and (4) the feasibility of providing the facility."[55] Would the Court have found a violation if Highlands had just developed the fourth and final mountain at Aspen and sought to initiate a four-mountain ticket arrangement, and Ski Co. then refused?

(d) Does *Aspen* suggest that monopolization exists in the following circumstances? (1) A monopolist refuses to license a patent[56] or share its research with rivals. (2) A monopolist opposes entry of a potential rival before a regulatory body.[57] (3) A monopolist refuses to repair rivals' machines, forcing them to make independent arrangements at higher costs. (Recall the analysis of services in *United Shoe*.) (4) A monopolist refuses to allow potential rivals to use excess capacity at its warehouse, which otherwise would remain idle. (Or consider the case where the capacity would otherwise be rented to a noncompetitor at a lower rate than the rival would pay. Or when it is used by its own subsidiary in another business, where it can be demonstrated that the gain to the subsidiary is less than the rival would pay.)[58] (5) A monopolist sports league refuses a franchise to a proposed new team.[59]

(e) Consider the *Aspen* Court's footnotes 9 and 22. If challenged by a skier, would you find the 6-day pass to be a violation of Sherman Act §1? If so, is the remedy described in footnote 9 sufficient to prevent the danger of price fixing?[60]

(f) Your client asks whether it would violate the antitrust laws to terminate an arrangement with competitors. The company president informs you that the purpose is to drive rivals out of business. You describe the rule in *Aspen* and inquire into any legitimate business justifications, asking whether the proposed new plan would be less costly. The president explains that they have explored many options, and all studies and consultants have indicated that the

---

55. MCI v. AT&T, 708 F.2d 1081 (7th Cir. 1983).

56. See ¶280.

57. See Ch. 2F.

58. Gamco v. Providence Fruit & Produce Bldg., 194 F.2d 484 (1st Cir.), cert. denied, 344 U.S. 317 (1952) (prima facie showing of purpose to monopolize demonstrated by refusal to lease space to a competing wholesaler).

59. Seattle Totems Hockey Club v. National Hockey League, 783 F.2d 1347 (9th Cir. 1986) (minor league team denied National Hockey League franchise; no fall in competition because plaintiff did not compete with league but sought to join it). See also Ch. 2E.

60. Two other issues are not addressed in this opinion. First, the question of market power was not raised on appeal. After studying Ch. 3B, consider whether Aspen should be viewed as the appropriate geographic market. Second, consider whether Ski Co.'s offering of a 6-day pass limited to its own mountains could be analyzed in a manner similar to that applied under Clayton Act §3, which is examined in Chs. 4B, 4C.

status quo is best (ignoring the competitive dimension), except for one report, which was discredited by staff and is inconsistent with all other reports. (1) Can you advise that termination would be legal? If not, can you suggest the company destroy all reports and memos except the discredited one, so that only it would be discovered in the event of litigation?[61] (If not, can you give the president a brief lecture on antitrust law that will make it clear that such selective document destruction would lead to success, despite illegality? See ¶315d.) (2) If the president had consulted you before the studies of alternatives were performed, should you have advised that the studies not be conducted, so there would be no record to contradict the assertion that the company believed alternatives were cost-effective? Or that no written records of any kind be made until the results were cleared with you?

325.   (a) Suppose that Alcoa possessed a lawful patent monopoly of aluminum ingot. It builds several fabrication plants for processing ingot into forms used by other firms (such as aluminum sheet or cable) or by ultimate consumers (such as kitchen utensils or window frames). Is such vertical integration itself a violation of Sherman Act §2?

(b) If the hypothetical Alcoa of ¶a may lawfully integrate into fabrication, may it lawfully refuse to sell ingot to independent fabricators? If not, what would be the appropriate remedy?

(c) Suppose Gotham City's only newspaper has consistently refused to accept advertising from the department store in a nearby town, just across the state border. Would such a refusal violate §2 of the Sherman Act if the newspaper (1) owns a department store that is Gotham's leading retail establishment[62] or (2) has no connection with any other enterprise?

(d) Suppose that the Alpha Company of ¶313a chooses to distribute its product solely through its own retail outlets staffed with its own employees. The current retail price to customers is $100 per unit. Independent retailer Rho, who is undoubtedly competent to distribute the product, sought to purchase that product from Alpha

61. Cf. United States v. Perlstein, 126 F.2d 789 (3d Cir.), cert. denied, 316 U.S. 678 (1942) (affirming conviction for conspiracy to obstruct future judicial proceeding by advising client to destroy documents if proceeding brought).

62. Six Twenty-Nine Productions v. Rollins Telecasting, 365 F.2d 478 (5th Cir. 1966); Packaged Programs v. Westinghouse Broadcasting Co., 255 F.2d 708 (3d Cir. 1958) (although difficult to prove, cause of action stated by allegation that city's only TV station refused, with intent to monopolize program production, to accept programs produced by independents); *Fishman*, note 50 (refusal to make stadium — an essential facility — available to plaintiff who was competing with defendant to purchase basketball franchise violates §2).

at a wholesale price. Alpha replied: "We would be delighted to sell you as much of our product as you may desire at our current price of $100. Please contact our nearest retail outlet. We neither need nor want any other outlets. We are happy to be and intend to remain the sole distributor of our important product for which there is no substitute." Should Rho be granted relief under Sherman Act §2? How would the *Otter Tail* or *Aspen* Court respond?[63]

(e) If Alpha already had an independent retailer in Rho's area, is it obliged to sell to Rho as well and at a similar wholesale price?[64]

(f) Could a producer of X-rated movies require a monopoly newspaper to accept advertisements over its moral objections?[65] Political advertisements?[66]

326. Sigma Company is an undoubted monopolist. Assume that its monopoly is lawful except insofar as the following facts suggest otherwise. Would Sigma be found to have violated Sherman Act §2 upon proof of any of the following facts?

(a) Omega Corporation once competed but became bankrupt five years ago when it could not match Sigma's superior innovative skill. (1) At the bankruptcy sale, Sigma made the high bid for Omega's plant. (2) As an aspect of that purchase, Mr. Omega promised that he would not reenter that market for five years. (3) Sigma has kept the Omega plant intact but idle over these five years. Phi told Sigma: "I am thinking about entering your market and would like to buy the Omega plant. Let's negotiate about the price and other terms." Sigma responded, "I refuse to discuss the

63. Most cases seem to decide in favor of the integrated firm — often because the plaintiff fails to prove a relevant market or show that the integrated firm has a market share sufficient for monopolization or even for attempted monopolization, the nonmonopolist is not shown to have had a specific intent to monopolize, there seems to be a legitimate business purpose for integration, or the plaintiff's theory of an intraenterprise conspiracy (see *Copperweld*, Ch. 2C) is rejected. And, in any event, courts usually find for defendants as long as the anticompetitive effects are not disproportionate to the legitimate business purposes of the self-distribution. See Areeda & Turner, note 1, ¶729. Most of these cases arise from a suit from a former retailer after the wholesaler (who possesses an exclusive territory) decides to switch to internal retailing. See, e.g., id. ¶729.7b (Supp. 1996).

64. Compare *Packard Motor*, Ch. 4A, and ¶409.

65. Homefinders v. Providence J. Co., 621 F.2d 441 (1st Cir. 1980) (monopoly newspaper may refuse misleading ad); America's Best Cinema Corp. v. Fort Wayne Newspapers, 347 F. Supp. 328 (N.D. Ind. 1972) (newspaper refusal reasonable). Cf. Home Placement Serv. v. Providence J. Co., 682 F.2d 274 (1st Cir. 1982) (distinguishing *Homefinders*: publisher did not show advertising was false or encouraged unauthorized listing; refusal was monopolization).

66. Cf. Columbia Broad. Sys. v. Democratic Natl. Comm., 412 U.S. 94 (1973) (broadcaster not obliged by Constitution or Communications Act to accept political advertising).

matter. Indeed, I might just reopen the Omega plant myself." Phi did not enter; Sigma still has not reopened the plant.

(b) Many of the largest buyers of this product are supplied by Sigma under long-term contracts providing that Sigma will supply each buyer's full requirements for three years.[67]

(c) Iota Corporation entered Sigma's market. Sigma became impressed with Ms. Bright who was Iota's imaginative and creative director of research. Bright left Iota and joined Sigma which offered her a larger salary and command of the elaborate and respected Sigma Research Laboratories.[68] Ms. Bright and all other Sigma research scientists are employed under 10-year contracts.[69] Compare ¶310b.

(d) The monopolized product is a computer consisting of a central processing unit (CPU) and certain peripheral equipment (PE) such as disk drives and printers. When the PE and the CPU have the same electronic interface, they are plug-compatible (PC) and can simply be plugged together.

Sigma redesigns its CPUs from time to time. Some functions previously performed by PE come to be performed within the CPU, and new CPUs often have a different electronic interface for PE. Independent PC/PE manufacturers complain that Sigma's redesigning excludes them from the PC/PE market by (1) reducing user need for independently supplied PE and (2) requiring independents to bear the delays, difficulties, and expense of discovering the new electronic interface and altering their own PE to match.[70]

---

67. See Ch. 4C.

68. See Universal Analytics v. MacNeal-Schwendler Corp., 707 F. Supp. 1170 (C.D. Cal. 1989), aff'd per curiam, 914 F.2d 1256 (9th Cir. 1990) (cause of action made out if hiring is solely to deprive of use, but not if part of motivation was to gain productive employee); Stifel, Nicolaus & Co. v. Dain, Kalman & Quail, 578 F.2d 1256 (8th Cir. 1978) (no dismissal of monopolization claim against broker hiring rival broker's employee until defendant's market power determined). Cf. Salerno v. American League of Prof. Baseball Clubs, 429 F.2d 1003, 1004 (2d Cir. 1970), cert. denied, 400 U.S. 1001 (1971) ("Wrongful discharge of an employee does not become an antitrust violation simply because the employer is a monopolist.").

69. Philadelphia World Hockey Club v. Philadelphia Hockey Club, 351 F. Supp. 462 (E.D. Pa. 1972) (reserve clause in player contracts one of several practices indicating that National Hockey League willfully acquired monopoly power).

70. California Computer Prods. v. IBM, 613 F.2d 727, 744 (9th Cir. 1979) (design changes reflect quality improvement; defendant not obligated to provide rivals with product for examining and copying); Transamerica Computer Co. v. IBM, 481 F. Supp. 965, 1002-1008 (N.D. Cal. 1979), aff'd, 698 F.2d 1377 (9th Cir.), cert. denied, 464 U.S. 955 (1983) (product improvements lawful although injuring rival and adopted primarily to minimize competition from independent PC/PE; unlawful, however, to slow down certain machine to point just short of speed at which rival PE could be attached: quality degradation solely for purpose of restrict-

(e) In January 1981, Iota announced that it was ready to begin immediate deliveries of its Model T. Trade publications emphasized its superiority over Sigma's standard Model A and reported intense buyer interest. Within a distressed Sigma, the staff concluded that Sigma could in all probability design, produce, and begin deliveries of an equally attractive Model B by January 1983, and perhaps some months sooner. Sigma's president told the staff of his confidence that they could do even better. He immediately announced Model B to the trade, promised deliveries beginning in September 1981, and began taking orders. Many buyers who had expressed interest in the Iota machine decided to wait. As it turned out, Sigma did not begin Model B deliveries until mid-1982.[71]

(f) Tau Company sought to build a plant whose product would compete with Sigma's product. Sigma urged the local zoning board to deny Tau the approval needed for the planned construction. After lengthy and costly proceedings, the zoning board denied Tau's request.[72]

(g) When Figma began making inroads on Sigma's market share, Sigma began advertising comparatively and would stress that "as compared with Brand *X*," Sigma's product (1) "is genuine Sigma," (2) "is best," (3) "is more reliable," (4) "contains *Z*," and (5) "is faster." Sigma salespeople have also been known to tell customers that (6) Figma is financially weak and might not remain in business for long and (7) Figma's product contains the harmful substance *Y*.[73]

327. AT&T divestiture.[74] The government challenged AT&T's vertical integration in two main respects: that AT&T's lawful local monopolies of telephone service were coupled with internal manu-

ing competition); ILC Peripherals Leasing Corp. v. IBM, 458 F. Supp. 423, 439 (N.D. Cal. 1978), aff'd, 636 F.2d 188 (9th Cir.), cert. denied, 452 U.S. 972 (1981) ("Where there is a difference of opinion as to the advantages of two alternatives which can both be defended from an engineering standpoint," the court would not allow itself to be "enmeshed in a technical inquiry into the justifiability of product innovations."); Telex Corp. v. IBM Corp., 367 F. Supp. 258, 355-356 (N.D. Okla. 1973), rev'd on other grounds, 510 F.2d 894 (10th Cir. 1975) (court not competent to design products; undue supervision would chill innovation); J. Ordover & R. Willig, An Economic Definition of Predation: Pricing and Product Innovation, 91 Yale L.J. 8 (1981) (arguing that predation can occur through excessive product innovation).

71. *ILC*, note 70, at 442 (no evidence suggesting that announcements were not honest and in good faith).

72. See *Omni*, Ch. 2F.

73. L.G. Balfour Co. v. FTC, 442 F.2d 1 (7th Cir. 1971).

74. United States v. AT&T, 552 F. Supp. 131 (D.D.C. 1982), aff'd mem. sub nom. Maryland v. United States, 460 U.S. 1001 (1983). See also the court's earlier decision denying the defendants' motion to dismiss at the conclusion of the government's case. 524 F. Supp. 1336 (D.D.C. 1981).

facture of telephone equipment and with internal provision of long distance service. After years of litigation, the parties reached a settlement that allowed AT&T to continue manufacturing equipment and providing long distance service but required it to divest the local operating companies' (LOCs) provision of local telephone service.[75]

Because the LOCs had purchased most of their telephone and other equipment from AT&T's Western Electric subsidiary, the vertical integration had reduced the marketing opportunities of rival equipment manufacturers — especially in earlier days when users were forbidden to connect noncompany equipment to telephone lines. Even if customers were allowed to connect their own equipment, the LOCs might favor Western Electric as a source of switching and other equipment.

Before divestiture, the LOCs had routed their customers' long distance calls through the AT&T network, and the company had opposed interconnection with such independent suppliers of long distance service as MCI or ITT. The growth of these independent suppliers using microwave and satellite transmission suggested that competition in long distance service was feasible. After divestiture, the customer would presumably purchase long distance service from the most economical supplier.

The government based its challenge on the competitive desirability of separating the natural monopoly of local telephone connections from other goods (equipment) or services (long distance) as to which competition was (1) possible and (2) likely to be impeded by integration. This theory called for excluding the divested LOCs from providing customers with equipment or from publishing the profitable yellow-page advertising medium. Accordingly, these functions were to be retained by AT&T and forbidden to the LOCs. But the district judge insisted otherwise, and the final judgment provided that the LOCs could provide (but not manufacture) terminal equipment to customers and would inherit the yellow pages. The

---

75. The settlement also ended a previous consent decree preventing AT&T from competing in any noncommunication business, such as the computer business.

On January 8, 1982, the same date as the announcement of the AT&T settlement, the government also dismissed the over decade-long case against IBM. See ¶141d. The case had its origin in the 1960s, as the first of many manufacturers of computers and related products brought suit. Control Data reached an early, substantial settlement. Most of the other private suits were litigated, and won by IBM. The Justice Department's suit had been initiated in 1969, and at the time the case was dropped the trial, one of the longest in history (in its seventh year), was near completion. The disputes in the case centered on the appropriate market in which to examine IBM's power and myriad practices alleged to be exclusionary. The hypotheticals in ¶¶326d-326e, are derived, in part, from some of the various challenges.

judge believed that the prospective additional revenue for the LOCs — implying somewhat lower local telephone rates — was more important than fidelity to the government's theory underlying any remedy against AT&T in the first place.

By 1996, it had become clear that a variety of industries and businesses had arisen that were capable of competing in the local telephone market (e.g., cable providers, cellular telephone companies), and market analysts were beginning to doubt whether the local telephone companies themselves were truly natural monopolies.[76] The Telecommunications Act of 1996 displaced the AT&T "modified final judgment," which had kept the LOCs out of the long distance market, and changed the way that the local market was regulated. Supporters of this new system point to the success of competition in the long-distance market, which they claim can now benefit the local market.[77] In exchange for losing control of their monopoly over local telephone customers, the LOCs will be able to participate in the long-distance market and compete against such established long-distance companies as AT&T, MCI, and Sprint. Although there will be increased competition between the various participants in the communications industry, the Act also requires a general duty to provide access and interconnection "with the facilities and equipment of other telecommunications carriers."[78]

Predatory Pricing

BARRY WRIGHT CORP. v. ITT GRINNELL CORP.
724 F.2d 227 (1st Cir. 1983)

BREYER, Circuit Judge. The question that this case presents is whether defendant Pacific Scientific Company ("Pacific") engaged in "exclusionary practices" in violation of the anti-monopoly law, Sherman Act §2. The practices at issue are embodied in agreements between Pacific and ITT Grinnell ("Grinnell"), under which Pacific agreed to sell its product (mechanical snubbers) to Grinnell at a specially low price and Grinnell agreed to take nearly all its snubber requirements from Pacific. The district court found that the relevant contract provisions did not violate the antitrust laws. We

76. See, e.g., D. Spulber, Deregulating Telecommunications, 12 Yale J. on Reg. 25, 31 (1995). See also Symposium, Recent Competition Issues in Telecommunications, 40 Antitr. Bull. 455 (1995).

77. Leasing the Loop: Telephone Service Resale in the Local Exchange, 134 Pub. Util. Fort. 19 (July 15, 1996).

78. 47 U.S.C. §251(a)(1).

agree with the district court on this matter, and on others less important; and we affirm its judgment. ⌡

I . . .

Pacific produces mechanical snubbers; they are shock absorbers used in building pipe systems for nuclear power plants. No other domestic firm makes mechanical snubbers; foreign mechanical snubbers do not satisfy Nuclear Regulatory Commission standards; and snubber users have found the closest substitute, namely, *hydraulic* snubbers, to be less reliable than the mechanical version. Thus, in 1976, Pacific's sales accounted for 47 percent of all snubbers sold; in 1977, 83 percent; in 1978, 84 percent; and in 1979, 94 percent.

Grinnell makes and installs nuclear plant pipe systems; it is a major snubber user. Its snubber purchases accounted for 51 percent of all mechanical snubbers and related hardware sold domestically in 1977; 52 percent in 1978; and 43 percent in 1979. By 1976, most of Grinnell's pipe system customers were requiring Grinnell to use mechanical snubbers. Recognizing Pacific's strong market position, Grinnell sought to develop an alternate mechanical snubber source. Hence, it entered into a contract with Barry Wright Corporation ("Barry"), the plaintiff here, under which it would help Barry develop a full mechanical snubber line. Grinnell agreed to contribute to Barry's development costs. It also agreed to use Barry as an exclusive source of supply between 1977 and 1979, promising to buy between $9 million and $15 million worth of snubbers during that period. Barry was to have its full line of six snubber sizes in production by the first quarter of 1977.

While waiting for Barry, Grinnell satisfied its current needs by buying mechanical snubbers from Pacific at Pacific's ordinary "discount" price — 20 percent below list. Pacific noticed that Grinnell's orders seemed small in relation to its likely needs. And, by September, 1976, Pacific realized that Grinnell was trying to develop its own supply source through Barry. In August, 1976, Pacific offered Grinnell a special price break — a 30 percent discount from list for small snubbers, 25 percent for larger ones — in return for a large $5.7 million order that would have met Grinnell's snubber needs through 1977. Grinnell, after tentatively accepting this proposal, consulted with Barry and then rejected Pacific's offer. Instead, it placed a smaller $1 million order at the standard 20 percent discount.

Barry could not meet the required January, 1977 production schedule. By mid-January, 1977, it told Grinnell that it would not be able to produce small snubbers until August, 1977 nor large ones until February, 1978. Grinnell then met with Pacific and (at the end of January, 1977) negotiated a $4.3 million snubber contract — enough snubbers to meet Grinnell's estimated needs for the next twelve months. Pacific gave Grinnell the large 30 percent/25 percent discounts. It also gave Grinnell an option — open until July, 1977 — to buy its 1978 requirements at the same prices (as long as Grinnell agreed to buy as much as in 1977). Grinnell, in turn, agreed to a non-cancellation clause that would have made it especially onerous for Grinnell to break the agreement.

Grinnell then told Barry that its production delays were unacceptable and that Barry had breached its development contract. Grinnell wanted Barry to continue its efforts, but it would not promise to buy more than $3.6 million worth of snubbers through 1979. Barry said this modification of the development contract was unjustified. It continued to try to develop snubbers. The extent of its progress is in dispute, but there is considerable evidence that it fell further behind its production schedules.

At the end of May, 1977, Grinnell and Pacific agreed further that Grinnell would buy $6.9 million worth of Pacific's snubbers for 1978 and $5 million for 1979. Grinnell predicted snubber "needs" of $6.9 million for each of the two years. On July 5, 1977 and July 14, 1977, Grinnell finalized the agreements for 1978 and 1979 by issuing purchase orders in these amounts. Pacific granted the special 30 percent/25 percent price discounts; and the contracts contained the special cancellation clause.

In June, 1977, Grinnell told Barry that their collaboration was at an end. Barry looked for other potential snubber buyers and then abandoned its snubber efforts. Subsequently, Barry brought this lawsuit against Pacific (and against Grinnell, as well, although Barry and Grinnell have reached a settlement). Barry charged that Pacific's efforts to sell snubbers to Grinnell and the terms of its contracts violated Sections 1 and 2 of the Sherman Act and Section 3 of the Clayton Act. . . .

II . . .

Monopolization has two elements: first the "possession of monopoly power in the relevant market" and, second, the "acquisition or maintenance of that power" by other than such legitimate means as patents, "superior product, business acumen, or historic accident." *Grinnell.* On this appeal, the parties do not dispute Pacific's monopoly power in the relevant market, which the district court identified as the domestic market for snubbers (whether mechanical or hydraulic). Nor do they dispute the legitimacy of Pacific's *acquisition* of this power. . . . Accepting these two assumptions, we turn to the issue that is in dispute, whether Pacific *maintained* its monopoly position against the threat of Barry's entry through improper means.

In this context, a practice, a method, a means, is "improper" if it is "exclusionary." *United Shoe.* To decide whether Pacific's conduct was exclusionary, we should ask whether its dealings with Grinnell went beyond the needs of ordinary business dealings, beyond the ambit of ordinary business skill, and "unnecessarily excluded competition" from the snubber market. . . . Professors Areeda and Turner have put the matter nicely: "'Exclusionary' conduct is conduct, other than competition on the merits or restraints reasonably 'necessary' to competition on the merits, that reasonably appears capable of making a significant contribution to creating or maintaining monopoly power." 3 P. Areeda and D. Turner, Antitrust Law ¶626 at 83 (1978). Was Pacific's conduct reasonable in light of its business needs or did it unreasonably restrict competition? . . . Barry points to three specific aspects of Pacific's conduct — its offer of special discounts to Grinnell, its insistence on a long-term large-volume contract, and its inclusion of the special non-cancellation clause — which it claims show that Pacific acted in an exclusionary manner.

A

Barry first attacks the special 30 percent/25 percent discounts that Pacific granted Grinnell. It argues that Pacific's discounted prices were unreasonably low. This argument founders, however, on the district court finding that these prices, while lower than normal, nonetheless generated revenues more than sufficient to cover the total cost of producing the goods to which they applied. Barry does not attack that finding; but, instead, it argues that price cutting by a monopolist may still prove unlawful, even if prices remain above total cost. While some circuits have accepted a form of Barry's argument, see, e.g., Transamerica Computer Co. v. International Business Machines Corp., 698 F.2d 1377 (9th Cir.), cert. denied, 104 S. Ct. 370 (1983); International Air Industries, Inc. v. American Excelsior Co., 517 F.2d 714, 724 (5th Cir. 1975), cert. denied, 424 U.S. 943 (1976), we do not.

To understand the basis of our disagreement, one must ask why the Sherman Act *ever* forbids price cutting. After all, lower prices help consumers. The competitive marketplace that the antitrust laws encourage and protect is characterized by firms willing and able to cut prices in order to take customers from their rivals. And, in an economy with a significant number of concentrated industries, price cutting limits the ability of large firms to exercise their "market power," see J. Bain, Industrial Organization ch. 5 (2d ed.

1968); F. Scherer, Industrial Market Structure and Economic Performance 56-70, 222-225 (2d ed. 1980); at a minimum it likely moves "concentrated market" prices in the "right" direction — towards the level they would reach under competitive conditions. See 2 P. Areeda & D. Turner, Antitrust Law ¶404; J. Bain, supra, at 118-23; F. Scherer, supra, ch. 5. Thus, a legal precedent or rule of law that prevents a firm from unilaterally cutting its prices risks interference with one of the Sherman Act's most basic objectives: the low price levels that one would find in well-functioning competitive markets. See, e.g., *Engineers.* . . .

Despite these considerations, courts have reasoned that it is sometimes possible to identify circumstances in which a price cut will make consumers worse off, not better off. See, e.g., Northeastern Telephone Co. v. American Telephone and Telegraph Co., 651 F.2d 76, 88 (2d Cir. 1981), cert. denied, 455 U.S. 943 (1982). Suppose, for example, a firm cuts prices to unsustainably low levels — price below "incremental" costs. Suppose it drives competitors out of business, and later on it raises prices to levels higher than it could have sustained had its competitors remained in the market. Without special circumstances there is little to be said in economic or competitive terms for such a price cut. Yet, how often firms engage in such "predatory" price cutting, whether they ever do so, and precisely when, is all much disputed — a dispute that is not surprising given the difficulties of measuring costs, discerning intent, and predicting future market conditions. See, e.g., Koller, The Myth of Predatory Pricing: An Empirical Study, 4 Antitrust L. & Econ. Rev. 105 (1971); McGee, Predatory Pricing Revisited, 23 J.L. & Econ. 289 (1980); Posner, Exclusionary Practices and the Antitrust Laws, 41 U. Chi. L. Rev. 506, 516-517 (1974); F. Scherer, supra, at 335-340.

Despite this dispute, there is general agreement that a profit maximizing firm might sometimes find it rational to engage in predatory pricing; it might do so if it knows (1) that it can cut prices deeply enough to outlast and to drive away all competitors, and (2) that it can then raise prices high enough to recoup lost profits (and then some) before new competitors again enter the market. See Areeda & Turner, Predatory Pricing and Related Practices Under Section 2 of the Sherman Act, 88 Harv. L. Rev. 697, 698-699 (1975) [hereafter cited as Areeda & Turner, Predatory Pricing]. There is also general agreement that the antitrust courts' major task is to set rules and precedents that can segregate the economically harmful price-cutting goats from the more ordinary price-cutting sheep, in a manner precise enough to avoid discouraging desirable price-cutting activity. See P. Areeda & D. Turner, Antitrust Law ¶¶711.1a-b, 714.1b, 714.5 (1982 Supp.).

Barry, of course, suggests that Pacific's price cut is a "goat," arguing that Pacific "intended" to drive Barry from the market place. Some courts have written as if one might look to a firm's "intent to harm" to separate "good" from "bad." See, e.g., D.E. Rogers Associates, Inc. v. Gardner-Denver Co., 718 F.2d 1431, 1435-36 (6th Cir. 1983); Forster Manufacturing Co. v. FTC, 335 F.2d 47 (1st Cir. 1964), cert. denied, 380 U.S. 906 (1965). But "intent to harm" without more offers too vague a standard in a world where executives may think no further than "Let's get more business," and long-term effects on consumers depend in large measure on competitors' responses. See Zerbe & Cooper, An Empirical and Theoretical Comparison of Alternative Predation Rules, 61 Tex. L. Rev. 655, 659-677 (1982). Moreover, if the search for intent means a search for documents or statements specifically reciting the likelihood of anticompetitive consequences or of subsequent opportunities to inflate prices, the knowledgeable firm will simply refrain from overt description. If it is meant to refer to a set of objective economic conditions that allow the court to "infer" improper intent, see, e.g., D.E. Rogers Associates, Inc. v. Gardner-Denver Co., 718 F.2d at 1436; cf. O. Hommel Corp. v. Ferro Corp., 659 F.2d 340, 347 (3d Cir. 1981), cert. denied, 455 U.S. 1017 (1982), then, using Occam's razor, we can slice "intent" away. Thus, most courts now find their standard, not in intent, but in the relation of the suspect price to the firm's costs. And, despite the absence of any perfect touchstone, modern antitrust courts look to the relation of price to "avoidable" or "incremental" costs as a way of segregating price cuts that are "suspect" from those that are not. . . .

test for price

One can understand the intuitive idea behind this test by supposing, for example, that a firm charges prices that fail to cover these "avoidable" or "incremental" costs — the costs that the firm would save by not producing the additional product it can sell at that price. Suppose further that the firm cannot show that this low price is "promotional," e.g., a "free sample." Nor can it show that it expects costs to fall when sales increase. Then one would know that the firm cannot rationally plan to maintain this low price; if it does not expect to raise its price, it would do better to discontinue production. Moreover, equally efficient competitors cannot permanently match this low price and stay in business. Further, competitive industries are typically characterized by prices that are roughly equal to, not below, "incremental" costs. See F. Scherer, supra, at 13-14; Areeda & Turner, Predatory Pricing at 702-703, 712. At a minimum, one would wonder why this firm would cut prices on "incremental production" below its "avoidable" costs unless it later expected to raise its prices and recoup its losses. When prices exceed incremental costs, one cannot argue that they must rise for the firm to stay in business. Nor will such prices have a tendency to exclude or eliminate equally efficient competitors. Moreover, a price cut that leaves prices above incremental costs was probably moving prices in the "right" direction — towards the competitive norm. See J. Bain, supra, at 14; Areeda & Turner, Predatory Pricing, at 704-707. These considerations have typically led courts to question, and often to forbid, price cuts below "incremental costs," (or "avoidable costs"), while allowing those where the resulting price is higher. See, e.g., Northeastern Telephone Co. v. American Telephone and Telegraph Co., 651 F.2d at 88; International Air Industries, Inc. v. American Excelsior Co., 517 F.2d at 723-724; cf. William Inglis & Sons Baking Co. v. ITT Continental Baking Co., 668 F.2d 1014, 10035-10036 (9th Cir. 1981) (price below average variable cost supports "inference" of predatory pricing), cert. denied, 459 U.S. 825 (1982).

In fact, the use of cost-based standards is more complicated than this brief discussion suggests. But, we need not explore here the arguments about how best to measure "incremental" or "avoidable" costs (e.g., whether "average variable cost" is an appropriate surrogate). Nor need we consider the theoretical difficulties that arise when prices fall *between* "incremental costs" and "average (total) costs," a circumstance that can arise either when production is at a level below full capacity and the firm lowers prices to levels that do not cover a "fair share" of fixed costs or when a plant is pushed beyond its "full" capacity at prices that do not cover the specially high costs of the extraordinary production levels. See, e.g., *Inglis*; Pacific Engineering and Production Co. v. Kerr-McGee Corp., 551 F.2d 790, 795-97 (10th Cir.), cert. denied, 434 U.S. 879 (1977); Areeda & Turner, Predatory Pricing, at 709-712; Scherer, Predatory Pricing and the Sherman Act: A Comment, 89 Harv. L. Rev. 869 (1976); Zerbe & Cooper, supra, at 681-84. Here we have a price that exceeds *both* "average cost" and "incremental cost" — that exceeds cost however plausibly measured. And as to those prices, "virtually every court and commentator agrees" that they are lawful, "perhaps conclusively, but at least presumptively." P. Areeda & D. Turner, Antitrust Law ¶711.1c at 118 (1982 Supp.).

Barry points, however, to a possible exception to this rule — an "exception" created by the Ninth Circuit making certain price cuts unlawful even when the resulting revenues exceed total costs. In *Inglis*, that circuit held that a price cut is unlawful if "the anticipated benefits of defendant's price depended on its tendency to discipline or eliminate competition and thereby enhance the firm's long-term ability to reap the benefits of monopoly power." In the Ninth Circuit's view, prices below "average variable costs" (a surrogate for "incremental costs") produce a presumption of "predatory pricing." When prices exceed "average variable cost," but are "below average total cost," the plaintiff must prove by a preponderance of the evidence that the defendant's pricing policy depends on its exclusionary or disciplinary tendency. And, in a case like this one — a case that the Ninth Circuit would describe as "prices above average total cost" — the plaintiff can still win if it proves "by clear and convincing evidence — i.e., that it is highly probably true — that the defendant's pricing policy was predatory," in the sense defined in *Inglis. Transamerica.*

The virtue of the Ninth Circuit test is that it recognizes an economic circumstance in which even "above total cost" price cutting might not be procompetitive and might, in theory, hurt the consumer. See *Transamerica.* For instance, if a dominant firm's costs are lower than its competitors', it could use an "above cost" price cut to drive out competition, and then later raise prices to levels higher than they otherwise would be. Moreover, if the price cut meant *less* profit for the firm *unless* (1) it drove out competitors *and* (2) higher prices later followed, the cut might be viewed as lying outside the range of normal, desirable, competitive processes. Even though such a price cut would only injure or eliminate firms that were less efficient than the price-cutters, one could argue that, other things being equal, their continued presence helps the competitive process (say, by constraining price rises) and may lead to greater efficiency in the future. Why should the antitrust laws not forbid this potentially harmful behavior? Indeed, economists have identified this type of pricing behavior (and certain other forms of above-cost pricing behavior) as potentially harmful, see, e.g., Brodley & Hay, Predatory Pricing: Competing Economic Theories and the Evolution of Legal Standards, 66 Cornell L. Rev. 738, 743-46 (1981); Scherer, supra (discussing other, more complex anticompetitive pricing strategies involving above-cost prices); Williamson, Predatory Pricing: A Strategic Welfare Analysis, 87 Yale L.J. 284 (1977) (same).

Nonetheless, while technical economic discussion helps to inform the antitrust laws, those laws cannot precisely replicate the economists' (sometimes conflicting) views. For, unlike economics, law is an administrative system the effects of which depend upon the content of rules and precedents only as they are applied by judges and juries in courts and by lawyers advising their clients. Rules that seek to embody every economic complexity and qualification may well, through the vagaries of administration, prove counter-productive, undercutting the very economic ends they seek to serve. Thus, despite the theoretical possibility of finding instances in which horizontal price fixing, or vertical price fixing, are economically justified, the courts have held them unlawful per se, concluding that the administrative virtues of simplicity outweigh the occasional "economic" loss.... Conversely, we must be concerned lest a rule or precedent that authorizes a search for a particular type of undesirable pricing behavior end up by discouraging legitimate price competition. Indeed, it is this risk that convinces us not to follow the Ninth Circuit's approach.

Thus, we believe we should not adopt the Ninth Circuit's exception because of the *combined effect* of the following considerations. For one thing, a price cut that ends up with a price exceeding total cost — in all likelihood a cut made by a firm with market power — is almost certainly moving price in the "right" direction (towards the level that would be set in a competitive marketplace). The antitrust laws very rarely reject such beneficial "birds in hand" for the sake of more speculative (future low-price) "birds in the bush." To do so opens the door to similar speculative claims that might seek to legitimate even the most settled unlawful practices. (Should a price-fixer be allowed to argue that a cartel will help weaker firms survive bad times, leaving them as a competitive force when times are good? Suppose the price-fixer offers to "prove it" by "clear and convincing evidence?" ...)

For another thing, the scope of the Ninth Circuit's test is vague. Is it meant to include, for example, "limit pricing" — the common practice of firms in concentrated industries not to price "too high" for fear of attracting new competition? See *Transamerica*; Areeda & Turner, Predatory Pricing, at 705-706. The "anticipated benefits" of such a price arguably depend "on its tendency to discipline or eliminate competition" thereby enhancing "the firm's long-term ability to reap the benefits of monopoly power." Does the test mean to include every common instance of a firm (with market power) deciding not to raise its prices? If it means to include either of these sorts of circumstances, the rule risks making of the antitrust laws a powerful force for price increases. But, if the rule does not mean to include these sorts of circumstances, which prices do, and which do not, fall within the test's proscription?

Further, even were the test more specific, it seems to us as a practical matter most difficult to distinguish in any particular case between a firm that is cutting price to "discipline" or to displace a rival and one cutting price "better to compete." No one would condemn a price cut designed to maximize profits in the short run, i.e., by increasing sales at the lower price, not by destroying competition and then raising prices. But the general troubles surrounding proof of firm costs, see, e.g., *Transamerica*; P. Areeda & D. Turner, Antitrust Law ¶¶711.1d, 715.2 (1982 Supp.), only hint at the difficulty of deciding whether or not a firm's price cut is profit-maximizing in the short-run, a determination that hinges not only on cost data, but also on elasticity of demand, competitors' responses to price shifts, and changes in unit costs with variations in production volume. Direct statements by firm executives concerning their expectations will probably not be found; and, one might ask, in light of uncertain and changing market conditions, how much will the firm itself know? One can foresee conflicting testimony by economic experts, with the eventual determination made, not by economists or accountants, but by a jury. Of course, one might claim that such are the dangers inherent in many antitrust cases. But the consequence of a mistake here is not simply to force a firm to forego legitimate business activity it wishes to pursue; rather, it is to penalize a procompetitive price cut, perhaps the most desirable activity (from an antitrust perspective) that can take place in a concentrated industry where prices typically exceed costs. See *Container; Hommel; Kerr-McGee;* 2 P. Areeda & D. Turner, Antitrust Law ¶¶404-05; J. Bain, supra, at 118-23; F. Scherer, supra, ch. 5.

Additionally, if private plaintiffs are allowed to attack the "above total cost disciplinary price," we are unlikely to lack for plaintiffs willing to make the effort. After all, even the most competitive of price cuts may hurt rivals; indeed, such may well be its object. And those rivals, if seriously damaged, may well bring suit, hoping or believing they can fit within the *Inglis/Transamerica* standard.

Finally, we ask ourselves what advice a lawyer, faced with the *Transamerica* rule, would have to give a client firm considering procompetitive price-cutting tactics in a concentrated industry. Would he not have to point out the risks of suit — whether ultimately successful or not — by an injured competitor claiming that the cut was "disciplinary?" Price cutting in concentrated industries seems sufficiently difficult to stimulate that we hesitate before embracing a rule that could, in practice, stabilize "tacit cartels" and further encourage interdependent pricing behavior. See 2 P. Areeda & D. Turner, Antitrust Law ¶404b3; F. Scherer, supra, at 190-193; Turner, Definition of Agreement under the Sherman Act: Conscious Parallelism and Refusals to Deal, 75 Harv. L. Rev. 655 (1962); cf. Hay & Kelley, An Empirical Survey of Price Fixing Conspiracies, 17 J.L. & Econ. 13, 20-24 (1974). This risk could be minimized only if the conditions imposed by the words "clear and convincing evidence" were so stringent that the claim could almost never be proved. But then, one might ask, would the *Transamerica* "exception" be worth the trouble? See *Transamerica* (Lucas, J., dissenting).

We reiterate that these considerations might not prove sufficient to make the difference were we dealing with a price that, although above average total costs, was *below* incremental costs — a price that in the absence of special circumstances proves unsustainable. But, here we deal with a price that is *above* both incremental and total cost.

In sum, we believe that such above-cost price cuts are typically sustainable; that they are normally desirable (particularly in concentrated industries); that the "disciplinary cut" is difficult to distinguish in practice; that it, in any event, primarily injures only higher cost competitors; that its presence may well be "wrongly" asserted in a host of cases involving legitimate competition; and that to allow its assertion threatens to "chill" highly desirable procompetitive price cutting. For these reasons, we believe that a precedent allowing this type of attack on prices that exceed both incremental and average costs would more likely interfere with the procompetitive aims of the antitrust laws than further them. Hence, we conclude that the Sherman Act does not make unlawful prices that exceed both incremental and average costs.

Even if we are wrong, however, and *Inglis* and *Transamerica* contain the correct legal standard, Barry would fail. Barry has not demonstrated by "clear and convincing evidence" that Pacific offered Grinnell an additional 5 or 10 percent price discount only because it wished to keep Barry out of the market. Rather, Pacific testified that the additional discount was related to additional cost savings. Grinnell's firm order for snubbers in 1977 was larger than the total volume of Pacific sales of snubbers in any previous year. Pacific had excess snubber capacity. The price discount, by securing the firm order, allowed Pacific to operate this capacity more efficiently, saved Pacific money, and thereby produced more profit than a higher price (without the firm order) could have done, without regard to any impact on Barry. At least there is evidence this was so — that this was the sort of price cut a firm would have made under competitive conditions in a fully competitive industry. And, the evidence in the record to this effect precludes the possibility of "clear and convincing evidence" to the contrary. Thus, even under the *Transamerica* test, Pacific's price cut would not be found anticompetitive or exclusionary.

B

Barry argues next that Pacific's "requirements contract" with Grinnell was exclusionary, that it was more restrictive of competition than legitimate business considerations could justify. The district court, however, disagreed. And so do we.

The antitrust problem that courts have found lurking in requirements contracts grows out of their tendency to "foreclose" other sellers from the market by "tying up" potential purchases of the buyer. Arguably, under certain circumstances substantial foreclosure might discourage sellers from entering, or seeking to sell in, a market at all, thereby reducing the amount of competition that would otherwise be available. Of course, the connection between "foreclosure" and lessened entry is somewhat distant, since it depends on how potential competitors perceive the foreclosure's likely effects on their opportunities. Moreover, virtually *every* contract to buy "forecloses" or "excludes" alternative sellers from *some* portion of the market, namely the portion consisting of what was bought. It is not surprising, then, that courts have judged the lawfulness of contracts to purchase not under per se rules but under a "rule of reason." *Tampa Electric.* . . . [W]e are to take into account both the extent of the foreclosure and the buyer's and seller's business justifications for the arrangement. We must look both to the severity of the foreclosure (a fact which, other things being equal, suggests anticompetitive harm) and the strength of the justifications in determining whether the "size" of the contract to purchase is reasonable.

Barry would like to characterize the agreements before us as consisting of a Grinnell promise to buy all its snubber requirements from Pacific for three years. And, if Barry correctly describes Grinnell as accounting for half the snubber market, this characterization suggests a three-year "foreclosure" of 50 percent of the relevant market. In terms of the case law, this sounds like a significant foreclosure. See *Standard [Stations].* . . . But this description considerably overstates the size of the foreclosure and its likely anticompetitive effect for several reasons.

First, Grinnell did not actually promise to buy all its requirements from Pacific; it entered into a contract for a fixed dollar amount. . . . This flexibility is important here, for it left Grinnell the legal power to buy small (and then in 1979, larger) amounts from Barry should they have become available.

Second, the Grinnell-Pacific contract was not a single three-year agreement. The district court found that the contract consummated in late January, 1977, bound Grinnell to take $4.3 million worth of snubbers — its estimated needs for the next twelve months. Grinnell then separately promised — in May 1977 — to buy $6.9 million worth of snubbers for 1978 (its estimated requirements) and $5 million for 1979 (considerably less than its estimated requirements). Even if we view the 1978 and 1979 purchases as a single agreement, the scope of this agreement's preclusive effect then tended over something less than Grinnell's expected requirements and lasted about two years.

Third, Grinnell's contract with Barry suggests that a snubber buyer typically places orders for snubbers well in advance of expected delivery. In fact, normally Grinnell would be required to place orders with Barry (once Barry developed the product) at least six months before delivery. Moreover, the record demonstrates the long delay that any new entrant would have to anticipate between the time it decided to enter the snubber market and the time it would be ready to deliver a product. Under these circumstances, a Grinnell decision to buy a year or two's worth of snubbers from Pacific *at one shot* instead of *from time to time* seems likely, as a practical matter, to have had, at most, limited anticompetitive effects.

At the same time, the record suggests the existence of legitimate business justifications for the agreements from the perspectives of both buyer and seller. For Grinnell, the contracts guaranteed a stable source of supply, and, perhaps, more important, they assured Grinnell a stable, favorable price. For Pacific, they allowed use of considerable excess snubber capacity; and they allowed production planning that was likely to lower costs. (At least Pacific executives testified as much and the record contains no refutation of this testimony.)

Finally, Grinnell is not a small firm that Pacific could likely bully into accepting a contract that might foreclose new competition. . . . To the contrary, it was Grinnell, not Pacific, that sought the extensions for 1978 and 1979. Moreover, Grinnell had every interest in promoting new competition. It agreed to provide Barry with several hundred thousand dollars expressly to develop a new source of supply. Grinnell could have obtained snubbers without placing such large orders had it given up the "special" extra 5 to 10 percent price discount, a matter of a few hundred thousand dollars per year. Had Grinnell believed that the long-term nature of the contracts significantly interfered with new entry, or inhibited the development of a new source of supply, it is difficult to understand why it would have sought the agreements.

In sum, in light of the nature of the contracts and the market, their fairly short time period, their business justifications, the characteristics of the parties, and their likely motives as revealed by their business interests, we believe that the district court could reasonably have concluded they were not "exclusionary."

C

Barry also argues that the "noncancellation" clauses were exclusionary. The clauses stated that "quantities [mentioned in the contract] . . . are considered to be minimum with pricing based accordingly. For this reason, full cancellation charges would apply if all or any portion of the requirements were cancelled or rescheduled by ITT Grinnell beyond [the contract period]." Those clauses, as the parties (and, we think, as the district court) interpreted them, would require Grinnell to pay the *entire* price of the yearly order (i.e. $4.3 million for 1977, $6.9 million for 1978, etc.) whether Grinnell took all, some or none of the snubbers that the order covered. The noncancellation clause thus acted as a powerful economic incentive for Grinnell to stick to its bargain; and Barry says this incentive was "too powerful" to the point where it is "exclusionary."

Of course, the parties to a contract have a right to collect damages for breach.... If the cancellation clause provides only for lawful liquidated damages, it is no more "exclusionary" than the underlying substantive agreement that it helps to enforce. But Barry argues that the cancellation clause is a "penalty" and that it therefore has no legitimate place in the substantive agreement.

We shall assume for the sake of argument that Barry is correct. If so, the clause *in principle* might have an unjustified anticompetitive effect. It might discourage a buyer from pursuing a course of action otherwise open to him under the law of contracts, namely to breach the purchase agreement, to pay damages, and to buy from a new entrant instead. While the presence of the clause could not legally *forbid* this course of action — as it would be unenforceable as a penalty at law — its presence does still threaten the buyer with the lawsuit that would be needed to prove that it is unenforceable. And it is this threat, and the consequent *additional* deterrence to the "breach and pay damages" course of action that constitutes the "unreasonably anticompetitive" aspect of the clause. Cf. *United Shoe* (lease provisions deterring early terminations are exclusionary).

This argument, while logical, strikes us as of virtually no practical importance in this case. Even if one heroically assumed that Grinnell might have wished to breach and to buy elsewhere in 1977, 1978 or 1979, it is virtually impossible to believe that the presence of this clause could have stopped it from doing so. Given Grinnell's size and the competence of its legal staff, it is most unlikely to have been deterred by Pacific's assertion of unusually high damages resting upon a legally invalid provision in the contract. (And, if the provision is not legally invalid — that is, if it does reasonably reflect Pacific's likely actual damages — then it is not, from an antitrust perspective, unreasonable.) This is simply to say that the anticompetitive consequence to which Barry might point is too remote, too speculative in the context of this case, to warrant classifying the clause as significantly anticompetitive. And, the district court's conclusion that its presence did not transform otherwise lawful purchase agreements into unlawful, exclusionary ones, is adequately supported.

III

If Pacific's challenged conduct is not "exclusionary," for purposes of Sherman Act §2, then a fortiori, it does not violate the other provisions of law that Barry cites.... [C]onduct that is not "exclusionary" is not "unreasonable." And we do not see how ordinar-

ily that conduct could be forbidden by Sherman Act §1's prohibition of "unreasonable" restraints of trade.... We see no conduct
here that is subject to any section 1-based rule of "per se" illegality....

328. (a) What do you suppose were Pacific's motivations for its
pricing actions? In light of the timing of its offers, do you think
it knew what effect Grinnell's acceptance would have on Barry's
prospects? If so, does that suggest predatory intent, and therefore
liability?

(b) Do you suspect Pacific's additional discounts continued into
the 1980's, after Barry's demise? If they did not, would that be a
justification for liability?

(c) If Pacific's discounted prices were undoubtedly below variable
or marginal cost, the court suggests it would have found liability. Do
you think Pacific could have been a successful predator in such
circumstances? Of what relevance are Grinnell's actions in considering this issue?

(d) The court was skeptical about inquiries into intent, in part
because "the knowledgeable firm will simply refrain from overt
description" and "[d]irect statements by firm executives concerning their expectations will probably not be found."[79] What role do
you suspect lawyers play in producing such a state of affairs? Should
the legal rules reflect such a reality, or should rules regulating
lawyers' conduct be altered? If the latter, how so? See ¶324f.

329. The Delta Corporation is an undoubted monopolist. Assume that its monopoly is lawful except insofar as the following facts
suggest otherwise. Would Delta be found to have violated Sherman
Act §2 upon any of the following proofs?

(a) Delta has persistently charged a monopoly price.

(b) Delta's price has been higher than a competitive price but
less than a monopoly price. It has charged a so-called limit price in
order to discourage new entry and thus maintain its monopoly.[80]

(c) Puny Products entered the market with a price below Delta's
price. Delta reduced its price to meet Puny's price. Alternatively,
Delta cut its price below Puny's.

(d) Would your ¶c analysis differ if Puny's price, which Delta met
or undercut, was shown to be less than Delta's short-run variable

79. For a contrasting view, see W. Comanor & H. Frech, Predatory Pricing and
the Meaning of Intent, 38 Antitr. Bull. 293 (1993).

80. For a discussion of limit pricing, see J. Roberts, Battles for Market Share:
Incomplete Information, Aggressive Strategic Pricing, and Competitive Dynamics,
in Advances in Economic Theory—Fifth World Congress (T. Bewley ed. 1987).

cost of production?[81] When Mr. Delta was asked why he had thus lowered the price, he responded, "Well, I had to do something, didn't I? Anyway, I'm buying time while I figure out some way to cut my costs. And who knows, I may make Puny reconsider whether it wants to be in this business."

(e) Is the test of predatory pricing that compares price and cost inconsistent with the mandate of such cases as *Trans-Missouri* and *Trenton Potteries* not to look into the reasonableness of prices?[82] If prices can be examined, why should the practices described in ¶¶a-b escape scrutiny?

(f) Delta reduced its price to competitive levels when Puny announced plans to make a product that would be competitive with Delta's product. Would your analysis differ (1) if Puny actually entered and the price remained at the competitive level? (2) If Puny abandoned its entry plan but Delta's price remained at the competitive level? (3) If Puny abandoned its plan and Delta then restored its price to the previous level? Would your analysis differ if Puny were a subsidiary of General Motors Corporation?

(g) If it could be shown in any of the above scenarios involving price reductions by Delta that it stood to lose more profits in scaring away or destroying Puny than it gained from not having to share a small slice of the market with such a competitor, should antitrust courts ignore such situations on the grounds that Delta,

---

81. Some readers may find a graphic illustration helpful.

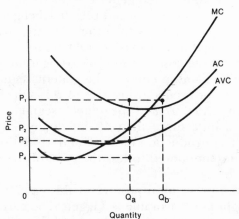

Illustrative cost curves are presented: average total (fixed plus variable) cost *AC*, average variable cost *AVC*, and marginal cost *MC*. Consider whether each price should be considered predatory by a monopolist producing at quantity level Q_a or, in the case of P_1, at quantity Q_b as well.

82. Reconsider this question after studying the discussion of market power in ¶¶336-337.

and firms like it, would not find it in their interest to engage in such tactics?

BROOKE GROUP LTD. v. BROWN & WILLIAMSON TOBACCO CORP.
509 U.S. 209 (1993)

Justice KENNEDY. . . . Liggett contends that Brown & Williamson cut prices on generic cigarettes below cost and offered discriminatory volume rebates to wholesalers to force Liggett to raise its own generic cigarette prices and introduce oligopoly pricing in the economy segment. We hold that Brown & Williamson is entitled to judgment as a matter of law.

I

In 1980, Liggett pioneered the development of the economy segment of the national cigarette market by introducing a line of "black and white" generic cigarettes. The economy segment of the market, sometimes called the generic segment, is characterized by its bargain prices and comprises a variety of different products: black and whites, which are true generics sold in plain white packages with simple black lettering describing their contents; private label generics, which carry the trade dress of a specific purchaser, usually a retail chain; branded generics, which carry a brand name but which, like black and whites and private label generics, are sold at a deep discount and with little or no advertising; and "Value-25s," packages of 25 cigarettes that are sold to the consumer some 12.5% below the cost of a normal 20-cigarette pack. By 1984, when Brown & Williamson entered the generic segment and set in motion the series of events giving rise to this suit, Liggett's black and whites represented 97% of the generic segment, which in turn accounted for a little more than 4% of domestic cigarette sales. Prior to Liggett's introduction of black and whites in 1980, sales of generic cigarettes amounted to less than 1% of the domestic cigarette market.

Because of the procedural posture of this case, we view the evidence in the light most favorable to Liggett. The parties are in basic agreement, however, regarding the central, historical facts. Cigarette manufacturing has long been one of America's most concentrated industries, see F. Scherer & D. Ross, Industrial Market Structure and Economic Performance 250 (3d ed. 1990) (hereinafter Scherer & Ross), and for decades, production has been dominated by six firms: R. J. Reynolds, Philip Morris, American Brands,

Lorillard, and the two litigants involved here, Liggett and Brown & Williamson. R. J. Reynolds and Philip Morris, the two industry leaders, enjoyed respective market shares of about 28% and 40% at the time of trial. Brown & Williamson ran a distant third, its market share never exceeding 12% at any time relevant to this dispute. Liggett's share of the market was even less, from a low of just over 2% in 1980 to a high of just over 5% in 1984.

The cigarette industry also has long been one of America's most profitable, in part because for many years there was no significant price competition among the rival firms. See Scherer & Ross 250-251; R. Tennant, American Cigarette Industry 86-87 (1950). List prices for cigarettes increased in lock-step, twice a year, for a number of years, irrespective of the rate of inflation, changes in the costs of production, or shifts in consumer demand. Substantial evidence suggests that in recent decades, the industry reaped the benefits of prices above a competitive level, though not through unlawful conduct of the type that once characterized the industry. See Tennant, supra, at 275; cf. *American Tobacco* (1946); *American Tobacco* (1911); Scherer & Ross, at 451.

By 1980, however, broad markets trends were working against the industry. Overall demand for cigarettes in the United States was declining, and no immediate prospect of recovery existed. As industry volume shrank, all firms developed substantial excess capacity. This decline in demand, coupled with the effects of nonprice competition, had a severe negative impact on Liggett. Once a major force in the industry, with market shares in excess of 20%, Liggett's market share had declined by 1980 to a little over 2%. With this meager share of the market, Liggett was on the verge of going out of business.

At the urging of a distributor, Liggett took an unusual step to revive its prospects: It developed a line of black and white generic cigarettes. When introduced in 1980, black and whites were offered to consumers at a list price roughly 30% lower than the list price of full-priced, branded cigarettes. They were also promoted at the wholesale level by means of rebates that increased with the volume of cigarettes ordered. Black and white cigarettes thus represented a new marketing category. The category's principal competitive characteristic was low price. Liggett's black and whites were an immediate and considerable success, growing from a fraction of a percent of the market at their introduction to over 4% of the total cigarette market by early 1984.

As the market for Liggett's generic cigarettes expanded, the other cigarette companies found themselves unable to ignore the economy segment. In general, the growth of generics came at the expense of the other firms' profitable sales of branded cigarettes. Brown & Williamson was hardest hit, because many of Brown & Williamson's brands were favored by consumers who were sensitive to changes in cigarette prices. Although Brown & Williamson sold only 11.4% of the market's branded cigarettes, 20% of the converts to Liggett's black and whites had switched from a Brown & Williamson brand. Losing volume and profits in its branded products, Brown & Williamson determined to enter the generic segment of the cigarette market. In July 1983, Brown & Williamson had begun selling Value-25s, and in the spring of 1984, it introduced its own black and white cigarette.

Brown & Williamson was neither the first nor the only cigarette company to recognize the threat posed by Liggett's black and whites and to respond in the economy segment. R. J. Reynolds had also introduced a Value-25 in 1983. And before Brown & Williamson introduced its own black and whites, R. J. Reynolds had repriced its "Doral" branded cigarette at generic levels. To compete with Liggett's black and whites, R. J. Reynolds dropped its list price on Doral about 30% and used volume rebates to wholesalers as an incentive to spur orders. Doral was the first competition at Liggett's price level.

Brown & Williamson's entry was an even greater threat to Liggett's dominance of the generic category. Unlike R. J. Reynolds' Doral, Brown & Williamson's product was also a black and white and so would be in direct competition with Liggett's product at the wholesale level and on the retail shelf. Because Liggett's and Brown & Williamson's black and whites were more or less fungible, wholesalers had little incentive to carry more than one line. And unlike R. J. Reynolds, Brown & Williamson not only matched Liggett's prices but beat them. At the retail level, the suggested list price of Brown & Williamson's black and whites was the same as Liggett's, but Brown & Williamson's volume discounts to wholesalers were larger. Brown & Williamson's rebate structure also encompassed a greater number of volume categories than Liggett's, with the highest categories carrying special rebates for orders of very substantial size. Brown & Williamson marketed its black and whites to Liggett's existing distributors as well as to its own full list of buyers, which included a thousand wholesalers who had not yet carried any generic products.

[In response,] Liggett increased its own wholesale rebates. This precipitated a price war at the wholesale level, in which Liggett five times attempted to beat the rebates offered by Brown & Williamson. At the end of each round, Brown & Williamson maintained a real advantage over Liggett's prices. Although it is undisputed that Brown & Williamson's original net price for its black and whites was above its costs, Liggett contends that by the end of the rebate war, Brown & Williamson was selling its black and whites at a loss. This rebate war occurred before Brown & Williamson had sold a single black and white cigarette.

[In suing Brown & Williamson,] Liggett claimed that Brown & Williamson's discriminatory volume rebates were integral to a scheme of predatory pricing, in which Brown & Williamson reduced its net prices for generic cigarettes below average variable costs. According to Liggett, these below-cost prices were not promotional but were intended to pressure it to raise its list prices on generic cigarettes, so that the percentage price difference between generic and branded cigarettes would narrow. Liggett explained that it would have been unable to reduce its wholesale rebates without losing substantial market share to Brown & Williamson; its only choice, if it wished to avoid prolonged losses on its principal product line, was to raise retail prices. The resulting reduction in the list price gap, it was said, would restrain the growth of the economy segment and preserve Brown & Williamson's supracompetitive profits on its branded cigarettes.

The trial began in the fall of 1989. By that time, all six cigarette companies had entered the economy segment. The economy segment was the fastest growing segment of the cigarette market, having increased from about 4% of the market in 1984, when the rebate war in generics began, to about 15% in 1989. Black and white generics had declined as a force in the economy segment as consumer interest shifted toward branded generics, but Liggett's overall volume had increased steadily to 9 billion generic cigarettes sold. Overall, the 2.8 billion generic cigarettes sold in 1981 had become 80 billion by 1989.

The consumer price of generics had increased along with output. For a year, the list prices for generic cigarettes established at the end of the rebate war remained stable. But in June of 1985, Liggett raised its list price, and the other firms followed several months later. The precise effect of the list price increase is difficult to assess, because all of the cigarette firms offered a variety of discounts, coupons, and other promotions directly to consumers on both generic and branded cigarettes. Nonetheless, at least some portion of the list price increase was reflected in a higher net price to the consumer.

In December 1985, Brown & Williamson attempted to increase its list prices, but retracted the announced increase when the other firms adhered to their existing prices. Thus, after Liggett's June 1985 increase, list prices on generics did not change again until the summer of 1986, when a pattern of twice yearly increases in tandem with the full-priced branded cigarettes was established. The dollar amount of these increases was the same for generic and full-priced cigarettes, which resulted in a greater percentage price increase in the less expensive generic cigarettes and a narrowing of the percentage gap between the list price of branded and black and white cigarettes, from approximately 38% at the time Brown & Williamson entered the segment, to approximately 27% at the time of trial. Also by the time of trial, five of the six manufacturers, including Liggett, had introduced so-called "subgenerics," a category of branded generic cigarette that sold at a discount of 50% or more off the list price of full-priced branded cigarettes.

After a 115-day trial involving almost 3000 exhibits and over a score of witnesses, the jury returned a verdict in favor of Liggett, finding on the special verdict form that Brown & Williamson had engaged in price discrimination that had a reasonable possibility of injuring competition in the domestic cigarette market as a whole. The jury awarded Liggett $49.6 million in damages, which the District Court trebled to $148.8 million. After reviewing the record, however, the District Court held that Brown & Williamson was entitled to judgment as a matter of law on three separate grounds: lack of injury to competition, lack of antitrust injury to Liggett, and lack of a causal link between the discriminatory rebates and Liggett's alleged injury. With respect to the first issue, which is the only one before us, the District Court found that no slowing of the growth rate of generics, and thus no injury to competition, was possible unless there had been tacit coordination of prices in the economy segment of the cigarette market by the various manufacturers. The District Court held that a reasonable jury could come to but one conclusion about the existence of such coordination among the firms contending for shares of the economy segment: It did not exist, and Brown & Williamson therefore had no reasonable possibility of limiting the growth of the segment.

The United States Court of Appeals for the Fourth Circuit affirmed. The Court of Appeals held that the dynamic of conscious parallelism among oligopolists could not produce competitive injury in a predatory pricing setting, which necessarily involves a price cut by one of the oligopolists. In the Court of Appeals' view, "[t]o rely on the characteristics of an oligopoly to assure recoupment of losses from a predatory pricing scheme after one oligopolist has made a competitive move is ... economically irrational."

We ... affirm.

II

A ...

Liggett contends that Brown & Williamson's discriminatory volume rebates to wholesalers threatened substantial competitive injury by furthering a predatory pricing scheme designed to purge competition from the economy segment of the cigarette market.

This type of injury, which harms direct competitors of the discriminating seller, is known as primary-line injury. . . . But whatever additional flexibility the Robinson-Patman Act standard may imply, the essence of the claim under either statute is the same: A business rival has priced its products in an unfair manner with an object to eliminate or retard competition and thereby gain and exercise control over prices in the relevant market.

Accordingly, whether the claim alleges predatory pricing under §2 of the Sherman Act or primary-line price discrimination under the Robinson-Patman Act, two prerequisites to recovery remain the same. First, a plaintiff seeking to establish competitive injury resulting from a rival's low prices must prove that the prices complained of are below an appropriate measure of its rival's costs.[1] See, e.g., *Cargill; Matsushita; Utah Pie; DuPont (Titanium).* . . . Although *Cargill* and *Matsushita* reserved as a formal matter the question " 'whether recovery should ever be available . . . when the pricing in question is above some measure of incremental cost,' " *Cargill* (quoting *Matsushita*), the reasoning in both opinions suggests that only below-cost prices should suffice, and we have rejected elsewhere the notion that above-cost prices that are below general market levels or the costs of a firm's competitors inflict injury to competition cognizable under the antitrust laws. See *ARCO.* . . . As a general rule, the exclusionary effect of prices above a relevant measure of cost either reflects the lower cost structure of the alleged predator, and so represents competition on the merits, or is beyond the practical ability of a judicial tribunal to control without courting intolerable risks of chilling legitimate price-cutting. See Areeda & Hovenkamp ¶¶714.2, 714.3; . . . *Cargill.*

Even in an oligopolistic market, when a firm drops its prices to a competitive level to demonstrate to a maverick the unprofitability of straying from the group, it would be illogical to condemn the price cut: The antitrust laws then would be an obstacle to the chain of events most conducive to a breakdown of oligopoly pricing and the onset of competition. Even if the ultimate effect of the cut is to induce or reestablish supracompetitive pricing, discouraging a price cut and forcing firms to maintain supracompetitive prices, thus depriving consumers of the benefits of lower prices in the interim, does not constitute sound antitrust policy. Cf. Areeda & Hovenkamp ¶¶714.2d, 714.2f; Areeda & Turner, Predatory Pricing and Related Practices under Section 2 of the Sherman Act, 88 Harv. L. Rev. 697, 708-709 (1975); Posner, Antitrust Law: An Economic Perspective, at 195, n.39.

1. Because the parties in this case agree that the relevant measure of cost is average variable cost, however, we again decline to resolve the conflict among the lower courts over the appropriate measure of cost. See *Cargill; Matsushita.*

The second prerequisite to holding a competitor liable under the antitrust laws for charging low prices is a demonstration that the competitor had a reasonable prospect, or, under §2 of the Sherman Act, a dangerous probability, of recouping its investment in below-cost prices. See *Matsushita*. "For the investment to be rational, the [predator] must have a reasonable expectation of recovering, in the form of later monopoly profits, more than the losses suffered." *Matsushita*. Recoupment is the ultimate object of an unlawful predatory pricing scheme; it is the means by which a predator profits from predation. Without it, predatory pricing produces lower aggregate prices in the market, and consumer welfare is enhanced. Although unsuccessful predatory pricing may encourage some inefficient substitution toward the product being sold at less than its cost, unsuccessful predation is in general a boon to consumers.

That below-cost pricing may impose painful losses on its target is of no moment to the antitrust laws if competition is not injured: It is axiomatic that the antitrust laws were passed for "the protection of competition, not competitors." *Brown Shoe*. Earlier this Term, we held in the Sherman Act §2 context that it was not enough to inquire "whether the defendant has engaged in 'unfair' or 'predatory' tactics"; rather, we insisted that the plaintiff prove "a dangerous probability that [the defendant] would monopolize a particular market." *Spectrum Sports*. Even an act of pure malice by one business competitor against another does not, without more, state a claim under the federal antitrust laws. . . .

For recoupment to occur, below-cost pricing must be capable, as a threshold matter, of producing the intended effects on the firm's rivals, whether driving them from the market, or, as was alleged to be the goal here, causing them to raise their prices to supracompetitive levels within a disciplined oligopoly. This requires an understanding of the extent and duration of the alleged predation, the relative financial strength of the predator and its intended victim, and their respective incentives and will. See 3 Areeda & Turner ¶711b. The inquiry is whether, given the aggregate losses caused by the below-cost pricing, the intended target would likely succumb.

If circumstances indicate that below-cost pricing could likely produce its intended effect on the target, there is still the further question whether it would likely injure competition in the relevant market. The plaintiff must demonstrate that there is a likelihood that the predatory scheme alleged would cause a rise in prices above a competitive level that would be sufficient to compensate for the amounts expended on the predation, including the time value of the money invested in it. . . . *Matsushita*.

Evidence of below-cost pricing is not alone sufficient to permit an inference of probable recoupment and injury to competition. Determining whether recoupment of predatory losses is likely requires an estimate of the cost of the alleged predation and a close analysis of both the scheme alleged by the plaintiff and the structure and conditions of the relevant market. Cf., e.g., Elzinga & Mills, Testing for Predation: Is Recoupment Feasible?, 34 Antitrust Bull. 869 (1989) (constructing one possible model for evaluating recoupment). If market circumstances or deficiencies in proof would bar a reasonable jury from finding that the scheme alleged would likely result in sustained supracompetitive pricing, the plaintiff's case has failed. In certain situations — for example, where the market is highly diffuse and competitive, or where new entry is easy, or the defendant lacks adequate excess capacity to absorb the market shares of his rivals and cannot quickly create or purchase new capacity — summary disposition of the case is appropriate. See, e.g., *Cargill.*

These prerequisites to recovery are not easy to establish, but they are not artificial obstacles to recovery; rather, they are essential components of real market injury. As we have said in the Sherman Act context, "predatory pricing schemes are rarely tried, and even more rarely successful," *Matsushita*, and the costs of an erroneous finding of liability are high. "[T]he mechanism by which a firm engages in predatory pricing — lowering prices — is the same mechanism by which a firm stimulates competition; because 'cutting prices in order to increase business often is the very essence of competition ... [,] mistaken inferences ... are especially costly, because they chill the very conduct the antitrust laws are designed to protect.'" *Cargill* (quoting *Matsushita*). It would be ironic indeed if the standards for predatory pricing liability were so low that antitrust suits themselves became a tool for keeping prices high.

B

Liggett does not allege that Brown & Williamson sought to drive it from the market but that Brown & Williamson sought to preserve supracompetitive profits on branded cigarettes by pressuring Liggett to raise its generic cigarette prices through a process of tacit collusion with the other cigarette companies. Tacit collusion, sometimes called oligopolistic price coordination or conscious parallelism, describes the process, not in itself unlawful, by which firms in a concentrated market might in effect share monopoly power, setting their prices at a profit-maximizing, supracompetitive level by recognizing their shared economic interest and their interdependence with respect to price and output decisions. See 2 Areeda & Turner ¶404; Scherer & Ross 199-208.

In *Matsushita*, we remarked upon the general implausibility of predatory pricing. *Matsushita* observed that such schemes are even more improbable when they require coordinated action among several firms. *Matsushita* involved an allegation of an express conspiracy to engage in predatory pricing. The Court noted that in addition to the usual difficulties that face a single firm attempting to recoup predatory losses, other problems render a conspiracy "incalculably more difficult to execute." In order to succeed, the conspirators must agree on how to allocate present losses and future gains among the firms involved, and each firm must resist powerful incentives to cheat on whatever agreement is reached.

However unlikely predatory pricing by multiple firms may be when they conspire, it is even less likely when, as here, there is no express coordination. Firms that seek to recoup predatory losses through the conscious parallelism of oligopoly must rely on uncertain and ambiguous signals to achieve concerted action. The signals are subject to misinterpretation and are a blunt and imprecise means of ensuring smooth cooperation, especially in the context of changing or unprecedented market circumstances. This anticompetitive minuet is most difficult to compose and to perform, even for a disciplined oligopoly.

From one standpoint, recoupment through oligopolistic price coordination could be thought more feasible than recoupment through monopoly: In the oligopoly setting, the victim itself has an economic incentive to acquiesce in the scheme. If forced to choose between cutting prices and sustaining losses, maintaining prices and losing market share, or raising prices and enjoying a share of supracompetitive profits, a firm may yield to the last alternative. Yet on the whole, tacit cooperation among oligopolists must be considered the least likely means of recouping predatory losses. In addition to the difficulty of achieving effective tacit coordination and the high likelihood that any attempt to discipline will produce an outbreak of competition, the predator's present losses in a case like this fall on it alone, while the later supracompetitive profits must be shared with every other oligopolist in proportion to its market share, including the intended victim. In this case, for example, Brown & Williamson, with its 11-12% share of the cigarette market, would have had to generate around $9 in supracompetitive profits for each $1 invested in predation; the remaining $8 would belong to its competitors, who had taken no risk.

Liggett suggests that these considerations led the Court of Appeals to rule out its theory of recovery as a matter of law. . . . To the extent that the Court of Appeals may have held that the interdependent pricing of an oligopoly may never provide a means for achieving recoupment and so may not form the basis of a primary-line injury claim, we disagree. A predatory pricing scheme designed to preserve or create a stable oligopoly, if successful, can injure consumers in the same way, and to the same extent, as one designed to bring about a monopoly. However unlikely that possibility may be as a general matter, when the realities of the market and the record facts indicate that it has occurred and was likely to have succeeded, theory will not stand in the way of liability. *Kodak.* . . . We decline to create a per se rule of nonliability for predatory price discrimination when recoupment is alleged to take place through supracompetitive oligopoly pricing. Cf. *Cargill.*

III

Although Liggett's theory of liability, as an abstract matter, is within the reach of the statute, we agree with the Court of Appeals and the District Court that Liggett was not entitled to submit its case to the jury. It is not customary for this Court to review the sufficiency of the evidence, but we will do so when the issue is properly before us and the benefits of providing guidance concerning the proper application of a legal standard and avoiding the systemic costs associated with further proceedings justify the required expenditure of judicial resources. See, e.g., *Aspen*; *Monsanto*; United States v. Pabst Brewing Co., 384 U.S. 546, 550-552 (1966). The record in this case demonstrates that the anticompetitive scheme Liggett alleged, when judged against the realities of the market, does not provide an adequate basis for a finding of liability.

A

Liggett's theory of competitive injury through oligopolistic price coordination depends upon a complex chain of cause and effect: Brown & Williamson would enter the generic segment with list prices matching Liggett's but with massive, discriminatory volume rebates directed at Liggett's biggest wholesalers; as a result, the net price of Brown & Williamson's generics would be below its costs; Liggett would suffer losses trying to defend its market share and wholesale customer base by matching Brown & Williamson's rebates; to avoid further losses, Liggett would raise its list prices on generics or acquiesce in price leadership by Brown & Williamson; higher list prices to consumers would shrink the percentage gap in retail price between generic and branded cigarettes; and this narrowing of the gap would make generics less appealing to the consumer, thus slowing the growth of the economy segment and reducing cannibalization of branded sales and their associated supracompetitive profits.

Although Brown & Williamson's entry into the generic segment could be regarded as procompetitive in intent as well as effect, the record contains sufficient evidence from which a reasonable jury could conclude that Brown & Williamson envisioned or intended this anticompetitive course of events. There is also sufficient evidence in the record from which a reasonable jury could conclude that for a period of approximately 18 months, Brown & Williamson's prices on its generic cigarettes were below its costs, and that this below-cost pricing imposed losses on Liggett that Liggett was unwilling to sustain, given its corporate parent's effort to locate a buyer for the company. Liggett has failed to demonstrate competitive injury as a matter of law, however, because its proof is flawed in a critical respect: The evidence is inadequate to show that in pursuing this scheme, Brown & Williamson had a reasonable prospect of recovering its losses from below-cost pricing through slowing the growth of generics. As we have noted, "[t]he success of any predatory scheme depends on maintaining monopoly power for long enough both to recoup the predator's losses and to harvest some additional gain." *Matsushita.*

No inference of recoupment is sustainable on this record, because no evidence suggests that Brown & Williamson — whatever its intent in introducing black and whites may have been — was likely to obtain the power to raise the prices for generic cigarettes above a competitive level. Recoupment through supracompetitive pricing in the economy segment of the cigarette market is an indispensable aspect of Liggett's own proffered theory, because a slowing of growth in the economy segment, even if it results from an increase in generic prices, is not itself anticompetitive. Only if those higher prices are a product of nonmarket forces has competition suffered. If prices rise in response to an excess of demand over supply, or segment growth slows as patterns of consumer preference become stable, the market is functioning in a competitive manner. Consumers are not injured from the perspective of the antitrust laws by the price increases; they are in fact causing them. Thus, the linchpin of the predatory scheme alleged by Liggett is Brown & Williamson's ability, with the other oligopolists, to raise prices above a competitive level in the generic segment of the market. Because relying on tacit coordination among oligopolists as a means of recouping losses from predatory pricing is "highly speculative," Areeda & Hovenkamp ¶711.2c, at 647, competent evidence is necessary to allow a reasonable inference that it poses an authentic threat to competition. The evidence in this case is insufficient to demonstrate the danger of Brown & Williamson's alleged scheme.

B

Based on Liggett's theory of the case and the record it created, there are two means by which one might infer that Brown & Wil-

liamson had a reasonable prospect of producing sustained supracompetitive pricing in the generic segment adequate to recoup its
predatory losses: first, if generic output or price information indicates that oligopolistic price coordination in fact produced supracompetitive prices in the generic segment; or second, if evidence
about the market and Brown & Williamson's conduct indicate that
the alleged scheme was likely to have brought about tacit coordination and oligopoly pricing in the generic segment, even if it did not
actually do so.

1

In this case, the price and output data do not support a reasonable inference that Brown & Williamson and the other cigarette
companies elevated prices above a competitive level for generic
cigarettes. Supracompetitive pricing entails a restriction in output.
See *NCAA*; *BMI*. ... In the present setting, in which output expanded at a rapid rate following Brown & Williamson's alleged predation, output in the generic segment can only have been restricted
in the sense that it expanded at a slower rate than it would have
absent Brown & Williamson's intervention. Such a counterfactual
proposition is difficult to prove in the best of circumstances; here,
the record evidence does not permit a reasonable inference that
output would have been greater without Brown & Williamson's
entry into the generic segment.

Following Brown & Williamson's entry, the rate at which generic
cigarettes were capturing market share did not slow; indeed, the
average rate of growth doubled. During the four years from 1980 to
1984 in which Liggett was alone in the generic segment, the segment gained market share at an average rate of 1% of the overall
market per year, from .4% in 1980 to slightly more than 4% of the
cigarette market in 1984. In the next five years, following the alleged predation, the generic segment expanded from 4% to more
than 15% of the domestic cigarette market, or greater than 2% per
year.

While this evidence tends to show that Brown & Williamson's
participation in the economy segment did not restrict output, it is
not dispositive. One could speculate, for example, that the rate of
segment growth would have tripled, instead of doubled, without
Brown & Williamson's alleged predation. But there is no concrete
evidence of this. Indeed, the only industry projection in the record
estimating what the segment's growth would have been without
Brown & Williamson's entry supports the opposite inference. In
1984, Brown & Williamson forecast in an important planning document that the economy segment would account for 10% of the total
cigarette market by 1988 if it did not enter the segment. In fact, in

1988, after what Liggett alleges was a sustained and dangerous anti-competitive campaign by Brown & Williamson, the generic segment accounted for over 12% of the total market. Thus the segment's output expanded more robustly than Brown & Williamson had estimated it would had Brown & Williamson never entered.

Brown & Williamson did note in 1985, a year after introducing its black and whites, that its presence within the generic segment "appears to have resulted in ... a slowing in the segment's growth rate." But this statement was made in early 1985, when Liggett itself contends the below-cost pricing was still in effect and before any anticompetitive contraction in output is alleged to have occurred. Whatever it may mean, this statement has little value in evaluating the competitive implications of Brown & Williamson's later conduct, which was alleged to provide the basis for recouping predatory losses.

In arguing that Brown & Williamson was able to exert market power and raise generic prices above a competitive level in the generic category through tacit price coordination with the other cigarette manufacturers, Liggett places its principal reliance on direct evidence of price behavior. This evidence demonstrates that the list prices on all cigarettes, generic and branded alike, rose to a significant degree during the late 1980s. From 1986 to 1989, list prices on both generic and branded cigarettes increased twice a year by similar amounts. Liggett's economic expert testified that these price increases outpaced increases in costs, taxes, and promotional expenditures. The list prices of generics, moreover, rose at a faster rate than the prices of branded cigarettes, thus narrowing the list price deferential between branded and generic products. Liggett argues that this would permit a reasonable jury to find that Brown & Williamson succeeded in bringing about oligopolistic price coordination and supracompetitive prices in the generic category sufficient to slow its growth, thereby preserving supracompetitive branded profits and recouping its predatory losses.

A reasonable jury, however, could not have drawn the inferences Liggett purposes. All of Liggett's data is based upon the list prices of various categories of cigarettes. Yet the jury had before it undisputed evidence that during the period in question, list prices were not the actual prices paid by consumers. As the market became unsettled in the mid-1980s, the cigarette companies invested substantial sums in promotional schemes, including coupons, stickers, and giveaways, that reduced the actual cost of cigarettes to consumers below list prices. This promotional activity accelerated as the decade progressed. Many wholesalers also passed portions of their volume rebates on to the consumer, which had the effect of further undermining the significance of the retail list prices. Especially in an oligopoly setting, in which price competition is most likely to take place through less observable and less regulable means than list prices, it would be unreasonable to draw conclusions about the existence of tacit coordination or supracompetitive pricing from data that reflects only list prices.

Even on its own terms, the list price data relied upon by Liggett to demonstrate a narrowing of the price differential between generic and full-priced branded cigarettes could not support the conclusion that supracompetitive pricing had been introduced into the generic segment. Liggett's gap data ignores the effect of "subgeneric" cigarettes, which were priced at discounts of 50% or more from the list prices of normal branded cigarettes. Liggett itself, while supposedly under the sway of oligopoly power, pioneered this development in 1988 with the introduction of its "Pyramid" brand. By the time of trial, five of the six major manufacturers offered a cigarette in this category at a discount from the full list price of at least 50%. Thus, the price difference between the highest priced branded cigarette and the lowest priced cigarettes in the economy segment, instead of narrowing over the course of the period of alleged predation as Liggett would argue, grew to a substantial extent. In June 1984, before Brown & Williamson entered the generic segment, a consumer could obtain a carton of black and white generic cigarettes from Liggett at a 38% discount from the list price of a leading brand; after the conduct Liggett complains of, consumers could obtain a branded generic from Liggett for 52% off the list price of a leading brand.

It may be that a reasonable jury could conclude that the cumulative discounts attributable to subgenerics and the various consumer promotions did not cancel out the full effect of the increases in list prices, and that actual prices to the consumer did indeed rise, but rising prices do not themselves permit an inference of a collusive market dynamic. Even in a concentrated market, the occurrence of a price increase does not in itself permit a rational inference of conscious parallelism or supracompetitive pricing. Where, as here, output is expanding at the same time prices are increasing, rising prices are equally consistent with growing product demand. Under these conditions, a jury may not infer competitive injury from price and output data absent some evidence that tends to prove that output was restricted or prices were above a competitive level. Cf. *Monsanto.*

Quite apart from the absence of any evidence of that sort, an inference of supracompetitive pricing would be particularly anomalous in this case, as the very party alleged to have been coerced into pricing through oligopolistic coordination denied that such coordination existed: Liggett's own officers and directors consistently denied that they or other firms in the industry priced their cigarettes through tacit collusion or reaped supracompetitive profits. Liggett seeks to explain away this testimony by arguing that its officers and directors are businesspeople who do not ascribe the same meaning to words like "competitive" and "collusion" that an economist would. This explanation is entitled to little, if any, weight. . . .

2

Not only does the evidence fail to show actual supracompetitive pricing in the generic segment, it also does not demonstrate its likelihood. At the time Brown & Williamson entered the generic segment, the cigarette industry as a whole faced declining demand and possessed substantial excess capacity. These circumstances tend to break down patterns of oligopoly pricing and produce price competition. See Scherer & Ross, 294, 315; 2 Areeda & Turner ¶404b2, at 275-276; 6 P. Areeda, Antitrust Law ¶1430e, at 181 (1986). The only means by which Brown & Williamson is alleged to have established oligopoly pricing in the face of these unusual competitive pressures is through tacit price coordination with the other cigarette firms.

Yet the situation facing the cigarette companies in the 1980s would have made such tacit coordination unmanageable. Tacit coordination is facilitated by a stable market environment, fungible products, and a small number of variables upon which the firms seeking to coordinate their pricing may focus. See generally Scherer & Ross 215-315; 6 P. Areeda, supra, ¶¶1428-1430. Uncertainty is an oligopoly's greatest enemy. By 1984, however, the cigarette market was in an obvious state of flux. The introduction of generic cigarettes in 1980 represented the first serious price competition in the cigarette market since the 1930s. See Scherer & Ross 250-251. This development was bound to unsettle previous expectations and patterns of market conduct and to reduce the cigarette firms' ability to predict each other's behavior.

The larger number of product types and pricing variables also decreased the probability of effective parallel pricing. When Brown & Williamson entered the economy segment in 1984, the segment included value-25s, black and whites, and branded generics. With respect to each product, the net price in the market was determined not only by list prices, but also by a wide variety of discounts and promotions to consumers, and by rebates to wholesalers. In order to coordinate in an effective manner and eliminate price competition, the cigarette companies would have been required, without communicating, to establish parallel practices with respect to each of these variables, many of which, like consumer stickers or coupons, were difficult to monitor. Liggett has not even alleged parallel behavior with respect to these other variables, and the inherent limitations of tacit collusion suggest that such multivariable coordination is improbable. See R. Dorfman, The Price System 99-100, and n.10 (1964); Scherer & Ross 279.

In addition, R. J. Reynolds had incentives that, in some respects, ran counter to those of the other cigarette companies. It is implausible that without a shared interest in retarding the growth of the economy segment, Brown & Williamson and its fellow oligopolists could have engaged in parallel pricing and raised generic prices above a competitive level. "[C]oordination will not be possible when any significant firm chooses, for any reason, to 'go it alone.'" 2 Areeda and Turner ¶404b2, at 276. It is undisputed — indeed it was conceded by Liggett's expert — that R. J. Reynolds acted without regard to the supposed benefits of oligopolistic coordination when it repriced Doral at generic levels in the spring of 1984 and that the natural and probable consequence of its entry into the generic segment was procompetitive. Indeed, Reynolds' apparent objective in entering the segment was to capture a significant amount of volume in order to regain its number one sales position in the cigarette industry from Phillip Morris. There is no evidence that R. J. Reynolds accomplished this goal during the period relevant to this case, or that its commitment to achieving that goal changed. Indeed, R. J. Reynolds refused to follow Brown & Williamson's attempt to raise generic prices in June 1985. The jury thus had before it undisputed evidence that contradicts the suggestion that the major cigarette companies shared a goal of limiting the growth of the economy segment; one of the industry's two major players concededly entered the segment to expand volume and compete.

Even if all the cigarette companies were willing to participate in a scheme to restrain the growth of the generic segment, they would not have been able to coordinate their actions and raise prices above a competitive level unless they understood that Brown & Williamson's entry into the segment was not a genuine effort to compete with Liggett. If even one other firm misinterpreted Brown & Williamson's entry as an effort to expand share, a chain reaction of competitive responses would almost certainly have resulted, and oligopoly discipline would have broken down, perhaps irretrievably. "[O]nce the trust among rivals breaks down, it is as hard to put back together again as was Humpty-Dumpty, and non-collusive behavior is likely to take over." Samuelson & Nordhaus, Economics, at 534.

Liggett argues that the means by which Brown & Williamson signaled its anticompetitive intent to its rivals was through its pricing structure. According to Liggett, maintaining existing list prices while offering substantial rebates to wholesalers was a signal to the other cigarette firms that Brown & Williamson did not intend to attract additional smokers to the generic segment by its entry. But a reasonable jury could not conclude that this pricing structure eliminated or rendered insignificant the risk that the other firms might misunderstand Brown & Williamson's entry as a competitive move. The likelihood that Brown & Williamson's rivals would have regarded its pricing structure as an important signal is low, given that Liggett itself, the purported target of the predation, was already using similar rebates, as was R. J. Reynolds in marketing its Doral branded generic. A Reynolds executive responsible for Doral testified that given its and Liggett's use of wholesaler rebates, Brown & Williamson could have competed effectively without them. And despite extensive discovery of the corporate records of R. J. Reynolds and Philip Morris, no documents appeared that indicated any awareness of Brown & Williamson's supposed signal by its principal rivals. Without effective signaling, it is difficult to see how the alleged predation could have had a reasonable chance of success through oligopoly pricing.

Finally, although some of Brown & Williamson's corporate planning documents speak of a desire to slow the growth of the segment, no objective evidence of its conduct permits a reasonable inference that it had any real prospect of doing so through anticompetitive means. It is undisputed that when Brown & Williamson introduced its generic cigarettes, it offered them to a thousand wholesalers who had never before purchased generic cigarettes. The inevitable effect of this marketing effort was to expand the segment, as the new wholesalers recruited retail outlets to carry generic cigarettes. Even with respect to wholesalers already carrying generics, Brown & Williamson's unprecedented volume rebates had a similar expansionary effect. Unlike many branded cigarettes, generics came with no sales guarantee to the wholesaler; any unsold stock represented pure loss to the wholesaler. By providing substantial incentives for wholesalers to place large orders, Brown & Williamson created strong pressure for them to sell more generic cigarettes. In addition, as we have already observed, many wholesalers passed portions of the rebates about which Liggett complains on to consumers, thus dropping the retail price of generics and further stimulating demand. Brown & Williamson provided a further, direct stimulus, through some $10 million it spent during the period of alleged predation placing discount stickers on its generic cartons to reduce prices to the ultimate consumer. In light of these uncontested facts about Brown & Williamson's conduct, it is not reasonable to conclude that Brown & Williamson threatened in a serious way to restrict output, raise prices above a competitive level, and artificially slow the growth of the economy segment of the national cigarette market.

To be sure, Liggett's economic expert explained Liggett's theory of predatory price discrimination and testified that he believed it created a reasonable possibility that Brown & Williamson could injure competition in the United States cigarette market as a whole. But this does not alter our analysis. When an expert opinion is not supported by sufficient facts to validate it in the eyes of the law, or when indisputable record facts contradict or otherwise render the opinion unreasonable, it cannot support a jury's verdict. Cf. *J. Truett Payne* (referring to expert economic testimony not based on "documentary evidence as to the effect of the discrimination on retail prices" as "weak" at best). Expert testimony is useful as a guide to interpreting market facts, but it is not a substitute for them. As we observed in *Matsushita*, "expert opinion evidence ... has little probative value in comparison with the economic factors" that may dictate a particular conclusion. Here, Liggett's expert based his opinion that Brown & Williamson had a reasonable prospect of recouping its predatory losses on three factors: Brown & Williamson's black and white pricing structure, corporate documents showing an intent to shrink the price differential between generic and branded cigarettes, and evidence of below-cost pricing. Because, as we have explained, this evidence is insufficient as a matter of law to support a finding of primary-line injury under the Robinson-Patman Act, the expert testimony cannot sustain the jury's verdict.

IV

We understand that the chain of reasoning by which we have concluded that Brown & Williamson is entitled to judgment as a matter of law is demanding. But a reasonable jury is presumed to know and understand the law, the facts of the case, and the realities of the market. We hold that the evidence cannot support a finding that Brown & Williamson's alleged scheme was likely to result in oligopolistic price coordination and sustained supracompetitive pricing in the generic segment of the national cigarette market. Without this, Brown & Williamson had no reasonable prospect of recouping its predatory losses and could not inflict the injury to competition the antitrust laws prohibit. The judgment of the Court of Appeals is affirmed.

Justice STEVENS, with whom Justice WHITE and Justice BLACKMUN join, dissenting. For a period of 18 months in 1984 and 1985, respondent Brown & Williamson Tobacco Corporation (B & W) waged a price war against petitioner, known then as Liggett & Meyers (Liggett). Liggett filed suit claiming that B & W's pricing practices violated the Robinson-Patman Act. After a 115-day trial, the jury agreed, and awarded Liggett substantial damages. . . .

Today, the Court [reviews] portions of the voluminous trial record, and comes to the conclusion that the evidence does not support the jury's finding that B & W's price discrimination "had a reasonable possibility of injuring competition."[2] In my opinion the evidence is plainly sufficient to support that finding.

I

The fact that a price war may not have accomplished its purpose as quickly or as completely as originally intended does not immunize conduct that was illegal when it occurred. . . . Assessing the pre-July 1984 evidence tending to prove that B & W was motivated by anticompetitive intent, the District Court observed that the documentary evidence was "more voluminous and detailed than any other reported case. This evidence not only indicates B & W wanted to injure Liggett, it also details an extensive plan to slow the growth of the generic cigarette segment." . . .

The rebate program was intended to harm Liggett and in fact caused it serious injury.[10] The jury found that Liggett had suffered actual damages of $49.6 million, an amount close to, but slightly

2. The jury gave an affirmative answer to the following special issue:

  1. Did Brown & Williamson engage in price discrimination that had a reasonable possibility of injuring competition in the cigarette market as a whole in the United States?

The jury made its finding after being instructed that "injury to competition" means

  the injury to consumer welfare which results when a competitor is able to raise and to maintain prices in a market or well-defined submarket above competitive levels. In order to injure competition in the cigarette market as a whole, Brown & Williamson must be able to create a real possibility of both driving out rivals by loss-creating price cutting and then holding on to that advantage to recoup losses by raising and maintaining prices at higher than competitive levels. You must remember that the Robinson-Patman Act was designed to protect competition rather than just competitors and, therefore, injury to competition does not mean injury to a competitor. Liggett & Myers can not satisfy this element simply by showing that they were injured by Brown & Williamson's conduct. To satisfy this element, Liggett & Myers must show, by a preponderance of the evidence, that Brown & Williamson's conduct had a reasonable possibility of injuring competition in the cigarette market and not just a reasonable possibility of injuring a competitor in the cigarette market.

10. By offering its largest discounts to Liggett's 14 largest customers, B & W not only put its "money where the volume is," but also applied maximum pressure to Liggett at a lesser cost to itself than would have resulted from a nondiscriminatory price cut.

larger than, the $48.7 million trading profit B & W had indicated it would forgo in order to discipline Liggett. To inflict this injury, B & W sustained a substantial loss. During the full 18-month period, B & W's revenues ran consistently below its total variable costs, with an average deficiency of approximately $0.30 per carton and a total loss on B & W black and whites of almost $15 million. That B & W executives were willing to accept losses of this magnitude during the entire 18 months is powerful evidence of their belief that prices ultimately could be "managed up" to a level that would allow B & W to recoup its investment.

At the end of 1985, the list price of branded cigarettes was $33.15 per carton, and the list price of black and whites, $19.75 per carton. Over the next four years, the list price on both branded and black and white cigarettes increased twice a year, by identical amounts. The June 1989 increases brought the price of branded cigarettes to $46.15 per carton, and the price of black and whites to $33.75 — an amount even higher than the price for branded cigarettes when the war ended in December 1985.[11] Because the rate of increase was higher on black and whites than on brandeds, the price differential between the two types of cigarettes narrowed, from roughly 40% in 1985 to 27% in 1989.

The expert economist employed by Liggett testified that the post-1985 price increases were unwarranted by increases in manufacturing or other costs, taxes, or promotional expenditures. To be sure, some portion of the volume rebates granted distributors was passed on to consumers in the form of promotional activity, so that consumers did not feel the full brunt of the price increases. Nevertheless, the record amply supports the conclusion that the post-1985 price increases in list prices produced higher consumer prices, as well as higher profits for the manufacturers.[12]

---

11. It is also true that these same years, other major manufacturers entered the generic market and expanded their generic sales. Their entry is entirely consistent with the possibility that lock-step increases in the price of generics brought them to a level that was supracompetitive, though lower than that charged on branded cigarettes.

12.

    Q Does this mean that the price increases, which you testified are happening twice a year, are used up in these consumer promotions?

    A Not by any stretch of the imagination. Although there has been an increase in the use of this type of promotional activity over the last four or five years, the increase in that promotional activity has been far outstripped by the list price increases. The prices go up by a lot; the promotional activity, indeed, does go up. But the promotional activity has not gone up by anywhere near the magnitude of the list price increases. Further, those price increases are not warranted by increasing costs, since the manufacturing costs of making cigarettes have remained roughly constant over the last five years.

The legal question presented by this evidence is whether the facts as they existed during and at the close of the 18-month period, and all reasonable inferences to be drawn from those facts, justified the finding by the jury that B & W's discriminatory pricing campaign "had a reasonable possibility of injuring competition."

II

The Sherman Act, the Clayton Act, and the Robinson-Patman Act all serve the purpose of protecting competition. Because they have a common goal, the statutes are similar in many respects.... The statutes do differ significantly with respect to one element of the violation, the competitive consequences of predatory conduct. Even here, however, the three statutes have one thing in common: Not one of them requires proof that a predatory plan has actually succeeded in accomplishing its objective. Section 1 of the Sherman Act requires proof of a conspiracy. It is the joint plan to restrain trade, however, and not its success, that is prohibited by §1. Nash v. United States, 229 U.S. 373, 378 (1913). Section 2 of the Sherman Act applies to independent conduct, and may be violated when there is a "dangerous probability" that an attempt to achieve monopoly power will succeed. *Swift.* The Clayton Act goes beyond the "dangerous probability" standard to cover price discrimination "where the effect of such discrimination may be to substantially lessen competition or tend to create a monopoly in any line of commerce." ...

III

After 115 days of trial, during which it considered 2,884 exhibits, 85 deposition excerpts, and testimony from 23 live witnesses, the jury deliberated for nine days and then returned a verdict finding that B & W engaged in price discrimination with a "reasonable possibility of injuring competition." The Court's contrary conclusion rests on a hodgepodge of legal, factual, and economic propositions that are insufficient, alone or together, to overcome the jury's assessment of the evidence.

First, as a matter of law, the Court reminds us that the Robinson-Patman Act is concerned with consumer welfare and competition, as opposed to protecting individual competitors from harm; "the antitrust laws were passed for the protection of competition, not competitors." For that reason, predatory price-cutting is not unlawful unless the predator has a reasonable prospect of recouping his investment from supracompetitive profits. The jury, of course, was so instructed, see n.2, supra, and no one questions that proposition here.

As a matter of fact, the Court emphasizes the growth in the generic segment following B & W's entry. As the Court notes, generics' expansion to close to 15% of the total market by 1988 exceeds B & W's own forecast that the segment would grow to only about 10%, assuming no entry by B & W. What these figures do not do, however, is answer the relevant question: whether the prices of generic cigarettes during the late 1980s were competitive or supracompetitive.

On this point, there is ample, uncontradicted evidence that the list prices on generic cigarettes, as well as the prices on branded cigarettes, rose regularly and significantly during the late 1980s, in a fashion remarkably similar to the price change patterns that characterized the industry in the 1970s when supracompetitive, oligopolistic pricing admittedly prevailed. Given its knowledge of the industry's history of parallel pricing, I think the jury plainly was entitled to draw an inference that these increased prices were supracompetitive.

The Court responds to this evidence dismissively, suggesting that list prices have no bearing on the question because promotional activities of the cigarette manufacturers may have offset such price increases. That response is insufficient for three reasons. First, the promotions to which the majority refers related primarily to branded cigarettes; accordingly, while they narrowed the differential between branded prices and black and white prices, they did not reduce the consumer price of black and whites. Second, the Courts speculation is inconsistent with record evidence that the semiannual list price increases were not offset by consumer promotions. See n.12, supra. See also [the Court's opinion] ("at least some portion of the list price increase was reflected in a higher net price to the consumer"). Finally, to the extent there is a dispute regarding the effect of promotional activities on consumer prices for generics, the jury presumably resolved that dispute in Liggett's favor, and the Court's contrary speculation is an insufficient basis for setting aside that verdict.[15] . . .

15. In finding an absence of actual supracompetitive pricing, the Court also relies on the testimony of Liggett executives, who stated that industry prices were fair. Illustrative is the following exchange:

Q I want to know — yes or no — sir, whether or not you say that the price you charged for branded cigarettes, which is the same price you say everybody else charged, was a fair and equitable price for that product to the American consumer.
A It's what the industry set, and based on that it's a fair price.

The problem with this testimony, and testimony like it, is that it relates to the period before the price war, as well as after, when there is no real dispute but that prices were supracompetitive. ("[T]he profits in the cigarette industry are the best of any industry I've been associated with, very much so.") Some of the testimony cited by the Court, for instance, is that of an outside director who served only from

Also as a matter of economics, the Court insists that a predatory pricing program in an oligopoly is unlikely to succeed absent actual conspiracy. Though it has rejected a somewhat stronger version of this proposition as a rule of decision, the Court comes back to the same economic theory, relying on the supposition that an "anti-competitive minuet is most difficult to compose and to perform, even for a disciplined oligopoly." . . . I would suppose, however, that the professional performers who had danced the minuet for 40 to 50 years would be better able to predict whether their favorite partners would follow them in the future than would an outsider, who might not know the difference between Haydn and Mozart.[18] In any event, the jury was surely entitled to infer that at the time of the price war itself, B & W reasonably believed that it could signal its intentions to its fellow oligopolists, assuring their continued cooperation.

Perhaps the Court's most significant error is the assumption that seems to pervade much of the final sections of its opinion: that Liggett had the burden of proving either the actuality of supracompetitive pricing, or the actuality of tacit collusion. . . . In my opinion, the jury was entitled to infer from the succession of price increases after 1985 — when the prices for branded and generic cigarettes increased every six months from $33.15 and $19.75, respectively, to $46.15 and $33.75 — that B & W's below-cost pricing actually produced supracompetitive prices, with the help of tacit collusion among the players. But even if that were not so clear, the jury would surely be entitled to infer that B & W's predatory plan, in which it invested millions of dollars for the purpose of achieving an admittedly anticompetitive result, carried a "reasonable possibility" of injuring competition.

Accordingly, I respectfully dissent.

1977 or 1978 until 1980; his belief in the competitiveness of his industry must be viewed against the "[s]ubstantial evidence suggest[ing] that in recent decades, the industry reaped the benefits of prices above a competitive level" to which the majority itself refers.

The jury was, of course, entitled to discount the probative force of testimony from executives to the effect that there was no collusion among tobacco manufacturers, and that they had appeared before a congressional committee to vouch for the competitive nature of their industry. The jury was also free to give greater weight to the documentary evidence presented, the inferences to be drawn therefrom, and the testimony of experts who agreed with the textbook characterization of the industry. . . .

18. Judge Easterbrook has made the same point:

   Wisdom lags far behind the market. . . . [L]awyers know less about the business than the people they represent. . . . The judge knows even less about the business than the lawyers.

Easterbrook, The Limits of Antitrust, 63 Tex. L. Rev. 1, 5 (1984).

330. (a) What must a plaintiff prove in a predatory pricing case? Should it be permissible for a jury to infer some elements from others (for example, to infer the possibility of recoupment from the existence of below-cost pricing)?

(b) What would have convinced the majority that recoupment was possible in *Brooke Group*? Were its arguments about the inadequacy of the plaintiff's proof convincing? What weight should be given to the plaintiff's concession that there was no collusion in pricing?

(c) If recoupment was not plausible, how can we explain Brown and Williamson's pricing? Of what relevance are documents indicating the defendant's intent?

(d) Of what relevance is the procedural posture, that a jury below had found a violation?[83]

Patent Accumulation

331. Patent accumulation: development and acquisition.[84] Patent accumulation in the hands of a monopolist presents a dilemma. On one hand, we certainly do not want to impede research, development, and innovation by all, including monopolists. Nor can we totally prevent a patentee from selling the use of its invention to an existing monopolist without sometimes depriving the patentee of any reward from that invention or without sometimes depriving the public of the best products at lowest cost. On the other hand, the more patents that a monopolist accumulates, whether from internal invention or from acquisition, the greater the impediment to competition. Some of the problems can be readily illustrated.

Consider first the simple case of 20 firms, each of which owns a patent that produces entirely equivalent products that no other firm can make without infringing these patents. If one firm ac-

---

83. Reconsider this question after studying *Kodak*, in Ch. 4B. One aspect of the Court's argument in *Brooke Group* and *Matsushita* is that predatory pricing schemes are rarely tried or successful. For some recent studies indicating that predation may be more plausible than others had previously suggested, see Y. Jung, J. Kagel & D. Levin, On the Existence of Predatory Pricing: An Experimental Study of Reputation and Entry Deterrence in the Chain-Store Game, 25 Rand J. Econ. 72 (1994); D. Weiman & R. Levin, Preying for Monopoly? The Case of Southern Bell Telephone Company, 1894-1912, 102 J. Pol. Econ. 103 (1994); R. Zerbe & M. Mumford, Does Predatory Pricing Exist?, Economic Theory and the Courts After *Brooke Group*, 41 Antitr. Bull. 949 (1996). For a brief survey of recent theoretical developments and a suggestion that courts have ignored them, see A. Klevorick, The Current State of the Law and Economics of Predatory Pricing, 83 Am. Econ. Assn. Papers & Proceedings 162 (May 1993).

84. See Areeda & Turner, note 1, ¶¶705-706.

quired the others, it would have a patent-protected monopoly, industry profits would be higher, and such incremental profits would provide both the incentive for the acquisitions and the source for paying the other firms a premium above competitive-market values for selling out.[85]

Now consider an otherwise lawful monopoly that rests on a single patent. Imagine that an individual invents and patents an exactly equivalent technology that can be practiced without infringing the monopolist's patent. The monopolist would pay more for it than anyone else because combining the new and old patents would preserve monopoly profits while any other buyer would merely have the prospect of (a share of) profits closer to the competitive level.[86]

The same reasoning illuminates the incentives for invention faced by an existing monopolist and a prospective new entrant. Imagine an existing monopoly resting on a patent that controls the relevant technology and that the scientific literature suggests that there may be a second way of achieving the very same result, without infringing the first patent. The monopolist will have the greater incentive to seek and patent the alternative technology, because success will preserve its monopoly profits while it would bring a new entrant only the prospect of (a share of) profits closer to the competitive level.[87]

The monopolist's relative incentive for invention and its opportunities to acquire inventions developed by outsiders are even greater for new inventions that cannot be practiced without infringing the monopolist's existing patents. Suppose, for example, that firm Alpha possesses hundreds or even thousands of patents relating to the new miracle fiber xlon and its manufacture. Many new patents in xlon technology will inevitably be improvements on existing patents. Because the improvements cannot be practiced without infringing Alpha's basic patents, only Alpha (or its licensees) can use the new patent. If, in addition, a corollary of Alpha's patent position is substantial dominance of the xlon market, Alpha may be the only firm able to utilize the new patent and thus the only one able to pay the inventor its full value. Thus, Alpha may be the most likely and desirable market for inventors with new patents. And, of

85. We have seen this phenomenon in ¶288 with regard to patent settlements.

86. Of course, monopoly profits would be maintained for the industry if the new entrant and the former monopolist tacitly coordinated prices at the perfectly monopolistic level for the duration of the patent.

87. See, e.g., R. Gilbert & D. Newberry, Preemptive Patenting and the Persistence of Monopoly, 72 Am. Econ. Rev. 514 (1982); C. Harris & J. Vickers, Patent Races and the Persistence of Monopoly, 33 J. Indus. Econ. 461 (1985).

course, every acquisition by Alpha of a patent lessens the possibility of competition from others. And even mere improvement patents may extend the period of Alpha's control beyond the 20 years of its basic patents.

Alpha's rivals may feel overwhelming pressure to invent around its patents. They may be discouraged from trying, however, if inventive effort seems less likely to produce new basic patents than improvement patents that cannot be practiced without Alpha's permission. Alpha would not be so dissuaded. As a by-product of its search for improvements or as a conscious object, Alpha may also find and patent the alternative methods of making xlon or similar fibers.

Alpha's large and possibly growing patent hoard blanketing xlon-type fibers and their technology confronts a new producer with the substantial possibility of an infringement suit. Even if all of Alpha's patents are relatively "weak," their sheer number threatens that one might be held valid and infringed. The newcomer, therefore, may feel compelled to make its peace with Alpha before committing substantial investments to the field.

332. The authorities on accumulation. This brief review of the limited authorities might just as well begin with the frequently cited Supreme Court dictum in *Hazeltine*[88] that "[t]he mere accumulation of patents, no matter how many, is not in itself illegal." In contrast, the Court in *Trans-Wrap*[89] observed that

88. Automatic Radio Mfg. Co. v. Hazeltine Res., 339 U.S. 827, 834 (1950). Ironically, the Court cited the contrasting *Trans-Wrap* opinion in support of this proposition.

89. Transparent-Wrap Mach. Corp. v. Stokes & Smith Co., 329 U.S. 637, 642, 644, 646-648 (1947). In *Trans-Wrap*, plaintiff granted defendant an exclusive license to make and sell a patented wrapping machine. Defendant agreed to assign to plaintiff improvement patents suitable for use in connection with the machine. The court of appeals condemned this grant-back provision as a patent abuse. Held: reversed. The patent statute expressly permits licenses and assignments and does not limit the consideration which may be paid for the assignment to any species or kind of property. "[W]e see no difference whether the consideration is services . . . or cash, or the right to use another patent." To be sure, the power to refuse a license is not a power to license on any terms. But an

> improvement patent, like the basic patent to which it relates, is a legalized monopoly for a limited period. The law permits both to be bought and sold. One who uses one patent to acquire another is not extending his patent monopoly to articles governed by the general law and as respects which neither monopolies nor restraints of trade are sanctioned. He is indeed using one legalized monopoly to acquire another legalized monopoly. . . . [T]he effect on the public interest would seem to be the same whether the licensee or the licensor owns the improvement patents.
>
> We are quite aware of the possibilities of abuse in the practice of licensing a patent on condition that the licensee assign all improvement patents to the licensor. Conceiv-

[h]e who acquires two patents acquires a double monopoly. As patents are added to patents a whole industry may be regimented. The owner of a basic patent might thus perpetuate his control over an industry long after the basic patent expired. Competitors might be eliminated and an industrial monopoly perfected and maintained.

Winslow,[90] one of the Court's earliest holdings, validated under Sherman Act §1 the creation of the United Shoe Company through the merger of three companies, each of which was dominant in different types of shoe machinery. The Court, through Justice Holmes, said,

> The machines are patented, making them is a monopoly in any case.... [As] they did not compete with one another, it is hard to see why the collective business should be any worse than its component parts.... [W]e can see no greater objection to one corporation manufacturing 70 percent of three noncompeting groups of patented machines collectively used for making a single product than to three corporations making the same proportion of one group each.

A further, more successful challenge to United Shoe was noted earlier in this section. As part of that case, the accumulation of more than 2000 shoe machinery patents was challenged by the government. United had acquired about 5 percent of them from outsiders in order to protect itself against infringements suits, to avoid blocking desirable developments, and to settle patent controversies. "But most of these purposes could have been served by nonexclusive licenses. Taking the further step of acquiring the patents ... buttressed United's market power. In some instances ... the acquisitions made it less likely that United would have competition."[91] The court referred to these acquisitions but did not seem to rely on them in finding a violation of §2.

In the *General Electric* case,[92] GE held the basic patents controlling the tungsten filament incandescent lamp. It conditioned its licenses to other lampmakers on their undertaking to grant back to GE nonexclusive licenses under any new patents they developed in the field. Since GE was also to have the power to sublicense others under such patents, GE's licensees would get little benefit from their own inventions and would therefore be dissuaded from re-

---

ably the device could be employed with the purpose or effect of violating the anti-trust laws. [But the antitrust issue was not raised or decided below.] We only hold that the inclusion in the license of the condition requiring the licensee to assign improvement patents is not per se illegal and unenforceable.

90. United States v. Winslow, 227 U.S. 202, 217 (1913).
91. *United Shoe*, 110 F. Supp. at 333.
92. United States v. GE (lamp monopoly), 82 F. Supp. 753 (D.N.J. 1949).

search. The district court held that GE's patent acquisitions had monopolized patents in violation of Sherman Act §2.

More recently, the Second Circuit upheld Xerox's acquisition of patents and its refusal to license them. It argued that an acquisition by a dominant competitor of a patent that resulted in monopoly power would violate Sherman Act §2, but such a prohibition was inapplicable where the acquisition preceded the development of the product, plain paper copying. In addition, it held that even a monopolist is permitted by the patent laws not to license its patents, and thus no liability arises under §2.[93]

333. Solely through its internal research, the *M* Corporation has achieved a strong patent position enabling it to control a specialized but large and important segment of the computer market. By any test, *M* holds monopoly power.

(a) Has it monopolized in violation of Sherman Act §2, or is its market success simply attributable to superior skill, foresight, and industry, together with a lawful patent monopoly?

(b) Would it make a difference if *M* had neither used nor licensed some of its patented inventions and thus suppressed them?[94] If no one had sought a license to use the suppressed inventions? If someone had requested a license? At what royalty rate? If *M* admitted that it had developed and patented the suppressed inventions with the sole object of foreclosing its competitors? Can *M* persuasively argue that the original invention was rewarded by a patent monopoly, which is merely preserved as the deserved reward for the second (and suppressed) invention? If not, why not?

(c) Ignore ¶b and suppose only that *M* admitted that it hoped to invest everything it had in its area and it realized that its old and new patents would tend to exclude competition. Has *M* monopolized? Is it realistic to base a finding of monopolization upon a showing of exclusionary purpose? Isn't all inventive effort looking toward patent protection designed to foreclose some possibility to competitors and thus exclusionary? Should §2 liability rest on findings of fact about the motivations with which research or patenting was undertaken?

(d) If *M* is inhibited by §2 from patenting its subsequent inventions, how can it protect itself against subsequent patent applicants? Should spending for research be regarded no more favorably than any other spending by a monopolist to reinforce its position? Or is

93. SCM Corp. v. Xerox Corp., 645 F.2d 1195 (2d Cir. 1981), cert. denied, 455 U.S. 1016 (1982).
94. See ¶280.

invention different because, inter alia, one must defend oneself from being excluded by others?

334. The M Corporation acquired a lawful monopoly of a certain segment of the computer industry through internal inventions that it has patented. Beta has developed a patent covering an alternative computer that might well satisfy M's segment of the computer market. Would M's acquisition of the Beta patent offend Sherman Act §2?[95]

(a) Would it matter if M does not use or license the acquired patent? What result when the acquired patent is actually used by M? Should we infer superiority from the fact that M is using the patent? Or would it do so whenever the acquired patent is merely equivalent to its existing technology? But would it be practical to demand clear proof of the acquired patent's superiority? Even if the acquired patent is demonstrably superior, does M's aggregation tend to impair competition?

(b) Would it encourage entry and stimulate competition to bar M from taking any interest in the new invention? Would it be consistent with the patent system to deny the patentee any opportunity to sell any interest in its patent to M? Would it be best to limit M to the acquisition of a nonexclusive license? How can one determine whether a nonexclusive license in form is in fact exclusive? Suppose M acquires superior technology under a nonexclusive license from the inventor in return for a royalty equal to a percentage of M's profits. If the licensor acts in its independent self-interest, will it license any others?

(c) How does the analysis differ, if at all, when the new patent is acquired from M's own licensee (under earlier patents) who had promised to grant back to M any patents developed within the licensed field? If M is denied the power to demand an exclusive grant-back, would it have granted the original license at all? What is the relevance of this question?

(d) In what respects should the analysis differ when the acquired patent is subservient to M's patents because it cannot be practiced without infringing M's patents? Can all of M's legitimate interests be satisfied with a nonexclusive license?

(e) How should the analysis differ, if at all, when the patent is acquired by M in the settlement of a bona fide dispute over the validity of the new patent, which would be competing with one of M's existing patents?[96]

---

95. Reexamine these questions under Clayton Act §7 after studying Ch. 5.
96. See ¶288.

3B. MONOPOLY POWER[1]

335. Introduction. Although the antitrust laws may condemn some conduct with little inquiry, as in the case of price fixing, market power is often crucial in antitrust analysis. Inquiry into the reasonableness of a particular restraint of trade may be made only after some demonstration of the defendant's market power. There are several reasons for such a threshold power requirement. First, judicial (and private) resources might otherwise be wasted investigating practices that cannot harm consumers in any event. Second, some practices may be detrimental only in the presence of market power (recall the discussion in *United Shoe*). These two reasons together are particularly important under Sherman Act §2, which deals with acts of individual firms. Absent a market power requirement, many common practices might be subject to review by antitrust courts. Third, the inevitable mistakes in appraising conduct can be minimized by examining it only where there is sufficient ground for anticompetitive concern.

Of course, the inquiry into market power is itself costly and subject to mistakes; thus courts, as in the case of price fixing, sometimes dispense with that inquiry. When practices are generally detrimental regardless of the circumstances, the error of greatest concern is failing to condemn the practice rather than overbroad prohibition. Moreover, to the extent some restraints only make business sense in the presence of sufficient power, explicit demonstration may be unnecessary.

This section explores the concept of market power in the context of the offense of monopolization, although it is largely applicable in other contexts as well. Nearly any departure from perfect competition implies some power. Thus, whenever the antitrust laws require a showing of market power, the courts must make a judgment of degree. Paragraph 336 begins the inquiry by defining market power more precisely and relating it to the concept of monopoly as used in Sherman Act §2. The relationship among various approaches to measuring market power is described in ¶337. Paragraph 338 examines the determinants of market power, many of which are considered in greater detail in ¶¶339-342. In the process, this discussion develops the concept of market definition that is so central to judi-

---

1. This discussion derives largely from IIA P. Areeda, H. Hovenkamp & J. Solow, Antitrust Law (1995); L. Kaplow, The Accuracy of Traditional Market Power Analysis and a Direct Adjustment Alternative, 95 Harv. L. Rev. 1817 (1982); W. Landes & R. Posner, Market Power in Antitrust Cases, 94 Harv. L. Rev. 937 (1981), each of which also addresses, to varying degrees, when market power is substantial and how much power is required to establish the monopolization offense.

cial inquiries into market power. Paragraph 343 summarizes the discussion, emphasizing points where confusion is common. This textual presentation is followed by government guidelines and two leading market power decisions in the monopolization context.

336.   Monopoly and market power. (a) *Defining monopoly in terms of market power*. Although the monopolization offense is routinely assumed to require market power in an economic sense, it is useful to trace the motivation for this approach. Sherman Act §2 does not speak of power or markets but merely condemns those "who shall monopolize ... any part of the trade or commerce among the several states, or with foreign nations." Conventional definitions of monopoly explicitly refer to *exclusive* possession or control. But §2 does not adopt this dictionary definition. It has been clear from the earliest days of the Sherman Act that one can be a monopolist and monopolize within the meaning of the statute without being the sole supplier of a product. Rather, the courts have defined the possession of monopoly power as the power to control price or to exclude competition. A dominant firm might possess such power even though it accounts for, say, only 90 percent of the sales of a product. Moreover, a firm accounting for 100 percent of such sales might lack power over price if customers are readily satisfied by substitute products or if new entry is very easy.[2]

This power to elevate prices above (and to restrict output below) competitive levels is called market power by economists (and, increasingly, by courts as well). It is possessed to some degree by every firm that is not constrained by perfect competition. But we have already seen that it does not appear to be the purpose of the Sherman Act to bring about a regime of perfect competition.[3] Under §2, only substantial market power will be deemed monopoly power. Thus, two problems face the courts: (1) How do we determine how much market power exists in a given case? (2) At what point on the spectrum between perfect competition and perfect monopoly should market power be deemed sufficient?[4] The factors

---

2. For example, consider a trucking company that offers the only regular delivery between two cities. Its 100 percent share may make it a literal monopoly, but it has hardly any power to exploit consumers because even modest price increases above the competitive level would induce shippers to telephone other trucking companies to arrange for them to haul the freight at a better price. After all, there are few industries in which the relevant capital stock is more mobile.

3. See ¶¶125-127.

4. This second formulation is itself overly simplistic, since a perfect monopolist can have no power or substantial power, depending on the circumstances.

described in ¶335 should determine, in principle, what threshold is appropriate in a given context.[5]

Although the ability to charge 50 percent more than the competitive price is generally understood to show market power and be of equal legal concern whether the product is steel or paper clips, the impact on consumer welfare varies. Even in markets of similar magnitude, the economic loss from a given excess of price over cost varies with the shape of demand and cost curves at monopoly and competitive levels of output, although these variations are typically too complex to be considered in antitrust litigation. Secondly, the assumed 50 percent excess impairs consumer welfare much more in the multibillion dollar steel market than in the far smaller clip market. Does this mean that society should be readier to control possible misbehavior in the larger market and thus to set a lower threshold of market power before doing so? (To put the same question from the opposite angle, should we insist on higher-than-usual power thresholds before intervening in smaller markets?) In favor of doing so, the cost and complexity of antitrust litigation does not rise proportionally with the economic stakes. On the other hand, varying the legal standard according to the absolute size of the market may overcomplicate the system. In addition, the social consequence of an erroneous condemnation may also be greater in the larger market.

(b) *The price of monopoly.*[6] Since market power is to serve as our measure of the evil effects of monopoly, we must begin by recalling the reasons that we object to monopoly and value competition. Monopoly, for example, produces economic inefficiency. In the formal model of perfect competition, the output of a commodity tends to expand until price falls to the point just equal to each firm's marginal cost of production, which, in equilibrium, will also equal long-run average cost (including normal profits but no more). Where a single firm controls the production of that commodity, the output will be smaller and price higher.[7] Thus, the monopolist profits at the expense of buyers, who are forced to pay more. Consumers unable to pay the monopolist's high price will spend their funds elsewhere and thus induce increased production of other commodities — commodities that consumers would not want under competitive pricing conditions. Thus, monopolistic limitations on output divert society's productive energies to less valued undertak-

5. Market power inquiries in contexts other than §2 will employ similar analysis as to the first question, but the appropriate answer to the second may differ substantially.

6. For a more detailed statement, see ¶¶112-113.

7. See ¶112a.

ings and thereby distort resource allocation away from the maximum satisfaction of consumer wants.

(c) *Market power as power over price.* Given this statement of the economic harms for monopoly, market power is measured by the extent to which price can be elevated above the competitive level, which corresponds to cost. Common statements of market power — the power to control price, the range of discretion, or choice that the firm possesses — are suggestive of this definition but leave some room for confusion. Such terms are meant to contrast the powerful firm with the perfectly competitive firm that has no choice but to match the market price. It cannot obtain more than its rivals charge, and it has no reason to take any less (because, by definition, the perfectly competitive firm is too small to have any impact on market price and thus can sell all it can produce at the going price). By contrast, a monopolist maximizes profits by choosing the price at which any further increase would cost it more in lost sales than it gains in increased profit on sales retained. Typically, there is only one such price that maximizes profits.[8] Thus, at least if the monopolist is a rational, profit-maximizing firm, it, like the perfect competitor, has only one choice. But the absence of discretion for a profit maximizer, is, of course, irrelevant. The evil of monopoly is that the profit-maximizing price, even if not truly discretionary, harms consumers and reduces economic efficiency, while that of the perfect competitor does not.[9]

(d) *Market power and the goals of the antitrust laws.* This definition of market power focuses entirely on competitive prices and economically efficient results. Is that narrow focus inconsistent with the broader social and political values that the antitrust laws are sometimes said to foster?[10] That question has not been much explored, but several answers are possible. First, the behavior of firms without market power might be thought too inconsequential to affect any of those broader purposes of the antitrust laws. Second, some would argue that the noneconomic motives for the legislation are less important than serving the economic function or that pursuing competitive prices and efficiency actually serves the broader objectives to the extent that Congress intended. Third, the difficulty of formulating standards to serve the broader objectives may leave the courts, by default, with those of the economic model of competi-

8. Id.
9. The monopolist that chooses not to charge the full monopoly price still exploits consumers and impairs efficient resource allocation. Even the monopolist that chooses the competitive price still has the power to do otherwise (although we may not be able to detect it when prices and profits are merely at the competitive level).
10. See *Alcoa*, Ch. 3A, and ¶¶117, 130, 505.

tion: allocative or productive efficiency, innovation, and consumer welfare. The last point, however, might still leave some room for these broader concerns — to whatever extent that can be articulated and sensibly applied — in setting the market power threshold for particular offenses, resolving uncertainties concerning market power in individual cases, defining the range of conduct that subjects firms to liability in the presence of market power, and limiting permissible defenses to such conduct.

337. Ways of measuring market power. (a) *Introduction.* Although we shall see that the conventional approach to measuring market power is to define a relevant market, the resulting market share merely offers a basis for *inferring* market power — that is, the degree to which price will be elevated above the competitive level. When the existence of monopoly is the issue, would it not be simpler to go directly to the ultimate question, that is, to ask whether and how much price is above cost? The remainder of this Paragraph notes the limitations on this approach and helps explain the role of the market definition concept.

(b) *Difficulty of direct measurement.* We seldom measure power directly because it is difficult to obtain and appraise the relevant data.[11] Although identifying the price is often straightforward, measuring the relevant cost is not. An alternative would be to ask whether the firm's profits on the product exceed the normal return to which they would be driven in a competitive equilibrium. Cost and profits involve many components buried within mounds of accounting information, where the books do not directly reflect economic concepts of cost and profit. Problems with overhead, inventories, depreciation, joint production costs, and allocations of charges within a conglomerate make such inquiries notoriously difficult.[12]

---

11. Recently some studies have attempted to show how market power could be directly measured. See D. Kamerschen & J. Kohler, Residual Demand Analysis of the Ready-to-Eat Breakfast Cereal Market, 38 Antitr. Bull. 903 (1993); D. Kamerschen & J. Park, An Alternative Approach to Market Structure and Market Price, 25 Applied Econ. 111 (1993); J. Baker & T. Bresnahan, Empirical Methods of Identifying and Measuring Market Power, 61 Antitr. L.J. 3 (1992); J. Baker & T. Bresnahan, Estimating the Residual Demand Curve Facing a Single Firm, 6 Intl. J. Indus. Org. 283 (1988). And courts have expressed a willingness to consider direct evidence of market power. See Rebel Oil Co. v. Atlantic Richfield Co., 51 F.3d 1421 (9th Cir.), cert. denied, 116 S. Ct. 515 (1995) (in predation case, market power may be shown by direct evidence of its exercise or by more common method of circumstantial evidence pertaining to market structure).

12. This problem was explored in ¶232a and is addressed further in the excerpt in ¶347, at note 107.

Even reliable measures of cost and profit may be misleading. If costs exceed the competitive level, so will prices that generate only normal profits. A monopolist's cost might be excessive because of diseconomies of scale, because significant costs are incurred in expanding or protecting its monopoly position, or because it is less careful in controlling costs due to the lack of competitive pressures. On the other hand, observed excess profits do not imply enduring market power when they are caused by short-run fluctuations, such as a recent increase in demand or a decrease in costs, in an otherwise competitive industry that has not yet fully adjusted to changed conditions.

This is not to suggest that cost and profit measures are never useful. When power is particularly great, large price-cost divergences might clearly emerge despite substantial ambiguity in the data. In other instances, a firm may face significant competition in one market and little in another. Significantly higher prices in one that cannot be explained by higher transportation or other costs suggests a significant price-cost divergence there.[13] Clear evidence of a substantial divergence does not merely suggest market power; it is the very definition of power.[14] When such evidence is unavailable, surrogates will be required.

Even when cost or profits are measured satisfactorily, the difficult task remains of judging how high a price-cost margin or profit level is excessive for the antitrust purpose at hand. But there is no way to avoid this judgment. Even such surrogates as market share are relevant only as indicators of a firm's ability to price significantly above the competitive level. There is no economically meaningful way to state that a given market share is excessive without connecting it somehow to a price-cost divergence that is deemed excessive.

(c) *Unexploited power.* Performance tests such as excess price-cost margins or profits obviously cannot detect market power that has not been exercised at all. Although unexercised power may seem

13. Similarly, price discrimination generally requires the existence of market power. See ¶285a. Because sales to those charged the lower price presumably cover cost — else it would be more profitable to forgo such sales — sales at the higher price must exceed cost by at least the amount of the price differential (adjusted for any cost differences).

14. Note two qualifications: If the divergence is not persistent, it is more likely to reflect a temporary disequilibrium rather than market power. Secondly, some excesses of price over cost reflect economic "rents" rather than market power. As a simple illustration, suppose that the defendant possesses a copper mine that can be worked at lower unit costs than other copper mines but whose output cannot be expanded beyond the present volume except at the same unit costs borne by rivals. The defendant will then be earning above-normal profits, but these are styled rents rather than market power because industry prices would be no lower if pieces of the mine were owned by numerous independent competitors.

harmless, its wrongful acquisition or maintenance affronts the goal of keeping market processes open and competitive. Moreover, the power that is unexercised today may be exploited tomorrow and waiting for its exercise would impose on antitrust courts the unwelcome burden of supervising prices from day to day.[15] Anyway, completely unexercised power is probably rare.

(d) *Prospective power.* Performance tests obviously cannot detect power that has not yet been attained and thus cannot aid antitrust efforts to control conduct leading to market power. For example, an antitrust court may judge a merger or joint venture before it is consummated and thus before it could have had any effect at all. Similarly, the attempts to monopolize considered in Chapter 3C often involve firms that do not yet have significant market power but hope to win it through improper behavior, which will be judged before its effects are apparent. In such cases, market shares may hint at the prospect of achieving market power through the challenged conduct.

(e) *Power inferred from conduct.* Conduct itself might illuminate the existence or prospect of market power. The refusal to sell machines in *United Shoe* might seem pointless unless United had market power to be protected.[16] Sustained below-cost pricing that cannot otherwise be explained makes no sense unless intended to win market power by destroying rivals because without such power the predator could never recoup the losses suffered during the predatory period. Once we are certain that the pricing is truly predatory, should we simply accept the defendant's own implicit judgment that its conduct will lead to market power?[17]

338. Determinants of market power. (a) *Buyer responsiveness determines seller's power.* The ability of a seller to charge more than a competitive price depends upon buyers' desire for its particular product. At the perfectly competitive extreme, buyers have no unique desire for any one seller's product: If one seller raises its price even a trifle above the competitive price, all buyers will purchase elsewhere. Generalizing broadly, we can say that the more massive is buyer response to small changes in price, the less is a firm's power, and the smaller is the opportunity for excess prices or profits or for distortions in resource allocation; the less is buyer

15. Recall the analysis of reasonable prices in *Trans-Missouri* and *Trenton Potteries* from Ch. 2A.
16. Cf. Pacific Mailing Equip. Corp. v. Pitney-Bowes, 499 F. Supp. 108 (N.D. Cal. 1980) (fact that defendant destroys all used machines above a certain age before disposing of them as scrap reinforces the inference of market power).
17. See *Brooke Group*, Ch. 3A; *Rebel Oil*, note 11.

response to price changes, the greater is the firm's power.[18] Of course, from the firm's viewpoint, it does not matter why customers turn away or where they turn but only the rate at which sales decrease when that firm raises its price.

The rate at which a defendant will lose sales as it raises price depends upon the range and attractiveness of the alternatives available to buyers. One alternative is simply to do without — an important alternative that affects the intensity of demand but that cannot be captured in any market definition.[19] The other alternatives can be conveniently grouped in three categories, which will be elaborated in subsequent Paragraphs. (1) Suppliers of the very same product in the same vicinity (current direct competitors). (2) Potential suppliers of that product to the defendant's customers. For example, firms making that product in adjacent areas may find it profitable to "export" it to the defendant's customers. Or firms making related products in the immediate or adjacent areas may be

---

18. In economic terms, the rate of decrease in sales in response to an increase in the firm's price (expressed in percentage terms) is the *firm's* elasticity of demand. We generally avoid that term here in order to minimize confusion with the more commonly used concept of the *industry* elasticity of demand, which refers to the rate of decrease in sales in response to an increase in the *industry* price level.

Consider the following illustration:

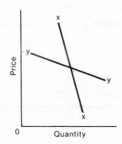 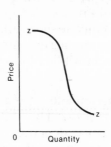

Demand functions *xx*, *yy*, and *zz* relate consumer purchases to price. Price is plotted vertically and sales quantity horizontally. On the assumption that more will be sold as price declines, the demand function for an industry's product slopes downward. A monopolist confronted with demand function *yy* has less power than one facing demand function *xx* because a given price increase costs it more sales in the former case than in the latter. Also note that a demand function can have different characteristics at different prices. Demand function *zz* is quite elastic (more like *yy*) at both high and low prices, but rather inelastic (more like *xx*) at intermediate prices.

19. Many of the customers driven away from product *A* will spend more of their funds on something else. If most of them turn to product *B*, that product would indeed be a substitute and the two products may belong in the same market. But if home cooks react to higher prices for electric mixers by stirring manually and spend their mixer money on holidays, movies, shirts, or gin, no market definition can reflect those choices.

readily able to convert their production to supply the defendant's customers. And new entrants not previously associated with the product or the territory might be induced to begin production. (3) Suppliers of substitute products. For example, if one vegetable becomes more expensive, consumers shift to others, or possibly to fruits.

It is apparent that market power and its determinants are all matters of degree. Even the most powerful monopolist will reach a point where a further price rise will drive enough buyers away to make the price increase unprofitable. At the other end of the spectrum, modest power is commonplace. The convenience grocery store may have some power over price due to a locational advantage, and one brand may command some distinctive consumer loyalty notwithstanding other roughly equivalent brands. Even other producers of the very same product may require some time before they could expand their output to satisfy customers turning away from a producer that increased its price. Some market power is virtually unavoidable, and will be exercised short of wholesale regulation of all prices, and thus is not a very enticing target for antitrust intervention. Sherman Act §2 is limited to cases where existing or prospective power is substantial.

(b) *Price at which buyers' alternatives are assessed.* Suppose that we need to assess the market power of the sole producer of the fabric xlon, that the competitive price of xlon is $1 per unit, and that a $1.01 price for that product would cause most xlon customers to buy the fabric ylon instead. On these assumptions, the ylon alternative guarantees consumers a competitive price for xlon. (As we shall see presently, the two fabrics would be put in the same market.) The same could be true at lower levels of substitution. Perhaps only 50 percent of xlon customers would shift in response to a 1¢ price increase, but that shift might suffice to make the price increase unprofitable.[20]

---

20. That some portion of the defendant's customers have no alternative and would pay $5 a unit would not give the defendant market power if it could not profitably cut back its production to satisfy only them. One might wonder why the defendant ever expanded output to the point where it earned only competitive returns rather than confining itself to earning monopoly profits at a lower level of output. Perhaps economies of scale in production entail very high unit costs at the lower level of production. Or perhaps it was only large scale production, promotion, and distribution that created the loyalty of the $5 customers. Or perhaps only by selling millions of units throughout the country was it possible to reach the few thousand who would pay dearly. (Of course, if the defendant could somehow identify those buyers and prevent them from buying from other customers, it could charge them $5 and would enjoy market power in that segment of its business. See ¶285a.)

Suppose now that the competitive price would again be $1, that the current price of xlon is $2, and again that a 1¢ price increase would cause most customers to shift to ylon. Although a tiny price increase causes a massive shift to ylon, it is obvious that the ylon alternative has not protected consumers from substantial exploitation. That the xlon firm could not profitably raise prices *above the level it has already set* is fully consistent with substantial market power, as demonstrated by the price-cost margin of 100 percent. Indeed, it would be astonishing if significant product substitution were not already taking place. If this firm could profitably raise prices further without losing even more sales, would it not already have done so? Of course, if this price-cost information were known, there would be no need to inquire into substitutes or define markets because we already would know that price substantially exceeds the competitive level. The lesson of these two examples is that the existence of significant substitution in the event of *further* price increases or even at the *current* price does not tell us whether the defendant *already* exercises significant market power.[21]

339. Market definition, the relevant market, and market share. Let us now consider the conventional inference of market power from a share of a relevant market. The present focus will be on the inclusion or exclusion of substitute products.

(a) *The market definition concept.* A vast number of firms might have some actual or potential effect on a defendant's behavior. Many of them, however, will not have a significant effect and we attempt to exclude them from the relevant market in which we appraise a defendant's power. We try to include in the relevant market only those suppliers—of the same or related product in the same or related geographic area—whose existence significantly restrains the defendant's power. This process of inclusion and exclusion is spoken of as market definition. Once the market is defined, we measure its dollar volume of sales.[22] This is the denominator. The numerator would then be the sales volume in that market of the defendant firm (or any other firm in which we are interested). The resulting percentage is the market share of that firm. Any given sales volume for the defendant (given numerator) will necessarily

21. If we actually know the elasticity of demand (that is, the degree of buyer responsiveness at present prices) and assume that the current price is at the profit-maximizing level, we could figure out the firm's marginal cost and then compare it with price, although the marginal cost thus inferred could differ from that at competitive levels of output. See Landes & Posner, note 1, at 939-943.

22. This is the usual measure, although other measures of the relative significance of firms may be used instead—such as physical units sold, rental revenues or placements, or plant capacity.

represent a larger share of a narrower market (smaller denominator) or a smaller share of a wider market (larger denominator). Larger shares are associated with greater power.

For example, the sole producer of canoes would have 100 percent of a canoe market but, say, 1 percent of a pleasure boat market. An either-or choice might mislead the tribunal because, although other boats are hardly perfect substitutes for canoes, there is doubtless some substitution. That is, the 1 percent number ordinarily associated with insignificance may well understate the canoe firm's power, while the 100 percent number ordinarily associated with great power may well overstate that firm's power. Thus, such all-or-nothing choices often generate misleading inferences even when the market chosen is best in that it mismeasures power less than any alternative. One hundred percent may be closer to the mark than 1 percent while still overstating greatly the canoe firm's power. Perhaps the careful observer would associate the firm's power with some typical situation in which a defendant has 80 percent of the market, but articulating the basis for such intuitions or rough judgments is difficult. Notwithstanding the accepted principle that market shares must be interpreted in their context, courts tend to focus on the share yielded by a market definition and then to assume that any percentage figure means the same thing in every industry. After all, that approach is more appealing to the judge (or advocate) who can defend one choice merely as more reasonable than a specified alternative or two.[23] Of course, it would be better to reason directly from the complex underlying factors affecting the existence and magnitude of a firm's ability to price above the com-

---

23. Some courts do not even select and defend a single, best market but declare that a certain larger market can be appropriate and, simultaneously, that a smaller submarket can be. For example, recall *Aspen,* Ch. 3A. In a portion of the case not reviewed by the Supreme Court, the trial court had permitted the jury to find — to oversimplify a bit — that the relevant geographic market in which to assess the Aspen Skiing Company's monopoly power was simultaneously western ski resorts generally (because most skiers on the Aspen slopes were not local residents but came from afar) and those in the town of Aspen alone (submarket). To say, however, that the former is a relevant market is to say that the Aspen firm's prices are determined (in the relevant degree) by its competition with western resorts generally; to say that Aspen is a relevant market is to say that the Aspen firm's prices are determined (in the relevant degree) by competition with other firms in Aspen alone. Both statements cannot simultaneously be true.

Perhaps, as in our canoe example, the court felt that the defendant's share of neither alleged market implied its actual degree of power and that the smaller one was closest to the truth. But then the smaller should be chosen and the larger rejected. One might even have the intuition that a number somewhere between the two numbers has the right connotation, but that would not justify choosing the smaller and larger simultaneously and then basing an inference of monopoly power on the smaller market alone.

petitive level. At the very least, we should adjust the inferences of power drawn from shares of the least-bad market upward or downward based on our appreciation of the imperfections of that market definition (and some other factors considered below).[24]

(b) *Market share and market power.* Once we have a firm's market share, we still need to determine what it implies about the existence or magnitude of that firm's ability to charge more than a competitive price. Assume that we have chosen the best possible market in which the complications we have noted are either absent or at normal background levels.

The starting point is the lay intuition that a firm with 100 percent of a market possesses market power. It almost surely has the power to restrict output and to charge more than the perfectly competitive firm. But how much more? Five or 500 percent? Such answers, never supplied, are essential if one is to infer market power from market share.

Suppose we knew that a given defendant could price 25 percent above the competitive level. It that enough? The relevant threshold of concern might, of course, be less when judging mergers than when trying to identify a single firm monopoly or perhaps less for some types of unilateral conduct than for others. You will see that the courts have emphasized power over price without indicating how much power we should be concerned about. Indeed, most judicial pronouncements on the proof of monopoly power embody little more than a vague perception that a very large market share sufficiently approximates total control as to be fairly regarded as a monopoly.

This perception recognizes that large firms can affect the market more readily than small ones. The 10 percent defendant might try to raise market prices by cutting its output in half. But its enormous percentage reduction affects the market by only 5 percent. Not only that, but the remaining firms would have to squeeze out only a trifle more output from their plants to offset the defendant's cutback. By contrast, a 90 percent defendant cutting its output by one-third would have a large impact on market supply that the remaining firms could not offset without quadrupling their output. Inferences of market power based on a defendant's market share rest, in part, on the assumption that rivals' ability to expand is roughly proportional to their market share. Indeed, a firm is likely to be more willing and able to increase its output — by employing excess capacity or otherwise — by a few percent than by a few hundred percent. Even a firm adding new capacity is somewhat more likely to double than to quadruple it.

24. See Kaplow, note 1, at 1826-1832.

It is thus apparent that the connection between market share and market power is very loose indeed, but the judicial focus on market shares can still be justified. When direct measurement and appraisal of economic performance is not feasible or would be misleading,[25] we must rely on such surrogates as market share and other elements of industry structure to determine whether and how much power over price exists. As a practical matter, the courts will generally regard shares of 90 percent as sufficient for unilateral monopolistic exploitation and shares of 5 or even 50 percent as insufficient. But even such rules of thumb leave an enormous range of uncertainty.

(c) *Group power.* Although we are focusing here on the power of a single firm in the monopolization context, other contexts require us to assess the market power of a group of firms. For example, a joint venture or merger between two widget firms might trouble us if widgets are a relevant market and if those 2 firms have a substantial share of it. And even if their combined market share is only, say, 20 percent, tacit oligopolistic collaboration might be more of a danger if there were four other firms with 20 percent each than if there were 20 other firms with 4 percent each. Thus, we will need to define markets in many non-monopoly cases as well. In doing so, it is often helpful to imagine that all the widget producers are controlled by a hypothetical firm and then to ask whether the hypothetical firm has the power to raise prices significantly above competitive levels.[26]

340. More about product market definition. (a) *Differentiated products, different brands.* Physically similar substances are not necessarily the same product. They may be differentiated by small differences in composition, distribution channel, or advertised brand name. Even physically and functionally identical items may be differentiated if consumers, whether wisely or not, suppose them to be different. As one instance, consumers accustomed to one brand might find switching costly.[27] Such differences can be small and large simultaneously; some smokers would walk a mile for a cigarette *C* while others would quickly shift to cigarette *L* in response to a fractional price change. Although buyers of differentiated products do not respond to relative price changes as rapidly and as massively as the buyers of homogeneous products, this may understate the importance of substitution. Suppose, for example, that

---

25. See ¶337.
26. See ¶344 and the government merger guidelines.
27. See P. Klemperer, Markets with Consumer Switching Costs, 102 Q.J. Econ. 93 (1987); M. Katz & C. Shapiro, Systems Competition and Network Effects, 8 J. Econ. Persp. 93 (Spring 1994).

cigarette C periodically sells 10 million units to smokers dedicated to its brand, 40 million to those who would shift to L in response to a 2¢ change in relative prices, and 50 million to those who would shift in response to any change in relative prices. If C wishes to increase its prices even slightly, it must sacrifice half its sales. If this is not a practicable choice, then the market is not limited to C's product alone.[28]

Product differentiation, like product substitution generally, is a matter of degree. For example, Coca-Cola might be unable to raise its prices significantly above cost without losing too much business to Pepsi, while a merged Coke and Pepsi might be able to profitably charge supracompetitive prices without losing too much business to weakly advertised brands.[29] Similarly, the price of a Rolls Royce or a Mercedes is not tightly constrained by Hyundai prices, although one doubts that any single brand of automobiles is totally unconstrained. Proper market boundaries will seldom be clear.

(b) *Physically different products.* Physically different products can be good or even perfect substitutes.[30] Purchasers of photocopying machines are probably indifferent between two machines of similar speed and quality employing altogether different technologies and would not pay more for one than the other. Trucks and barges between two points would be perfect substitutes for shippers at the waterfront who are indifferent to speed but imperfect substitutes for those shippers requiring the faster service of trucks. On the other hand, products with some (or substantial) physical similarity may not be good substitutes. Wine and milk may both quench thirst and bicycles and autos may both provide transportation, but they are rather poor substitutes for each other and each tends to have relatively little impact upon the other, at least within the price ranges at which these products customarily sell. Finally, even if gin had the same thermal properties as fuel oil, the enormous price differences between them would prevent anyone from regarding gin as a substitute for oil. This is not to say that similarities in physical characteristics or use are irrelevant but rather to emphasize that one can make few confident inferences from such features alone.

28. Observe that this market definition may be misleading because it says nothing about whether current prices substantially exceed costs for C or for other cigarette producers. See ¶338b.

29. See Coca-Cola Co., 5 Trade Reg. Rep. ¶23625 (FTC 1994) (name-brand soft drinks constitute separate market because five percent price increase would cause negligible shift to unbranded soft drinks).

30. See, e.g., Allen-Myland v. IBM, 33 F.3d 194 (3d Cir. 1994), cert. denied, 115 S. Ct. 684 (1994) (software and peripherals could be in same market if consumers perceived them as substitutes).

(c) *Elasticity versus cross-elasticity.* Cross-elasticity of demand —
mentioned explicitly in some of the cases addressing market
power — refers to the rate at which consumers change their consumption of one product in response to a price change for another.
Thus, the cross-elasticity between Coke and Pepsi may be high,
while that between Coke and wine is negligible. Reliable judgments
might be based on intuition in some cases or, when sufficient data
are available, on econometric techniques. When cross-elasticity is
high, the two products should be included in the same market.

But remember that market shares tell us relatively little about a
defendant's ability to charge more than a competitive price. Cross-
elasticity might be high and yet not high enough to subject the firm
to competitive discipline. It might be low for each of a variety of
alternative products that, in the aggregate, allow enough of the
defendant's customers to turn elsewhere that it cannot profitably
raise its price above the competitive level. Thus, the defendant with
50 percent of a market that includes the only notable substitute,
albeit a strong one, may have no less power — and could have
more — than a defendant with 90 percent of a market that does not
include dozens of weak substitutes. What constrains the defendant's
price is not the cross-elasticity of any particular product but the
willingness of buyers to purchase less from the firm in response to
its price increase — including their choice to do without the product or any of its obvious substitutes. That is, what matters is the
elasticity of demand faced by the defendant — the degree to which
its sales fall (for whatever reason) as its price rises.[31] If we could
measure that, we could dispense with market definition altogether.

At the very least, this discussion suggests that market share data
should be interpreted in light of the particular circumstances of
each case. Thus, where the defendant's product has one moderately
strong substitute with no others even close, a court that included it
within the market might nevertheless infer more market power
from say, a 60 percent share than it would from the same share of a
single-product market. Similarly, a court that declined to include
dozens of weak substitutes might infer much less power from a 60
percent share than it would from the same share of a typical single-
product market.

31. This so-called market elasticity is necessarily a sum of all the cross-elasticities
for literally every other product, each weighted by its importance in overall consumption. See note 18 and Kaplow, note 1, at 1829 n.52. Although difficult to
procure, econometric evidence of market elasticity is generally more readily and
reliably obtained than particular cross-elasticities. See, e.g., Baker & Bresnahan
(1988), note 11. See also D. Scheffman & P. Spiller, Econometric Market Delineation, 17 Mgmt. & Decision Econ. 165 (1996).

341. Geographic market definition. The most immediate constraint on defendant's pricing freedom is another producer of the very same product (or a very close substitute) located at the same place. That the latter firm is 5 or 5000 miles away would not matter at all if the product is transported cheaply, without any tariff or similar burdens, and is purchased by knowledgeable buyers who do not need local salespeople, service, or repairs and who have no prejudice against remote sources. If any of these conditions are absent, however, there are barriers to interregional trade, and it will be necessary to decide which remote firms should be included in the geographic dimension of the market.[32]

To simplify the discussion, we will assume that the defendant supplies 90 percent of local demand for a product in one region and that the remaining 10 percent is important from a geographically remote region.[33] To what extent is the defendant's power over price constrained by the remote firms?

This resembles the search for the producers of another product who adequately constrain the defendant producer of a different product. But unlike the extremely uncertain degree of product substitution, the geographic inquiry may tell us exactly how much price-affecting power is involved. The defendant will have the power, if otherwise profitable, to charge at least $1 per unit over the competitive level if transport from the other area costs $1 per unit and the remote firms have no offsetting advantage in raw material, labor, power, or other costs.[34]

More often, we will observe some transportation, tariff, or intangible barriers to interregional trade but be unable to appraise their significance without looking at price movements in the two areas or actual shipment patterns. Even if no product moves between the two areas, they still constitute a single market when prices in each respond directly to price changes in the other in the same way that prices among firms within a region respond to each other.[35]

Even if they are not a single market, the imports may mean that the remote firms constrain the defendant's power. The usual ap-

32. After completing this Paragraph, consider the significance of the fact recited in *Cement Institute*, Ch. 2D, that occasionally foreign cement had been imported and sold for prices below the delivered price of domestic cement. Does this suggest that the domestic price was above the competitive level?

33. It is convenient to speak of imports even if the second area lies within the United States rather than abroad.

34. We say "at least" because the remote firms may themselves be charging more than the competitive price level.

35. Note, however, that unrelated markets may respond in similar ways to common fluctuation in costs. For example, cement costs in New York and California may each fall by 10¢ per unit in response to the same technological improvement in both areas. This would not mean that the two states are in the same market.

proach is to include at least actual imports in the local market, just as we would another local 10 percent producer. Of course, that other 10 percent share does not necessarily disprove the defendant's power. For example, the other producer, whether local or remote, may suffer higher costs and thus survive in the local market only because the defendant has already priced at monopoly levels.[36] The remote firms might constrain the defendant more than another local producer because they are able to divert a large volume of their existing production to the local market in response to the defendant's price rise; another local producer can seldom expand output so greatly or so quickly.

That potential flood of imports, diverted from remote markets, might suggest that we should include in the local market not only the actual volume of imports but the full output or capacity of the remote firms. But this may significantly understate the power of the defendant. (1) Imports may have occurred only because its price exceeds the competitive level, which would make clear that actual or future imports do not prevent supracompetitive pricing. Of course, if we know that, we don't need any market definition. (2) Increased imports may be blocked by saturated transportation or distribution facilities or, in the case of foreign sources, by legal barriers imposed by the exporting or importing country. (3) In the case of differentiated products, differences in warranties, repair availability, quality, or brand name may impede any import flood from the remote region. The imported goods already in the local market may satisfy only a confined and not very expandable niche.[37] Such complications would have to be considered before including more remote output in the local market.[38]

36. See ¶338b.

37. To take an extreme example, the imports of Mercedes hardly means that vastly more of them would be sold even if domestic producers raised their prices substantially.

38. See Areeda et al., note 1, ¶552; Landes & Posner, note 1, at 963-972 (always include remote output); Kaplow, note 1, at 1835-1843 (criticizing willingness to include foreign production based on existence of some imports). Where transport costs, tariffs, and the like are not covered by the excess of the local price over the remote price, remote suppliers must be earning less on their exports than at home and thus would not export all of their output; the amount would depend upon the relative elasticities of demand in the two areas. Landes and Posner would include remote output even here because, for all we know, the remote price may exceed production costs enough that lower returns on exports would still earn at least competitive profits. Even so, export profits are less than those on home sales and therefore their diversion cannot be taken for granted. To be sure, remote firms with excess capacity can expand their exports without loss of home sales but persistent excess capacity cannot be assumed. As is so often the case, exclusion of remote output in this instance may underweight it, while inclusion may overweight

342.   Competitors, supply substitution, and entry. (a) *Expansion by immediate competitors.*] The demand for Alpha Company's product is obviously affected by the ability of its direct competitors to deliver the same product. But if the others are to limit Alpha's actions, they must be able to expand their production when Alpha increases its prices because consumers cannot turn to other suppliers if those suppliers are unable to expand their output. If idle capacity is not instantly available to substitute for Alpha's output, expansion by the other suppliers will at least take time, and immediate expansion, when possible, may be at greater unit cost as capacity limits are approached. Thus supply responses are often limited in the short run. Long-run possibilities may be virtually unlimited, but exploitation may occur in the interim and competitors may be reluctant to build substantial additional capacity if they fear that doing so will lead Alpha to restore its output, thereby driving the price down to, or even below, the long-run competitive level. Other factors may inhibit long-run increases in capacity. For a particular industry at a particular time, the capital necessary to finance expansion may not be forthcoming. Other necessary factors of production — skilled labor, raw materials, fabricated inputs, new production sites, distribution facilities — may be in short supply. And technological factors may preclude small additions to capacity — that is, to produce an extra ton of steel efficiently may require building a plant capable of producing 1 million tons. If prospective business gains are small relative to the minimum efficient scale of productive units, the other suppliers are not likely to expand in response to Alpha's price increase. In short, alternative suppliers will not necessarily restrain defendant's power significantly.

This is yet another respect in which market definition does not fully indicate market power. Although no court would exclude local producers of the identical product from the market, those producers will not constrain the defendant if they cannot expand. On the other hand, where massive expansion by smaller firms is feasible, even a very large firm will lack power over price.

(b) *Supply substitution.* Buyers may be able to turn to alternative suppliers not now producing the product in question. Existing firms in related lines might be able to produce defendant's product easily. Consider chemicals Y and Z, which are purchased by different buyers for entirely different uses; Y and Z are not interchangeable in use. Suppose that Chemco can produce and distribute chemicals Y and Z in any proportion simply by adding readily available ingredients to its existing processes and that Chemco has

it. Whichever course one takes, one should adjust inferences about the defendant's market power accordingly.

unused capacity. Even if it does not now produce Z, it limits the power of Z producers in the same way that another Z producer would.

(c) *Entry*. Similar to expansion by existing or related producers, but less immediate or certain, is entry by new firms. If buyers, after a time lag, can turn to suppliers not yet in existence, such potential competition restrains defendant. *P* may be the only pen producer at the moment, but it may have to forgo monopoly profits and content itself with a normal profit if a greater return would attract new firms into the pen business.

The strength of potential competition depends on the height of the barriers to entry, as discussed in ¶114. A plant of minimum efficient scale may add more capacity than the market can absorb or be so large as to discourage investors or lenders, and less than optimum scale may involve a significant cost disadvantage. The technology of the industry may demand patents, know-how, or technical skills that are not readily available. It may be difficult to obtain the requisite personnel, machinery, sites, raw materials, or other supplies. Distributors may be too committed to existing producers to undertake a new line. A generation of advertising may have created such overwhelming consumer attachment to existing brands as to preclude new entry except at prohibitive promotional costs. If these barriers to new entry are not great, potential competition can be a significant restraining force.

343. Summary of market power: unavoidable approximations. It cannot be emphasized too strongly that market definition and the defendant's market share give, at best, only a suggestion of defendant's market power. The boundaries of any product and geographic market are necessarily imprecise. The universe of existing producers, however broadly defined, cannot account for ease of entry by other firms. Nor do market shares speak of relative production costs, the expansion potential of other firms, their independence or dynamism, scope and direction of market changes, buyer power, or nonmarket forces. In addition, market power is intrinsically a matter of degree, which is often lost sight of by a process of market definition that either wholly includes or excludes substitutes at the initial stages of the assessment. But even if such problems are overcome, the power implications of any particular market share remain obscure. The courts have not stated how much power they believe to be associated with given market shares. Nor have they indicated how much power must be established as a prerequisite to a finding of liability. Market definition is customary and may provide a helpful first approximation but one should have no illusions about its meaning.

Imperfections in market definition coupled with the uncertain connections between the market shares we see and the market power we hope to infer might lead us to reexamine economic performance or conduct as direct indicators of a firm's power to charge supracompetitive prices. As we saw in ¶337b, antitrust courts and commentators have often felt overwhelmed by the many difficulties of measuring the excess of a firm's price over marginal cost or the excess of profits over competitive returns.[39] But would such measures be less reliable than inferences based on market definition and shares? That question should be considered as we work through the market power issues in this chapter and the remainder of the book. Now that we have seen the nature and difficulty of measuring market power, we should once again ask why, whether, and when antitrust law should insist on it.

This discussion hardly suggests that courts and litigants must construct demand and supply functions that would satisfy a rigorous economist. The fact is that decisions must be made even when available data are inconclusive. It is important, however, that we be sensitive to the inadequacies of the decisionmaking materials. To rely on crude approximations may not be ideal, but it is inevitable. Inadequate time, human frailty, and complexity force us to use rough estimates. What is unforgivable is to forget the crudity of such factfinding.

Finally, courts sometimes seem reluctant to find significant market power where the defendant's behavior creating such power appears commendable. But one must remember that market power does not itself create liability; it is, at most, a threshold requirement that must be satisfied before liability can be imposed. In some instances, society chooses to encourage invention by rewarding it with a patent that temporarily prevents competition. Similarly, we may promote superior skill, foresight, and industry by leaving undisturbed the power that results.

344. Market definition and measurement under 1992 government merger guidelines. In 1992, the Justice Department and Federal Trade Commission jointly promulgated new guidelines stating their enforcement intentions with respect to horizontal mergers which, like monopolization cases, require an appraisal of market

---

39. Refined measures of variable cost have been given a central role as surrogates for marginal cost in determining the existence of predation. Whether the errors in such measurements or possible divergences between variable cost and marginal cost make a similar approach substantially less reliable in the market power context, particularly in comparison to the alternatives, is difficult to determine a priori.

power. The market definition problem is not always identical for monopolization and merger purposes. In particular, monopolization cases ask whether the defendant already possesses market power, whereas merger cases ask in addition whether combining two firms will newly create market power or greater opportunities for express or tacit coordination that did not previously exist.[40] Nevertheless, many of the topics pursued in the merger guidelines illuminate the market definition process generally and therefore merit examination here.[41]

DEPARTMENT OF JUSTICE AND FEDERAL TRADE COMMISSION HORIZONTAL MERGER GUIDELINES
April 2, 1992

1. MARKET DEFINITION, MEASUREMENT AND CONCENTRATION

1.0 OVERVIEW

... A market is defined as a product or group of products and a geographic area in which it is produced or sold such that a hypothetical profit-maximizing firm, not subject to price regulation, that was the only present and future producer or seller of those products in that area likely would impose at least a "small but significant and nontransitory" increase in price, assuming the terms of sale of all other products are held constant. A relevant market is a group of products and a geographic area that is no bigger than necessary to satisfy this test. ... A firm is viewed as a participant if, in response to a "small but significant and nontransitory" price increase, it likely would enter rapidly into production or sale of a market product in the market's area, without incurring significant sunk costs of entry and exit. ...

1.1 PRODUCT MARKET DEFINITION ...

[T]he Agency[42] will begin with each product (narrowly defined) produced or sold by each merging firm and ask what would happen

40. See Chs. 2C, 5D.
41. See Ch. 5D for portions outlining the government's analysis of horizontal mergers.
42. The "Agency" refers to the Department of Justice and Federal Trade Commission. — eds.

if a hypothetical monopolist of that product imposed at least a "small but significant and nontransitory" increase in price, but the terms of sale of all other products remained constant. If, in response to the price increase, the reduction in sales of the product would be large enough that a hypothetical monopolist would not find it profitable to impose such an increase in price, then the Agency will add to the product group the product that is the next-best substitute for the merging firm's product.

In considering the likely reaction of buyers to a price increase, the Agency will take into account all relevant evidence, including, but not limited to, the following:

(1) evidence that buyers have shifted or have considered shifting purchases between products in response to relative changes in price or other competitive variables;
(2) evidence that sellers base business decisions on the prospect of buyer substitution between products in response to relative changes in price or other competitive variables;
(3) influence of downstream competition faced by buyers in their output markets; and
(4) the timing and costs of switching products.

The price increase question is then asked for a hypothetical monopolist controlling the expanded product group. In performing successive iterations of the price increase test, the hypothetical monopolist will be assumed to pursue maximum profits in deciding whether to raise the prices of any or all of the additional products under its control. This process will continue until a group of products is identified such that a hypothetical monopolist over that group of products would profitably impose at least a "small but significant and nontransitory" increase, including the price of a product of one of the merging firms. The Agency generally will consider the relevant product market to be the smallest group of products that satisfies this test.

In the above analysis, the Agency will use prevailing prices of the products of the merging firms and possible substitutes for such products, unless premerger circumstances are strongly suggestive of coordinated interaction, in which case the Agency will use a price more reflective of the competitive price....

In attempting to determine objectively the effect of a "small but significant and nontransitory" increase in price, the Agency, in most contexts, will use a price increase of five percent lasting for the foreseeable future. However, what constitutes a "small but significant and nontransitory" increase in price will depend on the nature of the industry, and the Agency at times may use a price increase that is larger or smaller than five percent.[43]

1.2 GEOGRAPHIC MARKET DEFINITION . . .

In defining the geographic market or markets affected by a merger, the Agency will begin with the location of each merging firm (or each plant of a multiplant firm) and ask what would happen if a hypothetical monopolist of the relevant product at that point imposed at least a "small but significant and nontransitory" increase in price, but the terms of sale at all other locations remained constant. If, in response to the price increase, the reduction in sales of the product at that location would be large enough that a hypothetical monopolist producing or selling the relevant product at the merging firm's location would not find it profitable to impose such an increase in price, then the Agency will add the location from which production is the next-best substitute for production at the merging firm's location. [The section 1.1 factors and approach are repeated here.]

1.3 IDENTIFICATION OF FIRMS THAT PARTICIPATE IN THE RELEVANT MARKET

1.31 Current Producers or Sellers. The Agency's identification of firms that participate in the relevant market begins with all firms that currently produce or sell in the relevant market. This includes vertically integrated firms to the extent that such inclusion accurately reflects their competitive significance in the relevant market prior to the merger. To the extent that the analysis under Section 1.1 indicates that used, reconditioned or recycled goods are included in the relevant market, market participants will include firms that produce or sell such goods and that likely would offer those goods in competition with other relevant products.

1.32 Firms That Participate Through Supply Response. In addition, the Agency will identify other firms not currently producing or selling the relevant product in the relevant area as participating in the relevant market if their inclusion would more accurately reflect probable supply responses. These firms are termed "uncommitted

43. The Guidelines also contain a discussion of product market definition in the presence of price discrimination, indicating that if a hypothetical monopolist can successfully target a group of buyers, the Agency will consider additional relevant products markets consisting of particular uses by groups of buyers who can successfully be targeted for a price increase. — eds.

entrants." These supply responses must be likely to occur within one year and without the expenditure of significant sunk costs of entry and exit, in response to a "small but significant and nontransitory" price increase. If a firm has the technological capability to achieve such an uncommitted supply response, but likely would not (e.g., because difficulties in achieving product acceptance, distribution, or production would render such a response unprofitable), that firm will not be considered to be a market participant. The competitive significance of supply responses that require more time or that require firms to incur significant sunk costs of entry and exit will be considered in entry analysis. . . .

If a firm has existing assets that likely would be shifted or extended into production and sale of the relevant product within one year, and without incurring significant sunk costs of entry and exit, in response to a "small but significant and nontransitory" increase in price for only the relevant product, the Agency will treat that firm as a market participant. In assessing whether a firm is such a market participant, the Agency will take into account the costs of substitution or extension relative to the profitability of sales at the elevated price, and whether the firm's capacity is elsewhere committed or elsewhere so profitably employed that such capacity likely would not be available to respond to an increase in price in the market. . . .

If new firms, or existing firms without closely related products or productive assets, likely would enter into production or sale in the relevant market within one year without the expenditure of significant sunk costs of entry and exit, the Agency will treat those firms as market participants.

1.4 CALCULATING MARKET SHARES

1.41 General Approach. The Agency normally will calculate market shares for all firms (or plants) identified as market participants in Section 1.3 based on the total sales or capacity currently devoted to the relevant market together with that which likely would be devoted to the relevant market in response to a "small but significant and nontransitory" price increase. Market shares can be expressed either in dollar terms through measurement of sales, shipments, or production, or in physical terms through measurement of sales, shipments, production, capacity, or reserves.

Market shares will be calculated using the best indicator of firms' future competitive significance. Dollar sales or shipments generally will be used if firms are distinguished primarily by differentiation of their products. Unit sales generally will be used if firms are distinguished primarily on the basis of their relative advantages in serving different buyers or groups of buyers. Physical capacity or reserves generally will be used if it is these measures that most effectively distinguish firms. Typically, annual data are used, but where individual sales are large and infrequent so that annual data may be unrepresentative, the Agency may measure market shares over a longer period of time.

In measuring a firm's market share, the Agency will not include its sales or capacity to the extent that the firm's capacity is committed or so profitably employed outside the relevant market that it would not be available to respond to an increase in price in the market. . . .

1.43   Special Factors Affecting Foreign Firms.   Market shares will be assigned to foreign competitors in the same way in which they are assigned to domestic competitors. However, if exchange rates fluctuate significantly, so that comparable dollar calculations on an annual basis may be unrepresentative, the Agency may measure market shares over a period longer than one year.

If shipments from a particular country to the United States are subject to a quota, the market shares assigned to firms in that country will not exceed the amount of shipments by such firms allowed under the quota. In the case of restraints that limit imports to some percentage of the total amount of the product sold in the United States (i.e., percentage quotas), a domestic price increase that reduced domestic consumption also would reduce the volume of imports into the United States. Accordingly, actual import sales and capacity data will be reduced for purposes of calculating market shares. Finally, a single market share may be assigned to a country or group of countries if firms in that country or group of countries act in coordination. . . .

UNITED STATES v. ALUMINUM CO.
OF AMERICA (ALCOA)
148 F.2d 416 (2d Cir. 1945)

Before L. HAND, SWAN, and A. HAND, Circuit Judges.
L. HAND, Circuit Judge. [The facts and discussion of liability are set forth in the excerpts in Chapter 3A.]

[B]

From 1902 onward until 1928 "Alcoa" was making ingot in Canada through a wholly owned subsidiary; so much of this as it imported into the United States it is proper to include with what it produced here. In the year 1912 the sum of these two items represented nearly ninety-one per cent of the total amount of "virgin" ingot available for sale in this country. This percentage varied year by year up to and including 1938: in 1913 it was about seventy-two per cent; in 1921 about sixty-eight per cent; in 1922 about seventy-two per cent; with these exceptions it was always over eighty per cent of the total and for the last five years 1934-1938 inclusive it averaged over ninety per cent. . . .

There are various ways of computing "Alcoa's" control of the aluminum market — as distinct from its production — depending upon what one regards as competing in that market. The judge figured its share — during the years 1929-1938, inclusive — as only about thirty-three per cent; to do so he included "secondary," and excluded that part of "Alcoa's" own production which it fabricated and did not therefore sell as ingot. If, on the other hand, "Alcoa's" total production, fabricated and sold, be included, and balanced against the sum of imported "virgin" and "secondary," its share of the market was in the neighborhood of sixty-four per cent for that period. The percentage we have already mentioned — over ninety — results only if we both include all "Alcoa's" production and exclude "secondary." That percentage is enough to constitute a monopoly; it is doubtful whether sixty or sixty-four per cent would be enough; and certainly thirty-three per cent is not. Hence it is necessary to settle what we shall treat as competing in the ingot market. That part of its production which "Alcoa" itself fabricates, does not of course ever reach the market as ingot; and we recognize that it is only when a restriction of production either inevitably affects prices, or is intended to do so, that it violates §1 of the Act. . . . However, even though we were to assume that a monopoly is unlawful under §2 only in case it controls prices, the ingot fabricated by "Alcoa," necessarily had a direct effect upon the ingot market. All ingot — with trifling exceptions — is used to fabricate intermediate, or end, products; and therefore all intermediate, or end, products which "Alcoa" fabricates and sells, pro tanto reduce the demand for ingot itself. . . . We cannot therefore agree that the computation of the percentage of "Alcoa's" control over the ingot market should not include the whole of its ingot production.

As to "secondary," . . . for certain purposes the industry will not accept it at all; but for those for which it will, the difference in price is ordinarily not very great; the judge found that it was between one and two cents a pound, hardly enough margin on which to base a monopoly. Indeed, there are times when all differential disappears, and "secondary" will actually sell at a higher price: i.e. when there is a supply available which contains just the alloy that a fabricator needs for the article which he proposes to make. Taking the industry as a whole, we can say nothing more definite than that, although "secondary" does not compete at all in some uses, (whether because of "sales resistance" only, or because of actual metallurgical inferiority), for most purposes it competes upon a substantial equality with "virgin." On these facts the judge found that "every pound of secondary or scrap aluminum which is sold in commerce displaces a pound of virgin aluminum which otherwise would, or might have been, sold." We agree: so far as "secondary" supplies the demand of such fabricators as will accept it, it increases the amount of "virgin" which must seek sale elsewhere; and it therefore results that the supply of that part of the demand which will accept only "virgin" becomes greater in proportion as "secondary" drives away "virgin" from the demand which will accept "secondary." (This is indeed the same argument which we used a moment ago to include in the supply that part of "virgin" which "Alcoa" fabricates; it is not apparent to us why the judge did not think it applicable to that item as well.) At any given moment therefore "secondary" competes with "virgin" in the ingot market; further, it can, and probably does, set a limit or "ceiling" beyond which the price of "virgin" cannot go, for the cost of its production will in the end depend only upon the expense of scavenging and reconditioning. It might seem for this reason that in estimating "Alcoa's" control over the ingot market, we ought to include the supply of "secondary," as the judge did. Indeed, it may be thought a paradox to say that anyone has the monopoly of a market in which at all times he must meet a competition that limits his price. We shall show that it is not.

In the case of a monopoly of any commodity which does not disappear in use and which can be salvaged, the supply seeking sale at any moment will be made up of two components: (1) the part which the putative monopolist can immediately produce and sell; and (2) the part which has been, or can be, reclaimed out of what he has produced and sold in the past. By hypothesis he presently controls the first of these components; the second he has controlled in the past, although he no longer does. During the period when he did control the second, if he was aware of his interest, he was guided, not alone by its effect at that time upon the market, but by his knowledge that some part of it was likely to be reclaimed and seek the future market. That consideration will to some extent always affect his production until he decides to abandon the business, or for some other reason ceases to be concerned with the future market. Thus, in the case at bar "Alcoa" always knew that the future supply of ingot would be made up in part of what it produced at the time, and, if it was as far-sighted as it proclaims itself, that consideration must have had its share in determining how much to produce. How accurately it could forecast the effect of present production upon the future market is another matter. Experience, no doubt, would help; but it makes no difference that it had to guess; it is enough that it had an inducement to make the best guess it could, and that it would regulate that part of the future supply, so far as it should turn out to have guessed right. The competition of "secondary" must therefore be disregarded, as soon as we consider the position of "Alcoa" over a period of years; it was as much within "Alcoa's" control as was the production of the "virgin" from which it had been derived.... [C]onsider the situation of the owner of the only supply of some raw material like iron ore. Scrap iron is a constant factor in the iron market; it is scavenged, remelted into pig, and sold in competition with newly smelted pig; an owner of the sole supply of ore must always face that competition and it will serve to put a "ceiling" upon his price, so far as there is enough of it. Nevertheless, no one would say that, even during the period while the pig which he has sold in the past can so return to the market, he does not have a natural monopoly. . . .

We conclude therefore that "Alcoa's" control over the ingot market must be reckoned at over ninety per cent; that being the proportion which its production bears to imported "virgin" ingot. If the fraction which it did not supply were the produce of domestic manufacture there could be no doubt that this percentage gave it a monopoly — lawful or unlawful, as the case might be. The producer of so large a proportion of the supply has complete control within certain limits. It is true that, if by raising the price he reduces the amount which can be marketed — as always, or almost always, happens — he may invite the expansion of the small producers who will try to fill the place left open; nevertheless, not only is there an inevitable lag in this, but the large producer is in a strong position to check such competition; and, indeed, if he has retained his old plant and personnel, he can inevitably do so. There are indeed limits to his power; substitutes are available for almost all commodities, and to raise the price enough is to evoke them. . . . Moreover, it is difficult and expensive to keep idle any part of a plant or of personnel; and any drastic contraction of the market will offer increasing temptation to the small producers to expand. But these limitations also exist when a single producer occupies the whole market: even then, his hold will depend upon his moderation in exerting his immediate power.

The case at bar is however different, because, for aught that appears there may well have been a practically unlimited supply of imports as the price of ingot rose. Assuming that there was no agreement between "Alcoa" and foreign producers not to import, they sold what could bear the handicap of the tariff and the cost of transportation. For the period of eighteen years — 1920-1937 — they sold at times a little above "Alcoa's" prices, at times a little under; but there was substantially no gross difference between what they received and what they would have received, had they sold uniformly at "Alcoa's" prices. While the record is silent, we may therefore assume — the plaintiff having the burden — that, had "Alcoa" raised its prices, more ingot would have been imported. Thus there is a distinction between domestic and foreign competition: the first is limited in quantity, and can increase only by an increase in plant and personnel; the second is of producers who, we must assume, produce much more than they import, and whom a rise in price will presumably induce immediately to divert to the American market what they have been selling elsewhere. It is entirely consistent with the evidence that it was the threat of greater foreign imports which kept "Alcoa's" prices where they were, and prevented it from exploiting its advantage as sole domestic producer; indeed, it is hard to resist the conclusion that potential imports did put a "ceiling" upon those prices. Nevertheless, within the limits afforded by the tariff and the cost of transportation, "Alcoa" was free to raise its prices as it chose, since it was free from domestic competition, save as it drew other metals into the market as substitutes. Was this a monopoly within the meaning of §2? The judge found that, over the whole half century of its existence, "Alcoa's" profits upon capital invested, after payment of income taxes, had been only about ten per cent, and, although the plaintiff puts this figure a little higher, the difference is negligible.... [I]t would be hard to say that "Alcoa" had made exorbitant profits on ingot, if it is proper to allocate the profit upon the whole business proportionately among all its products — ingot, and fabrications from ingot. A profit of ten per cent in such an industry, dependent, in part at any rate, upon continued tariff protection, and subject to the vicissitudes of new demands, to the obsolescence of plant and process — which can never be accurately gauged in advance — to the chance that substitutes may at any moment be discovered which will reduce the demand, and to the other hazards which attend all industry; a profit of ten per cent, so conditioned, could hardly be considered extortionate. [The next section of the opinion, reproduced in Chapter 3A, addresses whether modest profit levels constitute an excuse.]

582   *Monopoly Power*   ¶344

345.[44] (a) What is the effect on Alcoa's market share of including within the market that ingot that Alcoa produced, consumed internally, and sold in form of fabricated products? Does consistency require that the ingot content of imported fabrications also be included?

(b) In *Alcoa,* why did Judge Hand treat secondary aluminum as he did in determining Alcoa's market share? Do you agree with his reasons? Does the existence of scrap reduce Alcoa's present market power? To the same degree that an equivalent amount of new production by another producer would? Why or why not?[45]

(c) In *Alcoa,* Judge Hand said that a firm with 90 percent of the market would clearly have monopoly power if the remaining 10 percent were produced domestically. (1) In what respects is this statement sound or unsound? (2) In what respects might it be said that 10 percent occupancy of the market by imports limits Alcoa's power less than a 10 percent domestic producer would? (3) In what respects might it be said that 10 percent occupancy of the market by imports limits Alcoa more than a 10 percent domestic producer would?

(d) Do you agree with Judge Hand's treatment of imports? To facilitate your analysis, suppose the following simplified facts: that Alcoa's price averages about 20¢ per pound; that United States import taxes and transportation and handling charges from European mills average about 1¢ per pound; that annual imports provide about 10 percent of the United States's supply of virgin aluminum; and that Alcoa's profit is about 0.25¢ per pound and that this amounts to a 10 percent return on Alcoa's net investment. On these assumptions, does Alcoa possess monopoly power? In particular: (1) What did the court assume about the responsiveness of foreign suppliers to price changes within the United States?

---

44. A tabular view of approximate Alcoa percentage shares of the three possible markets discussed by Judge Hand follows. (* indicates not applicable.)

	Market		
	A	*B*	*C*
Alcoa virgin aluminum production	90	64	*
Alcoa virgin aluminum sales	*	*	33
Secondary aluminum sales	*	29	54
Imports	10	7	13
	100	100	100

45. Although not mentioned in Hand's analysis, earlier in the opinion he noted that a portion of the scrap was not recycled aluminum but rather was the remaining portion of new sheets from which patterns had been cut out. Is this relevant?

(2) Does the court's assumption imply that Alcoa lacks market power? Why or why not?[46]

(e) Were Alcoa's profits excessive? (1) Do we know? (2) If Alcoa's profits could be found to be reasonable, should this be a defense? (3) Whether or not low profits should be a defense to unlawful monopolization, might small profits imply that defendant's market power is small, or large profits imply that defendant's market power is large?

346. (a) Which of the following statements is true? What does each imply as to Alcoa's power? What are the legal implications of each? (1) Alcoa produces 90 percent of the virgin aluminum used within the United States. (2) Alcoa produces 64 percent of the aluminum (virgin and secondary) used within the United States. (3) Alcoa sells 33 percent of the raw aluminum (virgin and secondary) sold within the United States.

(b) Consider Judge Hand's now famous proclamation that 90 percent "is enough to constitute a monopoly"; 60 or 64 percent "is doubtful"; and 33 percent "certainly . . . is not" enough. Was he stating (1) how much market power is implied by a given market share or (2) how much market power is necessary for liability? Are these two questions different?

(c) Does he mean that a 90 percent share is always enough and that 33 percent is always insufficient? Does he rest on an underlying economic analysis or on a semantic definition of monopolization in Sherman Act §2? If the former, what data did he offer? What information and policy judgments are required to justify such a pronouncement?

UNITED STATES v. E.I. du PONT De
NEMOURS & CO. (CELLOPHANE)
351 U.S. 377 (1956)

Justice REED. [The government's appeal attacks the ruling that du Pont has not monopolized trade in cellophane, thereby violating Sherman Act §2. During the relevant period, du Pont produced almost 75 percent of cellophane sold in the United States, but cellophane constituted less than 20 percent of all flexible packaging material sales. The lower court found the latter to be the relevant

---

46. Would the United States automobile companies constitute a monopoly if they merged into one firm? (If not, should such a merger be permitted? See Ch. 5D on horizontal mergers.)

market and that competition from these other materials prevented du Pont from possessing monopoly power].

The ultimate consideration in such a determination is whether the defendants control the price and competition in the market for such part of trade or commerce as they are charged with monopolizing. Every manufacturer is the sole producer of the particular commodity it makes but its control in the above sense of the relevant market depends upon the availability of alternative commodities for buyers: i.e., whether there is a cross-elasticity of demand between cellophane and the other wrappings. This interchangeability is largely gauged by the purchase of competing products for similar uses considering the price, characteristics and adaptability of the competing commodities. . . .

Since the Government specifically excludes attempts and conspiracies to monopolize from consideration, a conclusion that du Pont has no monopoly power would obviate examination of [the lower court's findings that du Pont's acquisition of any such power was protected by patents and that any such power was acquired solely through du Pont's business expertise].

I. FACTUAL BACKGROUND

[du Pont's position originates with patent licensing agreements under which it obtained exclusive rights to operate in North and Central America. In 1930, Sylvania, a U.S. affiliate of a foreign producer not covered by these license agreements, began manufacturing in the United States. Since 1934, it has produced 25 percent of cellophane in the United States. Patent right negotiations resulted in du Pont licensing Sylvania in exchange for royalties and an effective limitation on Sylvania's production — a limitation dropped in 1945.]

Between 1928 and 1950, du Pont's sales of plain cellophane increased from $3,131,608 to $9,330,776. Moistureproof sales increased from $603,222 to $89,850,416, although prices were continuously reduced. It could not be said that this immense increase in use was solely or even largely attributable to the superior quality of cellophane or to the technique or business acumen of du Pont, though doubtless those factors were important. The growth was a part of the expansion of the commodity-packaging habits of business, a by-product of general efficient competitive merchandising to meet modern demands. The profits, which were large, apparently arose from this trend in marketing, the development of the industrial use of chemical research and production of synthetics, rather than from elimination of other producers from the relevant market. . . .

III. THE SHERMAN ACT, §2 — MONOPOLIZATION . . .

If cellophane is the "market" that du Pont is found to dominate, it may be assumed it does have monopoly power over that "market." Monopoly power is the power to control prices or exclude competition. It seems apparent that du Pont's power to set the price of cellophane has been limited only by the competition afforded by other flexible packaging materials. Moreover, it may be practically impossible for anyone to commence manufacturing cellophane without full access to du Pont's technique. However, du Pont has no power to prevent competition from other wrapping materials. The trial Court consequently had to determine whether competition from the other wrappings prevented du Pont from possessing monopoly power in violation of §2. Price and competition are so intimately entwined that any discussion of theory must treat them as one. It is inconceivable that price could be controlled without power over competition or vice versa. This approach to the determination of monopoly power is strengthened by this Court's conclusion in prior cases that, when an alleged monopolist has power over price and competition, an intention to monopolize in a proper case may be assumed.

If a large number of buyers and sellers deal freely in a standardized product, such as salt or wheat, we have complete or pure competition. Patents, on the other hand, furnish the most familiar type of classic monopoly. As the producers of a standardized product bring about significant differentiations of quality, design, or packaging in the product that permit differences of use, competition becomes to a greater or less degree incomplete and the producer's power over price and competition greater over his article and its use, according to the differentiation he is able to create and maintain. A retail seller may have in one sense a monopoly on certain trade because of location, as an isolated country store or filling station, or because no one else makes a product of just the quality or attractiveness of his product, as for example in cigarettes. Thus one can theorize that we have monopolistic competition in every nonstandardized commodity with each manufacturer having power over the price and production of his own product. However, this power that, let us say, automobile or soft-drink manufacturers have over their trademarked products is not the power that makes an illegal monopoly. Illegal power must be appraised in terms of the competitive market for the product.

Determination of the competitive market for commodities depends on how different from one another are the offered commodities in character or use, how far buyers will go to substitute one commodity for another. For example, one can think of building materials as in commodity competition but one could hardly say that brick competed with steel or wood or cement or stone in the meaning of Sherman Act litigation; the products are too different. This is the interindustry competition emphasized by some economists. . . . On the other hand, there are certain differences in the formulae for soft drinks but one can hardly say that each one is an illegal monopoly. Whatever the market may be, we hold that control of price or competition establishes the existence of monopoly power under §2. Section 2 requires the application of a reasonable approach in determining the existence of monopoly power just as surely as did §1. This of course does not mean that there can be a reasonable monopoly. Our next step is to determine whether du Pont has monopoly power over cellophane, that is, power over its price in relation to or competition with other commodities. The charge was monopolization of cellophane. The defense, that cellophane was merely a part of the relevant market for flexible packaging materials.

IV. THE RELEVANT MARKET

When a product is controlled by one interest, without substitutes available in the market, there is monopoly power. Because most products have possible substitutes, we cannot . . . give "that infinite range" to the definition of substitutes. Nor is it a proper interpretation of the Sherman Act to require that products be fungible to be considered in the relevant market.

The Government argues:

> We do not here urge that in *no* circumstances may competition of substitutes negative possession of monopolistic power over trade in a product. The decisions make it clear at the least that the courts will not consider substitutes other than those which are substantially fungible with the monopolized product and sell at substantially the same price.

But where there are market alternatives that buyers may readily use for their purposes, illegal monopoly does not exist merely because the product said to be monopolized differs from others. If it were not so, only physically identical products would be a part of the market. To accept the Government's argument, we would have to conclude that the manufacturers of plain as well as moisture-proof cellophane were monopolists, and so with films such as Pliofilm, foil, glassine, polyethylene, and Saran, for each of these wrapping materials is distinguishable. These were all exhibits in the case. New wrappings appear, generally similar to cellophane: is each a monopoly? What is called for is an appraisal of the "cross-elasticity" of demand in the trade.... In considering what is the relevant market for determining the control of price and competition, no more definite rule can be declared than that commodities reasonably interchangeable by consumers for the same purposes make up that "part of the trade or commerce," monopolization of which may be illegal. As respects flexible packaging materials, the market geographically is nationwide.

Industrial activities cannot be confined to trim categories. Illegal monopolies under §2 may well exist over limited products in narrow fields where competition is eliminated.[23] That does not settle the issue here. In determining the market under the Sherman Act, it is the use or uses to which the commodity is put that control. The selling price between commodities with similar uses and different characteristics may vary, so that the cheaper product can drive out the more expensive. Or, the superior quality of higher priced articles may make dominant the more desirable. Cellophane costs more than many competing products and less than a few. But whatever the price, there are various flexible wrapping materials that are bought by manufacturers for packaging their goods in their own plants or are sold to converters who shape and print them for use in the packaging of the commodities to be wrapped.

Cellophane differs from other flexible packaging materials. From some it differs more than from others. The basic materials from which the wrappings are made ... are aluminum, cellulose acetate, chlorides, wood pulp, rubber hydrochloride, and ethylene gas....

It may be admitted that cellophane combines the desirable elements of transparency, strength and cheapness more definitely than any of the others. Comparative characteristics have been noted thus:

> Moistureproof cellophane is highly transparent, tears readily but has high bursting strength, is highly impervious to moisture and gases, and is resistant to grease and oils. Heat sealable, printable, and adapted to use on wrapping machines, it makes an excellent packaging material for both display and protection of commodities.
>
> Other flexible wrapping materials fall into four major categories: (1) opaque nonmoistureproof wrapping *paper* designed primarily for convenience and protection in handling packages; (2) moistureproof *films* of varying degrees of transparency designed primarily either to protect, or to display and protect, the products they encompass; (3) nonmoistureproof transparent *films* designed primarily to display and to some extent protect, but which obviously do a poor protecting job where exclusion or retention of moisture is important; and (4) moistureproof *materials* other than films of varying

---

23. [The Court's footnote is reproduced in Ch. 3C, n.9.]

degrees of transparency (foils and paper products) designed to protect and display.[26] . . .

But, despite cellophane's advantages it has to meet competition
from other materials in every one of its uses. . . . Food products are
the chief outlet, with cigarettes next. The Government makes no
challenge to Finding 283 that cellophane furnishes less than 7% of
wrappings for bakery products, 25% for candy, 32% for snacks, 35%
for meats and poultry, 27% for crackers and biscuits, 47% for fresh
produce, and 34% for frozen foods. Seventy-five to eighty percent
of cigarettes are wrapped in cellophane. Thus, cellophane shares
the packaging market with others. The over-all result is that cellophane accounts for 17.9% of flexible wrapping materials, measured
by the wrapping surface.

Moreover a very considerable degree of functional interchangeability exists between these products. . . . It will be noted that except
as to permeability to gases, cellophane has no qualities that are not
possessed by a number of other materials. Meat will do as an example of interchangeability. Although du Pont's sales to the meat
industry have reached 19,000,000 pounds annually, nearly 35%, this
volume is attributed "to the rise of self-service retailing of fresh
meat." In fact, since the popularity of self-service meats, du Pont
has lost "a considerable proportion" of this packaging business to
Pliofilm. Pliofirm is more expensive than cellophane, but its superior physical characteristics apparently offset cellophane's price advantage. While retailers shift continually between the two, the trial
court found that Pliofilm is increasing its share of the business. One
further example is worth noting. Before World War II, du Pont
cellophane wrapped between 5 and 10% of baked and smoked
meats. The peak year was 1933. Thereafter du Pont was unable to
meet the competition of Sylvania and of greaseproof paper. Its sales
declined and the 1933 volume was not reached again until 1947. It
will be noted that greaseproof paper, glassine, waxed paper, foil
and Pliofilm are used as well as cellophane. Findings 209-210 show
the competition and 215-216 the advantages that have caused the
more expensive Pliofilm to increase its proportion of the business.

An element for consideration as to cross-elasticity of demand
between products is the responsiveness of the sales of one product
to price changes of the other. If a slight decrease in the price of
cellophane causes a considerable number of customers of other
flexible wrappings to switch to cellophane, it would be an indication that a high cross-elasticity of demand exists between them; that
the products compete in the same market. The court below held

26. Stocking and Mueller, The Cellophane Case, 45 Amer. Econ. Rev. 29, 48-49.

that the "[g]reat sensitivity of customers in the flexible packaging markets to price or quality changes" prevented du Pont from possessing monopoly control over price. The record sustains these findings.

We conclude that cellophane's interchangeability with the other materials mentioned suffices to make it a part of this flexible packaging material market.

The Government stresses the fact that the variation in price between cellophane and other materials demonstrates they are noncompetitive. As these products are all flexible wrapping materials, it seems reasonable to consider, as was done at the trial, their comparative cost to the consumer in terms of square area.... Findings as to price competition are set out in the margin.[29] Cellophane costs two or three times as much, surface measure, as its chief competitors for the flexible wrapping market, glassine and greaseproof papers. Other forms of cellulose wrappings and those from other chemical or mineral substances, with the exception of aluminum foil, are more expensive. The uses of these materials ... are largely to wrap small packages for retail distribution. The wrapping is a relatively small proportion of the entire cost of the article. Different producers need different qualities in wrappings and their need may vary from time to time as their products undergo change. But the necessity for flexible wrappings is the central and unchanging demand. We cannot say that these differences in cost gave

---

29.

132. The price of cellophane is today an obstacle to its sales in competition with other flexible packaging materials.

133. Cellophane has always been higher priced than the two largest selling flexible packaging materials, wax paper and glassine, and this has represented a disadvantage to sales of cellophane.

134. DuPont considered as a factor in the determination of its prices, the prices of waxed paper, glassine, greaseproof, vegetable parchment, and other flexible packaging materials.

135. DuPont, in reducing its prices, intended to narrow [the] price differential between cellophane and packaging papers, particularly glassine and waxed paper. The objective of this effort has been to increase the use of cellophane. Each price reduction was intended to open up new uses for cellophane, and to attract new customers who had not used cellophane because of its price.

[According to the district court, 118 F. Supp. 41, 82-84, the price per pound of moistureproof cellophane and its multiple of glassine and waxpaper prices in selected years were as follows:

	1924	1929	1934	1940	1949
Cellophane price	$2.51	$1.07	$0.48	$0.38	$0.48
Glassine multiple	—	7	4	—	2.2
Waxpaper multiple	—	—	4.5	—	3.2/4.1*

* For self-sealing and coated waxpaper, respectively.]

du Pont monopoly power over prices in view of the findings of fact on that subject.[31] ...

[T]he trial court found that du Pont could not exclude competitors even from the manufacture of cellophane, an immaterial matter if the market is flexible packaging material. Nor can we say that du Pont's profits, while liberal (according to the Government 15.9% net after taxes on the 1937-1947 average), demonstrate the existence of a monopoly without proof of lack of comparable profits during those years in other prosperous industries. Cellophane was a leader, over 17%, in the flexible packaging materials market. There is no showing that du Pont's rate of return was greater or less than that of other producers of flexible packaging materials.

The "market" which one must study to determine when a producer has monopoly power will vary with the part of commerce under consideration. The tests are constant. That market is composed of products that have reasonable interchangeability for the purposes for which they are produced — price, use and qualities considered. While the application of the tests remains uncertain, it seems to us that du Pont should not be found to monopolize cello-

---

31.

140. Some users are sensitive to the cost of flexible packaging materials; others are not. Users to whom cost is important include substantial business: for example, General Foods, Armour, Curtiss Candy Co., and smaller users in the bread industry, cracker industry, and frozen food industry. These customers are unwilling to use more cellophane because of its relatively high price, would use more if the price were reduced, and have increased their use as the price of cellophane has been reduced.

141. The cost factor slips accounts away from cellophane. This hits at the precarious users, whose profit margins on their products are low, and has been put in motion by competitive developments in the user's trade. Examples include the losses of business to glassine in candy bar wraps in the 30's, frozen food business to waxed paper in the late 40's, and recent losses to glassine in cracker packaging.

142. The price of cellophane was reduced to expand the market for cellophane. DuPont did not reduce prices for cellophane with intent of monopolizing manufacture or with intent of suppressing competitors.

143. DuPont reduced cellophane prices to enable sales to be made for new uses from which higher prices had excluded cellophane, and to expand sales. Reductions were made as sales volume and market conditions warranted. In determining price reductions, duPont considered [the] relationship between its manufacturing costs and proposed prices, [the] possible additional volume that might be gained by the price reduction, [and the] effect of price reduction upon the return duPont would obtain on its investment. It considered the effect its lowered price might have on the manufacture by others, but this possible result of a price reduction was never a motive for the reduction.

144. DuPont never lowered cellophane prices below cost, and never dropped cellophane prices temporarily to gain a competitive advantage.

145. As duPont's manufacturing costs declined, 1924 to 1935, duPont reduced prices for cellophane. When costs of raw materials increased subsequent to 1935, it postponed reductions until 1938 and 1939. Subsequent increases in cost of raw material and labor brought about price increases after 1947.

phane when that product has the competition and interchangeability with other wrappings that this record shows.
Affirmed.

[Chief Justice Warren and Justices Black and Douglas dissented. The dissent emphasized the following points of disagreement: (1) The majority quoted at length from an article by economists Stocking and Mueller but did not state their conclusion that du Pont had significant monopoly power in cellophane. In particular, the dissent emphasized evidence on du Pont's enormous profits, in contrast to its low profits on rayon, for which there was direct competition. (An excerpt from that article appears in ¶347.) (2) That buyers bought cellophane in increasing amounts despite cellophane's significantly higher price demonstrated that the alternatives were not close substitutes. (3) Prices of alleged substitutes did not respond to du Pont's substantial price reductions over time. (4) du Pont's internal memoranda indicated that it believed cellophane to constitute a distinct market. (5) du Pont's actions, particularly its efforts to lobby for a higher tariff on cellophane imports, indicated that dominance over cellophane conveyed market power. The dissenters concluded that du Pont had monopoly power and that its conduct constituted monopolization.][47]

347.   du Pont's profits. Consider the following excerpt from G. Stocking and W. Mueller, The Cellophane Case and the New Competition, 45 Am. Econ. Rev. 29, 57-62 (1955).[48]

As du Pont reduced cellophane prices, output and sales expanded rapidly.... In 1925 it earned, before taxes (operating earnings),[107]

47. Clark and Harlan, JJ., did not participate.
48. Reproduced by permission of the American Economic Association. Footnote references are to government (*GX*) and defendant (*DX*) exhibits.
107. Du Pont computes operating earnings for each operating division by deducting all of the expenses directly related to its operations from its sales. Among these expenses are production, selling, administration, and research expenditures conducted within and for the particular division. Du Pont calculates its rate of operating earnings on the basis of its working and fixed investment allocated to its cellophane operations.
Net cellophane earnings are calculated by allowing for federal income taxes, capital stock tax, franchise, state income, and foreign taxes, "B" bonus, and fundamental research by the chemicals department. Federal income and other taxes constituted the great bulk of these deductions: 90 per cent as early as 1935 (GX 490, p. 6506) and during the second world war practically all, when the company was paying large excess profits taxes. Consequently, cellophane operating earnings may be thought of as primarily representing earnings on total cellophane investment before taxes, and cellophane net earnings as earnings after taxes.
The problem of empirically determining profit rates is subject to many pit-

$779,000 on its cellophane operating investment. In 1934 it earned $6,000,000 and in 1940, $12,000,000. Although its annual rate of earnings before taxes declined somewhat from a high of 62.4 per cent in 1928, in only two years between 1923 and 1950 inclusive did the rate fall below 20 per cent. . . .]

Cellophane's earnings record offers persuasive if not convincing evidence that du Pont has had monopoly power in selling cellophane. A comparison of du Pont's earnings from cellophane with its earnings from rayon lends force to this conclusion.[113] Despite the dissimilarity of the end products, several factors justify the comparison. Cellophane and rayon stem from the same basic raw materials. Both are radical innovations. Both were initially manufactured under noncompetitive conditions and both enjoyed substantial tariff protection. The same business management produced both products. The French Comptoir shared in the management of both du Pont Cellophane and du Pont Rayon until 1929. Yerkes, president of du Pont Cellophane, was also president of du Pont Rayon. Presumably du Pont in controlling business policy for both companies was actu-

---

falls. However, the procedure used by du Pont to determine cellophane earnings is subject to fewer criticisms than are usually encountered in profit estimates. It is true that earnings may be understated somewhat because of expenditures not directly related to cellophane manufacture and sale as noted above. On the other hand, some might argue that actual earnings are overstated in some years and understated in others because operating investment is necessarily based in part on historical rather than replacement costs. This error is reduced by the fact that du Pont has increased its capacity periodically by substantial amounts, so that of its historical costs a substantial portion is always recent history. However, some of the most frequent and important shortcomings of profit estimates are not involved in our calculations; operating investment does not include assets capitalized in expectation of excess profits, nor has overcapacity broadened the investment base. Probably the most convincing argument as to the credibility of these earnings is that du Pont has no reason to delude itself as to what it is earning in making cellophane. The investment base which du Pont uses to calculate its rates of operating and net earnings is its estimate of the actual total investment involved in its cellophane operations. Such an investment base is considerably larger than that used by the Federal Trade Commission in its study, Rates of Return (after Taxes) for 516 Identical Companies in 25 Selected Manufacturing Industries, 1940, 1947-52 (Washington, D.C., 1954), which uses stockholders' investment as its base. If this base were used in calculating rates of cellophane earnings they would undoubtedly be greater for all years. For example, in 1935, the year before du Pont Cellophane was consolidated with du Pont, the latter's equity in du Pont Cellophane was only $9,696,000. GX 490, p. 6504. If this were used as a base upon which to calculate du Pont's rate of earnings in that year, instead of that actually used, . . . its rate of operating earnings would be about 60 per cent instead of 24.6 per cent.

113. Data are not available to compare du Pont's earnings from cellophane with the earnings of producers of other wrapping materials. These are without exception diversified firms producing a variety of products. However, the record discloses that in every year from 1935 through 1942 du Pont failed to cover costs in selling cellulose acetate film, which it sold in competition with two other concerns (GX 490 through GX 497).

ated by similar business motives. Both products have had several reasonably close substitutes. The production and consumption of both increased phenomenally. Cellophane and rayon have been similarly characterized by rapidly developing technology, rapid reduction in costs, and rapid decline in prices. The chief difference in the manufacture and sale of the two products significant to the course of profits apparently lies in the structure of the rayon and cellophane industries. Although rayon manufacture began in this country as a monopoly, rival firms came into the industry promptly. American Viscose Corporation began as the sole domestic producer of rayon shortly before the first world war and du Pont followed in 1920. By 1930 these concerns had eighteen rivals. As late as 1949 fifteen firms occupied the field. Although the four largest firms in recent years have usually accounted for about 70 per cent of the total output and although most of the firms have generally followed a price leader, Markham from his painstaking and exhaustive study concludes that freedom of entry and the pressure of substitute products have made the rayon industry workably or effectively competitive. The course of both du Pont's and the industry's rate of earnings supports this conclusion. . . . Federal Trade Commission data reveal that in 1920, when du Pont first produced rayon, American Viscose Corporation, until then the country's sole producer, realized 64.2 per cent on its investment. Although du Pont showed a loss in 1921, its rate of earnings rose to 38.9 per cent by 1923. Thereafter its rate of earnings and those of the industry declined until by 1929 they had fallen to 19.0 and 18.1 per cent, respectively. When six more firms entered the industry in 1930, average industry earnings fell to 5.0 per cent and du Pont suffered a loss of 0.9 per cent. During the following eight years du Pont averaged only 7.5 per cent on its rayon investment, and the industry as a whole put in a similar performance.

In striking contrast, du Pont with only a single rival in producing cellophane (and that rival's output closely geared to du Pont's) earned less than 20 per cent on its cellophane investment in only one depression year. From the beginning of the depression in 1929 through the succeeding recovery and the 1938 recession du Pont averaged 29.6 per cent before taxes on its cellophane investment. On its rayon investment it averaged only 6.3 per cent. . . .

Du Pont has used its power with foresight and wisdom. It has apparently recognized that it could increase its earnings by decreasing its costs and prices, by educating its potential customers to the benefits of wrapping their products in cellophane, by improving machinery for packaging, by helping converters and packagers solve their technical problems. It has built a better mousetrap and taught people how to use it.

But du Pont has not surrendered its monopoly power. Its strategy, cellophane's distinctive qualities, and the course of its prices and earnings indicate this. Du Pont's strategy was designed to protect a monopoly in the sale of a product it regarded as unique, and its pricing policies reflected the judgment of its executives on how best to maximize earnings. We think its earnings illustrate Knight's distinction between justifiable profits to the innovator and unjustifiable monopoly gains. They have been "too large" and have lasted "too long."

348. Consider the *Cellophane* Court's approach to substitution between cellophane and other flexible wrapping materials.

(a) Does the substantial overlap in end use suggest that the products should be considered to be in one market? What about products, like cigarettes, where cellophane was dominant — could du Pont be said to have monopoly power in this "submarket"?[49]

(b) Does the fact that cellophane commanded a significantly higher price than many of the alleged substitutes suggest that the markets were distinct? If so, how does one account for the overlap in end use?

(c) What of the fact that prices of other flexible wrapping materials did not respond to substantial decreases in the price of cellophane over time?

(d) If one believes that other flexible wrapping materials offer some nontrivial competition to cellophane, but are still far from perfect substitutes, what should one conclude about market definition? About market power?

(e) If one firm produced all televisions sold in the United States (assume trade barriers prevent all imports), would the *Cellophane* Court decide it did not have monopoly power because, for each important end use (for example, news, sports, and other entertainment), there was substantial competition from radio, newspapers, magazines, books, and live entertainment such that television accounted for no more than 40 percent of any segment?[50]

349. How should one view the market definition and market power inquiry in *Cellophane* in light of the following evidence, much

49. See ¶285a. Recall that, in *United Shoe*, it was found that United charged different mark-ups on different lines of machines, depending on the strength of competition.

50. See Yoder Bros. v. California-Florida Plant Corp., 537 F.2d 1347 (5th Cir.), cert. denied, 429 U.S. 1094 (1976) (ornamental plants rather than chrysanthemums relevant market); Science Prod. Co. v. Chevron Chem. Co., 384 F. Supp. 793 (N.D. Ill. 1974) (court refused to distinguish liquid fertilizers from dry fertilizers or garden chemicals from household insecticides). Also compare Affiliated Music Enter. v. Sesac, 268 F.2d 13 (2d Cir.), cert. denied, 361 U.S. 831 (1959), and International Boxing Club v. United States, 358 U.S. 242 (1959) (championship boxing is a relevant market for §2 purposes; revenues at least two or three times greater than from nonchampionship bouts involving same persons), with Twin City Sportservice v. Finley & Co., 512 F.2d 1264 (9th Cir. 1975) (food concessions at baseball parks part of the general concession franchise market even though baseball concessions are the richest segment of the industry).

noted by the dissent? Which evidence indicates market power, and how much power is indicated?

(a) du Pont made every effort to retain control over the manufacture and sale of cellophane. du Pont sought tariff protection from cellophane imports and tried to postpone domestic competition in cellophane.

(b) Internal memoranda indicated defendant's belief that the substitutes did not significantly compete with cellophane.

(c) du Pont earned enormous profits on cellophane but did not on rayon, which faced significant direct competition. (1) Were such accounting measures reliable? (2) Do high profits necessarily indicate market power? (3) What would the Court have to know about profits of other flexible wrapping material producers? (4) Should the Court have been reluctant to condemn du Pont for success?

(d) Should the Court have considered the alleged acts of monopolization when deciding the market power issue?

(e) Considering the factors in the preceding subparagraphs, do you find the inquiry directed at product substitution to be the most reliable indicator of monopoly power, or its absence, in this case? If not, how would you write the market definition portion of this opinion?[51] Would you have found that du Pont possessed monopoly power?

350. Granite for buildings is removed from quarries in rough form and then finished by granite fabricators before delivery to builders. The Darr Company of Darr, Vermont, possesses the only quarry supplying a so-called B-granite, which it generally fabricates itself. When the government decided to build several buildings in Washington, it specified B-granite, and accepted Plymouth's bid to supply the required "B-granite or equivalent" for $250,000. When the government refused to accept the substitute that had previously been accepted by other builders, Plymouth sought to purchase B-granite from Darr, which refused to sell any unfinished B-granite. Plymouth then managed, at inordinate cost, to find and quarry an acceptable substitute to fulfill its contract. Plymouth now sues Darr for treble damages on the ground that Darr unlawfully monopolized the supply of B-granite.

You are law clerk to the judge, who asks you to study and criticize the following draft:

> Although §2 condemns monopolization of "any part" of interstate commerce, this must mean "some appreciable part" of a market. Defendant's proofs show, and plaintiff does not deny, that other types

---

51. See *Rebel Oil*, note 11 (market power may be shown by direct evidence of its exercise). See also the discussion in *Indiana Dentists*, Ch. 2E, on the need to define a market when adverse competitive effects are present.

compete with B-granite. Although the instant builder was very particular, he could have availed himself, at some small aesthetic sacrifice, of the substitutes normally considered adequate. So small a market is not an appreciable part of commerce. Despite the conventional antitrust trappings with which the case has been draped, this is essentially a private squabble between two energetic Yankee businesses.

Should the judge issue this opinion? If not, what changes would you recommend?[52]

351. TrashKing stands accused of monopolizing the market for trash collection in Dallas. Its defense on the market power issue is that, despite its 100 percent market share, potential competition restrains its ability to price above a competitive level. Most obviously, trash collectors in Fort Worth — more than an hour's drive away, with largely rural area in between — could also arrange pickups in Dallas, although no trucks from one city currently pick up trash in the other. Although the distance may be too far to make this feasible, such firms could always station some of their trucks and drivers in Dallas. For that matter, other trucking enterprises, or anyone with an entrepreneurial spirit, could lease or purchase a few garbage trucks, hire some truck drivers, and begin bidding on trash removal contracts if they felt TrashKing was exploiting its customers.[53]

(a) Should the geographic market be defined to include trash collectors in Fort Worth? Or the product market to include other trucking firms in Dallas?

(b) If a narrow market definition is adopted, giving TrashKing a 100 percent share, what inference of market power should be made?

3C. ATTEMPT TO MONOPOLIZE[1]

352. Introduction. Attempt to monopolize is an elusive concept that will appear several times in this book. The topic is treated here because of its obvious relation to monopolization and market power. The initial focus of this section will be on various acts that might be considered sufficient basis for liability. This inquiry has

---

52. H.E. Fletcher Co. v. Rock of Ages Corp., 326 F.2d 13 (2d Cir. 1963); Acme Precision Prods. v. American Alloys Corp., 484 F.2d 1237 (8th Cir. 1973) (distinctive product interchangeable with inferior substitutes in 95 percent of its uses). See also ¶336a.

53. This illustration is based on the merger case, United States v. Waste Management, 743 F.2d 976 (2d Cir. 1984).

1. See IIIA P. Areeda & H. Hovenkamp, Antitrust Law ch. 8B (1996).

much in common with the study of acts of monopolization in Chapter 3A, boycotts in Chapter 2E, and many vertical restraints covered in Chapter 4.

353. Widgco manufactures widgets. In the last 10 years under the leadership of Gloria Gladstone, the president and major stockholder, Widgco has increased its share of the widget market from 4 to 36 percent. This result has been achieved by aggressive but nonpredatory price competition, development of a superior product by the company's research division, and imaginative advertising and sales promotion. President Gladstone has candidly stated her company's intentions: Widgco will continue its successful practices with the objective of capturing control of the widget market.

(a) Does Widgco exhibit a specific intent to gain a monopoly of the widget market?[2]

(b) If there is a substantial probability that Widgco may attain a monopoly, has Widgco attempted to monopolize?

(c) Should Widgco's conduct be proscribed by the Sherman Act?

(d) What additional elements are necessary to constitute an attempt to monopolize?[3]

LORAIN JOURNAL CO. v. UNITED STATES
342 U.S. 143 (1951)

Justice BURTON. . . . The principal question here is whether a newspaper publisher's conduct constituted an attempt to monopolize interstate commerce, justifying the injunction issued against it. . . .

From 1933 to 1948 the publisher [Lorain Journal Co.] enjoyed a substantial monopoly in Lorain of the mass dissemination of news and advertising, both of a local and national character. However, in 1948 [WEOL] was licensed . . . to establish and operate in Elyria, Ohio, eight miles south of Lorain, a radio station. . . .

2. See note 1 of *Fortner*, Ch. 4B, for a discussion of this issue.

3. Consider, in the common law of crime, these formulations the standard notion of attempt, which "consists of: (1) an intent to do an act or to bring about certain consequences which would in law amount to a crime; and (2) an act in furtherance of that intent which . . . goes beyond mere preparation." W. LaFave & A. Scott, Criminal Law 495 (2d ed. 1986). Consider also the well-known statement that "'factual impossibility' is no defense to a charge of attempt," id. at 512, and keep in mind that "[a]ttempts are cases of failure." G. Fletcher, Rethinking Criminal Law 131 (1978). Throughout this section, one should reflect on the general reasons attempts are often punishable independently of the related offense and on how attempts relate to monopolization and the rest of antitrust law.

2. *The publisher's attempt to regain its monopoly of interstate commerce by forcing advertisers to boycott a competing radio station violated §2.* The findings and opinion of the trial court describe the conduct of the publisher upon which the Government relies. The surrounding circumstances are important. The most illuminating of these is the substantial monopoly which was enjoyed in Lorain by the publisher from 1933 to 1948, together with a 99% coverage of Lorain families. Those factors made the Journal an indispensable medium of advertising for many Lorain concerns. Accordingly, its publisher's refusals to print Lorain advertising for those using WEOL for like advertising often amounted to an effective prohibition of the use of WEOL for that purpose. Numerous Lorain advertisers wished to supplement their local newspaper advertising with local radio advertising but could not afford to discontinue their newspaper advertising in order to use the radio.

WEOL's greatest potential source of income was local Lorain advertising. Loss of that was a major threat to its existence. The court below found unequivocally that appellants' conduct amounted to an attempt by the publisher to destroy WEOL and, at the same time, to regain the publisher's pre-1948 substantial monopoly over the mass dissemination of all news and advertising.

To establish this violation of §2 as charged, it was not necessary to show that success rewarded appellants' attempt to monopolize. The injunctive relief under §4 sought to forestall that success. While appellants' attempt to monopolize did succeed insofar as it deprived WEOL of income, WEOL has not yet been eliminated. The injunction may save it. "[W]hen that intent [to monopolize] and the consequent dangerous probability exist, this statute [the Sherman Act], like many others, and like the common law in some cases, directs itself against that dangerous probability as well as against the completed result." ...

Assuming the interstate character of the commerce involved, it seems clear that if all the newspapers in a city, in order to monopolize the dissemination of news and advertising by eliminating a competing radio station, conspired to accept no advertisements from anyone who advertised over that station, they would violate §§1 and 2 of the Sherman Act. ... It is consistent with that result to hold here that a single newspaper, already enjoying a substantial monopoly in its area, violates the "attempt to monopolize" clause of §2 when it uses its monopoly to destroy threatened competition.

The publisher claims a right as a private business concern to select its customers and to refuse to accept advertisements from whomever it pleases. We do not dispute that general right. "But the word 'right' is one of the most deceptive of pitfalls; it is so easy to slip from a qualified meaning in the premise to an unqualified one in the conclusion. Most rights are qualified.". . . The right claimed by the publisher is neither absolute nor exempt from regulation. Its exercise as a purposeful means of monopolizing interstate commerce is prohibited by the Sherman Act. The operator of the radio station, equally with the publisher of the newspaper, is entitled to the protection of that Act. "*In the absence of any purpose to create or maintain a monopoly,* the act does not restrict the long recognized right of trader or manufacturer engaged in an entirely private business, freely to exercise his own independent discretion as to parties with whom he will deal." (Emphasis supplied.) *Colgate.* See *Associated Press.* . . .

Affirmed.[4]

354. (a) Do you think the Journal earned more or less profit in the short run as a result of its restriction?[5] If the restriction was unprofitable, why was it imposed?[6] What must the Journal have expected to be its long-run effect?

(b) If the effect would be to put WEOL out of business, that might well have been to the disadvantage of advertisers. If so, why wouldn't they have been willing to make a short-run sacrifice by standing up to the Journal's tactics and advertising in WEOL alone, to ensure its continued existence? After all, once it became clear to the Journal that its tactics would fail, it would ultimately give in, permitting advertising to those who also used WEOL.

(c) Can you imagine any justifications for the Journal's behavior? Was *Lorain Journal* correctly decided? Observe that the objective sought by both the Journal and Widgco is the same: monopoly. If one is guilty of an unlawful attempt, why not the other? Is it enough to say that the competitive behavior is fair in the Widgco situation?

(d) Suppose that a market is found to be a natural monopoly, and a new firm enters trying to take the market from the incumbent for itself. Would all attempts to gain business be acts of attempted monopolization? Should there be no offense regardless of the acts, because monopoly is unavoidable?[7]

4. Clark and Minton, JJ., did not participate.
5. Consider whether advertisers would be willing to pay more, less, or the same to advertise in the Journal when they are required to forgo WEOL as when they are permitted to advertise on radio at their option.
6. Compare vertical integration, ¶321, and the questions on *Griffith,* ¶308. For an economic analysis, see T. Brennan, Refusing to Cooperate with Competitors: A Theory of Boycotts, 35 J.L. & Econ. 247 (1992).
7. See Union Leader Corp. v. Newspapers of New England, 180 F. Supp. 125 (D. Mass. 1959), aff'd in part and rev'd in part, 284 F.2d 582 (1st Cir. 1960), cert. denied, 365 U.S. 833 (1961) (finding attempted monopolization by entrant newspaper in a market that could support only one newspaper; some practices exonerated as amounting only to fair competition).

355.[8]   The single largest retailer in Amesville is the Webb Department Store. Webb is a community institution: the favorite rendezvous for those involved in business, shoppers, youngsters, and everyone else. Most of the citizens of Amesville pass through or near Webb several times weekly. Webb sells more toothpaste, clothes, appliances, and groceries than any other retailer in Amesville. More than 75 percent of Amesville clothing and appliance sales are made by Webb, which is concerned about the price-cutting activities of certain small appliance retailers. Webb informs the Quickshave Electric Razor Company that it cannot afford to continue to handle the Quickshaver unless it becomes the exclusive outlet in Amesville. Quickshave ceases to sell its razors to other Amesville dealers. Has Webb violated Sherman Act §2?

(a) Does a dealer's insistence on being an exclusive outlet show its intent to monopolize in the area within which it is to be the manufacturer's sole outlet? Would such an insistence nevertheless be justified by showing that the market could support only one outlet? Or by showing that no dealer would distribute this product unless it were an exclusive outlet? Is the basic inquiry not monopolistic intent but whether a monopoly is justifiable in the circumstances?

(b) If an exclusive outlet arrangement is justified for a newly entering dealer, when does a dealer's continuing insistence cease to be justifiable? Should a dealer who has invested large sums in building product goodwill be deprived of the fruits of its investment? Would a negative answer generally be sensible?

(c) What result when Webb shows that it had been losing money on the Quickshaver? Or that it had been earning less than a normal return?

(d) What result when Webb says that it earns less on its nonexclusive Quickshaver operation than it could earn by devoting the same counter space and energies to another product? Quickshaver accepted Webb's statement. Should the court? On what proofs?

(e) Is it ever a defense to actual or attempted monopolization in one area that some other use of capital would be more attractive in the absence of monopoly profits in the first undertaking?

(f) Does Webb have any duty to continue handling the Quickshaver? If not, and if Webb is prevented from stating its reasons to Quickshaver, will Quickshaver avoid the risk of losing Webb by playing it safe and unilaterally making Webb its sole outlet without waiting to be asked?

---

8. The issue in this Paragraph will be addressed further in Ch. 4A's discussion of sole outlets and territorial and customer restrictions. See particularly *Packard* and ¶409. One should also consider the material on vertical integration in ¶¶321-327.

(g) Is this case controlled by *Lorain Journal*—i.e., is there a relevant distinction between Lorain Journal refusing to deal with advertisers that dealt with competitor WEOL and Webb refusing to deal with manufacturers that deal with Webb's competitors?

356. *United States v. American Airlines*, 743 F.2d 1114 (5th Cir. 1984), cert. dismissed, 474 U.S. 1001 (1985). American Airlines and Braniff Airlines were in stiff competition for passengers flying through the Dallas-Fort Worth Airport, which the two airlines dominated at the time. American's president telephoned Braniff's president to propose that the two airlines end their price competition by raising fares 20 percent. Braniff not only declined American's offer but gave the government a tape recording of the telephone conversation.

(a) Did American violate Sherman Act §1?

(b) Should the court have found that American violated §2's prohibition against attempted monopolization? (It did.) What of the facts that American shared the market with Braniff (that is, it had no monopoly on its own) and that there was no prospect that the conspiracy, if formed, would have any effect on its market share? If this is a violation, would you also find liability if there were 10 airlines, each with one-tenth of the market, and American was caught on its first telephone call?

SPECTRUM SPORTS v. McQUILLAN
506 U.S. 447 (1993)

Justice WHITE. . . . The jury in this case returned a verdict finding that petitioners had monopolized, attempted to monopolize, and/or conspired to monopolize. The District Court entered a judgment ruling that petitioners had violated §2, and the Court of Appeals affirmed on the ground that petitioners had attempted to monopolize. The issue we have before us is whether the District Court and the Court of Appeals correctly defined the elements of that offense.

I

[Respondents were regional distributers of products made with sorbothane, an elastic shock-absorbing polymer that they used for making products such as a horseshoe pad and athletic shoe inserts. One of the petitioners, the S.I. Group, which owns all manufacturing and distribution rights to sorbothane, informed the McQuillans that they must sell their athletic distributorship to keep their equestrian distribution rights. The McQuillans refused to sell, were terminated, and Spectrum (a co-owner of which was the son of S.I. Group's president) became the national distributor of sorbothane athletic shoe inserts. Respondents sued and won a jury verdict on all their claims, including one under Sherman Act §2.]

The Court of Appeals for the Ninth Circuit affirmed the judgment in an unpublished opinion. The court expressly ruled that the trial court had properly instructed the jury on the Sherman Act claims and found that the evidence supported the liability verdicts as well as the damages awards on these claims. . . . On the §2 issue that petitioners present here, the Court of Appeals, noting that the jury had found that petitioners had violated §2 without specifying whether they had monopolized, attempted to monopolize, or conspired to monopolize, held that the verdict would stand if the evidence supported any one of the three possible violations of §2. The court went on to conclude that a case of attempted monopolization had been established.[4] The court rejected petitioners' argument that attempted monopolization had not been established because respondents had failed to prove that petitioners had a specific intent to monopolize a relevant market. The court also held that in order to show that respondents' attempt to monopolize was likely to succeed it was not necessary to present evidence of the relevant market or of the defendants' market power. In so doing, the Ninth Circuit relied on Lessig v. Tidewater Oil Co., 327 F.2d 459 (CA9), cert. denied, 377 U.S. 993 (1964), and its progeny. The Court of Appeals noted that these cases, in dealing with attempts to monopolize claims, had ruled that "if evidence of unfair or predatory conduct is presented, it may satisfy both the specific intent and dangerous probability elements of the offense, without any proof of relevant market or the defendant's market power." If, however, there is insufficient evidence of unfair or predatory conduct, there

---

4. The District Court's jury instructions were transcribed as follows:

In order to win on the claim of attempted monopoly, the Plaintiff must prove each of the following elements by a preponderance of the evidence: first, that the Defendants had a specific intent to achieve monopoly power in the relevant market; second, that the Defendants engaged in exclusionary or restrictive conduct in furtherance of its specific intent; third, that there was a dangerous probability that Defendants could sooner or later achieve [their] goal of monopoly power in the relevant market; fourth, that the Defendants' conduct occurred in or affected interstate commerce; and fifth, that the Plaintiff was injured in the business or property by the Defendants' exclusionary or restrictive conduct.

If the Plaintiff has shown that the Defendant engaged in predatory conduct, you may infer from that evidence the specific intent and the dangerous probability element of the offense without any proof of the relevant market or the Defendants' [market] power.

must be a showing of "relevant market or the defendant's market power." The court went on to find:

> There is sufficient evidence from which the jury could conclude that the S.I. Group and Spectrum Group engaged in unfair or predatory conduct and thus inferred that they had the specific intent and the dangerous probability of success and, therefore, McQuillan did not have to prove relevant market or the defendant's [market] power.

The decision below, and the *Lessig* line of decisions on which it relies, conflicts with holdings of courts in other Circuits. Every other Court of Appeals has indicated that proving an attempt to monopolize requires proof of a dangerous probability of monopolization of a relevant market. We granted certiorari to resolve this conflict among the Circuits. We reverse.

II

While §1 of the Sherman Act forbids contracts or conspiracies in restraint of trade or commerce, §2 addresses the actions of single firms that monopolize or attempt to monopolize, as well as conspiracies and combinations to monopolize. Section 2 does not define the elements of the offense of attempted monopolization. Nor is there much guidance to be had in the scant legislative history of that provision, which was added late in the legislative process. . . . The legislative history does indicate that much of the interpretation of the necessarily broad principles of the Act was to be left for the courts in particular cases. . . .

This Court first addressed the meaning of attempt to monopolize under §2 in Swift & Co. v. United States, 196 U.S. 375 (1905). The Court's opinion, written by Justice Holmes, contained the following passage:

> Where acts are not sufficient in themselves to produce a result which the law seeks to prevent — for instance, the monopoly — but require further acts in addition to the mere forces of nature to bring that result to pass, an intent to bring it to pass is necessary in order to produce a dangerous probability that it will happen. . . . But when that intent and the consequent dangerous probability exist, this statute, like many others and like the common law in some cases, directs itself against that dangerous probability as well as against the completed result.

The Court went on to explain, however, that not every act done with intent to produce an unlawful result constitutes an attempt. "It is a question of proximity and degree." *Swift* thus indicated that intent is necessary, but alone is not sufficient, to establish the dangerous probability of success that is the object of §2's prohibition of attempts.[7]

The Court's decisions since *Swift* have reflected the view that the plaintiff charging attempted monopolization must prove a dangerous probability of actual monopolization, which has generally required a definition of the relevant market and examination of market power. In Walker Process Equipment v. Food Machinery & Chemical Corp., 328 U.S. 172, 177 (1965), we found that the enforcement of a fraudulently obtained patent claim could violate the Sherman Act. We stated that, to establish monopolization or attempt to monopolize under §2 of the Sherman Act, it would be necessary to appraise the exclusionary power of the illegal patent claim in terms of the relevant market for the product involved. The reason was that "[w]ithout a definition of that market there is no way to measure [the defendant's] ability to lessen or destroy competition."

Similarly, this Court reaffirmed in *Copperweld* that "Congress authorized Sherman Act scrutiny of single firms only when they pose a danger of monopolization. Judging unilateral conduct in this manner reduces the risk that the antitrust laws will dampen the competitive zeal of a single aggressive entrepreneur." Thus, the conduct of a single firm, governed by §2, "is unlawful only when it threatens actual monopolization." See also *Lorain Journal*; *Griffith*; *American Tobacco* (1946).

The Courts of Appeals other than the Ninth Circuit have followed this approach. Consistent with our cases, it is generally required that to demonstrate attempted monopolization a plaintiff must prove (1) that the defendant has engaged in predatory or anticompetitive conduct with (2) a specific intent to monopolize and (3) a dangerous probability of achieving monopoly power. See Areeda & Turner, supra, at ¶820, p. 312. In order to determine whether there is a dangerous probability of monopolization, courts have found it necessary to consider the relevant market and the defendant's ability to lessen or destroy competition in that market.

Notwithstanding the array of authority contrary to *Lessig*, the Court of Appeals in this case reaffirmed its prior holdings. . . . We are not at all inclined, however, to embrace *Lessig*'s interpretation of §2, for there is little if any support for it in the statute or the case

---

7. Justice Holmes confirmed that this was his interpretation of *Swift* in Hyde v. United States, 225 U.S. 347, 387-388 (1912). In dissenting in that case on other grounds, the Justice, citing *Swift*, stated that an attempt may be found where the danger of harm is very great; however, "combination, intention and overt act may all be present without amounting to a criminal attempt. . . . There must be dangerous proximity to success."

law, and the notion that proof of unfair or predatory conduct alone is sufficient to make out the offense of attempted monopolization is contrary to the purpose and policy of the Sherman Act.

The *Lessig* opinion claimed support from the language of §2, which prohibits attempts to monopolize "any part" of commerce, and therefore forbids attempts to monopolize any appreciable segment of interstate sales of the relevant product. See United States v. Yellow Cab Co., 332 U.S. 218 (1947). The "any part" clause, however, applies to charges of monopolization as well as to attempts to monopolize, and it is beyond doubt that the former requires proof of market power in a relevant market. *Grinnell*; *Cellophane.*

In support of its determination that an inference of dangerous probability was permissible from a showing of intent, the *Lessig* opinion cited, and added emphasis to, this Court's reference in its opinion in *Swift* to "intent and the *consequent* dangerous probability." But any question whether dangerous probability of success requires proof of more than intent alone should have been removed by the subsequent passage in *Swift* which stated that "not every act that may be done with an intent to produce an unlawful result . . . constitutes an attempt. It is a question of proximity and degree."

The *Lessig* court also relied on [footnote 23] in *Cellophane* for the proposition that when the charge is attempt to monopolize, the relevant market is "not in issue." That footnote, which appeared in analysis of the relevant market issue in *Cellophane*, rejected the Government's reliance on several cases, noting that "the scope of the market was not in issue" in Story Parchment Co. v. Paterson Parchment Paper Co., 282 U.S. 555 (1931). That reference merely reflected the fact that, in *Story Parchment*, which was not an attempt to monopolize case, the parties did not challenge the definition of the market adopted by the lower courts. Nor was *Cellophane* itself concerned with the issue in this case.

It is also our view that *Lessig* and later Ninth Circuit decisions refining and applying it are inconsistent with the policy of the Sherman Act. The purpose of the Act is not to protect businesses from the working of the market; it is to protect the public from the failure of the market. The law directs itself not against conduct which is competitive, even severely so, but against conduct which unfairly tends to destroy competition itself. It does so not out of solicitude for private concerns but out of concern for the public interest. See, e.g., *Brunswick*; *Cargill*; *Brown Shoe*. Thus, this Court and other courts have been careful to avoid constructions of §2 which might chill competition, rather than foster it. It is sometimes difficult to distinguish robust competition from conduct with long-term anticompetitive effects; moreover, single-firm activity is unlike concerted activity covered by §1, which "inherently is fraught with anticompetitive risk." *Copperweld*. For these reasons, §2 makes the conduct of a single firm unlawful only when it actually monopolizes or dangerously threatens to do so. The concern that §2 might be applied so as to further anticompetitive ends is plainly not met by inquiring only whether the defendant has engaged in "unfair" or "predatory" tactics. Such conduct may be sufficient to prove the necessary intent to monopolize, which is something more than an intent to compete vigorously, but demonstrating the dangerous probability of monopolization in an attempt case also requires inquiry into the relevant product and geographic market and the defendant's economic power in that market.

III

We hold that petitioners may not be liable for attempted monopolization under §2 of the Sherman Act absent proof of a dangerous probability that they would monopolize a particular market and specific intent to monopolize. In this case, the trial instructions allowed the jury to infer specific intent and dangerous probability of success from the defendants' predatory conduct, without any proof of the relevant market or of a realistic probability that the defendants could achieve monopoly power in that market. In this respect, the instructions misconstrued §2, as did the Court of Appeals in affirming the judgment of the District Court. Since the affirmance of the §2 judgment against petitioners rested solely on the legally erroneous conclusion that petitioners had attempted to monopolize in violation of §2 and since the jury's verdict did not negate the possibility that the §2 verdict rested on the attempt to monopolize ground alone, the judgment of the Court of Appeals is reversed . . . and the case is remanded for further proceedings consistent with this opinion.

357. (a) Why does the Court in *Spectrum Sports* require independent proof of a dangerous probability of monopolizing a relevant market?[9] The jury was instructed (see note 4) that it may infer the

---

9. In considering the Court's discussion of precedent, footnote 23 from *Cellophane* is reproduced here.

The Government notes that the prohibitions of §2 of the Sherman Act have often been extended to producers of single products and to businesses of limited scope. But the cases to which the Government refers us were not concerned with the problem that is now before the Court. In Story Parchment Co. v. Paterson, 282 U.S. 555, a conspiracy to monopolize trade in vegetable parchment was held to be a violation of §2. Parchment paper is obviously no larger a part of commerce than cellophane. Recovery, however, was based on proven allegations of combination and conspiracy to

dangerous probability from the defendant's conduct. Is such an inference irrational?

(b) What was the defendant's conduct from which the jury might make the inference? Is it relevant that the plaintiff might have been terminated for the purpose of helping out the company president's son?

(c) How much market power must a plaintiff demonstrate in an attempted monopolization case? Should the required showing depend upon the defendant's conduct?[10]

(d) In price-fixing and some other Sherman Act §1 cases, demonstration of market power is not required, presumably motivated by concerns of judicial economy. Can one reconcile this approach with that required by the Court in attempted monopolization cases?

---

monopolize, and the scope of the market was not in issue. Similarly, Indiana Farmer's Guide Co. v. Prairie Farmer Publishing Co., 293 U.S. 268, ruled that a combination or conspiracy for the purpose of monopolizing the farm-paper business in the north central part of the Nation would be illegal by reason of the second section of the Sherman Act. *Lorain Journal,* a case not cited by the Government, was concerned with even a smaller geographical area (dissemination of news in a community and surrounding territory). But the Court held only that defendant had attempted to monopolize, not that he had in fact monopolized. Also, this Court found in United States v. Columbia Steel Co., 334 U.S. 495, that the "relevant competitive market" for determining whether there had been an unreasonable restraint of trade (or an attempt to monopolize) was the market for "rolled steel" products in an 11-state area. Women's dresses of "original design," *Fashion Originators' Guild;* "first run" motion pictures, United States v. Paramount Pictures, 334 U.S. 131; the news services of one news agency, *Associated Press,* and newspaper advertising as distinguished from other means of news dissemination, Times-Picayune Co. v. United States, 345 U.S. 594, have all been designated as parts of commerce. All four were concerned only with the question of whether there had been an attempt to monopolize....

10. Rebel Oil Co. v. Atlantic Richfield Co., 51 F.3d 1421, 1438 (9th Cir.), cert. denied, 116 S. Ct. 515 (1995) (most cases hold that less than a 30 percent market share is presumptively insufficient); M&M Medical Supplies v. Pleasant Valley Hosp., 981 F.2d 160, 168 (4th Cir. 1992) (en banc), cert. denied, 508 U.S. 972 (1993) (less than 30 percent market share should be presumptively rejected; 30 to 50 percent market share should usually be rejected absent "invidious" conduct that is "very likely to achieve monopoly"; greater than 50 percent market share is presumptively enough assuming the other qualifications are met); Advo v. Philadelphia Newspapers, 854 F. Supp. 367 (E.D. Pa. 1994), aff'd, 51 F.3d 1191 (3d Cir. 1995) (40 percent market share insufficient for attempted monopolization).

Chapter 4

Vertical Restraints

400. Prologue. Chapter 3A explored some aspects of vertical integration by monopolists. As you will recall from the discussion in ¶321, vertical integration consists of the combination in a single firm of various stages of production — such as mining iron ore, making ingot, transforming ingot into usable forms, fabricating end products, and distributing products through wholesalers and retailers to ultimate consumers. This chapter considers vertical relationships between otherwise independent firms, which necessarily arise whenever all stages in the production process are not fully integrated. Whether the firm chooses to integrate vertically or to conduct necessary vertical exchanges on the open market or through some, possibly elaborate, contractual arrangement will depend on the relative cost of each process. If internal direction is cheaper or simpler than market transactions, the firm will find it profitable to integrate; if market transactions are convenient and information cheap and reliable, integration with internal management and coordination by direction rather than price might be more costly, especially for the far-flung firm.[1] Actual business arrangements may have aspects of both. The single firm might be organized into divisions where each division is a profit center responsible for maximizing its own profits and therefore dealing with other divisions at arm's length, almost as if they were separate firms. On the other

---

1. R. Coase, The Nature of the Firm, 4 Economica 386 (1937); O. Williamson, The Vertical Integration of Production: Market Failure Considerations, 61 Am. Econ. Rev. 112 (1971); O. Williamson, The Economic Institutions of Capitalism (1985). For a challenge to this now-traditional characterization, see S. Grossman & O. Hart, The Costs and Benefits of Ownership: A Theory of Vertical and Lateral Integration, 94 J. Pol. Econ. 691 (1986); O. Hart, Firms, Contracts, and Financial Structure (1995). Related criticisms are made in a case study of the *AT&T* case by D. Evans and S. Grossman, Integration, in Breaking up Bell: Essays on Industrial Organization and Regulation (D. Evans ed. 1983). A survey of economics literature is provided in M. Katz, Vertical Contractual Relations, in 1 Handbook of Industrial Organization, (R. Schmalensee and R. Willig eds. 1989). Undergraduate texts include F.M. Scherer & D. Ross, Industrial Market Structure and Economic Performance, ch. 15 (3d ed. 1990); W.K. Viscusi, J. Vernon & J. Harrington, Economics of Regulation and Antitrust, ch. 8 (2d ed. 1995).

side, entirely separate firms may have very disparate bargaining strength or deal with each other through long-term contracts, such that their dealings resemble those within the integrated firm. To recognize this, it may sometimes be convenient to speak of "vertical integration by dependency or by contract."

In all events, the contracts or conditions of such vertical dealings may be of antitrust concern. They may restrain trade in violation of Sherman Act §1; they may violate Clayton Act §3; and, of course, they may offend Sherman Act §2. Section A examines seller-buyer, usually manufacturer-retailer, arrangements affecting retail level competition in sales of that manufacturer's product. Such restraints have their most direct (although not necessarily their only) effect on the conditions of *intra*brand competition; restraints explored in the rest of the Chapter are expressly directed toward *inter*brand competition. Section B explores tying arrangements, whereby a supplier refuses to supply one product unless its customer also accepts some other product from it, rather than from competitors. Section C concerns exclusive dealing arrangements under which, typically, a buyer purchases its requirements exclusively from a single supplier, effectively agreeing not to purchase from the supplier's competitors. The economic analysis developed here, particularly in sections B and C, continues the analysis of some issues from the monopolization discussion in Chapter 3 and is carried forward in the treatment of vertical integration by merger in Chapter 5. An additional aspect of vertical dealing, discriminatory pricing, is the subject of Chapter 6.

4A.   RESTRICTED DISTRIBUTION

401.   Introduction. A manufacturer may sell its product directly to ultimate consumers through its own employees, agents, or wholly owned subsidiaries. Most manufacturers, however, reach ultimate buyers through intermediate dealers.[2] When one considers the wide range of products sold in department stores, drug stores, and many other retail establishments, it is obvious that this pattern is inevitable, as it would be impractical in most cases to maintain an independent distribution system for each product, much less for each brand.

2. While there may be many levels — jobbers, wholesalers, retailers — this section will usually focus on a simple two-level distribution system: A manufacturer sells to a dealer who sells to the ultimate buyers.

The manufacturer-dealer relationship can involve many forms of vertical restraint. A manufacturer may seek to limit competition among dealers. It may, for example, limit their resale prices, separate them geographically so that there is little competition among them and maintain such separation through contracts limiting dealers to their territories or to specified customers, or regulate their advertising policies or other competitive behavior. In addition, if the manufacturer chooses to compete directly or indirectly with its dealers, it may seek to prevent or limit its dealers from competing with the manufacturer's own sales to consumers. Whatever the restraint, the competitive effects may depend on whether the dealers customarily handle only one product or the goods of one manufacturer (as do many automobile dealers) or many products or the goods of competing manufacturers (as the usual drugstore does). In all these cases, the restraint may be effected by unilateral decision (perhaps at the request of the dealer or its competitors), a refusal to sell (or buy) unless the other party behaves in a specified way, or express agreement. The question throughout is this: why — and how much — do we care about competition in the distribution of a single manufacturer's product? Of course, such restrictions of intrabrand competition might increase or decrease interbrand competition, as we shall analyze in this section. But we shall not pursue here the possible reduction of interbrand competition that might result when one manufacturer's product is distributed by an actual or potential rival manufacturer.[3]

The section begins by considering the permissible content of restraints. (1) May a manufacturer agree with its dealers on their resale prices? Although a negative answer is relatively clear, a change may be in the wind, and judicial reasoning about resale price maintenance influences the courts' approach to current disputes and uncertainties in other areas. (2) May a manufacturer lawfully agree to sell solely through a particular outlet or confine dealers to specified territories or to particular customers? In either case, Sherman Act §1 is applicable only if there is an unlawful agreement, which poses two further questions. (3) When is a dealer closely enough related to a manufacturer to be considered an agent whose pricing and other actions may lawfully be controlled? (4) Under what circumstances will a manufacturer's refusal to sell to dealers who do not comply with its desires be deemed an impermissible agreement where a contractual promise to comply would be unlawful?

---

3. See *Palmer*, Ch. 2B.

Resale Price Maintenance[4]

402. Manufacturer's interest in minimizing dealer profits. In the simplest case, a manufacturer would prefer its retailers' prices to be as low as possible. Higher retail prices increase retailers' profits and reduce sales, the latter being detrimental to the manufacturer. If, in fact, higher retail prices generated more aggregate profits, the manufacturer's preference would be to charge a higher wholesale price — reaping the profits itself — leaving a margin for retailers just sufficient to cover their costs (including a normal profit). Thus, the manufacturer would take into account its production and distribution costs and the prices of competing brands and set its wholesale price accordingly. If it sold exclusively to independent dealers, it might rely on competition among them to prevent them from raising the retail price in an effort to earn excess profits. If the dealers are few in number or if they have illegally combined horizontally, the retail price would be higher, unless the manufacturer also sells at retail (thereby providing the necessary competition itself) or has the power to fix *maximum* resale prices.[5] The

---

4. For economic treatments, see L. Telser, Why Should Manufacturers Want Fair Trade?, 3 J.L. & Econ. 86 (1960); H. Marvel & S. McCafferty, Resale Price Maintenance and Quality Certification, 15 Rand J. Econ. 346 (1984); W. Comanor, Vertical Price-Fixing, Vertical Market Restrictions, and the New Antitrust Policy, 98 Harv. L. Rev. 983 (1985); T. Gilligan, The Competitive Effects of Resale Price Maintenance, 17 Rand J. Econ. 544 (1986); P. Rey & J. Tirole, The Logic of Vertical Restraints, 76 Am. Econ. Rev. 921 (1986); A. Kleit, Efficiencies without Economists: The Early Years of Resale Price Maintenance, 59 So. Econ. J. 597 (1993). For an early debate about whether resale price maintenance increases distribution efficiency and thus promotes efficient resource allocation, see R. Bork, The Rule of Reason and the Per Se Concept: Price Fixing and Market Division, 75 Yale L.J. 373 (1966); J. Gould & B. Yamey, Professor Bork on Vertical Price-Fixing, 76 Yale L.J. 722 (1967); R. Bork, A Reply to Professors Gould and Yamey, 76 Yale L.J. 731 (1967).

5. This situation parallels that discussed in ¶321. A simple diagram will illustrate the point.

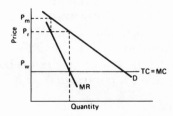

D is the demand curve for the manufacturer's product; MR is the marginal revenue curve derived from it. (For a fuller explanation, see ¶112.) Unit retailing costs, equal to $P_r - P_w$ (the competitive resale price minus the wholesale price),

essential point is this: Ordinarily, a manufacturer will maximize its profits by selling wholesale at a price satisfactory to itself and by encouraging maximum competition among dealers in order that their profit margins might be as low as possible, consistent with the continued performance of their distribution function. Excessive dealer profit resembles a tax on the product: It inflates the retail price and thus discourages sales without providing any countervailing benefit to the manufacturer.

This suggests that a rational manufacturer would prevent price competition among dealers by enforcing *minimum* retail prices — referred to as resale price maintenance — only if forced to do so by the dealers to serve their anticompetitive purposes. In that event, one could infer the existence of a dealer cartel and condemn the vertical price fix on standard horizontal grounds. But we shall see in the next Paragraph that a manufacturer might find that vertical price fixing contributes to the effective distribution of its product.

403. Manufacturer's reasons for limiting intrabrand competition among its dealers; procompetitive and anticompetitive effects.[6] Although we have just seen that a manufacturer's interests are ordinarily served best by intensive competition among dealers, manufacturers sometimes limit such competition and, therefore, we need to ask why they would do so. The following are the most familiar explanations, beginning with those that arguably make distribution more efficient and including anticompetitive reasons as well. Our main focus here is on resale price maintenance, by which

---

are assumed constant at *TC*. (More realistic cost assumptions would complicate the diagram without affecting the analysis.) When unit cost is constant, marginal cost (*MC*) is identical to it. The fully integrated producer would sell at retail to consumers at price P_r, which is indicated by the intersection of its *MC* and *MR* curves. Knowing that retailing costs equal $P_r - P_w$, it will set the wholesale price at P_w. If the retailers are fully competitive with each other, they will sell at their marginal cost P_r, which is P_w plus retailing costs. Observe that if the retailer is a monopolist or if the retailers have a price-fixing cartel, they will equate their marginal cost P_r with *MR* and thus set the higher price P_m. In summary, if dealers combine to set retail prices, the resulting price will (1) never be lower than the retail price that would be set by the manufacturer, (2) be the same when dealers and the manufacturer agree on the price that would maximize their total collective revenue and then divide the spoils, but (3) be higher in all other cases — i.e., when each behaves independently, taking as given the behavior of others.

6. This discussion is derived from VIII P. Areeda, Antitrust Law, ch. 16 (1989). For empirical evidence, see P. Hersch, The Effects of Resale Price Maintenance on Shareholder Wealth: The Consequences of *Schwegmann*, 42 J. Indus. Econ. (1994) (support for free-ridership, for dealer cartels, and somewhat for protection of product reputation); P. Ippolito, Resale Price Maintenance: Empirical Evidence from Litigation, 34 J.L. & Econ. 263 (1991) (only 10 to 13 percent of cases include allegations of horizontal collusion).

a manufacturer fixes the minimum resale prices of its dealers, but we also include restrictions on the territories within which a dealer may sell or on the customers to whom it may sell, as well as limitations on the manufacturer's appointment of additional dealers. This rather summary listing does not always distinguish sharply among these several forms of distribution restraint.[7] In each case, consider why a manufacturer might employ resale price maintenance or other restrictions on dealer competition rather than, say, requiring dealers by contract to provide specified services or providing such services (advertising for instance) itself.

(a) *Goodwill.* It is often said that a manufacturer may restrain distribution to achieve the goodwill of its dealers or to protect its own goodwill interest in its product. The dealer goodwill prized by every manufacturer is simply the dealer's willingness to handle the product and to do so in a favorable manner. It breaks down into the more specific arguments that follow. This is also true of the general defense offered for vertical distribution restraints, that they protect the manufacturer's goodwill in its brand. This turns out to be an argument about the services and image associated with the product.

(b) *Free riding.* The most common free-rider argument emphasizes costly services that some dealers provide but cannot charge for separately. For example, a manufacturer of stereo equipment understands that its sales will be enhanced by presale demonstration and explanation. Individual dealers providing such services, however, might find that customers take the free advice from them but purchase the product at a lower price from the next-door discounter or mail-order house, which has avoided the costs of listening rooms, trained salespeople, and the like. The full-service dealers bear costs that prevent them from matching these discount prices. If a significant fraction of consumers shop at the full-service outlet and purchase from a no-frills discounter, the manufacturer may find it difficult to induce dealers to offer such services. There is force to this argument, although free riding or other market failures need not impede effective distribution. As illustrated by parenthetical examples, unrestrained intrabrand competition does not lead to detrimental free riding when dealers provide no significant services (drug store selling toothpaste), the services they do provide (luxurious ambience) cannot be utilized by customers who patronize other dealers, the services are paid for separately (post-sale repair), the services provided are not brand specific (department store's general reputation), the services can be provided directly by the manufacturer (much advertising), or a sufficient number of consumers patronize the dealers from whom they receive the service.

7. Territorial and customer restraints are addressed further in ¶¶408, 410.

When free riding is a serious problem, resale price maintenance offers one possible solution for the manufacturer because the discounter can no longer lure consumers from the full-service store by offering lower prices. Of course, they will be able to free-ride somewhat, as some consumers will shop one day and purchase later from a store that did not provide the earlier services. Moreover, creative discounters may circumvent a proscription against price cutting by offering favorable credit, free delivery, or other inducements. Exclusive territories can also limit free riding, in this case by making it inconvenient for customers to browse at one store and purchase at another.

The provision of such additional services might sometimes be excessive. Although there is no reason to suppose that excess can be identified by antitrust tribunals, it is the case that such services often benefit the manufacturer at the expense of its competitors (advertising is an oft-noted example), making it unclear how much consumers benefit. And even when distribution restraints benefit consumers by controlling free riding, they may simultaneously harm competition and consumer welfare in other ways. Indeed, there may be equally effective means of assuring dealer services with fewer anticompetitive risks in the particular case or generally. This is not to say that distribution restraints are always or usually harmful, but to say only that one should approach free-rider justifications with caution.

(c) *Brand image: loss leaders.* Vertical price floors prevent discounting that, it was once commonly argued, would cheapen the brand and ultimately reduce sales. Although not impossible, raising product demand by raising the price seems rare, and, if accomplished by raising the wholesale price, is more in the manufacturer's interest. It was also argued that price floors were needed to stop discounters from selling a product below cost as a loss leader in order to attract customers who, once in the store, would buy other things at high prices. Not only would consumers then think the brand worth only the lower price, they would erroneously believe that the dealer's other prices were low as well, and other dealers would be unwilling to match the losing price and might abandon the product altogether. It has not been established, however, whether below-cost retailing that harms manufacturers or consumers occurs with any frequency.

(d) *Brand image: elite stores' "certification" of fashionability or quality.* Business talk of preserving a brand's image might be restated in terms of the fashion or quality signals emitted by high-priced, elite retailers, who might cease handling a brand that comes to be discounted by less prestigious stores. The elite store provides, in effect, an information service to consumers who believe, perhaps correctly, that such a retailer knows or even creates fashion or undertakes expensive testing, guaranteeing a high-quality inventory that preserves its own reputation. Consumers may appropriate this information without paying for it and buy from discount stores, which thus receive a free ride on the elite stores' expensive certifications. If such free riding deprives the latter of the reward for their efforts, they will cease to provide the service, the flow of information to consumers will decline, and sales of the brand will fall — much as in the case of presale services described in ¶b.

This argument appeals to defenders of resale price maintenance because it appears to explain the practice on products not requiring such tangible services as demonstration or repair, which are invoked by the usual free-rider argument. Notwithstanding some merit in this version of the image argument, the marketplace is full of free riding — on unpatentable innovations, for example — that has not been thought sufficient to warrant public prevention or even to allow private protection. Moreover, free riding may not substantially impair the flow of valuable information from elite dealers, primarily because they presumably profit from their own reputations for fashion or quality notwithstanding some free riding.[8] One might also question how many consumers shop in elite stores to determine which brands they carry, only to go to cut-rate outlets to make their purchases. Of course, the manufacturer who chooses resale price maintenance may think otherwise, but such manufacturers may in fact be the victims of elite dealers' power. Also, one might question whether society has too few fashion or quality goods, notwithstanding the present illegality of resale price maintenance.

(e) *Preference by multibrand dealers.* Where dealers handle numerous brands, resale price maintenance may increase a dealer's profit margin on a particular brand and thus encourage it to push that brand. When consumers are unable to judge quality for themselves on such products as nonprescription drugs, they may rely on dealers' recommendations. Consumers might believe that these recommendations are based on quality, although the recommendations are actually based on the dealer's high profit margin, which is protected by resale price maintenance from intrabrand competition. This private benefit for a manufacturer may increase its sales at the expense of rivals, but it results from misleading consumers

---

8. Limiting distribution to such elite stores is another arrangement explored in this section. In addition, manufacturers might directly purchase product endorsements or otherwise compensate elite stores for their association with products, although such payments might raise issues of price discrimination, explored in Ch. 6.

and thereby reduces their welfare. Moreover, if this practice is imitated by rival manufacturers, none will gain any relative advantage, but none may be willing to sacrifice its sales to others by abandoning it.[9]

(f) *Avoiding dealer concentration.* It is sometimes argued that, without resale price maintenance, the largest and most aggressive retailers would drive smaller merchants out of business, because either the larger firms behave predatorily or they are more efficient. A distribution restraint can prevent price cutting or otherwise prevent low-cost dealers from expanding their sales at the expense of less efficient dealers. Although high-cost distribution seems contrary to the manufacturer's interest, it might fear that it would become unduly dependent on a few super-efficient dealers who could either change their allegiance to its detriment or, by threatening to do so, bargain for a greater share of the brand's profits. In most instances, this would not motivate distribution restraints because the manufacturer's product will be only one of many carried by retailers. Thus, a single manufacturer's action is unlikely to affect the survival of any retailer, much less retailer market structure as a whole. Moreover, unless the result will be a highly concentrated retail market, more efficient distribution benefits manufacturers. And if excessive resale prices were the feared result, a manufacturer might (if it were legal) later set *maximums* for resale prices, unless it anticipated that dealer power would be too great to permit such a bargain.

(g) *Extensive availability.* The product might be one whose sales are less dependent on small price changes than on widespread and immediate availability. In order to have more dealers, one might imagine that a manufacturer would restrain the prices or territories of low-cost or potentially low-cost dealers in order to prevent them from achieving the large-scale operation that minimizes their costs, eliminates inefficient dealers, reduces resource use, and benefits consumers with lower prices. The motivating assumption is that sales may be larger with many dispersed dealers than with fewer low-cost and low-priced outlets because many consumers would thus benefit from the service of convenient access. But if consumers in fact desire convenience, even at a cost, resale price maintenance or other restrictions would generally be unnecessary, as consumers' demand would sustain the convenience outlets — for example, vending machine prices are well above those in a supermarket. If consumers would not pay the higher prices to sustain convenience outlets, the manufacturer would generally find that it could not increase sales to such consumers by imposing high prices through

9. The latter point is also suggested by the free-rider argument in ¶b and elite store certification in ¶d.

resale price maintenance. In addition, as noted in ¶f, limiting competition on one brand alone cannot sustain a dealer whose other brands or products are subject to such intense intrabrand competition as to make handling them unprofitable. Indeed, many convenience outlets are supported by a variety of brands and products such that resale price maintenance on one of them would make little difference.

(h) *Efficient territorial size.* Instead of promoting high-cost small-scale dealers, a manufacturer might use territorial or customer restraints to prevent invading dealers from depriving a dealer of the patronage necessary to allow it to operate at efficient scale. But restraints would be useful only if the efficient invading dealer failed to serve adequately the actual or potential customers of the rival that it weakened or ruined, and if the manufacturer's product line was a significant portion of the dealer's business.

(i) *Dealer specialization: product quality and price discrimination.* In order to serve the peculiar needs of certain customers, a manufacturer may appoint specialized dealers and restrict them from selling to regular customers or restrict regular dealers from selling to the special customers. The regular dealers may be ill-suited for this task or might deprive the specialists of necessary scale economies. More likely, price discrimination will be involved. The specialized dealers might receive a lower wholesale price to enable them to reach customers with more elastic demand — bulk buyers, for example. Unless fenced in by customer restraints, they might use those lower wholesale prices to sell to regular customers, undercutting regular dealers. Or it may be the regular dealers who receive a lower wholesale price in recognition of their higher unit costs of reselling the product one unit at a time — a margin that may well be unnecessarily large when bulk resales are made. Unless regular dealers are fenced out of the specialized channel, they might undersell the specialized dealers and thus force the price to bulk buyers even lower than the manufacturer thought necessary. The latter case is more likely to impair consumer welfare than the former, but the results of price discrimination generally are indeterminate.[10] In any event, there may be little point in prohibiting price discrimination that can be achieved by other lawful means. On the other hand, if a restraint were detrimental on other grounds, the same argument would counsel against accepting a defense for price discrimination.

(j) *Market penetration; price discrimination.* Territorial restraints might aid intensive market penetration. Fencing a dealer into an assigned territory forces it to find its profit there without distraction from possible sales elsewhere. Fencing other dealers out of its terri-

10. See ¶285b.

tory allows it to (1) survive although its area is too small for minimum-cost operation and (2) exploit those consumers who can be served at low cost but who are willing to pay the full list price. Such high-profit transactions — so-called "cream," which the restraint prevents others from skimming — may then subsidize no-profit or even negative-profit sales to low-value consumers, which the manufacturer may require by insisting that the dealer meet a minimum sales quota. Although encouraging more intensive dealer sales efforts seems generally legitimate, the pattern just described may involve price discrimination, which has the usual ambiguities: We cannot tell whether the gains from prohibiting restraints facilitating discrimination would generally offset the losses from sacrificing beneficial price discrimination plus the losses that result from channeling transactions into more costly alternatives. To the extent that there are adverse effects from price discrimination, interbrand competition moderates but does not eliminate them.

(k) *Product quality: safety, dealer responsibility.* When a product is offered in forms unsuitable for ordinary consumers — for example, an insecticide destined for professionals already familiar with the instructions and warnings necessary for home gardeners — a manufacturer may restrict dealers handling the professional package from reselling it to the home gardeners. Also, customer or territorial restraints may help assure that dealers know and keep track of their local customers — more than a remote dealer would. Such dealers will then be in a position to make sure that stale goods are retrieved, customers know how to use the product, and safety and product recall notices actually reach consumers. This is a genuine benefit, although one inapplicable to most consumer products.

(l) *Promote entry.* A "pioneer" dealer handling a new product or an existing product in a new region may be expected to make significant investments in cultivating demand, through advertising and product demonstration. Such a dealer may fear that its manufacturer will designate other dealers before it recovers its investment in developing the market for that brand. Such new dealers, unburdened by development costs, may drive the price down to their costs, taking a free ride on the pioneer's investment. Without distribution restraints, a new manufacturer may find no dealers willing to make the pioneering investment and may thus be dissuaded from entry. The restraint that makes such entry possible is thus procompetitive. The relevant restraint is more likely to regulate the manufacturer's appointment of new dealers or to limit other dealers' customers or territories than to specify price. Resale price maintenance does not guarantee the pioneering dealer that the price later specified by the manufacturer will be based on the pioneer's own earlier unrecovered costs of developing the market. Nor does it prevent the manufacturer from appointing other dealers who will divert sales from the pioneer before it has recovered that investment. In fact, if sufficient intrabrand (nonprice) competition among the dealers results, the entire margin may be competed away, again leaving no further recovery for the pioneer. The prospective pioneer who fears that the manufacturer will double-cross it by creating intrabrand competition once that becomes feasible but before its initial investment is recouped is thus unlikely to be reassured by the prospect of future resale price maintenance. Finally, much initial stimulus of demand may be done by the manufacturer directly, through national or regional advertising campaigns, thus alleviating the need to stimulate dealer investment. In any event, to allow a new entry defense to otherwise illegal competitive restraints, we need to decide when expansion by minor firms should be treated like initial entry and how long any special treatment should last. Somewhat more difficult is the situation of a weak manufacturer who may have a greater need than better-known rivals for the promotional and demonstration services stimulated by distribution restraints (justifying restraints) or who is more likely to be the victim of dealer power (favoring prohibition).

(m) *Promote interbrand competition; distribution restraints presumptively efficient?* The preceding arguments might be generally summarized in the claim that manufacturers restrict intrabrand competition in order to intensify interbrand competition. Similarly, the various arguments presented above, especially free-rider arguments, are particular versions of the more comprehensive argument that distribution restraints generally promote efficient distribution and thus improve consumer welfare. The argument builds on the truth that a rational manufacturer knows that its profits would necessarily decline if limiting intrabrand competition allowed its dealers to earn more than necessary for effective distribution. Such a manufacturer would not restrain intrabrand competition more than necessary to make its product more attractive to consumers through, for example, expanded dealer services. Although forceful, the argument needs to be qualified.

First, the manufacturer may mistake its own interest. Such mistakes doubtless occur, but we might well ignore this danger because the market tends to punish and therefore to induce correction of such mistakes.[11] Furthermore, judges or juries are generally no

---

11. Note, however, that in two of three case studies of resale price maintenance reported in Impact Evaluations of Federal Trade Commission Vertical Restraint Cases (R. Lafferty, R. Lande & J. Kirkwood eds. 1984), firms were found to have continued using resale price maintenance well after its use in establishing new products or brands had ceased, to the detriment of both manufacturers and consumers.

better equipped than a manufacturer to judge what best serves its business interest. The existence of mistakes, however, may explain occasional restraints that seem difficult to rationalize on other grounds and justify less deference to manufacturers' decisions when anticompetitive effects are possible, but uncertain.

Second, even if it is not mistaken, the manufacturer may restrain distribution because it wants to induce dealers to accept tie-ins or requirements contracts, it seeks to facilitate price coordination with rival manufacturers, or it is forced by powerful dealers or a dealer cartel to limit intrabrand competition, as noted in ¶¶n-p. If such cases could readily be distinguished from those enhancing interbrand competition, courts could simply prohibit restraints for the former and permit them for the latter. Because it is often difficult to discover the motivation for or likely effect of a given restraint, however, the formulation of presumptions and proof burdens will have to be guided by the perceived likelihood of the various possible outcomes and the magnitude of benefit or harm associated with each. In such instances, the existence of alternative, legal mechanisms will be important. For example, if most legitimate purposes served by restraints on intrabrand competition could be served almost as well in most instances by less restrictive alternatives that did not pose the same competitive dangers, there may be a strong argument for prohibition of the restraints, absent compelling evidence of an exception.

Third, the activities a manufacturer seeks to promote may lead to wasteful, excessive or entry-impeding levels of brand differentiation. Product variation, advertising, and point-of-sale services may be excessive in the sense of using more resources than some consumers desire and thus depriving them of the choice to obtain that product at a lower price without unwanted services.[12] Still, courts have no practical way to determine the excessiveness of services or product differentiation, in particular cases or generally, and some of the potentially adverse effects of product differentiation may be unavoidable attributes of a valuable competitive process. Furthermore, the services promoted by distribution restraints are neither more nor less detrimental when provided directly by the manufacturer itself. Yet the question remains whether prohibiting the restraints would sacrifice much consumer welfare.

(n) *Quid pro quo for other restraints foreclosing rival manufacturers.* A manufacturer might limit intrabrand competition among dealers in order to please them enough to accept a tie-in or exclusive dealer arrangement limiting their freedom to handle the products of rival

---

12. For a theoretical treatment of some of the issues, see A. Dixit & V. Norman, Advertising and Welfare, 9 Bell J. Econ. 1 (1978).

manufacturers. Of course, such tie-ins or exclusive dealing are not always substantially anticompetitive, and they can be appraised and prohibited by an antitrust court independently of the distribution restraint that accompanies them, as explored in Chapter 4B, 4C.

(o) *Coordination among manufacturers facilitated.*[13] Distribution restraints might aid express or tacit coordination among manufacturers. By eliminating or narrowing competition among all dealers, resale prices fixed industrywide could reduce dealer incentives to bargain for lower wholesale prices from manufacturers. By reducing or eliminating interbrand retail price competition, resale price maintenance reduces the incentive for and the destabilizing consequences of a wholesale price cut; notwithstanding service competition among dealers, a manufacturer has less reason to cut prices when dealers cannot pass on the price cut to consumers. By making manufacturer price decisions more visible, fixed retail prices help the manufacturers monitor each other's pricing decisions and thus discourage both the uncertainty and the secret price cuts that impede tacit coordination and undermine express cartels. See ¶¶229b, 230c. To be sure, manufacturer discounts may be visible enough without resale price maintenance, which may raise distribution costs — and thereby harm manufacturers — by preventing efficient dealers from expanding. But tacit coordination among manufacturers may need stabilizing devices to reduce uncertainty and support their supracompetitive prices.

Even if resale price maintenance contributes significantly to monitoring only in a few instances, the cumulative impact of these ways of facilitating collusion or coordination among manufacturers remains troubling. Although there is considerable dispute about the contribution of resale price maintenance to coordination among manufacturers, resale price maintenance might be presumed dangerous to competition among manufacturers when it covers a substantial portion of a concentrated market. This presumption, however, does not extend to customer and territorial restraints, which are less likely to aid manufacturer collaboration.

(p) *Masquerade for actual horizontal restraint among dealers or for exertion of dealer power.* The manufacturer may restrain intrabrand distribution not because it wants to but because powerful dealers or a dealer cartel force it to do so.[14] Although vertical in form, such a

13. Another theory is that resale price maintenance may facilitate the exercise of *unilateral* manufacturer power by preventing countervailing buyer power from lowering prices. See, e.g., D. O'Brien & G. Shaffer, Vertical Control with Bilateral Contracts, 23 Rand J. Econ. 299 (1992).

14. For an analysis of one way that resale price maintenance may facilitate anticompetitive pricing by retailers, see G. Shaffer, Slotting Allowances and Resale Price Maintenance: A Comparison of Facilitating Practices, 22 Rand J. Econ. 120 (1991).

coerced restraint on intrabrand competition is horizontal in substance. Although this is true and universally acknowledged to be a danger attending legal toleration of vertical restraints, some believe that such extractions are rare in occurrence, insignificant in magnitude, and both readily detected and remedied as illegal horizontal combinations among dealers. Dealer power, however, may not be so rare (particularly if the power of some individual dealers is taken into account[15]) and the antitrust rules controlling horizontal combination cannot themselves prevent all distribution restraints caused by dealer power or cartels. Such considerations are reinforced by taking into account the political forces responsible for fair trade legislation. See ¶405. Nevertheless, it is unclear what portion of distribution restraints can be explained by such power.

The remaining points are not additional reasons why a manufacturer might want to restrain competition, but a few additional considerations bearing on the legal analysis of distribution restraints.

(q) *Dealer freedom impaired.* We will see that the courts have been troubled by the intrusion of vertical restraints upon dealer freedom. Although distribution restraints protect some dealers from others, they interfere with a dealer's autonomy as an independent economic actor. This is undoubtedly true, although not obviously more so than such lawful contractual limitations on dealer freedom as quality or service requirements.

(r) *Less restrictive than lawful vertical integration.* Notwithstanding the possible anticompetitive incidents of distribution restraints, such restraints might be thought preferable to the manufacturer's alternative of vertical integration, distributing its product solely through its own employees. The presumptive legality of such vertical integration, at least for a nonmonopolist, might suggest that distribution restraints, which usually allow more intrabrand competition than vertical integration, should be equally lawful. There is some force to the argument, but two kinds of qualifications are necessary. First, the law's relative hospitality to what a manufacturer does for itself reflects the sheer ubiquity of unilateral action, which courts cannot hope to supervise and which the Sherman Act does not reach apart from monopolization or attempted monopolization. That evil results sometimes attend lawful vertical integration is not therefore reason to tolerate such results achieved via contractual restraints involving independent persons and subject to Sherman Act §1. Second, prohibition of the contractual restraint would be futile if it merely drove manufacturers toward vertical integration or another lawful alternative that achieves the same allegedly evil effect as the prohibited restraint, perhaps at greater cost. But

15. See ¶355.

vertical integration often will not be a viable business option, as is usually the case when the manufacturer's product is one of many carried by retail outlets.

(s) *Other manufacturer alternatives.* Of course, a manufacturer can often achieve its distribution objectives without restraining its deal-ers' freedom to set their own prices or to choose their own cus-tomers or territories. It can advertise or demonstrate the product itself or distribute it in part through its own employees. It can set a higher wholesale price but give a discount to those dealers that provide the services it desires. It might continue selling only to those dealers who provide such services, its contracts with dealers might require each of them to provide specified services, or, as most manufacturers do, it might simply rely on the market to provide the mix of services and prices desired by consumers. Per-haps the antitrust court should assume that the manufacturer would not have chosen distribution restraints unless the alternatives were less effective or more costly. But an alternative can be rejected by a profit-maximizing and error-free manufacturer as long as it is not superior to the restraint it adopted. It may not be common that one is clearly and significantly superior to the other. Indeed, both a restraint and its alternatives are likely to achieve a manufacturer's objectives only crudely. Finally, we must remember that the manu-facturer's choice might reflect an illegitimate interest in strengthen-ing a manufacturer cartel or an unwanted need to bow to dealer pressure.

(t) *Similarity to dealer cartel.* We conclude by emphasizing the con-cern that has led the courts to worry about a manufacturer's limita-tions on its dealers' prices, customers, or territories. Such restraints limit price or quality competition among resellers of a particular manufacturer's product as much as, or even more severely, than would a horizontal cartel among dealers. It is true that both hori-zontal and vertical restraints have the same type of effect, namely the limitation of intrabrand competition, and that manufacturers can compel dealer compliance more effectively than a cartel can police its members. But the dealer cartel is more anticompetitive than a vertical restraint because a manufacturer never shares the dealers' incentive to maximize dealer-level profits, which, when larger than necessary for effective distribution, harm the manufac-turer.[16]

---

16. See ¶402. Where the manufacturer itself competes with its dealers by selling directly to consumers, the ostensibly vertical restriction limits the dealers' horizon-tal competition with the manufacturer, but the manufacturer is not led to generate excess profits at the dealer level. Therefore, a dual distributing manufacturer's vertical restraint is not the same as a horizontal restraint.

DR. MILES MEDICAL CO. v. JOHN D. PARK
& SONS CO.
220 U.S. 373 (1911)

Justice HUGHES. . . . The complainant, a manufacturer of proprietary medicines which are prepared in accordance with secret formulas, presents by its bill a system, carefully devised, by which it seeks to maintain certain prices fixed by it for all the sales of its products both at wholesale and retail. Its purpose is to establish minimum prices at which sales shall be made by its vendees and by all subsequent purchasers who traffic in its remedies. Its plan [using contracts with wholesalers and retailers] is thus to govern directly the entire trade in the medicines it manufactures, embracing interstate commerce as well as commerce within the States respectively. . . .

The defendant is a wholesale drug concern which has refused to enter into the required contract, and is charged with procuring medicines for sale at "cut prices" by inducing those who have made the contracts to violate the restrictions. . . .

That these agreements restrain trade is obvious. . . . But it is insisted that the restrictions are not invalid either at common law or under the [Sherman Act] upon the following grounds, which may be taken to embrace the fundamental contentions for the complainant: (1) That the restrictions are valid because they relate to proprietary medicines manufactured under a secret process; and (2) that, apart from this, a manufacturer is entitled to control the prices on all sales of his own products.

First. . . . The secret process may be the subject of confidential communication and of sale or license to use with restrictions as to territory and prices. Fowle v. Park, 131 U.S. 88. . . . Here, however, the question concerns not the process of manufacture, but the manufactured product, an article of commerce. The complainant has not communicated its process in trust, or under contract, or executed a license for the use of the process with restrictions as to the manufacture and sale by the licensee to whom the communication is made. . . . It is also argued that, as the process is secret, no one else can manufacture the article. But this argument . . . implies that, if for any reason monopoly of production exists, it carries with it the right to control the entire trade of the produced article and to prevent any competition that otherwise might arise between wholesale and retail dealers. The principle would not be limited to secret processes, but would extend to goods manufactured by any one who secured control of the source of supply of a necessary raw material or ingredient. But, because there is monopoly of production, it certainly cannot be said that there is no public interest in maintaining freedom of trade with respect to future sales after the article has been placed on the market and the producer has parted with his title. Moreover, every manufacturer, before sale, controls the articles he makes. With respect to these, he has the rights of ownership and his dominion does not depend upon whether the process of manufacture is known or unknown, or upon any special advantage he may possess by reason of location, materials or efficiency. The fact that the market may not be supplied with the particular article, unless he produces it, is a practical consequence which does not enlarge his right of property in what he does produce. . . .

Second. We come, then, to the second question, whether the complainant, irrespective of the secrecy of its process, is entitled to maintain the restrictions by virtue of the fact that they relate to products of its own manufacture.

The basis of the argument appears to be that, as the manufacturer may make and sell, or not, as he chooses, he may affix conditions as to the use of the article or as to the prices at which purchasers may dispose of it. The propriety of the restraint is sought to be derived from the liberty of the producer.

But because a manufacturer is not bound to make or sell, it does not follow in case of sales actually made he may impose upon purchasers every sort of restriction. Thus a general restraint upon alienation is ordinarily invalid.

> The right of alienation is one of the essential incidents of a right of general property in movables, and restraints upon alienation have been generally regarded as obnoxious to public policy, which is best subserved by great freedom of traffic in such things as pass from hand to hand. General restraint in the alienation of articles, things, chattels, except when a very special kind of property is involved, such as a slave or an heirloom, have been generally held void. . . .

With respect to contracts in restraint of trade, the earlier doctrine of the common law has been substantially modified in adaptation to modern conditions. But the public interest is still the first consideration. To sustain the restraint, it must be found to be reasonable both with respect to the public and to the parties and that it is limited to what is fairly necessary, in the circumstances of the particular case, for the protection of the covenantee. Otherwise restraints of trade are void as against public policy. . . .

The present case is not analogous to that of a sale of good will, or of an interest in a business, or of the grant of a right to use a process of manufacture. The complainant has not parted with any interest in its business or instrumentalities of production. It has conferred no right by virtue of which purchasers of its products may compete with it. It retains complete control over the business in which it is engaged, manufacturing what it pleases and fixing such prices for its own sales as it may desire. Nor are we dealing with a single transaction, conceivably unrelated to the public interest. The agreements are designed to maintain prices, after the complainant has parted with the title to the articles, and to prevent competition among those who trade in them.

The bill asserts the importance of a standard retail price and alleges generally that confusion and damage have resulted from sales at less than the prices fixed. But the advantage of established retail prices primarily concerns the dealers. The enlarged profits which would result from adherence to the established rates would go to them and not to the complainant. It is through the inability of the favored dealers to realize these profits, on account of the described competition, that the complainant works out its alleged injury. If there be an advantage to a manufacturer in the maintenance of fixed retail prices, the question remains whether it is one which he is entitled to secure by agreements restricting the freedom of trade on the part of dealers who own what they sell. As to this, the complainant can fare no better with its plan of identical contracts than could the dealers themselves if they formed a combination and endeavored to establish the same restrictions, and thus to achieve the same result, by agreement with each other. If the immediate advantage they would thus obtain would not be sufficient to sustain such a direct agreement, the asserted ulterior benefit to the complainant cannot be regarded as sufficient to support its system.

But agreements or combinations between dealers, having for their sole purpose the destruction of competition and the fixing of prices, are injurious to the public interest and void. They are not saved by the advantages which the participants expect to derive from the enhanced price to the consumer. . . .

The complainant's plan falls within the principle which condemns contracts of this class. It, in effect, creates a combination for the prohibited purposes. . . . [The product] is an article of commerce and the rules concerning the freedom of trade must be held to apply to it. Nor does the fact that the margin of freedom is reduced by the control of production make the protection of what remains, in such a case, a negligible matter. And where commodities have passed into the channels of trade and are owned by dealers, the validity of agreements to prevent competition and to maintain prices is not to be determined by the circumstance whether they were produced by several manufacturers or by one, or whether they were previously owned by one or by many. The complainant having sold its product at prices satisfactory to itself, the public is entitled to whatever advantage may be derived from competition in the subsequent traffic. . . .

[A]ffirmed.

Justice HOLMES, dissenting. . . . There is no statute covering the case; there is no body of precedent that by ineluctable logic requires the conclusion to which the court has come. The conclusion is reached by extending a certain conception of public policy to a new sphere. On such matters we are in perilous country. I think that, at least, it is safe to say that the most enlightened judicial policy is to let people manage their own business in their own way, unless the ground for interference is very clear. . . . I think that we greatly exaggerate the value and importance to the public of competition in the production or distribution of an article (here it is only distribution), as fixing a fair price. What really fixes that is the competition of conflicting desires. . . . As soon as the price of something that we want goes above the point at which we are willing to give up other things to have that, we cease to buy it and buy something else. Of course, I am speaking of things that we can get along without. There may be necessaries that sooner or later must be dealt with like short rations in a shipwreck, but they are not Dr. Miles's medicines. . . . The Dr. Miles Medical Company knows better than we do what will enable it to do the best business. We must assume its retail price to be reasonable, for it is so alleged and the case is here on demurrer. . . . I cannot believe that in the long run the public will profit by this court permitting knaves to cut reasonable prices for some ulterior purpose of their own and thus to impair, if not to destroy, the production and sale of articles which it is assumed to be desirable that the public should be able to get. . . .

404. Why should antitrust law be concerned with vertical restraints in the distribution of a single product? To put the question in a more manageable form: Why did *Dr. Miles* hold as it did, and is its reasoning persuasive? More particularly:

(a) The Court seemed hostile to restraints on alienation. Why?

(b) Is the resale price provision ancillary to the seller's disposition of an interest by virtue of which the buyer competes with it? The Court thought not. Do you agree? Should the result be different if Dr. Miles also sold directly to ultimate consumers? Would it be legal for a manufacturer to dictate prices to its retailing division? (See *Copperweld*, Ch. 2C.)

(c) The Court suggested that the manufacturer had no independent interest in the resale price. Do manufacturers have any such interests that are legitimate and consistent with the premises of the antitrust laws? If so, are such interests furthered by permitting the manufacturer to fix resale prices? Can they be furthered in other ways?

(d) The Court declared that vertical price fixing "falls within the principle which condemns" horizontal price fixing. (1) In what sense is this true? Does it require the same legal result in the two situations?[17] (2) Could you hold, on *Interstate Circuit*[18] grounds, that the dealers had agreed among themselves to fix prices in violation of Sherman Act §1? (3) Does the existence of a vertical agreement permit or require an inference about the market power of the manufacturer's product? Would the existence of a horizontal agreement among the dealers allow an inference about their market power? (4) Does the manufacturer imposing vertical restraints have the same purpose as the dealer agreeing to horizontal restraints? Are manufacturers and dealers likely to desire the same resale price? If not, what differences would you expect? (5) If the manufacturer could persuade you that dealer-provided services were vital to the success of its product, would you allow it to require dealers to provide the required service? Would the dealers' horizontal agreement requiring such services be lawful? If not, does it follow that a vertical agreement with the same effect would be unlawful?

(e) What is the likely effect of resale price maintenance? On competition among manufacturers? On competition among retailers? On prices to the consumer? If some manufacturers use it? If all use it? In sum, what is the public interest, if any, in competition among dealers?

(f) Would the manufacturer have any legitimate reason for recommending a resale price even though it made no effort to enforce it?

(g) Would you find resale price maintenance on the following facts? Automobile dealers are required to pay a specified sum per car, matched by the manufacturer, for group or even individual dealer advertising approved by the manufacturer. Dealers were not given any advertising allowance for advertisements mentioning or implying that the dealer would sell at a price below that recommended by the manufacturer. The dealers' price and other advertising were not restricted.[19]

---

17. Consider Justice Holmes's statement in dissent that Dr. Miles "knows better than we do what will enable it to do the best business. We must assume its retail price to be reasonable, for it is so alleged and the case is here on demurrer." Is this view consistent with the horizontal price-fixing cases, particularly those decided before *Dr. Miles*?

18. See Ch. 2C; Sun Oil Co. v. FTC, 350 F.2d 624, 632 (7th Cir. 1965), cert. denied, 382 U.S. 982 (1966); Klein v. American Luggage Works, 206 F. Supp. 924 (D. Del. 1962), rev'd, 323 F.2d 787 (3d Cir. 1963).

19. See Nissan Antitr. Litigation, 577 F.2d 910 (5th Cir. 1978), cert. denied, 439 U.S. 1072 (1979) (affirming jury finding for defendant; dealers free to sell and did

405. Fair trade laws. Sherman Act §1 was amended in 1937 by the Miller-Tydings Act to exempt "agreements prescribing minimum prices for the resale of a [branded] commodity which . . . is in free and open competition with commodities of the same general class produced or distributed by others" when such agreements are lawful in the state of resale. The legislation was responsive to pressure by retailing groups[20] and was enacted one year after the Robinson-Patman Act, the subject of Chapter 6, which strengthened the Clayton Act's proscription against price discrimination, and only a few years after the Court's decision in *Appalachian Coals* from Chapter 2A.[21]

Vertical agreements, however, did not fully eliminate retail price competition, and many states enacted nonsigner provisions compelling all retailers to comply with the resale price contract executed by a single retailer in that state. But the Supreme Court held such nonconsensual arrangements outside the Miller-Tydings permission.[22] In response Congress enacted the McGuire Act, permitting the states to authorize a manufacturer to fix resale prices of nonsigners as well as signers. Then, after some 40 years of fair trade, Congress repealed the Miller-Tydings Act and the McGuire Act in 1975.[23] Nevertheless, the reader should know a little about the administration and operation of those statutes, both to understand occasional references in the cases and to see examples of resale price maintenance.

The federal permission for resale price maintenance under state law did not save horizontal agreements among producers, retailers, or, more generally, persons "in competition with each other."[24] Thus, a manufacturer selling at retail could not lawfully fix the prices of retailers in competition with it. The federal permission was also contingent on the existence of "free and open competition with commodities of the same general class." Because the presence of resale price maintenance indicates some market power, this contingency requires that courts either rule that free and open competition is lacking or attempt to assess the degree of power in the particular brand. The first course would have been inconsistent with the basic statutory permission for resale price maintenance, and the second was seldom taken. Usually the courts rendered the condition unimportant by holding it satisfied by a showing that two or more producers sold goods of the same general category.

sell at own prices; nothing "unreasonable per se about anchoring advertised prices to the manufacturer's suggested retail price").

20. See Areeda, note 6, ¶1604(b).
21. See ¶208.
22. Schwegmann Bros. v. Calvert Distillers Corp., 341 U.S. 384 (1951).
23. 89 Stat. 801 (1975). This is addressed further in ¶413a.
24. United States v. McKesson & Robbins, 351 U.S. 305, 312 (1956).

The extent of resale price maintenance declined over the fair trade years. Immediately after the enactment of the McGuire Act, only three states lacked fair trade legislation. Since then, numerous states repealed or held unconstitutional their resale price maintenance statutes or their nonsigner provisions. Even where price maintenance was lawful, moreover, it was often difficult to enforce,[25] and some manufacturers abandoned the practice because they were losing sales to competitors. According to one estimate, the value of items sold subject to maintained prices fell from a high of 10 percent of retail sales in 1959 to 4 percent in 1974.[26] But with federal repeal in 1975, state law can no longer immunize private resale price maintenance programs under the antitrust laws.[27] The continued propriety of the per se approach, however, has been challenged recently before the Supreme Court, although the issue was deemed not properly presented.[28]

406. *Albrecht v. The Herald Co.*, 390 U.S. 145, 152-153 (1968).[29] The Herald ceased selling its newspaper to Albrecht, who had been the publisher's exclusive distributor in an area of the city, when Albrecht insisted on continuing to charge readers *more* than the Herald's suggested retail price. The Supreme Court reversed a refusal to grant Albrecht's motion for judgment notwithstanding the verdict against it. The Court stated that

> schemes to fix maximum prices, by substituting the perhaps erroneous judgment of a seller for the forces of the competitive market, may severely intrude upon the ability of buyers to compete and survive in that market. Competition, even in a single product, is not cast in a single mold. Maximum prices may be fixed too low for the dealer to furnish services essential to the value which goods have for the consumer or to furnish services and conveniences which consumers desire and for which they are willing to pay. Maximum price fixing may channel distribution through a few large or specifically advantaged dealers who otherwise would be subject to significant nonprice competition. Moreover, if the actual price charged under a maximum price scheme is nearly always the fixed maximum price, which is increasingly likely as the maximum price approaches the actual cost of the dealer, the scheme tends to acquire all the attributes of an arrangement fixing minimum prices.

25. C. Fulda, Resale Price Maintenance, 21 U. Chi. L. Rev. 175 (1954).

26. What's "Fair" about State Fair-Trade Laws?, 39 Consumer Reports 783 (1974).

27. On the applicability of preemption and the "state action" doctrine to laws requiring adherence to retail prices, see ¶¶164-165.

28. See note 7 in *Monsanto*.

29. The portion of the Court's opinion addressing the existence of agreement is presented in ¶419.

In response to the argument that the price ceiling was necessary to prevent price gouging within the exclusive territories, the Court suggested that defendant's use of a questionably legal territorial scheme with pernicious consequences could not justify otherwise illegal price fixing.

Justices Stewart and Harlan's dissenting opinions distinguished *Kiefer-Stewart*[30] as involving a horizontal combination and justified the maximum price restraint as an appropriate limit on distributors' monopoly pricing in exclusive territories, which may be an economic necessity in an industry such as this. If not, then intrabrand competition would have prevented the plaintiff from raising prices. The plaintiff should not be allowed to enjoy the benefits of the exclusive territory and then obtain the court's aid in charging monopoly prices.

(a) Justice Douglas's concurring opinion stated that this was "a 'rule of reason' case." Did the Court hold the Herald's attempt to limit Albrecht's maximum resale price unlawful per se?

(b) Why do you suppose the Herald employed exclusive territories for distributing its newspapers? Should such reasons make the action permissible? If the exclusive territory is unlawful, should the plaintiff be awarded damages because the defendant interfered with the plaintiff's exploitation of his mini-monopoly?

(c) Given its exclusive territories, why would the Herald have insisted on establishing maximum resale prices? Are the *Dr. Miles* arguments against *minimum* resale price maintenance and the analysis of ¶¶402-403 applicable to *maximum* resale price restraints?

(d) Is a horizontal agreement fixing maximum prices unlawful? Why? Are the reasons for your answer applicable to a vertical agreement fixing maximum resale prices?[31]

(e) The defendant undoubtedly restricted the freedom of the plaintiff to do as he wished. Does that fact alone support the *Albrecht* result? May a manufacturer require a dealer to maintain a warehouse, devote certain resources to advertising, provide specified services to the public, or avoid certain abuses?[32] Is controlling such behavior distinguishable from controlling a high price?[33]

---

30. This case is discussed in the *Maricopa* opinion in Ch. 2B.

31. See *Maricopa*, Ch. 2B, and ¶¶210-211.

32. See Kestenbaum v. Falstaff Brewing Corp., 575 F.2d 564 (5th Cir. 1978), cert. denied, 440 U.S. 909 (1979) (such restraints lawful); Gordon v. Crown Cent. Petro. Corp., 423 F. Supp. 58 (N.D. Ga. 1976), aff'd mem., 564 F.2d 413 (5th Cir. 1977) (requirement of 24-hour service does not restrict competition); Gibson, 1980 Trade Reg. Rep. ¶21692 (FTC), aff'd, 682 F.2d 554 (5th Cir. 1982), cert. denied, 460 U.S. 1068 (1983) (quality control legitimate).

33. See *Sylvania*, reproduced later in this section, for more recent Supreme Court views on the relevance of restricting the "freedom of the trader."

(f) May a supplier increase the wholesale price to a dealer by the same amount as that dealer had increased the retail price to consumers?[34]

(g) May a manufacturer lawfully include in its national advertising a price to the consumer of $15 when the product is in fact sold through independent dealers?[35] Most dealers do in fact sell at that price. A few charge less and even fewer charge more. Dealers who would like to charge more encounter considerable consumer resistance.

407. *Atlantic Richfield Co. v. USA Petroleum Co.*, 495 U.S. 328 (1990). Atlantic Richfield (ARCO), an integrated oil company, marketed gasoline in the western United States through its own stations and also through ARCO-brand dealers. USA was an independent retailer, which bought gasoline from major petroleum companies, in competition with ARCO dealers. Its outlets typically were low-overhead, high-volume, "discount" stations. USA's complaint alleged that "ARCO and its co-conspirators have organized a resale price maintenance scheme, as a direct result of which competition that would otherwise exist among ARCO-branded dealers has been eliminated by agreement, and the retail price of ARCO-brand gasoline has been fixed, stabilized and maintained at artificially low and uncompetitive levels." In particular, the complaint charged that ARCO's vertical, maximum price-fixing scheme violated Sherman Act §1. The further allegation that ARCO's acts involved predatory pricing in violation of §2 was later withdrawn with prejudice, and the Supreme Court considered the case on the assumption that the pricing involved was not predatory (acknowledging that what constitutes a predatory price had not been defined by the Court). As noted in ¶146d, the Supreme Court held that USA did not suffer antitrust injury.

The Court began by discussing the basis for its *Albrecht* opinion (which it assumed, arguendo, correctly held that vertical, maximum price-fixing is per se illegal).

> [W]e found that a vertical, maximum price-fixing scheme was unlawful per se under §1 of the Sherman Act because it threatened to inhibit vigorous competition by the dealers bound by it and because it threatened to become a minimum price-fixing scheme.... In holding such a maximum-price vertical agreement illegal, we analyzed the manner in which it might restrain competition by dealers. First,

---

34. See Newberry v. Washington Post, 438 F. Supp. 470 (D.D.C. 1977) (unlawful).

35. Cf. Cokeley v. Tandy Corp., 1973 Trade Cas. ¶74342 (N.D. Cal.) (disappointed dealer's motion for summary judgment denied).

we noted that such a scheme, "by substituting the perhaps erroneous judgment of a seller for the forces of the competitive market, may severely intrude upon the ability of buyers to compete and survive in that market." We further explained that "[m]aximum prices may be fixed too low for the dealer to furnish services essential to the value which goods have for the consumer or to furnish services and conveniences which consumers desire and for which they are willing to pay." By limiting the ability of small dealers to engage in nonprice competition, a maximum price-fixing agreement might "channel distribution through a few large or specifically advantaged dealers." Finally, we observed that "if the actual price charged under a maximum price scheme is nearly always the fixed maximum price, which is increasingly likely as the maximum price approaches the actual cost of the dealer, the scheme tends to acquire all the attributes of an arrangement fixing minimum prices."

Thus, *Albrecht* held vertical, maximum price-fixing per se unlawful

> because of its potential effects on dealers and consumers, not because of its effect on *competitors*.... [USA] was *benefitted* rather than harmed if [ARCO's] pricing policies restricted ARCO sales to a few large dealers or prevented [ARCO's] dealers from offering services desired by consumers such as credit card sales. Even if the maximum price agreement ultimately had acquired all of the attributes of a minimum price-fixing scheme, [USA] still would not have suffered antitrust injury because higher ARCO prices would have worked to USA's advantage.... Indeed, the gravamen of [USA's] complaint — that the price-fixing scheme between [ARCO] and its dealers enabled those dealers to increase their sales — amounts to an assertion that the dangers with which we were concerned in *Albrecht* have *not* materialized in the instant case. In sum, [USA] has not suffered "*antitrust* injury," since its losses do not flow from the aspects of vertical, maximum price-fixing that render it illegal.... When a firm, or even a group of firms adhering to a vertical agreement, lowers prices but maintains them above predatory levels, the business lost by rivals cannot be viewed as an "anticompetitive" consequence of the claimed violation.... This is not *antitrust* injury; indeed, "cutting prices in order to increase business often is the very essence of competition." *Matsushita.* The antitrust laws were enacted for "the protection of *competition*, not *competitors*." *Brown Shoe* (emphasis in original). "To hold that the antitrust laws protect competitors from the loss of profits due to [nonpredatory] price competition would, in effect, render illegal any decision by a firm to cut prices in order to increase market share." *Cargill.*

The Court also rejected the argument that because, in a §1 case, the price agreement is itself illegal, all injuries resulting therefrom are "antitrust injuries."

Although a vertical, maximum price-fixing agreement is unlawful under §1 of the Sherman Act, it does not cause a competitor antitrust injury unless it results in predatory pricing. Antitrust injury does not arise for purposes of §4 of the Clayton Act, until a private party is adversely affected by an *anticompetitive* aspect of the defendant's conduct, see *Brunswick*; in the context of pricing practices, only predatory pricing has the requisite anticompetitive effect.... Low prices benefit consumers regardless of how those prices are set, and so long as they are above predatory levels, they do not threaten competition. Hence, they cannot give rise to antitrust injury.

The Court similarly was unconvinced by the claim that no antitrust injury need be shown where a per se violation is involved.

The per se rule is a method of determining whether §1 of the Sherman Act has been violated, but it does not indicate whether a private plaintiff has suffered antitrust injury and thus whether he may recover damages under §4 of the Clayton Act.... The purpose of the antitrust injury requirement is different. It ensures that the harm claimed by the plaintiff corresponds to the rationale for finding a violation of the antitrust laws in the first place, and it prevents losses that stem from competition from supporting suits by private plaintiffs for either damages or equitable relief. Actions per se unlawful under the antitrust laws may nonetheless have *some* procompetitive effects, and private parties might suffer losses therefrom.[36] See *Maricopa*; *Sylvania*.... The antitrust injury requirement ensures that a plaintiff can recover only if the loss stems from a competition-*reducing* aspect or effect of the defendant's behavior. The need for this showing is at least as great under the per se rule as under the rule of reason. Indeed, insofar as the per se rule permits the prohibition of efficient practices in the name of simplicity, the need for the antitrust injury requirement is underscored.

36. At this point, the Court added in a footnote:

When a manufacturer provides a dealer an exclusive area within which to distribute a product, the manufacturer's decision to fix a maximum resale price may actually protect consumers against exploitation by the dealer acting as a local monopolist. The manufacturer acts not out of altruism, of course, but out of a desire to increase its own sales — whereas the dealer's incentive, like that of any monopolist, is to reduce output and increase price. If an exclusive dealership is the most efficient means of distribution, the public is not served by forcing the manufacturer to abandon this method and resort to self-distribution or competing distributors. Vertical, maximum price-fixing thus may have procompetitive interbrand effects even if it is per se illegal because of its potential effects on dealers and consumers. See *Albrecht* (Harlan, J., dissenting).... Indeed, we acknowledged in *Albrecht* that "[m]aximum and minimum price fixing may have different consequences in many situations." The procompetitive potential of vertical maximum price restraint is more evident now than it was when *Albrecht* was decided, because exclusive territorial arrangements and other nonprice restrictions were unlawful per se in 1968.... Many commentators have identified procompetitive effects of vertical, maximum price-fixing....

Finally, the Court addressed the role of the antitrust injury requirement with respect to enforcement of the antitrust laws in this context.

> We decline to dilute the antitrust injury requirement here because we find that there is no need to encourage private enforcement by competitors of the rule against vertical, maximum price-fixing. If such a scheme causes the anticompetitive consequences detailed in *Albrecht*, consumers and the manufacturers' own dealers may bring suit. . . . [USA's] injury, moreover, is not "inextricably intertwined" with the antitrust injury that a dealer would suffer, *McCready*, and thus does not militate in favor of permitting [USA] to sue on behalf of [ARCO's] dealers. A competitor is not injured by the *anticompetitive* effects of vertical, maximum price-fixing, and does not have any incentive to vindicate the legitimate interests of a rival's dealer. . . . A competitor will not bring suit to protect the dealer against a maximum price that is set too low, inasmuch as the competitor would *benefit* from such a situation. Instead, a competitor will be motivated to bring suit only when the vertical restraint promotes interbrand competition between the competitor and the dealer subject to the restraint. In short, a competitor will be injured and hence motivated to sue only when a vertical, maximum price-fixing arrangement has a *procompetitive* impact on the market. Therefore, providing the competitor a cause of action would not protect the rights of dealers and consumers under the antitrust laws.

Justices Stevens and White dissented. They emphasized the following. (1) Only predatory prices are illegal under Sherman Act §2, which regulates unilateral behavior, but all prices set by conspiracies are illegal under §1, without regard to reasonableness. The Court does not disturb the rule that an agreement on maximum resale prices is per se illegal. Yet its argument that nonpredatory maximum resale prices do not cause antitrust injury to competitors exonerates behavior because of the reasonableness of the prices charged. (2) The conspiracy, even if nonpredatory, may drive competitors such as USA from business, as the plaintiff alleges. Because the plaintiff is the direct target of the alleged conspiracy, the plaintiff's injury is antitrust injury. "[Section] 1 is intended to forbid price-fixing conspiracies that are designed to drive competitors out of the market. See *Klor's*." A vertical maximum price-fixing arrangement ancillary to an exclusive distributorship, which might protect consumers from exploitation of dealer monopoly power, must be distinguished from an arrangement designed to drive competitors from the market. (3) Much of the Court's reasoning about what constitutes injury actionable by a competitor would apply even if the alleged conspiracy had been horizontal, involving only the retailers themselves, or, instead, the other major oil companies as well as ARCO. (4) Competitors' suits are required to deter such admittedly illegal behavior; one cannot rely solely on the conspiring dealers themselves to bring suit.

(a) In the *ARCO* case, the plaintiff loses despite being injured by a scheme that is deemed per se illegal. Why?[37]

(b) If only predatory pricing can cause "antitrust injury" to the plaintiff, why is it per se illegal to set maximum resale prices? (Does the Court's footnote suggest that *Albrecht* would be reversed today?) Who is injured? Is their injury an antitrust injury?

Sole Outlets; Territorial and Customer Limitations

408. Territorial limitations generally. (a) *Forms and degrees of limitations.* There are many different ways in which a manufacturer can insulate its dealers from competition with each other. (1) The dealers who are sole outlets in distinct geographic areas might focus on their respective territories and compete relatively little with each other except at the borders. And the greater the space separating the several dealers, the greater will be each dealer's freedom from intrabrand competition. (2) Whatever the distance between dealers, promises by each dealer to devote its best efforts or primary responsibility to developing and serving a particular territory may lead it to do just that and ignore marketing opportunities in adjoining territories. (3) There may be special incentives inducing a dealer to sell in its own area or disincentives for selling elsewhere. For example, the wholesale price might be lower for goods sold locally. Or the dealer selling in another's area might be required to compensate the latter in some way — such as for the cost of free warranty service on the "imported" goods. (4) The dealer's place of business might be agreed upon with the manufacturer. (5) The dealer might agree not to solicit business outside its designated territory or, more stringently, not to sell to buyers located elsewhere or to customers of a particular class.

(b) *Manufacturer motivations.*[38] In considering why a manufacturer would want to restrict intrabrand competition among those who distribute its product, recall ¶¶402-403. We saw that although a manufacturer would ordinarily prefer that intrabrand competi-

---

37. Review ¶146.

38. See P. Rey & J. Stiglitz, The Role of Exclusive Territories in Producers' Competition, 26 Rand J. Econ. 431 (1995). For evidence on the effects of exclusive territories, see T. Sass & D. Saurman, Mandated Exclusive Territories and Economic Efficiency: An Empirical Analysis of the Malt-Beverage Industry, 36 J.L. & Econ. 153 (1993).

tion eliminate any dealer excess profits, a dealer cartel might force it to limit intrabrand competition, or it might do so to maximize its own profits. Territorial or customer limitations might serve a manufacturer's interests in roughly the same ways as resale price maintenance. Product promotion remains relevant, not so much for the image associated with a high price (¶403c) but as the objective or result of encouraging each local dealer to engage in selling and promotional efforts without fear that an invading dealer will harvest the fruits of the local dealer's efforts (¶403b). Thus, avoiding free riders may be one of the principal objectives of customer and territorial limitations. Although interbrand price competition is not precluded by customer or territorial limitations, the objective and result may be to encourage more nonprice competition. Maintaining efficient territorial size and achieving market penetration (¶¶403h, 403j) might also be relevant. Perhaps a manufacturer would impose such a restriction in order to avoid dependence on a few superefficient dealers (¶403f) who would otherwise displace all other dealers, although such a motivation would seem rare. The concerns for elite stores' certification and having a large number of stores (¶¶403d, 403g) seem generally inapplicable. The manufacturer might be attempting price discrimination if purchasers in one area value a product more than do purchasers elsewhere. (Compare ¶403i.) Manufacturer liability for the product and subsequent recalls or service may lead it to insist that each dealer be in a position to see that the product is adequately installed and recalled if and when necessary (¶403k). Finally, the restrictions might contribute to the recruitment of dealers by new entrants and the goodwill of multi-product dealers (¶¶403e, 403*l*) or secure other restraints and reduce interbrand competition among manufacturers (¶¶403n, 403o).

In considering any possible motive for restricting intrabrand competition, we must ask whether the restriction actually serves the stated aim, whether the aim is a legitimate one that is consistent with the purposes of the antitrust laws, whether a less restrictive alternative can generally accomplish the same objective, whether desirable restrictions can be distinguished from undesirable ones, and what calculus or presumptions seem helpful to guide businesses and courts in judging these restraints.

PACKARD MOTOR CAR CO. v. WEBSTER MOTOR CAR CO.
243 F.2d 418 (D.C. Cir.), cert. denied, 355 U.S. 822 (1957)

EDGERTON, Chief Judge. Packard Motor Car Company and two of its officers appeal from a judgment for $570,000 in favor of Webster

Motor Car Company, a former Packard dealer in Baltimore, for alleged violation of the Sherman Anti-Trust Act. The essential facts are not disputed.

There were formerly four dealers in Packard cars in Baltimore. In 1953 there were three, of which Webster was one. The usual dealer contract in the automobile business, and the contract between Packard and Webster, were for one year, with no option of extension. It was the custom in the business to extend contracts, from year to year, "barring some reason for cancellation." Webster and Packard had extended their contracts from year to year a considerable number of times.

In 1953 Zell Motor Car Company, the largest of the three Baltimore dealers in Packard cars, told Packard that Zell was losing money and would quit unless Packard gave it an exclusive contract. Packard told Zell it would do so, and told Webster and the other Baltimore dealer that their contracts would not be renewed. After Webster protested and threatened suit, Packard offered Webster the usual one-year renewal but refused to promise more. Packard told Zell, in effect, that this would be Webster's last renewal. Webster declined Packard's offer, quit the business, and brought this suit.

The District Court submitted to the jury the question whether there was an unreasonable restraint of trade, and also whether there was an agreement or attempt to monopolize. The jury found for the plaintiff and awarded $190,000 damages, which the court trebled in accordance with the statute. Motions for judgment notwithstanding the verdict, and for a new trial, were denied. The court held that the jury had

> a right to reach the conclusion that an agreement on the part of the manufacturer with one of its own dealers to terminate the franchise of all competitors and to grant to him a monopoly within a certain area, is an agreement in unreasonable restraint of trade, or an agreement to monopolize.

We think the defendants were entitled to judgment. We agree substantially with Schwing Motor Co. v. Hudson Sales Co., D.C.D. Md. 1956, 138 F. Supp. 899, affirmed 4 Cir., 1956, 239 F.2d 176.

1. There was no monopoly, or attempt or conspiracy to monopolize, within the meaning of the Sherman Act. *Cellophane*, which had not been decided when the present case was tried, makes this clear. The Supreme Court there said: "this power that, let us say, automobile or soft-drink manufacturers have over their trademarked products is not the power that makes an illegal monopoly. Illegal power must be appraised in terms of the competitive market for the product." And the Court held that "In considering what is the relevant market for determining the control of price and competition . . .

commodities reasonably interchangeable by consumers for the same purposes make up that 'part of the trade or commerce,' monopolization of which may be illegal." The Court accordingly held that, although du Pont produced about 75% of the cellophane sold in this country, there was no monopoly, because "the relevant market" was flexible packaging materials, including such things as glassine, waxed paper, and foil, as well as cellophane, and cellophane accounted for only 17.9% of this market. Since there are other cars "reasonably interchangeable by consumers for the same purposes" as Packard cars and therefore in competition with Packards, an exclusive contract for marketing Packards does not create a monopoly. And there is no evidence of any attempt or conspiracy to create a monopoly, since there is no evidence of any attempt to get control of the relevant market.

2. There was no contract or conspiracy in restraint of trade within the meaning of the Sherman Act. As the court informed the jury, it has long been clear that only unreasonable restraints of trade are unlawful.... When an exclusive dealership "is not part and parcel of a scheme to monopolize and effective competition exists at both the seller and buyer levels, the arrangement has invariably been upheld as a reasonable restraint of trade. In short, the rule was virtually one of per se legality" until the District Court decided the present case. Of Packard's 1600 dealers, 1100 were the only Packard dealers in their cities, some of which were nearly as large as Baltimore, and such a ratio was typical in the automobile industry. The fact that any other dealers in the same product of the same manufacturer are eliminated does not make an exclusive dealership illegal; it is the essential nature of the arrangement. The fact that Zell asked for the arrangement does not make it illegal. Since the immediate object of an exclusive dealership is to protect the dealer from competition in the manufacturer's product, it is likely to be the dealer who asks for it.

The short of it is that a relatively small manufacturer, competing with large manufacturers, thought it advantageous to retain its largest dealer in Baltimore, and could not do so without agreeing to drop its other Baltimore dealers. To penalize the small manufacturer for competing in this way not only fails to promote the policy of the antitrust laws but defeats it....

[R]eversed....

BAZELON, Circuit Judge (dissenting).... From this evidence the jury could have found — as it apparently did — that Webster's elimination as a dealer resulted not from a unilateral decision by Packard in selecting its customers, but rather from an agreement between Packard and Zell to eliminate Zell's competitor and make

Zell the sole distributor of Packard cars in Baltimore; in simple terms, that it was an agreement which amounted to a combination or conspiracy to get rid of Webster.[1]

409. Consider the *Packard* situation. (a) Suppose that Packard had simply appointed Zell a distributor and had appointed no other Baltimore distributors. Suppose also that no agreement or understanding existed between Packard and Zell on whether Packard would designate any other Baltimore distributors. Would the Sherman Act have anything to say with respect to Packard's action?

(b) Should the result differ if Packard had established other Baltimore dealers and then had canceled those dealerships on its own motion and without agreement or consultation with anyone?[39]

(c) Suppose that Packard and Zell agreed that Packard would make Zell its sole outlet in Baltimore.[40] (1) Is this an agreement to boycott the other Baltimore dealers? Is it illegal?[41] (2) Can you infer a harmful effect on competition from this agreement as you can from a price-fixing agreement? (3) Do the effects in ¶¶a-b differ from those here? (4) Is a harmful effect on competition necessary to condemn a collective refusal to deal? (5) Are the reasons for harsh treatment of collective refusals to deal present here?

(d) Would your analysis of the arrangement differ if Packard had only promised to consult existing dealers before appointing any new dealers in the area, and Packard had rejected new applicants after Zell protested?

(e) Would your analysis be different had Packard been more successful and enjoyed a larger market share?

(f) Should the decision of reasonableness in the circumstances described in ¶¶a-e be left to the jury? What does *Packard* hold on this issue?

(g) Suppose the ruling against Packard were upheld, and the situation recurs in another city. (Alternatively, consider what injunctive relief would be appropriate for the victorious plaintiff.)

1. We are not called upon to decide whether §1 of the Sherman Act applies to a manufacturer who, after a discussion with one dealer, decides to make the latter his exclusive distributor, cutting off all others, for the purpose of improving the manufacturer's competitive position vis-à-vis more powerful manufacturers.... That is not this case.

39. E.g., Harron v. United Hosp. Center, 522 F.2d 1133, 1134 (4th Cir.) (per curiam), cert. denied, 424 U.S. 916 (1975) ("frivolous to urge that the employment of a single doctor to operate the radiology department of a hospital invokes the Sherman Act").

40. See Golden Gate Acceptance Corp. v. General Motors Corp., 597 F.2d 676, 678 (9th Cir. 1979) (summary judgment; consistently held that no violation "for a manufacturer to conspire with others to simply switch distributors").

41. Review the *Klors* decision and related cases in Ch. 2E.

Can the complaining dealer be forced to continue selling Packards? Would you force Packard to retain the other dealers and thus lose what may have been its most successful outlet? Should the Court ask whether the complaining dealer was bluffing? Can we know?

(h) What should be the result if Zell were also the sole Baltimore outlet for all other automobile manufacturers or for all other small manufacturers? In the actual case, might Zell be monopolizing or attempting to monopolize? Recall *Lorain Journal* and ¶355. Does the majority thus protect the "relatively small manufacturer, competing with large manufacturers"?

410. Customer limitations. A manufacturer may attempt to restrict the customers to whom its dealers may sell. Because many of the purposes and effects of such a restriction resemble those of territorial limitations,[42] this Paragraph is confined to a few aspects of customer restrictions.

(a) *Controlling resellers.* A manufacturer may sell only to wholesalers and yet be concerned with the quality or behavior of retailers. The manufacturer can limit the title "authorized dealer" to those it approves, but buyers dissatisfied with unapproved dealers may nevertheless blame the manufacturer. It might be in its interest, therefore, to require wholesalers to confine their sales to approved retailers. In this way, the manufacturer can assure that its product is handled only by competent dealers. The wholesaler may also want qualified dealers, but the manufacturer may have greater confidence in its own judgment or a stronger interest. Of course the manufacturer may be concerned not only with the retailer's competence but also with its price. In that event, the manufacturer might withdraw its approval from price-cutting or price-gouging dealers. Customer restrictions confining wholesalers to approved retailers are held to violate Sherman Act §1 when used in support of resale price maintenance.[43]

(b) *Allocating customers among dealers.* A manufacturer might wish to allocate different customers to different dealers. A cosmetics manufacturer, for example, might permit one wholesaler to sell only to drugstores and permit a different wholesaler to sell only to

42. A territorial limitation forbidding the dealer from selling to persons located outside a specified territory is, of course, a restriction on the customers to whom it may sell. A limitation on the location of the dealer's place of business tends to have the same effect. Thus, territorial limitations may be seen as a species of customer restriction. This Paragraph is concerned with nongeographic customer restrictions.

43. United States v. Bausch & Lomb Opt. Co., 321 U.S. 707, 721 (1944); United States v. Univis Lens Co., 316 U.S. 241, 251 (1942); Ethyl Gasoline Corp. v. United States, 309 U.S. 436 (1940).

beauty salons (which both use and resell the product). It might do so for any one of three reasons or for all of them: to limit competition or to facilitate price discrimination — reasons already explored in ¶403 and ¶408 — or to achieve efficient specialization. The exploitation of different distribution outlets may call for different techniques of promotion, servicing, and payment. Wholesalers experienced in dealing with beauty salons may be more effective in selling to them than would be drugstore wholesalers without such experience. Established specialists might confine themselves to their usual undertakings without the compulsion of a customer restriction. But the restriction might nevertheless seem necessary to the creation of a specialized class of wholesalers.[44]

(c) *Reserving customers to the manufacturer.* The manufacturer may wish to exclude dealers from selling to customers that it desires for itself. Its experience or resources may be necessary to sell and service some customers. Others may buy in such large quantities that the manufacturer can efficiently handle them directly and thus eliminate the cost of intermediate distribution. Yet, the dealer's cost may leave it a margin to compete with the manufacturer for such business because the dealer margin may well be predicated on a typical relationship between sales effort and sales volume and the sales effort required for bulk sales might be less (¶403i). Or perhaps sales to large national buyers offer substantial profits that the manufacturer prefers to keep for itself. At the same time, such bulk sales might be profitable at a very low price to a manufacturer with idle capacity. And the price concessions needed to win such sales may be beyond the dealer's means.

CONTINENTAL T.V. v. GTE SYLVANIA
433 U.S. 36 (1977)

Justice POWELL. . . . Franchise agreements between manufacturers and retailers frequently include provisions barring the retailers from selling franchised products from locations other than those specified in the agreements. This case presents important questions concerning the appropriate antitrust analysis of these restrictions

44. The restriction may also be necessary to avoid this Robinson-Patman Act problem: Servicing different outlets may require the specialist wholesaler to undertake certain operations not required of regular wholesalers. Thus, the manufacturer may have to give the specialists different prices, allowances, or services. Such differences create Robinson-Patman Act problems if the two wholesaler types compete at all with each other. Customer limitations prevent the two groups from competing for the same customers and thus eliminate the Robinson-Patman Act issue. See Chs. 6B, 6D.

under §1 of the Sherman Act and the Court's decision in United States v. Arnold, Schwinn & Co., 388 U.S. 365 (1967).

I

Respondent GTE Sylvania, Inc. (Sylvania) manufactures and sells television sets through its Home Entertainment Products Division. Prior to 1962, like most other television manufacturers, Sylvania sold its televisions to independent or company-owned distributors who in turn resold to a large and diverse group of retailers. Prompted by a decline in its market share to a relatively insignificant 1% to 2% of national television sales, Sylvania conducted an intensive reassessment of its marketing strategy, and in 1962 adopted the franchise plan challenged here. Sylvania phased out its wholesale distributors and began to sell its televisions directly to a smaller and more select group of franchised retailers. An acknowledged purpose of the change was to decrease the number of competing Sylvania retailers in the hope of attracting the more aggressive and competent retailers thought necessary to the improvement of the company's market position. To this end, Sylvania limited the number of franchises granted for any given area and required each franchise to sell his Sylvania products only from the location or locations at which he was franchised.[3] A franchise did not constitute an exclusive territory, and Sylvania retained sole discretion to increase the number of retailers in an area in light of the success or failure of existing retailers in developing their market. The revised marketing strategy appears to have been successful during the period at issue here, for by 1965 Sylvania's share of national television sales had increased to approximately 5%, and the company ranked as the Nation's eighth largest manufacturer of color television sets.

This suit is the result of the rupture of a franchiser-franchisee relationship [between Sylvania and Continental T.V., Inc. (Continental)] that had previously prospered under the revised Sylvania plan. [Sylvania, after a series of disputes, terminated Continental for having begun unauthorized expansion into the Sacramento market, which Sylvania thought to be adequately served by existing retailers.]

[Continental claims] that Sylvania had violated §1 of the Sherman Act by entering into and enforcing franchise agreements that prohibited the sale of Sylvania products other than from specified locations. At the close of evidence in the jury trial of Continental's claims, Sylvania requested the District Court to instruct the jury that

3. Sylvania imposed no restrictions on the right of the franchise to sell the products of competing manufacturers.

its location restriction was illegal only if it unreasonably restrained or suppressed competition. Relying on this Court's decision in United States v. Arnold, Schwinn & Co., the District Court rejected the proffered instruction in favor of the following one:

> Therefore, if you find by a preponderance of the evidence that Sylvania entered into a contract, combination or conspiracy with one or more of its dealers pursuant to which Sylvania exercised dominion or control over the products sold to the dealer, after having parted with title and risk to the products, you must find any effort thereafter to restrict outlets or store locations from which its dealers resold the merchandise which they had purchased from Sylvania to be a violation of Section 1 of the Sherman Act, regardless of the reasonableness of the location restrictions.

In answers to special interrogatories, the jury found that Sylvania had engaged "in a contract, combination or conspiracy in restraint of trade in violation of the antitrust laws with respect to location restrictions alone," and assessed Continental's damages at $591,505, which was trebled....

On appeal, the Court of Appeals for the Ninth Circuit, sitting en banc, reversed by a divided vote.... Contrasting the nature of the restrictions, their competitive impact, and the market shares of the franchisers in the two cases, the court concluded that Sylvania's location restriction had less potential for competitive harm than the restrictions invalidated in *Schwinn* and thus should be judged under the "rule of reason" rather than the per se rule stated in *Schwinn*....

II

A

We turn first to Continental's contention that Sylvania's restriction on retail locations is a per se violation of §1 of the Sherman Act as interpreted in *Schwinn*. The restrictions at issue in *Schwinn* were part of a three-tier distribution system comprising, in addition to Arnold, Schwinn & Co. (Schwinn), 22 intermediate distributors and a network of franchised retailers. Each distributor had a defined geographic area in which it had the exclusive right to supply franchised retailers. Sales to the public were made only through franchised retailers, who were authorized to sell Schwinn bicycles only from specified locations. In support of this limitation, Schwinn prohibited both distributors and retailers from selling Schwinn bicycles to nonfranchised retailers. At the retail level, therefore, Schwinn was able to control the number of retailers of its bicycles in any given area according to its view of the needs of that market.

As of 1967 approximately 75% of Schwinn's total sales were made under the "Schwinn Plan." Acting essentially as a manufacturer's representative or sales agent, a distributor participating in this plan forwarded orders from retailers to the factory. Schwinn then shipped the ordered bicycles directly to the retailer, billed the retailer, bore the credit risk, and paid the distributor a commission on the sale. Under the Schwinn Plan, the distributor never had title to or possession of the bicycles. The remainder of the bicycles moved to the retailers through the hands of the distributors. For the most part, the distributors functioned as traditional wholesalers with respect to these sales, stocking an inventory of bicycles owned by them to supply retailers with emergency and "fill-in" requirements. A smaller part of the bicycles that were physically distributed by the distributors were covered by consignment and agency arrangements that had been developed to deal with particular problems of certain distributors. Distributors acquired title only to those bicycles that they purchased as wholesalers; retailers, of course, acquired title to all of the bicycles sold by them.

In the District Court, the United States charged a continuing conspiracy by Schwinn and other alleged co-conspirators to fix prices, allocate exclusive territories to distributors, and confine Schwinn bicycles to franchised retailers. Relying on United States v. Bausch & Lomb Co., 321 U.S. 707 (1944), the Government argued that the nonprice restrictions were per se illegal as part of a scheme for fixing the retail prices of Schwinn bicycles. The District Court rejected the price-fixing allegation because of a failure of proof and held that Schwinn's limitation of retail bicycle sales to franchised retailers was permissible under §1. The court found a §1 violation, however, in "a conspiracy to divide certain borderline or overlapping counties in the territories served by four Midwestern cycle distributors." The court described the violation as a "division of territory by agreement between the distributors ... horizontal in nature," and held that Schwinn's participation did not change that basic characteristic. The District Court limited its injunction to apply only to the territorial restrictions on the resale of bicycles purchased by the distributors in their roles as wholesalers.

Schwinn came to this Court on appeal by the United States from the District Court's decision. Abandoning its per se theories, the Government argued that Schwinn's prohibition against distributors and retailers selling Schwinn bicycles to nonfranchised retailers was unreasonable under §1 and that the District Court's injunction against exclusive distributor territories should extend to all such restrictions regardless of the form of the transaction. The Government did not challenge the District Court's decision on price-fixing, and Schwinn did not challenge the decision on exclusive distributor territories.

The Court acknowledged the Government's abandonment of its per se theories and stated that the resolution of the case would require an examination of "the specifics of the challenged practices and their impact upon the marketplace in order to make a judgment as to whether the restraint is or is not 'reasonable' in the special sense in which §1 of the Sherman Act must be read for purposes of this type of inquiry." Despite this description of its task, the Court proceeded to articulate the following "bright line" per se rule of illegality for vertical restrictions: "Under the Sherman Act, it is unreasonable without more for a manufacturer to seek to restrict and confine areas or persons with whom an article may be traded after the manufacturer has parted with dominion over it." But the Court expressly stated that the rule of reason governs when "the manufacturer retains title, dominion, and risk with respect to the product, and the position and function of the dealer in question are, in fact, indistinguishable from those of an agent or salesman of the manufacturer."

Application of these principles to the facts of *Schwinn* produced sharply contrasting results depending upon the role played by the distributor in the distribution system. With respect to that portion of Schwinn's sales for which the distributors acted as ordinary wholesalers, buying and reselling Schwinn bicycles, the Court held that the territorial and customer restrictions challenged by the Government were per se illegal. But, with respect to that larger portion of Schwinn's sales in which the distributors functioned under the Schwinn Plan and under the less common consignment and agency arrangements, the Court held that the same restrictions should be judged under the rule of reason. The only retail restriction challenged by the Government prevented franchised retailers from supplying nonfranchised retailers. The Court apparently perceived no material distinction between the restrictions on distributors and retailers, for it held: that "The principle is, of course, equally applicable to sales to retailers, and the decree should similarly enjoin the making of any sales to retailers upon any condition, agreement or understanding limiting the retailer's freedom as to where and to whom it will resell the products." Applying the rule of reason to the restrictions that were not imposed in conjunction with the sale of bicycles, the Court had little difficulty finding them all reasonable in light of the competitive situation in "the product market as a whole."

B

In the present case, it is undisputed that title to the televisions passed from Sylvania to Continental. Thus, the *Schwinn* per se rule applies unless Sylvania's restriction on locations falls outside

Schwinn's prohibition against a manufacturer's attempting to restrict a "retailer's freedom as to where and to whom it will resell the products." As the Court of Appeals conceded, the language of *Schwinn* is clearly broad enough to apply to the present case. Unlike the Court of Appeals, however, we are unable to find a principled basis for distinguishing *Schwinn* from the case now before us.

Both Schwinn and Sylvania sought to reduce but not to eliminate competition among their respective retailers through the adoption of a franchise system. Although it was not one of the issues addressed by the District Court or presented on appeal by the Government, the Schwinn franchise plan included a location restriction similar to the one challenged here. These restrictions allowed Schwinn and Sylvania to regulate the amount of competition among their retailers by preventing a franchisee from selling franchised products from outlets other than the one covered by the franchise agreement. To exactly the same end, the Schwinn franchise plan included a companion restriction, apparently not found in the Sylvania plan, that prohibited franchised retailers from selling Schwinn products to nonfranchised retailers. In *Schwinn* the Court expressly held that this restriction was impermissible under the broad principle stated there. In intent and competitive impact, the retail-customer restriction in *Schwinn* is indistinguishable from the location restriction in the present case. In both cases the restrictions limited the freedom of the retailer to dispose of the purchased products as he desired. The fact that one restriction was addressed to territory and the other to customers is irrelevant to functional antitrust analysis and, indeed, to the language and broad thrust of the opinion in *Schwinn*. . . .

III

Sylvania argues that if *Schwinn* cannot be distinguished, it should be reconsidered. Although *Schwinn* is supported by the principle of stare decisis . . . we are convinced that the need for clarification of the law in this area justifies reconsideration. *Schwinn* itself was an abrupt and largely unexplained departure from White Motor Co. v. United States, 372 U.S. 253 (1963), where only four years earlier the Court had refused to endorse a per se rule for vertical restrictions. Since its announcement, *Schwinn* has been the subject of continuing controversy and confusion, both in the scholarly journals and in the federal courts. The great weight of scholarly opinion has been critical of the decision, and a number of the federal courts confronted with analogous vertical restrictions have sought to limit its reach. In our view, the experience of the past 10 years should be brought to bear on this subject of considerable commercial importance.

The traditional framework of analysis under §1 of the Sherman Act is familiar and does not require extended discussion.... [The rule of reason is] the prevailing standard of analysis.... Under this rule, the factfinder weighs all of the circumstances of a case in deciding whether a restrictive practice should be prohibited as imposing an unreasonable restraint on competition. Per se rules of illegality are appropriate only when they relate to conduct that is manifestly anticompetitive. As the Court explained in *Northern Pac. R. Co.*, "there are certain agreements or practices which because of their pernicious effect on competition and lack of any redeeming virtue are conclusively presumed to be unreasonable and therefore illegal without elaborate inquiry as to the precise harm they have caused or the business excuse for their use."

In essence, the issue before us is whether *Schwinn*'s per se rule can be justified under the demanding standards of *Northern Pac. R. Co.* The Court's refusal to endorse a per se rule in *White Motor Co.* was based on its uncertainty as to whether vertical restrictions satisfied those standards. Addressing this question for the first time, the Court stated: "We need to know more than we do about the actual impact of these arrangements on competition to decide whether they have such a 'pernicious effect on competition and lack ... any redeeming virtue' ... and therefore should be classified as per se violations of the Sherman Act." Only four years later the Court in *Schwinn* announced its sweeping per se rule without even a reference to *Northern Pac. R. Co.* and with no explanation of its sudden change in position. We turn now to consider *Schwinn* in light of *Northern Pac. R. Co.*

The market impact of vertical restrictions[18] is complex because of their potential for a simultaneous reduction of intrabrand competi-

---

18. As in *Schwinn*, we are concerned here only with nonprice vertical restrictions. The per se illegality of price restrictions has been established firmly for many years and involves significantly different questions of analysis and policy. As Justice White notes, some commentators have argued that the manufacturer's motivation for imposing vertical price restrictions may be the same as for nonprice restrictions. There are, however, significant differences that could easily justify different treatment. In his concurring opinion in *White Motor Co.*, Justice Brennan noted that, unlike nonprice restrictions, "[r]esale price maintenance is not designed to, but almost invariably does in fact, reduce price competition not only *among* sellers of the affected product, but quite as much *between* that product and competing brands." ... Furthermore, Congress recently has expressed its approval of a per se analysis of vertical price restrictions by repealing those provisions of the Miller-Tydings and McGuire Acts allowing fair trade pricing at the option of the individual States. Consumer Goods Pricing Act of 1975, 89 Stat. 801, amending 15 U.S.C. §§1, 45(a). No similar expression of congressional intent exists for nonprice restrictions.

tion and stimulation of interbrand competition.[19] Significantly, the Court in *Schwinn* did not distinguish among the challenged restrictions on the basis of their individual potential for intrabrand harm or interbrand benefit. Restrictions that completely eliminated intrabrand competition among Schwinn distributors were analyzed no differently than those that merely moderated intrabrand competition among retailers. The pivotal factor was the passage of title: All restrictions were held to be per se illegal where title had passed, and all were evaluated and sustained under the rule of reason where it had not. The location restriction at issue here would be subject to the same pattern of analysis under *Schwinn*.

It appears that this distinction between sale and nonsale transactions resulted from the Court's effort to accommodate the perceived intrabrand harm and interbrand benefit of vertical restrictions. The per se rule for sale transactions reflected the view that vertical restrictions are "so obviously destructive" of intrabrand competition that their use would "open the door to exclusivity of outlets and limitation of territory further than prudence permits."[21] Con-

---

19. Interbrand competition is the competition among the manufacturers of the same generic product — television sets in this case — and is the primary concern of antitrust law. The extreme example of a deficiency of interbrand competition is monopoly, where there is only one manufacturer. In contrast, intrabrand competition is the competition between the distributors — wholesale or retail — of the product of a particular manufacturer.

The degree of intrabrand competition is wholly independent of the level of interbrand competition confronting the manufacturer. Thus, there may be fierce intrabrand competition among the distributors of a product produced by a monopolist and no intrabrand competition among the distributors of a product produced by a firm in a highly competitive industry. But when interbrand competition exists, as it does among television manufacturers, it provides a significant check on the exploitation of intrabrand market power because of the ability of consumers to substitute a different brand of the same product.

21. The Court also stated that to impose vertical restrictions in sale transactions would "violate the ancient rule against restraints on alienation." This isolated reference has provoked sharp criticism from virtually all of the commentators on the decision, most of whom have regarded the Court's apparent reliance on the "ancient rule" as both a misreading of legal history and a perversion of antitrust analysis. . . .

We are similarly unable to accept Judge Browning's interpretation of *Schwinn*. In his dissent below he argued that the decision reflects the view that the Sherman Act was intended to prohibit restrictions on the autonomy of independent businessmen even though they have no impact on "price, quality, and quantity of goods and services." This view is certainly not explicit in *Schwinn*, which purports to be based on an examination of the "impact [of the restrictions] upon the marketplace." Competitive economies have social and political as well as economic advantages, see, e.g., *Northern Pac.*, but an antitrust policy divorced from market considerations would lack any objective benchmarks. . . . Although Justice White's opinion endorses Judge Browning's interpretation, it purports to distinguish *Schwinn* on grounds inconsistent with that interpretation.

versely, the continued adherence to the traditional rule of reason
for nonsale transactions reflected the view that the restrictions have
too great a potential for the promotion of interbrand competition
to justify complete prohibition.[22] The Court's opinion provides no
analytical support for these contrasting positions. Nor is there even
an assertion in the opinion that the competitive impact of vertical
restrictions is significantly affected by the form of the transaction.
Nonsale transactions appear to be excluded from the per se rule,
not because of a greater danger of intrabrand harm or a greater
promise of interbrand benefit, but rather because of the Court's
unexplained belief that a complete per se prohibition would be too
"inflexible."

Vertical restrictions reduce intrabrand competition by limiting
the number of sellers of a particular product competing for the
business of a given group of buyers. Location restrictions have this
effect because of practical constraints on the effective marketing
area of retail outlets. Although intrabrand competition may be reduced, the ability of retailers to exploit the resulting market may be
limited both by the ability of consumers to travel to other franchised
locations and, perhaps more importantly, to purchase the competing products of other manufacturers. None of these key variables,
however, is affected by the form of the transaction by which a
manufacturer conveys his products to the retailers.

Vertical restrictions promote interbrand competition by allowing
the manufacturer to achieve certain efficiencies in the distribution
of his products. These "redeeming virtues" are implicit in every
decision sustaining vertical restrictions under the rule of reason.
Economists have identified a number of ways in which manufacturers can use such restrictions to compete more effectively against
other manufacturers. See, e.g., Preston, Restrictive Distribution Arrangements: Economic Analysis and Public Policy Standards, 30 Law
& Contemp. Prob. 506, 511 (1965).[23] For example, new manufactur-

---

22. In that regard, the Court specifically stated that a more complete prohibition
"might severely hamper smaller enterprises resorting to reasonable methods of meeting the competition of giants and of merchandising through independent dealers."
The Court also broadly hinted that it would recognize additional exceptions to the
per se rule for new entrants in an industry and for failing firms, both of which were
mentioned in *White Motor* as candidates for such exceptions. The Court might have
limited the exceptions to the per se rule to these situations, which present the
strongest arguments for the sacrifice of intrabrand competition for interbrand competition. Significantly, it chose instead to create the more extensive exception for
nonsale transactions which is available to all businesses, regardless of their size,
financial health, or market share. This broader exception demonstrates even more
clearly the Court's awareness of the "redeeming virtues" of vertical restrictions.

23. Marketing efficiency is not the only legitimate reason for a manufacturer's
desire to exert control over the manner in which his products are sold and

ers and manufacturers entering new markets can use the restrictions in order to induce competent and aggressive retailers to make the kind of investment of capital and labor that is often required in the distribution of products unknown to the consumer. Established manufacturers can use them to induce retailers to engage in promotional activities or to provide service and repair facilities necessary to the efficient marketing of their products. Service and repair are vital for many products, such as automobiles and major household appliances. The availability and quality of such services affect a manufacturer's good will and the competitiveness of his product. Because of market imperfections such as the so-called "free rider" effect, these services might not be provided by retailers in a purely competitive situation, despite the fact that each retailer's benefit would be greater if all provided the services than if none did. . . .

Economists also have argued that manufacturers have an economic interest in maintaining as much intrabrand competition as is consistent with the efficient distribution of their products. Bork, The Rule of Reason and the Per Se Concept: Price Fixing and Market Division [II], 75 Yale L.J. 373, 403 (1966); Posner, supra, n.13, at 283, 287-288. Although the view that the manufacturer's interest necessarily corresponds with that of the public is not universally shared, even the leading critic of vertical restrictions concedes that *Schwinn*'s distinction between sale and nonsale transactions is essentially unrelated to any relevant economic impact. Comanor, Vertical Territorial and Customer Restrictions: White Motor and Its Aftermath, 81 Harv. L. Rev. 1419, 1422 (1968).[25] Indeed, to the extent that the form of the transaction is related to interbrand benefits, the Court's distinction is inconsistent with its articulated concern for the ability of smaller firms to compete effectively with larger ones. Capital require-

---

serviced. As a result of statutory and common-law developments, society increasingly demands that manufacturers assume direct responsibility for the safety and quality of their products. For example, at the federal level, apart from more specialized requirements, manufacturers of consumer products have safety responsibilities under the Consumer Product Safety Act, 15 U.S.C. §2051 et seq., and obligations for warranties under the Consumer Product Warranties Act, 15 U.S.C. §2301 et seq. Similar obligations are imposed by state law. See, e.g., Cal. Civ. Code Ann. §1790 et seq. The legitimacy of these concerns has been recognized in cases involving vertical restrictions. See, e.g., Tripoli Co. v. Wella Corp., supra, 425 F.2d 932 (CA3 1970).

25. Professor Comanor argues that the promotional activities encouraged by vertical restrictions result in product differentiation and, therefore, a decrease in interbrand competition. This argument is flawed by its necessary assumption that a large part of the promotional efforts resulting from vertical restrictions will not convey socially desirable information about product availability, price, quality, and services. Nor is it clear that a per se rule would result in anything more than a shift to less efficient methods of obtaining the same promotional effects.

ments and administrative expenses may prevent smaller firms from using the exception for nonsale transactions.[26] ...

We conclude that the distinction drawn in *Schwinn* between sale and nonsale transactions is not sufficient to justify the application of a per se rule in one situation and a rule of reason in the other. The question remains whether the per se rule stated in *Schwinn* should be expanded to include nonsale transactions or abandoned in favor of a return to the rule of reason. We have found no persuasive support for expanding the per se rule. As noted above, the *Schwinn* Court recognized the undesirability of "prohibit[ing] all vertical restrictions of territory and all franchising...."[27] And even Continental does not urge us to hold that all such restrictions are per se illegal.

We revert to the standard articulated in *Northern Pac. R. Co.*, and reiterated in *White Motor*, for determining whether vertical restrictions must be "conclusively presumed to be unreasonable and therefore illegal without elaborate inquiry as to the precise harm they have caused or the business excuse for their use." Such restrictions, in varying forms, are widely used in our free market economy. As indicated above, there is substantial scholarly and judicial authority supporting their economic utility. There is relatively little authority to the contrary.[28] Certainly, there has been no showing in this case, either generally or with respect to Sylvania's agreements, that vertical restrictions have or are likely to have a "pernicious effect on competition" or that they "lack ... any redeeming virtue."[29] Ac-

26. We also note that per se rules in this area may work to the ultimate detriment of the small businessmen who operate as franchisees. To the extent that a per se rule prevents a firm from using the franchise system to achieve efficiencies that it perceives as important to its successful operation, the rule creates an incentive for vertical integration into the distribution system, thereby eliminating to that extent the role of independent businessmen....

27. Continental's contention that balancing intrabrand and interbrand competitive effects of vertical restrictions is not a "proper part of the judicial function" is refuted by *Schwinn* itself. *Topco* is not to the contrary, for it involved a horizontal restriction among ostensible competitors.

28. There may be occasional problems in differentiating vertical restrictions from horizontal restrictions originating in agreements among the retailers. There is no doubt that restrictions in the latter category would be illegal per se, see, e.g., United States v. General Motors Corp., 384 U.S. 127 (1966); *Topco*, but we do not regard the problems of proof as sufficiently great to justify a per se rule.

29. The location restriction used by Sylvania was neither the least nor the most restrictive provision that it could have used.... Although distinctions can be drawn among the frequently used restrictions, we are inclined to view them as differences of degree and form.... We are unable to perceive significant social gain from channeling transactions into one form or another. Finally, we agree with the Court in *Schwinn* that the advantages of vertical restrictions should not be limited to the categories of new entrants and failing firms. Sylvania was faltering, if not failing, and we think it would be unduly artificial to deny it the use of valuable competitive tools.

cordingly, we conclude that the per se rule stated in *Schwinn* must be overruled. In so holding we do not foreclose the possibility that particular applications of vertical restrictions might justify per se prohibition under *Northern Pac. R. Co.* But we do make clear that departure from the rule of reason standard must be based upon demonstrable economic effect rather than — as in *Schwinn* — upon formalistic line drawing.

In sum, we conclude that the appropriate decision is to return to the rule of reason that governed vertical restrictions prior to *Schwinn.* When anticompetitive effects are shown to result from particular vertical restrictions they can be adequately policed under the rule of reason, the standard traditionally applied for the majority of anticompetitive practices challenged under §1 of the Act. Accordingly, the decision of the Court of Appeals is [a]ffirmed.

[Justice White concurred in the judgment. First, he distinguished *Schwinn* "because there is less potential for restraint of intrabrand competition and more potential for stimulating interbrand competition." Sylvania dealers were free, for example, to sell to price discounters in their own area or elsewhere, which would be especially important for competition when interbrand competition is weak. Furthermore, Sylvania "had an insignificant market share at the time it adopted its challenged distribution practice and enjoyed no consumer preference that would allow its retailers to charge a premium over other brands." Indeed, White saw "no doctrinal obstacle to excluding firms with such minimal market power as Sylvania from the reach of the *Schwinn* rule."

Second, White defended *Schwinn*'s distinction between sale and nonsale transactions because "independent businessmen should have the freedom to dispose of the goods they own as they see fit." In that connection he cited *Dr. Miles, GE, Albrecht,* and *Colgate* (each is considered elsewhere in this section).

> [W]hile according some weight to the businessman's interest in controlling the terms on which he trades in his own goods may be anathema to those who view the Sherman Act as directed solely to economic efficiency, this principle is without question more deeply embedded in our cases than the notions of "free rider" effects and distribution efficiencies borrowed by the majority from the "new economics of vertical relationships."

Third,

> It is common ground among the leading advocates of a purely economic approach to the question of distribution restraints that the economic arguments in favor of allowing vertical nonprice restraints

generally apply to vertical price restraints as well. . . . The effect, if not the intention, of the Court's opinion is necessarily to call into question the firmly established per se rule against price restraints.][45]

411. (a) What are the competitive dangers and redeeming virtues of territorial limitations on dealers? For simplicity, consider the "strict" territorial confinement agreement that prevents a dealer from soliciting or selling to anyone outside a specified area. Review each of the rationales raised in ¶¶402, 403, and 408, and *Sylvania*. With respect to each possible benefit, analyze the usual questions. (1) What exactly is the benefit claimed and how is it served by territorial limitations? (2) Is the claimed benefit consistent with antitrust policy and therefore legitimate? (3) Can legitimate ends be achieved in less restrictive ways? With respect to competitive dangers, assess (1) how territorial limitations serve anticompetitive purposes and (2) whether situations in which they are present can be distinguished from those involving no serious risk.

(b) Does a territorial restraint always injure competition because it necessarily restricts the freedom of the trader, who is subject to the restriction? See the *Sylvania* Court's note 21 and ¶406e.

(c) Appraise the argument made by some commentators that all restrictions on intrabrand competition imposed by a manufacturer in its own interest are legitimate because such a manufacturer would have no reason for doing so except to distribute its product in the most efficient manner.

(d) Which explanations are most consistent with the facts of *Sylvania*? What result should follow? Does *Sylvania* express a judgment about which of the justifications canvassed in ¶403 and ¶408 are legitimate under the Sherman Act or did it simply hold that the question of justification is open for consideration in each case?

(e) Does the magnitude or seriousness of the intrabrand restrictions depend on the manufacturer's market share? Would such a market share ordinarily reflect the degree to which that manufacturer's price is relatively unaffected by price changes on rival products?

---

45. Rehnquist, J., did not participate. Brennan and Marshall, JJ., dissented. On remand, the trial judge found the defendant's location restraint reasonable under either of two possible tests: (1) the detriment of lessened intrabrand competition did not outweigh the benefit of enhanced interbrand competition or (2) the restriction was intended to serve the manufacturer's own interests rather than the interests of any dealer cartel. The court emphasized Sylvania's faltering status, the absence of oligopoly (existence of more than 100 competing manufacturers), Sylvania's improved effectiveness as a competitor, and the less restrictive character of the locational restriction. 461 F. Supp. 1046 (N.D. Cal. 1978), aff'd, 694 F.2d 1132 (9th Cir. 1982).

(f) Should an intrabrand restriction imposed by a manufacturer to serve its own interests be treated differently than one imposed to serve dealer interests? If so, how can we tell whose interests are being served in the particular case? Suppose that the manufacturer imposes the restraint (1) without consultation, (2) after a request from one dealer, from several dealers individually, or from several dealers collectively, or (3) without consultation but takes later enforcement steps after complaints from dealers?

(g) Assuming that a horizontal restriction among dealers would violate the Sherman Act, what should be the status of a vertical restraint imposed on dealers where the manufacturer itself sells directly to consumers? The restraint might, for example, prevent dealers from selling in an area where the manufacturer sells to consumers.[46]

412. Consider *Sylvania*'s treatment of *Schwinn* and its adoption of a rule of reason approach.

(a) From your reading of the *Sylvania* majority and the summary of Justice White's concurrence, do you believe that a result for the defendant could have been reconciled with *Schwinn*?[47]

(b) Had *Schwinn* denied the existence of redeeming virtues for territorial restrictions? Why had *Schwinn* allowed restrictions when Schwinn retained "dominion" over the bicycles? (1) Because Schwinn may do what it wishes with respect to "its own goods"? (2) For some other reason? (3) Is the reason for permitting the restriction when Schwinn retains dominion absent when Schwinn sells the bicycles to distributors? (4) Can you explain or otherwise account for the *Schwinn* ruling? Reconsider these questions in connection with the subsection on "agency," which follows.

(c) What was the *Schwinn* Court's rationale for its virtual per se prohibition of customer and territorial restraints? Would per se prohibition be warranted by the difficulty of appraising these re-

---

46. A number of cases treat such arrangements as horizontal restraints, at least in part. E.g., Hobart Bros. Co. v. M.T. Gilliland, 471 F.2d 894 (5th Cir.), cert. denied, 412 U.S. 923 (1973); Pitchford Scientific Instruments Corp. v. Pepi, 531 F.2d 92 (3d Cir.), cert. denied, 426 U.S. 935 (1970); Interphoto Corp. v. Minolta Corp., 295 F. Supp. 711 (S.D.N.Y.), aff'd, 417 F.2d 621 (2d Cir. 1969). That approach was rejected in Krehl v. Baskin-Robbins Ice Cream Co., 1979 Trade Cas. ¶62806 (C.D. Cal.), aff'd, 664 F.2d 1348 (9th Cir. 1982); Abadir & Co. v. First Miss. Corp., 651 F.2d 422, reh'g denied, 656 F.2d 700 (5th Cir. 1981). See generally S. Altschuler, Sylvania, Vertical Restraints and Dual Distribution, 25 Antitr. Bull. 1 (1980).

47. Only Justice Brennan remained on the Court from the *Schwinn* majority, and he dissented in *Sylvania*. Similarly, Justice Stewart, who dissented in *Schwinn*, joined the *Sylvania* majority. Justice White, the only other remaining Justice, did not participate in *Schwinn*.

straints in particular cases because the relevant factual determinations cannot easily be made and because the relevant market circumstances change frequently?

(d) What is the *Sylvania* Court's standard for determining when to impose per se liability? How was that standard applied in *Sylvania?*

(e) What does it mean to say that the *Sylvania* restriction is governed by the rule of reason? In a footnote, the Court quoted the usual language from *Chicago Board of Trade,* reproduced in Chapter 2A. Is that language helpful? How should one determine reasonableness from the nature, purpose, and history of the restraint?

(f) After *Sylvania,* must the plaintiff prove (or the defendant disprove) that the challenged restraint had a net adverse effect on consumer welfare because the adverse effect on intrabrand competition outweighed the beneficial impact on interbrand competition? Would such a requirement be equivalent to per se toleration (or condemnation) of intraband restrictions?[48]

(g) Which party should have the burden of going forward with evidence on possible detriments to competition or on possibly redeeming virtues or on the adequacy or inadequacy of less restrictive alternatives? What should be the outcome of a case where the only evidence consists of one or more of the following proofs: (1) a territorial restriction on dealers, (2) defendant's market share in one area is 25 percent but its national share is 5 percent, (3) local selling efforts, which cannot be separately charged for, are not trivial, or (4) the only justification the defendant offered is proved to be insincere.[49]

48. See, e.g., R. Posner, The Rule of Reason and the Economic Approach: Reflections on the Sylvania Decision, 45 U. Chi. L. Rev. 1, 14 (1977) (the "content of the Rule of Reason is largely unknown; in practice, it is little more than a euphemism for nonliability"); A. Foer, The Political-Economic Nature of Antitrust, 27 St. Louis U. L.J. 331, 337-338 (1983) ("With only slight exaggeration, there is really only one thing one needs to know about the rule of reason: when the rule is applied, the defendant virtually always wins."); D. Ginsburg, Vertical Restraints: De Facto Legality, 60 Antitr. L.J. 67 (1991) (concluding that nonmonopolists have been effectively freed from antitrust regulation of vertical nonprice restraints).

49. Should a small market share be determinative? How small? See Assam Drug Co. v. Miller Brewing Co., 624 F. Supp. 411 (D.S.D. 1985), aff'd, 798 F.2d 311 (8th Cir. 1986) (summary judgment: defendant employing exclusive territories with 19 percent market share and two larger competitors did not possess market power). Whatever the market share, should an intrabrand restriction be presumptively lawful, at least in the absence of a reason to believe that it is designed to serve the interests of a horizontal dealer or a horizontal manufacturer cartel? If the latter determination is critical, how can it be made: when no other justification is offered or seems plausible or when plausible but inconclusive? For approaches tolerant of intrabrand restrictions, see Posner, note 48; R. Pitofsky, The Sylvania Case: Antitrust Analysis of Nonprice Vertical Restrictions, 78 Colum. L. Rev. 1 (1978). In *Krehl,* note 46, the court ruled that the defendant has no burden to show beneficial

413. Consider the implications of *Sylvania* for other restrictions on competition.

(a) Is minimum resale price maintenance now subject to the rule of reason?[50] What did the *Sylvania* Court say? Does the Court's statement in note 18 suggest that the repeal of fair trade in 1975 should be understood as Congress having decided the issue? Does that conclusion follow? (Recall the history, reviewed in ¶405.)

(b) Is there any distinction between the competitive effects of these practices? (1) Compare the justifications. (2) Compare the possible threats to intrabrand or interbrand competition. In the latter connection, make the comparison in the context of multibrand or single-brand dealers where many or few manufacturers use the device. In particular, compare few manufacturers using territorial limitations for single-brand dealers and most manufacturers using resale price maintenance for multibrand dealers.

(c) Is *maximum* resale price fixing now subject to the rule of reason — i.e., can *Albrecht* survive *Sylvania*?[51]

(d) Is a horizontal territorial agreement among the dealers themselves now subject to the rule of reason? (1) Might they have the same reasons for the horizontal restriction as Sylvania would have for a vertical restriction? (2) Is the vertical restriction likely to reduce competition any less than a horizontal territorial allocation among multibrand or single-brand dealers?

(e) Is *Sylvania* consistent with *Topco*, reproduced in Chapter 2B? Did *Topco* involve a horizontal or a vertical restraint? Suppose that several manufacturers of mattresses formed a joint venture to promote and make the "Sleepy" mattress and agreed that they would market mattresses of that brand only within specified non-overlapping territories. Would the justifications for the restraint be any less than those in *Sylvania?* Would the dangers to competition be any greater?[52]

economic effects in justification of a restraint, unless the plaintiff satisfies its burden of demonstrating a significant adverse impact on actual or potential intrabrand competition.

50. Consider Eastern Sci. Co. v. Wild Heerbrugg Instr., 572 F.2d 883, 886 (1st Cir.), cert. denied, 439 U.S. 833 (1978) (rule of reason governs requirement that out-of-territory sales be at or above list price because no worse than prohibition of external sales).

51. See Khan v. State Oil, 93 F.3d 1358, 1363 (7th Cir. 1996) ("Albrecht was unsound when decided, and is inconsistent with later decisions by the Supreme Court. It should be overruled. Someday, we expect, it will be." After discussing *Sylvania,* as well as other reasons to overrule *Albrecht,* the court nevertheless went on to apply *Albrecht* because they were bound by it.), cert. granted, 117 S. Ct. 941 (1997).

52. If rule of reason treatment for resale price maintenance and horizontal territorial restrictions follows from the justifications accepted in *Sylvania,* would the rule of reason also govern horizontal price fixing? Can the conclusion be rejected without also questioning the premise, and therefore the rationale for *Sylvania?*

Agency and Similar Relationships[53]

414. The Supreme Court cases. (a) *United States v. General Electric Co.*, 272 U.S. 476, 481-484, 488 (1926). General Electric (the company) had a series of contracts governing its distribution of lamps through so-called A agents and B agents. The contract

provides that the company is to maintain on consignment in the custody of the agent a stock of lamps, the sizes, types, classes and quantity of which, and the length of time which they are to remain in stock, to be determined by the company. The lamps consigned to the agents are to be kept in their respective places of business where they may be readily inspected and identified by the company. The consigned stock or any part of it is to be returned to the company as it may direct. The agent is to keep account books and records giving the complete information as to his dealings for the inspection of the company. All of the lamps in such consigned stock are to be and remain the property of the company until the lamps are sold, and the proceeds of all lamps are to be held in trust for the benefit and for the account of the company until fully accounted for. [These contracts specified the prices at which the agents would sell lamps to consumers. In addition, the] agent is to pay all expenses in the storage, cartage, transportation, handling, sale and distribution of lamps, and all expenses incident thereto and to the accounting therefor and to the collection of accounts created. This transportation does not include the freight for the lamps in the consignment from the company to the agent. [The contracts set a commission rate, and, although not specified in the contract,] the company has assumed all risk of fire, flood, obsolescence, and price decline, and carries whatever insurance is carried on the stocks of lamps in the hands of its agents, and pays whatever taxes are assessed.

[The question is] whether, in view of the arrangements made by the company with those who ordinarily and usually would be merchants buying from the manufacturer and selling to the public, such persons are to be treated as agents, or as owners of the lamps consigned to them under such contracts. If they are to be regarded really as purchasers, then the restriction as to the prices at which the sales are to be made is a restraint of trade and a violation of the Anti-Trust Law. [The court answered:] We find nothing in the form of the contracts and the practice under them which makes the so-called B and A agents anything more than genuine agents of the company, or the delivery of the stock to each agent anything more than a consignment to the agent for his custody and sale as such. [The Court concluded:] The owner of an article, patented or otherwise, is not violating the common law, or the Anti-Trust law, by seeking to

---

53. See VII P. Areeda, Antitrust Law ¶1473, 1473' (1986; Supp. 1996); J. Rahl, Control of an Agent's Prices, 61 Nw. U. L. Rev. 1 (1966).

dispose of his article directly to the consumer and fixing the price by which his agents transfer the title from him directly to such consumer.[54]

(b) *Simpson v. Union Oil Co.*, 377 U.S. 13, 16, 20-24, 26-27, 29 & n.2 (1964). Union Oil, pursuant to a consignment agreement, set retailers' prices for gasoline. Simpson was terminated for selling at a lower price and brought this suit. The arrangement provided that title remained in Union until the gas was sold to consumers. Union paid property taxes on gasoline in Simpson's possession. Simpson carried liability and property insurance, and was responsible for most losses. Simpson's compensation was by commission, and it paid costs of operation.

The Supreme Court stated that

> [i]f the "consignment" agreement achieves resale price maintenance in violation of the Sherman Act, it ... injure[s] interstate commerce by depriving independent dealers of the exercise of free judgment.... Dealers, like Simpson, are independent businessmen; and they have all or most of the indicia of entrepreneurs, except for price fixing.... Practically the only power they have to be wholly independent businessmen, whose service depends on their own initiative and enterprise, is taken from them by the proviso that they must sell their gasoline at prices fixed by Union Oil.... As we have said, an owner of an article may send it to a dealer who may in turn undertake to sell it only at a price determined by the owner.... When, however, a "consignment" device is used to cover a vast gasoline distribution system, fixing prices through many retail outlets, the antitrust laws prevent calling the "consignment" an agency....
>
> Union Oil correctly argues that the consignment in *[General Electric]* somewhat parallels the one in the instant case. The Court in the *General Electric* case did not restrict its ruling to patented articles; it, indeed, said that the use of the consignment device was available to the owners of articles "patented or otherwise." But whatever may be said of the *General Electric* case on its special facts, involving patents, it is not apposite to the special facts here. The Court in that case particularly relied on the fact that patent rights have long included licenses ... "for any royalty or upon any condition the performance of which is reasonably within the reward which the patentee by the grant of the patent is entitled to secure." That was the ratio decidendi of the *General Electric* case. We decline to extend it.

Justice Stewart's dissent argued that the agreements in the two cases "are virtually indistinguishable. Instead of expressly overruling *General Electric*, however, the Court seeks to distinguish that case upon the specious ground that its underpinnings rest on pat-

54. See also United States v. Masonite Corp., 316 U.S. 265, 279 (1942).

ent law." In a footnote, it was explained how the majority's quotations from that case referred "to a wholly separate second issue" relating to General Electric's license to Westinghouse, and thus was irrelevant.[55] "It is clear, therefore, that the Court today overrules *General Electric.*"[56]

415. (a) Is *General Electric* consistent with *Simpson*, or has the earlier case been effectively overruled, as Justice Stewart suggests?

(b) Even *Simpson* concedes that there is some agency exception to the rule in *Dr. Miles*. Why do you think that is? Is this a sensible rule? If so, is *Simpson*'s narrowing of the exception sound?[57]

(c) Multimillionaire Nelson Stonefellow, noted bibliophile, has fallen on hard times. He consigns portions of his library — which includes many duplicates — to numerous booksellers and reserves the power to fix the prices at which the books are sold. Does this arrangement offend Sherman Act §1? What would the *Simpson* Court have said?

(d) *B* Baker is "employed" by *T* Typewriter Company to operate a retail store rented by *T* from an independent landlord. *T* pays for utilities and the few necessary clerks. *B* receives as compensation a specified commission on each typewriter sale. The operating expenses of the outlet are deducted from *B*'s commissions. In the

55. That portion of *General Electric* is reproduced in Ch. 2G.

56. United States v. GE, 358 F. Supp. 731 (S.D.N.Y. 1973), held unlawful per se the very distribution system validated by the Supreme Court in 1926. The court reasoned that the earlier case was declared by the *Simpson* Court to rest on GE's patents which controlled light bulb production in 1926 but which no longer did. As to whether the earlier adjudication bound the government under the doctrine of res judicata, see ¶158.

57. You will recall that the more recent opinion in *Sylvania* addressed at great length the distinction drawn in *Schwinn*, which evaluated nonprice vertical restraints on independent dealers under the per se rule and restraints on agents under a rule of reason. Consider some of the statements in *Sylvania* in rejecting *Schwinn*'s per se rule:

> [*Schwinn*] provides no analytical support for these contrasting positions. Nor is there even an assertion in the opinion that the competitive impact of vertical restrictions is significantly affected by the form of the transaction. . . . [E]ven the leading critic of vertical restrictions concedes that *Schwinn*'s distinction between sale and nonsale transactions is essentially unrelated to any relevant economic impact.

Does *Sylvania* mean that the absence of an intervening sale to a dealer is always irrelevant? If it does, would *Dr. Miles*'s per se rule apply to prices dictated to local retail operations carried out by the manufacturer in a single corporate entity, and would *Sylvania*'s rule of reason (in contrast to per se legality) apply to such retail operations when the central office dictated territorial and customer limitations? If these implications are rejected (as *Copperweld* implies), what should one make of the quoted analysis in *Sylvania*?

unlikely event that *B*'s commissions are less than the expense, *B* is not obligated for those expenses. May *T* lawfully set the price at which *B* sells?[58]

(e) Sigma manufactures and distributes foods. Does it violate Sherman Act §1 in any of the following cases? (1) It utilizes the services of an individual Alpha, to solicit orders from hotels and other institutional buyers at prices set by Sigma.[59] (2) It utilizes the Beta company, which maintains a large place of business and employs many solicitors who seek orders for many manufacturers from institutional buyers at prices set by the manufacturers.[60] Would it make any difference if Beta maintained, on consignment, modest inventories of selected Sigma products for "emergency" supply to hotels? (3) Sigma sells directly to Gamma, which resells to various institutional buyers. Sigma also ships goods on consignment to Gamma, which delivers them at Sigma's direction to local outlets of certain national hotel chains, which negotiate and agree on the purchase price directly with Sigma.[61]

58. See, e.g., Hardwick v. Nu-Way Oil Co., 589 F.2d 806, 810 (5th Cir.), cert. denied, 444 U.S. 836 (1979) (plaintiff merely "a salaried part-time cashier" operating grocery store on own premises on which defendant oil company installed pumps and equipment, paid taxes and insurance on gasoline and equipment, and paid plaintiff a fixed salary without regard to price or volume of gasoline); Goldinger v. Boron Oil Co., 375 F. Supp. 400 (W.D. Pa. 1974), aff'd mem., 511 F.2d 1393 (3d Cir.), cert. denied, 423 U.S. 834 (1975) (commission manager is employee notwithstanding own hand tools, and payment of wages, operating insurance, and other day-to-day operating expenses before receipt of full commission seven weeks later; defendant oil company exercised extensive control over manager, owned real estate and major equipment of station, and paid commissions on quantity without regard to price); Roberts v. Exxon Corp., 427 F. Supp. 389 (W.D. La. 1976) (commission manager was really independent businessman; operated own garage on Exxon premises; no minimum income; bore risk of gasoline losses not attributable to acts of God).

59. Morrison v. Murray Biscuit Co., 797 F.2d 1430 (7th Cir. 1986) (*Simpson* permits price agreement with agents where brokerage arrangement is not a subterfuge or otherwise artificial or unnatural).

60. In Fuchs Sugars & Syrups v. AmStar Corp., 602 F.2d 1025, 1031 n.5 (2d Cir.), cert. denied, 444 U.S. 917 (1979), sugar brokers were said to possess none of the earmarks of an economic entity separate and distinct from the principal for whom they acted because they performed no function other than securing an offer from a buyer, had little discretion concerning price and other terms, and were not involved in the physical distribution of the product.

61. Greene v. General Foods Corp., 517 F.2d 635 (5th Cir. 1975), cert. denied, 424 U.S. 942 (1976) (rejecting argument that such a distributor was a mere agent, allowed a delivery allowance, on goods supplied from his general inventory to customers negotiating directly with manufacturer); Overhead Door Corp. v. Nordpal Corp., 1979 Trade Cas. ¶62595 (D. Minn. 1978) (no resale price fixing because only single sale from manufacturer to national customer ordering from manufacturer who ships to nearest distributor who installs product for a fee based

Refusal to Deal and Vertical Agreement[62]

416. The vertical agreement[63] puzzle. Perhaps the single most litigated issue under the antitrust laws is the existence or non-existence of a vertical agreement. The difficulty can be seen by considering the range of possibilities each involving attempts to secure compliance with resale prices dictated by Manufacturer *M*: (1) *M*'s contract with each retailer specifies that the retailer will adhere to prices established by *M*. (2) The contracts are at will and are silent as to price; *M* tells retailers that they should only accept the contract if they agree to adhere to specified retail prices and indicates that they will be terminated if they ever fail to comply; *M* terminates noncomplying retailers who fail to fall back into line after exhortations and demands but continues those retailers who respond favorably to such pressure. (3) The contracts are at will and silent as to price; *M* announces retail prices and that it will terminate all who do not comply; no discussions ever take place but when *M* discovers noncompliance, it always terminates. As is obvious from cases in this section, (1) is a clear agreement and thus illegal. The cases that follow indicate that (3) involves no agreement. Not surprisingly, most of the development and difficulty concerns whether cases in between, such as (2), involve agreements and thus are illegal.

In considering this material, it is useful to recall the cases from Chapter 2C concerning the existence of agreement in the horizontal context. Is the approach used here the same? Is the relationship between the existence of agreement and competitive evil the same in both contexts? How are the courts' decisions on agreement affected, if at all, by the rules determining when an agreement is unlawful?

UNITED STATES v. COLGATE & CO.
250 U.S. 300 (1919)

Justice McReynolds. [The district court had quashed an indictment charging that Colgate combined with wholesalers and retailers] "for the purpose and with the effect of procuring adherence

---

on sales price and paid by manufacturer in form of credit to distributor; manufacturer collects directly from purchaser).

62. See generally Areeda, note 53, ch. 14D; D. Turner, The Definition of Agreement Under the Sherman Act: Conscious Parallelism and Refusals to Deal, 75 Harv. L. Rev. 655 (1962).

63. Unless the context indicates otherwise, the shorthand term "agreement" designates the "contract, combination . . . or conspiracy" necessary to trigger Sherman Act §1 and also designates the "condition, agreement, or understanding" necessary to trigger Clayton Act §3, which is considered in Chs. 4B and 4C.

on the part of such dealers ... to resale prices fixed by the defendant. ..." Following this [in the indictment] is a summary of things done to carry out the purposes of the combination: Distribution among the dealers of letters, telegrams, circulars and lists showing uniform prices to be charged; urging them to adhere to such prices and notices, stating that no sales would be made to those ... not adhering thereto and placing their names upon "suspended lists"; requests to offending dealers for assurances and promises of future adherence to prices, which were often given; uniform refusals to sell to any who failed to give the same; [and] sales to those who did. ...

Our problem is to ascertain, as accurately as may be, what interpretation the trial court placed upon the indictment—not to interpret it ourselves; and then to determine whether, so construed, it fairly charges violation of the Sherman Act. ... [The trial court had declared that]

> The retailer, after buying, could, if he chose, give away his purchase, or sell it at any price he saw fit, or not sell it at all; his course in these respects being affected only by the fact that he might by his action incur the displeasure of the manufacturer, who could refuse to make further sales to him, as he had the undoubted right to do.

And we must conclude that, as interpreted below, the indictment does not charge Colgate & Company with selling its product to dealers under agreements which obligated the latter not to resell except at prices fixed by the company. ...

The purpose of the Sherman Act is to prohibit monopolies, contracts and combinations which probably would unduly interfere with the free exercise of their rights by those engaged, or who wish to engage, in trade and commerce—in a word to preserve the right of freedom to trade. In the absence of any purpose to create or maintain a monopoly, the act does not restrict the long recognized right of trader or manufacturer engaged in an entirely private business, freely to exercise his own independent discretion as to parties with whom he will deal. And, of course, he may announce in advance the circumstances under which he will refuse to sell. ...

Affirmed.

417. (a) What did the Court hold in *Colgate*? On what rationale?
(b) Which of the following amounts to a "contract, combination ... or conspiracy in restraint of trade" and what are the legal and economic differences among them? (1) *S* sells *R* who promises to resell at *x* price. (2) *S* sells to *R* subject to the stated condition that *R* resell at *x* price but that breach of the condition will not subject *R* to any suit. (3) *S* sells to *R* while declaring that it will cease selling to

any dealer who fails to resell at x price. (4) S sells generally with the suggestion that the preferable retail price is x and ceases to deal with Q who had occasionally resold at prices below x.

(c) In light of the allegation that there were "requests to offending dealers for assurances and promises of future adherence to prices, which were often given," where does *Colgate* appear to draw the line among the options in ¶b? Would the result have been different if these "assurances and promises . . . were . . . given" in writing? What if the oral assurances were enforceable contracts under state law?

(d) Would any of your ¶b answers differ if you were persuaded that R had previously sold at x price and would have continued doing so regardless of S's behavior?

(e) To what extent, if any, would overruling *Colgate* leave a manufacturer free to (1) suggest resale prices or (2) select and abandon dealers in its unrestrained discretion?

418.   *United States v. Parke, Davis & Co.*, 362 U.S. 29, 38-39, 44-47 (1960). The government sought injunctive relief against an alleged combination and conspiracy between Parke Davis and its wholesalers and retailers. Parke Davis had announced its continuing policy to sell only to wholesalers and retailers who maintained the resale prices specified by Parke Davis.

> [J]udicial inquiry is not to stop with a search of the record for evidence of purely contractual arrangements. The Sherman Act forbids combinations of traders to suppress competition. True, there results the same economic effect, as is accomplished by a prohibited combination to suppress price competition if each customer, although induced to do so solely by a manufacturer's announced policy, independently decides to observe specified resale prices. So long as *Colgate* is not overruled, this result is tolerated but only when it is the consequence of a mere refusal to sell in the exercise of the manufacturer's right "freely to exercise his own independent discretion as to parties with whom he will deal." [The Court noted that] Parke Davis used the refusal to deal with the wholesalers in order to elicit their willingness to deny Parke Davis products to retailers. [The] entire policy was tainted . . . when Parke Davis used it as the vehicle to gain the wholesalers' participation in the program to effectuate the retailers' adherence to the suggested retail prices. [It also found a conspiracy with retailers, concerning their suspension of advertising. Parke Davis] discussed the subject with Dart Drug. When Dart indicated willingness to go along the other retailers were approached and Dart's apparent willingness to cooperate was used as the lever to gain their acquiescence in the program. . . . In this manner Parke Davis sought assurances of compliance and got them, as well as the compliance itself. [The Court concluded that] if a manu-

facturer is unwilling to rely on individual self-interest to bring about
general voluntary acquiescence which has the collateral effect of
eliminating price competition, and takes affirmative action to
achieve uniform adherence by inducing each customer to adhere to
avoid such price competition, the customers' acquiescence is not
then a matter of individual free choice prompted alone by the desirability of the product.

Three Justices dissented in an opinion that emphasized that each
aspect of Parke Davis's action was unilateral, and each decision to
enforce as to any wholesaler or retailer was not dependent on the
acts of other wholesalers or retailers.

(a) Did Parke Davis engage in relevant actions beyond those of
Colgate, or does this decision narrow (or partially overrule) *Colgate?*

(b) *Parke Davis* states that vertical price determination "results
[in] the same economic effect" whether accomplished by a prohibited combination or independent action. If so, why did it not simply
overrule *Colgate?* If the effect is the same, would *Colgate*'s continued
vitality be consistent with decisions such as *Sylvania,* which overruled *Schwinn* on the ground that its formal distinction "between
sale and nonsale transactions is essentially unrelated to any relevant
impact"?

419.   *Albrecht v. The Herald Co.,* 390 U.S. 145, 147-150, 160-162
(1968). It sometimes happens that a dealer who has refused a
manufacturer's unlawful demands to agree on vertical restraints is
terminated and brings suit, seeking treble damages. Had the dealer
agreed, only later to withdraw, it could bring suit,[64] but some courts
have denied recovery where there was no agreement[65] or, in Clayton Act §3 cases, where there was no executed sale or lease.[66]
Albrecht illustrates the pressure to find an agreement in such situations. The Herald, as described in ¶406, insisted that Albrecht not
exceed its suggested retail price. In response to Albrecht's raising

64. In this circumstance, the dealer would not be barred from suit by its own
participation in the unlawful agreement. See ¶148.
65. See the several perplexed opinions in Quinn v. Mobil Oil Co., 375 F.2d 273
(1st Cir.), petition for cert. dismissed, 389 U.S. 801 (1967). Cornwell Quality Tools
Co. v. C.T.S. Co., 446 F.2d 825 (9th Cir.), cert. denied, 404 U.S. 1049 (1971),
declared that the situation described in the text was a prima facie violation of
Sherman Act §1.
66. Compare Alles Corp. v. Senco Prods., 329 F.2d 567 (6th Cir. 1964) (cause of
action stated although no contract entered into), with Amplex v. Outboard Marine
Corp., 380 F.2d 112 (4th Cir. 1967), cert. denied, 389 U.S. 1036 (1968) (executed
sale or agreement required for Sherman Act §1 or Clayton Act §3 violation);
Timken Roller Bearing Co. v. FTC, 299 F.2d 839 (6th Cir.), cert. denied, 371 U.S.
861 (1962); Leo J. Meyberg Co. v. Eureka Williams Corp., 215 F.2d 100 (9th Cir.),
cert. denied, 348 U.S. 875 (1954).

its price, the Herald "hired Milne Circulation Sales, Inc., which solicited readers for newspapers, to engage in telephone and house-to-house solicitation of all residents on" Albrecht's route. It then advertised the availability of this route. "Another carrier, George Kroner, took over the route knowing that respondent would not tolerate overcharging and understanding that he might have to return the route if [Albrecht] discontinued his pricing practice."

The amended complaint charged "only a combination between respondent and 'plaintiff's customers and/or Milne Circulation Sales, Inc., and/or George Kroner.'"[67] In assessing these allegations, the Court stated that Sherman Act §1

> covers combinations in addition to contracts and conspiracies, express or implied. The Court made this quite clear in United States v. Parke, Davis & Co., 362 U.S. 29 (1960), where it held that an illegal combination to fix prices results if a seller suggests resale prices and secures compliance by means in addition to "the mere announcement of his policy and the simple refusal to deal." [Thus,] there can be no doubt that a combination arose between respondent, Milne, and Kroner to force petitioner to conform to the advertised retail prices. . . . Milne's purpose was undoubtedly to earn its fee, but it was aware that the aim of the solicitation campaign was to force petitioner to lower his price. Kroner knew that respondent was giving him the customer list as part of a program to get petitioner to conform to advertised prices. . . .

In response, Justice Harlan's dissent argued that

> [n]either had any interest of his own in respondent's objective of setting a price ceiling. . . . The premise of §1 adjudication has always been that it is quite proper for a firm to set its own prices and determine its own territories. . . . A firm is not "combining" to fix its own prices or territory simply because it hires outside accountants, market analysts, advertisers by telephone or otherwise, or delivery boys. Once it is recognized that Kroner had no interest whatever in forcing his competitor to *lower* his price, and was merely being paid to perform a delivery job that respondent could have done itself, it is clear respondent's activity was in its essence unilateral. . . .
>
> The Court also suggests that, under *Parke Davis*, "petitioner could have claimed a combination between respondent and himself, at least as of the day he unwillingly complied with respondent's advertised price." . . . Obviously it makes no sense to deny recovery to a pressured retailer who resists temptation to the last and grant it to one who momentarily yields but is restored to virtue by the vision of

---

67. The Court noted that, since it found combinations as to the latter two, it did not have to reach the question of the alleged combination with the newspaper customers, although the Court stated that this claim "was not, however, a frivolous contention."

treble damages. It is not the momentary acquiescence but the punishment for refusing to acquiesce that does the damage on which recovery is based. The Court's difficulties on all of its theories stem from its unwillingness to face the ultimate conclusion at which it has actually arrived: it is unlawful for one person to dictate price floors or price ceilings to another; any pressure brought to bear in support of such dictation renders the dictator liable to any dictatee who is damaged. The reason for the Court's reluctance to state this conclusion bluntly is transparent: this statement of the matter takes no account of the absence of a combination or conspiracy.

Clearly, *Albrecht* reached quite far to find a conspiracy. More commonly, one finds allegations that the manufacturer conspired with other retailers or wholesalers to maintain prices. In *Albrecht*, which involved *maximum* prices, Justice Harlan argued that any agreements with other dealers were irrelevant to Albrecht, because "the effectiveness of a price ceiling imposed on one distributor does not depend upon the imposition of ceilings on other distributors, be they competitive or not." In fact, to the extent there is any competition among dealers, each would rather that the others be permitted to charge higher prices, whereas when minimum prices are maintained, price cutting by other dealers will be detrimental to dealers that adhere to the manufacturer's stated price. Dealer complaints in the latter context often give rise to allegations of conspiracy, as the following case suggests.

MONSANTO CO. v. SPRAY-RITE SERVICE CORP.

465 U.S. 752 (1984)

Justice POWELL.... This case presents a question as to the standard of proof required to find a vertical price-fixing conspiracy in violation of §1 of the Sherman Act.

I

Petitioner Monsanto Company manufactures chemical products, including agricultural herbicides.... Respondent Spray-Rite Service Corp. was engaged in the wholesale distribution of agricultural chemicals from 1955 to 1972.... Spray-Rite was a discount operation, buying in large quantities and selling at a low margin....

In October 1968, Monsanto declined to renew Spray-Rite's distributorship. At that time, Spray-Rite was the tenth largest out of approximately 100 distributors of Monsanto's primary corn herbicide....

Spray-Rite brought this action under §1 of the Sherman Act. It alleged that Monsanto and some of its distributors conspired to fix the resale prices of Monsanto herbicides. Its complaint further alleged that Monsanto terminated Spray-Rite's distributorship, adopted compensation programs and shipping policies, and encouraged distributors to boycott Spray-Rite in furtherance of this conspiracy. Monsanto denied the allegations of conspiracy, and asserted that Spray-Rite's distributorship had been terminated because of its failure to hire trained salesmen and promote sales to dealers adequately.

The case was tried to a jury. The District Court instructed the jury that Monsanto's conduct was per se unlawful if it was in furtherance of a conspiracy to fix prices. In answers to special interrogatories, the jury found that (i) the termination of Spray-Rite was pursuant to a conspiracy between Monsanto and one or more of its distributors to set resale prices, (ii) the compensation programs, areas of primary responsibility, and/or shipping policies were created by Monsanto pursuant to such a conspiracy, and (iii) Monsanto conspired with one or more distributors to limit Spray-Rite's access to Monsanto herbicides after 1968. The jury awarded $3.5 million in damages, which was trebled to $10.5 million. Only the first of the jury's findings is before us today.

The Court of Appeals for the Seventh Circuit affirmed.... In substance, the Court of Appeals held that an antitrust plaintiff can survive a motion for a directed verdict if it shows that a manufacturer terminated a price-cutting distributor in response to or following complaints by other distributors. This view brought the Seventh Circuit into direct conflict with a number of other Courts of Appeals. We granted certiorari to resolve the conflict. We reject the statement by the Court of Appeals for the Seventh Circuit of the standard of proof required to submit a case to the jury in distributor-termination litigation, but affirm the judgment under the standard we announce today.[6]

6. Monsanto also challenges another part of the Court of Appeals' opinion. It argues that the court held that the nonprice restrictions in this case — the compensation and shipping policies — would be judged under a rule of reason rather than a per se rule "'only if there is no allegation that the [nonprice] restrictions are part of a conspiracy to fix prices.'".... Read in context, the court's somewhat broad language fairly may be read to say that a plaintiff must prove, as well as allege, that the nonprice restrictions were in fact a part of a price conspiracy. Thus, later in its opinion the court notes that the District Court properly instructed the jury that "Monsanto's otherwise lawful compensation programs and shipping policies were per se unlawful *if undertaken as part of an illegal scheme to fix prices.*" ...

Monsanto does not dispute Spray-Rite's view that if the nonprice practices were proven to have been instituted as part of a price-fixing conspiracy, they would be subject to per se treatment. Instead, Monsanto argues that there was insufficient

II

This Court has drawn two important distinctions that are at the center of this and any other distributor-termination case. First, there is the basic distinction between concerted and independent action — a distinction not always clearly drawn by parties and courts. Section 1 of the Sherman Act requires that there be a "contract, combination ... or conspiracy" between the manufacturer and other distributors in order to establish a violation. Independent action is not proscribed. A manufacturer of course generally has a right to deal, or refuse to deal, with whomever it likes, as long as it does so independently. *Colgate*; cf. *Parke Davis*. Under *Colgate*, the manufacturer can announce its resale prices in advance and refuse to deal with those who fail to comply. And a distributor is free to acquiesce in the manufacturer's demand in order to avoid termination.

The second important distinction in distributor-termination cases is that between concerted action to set prices and concerted action on nonprice restrictions. The former have been per se illegal since the early years of national antitrust enforcement.... The latter are judged under the rule of reason, which requires a weighing of the relevant circumstances of a case to decide whether a restrictive practice constitutes an unreasonable restraint on competition....[7]

---

evidence to support the jury's finding that the nonprice practices were "created by Monsanto pursuant to" a price-fixing conspiracy. Monsanto failed to make its sufficiency-of-the-evidence argument in the Court of Appeals with respect to this finding, and the court did not address the point. We therefore decline to reach it....

In view of Monsanto's concession that a proper finding that nonprice practices were part of a price-fixing conspiracy would suffice to subject the entire conspiracy to per se treatment, *Sylvania* is not applicable to this case. In that case only a nonprice restriction was challenged. Nothing in our decision today undercuts the holding of *Sylvania* that nonprice restrictions are to be judged under the rule of reason. In fact the need to ensure the viability of *Sylvania* is an important consideration in our rejection of the Court of Appeals' standard of sufficiency of the evidence.

7. The Solicitor General (by brief only) and several other amici suggest that we take this opportunity to reconsider whether "contract[s], combination[s] ... or conspirac[ies]" to fix resale prices should always be unlawful. They argue that the economic effect of resale price maintenance is little different from agreements on nonprice restrictions.... They say that the economic objections to resale price maintenance that we discussed in *Sylvania* — such as that it facilitates horizontal cartels — can be met easily in the context of rule-of-reason analysis.

Certainly in this case we have no occasion to consider the merits of this argument. This case was tried on per se instructions to the jury. Neither party argued in the District Court that the rule of reason should apply to a vertical price-fixing conspiracy, nor raised the point on appeal. In fact, neither party before this Court presses the argument advanced by amici. We therefore decline to reach the question, and we decide the case in the context in which it was decided below and argued here.

While these distinctions in theory are reasonably clear, often they are difficult to apply in practice. In *Sylvania* we emphasized that the legality of arguably anticompetitive conduct should be judged primarily by its "market impact." But the economic effect of all of the conduct described above — unilateral and concerted vertical price setting, agreements on price and nonprice restrictions — is in many, but not all, cases similar or identical. And judged from a distance, the conduct of the parties in the various situations can be indistinguishable. For example, the fact that a manufacturer and its distributors are in constant communication about prices and marketing strategy does not alone show that the distributors are not making independent pricing decisions. A manufacturer and its distributors have legitimate reasons to exchange information about the prices and the reception of their products in the market. Moreover, it is precisely in cases in which the manufacturer attempts to further a particular marketing strategy by means of agreements on often costly nonprice restrictions that it will have the most interest in the distributors' resale prices. The manufacturer often will want to ensure that its distributors earn sufficient profit to pay for programs such as hiring and training additional salesmen or demonstrating the technical features of the product, and will want to see that "free-riders" do not interfere. . . . Thus, the manufacturer's strongly felt concern about resale prices does not necessarily mean that it has done more than the *Colgate* doctrine allows.

Nevertheless, it is of considerable importance that independent action by the manufacturer, and concerted action on nonprice restrictions, be distinguished from price-fixing agreements, since under present law the latter are subject to per se treatment and treble damages. On a claim of concerted price fixing, the antitrust plaintiff must present evidence sufficient to carry its burden of proving that there was such an agreement. If an inference of such an agreement may be drawn from highly ambiguous evidence, there is a considerable danger that the doctrines enunciated in *Sylvania* and *Colgate* will be seriously eroded.

The flaw in the evidentiary standard adopted by the Court of Appeals in this case is that it disregards this danger. Permitting an agreement to be inferred merely from the existence of complaints, or even from the fact that termination came about "in response to" complaints, could deter or penalize perfectly legitimate conduct. As Monsanto points out, complaints about price-cutters "are natural — and from the manufacturer's perspective, unavoidable — reactions by distributors to the activities of their rivals." Such complaints, particularly where the manufacturer has imposed a costly set of nonprice restrictions, "arise in the normal course of business and do not indicate illegal concerted action." Roesch, Inc. v. Star Cooler Corp., 671 F.2d 1168, 1172 (CA8 1982), on rehearing en banc, 712 F.2d 1235 (CA8 1983) (affirming district court judgment by an equally divided court). Moreover, distributors are an important source of information for manufacturers. In order to assure an efficient distribution system, manufacturers and distributors constantly must coordinate their activities to assure that their product will reach the consumer persuasively and efficiently. To bar a manufacturer from acting solely because the information upon which it acts originated as a price complaint would create an irrational dislocation in the market. See F. Warren-Boulton, Vertical Control of Markets 13, 164 (1978). In sum, "[t]o permit the inference of concerted action on the basis of receiving complaints alone and thus to expose the defendant to treble damage liability would both inhibit management's exercise of independent business judgment and emasculate the terms of the statute." Edward J. Sweeney & Sons, Inc. v. Texaco, Inc., 637 F.2d 105, 111, n.2 (CA3 1980), cert. denied, 451 U.S. 911 (1981).[8]

Thus, something more than evidence of complaints is needed. There must be evidence that tends to exclude the possibility that the manufacturer and nonterminated distributors were acting independently. As Judge Aldisert has written, the antitrust plaintiff should present direct or circumstantial evidence that reasonably tends to prove that the manufacturer and others "had a conscious commitment to a common scheme designed to achieve an unlawful objective." Edward J. Sweeney & Sons, supra, at 111; accord H.L. Moore Drug Exchange v. Eli Lilly & Co., 662 F.2d 935, 941 (CA2 1981), cert. denied, 459 U.S. 880 (1982); cf. *American Tobacco* (1946) (circumstances must reveal "a unity of purpose or a common design and understanding, or a meeting of minds in an unlawful arrangement").[9]

III

A

Applying this standard to the facts of this case, we believe there was sufficient evidence for the jury reasonably to have concluded

---

8. We do not suggest that evidence of complaints has no probative value at all, but only that the burden remains on the antitrust plaintiff to introduce additional evidence sufficient to support a finding of an unlawful contract, combination, or conspiracy.

9. The concept of "a meeting of the minds" or "a common scheme" in a distributor-termination case includes more than a showing that the distributor conformed to the suggested price. It means as well that evidence must be presented both that the distributor communicated its acquiescence or agreement, and that this was sought by the manufacturer.

that Monsanto and some of its distributors were parties to an "agreement" or "conspiracy" to maintain resale prices and terminate price-cutters. In fact there was substantial *direct* evidence of agreements to maintain prices. There was testimony from a Monsanto district manager, for example, that Monsanto on at least two occasions in early 1969, about five months after Spray-Rite was terminated, approached price-cutting distributors and advised that if they did not maintain the suggested resale price, they would not receive adequate supplies of Monsanto's new corn herbicide. When one of the distributors did not assent this information was referred to the Monsanto regional office, and it complained to the distributor's parent company. There was evidence that the parent instructed its subsidiary to comply, and the distributor informed Monsanto that it would charge the suggested price. Evidence of this kind plainly is relevant and persuasive as to a meeting of minds.[10]

An arguably more ambiguous example is a newsletter from one of the distributors to his dealer customers. The newsletter is dated October 1, 1968, just four weeks before Spray-Rite was terminated. It was written after a meeting between the author and several Monsanto officials, and discusses Monsanto's efforts to "ge[t] the 'market place in order.'" The newsletter reviews some of Monsanto's incentive and shipping policies, and then states that in addition "every effort will be made to maintain a minimum market price level." The newsletter relates these efforts as follows:

> In other words, we are assured that Monsanto's company-owned outlets will not retail at less than their suggested retail price to the trade as a whole. Furthermore, those of us on the distributor level are not likely to deviate downward on price to anyone as the idea is implied that doing this possibly could discolor the outlook for continuity as one of the approved distributors during the future upcoming seasons. So, none interested in the retention of this arrangement is likely to risk being deleted from this customer service opportunity. Also, as far as the national accounts are concerned, they are sure to recognize the desirability of retaining Monsanto's favor on a continuing basis by respecting the wisdom of participating in the suggested program in a manner assuring order on the retail level "playground" throughout the entire country. It is elementary that harmony can only come from following the rules of the game and that in case of dispute, the decision of the umpire is final.

10. In addition, there was circumstantial evidence that Monsanto sought agreement from the distributor to conform to the resale price. The threat to cut off the distributor's supply came during Monsanto's "shipping season" when herbicide was in short supply. The jury could have concluded that Monsanto sought this agreement at a time when it was able to use supply as a lever to force compliance.

It is reasonable to interpret this newsletter as referring to an agreement or understanding that distributors and retailers would maintain prices, and Monsanto would not undercut those prices on the retail level and would terminate competitors who sold at prices below those of complying distributors; these were "the rules of the game."[11]

B

If, as the courts below reasonably could have found, there was evidence of an agreement with one or more distributors to maintain prices, the remaining question is whether the termination of Spray-Rite was part of or pursuant to that agreement. It would be reasonable to find that it was, since it is necessary for competing distributors contemplating compliance with suggested prices to know that those who do not comply will be terminated. Moreover, there is some circumstantial evidence of such a link. Following the termination, there was a meeting between Spray-Rite's president and a Monsanto official. There was testimony that the first thing the official mentioned was the many complaints Monsanto had received about Spray-Rite's prices. In addition, there was reliable testimony that Monsanto never discussed with Spray-Rite prior to the termination the distributorship criteria that were the alleged basis for the action. By contrast, a former Monsanto salesman for Spray-Rite's area testified that Monsanto representatives on several occasions in 1965-1966 approached Spray-Rite, informed the distributor of complaints from other distributors — including one major and influential one — and requested that prices be maintained. Later that same year, Spray-Rite's president testified, Monsanto officials made explicit threats to terminate Spray-Rite unless it raised its prices.[13]

11. The newsletter also is subject to the interpretation that the distributor was merely describing the likely reaction to unilateral Monsanto pronouncements. But Monsanto itself appears to have construed the flyer as reporting a price-fixing understanding. Six weeks after the newsletter was written, a Monsanto official wrote its author a letter urging him to "correct immediately any misconceptions about Monsanto's marketing policies." The letter disavowed any intent to enter into an agreement on resale prices. The interpretation of these documents and the testimony surrounding them properly was left to the jury.

13. The existence of the illegal joint boycott after Spray-Rite's termination, a finding that the Court of Appeals affirmed and that is not before us, is further evidence that Monsanto and its distributors had an understanding that prices would be maintained, and that price-cutters would be terminated. This last [fact], however, is also consistent with termination for other reasons, and is probative only of the ability of Monsanto and its distributors to act in concert.

IV

We conclude that the Court of Appeals applied an incorrect standard to the evidence in this case. The correct standard is that there must be evidence that tends to exclude the possibility of independent action by the manufacturer and distributor. That is, there must be direct or circumstantial evidence that reasonably tends to prove that the manufacturer and others had a conscious commitment to a common scheme designed to achieve an unlawful objective. Under this standard, the evidence in this case created a jury issue as to whether Spray-Rite was terminated pursuant to a price-fixing conspiracy between Monsanto and its distributors. The judgment of the court below is affirmed.[68]

420. (a) Was there any doubt as to why the plaintiff was terminated? If not, what is the dispute about?

(b) Why did *Monsanto* hold that dealer complaints followed by termination were insufficient? Do you agree with this result? Under *Monsanto*, would the facts of *Colgate* or *Parke Davis* give rise to liability?

(c) The Court insists that the actions in *Monsanto* went beyond unilateral action. Which of the facts cited (other than the dealer complaints, which alone were held insufficient) suggest that Monsanto's action was not unilateral? If communications are not to be decisive, how can one determine when action (for example, terminating a price-cutting dealer) is unilateral?[69]

(d) The Court stated that "the economic effect of all the conduct described above — unilateral and concerted price-setting, agreements on price and nonprice restrictions — is in many, but not all, cases similar or identical." In that event, why did the Court adhere to the *Colgate* rule at all? Did it cite any respects in which *Colgate* situations were dissimilar? In the alternative, why did it not take the Solicitor General's suggestion (note 7) to reconsider *Dr. Miles* and overrule it, particularly if it also believed that price and nonprice restrictions are so often similar or identical?[70]

(e) Would you give the following advice to a (manufacturer) client?

> In dealing with dealer complaints, . . . a supplier should write a letter stating that it makes its decisions independently and it doesn't want to receive such letters. . . . [R]eturning such a letter to the complain-

---

68. Brennan, J., concurred; White, J., did not participate.

69. See Arnold Pontiac-GMC v. General Motors Corp., 786 F.2d 564 (3d Cir. 1986) (no summary judgment for defendant that denied dealership application because of evidence that group of dealers at meeting influenced denial decision).

70. See G. Robinson, Explaining Vertical Agreements: The *Colgate* Puzzle and Antitrust Method, 80 Va. L. Rev. 577 (1994).

ing dealer can be effective. However, don't try to destroy the complaint; another copy will always turn up.... In terminating a dealer, ... [write] a letter stating: "While we don't have to give a reason for the termination, you did not meet your quota." ... [T]his approach is risky if other dealers with similar quota shortfalls are not terminated.[71]

BUSINESS ELECTRONICS CORP. v. SHARP ELECTRONICS CORP.
485 U.S. 717 (1988)

Justice SCALIA.... Petitioner Business Electronics Corporation seeks review of a decision of the United States Court of Appeals for the Fifth Circuit holding that a vertical restraint is per se illegal under §1 of the Sherman Act only if there is an express or implied agreement to set resale prices at some level. We granted certiorari to resolve a conflict in the Courts of Appeals regarding the proper dividing line between the rule that vertical price restraints are illegal per se and the rule that vertical nonprice restraints are to be judged under the rule of reason.

I

In 1968, petitioner became the exclusive retailer in the Houston, Texas, area of electronic calculators manufactured by respondent Sharp Electronics Corporation. In 1972, respondent appointed Gilbert Hartwell as a second retailer in the Houston area. During the relevant period, electronic calculators were primarily sold to business customers for prices up to $1,000. While much of the evidence in this case was conflicting — in particular, concerning whether petitioner was "free riding" on Hartwell's provision of presale educational and promotional services by providing inadequate services itself — a few facts are undisputed. Respondent published a list of suggested minimum retail prices, but its written dealership agreements with petitioner and Hartwell did not obligate either to observe them, or to charge any other specific price. Petitioner's retail prices were often below respondent's suggested retail prices and generally below Hartwell's retail prices, even though Hartwell too

71. Distribution Seminar Speakers Differ on Current Vertical Law, Counseling, 48 Antitr. & Trade Reg. Rep. 716, 720 (April 25, 1985). The advice to dealers was "that, following a termination, a dealer should try to get the seller to articulate the reason for termination. Sometimes, a dealer can moot the reasons by curing the problem." It was further suggested that "threatening litigation ... [doesn't] scare anyone." See ¶324f.

sometimes priced below respondent's suggested retail prices. Hartwell complained to respondent on a number of occasions about petitioner's prices. In June 1973, Hartwell gave respondent the ultimatum that Hartwell would terminate his dealership unless respondent ended its relationship with petitioner within 30 days. Respondent terminated petitioner's dealership in July 1973.

Petitioner brought suit in the United States District Court for the Southern District of Texas, alleging that respondent and Hartwell had conspired to terminate petitioner and that such conspiracy was illegal per se under §1 of the Sherman Act. The case was tried to a jury. The District Court submitted a liability interrogatory to the jury that asked whether "there was an agreement or understanding between Sharp Electronics Corporation and Hartwell to terminate Business Electronics as a Sharp dealer because of Business Electronics' price cutting." ... The jury answered ... affirmatively and awarded $600,000 in damages....

The Fifth Circuit reversed, holding that ... to render illegal per se a vertical agreement between a manufacturer and a dealer to terminate a second dealer, the first dealer "must expressly or impliedly agree to set its prices at some level, though not a specific one. The distributor cannot retain complete freedom to set whatever price it chooses."

II

A ...

Since the earliest decisions of this Court interpreting [§1], we have recognized that it was intended to prohibit only unreasonable restraints of trade. *NCAA*; see, e.g., *Standard Oil*. Ordinarily, whether particular concerted action violates §1 of the Sherman Act is determined through case-by-case application of the so-called rule of reason — that is, "the factfinder weighs all of the circumstances of a case in deciding whether a restrictive practice should be prohibited as imposing an unreasonable restraint on competition." *Sylvania*. Certain categories of agreements, however, have been held to be per se illegal, dispensing with the need for case-by-case evaluation. We have said that per se rules are appropriate only for "conduct that is manifestly anticompetitive," id., *Northwest Wholesale*, quoting *BMI*. See also *Indiana Dentists* ("we have been slow ... to extend per se analysis to restraints imposed in the context of business relationships where the economic impact of certain practices is not immediately obvious"); *NCAA* ("Per se rules are invoked when surrounding circumstances make the likelihood of anticompetitive conduct so great as to render unjustified further examination of the challenged conduct"); *Engineers* (agreements are per se illegal only if their "nature and necessary effect are so plainly anticompetitive that no elaborate study of the industry is needed to establish their illegality").

Although vertical agreements on resale prices have been illegal per se since *Dr. Miles,* we have recognized that the scope of per se illegality should be narrow in the context of vertical restraints. In *Sylvania,* we refused to extend per se illegality to vertical nonprice restraints, specifically to a manufacturer's termination of one dealer pursuant to an exclusive territory agreement with another. We noted that especially in the vertical restraint context "departure from the rule-of-reason standard must be based on demonstrable economic effect rather than . . . upon formalistic line drawing." We concluded that vertical nonprice restraints had not been shown to have such a "'pernicious effect on competition'" and to be so "'lack[ing] [in] . . . redeeming value'" as to justify per se illegality. Id., quoting *Northern Pacific.* Rather, we found, they had real potential to stimulate interbrand competition, "the primary concern of antitrust law." . . .

Moreover, we observed that a rule of per se illegality for vertical nonprice restraints was not needed or effective to protect *intra*brand competition. First, so long as interbrand competition existed, that would provide a "significant check" on any attempt to exploit intrabrand market power. In fact, in order to meet that interbrand competition, a manufacturer's dominant incentive is to lower resale prices. Second, the per se illegality of vertical restraints would create a perverse incentive for manufacturers to integrate vertically into distribution, an outcome hardly conducive to fostering the creation and maintenance of small businesses.

Finally, our opinion in *Sylvania* noted a significant distinction between vertical nonprice and vertical price restraints. That is, there was support for the proposition that vertical price restraints reduce *inter*brand price competition because they "'facilitate cartelizing.'" The authorities cited by the Court suggested how vertical price agreements might assist horizontal price fixing at the manufacturer level (by reducing the manufacturer's incentive to cheat on a cartel, since its retailers could not pass on lower prices to consumers) or might be used to organize cartels at the retailer level. . . . Similar support for the cartel-facilitating effect of vertical nonprice restraints was and remains lacking.

We have been solicitous to assure that the market-freeing effect of our decision in *Sylvania* is not frustrated by related legal rules. In *Monsanto,* which addressed the evidentiary showing necessary to establish vertical concerted action, we expressed concern that "[i]f an inference of such an agreement may be drawn from highly ambiguous evidence, there is considerable danger that the doctrin[e] enunciated in *Sylvania* ... will be seriously eroded." We eschewed adoption of an evidentiary standard that "could deter or penalize perfectly legitimate conduct" or "would create an irrational dislocation in the market" by preventing legitimate communication between a manufacturer and its distributors.

Our approach to the question presented in the present case is guided by the premises of *Sylvania* and *Monsanto*: that there is a presumption in favor of a rule-of-reason standard; that departure from that standard must be justified by demonstrable economic effect, such as the facilitation of cartelizing, rather than formalistic distinctions; that interbrand competition is the primary concern of the antitrust laws; and that rules in this area should be formulated with a view towards protecting the doctrine of *Sylvania*. These premises lead us to conclude that the line drawn by the Fifth Circuit is the most appropriate one.

There has been no showing here that an agreement between a manufacturer and a dealer to terminate a "price cutter," without a further agreement on the price or price levels to be charged by the remaining dealer, almost always tends to restrict competition and reduce output. Any assistance to cartelizing that such an agreement might provide cannot be distinguished from the sort of minimal assistance that might be provided by vertical nonprice agreements like the exclusive territory agreement in *Sylvania*, and is insufficient to justify a per se rule. Cartels are neither easy to form nor easy to maintain. Uncertainty over the terms of the cartel, particularly the prices to be charged in the future, obstructs both formation and adherence by making cheating easier. Cf. *Maple Flooring*; see generally *Matsushita*. Without an agreement with the remaining dealer on price, the manufacturer both retains its incentive to cheat on any manufacturer-level cartel (since lower prices can still be passed on to consumers) and cannot as easily be used to organize and hold together a retailer-level cartel.[2]

The District Court's rule on the scope of per se illegality for vertical restraints would threaten to dismantle the doctrine of *Sylvania*. Any agreement between a manufacturer and a dealer to

---

2. The dissent's principal fear appears to be not cartelization at either level, but Hartwell's assertion of dominant retail power. This fear does not possibly justify adopting a rule of per se illegality. Retail market power is rare, because of the usual presence of interbrand competition and other dealers, see *Sylvania*, and it should therefore not be assumed but rather must be proved. ... Of course this case was not prosecuted on the theory, and therefore the jury was not asked to find, that Hartwell possessed such market power.

terminate another dealer who happens to have charged lower prices can be alleged to have been directed against the terminated dealer's "price cutting." In the vast majority of cases, it will be extremely difficult for the manufacturer to convince a jury that its motivation was to ensure adequate services, since price cutting and some measure of service cutting usually go hand in hand. Accordingly, a manufacturer that agrees to give one dealer an exclusive territory and terminates another dealer pursuant to that agreement, or even a manufacturer that agrees with one dealer to terminate another for failure to provide contractually obligated services, exposes itself to the highly plausible claim that its real motivation was to terminate a price cutter. Moreover, even vertical restraints that do not result in dealer termination, such as the initial granting of an exclusive territory or the requirement that certain services be provided, can be attacked as designed to allow existing dealers to charge higher prices. Manufacturers would be likely to forgo legitimate and competitively useful conduct rather than risk treble damages and perhaps even criminal penalties.

We cannot avoid this difficulty by invalidating as illegal per se only those agreements imposing vertical restraints that contain the word "price," or that affect the "prices" charged by dealers. Such formalism was explicitly rejected in *Sylvania*. As the above discussion indicates, all vertical restraints, including the exclusive territory agreement held not to be per se illegal in *Sylvania*, have the potential to allow dealers to increase "prices" and can be characterized as intended to achieve just that. In fact, vertical nonprice restraints only accomplish the benefits identified in *Sylvania* because they reduce intrabrand price competition to the point where the dealer's profit margin permits provision of the desired services. As we described it in *Monsanto*: "The manufacturer often will want to ensure that its distributors earn sufficient profit to pay for programs such as hiring and training additional salesmen or demonstrating the technical features of the product, and will want to see that 'freeriders' do not interfere." See also *Sylvania*.

The dissent erects a much more complex analytic structure, which ultimately rests, however, upon the same discredited premise that the only function this nonprice vertical restriction can serve is restraint of dealer-level competition. Specifically, the dissent's reasoning hinges upon its perception that the agreement between Sharp and Hartwell was a "naked" restraint—that is, it was not "ancillary" to any other agreement between Sharp and Hartwell. But that is not true, unless one assumes, contrary to *Sylvania* and *Monsanto*, and contrary to our earlier discussion, that it is not a quite plausible purpose of the restriction to enable Hartwell to provide better services under the sales franchise agreement.[3] From its faulty conclusion that what we have before us is a "naked" restraint, the dissent proceeds, by reasoning we do not entirely follow, to the further conclusion that it is therefore a horizontal rather than a vertical restraint. We pause over this only to note that in addition to producing what we think the wrong result in the present case, it introduces needless confusion into antitrust terminology. Restraints imposed by agreement between competitors have traditionally been denominated as horizontal restraints, and those imposed by agreement between firms at different levels of distribution as vertical restraints.[4]

Finally, we do not agree with petitioner's contention that an agreement on the remaining dealer's price or price levels will so

3. The conclusion of "naked" restraint could also be sustained on another assumption, namely, that an agreement is not "ancillary" unless it is designed to enforce a contractual obligation of one of the parties to the contract. The dissent appears to accept this assumption. It is plainly wrong. The classic "ancillary" restraint is an agreement by the seller of a business not to compete within the market. See Mitchel v. Reynolds, 1 P. Wms. 181, 24 Eng. Rep. 347 (1711); Restatement (Second) of Contracts §188(2)(a) (1981). That is not ancillary to any other contractual obligation, but, like the restraint here, merely enhances the value of the contract, or permits the "enjoyment of [its] fruits." *Addyston Pipe*; cf. Restatement (Second) of Contracts §§187, 188 (1981) (restraint may be ancillary to a "transaction *or relationship*") (emphasis added); R. Bork, The Antitrust Paradox 29 (1978) ... (vertical arrangements are ancillary to the "transaction of supplying and purchasing").

More important than the erroneousness of the dissent's common-law analysis of "naked" and "ancillary" restraints are the perverse economic consequences of permitting nonprice vertical restraints to avoid per se invalidity only through attachment to an express contractual obligation. ... In the precise case of a vertical agreement to terminate other dealers, for example, there is no conceivable reason why the existence of an exclusivity commitment by the manufacturer to the one remaining dealer would render anticompetitive effects less likely, or the procompetitive effects on services more likely — so that the dissent's line for per se illegality fails to meet the requirement of *Sylvania* that it be based on "demonstrable economic effect." If anything, the economic effect of the dissent's approach is perverse, encouraging manufacturers to agree to otherwise inefficient contractual provisions for the sole purpose of attaching to them efficient nonprice vertical restraints which, only by reason of such attachment, can avoid per se invalidity as "naked" restraints. The dissent's approach would therefore create precisely the kind of "irrational dislocation in the market" that legal rules in this area should be designed to avoid. *Monsanto*.

4. The dissent apparently believes that whether a restraint is horizontal depends upon whether its anticompetitive *effects* are horizontal, and not upon whether it is the product of a horizontal agreement. That is of course a conceivable way of talking, but if it were the language of antitrust analysis there would be no such thing as an unlawful vertical restraint, since all anticompetitive effects are by definition horizontal effects. ...

often follow from terminating another dealer "because of [its] price cutting" that prophylaxis against resale price maintenance warrants the District Court's per se rule. Petitioner has provided no support for the proposition that vertical price agreements generally underlie agreements to terminate a price cutter. That proposition is simply incompatible with the conclusion of *Sylvania* and *Monsanto* that manufacturers are often motivated by a legitimate desire to have dealers provide services, combined with the reality that price cutting is frequently made possible by "free riding" on the services provided by other dealers. The District Court's per se rule would therefore discourage conduct recognized by *Sylvania* and *Monsanto* as beneficial to consumers.

B

In resting our decision upon the foregoing economic analysis, we do not ignore common-law precedent concerning what constituted "restraint of trade" at the time the Sherman Act was adopted. But neither do we give that pre-1890 precedent the dispositive effect some would. The term "restraint of trade" in the statute, like the term at common law, refers not to a particular list of agreements, but to a particular economic consequence, which may be produced by quite different sorts of agreements in varying times and circumstances. The changing content of the term "restraint of trade" was well recognized at the time the Sherman Act was enacted. . . .

The Sherman Act adopted the term "restraint of trade" along with its dynamic potential. It invokes the common law itself, and not merely the static content that the common law had assigned to the term in 1890. . . . If it were otherwise, not only would the line of per se illegality have to be drawn today precisely where it was in 1890, but also case-by-case evaluation of legality (conducted where per se rules do not apply) would have to be governed by 19th-century notions of reasonableness. It would make no sense to create out of the single term "restraint of trade" a chronologically schizoid statute, in which a "rule of reason" evolves with new circumstances and new wisdom, but a line of per se illegality remains forever fixed where it was.

Of course the common law, both in general and as embodied in the Sherman Act, does not lightly assume that the economic realities underlying earlier decisions have changed, or that earlier judicial perceptions of those realities were in error. It is relevant, therefore, whether the common law of restraint of trade ever prohibited as illegal per se an agreement of the sort made here, and whether our decisions under §1 of the Sherman Act have ever expressed or necessarily implied such a prohibition.

With respect to this Court's understanding of pre-Sherman Act common law, petitioner refers to our decision in *Dr. Miles*. Though that was an early Sherman Act case, its holding that a resale price maintenance agreement was per se illegal was based largely on the perception that such an agreement was categorically impermissible at common law. As the opinion made plain, however, the basis for that common-law judgment was that the resale restriction was an unlawful restraint on alienation. *Dr. Miles*. . . . In the present case, of course, no agreement on resale price or price level, and hence no restraint on alienation, was found by the jury, so the common-law rationale of *Dr. Miles* does not apply. . . .

Petitioner's principal contention has been that the District Court's rule on per se illegality is compelled not by the old common law, but by our more recent Sherman Act precedents. First, petitioner contends that since certain horizontal agreements have been held to constitute price fixing (and thus to be per se illegal) though they did not set prices or price levels, see, e.g., Catalano v. Target Sales, 446 U.S. 643, 647-650 (1980) (per curiam), it is improper to require that a vertical agreement set prices or price levels before it can suffer the same fate. This notion of equivalence between the scope of horizontal per se illegality and that of vertical per se illegality was explicitly rejected in *Sylvania* — as it had to be, since a horizontal agreement to divide territories is per se illegal, see *Topco*, while *Sylvania* held that a vertical agreement to do so is not. . . .

Second, petitioner contends that per se illegality here follows from our two cases holding per se illegal a group boycott of a dealer because of its price cutting. See United States v. General Motors Corp., 384 U.S. 127 (1966); *Klor's*. This second contention is merely a restatement of the first, since both cases involved horizontal combinations — *General Motors*, at the dealer level, and *Klor's*, at the manufacturer and wholesaler levels. . . .

Third, petitioner contends, relying on *Albrecht* and *Parke Davis*, that our vertical price-fixing cases have already rejected the proposition that per se illegality requires setting a price or price level. We disagree. In *Albrecht*, the maker of the product formed a combination to force a retailer to charge the maker's advertised retail price. This combination had two aspects. Initially, the maker hired a third party to solicit customers away from the noncomplying retailer. This solicitor "was aware that the aim of the solicitation campaign was to force [the noncomplying retailer] to lower his price" to the suggested retail price. Next, the maker engaged another retailer who "undertook to deliver [products] at the suggested price" to the noncomplying retailer's customers obtained by the solicitor. This combination of maker, solicitor, and new retailer was held to be per se illegal. It is plain that the combination involved both an explicit agreement on resale price and an agreement to force another to adhere to the specified price.

In *Parke Davis*, a manufacturer combined first with wholesalers and then with retailers in order to gain "the retailers' adherence to its suggested minimum retail prices." The manufacturer also brokered an agreement among its retailers not to advertise prices below its suggested retail prices, which agreement was held to be part of the per se illegal combination. This holding also does not support a rule that an agreement on price or price level is not required for a vertical restraint to be per se illegal — first, because the agreement not to advertise prices was part and parcel of the combination that contained the price agreement, and second because the agreement among retailers that the manufacturer organized was a horizontal conspiracy among competitors.

In sum, economic analysis supports the view, and no precedent opposes it, that a vertical restraint is not illegal per se unless it includes some agreement on price or price levels.

Justices Stevens and White dissented. The dissent viewed the case as one in which the retailer coerced the manufacturer into terminating a competitive retailer because of the competitor's price competition, rather than one involving an attempt by the manufacturer to maintain an orderly and efficient system of distribution. Thus, the agreement should be deemed per se illegal. (1) Such an agreement is more properly viewed as a horizontal restraint, governed by United States v. General Motors Corp., 384 U.S. 127 (1966). That there was only one rather than many dealers pressuring the manufacturer should be irrelevant (as there is still a two-party agreement, between the single retailer and the manufacturer). (2) The majority's characterization of the agreement as a "nonprice vertical restriction" is "surely an oxymoron when applied to the agreement the jury actually found," which was that the agreement's purpose was to terminate the plaintiff because of its price cutting. (3) The agreement constituted a naked restraint, for it was not ancillary to any program of the manufacturer to provide for an efficient distribution system. The purpose posited by the majority — providing better services by maintaining Hartwell's profit margin — is not a valid one under the Sherman Act, as explained in *Engineers*. If such a pure anticompetitive purpose is permissible in this context, it seems it would be available in defense of simple horizontal price fixing as well. (4) The majority misapplies *Sylvania* in giving no weight to the value of intrabrand competition. *Sylvania* only indicated that sufficient procompetitive benefits with regard to interbrand competition, as might result when the manufacturer initiates vertical nonprice restraints, may justify agreements under the rule of reason. (5) There is no serious reason to fear unfounded suits. The plaintiff's burden under *Monsanto* to show an agreement rather than independent action and that pricing was the motivation for the agreement combined with the manufacturer's opportunity to proffer its motivations are sufficient. "[T]he majority exhibits little confidence in the judicial process as a means of ascertaining the truth."][72]

421. (a) The Court states that *Business Electronics* is about the dividing line between vertical price and nonprice restraints. Under that view, why isn't Sharp liable, because the termination was motivated by the retailer's price cutting? What reasons does the Court give for treating Sharp's actions as involving nonprice restraints? Are they persuasive?

(b) In what sense can we say that there was no price set by Sharp? What about Sharp's suggested retail prices? Under *Monsanto* and *Business Electronics*, taken together, what must a plaintiff show?[73]

(c) Does the possibility of dealer coercion justify a per se rule? If coercion is demonstrated in a particular case, should this be enough to establish a rule of reason violation?[74]

(d) Glove Co. manufactures gloves and sells them to two different retailers — Hand Co. and Bird Inc. Neither Hand nor Bird follows Glove's suggested retail prices. Bird consistently undercuts Hand's prices. Lately, Hand has been advertising a new policy to buy only "quality merchandise" — that is, merchandise from manufacturers who refuse to sell to discount stores. Hand sends a copy of the advertisement to Glove. Shortly afterward, Glove Co. terminates Bird. Is this a per se violation?[75] What if Hand had written on the advertisement "Lose the Bird, and we'll charge what you say"?

72. Kennedy, J., did not participate.
73. The reader should also consider whether the facts described in the *Business Electronics* opinion are sufficient to demonstrate *any* agreement under *Monsanto*. In the lower court opinion, 780 F.2d 1212 (5th Cir. 1986), the court refers to evidence that Business Electronics was not free riding, nor were its sales less than those of the complaining dealer. This evidence, in the court's view, eroded Sharp's claims that it independently terminated Business Electronics, allowing a jury to infer an agreement between Sharp and Hartwell.
74. When considering this question, it is useful to recall the facts in *Packard*.
75. See Burlington Coat Factory Warehouse v. Esprit de Corps, 769 F.2d 919 (2d Cir. 1985) (rejecting off-price retailer's order, after full-price retailer publicly announced that it would no longer do business with manufacturers who supplied off-price retailers, did not establish concerted action); Garment Dist. v. Belk Stores Services, 799 F.2d 905 (4th Cir. 1986), cert. denied, 486 U.S. 1005 (1988) (neither a distributor's decision to exclude manufacturer's goods from distributor's trade show nor a letter to that distributor acknowledging manufacturer's decision to terminate a second discounting distributor constituted evidence of agreement to fix prices).

4B. TYING ARRANGEMENTS

422. Introduction and variations. A tying arrangement exists when a producer of a desired product sells it only to those who also buy a second product from it. The manufacturer of can closing machines, for example, might sell them only to those who also buy cans from it. In the customary terminology, the manufacturer ties the sale of the tying product (can closing machine) to sales of the tied product (cans).

Although concerned with the narrowing of the buyer's freedom of choice, the courts' analysis of tie-ins has generally focused primarily on their effect on competition in the market for the tied product. The tie-in might foreclose other sellers of the tied product from an opportunity to compete for patronage on the independent merits of the tied product standing alone and without the intrusion of the tying product as an alien factor. Of course, some tie-ins would have so little impact on the market for the tied product as to be irrelevant to competition.[1]

A tying arrangement might be reflected in a formal agreement, such as a refusal to lease a can closing machine except on the stipulation that future can purchases will be from the same seller, or a package sale requiring the buyer to take both products simultaneously, such as the sale of a computer system and related software only as a package. Either the tying or tied product may be land, a patented or unpatented article, a patent license or other intangible, or a service. And either the tying or the tied product can be the subject of a sale, lease, or license. The seller may or may not have significant market power with respect to either product. Buyers might feel coerced by the tie, unconcerned about it, or even welcome it (in the sense that the package price makes the arrangement attractive relative to what otherwise would have been available). The tie might be compulsory or it might be voluntary in the sense that one is permitted to buy the tying product separately although its price will be less when both are taken together.

The tying arrangement will sometimes constitute monopolization or attempted monopolization under Sherman Act §2. A tying agreement can, of course, be an unreasonable restraint under §1. The statutory provision specifically addressed to the tying problem is

---

1. For an analysis of whether and how foreclosures impair competition in the market for the tied product, see IX P. Areeda, Antitrust Law, ch. 17A (1991; Supp. 1996); T. Krattenmaker & S. Salop, Anticompetitive Exclusion: Raising Rivals' Costs to Achieve Power over Price, 96 Yale L.J. 209 (1986). For a critical examination of the debate concerning the effects of tying and related practices, see L. Kaplow, Extension of Monopoly Power through Leverage, 85 Colum. L. Rev. 515 (1985). Other tying issues are addressed in X P. Areeda, Antitrust Law (1996).

Clayton Act §3. Before considering that statute, however, we pause on historic decisions limiting the use of a patented product to restrict competition on a second product. The order of topics is: (1) the seller's reasons for wanting a tie, (2) *International Salt, Northern Pacific*, and other cases developing the per se rule against tying arrangements under Clayton Act §3 and Sherman Act §1, (3) *Jerrold* and issues pertaining to the existence of defenses and the definition of a tying arrangement (i.e., should the package sale of a car body and engine be viewed as the tying of two products or the sale of a single product?), and (4) the more recent developments in *Fortner, Jefferson Parish*, and *Kodak* concerning the market power requirement in tying cases.

Lest the student think that tying is an isolated issue, it should be noted that this section is broadly relevant to other antitrust topics. The leverage issue permeates antitrust law. Most clearly, some of the issues raised here parallel those considered in Chapter 3's consideration of monopoly and attempted monopoly. The rationale of the tying decisions, moreover, is crucial to understanding the Clayton Act. The tying cases explore the relationship of Clayton Act §3 and Sherman Act §1, and this relationship is important to the treatment of exclusive dealing and mergers. Many of the other topics treated here simplify the next section, and Chapters 4B and 4C together greatly simplify the presentation of vertical mergers in Chapter 5C.

423. Business reasons for tying. Many possible uses and effects of tying arrangements will be considered in the course of this Chapter. At the very outset, however, it is important to understand some of the business purposes, both legitimate and monopolistic, that tying might serve. Several key concepts will be covered briefly but without the many possible qualifications, exceptions, variations, or technical details. Much of the analysis will be seen to parallel closely that presented with regard to vertical integration, in ¶321.[2]

(a) *Monopoly in the tied product.*[3] A second monopoly might be the seller's object. If a new bolt is always used together with a new nut, a

---

2. More detailed and technical treatments will be found in R. Blair & D. Kaserman, Law and Economics of Vertical Integration and Control (1983); F. Warren-Boulton, Vertical Control of Markets (1978); O. Hart & J. Tirole, Vertical Integration and Market Foreclosure, Brookings Papers on Economic Activity: Microeconomics 205 (1990); M. Katz, Vertical Contractual Relations, in 1 Handbook of Industrial Organization, (R. Schmalensee and R. Willig eds. 1989). Among the more influential earlier works are W. Bowman, Tying Arrangements and the Leverage Problem, 67 Yale L.J. 19 (1957); M. Burstein, A Theory of Full-Line Forcing, 55 Nw. U. L. Rev. 62 (1960).

3. Compare ¶321b.

monopolist of the former could use a tie to obtain a monopoly of the latter. But

> if the price of bolts were set by a monopolist and the price of nuts were set by competition, tying the sale of nuts and the sale of bolts would not increase the monopoly profit. . . . Where fixed proportions are involved, no revenue can be derived from setting a higher price for the tied product which could not have been made by setting the optimum price for the tying product. The imposition of a tie-in under these circumstances determines the identity of the seller, but the amount of the tied product actually sold will not differ at all from that which could be sold if the optimum price for the tying product were set.[4]

For example, imagine that the competitive price for nuts and bolts would be 5¢ each, whereas a combined nut-bolt monopolist would maximize profits at a price of 20¢ for each nut-bolt pair. A bolt monopolist, observing a competitive market for nuts priced at 5¢, could simply price its bolts at 15¢. The total profits (10¢ above what competition would bring) are the same as in the case of the combined nut-bolt monopolist, and consumers face the same total price of 20¢. Thus, in terms of short-run pricing strategy, the bolt monopolist who ties nuts and bolts and maximizes profits by charging 20¢ would face essentially the same situation, and make the same profit, as if it simply sold its bolts at a monopoly price of 15¢ and left consumers free to buy nuts from whichever supplier they wished.

Thus far, the analysis suggests that tying would neither be a desirable business practice nor a harmful one. Society might nevertheless be concerned over the resulting nut monopoly that eliminates competitive pressures toward cost reduction and innovation in nuts and that might impede new entry in bolts when that becomes possible. If there is then no independent seller of nuts, a new entrant into bolts would also have to make nuts. Such effects may seem remote in the nut-bolt situation, but suppose that a monopolist of cameras required buyers to take their film from it. Of course, whether a monopoly of the second product will result depends on the nature of the tied product. If, for example, the seller of a unique specialty paper product ties its paper to pencils, it can hardly expect to obtain a commanding position in the pencil market since most pencils would still be purchased separately.

The two products need not, of course, be used in fixed proportions, as in the nut-bolt illustration. The following two subparagraphs consider products used in variable proportions, where price and profits will be affected. In addition, if the market for the tied product is not perfectly competitive, in some instances tying might

---

4. Bowman, note 2, at 21-23.

be used strategically to exclude rivals.[5] Or tying might be used to alter the strategic interaction among firms selling the tied product to produce higher prices.[6]

(b) *More "efficient" pricing of tying product.* In selling intermediate product *A* to buyers engaged in further manufacture, the monopolist faces this problem: To charge the monopoly price for *A* could induce buyers to substitute product *B*, which is cheaper in dollars although less "efficient" in the sense that *B* would not be used at all if *A* were priced competitively at its marginal cost of production. To avoid such substitution, the monopolist would set *A*'s price closer to its competitive level if it could find another way to exploit its monopoly position. If every buyer needs at least a little of *A*, then the monopolist could get extra revenue by (1) selling *A* at a more or less competitive price and charging each buyer a lump-sum fee before dealing with it at all, (2) selling *A* competitively and forcing buyers to take a tied product *C* that, although available from other suppliers, has no substitute in the buyers' manufacturing process, and charging an elevated price for *C*, or (3) maintaining its monopoly price for *A* and forcing buyers to take from it all their requirements of *B* (or any other substitute for *A*) at a similarly elevated price. Of course, it is possible that preventing such devices would force the monopolist to lower its price of *A* toward competitive levels, with a beneficial effect on output and on consumer welfare as well.[7]

(c) *Price discrimination.* A tying arrangement may be a vehicle for price discrimination. The supplies consumed in the course of using the machine can serve as a so-called counting device to measure the intensity of use. For example:

[A] machine was invented for stapling buttons to high-button shoes, an operation formerly done by hand at higher cost. The patentee had a number of prospective customers for his machine, some of whom made a great many shoes, others only a few. The invention saved each user a fixed amount on each button attached. Thus the machine was worth more to the more intensive users. If the patentee attempted to sell it at different prices to the different users, however, he would have encountered two problems. To determine in advance how intensively each buyer would use the machine would have been difficult; to prevent those who paid a low price from reselling to those who paid a high price might have proved impossible. A tie-in

5. See M. Whinston, Tying, Foreclosure, and Exclusion, 80 Am. Econ. Rev. 837 (1990).

6. See D. Seidmann, Bundling as a Facilitating Device: A Reinterpretation of Leverage Theory, 58 Economica 491 (1991).

7. See Blair & Kaserman, note 2; F.M. Scherer, The Economics of Vertical Control, 52 Antitr. L.J. 687 (1983).

would resolve these difficulties. The machine might be sold at cost, on condition that the unpatented staples used in the machine be bought from the patentee. Through staple sales, the patentee could obtain a device for measuring the intensity with which his customers used the machines. Hence by charging a higher than competitive price for the staples, the patentee could receive the equivalent of a royalty from his patented machines.[8]

Observe that use of a tying device in this situation is totally independent of any desire on the seller's part to achieve power in the market for the tied good. In addition, one should note that the ability to price discriminate presumes some degree of market power in the tying product, for if such power did not exist, buyers would purchase it elsewhere without the tie-in. Finally, keep in mind that such price discrimination is typically accomplished directly, by charging a royalty.

A common variation is designed to appeal to the risk-averse user who is not sure how much it would use the machine — such as a computer or copier — and is therefore unwilling to commit itself to paying a substantial price or rental. The seller might set a relatively low rental or price but require the user to buy all consumable supplies from it, at profitable prices.[9]

A tie-in of auxiliary equipment could work in much the same way. The sole maker of an amplifier useful both in homes and in theaters might sell it at a uniform price but require buyers to purchase their speakers from it. It would then charge a very high price for speakers suitable for theater use.

It should be remembered that price discrimination might reduce use and output, merely appropriate consumer surplus without affecting output, or extend use and output by making the product available to those only willing to pay less than the uniform price that would prevail if discrimination were not possible or permissible.[10]

(d) *Disguising price.* When two products are sold as a package, or otherwise tied together, the seller's receipts and buyer's payments necessarily reflect the aggregate transaction and are not obviously apportionable among the components. This explains how a tie can be used to evade price control, manipulate the computation base for royalties or taxes, conceal the true price of using the tying or

8. Bowman, note 2, at 23. See ¶285.
9. In yet another variation, the seller requires the low-price buyer of product *A* to take its requirements, at the regular market price, of a product *B*, which is not readily resaleable. Because the buyer will not want to accumulate excess amounts of *B*, it will be discouraged from buying excess *A* to resell to those being charged the higher price.
10. See ¶285b.

tied product, undercut minimum price regulation, and undercut and thereby weaken rigid oligopoly pricing. Consider these somewhat more concrete illustrations. (1) Sigma's product *A* is in short supply, but it is prevented by government regulations (or otherwise) from raising its price. It sells *A* at the specified price but insists that buyers also take product *B* from it at a profitable price.[11] (2) Sigma is obliged to pay royalties or taxes based on the price of product *A*. It sells *A* at a relatively low price but insists that buyers take product *B* from it at a profitable price. (3) Sigma sells or leases its machine for a nominal sum to buyers who later buy necessary supplies or repair parts at a profitable price. Once the buyer has the machine, it will tend to use it and keep it functioning. (4) Sigma is subject to minimum price control on product *B*. It sells a related product *A* at a bargain price to those who also buy *B* from it at the established price. (5) Sigma might feel restrained from cutting the product *B* price, not by law but by consideration of oligopolistic interdependence, as discussed in Chapter 2C. Selling product *A* at a bargain price when tied to *B* at the prevailing oligopoly price will not bring the general *B* price down whenever the tied transactions are sufficiently few to escape notice by rival oligopolists.

(e) *Cost savings; full-line representation.* A package sale might save costs. Two components might be made and marketed more cheaply when incorporated in an appliance than when made and marketed separately. The owner of many patents might reduce the costs of administration and policing by licensing its patents as a package rather than individually. Or a manufacturer's costs of supplying and servicing dealers might be lower when each dealer handles its full line of products than when more numerous dealers each handle only a portion of its line. In each case, however, the seller precluded from tying may offer the package at a price lower than the sum of the prices of each component by an amount that reflects the cost savings, leaving consumers free to choose combinations at prices that reflect actual costs. An alternative motivation arises when the manufacturer believes that its full line will be adequately represented before the public only if it requires dealers to handle the full line.

(f) *Quality control or improvement.* A machine maker might oblige buyers or users to take their repair service, supplies, or auxiliary equipment from it in order to assure the successful operation of the machine. Or, to avoid consumer ill will, a manufacturer might obli-

---

11. "Profitable price" for the tied product designates either (1) a price enhanced above the usually prevailing price for that product or (2) the prevailing price when (a) that price is already at monopoly or oligopoly level and (b) the buyer would not otherwise buy the tied product at that price from this seller.

gate a dealer to use its financing, repair parts, or ancillary services to assure that consumers will not be harmed by onerous financing, faulty repair, or poor service. Courts may be dubious of this rationale, however, because the option often exists for the manufacturer simply to inform consumers of problems or, if it is believed they may make mistakes that will damage the manufacturer's goodwill, it can insist on specifications for products or service. A related motivation involves requiring product users to take service from the manufacturer so that it can quickly learn about difficulties with the product and take steps to improve it.

(g) *Summary.* The reader will observe that the economic effects of tying can be highly diverse. Some harms and benefits are suggested here without assessing the net results of allowing or condemning tying arrangements. Nor has this Paragraph considered in any depth, particularly with respect to pricing motivations, the less restrictive alternatives by which a seller might achieve any of the objectives that might be considered legitimate. We now turn to these several questions and to the legal doctrines. A bit of history comes first.

424. Development in patent cases. (a) *Motion Picture Patents Co. v. Universal Film Manufacturing Co.*, 243 U.S. 502, 513, 517-518, 520 (1917). Plaintiff possessed the patent on motion picture projectors, which it sold to defendant subject to the stated condition imprinted on the machine that it was licensed for use only to project certain motion pictures involving now-expired patents. Plaintiff sued for infringement when this condition was violated. The Court ruled that the patent was not infringed and the restriction was ineffective. The patentee "should not be permitted by legal devices to impose an unjust charge upon the public in return for the use of it." The suggestion that the public benefited by the patentee's selling the machine near cost, making its profit from the sale of supplies used with the machine,

> instead of commending, is the clearest possible condemnation of, the practice adopted, for it proves that under color of its patent the owner intends to and does derive its profit, not from the invention on which the law gives it a monopoly but from the unpatented supplies with which it is used and which are wholly without the scope of the patent monopoly, thus in effect extending the power to the owner of the patent to fix the price to the public of the unpatented supplies as effectively as he may fix the price on the patented machine. We are confirmed in the conclusion which we are announcing by the fact that since the decision of Henry v. Dick Co., 224 U.S. 1, [which reached the opposite conclusion, the Clayton Act was enacted].... Our conclusion renders it unnecessary to make the

application of this statute to the case at bar ... but it must be accepted by us as a most persuasive expression of the public policy of our country with respect to the question before us.

The dissent suggested that the public benefited from the restricted license as compared with the patentee's keeping the device wholly out of use.

The supposed contravention of public interest sometimes is stated as an attempt to extend the patent law to unpatented articles, which of course it is not, and more accurately as a possible domination to be established by such means. But the domination is one only to the extent of the desire for the ... film feeder, and if the owner prefers to keep ... the feeder unless you will buy his ... films, I cannot see in allowing him the right to do so anything more than an ordinary incident of ownership.

(b) *Later elaboration.* The basic issue presented by *Motion Picture Patents* arises in many technical variations. Later cases made it clear that the basic rule extended to related contexts as well. *Carbice*[12] condemned an arrangement under which the plaintiff conditioned the use of its patented containers (manufactured by others) on purchasing needed dry ice from plaintiff. *Motion Picture Patents* was held to control notwithstanding the fact that "the unpatented refrigerant is one of the necessary elements of the patented product" which is a combination of unpatentable elements. The plaintiff in *Leitch*[13] permitted only those purchasing its unpatented emulsion to use its patented products. The Court held that *Motion Picture Patents* and *Carbice* condemn "every use of a patent as a means of obtaining a limited monopoly of unpatented material." This rule "applies whether the patent be for a machine, a product, or a process. It applies whatever the nature of the device by which the owner of the patent seeks to effect such unauthorized extension of the monopoly." *Morton Salt*[14] involved a patentee that licensed its machine on the condition that it be used only in connection with its salt. Although the defendant sold a machine that infringed the plaintiff's patent, the Court refused to enjoin the infringement "at least until it has been made to appear that the improper practice has been abandoned and that the consequences of the misuse of the patent have been dissipated."

(c) *Tying by patentees and the antitrust laws.* Without relying on the Sherman Act or the Clayton Act, each of these cases found the tying of unpatented products to the use of patented products or pro-

---

12. Carbice Corp. v. American Patents Dev. Corp., 283 U.S. 27, 33 (1931).
13. Leitch Mfg. Co. v. Barber Co., 302 U.S. 458, 463 (1938).
14. Morton Salt Co. v. G. S. Suppiger Co., 314 U.S. 488, 493 (1942).

cesses to be an unlawful extension of the patent monopoly. Typically, the issue was raised in defense to infringement actions. As later cases in this section, beginning with *International Salt*, will indicate, such tying has been held to violate the antitrust laws as well. What rules governing tying are appropriate is the subject of the remainder of this section. You should, however, consider how, if at all, the issue should be viewed differently when the tying arrangement involves the exploitation of a patent.[15]

425. Tying under the Clayton Act. The Clayton Act of 1914, like the other antitrust enactments, is somewhat vague. It is, to be sure, more specific than the Sherman Act and singles out price discrimination in §2, tying and related practices in §3, and mergers in §7. This specificity, however, is somewhat illusory, for each section[16] condemns the named practice only where the effect "may be to substantially lessen competition or tend to create a monopoly." It is usually said that the Clayton Act is more prohibitive than the Sherman Act for otherwise it would be superfluous and that it is designed to catch anticompetitive actions "in their incipiency" before they "ripen" into Sherman Act violations. See ¶132. The meaning of these statements will be explored here and in Chapter 5.

CLAYTON ACT §3

It shall be unlawful for any person engaged in commerce, in the course of such commerce, to lease or make a sale or contract for sale of goods, wares, merchandise, machinery, supplies, or other commodities, whether patented or unpatented, for use, consumption, or resale within the United States or any Territory thereof or the District of Columbia or any insular possession or other place under the jurisdiction of the United States, or fix a price charged therefor, or discount from, or rebate upon, such price, on the condition, agreement, or understanding that the lessee or purchaser thereof shall not use or deal in the goods, wares, merchandise, machinery, supplies, or other commodities of a competitor or competitors of the lessor or seller, where the effect of such lease, sale, or contract for sale or such condition, agreement, or under-

---

15. The dissent in *Motion Picture Patents* suggested that since patentees may legally keep their device wholly out of use, the lesser restriction involved with tying should be deemed permissible, an argument addressed in ¶277b. Note that a similar argument can be made with respect to any firm employing a tying arrangement in connection with selling or leasing a product.

16. Section 2, as amended by the Robinson-Patman Act, has a broader reach. See Ch. 6.

standing may be to substantially lessen competition or tend to create a monopoly in any line of commerce.

426. Initial coverage. Before exploring which circumstances satisfy the effects clause, consider the initial coverage of §3. When is there a condition "that the lessee or purchaser ... shall not use or deal in the goods ... of a competitor ... of the lessor or seller"?

(a) *United Shoe Machinery Corp. v. United States*, 258 U.S. 451, 456-457 (1922). The Court affirmed an injunction under §3 against the conditions on which defendant leased its shoe making machines to shoe manufacturers:

> (1) the restricted use clause, which provides that the leased machinery shall not, nor shall any part thereof, be used upon shoes, etc., or portions, thereof, upon which certain other operations have not been performed on other machines of the defendants; (2) the exclusive use clause, which provides that if the lessee fails to use exclusively machinery of certain kinds made by the lessor, the lessor shall have the right to cancel the right to use all such machinery so leased; (3) the supplies clause, which provides that the lessee shall purchase supplies exclusively from the lessor; (4) the patent insole clause, which provides that the lessee shall only use machinery leased on shoes which have had certain other operations performed upon them by the defendant's machines; (5) the additional machinery clause, which provides that the lessee shall take all additional machinery for certain kinds of work from the lessor or lose his right to retain the machines which he has already leased; (6) the factory output clause, which requires the payment of a royalty on shoes operated upon by machines made by competitors; (7) the discriminatory royalty clause, providing lower royalty for lessees who agree not to use certain machinery on shoes lasted on machines other than those leased from the lessor. . . .
>
> While the clauses enjoined do not contain specific agreements not to use the machinery of a competitor of the lessor, the practical effect of these drastic provisions is to prevent such use. We can entertain no doubt that such provisions as were enjoined are embraced in the broad terms of the Clayton Act, which cover all conditions, agreements or understandings of this nature. That such restrictive and tying agreements must necessarily lessen competition and tend to monopoly is, we believe, equally apparent. When it is considered that the United Company occupies a dominating position in supplying shoe machinery of the classes involved, these covenants, signed by the lessee and binding upon him effectually prevent him from acquiring the machinery of a competitor of the lessor except at the risk of forfeiting the right to use the machines furnished by the United Company which may be absolutely essential to the prosecution and success of his business.

696 Tying Arrangements ¶426

(b) *Other situations.* The preceding case holds that §3 does not require a formalized undertaking by the buyer (or lessee) to refrain from using the goods of the seller's competitors. Section 3 will be applied to arrangements that have the practical effect of precluding the buyer from using other suppliers. Should §3 be applied, however, when the buyer or lessee is not entirely foreclosed from competing suppliers? Suppose, for example, that a buyer uses several riveting machines purchased or leased from competing suppliers and that it agrees to use each machine only with rivets purchased from its manufacturer. Section 3 has been applied in several such cases.[17]

(c) *Goods.* Clayton Act §3 applies only to transactions in which both the tying and tied products are "goods, wares, merchandise, machinery, supplies, or other commodities." Do these words cover such things as land, repair or installation services, money or credit, or patent or copyright licenses? Later cases in this chapter bear on the answer.[18]

INTERNATIONAL SALT CO. v. UNITED STATES
332 U.S. 392 (1947)

Justice JACKSON. . . . The Government brought this civil action to enjoin the International Salt Company, appellant here, from carrying out provisions of the leases of its patented machines to the effect that lessees would use therein only International's salt products. The restriction is alleged to violate §1 of the Sherman Act, and §3 of the Clayton Act. Upon appellant's answer and admissions of fact, the Government moved for summary judgment under Rule 56 of the Rules of Civil Procedure, upon the ground that no issue as to a material fact was presented and that, on the admissions, judgment followed as matter of law. Neither party submitted affidavits. Judgment was granted and appeal was taken directly to this Court.

It was established by pleadings or admissions that the International Salt Company is engaged in interstate commerce in salt, of which it is the country's largest producer for industrial uses. It also owns patents on two machines for utilization of salt products. One, the "Lixator," dissolves rock salt into a brine used in various industrial processes. The other, the "Saltomat," injects salt, in tablet

17. E.g., Thomson Mfg. Co. v. FTC, 150 F.2d 952 (1st Cir.), cert. denied, 326 U.S. 776 (1945); Signode Steel Strapping Co. v. FTC, 132 F.2d 48 (4th Cir. 1942). See also ¶429.

18. And see United States v. Investors Divers. Servs., 102 F. Supp. 645, 647 (D. Minn. 1951).

form, into canned products during the canning process. The principal distribution of each of these machines is under leases which, among other things, require the lessees to purchase from appellant all unpatented salt and salt tablets consumed in the leased machines. . . . In 1944, appellant sold approximately 119,000 tons of salt, for about $500,000, for use in these machines.

The appellant's patents confer a limited monopoly of the invention they reward. From them appellant derives a right to restrain others from making, vending or using the patented machines. But the patents confer no right to restrain use of, or trade in, unpatented salt. By contracting to close this market for salt against competition, International has engaged in a restraint of trade for which its patents afford no immunity from the antitrust laws. . . .

Appellant contends, however, that summary judgment was unauthorized because it precluded trial of alleged issues of fact as to whether the restraint was unreasonable within the Sherman Act or substantially lessened competition or tended to create a monopoly in salt within the Clayton Act. We think the admitted facts left no genuine issue. Not only is price-fixing unreasonable, per se . . . but also it is unreasonable, per se, to foreclose competitors from any substantial market. *Fashion Originators' Guild.* The volume of business affected by these contracts cannot be said to be insignificant or insubstantial and the tendency of the arrangement to accomplishment of monopoly seems obvious. Under the law, agreements are forbidden which "tend to create a monopoly," and it is immaterial that the tendency is a creeping one rather than one that proceeds at full gallop; nor does the law await arrival at the goal before condemning the direction of the movement.

Appellant contends, however, that the "Lixator" contracts are saved from unreasonableness and from the tendency to monopoly because they provided that if any competitor offered salt of equal grade at a lower price, the lessee should be free to buy in the open market, unless appellant would furnish the salt at an equal price; and the "Saltomat" agreements provided that the lessee was entitled to the benefit of any general price reduction in lessor's salt tablets. The "Lixator" provision does, of course, afford a measure of protection to the lessee, but it does not avoid the stifling effect of the agreement on competition. The appellant had at all times a priority on the business at equal prices. A competitor would have to undercut appellant's price to have any hope of capturing the market, while appellant could hold that market by merely meeting competition. We do not think this concession relieves the contract of being a restraint of trade, albeit a less harsh one than would result in the absence of such a provision. The "Saltomat" provision obviously has no effect of legal significance since it gives the lessee nothing more than a right to buy appellant's salt tablets at appellant's going price. All purchases must in any event be of appellant's product.

Appellant also urges that since under the leases it remained under an obligation to repair and maintain the machines, it was reasonable to confine their use to its own salt because its high quality assured satisfactory functioning and low maintenance cost. The appellant's rock salt is alleged to have an average sodium chloride content of 98.2%. Rock salt of other producers, it is said, "does not run consistent in sodium chloride content and in many instances runs as low as 95% of sodium chloride." This greater percentage of insoluble impurities allegedly disturbs the functioning of the "Lixator" machine. A somewhat similar claim is pleaded as to the "Saltomat."

Of course, a lessor may impose on a lessee reasonable restrictions designed in good faith to minimize maintenance burdens and to assure satisfactory operation. We may assume, as matter of argument, that if the "Lixator" functions best on rock salt of average sodium chloride content of 98.2%, the lessee might be required to use only salt meeting such a specification of quality. But it is not pleaded, nor is it argued, that the machine is allergic to salt of equal quality produced by anyone except International. If others cannot produce salt to reasonable specifications for machine use, it is one thing; but it is admitted that, at times, at least, competitors do offer such a product. They are, however, shut out of the market by a provision that limits it, not in terms of quality, but in terms of a particular vendor. Rules for use of leased machinery must not be disguised restraints of free competition, though they may set reasonable standards which all suppliers must meet. . . .

[A]ffirmed.[19]

427. (a) What is the economic significance of a tie-in when each product is sold in perfectly competitive markets? Suppose that a seller of corn will not sell to any buyer who does not also take its wheat. What is the likely economic effect?

---

19. Frankfurter, Reed, and Burton, JJ., agreed with the portion of the opinion reproduced here but dissented with respect to the terms of the decree. See J. Peterman, The International Salt Case, 22 J.L. & Econ. 351 (1979): about 10 percent of International's total shipments of rock salt were for use in Lixators; this amounted to about 4 percent of the total rock salt consumed in areas where International sold. A quality-control motivation seems unlikely because International did not restrict machine users in areas where it did not itself sell salt. Nor was a "metering" explanation likely where the competitive conditions clause required International to sell salt at the market price. (See ¶423c.)

(b) Suppose that the sole manufacturer of can-closing machinery sells or leases its machinery to canners only on condition that they buy their cans from it. What is the likely economic effect in the can market?

(c) Suppose that the tied product in the previous question is not cans but sugar and the canners account for a fraction of 1 percent of all sugar consumed. (1) What is the likely effect in the sugar market? (2) Is the arrangement legal under the rule of *International Salt*? (3) Are buyers "coerced"?[20]

(d) Why might International Salt have imposed this tying arrangement? Do any of the grounds in ¶423 provide likely explanations?

(e) Are there any grounds for condemning tying arrangements with trivial economic effects in the market for the tied product? Is *International Salt* true to the statute? What reasons does it give for condemning the practice?

NORTHERN PACIFIC RAILWAY CO.
v. UNITED STATES
356 U.S. 1 (1958)

Justice BLACK. . . . In 1864 and 1870 Congress granted the predecessor of the Northern Pacific Railway Company approximately forty million acres of land in several Northwestern States and Territories to facilitate its construction of a railroad line. . . . In a large number of its sales contracts and most of its lease agreements [involving this land] the Railroad had inserted "preferential routing" clauses which compelled the grantee or lessee to ship over its lines all commodities produced or manufactured on the land, provided that its rates (and in some instances its service) were equal to those of competing carriers. Since many of the goods produced on the lands subject to these "preferential routing" provisions are shipped from one State to another the actual and potential amount of interstate commerce affected is substantial. Alternative means of transportation exist for a large portion of these shipments including the facilities of two other major railroad systems. . . . [The district court granted summary judgment on the Government's claim under Sherman Act §1.]

---

20. In Aqua Flame v. Imperial Fountains, 463 F. Supp. 736 (N.D. Tex. 1979), $75,000 of commerce in the tied product was sufficient to make a tie unlawful. Yentsch v. Texaco, 630 F.2d 46 (2d Cir. 1980), doubted that $15,000 was substantial.

Although [Sherman Act §1] is literally all-encompassing, the courts have construed it as precluding only those contracts or combinations which "unreasonably" restrain competition. *Standard Oil; Chicago Board of Trade.* However, there are certain agreements or practices which because of their pernicious effect on competition and lack of any redeeming virtue are conclusively presumed to be unreasonable and therefore illegal without elaborate inquiry as to the precise harm they have caused or the business excuse for their use. This principle of per se unreasonableness not only makes the type of restraints which are proscribed by the Sherman Act more certain to the benefit of everyone concerned, but it also avoids the necessity for an incredibly complicated and prolonged economic investigation into the entire history of the industry involved, as well as related industries, in an effort to determine at large whether a particular restraint has been unreasonable — an inquiry so often wholly fruitless when undertaken. Among the practices which the courts have heretofore deemed to be unlawful in and of themselves are price fixing, *Socony;* division of markets, *Addyston Pipe & Steel;* group boycotts, *Fashion Originators' Guild;* and tying arrangements, *International Salt.*

For our purposes a tying arrangement may be defined as an agreement by a party to sell one product but only on the condition that the buyer also purchases a different (or tied) product, or at least agrees that he will not purchase that product from any other supplier. Where such conditions are successfully exacted competition on the merits with respect to the tied product is inevitably curbed. Indeed "tying agreements serve hardly any purpose beyond the suppression of competition." *Standard [Stations].* They deny competitors free access to the market for the tied product, not because the party imposing the tying requirements has a better product or a lower price but because of his power or leverage in another market. At the same time buyers are forced to forego their free choice between competing products. For these reasons "tying agreements fare harshly under the laws forbidding restraints of trade." Times-Picayune Publishing Co. v. United States, 345 U.S. 594, 606. They are unreasonable in and of themselves whenever a party has sufficient economic power with respect to the tying product to appreciably restrain free competition in the market for the tied product and a "not insubstantial" amount of interstate commerce is affected. *International Salt.* Cf. United States v. Paramount Pictures, 334 U.S. 131, 156-159; *Griffith.* Of course where the seller has no control or dominance over the tying product so that it does not represent an effectual weapon to pressure buyers into taking the tied item any restraint of trade attributable to such tying arrangements would obviously be insignificant at most. As a simple example, if one of a dozen food stores in a community were to refuse to sell flour unless the buyer also took sugar it would hardly tend to restrain competition in sugar if its competitors were ready and able to sell flour by itself.

In this case we believe the district judge was clearly correct in entering summary judgment declaring the defendant's "preferential routing" clauses unlawful restraints of trade. We wholly agree that the undisputed facts established beyond any genuine question that the defendant possessed substantial economic power by virtue of its extensive landholdings which it used as leverage to induce large numbers of purchasers and lessees to give it preference, to the exclusion of its competitors, in carrying goods or produce from the land transferred to them. Nor can there be any real doubt that a "not insubstantial" amount of interstate commerce was and is affected by these restrictive provisions.

[Defendant's] land was strategically located in checkerboard fashion amid private holdings and within economic distance of transportation facilities. Not only the testimony of various witnesses but common sense makes it evident that this particular land was often prized by those who purchased or leased it and was frequently essential to their business activities. In disposing of its holdings the defendant entered into contracts of sale or lease covering at least several million acres of land which included "preferential routing" clauses. The very existence of this host of tying arrangements is itself compelling evidence of the defendant's great power, at least where, as here, no other explanation has been offered for the existence of these restraints. The "preferential routing" clauses conferred no benefit on the purchasers or lessees. While they got the land they wanted by yielding their freedom to deal with competing carriers, the defendant makes no claim that it came any cheaper than if the restrictive clauses had been omitted. In fact any such price reduction in return for rail shipments would have quite plainly constituted an unlawful rebate to the shipper. So far as the Railroad was concerned its purpose obviously was to fence out competitors, to stifle competition. . . . In short, we are convinced that the essential prerequisites for treating the defendant's tying arrangements as unreasonable "per se" were conclusively established below and that the defendant has offered to prove nothing there or here which would alter this conclusion.

In our view *International Salt*, which has been unqualifiedly approved by subsequent decisions, is ample authority for affirming the judgment below. . . . [W]e affirmed unanimously a summary judgment finding the defendant guilty of violating §1 of the Sherman Act. The Court ruled that it was "unreasonable, per se, to foreclose competitors from any substantial market" by tying arrangements.

As we later analyzed the decision, "it was not established that equivalent machines were unobtainable, it was not indicated what proportion of the business of supplying such machines was controlled by defendant, and it was deemed irrelevant that there was no evidence as to the actual effect of the tying clauses upon competition." *Standard [Stations].*

The defendant attempts to evade the force of *International Salt* on the ground that the tying product there was patented while here it is not. But we do not believe this distinction has, or should have, any significance. In arriving at its decision in *International Salt* the Court placed no reliance on the fact that a patent was involved nor did it give the slightest intimation that the outcome would have been any different if that had not been the case. If anything, the Court held the challenged tying arrangements unlawful despite the fact that the tying item was patented, not because of it. "By contracting to close this market for salt against competition, International has engaged in a restraint of trade for which its patents afford no immunity from the antitrust laws." Nor have subsequent cases confined the rule of per se unreasonableness laid down in *International Salt* to situations involving patents. Cf. *Griffith.* ...[8]

While there is some language in the *Times-Picayune* opinion which speaks of "monopoly power" or "dominance" over the tying product as a necessary precondition for application of the rule of per se unreasonableness to tying arrangements, we do not construe this general language as requiring anything more than sufficient economic power to impose an appreciable restraint on free competition in the tied product (assuming all the time, of course, that a "not insubstantial" amount of interstate commerce is affected). ...

The defendant contends that its "preferential routing" clauses are subject to so many exceptions and have been administered so leniently that they do not significantly restrain competition. It points out that these clauses permit the vendee or lessee to ship by competing carrier if its rates are lower (or in some instances if its service is better) than the defendant's. Of course if these restrictive provisions are merely harmless sieves with no tendency to restrain competition, as the defendant's argument seems to imply, it is hard to understand why it has expended so much effort in obtaining them in vast numbers and upholding their validity, or how they are

---

8. Of course it is common knowledge that a patent does not always confer a monopoly over a particular commodity. Often the patent is limited to a unique form or improvement of the product and the economic power resulting from the patent privileges is slight. As a matter of fact, the defendant in *International Salt* offered to prove that competitive salt machines were readily available that were satisfactory substitutes for its machines (a fact the Government did not controvert), but the Court regarded such proof as irrelevant.

of any benefit to anyone, even the defendant. But however that may be, the essential fact remains that these agreements are binding obligations held over the heads of vendees which deny defendant's competitors access to the fenced-off market on the same terms as the defendant. . . .

Affirmed.

Justice HARLAN, whom Justice FRANKFURTER and Justice WHITTAKER join, dissenting. . . . The District Court should have taken evidence of the relative strength of appellants' landholdings vis-à-vis that of others in the appropriate market for land of the types now or formerly possessed by appellants, of the "uniqueness" of appellants' landholdings in terms of quality or use to which they may have been put, and of the extent to which the location of the lands on or near the Northern Pacific's railroad line, or any other circumstances, put the appellants in a strategic position as against other sellers and lessors of land. Short of such an inquiry I do not see how it can be determined whether the appellants occupied such a dominant position in the relevant land market, cf. *du Pont [Cellophane]*, as to make these tying clauses illegal per se under the Sherman Act.

Explanation for the Court's failure to remand with instructions to pursue such an inquiry apparently lies in part in its statement that the "very existence of this host of tying arrangements is itself compelling evidence of the defendant's great power" over the land market. I do not deny that there may be instances where economic coercion by a vendor may be inferred, without any direct showing of market dominance, from the mere existence of the tying arrangements themselves, as where the vendee is apt to suffer economic detriment from the tying clause because precluded from purchasing a tied product at better terms or of a better quality elsewhere. But the tying clauses here are not cast in such absolute terms. The record indicates that a large majority of appellants' lands were close to the Northern Pacific lines and thus vendees or lessees of these lands might be expected to utilize Northern Pacific as a matter of course. Further, substantially all the tying clauses, as found by the District Court, contained provisos leaving the vendee or lessee free to ship by other railroads when offered either lower rates or superior service. In these circumstances it would appear that the inclusion of the tying clauses in contracts or leases might have been largely a matter of indifference to at least many of the purchasers or lessees of appellants' land, and hence that more is needed than the tying clauses themselves to warrant the inference that acceptance of the tying clauses resulted from coercion exercised by appellants through their position in the land market.

Particularly in view of the Court's affirmance of a judgment based on so inadequate a record, I have further difficulty with the opinion in its treatment of *International Salt,* the decision on which the Court principally relies. The Court regards that case as making irrelevant proof of market dominance in the tying interest, but it seems to me that *Times-Picayune,* has laid to rest all doubt as to the need for clear proof on this issue. In fact that case considered that ... *International Salt* simply treated a patent as the equivalent of proof of market control. . . .

Finally, the Court leaves in unsettling doubt the future effect of its statement that the use of the word "dominance" in *Times-Picayune* implies no more of a showing of market dominance than "sufficient economic power to impose an appreciable restraint on free competition in the tied product." As an abstraction one can hardly quarrel with this piece of surgery, for I do not claim that a monopoly in the sense of §2 of the Sherman Act must be shown over a tying product. As already indicated, I should think that a showing of "sufficient economic power" in cases of this kind could be based upon a variety of factors, such as significant percentage control of the relevant market, desirability of the product to the purchaser, use of tying clauses which would be likely to result in economic detriment to vendees or lessees, and such uniqueness of the tying product as to suggest comparison with a monopoly by patent. . . .[21]

428. Is *Northern Pacific* an a fortiori application of *International Salt?*

(a) Is it relevant that the *Northern Pacific* tying product, unlike that of *International Salt,* was unpatented?

(b) What further proof would have satisfied Justice Harlan? Was the proof sought by Justice Harlan required in *International Salt?* If not, why does Justice Harlan demand it here?

(c) Does Sherman Act §1 provide the defendant with a more favorable standard of legality than Clayton Act §3? Why? Why not?[22] If it doesn't, why was the Clayton Act enacted?[23] (And why was this case brought under the Sherman Act rather than the Clayton Act?)

---

21. Clark, J., did not participate. See F. Cummings & W. Ruhter, The Northern Pacific Case, 22 J.L. & Econ. 329, 342, 350 (1979): "When a buyer or lessee did not use Northern Pacific, the contract compelled him to disclose the lower rates or better service available elsewhere. If he was uncooperative in *reporting,* the traffic clauses would have given Northern Pacific grounds for legal action. . . ." Thus, the traffic clauses aided Northern Pacific "in detecting whether other railroads were adhering to rate and service standards."

22. See the *Times-Picayune* excerpt, note 31.

23. See ¶132.

(d) Suppose for the moment that §3 did not exist and that there is no precedent in the tying area. How would you analyze the *Northern Pacific* situation under §1? (Be sure to take into account the agreement's proviso that shippers must use Northern Pacific only when its rates, and in some instances its services, are equal to those of competing carriers.) Why do you think Northern Pacific included this clause? What effects made the Court hostile to it?

429. Coercion to purchase related products. *Atlantic*[24] and *Texaco*[25] both involved challenges under §5 of the Federal Trade Commission Act to arrangements under which oil companies undertook to induce their dealers (the service stations were independently owned) to purchase tires, batteries, and accessories (TBA) from a designated company which paid commissions to the oil companies. In both cases, the Supreme Court upheld the Commission's finding of violations. The *Atlantic* Court stated that

> the Commission was warranted in finding that the effect of the plan was *as though* Atlantic had agreed with Goodyear to require its dealers to buy Goodyear products and had done so.... Goodyear complains that there is no evidence of the economic power of many of the companies with which it has sales-commission plans.

But there would be "little point in paying substantial commissions to oil companies were it not for their ability to exert power over their wholesalers and dealers." In *Texaco,* there was "considerably less" evidence regarding coercive practices, but the Court had little difficulty finding "that Texaco's dominant economic power was used in a manner which tended to foreclose competition in the marketplace of TBA. The sales-commissions system for marketing TBA is inherently coercive."

(a) Should these arrangements have been condemned? Are they different in practice from tying arrangements?

(b) Would Atlantic or Texaco have been prevented from making or purchasing TBA to be resold by their dealers? If not, should the commission arrangement have been permitted?

430. Voluntary ties. A tie might be voluntary in two quite different senses: (1) a buyer chooses freely whether to take the tying product separately at one price or to take it at a lower price in connection with the tied product or (2) the buyer chooses, without any price advantage or price sanction although perhaps with per-

---

24. Atlantic Ref. Co. v. FTC, 381 U.S. 357, 370, 375-376 (1965).
25. FTC v. Texaco, 393 U.S. 223, 228-229 (1968).

suasion, to take both products. A brief word about each may be helpful.

(a) *Unrestrained choice.* It should be obvious that nothing in antitrust law or policy forbids a person from purchasing two products from a single supplier. Nor is the supplier forbidden from offering two products to a single customer or from normal persuasion. Of course, the buyer might in fact have agreed to buy its requirements of a second product, or the seller might have provided the first product only on condition that the second product would also be taken by the customer. Thus, we must distinguish truly voluntary conduct from improperly coerced conduct. We already examined that problem in Chapter 4A[26] and often cited tying and exclusive dealing cases indiscriminately with restricted distribution cases on the vertical agreement issue.

(b) *Preferential price.* We now turn to situations in which the seller simultaneously offers product *A* (1) separately at one price and (2) at a lower price when taken with product *B*. This kind of voluntary tie is not necessarily excluded from Clayton Act §3 which embraces those who "fix a price . . . or discount . . . or rebate . . . on the condition, agreement, or understanding that the lessee or purchaser . . . not use . . . the goods . . . of a competitor."

The *Northern Pacific* court observed that the defendant had not claimed that it sold its land more cheaply with the restrictive clause than it would have sold the land without the clause. Would or should the result be different if the defendant had made and substantiated such a claim? Consider the same issue on the facts of *Fortner*, below.

431. *United States v. Loew's*, 371 U.S. 38, 45 & n.4 (1962). The Court found illegal under Sherman Act §1 a block booking arrangement, under which the license of one or more feature films to television stations was conditioned upon acceptance of a package ("block") containing one or more unwanted or inferior films. The Court recited the test from *Northern Pacific* and indicated that "[t]he requisite economic power is presumed when the tying product is patented or copyrighted." The fact that there are other feature films and other programming available for television did not upset this conclusion, as each copyrighted film subject to block

---

26. Note that *Colgate* might be less of an obstacle to reaching unilaterally imposed tying than it might be to reaching unilaterally imposed distribution restraints. Clayton Act §3 is satisfied not only by an "agreement" but also by a "condition" or "understanding." See VII P. Areeda, Antitrust Law ¶1460 (1986; Supp. 1996).

booking was deemed unique.[27] Much of the opinion addressed the decree. Of particular interest, the Government and Court agreed in principle that only non-cost-justified price differentials between the package price and prices for individual films should be prohibited, although there was some dispute as to which costs were relevant. The Court permitted all legitimate cost justifications for quantity discounts whereas the government sought to make savings in distribution costs the only permissible basis for price differences.

(a) How would you expect the *Loew's* decree to operate in practice? What legitimate cost justifications might exist, and how might they be measured?[28]

(b) Huntington Collector has over the years acquired an extremely valuable collection of paintings. The collection also includes a number of unimportant but not valueless works by unknown artists. In order to finance his other activities, Collector proposes to sell his entire collection as a package to the highest bidder over $10 million. Collector is troubled, however, for he recently happened to read the *Loew's* decision. He asks you whether his proposed sale is distinguishable from *Loew's* and whether it is an unlawful tie-in.[29]

(c) Reconsider the tying aspect of *BMI* from Chapter 2B: Many owners of copyrighted compositions grant a nonexclusive license to ASCAP, which licenses those who wish to perform a copyrighted work. ASCAP grants only a "blanket" license, which permits a licensee to use the entire ASCAP repertoire in return for a royalty based on the licensee's revenues. Is ASCAP engaged in tying? Is it

27. In a footnote, the Court added:

Since the requisite economic power may be found on the basis of either uniqueness or consumer appeal, and since market dominance in the present context does not necessitate a demonstration of market power in the sense of §2 of the Sherman Act, it should seldom be necessary in a tie-in case to embark upon a full-scale factual inquiry into the scope of the relevant market for the tying product and into the corollary problem of the seller's percentage share in that market.

Does this view survive *Fortner* and *Jefferson Parish?*
28. See Ch. 6C (cost justification defense to price discrimination challenges). The pricing in *Loew's* might have been motivated because it permits the seller to obtain maximum revenues where it cannot easily discriminate in price. Suppose, for example, that each of two buyers wants products A and B, that one would pay $4 for A and $6 for B, and that the other's preferences are exactly opposite. The seller could sell both products to each at $4 prices, for total revenues of $16. A package price of $10, however, would appeal to both buyers and would yield the seller $20. See G. Stigler, The Organization of Industry 165-166 (1968).
29. See United States v. Loew's, 1972 Trade Cas. ¶74017 (S.D.N.Y.) (decree against block booking does not prohibit block license of 8 or 12 movies based on classical theme for exhibition in a single theater on two regularly scheduled days per month; public subscription for whole series solicited).

relevant that individual copyright-holders who wish to grant a license to perform an individual composition are free to do so, in light of the Court's suggestion that this was often infeasible? What is a cost-justified price for the package? Should one compare the license price for each of the individual compositions? Is it relevant that those securing blanket licenses will use only a fraction of the licensed compositions?[30]

432. Everybody in Amesville reads the Morning Lever, which is the city's only morning newspaper. Everybody in Amesville also reads one of the two evening newspapers, Tide and Time, which have roughly equal circulation. Lever and Tide are both owned by LeverTide and published in a single plant. The advertising revenue of each newspaper is roughly proportional to its share of total circulation — 50 percent for the Lever and 25 percent each for Tide and Time. Advertising space is not sold separately in the Lever; advertisers wishing to purchase space in the Lever must also purchase identical space in the Tide.[31]

(a) Is Lever's action an attempt to monopolize in violation of Sherman Act §2? Is this case similar to *Lorain Journal* from Chapter 3C? Does Lever have monopoly power? What is its market share? If Lever has monopoly power, is it monopolizing in violation of Sherman Act §2? Is this case similar to *Griffith* from Chapter 3A?

(b) Is Lever's arrangement subject to Clayton Act §3?

30. F.E.L. Pubs. v. Catholic Bishop of Chicago, 739 F.2d 284 (7th Cir. 1982) (relying on *BMI*, finds license charging same fee regardless of number of songs copied not an unlawful tie; cites transaction cost and monitoring savings; argues that blanket license is a unique, distinct, single product).

31. These facts are essentially those of Times-Picayune Publishing Co. v. United States, 345 U.S. 594, 608-609 (1953), which reversed by a 5-4 vote a finding that Sherman Act §1 was violated, emphasizing that the morning paper did not have a dominant market position, that there was no forced purchase of a distinct tied product since advertising space was indistinguishable to advertisers, and that advertising in both papers substantially reduced costs.

In addressing the statutes, the Court stated:

> When the seller enjoys a monopolistic position in the market for the "tying" product, *or* if a substantial volume of commerce in the "tied" product is restrained, a tying arrangement violates the narrower standards expressed in §3 of the Clayton Act because from either factor the requisite potential lessening of competition is inferred. And because for even a lawful monopolist it is "unreasonable, per se, to foreclose competitors from any substantial market," a tying arrangement is banned by §1 of the Sherman Act whenever *both* conditions are met. In either case, the arrangement transgresses §5 of the Federal Trade Commission Act, since minimally that section registers violations of the Clayton and Sherman Acts.

Queries: Do you agree with the role ascribed to a monopolistic position in the market for the tying product in these tests? Are these tests consistent with *International Salt*? Do they survive *Northern Pacific*?

(c) Advertisers in Lever do not have to place evening advertising exclusively with Tide but may advertise in Time as well. Is this fact relevant to the application of Clayton Act §3 or Sherman Act §1?

(d) Does the Lever arrangement constitute tying? Is it unlawful under §1? How do you assess the relevant competitive threats, redeeming virtues, and less restrictive alternatives?

(e) Would your answers to the preceding questions differ if Lever accepted advertising separately in the two papers but charged almost as much for an advertisement in the Lever alone as for an advertisement in both the Lever and the Tide? Suppose that Lever could show that all the difference between the package price and the individual prices is accounted for by cost savings resulting from the single setting of type for both newspapers. Suppose not.

(f) If the arrangement is illegal, what should an injunction provide? Is *Loew's* helpful to your answer?

433. Delta Company is the sole producer of can closing machinery and "gives" its machines to canners who buy their can requirements from Delta.

(a) Does Clayton Act §3 apply? Would the Sherman Act §1 test of legality be significantly different?

(b) Is the arrangement lawful if Delta does not otherwise lease or sell the machine?

(c) Is the arrangement lawful if Delta leases or sells the machine at a price to those who use its competitors' cans? (1) If Delta's can prices are competitive? What economic effect? (2) If Delta's can prices are higher than those of its competitors? What economic effect?

(d) If Delta leases the machine at a standard fee to all canners and gives a discount only to those who use its cans exclusively, what would the economic effect be?

(e) Assume that each Delta machine closes 100,000 cases of cans annually and that the prevailing price for cans is \$1.10 per case; note that $100,000 \times 10¢ = \$10,000$. Compare two situations: (1) Delta leases each machine for \$10,000 annually and sells cans profitably for \$1.00 per case; (2) Delta charges \$1.10 per case of cans and offers users the choice of renting a machine for (i) \$10,000 or (ii) 1¢ when coupled with the canner's promise to buy its can requirements from Delta. Is there any doubt about the legality of the first situation? Do its economic effects differ from those of the second? Has Delta violated the Clayton Act in the second situation? Why might Delta offer the second option? Why might it offer *only* the second?

434. Mandatory package licensing of patents. (a) *Patentee's reasons.* A patentee might prefer to license its patents as a package for

several reasons. (1) The administrative costs per patent of negotiating, licensing, and bookkeeping are reduced for package transactions covering several patents. (2) Detecting the unlicensed use of
each patent might be difficult. Consider, for example, the product
that can be made inefficiently without process patent *Y* but that
cannot be made at all without process patent *X.* Inspection of the
finished product might not disclose whether patent *Y* had been
used. In that case, the holder of both patents would suspect that a
licensee of the *X* patent alone might also practice the other patent.
To avoid the obvious difficulties of detecting the infringement of
the *Y* patent, the patentee would like to require the licensee to take
both. (3) The package might be easier to price than the individual
patents whenever the value of the whole to licensees generally is
more readily ascertainable than the value of each patent individually.[32] (4) A defendant patentee might possess both an important
patent and a lesser patent for which there is an adequate alternative
patent held by another. It can force both patents on a licensee who
wants both the important patent and either the defendant's or the
alternative lesser patent. The package price would not exceed
the value of the important patent alone plus the market price for
the alternative lesser patent.[33] (5) It is sometimes argued that the
licensee of a package would be discouraged from litigating
the validity of any invalid patent within the package.[34] Although the
licensee is not estopped from challenging the validity of a licensed
patent,[35] its incentive to do so might be reduced. If the same price
must be paid for the package as for one or a few patents, it would
have no incentive to litigate the validity of any one patent. And even
if each patent is of questionable validity, a substantial likelihood

32. With respect to the patentee's returns or the licensee's costs, the following
points may be noted. First, a patentee controlling a valid patent essential to the
production of an article could set a royalty that would extract the same monopoly
profit that it could earn were it the sole producer of that article. One truly essential
patent gives it that control; a hundred additional patents on that product do not
increase its control (although, of course, they might well diminish the likelihood
that others would find a way around the patent). Second, an undesired patent in a
package will not increase the licensee's willingness to pay. And packaging two
desired patents will not increase the licensee's willingness to pay more than it
would pay in the aggregate for both. Third, packaging might, however, increase
the patentee's returns where price discrimination is not customary or convenient.
See ¶423c.

33. A variant would involve the case where no substitute yet existed for the lesser
patent, but there was a significant prospect it would be invented around. Requiring
a combined license might deter invention of substitutes for the lesser patent.

34. See American Securit Co. v. Shatterproof Glass Corp., 268 F.2d 769, 777 (3d
Cir.), cert. denied, 361 U.S. 902 (1959); International Mfg. Co. v. Landon, 336 F.2d
723, 731 (9th Cir. 1964), cert. denied, 379 U.S. 988 (1965).

35. See ¶185.

that at least one would prove valid could discourage it from challenging the validity of any patent.

(b) *General rule.* It now seems clear that the refusal to license a patent except as part of a package is ordinarily unlawful.[36]

(c) *Related patents.* In *International Mfg.*,[37] plaintiff's alleged mandatory package licensing of two patents was held to be neither a patent misuse nor an antitrust violation for three reasons. (1) Because the two patents had been held valid and blocking (i.e., one could not be used without the other), the licensee was not required to take more than it needed to make a non-infringing product. (2) The package did not seem to the court to involve a tie because it believed that mutually blocking patents comprise a single product. (3) The package seemed necessary to protect the patentee because the court thought that a license of one patent would convey an implied license of the blocking patents as well.[38]

(d) *Identifying a mandatory package.*[39] Contrast two extremes: a holder of 10 patents offers to license (1) one for $10 or all for $10 or (2) each for $1 and all for $9 where the package is shown to save the patentee $1 in bookkeeping costs as compared with 10 individual licenses. In the second case, the licensee might well have an incentive to take the package from this patentee rather than to deal at greater cost with 10 different patentees, but this arrangement would be lawful.[40] The pricing arrangement in the first case, however, would usually be found indistinguishable from a mandatory package license.[41] Because there may be cost savings in packaging

36. Hazeltine Research v. Zenith Radio Corp., 239 F. Supp. 51, 77 (N.D. Ill. 1965), aff'd on this point, 388 F.2d 25 (7th Cir. 1967), rev'd on other grounds, 395 U.S. 100 (1969); *American Securit*, note 34, at 777 (One "invention is what the patent grant protects . . . not that invention plus some embellishment, improvement, or alternative product or process, which also happens to be patented." Mandatory package licensing "employs one patent as a lever to compel the acceptance of a license under another.").

37. *International Mfg.*, note 34.

38. See also North Am. Philips Co. v. Stewart Engr. Co., 319 F. Supp. 335 (N.D. Cal. 1970) (licensing three blocking or interlocking patents as a package not a misuse; no evidence that anyone had requested an individual license).

39. See also ¶430a.

40. See the decree in *Loew's*.

41. This arrangement would not be equivalent to a mandatory package where the value of each patent to the licensee was at least $10 and the additional patents did not increase that value. For example, each patent might be an alternative to the others such that the licensee could use only one patent at a time. Or $10 might be the monopoly value of controlling the licensee's production through one key patent such that the patentee cannot charge more for the package than for one. See Technograph Printed Circuits, Ltd. v. Bendix Aviation Corp., 218 F. Supp. 1, 49 (D. Md. 1963), aff'd, 327 F.2d 497 (4th Cir.), cert. denied, 379 U.S. 826 (1964)

and the different patents will have different values, the relationship between the package rates and individual rates may not be very revealing. The courts have tended to speak vaguely of prohibiting individual patent license rates "so disproportionate to the package rate as to amount to economic coercion."[42]

435. Patent royalty base. (a) *Duration of payments.* The Supreme Court has found patent misuse where a license required royalty payments beyond the life of the licensed patent.[43] Other courts have found patent misuse in a package license that extended beyond the life of one patent in the package and failed to reduce royalties as patents expired.[44] A contrary conclusion was reached where the patentee had demonstrated "a willingness to license any or all patents under reasonable, negotiated terms" and where the licensee had the option of terminating the agreement after a key patent had expired; the court distinguished coercion from freedom of choice.[45]

(b) *Sale price of unpatented products.* Royalties for the use of a patent are sometimes based on the sales price of a finished product

---

(package licensing may not be a misuse if the royalty charged for the package does not exceed the fair price for any one of the patents in the package).

42. *Hazeltine* (1967), note 36, at 39. The court approved a royalty schedule charging 50 percent of the package rate for one patent, 80 percent for two patents, and 100 percent for 3 or more patents. There were more than 500 patents in the package, but only three seemed in general use. That eight television manufacturers had taken a license for a single patent indicated to the court that the patentee's schedule was commercially reasonable. See also United States v. Westinghouse Elec. Corp., 471 F. Supp. 532, 545 (N.D. Cal. 1978), aff'd in part, rev'd in part on other grounds, 648 F.2d 642 (9th Cir. 1981) (no illegal tie "if the buyer is free to select wanted products and to reject the rest, even though the buyer has to pay a higher price for each product than if he had taken the entire package"); Mobil Oil Corp. v. W. R. Grace & Co., 367 F. Supp. 207 (D. Conn. 1973) (defined field license for 8.4 percent covering about 40 patents or 7 percent covering 5 patents reasonable in view of continuous policing required to assure no infringement of closely intertwined patents).

43. Brulotte v. Thys Co., 379 U.S. 29 (1964). See also Veltman v. Norton Simon, 425 F. Supp. 774 (S.D.N.Y. 1977) (royalty payments after patent expiration unlawful unless clearly designed as deferred compensation for pre-expiration use or as compensation for continuing supply of know-how or something other than patent itself). Compare Aronson v. Quick Point Pencil Co., 440 U.S. 257 (1979) (*Brulotte* rule inapplicable to agreement requiring 5 percent royalty if patent issues but 2.5 percent forever if no patent issues on the invention within five years).

44. E.g., Rocform Corp. v. Acitelli-Standard Concrete Wall, 367 F.2d 678 (6th Cir. 1966); *American Securit*, note 34, at 777. Is this result sound? Compare note 41.

45. Well Surveys v. Perfo-Log, 396 F.2d 15, 18 (10th Cir.), cert. denied, 393 U.S. 951 (1968). See also Congoleum Indus. v. Armstrong Cork Co., 366 F. Supp. 220, 236 (E.D. Pa. 1973), aff'd, 510 F.2d 334 (3d Cir.), cert. denied, 421 U.S. 988 (1975).

not covered by the patent. For example, a licensee might be permitted to use a patented component in return for a royalty of a specified percentage of the sales price of the finished product. Indeed, the license may require that royalty payment even though the patent is not used on all of the finished products. Although not condemning such payments absolutely, *Zenith* held "that conditioning the grant of a patent license upon payment of royalties on products which do not use the teaching of the patent does amount to patent misuse."[46] The Court addressed the situation

> where the patentee refuses to license on any other basis and leaves the licensee with the choice between a license so providing and no license at all. . . . [P]atent misuse inheres in a patentee's insistence on a percentage-of-sales royalty, regardless of use, and his rejection of licensee proposals to pay only for actual use.[47]

Justice Harlan dissented in *Zenith*. He thought the Court's test uncertain and difficult to apply. He also wondered about the rationale for judicial concern. There was the possibility of overreaching by Hazeltine, but there was no evidence that Zenith could not take care of itself. Beyond this, he saw two possibly undesirable effects.

> First . . . employment of such provisions may tend to reduce the licensee's incentive to substitute other, cheaper "inputs" for the patented item in producing an unpatented end-product. Failure of the licensee to substitute will, it is said, cause the price of the end-product to be higher and its output lower than would be the case if substitution had occurred. Second, it is suggested that under certain conditions a percentage-of-sales royalty arrangement may enable the patentee to garner for himself elements of profit, above the norm for the industry or economy, which are properly attributable not to the licensee's use of the patent but to other factors which cause the licensee's situation to differ from one of "perfect competition," and that this cannot occur when royalties are based upon use. If accepted, this economic analysis would indicate that percentage-of-sales royalties should be entirely outlawed.[48]

436. *International Business Machines Corp. v. United States*, 298 U.S. 131 (1936). IBM manufactured certain machines that sorted

---

46. Zenith Radio Corp. v. Hazeltine Research, 395 U.S. 100, 135 (1969).
47. Id. at 135, 139.
48. Id. at 145. Compare Plastic Contact Lens Co. v. W.R.S. Contact Lens Labs., 330 F. Supp. 441 (S.D.N.Y. 1970) (no credible proof of "conditioning" where patentee had offered licensees a choice between percentage-of-sale royalty or a higher royalty rate limited to patented items), with Glen Mfg. v. Perfect Fit Indus., 324 F. Supp. 1133 (S.D.N.Y. 1971) (royalty structure unnecessary and for sole benefit of patentee rather than for mutual convenience of parties). See L. Kaplow, The Patent-Antitrust Intersection: A Reappraisal, 97 Harv. L. Rev. 1813 (1984).

cards according to the holes punched in them to reflect certain information. The cards were not of unusual composition, although they had to be of a precise thickness and free of imperfections that might jam the machine. IBM leased the machine with the condition that users purchase their requirements of blank cards from itself. The condition was held to violate Clayton Act §3. IBM had 81 percent of the market for such cards, with one competitor supplying the remaining 19 percent, and it derived substantial profits from sales of cards. IBM asserted that the tying requirement was necessary to protect its goodwill, as the machines might malfunction if cards not meeting minute tolerances were used. The Court rejected this defense, as "[t]here is no contention that others ... cannot meet these requirements. It affirmatively appears, by stipulation, that others are capable of manufacturing [suitable] cards...." The Government, in fact, paid a 15 percent higher rental in exchange for being permitted to make its own cards. IBM could have warned consumers of the dangers of using improper cards or conditioned leases upon the use of cards conforming to necessary specifications.

(a) Can one apply to *IBM* the analysis of ¶433, which suggests that such tying arrangements may have no effect? If not, why not? If so, what result does it suggest?

(b) Why do you suppose IBM employed this arrangement? What do you infer from its special arrangement with the Government? Do its likely motives suggest that it was appropriate for the tie to have been deemed illegal?

UNITED STATES v. JERROLD ELECTRONICS CORP.

187 F. Supp. 545 (E.D. Pa. 1960), aff'd per curiam,
365 U.S. 567 (1961)

VAN DUSEN, District Judge. [Jerrold was organized in 1948 to make and sell a television booster to improve television reception in fringe areas by amplifying the weak signals available there. Jerrold then branched out into master antenna systems, which enable a single antenna to serve a number of television receivers. Its developments, service, manufacture, and operations became increasingly sophisticated and now embrace community antenna systems for towns remote from any television transmitting station. Such systems may include antenna construction quite remote from the town served, amplification of the received signal, conversion to a channel different from that received, and transmission by cable or microwave relay to the town center and then by cable directly to subscribers' homes.

Jerrold sells whole systems; it does not sell separate parts. It sells its system only on condition that Jerrold install and service the system. Many of its contracts provide for the exclusive use of Jerrold equipment whenever extra capacity is to be added to the system and forbid the installation of any additional equipment without Jerrold's approval.

The government attacked these arrangements as unlawful tie-ins in violation of Sherman Act §1 and Clayton Act §3.]

III-A. SERVICE CONTRACTS . . .

The Government concedes that §3 of the Clayton Act does not apply to this situation because that section, by its terms, only concerns "goods, wares, merchandise, machinery, supplies, or other commodities." It does not apply to tie-ins involving services. [The government invokes Sherman Act §1 as applied in *Northern Pacific*, which held tying agreements] ". . . unreasonable in and of themselves whenever a party has sufficient economic power with respect to the tying product to appreciably restrain free competition in the market for the tied product and a 'not insubstantial' amount of interstate commerce is affected." . . .

[The latter condition is clearly met. While the standard of sufficient economic power is elusive, it is easily satisfied in this case.] Jerrold admits that, as to the sale of complete community television antenna systems, it was an undoubted leader up until mid-1954, and more than a majority of the new systems from 1950 to mid-1954 were purchased from it. . . . The Supreme Court also stated in the *Northern Pacific* case that the requisite economic power can be inferred from the very existence of the tying clauses where no other explanation for their use is offered. The majority of the court appears to feel that this explanation must include a showing of some benefit conferred upon the purchasers in return for their sacrifice of a free choice of alternatives, but also considered the seller's motive.[12] This is an extremely difficult burden to meet and, in the opinion of this court, it has not been satisfied by the evidence offered by the defendants in the case at bar. Another fact from which economic power can be inferred is the desirability of the tying product to the purchaser. . . . Jerrold's highly specialized head end equipment was the only equipment available which was designed to meet all of the varying problems arising at the antenna site. It was

---

12. Much of the evidence objected to by the Government under its theory of per se unreasonableness was admissible for this purpose.

thus in great demand by system operators. This placed Jerrold in a strategic position and gave it the leverage necessary to persuade customers to agree to its service contracts. This leverage constitutes "economic power" sufficient to invoke the doctrine of per se unreasonableness.

While the trial judge is of the opinion that the Government has established both of the prerequisites necessary for treating Jerrold's policy and practice of selling its community equipment only in conjunction with a service contract as unreasonable, per se, under the *Northern Pacific* decision, he does not believe that the inquiry must end there in view of the rather unique circumstances involved in this particular case. Any judicially, as opposed to legislatively, declared per se rule is not conclusively binding on this court as to any set of facts not basically the same as those in the cases in which the rule was applied. In laying down such a rule, a court would be, in effect, stating that in all the possible situations it can think of, it is unable to see any redeeming virtue in tying arrangements which would make them reasonable. The Supreme Court of the United States did not purport in the *Northern Pacific* case to anticipate all of the possible circumstances under which a tying arrangement might be used. Therefore, while the per se rule should be followed in almost all cases, the court must always be conscious of the fact that a case might arise in which the facts indicate that an injustice would be done by blindly accepting the per se rule. In this case, the court felt that the facts asserted by the defendants in their pre-trial statement and trial brief warranted hearing their testimony and argument on the issue of reasonableness. It was partly influenced in this decision by the fact that the history of the industry was brief, and the position of the defendants did not seem to require a prolonged economic investigation — factors which the Supreme Court felt justified the per se rule. . . .

[Defendant] envisioned widespread chaos if Jerrold simply sold its community equipment to anyone who wanted it. This fear was based on more than mere speculation. Experience with the less complicated dealer and apartment systems bolstered their view, as did the history of community systems installed by operators on their own with Jerrold's standard equipment obtained from its *M* distributors. A rash of systems with unsatisfactory pictures could not be tolerated. The amount of capital necessary to start a system was substantial. Interest would wane rapidly if the systems installed did not consistently produce satisfactory results. Not only Jerrold's reputation but the growth of the entire industry was at stake during the development period. In addition to its reputation, Jerrold was also dependent upon successful system operation for payment. Many operators were not in a position to pay cash for the necessary equipment and the risks were such that outside financing could not be obtained. Therefore, payment was often contingent on the success of the system. It appeared that it was cheaper and more practical to insure that a system was properly installed in the first place than to attempt to get it operating once it was strung up. Furthermore, as has already been noted, use of existing utility poles was an important cost and public relations favor. The utility companies were reluctant to have men of unknown ability working on their poles. . . .

The Government does not dispute the reasonableness of the contracts for services but objects to the fact that they were compulsory. The crucial question, therefore, is whether Jerrold could have accomplished the ends it sought without requiring the contracts. It has been suggested that Jerrold could have accomplished the same results by addressing the persuasive argument it made to this court to its customers and leaving use of the contracts on a voluntary basis. . . . This argument assumes that Jerrold and the industry could survive the "transitory disloyalties" this approach would entail. Jerrold's service was costly and many operators, because of their limited finances, preferred to do-it-themselves and save the expense. Furthermore, Jerrold's limited facilities required that they only commit themselves to a certain amount of work. If Jerrold's equipment was available without a contract, many impatient operators probably would have attempted to install their systems without assistance. Consequently, unless Jerrold instituted a policy of compulsory service, it could expect many operators to buy its equipment without a contract, despite the strong reasons for having one, and the effort spent to present them. Jerrold's supply of equipment was limited. Unrestricted sales would have resulted in much of this equipment going into systems where prospects of success were at best extremely doubtful. . . . For these reasons, this court concludes that Jerrold's policy and practice of selling its community equipment only in conjunction with a service contract was reasonable and not in violation of §1 of the Sherman Act at the time of its inception. . . .

The court's conclusion is based primarily on the fact that the tie-in was instituted in the launching of a new business with a highly uncertain future. As the industry took root and grew, the reasons for the blanket insistence on a service contract disappeared. The development of the community antenna industry throughout the country was not uniform. It advanced and became established most rapidly in the East, particularly in Pennsylvania. Progress was slower in the Northwest and Southwest. Thus, when the reasons for this policy ceased to exist in the East, there were still good reasons for its continuance in other areas. Oral reports of successful systems 3,000 miles away are not as convincing as a number of failures nearby. Jerrold recognized this fact and abandoned its policy gradually. In March 1954, it dropped the policy as a general rule and thereafter applied it on an area-by-area and case-by-case basis. . . . On the present record, it would be a matter of speculation to determine when Jerrold's policy was no longer justified in various areas of the country. In view of the *Northern Pacific* case, it would seem that Jerrold has the burden on this point. . . . [W]hile Jerrold has satisfied this court that its policy was reasonable at its inception, it has failed to satisfy us that it remained reasonable throughout the period of its use, even allowing it a reasonable time to recognize and adjust its policies to changing conditions. . . .

III-B. FULL SYSTEM SALES . . .

Since this aspect of Jerrold's activity involves the tying of goods to goods, §3 of the Clayton Act, as well as §1 of the Sherman Act, is applicable. . . . The difficult question raised by the defendant is whether this should be treated as a case of tying the sale of one product to the sale of another product or merely as the sale of a single product. It is apparent that, as a general rule, a manufacturer cannot be forced to deal in the minimum product that could be sold or is usually sold. On the other hand, it is equally clear that one cannot circumvent the antitrust laws simply by claiming that he is selling a single product. The facts must be examined to ascertain whether or not there are legitimate reasons for selling normally separate items in a combined form to dispel any inferences that it is really a disguised tie-in.

There are several facts presented in this record which tend to show that a community television antenna system cannot properly be characterized as a single product. Others who entered the community antenna field offered all of the equipment necessary for a complete system, but none of them sold their gear exclusively as a single package as did Jerrold. The record also establishes that the number of pieces in each system varied considerably so that hardly any two versions of the alleged product were the same. Furthermore, the customer was charged for each item of equipment and not a lump sum for the total system. Finally, while Jerrold had cable and antennas to sell which were manufactured by other concerns, it only required that the electronic equipment in the system be bought from it.

In rebuttal, it must first be noted that the attitude of other manufacturers, while relevant, is hardly conclusive. Equally significant is the fact that the record indicates that some customers were interested in contracting for an installed system and not in building their own. Secondly, it was the job the system was designed to accomplish which dictated that each system be "custom made" in the sense that there were variations in the type and amount of equipment in each system. This, in turn, explains determining cost on a piece by piece, rather than a lump sum, basis. Finally, while the non-electronic equipment could be ordered from other sources and the system would be useless without the antenna and connecting cable, it is generally agreed that the electronic equipment is the most vital element in the system and Jerrold was still in charge of assembling all of the equipment into a functioning system.

Balancing these considerations only, the defendants' position would seem to be highly questionable.... [But] the court concludes that Jerrold's policy of full system sales was a necessary adjunct to its policy of compulsory service and was reasonably regarded as a product as long as the conditions which dictated the use of the service contract continued to exist. As the circumstances changed and the need for compulsory service contracts disappeared, the economic reasons for exclusively selling complete systems were eliminated. Absent these economic reasons, the court feels that a full system was not an appropriate sales unit.... The court concludes that the defendants' policy of selling full systems only was lawful at its inception but constituted a violation of §1 of the Sherman Act and §3 of the Clayton Act during part of the time it was in effect.[49]

437. (a) Is *Jerrold* consistent with *International Salt?* With *Northern Pacific?*

(b) Do *Jerrold, International Salt,* and *Northern Pacific,* taken together, stand for the proposition that tying agreements are unlawful per se but not all the time?[50] Is that proposition self-contradictory? Compare ¶215.

(c) The *IBM* Court stated that "[t]he Clayton Act names no exception to its prohibition of monopolistic tying clauses." What then is the warrant for permitting the *Jerrold* tying contract? Is *Jerrold*'s disposition of the service consistent with *IBM?*

(d) If there were otherwise an unlawful tie-in requiring a fast food franchisee to take its ingredients from the franchisor, could the tie be defended on the ground that it guarantees the product

49. The court's discussion of additional restraints is omitted. — eds.

50. Cf. Brown Shoe Co. v. United States, 370 U.S. 294, 330 (1962) ("unless the tying device is employed by a small company in an attempt to break into a market ... [it] can rarely be harmonized with the strictures of the antitrust laws"); White Motor Co. v. United States, 372 U.S. 253, 262 (1963) ("Tying arrangements ... may fall in that [per se] category, though not necessarily so.").

quality that consumers associate with the trademark and that gives the trademark its value?[51]

(e) Sigma Corporation leases its copying machines at a specified rental. There is no extra charge for repair service. Lessees are urged to use Sigma supplies with the machine because "Sigma supplies are best." The repair contract is expressly inapplicable to repairs necessitated by the use of non-Sigma supplies. That contract also authorizes Sigma to suspend the service agreement altogether when non-Sigma supplies are used.[52] Legal under *Jerrold*?

438. For a tying problem to exist, there must be two products. Deciding whether a transaction involves one product or two will often determine the result. Note that such definitional questions are particularly crucial in all the per se or near-per se areas where characterization often dictates the legal result. (Recall the statement in *BMI* that "it is necessary to characterize the challenged conduct as falling within or without that category of behavior to which we apply the label 'per se pricing fixing.'")

(a) In *Jerrold*, are several products tied together or does the whole system constitute a single product? What factors did the court consider? How did the court resolve the question? Do you agree with its disposition?[53]

(b) Is a delivered product a single product or a tie of the product and the delivery service?[54]

51. See Siegel v. Chicken Delight, 448 F.2d 43, 51 (9th Cir. 1971), cert. denied, 405 U.S. 955 (1972) (rejecting the defense upon a jury finding that there were other practical and less restrictive ways for the franchisor to protect its goodwill); Chock Full O'Nuts Corp., 83 F.T.C. 575, 643-656 (1973) (defense established on coffee blended according to supplier's taste and on goods baked by supplier but not on goods that could be produced by the licensees). Note that the owner of a trademark is obliged to supervise its licensees' quality through specifications, testing, or inspection in order to protect the trademark. Société Comptoir de l'Industrie Cotonnière Etablissements Boussac v. Alexander's Dept. Stores, 299 F.2d 33 (2d Cir. 1962); du Pont v. Celanese Corp., 167 F.2d 484 (3d Cir. 1948). In Data Gen. Corp. Antitr. Litigation, 490 F. Supp. 1089 (N.D. Cal. 1980) (for subsequent history as to other issues, see note 71), quality control justifications were rejected because of the availability of such less restrictive alternatives as minimum specifications (which, to be sure, might compromise trade secrets) or lesser warranties or service when goods from other sources are used; the defense that a tie was necessary to recover development costs was rejected in principle. Compare the arrangement under which service was bundled with machine leases in *United Shoe*, Ch. 3A.

52. See Advance Bus. Sys. v. SCM Corp., 415 F.2d 55 (4th Cir. 1969), cert. denied, 397 U.S. 920 (1970) (unlawful per se; no "legitimate purpose").

53. See also *Data General*, note 51 (computer and operating system software were separate products where often sold separately and not in fixed proportions).

54. See Anderson Foreign Motors v. New England Toyota Distrib., 475 F. Supp. 973 (D. Mass. 1979) (probable success for dealer complaining that supplier de-

(c) Can you distinguish *Jerrold* from the following situations: (1) Tau Television Manufacturing Company makes color television sets incorporating a superior picture tube of its design and manufacture. Other set manufacturers have asked Tau to sell its picture tube to them. Tau refuses to sell the tube except as part of its complete television set.[55] (2) An automobile manufacturer always delivers its automobiles with a radio installed as standard equipment.[56] (3) IBM manufactures a central processing unit (CPU) that has some internal memory capacity. It also sells external tape and disk memory that is plugged into the CPU. Independent manufacturers of plug-in memory devices complain that IBM tied memory devices to the CPU when it redesigned the CPU to have more internal memory.[57]

439. Consider the following possible tie-in claims with several questions in mind. (1) Do you see two products tied together or only one product? (2) Is the arrangement reasonable or otherwise justifiable? (3) Is competition likely to be adversely affected in any nontrivial way? You may sometimes find that you cannot respond to the first question without previously answering the second question; you may also find that resolving the second question depends in turn on the third inquiry.

(a) Defendant owns the "Ritz" trademark under which its several restaurants conduct business. It also franchises independent firms to conduct business under the trademark in return for a license fee based on a portion of the franchisee's revenues. (1) The franchisee is obliged to pay a specified sum for national advertising placed by Ritz. Is there a tie-in of advertising to the trademark? (2) The franchisee is required to deposit $15,000 with the franchisor for

---

livers cars on own trucks and charges dealers for delivery service; separate price for car and delivery; self-delivery not necessary for timely delivery).

55. ILC Peripherals Leasing Corp. v. IBM, 448 F. Supp. 228 (N.D. Cal. 1978), aff'd, 636 F.2d 1188 (9th Cir. 1980), cert. denied, 452 U.S. 972 (1981) (head/disk assembly and disk drive form one product because satisfies recognized consumer need, saves cost, and normally used together; others, including plaintiff, market their versions in similar fashion); Northwest Controls v. Outboard Marine Corp., 333 F. Supp. 493 (D. Del. 1971) (outboard motor distinct from remote control cables to operate it; previously sold separately; identical cables sold separately with certain motors).

56. See Automatic Radio Mfg. Co. v. Ford Motor Co., 390 F.2d 113 (1st Cir.), cert. denied, 391 U.S. 914 (1968) (denying preliminary injunction against auto manufacturer delivering new cars either with radio installed or with dashboard lacking provisions for dealer-installed radio).

57. Telex Corp. v. IBM, 367 F. Supp. 258 (D. Okla. 1973) rev'd on other grounds, 510 F.2d 894 (10th Cir. 1975) (court not qualified to decide upon proper machine design; attempting to do so would chill innovation).

which Ritz gives a non-interest-bearing note. Is the loan or note a product tied to the franchise?[58] (3) Franchisees resell a line of frozen foods made by Ritz and bearing its name. The franchisee wishes to buy identical foods from other sources and sell them under Ritz's name. Ritz refuses such permission. Is there a tie of the food to the Ritz trademark/franchise?[59] (4) Each franchisee makes foods on its own premises according to methods dictated by the franchise agreement. The franchisee is obliged by the contract to purchase its raw materials, certain seasoning mixes, and various other supplies, such as napkins, from Ritz. Any tie?[60]

(b) Assuming that Ritz is engaged in a tie in ¶a4, would it escape liability in the following situations: (1) Ritz does not itself supply the tied items but merely designates a supplier whom franchisees are obligated to patronize. Would it make any difference if Ritz received a fee or rebate from that supplier?[61] (2) Ritz requires fran-

---

58. See Kypta v. McDonald's Corp., 1979 Trade Cas. ¶62827, at 78781 (S.D. Fla. 1979) ("note is not a second product that is sold by [defendant] in competition with others, but is simply a condition of the lease, and evidences security for the franchisee's performance"), aff'd, 671 F.2d 1282 (11th Cir.) (cites *Fortner* for the proposition that "as long as the overall price is competitive then no harm has been incurred"; plaintiff did not show economic loss from the arrangement), cert. denied, 459 U.S. 857 (1982).

59. See California Glazed Prods. v. Burns & Russel Co., 708 F.2d 1423 (9th Cir.), cert. denied, 464 U.S. 938 (1983) (a trademark and the product it describes are a single product for tie-in purposes in ordinary distribution arrangements, by contrast with the so-called business format system franchises); Krehl v. Baskin-Robbins Ice Cream Co., 1979 Trade Cas. ¶62806 (C.D. Cal.) (trademark not distinct product from ice cream manufactured by trademark owner and resold as such by dealer; plaintiff has burden of showing two products; distinguishing *Siegel*, note 51, trademark as identifying marketing format rather than particular goods).

60. Several earlier cases doubted that the trademark and the supplies were separable products. Susser v. Carvel Corp., 332 F.2d 505 (2d Cir. 1964), cert. dismissed, 381 U.S. 125 (1965); Carvel Corp., 68 F.T.C. 128 (1965). But the later decisions are of the opposite view. E.g., *Siegel* and *Chock Full*, note 51.

61. Such arrangements often have not been distinguished from ties. E.g., Milsen Co. v. Southland Corp., 454 F.2d 363 (7th Cir. 1972); Falls Church Bratwursthaus v. Bratwursthaus Mgmt. Corp., 354 F. Supp. 1237 (E.D. Va. 1973). Kenner v. Sizzler Family Steak Houses, 597 F.2d 453, 456 (5th Cir. 1979), considered a franchisor's requirement that the franchisee use a particular building contractor familiar with company design. "There is no illegal tying arrangement where a 'tying' company has absolutely no interest in the sales of a third company whose products are favored by the tie-in." See Carl Sandburg Village Condo. Assn. v. First Condo. Dev. Co., 758 F.2d 203 (7th Cir. 1985) (condominium developer's sale of units subject to a two-year management contract with an unaffiliated company not an unlawful tie; no economic interest in sales of the tied product); Martino v. McDonald's Sys., 625 F. Supp. 356 (N.D. Ill. 1985) (McDonald's required franchisees to purchase Coca-Cola; economic benefit to McDonald's insufficient to establish per se violation; no invasion of second market).

chisees to buy from any of 100 approved sources.[62] May designated sources be required to pay a royalty for making patented items or using secret formulas?[63] (3) Ritz has not yet designated any other source but stands ready to approve other sources on request.[64]

(c) Ritz selected land for future construction and built some stores for dispensing its frozen food line and some completely equipped restaurants. (1) Ritz leases a store to an operator and requires it to sell the Ritz frozen food line. Are the foods tied to the lease or trademark?[65] (2) Ritz franchises the plaintiff to operate a Ritz restaurant on a site leased from Ritz. Are land and trademark/franchise tied?[66] (3) Ritz sells a restaurant, which it has operated itself, to a new franchisee. Has Ritz tied the trademark to building/equipment/land? Would your answer differ if Ritz's usual mode of franchising was to build the facilities and then sell them to a franchisee?[67]

62. See Miller v. International Dairy Queen, 1979 Trade Cas. ¶62593 (D. Minn.) (no tie where franchisor authorized more than 100 suppliers nationally and stands ready to designate more).

63. In Ohio-Sealy Mattress Mfg. Co. v. Sealy, 585 F.2d 821 (7th Cir. 1978), cert. denied, 440 U.S. 930 (1979), the defendant required licensees to comply with certain specifications in manufacturing a trademarked mattress. The specifications included mattress springs manufactured by the defendant and others with royalty-paying licenses from the defendant. The court regarded this arrangement as an unlawful tie without considering whether the patented springs were vital to mattress quality or image.

64. See Kentucky Fried Chicken Corp. v. Diversified Packaging Corp., 549 F.2d 368 (5th Cir. 1977) (no tie where contract forbids franchisor from "unreasonably withholding" its approval); Smith v. Denny's Restaurant, 62 F.R.D. 459 (N.D. Cal. 1974) (no tie unless approval unjustifiably withheld); Polytechnic Data Corp. v. Xerox Corp., 362 F. Supp. 1 (N.D. Ill. 1973) (machine lease forbids attachments not tested and listed by Underwriter's Labs; lessor demonstrated good faith by providing an interface for attachments made by others; no tie).

65. See Davison v. Crown Cent. Petro. Corp., 1977 Trade Cas. ¶61277 (D. Md. 1976) (supplier privileged to prevent sales of rival gasoline through tanks and premises it owns).

66. A similar tying claim was rejected in Principe v. McDonald's Corp., 631 F.2d 303 (4th Cir. 1980), cert. denied, 451 U.S. 970 (1981) (trademark license, building lease, and security deposit are, as matter of law, single product — the franchise — because challenged aggregation essential to system's formula for success: scientific site selection, site continuity, building style exclusivity, franchisee selection based on management ability alone, and quasi-partnership); Kypta v. McDonald's Corp., 1980 Trade Cas. ¶63267 (S.D. Fla.), aff'd, 671 F.2d 1282 (11th Cir.), cert. denied, 459 U.S. 857 (1982) (single authorization to operate specific McDonald's-built restaurant rather than tie of franchise name and facility; not provable that alternative location more profitable or that price paid exceeded fair value of license). Query: if a tie were found in such cases, who would have been foreclosed from what?

67. These are often called turnkey franchises because the franchisee can begin business immediately after accepting a key and opening the building door. North-

(d) On mortgage loans, a bank requires the borrower to pay a fee for the bank's legal work in connection with a mortgage. Is the bank tying legal services to mortgage loans? If the bank waives the fee when the borrower engages a bank-approved lawyer for all legal work in connection with the mortgage, is there any tie?[68]

(e) A professional football team sells a season ticket to all of its games. It recently raised the price and included two preseason exhibition games. Tickets to individual games are available, but the demand is very heavy. For that reason, many fans buy the season ticket.[69]

UNITED STATES STEEL CORP. v.
FORTNER ENTERPRISES
429 U.S. 610 (1977)

Justice STEVENS. . . . In exchange for respondent's promise to purchase prefabricated houses to be erected on land near Louisville, Ky., petitioners agreed to finance the cost of acquiring and developing the land. Difficulties arose while the development was in progress, and respondent (Fortner) commenced this treble-damages action, claiming that the transaction was a tying arrangement forbidden by the Sherman Act. Fortner alleged that competition for prefabricated houses (the tied product) was restrained by petitioners' abuse of power over credit (the tying product). A summary judgment in favor of petitioners was reversed by this Court. *Fortner Enterprises v. United States Steel Corp.*, 394 U.S. 495 [1969]

---

ern v. McGraw-Edison Co., 542 F.2d 1336, 1347 (8th Cir. 1976), cert. denied, 429 U.S. 1097 (1977), condemned the package sale of a dry-cleaning franchise and equipment even though the name "Arnold Palmer Cleaning Center" hardly dominated the dry-cleaning field and "[e]ven if franchisees' convenience would be best served by such an arrangement." Beefy Trail v. Beefy King Intl., 348 F. Supp. 799 (M.D. Fla. 1972), thought it reasonable to sell a going business as a whole but ruled that the jury must decide whether a particular sale was part of an intentional course of conduct to evade the proscription against tying.

68. Foster v. Maryland State Sav. & Loan Assn., 590 F.2d 928 (D.C. Cir. 1978), cert. denied, 439 U.S. 1071 (1979) (summary judgment for defendant: fee is incidental and inseparable part of loan purchase rather than purchase of separate product). See also Sibley v. Federal Land Bank, 597 F.2d 459 (5th Cir.), cert. denied, 444 U.S. 941 (1979) (approving bank's substantial reduction in fees when choosing counsel from list of lawyers whose title certification it would accept as final in granting mortgage loans).

69. See Coniglio v. Highland Servs., 495 F.2d 1286 (2d Cir.), cert. denied, 419 U.S. 1022 (1974) (two products but no foreclosure of competitors: no rival football team and broader entertainment market rejected); Driskill v. Dallas Cowboys Football Club, 498 F.2d 321 (5th Cir. 1974) (even if tie, no rival preseason professional football games in Dallas that could be adversely affected).

(*Fortner I*). We held that the agreement affected a "not in-substantial" amount of commerce in the tied product and that Fortner was entitled to an opportunity to prove that petitioners possessed "appreciable economic power" in the market for the tying product. . . .[1] . . .

I . . .

[U.S. Steel sells] two separate products — credit and prefabricated houses. The credit extended to Fortner was not merely for the price of the homes. Petitioners agreed to lend Fortner over $2,000,000 in exchange for Fortner's promise to purchase the components of 210 homes for about $689,000. The additional borrowed funds were intended to cover Fortner's cost of acquiring and developing the vacant real estate, and the cost of erecting the houses.

The impact of the agreement on the market for the tied product (prefabricated houses) is not in dispute. On the one hand, there is no claim — nor could there be — that the Home Division had any dominance in the prefabricated housing business. The record indi-cates that it was only moderately successful, and that its sales repre-sented a small fraction of the industry total. On the other hand, we have already held that the dollar value of the sales to respondent was sufficient to meet the "not insubstantial" test described in earlier cases. We therefore confine our attention to the source of the tying arrangement — petitioners' "economic power" in the credit market.

1. . . . In *Fortner I*, the Court noted that Fortner also alleged a §2 violation, namely, that petitioners "conspired together for the purpose of . . . acquiring a monopoly in the market for prefabricated houses." The District Court held that a §2 violation had been proved. Although the Court of Appeals did not reach this issue, a remand is unnecessary. It is clear that neither the District Court's findings of fact nor the record supports the conclusion that §2 was violated. The District Court found only that "the defendants did combine or conspire to *increase sales* of prefabricated house packages by United States Steel Corporation by the making of loans to numerous builders containing the tie-in provision" and that "the sole purpose of the loan programs of the Credit Corporation was specifically and deliberately to *increase the share of the market* of United States Steel Corporation in prefabricated house packages. . . ." (emphasis added). But "increasing sales" and "increasing market share" are normal business goals, not forbidden by §2 without other evidence of an intent to monopolize. The evidence in this case does not bridge the gap between the District Court's findings of intent to increase sales and its legal conclusion of conspiracy to monopolize. Moreover, petitioners did not have a large market share or dominant market position. No inference of intent to monopolize can be drawn from the fact that a firm with a small market share has engaged in nonpredatory competitive conduct in the hope of increasing sales. Yet as we conclude, that is all the record in this case shows.

II

The evidence supporting the conclusion that the Credit Corp. had appreciable economic power in the credit market relates to four propositions: (1) [petitioners] were owned by one of the Nation's largest corporations; (2) petitioners entered into tying arrangements with a significant number of customers in addition to Fortner; (3) the Home Division charged respondent a noncompetitive price for its prefabricated homes; and (4) the financing provided to Fortner was "unique," primarily because it covered 100% of Fortner's acquisition and development costs.

The Credit Corp. [subsidiary of U.S. Steel] was established in 1954 to provide financing for customers of the Home Division. The United States Steel Corp. not only provided the equity capital, but also allowed the Credit Corp. to use its credit in order to borrow money from banks at the prime rate. . . .

The Credit Corp.'s loan policies were primarily intended to help the Home Division sell its products. It extended credit only to customers of the Home Division, and over two-thirds of the Home Division customers obtained such financing. With few exceptions, all the loan agreements contained a tying clause comparable to the one challenged in this case. Petitioner's home sales in 1960 amounted to $6,747,353. Since over $4,600,000 of these sales were tied to financing provided by the Credit Corp., it is apparent that the tying arrangement was used with a number of customers in addition to Fortner.

The least expensive house package that Fortner purchased from the Home Division cost about $3,150. . . . Whether the price differential was as great as 15% is not entirely clear, but the record does support the conclusion that the contract required Fortner to pay a noncompetitive price for petitioners' houses. . . .

Dr. Masten testified that mortgage loans equal to 100% of the acquisition and development cost of real estate were not otherwise available in the Kentucky area; that even though Fortner had a deficit of $16,000, its loan was not guaranteed by a shareholder, officer, or other person interested in its business; and that the interest rate of 6% represented a low rate under prevailing economic conditions. Moreover, he explained that the stable price levels at the time made the risk to the lender somewhat higher than would have been the case in a period of rising prices. Dr. Masten concluded that the terms granted to respondent by the Credit Corp. were so unusual that it was almost inconceivable that the funds could have been acquired from any other source. It is a fair summary of his testimony, and of the District Court's findings, to say that the loan was unique because the lender accepted such a high risk and the borrower assumed such a low cost.

The District Court also found that banks and federally insured savings and loan associations generally were prohibited by law from making 100% land acquisition and development loans, and "that other conventional lenders would not have made such loans at the time in question since they were not prudent loans due to the risk involved."

Accordingly, the District Court concluded "that ... the Credit Corporation did possess sufficient economic power or leverage to effect such restraint."

III

Without the finding that the financing provided to Fortner was "unique," it is clear that the District Court's findings would be insufficient to support the conclusion that the Credit Corporation possessed any significant economic power in the credit market.

Although the Credit Corp. is owned by one of the Nation's largest manufacturing corporations, there is nothing in the record to indicate that this enabled it to borrow funds on terms more favorable than those available to competing lenders, or that it was able to operate more efficiently than other lending institutions. In short, the affiliation between the petitioners does not appear to have given the Credit Corp. any cost advantage over its competitors in the credit market. Instead, the affiliation was significant only because the Credit Corp. provided a source of funds to customers of the Home Division. That fact tells us nothing about the extent of petitioner's economic power in the credit market.

The same may be said about the fact that loans from the Credit Corp. were used to obtain house sales from Fortner and others. In some tying situations a disproportionately large volume of sales of the tied product resulting from only a few strategic sales of the tying product may reflect a form of economic "leverage" that is probative of power in the market for the tying product. If, as some economists have suggested, the purpose of a tie-in is often to facilitate price discrimination, such evidence would imply the existence of power that a free market would not tolerate.[7] But in this case Fortner was only required to purchase houses for the number of lots for which it received financing. The tying product produced no commitment from Fortner to purchase varying quantities of the tied product over an extended period of time. This record, therefore, does not

---

7. See Bowman, Tying Arrangements and the Leverage Problem, 67 Yale L.J. 19 (1957).

describe the kind of "leverage" found in some of the Court's prior decisions condemning tying arrangements.[8]

The fact that Fortner — and presumably other Home Division customers as well — paid a noncompetitive price for houses also lends insufficient support to the judgment of the lower court. Proof that Fortner paid a higher price for the tied product is consistent with the possibility that the financing was unusually inexpensive and that the price for the entire package was equal to, or below, a competitive price. And this possibility is equally strong even though a number of Home Division customers made a package purchase of homes and financing.[10]

The most significant finding made by the District Court related to the unique character of the credit extended to Fortner. This finding is particularly important because the unique character of the tying product has provided critical support for the finding of illegality in prior cases. Thus, the statutory grant of a patent monopoly in *International Salt*; the copyright monopolies in United States v. Paramount Pictures, Inc., 334 U.S. 131, and *Loew's*; and the extensive land holdings in *Northern Pacific*,[11] represented tying products that the Court regarded as sufficiently unique to give rise to a presumption of economic power.[12]

As the Court plainly stated in its prior opinion in this case, these decisions do not require that the defendant have a monopoly or even a dominant position throughout the market for a tying product. They do, however, focus attention on the question whether the seller has the power, within the market for the tying product, to raise prices or to require purchasers to accept burdensome terms

8. See, e.g., United Shoe Machinery Corp. v. United States, 258 U.S. 451; *IBM*; *International Salt*. In his article in the 1969 Supreme Court Review 16, Professor Dam suggests that this kind of leverage may also have been present in *Northern Pacific*.

10. Relying on Advance Business Systems & Supply Co. v. SCM Corp., 415 F.2d 55 (4th Cir. 1969), cert. denied, 397 U.S. 920, Fortner contends that acceptance of the package by a significant number of customers is itself sufficient to prove the seller's economic power. But this approach depends on the absence of other explanations for the willingness of buyers to purchase the package.... [T]his case differs from *Northern Pacific* because use of the tie-in in this case can be explained as a form of price competition in the tied product, whereas that explanation was unavailable to the Northern Pacific Railway.

11. The Court in *Northern Pacific* concluded that the railroad "possessed substantial economic power by virtue of its extensive landholdings." ...

12.

Since one of the objectives of the patent laws is to reward uniqueness, the principle of these cases was carried over into antitrust law on the theory that the existence of a valid patent on the tying product, without more, establishes a distinctiveness sufficient to conclude that any tying arrangement involving the patented product would have anti-competitive consequences. [*Loew's*.]

that could not be exacted in a completely competitive market.[13] In short, the question is whether the seller has some advantage not shared by his competitors in the market for the tying product.

Without any such advantage differentiating his product from that of his competitors, the seller's product does not have the kind of uniqueness considered relevant in prior tying-clause cases.[14] The Court made this point explicitly when it remanded this case for trial:

> We do not mean to accept petitioner's apparent argument that market power can be inferred simply because the kind of financing terms offered by a lending company are "unique and unusual." We do mean, however, that uniquely and unusually advantageous terms can reflect a creditor's unique economic advantages over his competitors.

An accompanying footnote explained:

> Uniqueness confers economic power only when other competitors are in some way prevented from offering the distinctive product themselves. Such barriers may be legal, as in the case of patented and copyrighted products, e.g., *International Salt*; *Loew's*, or physical, as when the product is land, e.g., *Northern Pacific*. It is true that the barriers may also be economic, as when competitors are simply unable to produce the distinctive product profitably, but the uniqueness test in such situations is somewhat confusing since the real

13. "Accordingly, the proper focus of concern is whether the seller has the power to raise prices, or impose other burdensome terms such as a tie-in with respect to any appreciable number of buyers within the market."

Professor Dam correctly analyzed the burden of proof imposed on Fortner by this language. In his article in the 1969 Supreme Court Review 25-26, he reasoned:

> One important question in interpreting the *Fortner* decision is the meaning of this language. Taken out of context, it might be thought to mean that, just as the "host of tying arrangements" was "compelling evidence" of "great power" in *Northern Pacific*, so the inclusion of tie-in clauses in contracts with "any appreciable numbers of buyers" establishes market power. But the passage read in context does not warrant this interpretation. For the immediately preceding sentence makes clear that market power in the sense of power over price must still exist. If the price could have been raised but the tie-in was demanded in lieu of the higher price, then — and presumably only then — would the requisite economic power exist. Thus, despite the broad language available for quotation in later cases, the treatment of the law on market power is on close reading not only consonant with the precedents but in some ways less far-reaching than *Northern Pacific* and *Loew's*, which could be read to make actual market power irrelevant. [Footnotes omitted.]

14. One commentator on *Fortner I* noted:

> The Court's uniqueness test is adequate to identify a number of situations in which this type of foreclosure is likely to occur. Whenever there are some buyers who find a seller's product uniquely attractive, and are therefore willing to pay a premium above the price of its nearest substitute, the seller has the opportunity to impose a tie to some other good. [Note, The Logic of Foreclosure: Tie-in Doctrine after Fortner v. U.S. Steel, 79 Yale L.J. 86, 93-94 (1969).]

source of economic power is not the product itself but rather the seller's cost advantage in producing it.

Quite clearly, if the evidence merely shows that credit terms are unique because the seller is willing to accept a lesser profit — or to incur greater risks — than its competitors, that kind of uniqueness will not give rise to any inference of economic power in the credit market. Yet this is, in substance, all that the record in this case indicates.

The unusual credit bargain offered to Fortner proves nothing more than a willingness to provide cheap financing in order to sell expensive houses.[15] Without any evidence that the Credit Corp. had some cost advantage over its competitors — or could offer a form of financing that was significantly differentiated from that which other lenders could offer if they so elected — the unique character of its financing does not support the conclusion that petitioners had the kind of economic power which Fortner had the burden of proving in order to prevail in this litigation.

The judgment of the Court of Appeals is reversed.

Chief Justice BURGER, with whom Justice REHNQUIST joins, concurring.

I concur in the Court's opinion and write only to emphasize what the case before us does *not* involve; I join on the basis of my understanding of the scope of our holding. Today's decision does not implicate ordinary credit sales of only a single product and which therefore cannot constitute a tying arrangement subject to per se scrutiny under §1 of the Sherman Act. In contrast to such transactions, we are dealing here with a peculiar arrangement expressly found by the Court in *Fortner I* to involve two separate products sold by two separate corporations. Consequently, I read the Court's assumption that a tie-in existed in this case, required as it is by the law of the case, to cast no doubt on the legality of credit financing by manufacturers or distributors.

440. (a) Under *Fortner*, is the ordinary credit sale suspect? If U.S. Steel granted credit on advantageous terms to house buyers,

---

15. The opinion of the Court in *Fortner I* notes that smaller companies might not have the "financial strength to offer credit comparable to that provided by larger competitors under tying arrangements." Fortner's expert witness was unaware of the financing practices of competing sellers of prefabricated homes, but there is nothing to suggest that they were unable to offer comparable financing if they chose to do so.

would that be undesirable? Would the existence of advantageous terms imply that the company had a competitive advantage in granting credit or market power with respect to credit?

(b) Are you persuaded by U.S. Steel's argument that any especially attractive features of its credit could be translated into a price adjustment on its houses? Does that possibility eliminate any cause for concern? Could there be a predatory pricing challenge?[70] If the credit arrangement amounts to a price cut, why didn't U.S. Steel grant it directly in the first place?

(c) Might the *Fortner* arrangement facilitate Mr. Fortner's entry into real estate development? Would that be beneficial? What is likely to be the consequence of condemning the *Fortner* arrangement? Would such a consequence serve the public interest? Would Fortner have been better off under such circumstances? If not, should that be decisive as to the legality of the arrangement? As to Fortner's ability to collect damages? See ¶441.

(d) Can we infer the existence of power in the tying product from the fact that the buyer accepts the tie? Would the results in *Northern Pacific* and the Court's other decisions, such as *International Salt* and *Loew's*, be unchanged after *Fortner*?

(e) Is a tie-in lawful when the defendant's competitors in the tied product are capable of offering the same combination of products?

(f) After *Fortner*, must the plaintiff always prove power in the tying product in order to establish an unlawful tie? How much power? What would Mr. Fortner have had to prove in order to prevail?[71]

---

70. Cf. Consolidated Term. Sys. v. ITT World Communications, 535 F. Supp. 225 (S.D.N.Y. 1982) (interpreting challenge by competitor in market for tying product as essentially a predatory pricing claim, which was rejected for lack of market power).

71. Phillips v. Crown Cent. Petro. Corp., 602 F.2d 616, 629 (4th Cir. 1979), cert. denied, 444 U.S. 1074 (1980), reversed a finding that a supplier tied motor oil to a franchise. The lower court had not identified the tying product or its power. If the station lease is the tying product, it is not shown that defendant has any power in real estate. If gasoline is the tying product, defendant's four percent market share is insufficient. The court commented that a 10 percent share is "very close to the minimum permissible." In Spartan Grain & Mill Co. v. Ayers, 581 F.2d 419, 427-428 (5th Cir. 1978), cert. denied, 444 U.S. 831 (1979), the court required a showing of power in the tying product. If the supplier "had effective competitors in this field, economic power would not have been shown, even though *all* the [suppliers would] be more sophisticated and powerful" than the buyers. In *Data General*, note 51, the defendant was granted judgment notwithstanding the verdict because it lacked power, even in the submarket of its software, to be free of competitive pressures. 529 F. Supp. 801 (N.D. Cal. 1981). The appellate court reversed, 734 F.2d 1336 (9th Cir. 1984), stating that, even after *Fortner* and *Jefferson Parish*, all that is necessary is enough power to induce purchase of the tied product

441. Coping with noninjurious ties.[72] In *Siegel*,[73] a franchisor charged no fee for the use of its name and methods but required franchisees to buy certain cooking utensils, cooking mixes, and paper packaging materials from it at specified prices. These prices included an incremental amount above prevailing market prices for similar items. This was held to be an unlawful tie upon a jury finding that there were other practical and less restrictive ways for the franchisor to protect its goodwill. Although actual effects in the markets for the tied products were doubtlessly very small, plaintiff franchisees were awarded three times the incremental amounts they had paid for supplies.[74] The district court rejected the defendant's claim that damages be offset by the reasonable value of the franchise. The court of appeals reversed and remanded on this point, but it was unwilling to accept the franchisor's argument that the franchisees suffered no injury because they would not have paid a greater increment for the tied items than the franchise was worth to them. The court disagreed on two grounds: that (1) what the franchisee would have paid for the franchise was a question of fact to be determined upon trial and (2) defendant's position would preclude all tie-in purchasers from recovering.

These reasons invite two questions. First, how can the value of the franchise be rationally determined except by reference to what franchisees have demonstrated a willingness to pay? What reason is there to believe the franchisee would have paid less in the absence

---

not on its merits. Two Justices in the *Jefferson Parish* majority dissented from the denial of certiorari. 473 U.S. 908 (1985).

Compare Will v. Comprehensive Accounting Corp., 776 F.2d 665, 673 (7th Cir. 1985), cert. denied, 475 U.S. 1129 (1986) (possibility that accounting franchisor required franchisees to use its data processing services not illegal because no market power over tying product; franchisor was a "pygmy among the large national firms"); Yentsch v. Texaco, 630 F.2d 46, 58 (2d Cir. 1980) (*Fortner* requires power in tying product; no power without significant advantage over rival suppliers); and Cash v. Arctic Circle, 85 F.R.D. 618 (E.D. Wash. 1979) (power in tying product will not be inferred from the mere existence of trademark), with Esposito v. Mr. Softee, 1980 Trade Cas. ¶63089 (E.D.N.Y. 1979), aff'd, 742 F.2d 1445 (2d Cir. 1983), cert. denied, 465 U.S. 1026 (1984) (sufficient economic power in franchise inferred from fact that 94 of the 110 licensed mobile vendors of ice cream in the Queens-Nassau area of New York City are Mr. Softee dealers); and Ware v. Trailer Mart, 623 F.2d 1150 (6th Cir. 1980) (dictum: appreciable economic power over tying product unnecessary to establish tie violating rule of reason).

72. See P. Areeda, Antitrust Violations Without Damage Recoveries, 89 Harv. L. Rev. 1127 (1976).

73. Compare *Siegel*, note 51, with *Kypta*, note 66, at 1285 (*Siegel* requires for injury "that payments for both the tied and tying products exceeded their combined fair market value").

74. That the plaintiffs had freely joined in the unlawful franchise agreement did not bar their recovery. See ¶148.

of a tie?[75] If the tying arrangement served as a metering device to facilitate price discrimination, see ¶423c, higher volume franchisees might have suffered damages relative to what would have been charged as a lump sum franchise fee, whereas lower volume outlets might have paid less than they would have been charged in the absence of the tying arrangement.[76] Consider the various motivations for tying described in ¶423 and determine what damages are suffered, in principle, by buyers in each situation. If the theory of damages depends on the motivation, must the court or jury decide the purpose and effect of the tying arrangements for purposes of assessing damages (even if such a finding is unnecessary to liability under the per se rule, and thus to the availability of injunctive relief)?

Second, should there be a recovery by a tie-in purchaser who was not in fact injured by the form in which the franchisor chose to take its reward?[77] Denying damages would mean, of course, that the franchisee would not sue the wrongdoer. Should such a result be considered desirable?[78] One could instead rely on foreclosed suppliers or potential entrants to bring suit based on the injury to competition. In considering whether one should rely exclusively on this alternative, one must ask how damages would be determined in such cases and whether such damages, or the prospect of an injunction against future violations, would provide sufficient incentives for such suits to be brought.

JEFFERSON PARISH HOSPITAL
DISTRICT NO. 2 v. HYDE
466 U.S. 2 (1984)

Justice STEVENS. . . . In July 1977, respondent Edwin G. Hyde, a board certified anesthesiologist, applied for admission to the medi-

---

75. *Mr. Softee*, note 71 (no injury where plaintiff does not prove it would have been able to purchase at a lower price in the absence of the tie).

76. It is generally assumed that a royalty based on the franchisee's revenues is lawful. Should a tying arrangement that accomplishes the same result be deemed illegal?

77. Cf. Central Chem. Corp. v. Agrico Chem. Co., 531 F. Supp. 333 (D. Md. 1982), aff'd, 1985 Trade Cas. ¶66753 (4th Cir.) (suggesting that because customers are not injured by foreclosure of competition in the tied product, they lack standing on the issue).

78. Whenever a legal rule condemns conduct regardless of significant effects, society may need a mechanism for disregarding the trivial. De minimis rules are one way, but they may complicate inquiries unnecessarily. Prosecutory discretion is another route: the government can ignore the trivial.

734 Jefferson Parish Hospital ¶441

cal staff of East Jefferson Hospital. The credentials committee and the medical staff executive committee recommended approval, but the hospital board denied the application because the hospital was a party to a contract providing that all anesthesiological services required by the hospital's patients would be performed by Roux & Associates. . . . Respondent then commenced this action seeking a declaratory judgment that the contract is unlawful and an injunction ordering petitioners to appoint him to the hospital staff. . . . [T]he District Court [after a full trial] denied relief, finding that the anticompetitive consequences of the Roux contract were minimal and outweighed by benefits in the form of improved patient care. . . . The Court of Appeals reversed because it was persuaded that the contract was illegal "per se." We . . . reverse.

I . . .

The contract provided that any anesthesiologist designated by Roux would be admitted to the hospital's medical staff. . . . The hospital agreed to "restrict the use of its anesthesia department to Roux & Associates and [that] no other persons, parties or entities shall perform such services within the Hospital for the ter[m] of this contract." . . .

In 1976, a second written contract was executed containing most of the provisions of the 1971 agreement. Its term was five years and the clause excluding other anesthesiologists from the hospital was deleted; the hospital nevertheless continued to regard itself as committed to a closed anesthesiology department. . . . There are at least 20 hospitals in the New Orleans metropolitan area and about 70 per cent of the patients living in Jefferson Parish go to hospitals other than East Jefferson. . . .

II . . .

It is far too late in the history of our antitrust jurisprudence to question the proposition that certain tying arrangements pose an unacceptable risk of stifling competition and therefore are unreasonable "per se." . . .

It is clear, however, that not every refusal to sell two products separately can be said to restrain competition. If each of the products may be purchased separately in a competitive market, one seller's decision to sell the two in a single package imposes no unreasonable restraint on either market, particularly if competing suppliers are free to sell either the entire package or its several parts. . . .[18] Buyers often find package sales attractive; a seller's decision to offer such packages can merely be an attempt to compete effectively — conduct that is entirely consistent with the Sherman Act. . . .

Our cases have concluded that the essential characteristic of an invalid tying arrangement lies in the seller's exploitation of its control over the tying product to force the buyer into the purchase of a tied product that the buyer either did not want at all, or might have preferred to purchase elsewhere on different terms. When such "forcing" is present, competition on the merits in the market for the tied item is restrained and the Sherman Act is violated. . . .

Accordingly, we have condemned tying arrangements when the seller has some special ability — usually called "market power" — to force a purchaser to do something that he would not do in a competitive market. . . .[20] When "forcing" occurs, our cases have found the tying arrangement to be unlawful.

Thus, the law draws a distinction between the exploitation of market power by merely enhancing the price of the tying product, on the one hand, and by attempting to impose restraints on competition in the market for a tied product, on the other. When the seller's power is just used to maximize its return in the tying product market, where presumably its product enjoys some justifiable advantage over its competitors, the competitive ideal of the Sherman Act is not necessarily compromised. But if that power is used to impair competition on the merits in another market, a potentially inferior product may be insulated from competitive pressures. This impairment could either harm existing competitors or create barriers to entry of new competitors in the market for the tied product, *Fortner I,* and can increase the social costs of market power by facilitating price discrimination, thereby increasing monopoly profits over what they would be absent the tie, *Fortner.* And from the standpoint of the consumer — whose interests the statute was especially intended to serve — the freedom to select the best bargain in

18. Thus, we have held that a seller who ties the sale of houses to the provision of credit simply as a way of effectively competing in a competitive market does not violate the antitrust laws. "The unusual credit bargain offered to Fortner proves nothing more than a willingness to provide cheap financing in order to sell expensive houses." *Fortner.*

20. This type of market power has sometimes been referred to as "leverage." Professors Areeda and Turner provide a definition that suits present purposes. " 'Leverage' is loosely defined here as a supplier's ability to induce his customer for one product to buy a second product from him that would not otherwise be purchased solely on the merit of that second product." 5 P. Areeda & D. Turner, Antitrust Law ¶1134a, p. 202 (1980).

the second market is impaired by his need to purchase the tying product, and perhaps by an inability to evaluate the true cost of either product when they are available only as a package. In sum, to permit restraint of competition on the merits through tying arrangements would be, as we observed in *Fortner*, to condone "the existence of power that a free market would not tolerate."

Per se condemnation — condemnation without inquiry into actual market conditions — is only appropriate if the existence of forcing is probable. Thus, application of the per se rule focuses on the probability of anticompetitive consequences. Of course, as a threshold matter there must be a substantial potential for impact on competition in order to justify per se condemnation. If only a single purchaser were "forced" with respect to the purchase of a tied item, the resultant impact on competition would not be sufficient to warrant the concern of antitrust law. It is for this reason that we have refused to condemn tying arrangements unless a substantial volume of commerce is foreclosed thereby.... Similarly, when a purchaser is "forced" to buy a product he would not have otherwise bought even from another seller in the tied product market, there can be no adverse impact on competition because no portion of the market which would otherwise have been available to other sellers has been foreclosed.

Once this threshold is surmounted, per se prohibition is appropriate if anticompetitive forcing is likely. For example, if the government has granted the seller a patent or similar monopoly over a product, it is fair to presume that the inability to buy the product elsewhere gives the seller market power.... Any effort to enlarge the scope of the patent monopoly by using the market power it confers to restrain competition in the market for a second product will undermine competition on the merits in that second market. Thus, the sale or lease of a patented item on condition that the buyer make all his purchases of a separate tied product from the patentee is unlawful....

The same strict rule is appropriate in other situations in which the existence of market power is probable. When the seller's share of the market is high ... or when the seller offers a unique product that competitors are not able to offer, ... the Court has held that the likelihood that market power exists and is being used to restrain competition in a separate market is sufficient to make per se condemnation appropriate.... When, however, the seller does not have either the degree or the kind of market power that enables him to force customers to purchase a second, unwanted product in order to obtain the tying product, an antitrust violation can be established only by evidence of an unreasonable restraint on competition in the relevant market....

In sum, any inquiry into the validity of a tying arrangement must focus on the market or markets in which the two products are sold, for that is where the anticompetitive forcing has its impact. Thus, in this case our analysis of the tying issue must focus on the hospital's sale of services to its patients, rather than its contractual arrangements with the providers of anesthesiological services. In making that analysis, we must consider whether petitioners are selling two separate products that may be tied together, and, if so, whether they have used their market power to force their patients to accept the tying arrangement.

III

The hospital has provided its patients with a package that includes the range of facilities and services required for a variety of surgical operations. At East Jefferson Hospital the package includes the services of the anesthesiologist.[28] Petitioners argue that the package does not involve a tying arrangement at all — that they are merely providing a functionally integrated package of services. . . .

Our cases indicate, however, that the answer to the question whether one or two products are involved turns not on the functional relation between them, but rather on the character of the demand for the two items. In Times-Picayune Publishing Co. v. United States, 345 U.S. 594 (1953), the Court held that a tying arrangement was not present because the arrangement did not link two distinct markets for products that were distinguishable in the eyes of buyers. In *Fortner I*, the Court concluded that a sale involving two independent transactions, separately priced and purchased from the buyer's perspective, was a tying arrangement. These cases make it clear that a tying arrangement cannot exist unless two separate product markets have been linked.

The requirement that two distinguishable product markets be involved follows from the underlying rationale of the rule against tying. The definitional question depends on whether the arrangement may have the type of competitive consequences addressed by the rule. The answer to the question whether petitioners have utilized a tying arrangement must be based on whether there is a possibility that the economic effect of the arrangement is that condemned by the rule against tying — that petitioners have foreclosed

---

28. It is essential to differentiate between the Roux contract and the legality of the contract between the hospital and its patients. The Roux contract is nothing more than an arrangement whereby Roux supplies all of the hospital's needs for anesthesiological services. That contract raises only an exclusive dealing question. The issue here is whether the hospital's insistence that its patients purchase anesthesiological services from Roux creates a tying arrangement.

competition on the merits in a product market distinct from the market for the tying item.[34] Thus, in this case no tying arrangement can exist unless there is a sufficient demand for the purchase of anesthesiological services separate from hospital services to identify a distinct product market in which it is efficient to offer anesthesiological services separately from hospital services.

Unquestionably, the anesthesiological component of the package offered by the hospital could be provided separately and could be selected either by the individual patient or by one of the patient's doctors if the hospital did not insist on including anesthesiological services in the package it offers to its customers. As a matter of actual practice, anesthesiological services are billed separately from the hospital services petitioners provide. There was ample and uncontroverted testimony that patients or surgeons often request specific anesthesiologists to come to a hospital and provide anesthesia, and that the choice of an individual anesthesiologist separate from the choice of a hospital is particularly frequent in respondent's specialty, obstetric anesthesiology.... The record amply supports the conclusion that consumers differentiate between anesthesiological services and the other hospital services provided by petitioners.[39] ...

Nevertheless, ... [o]nly if patients are forced to purchase Roux's services as a result of the hospital's market power would the arrangement have anticompetitive consequences. If no forcing is present, patients are free to enter a competing hospital and to use another anesthesiologist instead of Roux.[41] The fact that peti-

---

34. Of course, the Sherman Act does not prohibit "tying," it prohibits "contract[s] ... in restraint of trade." Thus, in a sense the question whether this case involves "tying" is beside the point. The legality of petitioners' conduct depends on its competitive consequences, not on whether it can be labeled "tying." If the competitive consequences of this arrangement are not those to which the per se rule is addressed, then it should not be condemned irrespective of its label.

39. ... Therefore, the *Jerrold* analysis indicates that there was a tying arrangement here. *Jerrold* also indicates that tying may be permissible when necessary to enable a new business to break into the market. Assuming this defense exists, and assuming it justified the 1971 Roux contract in order to give Roux an incentive to go to work at a new hospital with an uncertain future, that justification is inapplicable to the 1976 contract, since by then Roux was willing to continue to service the hospital without a tying arrangement.

41. ... Without evidence that petitioners are using market power to force Roux upon patients there is no basis to view the arrangement as unreasonably restraining competition whatever the reasons for its creation. Conversely, with such evidence, the per se rule against tying may apply. Thus, we reject the view of the District Court that the legality of an arrangement of this kind turns on whether it was adopted for the purpose of improving patient care.

tioner's patients are required to purchase two separate items is only the beginning of the appropriate inquiry.[42]

IV

The question remains whether this arrangement involves the use of market power to force patients to buy services they would not otherwise purchase. Respondent's only basis for invoking the per se rule against tying and thereby avoiding analysis of actual market conditions is by relying on the preference of persons residing in Jefferson Parish to go to East Jefferson, the closest hospital. A preference of this kind, however, is not necessarily probative of significant market power.

Seventy per cent of the patients residing in Jefferson Parish enter hospitals other than East Jefferson. Thus East Jefferson's "dominance" over persons residing in Jefferson Parish is far from overwhelming. The fact that a substantial majority of the parish's residents elect not to enter East Jefferson means that the geographic data does not establish the kind of dominant market position that obviates the need for further inquiry into actual competitive conditions. The Court of Appeals acknowledged as much; it recognized that East Jefferson's market share alone was insufficient as a basis to infer market power, and buttressed its conclusion by relying on "market imperfections" that permit petitioners to charge noncompetitive prices for hospital services: the prevalence of third party payment for health care costs reduces price competition, and a lack of adequate information renders consumers unable to evaluate the quality of the medical care provided by competing hospitals. While these factors may generate "market

---

42. Petitioners argue and the District Court found that the exclusive contract had what it characterized as procompetitive justifications in that an exclusive contract ensures 24-hour anesthesiology coverage, enables flexible scheduling, and facilitates work routine, professional standards, and maintenance of equipment. The Court of Appeals held these findings to be clearly erroneous since the exclusive contract was not necessary to achieve these ends. Roux was willing to provide 24-hour coverage even without an exclusive contract and the credentials committee of the hospital could impose standards for staff privileges that would ensure staff would comply with the demands of scheduling, maintenance, and professional standards. In the past, we have refused to tolerate manifestly anticompetitive conduct simply because the health care industry is involved.... We have also uniformly rejected similar "goodwill" defenses for tying arrangements, finding that the use of contractual quality specifications are generally sufficient to protect quality without the use of a tying arrangement.... Since the District Court made no finding as to why contractual quality specifications would not protect the hospital, there is no basis for departing from our prior cases here.

power" in some abstract sense, they do not generate the kind of market power that justifies condemnation of tying.

Tying arrangements need only be condemned if they restrain competition on the merits by forcing purchases that would not otherwise be made. A lack of price or quality competition does not create this type of forcing. If consumers lack price consciousness, that fact will not force them to take an anesthesiologist whose services they do not want—their indifference to price will have no impact on their willingness or ability to go to another hospital where they can utilize the services of the anesthesiologist of their choice. Similarly, if consumers cannot evaluate the quality of anesthesiological services, it follows that they are indifferent between certified anesthesiologists even in the absence of a tying arrangement—such an arrangement cannot be said to have foreclosed a choice that would have otherwise been made "on the merits." ...[47] ...

V

In order to prevail in the absence of per se liability, respondent has the burden of proving that the Roux contract violated the Sherman Act because it unreasonably restrained competition. That burden necessarily involves an inquiry into the actual effect of the exclusive

47. Nor is there an indication in the record that petitioners' practices have increased the social costs of their market power. Since patients' anesthesiological needs are fixed by medical judgment, respondent does not argue that the tying arrangement facilitates price discrimination. Where variable-quantity purchasing is unavailable as a means to enable price discrimination, commentators have seen less justification for condemning tying.... While tying arrangements like the one at issue here are unlikely to be used to facilitate price discrimination, they could have the similar effect of enabling hospitals "to evade price control in the tying product through clandestine transfer of the profit to the tied product...." Insurance companies are the principal source of price restraint in the hospital industry; they place some limitations on the ability of hospitals to exploit their market power. Through this arrangement, petitioners may be able to evade that restraint by obtaining a portion of the anesthesiologists' fees and therefore realize a greater return than they could in the absence of the arrangement. This could also have an adverse effect on the anesthesiology market since it is possible that only less able anesthesiologists would be willing to give up part of their fees in return for the security of an exclusive contract. However, there are no findings of either the District Court or the Court of Appeals which indicate that this type of exploitation of market power has occurred here. The Court of Appeals found only that Roux's use of nurse anesthetists increased its and the hospital's profits, but there was no finding that nurse anesthetists might not be used with equal frequency absent the exclusive contract. Indeed, the District Court found that nurse anesthetists are utilized in all hospitals in the area. Moreover, there is nothing in the record which details whether this arrangement has enhanced the value of East Jefferson's market power or harmed quality competition in the anesthesiology market.

contract on competition among anesthesiologists. This competition takes place in a market that has not been defined. The market is not necessarily the same as the market in which hospitals compete in offering services to patients; it may encompass competition among anesthesiologists for exclusive contracts such as the Roux contract and might be statewide or merely local. There is, however, insufficient evidence in this record to provide a basis for finding that the Roux contract, as it actually operates in the market, has unreasonably restrained competition. The record sheds little light on how this arrangement affected consumer demand for separate arrangements with a specific anesthesiologist. The evidence indicates that some surgeons and patients preferred respondent's services to those of Roux, but there is no evidence that any patient who was sophisticated enough to know the difference between two anesthesiologists was not able to go to a hospital that would provide him with the anesthesiologist of his choice.

In sum, all that the record establishes is that the choice of anesthesiologists at East Jefferson has been limited to one of the four doctors who are associated with Roux and therefore have staff privileges.[51] Even if Roux did not have an exclusive contract, the range of alternatives open to the patient would be severely limited by the nature of the transaction and the hospital's unquestioned right to exercise some control over the identity and the number of doctors to whom it accords staff privileges. If respondent is admitted to the staff of East Jefferson, the range of choice will be enlarged from four to five doctors, but the most significant restraints on the patient's freedom to select a specific anesthesiologist will nevertheless remain. Without a showing of actual adverse effect on competition, respondent cannot make out a case under the antitrust laws, and no such showing has been made.

VI

Petitioners' closed policy may raise questions of medical ethics, and may have inconvenienced some patients who would prefer to have their anesthesia administered by someone other than a member of Roux & Associates, but it does not have the obviously unreasonable impact on purchasers that has characterized the tying arrangements that this Court has branded unlawful. There is no evidence that the

51. The effect of the contract has, of course, been to remove the East Jefferson Hospital from the market open to Roux's competitors. Like any exclusive-requirements contract, this contract could be unlawful if it foreclosed so much of the market from penetration by Roux's competitors as to unreasonably restrain competition in the affected market, the market for anesthesiological services. . . . However, respondent has not attempted to make this showing.

742 Jefferson Parish Hospital ¶441

price, the quality, or the supply or demand for either the "tying product" or the "tied product" involved in this case has been adversely affected by the exclusive contract between Roux and the hospital. It may well be true that the contract made it necessary for Dr. Hyde and others to practice elsewhere, rather than at East Jefferson. But there has been no showing that the market as a whole has been affected at all by the contract. Indeed, as we previously noted, the record tells us very little about the market for the services of anesthesiologists. Yet that is the market in which the exclusive contract has had its principal impact. There is simply no showing here of the kind of restraint on competition that is prohibited by the Sherman Act. . . .

Justice BRENNAN, with whom Justice MARSHALL joins, concurring. As the opinion for the Court demonstrates, we have long held that tying arrangements are subject to evaluation for per se illegality under §1 of the Sherman Act. Whatever merit the policy arguments against this long-standing construction of the Act might have, Congress, presumably aware of our decisions, has never changed the rule by amending the Act. In such circumstances, our practice usually has been to stand by a settled statutory interpretation and leave the task of modifying the statute's reach to Congress. . . . I see no reason to depart from that principle in this case and therefore join the opinion and judgment of the Court.

Justice O'CONNOR, with whom Chief Justice BURGER, Justice POWELL, and Justice REHNQUIST join, concurring in the judgment. . . . I concur in the Court's decision to reverse but write separately to explain why I believe the Hospital-Roux contract, whether treated as effecting a tie between services provided to patients, or as an exclusive dealing arrangement between the Hospital and certain anesthesiologists, is properly analyzed under the rule of reason.

I . . .

The court has on occasion applied a per se rule of illegality in actions alleging tying in violation of §1 of the Sherman Act. *International Salt.* Under the usual logic of the per se rule, a restraint on trade that rarely serves any purposes other than to restrain competition is illegal without proof of market power or anti-competitive effect. . . . In deciding whether an economic restraint should be declared illegal per se,

> the probability that anticompetitive consequences will result from a
> practice and the severity of those consequences [is] balanced against

its procompetitive consequences. Cases that do not fit the generalization may arise, but a per se rule reflects the judgment that such cases are not sufficiently common or important to justify the time and expense necessary to identify them. *Sylvania.* See also *Maricopa.*

Some of our earlier cases did indeed declare that tying arrangements serve "hardly any purpose beyond the suppression of competition." . . . However, this declaration was not taken literally even by the cases that purported to rely upon it. In practice, a tie has been illegal only if the seller is shown to have "sufficient economic power with respect to the tying product to appreciably restrain free competition in the market for the tied product. . . ." . . . Without "control or dominance over the tying product," the seller could not use the tying product as "an effectual weapon to pressure buyers into taking the tied item," so that any restraint of trade would be "insignificant." The Court has never been willing to say of tying arrangements, as it has of price-fixing, division of markets, and other agreements subject to per se analysis, that they are always illegal, without proof of market power or anticompetitive effect.

The "per se" doctrine in tying cases has thus always required an elaborate inquiry into the economic effects of the tying arrangement.[1] As a result, tying doctrine incurs the costs of a rule-of-reason approach without achieving its benefits: the doctrine calls for the extensive and time-consuming economic analysis characteristic of the rule of reason, but then may be interpreted to prohibit arrangements that economic analysis would show to be beneficial. Moreover, the per se label in the tying context has generated more confusion than coherent law because it appears to invite lower courts to omit the analysis of economic circumstances of the tie that has always been a necessary element of tying analysis.

The time has therefore come to abandon the "per se" label and refocus the inquiry on the adverse economic effects, and the potential economic benefits, that the tie may have. The law of tie-ins will thus be brought into accord with the law applicable to all other allegedly anticompetitive economic arrangements, except those few horizontal or quasi-horizontal restraints that can be said to have no economic justification whatsoever.[2] This change will rationalize rather than abandon tie-in doctrine as it is already applied.

1. This inquiry has been required in analyzing both the prima facie case and affirmative defenses. Most notably, *Jerrold* upheld a requirement that buyers of television systems purchase the complete system, as well as installation and repair service, on the grounds that the tie assured that the systems would operate and thereby protected the seller's business reputation.

2. Tying law is particularly anomalous in this respect because arrangements largely indistinguishable from tie-ins are generally analyzed under the rule of reason. For example, the "per se" analysis of tie-ins subjects restrictions on a franchisee's freedom to purchase supplies to a more searching scrutiny than re-

II

Our prior opinions indicate that the purpose of tying law has been to identify and control those tie-ins that have a demonstrable exclusionary impact in the tied product market . . . or that abet the harmful exercise of market power that the seller possesses in the tying product market. Under the rule of reason tying arrangements should be disapproved only in such instances.

Market power in the *tying* product may be acquired legitimately (e.g., through the grant of a patent) or illegitimately (e.g., as a result of unlawful monopolization). In either event, exploitation of consumers in the market for the tying product is a possibility that exists and that may be regulated under §2 of the Sherman Act without reference to any tying arrangements that the seller may have developed. The existence of a tied product normally does not increase the profit that the seller with market power can extract from sales of the *tying* product. . . .

Tying may be economically harmful primarily in the rare cases where power in the market for the tying product is used to create *additional* market power in the market for the *tied* product.[4] The antitrust law is properly concerned with tying when, for example, the flour monopolist threatens to use its market power to acquire additional power in the sugar market, perhaps by driving out competing sellers of sugar, or by making it more difficult for new sellers to enter the sugar market. But such extension of market power is unlikely, or poses no threat of economic harm, unless the two markets in question and the nature of the two products tied satisfy three threshold criteria.

---

strictions on his freedom to sell his products. Compare, e.g., Siegel v. Chicken Delight, Inc., 448 F.2d 43 (CA9 1971), cert. denied, 405 U.S. 955 (1972), with *Sylvania*. And exclusive contracts, that, like tie-ins, require the buyer to purchase a product from one seller, are subject only to the rule of reason.

4. Tying might be undesirable in two other instances but the hospital-Roux arrangement involves neither one.

In a regulated industry a firm with market power may be unable to extract a supercompetitive profit because it lacks control over the prices it charges for regulated products or services. Tying may then be used to extract that profit from sale of the unregulated, tied products or services. . . .

Tying may also help the seller engage in price discrimination by "metering" the buyer's use of the tying product. Cf. *IBM*; *International Salt*. . . . Price discrimination may, however, *decrease* rather than increase the economic costs of a seller's market power. . . . *Fortner* did not hold that price discrimination in the form of a tie-in is always economically harmful; that case indicated only that price discrimination may indicate market power in the tying product market. But there is no need in this case to address the problem of price discrimination facilitated by tying. The discussion herein is aimed only at tying arrangements as to which no price discrimination is alleged.

First, the seller must have power in the tying product market.[6] ...[7] ... Second, there must be a substantial threat that the tying seller will acquire market power in the tied-product market. No such threat exists if the tied-product market is occupied by many stable sellers who are not likely to be driven out by the tying, or if entry barriers in the tied product market are low.... If, on the other hand, the tying arrangement is likely to erect significant barriers to entry into the tied-product market, the tie remains suspect. Atlantic Refining Co. v. FTC, 381 U.S. 357, 371 (1965).

Third, there must be a coherent economic basis for treating the tying and tied products as distinct. All but the simplest products can be broken down into two or more components that are "tied together" in the final sale. Unless it is to be illegal to sell cars with engines or cameras with lenses, this analysis must be guided by some limiting principle. For products to be treated as distinct, the tied product must, at a minimum, be one that some consumers might wish to purchase separately *without also purchasing the tying product*.[8] When the tied product has no use other than in conjunction with the tying product, a seller of the tying product can acquire

6. The Court has failed in the past to define how much market power is necessary, but in the context of this case it is inappropriate to attempt to resolve that question. In *International Salt* the Court assumed that a patent conferred market power and therefore sufficiently established "the tendency of the arrangement to accomplishment of monopoly." In its next tying case, *Times-Picayune*, the Court distinguished *International Salt* in part by finding that there was no market "dominance," after a careful consideration of the relevant market. Then, in *Northern Pacific* the Court required only a minimal showing of market power. More recently, in *Fortner*, the Court conducted a more extensive analysis of whether the tie was actually an exercise of market power, considering such factors as the size and profitability of the firm seeking to impose the tie, the character of the tying product, and the effects of the tie — the price charged for the products, the number of customers affected, the functional relation between the tied and tying product.

7. A common misconception has been that a patent or copyright, a high market share, or a unique product that competitors are not able to offer suffice to demonstrate market power. While each of these three factors might help to give market power to a seller, it is also possible that a seller in these situations will have no market power: for example, a patent holder has no market power in any relevant sense if there are close substitutes for the patented product. Similarly, a high market share indicates market power only if the market is properly defined to include all reasonable substitutes for the product....

8. Whether the tying product is one that consumers might wish to purchase without the tied product should be irrelevant. Once it is conceded that the seller has market power over the tying product it follows that the seller can sell the tying product on noncompetitive terms. The injury to consumers does not depend on whether the seller chooses to charge a supercompetitive price, or charges a competitive price but insists that consumers also buy a product that they do not want.

no *additional* market power by selling the two products together. If sugar is useless to consumers except when used with flour, the flour seller's market power is projected into the sugar market whether or not the two products are actually sold together; the flour seller can exploit what market power it has over flour with or without the tie. . . .

Even when the tied product does have a use separate from the tying product, it makes little sense to label a package as two products without also considering the economic justifications for the sale of the package as a unit. When the economic advantages of joint packaging are substantial the package is not appropriately viewed as two products, and that should be the end of the tying inquiry. The lower courts largely have adopted this approach.[10] . . .

These three conditions — market power in the tying product, a substantial threat of market power in the tied product, and a coherent economic basis for treating the products as distinct — are only threshold requirements. Under the rule of reason a tie-in may prove acceptable even when all three are met. Tie-ins may entail economic benefits as well as economic harms, and if the threshold requirements are met these benefits should enter the rule of reason balance.

> [Tie-ins] may facilitate new entry into fields where established sellers have wedded their customers to them by ties of habit and custom. *Brown Shoe*. . . . They may permit clandestine price cutting in products which otherwise would have no price competition at all because of fear of retaliation from the few other producers dealing in the market. They may protect the reputation of the tying product if failure to use the tied product in conjunction with it may cause it to misfunction. . . . [Citing] Pick Mfg. Co. v. General Motors Corp., 80 F.2d 641 (C.A. 7 1935), aff'd, 299 U.S. 3 (1936). And, if the tied and tying products are functionally related, they may reduce costs through economies of joint production and distribution. *Fortner I*, 394 U.S., at 514 n.9 (White, J., dissenting).

. . . A tie-in should be condemned only when its anticompetitive impact outweighs its contribution to efficiency.

---

10. The examination of the economic advantages of tying may properly be conducted as part of the rule-of-reason analysis, rather than at the threshold of the tying inquiry. This approach is consistent with this Court's occasional references to the problem. . . . These cases indicate that consideration of whether a buyer might prefer to purchase one component without the other is one of the factors in tying analysis and, more generally, that economic analysis rather than mere conventional separability into different markets should determine whether one or two products are involved in the alleged tie.

III

Application of these criteria to the case at hand is straightforward. Although the issue is in doubt, we may assume that the Hospital does have market power in the provision of hospital services in its area. . . .

Second, in light of the Hospital's presumed market power, we may also assume that there is a substantial threat that East Jefferson will acquire market power over the provision of anesthesiological services in its market. By tying the sale of anesthesia to the sale of other hospital services the Hospital can drive out other sellers of those services who might otherwise operate in the local market. The Hospital may thus gain local market power in the provision of anesthesiology; anesthesiological services offered in the Hospital's market, narrowly defined, will be purchased only from Roux, under the Hospital's auspices.

But the third threshold condition for giving closer scrutiny to a tying arrangement is not satisfied here: there is no sound economic reason for treating surgery and anesthesia as separate services. Patients are interested in purchasing anesthesia only in conjunction with hospital services, so the Hospital can acquire no *additional* market power by selling the two services together. Accordingly, the link between the Hospital's services and anesthesia administered by Roux will affect neither the amount of anesthesia provided nor the combined price of anesthesia and surgery for those who choose to become the Hospital's patients. In these circumstances, anesthesia and surgical services should probably not be characterized as distinct products for tying purposes.

Even if they are, the tying should not be considered a violation of §1 of the Sherman Act because tying here cannot increase the seller's already absolute power over the volume of production of the tied product, which is an inevitable consequence of the fact that very few patients will choose to undergo surgery without receiving anesthesia. The hospital-Roux contract therefore has little potential to harm the patients. On the other side of the balance, the District Court found, and the Court of Appeals did not dispute, that the tie-in conferred significant benefits upon the hospital and the patients that it served.

The tie-in improves patient care and permits more efficient hospital operation in a number of ways. From the viewpoint of hospital management, the tie-in ensures 24 hour anesthesiology coverage, aids in standardization of procedures and efficient use of equipment, facilitates flexible scheduling of operations, and permits the hospital more effectively to monitor the quality of anesthesiological services. Further, the tying arrangement is advantageous to patients because, as the District Court found, the closed anesthesiology department places upon the hospital, rather than the individual patient, responsibility to select the physician who is to provide anesthesiological services. The hospital also assumes the responsibility that the anesthesiologist will be available, will be acceptable to the surgeon, and will provide suitable care to the patient. In assuming these responsibilities — responsibilities that a seriously ill patient frequently may be unable to discharge — the hospital provides a valuable service to its patients. And there is no indication that patients were dissatisfied with the quality of anesthesiology that was provided at the hospital or that patients wished to enjoy the services of anesthesiologists other than those that the hospital employed. Given this evidence of the advantages and effectiveness of the closed anesthesiology department, it is not surprising that, as the District Court found, such arrangements are accepted practice in the majority of hospitals of New Orleans and in the health care industry generally. Such an arrangement, which has little anticompetitive effect and achieves substantial benefits in the provision of care to patients, is hardly one that the antitrust law should condemn.[13] This conclusion reaffirms our threshold determination that the joint provision of hospital services and anesthesiology should not be viewed as involving a tie between distinct products, and therefore should require no additional scrutiny under the antitrust law.

IV

Whether or not the hospital-Roux contract is characterized as a tie between distinct products, the contract unquestionably does constitute exclusive dealing. Exclusive-dealing arrangements are independently subject to scrutiny under §1 of the Sherman Act, and are also analyzed under the rule of reason. *Tampa Electric.*

The hospital-Roux arrangement could conceivably have an adverse effect on horizontal competition among anesthesiologists, or among hospitals. Dr. Hyde, who competes with the Roux anesthesiologists, and other hospitals in the area, who compete with East Jefferson, may have grounds to complain that the exclusive contract stifles horizontal competition and therefore has an adverse, albeit indirect, impact on consumer welfare even if it is not a tie.

---

13. The Court of Appeals disregarded the benefits of the tie because it found that there were less restrictive means of achieving them. In the absence of an adequate basis to expect any harm to competition from the tie-in, this objection is simply irrelevant.

Exclusive-dealing arrangements may, in some circumstances, create or extend market power of a supplier or the purchaser party to the exclusive-dealing arrangement, and may thus restrain horizontal competition. Exclusive dealing can have adverse economic consequences by allowing one supplier of goods or services unreasonably to deprive other suppliers of a market for their goods, or by allowing one buyer of goods unreasonably to deprive other buyers of a needed source of supply. In determining whether an exclusive-dealing contract is unreasonable, the proper focus is on the structure of the market for the products or services in question — the number of sellers and buyers in the market, the volume of their business, and the ease with which buyers and sellers can redirect their purchases or sales to others. Exclusive dealing is an unreasonable restraint on trade only when a significant fraction of buyers or sellers are frozen out of a market by the exclusive deal. *Standard Stations.* When the sellers of services are numerous and mobile, and the number of buyers is large, exclusive-dealing arrangements of narrow scope pose no threat of adverse economic consequences. To the contrary, they may be substantially procompetitive by ensuring stable markets and encouraging long-term, mutually advantageous business relationships.

At issue here is an exclusive dealing arrangement between a firm of four anesthesiologists and one relatively small hospital. There is no suggestion that East Jefferson Hospital is likely to create a "bottleneck" in the availability of anesthesiologists that might deprive other hospitals of access to needed anesthesiological services, or that the Roux associates have unreasonably narrowed the range of choices available to other anesthesiologists in search of a hospital or patients that will buy their services. Cf. *Associated Press.* A firm of four anesthesiologists represents only a very small fraction of the total number of anesthesiologists whose services are available for hire by other hospitals, and East Jefferson is one among numerous hospitals buying such services. Even without engaging in a detailed analysis of the size of the relevant markets we may readily conclude that there is no likelihood that the exclusive-dealing arrangement challenged here will either unreasonably enhance the hospital's market position relative to other hospitals, or unreasonably permit Roux to acquire power relative to other anesthesiologists. Accordingly, this exclusive dealing arrangement must be sustained under the rule of reason. . . .

442. (a) What ground does the *Jefferson Parish* concurrence offer for eliminating the per se rule? Do you agree that the "Court has *on occasion* applied a per se rule" to tying? How would application of the rule of reason change the Court's approach? (Consider the extent to which the disagreements between the two opinions can be traced to the difference in rules.)

(b) What do each of the opinions suggest to be the harms of tying?[79]

(c) Was there sufficient market power in *Jefferson Parish* to give rise to the harms in ¶b? How much market power is deemed necessary by the majority?[80] The concurrence notes that such arrangements are practiced by many (most?) hospitals. What implication, if any, does this have for the market power issue?

(d) How does each opinion decide the "two product" issue? Which test do you find most persuasive? Would the result be different if all the anesthesiologists were the Hospital's full-time employees?[81]

(e) What were the redeeming virtues of the practice? Is majority footnote 42 or concurrence footnote 13 more convincing? What was the relationship between the exclusivity of the arrangement and the alleged virtues?

(f) Why do you suppose East Jefferson adopted this arrangement? Was it trying to gain monopoly power in the market for anesthesiologists? To control the quality of doctors practicing on its premises (and thus avoid malpractice suits)? Was it giving in to hidden channels of pressure by some groups of doctors who may, at least in part, dictate hospital policy in their self-interest? What would be the implications of each purpose for the legality of the practice? Did either opinion think it necessary to determine the most plausible explanation? (See majority, footnote 41.)

79. Some lower courts have interpreted *Jefferson Parish* as requiring a further threshold to per se illegality: that the plaintiff prove a substantial danger that the seller will acquire market power in the tied product as a result of the tie. *Carl Sandburg*, note 61; Smith Mach. Co. v. Hesston Corp., 1987 Trade Cas. ¶67563 (D.N.M.). For a criticism of the Court's taking an excessively narrow approach to the ways in which competition can be adversely affected, see W.D. Slawson, A New Concept of Competition: Reanalyzing Tie-in Doctrine after Hyde, 30 Antitr. Bull. 257 (1985).

80. Compare *Data General* (1984), note 71 (finding adequate market power under *Jefferson Parish* where defendant's operating system software was tied to purchases of central processing units of its computer system; copyright of software created presumption of market power, and evidence showed that many customers were "locked in" to defendant's operating system through substantial subsequent investments in applications software), with A.I. Root Co. v. Computer/Dynamics, 806 F.2d 673 (6th Cir. 1986) (rejecting presumption of market power from copyright, and finding no evidence that operating system involved was particularly unique or desirable).

81. McMorris v. Williamsport Hosp., 597 F. Supp. 899 (N.D. Pa. 1984) (hospital's nuclear medicine department closed to outsiders, its full-time employee having exclusive control; defendant's summary judgment motion denied, but two-product question is stated to be closer than in *Jefferson Parish*).

EASTMAN KODAK CO. v. IMAGE
TECHNICAL SERVICES
504 U.S. 451 (1992)

Justice BLACKMUN. . . . This is yet another case that concerns the standard for summary judgment in an antitrust controversy. The principal issue here is whether a defendant's lack of market power in the primary equipment market precludes — as a matter of law — the possibility of market power in derivative aftermarkets.

Petitioner Eastman Kodak Company manufactures and sells photocopiers and micrographic equipment. Kodak also sells service and replacement parts for its equipment. Respondents are 18 independent service organizations (ISOs) that in the early 1980s began servicing Kodak copying and micrographic equipment. Kodak subsequently adopted policies to limit the availability of parts to ISOs and to make it more difficult for ISOs to compete with Kodak in servicing Kodak equipment. . . .

I

A

Because this case comes to us on petitioner Kodak's motion for summary judgment, "[t]he evidence of [respondents] is to be believed, and all justifiable inferences are to be drawn in [their] favor." Anderson v. Liberty Lobby, Inc., 457 U.S. 242, 255 (1986); *Matsushita*. Mindful that respondents' version of any disputed issue of fact thus is presumed correct, we begin with the factual basis of respondents' claims. See *Maricopa*.

Kodak manufactures and sells complex business machines — as relevant here, high-volume photocopier and micrographics equipment. Kodak equipment is unique; micrographic software programs that operate on Kodak machines, for example, are not compatible with competitors' machines. Kodak parts are not compatible with other manufacturers' equipment, and vice versa. Kodak equipment, although expensive when new, has little resale value.

Kodak provides service and parts for its machines to its customers. It produces some of the parts itself; the rest are made to order for Kodak by independent original-equipment manufacturers (OEMs). Kodak does not sell a complete system of original equipment, lifetime service, and lifetime parts for a single price. Instead, Kodak provides service after the initial warranty period either through annual service contracts, which include all necessary parts, or on a per-call basis. It charges, through negotiations and bidding, different prices for equipment, service and parts for different customers. Kodak provides 80% to 95% of the service for Kodak machines.

Beginning in the early 1980s, ISOs began repairing and servicing Kodak equipment. They also sold parts and reconditioned and sold used Kodak equipment. Their customers were federal, state, and local government agencies, banks, insurance companies, industrial enterprises, and providers of specialized copy and microfilming services. ISOs provide service at a price substantially lower than Kodak does. Some customers found that the ISO service was of higher quality.

Some of the ISOs' customers purchase their own parts and hire ISOs only for service. Others choose ISOs to supply both service and parts. ISOs keep an inventory of parts, purchased from Kodak or other sources, primarily the OEMs.

In 1985 and 1986, Kodak implemented a policy of selling replacement parts for micrographic and copying machines only to buyers of Kodak equipment who use Kodak service or repair their own machines.

As part of the same policy, Kodak sought to limit ISO access to other sources of Kodak parts. Kodak and the OEMs agreed that the OEMs would not sell parts that fit Kodak equipment to anyone other than Kodak. Kodak also pressured Kodak equipment owners and independent parts distributors not to sell Kodak parts to ISOs. In addition, Kodak took steps to restrict the availability of used machines.

Kodak intended, through these policies, to make it more difficult for ISOs to sell service for Kodak machines. It succeeded. ISOs were unable to obtain parts from reliable sources, and many were forced out of business, while others lost substantial revenue. Customers were forced to switch to Kodak service even though they preferred ISO service.

B

In 1987, the ISOs filed the present action in the District Court, alleging, inter alia, that Kodak had unlawfully tied the sale of service for Kodak machines to the sale of parts, in violation of §1 of the Sherman Act, and had unlawfully monopolized and attempted to monopolize the sale of service for Kodak machines, in violation of §2 of that Act.

Kodak filed a motion for summary judgment before respondents had initiated discovery. The District Court permitted respondents to file one set of interrogatories and one set of requests for production of documents, and to take six depositions. Without a hearing, the District Court granted summary judgment in favor of Kodak.

As to the §1 claim, the court found that respondents had provided no evidence of a tying arrangement between Kodak equipment and service or parts. The court, however, did not address respondents' §1 claim that is at issue here. Respondents allege a tying arrangement not between Kodak *equipment* and service, but between Kodak *parts* and service. As to the §2 claim, the District Court concluded that although Kodak had a "natural monopoly over the market for parts it sells under its name," a unilateral refusal to sell those parts to ISOs did not violate §2.

The Court of Appeals for the Ninth Circuit, by a divided vote, reversed. With respect to the §1 claim, the court first found that whether service and parts were distinct markets, and whether a tying arrangement existed between them were disputed issues of fact. Having found that a tying arrangement might exist, the Court of Appeals considered a question not decided by the District Court: was there "an issue of material fact as to whether Kodak has sufficient economic power in the tying product market [parts] to restrain competition appreciably in the tied product market [service]." The court agreed with Kodak that competition in the equipment market might prevent Kodak from possessing power in the parts market, but refused to uphold the District Court's grant of summary judgment "on this theoretical basis" because "market imperfections can keep economic theories about how consumers will act from mirroring reality." Noting that the District Court had not considered the market power issue, and that the record was not fully developed through discovery, the court declined to require respondents to conduct market analysis or to pinpoint specific imperfections in order to withstand summary judgment. . . .

As to the §2 claim, the Court of Appeals concluded that sufficient evidence existed to support a finding that Kodak's implementation of its parts policy was "anticompetitive" and "exclusionary" and "involved a specific intent to monopolize." It held that the ISOs had come forward with sufficient evidence, for summary judgment purposes, to disprove Kodak's business justifications. . . .

II

A tying arrangement is "an agreement by a party to sell one product but only on the condition that the buyer also purchases a different (or tied) product, or at least agrees that he will not purchase that product from any other supplier." *Northern Pacific.* Such an arrangement violates §1 of the Sherman Act if the seller has "appreciable economic power" in the tying product market and if the arrangement affects a substantial volume of commerce in the tied market. *Fortner Enterprises, Inc. v. United States Steel Corp.,* 394 U.S. 495, 503 (1969).

Kodak did not dispute that its arrangement affects a substantial volume of interstate commerce. It, however, did challenge whether its activities constituted a "tying arrangement" and whether Kodak exercised "appreciable economic power" in the tying market. We consider these issues in turn.

A

For the respondents to defeat a motion for summary judgment on their claim of a tying arrangement, a reasonable trier of fact must be able to find, first, that service and parts are two distinct products, and, second, that Kodak has tied the sale of the two products.

For service and parts to be considered two distinct products, there must be sufficient consumer demand so that it is efficient for a firm to provide service separately from parts. *Jefferson Parish.* Evidence in the record indicates that service and parts have been sold separately in the past and still are sold separately to self-service equipment owners. Indeed, the development of the entire high-technology service industry is evidence of the efficiency of a separate market for service.

Kodak insists that because there is no demand for parts separate from service, there cannot be separate markets for service and parts. By this logic, we would be forced to conclude that there can never be separate markets, for example, for cameras and film, computers and software, or automobiles and tires. That is an assumption we are unwilling to make. "We have often found arrangements involving functionally linked products at least one of which is useless without the other to be prohibited tying devices." *Jefferson Parish.*

Kodak's assertion also appears to be incorrect as a factual matter. At least some consumers would purchase service without parts, because some service does not require parts, and some consumers, those who self-service for example, would purchase parts without service. Enough doubt is cast on Kodak's claim of a unified market that it should be resolved by the trier of fact.

Finally, respondents have presented sufficient evidence of a tie between service and parts. The record indicates that Kodak would sell parts to third parties only if they agreed not to by service from ISOs.[8]

8. In a footnote, Kodak contends that this practice is only a unilateral refusal to deal, which does not violate the antitrust laws. Assuming, arguendo, that Kodak's refusal to sell parts to any company providing service can be characterized as a unilateral refusal to deal, its alleged sale of parts to third parties on condition that they buy service from Kodak is not.

B

Having found sufficient evidence of a tying arrangement, we consider the other necessary feature of an illegal tying arrangement: appreciable economic power in the tying market. Market power is the power "to force a purchaser to do something that he would not do in a competitive market." *Jefferson Parish*. It has been defined as "the ability of a single seller to raise price and restrict output." *Fortner; Cellophane*. The existence of such power ordinarily is inferred from the seller's possession of a predominant share of the market. *Jefferson Parish;* Times-Picayune Publishing Co. v. United States, 345 U.S. 594, 611-613 (1953).

Respondents contend that Kodak has more than sufficient power in the parts market to force unwanted purchases [in] the tied market, service. Respondents provide evidence that certain parts are available exclusively through Kodak. Respondents also assert that Kodak has control over the availability of parts it does not manufacture. According to respondents' evidence, Kodak has prohibited independent manufacturers from selling Kodak parts to ISOs, pressured Kodak equipment owners and independent parts distributors to deny ISOs the purchase of Kodak parts, and taken steps to restrict the availability of used machines.

Respondents also allege that Kodak's control over the parts market has excluded service competition, boosted service prices, and forced unwilling consumption of Kodak service. Respondents offer evidence that consumers have switched to Kodak service even though they preferred ISO service, that Kodak service was of higher price and lower quality than the preferred ISO service, and that ISOs were driven out of business by Kodak's policies. Under our prior precedents, this evidence would be sufficient to entitle respondents to a trial on their claim of market power.

Kodak counters that even if it concedes monopoly *share* of the relevant parts market, it cannot actually exercise the necessary market *power* for a Sherman Act violation. This is so, according to Kodak, because competition exists in the equipment market. Kodak argues that it could not have the ability to raise prices of service and parts above the level that would be charged in a competitive market because any increase in profits from a higher price in the aftermarkets at least would be offset by a corresponding loss in profits from lower equipment sales as consumers began purchasing equipment with more attractive service costs.

Kodak does not present any actual data on the equipment, service, or parts markets. Instead, it urges the adoption of a substantive legal rule that "equipment competition precludes any finding of monopoly power in derivative aftermarkets." Kodak argues that such a rule would satisfy its burden as the moving party of showing "that there is no genuine issue as to any material fact" on the market power issue.[11]

Legal presumptions that rest on formalistic distinctions rather than actual market realities are generally disfavored in antitrust law. This Court has preferred to resolve antitrust claims on a case-by-case basis, focusing on the "particular facts disclosed by the record." *Maple Flooring*; *Cellophane*; *Sylvania* (White, J., concurring in judgment).[12] In determining the existence of market power, and specifically the responsiveness of the sales of one product to price changes of the other, *Cellophane*, this Court has examined closely the economic reality of the market at issue.

Kodak contends that there is no need to examine the facts when the issue is market power in the aftermarkets. A legal presumption against a finding of market power is warranted in this situation, according to Kodak, because the existence of market power in the service and parts markets absent power in the equipment market "simply makes no economic sense," and the absence of a legal presumption would deter procompetitive behavior. *Matsushita*.

Kodak analogizes this case to Matsushita where a group of American corporations that manufactured or sold consumer electronic products alleged that their 21 Japanese counterparts were engaging in a 20-year conspiracy to price below cost in the United States in the hope of expanding their market share sometime in the future. After several years of detailed discovery the defendants moved for summary judgment. Because the defendants had every incentive not to engage in the alleged conduct which required them to sustain losses for decades with no foreseeable profits, the Court found an "absence of any rational motive to conspire." In that context, the Court determined that the plaintiffs' theory of predatory pricing makes no practical sense, was "speculative" and was not "reasonable." Accordingly, the Court held that a reasonable jury could not return a verdict for the plaintiffs and that summary judgment would be appropriate against them unless they came forward with more persuasive evidence to support their theory.

---

11. Kodak argues that such a rule would be per se, with no opportunity for respondents to rebut the conclusion that market power is lacking in the parts market....

As an apparent second-best alternative, Kodak suggests elsewhere in its brief that the rule would permit a defendant to meet its summary judgment burden under Fed. Rule Civ. Proc. 56(c); the burden would then shift to the plaintiffs to "prove ... that there is a specific reason to believe that normal economic reasoning does not apply."

12. See generally *Business Electronics*; *Indiana Dentists*; *NCAA*; *Sylvania*.

The Court's requirement in *Matsushita* that the plaintiffs' claims make economic sense did not introduce a special burden on plaintiffs facing summary judgment in antitrust cases. The Court did not hold that if the moving party enunciates *any* economic theory supporting its behavior, regardless of its accuracy in reflecting the actual market, it is entitled to summary judgment. *Matsushita* demands only that the nonmoving party's inferences be reasonable in order to reach the jury, a requirement that was not invented, but merely articulated, in that decision. If the plaintiff's theory is economically senseless, no reasonable jury could find in its favor, and summary judgment should be granted.

Kodak, then, bears a substantial burden in showing that it is entitled to summary judgment. It must show that despite evidence of increased prices and excluded competition, an inference of market power is unreasonable. To determine whether Kodak has met that burden, we must unravel the factual assumptions underlying its proposed rule that lack of power in the equipment market necessarily precludes power in the aftermarkets.

The extent to which one market prevents exploitation of another market depends on the extent to which consumers will change their consumption of one product in response to a price change in another, i.e., the "cross-elasticity of demand." See *Cellophane*; P. Areeda & L. Kaplow, Antitrust Analysis ¶342(c) (4th ed. 1988).[15] Kodak's proposed rule rests on a factual assumption about the cross-elasticity of demand in the equipment and aftermarkets: "If Kodak raised its parts or service prices above competitive levels, potential customers would simply stop buying Kodak equipment. Perhaps Kodak would be able to increase short term profits through such a strategy, but at a devastating cost to its long term interests." Kodak argues that the Court should accept, as a matter of law, this "basic economic realit[y]" that competition in the

---

15. What constrains the defendant's ability to raise prices in the service market is "the elasticity of demand faced by the defendant — the degree to which its sales fall . . . as its price rises." P. Areeda & L. Kaplow, Antitrust Analysis ¶342(c) (4th ed. 1988).

Courts usually have considered the relationship between price in one market and demand in another in defining the relevant market. Because market power is often inferred from market share, market definition generally determines the result of the case. Pitofsky, New Definitions of Relevant Market and the Assault on Antitrust, 90 Colum. L. Rev. 1805, 1806-1813 (1990). Kodak chose to focus on market power directly rather than arguing that the relationship between equipment and service and parts is such that the three should be included in the same market definition. Whether considered in the conceptual category of "market definition" or "market power," the ultimate inquiry is the same — whether competition in the equipment market will significantly restrain power in the service and parts markets.

equipment market necessarily prevents market power in the aftermarkets.

Even if Kodak could not raise the price of service and parts one cent without losing equipment sales, that fact would not disprove market power in the aftermarkets. The sales of even a monopolist are reduced when it sells goods at a monopoly price, but the higher price more than compensates for the loss in sales. Areeda & Kaplow, at ¶¶112 and 340(a). Kodak's claim that charging more for service and parts would be "a short-run game" is based on the false dichotomy that there are only two prices that can be charged — a competitive price or a ruinous one. But there could easily be a middle, optimum price at which the increased revenues from the higher-priced sales of service and parts would more than compensate for the lower revenues from lost equipment sales. The fact that the equipment market imposes a restraint on prices in the aftermarkets by no means disproves the existence of power in those markets. See Areeda & Kaplow, at ¶340(b) ("[T]he existence of significant substitution in the event of *further* price increases or even at the *current* price does not tell us whether the defendant *already* exercises significant market power") (emphasis in original). Thus, contrary to Kodak's assertion, there is no immutable physical law — no "basic economic reality" — insisting that competition in the equipment market cannot coexist with market power in the aftermarkets.

We next consider the more narrowly drawn question: Does Kodak's theory describe actual market behavior so accurately that respondents' assertion of Kodak market power in the aftermarkets, if not impossible, is at least unreasonable?[18] Cf. *Matsushita.*

To review Kodak's theory, it contends that higher service prices will lead to a disastrous drop in equipment sales. Presumably, the theory's corollary is to the effect that low service prices lead to a

---

18. Although Kodak repeatedly relies on *Sylvania* as support for its factual assertion that the equipment market will prevent exploitation of the service and parts markets, the case is inapposite. In *Sylvania*, the Court found that a manufacturer's policy restricting the number of retailers that were permitted to sell its product could have a procompetitive effect. The Court also noted that any negative effect of exploitation of the intrabrand market (the competition between retailers of the same product) would be checked by competition in the interbrand market (competition over the same generic product) because consumers would substitute a different brand of the same product. Unlike *Sylvania*, this case does not concern vertical relationships between parties on different levels of the same distribution chain. In the relevant market, service, Kodak and the ISOs are direct competitors; their relationship is horizontal. The interbrand competition at issue here is competition over the provision of service. Despite petitioner's best effort, repeating the mantra "interbrand competition" does not transform this case into one over an agreement the manufacturer has with its dealers that would fall under the rubric of *Sylvania.*

dramatic increase in equipment sales. According to the theory, one would have expected Kodak to take advantage of lower-priced ISO service as an opportunity to expand equipment sales. Instead, Kodak adopted a restrictive sales policy consciously designed to eliminate the lower-priced ISO service, an act that would be expected to devastate either Kodak's equipment sales or Kodak's faith in its theory. Yet, according to the record, it has done neither. Service prices have risen for Kodak customers, but there is no evidence or assertion that Kodak equipment sales have dropped.

Kodak and the United States [as amicus] attempt to reconcile Kodak's theory with the contrary actual results by describing a "marketing strategy of spreading over time the total cost to the buyer of Kodak equipment." In other words, Kodak could charge subcompetitive prices for equipment and make up the difference with supracompetitive prices for service, resulting in an overall competitive price. This pricing strategy would provide an explanation for the theory's descriptive failings — if Kodak in fact had adopted it. But Kodak never has asserted that it prices its equipment or parts subcompetitively and recoups its profits through service. Instead, it claims that it prices its equipment comparably to its competitors, and intends that both its equipment sales and service divisions be profitable. Moreover, this hypothetical pricing strategy is inconsistent with Kodak's policy toward its self-service customers. If Kodak were underpricing its equipment, hoping to lock in customers and recover its losses in the service market, it could not afford to sell customers parts without service. In sum, Kodak's theory does not explain the actual market behavior revealed in the record.

Respondents offer a forceful reason why Kodak's theory, although perhaps intuitively appealing, may not accurately explain the behavior of the primary and derivative markets for complex durable goods: the existence of significant information and switching costs. These costs could create a less responsive connection between service and parts prices and equipment sales.

For the service-market price to affect equipment demand, consumers must inform themselves of the total cost of the "package" — equipment, service, and parts — at the time of purchase; that is, consumers must engage in accurate lifecycle pricing. Lifecycle pricing of complex, durable equipment is difficult and costly. In order to arrive at an accurate price, a consumer must acquire a substantial amount of raw data and undertake sophisticated analysis. The necessary information would include data on price, quality, and availability of products needed to operate, upgrade, or enhance the initial equipment, as well as service and repair costs, including estimates of breakdown frequency, nature of repairs, price of service and parts, length of "downtime" and losses incurred from downtime.

Much of this information is difficult — some of it impossible — to acquire at the time of purchase. During the life of a product, companies may change the service and parts prices, and develop products with more advanced features, a need for repair, or new warranties. In addition, the information is likely to be customer-specific; lifecycle costs will vary from customer to customer with the type of equipment, degrees of equipment use, and costs of downtime.

Kodak acknowledges the cost of information, but suggests, again without evidentiary support, that customer information needs will be satisfied by competitors in the equipment markets. It is a question of fact, however, whether competitors would provide the necessary information. A competitor in the equipment market may not have reliable information about the lifecycle costs of complex equipment it does not service or the needs of customers it does not serve. Even if competitors had the relevant information, it is not clear that their interests would be advanced by providing such information to consumers. See 2 P. Areeda & D. Turner, Antitrust Law, ¶404b1 (1978).[21]

Moreover, even if consumers were capable of acquiring and processing the complex body of information, they may choose not to do so. Acquiring the information is expensive. If the costs of service are small relative to the equipment price, or if consumers are more concerned about equipment capabilities than service costs, they may not find it cost-efficient to compile the information. Similarly, some consumers, such as the Federal Government, have purchasing systems that make it difficult to consider the complete cost of the "package" at the time of purchase. State and local governments often treat service as an operating expense and equipment as a capital expense, delegating each to a different department. These governmental entities do not lifecycle price, but rather choose the lowest price in each market. See Brief for National Association of

21. To inform consumers about Kodak, the competitor must be willing to forgo the opportunity to reap supracompetitive prices in its own service and parts markets. The competitor may anticipate that charging lower service and parts prices and informing consumers about Kodak in the hopes of gaining future equipment sales will cause Kodak to lower the price on its service and parts, cancelling any gains in equipment sales to the competitor and leaving both worse off. Thus, in an equipment market with relatively few sellers, competitors may find it more profitable to adopt Kodak's service and parts policy than to inform the consumers. See 2 P. Areeda & D. Turner, Antitrust Law ¶404b1 (1978); App. 177 (Kodak, Xerox, and IBM together have nearly 100% of relevant market).

Even in a market with many sellers, any one competitor may not have sufficient incentive to inform consumers because the increased patronage attributable to the corrected consumer beliefs will be shared among other competitors. Beales, Craswell & Salop, 24 J. Law & Econ., at 503-504, 506.

State Purchasing Officials, et al., as Amici Curiae; Brief for State of Ohio et al., as Amici Curiae.

As Kodak notes, there likely will be some large-volume, sophisticated purchasers who will undertake the comparative studies and insist, in return for their patronage, that Kodak charge them competitive lifecycle prices. Kodak contends that these knowledgeable customers will hold down the package price for all other customers. There are reasons, however, to doubt that sophisticated purchasers will ensure that competitive prices are charged to unsophisticated purchasers, too. As an initial matter, if the number of sophisticated customers is relatively small, the amount of profits to be gained by supracompetitive pricing in the service market could make it profitable to let the knowledgeable consumers take their business elsewhere. More importantly, if a company is able to price-discriminate between sophisticated and unsophisticated consumers, the sophisticated will be unable to prevent the exploitation of the uninformed. A seller could easily price-discriminate by varying the equipment/parts/service package, developing different warranties, or offering price discounts on different components.

Given the potentially high cost of information and the possibility a seller may be able to price-discriminate between knowledgeable and unsophisticated consumers, it makes little sense to assume, in the absence of any evidentiary support, that equipment-purchasing decisions are based on an accurate assessment of the total cost of equipment, service, and parts over the lifetime of the machine.

Indeed, respondents have presented evidence that Kodak practices price-discrimination by selling parts to customers who service their own equipment, but refusing to sell parts to customers who hire third-party service companies. Companies that have their own service staff are likely to be high-volume users, the same companies for whom it is most likely to be economically worthwhile to acquire the complex information needed for comparative lifecycle pricing.

A second factor undermining Kodak's claim that supracompetitive prices in the service market lead to ruinous losses in equipment sales is the cost to current owners of switching to a different product. See Areeda & Turner, at ¶519a. If the cost of switching is high, consumers who already have purchased the equipment, and are thus "locked in," will tolerate some level of service-price increases before changing equipment brands. Under this scenario, a seller profitably could maintain supracompetitive prices in the aftermarket if the switching costs were high relative to the increase in service prices, and the number of locked-in customers were high relative to the number of new purchasers.

Moreover, if the seller can price-discriminate between its locked-in customers and potential new customers, this strategy is even more likely to prove profitable. The seller could simply charge new customers below-marginal cost on the equipment and recoup the charges in service, or offer packages with life-time warranties or long-term service agreements that are not available to locked-in customers.

Respondents have offered evidence that the heavy initial outlay for Kodak equipment, combined with the required support material that works only with Kodak equipment, makes switching costs very high for existing Kodak customers. And Kodak's own evidence confirms that it varies the package price of equipment/parts/service for different customers.

In sum, there is a question of fact whether information costs and switching costs foil the simple assumption that the equipment and service markets act as pure complements to one another.[24]

We conclude, then, that Kodak has failed to demonstrate that respondents' inference of market power in the service and parts markets is unreasonable, and that, consequently, Kodak is entitled to summary judgment. It is clearly reasonable to infer that Kodak has market power to raise prices and drive out competition in the aftermarkets, since respondents offer direct evidence that Kodak did so. It is also plausible, as discussed above, to infer that Kodak chose to gain immediate profits by exerting that market power where locked-in customers, high information costs, and discriminatory pricing limited and perhaps eliminated any long-term loss. Viewing the evidence in the light most favorable to respondents, their allegations of market power "mak[e] . . . economic sense." Cf. *Matsushita*.

Nor are we persuaded by Kodak's contention that it is entitled to a legal presumption on the lack of market power because, as in *Matsushita*, there is a significant risk of deterring procompetitive conduct. Plaintiffs in *Matsushita* attempted to prove the antitrust conspiracy "through evidence of rebates and other price-cutting activities." Because cutting prices to increase business is "the very essence of competition," the Court was concerned that mistaken inferences would be "especially costly," and would "chill the very conduct the antitrust laws are designed to protect." See also *Mon-*

---

24. The dissent disagrees based on its hypothetical case of a tie between equipment and service. "The only thing lacking" to bring this case within the hypothetical case, states the dissent, "is concrete evidence that the restrictive parts policy was . . . generally known." But the dissent's "only thing lacking" is the crucial thing lacking — evidence. Whether a tie between parts and service should be treated identically to a tie between equipment and service, as the dissent and Kodak argue, depends on whether the equipment market prevents the exertion of market power in the parts market. Far from being "anomalous," requiring Kodak to provide evidence on this factual question is completely consistent with our prior precedent.

santo (permitting inference of concerted action would "deter or penalize perfectly legitimate conduct"). But the facts in this case are just the opposite. The alleged conduct — higher service prices and market foreclosure — is facially anticompetitive and exactly the harm that antitrust laws aim to prevent. In this situation, *Matsushita* does not create any presumption in favor of summary judgment for the defendant.

Kodak contends that, despite the appearance of anticompetitiveness, its behavior actually favors competition because its ability to pursue innovative marketing plans will allow it to compete more effectively in the equipment market. A pricing strategy based on lower equipment prices and higher aftermarket prices could enhance equipment sales by making it easier for the buyer to finance the initial purchase. It is undisputed that competition is enhanced when a firm is able to offer various marketing options, including bundling of support and maintenance service with the sale of equipment. Nor do such actions run afoul of the antitrust laws. But the procompetitive effect of the specific conduct challenged here, eliminating all consumer parts and service options, is far less clear.[28]

We need not decide whether Kodak's behavior has any procompetitive effects and, if so, whether they outweigh the anticompetitive effects. We note only that Kodak's service and parts policy is simply not one that appears always or almost always to enhance competition, and therefore to warrant a legal presumption without any evidence of its actual economic impact. In this case, when we weigh the risk of deterring procompetitive behavior by proceeding to trial against the risk that illegal behavior go unpunished, the balance tips against summary judgment. Cf. *Matsushita.* . . .[29]

---

28. Two of the largest consumers of service and parts contend that they are worse off when the equipment manufacturer also controls service and parts. See Brief for State Farm Mutual Automobile Insurance Company et al. as Amici Curiae; Brief for State of Ohio et al. as Amici Curiae.

29. The dissent urges a radical departure in this Court's antitrust law. It argues that because Kodak has only an "inherent" monopoly in parts for its equipment, the antitrust laws do not apply to its efforts to expand that power into other markets. The dissent's proposal to grant per se immunity to manufacturers competing in the service market would exempt a vast and growing sector of the economy from antitrust laws. Leaving aside the question whether the Court has the authority to make such a policy decision, there is no support for it in our jurisprudence or the evidence in this case.

Even assuming, despite the absence of any proof from the dissent, that all manufacturers possess some inherent market power in the parts market, it is not clear why that should immunize them from the antitrust laws in another market. The Court has held many times that power gained through some natural and legal advantage such as a patent, copyright, or business acumen can give rise to liability if "a seller exploits his dominant position in one market to expand his empire into

III

Respondents also claim that they have presented genuine issues for trial as to whether Kodak has monopolized or attempted to monopolize the service and parts markets in violation of §2 of the Sherman Act. "The offense of monopoly under §2 of the Sherman Act has two elements: (1) the possession of monopoly power in the relevant market and (2) the willful acquisition or maintenance of that power as distinguished from growth or development as a consequence of a superior product, business acumen, or historic accident." *Grinnell.*

A

The existence of the first element, possession of monopoly power, is easily resolved. As had been noted, respondents have presented a triable claim that service and parts are separate markets, and that Kodak has the "power to control prices or exclude competition" in service and parts. *Cellophane.* Monopoly power under §2 requires, of course, something greater than market power under §1. See *Fortner I,* 394 U.S., at 502. Respondents' evidence that

the next." Times-Picayune Publishing Co. v. United States, 345 U.S. 594, 611 (1953); see, e.g., *Northern Pacific*; United States v. Paramount Pictures; Leitch Mfg. Co. v. Barber Co., 302 U.S. 458, 463 (1938). Moreover, on the occasions when the Court has considered tying in derivative aftermarkets by manufacturers, it has not adopted any exception to the usual antitrust analysis, treating derivative aftermarkets as it has every other separate market. See *International Salt*; *IBM*; United Shoe Machinery Co. v. United States, 258 U.S. 451 (1922). Our past decisions are reason enough to reject the dissent's proposal. See Patterson v. McLean Credit Union, 491 U.S. 164, 172-173 (1989) ("Considerations of stare decisis have special force in the area of statutory interpretation, for here, unlike in the context of constitutional interpretation, the legislative power is implicated, and Congress remains free to alter what we have done").

Nor does the record in this case support the dissent's proposed exemption for aftermarkets. The dissent urges its exemption because the tie here "does not permit the manufacturer to project power over a class of consumers distinct from that which it is already able to exploit (and fully) without the inconvenience of the tie." Beyond the dissent's obvious difficulty in explaining why Kodak would adopt this expensive tying policy if it could achieve the same profits more conveniently through some other means, respondents offer an alternative theory, supported by the record, that suggests Kodak is able to exploit some customers who in the absence of the tie would be protected from increases in parts prices by knowledgeable customers.

At bottom, whatever the ultimate merits of the dissent's theory, at this point it is mere conjecture. Neither Kodak nor the dissent have provided any evidence refuting respondents' theory of forced unwanted purchases at higher prices and price discrimination. While it may be, as the dissent predicts, that the equipment market will prevent any harms to consumers in the aftermarkets, the dissent never makes plain why the Court should accept that theory on faith rather than requiring the usual evidence needed to win a summary judgment motion.

Kodak controls nearly 100% of the parts market and 80% to 95% of the service market, with no readily available substitutes, is, however, sufficient to survive summary judgment under the more stringent monopoly standard of §2. . . .

Kodak also contends that, as a matter of law, a single brand of a product or service can never be a relevant market under the Sherman Act. We disagree. The relevant market for antitrust purposes is determined by the choices available to Kodak equipment owners. See *Jefferson Parish*. Because service and parts for Kodak equipment are not interchangeable with other manufacturers' service and parts, the relevant market from the Kodak-equipment owner's perspective is composed of only those companies that service Kodak machines. See *Cellophane* (the "market is composed of products that have reasonable interchangeability"). This Court's prior cases support the proposition that in some instances one brand of a product can constitute a separate market. See *NCAA*; International Boxing Club of New York, Inc. v. United States, 358 U.S. 242, 249-252 (1959); *IBM*. The proper market definition in this case can be determined only after a factual inquiry into the "commercial realities" faced by consumers. *Grinnell*.

B

The second element of a §2 claim is the use of monopoly power "to foreclose competition, to gain a competitive advantage, or to destroy a competitor." *Griffith*. If Kodak adopted its parts and service policies as part of a scheme of willful acquisition or maintenance of monopoly power, it will have violated §2. *Grinnell*; *Alcoa*; *Aspen*.[32]

As recounted at length above, respondents have presented evidence that Kodak took exclusionary action to maintain its parts monopoly and used its control over parts to strengthen its monopoly share of the Kodak service market. Liability turns, then, on whether "valid business reasons" can explain Kodak's actions. *Aspen*; *Alcoa*. Kodak contends that it has three valid business justifications for its actions: "(1) to promote interbrand equipment competition by allowing Kodak to stress the quality of its service; (2) to improve asset management by reducing Kodak's inventory costs; and (3) to prevent ISOs from free riding on Kodak's capital investment in equipment, parts and service." Factual questions exist,

---

32. It is true that as a general matter a firm can refuse to deal with its competitors. But such a right is not absolute; it exists only if there are legitimate competitive reasons for the refusal. See *Aspen*.

however, about the validity and sufficiency of each claimed justification, making summary judgment inappropriate.

Kodak first asserts that by preventing customers from using ISOs, "it [can] best maintain high quality service for its sophisticated equipment" and avoid being "blamed for an equipment malfunction, even if the problem is the result of improper diagnosis, maintenance or repair by an ISO." Respondents have offered evidence that ISOs provide quality service and are preferred by some Kodak equipment owners. This is sufficient to raise a genuine issue of fact. See *IBM* (rejecting IBM's claim that it had to control the cards used in its machines to avoid "injury to the reputation of the machines and the good will of" IBM in the absence of proof that other companies could not make quality cards); *International Salt* (rejecting International Salt's claim that it had to control the supply of salt to protect its leased machines in the absence of proof that competitors could not supply salt of equal quality).

Moreover, there are other reasons to question Kodak's proffered motive of commitment to quality service; its quality justification appears inconsistent with its thesis that consumers are knowledgeable enough to lifecycle price, and its self-service policy. Kodak claims the exclusive-service contract is warranted because customers would otherwise blame Kodak equipment for breakdowns resulting from inferior ISO service. Thus, Kodak simultaneously claims that its customers are sophisticated enough to make complex and subtle lifecycle-pricing decisions, and yet too obtuse to distinguish which breakdowns are due to bad equipment and which are due to bad service. Kodak has failed to offer any reason why informational sophistication should be present in one circumstance and absent in the other. In addition, because self-service customers are just as likely as others to blame Kodak equipment for breakdowns resulting from (their own) inferior service, Kodak's willingness to allow self-service casts doubt on its quality claim. In sum, we agree with the Court of Appeals that respondents "have presented evidence from which a reasonable trier of fact could conclude that Kodak's first reason is pretextual."

There is also a triable issue of fact on Kodak's second justification — controlling inventory costs. As respondents argue, Kodak's actions appear inconsistent with any need to control inventory costs. Presumably, the inventory of parts needed to repair Kodak machines turns only on breakdown rates, and those rates should be the same whether Kodak or ISOs perform the repair. More importantly, the justification fails to explain respondents' evidence that Kodak forced OEMs, equipment owners, and parts brokers not to sell parts to ISOs, actions that would have no effect on Kodak's inventory costs.

Nor does Kodak's final justification entitle it to summary judgment on respondents' §2 claim. Kodak claims that its policies prevent ISOs from "exploit[ing] the investment Kodak has made in product development, manufacturing and equipment sales in order to take away Kodak's service revenues." Kodak does not dispute that respondents invest substantially in the service market, with training of repair workers and investment in parts inventory. Instead, according to Kodak, the ISOs are free-riding because they have failed to enter the equipment and parts markets. This understanding of free-riding has no support in our caselaw.[33] To the contrary, as the Court of Appeals noted, one of the evils proscribed by the antitrust laws is the creation of entry barriers to potential competitors by requiring them to enter two markets simultaneously. *Jefferson Parish*; *Fortner*. . . .

IV

In the end, of course, Kodak's arguments may prove to be correct. It may be that its parts, service, and equipment are components of one unified market, or that the equipment market does discipline the aftermarkets so that all three are priced competitively overall, or that any anticompetitive effects of Kodak's behavior are outweighed by its competitive effects. But we cannot reach these conclusions as a matter of law on a record this sparse. Accordingly, the judgment of the Court of Appeals denying summary judgment is affirmed.

[Justices Scalia, O'Connor, and Thomas dissented. The dissent focused on the defendant's lack of power in the interbrand market for its equipment. It argued that the market power requirements for the per se rule against tying and for the offense of monopolization needed a more substantial threshold than the majority offered, for "the sort of power condemned by the Court today is possessed by every manufacturer of durable goods with distinctive parts." It further noted: (1) Had Kodak included a lifetime parts and service warranty with all original equipment or had it "consistently pursued

33. Kodak claims that both *Sylvania* and *Monsanto* support its free-rider argument. Neither is applicable. In both *Sylvania* and *Monsanto* the Court accepted free-riding as a justification because without restrictions a manufacturer would not be able to induce competent and aggressive retailers to make the kind of investment of capital and labor necessary to distribute the product. In *Sylvania* the relevant market level was retail sale of televisions and in *Monsanto* retail sales of herbicides. Some retailers were investing in those markets; others were not, relying, instead, on the investment of the other retailers. To be applicable to this case, the ISOs would have to be relying on Kodak's investment in the service market; that, however, is not Kodak's argument.

an announced policy of limiting parts sales in the manner alleged in this case, so that customers bought with the knowledge that after-market support could be obtained only from Kodak," the tying product would have been the original equipment and the plaintiff's claim would have failed. (2) "As implemented, the Kodak arrangement challenged in this case may have implicated truth-in-advertising or other consumer protection concerns, but those concerns do not alone suggest an antitrust prohibition." That there may be some irrational consumers is not sufficient reason to apply antitrust doctrine. Informational deficiencies of the sort that might be present in this case are commonplace and do not suggest the "exercise of market power in any sense relevant to the antitrust laws." (3) The leverage from the parts market to the service market is of no practical consequence "because of the perfect identity between the consumers in each of the subject aftermarkets." "If Kodak desired to exploit its circumstantial power over this wretched class by pressing them up to the point where the cost to each consumer of switching equipment brands barely exceeded the cost of retaining Kodak equipment and remaining subject to Kodak's abusive practices, it could plainly do so without the inconvenience of a tie, through supracompetitive parts pricing alone." (4) "In the absence of interbrand power, a manufacturer's bundling of aftermarket products may serve a multitude of legitimate purposes. . . ." The interbrand market will punish the manufacturer for intrabrand restraints not in consumers' interest.][82]

443. (a) In tying cases, the plaintiff must show market power. What, precisely, must the defendant have the power to do?[83] How is this question answered in *Kodak?*

(b) The Court expresses concern for buyers who may not take into account costs over the entire life-cycle of buying a Kodak machine. Is this "antitrust injury"?[84] Would it be an antitrust violation if Kodak, instead of tying, designed machines that more frequently required new parts, which consumers would have to buy from Kodak at inflated prices?[85]

---

82. On remand, a jury found a §2 violation and determined damages to be $23.9 million. Image Technical Service v. Eastman Kodak Co. (N.D. Cal. 1995), discussed in 69 Antitr. & Trade Reg. Rep. 441 (1995).

83. One answer would be the power to raise prices, as in monopolization and horizontal merger cases. Consider how the answer in the tying cases differs, if at all, from that in these other contexts.

84. See ¶146.

85. For an economic analysis of *Kodak,* see C. Shapiro, Aftermarkets and Consumer Welfare: Making Sense of *Kodak,* 63 Antitr. L.J. 483 (1995).

(c) Given that (under the Court's theory) Kodak has a monopoly over the supply of its unique parts, why does it tie parts to service rather than simply raising the prices on its parts but making them available to anyone?

(d) Can you reconcile the Court's acceptance of the plaintiff's theory at the time of Kodak's motion for summary judgment with the Court's reversal of the jury verdict in *Brooke Group*?

4C. EXCLUSIVE DEALING

444. Introduction. This section, like the preceding one, concerns arrangements under which a buyer does not use or deal in the goods of the seller's competitors. When, for example, one buys a seller's cans exclusively in order to obtain that seller's can closing machine, we speak of tying arrangements. If the buyer agrees to take its can requirements exclusively from one seller without regard to any other (or tying) product, we usually speak of exclusive dealing contracts. Although a tying agreement is a particular kind of exclusive dealing, the latter term usually refers only to nontying exclusive dealing arrangements. In all events, both invoke Clayton Act §3 and its concern with coercing buyers and foreclosing a rival's opportunities.[1]

445. Partial requirements contracts. Before examining the application of §3's effects clause to exclusive dealing arrangements, consider again the initial coverage of §3. When is there a condition "that the lessee or purchaser . . . shall not use or deal in the goods . . . of a competitor . . . of the lessor or seller"? Consider an agreement binding a dealer to purchase 80 percent of its requirements from a particular seller. Or suppose that the dealer is obliged to purchase a definite quantity that, upon inquiry, amounts to 80 percent of its average annual purchases. If Clayton Act policy embraces this situation, the language of §3 need not preclude its application. Compare ¶426. At the other extreme, consider the buyer needing only one unit of a product. Any contract with any seller necessarily entails that other sellers no longer have the opportunity to deal with that buyer. Both sorts of examples illustrate the

---

1. For an analysis of the effects of exclusive dealing, see IV P. Areeda & D. Turner, Antitrust Law, ch. 10A (1980; Supp. 1996), where this subject is developed in the context of vertical mergers. See generally M. Katz, Vertical Contractual Relations, in 1 Handbook of Industrial Organization, (R. Schmalensee & R. Willig eds. 1989); T. Krattenmaker & S. Salop, Anticompetitive Exclusion: Raising Rivals' Costs to Achieve Power over Price, 96 Yale L.J. 209 (1986).

rather obvious point, which emerges in the cases, that foreclosure is a matter of degree.

446. Objects of exclusive dealing. The purposes of exclusive dealing arrangements are too varied for comprehensive statement. But several recurrent and broadly suggestive reasons will alert the student to some of the interests at stake. This Paragraph does not seek to weigh these interests but only to develop some possible functions of exclusive dealing.[2]

(a) *Preempting outlets.* Exclusive dealing arrangements might foreclose the market opportunities of the seller's competitors. For example, if all food canners agree to buy exclusively from giant canmaker Alpha, there would be no customers left for Alpha's rivals. Alternatively, if a firm with a very large market share enters into exclusive arrangements with dealers, other firms might find it difficult to distribute their product because their sales are not alone sufficient to support separate dealerships. In addition, such foreclosure can have an important effect on potential entrants, who would be deterred by the absence of selling prospects. These examples invite two further points. First, while all buyers might conceivably choose to make each purchase from the large firm in any event, that possibility does not dissolve our concern with the contractual limitation on their future freedom of choice. Second, if only a portion of the buyers were covered, it would not have the same obvious impact on rivals, but it might limit their opportunities to some degree. Whether the resultant "clog on competition" is socially serious is another question, depending on the extent to which rivals are deprived of opportunities necessary to permit them to operate at an efficient scale and in sufficient numbers to guarantee workable competition.[3]

(b) *Assured markets or prices for sellers and buyers.*[4] When dealers or users with fairly stable requirements agree to buy exclusively from Beta, it is assured of fairly stable sales and can therefore plan its production and distribution operations with greater precision and efficiency. If total industry sales fluctuate widely, reserving the sta-

2. An exclusive dealing arrangement might have horizontal implications where a manufacturer abandons its own direct distribution after agreeing to supply the requirements of a distributor who is a potential entrant into manufacturing.
3. See P. Aghion & P. Bolton, Contracts as a Barrier to Entry, 77 Am. Econ. Rev. 388 (1987); K. Spier & M. Whinston, On the Efficiency of Privately Stipulated Damages for Breach of Contract: Entry Barriers, Reliance and Renegotiation, 26 Rand J. Econ. 180 (1995).
4. See P. Bolton & M. Whinston, Incomplete Contracts, Vertical Integration, and Supply Assurance, 60 Rev. Econ. Studies 121 (1993).

ble customers for Beta tends to aggravate the instability confronting its rivals and may increase their costs. But whether Beta will thereby gain an unfair advantage over them is unclear. The stable buyers may require Beta to share its cost savings with them as a condition to conferring the benefit on Beta rather than on Beta's competitors. In any event, Beta cannot expand its market share without entering the more volatile sector.

Buyers also may seek greater certainty. Some may wish a fixed price for a key portion of the year. Others may wish assurance of regular and frequent deliveries obviating the expense and trouble of maintaining inventories. A seller's promise satisfying any of these buyers would not itself raise a §3 issue, but the seller's price for such promises may be an undertaking by the buyer to purchase its requirements from that seller. The seller, to be sure, might have the alternative of charging a higher price in return for these promises, but contracts that guarantee price with no indication of quantity invite disaster. One who promises a specific future price for a potentially unlimited quantity will be ruined if market prices rise above the contract price; the buyer could purchase unlimited quantities, reselling what it does not need and pocketing the difference. And if the market price is lower than the contract price, the buyer would turn to the market, buying nothing under the contract. The fixed price contract thus usually specifies either a certain quantity (for example, a contract to deliver a thousand bushels of wheat next July, at $5 per bushel) or some standard (such as the buyer's own requirements).

(c) *Promoting dealer loyalty.* One of the most persistent impulses toward exclusive dealing is to make the dealer dependent on the manufacturer, thus giving the latter the exclusive benefit of the dealer's energies. Such a motivation is similar to some of those suggested in connection with intrabrand vertical restraints in ¶403j and ¶408b. When a dealer's fortunes depend entirely on the success of a single product or a single brand, it will promote that product or brand intensively. Dealers handling color television sets (or one brand) exclusively, for example, might promote and service televisions (or that brand) more intensively than would general appliance dealers. Similarly, manufacturers who promote a product and develop a brand image at great expense may be concerned that dealers will divert prospective customers to other brands if exclusive dealerships are not employed. Of course, a manufacturer's private interest is not necessarily the same as the social interest. The exclusive arrangement might impair competition in ways explored above. And even if it does not clog competition substantially, more intensive selling efforts might not be welcomed by those who feel that promotional and selling efforts are generally excessive and wasteful in our economy.[5] As with intrabrand vertical restraints, competing brands may engage in substantial expenditures that largely shuffle customers from one seller to another. The potential procompetitive benefits of exclusive dealing seem strongest in at least two cases.[6] First, exclusive dealing and the resulting dealer loyalty might facilitate the entry of a new brand and thereby intensify market competition. Second, a relatively weak brand might survive and compete only when there are dealers dedicated to it exclusively.

These issues raise two additional questions. (1) Is exclusive dealing necessary to achieve the asserted end? While dealers might dedicate themselves to the brand without being contractually bound to do so, this seems unlikely for a weak brand. Alternatively, the manufacturer might use a sales quota or incentive plan to induce dealer efforts in its behalf. Most obviously, one may reduce the wholesale price or offer commissions for additional sales. Of course, such alternatives also might foreclose competing sellers, although probably not as much. (2) If a brand remains weak over an extended period, would its dependence on exclusive arrangements for its continued survival mean that resources are being "artificially" diverted from more appropriate uses? Perhaps we may conclude that (i) as long as a dealer earns a sufficient return, involvement with the weak brand is economically justified, but (ii) without being pushed by the exclusive arrangement to promote the weak brand, dealers might be content to handle established brands, with the result that market competition would be less.

Related issues of dealer loyalty arise when the manufacturer-dealer relationship is more complex than that of seller-buyer. The manufacturer may finance, train, or advise the dealer, supply or maintain the retail premises, and assist in various ways in the operation of the dealership. Such a manufacturer would resent having these efforts benefit its competitors — a free-rider problem analogous to that described in ¶403b. To guard against that danger, it may insist that the dealer agree to handle its brand exclusively. Even without such an agreement, the dealer and manufacturer may think of themselves as engaged in a joint undertaking to compete with other brands. Thus, exclusive dealing can approach vertical integration, and some arrangements are referred to as "integration by

---

5. See ¶116.

6. One can imagine several other cases — of uncertain occurrence — in which the intensification of dealer selling effort would serve the public interest. If, for example, a relatively small community could support either one multibrand dealer or several smaller single-brand dealers, exclusive dealing would effect greater retail competition for sales of that product in that community.

contract." Many of the effects explored in the rest of this Paragraph suggest a similar interpretation.[7]

(d) *Other cost savings.* Exclusive dealing contracts may eliminate or reduce selling expenses. For example, transactions may be fewer in number and larger in volume. Such savings of economic resources are generally desirable, especially when the cost savings are offered to buyers who choose voluntarily whether or not to take lower prices and exclusive dealing. It is not clear, however, the extent to which such savings generally depend upon a contractual limitation on the buyer's or seller's ability to turn elsewhere if circumstances change. For example, a simple pattern of regular, repeated buying from the same seller, in large quantities, would tend to produce similar savings.

STANDARD OIL CO. OF CALIFORNIA (STANDARD STATIONS) v. UNITED STATES
337 U.S. 293 (1949)

Justice FRANKFURTER. . . . The Standard Oil Company of California . . . sells through its own service stations, to the operators of independent service stations, and to industrial users. It is the largest seller of gasoline in the [Western] area. In 1946 its combined sales amounted to 23% of the total taxable gallonage sold there in that year: sales by company-owned service stations constituted 6.8% of the total, sales under exclusive dealing contracts with independent service stations, 6.7% of the total; the remainder were sales to industrial users. Retail service-station sales by Standard's six leading competitors absorbed 42.5% of the total taxable gallonage; the remaining retail sales were divided between more than seventy small companies. It is undisputed that Standard's major competitors employ similar exclusive dealing arrangements. In 1948 only 1.6% of retail outlets were what is known as "split-pump" stations, that is, sold the gasoline of more than one supplier.

Exclusive supply contracts with Standard had been entered into, as of March 12, 1947, by the operators of 5,937 independent stations, or 16% of the retail gasoline outlets in the Western area. . . . Some outlets are covered by more than one contract so that in all about 8,000 exclusive supply contracts are here in issue. . . . Of the written agreements, 2,712 were for varying specified terms; the rest were effective from year to year but terminable "at the end of the first 6 months of any contract year, or at the end of any such year,

---

7. Recall from ¶423 how the analysis of many effects of tying arrangements paralleled that applicable to vertical integration, discussed in ¶321.

by giving to the other at least 30 days prior thereto written notice...." ...

The District Court held that the requirement of showing an actual or potential lessening of competition or a tendency to establish monopoly was adequately met by proof that the contracts covered "a substantial number of outlets and a substantial amount of products, whether considered comparatively or not." Given such quantitative substantiality, the substantial lessening of competition — so the court reasoned — is an automatic result, for the very existence of such contracts denies dealers opportunity to deal in the products of competing suppliers and excludes suppliers from access to the outlets controlled by those dealers. Having adopted this standard of proof, the court excluded as immaterial testimony bearing on "the commercial merits or demerits of the present system as contrasted with a system which prevailed prior to its establishment and which would prevail if the court declared the present arrangement [invalid]." The court likewise deemed it unnecessary to make findings, on the basis of evidence that was admitted, whether the number of Standard's competitors had increased or decreased since the inauguration of the requirements-contract system, whether the number of their dealers had increased or decreased, and as to other matters which would have shed light on the comparative status of Standard and its competitors before and after the adoption of that system. . . .

[The Court discusses some of the earlier §3 cases which seemed to indicate the importance of "some sort of showing as to the actual or probable economic consequences"; such power cannot, as a matter of law, be attributed to the defendant. If the test of the *International Salt* case is to be applied, however,] the showing that Standard's requirements contracts affected a gross business of $58,000,000 comprising 6.7% of the total in the area goes far toward supporting the inference that competition has been or probably will be substantially lessened.[8]

In favor of confining the standard laid down by the *International Salt* case to tying agreements, important economic differences may be noted. Tying agreements serve hardly any purpose beyond the suppression of competition. The justification most often advanced in their defense — the protection of the good will of the manufacturer of the tying device — fails in the usual situation because

---

8. It may be noted in passing that the exclusive supply provisions for tires, tubes, batteries, and other accessories which are a part of some of Standard's contracts with dealers who have also agreed to purchase their requirements of petroleum products should perhaps be considered, as a matter of classification, tying rather than requirements agreements.

specification of the type and quality of the product to be used in connection with the tying device is protection enough. If the manufacturer's brand of the tied product is in fact superior to that of competitors, the buyer will presumably choose it anyway. The only situation, indeed, in which the protection of good will may necessitate the use of tying clauses is where specifications for a substitute would be so detailed that they could not practicably be supplied. In the usual case only the prospect of reducing competition would persuade a seller to adopt such a contract and only his control of the supply of the tying device, whether conferred by patent monopoly or otherwise obtained, could induce a buyer to enter one.... The existence of market control of the tying device, therefore, affords a strong foundation for the presumption that it has been or probably will be used to limit competition in the tied product also.

Requirements contracts, on the other hand, may well be of economic advantage to buyers as well as to sellers, and thus indirectly of advantage to the consuming public. In the case of the buyer, they may assure supply, afford protection against rises in price, enable long-term planning on the basis of known costs,[9] and obviate the expense and risk of storage in the quantity necessary for a commodity having a fluctuating demand. From the seller's point of view, requirements contracts may make possible the substantial reduction of selling expenses, give protection against price fluctuations, and — of particular advantage to a newcomer to the field to whom it is important to know what capital expenditures are justified — offer the possibility of a predictable market.... They may be useful, moreover, to a seller trying to establish a foothold against the counterattacks of entrenched competitors.... Since these advantages of requirements contracts may often be sufficient to account for their use, the coverage by such contracts of a substantial amount of business affords a weaker basis for the inference that competition may be lessened than would similar coverage by tying clauses, especially where use of the latter is combined with market control of the tying device. A patent, moreover, although in fact there may be many competing substitutes for the patented article, is at least prima facie evidence of such control. And so we could not dispose of this case merely by citing *International Salt.*

Thus, even though the qualifying clause of §3 is appended without distinction of terms equally to the prohibition of tying clauses and of requirements contracts, pertinent considerations support, certainly as a matter of economic reasoning, varying standards as to

9. This advantage is not conferred by Standard's contracts, each of which provides that the price to be paid by the dealer is to be the "Company's posted price to its dealers generally at time and place of delivery."

each for the proof necessary to fulfill the conditions of that clause. If this distinction were accepted, various tests of the economic usefulness or restrictive effect of requirements contracts would become relevant. Among them would be evidence that competition has flourished despite use of the contracts, and under this test much of the evidence tendered by appellant in this case would be important.... Likewise bearing on whether or not the contracts were being used to suppress competition, would be the conformity of the length of their term to the reasonable requirements of the field of commerce in which they were used.... Still another test would be the status of the defendant as a struggling newcomer or an established competitor. Perhaps most important, however, would be the defendant's degree of market control, for the greater the dominance of his position, the stronger the inference that an important factor in attaining and maintaining that position has been the use of requirements contracts to stifle competition rather than to serve legitimate economic needs....

Yet serious difficulties would attend the attempt to apply these tests. We may assume, as did the court below, that no improvement of Standard's competitive position has coincided with the period during which the requirements-contract system of distribution has been in effect. We may assume further that the duration of the contracts is not excessive and that Standard does not by itself dominate the market. But Standard was a major competitor when the present system was adopted, and it is possible that its position would have deteriorated but for the adoption of that system. When it is remembered that all the other major suppliers have also been using requirements contracts, and when it is noted that the relative share of the business which fell to each has remained about the same during the period of their use, it would not be farfetched to infer that their effect has been to enable the established suppliers individually to maintain their own standing and at the same time collectively, even though not collusively, to prevent a late arrival from wresting away more than an insignificant portion of the market. If, indeed, this were a result of the system, it would seem unimportant that a short-run by-product of stability may have been greater efficiency and lower costs, for it is the theory of the antitrust laws that the long-run advantage of the community depends upon the removal of restraints upon competition....

Moreover, to demand that bare inference be supported by evidence as to what would have happened but for the adoption of the practice that was in fact adopted or to require firm prediction of an increase of competition as a probable result of ordering the abandonment of the practice, would be a standard of proof if not virtually impossible to meet, at least most ill-suited for ascertainment by courts.[13] Before the system of requirements contracts was instituted, Standard sold gasoline through independent service-station operators as its agents, and it might revert to this system if the judgment below were sustained. Or it might, as opportunity presented itself, add service stations now operated independently to the number managed by its subsidiary, Standard Stations, Inc. From the point of view of maintaining or extending competitive advantage, either of these alternatives would be just as effective as the use of requirements contracts, although of course insofar as they resulted in a tendency to monopoly they might encounter the antimonopoly provisions of the Sherman Act. . . . As appellant points out, dealers might order petroleum products in quantities sufficient to meet their estimated needs for the period during which requirements contracts are now effective, and even that would foreclose competition to some degree. So long as these diverse ways of restricting competition remain open, therefore, there can be no conclusive proof that the use of requirements contracts has actually reduced competition below the level which it would otherwise have reached or maintained.

We are dealing here with a particular form of agreement specified by §3 and not with different arrangements, by way of integration or otherwise, that may tend to lessen competition. To interpret that section as requiring proof that competition has actually diminished would make its very explicitness a means of conferring immunity upon the practices which it singles out. Congress has authoritatively determined that those practices are detrimental where their effect may be to lessen competition. It has not left at large for determination in each case the ultimate demands of the "public interest." . . . Though it may be that such an alternative to the present system as buying out independent dealers and making them dependent employees of Standard Stations, Inc., would be a greater detriment to the public interest than perpetuation of the system, this is an issue, like the choice between greater efficiency and freer competition, that has not been submitted to our decision. We are faced, not with a broadly phrased expression of general policy, but merely a broadly phrased qualification of an otherwise narrowly directed statutory provision.

13. The dual system of enforcement provided for by the Clayton Act must have contemplated standards of proof capable of administration by the courts as well as by the Federal Trade Commission and other designated agencies. . . . Our interpretation of the Act, therefore, should recognize that an appraisal of economic data which might be practicable if only the latter were faced with the task may be quite otherwise for judges unequipped for it either by experience or by the availability of skilled assistance.

In this connection it is significant that the qualifying language was not added until after the House and Senate bills reached Conference. The conferees responsible for adding that language were at pains, in answering protestations that the qualifying clause seriously weakened the section, to disclaim any intention seriously to augment the burden of proof to be sustained in establishing violation of it. It seems hardly likely that, having with one hand set up an express prohibition against a practice thought to be beyond the reach of the Sherman Act, Congress meant, with the other hand, to reestablish the necessity of meeting the same tests of detriment to the public interest as that Act has been interpreted as requiring. Yet the economic investigation which appellant would have us require is of the same broad scope as was adumbrated with reference to unreasonable restraints of trade in *Chicago Board of Trade.* To insist upon such an investigation would be to stultify the force of Congress' declaration that requirements contracts are to be prohibited wherever their effect "may be" to substantially lessen competition. If in fact it is economically desirable for service stations to confine themselves to the sale of the petroleum products of a single supplier, they will continue to do so though not bound by contract, and if in fact it is important to retail dealers to assure the supply of their requirements by obtaining the commitment of a single supplier to fulfill them, competition for their patronage should enable them to insist upon such an arrangement without binding them to refrain from looking elsewhere.

We conclude, therefore, that the qualifying clause of §3 is satisfied by proof that competition has been foreclosed in a substantial share of the line of commerce affected. It cannot be gainsaid that observance by a dealer of his requirements contract with Standard does effectively foreclose whatever opportunity there might be for competing suppliers to attract his patronage, and it is clear that the affected proportion of retail sales of petroleum products is substantial. In view of the widespread adoption of such contracts by Standard's competitors and the availability of alternative ways of obtaining an assured market, evidence that competitive activity has not actually declined is inconclusive. Standard's use of the contracts creates just such a potential clog on competition as it was the purpose of §3 to remove wherever, were it to become actual, it would impede a substantial amount of competitive activity.

Since the decree below is sustained by our interpretation of §3 of the Clayton Act, we need not go on to consider whether it might also be sustained by §1 of the Sherman Act. . . .

Affirmed.

[Chief Justice Vinson and Justices Jackson and Burton dissented: The courts are obliged by the statute to hear evidence and make a judgment about competitive effects. If legality must be determined without evidence, they would find the arrangements lawful, apparently on the ground that exclusive dealing is a necessary or appropriate quid pro quo for defendant's relieving service stations of the need to maintain substantial inventories.

Justice Douglas feared that the Court's ruling would encourage refiners to replace independent small-business service stations with their own outlets and employees. He assumed that the Court would unwisely hold such vertical integration lawful. On that assumption, he dissented.]

447. (a) Does the *Standard Stations* Court rely primarily on the substantiality of the dollar volume of business foreclosed? Does the Court, in effect, condemn any foreclosure that is not de minimis? What reasons does it give for its approach with regard to proof of competitive impact?

(b) The government had alleged that the challenged arrangements created substantial barriers to entry by new oil producers and to expansion by existing smaller producers. Choice retail outlets were effectively preempted; dealers would be unlikely to market new or lesser brands if they had to give up a major brand to do it, and thus newcomers could not be sure of operating at an efficient scale. (1) Are these possibilities inherent in exclusive dealing arrangements favoring substantial sellers? (2) How are they related to the dollar volume or percentage share of the trade covered by the exclusive dealing agreement?

(c) What is the Court's rule? Assess the reasons offered in support of it.

448. Proposition: *Standard Stations* misconceived the issue before it; the so-called exclusive dealing agreement is nothing less than a tying arrangement by which Standard exploits a dealer's desire to sell some Standard gas to force the dealer to forgo other brands. Do you agree? Consider the following.

(a) Upsilon Company is the only manufacturer of a full line of motorcycles. It faces no competition in its heavy duty motorcycle but significant competition in the lighter weight variety. It sells only to dealers who agree to handle Upsilon products exclusively. Is the arrangement lawful or unlawful?

(b) Essence Oil Company leases a valuable site to Smith on condition that Smith sell Essence oil exclusively at this site. Can you distinguish *Northern Pacific*?

(c) Compare *Standard Stations* with the preceding cases. Do you accept the proposition stated at the outset of this Paragraph? Why or why not?

(d) How did the Court distinguish exclusive dealing and tying cases? How did it deal with the fact that the same statutory language applies to both?

449. *Federal Trade Commission v. Motion Picture Advertising Service Co.*, 344 U.S. 392, 393 (1953). The Supreme Court found a Sherman Act violation, and therefore a violation of §5 of the Federal Trade Commission Act, where defendant "and three other companies . . . together had exclusive arrangements for advertising films with approximately three-fourths of the total number of theatres in the United States which display advertising films for compensation. Respondent had exclusive contracts with almost 40 percent of the theatres in the area where it operates." Justice Frankfurter, who wrote *Standard Stations*, dissented because the majority had aggregated the exclusive contracts of competitors to reach a share of 75 percent. In the absence of a conspiracy, he would not aggregate the shares to determine a large foreclosure. He distinguished *Standard Stations* on the grounds that Standard was the largest seller in its market and had the power to coerce dealers; by contrast, some theaters insisted on exclusivity in handling an ancillary aspect of their business.

450. Twenty-five competitors have roughly equal market shares. In 1950, three of these companies individually began to distribute only through exclusive dealers. Full trials of all the relevant facts resulted in determinations, affirmed by the Supreme Court, that these arrangements offended none of the antitrust laws. Over the intervening years, 17 other companies have come to use only exclusive dealers. The twenty-first firm, the Hardcase Company, now agrees with dealers that they will handle its products exclusively.

(a) The government alleges that Hardcase's action forecloses a substantial share of the market in violation of Clayton Act §3. What is the degree of foreclosure — 84 percent, 20 percent (i.e., 4 of the 20 percent remaining prior to Hardcase's actions), or 4 percent? What result?[8] Can you reconcile Justice Frankfurter's *Motion Picture Advertising Services* dissent with his *Standard Stations* opinion? What would those who concurred in *Jefferson Parish* say about this situation?

(b) Given what happened afterward, were the 1950 decisions wrong? Assuming that the 1950 foreclosures were not troublesome standing alone, should they have been condemned nevertheless on the ground that they might initiate a trend that would result in a troublesome degree of foreclosure?

8. Compare the discussion of incipiency in *Brown Shoe*, reproduced in Ch. 5D.

451. *Tampa Electric Co. v. Nashville Coal Co.*, 365 U.S. 320,
327-329, 333 (1961). Tampa Electric planned to build a new generating plant, which was, unlike all other power plants in the area, to
be designed to burn coal. It contracted with Nashville Coal to
supply its coal requirements for 20 years. When Nashville declined
to perform, Tampa sued to have the contract declared valid, but
Nashville was successful in winning summary judgment on the
ground that the undisputed facts showed a violation of Clayton Act
§3. The Supreme Court reversed.

> [A]n exclusive-dealing arrangement . . . does not violate the sec-
> tion unless the court believes it probable that performance of the
> contract will foreclose competition in a substantial share of the line
> of commerce affected. Following the guidelines of earlier decisions,
> certain considerations must be taken. *First*, the line of commerce . . .
> involved must be determined. . . . *Second*, the area of effective compe-
> tition in the known line of commerce must be charted by careful
> selection of the market area in which the seller operates, and to
> which the purchaser can practicably turn for supplies. . . . *Third*, and
> last, the competition foreclosed by the contract must be found to
> constitute a substantial share of the relevant market. That is to say,
> the opportunities for other traders to enter into or remain in that
> market must be significantly limited. . . . To determine substantiality
> in a given case, it is necessary to weigh the probable effect of the
> contract on the relevant area of effective competition, taking into
> account the relative strength of the parties, the proportionate vol-
> ume of commerce involved in relation to the total volume of com-
> merce in the relevant market area, and the probable immediate and
> future effects which pre-emption of that share of the market might
> have on effective competition therein. It follows that a mere showing
> that the contract itself involves a substantial number of dollars is
> ordinarily of little consequence.

The relevant geographic market was deemed to be the Appalachian coal area, where the share foreclosed by the requirements
contract was less than 1 percent, rather than a region limited to
portions of Georgia and Florida, where the contract covered 18
percent of the tonnage sold. The Court explained its selection as
reflecting the region in which sellers compete for the buyers' business. A share "less than 1%, is, conservatively speaking, quite insubstantial." Courts have not declared requirements contracts to be
illegal per se. This case, unlike prior cases, did not involve a seller
with a dominant position in the market, an industrywide practice of
relying upon exclusive contracts, or a tying arrangement. The Court
also noted the possible economic benefits of such contracts, such as
assuring the buyer of its supply and reducing sales expenses of the
seller, as well as protecting it against price fluctuations.

(a) Does *Tampa Electric* properly measure the foreclosure resulting from the requirements contract? What is the relevant market?
Why?

(b) Does *Tampa Electric* mean that very small foreclosures are not
substantial? Does it mean anything more?

(c) To what did the Court look in order to gauge the probable
effect on competition? Appraise each factor noted by the Court.
The opinion speaks of the relative strength of the firms. How is this
relevant to the Clayton Act?

(d) Is *Tampa Electric* faithful to *Standard Stations?* How would you
state the teaching of *Standard Stations* in the light of *Motion Picture
Advertising Services* and *Tampa Electric?*[9]

452. Healthsource, a health maintenance organization, functions as both a provider of care and as an insurer. Healthsource
uses contracts with 40 percent of the region's doctors to provide
care for its customers. These contracts are exclusive, forbidding
doctors from providing care under other health plans. Is this a
violation? Does it matter whether the contracts can be canceled on
180 days' notice? 30 days' notice?[10]

453. Nu Company manufactures a multivitamin and mineral
food supplement that it distributes through 80,000 independent

9. See Magnus Petro. Co. v. Skelly Oil Co., 599 F.2d 196 (7th Cir.), cert. denied,
444 U.S. 916 (1979)(reversing jury verdict for plaintiff failing to define market;
industry appeared competitive); Dillon Mat. Handling v. Albion Indus., 567 F.2d
1299 (5th Cir.), cert. denied, 439 U.S. 832 (1978)(jury verdict for plaintiff set
aside; failure to establish market effect; also, no exclusive dealing condition, agreement, or understanding); United States v. Dairymen, 1983 Trade Cas. ¶65651
(W.D. Ky.), aff'd, 758 F.2d 654 (6th Cir.), cert. denied, 474 U.S. 822 (1985) (one-
year exclusive dealing contracts unlawful where imposed by defendant having 60%
market share); American Passage Media Corp. v. Cass Communications, 1985
Trade Cas. ¶66358 (W.D. Wash.), 750 F.2d 1470 (9th Cir. 1985)(preliminary
injunction against exclusive contracts with many college newspapers where defendant sells more than 80% of national advertising, not all through exclusive arrangements, to such newspapers); United States v. Standard Oil Co. (Cal.), 362 F.
Supp. 1331 (N.D. Cal.), aff'd mem., 412 U.S. 924 (1973)(long-term requirements
contracts with American Samoa's three main users unlawful).

10. See U.S. Healthcare v. Healthsource, 986 F.2d 589 (1st Cir. 1993). The court
noted that, although the optional plan might not necessarily be considered an
exclusive dealing arrangement, the arrangement could still be unreasonable as a
restraint of trade. The court remarked that while 180 days might be problematic,
the 30-day version would be close to a de minimis constraint. Also, compare the
Justice Department and Federal Trade Commission's 1996 Statements of Antitrust
Enforcement Policy in Health Care, discussed in ¶223, which provide a safety zone
(indicating that the government will not make a challenge absent extraordinary
circumstances) for exclusive physician network joint ventures that involve no more
than 20 percent of the physicians in the relevant geographic market.

contractors who buy from Nu and sell to the public on a door-to-door basis. Each distributor agrees not to deal in the goods of any Nu competitor and not to solicit Nu customers for any such competitor within two years of terminating relations with Nu. Nu sales in 1958 accounted for 61 percent of direct house-to-house sales of vitamin concentrates and 8 percent of retail sales of vitamin concentrates sold through all types of outlets.

(a) Has Nu violated Clayton Act §3?[11]

(b) Assuming that the described arrangement is unlawful, would the result be different in each of the following situations? (1) Nu gives each distributor a two-week training course on how to sell the vitamin concentrate. (2) The distributors contract to serve as Nu's agents and subject to Nu's directions. (3) Nu finances the distributors' samples, automobiles, and other operating costs on exceedingly favorable terms.

454. Omega Office Machines Corporation sells its popular equipment to independent office supply dealers. Omega's catalogue states its conviction that consumers do not receive adequate advice and service from dealers who fail to specialize in one manufacturer's equipment. Omega has therefore made clear that it will not supply those dealers discovered by its own independent investigations to be selling competing lines. Omega's sales account for 15 percent of national sales of such equipment although its machinery is the sole equipment available in some communities which can support only one dealer.

(a) Would the government prevail against Omega if there were express agreements by some dealers that they would not sell competing machines?

(b) Would the government prevail on the facts stated?

(c) If either government suit could succeed, would a competitor of Omega also prevail?

(d) If a competitor could prevail over Omega in either situation, would a dealer cut off by Omega for selling competing goods also prevail?

(e) Would your answers differ if Omega merely encouraged dealers to handle its line exclusively? (1) If most dealers did not in fact

---

11. Compare Mytinger & Casselberry v. FTC, 301 F.2d 534 (D.C. Cir. 1962) (violation where the contracts preempted 80,700 outlets throughout the United States and thereby controlled a substantial share of commerce), with H.F. & S. Co. v. American Standard, 336 F. Supp. 110 (D. Kan. 1972) (no violation when the market was highly competitive and there was no dangerous probability of foreclosure — though defendant's market share was 75 percent of the local sales), and Rural Gas Serv., 59 F.T.C. 912 (1961).

handle competing lines? (2) If some dealers who had handled competing lines had been dropped by Omega?

455. Review the opinion in *Barry Wright* from Chapter 3A, particularly sections *B* and *C* dealing with the alleged requirements contract and the noncancellation clauses.

(a) Do these provisions violate Clayton Act §3? How does the foreclosure in *Barry Wright* compare with that in *Standard Stations*?

(b) Why did the *Barry Wright* court approve the challenged arrangement? Is its reasoning persuasive? What facts distinguish that case from *Standard Stations*?

Chapter 5

Mergers: Horizontal, Vertical, and Conglomerate[1]

500. Prologue. Antitrust analysis customarily uses the word "merger" to describe a permanent union of previously separate enterprises. Whether the union is effected by an exchange of stock or an acquisition of assets was relevant to the applicability of Clayton Act §7 as originally enacted, but it is not usually significant today. Generally, we may speak interchangeably of mergers, consolidations, acquisitions, amalgamations, or other forms of union that replace independent decisionmaking institutions with a unified system of control.

Mergers are usually classified according to the market relationship of the merging parties: horizontal mergers involve parties that are competitors; vertical mergers, parties that are or could become buyer and seller; and conglomerate mergers, every other case. Conglomerate mergers themselves can be categorized in a similar manner: Some of them may have effects resembling those of horizontal or vertical mergers, while others do not. These three categories are the particular subjects of Sections C, D, and E. These topics are preceded in Section A by a discussion of concentration and the motives for mergers. Section B then provides the history of the relevant statutes, Sherman Act §1 and Clayton Act §7.

5A. COMPETITIVE EFFECTS

501. Size and diversification. A horizontal merger eliminates competition between the merging parties, and a vertical merger may have the foreclosure effects suggested in ¶321 and Chapter 4. In addition to these conventional concerns, there are some more elusive varieties of competitive effects that may result from horizontal, vertical, and conglomerate mergers. The effects considered here might be loosely grouped into three overlapping categories: (1) less-competitive market structure, (2) increased opportunity for

1. See IV-V P. Areeda & D. Turner, Antitrust Law (1980; Supp. 1996).

anticompetitive behavior, and (3) desirable and undesirable
"efficiencies." Many of the details are left to the cases and problems. Here, we briefly consider levels of concentration in the economy and some of the many reasons firms merge.

502. The extent of concentration.[2] A horizontal merger eliminates a competitor and concentrates the market power of two firms
in the hands of one. This concentration process is, of course, the
classic merger problem. Vertical and conglomerate mergers also
may be feared because of their potential impact on concentration
in the long run. Although these basic issues are treated in later
sections, it is helpful at this point to have some idea of the actual
degree of market concentration in different industries.

Within a product or industry class, market concentration historically has been expressed as the share of industry shipments accounted for by the largest four firms. Such "concentration ratios,"
however, reveal a limited amount of information because they do
not describe the relative power of the individual firms within the
top group or the distribution or character of the other firms. Thus,
it has become common to make reference, in addition or instead,
to the Herfindahl-Hirschman Index (HHI), which takes all of these
factors into account.[3] Indeed, the government's horizontal merger
guidelines, discussed below, make use of the HHI rather than traditional concentration ratios.[4]

Many market concentration measurements are based on data
compiled by the U.S. Census Bureau. Using these statistics introduces additional distortions because the census classifications are
not necessarily defined in a meaningful way from the perspective of
economic theory and antitrust concerns. Products that are not close
substitutes are sometimes included in the same industry, while
products that are close substitutes are sometimes separated into
different industries.[5] Additionally, the Bureau's national data cannot reveal effects within separable geographic markets. Nevertheless, it is useful to examine the Bureau's data because they are

2. For additional data and discussion, see F.M. Scherer & D. Ross, Industrial
Market Structure and Economic Performance, ch. 3 (3d ed. 1990).
3. As will be explained in the government merger guidelines, in Ch. 5D, the
HHI is the sum of the squares, expressed in percentages, of the individual market
shares of all of the participants. For example, if there are 10 firms, each with a 10
percent share, each firm contributes 10^2, or 100, to the index, for a total HHI of
1000.
4. Excerpts from the government merger guidelines appear in Chs. 3B and 5D.
5. The Bureau uses a system of categories to classify industrial firms and products. The broadest categories are very comprehensive (e.g., industrial machinery
and equipment); such categories are identified by two-digit numbers (e.g., 35) and
are thus known as two-digit industries. Each such industry is further subdivided
into many four-digit industries (e.g., construction and mining machinery, 3531).

TABLE 1
Concentration of Selected Manufacturing Industries

Industry	Value of 1987 Shipments (billions)	Market Concentration	
		1987 4-firm Concentration (1967 in parentheses)	1987 HHI[7]
Cigarettes	17.4	92(81)	undisclosed
Motor Vehicles and Car Bodies	133.3	90(92)	undisclosed
Automotive Stampings	15.3	59(n/a)	1,183
Men's and Boys' Trousers and Slacks	6.0	57(n/a)	1,264
Blast Furnaces and Steel Mills	15.8	44(48)	607
Electronic Computers	33.6	43(n/a)	693
Semiconductors and Related Devices	19.8	40(47)	539
Broadwoven Fabric Mills: Manmade Fiber, Silk	8.0	35(46)	430
Paper Mills	18.9	33(26)	432
Petroleum Refining	118.2	32(n/a)	435
Industrial Organic Chemicals (other)	41.8	31(45)	376
Bottled and Canned Soft Drinks	21.8	30(13)	332
Search and Navigation Equipment	36.3	29(n/a)	401
Leather Tanning and Finishing	2.2	28(20)	323
Wood Household Furniture	8.0	20(n/a)	150
Sawmills and Planing Mills, General	17.4	15(11)	84
Sporting and Athletic Goods (other)	5.1	13(27)	94
Ready-mixed Concrete	13.0	8(6)	25
Commercial Printing, Lithographic	32.8	7(5)	22
Plastics Products (other)	33.8	6(n/a)	16

Source: U.S. Bureau of the Census, Concentration Ratios in Manufacturing, in 1987 Census of Manufactures, Table 4 (1992).

available and so widely used. (In merger filings and litigated merger cases, the parties are free to and do, in fact, use other sources, often based on data compiled for a particular industry by a trade organization or government agency.)

Table 1 provides the four-firm concentration ratios and the HHI for 20 illustrative industries.[6] As indicated by Table 1, the simple concentration ratios correlate fairly well with the HHI. Although

6. Table 1 includes the largest manufacturing industries, measured by value of shipments, for each of the 20 SIC product categories. Note that Table 1 is confined to manufacturing industries (which is all that is covered by the relevant census data), whereas much of the economy consists of other activities, notably agriculture, mining, construction, wholesale and retail trade, finance, insurance, real estate, communications, transportation, and government employment.

7. Herfindahl-Hirschman Index for 50 largest companies. (Very small firms add a trivial amount to the HHI.)

comparisons over time are not entirely reliable, there seems to be little significant movement in market concentration within industry groups as well as within product classes.

503.   Merger reasons.[8] Here we note the most common reasons for mergers. Some are clearly contrary to antitrust policy while some may serve it. Many are neutral. In any event, motivation may bear on a particular merger's effects.

(a) *Anticompetitive reasons.* During the late 1880s and the early years of this century, multiple acquisitions were often made within a single market in order to achieve monopoly. The characteristic acquisition of the 1920s was also horizontal and often with the hope of creating or strengthening an oligopoly. The merger movement of the 1940s was more diverse, and the largest mergers of the 1960s were conglomerate in character, although many acquisitions concerned a related product (product extension merger) or the same product in a different geographic market (market extension merger). The mergers of the 1980s, often the result of hostile takeovers, involved some horizontal combinations among the largest firms in an industry and some purely conglomerate combinations. To the extent that the parties propose to impair competition, antitrust policy would happily obstruct them. Many of the horizontal and vertical issues are already quite familiar from earlier chapters, and additional fears associated with all large mergers will be explored in Chapter 5E, which addresses conglomerate acquisitions.

(b) *Easier expansion or entry.* The acquiring company might be buying needed personnel, facilities, or patents. It is undoubtedly faster to buy a going business than to build one from the ground up. And where the acquiring firm is in a different line of work, merger is cheaper than independent entry with its costs of starting up, recruiting and teaching management and other personnel, advertising, and creating the necessary distribution facilities. It may be especially cheaper to acquire a going enterprise than to invent around critical patents or to obtain independent access to scarce personnel or other resources.

Speed and economy for the acquirer, however, are not in themselves beneficial to society. Merely transferring the ownership of an activity from one firm to another is, at best, socially neutral and may, of course, be harmful when it eliminates a significant competitor or otherwise threatens competition. Such a transfer would be socially beneficial where it induces or facilitates competition that would not otherwise occur. For example, an acquirer who would

8. See Scherer & Ross, note 2, ch. 5; W.K. Viscusi, J. Vernon & J. Harrington, Economics of Regulation and Antitrust, ch. 7 (2d ed. 1995).

not have entered independently may revitalize and expand the acquired firm into a more vigorous competitor. But standing alone, the private advantage in buying rather than building is not a gain for the economy.

(c) *Operating efficiencies and scale economies.* Reduced use of resources may be the object of the merging parties. These have already been discussed in ¶119. But several points are worth restating.

First, plant-level economies would on occasion be achieved through merger in the short run, but only to the extent the larger entity will be able to construct larger plants in the future than would have been possible if the firms had remained independent.

Second, integrating two different companies into one can produce inefficiencies both at the plant and the upper management levels, as many believe is demonstrated by certain railroad mergers of the 1960s that led to bankruptcy and by many conglomerate spinoffs in subsequent decades.

Third, the large and diversified firm may have a larger internal pool of retained earnings on which to draw. Its divisions might thus be able to obtain capital more cheaply than on the general capital market because the internal transfer requires fewer lawyers, investigators, and other transaction costs. The multiproduct firm might also allocate capital more effectively internally — although not necessarily more cheaply to the borrowing division — than the single-product firm would.

Fourth, marketing economies may be present although they are particularly difficult to identify or appraise with assurance in most instances.

Fifth, many facilities or services requiring relatively "large" scale can in fact be purchased at low unit costs on the open market. For example, the larger firm might provide its own internal legal or computing services; the smaller firm can hire these services as necessary at comparable costs. Of course, this will not necessarily be true of all management services or of all necessary research and development.

(d) *Financial gains without new efficiencies.* A merger might benefit the parties without reducing resource use. First is the appearance of growth. Second are unused tax shields. For example, a firm might have a tax loss carryforward, an investment credit exceeding taxable income, or more depreciation than income. It may acquire or be acquired by another firm with offsetting income and thus effect a saving in federal income tax.

Third is unused capital. Some mergers may simply be an outlet for unused capital, including profits that the firm chooses neither to pay to its owners nor to hold as portfolio investments. Or an outsider might take over the corporation with surplus capital, highly liquid resources, large cash flow relative to net earnings, or unused borrowing power, especially when the company's stock does not fully reflect its asset values.

Fourth is diversification. Where the merging firms occupy somewhat different markets, the merger may achieve for the parties the diversification of risk. One might, to be sure, ask whether such diversification is a significant social benefit. Each market operation should, of course, be judged on its own merits and pay its own "true" cost. To minimize risk through diversification, however, does not imply the subsidization of inefficient operations unable to pay their own way. Business firms do not usually set out to lose money or continue operations less profitable than available alternatives. In addition there is a social gain from minimizing disruptions. By contrast, diversification within the enterprise is not the only, or even the most important, way to reduce risks borne by investors, who can usually diversify their investments across several enterprises involved in widely differing activities.

(e) *Management goals.* Merger may serve the interest of a corporation's management more than it serves its shareholders. The selling management might want to be part of a larger, more diversified, and perhaps stronger enterprise. The acquiring management might be seeking growth for its own sake and be willing to sacrifice profits to achieve it. Management prestige may depend substantially on the size of the establishment, apart from the firm's profit rate. Firm size, moreover, might bring increased emoluments and perquisites to management even if it does not bring increased profits to the shareholders. Indeed, there is evidence that many previous acquisitions of active conglomerates have not fared particularly well in profitability and in the end acquirers have chosen to divest previously acquired subsidiaries;[9] from this,

---

9. See D. Ravenscraft & F.M. Scherer, Mergers, Sell-Offs, and Economic Efficiency (1987). One compilation of the evidence has found that

> [m]ergers led to a reduction in the profitability of the merging firms and a slowdown in their rate of growth in size.... This deterioration in operating performance of the acquiring companies was also reflected in a deterioration in the relative performance of their common shares. Stockholders who purchased common shares in a firm making an acquisition one year before the acquisition and sold them three years thereafter did either no better or significantly worse than shareholders holding reasonable alternative shares over the same time periods.

D. Mueller, The United States, 1962-1972, in The Determinants and Effects of Mergers: An International Comparison 297 (D. Mueller ed. 1980). See also A. Hughes, D. Mueller & A. Singh, Competition Policy in the 1980s: The Implications of the International Merger Wave, in id. at 324 (noting lack of profitability in seven countries studied). For the view that concentration and mergers are best (and almost exclusively) explained on grounds of efficiency, see Y. Brozen, Concentration, Mergers, and Public Policy 356-357 (1982).

some have argued that such active acquirers sacrificed profits for growth.[10]

(f) *Substituting better management.* A merger might succeed in transferring a business to better hands. Such new blood could produce more efficient operations and more vigorous competition. Some mergers are so motivated. An acquirer might see great gains in taking over a company from bad management that has failed to exploit available profit opportunities. This explanation is offered for many corporate takeovers, where incumbent management has been unwilling to give up control voluntarily. Or the owners of a firm, whether in decline or not, may decide they are not ready to meet the future with existing arrangements. Or a retiring owner-entrepreneur may lack confidence in successors within the firm. To transfer economic activities into better hands on these accounts is socially beneficial.

A similar point might be made about managerial control and accountability. Management is supposed to be accountable to shareholders who ultimately control the enterprise. There clearly is some such accountability notwithstanding the dispersal of ownership in publicly held corporations. But dispersed shareholders do not exercise the degree of supervision exerted by the top holding company management of a large conglomerate. Indeed, even the threat of a takeover by the large conglomerate may exert pressure on management to act as if it were more closely supervised by its shareholders.

(g) *Defensive mergers.*[11] Several kinds of defensive merger deserve separate mention. First, a firm may lack, or fear that it lacks, either sufficient scale to be efficient or sufficient resistance to rivals' unfair practices or advantages. Second, a firm may merge with a favored party in order to prevent an uncongenial takeover. Third, and most general, is ease of exit. The retiring entrepreneur may prefer the security of portfolio diversification. Or a firm may be impelled toward merger by the fact or fear of relative decline. The actual or prospective difficulties might be in management, research, marketing, capital, labor, or anything else that affects a firm's fortunes. Sale of the company as a going business may cause minimum disruption to owners, managers, suppliers, customers, employees, and communities. To facilitate exit when it is desired may indeed facilitate entry because the likelihood of exit with minimum loss or maximum gain reduces the risk and increases the attractiveness of entering a market.

10. D. Mueller, A Cross-National Comparison of Results, in The Determinants and Effects of Mergers, note 9, at 313-314.
11. See D. Greer, Acquiring in Order to Avoid Acquisition, 31 Antitr. Bull. 155 (1986).

(h) *The net reckoning.* This Paragraph has indicated some of the motivations for mergers. Some seem to serve only the parties' interests. Others serve society as well. Perhaps all can be said to reflect the social interest in a free market in stocks, assets, and whole companies. The market is the means by which economic units transfer resources from less to more efficient hands, for their mutual benefit. This is not to say that every exchange necessarily benefits society at large. But it is to say that the process of free exchange can facilitate entry via merger, effect graceful exit and thereby make original entry somewhat more likely, and generally contribute to more efficient production and distribution.

It is also true, however, that free exchange might lessen competition among significant competitors, creating market power, preempting supplies or markets to the detriment of competition, or threatening the economy or the polity in other ways. On that account, antitrust law does not allow completely unconstrained exchange.

The important point is that neither social harm nor social benefit will be precisely identifiable or quantifiable in every case. Yet, the lawmaker or interpreter must take care to remember the general benefits of a free market in capital assets. It would be wrong to suppose that nothing would be lost to society by, for example, presumptively condemning all mergers. Nor can one avoid the problem by permitting only those mergers with provable effects of social benefit. One cannot, for example, quantify in any particular case the general benefit of takeovers in disciplining remote corporate managers. To be sure, any loss from a presumptive condemnation might be outweighed by the gains of doing so. These concerns will now be pursued.

5B. INTRODUCTION TO MERGER LAW

504. Early Sherman Act cases. The starting point for the Sherman Act's legal attack on the great trusts and combines was the classic manifestation of anticompetitive conduct, the substantial horizontal merger.

(a) *Northern Securities Co. v. United States,* 193 U.S. 197 (1904). The Supreme Court faced the unification of the Great Northern Railroad and the Northern Pacific Railroad, two parallel railroads across the northern tier of the western United States. In holding this union to be a combination in restraint of trade forbidden by §1, the Court examined neither the degree to which the carriers' routes actually competed nor the competition of other railroads.

Comment. In one important respect the *Northern Securities* decision might be seen as a historical anomaly. The Court supported its result only by relying on the notion, from which it had not yet extricated itself, that the §1 prohibition of "every" combination restraining trade allowed no exceptions — except that a restraint tolerated at common law would not be considered a §1 restraint at all. The Court also tried for a while to exclude indirect restraints. Then the 1911 *Standard Oil* decision announced what has come to be known as the rule of reason: §1 condemns only unreasonable restraints (with the understanding that some restraints are inherently unreasonable). Although the formation of the Standard Oil Company through mergers was itself condemned, that case also exhibited predatory practices, subjective monopolistic purpose, and resulting monopoly power. Nevertheless, subsequent railroad mergers were handled in much the same manner as the *Northern Securities* case.

(b) *United States v. Union Pacific Railroad Co.,* 226 U.S. 61, 88 (1912). The Union Pacific railroad operated from Omaha and Kansas City to Denver and Ogden (Utah) and to Seattle and Portland. Union Pacific trains also operated from Ogden to San Francisco over Central Pacific lines and east from Omaha to Chicago via various connecting lines. Union Pacific acquired 46 percent of the stock of the Southern Pacific, which operated from Portland to San Francisco, Los Angeles, El Paso, Galveston, and New Orleans. The Southern Pacific operated ships between New Orleans and New York and also controlled the Central Pacific railroad. Unlike *Northern Securities,* these railroads were not parallel. Although they were competitive transcontinental systems (or parts thereof), there were several other transcontinental systems. Held: "The consolidation of two great competing systems" is an unlawful restraint of trade "in destroying or greatly abridging the ... competition theretofore existing." While "this competitive traffic ... was a comparatively small part of the sum total of all" their traffic, it was nevertheless "large in volume, amounting to many millions of dollars."

Comment. Although the Court followed a similar approach in *Southern Pacific,*[1] the railroad cases were not typical. Thousands of mergers were never attacked, and some notable combinations survived challenge.

(c) *United States v. United States Steel Corp.,* 251 U.S. 417 (1920). United States Steel Corp. was the product of mergers of previously independent steel companies that had an 80 to 95 percent market share of some products. Its overall share of iron and steel products, however, had declined to 40 percent at the time of the suit. Al-

---

1. United States v. Southern Pacific Co., 259 U.S. 214 (1922).

though the mergers were undertaken with the intent of gaining monopoly control over the industry, the Court absolved the steel company of §1 and §2 violations. The Court believed that the company had not achieved its purpose and had subsequently abandoned it.[2]

(d) *United States v. Columbia Steel Co.*, 334 U.S. 495, 510, 525, 537 (1948). The Court rejected the government's Sherman Act challenge to the acquisition of Consolidated (C) by U.S. Steel (USS), which was the largest producer of steel ingot and rolled steel in the nation. USS also fabricated and sold certain steel fabrications in competition with C. Although the Court accepted the finding that their shares in the western fabrication market adopted by the Court were 13 and 11 percent, respectively, it seemed to doubt the significance of those numbers in view of national competition and a substantial growth trend for western fabrications and therefore found no unreasonable trade restraint.

The merger was also vertical because C purchased rolled steel (mainly in the form of "shapes and plates") from such producers as USS. The Court first declared that "vertical integration, as such, without more, cannot be held violative of the Sherman Act." Nor did the merger unreasonably foreclose the selling opportunities of rival producers of rolled steel, for C's purchases accounted for only 3 percent of that market.[3] To the Court, the merger seemed motivated by the normal business purpose of securing an outlet for USS's planned increase in rolled steel capacity. The four dissenting Justices found this purpose impermissible, for "competition is never more irrevocably eliminated than by buying the customer for whose business the industry has been competing."

Comment. The Justices were seldom farther apart than in this case. On the vertical issue, the dissenters were apparently ready to condemn a vertical merger foreclosing only a small market share on the ground that it permitted USS to gain control of C's sales for which it previously had to compete. On the horizontal issue, the Court did not succeed in explaining the reasonableness of a combined 24 percent market share in favor of the largest firm in an industry not noted for competition. This victory for the merging parties was used to show the need for tougher antimerger standards and new legislation. To many observers, it was another case in which a court "mistakenly" allowed the creation or reinforcement

2. See also ¶303d.

3. Although C purchased 13 percent of the "shapes and plates" used in the western market, the Court refused to limit the market to that particular form of rolled steel because of evidence that any foreclosed sellers of rolled steel "can make other products interchangeably with shapes and plates."

of anticompetitive oligopoly. The impulse to avoid such "mistakes" may help explain the Supreme Court's hostility to mergers during the 1960s.

CLAYTON ACT §7

[Original 1914 language deleted or replaced by the 1950 or 1980 amendments is bracketed; language added by the 1950 or 1980 amendments is italicized.][4]

No [corporation] *person* engaged in commerce *or in any activity affecting commerce* shall acquire, directly or indirectly, the whole or any part of the stock or other share capital *and no* [*corporation*] *person subject to the jurisdiction of the Federal Trade Commission shall acquire the whole or any part of the assets* of another [corporation] *person* engaged also in commerce *or in any activity affecting commerce,* where *in any line of commerce or in any activity affecting commerce in any section of the country,* the effect of such acquisition may be *substantially* to [substantially] lessen competition [between the corporation whose stock is so acquired and the corporation making the acquisition, or to restrain such commerce in any section or community], or to tend to create a monopoly [of any line of commerce]. . . .

505. Legislative history of amended §7. (a) *Brown Shoe Co. v. United States,* 370 U.S. 294, 312-323 (1962). The following discussion of the legislative history of §7, as amended in 1950, is taken from the majority opinion in the first major case applying the revised statute.

As enacted in 1914, §7 of the original Clayton Act prohibited the acquisition by one corporation of the *stock* of another corporation when such acquisition would result in a substantial lessening of competition *between the acquiring and the acquired* companies, or tend to create a monopoly in any line of commerce. The Act did not, by its explicit terms, or as construed by this Court, bar the acquisition by one corporation of the *assets* of another. Nor did it appear to preclude the acquisition of stock in any corporation other than a direct competitor. Although proponents of the 1950 amendments to the Act suggested that the terminology employed in these provisions was the result of accident or an unawareness that the acquisition of assets could be as inimical to competition as stock acquisition, a review of the legislative history of the original Clayton Act fails to support such views. The possibility of asset acquisition was discussed,

---

4. The 1950 amendment substantively changed the statute, while the 1980 amendment merely expanded "corporation" to "person" and "commerce" to "any activity affecting commerce."

but was not considered important to an Act then conceived to be directed primarily at the development of holding companies and at the secret acquisition of competitors through the purchase of all or parts of such competitors' stock.

It was, however, not long before the Federal Trade Commission recognized deficiencies in the Act as first enacted. Its Annual Reports frequently suggested amendments, principally along two lines: first, to "plug the loophole" exempting asset acquisitions from coverage under the Act, and second, to require companies proposing a merger to give the Commission prior notification of their plans. The Final Report of the Temporary National Economic Committee also recommended changes focusing on these two proposals. Hearings were held on some bills incorporating either or both of these changes but, prior to the amendments adopted in 1950, none reached the floor of Congress for plenary consideration. Although the bill that was eventually to become amended §7 was confined to embracing within the Act's terms the acquisition of assets as well as stock, in the course of the hearings conducted in both the Eightieth and Eighty-first Congresses, a more far-reaching examination of the purposes and provisions of §7 was undertaken. A review of the legislative history of these amendments provides no unmistakably clear indication of the precise standards the Congress wished the Federal Trade Commission and the courts to apply in judging the legality of particular mergers. However, sufficient expressions of a consistent point of view may be found in the hearings, committee reports of both the House and Senate and in floor debate to provide those charged with enforcing the Act with a usable frame of reference within which to evaluate any given merger.

The dominant theme pervading congressional consideration of the 1950 amendments was a fear of what was considered to be a rising tide of economic concentration in the American economy. Apprehension in this regard was bolstered by the publication in 1948 of the Federal Trade Commission's study on corporate mergers. Statistics from this and other current studies were cited as evidence of the danger to the American economy in unchecked corporate expansions through mergers.[27] Other considerations cited in support of the bill were the desirability of retaining "local control" over industry and the protection of small businesses. Throughout the recorded discussion may be found examples of Congress' fear not only of accelerated concentration of economic power on economic

---

27. .... The House Report on the amendments summarized its view of the situation:

> That the current merger movement [during the years 1940-1947] has had a significant effect on the economy is clearly revealed by the fact that the asset value of the companies which have disappeared through mergers amounts to 5.2 billion dollars, or no less than 5.5 per cent of the total assets of all manufacturing corporations — a significant segment of the economy to be swallowed up in such a short period of time. H.R. Rep. No. 1191, 81st Cong., 1st Sess. 3.

grounds, but also of the threat to other values a trend toward concentration was thought to pose.

What were some of the factors, relevant to a judgment as to the validity of a given merger, specifically discussed by Congress in redrafting §7?

First, there is no doubt that Congress did wish to "plug the loophole" and to include within the coverage of the Act the acquisition of assets no less than the acquisition of stock.

Second, by the deletion of the "acquiring-acquired" language in the original text, it hoped to make plain that §7 applied not only to mergers between actual competitors, but also to vertical and conglomerate mergers whose effect may tend to lessen competition in any line of commerce in any section of the country.

Third, it is apparent that a keystone in the erection of a barrier to what Congress saw was the rising tide of economic concentration, was its provision of authority for arresting mergers at a time when the trend to a lessening of competition in a line of commerce was still in its incipiency. Congress saw the process of concentration in American business as a dynamic force; it sought to assure the Federal Trade Commission and the courts the power to brake this force at its outset and before it gathered momentum.[32]

Fourth, and closely related to the third, Congress rejected, as inappropriate to the the problem it sought to remedy, the application to §7 cases of the standards for judging the legality of business combinations adopted by the courts in dealing with cases arising under the Sherman Act, and which may have been applied to some early cases arising under original §7.[33]

32. That §7 of the Clayton Act was intended to reach incipient monopolies and trade restraints outside the scope of the Sherman Act was explicitly stated in the Senate Report on the original Act. S. Rep. No. 698, 63d Cong., 2d Sess. 1. See *du Pont [GM]*. This theme was reiterated in congressional consideration of the amendments adopted in 1950, and found expression in the final House and Senate Reports on the measure. H.R. Rep. No. 1191, 81st Cong., 1st Sess. 8 ("Acquisitions of stock or assets have a cumulative effect, and control of the market . . . may be achieved not in a single acquisition but as the result of a series of acquisitions. The bill is intended to permit intervention in such a cumulative process when the effect of an acquisition may be a significant reduction in the vigor of competition."). . . .

33. . . . The House Judiciary Committee's 1949 Report supported this concept unanimously although five of the nine members who had dissented two years earlier in H.R. Rep. No. 596 were still serving on the Committee. H.R. Rep. No. 1191, 81st Cong., 1st Sess. 7-8. The Senate Report was explicit:

The committee wish to make it clear that the bill is not intended to revert to the Sherman Act test. The intent here . . . is to cope with monopolistic tendencies in their incipiency and well before they have attained such effects as would justify a Sherman Act proceeding. . . . [The] various additions and deletions — some strengthening and others weakening the bill — are not conflicting in purpose and effect. They merely are different steps toward the same objective, namely, that of framing a bill which, though dropping portions of the so-called Clayton Act test that have no economic significance [the reference would appear to be primarily to the "acquiring-acquired" standard of the original Act], reaches far beyond the Sherman Act. S. Rep. No. 1775, 81st Cong., 2d Sess. 4-5.

Fifth, at the same time that it sought to create an effective tool for preventing all mergers having demonstrable anticompetitive effects, Congress recognized the stimulation to competition that might flow from particular mergers. When concern as to the Act's breadth was expressed, supporters of the amendments indicated that it would not impede, for example, a merger between two small companies to enable the combination to compete more effectively with larger corporations dominating the relevant market, nor a merger between a corporation which is financially healthy and a failing one which no longer can be a vital competitive factor in the market. The deletion of the word "community" in the original Act's description of the relevant geographic market is another illustration of Congress' desire to indicate that its concern was with the adverse effects of a given merger on competition only in an economically significant "section" of the country. Taken as a whole, the legislative history illuminates congressional concern with the protection of *competition*, not *competitors*, and its desire to restrain mergers only to the extent that such combinations may tend to lessen competition.

Sixth, Congress neither adopted nor rejected specifically any particular tests for measuring the relevant markets, either as defined in terms of product or in terms of geographic locus of competition, within which the anticompetitive effects of a merger were to be judged. Nor did it adopt a definition of the word "substantially," whether in quantitative terms of sales or assets or market shares or in designated qualitative terms, by which a merger's effects on competition were to be measured.[36]

---

36. The House Report on H.R. 2734 stated that two tests of illegality were included in the proposed Act: whether the merger substantially lessened competition or tended to create a monopoly. It stated that such effects could be perceived through findings, for example, that a whole or material part of the competitive activity of an enterprise, which had been a substantial factor in competition, had been eliminated; that the relative size of the acquiring corporation had increased to such a point that its advantage over competitors threatened to be "decisive"; that an "undue" number of competing enterprises had been eliminated; or that buyers and sellers in the relevant market had established relationships depriving their rivals of a fair opportunity to compete. H.R. Rep. No. 1191, 81st Cong., 1st Sess. 8. Each of these standards, couched in general language, reflects a conscious avoidance of exclusively mathematical tests even though the case of *Standard [Stations]*, said to have created a "quantitative substantiality" test for suits arising under §3 of the Clayton Act, was decided while Congress was considering H.R. 2734. Some discussion of the applicability of this test to §7 cases ensued, see, e.g., S. Hearings on H.R. 2734, at 31-32, 169-172; S. Rep. No. 1775, 81st Cong., 2d Sess. 21; 96 Cong. Rec. 16443, but this aspect of the *Standard [Stations]* decision was neither specifically endorsed nor impugned by the bill's supporters. However, the House Judiciary Committee's Report, issued two months after *Standard [Stations]* had been decided, remarked that the tests of illegality under the new Act were intended to be "similar to those which the courts have applied in interpreting the

Seventh, while providing no definitive quantitative or qualitative tests by which enforcement agencies could gauge the effects of a given merger to determine whether it may "substantially" lessen competition or tend toward monopoly, Congress indicated plainly that a merger had to be functionally viewed, in the context of its particular industry. That is, whether the consolidation was to take place in an industry that was fragmented rather than concentrated, that had seen a recent trend toward domination by a few leaders or had remained fairly consistent in its distribution of market shares among the participating companies, that had experienced easy access to markets by suppliers and easy access to suppliers by buyers or had witnessed foreclosure of business, that had witnessed the ready entry of new competition or the erection of barriers to prospective entrants, all were aspects, varying in importance with the merger under consideration, which would properly be taken into account.[38]

Eighth, Congress used the words "*may be* substantially to lessen competition" (emphasis supplied), to indicate that its concern was with probabilities, not certainties.[39] Statutes existed for dealing with clear-cut menaces to competition; no statute was sought for dealing with ephemeral possibilities. Mergers with a probable anticompetitive effect were to be proscribed by this Act.

---

same language as used in other sections of the Clayton Act." H.R. Rep. No. 1191, 81st Cong., 1st Sess. 8.

38. Subsequent to the adoption of the 1950 amendments, both the Federal Trade Commission and the courts have, in the light of Congress' expressed intent, recognized the relevance and importance of economic data that places any given merger under consideration within an industry framework almost inevitably unique in every case. Statistics reflecting the shares of the market controlled by the industry leaders and the parties to the merger are, of course, the primary index of power; but only a further examination of the particular market — its structure, history and probable future — can provide the appropriate setting for judging the probable anticompetitive effect of the merger....

39. In the course of both the Committee hearings and floor debate, attention was occasionally focused on the issue of whether "possible," "probable" or "certain" anticompetitive effects of a proposed merger would have to be proven to establish a violation of the Act. Language was quoted from prior decisions of the Court in antitrust cases in which each of these interpretations of the word "may" was suggested as appropriate.... The final Senate Report on the question was explicit on the point:

> The use of these words ["may be"] means that the bill, if enacted, would not apply to the mere possibility but only to the reasonable probability of the prescribed [sic] effect.... The words "may be" have been in section 7 of the Clayton Act since 1914. The concept of reasonable probability conveyed by these words is a necessary element in any statute which seeks to arrest restraints of trade in their incipiency and before they develop into full-fledged restraints violative of the Sherman Act. A requirement of certainty and actuality of injury to competition is incompatible with any effort to supplement the Sherman Act by reaching incipient restraints. S. Rep. No. 1775, 81st Cong., 2d Sess. 6....

(b) D. Bok, Section 7 of the Clayton Act and the Merging of Law and Economics, 74 Harv. L. Rev. 226, 234-237 (1960).[5]

One fortunate aspect of the legislative history is the singleness of mind with which most proponents of the bill defended their handiwork. From the committee reports, and still more from the debates, there emerges a common definition of the problem at hand, a common philosophy as to its import, and a common notion, on a very general plane, of what the new act could do about it. The bill was pushed through on the basis of certain fundamental assertions of fact which were repeatedly hammered home by the many legislators who spoke in its behalf. First, it was pointed out that concentration had reached very high levels in America — 445 corporations were said to own 51 per cent of the country's gross assets, and in many important industries the great bulk of the business lay in the hands of three or four firms. Second, stress was placed on the assertion that concentration was still increasing. Third, it was emphasized that mergers had traditionally played an important part in the process of concentration; in critical industries like steel, for example, much of the growth of the largest companies was attributed to mergers. The fourth basic premise was that the country was in the midst of a new wave of mergers in which little businesses were being absorbed in large numbers by big firms. In this way, competitive, small-business industries such as textiles were steadily being transformed by mergers into oligopolies. In the same vein, much was made of the fact that over 90 per cent of the 2,500 firms acquired from 1940 to 1947 had assets under five million dollars while 70 per cent of these firms were acquired by firms with assets of over five million. The last important point was that mergers continued to play an important role because the Congress which enacted the original section 7 had overlooked the possibility that acquisitions could be consummated by purchases of assets as well as by buying stock.

This situation was appraised in the same Jeffersonian, egalitarian fashion by almost all who spoke for the bill. Various legislators anticipated [the argument] that big business begets big labor unions.... In the minds of the congressmen, the growth of these large economic groups could lead only to increasing government control; freedom would corrode and the nation would drift into some form of totalitarianism. It was hardly a surprise, of course, to find a finger pointed at Adolf Hitler and Karl Marx, for they were no strangers to debates on antitrust legislation.... The ill effects of big business on initiative and individuality were forcefully described. There were arguments that concentration narrowed the opportunity to have one's own business, depressed local initiative and civic responsibility, and diminished the scope of entrepreneurship by forcing small businesses to become ever more subject to the dictates of large concerns.

To anyone used to the preoccupation of professors and administrators with the economic consequences of monopoly power, the curious aspect of the debates is the paucity of remarks having to do with the effects of concentration on prices, innovation, distribution, and efficiency. To be sure, there were allusions to the need for preserving competition. But competition appeared to possess a strong socio-political connotation which centered on the virtues of the small entrepreneur to an extent seldom duplicated in economic literature.

506. Market definition; multiple markets involved. (a) *Importance; monopoly and merger compared.* However wide or narrow the range of inquiry for appraising a merger, market definition is frequently critical. For example, viewed in a wider product or geographic market than the minimum necessary to include the merging firms, a merger will appear to have a less significant effect. In contrast, when the products or regions of the merging firms differ, a definition wide enough to bring the merging firms into the same market makes the merger horizontal and thus more likely to be seen as troublesome.

The techniques of market definitions are fundamentally similar in monopoly and merger cases.[6] What differs is the magnitude or degree of certainty about power that is necessary to trigger the legal rule. Also, in monopoly cases, we usually ask whether the defendant already has monopoly power. In horizontal merger cases, we ask whether the firm that results from the merger will acquire individual power over price and, if not, whether the resulting increase in market concentration will create (or reinforce) oligopoly and the danger of anticompetitive tacit price coordination.[7] Such predictions about the future are somewhat more speculative than inferences about the past. At the same time, less precise inferences seem more tolerable in merger than in monopoly cases. We need to be quite sure about a single firm's monopoly power before breaking it up or substantially limiting its behavior in ways that might weaken competition if it were not really a monopolist. By contrast, we more willingly enjoin mergers after less precise prediction of the merged firm's power or of the likelihood of tacit price coordination. Because antitrust law has no control over the anticompetitive pricing of monopolies and questionable control over that of oligopolies once they come into existence, §7 serves a prophylactic purpose of preventing the initial creation or the reinforcement of monopolies or anticompetitive oligopolies. One might be inclined, therefore, to accept less exacting market definitions in merger than in monopoly

6. Some differences were noted in ¶339c.
7. See ¶¶228-231.

cases and perhaps to err, when in genuine doubt, in the direction of predicting monopoly or oligopoly behavior. Refinement of such an approach depends on the resolution of the several interconnected questions posed in ¶507.

(b) *Multiple markets.* Where several different markets are affected by a single merger, three issues are present. (1) Are anticompetitive effects in one market sufficient to condemn the whole merger? The answer is affirmative.[8] Of course, if the tribunal can tailor its remedy to eliminate that anticompetitive effect while leaving the rest of the merger intact, it will do so. (2) Where the merger must stand or fall as a whole, can an anticompetitive effect in one market be redeemed by a procompetitive effect in a different market? The answer is negative.[9] (3) Should different low-order possibilities of competitive harm in each of several markets (or even within a single market) be cumulated somehow to condemn the merger? Notwithstanding an occasional suggestion of an affirmative answer,[10] the general answer has tended to be negative — at least in the context of decisions that set condemnation thresholds so low that a merger failing to surpass them is likely to be harmless.[11] At higher and less prohibitive thresholds, a different answer might be appropriate.

507. Effects clause: general issues. A covered acquisition is not automatically unlawful because §7 forbids only those mergers that may substantially lessen competition or tend to create a monopoly. What satisfies the effects clause is the subject of the remainder of this chapter. At the outset, however, five points are worth emphasizing.

First, the legislative history makes clear that §7 is intended to control mergers before they have the actual effect of reducing competition. Unfortunately, neither the statutory language nor the legislative history reveals the criteria by which this prophylactic approach is to be applied.

Second, predictions about the future consequences of a particular merger might be attempted by weighing every economic detail which bears on the question. It is very difficult, however, to know which details are relevant in each situation, to know the implications of each such fact, and to reach any net evaluation.

Third, "simple" or "arbitrary" rules might be formulated to decide the presumptive legality or illegality of a merger. Such rules would

8. See *Brown Shoe* and *Philadelphia Bank*, Ch. 5D.

9. See *Philadelphia Bank*, Ch. 5D.

10. United States v. Wilson Sporting Goods Co., 288 F. Supp. 543, 563 (N.D. Ill. 1968); L. Preston, A Probabilistic Approach to Conglomerate Mergers, 44 St. John L. Rev. 341, 343 (spec. ed. 1970).

11. See V P. Areeda & D. Turner, Antitrust Law ¶1147 (1980; Supp. 1996).

focus on what are thought to be the key factors in appraising a market, with no pretense of considering everything that might be relevant. The use of such simple rules is neither compelled nor forbidden by the statute or its legislative history. Compare the evolution and use of per se rules under Sherman Act §1 and Clayton Act §3.

Fourth, the sensible formulation of any set of presumptions or rules of thumb governing mergers depends on judgments about at least four matters. (1) What size mergers in what circumstances are likely to impair competition? For example, would one or more similar mergers reducing the number of significant firms in a market to 12 or 10 lead to oligopolistic pricing? (2) Should the antitrust tribunal prevent a merger that would not itself threaten to impair competition, if possible subsequent mergers of the same size would do so? Suppose, for example, that the tribunal concluded that fewer than 12 firms of comparable size would be undesirable. Should that tribunal prevent the first merger of two 5-percent firms in a market of twenty 5-percent firms? (3) What would society lose as a result of prohibiting mergers of a given magnitude? Obviously, the smaller the firms whose merger would be forbidden, the greater the danger that the law would prevent them from achieving necessary economies of scale in production. Similarly, the higher the threshold of prohibition, the less society need worry about obstructing efficient production and the less the need for any "efficiencies defense" for presumptively unlawful mergers. (4) What "defenses" will be realistically made available to merging firms? As the defenses are more generous, it is less likely that economic efficiency will be impaired even if rather modest mergers are presumptively unlawful. The general point is that the answer to any one of these questions depends on the answers to the others.

Fifth, the failure of Congress to decide any of these questions is matched by that of the professional students of industrial organization. Neither economic theory nor empirical study provides clear answers. Only rough judgments are available, and those must be considered tentative and subject to revision in the light of further knowledge or improved understanding.

508. Acquisitions covered.[12] (a) *Person in or affecting commerce.* Until 1980, Clayton Act §7 applied only to acquisitions involving two "corporations ... in commerce." Thus, noncorporate businesses were immune from §7, as were corporations not engaged in interstate or foreign commerce. A 1980 amendment expanded §7 in two respects. It now applies to "persons" rather than merely to "corporations." And it now embraces those engaged "in any activity

---

12. The issues noted in the Paragraph are analyzed in id. ch. 12.

affecting commerce." In addition, the Sherman Act and the FTC Act are fully applicable to any merger "affecting commerce," whether or not each merging firm is a corporation or is itself "in commerce."[13]

(b) *Acquire.* Ordinarily, there is little difficulty in identifying an acquisition for §7 purposes. It would probably not include an offer to buy (which, nevertheless, could be enjoined if acceptance would involve an unlawful merger). Nor would it include a mere contingent security interest in stock or assets, at least not until that interest would affect competitive behavior of the borrower. On the other hand, a lease of assets or a contract right or option to purchase stock or assets falls clearly within the embrace of §7.

(c) *Partial asset acquisition.* Since its 1950 amendment, §7 reaches asset acquisitions as well as stock acquisition, whether whole or partial. Nevertheless, not all partial asset acquisitions are covered. For example, one firm's purchase of a typewriter has nothing to do with the purposes of §7. Neither does a firm's purchase of an office building for its own use. The acquisition of a nonexclusive patent license also does not seem to implicate any §7 policy. Of course, there may be circumstances where the acquisition of a patent or trademark is, in effect, the acquisition of a going business and, therefore, is covered by §7.[14] We cannot pursue the issue here, although it may be helpful to suggest that (1) the asset clause is limited to the acquisition of "a going (even though failing) concern, or its equivalent, involving a relatively immediate and relatively permanent transfer of market share from one to another corporation," (2) the statute is "not intended to ration — or otherwise to displace the market for — most goods and services, no matter how scarce," and (3) in any event the "effects test of Clayton Act §7 must be applied with very sensitive regard for any differences

---

13. See ¶167 on the meaning of "in commerce" and ¶166 for the broader concept of "affecting commerce." Note the peculiarity of §7's asset clause that covers only acquisitions by persons subject to FTC jurisdiction. Until 1980, this was broader than the stock acquisitions clause because 1975 FTC Act amendments embrace persons "in or *affecting* commerce" (emphasis added). However, it is narrower because certain banks, common carriers, and stockyards are not subject to FTC jurisdiction.

14. Automated Bldg. Components v. Trueline Truss Co., 318 F. Supp. 1252 (D. Or. 1970) (patent application); Western Geophys., Co. v. Bolt Assocs., 305 F. Supp. 1248 (D. Conn. 1969) (exclusive patent license); United States v. Lever Bros. Co., 216 F. Supp. 887 (S.D.N.Y. 1963) (trademark); United States v. Columbia Pictures Corp., 189 F. Supp. 153 (S.D.N.Y. 1960) (exhibition right). Cf. United States v. ITT Continental Baking Co., 485 F.2d 16 (10th Cir. 1973) (customer lists and sales routes), rev'd on other grounds, 420 U.S. 223 (1974).

between a covered asset acquisition and the ordinary 'merger' to which the statute is addressed at its core."[15]

(d) *Partial stock acquisition.* Control or steps toward control should be treated as a full merger. The acquisition of a noncontrolling interest with no apparent intention even to influence the corporation's management might be regarded as an immune acquisition solely for investment.[16] If membership on the board of directors is contemplated, however, the acquisition would no longer seem to be solely for investment.[17] In the horizontal context especially, a substantial investment in a rival might affect each company's zeal or perhaps ability to compete.[18]

(e) *Joint ventures.* Joint venture arrangements often involve joint ownership or control of assets in one form or another. Although they involve the creation of a new entity, §7 concerns might be raised, and the Supreme Court has applied the statute in this context.[19] After studying this chapter, it would be useful to reexamine the discussion of joint ventures in Chapter 2B.

509. Procedural matters. (a) *Remedies.*[20] The usual remedy for an unlawful merger is divestiture. Preliminary injunctions are also available to the Justice Department, the FTC, and private plaintiffs. Rather than enjoin the merger, the court may allow its consummation but require that the acquired company be "held separate" as a going concern to facilitate its divestiture should the merger be held unlawful. In addition, several cases have suggested that rescission of a consummated merger might be available and, therefore, that the selling corporation may properly be made a party to a suit attacking a merger.[21]

(b) *Premerger notification.* Clayton Act §7A, enacted in 1976, requires advance notice to the government of large mergers. Notice must be given where (1) the acquiring company has total assets or annual sales of at least $100 million and (2) the acquired company has assets of at least $10 million or, in the case of acquired manufac-

15. Areeda & Turner, note 11, ¶1202a.
16. See the third paragraph of §7, as reproduced in the Appendix; United States v. Tracinda Inv. Corp., 477 F. Supp. 1093, 1100 (C.D. Cal. 1979).
17. E.g., Hamilton Watch Co. v. Benrus Watch Co., 114 F. Supp. 307, 317 (D. Conn.), aff'd, 206 F.2d 738 (2d Cir. 1953).
18. F&M Schaefer Corp. v. C. Schmidt & Sons, 597 F.2d 814, 818 (2d Cir. 1979).
19. See ¶532c.
20. See ¶¶139, 140.
21. United States v. Coca-Cola Bottling Co., 575 F.2d 222 (9th Cir.), cert. denied, 439 U.S. 959 (1978). See Palmer News v. ARA Servs., 476 F. Supp. 1176 (D. Kan. 1979); Note, Section 7 Clayton Act Remedies — The Rescission Decision, 64 Cornell L. Rev. 736 (1979).

turing firms, annual net sales of $10 million or more. The transaction is covered only if the acquiring company would hold either more than $15 million worth or at least 15 percent of the voting securities or assets of the acquired company.[22]

Such acquisitions may be consummated 30 days (or 15 days in the case of a cash tender offer) after completed notice is filed. This waiting period may be extended by an additional 20 days (or 10 days on cash tender offers) by the appropriate government agency demanding supplementary information. It may be extended even further by the court.

Upon notification, the government will assess the merger in accordance with its published guidelines.[23] In practice, mergers that are not challenged by the government at the premerger notification stage usually will not be challenged by private parties or states. On the other hand, mergers that are challenged will often be dropped by the parties or restructured (by selling assets that raise concerns) to satisfy the government.[24] Consequently, the outcome of the premerger notification process normally will be the *de facto* final determination on the permissibility of a merger. In 1996 the government received 3094 premerger notifications, initiated investigation of 186 of the proposed mergers, and filed complaints in 9 cases.[25]

5C. VERTICAL MERGERS

510. Introduction. Merger cases do not split cleanly into vertical and nonvertical problems. These materials separate the two types only so far as pedagogically convenient; remember, therefore, that vertical mergers cannot be understood without a consideration of Chapter 5 as a whole.

Vertical mergers were not thought to be covered by Clayton Act §7 before the 1950 amendment. And, although the Sherman Act applied, there were few cases dealing with vertical integration in any

22. 16 C.F.R. §802.20 broadens somewhat these exceptions for small acquisitions. For a detailed discussion of transactions subject to the premerger notification rules, see 2 M. Ginsburg & J. Levin, Mergers, Acquisitions, and Buyouts: A Transactional Analysis of the Governing Tax, Legal, and Accounting Considerations §1507 (1997).

23. See ¶527.

24. See M. Coate, A. Kleit & R. Bustamante, Fight, Fold or Settle?: Modelling the Reaction to FTC Merger Challenges, 33 Econ. Inquiry 537 (1995).

25. Department of Justice, Antitrust Division, Workload Statistics FY 1987-1996, in 72 Antitr. & Trade Reg. Rep. 117 (1997).

form. These early cases, even those in which there had in fact been a merger, tended to examine the problem not in terms of the merger but rather in terms of vertical integration as such. Three major vertical cases utilizing this approach and the surprising *du Pont (GM)* case are summarized as an introduction, followed by the vertical aspects of *Brown Shoe*, the Supreme Court's first discussion of amended §7.

511. Early development. (a) *Sherman Act cases.* In *Yellow Cab,*[1] Checker Cab Manufacturing Corporation had, over time, acquired control of local taxi cab operating companies. Checker required these subsidiary companies to purchase their vehicles from it. The government charged that the Sherman Act was violated by depriving the operating companies of their choice of vehicles and depriving General Motors, Ford, and other auto manufacturers of the opportunity to sell to those operators. The trial court dismissed the complaint, but the Supreme Court reversed, holding that a violation would be established if, as the complaint alleged, Checker's power over the cab companies "was not obtained by normal expansion to meet the demands of a business growing as a result of superior and enterprising management, but by deliberate, calculated purchase for control." A finding on remand that there was no design or motive to suppress competition was affirmed as not being clearly erroneous.[2]

Paramount[3] was a wide ranging government attack on the movie distribution system as it existed through World War II. The government objected to the vertical integration of the major studios into production, distribution, and exhibition in wholly or partially owned theaters. In addition, the government alleged that the major studios favored each other over independents — exhibiting each other's movies in their theaters rather than movies produced by others and licensing first run movies to each other's theaters rather than to independent theaters. Also challenged were a variety of other practices — such as licensing films as a package rather than singly — which allegedly oppressed independent exhibitors and tended to exclude independent producers from access to theaters. The Court rejected the government's contention that "vertical integration of producing, distributing, and exhibiting motion pictures is illegal per se." The Sherman Act is violated if integration constitutes "a calculated scheme to gain control over an appreciable segment of the market and to restrain or suppress competition,

1. United States v. Yellow Cab Co., 332 U.S. 218, 227-228 (1947).
2. United States v. Yellow Cab Co., 338 U.S. 338 (1949).
3. United States v. Paramount Pictures, 334 U.S. 131, 173-174 (1948).

rather than an expansion to meet legitimate business needs." The Court indicated that one factor to be considered was "the leverage on the market which the particular vertical integration creates or makes possible." Divestiture was ordered on remand.[4] Although *Paramount* did challenge the way that movies were produced, the resulting divestiture coupled with the advent of television led to the reorganization of production as well. The old studio system with a large stable of actors, directors, writers, and technicians had generated a large annual output of movies. Today, far fewer films are made, and each requires the producers to assemble the necessary creative and technical talent.

In *A&P*,[5] the government successfully challenged a grocery store chain's attempts to obtain special discounts from suppliers by threatening to cease dealing with them, substituting its own supply or manufacture where necessary. In several instances, A&P did create its own manufacturing and processing divisions. One fruit and vegetable subsidiary purchased for A&P and also acted as a broker for small grocers. It kept the best for A&P and profited on its external sales. The lower court stated that this integration meant that "defendants purchased merchandise at prices they would not otherwise have obtained, at prices less than those of competitors, with a resulting handicap to competitors." The appeals court affirmed, finding that A&P was able to obtain "preferential discounts not by force of its large purchasing power . . . but through its abuse of that power by the threats to boycott suppliers . . . and by threats to go into the manufacturing and processing business itself."[6]

These cases did not offer any extensive or penetrating discussion of the virtues or vices of vertical integration by merger or otherwise. Nor did they consider how one might measure or otherwise assess the significance of any anticompetitive threats that might occur. In light of ¶321 and Chapter 4C, how would you evaluate the threats to competition posed by Checker's sale of cabs to its affiliated operating companies, Paramount's exhibition of its movies in affiliated theaters, or A&P's brokerage or self-processing of certain grocery items?

(b) *United States v. E.I. du Pont de Nemours & Co. (General Motors)*, 353 U.S. 586, 607 (1957). du Pont acquired a 23 percent stock interest in General Motors in 1917-1919, and supplied a large portion of finishes (two-thirds) and fabrics (more than one-third) used

---

4. 85 F. Supp. 881 (S.D.N.Y. 1949).

5. United States v. New York Great Atl. & Pac. Tea Co., 67 F. Supp. 626, 663 (E.D. Ill. 1946), aff'd, 173 F.2d 79, 83 (7th Cir. 1949).

6. See Ch. 6D for the application of the Robinson-Patman Act to attempts to secure preferential prices. For criticism of *A&P*, see M. Adelman, A&P — A Study in Price-Cost Behavior and Public Policy (1959).

by GM in making automobiles. Upon suit by the government in 1949, the Supreme Court ruled that du Pont's holding of GM stock violated Clayton Act §7. The Court reasoned as follows: (1) Although unamended §7 applied to a lessening of competition between the acquiring and acquired companies, its "tend to create a monopoly" language applied to vertical mergers, contrary to the view most held before this case. (2) Although the second paragraph of §7[7] exempts acquisitions of stock "solely for investment," that exemption does not save those who use the stock "to bring about, or in attempting to bring about, the substantial lessening of competition." (3) There is no barrier to challenging this stock holding now, and its legality depends on "whether, at the time of suit, there was a reasonable probability that the acquisition is likely to result in the condemned restraints."[8] (4) Although GM's operating divisions claim to purchase their finishes and fabrics solely on the basis of price and quality, some of them purchase nothing from du Pont, and other auto producers sometimes purchase significant amounts of these products from du Pont, the Court attributed GM's purchases to du Pont's ownership of its stock. (5) Although the bulk of du Pont's sales of the finishes and fabrics it sells to GM are sold to customers other than GM and mainly for nonautomobile use, the relevant market is *automobile* finishes and fabrics. (6) The foreclosure is substantial. Even though GM buys only 3.5 and 1.6 percent, respectively, of industrial finishes and fabrics, it buys about half of its own requirements of these products from du Pont. Given that GM then accounted for about half the automobiles sold, the foreclosure of the automobile finish and fabric market was substantial.

BROWN SHOE CO. v. UNITED STATES
370 U.S. 294 (1962)

Chief Justice WARREN. . . . [T]he Government contended that the effect of the merger of Brown — the third largest seller of shoes by dollar volume in the United States, a leading manufacturer of men's, women's, and children's shoes, and a retailer with over 1,230 owned, operated or controlled retail outlets — and Kinney — the eighth largest company, by dollar volume, among those primarily engaged in selling shoes, itself a large manufacturer of shoes, and a

---

7. See the full text reprinted in the Appendix.
8. See V P. Areeda & D. Turner, Antitrust Law ¶1205 (1980; Supp. 1996), concluding that (1) noncontrolling acquisitions may be appraised at any time and (2) controlling and especially total acquisitions should be judged as of the time of acquisition, except that current data may reveal the true situation at the time of merger and is always relevant to the propriety of present-day equitable relief.

retailer with over 350 retail outlets — "may be substantially to lessen competition or to tend to create a monopoly" by eliminating actual or potential competition in the production of shoes for the national wholesale shoe market and in the sale of shoes at retail in the Nation, by foreclosing competition from "a market represented by Kinney's retail outlets whose annual sales exceed $42,000,000," and by enhancing Brown's competitive advantage over other producers, distributors and sellers of shoes. . . .

[The 24 largest shoe manufacturers produced 35 percent of the nation's shoes; the top 4 produced 23 percent. There are 70,000 retail outlets; of these, 20,000 are so-called shoe stores that derive at least half their gross receipts from shoe sales. The District Court found a "definite trend" (1) for shoe manufacturers to acquire retail outlets — for example, nine independent chains, operating 1,114 stores, were acquired by large firms between 1950 and 1956; (2) for such manufacturers to supply an ever increasing percentage of the acquired outlets' shoes, thereby foreclosing other manufacturers; and (3) for the number of manufacturing plants to diminish — dropping 10 percent, from 1,077 to 970 between 1947 and 1954.

Brown had contributed to these trends, acquiring all its retail outlets since 1951 and also seven manufacturing companies, making it fourth largest, with a 4 percent share. Kinney is the largest family-style retail shoe chain, with over 400 stores in 270 cities, selling 1.2 percent of national dollar volume and 1.6 percent of national pairage. Its four plants gave it a 0.5 percent share of production, making it the twelfth largest manufacturer. Although Kinney had bought no shoes from Brown at the time of the merger, by 1957 Brown was its largest supplier, providing 7.9 percent of Kinney's needs.]

The Vertical Aspects of the Merger

Economic arrangements between companies standing in a supplier-customer relationship are characterized as "vertical." The primary vice of a vertical merger or other arrangement tying a customer to a supplier is that, by foreclosing the competitors of either party from a segment of the market otherwise open to them, the arrangement may act as a "clog on competition," *Standard Stations*, which "deprive[s] . . . rivals of a fair opportunity to compete."[40] H.R. Rep.

___

40. In addition, a vertical merger may disrupt and injure competition when those independent customers of the supplier who are in competition with the merging customer, are forced either to stop handling the supplier's lines, thereby jeopardizing the goodwill they have developed, or to retain the supplier's lines, thereby forcing them into competition with their own supplier. . . .

No. 1191, 81st Cong., 1st Sess. 8. Every extended vertical arrangement by its very nature, for at least a time, denies to competitors of the supplier the opportunity to compete for part or all of the trade of the customer-party to the vertical arrangement. However, the Clayton Act does not render unlawful all such vertical arrangements, but forbids only those whose effect "may be substantially to lessen competition, or to tend to create a monopoly" "in any line of commerce in any section of the country." Thus, as we have previously noted, "[d]etermination of the relevant market is a necessary predicate to a finding of a violation of the Clayton Act because the threatened monopoly must be one which will substantially lessen competition 'within the area of effective competition.' Substantiality can be determined only in terms of the market affected." The "area of effective competition" must be determined by reference to a product market (the "line of commerce") and a geographic market (the "section of the country").

THE PRODUCT MARKET

The outer boundaries of a product market are determined by the reasonable interchangeability of use or the cross-elasticity of demand between the product itself and substitutes for it.[42] However, within this broad market, well-defined submarkets may exist which, in themselves, constitute product markets for antitrust purposes. *du Pont [GM]*. The boundaries of such a submarket may be determined by examining such practical indicia as industry or public recognition of the submarket as a separate economic entity, the product's peculiar characteristics and uses, unique production facilities, distinct customers, distinct prices, sensitivity to price changes, and specialized vendors. Because §7 of the Clayton Act prohibits any merger which may substantially lessen competition "in *any* line of commerce" (emphasis supplied), it is necessary to examine the effects of a merger in each such economically significant submarket to determine if there is a reasonable probability that the merger will substantially lessen competition. If such a probability is found to exist, the merger is proscribed.

Applying these considerations to the present case, we conclude that the record supports the District Court's finding that the relevant lines of commerce are men's, women's, and children's shoes.

42. The cross-elasticity of production facilities may also be an important factor in defining a product market within which a vertical merger is to be viewed.... However, the District Court made but limited findings concerning the feasibility of interchanging equipment in the manufacture of nonrubber footwear. At the same time, the record supports the court's conclusion that individual plants generally produced shoes in only one of the product lines the court found relevant.

These product lines are recognized by the public; each line is manufactured in separate plants; each has characteristics peculiar to itself rendering it generally noncompetitive with the others; and each is, of course, directed toward a distinct class of customers.

[In a brief discussion of possible submarkets, the Court rejected the defendant's contentions that the district court failed "to recognize sufficiently 'price/quality' and 'age/sex' distinctions in shoes." The Court found that subdividing the market further than men's, women's, and children's shoes would be "impractical" and "unwarranted."]

The Geographic Market . . .

[T]he relevant geographic market is the entire Nation. The relationships of product value, bulk, weight and consumer demand enable manufacturers to distribute their shoes on a nationwide basis, as Brown and Kinney, in fact, do. . . .

The Probable Effect of the Merger

Once the area of effective competition affected by a vertical arrangement has been defined, an analysis must be made to determine if the effect of the arrangement "may be substantially to lessen competition, or to tend to create a monopoly" in this market.

Since the diminution of the vigor of competition which may stem from a vertical arrangement results primarily from a foreclosure of a share of the market otherwise open to competitors, an important consideration in determining whether the effect of a vertical arrangement "may be substantially to lessen competition, or to tend to create a monopoly" is the size of the share of the market foreclosed. However, this factor will seldom be determinative. If the share of the market foreclosed is so large that it approaches monopoly proportions, the Clayton Act will, of course, have been violated; but the arrangement will also have run afoul of the Sherman Act. And the legislative history of §7 indicates clearly that the tests for measuring the legality of any particular economic arrangement under the Clayton Act are to be less stringent than those used in applying the Sherman Act. On the other hand, foreclosure of a de minimis share of the market will not tend "substantially to lessen competition."

Between these extremes, in cases such as the one before us, in which the foreclosure is neither of monopoly nor de minimis proportions, the percentage of the market foreclosed by the vertical arrangement cannot itself be decisive. In such cases, it becomes necessary to undertake an examination of various economic and historical factors in order to determine whether the arrangement under review is of the type Congress sought to proscribe.

A most important such factor to examine is the very nature and purpose of the arrangement.[48] Congress not only indicated that "the tests of illegality [under §7] are intended to be similar to those which the courts have applied in interpreting the same language as used in other sections of the Clayton Act," but also chose for §7 language virtually identical to that of §3 of the Clayton Act, which had been interpreted by this Court to require an examination of the interdependence of the market share foreclosed by, and the economic purpose of, the vertical arrangement. Thus, for example, if a particular vertical arrangement, considered under §3, appears to be a limited term exclusive-dealing contract, the market foreclosure must generally be significantly greater than if the arrangement is a tying contract before the arrangement will be held to have violated the Act. Compare *Tampa Electric* and *Standard Stations* with *International Salt*. The reason for this is readily discernible. The usual tying contract forces the customer to take a product or brand he does not necessarily want in order to secure one which he does desire. Because such an arrangement is inherently anticompetitive, we have held that its use by an established company is likely "substantially to lessen competition" although only a relatively small amount of commerce is affected. . . . Thus, unless the tying device is employed by a small company in an attempt to break into a market, cf. Harley-Davidson Motor Co., 50 F.T.C. 1047, 1066, the use of a tying device can rarely be harmonized with the strictures of the antitrust laws, which are intended primarily to preserve and stimulate competition. . . . On the other hand, requirement contracts are frequently negotiated at the behest of the customer who has chosen the particular supplier and his product upon the basis of competitive merit. . . . Of course, the fact that requirement contracts are not inherently anticompetitive will not save a particular agreement if, in fact, it is likely "substantially to lessen competition, or to tend to create a monopoly." E.g., *Standard Stations*. Yet a requirement contract may escape censure if only a small share of the market is involved, if the purpose of the agreement is to insure to the customer a sufficient supply of a commodity vital to the customer's trade or to insure to the supplier a market for his output

---

48. Although it is "unnecessary for the Government to speculate as to what is in the 'back of the minds' of those who promote a merger," H.R. Rep. No. 1191, 81st Cong., 1st Sess. 8, evidence indicating the purpose of the merging parties, where available, is an aid in predicting the probable future conduct of the parties and thus the probable effects of the merger.

and if there is no trend toward concentration in the industry. *Tampa Electric.* Similar considerations are pertinent to a judgment under §7 of the Act.

The importance which Congress attached to economic purpose is further demonstrated by the Senate and House Reports on H.R. 2734, which evince an intention to preserve the "failing company" doctrine of International Shoe Co. v. Federal Trade Comm'n, 280 U.S. 291. Similarly, Congress foresaw that the merger of two large companies or a large and a small company might violate the Clayton Act while the merger of two small companies might not, although the share of the market foreclosed be identical, if the purpose of the small companies is to enable them in combination to compete with larger corporations dominating the market.

The present merger involved neither small companies nor failing companies.... Not only was Brown one of the leading manufacturers of men's, women's, and children's shoes, but Kinney, with over 350 retail outlets, owned and operated the largest independent chain of family shoe stores in the Nation. Thus, in this industry, no merger between a manufacturer and an independent retailer could involve a larger potential market foreclosure. Moreover, it is apparent both from past behavior of Brown and from the testimony of Brown's President, that Brown would use its ownership of Kinney to force Brown shoes into Kinney stores. Thus, in operation this vertical arrangement would be quite analogous to one involving a tying clause.[55]

Another important factor to consider is the trend toward concentration in the industry. It is true, of course, that the statute prohibits a given merger only if the effect of *that* merger may be substantially to lessen competition. But the very wording of §7 requires a prognosis of the probable *future* effect of the merger.

The existence of a trend toward vertical integration, which the District Court found, is well substantiated by the record. Moreover, the court found a tendency of the acquiring manufacturers to become increasingly important sources of supply for their acquired outlets. The necessary corollary of these trends is the foreclosure of independent manufacturers from markets otherwise open to them. And because these trends are not the product of accident but are rather the result of deliberate policies of Brown and other leading shoe manufacturers, account must be taken of these facts in order to predict the probable future consequences of this merger. It is

55. Moreover, ownership integration is a more permanent and irreversible tie than is contract integration. See Kessler and Stern, Competition, Contract, and Vertical Integration, 69 Yale L.J. 1, 78 (1959).

against this background of continuing concentration that the present merger must be viewed.

Brown argues, however, that the shoe industry is at present composed of a large number of manufacturers and retailers, and that the industry is dynamically competitive. But remaining vigor cannot immunize a merger if the trend in that industry is toward oligopoly.... It is the probable effect of the merger upon the future as well as the present which the Clayton Act commands the courts and the Commission to examine.

Moreover, as we have remarked above, not only must we consider the probable effects of the merger upon the economics of the particular markets affected but also we must consider its probable effects upon the economic way of life sought to be preserved by Congress. Congress was desirous of preventing the formation of further oligopolies with their attendant adverse effects upon local control of industry and upon small business. Where an industry was composed of numerous independent units, Congress appeared anxious to preserve this structure. The Senate Report, quoting with approval from the Federal Trade Commission's 1948 report on the merger movement, states explicitly that amended §7 is addressed, inter alia, to the following problem:

> Under the Sherman Act, an acquisition is unlawful if it creates a monopoly or constitutes an attempt to monopolize. Imminent monopoly may appear when one large concern acquires another, but it is unlikely to be perceived in a small acquisition by a large enterprise. As a large concern grows through a series of such small acquisitions, its accretions of power are individually so minute as to make it difficult to use the Sherman Act tests against them.... Where several large enterprises are extending their power by successive small acquisitions, the cumulative effect of their purchases may be to convert an industry from one of intense competition among many enterprises to one in which three or four large concerns produce the entire supply. S. Rep. No. 1775, 81st Cong., 2d Sess. 5. And see H.R. Rep. No. 1191, 81st Cong., 1st Sess. 8.

The District Court's findings, and the record facts ... convince us that the shoe industry is being subjected to just such a cumulative series of vertical mergers which, if left unchecked, will be likely "substantially to lessen competition."

We reach this conclusion because the trend toward vertical integration in the shoe industry, when combined with Brown's avowed policy of forcing its own shoes upon its retail subsidiaries, may foreclose competition from a substantial share of the markets for men's, women's, and children's shoes, without producing any countervailing competitive, economic, or social advantages....

Affirmed.

Justice HARLAN. . . . Brown contends that even if these anticompetitive effects are probable, they touch upon an insignificant share of the market and are not, therefore, "substantial" within the meaning of §7. Our decision in *Tampa Electric* is cited as authority for the proposition that a foreclosure of about 1 percent of the relevant market is necessarily insubstantial. But the opinion in *Tampa Electric* carefully noted that "substantiality in a given case" depends on a variety of factors. Two of the considerations that were mentioned were "the relative strength of the parties" and "the probable immediate and future effects which preemption of that share of the market might have on effective competition therein." When, as here, the foreclosure of what may be considered a small percentage of retailers' purchases may be caused by the combination of the country's third largest seller of shoes with the country's largest family-style shoe store chain, and when the volume of the latter's purchases from independent manufacturers in various parts of the country is large enough to render it probable that these suppliers, if displaced, will have to fall by the wayside, it cannot, in my opinion, be said that the effect on the shoe industry is "remote" or "insubstantial."

I reach this result without considering the findings of the District Court respecting the trend in the shoe industry towards "oligopoly" and vertical integration. The statistics in the record fall short of convincing me that any such trend exists. I consider the District Court's judgment warranted apart from these findings. . . .[9]

512. If a series of vertical acquisitions had not altered the level of concentration at the manufacturing or retailing levels, should the Court have decided the case differently? That is, assuming that in a particular case vertical foreclosure is not accompanied by increased concentration at either the manufacturing or distribution level, why should we be concerned with the foreclosure?[10] Would such a vertical merger have any anticompetitive effect? Consider the following situations.

9. Clark, J., concurred separately. Harlan, J., dissented on jurisdictional grounds but concurred in the result on the merits (the latter statement appearing in text). Frankfurter and White, JJ., did not participate. An additional consideration bearing on the vertical aspect of the merger is included in the Court's discussion, reproduced in the next section, of the horizontal aspect of the Brown-Kinney merger. For a critical analysis of the facts of *Brown Shoe*, see J. Peterman, The Brown Shoe Case, 18 J.L. & Econ. 81 (1975).

10. See IV Areeda & Turner, note 8, ch. 10A; M. Klass & M. Salinger, Do New Theories of Vertical Foreclosure Provide Sound Guidance for Consent Agreements in Vertical Merger Cases?, 40 Antitr. Bull. 667 (1995); M. Riordan & S. Salop, Evaluating Vertical Mergers: A Post-Chicago Approach, 63 Antitr. L.J. 513 (1995).

(a) Suppose that one of many sellers of a product merges with one of many buyers of that product. What is the significance of the vertical foreclosure?

(b) Suppose that there are 10 sellers and 10 buyers of a product. If all paired off, what would happen to entry barriers? If only some paired off?[11]

(c) Suppose that firm *P*, with relatively few competitors, sells about one-third of product *Z* and that firm *Q* buys about one-third of product *Z* (which is also purchased by numerous smaller firms). How might the merger of *P* and *Q* reduce the competitive pressures on the *Z* sellers?

(d) In *Brown Shoe*, was there significant vertical foreclosure? How is the "trend" toward vertical acquisitions relevant to your conclusion?

(e) The Court discussed how §7 was designed to prevent concentration and avoid oligopoly. How does the vertical aspect of the *Brown Shoe* merger affect concentration in any relevant market?

(f) How do you determine whether any particular merger will lessen competition? Is the *Standard Stations* test to be applied to vertical mergers? The test of *International Salt*? What does *Brown Shoe* say?

(g) *Brown Shoe* emphasized the Clayton Act's purpose to arrest mergers "at a time when the trend to a lessening of competition ... was still in its incipiency." When is that? How does this notion help the Court to resolve the case?

(h) The Court said, as is often said, that intent is considered as an aid to predicting future conduct and thus probable effect. In what sense, if any, is this true? Does the Court's view of the legitimacy of Tampa Electric's purpose distinguish that case from the shoe merger? To whatever extent *Brown Shoe* is concerned with purpose, does the Court identify any of the purposes that it would consider sufficiently legitimate to weigh in the scale of legality?

513. Vertical mergers under 1984 government guidelines.[12]
(a) *Entry barriers raised.* A vertical merger might increase entry barriers if three "necessary (but not sufficient)" conditions are satis-

11. See United States Steel Corp., 74 F.T.C. 1270, 1295, 1297, 1300 (1968), rev'd on other grounds, 426 F.2d 592 (6th Cir. 1970) (remanding for consideration of the failing company defense, see ¶525), order on remand, 81 F.T.C. 629 (1972) (ordering divestiture).

12. 49 Fed. Reg. 26823 (1984). The 1992 Horizontal Merger Guidelines, discussed in ¶527 suggest that the 1984 guidelines remain in effect for nonhorizontal mergers. Note the absence of any reference to foreclosure of markets, as such, in the 1984 guidelines, which stands in contrast to the 1968 guidelines that examined entry barriers in such terms.

fied. "First, the degree of vertical integration between the two markets must be so extensive that entrants to one market (the 'primary market') also would have to enter the other market (the 'secondary market') simultaneously." Challenge is unlikely "where postmerger sales (purchases) by unintegrated firms in the secondary market would be sufficient to service two minimum-efficient-scale plants in the primary market." Challenge is increasingly likely as unintegrated capacity is less.

"Second, the requirement of entry at the secondary level must make entry at the primary level significantly more difficult and less likely to occur." Challenge is unlikely "if entry at the secondary level is easy." Even if such entry is not possible, the government will not proceed unless "the need for secondary market entry significantly increases the costs (which may take the form of risks) of primary market entry." For example, the incremental capital needed might become a barrier if entry into the secondary market would require either substantially different skills than entry into the primary market or a high percentage of specialized and long-lived capital assets. Furthermore, "if the capacity of a minimum-efficient-scale plant in the secondary market were significantly greater than the needs of a minimum-efficient-scale plant in the primary market" and if there were no readily available buyers for the excess, "entrants would have to choose between inefficient operation at the secondary level . . . or a larger than necessary scale at the primary level. Either of these effects could cause a significant increase in the operating costs of the entering firm."

Third, "the structure and other characteristics of the primary market must be otherwise so conducive to non-competitive performance that the increased difficulty of entry is likely to affect its performance." Challenge is unlikely unless the HHI (as defined in the excerpt of the horizontal merger guidelines in Chapter 5D) exceeds 1800 or, with smaller numbers, if "effective collusion is particularly likely. . . . [T]he Department is increasingly likely to challenge a merger that meets the other criteria set forth above as the concentration increases."

(b) *Vertical mergers facilitating collusion.* Because retail prices are "generally more visible than prices in upstream markets," widespread vertical integration might increase the ability of oligopolists to monitor each other's prices. The government may consider a challenge if the HHI satisfies the test in ¶a and "a large percentage of the upstream product would be sold through vertically-integrated retail outlets after the merger."

Because rivalry for the patronage of a particularly attractive buyer may impede oligopolistic price coordination, the government may consider challenging the acquisition of a firm that "differs substantially in volume of purchases or other relevant characteristics from the other firms in its market" where the upstream HHI satisfies the test in ¶a.

(c) *Evasion of rate regulation.* "Monopoly public utilities subject to rate regulation" might acquire a supplier and then purchase from itself at arbitrarily inflated prices that might escape detection by the regulator, especially where "there is no independent market for the product (or service) purchased from the affiliate.... The Department will consider challenging mergers that create substantial opportunities for such abuses."

(d) *Efficiencies.* "An extensive pattern of vertical integration may constitute evidence that substantial economies are afforded by vertical integration. Therefore, the Department will give relatively more weight to expected efficiencies in determining whether to challenge a vertical merger than in determining whether to challenge a horizontal merger."

514. Coolair Corporation manufactures window air conditioning units of various sizes designed to cool one or a few contiguous rooms to some predetermined temperature. Each air conditioner therefore includes a comfort control designed to sense temperature conditions and, at appropriate intervals, start and stop the machine's cooling system. Coolair's revenues amount to about 6 percent of national sales of such units. There are seven other producers, of which the largest two account for about 49 percent of industry sales. Each of the two largest firms makes its own comfort controls. The other six producers purchase comfort controls from Thermo Company or Robot. Robot is a large diversified producer of thermostatic, timing, and control devices for many purposes. Thermo has been making about one-third and Robot about two-thirds of the sales to the six manufacturers. Recently Coolair acquired Thermo's stock, provided it with additional funds for plant expansion, and agreed to use Thermo devices exclusively. Thermo contracted to supply its devices to Coolair at cost and to give Coolair priority in the event of a short supply.

(a) What are the effects of the merger in the comfort control market? Does the vertical merger substantially lessen competition in the control market by foreclosing outlets to Thermo's competitor? (1) What is the economic relevance of the exclusive use contract? (2) Is the relevant market comfort controls for room air conditioners? Thermostatic controls for all cooling machines? All thermostats? All control devices? (3) If the proper market is room air conditioner controls, what is the degree of foreclosure? (4) Should the acquisition of a supplier be treated any differently from the acquisition of a customer? (5) Would it be relevant if both

Thermo and Robot had previously behaved monopolistically? (6) Is it relevant that some of Coolair's competitors are already integrated?

(b) Analyze the impact of the merger on Coolair's air conditioner competitors. (1) Would you suppose that Coolair would preempt Thermo's output of controls to the detriment of its competitors? (2) Suppose that Thermo sells all of its output to Coolair. What is the impact on Coolair's competitors if Robot could readily produce a sufficient number of controls to meet the demand of all air conditioner producers? (3) Will Coolair obtain an unfair advantage over its competitors by acquiring controls at cost while they must pay the market price? (4) Could Coolair undersell its air conditioner competitors by lowering air conditioner prices with compensatory increases in the price of controls? (5) Suppose that Thermo had a legal patent monopoly of all comfort controls. Would the vertical integration be likely to lessen competition in the air conditioner market? (6) Does this vertical merger impose any additional barriers to entry into the air conditioner market?

(c) Has Coolair violated Clayton Act §7?[13]

515. Ajax Corporation is 1 of 10 producers of a complex machine used in drilling oil wells. Ajax accounts for about 30 percent of the market; the other nine have shares ranging from 5 to 10 percent. Two of the producers first entered the industry within the past 5 years. Competition in price and quality has been vigorous; none of the producers has persistently earned abnormally high profits. Annual industry sales have been rising at a rate of about 5 percent; total sales in 1969 were around 100,000 units.

At the moment, each machine producer manufactures its own requirements of a vital component. Although costs vary somewhat among the producers, the cost of the component is believed to average around $3,000, or nearly one-third of the cost of the finished machine.

---

13. A vertical merger was upheld in Fruehauf Corp. v. FTC, 603 F.2d 345 (2d Cir. 1979) (5.8 percent foreclosure insubstantial). Earlier cases often found vertical mergers to be illegal. E.g., Ash Grove Cement Co. v. FTC, 577 F.2d 1368 (9th Cir.), cert. denied, 439 U.S. 982 (1978) (portland cement producer acquired two customers accounting for 10.2 and 3.1 percent of local purchases of that product); Heatransfer Corp. v. Volkswagenwerk, 553 F.2d 964, 980-981 (5th Cir. 1977), cert. denied, 434 U.S. 1087 (1978) (VW acquired auto air conditioner maker). The attitude of modern courts has been that vertical integration is usually procompetitive and not of antitrust concern. See, e.g., Reazin v. BlueCross & BlueShield of Kansas, 663 F. Supp. 1360, 1489 (D. Kan. 1987), aff'd, 899 F.2d 951 (10th Cir.), cert. denied, 497 U.S. 1005 (1990); Jack Walters & Sons Corp. v. Morton Building, 737 F.2d 698, 710 (7th Cir.), cert. denied, 469 U.S. 1018 (1984).

Recent innovations in automated production techniques have made it possible to produce this component at an estimated cost of $1,000 per unit in a single plant of most efficient size operating at its capacity of 150,000 units annually, or around $1,500 per unit operating at an output level of 100,000 units annually. Minimum costs per unit for new but smaller plants operating at full capacity are estimated as follows: (a) 100,000 unit annual capacity: $1,700, (b) 80,000 unit annual capacity: $2,000, (c) 50,000 unit annual capacity: $2,500.

In response to this development, Electric Company (ECO), a general manufacturer of a variety of machine parts, has notified the 10 machine producers that it will build a new plant of 150,000 unit annual capacity to make this component if individual producers currently accounting in the aggregate for at least 80,000 annual machine sales make advance commitments to purchase their requirements of the component from ECO for five years.

Ajax has notified the other nine machine producers that it is willing to build a 150,000 unit plant and to supply all buyer component orders at a price significantly below current component costs. Ajax stated it was prepared to do this without any advance commitments on the buyers' part.

The other nine producers, having discussed the matter among themselves, have jointly notified both ECO and Ajax that they would consider either proposal and enter into five-year requirements contracts with either company, if ECO or Ajax would agree to sell the component at a "reasonable" price derived from an explicit formula. The formula would be negotiated among the parties before any commitments were made, and either ECO or Ajax would have to be satisfied that the formula would permit it to recover its investment in five years (which is concededly reasonable in this industry) and to earn a fair rate of return during that period.

The other nine producers have also sent a separate letter to Ajax proposing, in the alternative, that all ten producers create a jointly owned subsidiary to build the new plant and to supply their component requirements, each producer to be entitled to a minimum ownership participation in proportion to its average market share over the past five years.

While Ajax and the other nine producers have divergent interests in some respects, all are primarily interested in getting the component as cheaply as possible, and in avoiding or minimizing antitrust risks. They collectively seek antitrust advice.

Assess the antitrust risks involved in the various proposed courses of action and advise the ten producers what they should do. You may find it useful to analyze the proposals in the following order: (1) ECO's original proposal and Ajax's original proposal. (2) The proposed undertaking between the nine producers and either ECO or Ajax. (3) The proposed joint venture.

5D. HORIZONTAL MERGERS[1]

516. Consider the following argument: Horizontal mergers should be deemed per se illegal *under Sherman Act §1.* Surely there is a "contract, combination ... or conspiracy." *Socony* held price-fixing agreements to be per se illegal, without regard to the market power of the involved parties. After a merger, the previously separate entities have their prices set by a single authority (or at least there is the power to do so).[2] Moreover, a merger allows more ready enforcement of established prices ("cheating" subordinates can simply be fired) and tends to be more permanent.[3] Therefore, the conclusion follows a fortiori from the rule against price fixing.

Evaluate this argument. Although ¶504 indicated that some early mergers were invalidated under Sherman Act §1, the suggested interpretation has never been accepted. Why not? Should the suggested approach have been taken?

517. (a) Is monopoly power necessary to a violation of §7? Or is the possibility of some competitive impact sufficient to invoke the prohibition? If the latter, how much impact is necessary? In addressing this question, consider how competition is affected by horizontal mergers.

(b) Is sufficient impact present in the following cases? Percentage figures refer to shares of an appropriate market that has no unusual features such as costless new entry. (1) The original formation of United States Steel Company. (2) The union of two 0.5-percent firms in a more-or-less perfectly competitive industry. (3) The union of two 5-percent firms in an industry of three 10-percent firms and 12 surviving 5-percent firms. Is price competition likely to be reduced? (4) The union of two 10-percent firms in an industry with four 20-percent firms. Is oligopoly pricing any more likely? (5) The union of two 10-percent firms in an industry with eight other 10-percent firms. Is any change in the character of competi-

1. See ABA Antitrust Section, Monograph No. 12, Horizontal Mergers: Law and Policy (1986).
2. See *Copperweld,* Ch. 2C.
3. In *Philadelphia Bank,* reproduced later in this section, the Court indicated that Clayton Act §3 cases were "highly suggestive in the present context, for ... integration by merger is more suspect than integration by contract, because of the greater permanence of the former."

tion likely? (6) The union of a 30-percent firm and a 5-percent firm in an industry with five 3-percent firms and 50 smaller ones. (7) The union of a 10-percent firm and a 1-percent firm (which is the industry maverick, both in price cutting and innovation) where there are eight other 10-percent firms and nine other 1-percent firms.

(c) What market conditions might be relevant to minimize or magnify the significance of an increase in concentration inherent in a horizontal merger? Recall your analyses of market definition and market power; market share, whether large or small, cannot automatically be translated into substantial market power or its absence.

BROWN SHOE CO. v. UNITED STATES
370 U.S. 294 (1962)

Chief Justice WARREN. [The facts are set forth in the excerpt at pages 809-810, above.] An economic arrangement between companies performing similar functions in the production or sale of comparable goods or services is characterized as "horizontal." The effect on competition of such an arrangement depends, of course, upon its character and scope. Thus, its validity in the face of the antitrust laws will depend upon such factors as: the relative size and number of the parties to the arrangement; whether it allocates shares of the market among the parties; whether it fixes prices at which the parties will sell their product; or whether it absorbs or insulates competitors. Where the arrangement effects a horizontal merger between companies occupying the same product and geographic market, whatever competition previously may have existed in that market between the parties to the merger is eliminated. Section 7 of the Clayton Act, prior to its amendment, focused upon this aspect of horizontal combinations by proscribing acquisitions which might result in a lessening of competition between the acquiring and the acquired companies. The 1950 amendments made plain Congress' intent that the validity of such combinations was to be gauged on a broader scale: their effect on competition generally in an economically significant market.

Thus, again, the proper definition of the market is a "necessary predicate" to an examination of the competition that may be affected by the horizontal aspects of the merger. The acquisition of Kinney by Brown resulted in a horizontal combination at both the manufacturing and retailing levels of their businesses. Although the District Court found that the merger of Brown's and Kinney's *manufacturing* facilities was economically too insignificant to come within the prohibitions of the Clayton Act, the Government has not appealed from this portion of the lower court's decision. Therefore, we have no occasion to express our views with respect to that finding. On the other hand, appellant does contest the District Court's finding that the merger of the companies' *retail* outlets may tend substantially to lessen competition.

THE PRODUCT MARKET . . .

In [the vertical merger section] of this opinion we hold that the District Court correctly defined men's, women's, and children's shoes as the relevant lines of commerce in which to analyze the vertical aspects of the merger. For the reasons there stated we also hold that the same lines of commerce are appropriate for considering the horizontal aspects of the merger.

THE GEOGRAPHIC MARKET . . .

[A]lthough the geographic market in some instances may encompass the entire Nation, under other circumstances it may be as small as a single metropolitan area. . . . The fact that two merging firms have competed directly on the horizontal level in but a fraction of the geographic markets in which either has operated, does not, in itself, place their merger outside the scope of §7. . . . [65]

The District Court found that the effects of this aspect of the merger must be analyzed in every city with a population exceeding 10,000 and its immediate contiguous surrounding territory in which both Brown and Kinney sold shoes at retail through stores they either owned or controlled. By this definition of the geographic market, less than one-half of all the cities in which either Brown or Kinney sold shoes through such outlets are represented. The appellant recognizes that if the District Court's characterization of the relevant market is proper, the number of markets in which both Brown and Kinney have outlets is sufficiently numerous so that the validity of the entire merger is properly judged by testing its effects in those markets. However, it is appellant's contention that the areas of effective competition in shoe retailing were improperly defined by the District Court. It claims that such areas should, in some

---

65. To illustrate: If two retailers, one operating primarily in the eastern half of the Nation, and the other operating largely in the West, competed in but two mid-Western cities, the fact that the latter outlets represented but a small share of each company's business would not immunize the merger in those markets in which competition might be adversely affected. On the other hand, that fact would, of course, be properly considered in determining the equitable relief to be decreed. Cf. *Jerrold.*

cases, be defined so as to include only the central business districts of large cities, and in others, so as to encompass the "standard metropolitan areas" within which smaller communities are found. It argues that any test failing to distinguish between these competitive situations is improper.

We believe, however, that the record fully supports the District Court's findings that shoe stores in the outskirts of cities compete effectively with stores in central downtown areas, and that while there is undoubtedly some commercial intercourse between smaller communities within a single "standard metropolitan area," the most intense and important competition in retail sales will be confined to stores within the particular communities in such an area and their immediate environs.

We therefore agree that the District Court properly defined the relevant geographic markets in which to analyze this merger as those cities with a population exceeding 10,000 and their environs in which both Brown and Kinney retailed shoes through their own outlets. Such markets are large enough to include the downtown shops and suburban shopping centers in areas contiguous to the city, which are the important competitive factors, and yet are small enough to exclude stores beyond the immediate environs of the city, which are of little competitive significance.

THE PROBABLE EFFECT OF THE MERGER

Having delineated the product and geographic markets within which the effects of this merger are to be measured, we turn to an examination of the District Court's finding that as a result of the merger competition in the retailing of men's, women's, and children's shoes may be lessened substantially in those cities in which both Brown and Kinney stores are located. . . .

Although Brown objects to some details in the Government's computations used in drafting [its] exhibits, appellant cannot deny the correctness of the more general picture they reveal. . . . They show, for example, that during 1955 in 32 separate cities, ranging in size and location from Topeka, Kansas, to Batavia, New York, and Hobbs, New Mexico, the combined share of Brown and Kinney sales of women's shoes (by unit volume) exceeded 20%. In 31 cities — some the same as those used in measuring the effect of the merger in the women's line — the combined share of children's shoes sales exceeded 20%; in 6 cities their share exceeded 40%. In Dodge City, Kansas, their combined share of the market for women's shoes was over 57%; their share of the children's shoe market in that city was 49%. In the 7 cities in which Brown's and Kinney's combined shares of the market for women's shoes were greatest (ranging from 33% to 57%) each of the parties alone, prior to the merger, had captured substantial portions of those markets (ranging from 13% to 34%); the merger intensified this existing concentration. In 118 separate cities the combined shares of the market of Brown and Kinney in the sale of one of the relevant lines of commerce exceeded 5%. In 47 cities, their share exceeded 5% in all three lines.

The market share which companies may control by merging is one of the most important factors to be considered when determining the probable effects of the combination on effective competition in the relevant market. In an industry as fragmented as shoe retailing, the control of substantial shares of the trade in a city may have important effects on competition. If a merger achieving 5% control were now approved, we might be required to approve future merger efforts by Brown's competitors seeking similar market shares. The oligopoly Congress sought to avoid would then be furthered and it would be difficult to dissolve the combinations previously approved. Furthermore, in this fragmented industry, even if the combination controls but a small share of a particular market, the fact that this share is held by a large national chain can adversely affect competition. Testimony in the record from numerous independent retailers, based on their actual experience in the market, demonstrates that a strong, national chain of stores can insulate selected outlets from the vagaries of competition in particular locations and that the large chains can set and alter styles in footwear to an extent that renders the independents unable to maintain competitive inventories. A third significant aspect of this merger is that it creates a large national chain which is integrated with a manufacturing operation. The retail outlets of integrated companies, by eliminating wholesalers and by increasing the volume of purchases from the manufacturing division of the enterprise, can market their own brands at prices below those of competing independent retailers. Of course, some of the results of large integrated or chain operations are beneficial to consumers. Their expansion is not rendered unlawful by the mere fact that small independent stores may be adversely affected. It is competition, not competitors, which the Act protects. But we cannot fail to recognize Congress' desire to promote competition through the protection of viable, small, locally owned businesses. Congress appreciated that occasional higher costs and prices might result from the maintenance of fragmented industries and markets. It resolved these competing considerations in favor of decentralization. We must give effect to that decision.

Other factors to be considered in evaluating the probable effects of a merger in the relevant market lend additional support to the

District Court's conclusion that this merger may substantially lessen competition. One such factor is the history of tendency toward concentration in the industry.[72] As we have previously pointed out, the shoe industry has, in recent years, been a prime example of such a trend. Most combinations have been between manufacturers and retailers, as each of the larger producers has sought to capture an increasing number of assured outlets for its wares. Although these mergers have been primarily vertical in their aim and effect, to the extent that they have brought even greater numbers of retail outlets within fewer and fewer hands, they have had an additional important impact on the horizontal plane. By the merger in this case, the largest single group of retail stores still independent of one of the large manufacturers was absorbed into an already substantial aggregation of more or less controlled retail outlets. As a result of this merger, Brown moved into second place nationally in terms of retail stores directly owned. Including the stores on its franchise plan, the merger placed under Brown's control almost 1,600 shoe outlets, or about 7.2% of the Nation's retail "shoe stores" as defined by the Census Bureau, and 2.3% of the Nation's total retail shoe outlets. We cannot avoid the mandate of Congress that tendencies toward concentration in industry are to be curbed in their incipiency, particularly when those tendencies are being accelerated through giant steps striding across a hundred cities at a time. In the light of the trends in this industry we agree with the Government and the court below that this is an appropriate place at which to call a halt.

At the same time appellant has presented no mitigating factors, such as the business failure or the inadequate resources of one of the parties that may have prevented it from maintaining its competitive position, nor a demonstrated need for combination to enable small companies to enter into a more meaningful competition with those dominating the relevant markets. On the basis of the record before us, we believe the Government sustained its burden of proof. We hold that the District Court was correct in concluding that this merger may tend to lessen competition substantially in the retail sale of men's, women's, and children's shoes in the overwhelming

72. .... A company's history of expansion through mergers presents a different economic picture than a history of expansion through unilateral growth. Internal expansion is more likely to be the result of increased demand for the company's products and is more likely to provide increased investment in plants, more jobs and greater output. Conversely, expansion through merger is more likely to reduce available consumer choice while providing no increase in industry capacity, jobs or output. It was for these reasons, among others, Congress expressed its disapproval of successive acquisitions. Section 7 was enacted to prevent even small mergers that added to concentration in an industry. ...

majority of those cities and their environs in which both Brown and Kinney sell through owned or controlled outlets. . . .
Affirmed.[4]

518. (a) Apart from the fact that market shares were not trivial, upon what did the *Brown Shoe* Court base its conclusions concerning the horizontal aspects of the merger?

(b) Did the *Brown Shoe* Court find a concentration trend in the relevant retail markets? What evidence bears on this question?

(c) Suppose there had been a concentration trend. Would the significance of that trend depend in any way on whether it had resulted from internal growth or from merger?

(d) Should the §3 test be applied to mergers? Is the *Standard Stations* test applied to horizontal mergers? What does *Brown Shoe* say?

(e) Proposition: If a merger between X and Y were now approved, one would have to approve subsequent mergers effecting an equivalent increase in concentration; because the statute would have us stop such a process in its incipiency, §7 condemns all the mergers of ¶517b. (1) Did *Brown Shoe* assert this proposition or any part of it? (2) Is the proposition or any part of it sound? Compare ¶450.

(f) Could you conclude that *Brown Shoe* stands for any or all of the following propositions? (1) Effects can be presumed from a series of acquisitions. Rebuttable? How? (2) Smoke implies fire: a number of mergers in an industry must ultimately portend a change in the character of the industry. (3) The loss of numerous small units is within the statutory ban regardless of actual or potential effects on competition in the market. (4) Some other propositions?

519. Consider the *Brown Shoe* Court's comments concerning the values to be promoted by or considered in enforcement of §7.

(a) What does the Court have in mind by "competition"? Does it speak to a process or a result? What process? What result? The Court's statement that "[i]t is competition, not competitors, which the Act protects" is often cited. What does it mean in light of the remainder of the paragraph (beginning "But . . .") that follows?

(b) Note the use of the efficiency issue in *Brown Shoe,* not as a defense, but as a reason for questioning the merger. (1) Was it established that the merging companies would be able to cut the cost of distributing shoes? (2) If that were to occur, would it be undesirable? (3) If the result is undesirable, can it be prevented by

---

4. Clark, J., concurred separately. Harlan, J., dissented on jurisdictional grounds but concurred in the result on vertical grounds. Frankfurter and White, JJ., did not participate.

§7? Can it be made more difficult? If not, should a merger be prohibited solely on this ground?

(c) What would be the practical consequence of the acceptance in principle of at least some efficiency defenses in justification of at least some mergers?[5] (1) Would you expect to see a different result in very many merger cases? (2) Apart from any difference in outcome, would you expect to see any difference in the conduct and content of merger litigation? (3) Should any efficiency defense be rejected categorically and in principle on the ground that internal growth is a preferable and reasonable alternative?

(d) Would consumers be better off as a result of mergers that enhanced efficiency but decreased competition? Should this consideration determine whether an efficiency defense should be permitted?

(e) Do the relevant statutes say anything about efficiency as a possible justification for mergers or other conduct possibly impairing competition? It is generally assumed that the legislative histories of the relevant statutes include little reference to efficiency. Would it follow that efficiency considerations have no place in the application of §7?[6] How does your answer in ¶516 bear on this question?

(f) In the light of *Brown Shoe* and your own reasoning, how would you appraise the efficiency "defense" in the following cases? (1) Firm *A* has an effective but expensive management team that is efficient enough to manage a firm twice as large. To this end, firm *B* is acquired. (2) Firm *C* possesses especially useful market outlets, important patents, and active dynamic management. Firm *D* finds itself in great need of these resources. *D* acquires *C*.

UNITED STATES v. PHILADELPHIA
NATIONAL BANK
374 U.S. 321 (1963)

Justice BRENNAN. . . . We reverse the judgment of the District Court. We hold that the merger of appellees is forbidden by §7 of the Clayton Act and so must be enjoined; we need not, and there-

5. See J. Brodley, Proof of Efficiencies in Mergers and Joint Ventures, 64 Antitr. L.J. 575 (1996).

6. In addition to *Brown Shoe*, consider the discussion of this issue in *Clorox*, Ch. 5E, and recall the *Alcoa* statement favoring small units "in spite of possible cost." Contrast the Court's observation in *Sylvania*, Ch. 4A, at n.21: "Competitive economies have social and political as well as economic advantages . . . but an antitrust policy divorced from market considerations would lack any objective benchmarks." In each instance, consider precisely what argument is being accepted or rejected and what reasons these courts offer for their conclusions.

fore do not, reach the further question of alleged violation of §1 of the Sherman Act. . . .

[Philadelphia National Bank (PNB) and Girard are the second and third largest commercial banks in the Philadelphia metropolitan area, consisting of the City and three contiguous counties in Pennsylvania. PNB, with assets over one billion dollars, was the twenty-first largest bank in the country. If the merger is consummated, the resulting bank will be the area's largest, having approximately 35 percent of area banks' total assets, deposits, and net loans. With the next largest, the combined share would be 58 percent, and the top four would have 78 percent. The largest banks have achieved their size through mergers, and since 1947 the number of banks has fallen from 108 to 42.]

We have no difficulty in determining the "line of commerce" (relevant product or services market) and "section of the country" (relevant geographical market) in which to appraise the probable competitive effects of appellees' proposed merger. We agree with the District Court that the cluster of products (various kinds of credit) and services (such as checking accounts and trust administration) denoted by the term "commercial banking" composes a distinct line of commerce. Some commercial banking products or services are so distinctive that they are entirely free of effective competition from products or services of other financial institutions; the checking account is in this category. Others enjoy such cost advantages as to be insulated within a broad range from substitutes furnished by other institutions. For example, commercial banks compete with small-loan companies in the personal-loan market; but the small-loan companies' rates are invariably much higher than the banks', in part, it seems, because the companies' working capital consists in substantial part of bank loans. Finally, there are banking facilities which, although in terms of cost and price they are freely competitive with the facilities provided by other financial institutions, nevertheless enjoy a settled consumer preference, insulating them, to a marked degree, from competition; this seems to be the case with savings deposits. In sum, it is clear that commercial banking is a market "sufficiently inclusive to be meaningful in terms of trade realities." . . .

We part company with the District Court on the determination of the appropriate "section of the country." The proper question to be asked in this case is not where the parties to the merger do business or even where they compete, but where, within the area of competitive overlap, the effect of the merger on competition will be direct and immediate. . . . This depends upon "the geographic structure of supplier-customer relations." . . . In banking, as in most service industries, convenience of location is essential to effective competition. Individuals and corporations typically confer the bulk of their patronage on banks in their local community; they find it impractical to conduct their banking business at a distance.... The factor of inconvenience localizes banking competition as effectively as high transportation costs in other industries.... Therefore, since, as we recently said in a related context the "area of effective competition in the known line of commerce must be charted by careful selection of the market area in which the seller operates, *and to which the purchaser can practicably turn for supplies,*" *Tampa Electric*; see *Standard Stations*, the four-county area in which appellees' offices are located would seem to be the relevant geographical market.... In fact, the vast bulk of appellees' business originates in the four-county area. Theoretically, we should be concerned with the possibility that bank offices on the perimeter of the area may be in effective competition with bank offices within; actually, this seems to be a factor of little significance.

We recognize that the area in which appellees have their offices does not delineate with perfect accuracy an appropriate "section of the country" in which to appraise the effect of the merger upon competition. Large borrowers and large depositors, the record shows, may find it practical to do a large part of their banking business outside their home community; very small borrowers and depositors may, as a practical matter, be confined to bank offices in their immediate neighborhood; and customers of intermediate size, it would appear, deal with banks within an area intermediate between these extremes. So also, some banking services are evidently more local in nature than others. But that in banking the relevant geographical market is a function of each separate customer's economic scale means simply that a workable compromise must be found: some fair intermediate delineation which avoids the indefensible extremes of drawing the market either so expansively as to make the effect of the merger upon competition seem insignificant, because only the very largest bank customers are taken into account in defining the market, or so narrowly as to place appellees in different markets, because only the smallest customers are considered. We think that the four-county Philadelphia metropolitan area, which state law apparently recognizes as a meaningful banking community in allowing Philadelphia banks to branch within it, and which would seem roughly to delineate the area in which bank customers that are neither very large nor very small find it practical to do their banking business, is a more appropriate "section of the country" in which to appraise the instant merger than any larger or smaller or different area.... We are helped to this conclusion by the fact that the three federal banking agencies regard the area in which banks have their offices as an "area of effective competition."

Not only did the FDIC and FRB, in the reports they submitted to the Comptroller of the Currency in connection with appellees' application for permission to merge, so hold, but the Comptroller, in his statement approving the merger, agreed: "With respect to the effect upon competition, there are three separate levels and effective areas of competition involved. These are the national level for national accounts, the regional or sectional area, and the local area of the City of Philadelphia and the immediately surrounding area."

Having determined the relevant market, we come to the ultimate question under §7: whether the effect of the merger "may be substantially to lessen competition" in the relevant market. Clearly, this is not the kind of question which is susceptible of a ready and precise answer in most cases. It requires not merely an appraisal of the immediate impact of the merger upon competition, but a prediction of its impact upon competitive conditions in the future; this is what is meant when it is said that the amended §7 was intended to arrest anticompetitive tendencies in their "incipiency." . . . Such a prediction is sound only if it is based upon a firm understanding of the structure of the relevant market; yet the relevant economic data are both complex and elusive. . . . And unless businessmen can assess the legal consequences of a merger with some confidence, sound business planning is retarded. . . . So also, we must be alert to the danger of subverting congressional intent by permitting a too-broad economic investigation. *Standard Stations.* And so in any case in which it is possible, without doing violence to the congressional objective embodied in §7, to simplify the test of illegality, the courts ought to do so in the interest of sound and practical judicial administration. . . . This is such a case.

We noted in *Brown Shoe* that "[t]he dominant theme pervading congressional consideration of the 1950 amendments [to §7] was a fear of what was considered to be a rising tide of economic concentration in the American economy." This intense congressional concern with the trend toward concentration warrants dispensing, in certain cases, with elaborate proof of market structure, market behavior, or probable anticompetitive effects. Specifically, we think that a merger which produces a firm controlling an undue percentage share of the relevant market, and results in a significant increase in the concentration of firms in that market, is so inherently likely to lessen competition substantially that it must be enjoined in the absence of evidence clearly showing that the merger is not likely to have such anticompetitive effects. . . .

Such a test lightens the burden of proving illegality only with respect to mergers whose size makes them inherently suspect in light of Congress' design in §7 to prevent undue concentration.

Furthermore, the test is fully consonant with economic theory. That "[c]ompetition is likely to be greatest when there are many sellers, none of which has any significant market share," is common ground among most economists, and was undoubtedly a premise of congressional reasoning about the antimerger statute.

The merger of appellees will result in a single bank's controlling at least 30% of the commercial banking business in the four-county Philadelphia metropolitan area. Without attempting to specify the smallest market share which would still be considered to threaten undue concentration, we are clear that 30% presents that threat.[41] Further, whereas presently the two largest banks in the area (First Pennsylvania and PNB) control between them approximately 44% of the area's commercial banking business, the two largest after the merger (PNB-Girard and First Pennsylvania) will control 59 percent. Plainly, we think, this increase of more than 33 percent in concentration must be regarded as significant.

Our conclusion that these percentages raise an inference that the effect of the contemplated merger of appellees may be substantially to lessen competition is not an arbitrary one, although neither the terms of §7 nor the legislative history suggests that any particular percentage share was deemed critical. The House Report states that the tests of illegality under amended §7 "are intended to be similar to those which the courts have applied in interpreting the same language as used in other sections of the Clayton Act." . . . Accordingly, we have relied upon decisions under these other sections in applying §7. . . . In *Standard Stations,* . . . this Court held violative of §3 of the Clayton Act exclusive contracts whereby the defendant company, which accounted for 23% of the sales in the relevant market and, together with six other firms, accounted for 65% of such sales, maintained control over outlets through which approximately 7% of the sales were made. In *Motion Picture Adv. Serv.,* we held unlawful, under §1 of the Sherman Act and §5 of the Federal

41. Kaysen and Turner [Antitrust Policy (1959)] suggest that 20% should be the line of prima facie unlawfulness; Stigler [Mergers and Preventive Antitrust Policy, 104 U. Pa. L. Rev. 176 (1955)] suggests that any acquisition by a firm controlling 20% of the market after the merger is presumptively unlawful; Markham [Merger Policy under the New §7, 43 Va. L. Rev. 489 (1957)] mentions 25%. Bok's [Section 7 of the Clayton Act and the Merging of Law and Economics, 74 Harv. L. Rev. 226 (1960)] principal test is increase in market concentration, and he suggests a figure of 7% or 8%. We intimate no view on the validity of such tests for we have no need to consider percentages smaller than those in the case at bar, but we note that such tests are more rigorous than is required to dispose of the instant case. Needless to say, the fact that a merger results in a less-than-30% market share, or in a less substantial increase in concentration than in the instant case, does not raise an inference that the merger is *not* violative of §7. See, e.g., *Brown Shoe.*

Trade Commission Act, rather than under §3 of the Clayton Act, exclusive arrangements whereby the four major firms in the industry had foreclosed 75% of the relevant market; the respondent's market share, evidently, was 20%. . . . In the instant case, by way of comparison, the four largest banks after the merger will foreclose 78% of the relevant market. And in Standard Fashion Co. v. Magrane-Houston Co., 258 U.S. 346, the Court held violative of §3 a series of exclusive contracts whereby a single manufacturer controlled 40% of the industry's retail outlets. Doubtless these cases turned to some extent upon whether "by the nature of the market there is room for newcomers." . . . But they remain highly suggestive in the present context, for . . . integration by merger is more suspect than integration by contract, because of the greater permanence of the former. The market share and market concentration figures in the contract-integration cases, taken together with scholarly opinion, support, we believe, the inference we draw in the instant case from the figures disclosed by the record.

There is nothing in the record of this case to rebut the inherently anticompetitive tendency manifested by these percentages. There was, to be sure, testimony by bank officers to the effect that competition among banks in Philadelphia was vigorous and would continue to be vigorous after the merger. We think, however, that the District Court's reliance on such evidence was misplaced. This lay evidence on so complex an economic-legal problem as the substantiality of the effect of this merger upon competition was entitled to little weight, in view of the witnesses' failure to give concrete reasons for their conclusions.[43]

Of equally little value, we think, are the assurances offered by appellees' witnesses that customers dissatisfied with the services of the resulting bank may readily turn to the 40 other banks in the Philadelphia area. In every case short of outright monopoly, the disgruntled customer has alternatives; even in tightly oligopolistic markets, there may be small firms operating. A fundamental purpose of amending §7 was to arrest the trend toward concentration, the *tendency* to monopoly, before the consumer's alternatives disappeared through merger, and that purpose would be ill served if the law stayed its hand until 10, or 20, or 30 more Philadelphia banks were absorbed. This is not a fanciful eventuality, in view of the

---

43. The fact that some of the bank officers who testified represented small banks in competition with appellees does not substantially enhance the probative value of their testimony. The test of a competitive market is not only whether small competitors flourish but also whether consumers are well served. . . . In an oligopolistic market, small companies may be perfectly content to follow the high prices set by the dominant firms, yet the market may be profoundly anticompetitive.

strong trend toward mergers evident in the area; and we might note also that entry of new competitors into the banking field is far from easy.

So also, we reject the position that commercial banking, because it is subject to a high degree of governmental regulation, or because it deals in the intangibles of credit and services rather than in the manufacture or sale of tangible commodities, is somehow immune from the anticompetitive effects of undue concentration. Competition among banks exists at every level — price, variety of credit arrangements, convenience of location, attractiveness of physical surroundings, credit information, investment advice, service charges, personal accommodations, advertising, miscellaneous special and extra services — and it is keen; on this appellees' own witnesses were emphatic. There is no reason to think that concentration is less inimical to the free play of competition in banking than in other service industries. On the contrary, it is in all probability more inimical. For example, banks compete to fill the credit needs of businessmen. Small businessmen especially are, as a practical matter, confined to their locality for the satisfaction of their credit needs. If the number of banks in the locality is reduced, the vigor of competition for filling the marginal small business borrower's needs is likely to diminish. At the same time, his concomitantly greater difficulty in obtaining credit is likely to put him at a disadvantage vis-à-vis larger businesses with which he competes. In this fashion, concentration in banking accelerates concentration generally.

We turn now to three affirmative justifications which appellees offer for the proposed merger. The first is that only through mergers can banks follow their customers to the suburbs and retain their business. This justification does not seem particularly related to the instant merger, but in any event it has no merit. There is an alternative to the merger route: the opening of new branches in the areas to which the customers have moved — so-called de novo branching. Appellees do not contend that they are unable to expand thus, by opening new offices rather than acquiring existing ones, and surely one premise of an antimerger statute such as §7 is that corporate growth by internal expansion is socially preferable to growth by acquisition.

Second, it is suggested that the increased lending limit of the resulting bank will enable it to compete with the large out-of-state banks, particularly the New York banks, for very large loans. We reject this application of the concept of "countervailing power." Cf. Kiefer-Stewart Co. v. Joseph E. Seagram & Sons, 340 U.S. 211. If anticompetitive effects in one market could be justified by procompetitive consequences in another, the logical upshot would be that every firm in an industry could, without violating §7, embark on a series of mergers that would make it in the end as large as the industry leader. For if all the commercial banks in the Philadelphia area merged into one, it would be smaller than the largest bank in New York City. This is not a case, plainly, where two small firms in a market propose to merge in order to be able to compete more successfully with the leading firms in that market. Nor is it a case in which lack of adequate banking facilities is causing hardships to individuals or businesses in the community. The present two largest banks in Philadelphia have lending limits of $8,000,000 each. The only businesses located in the Philadelphia area which find such limits inadequate are large enough readily to obtain bank credit in other cities.

This brings us to appellees' final contention, that Philadelphia needs a bank larger than it now has in order to bring business to the area and stimulate its economic development. We are clear, however, that a merger the effect of which "may be substantially to lessen competition" is not saved because, on some ultimate reckoning of social or economic debits and credits, it may be deemed beneficial. A value choice of such magnitude is beyond the ordinary limits of judicial competence, and in any event has been made for us already, by Congress when it enacted the amended §7. Congress determined to preserve our traditionally competitive economy. It therefore proscribed anticompetitive mergers, the benign and the malignant alike, fully aware, we must assume, that some price might have to be paid.

In holding as we do that the merger of appellees would violate §7 and must therefore be enjoined, we reject appellees' pervasive suggestion that application of the procompetitive policy of §7 to the banking industry will have dire, although unspecified, consequences for the national economy. . . . The fact that banking is a highly regulated industry critical to the Nation's welfare makes the play of competition not less important but more so. At the price of some repetition, we note that if the businessman is denied credit because his banking alternatives have been eliminated by mergers, the whole edifice of an entrepreneurial system is threatened; if the costs of banking services and credit are allowed to become excessive by the absence of competitive pressures, virtually all costs, in our credit economy, will be affected; and unless competition is allowed to fulfill its role as an economic regulator in the banking industry, the result may well be even more governmental regulation. Subject to narrow qualifications, it is surely the case that competition is our fundamental national economic policy, offering as it does the only alternative to the cartelization or governmental regimentation of large portions of the economy. . . . There is no warrant for declining to enforce it in the instant case. . . .[7]

520. Do you agree with the Court's product and geographic market definitions in *Philadelphia Bank*?[8]

521. (a) What is the "undue" percentage share or the "significant" increase in concentration that condemns the merger? Are these conditions alternative or cumulative?[9]

(b) Would *Philadelphia Bank* dictate a different result in *Brown Shoe*? Does the shoe merger produce a "firm controlling an undue percentage share of the relevant market" or result "in a significant increase in the concentration of firms in that market"? Why do plaintiffs attacking or courts condemning mergers involving market shares higher than in *Brown Shoe* but lower than in *Philadelphia Bank* so often cite the latter rather than the former?

(c) Is the *Philadelphia Bank* invocation of Clayton Act §3 and its use of §3 cases consistent with the approach of *Brown Shoe*? What does the Court have in mind when it uses the language of foreclosure to describe this horizontal merger?

522. Do you agree with the *Philadelphia Bank* disposition of the second and third "affirmative justifications"? In particular:

7. Harlan, Stewart, and Goldberg, JJ., dissented from the Court's holding that §7 applied to the bank merger. White, J., did not participate.

Much of the reaction to *Philadelphia Bank* reflected surprise over the Court's application of §7, which did not appear to be covered by the 1950 Amendment. Congress responded in 1966 with legislation exempting bank mergers from §1 and §7 (not from §2), but permitting attack within 30 days of banking authorities' approval of a merger under a standard similar to §7, with a proviso directing courts to approve mergers whose anticompetitive effects "are clearly outweighed in the public interest by the probable effect of the transaction in meeting the convenience and needs of the community served." 80 Stat. 7 (1966), as amended, 12 U.S.C. §1828(c) (1987). In United States v. Third Natl. Bank in Nashville, 390 U.S. 171, 189 (1968), the Supreme Court, finding a violation under a standard §7 approach, reversed and remanded for further demonstration in support of the three trial court findings of benefits from the merger. See also United States v. Citizens and Southern Natl. Bank, 422 U.S. 86 (1975) (no §7 violation because state law precluded preexisting competition).

8. For a recent discussion of market definition in bank merger cases, see M. Guerin-Calvert, Key Issues in Antitrust Analysis of Bank Mergers, 858 Practicing Law Institute Corporate Law and Practice Course Handbook Series (1994).

9. See United States v. Tidewater Marine Serv., 284 F. Supp. 324 (E.D. La. 1968) (*Philadelphia Bank* presumption not controlling where clear showing of vigorous competition and no likely anticompetitive effect; defendant nevertheless accepted consent decree, 1971 Trade Cas. ¶73705).

(a) Is this a case, as the Court says, of "countervailing power"? Is it a sufficient answer to say with the Court that borrowers large enough to be affected by existing lending limits can get credit elsewhere? Is internal growth a real alternative for PNB?

(b) With respect to the alleged contribution of a larger bank to Philadelphia's economic development, the Court says that this cannot be a defense in this case because the statute requires the condemnation of a merger tending substantially to lessen competition. Is the Court's reasoning sound? As applied to this case?

(c) In similar fashion, the Court observes that any ultimate reckoning of social or economic debits and credits is beyond the ordinary limits of judicial competence. Is that a sufficient answer to the defense's claim? Why or why not?

(d) Would these affirmative justifications be excluded under the *Engineers* formulation? Should that rule for applying the Sherman Act be relevant for §7?

523. *United States v. Continental Can Co.*, 378 U.S. 441, 453 (1964). The Supreme Court condemned a merger of the country's second largest can producer (33 percent share) with the nation's third largest producer of glass containers (10 percent share). The Court noted specific instances where cans and bottles had been and continued to be in confrontation with each other for the patronage of producers of particular end-use products such as baby food, soft drinks, and beer.[10]

> In our view there is and has been a rather general confrontation between metal and glass containers and competition between them for the same end uses which is insistent, continuous, effective and quantitywise very substantial. Metal has replaced glass and glass has replaced metal as the leading container for some important uses; both are used for other purposes; each is trying to expand its share of the market at the expense of the other; and each is attempting to preempt for itself every use for which its product is physically suitable, even though some such uses have traditionally been regarded as the exclusive domain of the competing industry.

---

10. Rather than merely noting substitution possibilities in end-use markets for the purpose of determining whether bottles and cans are in the same market, consider defining each end-use — for example, beer containers — to be a separate market. Is such a market definition appropriate? Is it more precise than the Court might have thought necessary? Would it matter if the same type of can or bottle were used for many end products? If the merging companies were not currently direct competitors in the beer market, would there be no competitive threat in that market from the merger? Are producer shares in particular end-use markets likely to be stable?

It thus looked to a market consisting of bottles and cans —
ignoring, for example, plastic containers — in which the two firms
possessed 22 percent and 3 percent, whereupon the Court invoked
the *Philadelphia Bank* presumption that condemned mergers resulting in a significant increase in concentration and a firm controlling
an undue percentage of the market. Both can and bottle production were relatively concentrated. The two largest can firms accounted for 70 percent of can sales, while the three largest bottle
makers accounted for 55 percent of bottle sales. The Court seemed
to fear that the merger would reduce competition between cans
and bottles and would also reduce innovation.

(a) How should the *Philadelphia Bank* presumption be applied to
such hybrid markets? Is the danger to competition the same in *Continental Can* as it was in *Philadelphia Bank*? Is the level of danger
reflected in the market share numbers used by the Court? Is there any
sensible way to apply a presumption, thereby avoiding a more detailed inquiry into the competitive impact of interindustry mergers?[11]

(b) If the Court erred in resting on the *Philadelphia Bank* presumption, did it reach the wrong result in *Continental Can*? Did the
mergers significantly threaten competition? In *Continental Can,* for
example, might the merger reduce bottle-can competition? Might
the *Continental Can* Court have feared any possible changes for the
worse when both industries were so highly concentrated?

(c) Do *Philadelphia-Bank*-like presumptions produce significantly
fewer reliable results than *Brown Shoe*'s examination of all relevant
factors? Was *Brown Shoe*'s condemnation of the rather modest
market share merger any more satisfying? For most cases, actual
or prospective effects cannot be confidently established with the
naked eye, laboratory tests, or economics. While predictions are
sometimes possible, we are often reduced to the simple textbook
proposition that the larger the number of competitors, the greater
is the likelihood of competition, other things being equal.

UNITED STATES v. VON'S GROCERY CO.
384 U.S. 270 (1966)

Justice BLACK. [In March, 1960, when Von's, a grocery chain,
sought to merge with Shopping Bag, a competing chain, the Justice
Department brought suit under Clayton Act §7.] The market in-

---

11. The government brief in *Continental Can* had suggested that interindustry
mergers be forbidden when there is substantial competition between those industries, one or both industries are highly concentrated, and each of the merging
firms is dominant in its own industry.

volved here is the retail grocery market in the Los Angeles area. In 1958 Von's retail sales ranked third in the area and Shopping Bag's ranked sixth. In 1960 their sales together were 7.5% of the total two and one-half billion dollars of retail groceries sold in the Los Angeles market each year. For many years before the merger both companies had enjoyed great success as rapidly growing companies. From 1948 to 1958 the number of Von's stores in the Los Angeles area practically doubled from 14 to 27, while at the same time the number of Shopping Bag's stores jumped from 15 to 34. During that same decade, Von's sales increased four fold and its share of the market almost doubled while Shopping Bag's sales multiplied seven times and its share of the market tripled. The merger of these two highly successful, expanding and aggressive competitors created the second largest grocery chain in Los Angeles with sales of almost $172,488,000 annually. In addition the findings of the District Court show that the number of owners operating single stores in the Los Angeles retail grocery market decreased from 5,365 in 1950 to 3,818 in 1961. By 1963, three years after the merger, the number of single-store owners had dropped still further to 3,590. During roughly the same period, from 1953 to 1962, the number of chains with two or more grocery stores increased from 96 to 150. While the grocery business was being concentrated into the hands of fewer and fewer owners, the small companies were continually being absorbed by the larger firms through mergers. . . . [I]n the period from 1949 to 1958 nine of the top 20 chains acquired 126 stores from their smaller competitors. . . . Moreover, a table prepared by the Federal Trade Commission . . . shows that acquisitions and mergers in the Los Angeles retail grocery market have continued since the merger. These facts alone are enough to cause us to conclude contrary to the District Court that the Von's-Shopping Bag merger did violate §7. According, we reverse. . . .[12]

Justice WHITE, concurring. As I read the Court's opinion, which I join, it does not hold that in any industry exhibiting a decided

---

12. Most of the remainder of the majority's opinion addressed the history of the antitrust laws, emphasizing the objective of protecting small business. The Court quoted from *Trans-Missouri* the reference to powerful combinations restraining competition "by driving out of business the small dealers and worthy men whose lives have been spent therein" and noted Judge Hand's statement in *Alcoa* concerning the Sherman Act's purpose of protecting "for its own sake and in spite of possible cost, an organization of industry in small units which can effectively compete with each other." Finally, it noted the legislative history recounted in ¶505. After these recitations, the Court stated: "The facts of this case present exactly the threatening trend toward concentration which Congress wanted to halt." — eds.

trend towards concentration, any merger between competing firms violates §7 unless saved by the failing company doctrine; nor does it declare illegal each and every merger in such an industry where the resulting firm has as much as a 7.5% share of the relevant market. But here, in 1958 before the merger, the largest firm had 8% of the sales, Von's was third with 4.7% and Shopping Bag was sixth with 4.2%. The four largest firms had 24.4% of the market, the top eight had 40.9% and the top 12 had 48.8% as compared with 25.9%, 33.7% and 38.8% in 1948. All but two of the top 10 firms in 1958 were very probably also among the top 10 in 1948 or had acquired a firm that was among the top 10. Further, all but three of the top 10 had increased their market share between 1948 and 1958 and those which gained gained more than the three lost. Also, although three companies declined in market share their total sales increased in substantial amounts.

Given a trend towards fewer and fewer sellers which promises to continue, it is clear to me that where the eight leading firms have over 40% of the market, any merger between the leaders or between one of them and a lesser company is vulnerable under §7, absent some special proof to the contrary. . . .

Justice STEWART, with whom Justice HARLAN joins, dissenting. . . . The Court rests its conclusion on the "crucial point" that, in the 11-year period between 1950 and 1961, the number of single-store grocery firms in Los Angeles decreased 29% from 5,365 to 3,818. Such a decline should, of course, be no more than a fact calling for further investigation of the competitive trend in the industry. For the Court, however, that decline is made the end, not the beginning, of the analysis. In the counting-of-heads game played today by the Court, the reduction in the number of single-store operators becomes a yardstick for automatic disposition of cases under §7. . . .

Section 7 was never intended by Congress for use by the Court as a charter to roll back the supermarket revolution. Yet the Court's opinion is hardly more than a requiem for the so-called "Mom and Pop" grocery stores . . . that are now economically and technologically obsolete in many parts of the country. . . .

[The opinion discusses the evidence indicating that although the combined shares of the top 20 firms increased from 47% to 57% between 1948 and 1958, the shares of the top 5 firms fell; 7 of 1958's top 20 had not even been in existence in 1948. Between 1953 and 1962 the number of chain stores in business increased from 96 to 150 with 173 new entries and 119 exits.]

With regard to the "plight" of the small businessman, the record is unequivocal that his competitive position is strong and secure in the Los Angeles retail grocery industry. . . . The vitality of these independents is directly attributable to the recent and spectacular growth in California of three large cooperative buying organizations.... In the face of the substantial assistance available to independents through membership in such cooperatives, the Court's implicit equation between the market power and the market share resulting from the present merger seems completely invalid.

Moreover, it is clear that there are no substantial barriers to market entry. The record contains references to numerous highly successful instances of entry with modest initial investments. Many of the stores opened by new entrants were obtained through the disposition of unwanted outlets by the chains; frequently the new competitors were themselves chain-store executives who had resigned to enter the market on their own. Enhancing free access to the market is the absence of any such restrictive factors as patented technology, trade secrets, or substantial product differentiation.

Numerous other factors attest to the pugnacious level of grocery competition in Los Angeles, all of them silently ignored by the Court in its emphasis solely on the declining number of single-store competitors in the market. 3,590 single-store firms is a lot of grocery stores. The large number of separate competitors and the frequent price battles between them belie any suggestion that price competition in the area is even remotely threatened by a descent to the sort of consciously interdependent pricing that is characteristic of a market turning the corner toward oligopoly....

[T]he Court pronounces its work consistent with the line of our decisions under §7 since the passage of the 1950 amendment. The sole consistency that I can find is that under §7, the Government always wins. The only precedent that is even within sight of today's holding is *Philadelphia Bank.* In that case, in the interest of practical judicial administration, the Court proposed a simplified test of merger illegality.... The merger between Von's and Shopping Bag produced a firm with 1.4% of the grocery stores and 7.5% of grocery sales in Los Angeles, and resulted in an increase of 1.1% in the market share enjoyed by the two largest firms in the market and 3.3% in the market share of the six largest firms. The former two figures are hardly the "undue percentage" of the market, nor are the latter two figures the "significant increase" in concentration, that would make this merger inherently suspect under the standard of *Philadelphia Bank.*...[13]

524. (a) The *Von's* Court states: "These facts alone are enough to cause us" to condemn the merger. Which facts? Do the Court's statistics show that the present market is becoming significantly

13. Fortas, J., did not participate.

concentrated? Does the first sentence of Justice White's concurrence correctly state the holding of the case?

(b) What is the result of *Continental Can* and *Von's?* Do they imply a rule of per se or presumptive illegality? For anyone the government chooses to prosecute or only for large firms or industry leaders? Is any merger between competing firms in an industry exhibiting a "trend" toward concentration violative of §7? What possible defenses are left after *Von's?*

(c) After *Von's,* need the government show more than substantial dollar volume? How much more?[14]

(d) Is this line of cases consistent with the legislative history of amended §7, as described in ¶505? Did Congress intend "to roll back the supermarket revolution," as the dissent argues the majority is doing?

(e) Can it be argued that although Von's itself would not have overwhelming power as a result of the merger, and although the market is not yet overly concentrated, the best method of preserving competition is to stop aggressive growth by merger before the initial problems of concentration begin? How does the state of antitrust law concerning oligopoly pricing and monopolization bear on this issue?

525. The failing company defense.[15] In its *International Shoe* decision of 1930,[16] the Supreme Court created what has become known as the failing company defense, which has been referred to approvingly in subsequent House and Senate reports accompanying the 1950 and subsequent amendments to Clayton Act §7. In that case, the Court found no §7 violation where the acquired company's "resources [were] so depleted and the prospect of rehabilitation so remote that it faced the grave probability of a business failure." The Court also noted that there was "no other prospective purchaser" of the failing firm. In its 1969 *Citizen Publishing* decision,[17] which involved a two-firm market where the arrangement

14. In United States v. Pabst Brewing Co., 384 U.S. 546 (1966), an opinion noted more for the geographic market definition issue that the case presented, the majority opinion indicated that, given a trend toward concentration, the market shares were high enough to establish a §7 violation in all markets addressed, including the nation as a whole, where the post-merger share was 4.49 percent.

15. See IV P. Areeda & D. Turner, Antitrust Law ¶¶924-925 (legislative history; competitive effects), ¶926 (failure defined), and ¶¶927-931 (preferred purchasers: when required, who is preferable, how diligent the search, and low or piecemeal offers) (1980; Supp. 1996).

16. International Shoe Co. v. Federal Trade Commn., 280 U.S. 291, 302 (1930).

17. Citizen Pub. Co. v. United States, 394 U.S. 131, 138 (1969).

between the parties created an effective monopoly,[18] the Court denied the defense because the acquiring (or otherwise controlling) firm was not "the only available purchaser." No effort had been made to sell the allegedly failing firm; its properties had not been put in the hands of a broker. Moreover the "prospects of reorganization" of that firm under the Bankruptcy Act "would have had to be dim or nonexistent to make the failing company doctrine applicable to this case."

Two possible rationales have been offered for the failing firm defense: that (1) the failing firm's contribution to competition is so modest that its absorption by a rival would not reduce competition significantly or (2) merger is preferable to failure from the viewpoint of the investors, employees, customers, and communities involved. Moreover, the prospect of graceful exit after failure might reduce entry barriers to some extent.

(a) Can the acquisition of a failing firm impair competition significantly? For simplicity consider a market with only two firms or a market with five firms and compare the state of competition after failure if a merger were allowed or prohibited. What happens to the assets and business of a failed firm? If a firm's failure were certain, why would its assets be of value to the other firm(s)?[19]

(b) Is the defense absolute or is it merely a factor to be weighed in assessing the competitive effects of a merger?[20]

(c) Is a failing company one that is insolvent? One suffering persistent losses or marked sales decline? Unable to obtain new capital for modernization? Unable to achieve efficiencies now enjoyed by rivals without the merger? A failing division or subsidiary of an otherwise successful firm? A firm whose withdrawal from the market (for whatever reason) is probable? Does *Brown Shoe* shed any light on this question?

---

18. The market had two newspapers which entered a "joint operating agreement" that left the two papers editorially independent but combined their printing, distribution, and selling of advertising such as to eliminate any price competition between them. Subsequent legislation exempts from the antitrust laws such joint operating agreements when not more than one of the papers involved "was likely to remain or become a financially sound publication." Post-enactment arrangements enjoy the exemption only upon prior approval of the Justice Department and a finding of "probable danger of financial failure." Newspaper Preservation Act, 84 Stat. 466 (1970), 15 U.S.C. §§1801-1804.

19. For an assessment of the efficiency of the failing company defense that focuses on the trade-off between increased market power and reduced productive capacity, see T. Campbell, The Efficiency of the Failing Company Defense, 63 Tex. L. Rev. 251 (1984).

20. United States Steel Corp. v. FTC, 426 F.2d 592 (6th Cir. 1970) (defense absolute if all its requirements are met).

(d) Should the failing company defense always be contingent on dim prospects for reorganization under the Bankruptcy laws or only where a monopoly (or other very substantial anticompetitive threat) would result from the merger? Should the defense always or only sometimes be contingent on a showing that there was no preferred purchaser?

(e) Assume that Kinney had been considered a "failing company" in *Brown Shoe* and that it had received merger offers from (1) Brown, (2) a larger shoe manufacturer that had no retail outlets, (3) Sears Roebuck & Co., and (4) General Motors. Which merger should antitrust law prefer? Rank them in order.

(f) Assume that your preferred merger partners offered to pay $8 million in cash for Kinney but that your last two choices offered $10 million and $12 million. Would the courts permit Kinney to sell to the highest bidder? Should they?[21]

UNITED STATES v. GENERAL DYNAMICS CORP.
415 U.S. 486 (1974)

Justice STEWART. [The Court affirmed the lower court's approval under §7 of the merger, ultimately into General Dynamics, of Freeman Coal Mining Corp. and United Electric Coal Companies. Freeman's parent had gradually acquired stock in United, attaining more than 34 percent and effective control by 1959. Freeman mined coal in deep shafts while United strip-mined. Shares of sales within Illinois and the so-called Eastern Interior Coal Province (EICP) were as follows:

	Illinois		EICP	
	1959	1967	1959	1967
Freeman	15	13	8	7
United	8	9	5	4
Largest four	55*	75	43*	63
Largest ten	84*	98	66*	91

* 1957 data

The district court found that the relevant product market was energy rather than coal alone. The geographic market was held to be (1) four so-called Freight Rate Districts (used by the Interstate Commerce Commission for rail rates) in the area served by the

21. Cf. ¶331.

defendant, (2) purchases by Commonwealth Edison that bought coal and generated electricity throughout the region, and (3) the "Chicago Control Region," which was subject to special pollution regulations governing the type of fuels that could be used. The Supreme Court majority did not find it necessary to choose a product or geographic market.]

In prior decisions involving horizontal mergers between competitors, this Court has found prima facie violations of §7 of the Clayton Act from aggregate statistics of the sort relied on by the United States in this case. . . .

The effect of adopting this approach to a determination of a "substantial" lessening of competition is to allow the Government to rest its case on a showing of even small increases of market share or market concentration in those industries or markets where concentration is already great, or has been recently increasing, since "if concentration is already great, the importance of preventing even slight increases in concentration and so preserving the possibility of eventual deconcentration is correspondingly great." United States v. Aluminum Co. of America, 377 U.S. 271, 279 [*Rome Cable*], citing *Philadelphia Bank*.

While the statistical showing proffered by the Government in this case, the accuracy of which was not discredited by the District Court or contested by the appellees, would under this approach have sufficed to support a finding of "undue concentration" in the absence of other considerations, the question before us is whether the District Court was justified in finding that other pertinent factors affecting the coal industry and the business of the appellees, mandated a conclusion that no substantial lessening of competition occurred or was threatened by the acquisition of United Electric. We are satisfied that the court's ultimate finding was not in error.

In *Brown Shoe,* we cautioned that statistics concerning market share and concentration, while of great significance, were not conclusive indicators of anticompetitive effects. . . . In this case, the District Court assessed the evidence of the "structure, history and probable future" of the coal industry, and on the basis of this assessment found no substantial probability of anticompetitive effects from the merger.

Much of the District Court's opinion was devoted to a description of the changes that have affected the coal industry since World War II. . . . [T]o a growing extent since 1954, the electric utility industry has become the mainstay of coal consumption. . . . [M]ost significantly, the court found that to an increasing degree, nearly all coal sold to utilities is transferred under long-term requirements contracts, under which coal producers promise to meet utilities' coal consumption requirements for a fixed period of time, and at predetermined prices. . . .

Because of these fundamental changes in the structure of the market for coal, the District Court was justified in viewing the statistics relied on by the Government as insufficient to sustain its case. Evidence of past production does not, as a matter of logic, necessarily give a proper picture of a company's future ability to compete. In most situations, of course, the unstated assumption is that a company that has maintained a certain share of a market in the recent past will be in a position to do so in the immediate future. Thus, companies that have controlled sufficiently large shares of a concentrated market are barred from merger by §7 not because of their past acts, but because their past performances imply an ability to continue to dominate with at least equal vigor. In markets involving groceries or beer, as in *Von's Grocery* and *Pabst,* statistics involving annual sales naturally indicate the power of each company to compete in the future. Evidence of the amount of annual sales is relevant as a prediction of future competitive strength, since in most markets distribution systems and brand recognition are such significant factors that one may reasonably suppose that a company which has attracted a given number of sales will retain that competitive strength.

In the coal market, as analyzed by the District Court, however, statistical evidence of coal *production* was of considerably less significance. The bulk of the coal produced is delivered under long-term requirements contracts, and such sales thus do not represent the exercise of competitive power but rather the obligation to fulfill previously negotiated contracts at a previously fixed price. The focus of competition in a given time frame is not on the disposition of coal already produced but on the procurement of new long-term supply contracts. In this situation, a company's past ability to produce is of limited significance, since it is in a position to offer for sale neither its past production nor the bulk of the coal it is presently capable of producing, which is typically already committed under a long-term supply contract. A more significant indicator of a company's power effectively to compete with other companies lies in the state of a company's uncommitted reserves of recoverable coal. A company with relatively large supplies of coal which are not already under contract to a consumer will have a more important influence upon competition in the contemporaneous negotiation of supply contracts than a firm with small reserves, even though the latter may presently produce a greater tonnage of coal. In a market where the availability and price for coal are set by long-term contracts rather than immediate or short-term purchases and sales, reserves rather than past production are the best measure of a company's ability to compete.

The testimony and exhibits in the District Court revealed that United Electric's coal reserve prospects were "unpromising." United's relative position of strength in reserves was considerably weaker than its past and current ability to produce. While United ranked fifth among Illinois coal producers in terms of annual production, it was 10th in reserve holdings, and controlled less than 1% of the reserves held by coal producers in Illinois, Indiana, and western Kentucky.... Even more significantly, the District Court found that of the 52,033,304 tons of currently mineable reserves in Illinois, Indiana, and Kentucky controlled by United, only four million tons had not already been committed under long-term contracts.... In addition, the District Court found that "United Electric has neither the possibility of acquiring more [reserves] nor the ability to develop deep coal reserves," and thus was not in a position to increase its reserves to replace those already depleted or committed....

Irrespective of the company's size when viewed as a producer, its weakness as a competitor was properly analyzed by the District Court and fully substantiated that court's conclusion that its acquisition by Material Service would not "substantially ... lessen competition...." The validity of this conclusion is not undermined, we think, by the three-faceted attack made upon it by the Government in this Court — to which we now turn.

First, the Government urges that the court committed legal error by giving undue consideration to facts occurring after the effective acquisition in 1959....

In this case, the District Court relied on evidence relating to changes in the patterns and structure of the coal industry and in United Electric's coal reserve situation after the time of acquisition in 1959. Such evidence could not reflect a positive decision on the part of the merged companies to deliberately but temporarily refrain from anticompetitive actions, nor could it reasonably be thought to reflect less active competition than that which might have occurred had there not been an acquisition in 1959.... And, unlike evidence showing only that no lessening of competition has yet occurred, the demonstration of weak coal resources necessarily and logically implied that United Electric was not merely disinclined but unable to compete effectively for future contracts. Such evidence went directly to the question of whether future lessening of competition was probable, and the District Court was fully justified in using it.

Second, the Government contends that reliance on depleted and committed resources is essentially a "failing company" defense which must meet the strict limits placed on that defense by this Court's decisions....

The Government asserts that United Electric was a healthy and thriving company at the time of the acquisition and could not be considered on the brink of failure, and also that the appellees have not shown that [Freeman's parent] was the only available acquiring company. These considerations would be significant if the District Court had found no violation of §7 by reason of United Electric's being a failing company, but the District Court's conclusion was not, as the Government suggests, identical with or even analogous to such a finding. The failing-company defense presupposes that the effect on competition and the "loss to [the company's] stockholders and injury to the communities where its plants were operated" . . . will be less if a company continues to exist even as a party to a merger than if it disappears entirely from the market. It is, in a sense, a "lesser of two evils" approach, in which the possible threat to competition resulting from an acquisition is deemed preferable to the adverse impact on competition and other losses if the company goes out of business. The appellees' demonstration of United's weak reserves position, however, proved an entirely different point. Rather than showing that United would have gone out of business but for the merger with [Freeman's parent], the finding of inadequate reserves went to the heart of the Government's statistical prima facie case based on production figures and substantiated the District Court's conclusion that United Electric, even if it remained in the market, did not have sufficient reserves to compete effectively for long-term contracts. The failing company defense is simply inapposite to this finding and the failure of the appellees to meet the prerequisites of that doctrine did not detract from the validity of the court's analysis.

Finally, the Government contends that the factual underpinning of the District Court's opinion was not supported by the evidence contained in the record, and should be re-evaluated by this Court. . . . Suffice it to say that we find the controlling findings and conclusions contained in the District Court's careful and lengthy opinion to be supported by the evidence in the record and not clearly erroneous.

One factual claim by the Government, however, goes to the heart of the reasoning of the District Court and thus is worthy of explicit note here. The Government asserts that the paucity of United Electric's coal reserves could not have the significance perceived by the District Court, since all companies engaged in extracting minerals at some point deplete their reserves and then acquire new reserves or the new technology required to extract more minerals from their existing holdings. United Electric, the Government suggests, could at any point either purchase new strip reserves or acquire the expertise to recover currently held deep reserves.

But the District Court specifically found new strip reserves not to be available:

> Evidence was presented at trial by experts, by state officials, by industry witnesses and by the Government itself indicating that economically mineable strip reserves that would permit United Electric to continue operations beyond the life of its present mines are not available. The Government failed to come forward with any evidence that such reserves are *presently* available.

In addition, there was considerable testimony at trial, apparently credited by the District Court, indicating that United Electric and others had tried to find additional strip reserves not already held for coal production, and had been largely unable to do so.

Moreover, the hypothetical possibility that United Electric might in the future acquire the expertise to mine deep reserves proves nothing — or too much. As the Government pointed out in its brief and at oral argument, in recent years a number of companies with no prior experience in extracting coal have purchased coal reserves and entered the coal production business in order to diversify and complement their current operations. The mere possibility that United Electric, in common with all other companies with the inclination and the corporate treasury to do so, could someday expand into an essentially new line of business does not depreciate the validity of the conclusion that United Electric at the time of the trial did not have the power to compete on a significant scale for the procurement of future long-term contracts, nor does it vest in the production statistics relied on by the Government more significance than ascribed to them by the District Court. . . .

Since we agree with the District Court that the Government's reliance on production statistics in the context of this case was insufficient, it follows that the judgment before us may be affirmed without reaching the issues of geographic and products markets.

[Justices Douglas, Brennan, White, and Marshall dissented. (1) The product market is coal, whose sales are effectively limited to utilities and similar buyers for whom its cost is considerably lower than any other fuel (except interruptible natural gas). (2) The geographic market was too narrowly drawn by the lower court. Freight Rate District (FRD) rates do not apply to barges or unit trains. And each firm sold about a quarter of its output in the other's FRD. EICP is a market because each firm could supply any point there while other producing regions are too remote. Illinois is also a relevant submarket because each merging firm had sold the bulk of its output there. (3) The findings with respect to United Electric's contribution to competition amount to a "failing company" defense, which requires proof of failure and the absence of a preferable purchaser — neither of which has been established. (4) The dissent explicitly agreed "that uncommitted reserves or sales of previously admitted coal would be preferable indicia of competitive strength." But the claim concerning United's weak reserve position improperly referred to time-of-trial, rather than time-of-acquisition evidence. In 1968 (two years before trial but just after the filing of the government's complaint), 21 million tons of United's reserves were committed. There was no finding that adequate reserves did not exist in 1959 (the time of the merger) or in 1967 (the time the complaint was filed). (5) United was not merely one company of many that might expand into a new line of business — deep mining. At the time of the merger, it already had 27 million tons of deep reserves and had been engaged in deep mining five years previously. United would only have to regain "expertise it once had to extract reserves it already owned for sale in a market where it already had a good name."]

526. (a) What are the relevant product and geographic markets in which to appraise the *General Dynamics* merger?

(b) Do you agree with the *General Dynamics* result? Was the merger's effect upon existing competition insubstantial?

(c) Are the dissent's figures concerning post-acquisition sales persuasive? If the dissent is right, what, if any, relief is appropriate given that available reserves have in fact been committed?

(d) Although perhaps an insubstantial present competitor, was United Electric a significant potential competitor, due to its potential to engage in deep mining? Was United, in relevant respects, like "all other companies with the inclination and the corporate treasury," and would expanding into deep mining involve entering "essentially [a] new line of business," as the majority suggests? Reconsider your answer after studying Chapter 5E.

(e) Many (not all) interpreted *General Dynamics* as heralding a new era in the Court's approach toward mergers (and toward antitrust more generally). Should *General Dynamics* be understood to redefine the elements of prima facie illegality in horizontal merger cases or to recognize an affirmatively proved rebuttal to a prima facie case? Does its approach affect any of the Court's earlier merger cases presented in this Chapter?[22]

22. Note that the majority of five in *General Dynamics* consisted of the four Justices that had been appointed subsequent to the earlier merger decisions (bringing into existence the "Burger Court") and Justice Stewart, who wrote this opinion and the *Von's* dissent complaining that "[t]he sole consistency that I can find is that under §7, the Government always wins." The four *General Dynamics* dissenters had been in the majority of the "Warren Court" merger decisions examined earlier in this Chapter.

(f) Would or should the "*General Dynamics* defense" save an otherwise unlawful merger with a firm (1) losing its only available component supplier because the latter was to use all its production internally, (2) losing market share as a result of poor product acceptance, (3) suffering losses as a result of poor management, or (4) needing new capital to exploit a product that would ultimately be successful?

527. Horizontal mergers under the government guidelines.[23] Government enforcement is critical in the merger area because few private parties have the incentive and standing to sue. Customers or suppliers who object to a horizontal merger have the standing to seek an injunction against the threatened injury that would result from a significant diminution of competition in the market. Because that injury is prospective and problematical in most merger cases, there would be no present damage to be trebled. Competitors might have the incentive to block efforts by their rivals to grow larger through merger, but the usual reason for condemning a horizontal merger — that oligopolists will raise their prices — helps rather than hurts competitors, who are always happy to see higher prices charged by their rivals. If the merger produces greater efficiency, less efficient rivals will suffer, but the Supreme Court has clearly held that such a loss is not one that the antitrust laws are intended to prevent. Thus, the competitor will be denied standing unless it can show that the merger creates a realistic potential for predatory pricing or perhaps for some of the arguable evils, such as reciprocity, considered in Chapter 5E.[24]

To carry out its paramount role in enforcing antitrust merger policy, the Justice Department issued merger guidelines in 1968 to inform those contemplating mergers of the conditions likely to produce a government challenge. Generally in line with the 1960s judicial decisions, those guidelines noted various combinations of market shares that would be challenged.

The Justice Department issued new and more lenient guidelines in 1982, which it modified slightly in the direction of greater leniency in 1984.[25] The government challenged very few acquisitions

23. 57 Fed. Reg. 41552 (1992). For economic analysis of horizontal mergers that bears on the methods used in the merger guidelines, see J. Farrell & C. Shapiro, Horizontal Mergers: An Equilibrium Analysis, 80 Am. Econ. Rev. 107 (1990); G. Hay & G. Werden, Horizontal Mergers: Law, Policy, and Economics, 83 Am. Econ. Assn. Papers & Proc. 173 (May 1993); R. Willig, Merger Analysis, Industrial Organization Theory, and Merger Guidelines, Brookings Papers on Econ. Activity: Microeconomics 281 (1991).

24. See ¶146.

25. Professor Fox applied the new guidelines — as promulgated in 1982 and before 1984 amendments made them somewhat more hospitable to mergers — to prior Supreme Court cases that held mergers to be illegal and concluded that the government probably would not have sued in a number of historic cases,

during the 1980s. Not only have multibillion dollar conglomerate mergers been approved, but many substantial horizontal mergers have been allowed as well.[26]

In 1992, the Justice Department and Federal Trade Commission jointly issued horizontal merger guidelines, superseding the (rather similar) 1984 Justice Department Guidelines and prior FTC statements on the issues addressed. (Portions relevant to horizontal mergers are excerpted here. Portions on market definition and measurement appear in Chapter 3B.) In 1997, these agencies revised section 4 on efficiencies.

DEPARTMENT OF JUSTICE AND FEDERAL TRADE COMMISSION HORIZONTAL MERGER GUIDELINES
April 2, 1992; April 8, 1997

0. PURPOSE, UNDERLYING POLICY ASSUMPTIONS AND OVERVIEW

These Guidelines outline the present enforcement policy of the Department of Justice and the Federal Trade Commission (the "Agency") concerning horizontal acquisitions and mergers ("mergers") subject to section 7 of the Clayton Act, to section 1 of the Sherman Act, or to section 5 of the FTC Act. They describe the analytical framework and specific standards normally used by the Agency in analyzing mergers. . . .

The Guidelines are designed primarily to articulate the analytical framework the Agency applies in determining whether a merger is likely substantially to lessen competition, not to describe how the Agency will conduct the litigation of cases that it decides to bring. . . .

The unifying theme of the Guidelines is that mergers should not be permitted to create or enhance market power or to facilitate its exercise. Market power to a seller is the ability profitably to maintain prices above competitive levels for a significant period of time. In some circumstances, a sole seller (a "monopolist") of a product with no good substitutes can maintain a selling price that is above the level that would prevail if the market were competitive. Similarly, in some circumstances, where only a few firms account for

including *Brown Shoe, Von's,* and *General Dynamics.* E. Fox, The New Merger Guidelines — A Blueprint for Microeconomic Analysis, 27 Antitr. Bull. 519, 590-591 (1982).

26. See 20 Mergers & Acquisitions 45 (Jan./Feb. 1986); E.W. Eckard, The Impact of the 1980's Merger Movement on U.S. Industrial Concentration, 40 Antitr. Bull. 397 (1995).

most of the sales of a product, those firms can exercise market power, perhaps even approximating the performance of a monopolist, by either explicitly or implicitly coordinating their actions. Circumstances also may permit a single firm, not a monopolist, to exercise market power through unilateral or non-coordinated conduct — conduct the success of which does not rely on the concurrence of other firms in the market or on coordinated responses by those firms. In any case, the result of the exercise of market power is a transfer of wealth from buyers to sellers or a misallocation of resources.[27] . . .

The Guidelines describe the analytical process that the Agency will employ in determining whether to challenge a horizontal merger. *First,* the Agency assesses whether the merger would significantly increase concentration and result in a concentrated market, properly defined and measured. *Second,* the Agency assesses whether the merger, in light of market concentration and other factors that characterize the market, raises concern about potential adverse competitive effects. *Third,* the Agency assesses whether entry would be timely, likely and sufficient either to deter or to counteract the competitive effects of concern. *Fourth,* the Agency assesses any efficiency gains that reasonably cannot be achieved by the parties through other means. *Finally,* the Agency assesses whether, but for the merger, either party to the transaction would be likely to fail, causing its assets to exit the market. The process of assessing market concentration, potential adverse competitive effects, entry, efficiency and failure is a tool that allows the Agency to answer the ultimate inquiry in merger analysis: whether the merger is likely to create or enhance market power or to facilitate its exercise.

1. MARKET DEFINITION, MEASUREMENT AND CONCENTRATION[28] . . .

1.5 CONCENTRATION AND MARKET SHARES

Market concentration is a function of the number of firms in a market and their respective market shares. As an aid to the interpretation of market data, the Agency will use the Herfindahl-Hirschman Index ("HHI") of market concentration. The HHI is calculated by summing the squares of the individual market shares

27. The Guidelines also discuss the exercise of market power by buyers (whether a single firm or a coordinating group of buyers), indicating that such exercise of power "has adverse affects comparable to those associated with the exercise of market power by sellers. In order to assess potential monopsony concerns, the Agency will apply an analytical framework analogous to the framework of these Guidelines." — eds.
28. Excerpts from the earlier parts of section 1 appear in Ch. 3B. — eds.

of all the participants.[17] Unlike the four-firm concentration ratio, the HHI reflects both the distribution of the market shares of the top four firms and the composition of the market outside the top four firms. It also gives proportionately greater weight to the market shares of the larger firms, in accord with their relative importance in competitive interactions. . . .

In evaluating horizontal mergers, the Agency will consider both the post-merger market concentration and the increase in concentration resulting from the merger.[18] Market concentration is a useful indicator of the likely potential competitive effect of a merger. The general standards for horizontal mergers are as follows:

(a) Post-Merger HHI Below 1000. The Agency regards markets in this region to be unconcentrated. Mergers resulting in unconcentrated markets are unlikely to have adverse competitive effects and ordinarily require no further analysis.

(b) Post-Merger HHI Between 1000 and 1800. The Agency regards markets in this region to be moderately concentrated. Mergers producing an increase in the HHI of less than 100 points in moderately concentrated markets post-merger are unlikely to have adverse competitive consequences and ordinarily require no further analysis. Mergers producing an increase in the HHI of more than 100 points in moderately concentrated markets post-merger potentially raise significant competitive concerns depending on the factors set forth in Sections 2-5 of the Guidelines.

(c) Post-Merger HHI Above 1800. The Agency regards markets in this region to be highly concentrated. Mergers producing an increase in the HHI of less than 50 points, even in highly concentrated markets post-merger, are unlikely to have adverse competitive consequences and ordinarily require no further analysis. Mergers producing an increase in the HHI of more than 50 points in highly concentrated markets post-merger potentially raise significant com-

---

17. For example, a market consisting of four firms with market shares of 30 percent, 30 percent, 20 percent and 20 percent has an HHI of 2600 ($30^2 + 30^2 + 20^2 + 20^2 = 2600$). The HHI ranges from 10,000 (in the case of a pure monopoly) to a number approaching zero (in the case of an atomistic market). Although it is desirable to include all firms in the calculation, lack of information about small firms is not critical because such firms do not affect the HHI significantly.

18. The increase in concentration as measured by the HHI can be calculated independently of the overall market concentration by doubling the product of the market shares of the merging firms. For example, the merger of firms with shares of 5 percent and 10 percent of the market would increase the HHI by 100 ($5 \times 10 \times 2 = 100$). The explanation for this technique is as follows: In calculating the HHI before the merger, the market shares of the merging firms are squared individually: $(a)^2 + (b)^2$. After the merger, the sum of those shares would be squared: $(a + b)^2$, which equals $a^2 + 2ab + b^2$. The increase in the HHI therefore is represented by $2ab$.

petitive concerns, depending on the factors set forth in Sections 2-5 of the Guidelines. Where the post-merger HHI exceeds 1800, it will be presumed that mergers producing an increase in the HHI of more than 100 points are likely to create or enhance market power or facilitate its exercise. The presumption may be overcome by a showing that factors set forth in Sections 2-5 of the Guidelines make it unlikely that the merger will create or enhance market power or facilitate its exercise, in light of market concentration and market shares.

[Market share and market concentration data sometimes understate or overstate the likely impact of a merger. Examples include changing market conditions and the degree of difference between products and locations in the market and substitutes outside the market.]

2. THE POTENTIAL ADVERSE COMPETITIVE EFFECTS OF MERGERS . . .

2.1 LESSENING OF COMPETITION THROUGH COORDINATED INTERACTION

A merger may diminish competition by enabling the firms selling in the relevant market more likely, more successfully, or more completely to engage in coordinated interaction that harms consumers. Coordinated interaction is comprised of actions by a group of firms that are profitable for each of them only as a result of the accommodating reactions of the others. This behavior includes tacit or express collusion, and may or may not be lawful in and of itself.

Successful coordinated interaction entails reaching terms of coordination that are profitable to the firms involved and an ability to detect and punish deviations that would undermine the coordinated interaction. Detection and punishment of deviations ensure that coordinating firms will find it more profitable to adhere to the terms of coordination than to pursue short-term profits from deviating, given the costs of reprisal. In this phase of the analysis, the Agency will examine the extent to which post-merger market conditions are conducive to reaching terms of coordination, detecting deviations from those terms, and punishing such deviations. . . .

Market conditions may be conducive to or hinder reaching terms of coordination. For example, reaching terms of coordination may be facilitated by product or firm homogeneity and by existing practices among firms, practices not necessarily themselves antitrust violations, such as standardization of pricing or product variables on which firms could compete. Key information about rival firms and the market may also facilitate reaching terms of coordination. . . .

Where market conditions are conducive to timely detection and punishment of significant deviations, a firm will find it more profitable to abide by the terms of coordination than to deviate from them. Deviation from the terms of coordination will be deterred where the threat of punishment is credible. Credible punishment, however, may not need to be any more complex than temporary abandonment of the terms of coordination by other firms in the market.

Where detection and punishment likely would be rapid, incentives to deviate are diminished and coordination is likely to be successful. The detection and punishment of deviations may be facilitated by existing practices among firms, themselves not necessarily antitrust violations, and by the characteristics of typical transactions. For example, if key information about specific transactions or individual price or output levels is available routinely to competitors, it may be difficult for a firm to deviate secretly. If orders for the relevant product are frequent, regular and small relative to the total output of a firm in a market, it may be difficult for the firm to deviate in a substantial way without the knowledge of rivals and without the opportunity for rivals to react. If demand or cost fluctuations are relatively infrequent and small, deviations may be relatively easy to deter. . . .

Where large buyers likely would engage in long-term contracting, so that the sales covered by such contracts can be large relative to the total output of a firm in the market, firms may have the incentive to deviate. However, this only can be accomplished where the duration, volume and profitability of the business covered by such contracts are sufficiently large as to make deviation more profitable in the long term than honoring the terms of coordination, and buyers likely would switch suppliers.[29] . . .

2.2 LESSENING OF COMPETITION THROUGH UNILATERAL EFFECTS

[The Guidelines focus on the case of mergers involving differentiated products. The analysis can be illustrated by supposing that a market contains six firms with substantial product differentiation. The products of four of them differ modestly from each other but substantially from those of the other two firms. The products of the latter two firms differ only modestly from each other. Although the two firms that are nearest each other in product space "compete" with each other and with everyone in the same market, the degree of competition varies with their proximity. Merging the two proximate firms eliminates the closest competition that each has faced

---

29. The Guidelines also discuss acquisitions of maverick firms. — eds.

and may enable them to raise prices to those customers with a particular preference for their products, regardless of whether the other firms raise their prices.

In determining whether to challenge mergers under this theory, the Agency will consider several factors. *First*, substantial unilateral price elevation in a market for differentiated products requires that there be a significant share of sales in the market accounted for by consumers who regard the products of the merging firms as their first and second choices, and that repositioning of the non-parties' product lines to replace the localized competition lost through the merger be unlikely.

Second, the price rise will be greater the closer substitutes are the products of the merging firms, i.e., the more the buyers of one product consider the other product to be their next choice.

Third, although the general market concentration thresholds for challenging horizontal mergers do not apply so readily under this theory, as a rough generalization mergers will be subject to challenge where they fall outside the "safe harbor" provisions of those thresholds and the market share of the merger participants exceeds 35 percent. This latter figure, it is noted, may overstate or understate the competitive significance of the merger, depending on the degree of similarity in the products of the two merging firms and their joint similarity to the products of the others.

Fourth, as it is more difficult and costly for nonparticipants to the merger in the product differentiated market to re-configure their products so as to compete more directly with the post-merger firm, the competitive effects of the merger increase and challenge is more likely.

Under a different theory, the Agency may also challenge mergers when non-merging rivals have binding capacity constraints that prevent them from increasing their own output significantly in response to the merged firm's output reduction to levels below the total output of the two pre-merger firms. Such a merger is most likely to be challenged where such capacity constraints are unlikely to be removed within two years or existing excess capacity is significantly more costly to use than capacity currently in production, and where the merging parties account for at least 35 percent of the market.]

3. ENTRY ANALYSIS

A merger is not likely to create or enhance market power or to facilitate its exercise, if entry into the market is so easy that market participants, after the merger, either collectively or unilaterally could not profitably maintain a price increase above premerger levels. Such entry likely will deter an anticompetitive merger in its incipiency, or deter or counteract the competitive effects of concern.

Entry is that easy if entry would be timely, likely, and sufficient in its magnitude, character and scope to deter or counteract the competitive effects of concern. In markets where entry is that easy (i.e., where entry passes these tests of timeliness, likelihood, and sufficiency), the merger raises no antitrust concern and ordinarily requires no further analysis.

The committed entry treated in this Section is defined as new competition that requires expenditure of significant sunk costs of entry and exit. . . .

The Agency generally will consider timely only those committed entry alternatives that can be achieved within two years from initial planning to significant market impact. . . .

An entry alternative is likely if it would be profitable at premerger prices, and if such prices could be secured by the entrant. The committed entrant will be unable to secure prices at premerger levels if its output is too large for the market to absorb without depressing prices further. Thus, entry is unlikely if the minimum viable scale is larger than the likely sales opportunity available to entrants. . . .

Inasmuch as multiple entry generally is possible and individual entrants may flexibly choose their scale, committed entry generally will be sufficient to deter or counteract the competitive effects of concern whenever entry is likely [as just stated]. However, entry, although likely, will not be sufficient if, as a result of incumbent control, the tangible and intangible assets required for entry are not adequately available for entrants to respond fully to their sales opportunities. . . .

4. EFFICIENCIES

Competition usually spurs firms to achieve efficiencies internally. Nevertheless, mergers have the potential to generate significant efficiencies by permitting a better utilization of existing assets, enabling the combined firm to achieve lower costs in producing a given quantity and quality than either firm could have achieved without the proposed transaction. Indeed, the primary benefit of mergers to the economy is their potential to generate such efficiencies. . . .

The Agency will consider only those efficiencies likely to be accomplished with the proposed merger and unlikely to be accomplished in the absence of either the proposed merger or another means having comparable anticompetitive effects. These are termed *merger-specific efficiencies*. Only alternatives that are practical in the business situation faced by the merging firms will be considered in making this determination; the Agency will not insist upon a less restrictive alternative that is merely theoretical.

Efficiencies are difficult to verify and quantify, in part because much of the information relating to efficiencies is uniquely in the possession of the merging firms. Moreover, efficiencies projected reasonably and in good faith by the merging firms may not be realized. Therefore, the merging firms must substantiate efficiency claims so that the Agency can verify by reasonable means the likelihood and magnitude of each asserted efficiency, how and when each would be achieved (and any costs of doing so), how each would enhance the merged firm's ability and incentive to compete, and why each would be merger-specific. Efficiency claims will not be considered if they are vague or speculative or otherwise cannot be verified by reasonable means.

Cognizable efficiencies are merger-specific efficiencies that have been verified and do not arise from anticompetitive reductions in output or service. Cognizable efficiencies are assessed net of costs produced by the merger or incurred in achieving those efficiencies.

The Agency will not challenge a merger if cognizable efficiencies are of a character and magnitude such that the merger is not likely to be anticompetitive in any relevant market. To make the requisite determination, the Agency considers whether cognizable efficiencies likely would be sufficient to reverse the merger's potential to harm consumers in the relevant market, e.g., by preventing price increases in that market. . . .

In the Agency's experience, efficiencies are most likely to make a difference in merger analysis when the likely adverse competitive effects, absent the efficiencies, are not great. Efficiencies almost never justify a merger to monopoly or near-monopoly.

The Agency has found that certain types of efficiencies are more likely to be cognizable and substantial than others. For example, efficiencies resulting from shifting production among facilities formerly owned separately, which enable the merging firms to reduce the marginal cost of production, are more likely to be susceptible to verification, merger-specific, and substantial, and are less likely to result from anticompetitive reductions in output. Other efficiencies, such as those relating to research and development, are potentially substantial but are generally less susceptible to verification and may be the result of anticompetitive output reductions. Yet others, such as those relating to procurement, management, or capital cost are less likely to be merger-specific or substantial, or may not be cognizable for other reasons.

5. FAILURE AND EXITING ASSETS . . .

A merger is not likely to create or enhance market power or facilitate its exercise if the following circumstances are met: (1) the allegedly failing firm would be unable to meet its financial obligations in the near future; (2) it would not be able to reorganize successfully under Chapter 11 of the Bankruptcy Act; (3) it has made unsuccessful good-faith efforts to elicit reasonable alternative offers of acquisition of the assets of the failing firm[36] that would both keep its tangible and intangible assets in the relevant market and pose a less severe danger to competition than does the proposed merger; and (4) absent the acquisition, the assets of the failing firm would exit the relevant market.[30] . . .

528. Hospital mergers. The recent wave of hospital mergers illustrates the industry-specific nature of antitrust analysis and the particular difficulties encountered in assessing the effects of new types of mergers. Many of the recent court cases on horizontal mergers have involved hospitals.[31] Consider the following recurring issues.

(a) What is the relevant product market in a hospital merger? Some hospitals (often teaching hospitals in larger cities) provide a broad range of primary, secondary, and tertiary care services, while smaller community hospitals provide only a subset of these services. Some services are provided only by hospitals, while others are also provided elsewhere (in clinics, doctors' offices, independent laboratories). To what extent should these types of care be considered separate product markets?[32]

(b) How should the geographic market be defined in a hospital merger? As the region from which most of the merging hospitals' patients reside? The hospitals to which most people from that region go for services? What about more distant hospitals in large

36. Any offer to purchase the assets of the failing firm for a price above the liquidation value of those assets — the highest valued use outside the relevant market or equivalent offer to purchase the stock of the failing firm — will be regarded as a reasonable alternative offer.

30. The Guidelines indicate that failing divisions will be treated similarly to failing firms. — eds.

31. For a discussion of other recent cases, see P. Areeda & H. Hovenkamp, Antitrust Law ¶917.1b (Supp. 1996).

32. The relevant product market is generally less controversial than the relevant geographic market, and often it is limited to general acute-care inpatient hospital services. See, e.g., FTC v. Freeman Hospital, 69 F.3d 260, 268 (8th Cir. 1995); FTC v. University Health Services, 938 F.2d 1206, 1211 (11th Cir. 1991); United States v. Mercy Health Services, 902 F. Supp. 968, 975 (N.D. Iowa 1995); United States v. Rockford Memorial Corp., 898 F.2d 1278, 1284 (7th Cir. 1990), cert. denied, 498 U.S. 920 (1990) (court rejects substitutability of inpatient and outpatient services).

cities that are frequented by a small but nontrivial fraction of those who live near the merging hospitals?[33]

(c) The government has investigated 13 percent and challenged less than 4 percent of the nearly 400 hospital mergers from the 1980s to the early 1990s.[34] Yet a substantial portion of these mergers occurred in markets that were, when measured against the 1992 horizontal merger guidelines, already highly concentrated and involved substantial increases in the HHI. Can this be justified by unusually high scale economies in this industry or by the existence of many failing hospitals? Should efficiencies be given greater weight due to the government's desire to control health care costs?[35]

(d) Should there be less strict scrutiny of mergers by nonprofit hospitals whose boards consist of community representatives with an interest in controlling health care costs?[36]

529. Fox is an independent oil refining company, selling primarily in New Mexico. Unlike major oil companies, which own their own distribution networks, independents normally sell to independently owned gasoline wholesalers and service stations. Their gasoline is marketed under many different brand names, usually at a price somewhat lower than that charged by majors. Fox's main asset is a refinery located at Artesia, New Mexico. The refinery is 35

33. If for no other reason than the availability of data, parties often examine existing patient flows, but this common technique has been criticized in *Freeman,* note 32, and *Mercy,* note 32, as presenting only a static picture, failing to indicate the possible competitive responses from other hospitals, third party payers, and consumers.

34. United States General Accounting Office, Health Care: Federal and State Antitrust Actions Concerning the Health Care Industry (Aug. 1994), at 2. See also Janet L. McDavid, Antitrust Analysis of Hospital Mergers, in Health Care Reform and Antitrust 1994, at 369, 378 (PLI Comm. Law and Practice Course Handbook Series No. 694, 1994).

35. See McDavid, note 34, at 381 (in practice, efficiency defenses are more often accepted in hospital mergers than in other transactions). In 1993 the Department of Justice and the FTC issued a joint health care antitrust enforcement policy statement, which was most recently revised in 1996. U.S. Department of Justice and Federal Trade Commission, Statements of Antitrust Enforcement Policy in Health Care, 71 Antitr. & Trade Reg. Rep. (BNA) No. 1777, at S-1 (August 29, 1996). The statement establishes an antitrust safety zone: the government is extremely unlikely to challenge any merger between two general acute-care hospitals where one of the hospitals has fewer than 100 licensed beds and an average daily census below 40 patients. (Other aspects of this policy statement are discussed in ¶223.)

36. See FTC v. Butterworth Health Corp., 1996-2 Trade Cas. (CCH) ¶71571 (W.D. Mich. 1996) (despite proof that merged entity would have substantial market power, permitting merger under decree committing defendants not to increase prices; citing following study for proposition that nonprofit hospitals with community boards are unlikely to raise prices; W. Lynk, Nonprofit Hospital Mergers and the Exercise of Market Power, 38 J.L. & Econ. 437 (1995).

years old. Some of its refining equipment can no longer be used, leaving it with a few extra storage tanks. And, because of outdated equipment, Fox has been earning low profits for several years.

Texaco is a major oil company, selling nationwide, through wholly owned wholesalers and service stations. It sells under the Texaco brand name. Texaco owns a modern refinery at Artesia.

There is evidence that Texaco and other majors operating in New Mexico have been very reluctant to sell gasoline to independent distributors.

Most of the gasoline sold in New Mexico is produced in refineries that are either located in New Mexico or located along a pipeline that runs through New Mexico and several nearby states. Shipping gasoline into New Mexico by truck is considerably more expensive than bringing it in by pipe. Many refineries located outside New Mexico, but on the New Mexico pipeline, sell much of their output in other states.

The total sales of gasoline in New Mexico for last year and the refining capacities of refineries located in New Mexico or on New Mexico pipelines are as follows: (*Indicates a major; the others are independents.)

Sales Rank	Refining Company	Sales Share	Capacity Share	Capacity Rank
*1	Sotex	23	21	2
2	El Paso	20	10	5
*3	Texaco	19	13	3
*4	Phillips	5	30	1
5	Shamrock	5	11	4
6	Fox	5	2	7
*7	Tiger	3	1.1	8
8	Cosden	3	—	—
9	Famariss	2	0.6	10
*10	Gulf	2	—	—
	Others	13	11.3	

Of the 378 million gallons of gasoline sold in New Mexico last year, 250 million, or 65 percent, were sold by major, integrated oil companies, while 128 million, or 35 percent, were supplied by independent refiners.

Texaco has just acquired all the assets of Fox. Texaco informed its stockholders that this purchase will enable it to economize by using Fox's extra storage facilities to store refined gasoline during periods of excess production. And, the total volume of Fox plus Texaco production is sufficient to justify building an additional new pipeline spur connecting the two adjacent refineries to the main pipeline.

Your superior in the Department of Justice has just learned of the Texaco-Fox acquisition and asks you to prepare a memo suggesting whether or not the Department should attack it.[37] How would this merger have fared before the Supreme Court in 1968? Under the 1992 Guidelines?

530. Interlocking directorates.[38] Under Clayton Act §8 "No person shall, at the same time, serve as a director or officer in any two corporations . . . that are . . . engaged in whole or in part in commerce; and . . . by virtue of their business and location of operation, competitors, so that the elimination of competition by agreement between them would constitute a violation of any of the antitrust laws. . . ." Section 8 applies only where "each of the corporations has capital, surplus, and undivided profits aggregating more than $10,000,000 as adjusted. . . ."[39] In addition to excluding application where the corporations are banks, banking associations, and trust companies, §8 creates "de minimis" exceptions for cases in which the competitive overlap is insignificant.

The first judicial construction of §8 took place in 1953 in *Sears*.[40] The defendant argued that §8 required a showing that the hypothetical merger between the two firms would violate §7. The court rejected that test, stating that the only purpose of the clause was to ensure that the acts involved were in interstate commerce, and adopted a "per se" rule requiring only a showing that the two firms are or have been competitors and that the dollar amount is sufficient to invoke the Act.[41]

5E. CONGLOMERATE MERGERS[1]

531. The conglomerate problem. Although neither conventionally horizontal nor vertical, a merger might impair competition in several ways, as explored in this section. For example, an acquisition

37. The facts in the text are based in part on United States v. Continental Oil Co., 1967 Trade Cas. ¶72292 (D.N.M.), aff'd per curiam, 393 U.S. 79 (1968).

38. See V Areeda & Turner, note 15, ch. 13; R. Burt, Corporate Profits and Cooptation: Networks of Market Constraints and Directorate Ties in the American Economy (1983).

39. This jurisdictional threshold amount is adjusted each year by an amount equal to the annual percentage increase in gross national product over the base year of 1989.

40. United States v. Sears, Roebuck & Co., 111 F. Supp. 614 (S.D.N.Y. 1953).

41. To similar effect is Protectoseal Co. v. Barancik, 484 F.2d 585 (7th Cir. 1973).

1. See V P. Areeda & D. Turner, Antitrust Law, ch. 11 (1980; Supp. 1996).

in one market by a potential entrant — that is, by a firm that is not in that market but that, in the absence of the merger, might have entered it — has something in common with a horizontal merger between actual competitors. Vertical issues are posed when one merging firm supplies customers who in turn sell to the other merger partner, raising the potential for "reciprocal dealing." Or a corporate giant's entry through merger into a market might create new opportunities for price leadership or predatory discipline against smaller firms in that market. Or perhaps conglomerates touching each other in various markets might refrain from competing aggressively in one market lest its conglomerate rival disrupt a different market that they both inhabit. At the most general level, some fear the concentration of assets into few hands produced by all large mergers on the ground that the concentration of economic forces and decisionmaking units narrows the economic choice of individuals and upsets democratic political processes.

The initial, and usually determinative, questions to be asked about any conglomerate merger are the same ones posed throughout this book: How is or might competition be affected, what are the likely consequences of allowing or forbidding the challenged conduct, what type and magnitude of impact are relevant under Clayton Act §7 and the antitrust laws generally, and how should the law deal with our inevitable uncertainty about the presence or absence of such effects and their substantiality? The cases that condemn mergers on the basis of rather remote possibilities of impaired competition may be impelled by a fear of asset aggregation as such, especially when very large firms are involved, even though such aggregation is not the stated basis for the plaintiff's challenge or the court's decision.

This section begins with a textual discussion of many of the problems. The *Clorox* case then illustrates a number of them. The *Consolidated Foods* decision exemplifies the reciprocity issue. One of the challenges to ITT's several hundred acquisitions adds the asset aggregation question and closes the chapter.

532. Eliminating potential competition.[2] (a) *Generally.* Consider two merging firms that produce different products, such as clothes washing machines and dishwashers. Alternatively, consider two firms that produce the same product in neighboring, but distinct, geographic markets. Such firms are not actual competitors. Yet, in

2. See id. ch. 11B-2; J. Brodley, Potential Competition Mergers: A Structural Synthesis, 87 Yale L.J. 1 (1977); T. Dunfee & L. Stern, Potential Competition Theory as an Antimerger Tool Under Section 7 of the Clayton Act: A Decision Model, 69 Nw. U.L. Rev. 821 (1975).

the absence of the merger, one might expand internally to enter the other's market. In that sense, they are potential competitors. Their merger precludes their own later independent entry and, to that extent, eliminates the potential competition that might previously have influenced existing producers or the competition that might otherwise have developed in the future. This result would not be dangerous if the firm in question was a relatively unlikely entrant, the market was competitive enough to make the elimination of potential competitors immaterial, or the number of remaining potential entrants was so large as to make the elimination of one potential entrant insignificant.

It is useful to distinguish two aspects of potential competition. The first is the prospect of actual future entry, which would then augment competition. That augmentation would be important in a market inhabited by only a few sellers. This possible future effect is described in the cases as "actual potential entry" — not because it has occurred but because the market would benefit only when entry actually occurs. Of course, the significance of eliminating such a future entrant depends not only on the likelihood of its occurrence but also on its timing, size, scope, and intensity. Note also that if a potential entrant, instead of merging, had entered as a very minor rival, its subsequent merger with at least some other market inhabitants would be allowed by prevailing horizontal merger doctrine.

Second, the possibility of future entry may act as a present competitive force. Incumbent firms may fear that high profits would attract new entry or that poor quality or service would create easy opportunities for new entrants to establish themselves. To discourage such new entry, a market's existing inhabitants might charge less (or serve more) than short-run profit maximization would dictate if the possibility of new entry could be disregarded. The fear of potential entry, moreover, will put additional pressure on existing sellers to keep their production costs down because high costs, unlike high prices, could not be quickly reduced to meet the threat of new competition. This concern is expressed in some cases as "perceived potential entry" because the outside firm's impact depends not on any actual entry in the future but on the present perception by incumbent firms that entry would occur if they were insufficiently competitive.

The Supreme Court's earlier potential competition decisions did not distinguish sharply between these two kinds of effects. When it came to do so, it ruled that the present effect was clearly a matter of statutory concern but explicitly reserved the question whether potential future effects are covered by §7 at all.[3] Moreover, the Court

3. United States v. Falstaff Brewing Corp., 410 U.S. 526 (1973).

has stressed that a firm can have a present effect if it is perceived by market incumbents as a potential entrant, even if a court believed that the firm would not actually enter.[4] As a starting point for a factual inquiry, however, such perceptions would match the objective likelihood of entry. It should be noted, however, that the more successful is the perception of potential entry in producing competitive behavior in the present, the less likely it is that actual entry in the future will occur.[5] Both aspects of potential entry are, of course, only of concern if the market is not otherwise competitively structured.

(b) *The relationship between potential and actual competition.* Potential competition may shade into actual competition, as an outsider's preparations to enter may be indistinguishable from actual competition. This is nicely illustrated by *El Paso*.[6] At the time of its acquisition of Pacific Northwest Pipeline Corporation, El Paso Natural Gas Company was the only out-of-state natural gas supplier to southern California. Just before the acquisition, Pacific Northwest, owner of the only other important interstate pipeline west of the Rocky Mountains, had made strenuous efforts to obtain contracts for the sale of natural gas to meet new demands in the California market. Although Pacific failed to win those contracts, El Paso secured them only by substantially reducing its previously quoted price and by improving its service. Thus, the acquisition of Pacific Northwest removed not merely a potential, but also an actual competitor, even though its probable future influence on the California natural gas market was not certain.

In addition, potential entry may be so imminent and the potential entrants so precisely defined as already to be in the same market as the acquired firm. For example, if producers of home or restaurant dishwashers could effortlessly produce and distribute the other product, they are in the same market,[7] and a merger between a maker of home machines and a maker of restaurant machines is horizontal. Similarly horizontal is a merger between two firms making the same product in different regions if transportation costs are sufficiently low. Because the question whether two products or two regions form a single market is one of degree, the difference between potential-competition conglomerate mergers and horizontal mergers will sometimes be quite small.

4. Id.
5. Thus, for example, potential entrants may indicate that entry would be unprofitable precisely because the industry is currently behaving rather competitively, encouraged to do so out of the fear that otherwise such potential competitors would find entry attractive.
6. United States v. El Paso Natural Gas Co., 376 U.S. 651 (1964).
7. See ¶339b.

(c) *Potential competition and joint ventures.* In *Penn-Olin,*[8] the Supreme Court held that §7 applied to the formation of a jointly owned new corporation to make sodium chlorate in the Southeast. The parents were Pennsalt, which made sodium chlorate in the northwest, and Olin, which had purchased and used that product, had a patent for putting it to certain uses, and had acted as a middleman in selling the chemical. The Court said that "the same considerations apply to joint ventures as to mergers," although acknowledging that the application would have to take account of the difference that joint ventures create a new competitive force while mergers eliminate a market participant. Although the trial court had found that both parents would not otherwise have entered sodium chlorate production in the southeast, the Court remanded for a determination whether one might have entered while the other remained as a significant potential competitor.[9] Query: Is this a more stringent test than would be used to determine the reasonableness of the joint venture under Sherman Act §1? If not, why bother to use §7? If so, what policy or purpose of §7 calls for a more stringent appraisal of joint ventures?

533. Predation, pricing discipline, and the powerful firm.
(a) *Predation.* It is often feared that a powerful firm may have the will and the power to destroy its rivals. Predatory pricing is the most noted means. Variants might involve, for example, giving premiums, increasing product quality, multiplying product variations, or expanding advertising. Chapter 3A explored such issues, emphasizing the importance and difficulty of distinguishing predatory behavior from hard competition.

Given that proved predation violates Sherman Act §2 as well as FTC Act §5; how should the prospect of predation affect the evaluation of a merger? First, it is often said that the purpose of the antimerger laws is to prevent anticompetitive results "in their incipiency" — that is, before they occur. As we have seen, this prophylactic purpose has led to the prohibition of mergers with little

8. United States v. Penn-Olin Chem. Co., 378 U.S. 158, 170 (1964).
9. Douglas and Black, JJ., dissented, suggesting that the joint venture, being akin to an agreement to divide the market, indicated a §7 violation, making the remand unnecessary. Harlan and White, JJ., dissented. On remand, the trial judge held the venture lawful. 246 F. Supp. 917, 919 (D. Del. 1965), aff'd by an equally divided court, 389 U.S. 308 (1967). He was not persuaded that either Pennsalt or Olin would otherwise have entered independently. Nor, had one entered, did he think it reasonably probable that the other would have maintained such continued interest in the market to make it "a significant potential competitor." He thus did not have to face the third question which defendants insisted was essential to condemnation: whether the venture probably substantially lessened competition as compared with individual entry by one and potential interest by the other.

immediate potential for impairing competition. But unlike the "inherent" anticompetitive tendency of a horizontal merger eliminating competition between the merging parties or a vertical merger possibly foreclosing rivals from supply or marketing opportunities, the likelihood of predation is typically more speculative and not an inherent tendency of any merger. On the other hand, predatory or disciplinary activities can be difficult to detect or prove. Actual predation may therefore escape detection or, if detected, be burdensome to prosecute. Those social costs might be reduced by prohibiting those mergers that substantially increase the likelihood of predatory or disciplinary pricing.

How might a merger increase the likelihood of predation? Some commentators and courts seem to assume that big or multiproduct firms necessarily threaten to use predatory prices. The multiproduct firm is capable, it is said, of cross-subsidizing predatory prices in one market with profit, especially monopoly profit, from other products. Mergers are said to facilitate this process. Vertical mergers may allow the firm to use profits from one stage to subsidize what amounts to predation at another, or conglomerates may use profits from one division to finance predatory action by another. Although funds are needed to finance below-cost pricing, the simple availability of such funds is hardly sufficient. And the origin of those resources is irrelevant: whether competitive or monopoly profits from a different vertical level, related markets, government bonds, inherited wealth, or elsewhere. Mergers most plausibly increase the prospect of predation either when a horizontal merger brings a firm within reach of monopoly; where predation against, for example, the merger partner, would not previously have been plausible; or when a merger substantially increases the resources of a firm relative to its rivals in one market so as to enable it to outlast them in a below-cost price war, which previously looked promising but for the lack of resources with which to undertake the endeavor.

Of course, it remains speculative whether a firm would choose to engage in illegal predatory or disciplinary activities even when, if undetected, it could profitably do so. Whether such speculation is worthwhile either as antitrust policy or as an interpretation of existing antimerger statutes can be decided by the reader after reflecting upon the remainder of this section. But one could well ignore the predation danger in a market where the defendant could not outlast its rivals or where outlasting the rivals would not lead to those substantial monopoly profits that would compensate a predator for the cost of its predation.

(b) *Pricing discipline or leadership.* A large or rich firm might temporarily lower its prices or raise its spending in order to punish and thus to discipline its rivals for failing to follow its pricing or otherwise competing too strenuously. Such actions seem more plausible than outright predation because disciplinary pricing is likely to cost less than destroying one's rivals and the actor's intent would be less obvious and thus more difficult to catch under §2. In short, this is a somewhat more troublesome possibility that shades into the issues addressed in ¶535.

Perhaps the mere entry of a giant into a world of commercial pygmies may induce the latter to cease competing because of fear that the giant will behave predatorily or discipline them. Note that no actual predatory conduct or disciplinary threat is necessary; the defendant's characteristics alone may be sufficient to induce fear in smaller rivals. In addition, the newly entering giant may become the natural focus for price leadership among firms that, although relatively few in number, had not previously found stable and effective mechanisms for collective monopolization in the absence of an express agreement.

534. Possible cost savings. (a) *Introduction.* If a merger reduces costs, should the savings justify an otherwise unlawful merger? The answer might vary of course, with the nature, clarity, and magnitude of the savings relative to the nature, clarity, and magnitude of the apparent threat to competition that makes the merger otherwise unlawful. The opposite question has also arisen: are some or all cost savings grounds for condemning an otherwise unobjectionable merger? That question arises because some courts have viewed some kinds of cost savings as an "unfair advantage" whose possessor can use to force smaller rivals out of the market. We begin by identifying some of the cost savings that might result from large size or multimarket operation and especially those that might result from mergers. We also ask whether some cost savings are good and others bad, or at least not demonstrably desirable. We begin with more conventional economies and proceed to more speculative claims.

(b) *Production and distribution efficiencies.* Reduced production costs are generally thought desirable. Evidence on the extent of scale economies and their relationship to market concentration is discussed in ¶119. Most analysts regard distribution economies as equally desirable, if harder to prove, although the Supreme Court suggested that such economies in *Brown Shoe* constituted an additional factor making the merger illegal. There, you recall, a shoe manufacturer acquired a retail shoe chain and would thereafter, the Court supposed, be able to reach consumers with fewer middlemen, lower costs, and therefore lower prices. The Court seemed to fear injury to smaller rivals operating at higher costs and charging consumers higher prices. The Court said nothing about consumers in that case, suggesting that it had not considered the efficiency question carefully.

(c) *Resources generally.* In condemning Kennecott Copper's acquisition of Peabody, the largest coal producer, the Federal Trade Commission and the appellate court relied in part on Kennecott's resources:

> The Commission reasoned that it was likely that this "deep pocket" of funds would be employed to acquire vast coal reserves and massive mining developments to enable Kennecott to compete for long-term utility supply contracts and thus to gain more market share.... [I]t was reasonable for the Commission to conclude that Kennecott would use its immense resources to gain for Peabody, already the number one producer in the industry, an even larger share of the market which promises to be a concentrated one in a relatively short period of time.[10]

If the acquisitions of "vast coal reserves" or "massive mining developments" are prudent steps for a profit-oriented coal producer, one must ask what would prevent other coal producers from taking these steps. Indeed, many other coal producers are affiliated with enterprises as large as or larger than Kennecott.

(d) *Capital costs.* Up to some point, there seems to be an inverse correlation between business size and the capital costs represented by interest on bank loans. The large and diversified firm presents fewer risks to investors[11] and seeks funds in a more competitive financial market; the smaller business can appeal only to a narrower range of financial sources. In addition, larger firms generate funds internally that may be applied to other divisions engaging in activities about which the firm has high expectations but is unable to sell to outside investors.[12]

(e) *Advertising.*[13] Substantial quantity discounts are sometimes offered by advertising media, with the result that giant advertisers may pay significantly less per advertisement than do their smaller competitors. And some promotional devices, such as sales contests, may be feasible only at a certain minimum scale of operation. In addition, a large firm's promotional resources might be effectively focused on a particular product or region at less cost than that for which a smaller company could obtain similar services. These are,

10. Kennecott Copper Corp. v. FTC, 467 F.2d 67, 78 (10th Cir. 1972), cert. denied, 416 U.S. 909 (1974).

11. Such benefits are likely to be modest because, as noted in ¶503d, investors can diversify.

12. This problem can arise because some information is difficult to convey credibly or at low cost and it may be strategic to keep hidden other information, such as new product or marketing ideas.

13. See ¶116.

of course, mere possibilities. Large-scale promotions may not help to sell some products, and smaller firms may have effective alternative means of exposure. And any promotional savings by the large firm will not necessarily be significant in relation to overall production or marketing costs.

Advertising efficiencies may be regarded unfavorably because heavy advertising can be wasteful. Advertising may not only waste resources but may also increase entry barriers by confronting new entrants with the entrenched goodwill of years of advertising. In any event, if promotional activities are important to the sale of a particular product, and the large advertiser obtains substantial quantity discounts amounting to a significant net cost advantage, then the smaller competitors must either affiliate with similarly large firms or suffer a competitive disadvantage. But it must be admitted that the implications of all this are far from clear. Are we ready to declare advertising undesirable and socially wasteful? In all cases? In some cases? Should the antitrust laws, which generally ignore advertising, condemn a merger that threatens to affect the outcome of competitive rivalry through wasteful promotional advantage? Is there any more of a conceptual problem in condemning mergers on grounds relating to advertising, which is not generally regulated by the antitrust laws, than in condemning mergers to monopoly when mere monopoly is legal?

(f) *Extending brand recognition and prestige.* If GM's Cadillac Division acquires a large number of restaurants, the use of the Cadillac name might confer a competitive advantage. For example, the cost of national advertising of a restaurant chain might be less than the combined cost to regional competitors of advertising in several separate markets. Or the prestige of the Cadillac name might be significant for consumers unfamiliar with particular restaurants; indeed, for a mobile public, the recognition of even a less prestigious but familiar name in a faraway place may be sufficient to induce patronage. Finally, consumers might patronize Cadillac restaurants because their prior dealings with GM have all been satisfactory. Of course, smaller competitors may be able to minimize these effects by adopting a single name that can be promoted nationally, affiliating with another nationally known company, or otherwise increasing their promotional activities.[14] In this sense, there is much in common with the advertising advantages considered above. But while consumers might rely unduly on a name, they do need quality information and, in the absence of convenient and objective data, may prefer a recognized name over a random guess. In addition,

14. Recall *Topco*, from Ch. 2B.

this recognition might increase the concern for quality by firms seeking a generally favorable reputation for the long run.

(g) *Transferred leverage.* Suppose that a manufacturer has some measure of economic power with respect to those who deal in its popular product. If that manufacturer acquires another producer whose product is distributed through the same channel, the leverage of the first product may induce greater acceptance of the second than its competitive merits would warrant.

(h) *Wide-line coverage.* The greater a seller's ability to satisfy a buyer's varied needs, the more likely is the seller to retain that buyer's patronage. Although this much is axiomatic, its significance is questionable. In *Continental Can,* ¶523, a can maker acquired a glass container manufacturer. Thereafter, a customer content with Continental cans might, other things equal, buy its jars from Continental as well. Conceivably, other jar makers might be unable to lure the customer away from the merged firm, even though, absent the merger, all jar manufacturers would be on an equal footing. In that event, other container firms may be driven into similar wide-line arrangements. But perhaps it is equally conceivable that the attempt to lure customers away from a wide-line company will mean more intensive price competition. Still, it may remain possible that the wide-line company gains goodwill amounting to a priority on the business, at least when prices and other circumstances are equal. A clog on competition is not implausible, but plausibility is not significance.

535. Extending the area of oligopolistic interdependence.[15] Oligopolistic sellers predicate their pricing and other competitive decisions on estimates and assumptions about the possible responses of rivals. See ¶¶228-231. Substantial rivalry and workably competitive results can occur in so-called oligopolistic markets because of competitive pressures, uncertainty, and the absence of completely identical interests among the several rivals. On the other hand, oligopolists can and sometimes do behave in almost the same way as true monopolists, particularly when there is sufficient threat that rivals will readily detect price cuts and respond effectively.

The acquisition by national seller *N* of local seller *L* might facilitate oligopoly pricing in the following way: While an independent *L* might cut prices whenever it thought it had an advantage in the

15. See Areeda & Turner, note 1, ¶1114; B.D. Bernheim & M. Whinston, Multimarket Contact and Collusive Behavior, 21 Rand J. Econ. 1 (1990). For empirical evidence, see W. Evans and I. Kessides, Living by the "Golden Rule": Multimarket Contact in the U.S. Airline Industry, 108 Q.J. Econ. 341 (1994); K. Hughes and C. Oughton, Diversification, Multi-market Contact and Profitability, 60 Economica 203 (1993).

local market, N might not do so if a rival in that market also confronted N in a second market where it could retaliate by pressing an advantage it had there or by otherwise causing substantial injury to N at little cost to itself. Thus, as the product and geographic areas in which oligopolists encounter each other widen, their interdependence becomes greater, so each comes to have more to lose from any move, which in turn might make any price initiative increasingly unlikely.

The anticompetitive effects just outlined assume that the national firms confront each other in markets that are oligopolistic but subject to potential disruption by N or by its national (or multimarket) rivals. The latter must be capable of retaliating in another such market, and N must stand to lose significantly in the event of such retaliation. Whether proof of such elements should be required to justify condemnation on such grounds is a more difficult question. But it should be noted that anticompetitive effects are not the necessary consequence of multimarket operations.

FEDERAL TRADE COMMISSION v. PROCTER & GAMBLE CO. (CLOROX)
386 U.S. 568 (1967)

Justice DOUGLAS. [The Federal Trade Commission found that Procter & Gamble's 1957 acquisition of the assets of Clorox Chemical Co. violated §7 in that it] might substantially lessen competition or tend to create a monopoly in the production and sale of household liquid bleaches. . . . The Court of Appeals for the Sixth Circuit reversed. . . . We find that the Commission's findings were amply supported by the evidence. . . .

It is agreed that household liquid bleach is the relevant line of commerce. . . . It is a distinctive product with no close substitutes. . . . The relevant geographical market is the Nation and a series of regional markets. Because of high shipping costs and low sales price, it is not feasible to ship the product more than 300 miles from its point of manufacture. Most manufacturers are limited to competition within a single region since they have but one plant. Clorox is the only firm selling nationally; it has 13 plants distributed throughout the Nation. Purex, Clorox's closest competitor in size, does not distribute its bleach in the northeast or mid-Atlantic States; in 1957, Purex's bleach was available in less than 50% of the national market.

At the time of the acquisition, Clorox was the leading manufacturer of household liquid bleach, with 48.8% of the national sales — annual sales of slightly less than $40,000,000. Its market share had been steadily increasing for the five years prior to the merger. Its nearest rival was Purex, which manufactures a number of products other than household liquid bleaches, including abrasive cleaners, toilet soap, and detergents. Purex accounted for 15.7% of the household liquid bleach market. The industry is highly concentrated; in 1957, Clorox and Purex accounted for almost 65% of the Nation's household bleach sales, and, together with four other firms, for almost 80%. The remaining 20% was divided among over 200 small producers. Clorox had total assets of $12,000,000; only eight producers had assets in excess of $1,000,000 and very few had assets of more than $75,000.

In light of the territorial limitations on distribution, national figures do not give an accurate picture of Clorox's dominance in the various regions. Thus, Clorox's seven principal competitors did no business in New England, the mid-Atlantic States, or metropolitan New York. Clorox's share of the sales in those areas was 56%, 72%, and 64% respectively. Even in regions where its principal competitors were active, Clorox maintained a dominant position. Except in metropolitan Chicago and the west-central States Clorox accounted for at least 39%, and often a much higher percentage, of liquid bleach sales.

Since all liquid bleach is chemically identical, advertising and sales promotion are vital. In 1957 Clorox spent almost $3,700,000 on advertising, imprinting the value of its bleach in the mind of the consumer. In addition, it spent $1,700,000 for other promotional activities. The Commission found that these heavy expenditures went far to explain why Clorox maintained so high a market share despite the fact that its brand, though chemically indistinguishable from rival brands, retailed for a price equal to or, in many instances, higher than its competitors.

Procter is a large, diversified manufacturer of low-price, high-turnover household products sold through grocery, drug, and department stores. Prior to its acquisition of Clorox, it did not produce household liquid bleach. Its 1957 sales were in excess of $1,100,000,000 from which it realized profits of more than $67,000,000; its assets were over $500,000,000. Procter has been marked by rapid growth and diversification. It has successfully developed and introduced a number of new products. Its primary activity is in the general area of soaps, detergents, and cleansers; in 1957, of total domestic sales, more than one-half (over $500,000,000) were in this field. Procter was the dominant factor in this area. It accounted for 54.4% of all packaged detergent sales. The industry is heavily concentrated — Procter and its nearest competitors, Colgate-Palmolive and Lever Brothers, account for 80% of the market.

In the marketing of soaps, detergents, and cleansers, as in the marketing of household liquid bleach, advertising and sales promotion are vital. In 1957, Procter was the Nation's largest advertiser, spending more than $80,000,000 on advertising, and an additional $47,000,000 on sales promotion. Due to its tremendous volume, Procter receives substantial discounts from the media. As a multi-product producer Procter enjoys substantial advantages in advertising and sales promotion. Thus, it can and does feature several products in its promotions, reducing the printing, mailing, and other costs for each product. It also purchases network programs on behalf of several products, enabling it to give each product network exposure at a fraction of the cost per product that a firm with only one product to advertise would incur.

Prior to the acquisition, Procter was in the course of diversifying into product lines related to its basic detergent-soap-cleanser business. Liquid bleach was a distinct possibility since packaged detergents — Procter's primary product line — and liquid bleach are used complementarily in washing clothes and fabrics, and in general household cleaning. As noted by the Commission:

> ... Household cleaning agents in general, like household liquid bleach, are low-cost, high-turnover household consumer goods marketed chiefly through grocery stores and pre-sold to the consumer by the manufacturer through mass advertising and sales promotions. Since products of both parties to the merger are sold to the same customers, at the same stores, and by the same merchandising methods, the possibility arises of significant integration at both the marketing and distribution levels. . . .

The Commission found that the substitution of Procter with its huge assets and advertising advantages for the already dominant Clorox would dissuade new entrants and discourage active competition from the firms already in the industry due to fear of retaliation by Procter. The Commission thought it relevant that retailers might be induced to give Clorox preferred shelf space since it would be manufactured by Procter, which also produced a number of other products marketed by the retailers. There was also the danger that Procter might underprice Clorox in order to drive out competition, and subsidize the underpricing with revenue from other products. The Commission carefully reviewed the effect of the acquisition on the structure of the industry, noting that "[t]he practical tendency of the . . . merger . . . is to transform the liquid bleach industry into an arena of big business competition only, with the few small firms that have not disappeared through merger eventually falling by the wayside, unable to compete with their giant rivals." Further, the merger would seriously diminish potential competition by eliminating Procter as a potential entrant into the industry. Prior to the merger, the Commission found, Procter was the most likely prospective entrant, and absent the merger would have remained on the periphery, restraining Clorox from exercising its market power. If Procter had actually entered, Clorox's dominant position would have been eroded and the concentration of the industry reduced. The Commission stated that it had not placed reliance on post-acquisition evidence in holding the merger unlawful. . . .

The anticompetitive effects with which this product-extension merger is fraught can easily be seen: (1) the substitution of the powerful acquiring firm for the smaller, but already dominant, firm may substantially reduce the competitive structure of the industry by raising entry barriers and by dissuading the smaller firms from aggressively competing; (2) the acquisition eliminates the potential competition of the acquiring firm.

The liquid bleach industry was already oligopolistic before the acquisition, and price competition was certainly not as vigorous as it would have been if the industry were competitive. Clorox enjoyed a dominant position nationally, and its position approached monopoly proportions in certain areas. The existence of some 200 fringe firms certainly does not belie that fact. Nor does the fact, relied upon by the court below, that, after the merger, producers other than Clorox "were selling more bleach for more money than ever before." In the same period, Clorox increased its share from 48.8% to 52%. The interjection of Procter into the market considerably changed the situation. There is every reason to assume that the smaller firms would become more cautious in competing due to their fear of retaliation by Procter. It is probable that Procter would become the price leader and that oligopoly would become more rigid.

The acquisition may also have the tendency of raising the barriers to new entry. The major competitive weapon in the successful marketing of bleach is advertising. Clorox was limited in this area by its relatively small budget and its inability to obtain substantial discounts. By contrast, Procter's budget was much larger; and, although it would not devote its entire budget to advertising Clorox, it could divert a large portion to meet the short-term threat of a new entrant. Procter would be able to use its volume discounts to advantage in advertising Clorox. Thus, a new entrant would be much more reluctant to face the giant Procter than it would have been to face the smaller Clorox.[3]

3. The barriers to entry have been raised both for entry by new firms and for entry into new geographical markets by established firms. The latter aspect is demonstrated by Purex's lesson in Erie, Pennsylvania. In October 1957, Purex selected Erie, Pennsylvania — where it had not sold previously — as an area in

Possible economies cannot be used as a defense to illegality. Congress was aware that some mergers which lessen competition may also result in economies but it struck the balance in favor of protecting competition. See *Brown Shoe.*

The Commission also found that the acquisition of Clorox by Procter eliminated Procter as a potential competitor. The Court of Appeals declared that this finding was not supported by evidence because there was no evidence that Procter's management had ever intended to enter the industry independently and that Procter had never attempted to enter. The evidence, however, clearly shows that Procter was the most likely entrant. Procter had recently launched a new abrasive cleaner in an industry similar to the liquid bleach industry, and had wrested leadership from a brand that had enjoyed even a larger market share than had Clorox. Procter was engaged in a vigorous program of diversifying into product lines closely related to its basic products. Liquid bleach was a natural avenue of diversification since it is complementary to Procter's products, is sold to the same customers through the same channels, and is advertised and merchandised in the same manner. Procter had substantial advantages in advertising and sales promotion, which, as we have seen, are vital to the success of liquid bleach. No manufacturer had a patent on the product or its manufacture, necessary information relating to manufacturing methods and processes was readily available, there was no shortage of raw material, and the machinery and equipment required for a plant of efficient capacity were available at reasonable cost. Procter's management was experienced in producing and marketing goods similar to liquid bleach. Procter had considered the possibility of independently entering but decided against it because the acquisition of Clorox would enable Procter to capture a more commanding share of the market.

It is clear that the existence of Procter at the edge of the industry exerted considerable influence on the market. First, the market behavior of the liquid bleach industry was influenced by each firm's predictions of the market behavior of its competitors, actual and potential. Second, the barriers to entry by a firm of Procter's size

---

which to test the salability, under competitive conditions, of a new bleach. The leading brands in Erie were Clorox with 52% and the "101" brand, sold by Gardner Manufacturing Company, with 29% of the market. Purex launched an advertising and promotional campaign to obtain a broad distribution in a short time, and in five months captured 33% of the Erie market. Clorox's share dropped to 35% and 101's to 17%. Clorox responded by offering its bleach at reduced prices, and then added an offer of a $1-value ironing board cover for 50¢ with each purchase of Clorox at the reduced price. It also increased its advertising with television spots. The result was to restore Clorox's lost market share and, indeed, to increase it slightly. Purex's share fell to 7%. . . .

and with its advantages were not significant. There is no indication that the barriers were so high that the price Procter would have to charge would be above the price that would maximize the profits of the existing firms. Third, the number of potential entrants was not so large that the elimination of one would be insignificant. Few firms would have the temerity to challenge a firm as solidly entrenched as Clorox. Fourth, Procter was found by the Commission to be the most likely entrant. These findings of the Commission were amply supported by the evidence.

The judgment of the Court of Appeals is reversed and remanded with instructions to affirm and enforce the Commission's order.

[Justice Harlan concurred: (1) The majority merely assumed that smaller firms would become more cautious in competing because they would fear retaliation by Procter. But this does not rise to a reasonable probability. Indeed, smaller firms might compete more aggressively lest Procter ultimately absorb their markets. (2) The loss of Procter as an actual competitor is not an issue because the FTC "expressly refused to find a reasonable probability that Procter would have entered this market on its own." (3) The FTC was entitled on this record to regard the market as oligopolistic and to ignore the many smaller firms who had not been proved by Procter to price at cost and thereby to impose an effective ceiling on market prices. Potential competition and the conditions of entry may therefore be regarded as determinative in this case. (4) The majority's analysis does not show that Procter's advertising capability would increase barriers to entry of a nationally advertised bleach beyond their already formidable level, which dissuaded even Procter from independent entry. Furthermore, entry was easy for unadvertised bleaches, and the majority has not shown why such competition was either unimportant or likely to be reduced by the merger. (5) Nevertheless, the FTC was entitled to conclude that Procter's advertising advantages and its ability to mobilize and utilize large financial resources would effect a substantial change in the conditions of entry. And Procter itself, as a potential entrant, might have faced fewer barriers to entry than others. (6) Efficiencies bear on the vigor of competition, and it is competition rather than inefficient competitors that the antitrust laws protect. Advertising efficiencies are as valuable as other cost savings. Although advertising may be used to create irrational brand preferences and to mislead consumers, advertising is an element of the product, and it is up to consumers to make the relevant choices. Procter, however, has merely shown dollar savings, not resource savings.][16]

16. Stewart and Fortas, JJ., did not participate.

536. Do you agree with the result and reasoning of the *Clorox* decision?

(a) Does the merger create any promotional economies? Should any such economies constitute a defense in the view of the majority or of Justice Harlan? In your view? Would bleach rivals be significantly disadvantaged?

(b) Procter is a much larger firm than any bleach producer (including the previously independent Clorox). Does Procter's acquisition (1) increase the danger of price leadership in liquid bleach, (2) reduce the opportunities or competitive vigor of bleach rivals, or (3) increase the danger of predation by the dominant bleach firm?

(c) Consider the barriers to the entry of new firms into the bleach business. (1) What is the competitive relevance of any such barriers — generally and in this business? (2) How high are the barriers to entry into the bleach business? (3) Could Procter's acquisition increase those barriers?

(d) Consider the potential competition issue. (1) Was Procter a potential entrant? Is it likely that Procter would have entered the bleach business independently? When? If it had conducted an internal study indicating that entry was not currently profitable, and would continue to be unprofitable given current prices, is any anticompetitive danger alleviated? (2) Assume that Procter was a potential entrant eliminated by its merger with Clorox. Does it follow that the likelihood of potential entry was significantly reduced — either necessarily or in this case? (3) Assume that the likelihood of potential entry was reduced by the merger. Would adverse competitive effects tend to follow — either necessarily or in this case?

(e) Of what relevance is the fact that Clorox bleach was chemically identical to that of its competitors, yet often sold at a substantial premium?

(f) What would have been the competitive effect if Proctor had entered independently? Or if it had acquired a small bleach company as a base for expansion?

(g) Suppose that, after the *Clorox* decision, Procter asked you whether it could lawfully acquire (1) Rome Cable Corp. or (2) Von's Grocery Co. What questions would you ask? What advice would you give?

(h) Suppose that the second and third largest bleach producers proposed to merge. May they cite *Clorox* and argue that the existence of potential competition minimizes the competitive significance of their merger?[17]

---

17. See United States v. Waste Mgmt., 743 F.2d 976 (2d Cir. 1984) (prima facie illegality rebutted by ease of entry, emphasizing Supreme Court's potential compe-

537. Subsequent potential competition decisions. Numerous subsequent cases developed in greater detail the reach of the potential competition doctrine, often in contexts where the relationship between the business of the acquiring and acquired firms was closer than in *Clorox*. In each instance, consider the theory under which the merger is arguably anticompetitive, determine the prerequisites that should be required for proof of the claim, and assess the plausibility of their having been met in the cases presented.

(a) *The toehold doctrine.* Starting with *Bendix*, considered in ¶b, the Federal Trade Commission and the courts began considering the circumstances in which an acquisition of a market's leading firm by a potential entrant should be banned on the ground that it would be preferable if the outside firm made a smaller — or toehold — acquisition. As with any potential competition case, the market would have to pose sufficient anticompetitive proclivities and have a sufficient shortage of potential entrants such that the loss of an opportunity to enhance competition would be worrisome. In addition, this doctrine, at least in principle, would require that an appropriate toehold be available and that its acquisition offer a meaningful prospect of increasing competition beyond any positive effect from the actual merger. The Supreme Court has not ruled on this doctrine, but the appeals court opinions in *Bendix* and another case[18] were sympathetic. In practice, its major use has been defensive, as a number of tribunals have appeared willing to tolerate the conglomerate acquisition of a mere toehold.

(b) *Bendix Corp.*, 77 F.T.C. 731, 831 (1970), vacated on procedural grounds, 450 F.2d 534 (6th Cir. 1971), consent order, 84 F.T.C. 1291 (1974). The Federal Trade Commission condemned an acquisition on potential entry grounds even though the acquiring firm was not found to be a probable de novo entrant into the acquired firm's market, where concentration was high (the top four firms had more than 80 percent of the sales) and competition weak. The Commission found it sufficient that Bendix would have entered through a smaller acquisition. The Commission found that Bendix would in fact have entered the market in one manner or another and had expressly considered merger with many smaller competitors before acquiring the third largest competitor. Bendix internal memoranda suggested it could build the business of such alternative partners and, within a few years, make sales and receive profits comparable to the second or third largest firms in the industry. The merger was seen as eliminating Bendix as a potential com-

---

tition cases and *General Dynamics'* holding that market shares may be misleading as to actual competitive effect).

18. *Kennecott*, note 10 (enforcement order).

petitor. While there were some other prospects for entry and enhanced competition, the Commission found them unlikely, at least in the near future, to transform the market radically. Entry barriers were thought to be significant for other prospective entrants, a conclusion supported by minimal actual entry during a period of high profits and sales growth. Bendix's significant resources and extensive experience in related markets were thought to place it in a particularly good position to succeed. "Bendix was among the most likely of a limited number of possible entrants capable of making a significant entry by acquisition and expansion of a smaller firm."

(c) *United States v. Falstaff Brewing Corp.*, 410 U.S. 526, 532-533 (1973). The government challenged Falstaff's acquisition of Narragansett, the largest seller of beer in New England, with 20 percent of the market. The four largest producers' share, which had been rising, was 61.3 percent in the year of the acquisition. Narragansett was a regional producer. Falstaff was one of the few large brewers (it was the nation's fourth largest) that did not yet sell in New England and, of that group, it was the largest and had the closest brewery. Falstaff had publicly expressed its desire to cover the nation, and it acquired Narragansett only after considering several prospects of entering the Northeast by acquisition. The lower court had found that the market was competitive and Falstaff would not have entered the Northeast de novo. The Supreme Court held that the district court had misapplied the potential competition doctrine, requiring a remand. "The error lay in the assumption that because Falstaff, as a matter of fact, would never have entered the market de novo, it could in no sense be considered a potential competitor." The question was not what Falstaff's internal decisions would have been "but whether, given its financial capabilities and conditions in the New England market, it would be reasonable to consider it a potential entrant into that market." Falstaff could well have been perceived as a potential entrant, and thus exert a current competitive effect. The Court expressly reserved the toehold question — whether a merger could be prohibited only on the ground that de novo or toehold entry would have been possible and superior, even where the merger would produce no direct effect on competition and the potential entrant had no current influence in the marketplace.[19]

19. *Falstaff* was a plurality opinion (of three of the seven participating Justices), the remand being supported by two Justices who, in varying respects, would have gone further. Justice Marshall's opinion emphasized the need to judge potential entry with objective data — on the assumption that firms will do what is profitable — rather than by management's subjective, potentially self-serving statements.

On remand, 383 F. Supp. 1020 (D.R.I. 1974), the court found (1) no subjective

(d) *United States v. Marine Bancorporation*, 418 U.S. 602, 639-640 (1974). NBC (a subsidiary of Marine Bancorporation), the second largest bank in Washington state, operating in Seattle and the west, acquired the ninth largest bank, operating in Spokane and the east. The Court doubted that NBC was an actual or perceived potential entrant into Spokane primarily because state law prohibited NBC from establishing de novo branches in Spokane. Although there was the possibility that the state's laws could be partially circumvented, the law would still not allow NBC to branch from a newly formed bank in Spokane once such bank was acquired by NBC. Similarly, if NBC acquired existing small Spokane banks, it would face the same legal barriers to expansion. "Rational commercial bankers in Spokane ... are aware of the regulatory barriers that render NBC an unlikely or an insignificant potential entrant.... In the light of those barriers, it is improbable that NBC exerts any meaningful procompetitive influence over Spokane Banks by 'standing in the wings.'" Because these barriers "strongly" suggest "that NBC would not develop into a significant participant in the Spokane market," the Court found it unnecessary to decide the question reserved in *Falstaff*: whether the elimination of a significant future addition to the market was covered by the statute.

538. Conglomerate mergers under 1984 government guidelines.[20] The 1984 merger guidelines considered conglomerate mergers only in terms of the elimination of specific potential entrants. The rationale is that stated in ¶532. "Because of the close relationship between perceived potential competition [or present effects] and actual potential competition [or future effects], the Department will [use] a single structural analysis...."

Market concentration. "The Department is unlikely to challenge ... unless overall concentration of the acquired firm's market is above 1800 HHI," although a lower number will suffice if effective collusion in the market is especially likely. "Other things being equal, the Department is increasingly likely to challenge a merger as this threshold is exceeded."

Entry conditions. Challenge is unlikely "when new entry into the acquired firm's market can be accomplished by firms without any specific entry advantages."

___

or objective evidence that Falstaff would have entered independently or that existing firms thought it would and (2) no evidence that that market was noncompetitive or that Falstaff influenced it.

20. 49 Fed. Reg. 26823 (1984). The 1992 Horizontal Merger Guidelines, discussed in ¶527, indicate that the 1984 government guidelines still apply to conglomerate mergers.

884   *Conglomerate Mergers*   ¶538

Other acquirers. The government "is unlikely to challenge a potential competition merger if the entry advantage ascribed to the acquiring firm (or another advantage of comparable importance) is also possessed by three or more other firms."

Other factors. (1) Challenge is possible when the merger eliminates a firm whose probable entry "is particularly strong," as indicated, for example, by "significant investments demonstrating an actual decision to enter." Such a firm may be treated as if it were already in the market at a scale indicated by "the firm's own documents or the minimum efficient scale in the industry," and its merger may be treated "much as ... a horizontal merger." (2) Challenge is unlikely "when the acquired firm has a market share of five percent or less." Challenge is increasingly likely with higher shares and certain at 20 percent (assuming that the other conditions for challenge are satisfied). (3) Efficiency and failing company defenses will be considered.

Under the 1982 version of these guidelines, one commentator[21] concluded that the Justice Department would have sued in *El Paso* and *Clorox* but would not have sued in *Consolidated Foods, Ford, Penn-Olin, Pabst, Falstaff,* and *Connecticut National Bank.*[22] The Supreme Court held the first four mergers illegal and indicated that the last four might be if certain facts were found.

539. Tidewater Oil Co., Phillips Petroleum Co., and Standard Oil Co. of New Jersey (Exxon) have submitted two related merger and acquisition agreements, described below, to the Department of Justice for review. You are asked to advise whether the proposed agreements violate the antitrust laws in any respects, stating your reasons. You are supplied with the following facts.[23]

(a) *The firms involved.* (1) Tidewater Oil Co. refines and sells gasoline in five far western states, principally in California. About 60 percent of its retail sales of Tidewater brand gasoline are made through Tidewater-owned stations, the balance through independent stations on requirements contracts terminable by either party on three months' notice. (2) Phillips sells gasoline at retail in all states except California. It is the fifth largest seller nationwide, and the largest not already selling in California. (3) Exxon sells gasoline in all states. It is the largest seller nationwide.

21. Fox, Ch. 5D, note 25.
22. Ford Motor Co. v. United States, 405 U.S. 562 (1972); United States v. Pabst Brewing Co., 384 U.S. 546 (1966); United States v. Connecticut Natl. Bank, 418 U.S. 656 (1974).
23. United States v. Phillips Petro. Co., 367 F. Supp. 1226 (C.D. Cal. 1973), aff'd mem., 418 U.S. 906 (1974).

(b) *Market data.* (1) Tidewater's market shares in the four far western states other than California have been 2 percent or less. Phillips's and Exxon's shares in those states do not exceed 8 percent. (2) In 1971, California retail gasoline sales of Socal, Union, Tidewater, Atlantic-Richfield, and Texaco each exceeded 10 percent of the market; Conoco and Exxon each sold 5 percent; independent chains sold 9 percent.

(c) *Background facts.* (1) With its market share having declined 2 percent in each of the past two years, Tidewater's profits have also steadily declined. It reported a small loss for the fourth quarter of 1971. An outside consulting firm, retained in early 1971 to study the company's situation, reported that the prospects for future improvement were poor because of an apparent consumer trend toward national brands. The firm recommended that Tidewater seek to sell out to, or merge with, another oil company. (2) Intensive efforts turned up only one firm offer in addition to the Phillips proposal described in ¶d: an offer by Sun Oil Company, a Midwest producer and marketer, to purchase the Tidewater stock for $25 million in Sun stock. (3) Difficulties in obtaining retail station outlets appear to be a substantial barrier to entry and growth in gasoline markets. Exxon first entered the California market in 1960. Its share of California sales did not reach 2 percent until 1967.

(d) *The agreements.* (1) Early in 1972, Tidewater stockholders ratified an agreement to exchange their stock for $100 million worth of stock in Phillips Petroleum Co. (2) Shortly before that time, Phillips agreed with Exxon that, contingent on consummation of the Tidewater transaction: (i) Phillips would sell to Exxon one-half of the owned California stations obtained from Tidewater (the list of actual stations being specified). (ii) Phillips would assign to Exxon one-half of the contract California stations (again specified). (iii) Neither would solicit the other's ex-Tidewater contract stations for a period of two years. (iv) For a period of three years, Exxon would have an option to purchase and at Phillips' election would be required to purchase, up to one-half of the output of the ex-Tidewater refineries. (3) If the agreements are consummated, Exxon intends to convert all acquired stations — owned or on contract — to its own brand. Phillips intends at the outset to convert all acquired California stations to "Phillips-Tidewater." Depending on later market analysis, it may gradually phase out the Tidewater name.

540. Reciprocity.[24] (a) *Generally.* Reciprocity is the practice by which a firm buys only from those who buy from it. An automobile

---

24. See Areeda & Turner, note 1, ¶¶1128-1133.

company, for example, may purchase steel only from steelmakers using its vehicles. A firm may increase the likelihood of reciprocity by diversifying — through merger or internal expansion — into products that its suppliers buy. Suppose, for example, that most of G's suppliers use liquid carbon dioxide (lcd). If G, a large defense contractor, acquires lcd-producer L, G might condition its purchases from its suppliers on their buying lcd from L. Of course, the suppliers might ignore G's demand if they are indifferent to the loss of its patronage. Remember, however, that it may take very little to induce suppliers to buy from L when its price, quality, and service are as good as its rivals'. Even so, the results might be unimportant. If G's suppliers do not represent a significant share of the lcd market, their purchasing entirely from L would not significantly foreclose the marketing opportunities of L's rivals.[25]

(b) *Purposes.* The reasons for using reciprocity are akin to those for tying, as discussed in ¶423. As with tying, the device does not itself increase the market power of its practitioners, but it might allow more effective exploitation of existing power or pose some dangers concerning future competitive prospects in the affected industries. Reciprocity might be a disguised form of price competition. As considered in Chapter 6, for example, the Robinson-Patman Act might inhibit a seller from lowering its price to a particular defendant buyer with monopsony power. Instead, the seller might buy some or all of its requirements of the defendant's product at a price profitable to the defendant. Minimum price control imposed by government or by such cartels as the New York Stock Exchange might similarly be evaded. The seller, who is forbidden from reducing the selling price for its product or service, might compete by paying a higher price or accepting lower quality goods than it otherwise would. The oligopolistic seller might do the same. A price cut might simply invite similar demands from other customers or induce general price reductions by rival oligopolists. And when other things are equal and both the buying and selling markets are oligopolistic, each firm might manipulate its patronage as a form of nonprice rivalry. It is also possible that buyers and sellers might deal with each other on a reciprocal basis in order to eliminate certain buying and selling expenses. Transaction costs might possibly fall, for example, if reciprocity replaced such forms of winning patronage as expensive entertainment.

25. These are the basic facts of United States v. General Dynamics Corp., 258 F. Supp. 36 (S.D.N.Y. 1966), which condemned the *L-G* merger. *L* accounted for about 35 to 40 percent of its market, which had a four-firm concentration ratio of about 75 percent. Its sales to *G*'s major accounts represented about 5 percent of the market. The court emphasized that *L*'s market share had been declining until the merger, which *L* welcomed in the hope of practicing reciprocity.

We do not purport to say with assurance whether such "virtues" are sufficiently redeeming, whether condemning reciprocity would stiffen cartel and oligopoly behavior, or whether eliminating reciprocity would channel rivalry into the open where it would be more intense and afford all sellers an equal opportunity to win patronage on the merits and without diversion from an "alien factor."

(c) *Relevant questions.* To appraise the potential for harmful reciprocity in a given situation, one should ask at least three questions. (1) Does the defendant engage in reciprocity or is it likely to attempt it? (2) Would any such attempt be successful? The answer may depend on the relative importance of the defendant to its suppliers as well as on a host of market circumstances. (3) Even if reciprocity is successfully practiced by the defendant, would rivals be foreclosed from a significant portion of the relevant market? The answer will be strongly influenced by the share of that market represented by the purchases of those who also sell to the defendant.

(d) *Agreements.* An express reciprocity agreement may violate Sherman Act §1 on reasoning analogous to that condemning tying agreements. (Consider why Clayton Act §3 would not be applicable to reciprocity as it is to tying and exclusive dealing.) And the Supreme Court seemed to say so in *Consolidated Foods,* which follows.[26] In the absence of an express agreement, a tacit agreement might perhaps be inferred from the fact of reciprocal dealing or from the maintenance by each firm of careful records relating their transactions to each other.[27] Of course, a supplier might voluntarily purchase from a potential customer in the hope that the latter would note the fact and purchase from it. But even informal arrangements may require detectable recordkeeping, at least when the transactions are numerous.

(e) *Mergers.* Suppose that a particular merger creates a noticeable possibility of reciprocity. If the reciprocity that might occur would be insubstantial, we could tolerate a merger even if unsure of our ability to detect and condemn reciprocity in the concrete. And the greater our assurance that §1 can catch reciprocity, the greater should be our insistence on a substantial competitive danger before preventing a merger. But the criteria of substantiality are far from clear.

26. See also Betaseed v. U & I, 681 F.2d 1203 (9th Cir. 1982).
27. Carlson Cos. v. Sperry & Hutchison Co., 1974 Trade Cas. ¶75153, at 97172-97173 (D. Minn.) ("[i]nferences of reciprocity can be drawn from the bare fact" of mutual dealing for the purpose of denying defendant's motion for summary judgment); United States v. Airco, 386 F. Supp. 915 (S.D.N.Y. 1974) (no illegal dealings inferred from mutual dealings, supplying sales data to purchasing officials, internal language of reciprocity, actual consideration in purchases of potential sales, and membership in "trade relations" association).

FEDERAL TRADE COMMISSION
v. CONSOLIDATED FOODS CORP.
380 U.S. 592 (1965)

Justice DOUGLAS. [Consolidated, a large food processor and distributor, acquired Gentry, Inc., a manufacturer of dehydrated onion and garlic. The FTC held that the acquisition violated §7 because of the danger of reciprocity which "may be substantially to lessen competition." The court of appeals set aside the Commission's order. Reciprocity] made possible by such an acquisition is one of the congeries of anticompetitive practices at which the antitrust laws are aimed. The practice results in "an irrelevant and alien factor" intruding into the choice among competing products, creating at the least "a priority on the business at equal prices." *International Salt; Northern Pacific.* Reciprocal trading may ensue not from bludgeoning or coercion but from more subtle arrangements. A threatened withdrawal of orders if products of an affiliate cease being bought, as well as a conditioning of future purchases on the receipt of orders for products of that affiliate is an anticompetitive practice. Section 7 of the Clayton Act is concerned "with probabilities, not certainties." *Brown Shoe.* . . . Reciprocity in trading as a result of an acquisition violates §7, if the probability of a lessening of competition is shown. We turn then to that, the principal, aspect of the present case.

Consolidated is a substantial purchaser of the products of food processors who in turn purchase dehydrated onion and garlic for use in preparing and packaging their food. Gentry, which as noted is principally engaged in the manufacture of dehydrated onion and garlic, had in 1950, immediately prior to its acquisition by Consolidated, about 32% of the total sales of the dehydrated garlic and onion industry and, together with its principal competitor, Basic Vegetable Products, Inc., accounted for almost 90% of the total industry sales. The remaining 10% was divided between two other firms. By 1958 the total industry output of both products had doubled, Gentry's share rising to 35% and the combined share of Gentry and Basic remaining at about 90%.

After the acquisition Consolidated (though later disclaiming adherence to any policy of reciprocity) did undertake to assist Gentry in selling. An official of Consolidated wrote as follows to its distributing divisions: "Oftentimes, it is a great advantage to know when you are calling on a prospect, whether or not that prospect is a supplier of someone within your own organization. Everyone believes in reciprocity providing all things are equal. . . ."

Food processors who sold to Consolidated stated they would give their onion and garlic business to Gentry for reciprocity reasons if it could meet the price and quality of its competitors' products. . . .

Some suppliers responded and gave reciprocal orders. Some who first gave generous orders later reduced them or abandoned the practice. It is impossible to recreate the precise anatomy of the market arrangements following the acquisition, though respondent offers a factual brief seeking to prove that "reciprocity" either failed or was not a major factor in the post-acquisition history.

The Commission found, however, that "merely as a result of its connection with Consolidated, and without any action on the latter's part, Gentry would have an unfair advantage over competitors enabling it to make sales that otherwise might not have been made." . . .

The Commission found that Basic's product was superior to Gentry's — as Gentry's president freely and repeatedly admitted. Yet Gentry, in a rapidly expanding market, was able to increase its share of onion sales by 7% and to hold its losses in garlic to a 12% decrease. Thus the Commission was surely on safe ground in reaching the following conclusion:

> If reciprocal buying creates for Gentry a protected market, which others cannot penetrate despite superiority of price, quality, or service, competition is lessened whether or not Gentry can expand its market share. It is for this reason that we reject respondent's argument that the decline in its share of the garlic market proves the ineffectiveness of reciprocity. We do not know that its share would not have fallen still farther, had it not been for the influence of reciprocal buying. This loss of sales fails to refute the likelihood that Consolidated's reciprocity power, which it has shown a willingness to exploit to the full, will not immunize a substantial segment of the garlic market from normal quality, price, and service competition.

. . . Reversed.

Justice STEWART, concurring in the judgment. . . . Clearly the opportunity for reciprocity is not alone enough to invalidate a merger under §7. The Clayton Act was not passed to outlaw diversification. Yet large scale diversity of industrial interests almost always presents the possibility of some reciprocal relationships. Often the purpose of diversification is to acquire companies whose present management can benefit from the technical skills and sales acumen of the acquiring corporation. . . .

The record in this case is sorely incomplete, and a reviewing court is given little guidance in determining why this merger should be voided, if reciprocity-creating mergers are not per se invalid. Yet our responsibility to the Commission — to respect its findings where there is evidence to support them — requires close scrutiny of the record before its conclusions are upset. I think the record contains just enough to support invalidation of the merger, but because of evidence not referred to in the Court's opinion.

The food processing industry is composed basically of two classes of manufacturers. One class, which includes such processors as Armour and Swift, has built significant brand names commanding consumer acceptance of their products. For such companies, exposure at the retail market is assured. Consolidated Foods, as the wholesaler, is sufficiently dependent on such processors that its economic power over this class is minimal. It cannot readily strong-arm Armour into purchasing dehydrated onions from Gentry at the pain of losing Consolidated's favor. A second class incorporates the smaller processors in the industry. Many of these sell their product to Consolidated in bulk, for packaging under house labels of Consolidated divisions. Many of the products which these processors package under their own labels are not so widely known; they rely on the wholesaler to persuade supermarkets to try them on their counters. These processors are susceptible to the subtle pressures of reciprocity.

My reading of the record persuades me that most of the processors in this second class shifted their buying from Basic to Gentry, though the extent of that shift varied from company to company. It is true that testimony from the purchasing agents of many of these companies attributed the shift to other causes. However, the pattern of movement in this class, when contrasted to the lack of a pattern among the major processors, seems to me sufficient to support the Commission's conclusion that these shifts were in response to the influence of reciprocity, whether express or "tacitly accommodative." The pattern is relevant because the independent processors are substantial purchasers in the dehydrated onion and garlic market. Furthermore, this pattern confirms what was assumed by the Commission: that Consolidated has the power to influence the purchases by a substantial segment of its suppliers. Some of the independent processors have failed, and others have merged with large processors leading to greater concentration in the food processing industry. The Commission could, therefore, have fairly concluded that the inhibitory effects of reciprocity in this situation marked this merger with illegality. . . .[28]

541. (a) One of the issues that frequently arises in merger cases is the weight to be given to evidence of actual conduct after the merger. Because, prior to the enactment of premerger notification in 1976,[29] antitrust suits or FTC proceedings were seldom initiated immediately and tried quickly, the merged company may have operated for several years before the tribunal's decision. Even today, late

28. Harlan, J., concurred separately.
29. See ¶509b.

attacks still occur. The FTC has argued that no weight ought to be given the absence of anticompetitive conduct during the early post-acquisition period because the defendant would be on its best behavior pending disposition of its case. In *Consolidated Foods* (in a portion of the opinion omitted here), the Court, while admitting that such evidence had some relevance, refused to give it much weight because that would be to allow the defendant a "free trial" period. Justice Stewart disagreed strongly, maintaining that such evidence was the best available indicia of market effects. Which, if any, of these positions is correct?[30]

(b) What is Justice Stewart's disagreement with the rest of the Court? Is he correct? Why?

(c) *Consolidated Foods* also stated that reciprocity is "one of the congeries of anticompetitive practices at which the antitrust laws are aimed." Does every acquisition that makes reciprocity possible violate §7? What defenses might be available?

542. Phi Petroleum Company produces, refines, and distributes gasoline under its well-known name through gasoline stations located throughout the country. It accounts for about 10 percent of the gasoline sold in the United States. Phi stations also account for about 10 percent of the national sales of that portion of tires, batteries, and automobile accessories sold through gasoline stations.

Phi sells its gasoline to independent businesses; about half of these stations are owned by Phi and leased to the operators on three-month leases. The remaining Phi stations are owned entirely by their operators. Each contract between Phi and a station expressly provides that the station is free to handle the products of any supplier.

Theta Tire Corporation manufactures automobile tires that it sells to numerous wholesalers, retailers (including department stores, automotive supply stores, and some who sell tires alone), and gasoline service stations. Theta does not sell to automobile manufacturers, who purchase tires used as original equipment on their new cars entirely from the five largest tire manufacturers. In addition to the largest five and Theta, there are 10 smaller producers. The following table lists percentage shares of national tire sales (dollar value) in each of several categories. To reflect the importance of each category to the industry, the first line lists in italics the percentage of total industry sales accounted for by each category.

---

30. See ¶511b. Also recall the discussion of this issue in *General Dynamics*, Ch. 5D.

	Bus & Truck Tires 4	Original Equip- ment 48	*Passenger Car Tires* *Replacement Tires* Gas Stations 24	Other 24	Replace- ment Total 48	Total 100
"*Importance*"						
Five largest	90	100	12	88	50	76
Theta	2	0	2	10	6	3
Ten smallest	8	0	86	2	44	21
Total	100	100	100	100	100	100

Phi acquired Theta and invited stations handling its gasoline to purchase Theta tires, which are offered at favorable prices that reflect the economies resulting from single billing of stations for both their gas and tires and from combining deliveries of gasoline and tires. Because Phi's gasoline trucks now carry a small but varied range of tires, it is possible for each service station to purchase economically even one or two tires of the sizes necessary to round out its inventory or to meet the special needs of customers.

The government has attacked this acquisition under Clayton Act §7. What result? Why?

543.   *United States v. International Telephone & Telegraph Corp.*, 324 F. Supp. 19, 24, 30, 46 n.209, 47-48, 51, 52-54 (D. Conn. 1970). ITT, a conglomerate, was the ninth largest industrial corporation, with 1969 employment of 353,000, revenues of about $5.5 billion, net income of $234 million, and assets of $5.2 billion. During the 1960s, ITT had acquired 85 domestic and 60 foreign companies. The government had challenged three of ITT's most recent acquisitions. The subject of this trial was Grinnell, the 268th largest industrial corporation. Also of importance was the ITT-Hartford merger; Hartford was the sixth largest property and liability insurance company, with 1968 premiums of $969 million and assets of $1.9 billion. In the case of both mergers, ITT paid premiums substantially above market price to shareholders of the acquired companies.

(a) *Claims concerning Grinnell's dominance and the competitive advantages it would gain through the merger.* The court began by noting:

> The law is well settled that when a company which is the dominant competitor in a relatively oligopolistic market is acquired by a much larger company, such acquisition violates Section 7 of the Clayton Act if the acquired company gains marketing and promotional competitive advantages from the merger which will further entrench its position of dominance by raising barriers to entry to the relevant

markets and by discouraging smaller competitors from aggressively competing. The effect of such a merger will be substantially to lessen competition.

The court cited *Clorox* and subsequent lower court cases. The court, however, was "left with the unusually firm conviction that Grinnell, although a large and leading competitor, clearly is not a *dominant* competitor within the recognized meaning of that term in the antitrust field." Grinnell is a maker and installer of automatic sprinkler devices and systems and power piping systems (the latter used by utilities and in industry, and designed to withstand extremely high temperatures and pressures). In each of these markets, the court found that, even when Grinnell was the largest firm, it had significant competitors and shares ranging only to 25 percent.[31] In addition, Grinnell's share in many of these markets was declining, and important competitors were gaining ground. The fact that Grinnell was involved in both manufacturing and installation was not seen as giving it any significant advantage.

Accepting arguendo the possibility that Grinnell was dominant, the court found that the merger would not give it any marketing or promotional advantages. The government's allegation that the merger would give rise to package or system selling of sprinkler systems with other construction products was dismissed because Grinnell had not engaged in this practice during the year since the merger was consummated and because general contractors invite and receive separate bids for sprinklers in any event. Advantages through affiliation with Hartford, also being acquired by ITT, were deemed insignificant and speculative, as insurance companies were not in fact a significant source of business for the sprinkler industry, sprinkler work was subject to competitive bidding, and Hartford had only a 2.4 percent share of the sprinkler risk market. Access to ITT's financial resources was unimportant as Grinnell already had sufficient resources to offer credit where necessary. Similarly, ITT was not an important factor in Grinnell's potential for foreign expansion, as Grinnell had, prior to the merger, expanded into Europe on its own. Direct vertical foreclosure of ITT purchases was de minimis.

Finally, and most importantly, the court focused on and rejected the government's allegations of reciprocity. ITT's purchases from suppliers constituted but a small fraction of the latter's sales, suggesting that ITT lacked the power to force them to buy from Grinnell. Furthermore, most sprinkler systems were sold through

---

31. One exception was for automatic sprinkler systems in the Utah submarket, where the share was 44.3 percent. Other indications noted in text were sufficient, in the court's judgment, to dispose of this instance.

competitive bidding. The government did present some evidence of past reciprocity between Grinnell and certain steel companies, in one case involving linkage with an ITT subsidiary. But the court found these instances to be "exceptions which ... prove the rule." The cited instances were in the past and subject to a consent decree. ITT was not prone to reciprocity because it was organized into profit centers, each of which acted independently, in its own interest. Evidence suggested that ITT did not maintain the records necessary to facilitate reciprocity, and ITT had a written policy against the practice. In all, the court found that the alleged marketing and promotional advantages, "neither separately nor cumulatively [would] result in a substantial lessening of competition."

(b) *The economic concentration claim.* Throughout the proceedings in this case, the government had challenged the rise in economic concentration resulting from the merger. At the trial, the court sustained objections against admitting the government's offer of expert testimony on this issue. It explained:

> The new twist to the government's economic concentration claim is that in the wake of a "trend among large diversified industrial firms to acquire other large corporations," it can be established that "anticompetitive consequences will appear in numerous though *undesignated individual 'lines of commerce.'*" (Emphasis added.)
>
> The Court's short answer to this claim ... is that the legislative history, the statute itself and the controlling decisional law all make it clear beyond a peradventure of a doubt that in a Section 7 case the alleged anticompetitive effects of a merger must be examined in the context of *specific product and geographic markets*; and the determination of such markets is a necessary predicate to a determination of whether there has been a substantial lessening of competition within an area of effective competition. To ask the Court to rule with respect to alleged anticompetitive consequences in *undesignated lines of commerce* is tantamount to asking the Court to engage in judicial legislation. This the Court most emphatically refuses to do.
>
> Recognition of the trend toward economic concentration in American industry, including extensive conglomerate merger activity in recent years, is not exactly new. The government points out that the trend during the last two decades toward concentration of assets in the hands of fewer and larger corporate entities, together with an increasing diversification of those firms which primarily control the assets, has resulted in certain anticompetitive effects, among which are increased opportunities for business reciprocity and reciprocity effect.... [T]he government contends that the most important anticompetitive effect of the trend toward conglomeration by merger is "conglomerate interdependence and forebearance," meaning "a system in which competitors respond to each other and to their own needs rather than to the impersonal disciplining forces of the market in general." From this the government concludes that "'trade

engaged in by large diversified industrial firms' describes a combination of many 'lines of commerce.' "

The legislative history of the 1950 amendments to Section 7 of the Clayton Act reflects a concern on the part of Congress about the rising tide of economic concentration in American industry caused by all types of mergers, including conglomerate mergers. . . . But the legislative history also indicates that Section 7 as amended was not intended to proscribe all mergers which result in economic concentration. The House Report recommending passage of amended Section 7 concluded that: "the purpose of the bill [H.R. 2734] is to protect competition *in each line of commerce* in each section of the country." (Emphasis added.) Similarly, the Senate Report stated that: "It is intended that acquisitions which substantially lessen competition, as well as those which tend to create a monopoly, will be unlawful *if they have the specified effect in any line of commerce,* whether or not that line of commerce is a large part of the business of any of the corporations involved in the acquisition." (Emphasis added.)

Amended Section 7 as enacted is specific in barring a merger only "where in any line of commerce in any section of the country, the effect of such acquisition may be substantially to lessen competition."

Even if the legislative history and the amended statute on its face were not as clear as the Court believes, the decisional law uniformly has emphasized the importance of defining the specific product market or line of commerce in which alleged anticompetitive effects of a merger are to be measured. [The court quotes from *Brown Shoe* on this point.]

The Court declines the government's invitation to indulge in an expanded reading of the statutory language and holds that the statute means just what it says. It proscribes only those mergers the effect of which "may be substantially to lessen competition"; it commands that the alleged anticompetitive effects be examined in the context of specific product and geographic markets; and it does not proscribe those mergers the effect of which may be substantially to increase economic concentration.

Whatever may be the merits of the arguments as a matter of social and economic policy in favor of, or opposed to, a standard for measuring the legality of a merger under the antitrust laws by the degree to which it may increase economic concentration rather than by the degree to which it may lessen competition, that is beyond the competence of the Court to adjudicate. . . . [I]f that standard is to be changed, it is fundamental under our system of government that any decision to change the standard be made by the Congress and not by the courts. . . .

(c) *The settlements.*[32] The government had lost this and other nearly contemporaneous attacks on conglomerate mergers in the

_____

32. Extended discussions of each round of filing of briefs, ITT's lobbying of the government, and discussions and encounters among administration officials, some

trial courts. The Assistant Attorney General for Antitrust, who was significantly responsible for initiating the campaign against large conglomerate mergers, sought to appeal this case to the Supreme Court.[33] Notwithstanding weaknesses in the record and the trial opinion rejecting all the government's claims, the Solicitor General eventually approved the appeal.[34] ITT, apparently fearful that the Supreme Court would reverse, undertook serious efforts to persuade the government to drop the appeal or settle the case.[35] For a while, this effort proved unsuccessful, as the Assistant Attorney General was adamant in rejecting even substantial settlement offers; his goal from the outset had been to get a Supreme Court opinion in the area.

Ultimately, after repeated contacts with higher administration officials — ITT's chairman alone had personally spoken with numerous cabinet members, the government's leading economic advisors, and some of the President's closest assistants — and many extensions in the deadline to perfect the appeal, the government accepted a settlement along the lines ITT had offered earlier. The government defended the settlement largely on grounds it had previously rejected concerning the financial hardship additional relief would impose on ITT.[36] ITT was allowed to retain Hartford, its primary objective, but it had to divest about $1 billion in assets and forgo for ten years (in the absence of Justice Department or court approval) any domestic acquisition of companies with assets

---

appearing on former President Nixon's tapes, can be found in R. Goolrick, Public Policy Toward Corporate Growth: The ITT Merger Cases (1978); W. Mueller, The ITT Settlement: A Deal with Justice, 1 Ind. Org. Rev. 67 (1973) (Mueller was the government's economic expert in the conglomerate merger cases). Most of the detail summarized in the text, without citation, can be found in these sources.

33. At the time, appeal was directly to the Supreme Court under the expediting act. See ¶155.

34. Not only had the government failed to introduce much evidence in the case, but the trial judge had found virtually every factual issue, large or small, against the government. The court had even devoted a brief, separate section of its opinion to the "credibility of witnesses," where it found that, despite the presence of many stipulated and undisputed facts as well as documentary evidence, "on almost every critical issue in this case . . . it has been necessary for the Court to resolve questions of credibility and to determine the appropriate weight to be given to testimony of the trial witnesses."

35. Earlier, ITT had attempted unsuccessfully to speed up congressional repeal of the expediting act. Had repeal come soon enough, the ITT case would have been reviewed by the Court of Appeals before getting to the Supreme Court. By that time, government zeal might have cooled or the composition of the Court might have changed favorably.

36. Views on the merits of the settlement varied widely. See Goolrick, note 32, at 146-150.

over $100 million, with sales exceeding $25 million where the acquired firm had 15 percent of a concentrated, significant market, with assets over $10 million in the insurance industry, or engaged in the automatic sprinkler business.[37] This relief was clearly significant — obviously far more than the trial court had given but far less than the government had originally sought and, until then, demanded.

The ITT merger cases are most known outside antitrust circles for the political controversy they generated. Not long after the settlement was announced and well in advance of the 1972 presidential elections, it became known that, over a period roughly corresponding to that of the post-trial settlement negotiations, ITT had committed several hundred thousand dollars to assist in financing the forthcoming Republican convention. Although it has never been established whether there was any direct connection between that commitment and the settlement, some of the officials involved in the former had been involved in the latter.[38] In any event, the lobbying efforts and settlement in the ITT merger cases was the most cited occasion for the enactment in 1974 of an amendment to the Clayton Act that requires the government to publicize in advance its basis for antitrust settlements and also requires court approval of such settlements.[39]

544. (a) Suppose that the *ITT* appeal had gone forward. What would or should the Supreme Court have ruled with respect to (1) The reciprocity issue? (2) The other claims of unfair advantage? Should the government's inability to prove that reciprocity would result be decisive? If not, what likelihood must be demonstrated?

(b) Why would ITT have been willing to pay huge premiums for Grinnell and other companies it acquired if no such advantages were to be obtained, and if it operated its acquisitions, as the court accepts, as independent profit centers — i.e., almost as though they were separate companies? What other (lawful) advantages might ITT have sought from its mergers?

(c) Do you agree with the lower court's resolution of the "economic concentration" issue? Are there interpretations of the

---

37. See 1971 Trade Cas. ¶¶73665, 73666 (D. Conn.), 1971 Trade Cas. ¶73667 (N.D. Ill.).

38. The cover-up concerning events relating to the contribution and settlement during the subsequent congressional investigation led both to criminal investigations (and one guilty plea) and to one of the bills of impeachment against President Nixon, and they are now remembered as part of the Watergate scandal.

39. See ¶¶141c-d.

statute that would justify a broader reach, along the lines advocated by the government?[40]

(d) Can antitrust law address such concerns relating to aggregate concentration?[41] Can you formulate a rule that would deal with "undue" asset concentration? What do you make of the fact that two of the cases most noted for language concerning size per se — *Alcoa* and *Brown Shoe* — are also two of the opinions most known for their emphasis on the need to engage in careful market delineation, apparently along economic lines?

545. Conglomerate mergers: past, present, and future.

The decade of the 1960s represented a continuation of the rapid rate of merger activity which prevailed between 1950 and 1959. . . . In 1965 . . . the number topped 1,000 and skyrocketed to the high of the decade, 2,407 in 1968, before dropping. The net effect of this activity was that by 1969 more than ten times as many mergers were occurring annually as in 1950 — 2,397 compared with 219. . . . By 1971, the level of merger activity had fallen . . . to an estimated 1,011 or less than half the number in 1969. The vast majority of these mergers represents the disappearance of relatively small firms. . . . Although relatively small in number, "large" mergers [those in which the acquired company had assets of $10 million or more] account for by far the greatest portion of all acquired assets. . . . [T]his series peaked during 1968 and has declined continuously since then. This does not necessarily mean that high levels of merger activity are a phenomenon of the past, however. Typically, merger activity has followed a cyclical pattern with major peaks occurring around 1899, 1929, and 1968. There is no reason to believe that merger activity may not rise to equally high or higher levels in the future.[42]

Indeed, later data show a resurgence of acquisitions in the late 1970s and a further increase in the 1980s, followed by a decline in the early 1990s.[43]

In the past, conglomerate merger legislation had been proposed. The 1968 White House Task Force would have prohibited a "large firm" (one with $250 million in assets or $500 million in annual sales) from acquiring a leading firm (one of the largest four firms

40. For a broader reading of existing statutes, see H. Blake, Conglomerate Mergers and the Antitrust Laws, 73 Colum. L. Rev. 462 (1973).

41. Could one argue that the *ITT* settlement process demonstrates the futility of attempting to use the law to limit the size and thereby the political influence of large corporations?

42. Federal Trade Commission Staff, Conglomerate Merger Performance: An Empirical Analysis of Nine Corporations 14, 15, 18 (1972).

43. Economic Report of the President 417 (1993).

with more than 10 percent of a market with a four-firm concentration ratio of 50 percent or more); the latter would also have been prohibited from acquiring the former.[44] S. 600, introduced in 1979, would have prevented mergers between firms with individual sales or assets exceeding $2 billion; any acquisitions by one such firm of another firm with 20 percent or more of a market involving more than $100 million would also have been restricted.[45]

A significant challenge to conglomerate mergers — whether through legislation or the courts — has never materialized. The 1984 merger guidelines[46] accept efficiencies as a defense to conglomerate mergers and eliminate all reasons for challenging conglomerate mergers except for potential competition. As a result of these guidelines, challenges to conglomerate mergers are now infrequent.[47]

---

44. White House Task Force Report on Antitrust Policy (1968).

45. S. 600, 96th Cong., 1st Sess. (1979). On the case for and against the bill, compare J. Brodley, Limiting Conglomerate Mergers: The Need for Legislation, 40 Ohio St. L.J. 867 (1979), with D. Baker & K. Grimm, S. 600 — An Unnecessary and Dangerous Foray into Classic Populism, id. at 847. See generally Recent Proposals to Restrict Conglomerate Mergers (American Enterprise Institute 1981); R. Blair & R. Lanzillotti, eds., The Conglomerate Corporation (1981).

46. See ¶538.

47. See Areeda & Turner, note 1.

Chapter 6

Discrimination Under the Robinson-Patman Act

600. Prologue. We have already seen instances in which a seller employs vertical integration or tying in order to maximize profits by charging some users of the product more than others.[1] Although such price discrimination in some instances has the beneficial effect of making the product more widely available,[2] the higher price might seem objectionable as monopolistic exploitation, regardless of whether output is increased. But these are not the concerns of Clayton Act §2, as amended by the Robinson-Patman Act of 1936, which is expressly directed at price discrimination. This statute focuses not immediately on consumers but on the rivals of the discriminating seller or of the buyer receiving lower prices.

Its two major concerns are the effects of price discrimination on competition at the seller's level (the so-called primary line) and at the buyer's level (the secondary line). The former is illustrated by the national seller that reduces prices in a single area with the purpose or effect of destroying a local rival, thus engaging in predatory pricing. Secondary-line injury arises when a powerful firm buying supplies at favorable prices thereby gains a decisive advantage over its competitors that are forced to pay higher prices for their supplies.

The chapter begins by exploring the core provision of the statute, §2(a)'s proscription against price discrimination. After some introductory discussion of the statute's requirements and its history, Chapters 6A and 6B address, respectively, primary- and secondary-line injury. The following section explores the two main statutory defenses — that the seller's price differential was fully justified by differences in the cost of serving different buyers and that the seller's lower price was merely a good faith attempt to meet the equally low price of competitors. Chapter 6D addresses supplementary provisions of the statute, which make buyers liable for inducing or receiving unlawful price preferences and which extend seller liability to brokerage and to promotional allowances and services

---

1. See ¶¶321 (vertical integration), 423 (tying).
2. See ¶285b.

that may have effects similar to those arising from price differences.[3]

ROBINSON-PATMAN ACT §2(a) AND §2(b)[4]

§2(a) It shall be unlawful for any person engaged in commerce, in the course of such commerce, either directly or indirectly, to discriminate in price between different purchasers of commodities of like grade and quality, where either or any of the purchases involved in such discrimination are in commerce, where such commodities are sold for use, consumption, or resale within the United States or any Territory thereof or the District of Columbia or any insular possession or other place under the jurisdiction of the United States, and where the effect of such discrimination may be substantially to lessen competition or tend to create a monopoly in any line of commerce, or to injure, destroy, or prevent competition with any person who either grants or knowingly receives the benefit of such discrimination, or with customers of either of them: *Provided*, That nothing herein contained shall prevent differentials which make only due allowance for differences in the cost of manufacture, sale, or delivery resulting from the differing methods or quantities in which such commodities are to such purchasers sold or delivered: *Provided, however*, That the Federal Trade Commission may, after due investigation and hearing to all interested parties, fix and establish quantity limits, and revise the same as it finds necessary, as to particular commodities or classes of commodities, where it finds that available purchasers in greater quantities are so few as to render differentials on account thereof unjustly discriminatory or promotive of monopoly in any line of commerce; and the foregoing shall then not be construed to permit differentials based on differences in quantities greater than those so fixed and established: *And provided further*, That nothing herein contained shall prevent persons engaged in selling goods, wares, or merchandise in

3. There is an extensive secondary literature on the Robinson-Patman Act. A good text is F. Rowe, Price Discrimination under the Robinson-Patman Act (1962; Supp. 1964). Examinations with emphasis on economic issues include C. Edwards, The Price Discrimination Law (1959); R. Posner, The Robinson-Patman Act (1976); K. Dam, The Economics and Law of Price Discrimination: Herein of Three Regulatory Schemes, 31 U. Chi. L. Rev. 1 (1963). For an analysis of the act and policy alternatives, see U.S. Justice Dept. Antitrust Division, Report on the Robinson-Patman Act (1977); ABA Antitrust Section, Monograph No. 4, The Robinson-Patman Act: Policy and Law (vol. 1, 1980; vol. 2, 1983).

4. This is Clayton Act §2 as amended by the Robinson-Patman Act. Additional provisions of the Robinson-Patman Act and the original Clayton Act §2 are reproduced in the Appendix.

commerce from selecting their own customers in bona fide transactions and not in restraint of trade: *And provided further*, That nothing herein contained shall prevent price changes from time to time where in response to changing conditions affecting the market for or the marketability of the goods concerned, such as but not limited to actual or imminent deterioration of perishable goods, obsolescence of seasonal goods, distress sales under court process, or sales in good faith in discontinuance of business in the goods concerned.

(b) Upon proof being made, at any hearing on a complaint under this section, that there has been discrimination in price or services or facilities furnished, the burden of rebutting the prima facie case thus made by showing justification shall be upon the person charged with a violation of this section, and unless justification shall be affirmatively shown, the Commission is authorized to issue an order terminating the discrimination: *Provided, however*, That nothing herein contained shall prevent a seller rebutting the prima-facie case thus made by showing that his lower price or the furnishing of services or facilities to any purchaser or purchasers was made in good faith to meet an equally low price of a competitor, or the services or facilities furnished by a competitor.

601.   General requirements of §2(a). The detailed language preceding the provisos of §2(a) should be examined:

(a) *"Unlawful for any person engaged in commerce [to discriminate] in the course of such commerce . . . where either or any of the purchases involved in such discrimination are in commerce."* It is generally accepted that the Sherman Act applies whenever interstate commerce is affected.[5] To trigger the Robinson-Patman Act, however, the seller must itself be "engaged in [interstate] commerce," the discrimination must occur "in the course of such commerce," and one of the sales must be "in commerce."[6] The latter requirement seems to include the other two. If one of the sales involved in the discrimination is "in commerce," then the seller is engaged in commerce and the discrimination has occurred in the course thereof. Thus, the basic jurisdictional question is whether one of the sales involved in a price discrimination crossed a state boundary. Where a firm produces goods in one state and ships them to its warehouse in a

---

5. See ¶166.
6. General Chems. v. Exxon Chem. Co., 625 F.2d 1231 (5th Cir. 1980) (summary judgment against plaintiff buyer where no evidence that favored buyer sold other than abroad); see ¶167. Note that a later clause of §2(a) expressly excludes sales for foreign use or resale.

second state, its later sales within the second state are "in commerce."[7] The many variations will not be pursued here.[8]

Section 2(a) has no application to the defendant without interstate sales, but even interstate sales at different prices will not necessarily confer jurisdiction. Where secondary-line injury is alleged, the victim is a disfavored buyer competing with a favored buyer from the same seller; because the substantive test of competitive injury focuses only on the defendant's sales to the victim and the victim's competitors, most courts demand that one of those sales be interstate.[9] Where primary-line injury is involved, the victim is a competitor of the defendant — perhaps a local rival facing low prices by a national defendant maintaining higher prices elsewhere; there is jurisdiction when either the low-price sale in the victim's area or the high-price sale elsewhere is interstate.[10]

(b) *"Either directly or indirectly to discriminate in price."* In economic or philosophical discourse, discrimination has many subtle overtones. As used in §2(a), however, the Supreme Court has held that "a price discrimination within the meaning of that provision is merely a price difference."[11] In determining price, discounts for quantity purchases or prompt payment, for example, are taken into account. What the buyer pays the seller is usually regarded as the "price" for purposes of this statute. Minor differences may be ignored.

Indirect price discrimination, which is expressly covered by §2(a), has an uncertain scope. It might embrace any difference in the way a supplier treats different customers — credit, return privileges, delivery speed, general attentiveness — because each element of a transaction or relationship has a theoretical monetary equivalent. But the courts have hesitated to appraise all aspects of a relationship. Credit and delivery charges have more readily been seen as indirect price discrimination[12] than have such matters as allocation of short supply or promptness of delivery.[13]

---

7. Standard Oil Co. v. FTC, 340 U.S. 231, 237 (1951).

8. See Rowe, note 3, §4.9; I P. Areeda & D. Turner, Antitrust Law ¶233b (1978).

9. E.g., Mayer Paving & Asphalt Co. v. General Dynamics Corp., 486 F.2d 763 (7th Cir. 1973), cert. denied, 414 U.S. 1146 (1974).

10. E.g., Moore v. Mead's Fine Breads, 348 U.S. 115, 119 (1954) ("profits made in interstate activities would underwrite the losses of local price-cutting campaigns"); Gulf Oil Corp. v. Copp Paving Co., 419 U.S. 186 (1974).

11. FTC v. Anheuser-Busch, 363 U.S. 536, 549 (1960); *Texaco*, Ch. 6B.

12. E.g., Craig v. Sun Oil Co., 515 F.2d 221, 224 (10th Cir. 1975), cert. denied, 429 U.S. 829 (1976) (discriminatory credit terms in "extreme circumstances" can violate §2(a)). Such discrimination, however, does not violate §2(e), whose prohibition of discriminatory services is held to be limited to promotional or merchandising services.

13. Most courts dealing with the question have ruled discrimination in such matters to be outside the Robinson-Patman Act, including both §2(a) and §2(e).

The existence of discrimination also may depend on the availability of the lower price or superior term. For example, a supplier selling single bars of soap at 50¢ or two for 80¢ may in fact be charging different customers either 40¢ or 50¢ per bar. Those who pay the higher price, however, are not seen as the victims of any price discrimination because the lower price was equally available to them. But if the lower price were offered only on purchases of 10 million bars annually — a volume reached only by a few gigantic distributors — it would not be considered "functionally available" to all and therefore would be held to be a price discrimination.[14]

(c) *"Between different purchasers."* A seller cannot violate §2(a) unless it has sold similar commodities to at least two different purchasers. Thus, the Act does not apply to leases or other transactions without a purchaser. Nor is it applied to a seller who sells to one customer while refusing to sell to another; the would-be buyer is usually held not to be a purchaser. This interpretation is reinforced by the third proviso to §2(a) when a seller refuses to sell on any terms, but it may seem incorrect when a seller refuses to sell except on discriminatory terms that the would-be buyer refuses to accept.

Where a parent and its subsidiary are involved, two different questions can arise. First, is the subsidiary a purchaser (at a "low price") from the parent, such that an outsider buying from the parent appears to be the victim of a price discrimination? The courts increasingly responded with a negative answer, especially where the subsidiary is actively controlled by the parent. Second, should affiliated corporations selling at different prices be seen as a single discriminating seller? Although there is little authority on this question, the courts probably would not allow a seller to practice otherwise unlawful discrimination through the simple formality of using two selling corporations. The answers suggested for both questions are reinforced by the Supreme Court's *Copperweld* holding that a parent and its wholly owned subsidiary comprise a single unit that is incapable of conspiring with itself for purposes of Sherman Act §1.[15]

A different question concerns the so-called indirect purchaser. Consider the plaintiff *P* who would like to purchase directly from manufacturer *M* and to compete with *M*'s dealer *D*. When *M* refuses to sell to *P* at the single price it charges its dealers, *P* may feel impelled to buy the product from *D* and obviously at a higher price than *M* charged. Because *M* itself is selling at a uniform price, there is no price discrimination to trigger §2(a) unless *P* can somehow be regarded as a "purchaser" from *M*. Several cases have characterized *P* as an indirect "purchaser" where *M* dealt directly with *P* although

14. See *Morton Salt*, Ch. 6B and ¶607.
15. See Ch. 2C.

formally selling only to *D* or where *M* controlled the terms of the *D-P* deal. The Supreme Court has protected persons not buying directly from *M*. It may be noted here that *P* is generally not held to be a purchaser for §2(a) purposes.

Finally, at least two kinds of purchasers raise special questions for Robinson-Patman Act purposes. First, a 1938 statute excludes non-profit institutions from the reach of the Act,[16] although the exclusion does not extend to resales by such institutions in competition with normal commercial establishments purchasing from the same supplier at higher prices.[17] Second, the Supreme Court has held that purchases by state agencies for resale are not exempted from the Act[18] — either with regard to §2(a) or buyer liability under §2(f) — although the Court did not reach the question whether purchases for use in traditional government functions were covered.[19] The Court noted that states are persons within antitrust provisions such as those allowing injured persons to collect damages for antitrust violations. Not only is there no specific exemption for states in the Robinson-Patman Act, but its legislative history demonstrates concern for small retailers competing with large organizations receiving preferential prices. For the Court, the state is the largest organization of all. For the four dissenters, states are not within the chain store rationale of the statute, and one of them declined to see state resale as being in general competition with retailers.

(d) *"Of commodities of like grade and quality."* Section 2(a), like Clayton Act §3, applies only to transactions in "commodities," which are customarily understood to exclude services and such intangibles as newspaper or broadcast advertising. A seller does not violate the Act unless it charges different prices for goods of "like grade and quality." Physical differences without commercial significance do not oust the statute. But §2(a) does not apply to sales of goods with physical differences substantial enough to affect their acceptability to buyers. Physically identical goods carrying different brand names have presented a problem. Although consumers do in fact value brand names, the Supreme Court has held that brand differences do not insulate from the statute goods that are otherwise of like grade and quality.[20]

In addition to the explicit requirement of "commodities of like grade and quality," there would seem to be an implicit requirement that the allegedly discriminatory transactions be comparable at least

16. 52 Stat. 446 (1938), 15 U.S.C. §13c.
17. Abbott Labs. v. Portland Retail Druggist Assn., 425 U.S. 1 (1976).
18. Jefferson County Pharm. Assn. v. Abbott Labs., 460 U.S. 150 (1983).
19. Id. at 153-154 & n.6.
20. *Borden,* ¶612.

in some respects. The issue is complex, because nonprice identity is clearly not a prerequisite. For example, different prices on large and small volumes are considered a price discrimination, as we shall see in *Morton Salt*. But, different prices on sales widely separated in time are not treated as a price discrimination. Also outside the statute, according to one court, is the seller accepting the highest secret bid from time to time.[21] One might also question whether a covered price discrimination should be found where a supplier sells at a lower price on a long-term requirements contract than on spot market sales.

(e) *"Where the effect of such discrimination may be substantially [I] to lessen competition or tend to create a monopoly in any line of commerce, or [II] to injure, destroy or prevent competition with" [A] the discriminating seller, or [B₁] the knowing[22] and benefited recipient, or [B₂] customers of the discriminating seller, or [C] customers of the knowing and benefited recipient.* Clause I repeats the effects language of Clayton Act §3 and §7. Clause II, unique to the Robinson-Patman Act, is paraphrased to emphasize its focus on so-called primary-line injury to competitors of the seller [A], secondary-line injury to competitors of the buyer [B], and tertiary-line injury to competitors of the buyer's customers [C]. These concepts are explored in Sections A and B.[23]

(f) *Standing and damages.* In some instances, as we shall see, it is quite easy to show a price discrimination that is prima facie unlawful. And that is all that need be shown in a government suit or FTC proceeding. The treble-damage plaintiff, however, must also establish standing to sue and prove damages.

General principles relating to standing were stated at ¶¶144-146. More specific applications depend on the substantive rules considered below. But one pervasive point can be emphasized. The plaintiff need not have purchased from the defendant in order to have standing. For example, a retailer buying from a wholesaler may have standing to sue the manufacturer who is charging that wholesaler more than a rival retailer to whom the manufacturer sells directly. Moreover, in primary-line cases, as with predatory pricing, a proper private plaintiff is a rival of the defendant.

---

21. Hancock Paper Co. v. Champion Intl. Corp., 424 F. Supp. 285 (E.D. Pa. 1976) (seller has no choice but to accept bid price; condemnation would end competitive bidding which is not statutory purpose).

22. See *Automatic Canteen*, ¶623.

23. We do not consider here Robinson-Patman Act §3, which declares it criminal to discriminate geographically or to sell at "unreasonably low prices" where either is done "for the purpose of destroying competition or eliminating a competitor." (Additional provisions of §3 are noted in the Appendix and are discussed in Rowe, note 3, ¶15.3.)

Damage issues are not necessarily distinctive. In primary-line cases, the plaintiff must prove the loss of profits resulting from the defendant's unlawfully low price. What may be distinctive is the secondary-line damage issue. Because, as we shall see, secondary-line illegality may follow simply from the existence of a price discrimination, it had sometimes been suggested that the disfavored buyer's damage is the excess it paid the seller above the lower price paid by the competing favored buyer, but the Supreme Court has settled the issue by insisting on more particular proof of injury.[24] For example, the plaintiff might show that the favored purchaser actually used the buying preference to draw sales or profits from the plaintiff.

602. The development of §2. (a) *The original provision.* The Supreme Court has explained that §2(a), "when originally enacted as part of the Clayton Act in 1914, was born of a desire by Congress to curb the use by financially powerful corporations of localized price-cutting tactics which had gravely impaired the competitive position of other sellers."[25] The House Judiciary Committee had explained that §2(a) was expressly designed to forbid

> a common and widespread unfair trade practice whereby certain great corporations and also certain smaller concerns, which seek to secure a monopoly ... by aping the methods of the great corporations, have ... [sold] at a less price in the particular communities where their rivals are engaged in business than at other places throughout the country.[26]

(b) *Background of the 1936 legislation.*[27] Clayton Act §2, as originally enacted, was understood to be concerned mainly or even exclusively with price discrimination's effects upon the seller's competitors. Although the Court came to hold buyer-level competition within the statute's protection, the original enactment immunized quantity discounts and thus seemed impotent to control the granting of preferential prices to mass buyers. The mass-buying chain stores and mail order houses grew greatly after World War I and seemed to imperil independent businesses. The chains often purchased directly from manufacturers, dispensed with ordinary whole-

---

24. J. Truett Payne v. Chrysler Motors Corp., 451 U.S. 557 (1981). See Allen Pen Co. v. Springfield Photo Mount Co., 653 F.2d 17 (1st Cir. 1981); Distributing Corp. v. Singer Co., 543 F. Supp. 1033 (D. Kan. 1982) (summary judgment for defendant on damages; preferred buyer failed to capture any sales and plaintiff's sales and profits rose).

25. *Anheuser-Busch,* note 11, at 543.

26. H.R. Rep. No. 627, 63d Cong., 2d Sess. 8 (1914).

27. See generally Rowe, note 3, at 3-10 (political background), 11-23 (broad legislative history).

salers, and undersold independent retailers. The traditional merchants, threatened with extinction, fought back. While many states acted by imposing special taxes on chain stores, the Federal Trade Commission undertook an extensive investigation of the chain store problem.

The Commission concluded[28] that the independents would continue to lose ground as long as the chains continued to offer lower prices to consumers. Because the chains' competitive advantage was partly attributed to discriminatory concessions from suppliers,[29] the FTC proposed that §2 be tightened. The Robinson-Patman enactment exceeded the Commission's recommendations and

> superimposed more stringent prohibitions on the existing framework of §2 of the Clayton Act, expressly enumerated conspicuous types of secret concessions, and penalized the discriminatory discounts on which mass buyers were suspected to thrive. The design of the Robinson-Patman amendments was to facilitate proof of the substantive violation while narrowing the availability of statutory exceptions for justifying price differentials challenged under the Act.[30]

These attitudes were prevalent in the 1930s. Competition was often seen to threaten the survival of small businesses and even of all businesses. We have already seen some evidence of this in the Supreme Court's *Appalachian Coals* decision[31] and in the enactment of fair trade legislation.[32] Other legislation, such as the Motor Carrier Act of 1935,[33] which subjected the emerging and highly competitive trucking industry to regulated price fixing and entry, reflected similar concerns.

(c) *Other antitrust statutes compared.* Unlike the open-ended Federal Trade Commission Act §5 and the Sherman Act, Clayton Act §2, §3, and §7 each address a specific practice. In its original form, §2's coverage and effects clause paralleled that of the other Clayton Act provisions, but the 1936 amendments widened its effects clause and added several more categorical provisions (to be examined in Section D) that are not found elsewhere in antitrust legislation.

---

28. Federal Trade Commission, Final Report on the Chain Store Investigation, S. Doc. No. 4, 74th Cong., 1st Sess. 85-86 (1935).

29. M. Adelman, Price Discrimination as Treated in the Attorney General's Report, 104 U. Pa. L. Rev. 222, 232 (1955), said that the FTC's own data showed that gains from preferential prices accounted for only 15 percent of the chains' price advantage, the rest being attributable to operational efficiencies.

30. Report of the Attorney General's National Committee to Study the Antitrust Laws 156 (1955).

31. See ¶208.

32. See ¶405.

33. 49 Stat. 543.

6A.   PRIMARY-LINE INJURY

603.   The diversion test. Examine the effects clause of §2(a). What must be shown to satisfy it when primary-line discrimination is in issue? In its early *Moss*[34] decision under the statute, the Federal Trade Commission argued that a seller who charges different customers different prices violates §2(a) unless it affirmatively proves the absence of any harm to competition. A distinguished panel — Judges L. Hand, A. Hand, and Clark — accepted the FTC's reading of the statute.

> It is true that §2(a) makes price discrimination unlawful only in case it lessens, or tends to prevent, competition with the merchant who engages in the practice; and that no doubt means that the lower price must prevent, or tend to prevent, competitors from taking business away from the merchant which they might have got, had the merchant not lowered his price below what he was charging elsewhere. But that is often hard to prove; the accuser must show that there were competitors whom the higher of the two prices would, or might, not have defeated, but who could not meet the lower. Hence Congress [in §2(b)] adopted the common device in such cases of shifting the burden of proof to anyone who sets two prices, and who probably knows why he has done so, and what has been the result. If he can prove that the lower price did not prevent or tend to prevent anyone from taking away the business; he will succeed, for the accuser will not then have brought him within the statute at all.

The *Moss* holding was followed in some Second Circuit cases but not elsewhere.[35] In *Moss* itself and thereafter, the Federal Trade Commission took the position that "counsel supporting the complaint has the burden of proof to establish the necessary competitive injury. . . . '[T]he Commission has always construed the Act to require it as a part of its affirmative case to present evidence that a discrimination may lessen or tend to injure competition.' "[36] The Commission purported to find such injury in *Moss*, but that finding seemed to be an inference from the admitted fact that Moss had sold at different prices and had won customers away from its competitors.[37] Although it does not appear in the Commission's opinion, "there are said to be more than 70 . . . manufacturers [like Moss] in New York City alone. . . . [Moss] employed about 19 persons."[38]

---

34. Moss v. FTC, 148 F.2d 378, 379 (2d Cir.), cert. denied, 326 U.S. 734 (1945).
35. Anheuser-Busch v. FTC, 289 F.2d 835 (7th Cir. 1961).
36. General Foods Corp., 50 F.T.C. 885, 890 (1954).
37. 36 F.T.C. 640, 648-649 (1943).
38. Edwards, note 3, at 477.

In addition to placing the burden of proof on the discriminating seller, the *Moss* court seemed to indicate that the mere diversion of business away from rivals constituted sufficient injury to competition to violate the statute. The court indicated that injury would be shown by proof "that there were competitors whom the higher of the two prices would, or might, not have defeated, but who could not meet the lower." Does every discriminatorily low price satisfy this test? A defendant lowers price for the very purpose of defeating a competitor, hoping that ignorance of the price cut or other factors will prevent that competitor from matching the price cut.

Moss engaged in haphazard price discrimination, reducing its price in the course of bargaining with particular potential customers. Is price discrimination in Moss's circumstances, or generally, undesirable? Consider the next problem.

604. Suppose that all steel producers usually charge more-or-less identical list prices on steel wire used to reinforce concrete in buildings. Even on construction projects requiring the submission of sealed bids, the steel companies nearly always bid their list prices. Recently, Maverick Steel Corporation won several very large contracts at prices substantially below the list price charged on most of its sales. Maverick, which supplies about 10 percent of the market, makes the remainder of its sales at list price.

(a) Has Maverick discriminated in price? If so, is the discrimination unlawful under *Moss*? Would the Commission find the prohibited injury to competition? If all questions are answered affirmatively, is sealed bidding illegal?[39]

(b) What is the effect of Maverick's behavior on the steel wire market? Are the likely results harmful?

(c) If Maverick frequently repeats the described behavior, how will its rivals respond? Is the result likely to be socially desirable?

(d) If Maverick's behavior is held unlawful, what are the possible or probable effects on its future pricing decisions? Would the consequences in the steel wire market be desirable?

(e) How is Moss different from Maverick? Does the difference call for different legal results?

(f) Would you hold that Moss or Maverick has violated the statute?

605. *Utah Pie Co. v. Continental Baking Co.*, 386 U.S. 685 (1967). The plaintiff was a local Salt Lake City company that had entered the frozen pie business. The defendants were national firms that supplied the Salt Lake City market from plants in California. The

39. Consider the buyer's liability after examining Ch. 6D.

plaintiff set prices below defendants' and succeeded in capturing a majority of the market. In response, the defendants lowered their prices, sometimes selling at prices below those they charged in markets closer to their plants in California (despite the significant freight costs of selling in Salt Lake City) and also below various measures of costs. Plaintiff, who had to lower its prices and still suffered a loss in market share, sued. The Supreme Court held that there was sufficient basis for the jury's finding of liability.

> There was ample evidence to show that each of the respondents contributed to what proved to be a deteriorating price structure . . . and each of the respondents in the course of the ongoing price competition sold frozen pies in the Salt Lake market lower than it sold pies of like grade and quality in other markets considerably closer to its plants. . . . [T]he Court of Appeals placed heavy emphasis on the fact that Utah Pie constantly increased its sales volume and continued to make a profit. But we disagree with its apparent view that there is no reasonably possible injury to competition as long as the volume of sales in a particular market is expanding and at least some of the competitors in the market continue to operate at a profit. Nor do we think that the Act only comes into play to regulate the conduct of price discriminators when their discriminatory prices consistently undercut other competitors. . . . We believe that the Act reaches price discrimination that erodes competition as much as it does price discrimination that is intended to have immediate destructive impact. In this case, the evidence shows a drastically declining price structure which the jury could rationally attribute to continued or sporadic price discrimination. . . .

(a) How is the existence of price *discrimination*, in contrast with *low* prices, relevant to liability in *Utah Pie*? How does discrimination per se bear on the competitive danger?

(b) If a geographic price difference producing harm to local competitors creates liability, must the national pie companies either charge uniform national prices or stay out of Salt Lake City?[40] Would prices have been higher or lower in Salt Lake City? How might the permissibility of local price cutting by national firms affect the prospects of entry by small, local firms?

606.   *Brooke Group Ltd. v. Brown & Williamson Tobacco Corp.*, 509 U.S. 209 (1993). It was alleged that the defendant cigarette com-

---

40. After studying Ch. 6C, consider why a meeting competition defense would not have saved the defendants' conduct in *Utah Pie*. See Anheuser-Busch, 54 F.T.C. 277, 302 (1957), rev'd on other grounds, 289 F.2d 835 (7th Cir. 1961) ("The reduction from the premium price to match the prices of the regional beers . . . was not a meeting of competition. The effect was to undercut competition.").

pany had lowered its prices below cost, in a discriminatory manner, so as to discipline the plaintiff (Liggett) to raise its prices so that all producers could enjoy higher profits. Most of the opinion, which is reproduced in Chapter 3A, contains the facts, the Supreme Court's discussion of the prerequisites for predatory pricing cases under the Sherman Act and Robinson-Patman Act, and the Court's analysis of whether there was sufficient evidence from which a jury could find a violation. Because the complaint alleged price discrimination under the Robinson-Patman Act, the Court took the occasion to discuss the Act's primary-line prohibition and its relationship to Sherman Act §2 predation claims.

> Although we have reiterated that "'a price discrimination within the meaning of [this] provision is merely a price difference,'" *Texaco*, the statute as a practical matter could not, and does not, ban all price differences charged to "different purchasers of commodities of like grade and quality." Instead, the statute contains a number of important limitations, one of which is central to evaluating Liggett's claim: By its terms, the Robinson-Patman Act condemns price discrimination only to the extent that it threatens to injure competition. The availability of statutory defenses permitting price discrimination when it is based on differences in costs, §13(a), "changing conditions affecting the market for or the marketability of the goods concerned," ibid., or conduct undertaken "in good faith to meet an equally low price of a competitor," §13(b); Standard Oil Co. v. FTC, 340 U.S. 231, 250 (1951), confirms that Congress did not intend to outlaw price differences that result from or further the forces of competition. Thus, "the Robinson-Patman Act should be construed consistently with broader policies of the antitrust laws." *A&P*. See also Automatic Canteen Co. of America v. FTC, 346 U.S. 61, 63, 74 (1953)....
>
> We last addressed primary line injury over 25 years ago, in *Utah Pie*.... *Utah Pie* has often been interpreted to permit liability for primary-line price discrimination on a mere showing that the defendant intended to harm competition or produced a declining price structure.... *Utah Pie* was an early judicial inquiry in this area and did not purport to set forth explicit, general standards for establishing a violation of the Robinson-Patman Act.... There are, to be sure, differences between the two statutes. For example, we interpret §2 of the Sherman Act to condemn predatory pricing when it poses "a dangerous probability of actual monopolization," *Spectrum Sports*, whereas the Robinson-Patman Act requires only that there be "a reasonable possibility" of substantial injury to competition before its protections are triggered. *Falls City*. But whatever additional flexibility the Robinson-Patman Act standard may imply, the essence of the claim under either statute is the same: A business rival has priced its products in an unfair manner with an object to eliminate or retard competition and thereby gain and exercise control over prices in the relevant market.

Accordingly, whether the claim alleges predatory pricing under §2 of the Sherman Act or primary-line price discrimination under the Robinson-Patman Act, two prerequisites to recovery remain the same. First, a plaintiff seeking to establish competitive injury resulting from a rival's low prices must prove that the prices complained of are below an appropriate measure of its rival's costs. . . .

The second prerequisite to holding a competitor liable under the antitrust laws for charging low prices is a demonstration that the competitor had a reasonable prospect, or, under §2 of the Sherman Act, a dangerous probability, of recouping its investment in below-cost prices. . . .

The Court resolved the defendant's claim that there could not, as a matter of law, be a primary-line injury in an oligopolistic market, as follows:

The Robinson-Patman Act, which amended §2 of the original Clayton Act, suggests no exclusion from coverage when primary-line injury occurs in an oligopoly setting. Unlike the provisions of the Sherman Act, which speak only of various forms of express agreement and monopoly, the Robinson-Patman Act is phrased in broader, disjunctive terms, prohibiting price discrimination "where the effect of such discrimination may be substantially to lessen competition or tend to create a monopoly." For all the words of the Act to carry adequate meaning, competitive injury under the Act must extend beyond the monopoly setting. . . . The language referring to a substantial lessening of competition was part of the original Clayton Act §2, and the same phrasing appears in §7 of that Act. In the §7 context, it has long been settled that excessive concentration, and the oligopolistic price coordination it portends, may be the injury to competition the Act prohibits. See, e.g., *Philadelphia National Bank*. . . . We decline to create a per se rule of nonliability for predatory price discrimination when recoupment is alleged to take place through supracompetitive oligopoly pricing. Cf. *Cargill*.

The dissenters suggested a somewhat greater difference between the reach of the Robinson-Patman Act and that of the Sherman Act.

The Sherman Act, the Clayton Act, and the Robinson-Patman Act all serve the purpose of protecting competition. Because they have a common goal, the statutes are similar in many respects. . . . The statutes do differ significantly with respect to one element of the violation, the competitive consequences of predatory conduct. Even here, however, the three statutes have one thing in common: Not one of them requires proof that a predatory plan has actually succeeded in accomplishing its objective. Section 1 of the Sherman Act requires proof of a conspiracy. It is the joint plan to restrain trade, however, and not its success, that is prohibited by §1. . . . Section 2 of the Sherman Act applies to independent conduct, and may be violated when there is a "dangerous probability" that an attempt to achieve monopoly power will succeed. *Swift*. The Clayton Act goes beyond the "dangerous probability" standard to cover price discrimination "where the effect of such discrimination may be to substantially lessen competition or tend to create a monopoly in any line of commerce."

The element of competitive injury as defined in the Robinson-Patman Act is broader still. See S. Rep. No. 1502, 74th Cong., 2d Sess., 4 (1936) (Act substantially broadens similar clause of Clayton Act). The Robinson-Patman Act was designed to reach discriminations "in their incipiency, before the harm to competition is effected. It is enough that they 'may' have the proscribed effect." Corn Products Refining Co. v. FTC, 324 U.S. 726, 738 (1945). Or, as the Report of the Senate Judiciary Committee on the proposed Act explained, "to catch the weed in the seed will keep it from coming to flower."

Accordingly, our leading case concerning discriminatory volume rebates described the scope of the Act as follows: "There are specific findings that such injuries had resulted from respondent's discounts, although the statute does not require the Commission to find that injury has actually resulted. The statute requires no more than that the effect of the prohibited price discriminations 'may be substantially to lessen competition ... or to injure, destroy, or prevent competition.' After a careful consideration of this provision of the Robinson-Patman Act, we have said that 'the statute does not require that the discrimination must in fact have harmed competition, but only that there is a reasonable possibility that they "may" have such an effect.' Corn Products Co. v. Federal Trade Commn., 324 U.S. 726, 742." *Morton Salt.* See also *Falls City* ("In keeping with the Robinson-Patman Act's prophylactic purpose, §2(a) does not require that the discrimination must in fact have harmed competition (internal quotation marks omitted).").

In the light of the Court's analysis of the facts in *Brooke Group* and its ultimate conclusion that the plaintiff did not offer sufficient evidence from which a jury could find the defendant liable (see Chapter 3A), how much difference actually remains between the Sherman Act and the Robinson-Patman Act, as applied to predatory pricing?

6B. SECONDARY-LINE INJURY

FEDERAL TRADE COMMISSION v.
MORTON SALT CO.
334 U.S. 37 (1948)

Justice BLACK. ... Respondent sells its finest brand of table salt, known as Blue Label, on what it terms a standard quantity discount system available to all customers. Under this system the purchasers pay a delivered price and the cost to both wholesale and retail purchasers of this brand differs according to the quantities bought. These prices are as follows, after making allowance for rebates and discounts:

	Per case
Less-than-carload purchases	$1.60
Carload purchases	1.50
5,000-case purchases in any consecutive 12 months	1.40
50,000-case purchases in any consecutive 12 months	1.35

Only five companies have ever bought sufficient quantities of respondent's salt to obtain the $1.35 per case price. These companies could buy in such quantities because they operate large chains of retail stores in various parts of the country. As a result of this low price these five companies have been able to sell Blue Label salt at retail cheaper than wholesale purchasers from respondent could reasonably sell the same brand of salt to independently operated retail stores, many of whom competed with the local outlets of the five chain stores. . . .

First. Respondent's basic contention, which it argues this case hinges upon, is that its "standard quantity discounts, available to all on equal terms, as contrasted, for example, to hidden or special rebates, allowances, prices or discounts, are not discriminatory within the meaning of the Robinson-Patman Act." Theoretically, these discounts are equally available to all, but functionally they are not. For as the record indicates (if reference to it on this point were necessary) no single independent retail grocery store, and probably no single wholesaler, bought as many as 50,000 cases . . . of table salt in one year. Furthermore, the record shows that, while certain purchasers were enjoying one or more of respondent's standard quantity discounts, some of their competitors made purchases in such small quantities that they could not qualify for any of respondent's discounts, even those based on carload shipments. The legislative history of the Robinson-Patman Act makes it abundantly clear that Congress considered it to be an evil [permitted by §2 as originally enacted in 1914] that a large buyer could secure a competitive advantage over a small buyer solely because of the large buyer's quantity purchasing ability. The Robinson-Patman Act was passed to deprive a large buyer of such advantages except to the extent that a lower price could be justified by reason of a seller's diminished costs due to quantity manufacture, delivery or sale, or by reason of the seller's good faith effort to meet a competitor's equally low price. . . . [R]espondent's standard quantity discounts are discriminatory within the meaning of the Act, and are prohibited by it whenever they have the defined effect on competition. . . .

Second. [The Commission does not have the burden of proving that respondent's quantity discount differentials were not cost justified. General rules of statutory construction, the express language of §2(b), and the legislative history clearly indicate that the burden lies with the defendant.] [13] . . .

Third. It is argued that the findings fail to show that respondent's discriminatory discounts had in fact caused injury to competition. There are specific findings that such injuries had resulted from respondent's discounts, although the statute does not require the Commission to find that injury has actually resulted. . . . [W]e have said that "the statute does not require that the discriminations must in fact have harmed competition, but only that there is a reasonable possibility that they 'may' have such an effect." Corn Products Co. v. Federal Trade Comm'n, 324 U.S. 726, 742. Here the Commission found what would appear to be obvious, that the competitive opportunities of certain merchants were injured when they had to pay respondent substantially more for their goods than their competitors had to pay. The findings are adequate.

Fourth. It is urged that the evidence is inadequate to support the Commission's findings of injury to competition. As we have pointed out, however, the Commission is authorized by the Act to bar discriminatory prices upon the "reasonable possibility" that different prices for like goods to competing purchasers may have the defined effect on competition. That respondent's quantity discounts did result in price differentials between competing purchasers sufficient in amount to influence their resale price of salt was shown by evidence. This showing in itself is adequate to support the Commission's appropriate findings that the effect of such price discriminations "may be substantially to lessen competition . . . and to injure, destroy and prevent competition." . . .

It is also argued that respondent's less-than-carload sales are very small in comparison with the total volume of its business and for that reason we should reject the Commission's finding that the effect of the carload discrimination may substantially lessen competition and may injure competition between purchasers who are granted and those who are denied this discriminatory discount. To support this argument, reference is made to the fact that salt is a small item in most wholesale and retail businesses and in consumers' budgets. For several reasons we cannot accept this contention.

13. See *Moss*, holding that proof of a price differential in itself constituted "discrimination in price," where the competitive injury in question was between sellers. See also *Cement Institute*.

There are many articles in a grocery store that, considered separately, are comparatively small parts of a merchant's stock. Congress
intended to protect a merchant from competitive injury attributable to discriminatory prices on any or all goods sold in interstate
commerce, whether the particular goods constituted a major or
minor portion of his stock. Since a grocery store consists of many
comparatively small articles, there is no possible way effectively to
protect a grocer from discriminatory prices except by applying the
prohibitions of the Act to each individual article in the store.

Furthermore, in enacting the Robinson-Patman Act Congress was
especially concerned with protecting small businesses which were
unable to buy in quantities, such as the merchants here who purchased in less-than-carload lots. To this end it undertook to
strengthen this very phase of the old Clayton Act. The committee
reports on the Robinson-Patman Act emphasized a belief that §2 of
the Clayton Act had "been too restrictive in requiring a showing of
general injury to competitive conditions. ..." The new provision,
here controlling, was intended to justify a finding of injury to competition by a showing of "injury to the competitor victimized by the
discrimination." Since there was evidence sufficient to show that the
less-than-carload purchasers might have been handicapped in competing with the more favored carload purchasers by the differential
in price established by respondent, the Commission was justified in
finding that competition might have thereby been substantially lessened or have been injured within the meaning of the Act.

Apprehension is expressed in this Court that enforcement of the
Commission's order against respondent's continued violations of
the Robinson-Patman Act might lead respondent to raise table salt
prices to its carload purchasers. Such a conceivable, though, we
think, highly improbable contingency, could afford us no reason
for upsetting the Commission's findings and declining to direct
compliance with a statute passed by Congress. ...

Reversed.

[Justices Jackson and Frankfurter dissented in part. They objected to the "reasonable possibility" language in the Court's interpretation of §2's effect clause. Nevertheless, they agreed that the
cumulative quantity discounts on Blue Label salt were prima facie
unlawful. But they regarded the discount of 10¢ per case of salt
delivered in carload lots as relatively small and obviously related, in
some degree, to differences in the cost of handling less-than-
carload lots. Because most buyers (99.9 percent of Morton's sales)
were able to take advantage of this discount, the requisite competitive effect seemed unlikely to the dissenters.]

607. (a) In *Morton Salt*, had the seller treated its customers differently? Consider whether the following sellers have discriminated within the meaning of §2(a): (1) The first seller permits some buyers to pay within 30 days of delivery but requires competing buyers to pay within 10 days. (2) The second seller permits all buyers to pay within 30 days but offers a special discount for payment within 10 days. (3) If the second seller has not discriminated, has the salt company?

(b) Examine carefully the effects clause of §2(a). Was there any showing that Morton's discrimination affected "competition with any person who ... knowingly receives the benefit of such discrimination"? If not, are there other portions of the effects clause that bear on the *Morton Salt* situation?

(c) How were the requisite competitive effects established in *Morton Salt*? Consider: (1) Are you persuaded by the dissent's view of the discount for purchases in carload lots? (2) What harm to competitors or to competition had in fact occurred? (3) Is actual competitive injury necessary for illegality? What is the standard of illegality? (4) Upon what evidence of competitive injury did the Court rely?[1]

(d) Would or should the *Morton Salt* result be applied in the following circumstances? (1) The price discrimination is not reflected in the favored buyer's resale price. (2) The favored buyer has not increased its share of the resale market. (3) Many of the buyers who were discriminated against testified that they were not injured, and the parties stipulated that all the seller's customers would so testify if called. (4) A seller is shown to have discriminated in price among competing purchasers; there is no proof of any kind on competitive impact. (5) A seller of carbon paper discriminates in price in its sales to the three major automobile companies. (6) A seller of iron ore sells at discriminatory prices to competing steel producers.

(e) Suppose that most grocery suppliers discriminated against smaller buyers with the result that many of the smaller buyers were unable to survive in competition with the favored buyers. In that event, would the §2(a) effects clause be unequivocally satisfied? Argue the negative. Where do you come out?

1. FTC Adv. Opinion Dig. No. 253, 73 F.T.C. 1337 (1968): The Commission approved the grant of extended credit for five years to new businesses located in urban ghettos and run by proprietors residing there but denied credit to older ghetto firms, new ghetto firms with outside proprietors, and other firms generally. It doubted that there would be any substantial competition between favored and disfavored customers. Is this opinion consistent with *Morton Salt*?

608. Prudential Salt Company supplies about 10 percent of the country's table salt in competition with five larger rivals who produce about 80 percent of the national supply. Although they all have excess capacity, their list prices, which are identical, have not been altered. Recently, Prudential was approached by Colossal Wholesalers, which offered to give Prudential its patronage at a price 8 percent below the published list price. Colossal promised to keep such a discount secret. Prudential concludes that the arrangement would be highly profitable and grants the discount.

(a) If Prudential continues to sell to Colossal's competitors at list price, would it offend §2(a)?

(b) If the proposed arrangement is held unlawful, what are the possible or probable effects on Prudential's pricing behavior? Would the consequences in the salt market be desirable?[2]

609. The price-cost relationship; delivered prices. (a) *Generally.* Under the statute, the first proviso of §2(a) saves those price differences that reflect certain cost savings of the seller. The limited usefulness in practice of that defense will be noted briefly in Chapter 6C. Here we pose a different question: *Must* the seller give buyers the benefit of cost savings attributable to its dealings with them? The question might seem fanciful if principle and precedent did not thrust it forward. In principle, unequal treatment for those similarly situated may be no more discriminatory than equal treatment for those differently situated. To charge cash and credit customers the same price is, economically speaking, to discriminate against the former. To charge buyers at the plant the same price as for delivery to remote buyers discriminates against the former. Perhaps the law can avoid calling such equal prices discriminatory by focusing on equal availability. Thus, if credit or delivery is available to all, we might remain indifferent to economic discrimination resulting from the buyer's preference to pay cash or to pick up its goods. But consider the seller who charges remote buyers the same delivered price paid by nearby customers. The remote and nearby buyers pay the same sum for different economic packages. Whether this economic discrimination is a discrimination within the meaning of §2(a) depends on one's reading of the basing point and related cases.

(b) *Basing point pricing.*[3] In a single basing point system, the seller charges each buyer a delivered price that reflects a base charge plus

---

2. See D. O'Brien & G. Shaffer, The Welfare Effects of Forbidding Discriminatory Discounts: A Secondary Line Analysis of Robinson-Patman, 10 J.L. Econ. & Org. 296 (1994).

3. Review ¶250.

transportation (usually rail freight charges) between the base and the buyer's premises. Variously located buyers will therefore pay different delivered prices. If these buyers compete and the differential is significant, there could be a §2(a) price discrimination with the proscribed competitive impact. If the seller is located at the basing point, however, the differential among buyers will reflect the seller's actual transportation costs attributable to each shipment. In that event, §2(a)'s cost justification proviso will make the discrimination lawful. But where the seller ships goods from a plant that is not located at the basing point, its varying delivered prices will not reflect its actual transportation costs and will be unlawful unless saved by some other defense. And it was so held in *Corn Products*,[4] where the seller sold glucose from both its Chicago and Kansas City factories at a Chicago-plus price consisting of a base price plus transportation from Chicago. The cost justification defense was not available for sales from the Kansas City plant, and injury to competing candy manufacturers purchasing glucose was inferred from the price differentials: Chicago candy makers received an advantage over their Kansas City competitors, and this advantage was not attributable to relative proximity to glucose manufacturers.

(c) *Varying net receipts.* The *Corn Products* Court also spoke of varying net returns to the seller.[5] Different sales will obviously produce different net receipts (that is, price minus actual transportation costs) whenever delivered prices do not reflect actual transportation charges paid by the seller. Net returns were emphasized in *Cement Institute.*[6] The Supreme Court also described the pricing system in terms of varying mill nets and agreed that there was an unlawful price discrimination.[7]

(d) *Implications of the net receipts test.* If different net receipts are a §2(a) price discrimination, then two sales at equal prices can violate the statute when the seller's costs are not identical for the two transactions. That result might be resisted on three grounds. First, the statute's concern with differences in "price" does not compel concern with variations in the seller's profit. Second, there is no indication in the legislative history or elsewhere that the original or amended §2 was designed to compel sellers to vary their prices according to their costs.[8] Third, such compulsion would be impracticable to administer. Perhaps for these reasons, both the courts and the Commission have assumed that equal delivered prices are

4. Corn Prods. Ref. Co. v. FTC, 324 U.S. 726 (1945).
5. Id. at 733.
6. Cement Inst., 37 F.T.C. 87, 256 (1943).
7. *Cement Institute*, 333 U.S. at 721-724.
8. See F. Rowe, Price Discrimination under the Robinson-Patman Act 88 (1962; Supp. 1964).

generally exempt from §2(a). In *Staley*, the Supreme Court held a basing point pricing system unlawful and then said: "But it does not follow that respondents ... may not maintain a uniform delivered price at all points of delivery, for in that event there is no discrimination in price."[9] The Commission's disposition of later cases, moreover, reflects a similar view. While it might be practicable to exclude from price delivery charges paid to independent carriers without thereby investigating every cost within the seller's own integrated operation, the authorities have apparently come to focus on final prices paid by the buyer to the seller as the usual measure of price for §2(a).

TEXACO v. HASBROUCK
496 U.S. 543 (1990)

Justice STEVENS.... Petitioner (Texaco) sold gasoline directly to respondents and several other retailers in Spokane, Washington, at its retail tank wagon prices (RTW) while it granted substantial discounts to two distributors. During the period between 1972 and 1981, the stations supplied by the two distributors increased their sales volume dramatically, while respondents' sales suffered a corresponding decline. Respondents filed an action against Texaco ... alleging that the distributor discounts violated §2(a) of the [Robinson-Patman] Act. Respondents recovered treble damages, and the Court of Appeals for the Ninth Circuit affirmed the judgment. We granted certiorari to consider Texaco's contention that legitimate functional discounts do not violate the Act because a seller is not responsible for its customers' independent resale pricing decisions. While we agree with the basic thrust of Texaco's argument, we conclude that in this case it is foreclosed by the facts of record.

I

Given the jury's general verdict in favor of respondents, disputed questions of fact have been resolved in their favor. There seems, moreover, to be no serious doubt about the character of the market, Texaco's pricing practices, or the relative importance of Texaco's direct sales to retailers ("through put" business) and its sales to distributors. The principal disputes at trial related to questions of causation and damages.

Respondents are 12 independent Texaco retailers. They displayed the Texaco trademark, accepted Texaco credit cards, and

9. FTC v. A.E. Staley Mfg. Co., 324 U.S. 746, 757 (1945).

bought their gasoline directly from Texaco. Texaco delivered the gasoline to respondents' stations.

The retail gasoline market in Spokane was highly competitive throughout the damages period, which ran from 1972 to 1981. Stations marketing the nationally advertised Texaco gasoline competed with other major brands as well as with stations featuring independent brands. Moreover, although discounted prices at a nearby Texaco station would have the most obvious impact on a respondent's trade, the cross-city traffic patterns and relatively small size of Spokane produced a city-wide competitive market. Texaco's through put sales in the Spokane market declined from a monthly volume of 569,269 gallons in 1970 to 389,557 gallons in 1975. Texaco's independent retailers' share of the market for Texaco gas declined from 76% to 49%. Seven of the respondents' stations were out of business by the end of 1978.

The respondents tried unsuccessfully to increase their ability to compete with lower priced stations. Some tried converting from a full service to self-service stations. Two of the respondents sought to buy their own tank trucks and haul their gasoline from Texaco's supply point, but Texaco vetoed that proposal.

While the independent retailers struggled, two Spokane gasoline distributors supplied by Texaco prospered. Gull Oil Company (Gull) had its headquarters in Seattle and distributed petroleum products in four western States under its own name. In Spokane it purchased its gas from Texaco at prices that ranged from six to four cents below Texaco's RTW price. Gull resold that product under its own name; the fact that it was being supplied by Texaco was not known by either the public or the respondents. In Spokane, Gull supplied about 15 stations; some were "consignment stations" and some were "commission stations." In both situations Gull retained title to the gasoline until it was pumped into a motorist's tank. In the consignment stations, the station operator set the retail prices, but in the commission stations Gull set the prices and paid the operator a commission. Its policy was to price its gasoline at a penny less than the prevailing price for major brands. Gull employed two truck drivers in Spokane who picked up product at Texaco's bulk plant and delivered it to the Gull stations. It also employed one supervisor in Spokane. Apart from its trucks and investment in retail facilities, Gull apparently owned no assets in that market. At least with respect to the commission stations, Gull is fairly characterized as a retailer of gasoline throughout the relevant period.

The Dompier Oil Company (Dompier) started business in 1954 selling Quaker State Motor Oil. In 1960 it became a full line distributor of Texaco products, and by the mid-1970s its sales of gasoline represented over three-quarters of its business. Dompier purchased

Texaco gasoline at prices of 3.95¢ to 3.65¢ below the RTW price. Dompier thus paid a higher price than Gull, but Dompier, unlike Gull, resold its gas under the Texaco brand names. It supplied about eight to ten Spokane retail stations. In the period prior to October 1974, two of those stations were opened by the president of Dompier but the others were independently operated. In the early 1970s, Texaco representatives encouraged Dompier to enter the retail business directly, and in 1974 and 1975 it acquired four stations. Dompier's president estimated at trial that the share of its total gasoline sales made at retail during the middle 1970s was "probably 84 to 90 percent."

Like Gull, Dompier picked up Texaco's product at the Texaco bulk plant and delivered directly to retail outlets. Unlike Gull, Dompier owned a bulk storage facility, but it was seldom used because its capacity was less than that of many retail stations. Again unlike Gull, Dompier received from Texaco the equivalent of the common carrier rate for delivering the gasoline product to the retail outlets. Thus, in addition to its discount from the RTW price, Dompier made a profit on its hauling function.

The stations supplied by Dompier regularly sold at retail at lower prices than respondents'. Even before Dompier directly entered the retail business in 1974, its customers were selling to consumers at prices barely above the RTW price. Dompier's sales volume increased continuously and substantially throughout the relevant period. Between 1970 and 1975 its monthly sales volume increased from 155,152 gallons to 462,956 gallons; this represented an increase from 20.7% to almost 50% of Texaco's sales in Spokane.

There was ample evidence that Texaco executives were well aware of Dompier's dramatic growth and believed that it was attributable to "the magnitude of the distributor discount and the hauling allowance." In response to complaints from individual respondents about Dompier's aggressive pricing, however, Texaco representatives professed that they "couldn't understand it."

II

Respondents filed suit against Texaco in July 1976. After a four week trial, the jury awarded damages measured by the difference between the RTW price and the price paid by Dompier. As we subsequently decided in J. Truett Payne Co. v. Chrysler Motors Corp., 451 U.S. 557 (1981), this measure of damages was improper. Accordingly, ... the Court of Appeals for the Ninth Circuit remanded the case for a new trial.

At the second trial, Texaco contended that the special prices to Gull and Dompier were justified by cost savings, were the product of a good faith attempt to meet competition, and were lawful "functional discounts." The District Court withheld the cost justification defense from the jury because it was not supported by the evidence and the jury rejected the other defenses. It awarded respondents actual damages of $449,900. The jury apparently credited the testimony of respondents' expert witness who had estimated what the respondents' profits would have been if they had paid the same prices as the four stations owned by Dompier.

In Texaco's motion for judgment notwithstanding the verdict, it claimed as a matter of law that its functional discounts did not adversely affect competition within the meaning of the Act because any injury to respondents was attributable to decisions made independently by Dompier. The District Court denied the motion. In an opinion supplementing its oral ruling denying Texaco's motion for a directed verdict, the Court assumed, arguendo, that Dompier was entitled to a functional discount, even on the gas that was sold at retail,[9] but nevertheless concluded that the "presumed legality of functional discounts" had been rebutted by evidence that the amount of the discounts to Gull and Dompier was not reasonably related to the cost of any function that they performed.

The Court of Appeals affirmed. It reasoned:

> As Supreme Court long ago made clear, and recently reaffirmed, there may be a Robinson-Patman violation even if the favored and disfavored buyers do not compete, so long as the customers of the favored buyer compete with the disfavored buyer or its customers. *Morton Salt; Perkins; Falls City.* Despite the fact that Dompier and Gull, at least in their capacities as wholesalers, did not compete directly with Hasbrouck, a section 2(a) violation may occur if (1) the discount they received was not cost-based and (2) all or a portion of it was passed on by them to customers of theirs who competed with Hasbrouck. *Morton Salt; Perkins;* see 3 E. Kintner & J. Bauer, §22.14.
>
> Hasbrouck presented ample evidence to demonstrate that . . . the services performed by Gull and Dompier were insubstantial and did not justify the functional discount.

The Court of Appeals concluded its analysis by observing:

> To hold that price discrimination between a wholesaler and a retailer could *never* violate the Robinson-Patman Act would leave immune from antitrust scrutiny a discriminatory pricing procedure that

9. While there is a serious question as to whether Dompier was entitled to a "functional discount" on the gas it *resold at retail,* compare *Mueller* (entitlement to functional discount based on resale level) with *Doubleday and Co.,* 52 F.T.C. 169 (1955) (entitlement to functional discount based on level of purchase), the court assumes, arguendo, that the mere fact that Dompier retailed the gas does not preclude a "functional discount."

can effectively serve to harm competition. We think such a result would be contrary to the objectives of the Robinson-Patman Act.

III

It is appropriate to begin our consideration of the legal status of functional discounts[11] by examining the language of the Act.... The Act contains no express reference to functional discounts.[12] It does contain two affirmative defenses that provide protection for two categories of discounts — those that are justified by savings in the seller's cost of manufacture, delivery or sale, and those that represent a good faith response to the equally low prices of a competitor.... As the case comes to us, neither of those defenses is available to Texaco.

In order to establish a violation of the Act, respondents had the burden of proving four facts: (1) that Texaco's sales to Gull and Dompier were made in interstate commerce; (2) that the gasoline sold to them was of the same grade and quality as that sold to respondents; (3) that Texaco discriminated in price as between Gull and Dompier on the one hand and respondents on the other; and (4) that the discrimination had a prohibited effect on competition. Moreover, for each respondent to recover damages, he had the burden of proving the extent of his actual injuries. *J. Truett Payne.*

The first two elements of respondents' case are not disputed in this Court,[14] and we do not understand Texaco to be challenging the sufficiency of respondents' proof of damages. Texaco does ar-

11. In their brief as amici curiae, the United States and the Federal Trade Commission suggest the following definition of "functional discount," which is adequate for our discussion: "A functional discount is one given to a purchaser based on its role in the supplier's distributive system, reflecting, at least in a generalized sense, the services performed by the purchaser for the supplier."

12. The legislative history indicates that earlier drafts of the Act did include such a proviso.... The deletion of this exception for functional discounts has ambiguous significance. It may be, as one commentator has suggested, that the circumstances of the Act's passage "must have conveyed to the congressional mind the realization that the judiciary and the FTC would view what had occurred as a narrowing of the gates through which the functional classification plan of a seller had to pass to come within the law." ... In any event, the deletion in no way detracts from the blunt direction of the statutory text, which indicates that any price discrimination substantially lessening competition will expose the discriminator to liability, regardless of whether the discriminator attempts to characterize the pricing scheme as a functional discount.

14. Texaco has not contested here the proposition that branded gas and unbranded gas are of like grade and quality. See *FTC v. Borden Co.* ("the economic factors inherent in brand names and national advertising should not be considered in the jurisdictional inquiry under the statutory 'like grade and quality' test").

gue, however, that although it charged different prices, it did not "discriminate in price" within the meaning of the Act, and that, at least to the extent that Gull and Dompier acted as wholesalers, the price differentials did not injure competition. We consider the two arguments separately.

IV

Texaco's first argument would create a blanket exemption for all functional discounts. Indeed, carried to its logical conclusion, it would exempt all price differentials except those given to competing purchasers.... In the context of a statute that plainly reveals a concern with competitive consequences at different levels of distribution, and carefully defines specific affirmative defenses, it would be anomalous to assume that the Congress intended the term "discriminate" to have such a limited meaning. In *Anheuser-Busch* we rejected an argument identical to Texaco's in the context of a claim that a seller's price differential had injured its own competitors — a so called "primary line" claim. The reasons we gave for our decision in *Anheuser-Busch* apply here as well....

> The trouble with respondent's arguments is not that they are necessarily irrelevant in a §2(a) proceeding, but that they are misdirected when the issue under consideration is solely whether there has been a price discrimination. We are convinced that, whatever may be said with respect to the rest of §§2(a) and 2(b) — and we say nothing here — there are no overtones of business buccaneering in the §2(a) phrase "discriminate in price." Rather, a price discrimination within the meaning of that provision is merely a price difference.

After noting that this view was consistent with our precedents, we added:

> the statute itself spells out the conditions which make a price difference illegal or legal, and we would derange this integrated statutory scheme were we to read other conditions into the law by means of the nondirective phrase, "discriminate in price." Not only would such action be contrary to what we conceive to be the meaning of the statute, but, perhaps because of this, it would be thoroughly undesirable. As one commentator has succinctly put it, "Inevitably every legal controversy over any price difference would shift from the detailed governing provisions — 'injury,' cost justification, 'meeting competition,' etc. — over into the 'discrimination' concept of ad hoc resolution divorced from specifically pertinent statutory text." Rowe, Price Differentials and Product Differentiation: The Issues Under the Robinson-Patman Act, 66 Yale L.J. 1, 38.

Since we have already decided that a price discrimination within the meaning of §2(a) "is merely a price difference," we must reject Texaco's first argument.

V

In *Morton Salt*, we held that an injury to competition may be inferred from evidence that some purchasers had to pay their supplier "substantially more for their goods than their competitors had to pay." See also *Falls City*. Texaco, supported by the United States and the Federal Trade Commission as amici curiae (the Government), argues that this presumption should not apply to differences between prices charged to wholesalers and those charged to retailers. Moreover, they argue that it would be inconsistent with fundamental antitrust policies to construe the Act as requiring a seller to control his customers' resale prices. The seller should not be held liable for the independent pricing decisions of his customers. As the Government correctly notes, this argument endorses the position advocated 35 years ago in the Report of the Attorney General's National Committee to Study the Antitrust Laws (1955).

After observing that suppliers ought not to be held liable for the independent pricing decisions of their buyers,[16] and that without functional discounts distributors might go uncompensated for services they performed,[17] the Committee wrote:

> The Committee recommends, therefore, that suppliers granting functional discounts either to single-function or to integrated buyers should not be held responsible for any consequences of their customers' pricing tactics. Price cutting at the resale level is not in fact,

16.

In the Committee's view, imposing on any dual supplier a legal responsibility for the resale policies and prices of his independent distributors contradicts basic antitrust policies. Resale-price fixing is incompatible with the tenets of a free and competitive economy. What is more, the arrangements necessary for policing, detecting, and reporting price cutters may be illegal even apart from the resale-price agreement itself. And even short of such arrangements, a conscious adherence in a supplier's sales to retail customers to the price quotations by independent competing distributors is hardly feasible as a matter of business operation, or safe as a matter of law.

17.

In our view, to relate discounts or prices solely to the purchaser's resale activities without recognition of his buying functions thwarts competition and efficiency in marketing. It compels affirmative discrimination *against* a substantial class of distributors, and hence serves as a penalty on integration. If a businessman actually fulfills the wholesale function by relieving his suppliers of risk, storage, transportation, administration, etc., his performance, his capital investment, and the saving to his suppliers, are unaffected by whether he also performs the retailing function, or any number of other functions. A legal rule disqualifying him from discounts recognizing wholesaling functions actually performed compels him to render these functions free of charge.

and should not be held in law, "the effect of" a differential that merely accords due recognition and reimbursement for actual marketing functions. The price cutting of a customer who receives this type of differential results from his own independent decision to lower price and operate at a lower profit margin per unit. The legality or illegality of this price cutting must be judged by the usual legal tests. In any event, consequent injury or lack of injury should not be the supplier's legal concern.

On the other hand, the law should tolerate no subterfuge. For instance, where a wholesaler-retailer *buys* only part of his goods as a wholesaler, he must not claim a functional discount on all. Only to the extent that a buyer *actually* performs certain functions, assuming all the risk, investment, and costs involved, should he legally qualify for a functional discount. Hence a distributor should be eligible for a discount corresponding to any part of the function he actually performs on that part of the goods for which he performs it.

We generally agree with this description of the legal status of functional discounts. A supplier need not satisfy the rigorous requirements of the cost justification defense in order to prove that a particular functional discount is reasonable and accordingly did not cause any substantial lessening of competition between a wholesaler's customers and the supplier's direct customers.[18] The record in this case, however, adequately supports the finding that Texaco violated the Act.

The hypothetical predicate for the Committee's entire discussion of functional discounts is a price differential "that merely accords due recognition and reimbursement for actual marketing functions." Such a discount is not illegal. In this case, however, both the District Court and the Court of Appeals concluded that even without viewing the evidence in the light most favorable to the respondents, there was no substantial evidence indicating that the discounts to Gull and Dompier constituted a reasonable reimbursement for the value to Texaco of their actual marketing functions. Indeed, Dompier was separately compensated for its hauling func-

18. In theory, a supplier could try to defend a functional discount by invoking the Act's cost justification defense, but the burden of proof with respect to the defense is upon the supplier, and interposing the defense "has proven difficult, expensive, and often unsuccessful." 3 E. Kintner & J. Bauer, Federal Antitrust Law, §23.19, pp. 366-367 (1983)....

Discounters will therefore likely find it more useful to defend against claims under the Act by negating the causation element in the case against them: a legitimate functional discount will not cause any substantial lessening of competition. The concept of substantiality permits the causation inquiry to accommodate a notion of economic reasonableness with respect to the pass-through effects of functional discounts, and so provides a latitude denied by the cost-justification defense....

tion, and neither Gull nor Dompier maintained any significant storage facilities.

Despite this extraordinary absence of evidence to connect the discount to any savings enjoyed by Texaco, Texaco contends that the decision of the Court of Appeals cannot be affirmed without departing "from established precedent, from practicality, and from Congressional intent." This argument assumes that holding suppliers liable for a gratuitous functional discount is somehow a novel practice. That assumption is flawed.

As we have already observed, the "due recognition and reimbursement" concept endorsed in the Attorney General's Committee's study would not countenance a functional discount completely untethered to either the supplier's savings or the wholesaler's costs. The longstanding principle that functional discounts provide no safe harbor from the Act is likewise evident from the practice of the Federal Trade Commission, which has, while permitting legitimate functional discounts, proceeded against those discounts which appeared to be subterfuges to avoid the Act's restrictions. . . .

Most of these cases involve discounts made questionable because offered to "complex types of distributors" whose "functions became scrambled." Doubleday & Co., 52 F.T.C., at 208. This fact is predictable: manufacturers will more likely be able to effectuate tertiary line price discrimination through functional discounts to a secondary line buyer when the favored distributor is vertically integrated. Nevertheless, this general tendency does not preclude the possibility that a seller may pursue a price discrimination strategy despite the absence of any discrete mechanism for allocating the favorable price discrepancy between secondary and tertiary line recipients.[23]

---

23. The seller may be willing to accept any division of the price difference so long as some significant part is passed on to the distributor's customers. Although respondents here did not need to show any benefit to Texaco from the price discrimination scheme in order to establish a violation of the Act, one possibility is indicated by the brief filed amicus curiae by the Service Station Dealers of America (SSDA), an organization representing both stations supplied by independent jobbers and stations supplied directly by sellers. SSDA suggests that an indirect price discount to competitors may be used to force directly supplied franchisees out of the market, and so to circumvent federal restrictions upon the termination of franchise agreements. See 92 Stat. 324-332, 15 U.S.C. §§2801-2806.

One would expect that — absent a safe harbor rule making functional discounts a useful means to engage in otherwise unlawful price discrimination — excessive functional discounts of the sort in evidence here would be rare. As the Government correctly observes, "[t]his case appears to reflect rather anomalous behavior on the part of the supplier." See also Brief for United States as Amicus Curiae 15 (filed May 16, 1989) ("market forces should tend to discourage a supplier from offering independent wholesalers discounts that would allow them to undercut the supplier's own retail customers").

Indeed, far from constituting a novel basis for liability under the Act, the fact pattern here reflects conduct similar to that which gave rise to *Perkins*. Perkins purchased gas from Standard, and was both a distributor and a retailer. He asserted that his retail business had been damaged through two violations of the Act by Standard: first, Standard had sold directly to its own retailers at a price below that charged to Perkins; and second, Standard had sold to another distributor, Signal, which sold gas to Western Hyway, which in turn sold gas to Regal, a retailer in competition with Perkins. The question presented was whether the Act — which refers to discriminators, purchasers, and their customers — covered injuries to competition between purchasers and the customers of purchasers. We held that a limitation excluding such "fourth level" competition would be "wholly an artificial one." We reasoned that from "Perkins' point of view, the competitive harm done him by Standard is certainly no less because of the presence of an additional link in this particular distribution chain from the producer to the retailer." The same may justly be said in this case. The additional link in the distribution chain does not insulate Texaco from liability if Texaco's excessive discount otherwise violated the Act.

Nor should any reader of the commentary on functional discounts be much surprised by today's result. Commentators have disagreed about the extent to which functional discounts are generally or presumptively allowable under the Robinson-Patman Act. They nevertheless tend to agree that in exceptional cases what is nominally a functional discount may be an unjustifiable price discrimination entirely within the coverage of the Act. Others, like Frederick Rowe, have asserted the legitimacy of functional discounts in more sweeping terms, but even Rowe concedes the existence of an "exception to the general rule." F. Rowe, Price Discrimination Under the Robinson-Patman Act 174, n.7 (1962); id., at 195-205.

We conclude that the commentators' analysis, like the reasoning in *Perkins* and like the Federal Trade Commission's practice, renders implausible Texaco's contention that holding it liable here involves some departure from established understandings. Perhaps respondents' case against Texaco rests more squarely than do most functional discount cases upon direct evidence of the seller's intent to pass a price advantage through an intermediary. This difference, however, hardly cuts in Texaco's favor. In any event, the evidence produced by respondents also shows the scrambled functions which have more frequently signaled the illegitimacy under the Act of what is alleged to be a permissible functional discount. Both Gull and Dompier received the full discount on all their purchases even though most of their volume was resold directly to consumers. The extra margin on those sales obviously enabled them to price aggressively in both their retail and their wholesale marketing. To the extent that Dompier and Gull competed with respondents in the retail market, the presumption of adverse effect on competition recognized in the *Morton Salt* case becomes all the more appropriate. Their competitive advantage in the market also constitutes evidence tending to rebut any presumption of legality that would otherwise apply to their wholesale sales.

The evidence indicates, moreover, that Texaco affirmatively encouraged Dompier to expand its retail business and that Texaco was fully informed about the persistent and marketwide consequences of its own pricing policies. Indeed, its own executives recognized that the dramatic impact on the market was almost entirely attributable to the magnitude of the distributor discount and the hauling allowance. Yet at the same time that Texaco was encouraging Dompier to integrate downward, and supplying Dompier with a generous discount useful to such integration, Texaco was inhibiting upward integration by the respondents: two of the respondents sought permission from Texaco to haul their own fuel using their own tank-wagons, but Texaco refused. The special facts of this case thus make it peculiarly difficult for Texaco to claim that it is being held liable for the independent pricing decisions of Gull or Dompier.

As we recognized in *Falls City*, "the competitive injury component of Robinson-Patman Act violation is not limited to the injury to competition between the favored and the disfavored purchaser; it also encompasses the injury to competition between their customers." This conclusion is compelled by the statutory language, which specifically encompasses not only the adverse effect of price discrimination on persons who either grant or knowingly receive the benefit of such discrimination, but also on "customers of either of them." Such indirect competitive effects surely may not be presumed automatically in every functional discount setting, and, indeed, one would expect that most functional discounts will be legitimate discounts which do not cause harm to competition. At the least, a functional discount that constitutes a reasonable reimbursement for the purchasers' actual marketing functions will not violate the Act. When a functional discount is legitimate, the inference of injury to competition recognized in the *Morton Salt* case will simply not arise. Yet it is also true that not every functional discount is entitled to a judgment of legitimacy, and that it will sometimes be possible to produce evidence showing that a particular functional discount caused a price discrimination of the sort the Act prohibits. When such anti-competitive effects are proved — as we believe they were in this case — they are covered by the Act.[30]

---

30. The parties do not raise, and we therefore need not address, the question whether the inference of injury to competition might also be negated by evidence

VI

At the trial respondents introduced evidence describing the diversion of their customers to specific stations supplied by Dompier. Respondents' expert testimony on damages also focused on the diversion of trade to specific Dompier-supplied stations. The expert testimony analyzed the entire damages period, which ran from 1972 and 1981 and included a period prior to 1974 when Dompier did not own any retail stations (although the jury might reasonably have found that Dompier controlled the Red Carpet station from the outset of the damages period). Moreover, respondents offered no direct testimony of any diversion to Gull and testified that they did not even know that Gull was being supplied by Texaco. Texaco contends that by basing the damages award upon an extrapolation from data applicable to Dompier-supplied stations, respondents necessarily based the award upon the consequences of pricing decisions made by independent customers of Dompier. Texaco argues that the damages award must therefore be judged excessive as a matter of law.

Even if we were to agree with Texaco that Dompier was not a retailer throughout the damages period, we could not accept Texaco's argument. Texaco's theory improperly blurs the distinction between the liability and the damages issues. The proof established that Texaco's lower prices to Gull and Dompier were discriminatory throughout the entire nine-year period; that at least Gull, and apparently Dompier as well, was selling at retail during that entire period; that the discounts substantially affected competition throughout the entire market; and that they injured each of the respondents. There is no doubt that respondents' proof of a continuing violation of the Act throughout the nine-year period was sufficient. Proof of the specific amount of their damages was necessarily less precise. Even if some portion of some of respondents' injuries may be attributable to the conduct of independent retailers, the expert testimony nevertheless provided a sufficient basis for an acceptable estimate of the amount of damages. We have held that a plaintiff may not recover damages merely by showing a violation of the Act; rather, the plaintiff must also "make some showing of actual injury attributable to something the antitrust laws were designed to prevent. *Perkins* (plaintiff 'must, of course, be able to show a causal connection between the price discrimination in violation of the Act and the injury suffered')." *J. Truett Payne*. At the same time, however, we reaffirmed our "traditional rule excusing antitrust plaintiffs from an unduly rigorous standard of proving antitrust

---

that disfavored buyers could make purchases at a reasonable discount from favored buyers.

injury." See also Zenith Radio Corp. v. Hazeltine Research, 395 U.S. 100, 123-124 (1969); Bigelow v. RKO Radio Pictures, 327 U.S. 251, 264-265 (1946).[31] Moreover, as we have noted, Texaco did not object to the instructions to the jury on the damages issue. A possible flaw in the jury's calculation of the amount of damages would not be an appropriate basis for granting Texaco's motion for a judgment notwithstanding the verdict.

The judgment is affirmed. . . .

[There were two opinions concurring in the result. Justice White objected to the portion of the Court's opinion that "declares that a price differential that merely accords due recognition and reimbursement for actual marketing functions not only does not trigger the presumption of an injury to competition, see *Morton Salt*, but also announces that '[s]uch a discount is not illegal.' There is nothing in the Act to suggest such a defense. . . . " Under the Court's analysis, a "retailer charged a higher price than a distributor who is given what the Court would call a legitimate discount is entirely foreclosed, even though he . . . could prove that the distributor sells to his customers at a price lower than the plaintiff retailer pays Texaco and that those customers of the distributor undersell the plaintiff and have caused plaintiff's business to fail." Such injury is squarely covered by the Act. The Court's only justification is that, if the discount is legitimate, the injury is caused by the distributor's discount, even though Texaco's discount is what makes this possible. Despite contrary indications from the Attorney General's Committee and the FTC, "I doubt that at this late date we should attempt to set the matter right [in the absence of Congressional attention], at least not in a case that does not require us to define what a legitimate functional discount is."

Justices Scalia and Kennedy also would not "adopt the Court's reasoning, which seems to create an exemption for functional discounts that are 'reasonable' even though prohibited by the text of the Act." The argument of the petitioner and the United States as amicus that functional discounts should be exempted even if they cannot be shown to be cost-based because they constitute an effi-

---

31. In *J. Truett Payne*, we quoted with approval the following passage:

Damage issues in these cases are rarely susceptible of the kind of concrete, detailed proof of injury which is available in other contexts. The Court has repeatedly held that in the absence of more precise proof, the factfinder may "conclude as a matter of just and reasonable inference from the proof of defendants' wrongful acts and their tendency to injure plaintiffs' business, and from the evidence of the decline in prices, profits and values, not shown to be attributable to other causes, that defendants' wrongful acts had caused damage to the plaintiffs." . . .

Zenith Radio Corp. v. Hazeltine Research, 395 U.S., at 123-124.

cient and legitimate commercial practice should be addressed to Congress. The opinion goes on to suggest that a functional discount would be unlikely to subvert the purposes of the Act even if it is not commensurate with savings by the supplier so long as it is commensurate with costs incurred by the wholesaler in performing services, because such a discount would not be passed on to the wholesaler's customer. Even so, such a functional discount would have to be cost justified in at least one of these respects to be deemed "reasonable." The only plausible argument for generally finding that functional discounts could not be a probable cause of competitive injury would be that if the market were fully functionally divided, no retailers would compete with wholesalers and all competing retailers would have the opportunity to obtain the same price from wholesalers. But since the argument was not raised, it should not be decided in this case.]

610. (a) Why should functional discounts ever be permitted? If they are allowed, why not insist that the requirements of the cost justification defense be satisfied? How does the *Texaco* Court avoid insisting upon the strict requirements of the defense?

(b) Given that functional discounts are held not to be a violation, why does the defendant lose? Because its discounts are not cost justified?

(c) Why might Texaco have given these discounts if, indeed, they were not cost justified? Will a seller typically profit from offering such discounts?

611. Seller Sigma refines gasoline and makes interstate sales directly to retailer Alpha at a price of 92 per unit. It sells gasoline to wholesaler White at a price of 90. White resells at a price of 92 to retailer Beta, who competes with Alpha. Assume that no statutory proviso applies.

(a) Is there any price discrimination? What are the competitive effects? Do they indicate that Sigma has violated the statute?

(b) Suppose that 5 percent of White's sales are directly to consumers and that all sales to consumers seem to be made at 95. Are there any effects indicating that Sigma has violated the statute?

(c) If Sigma seems to be violating §2(a) in ¶b, how can it extricate itself?

(d) Suppose that White resells to Beta at a price of 91. Are there any effects indicating that Sigma has violated §2(a)?

(e) If Sigma seems to be violating §2(a) in ¶d, how can it avoid the violation consistent with its own business needs and with the antitrust laws generally?

612. ***Federal Trade Commission v. Borden Co.***, 383 U.S. 637, 644, 646, 659-660 & n.17 (1966). Borden sold evaporated milk under its own nationally advertised brand. It also sold chemically identical milk bearing the private brand labels of the buyers; the private label product is sold for a lower price by Borden, wholesalers, and retailers. The Court held these products to be "of like grade and quality" within the meaning of §2(a). First, neither the statutory words nor their legislative history clearly requires like brands. Second, to hold otherwise would permit sellers to deny some buyers the lower-priced brand and thus seriously injure them. Third, the contrary holding would permit the seller to escape the Act whenever it succeeds "in selling some unspecified amount of each product to some unspecified portion of his customers, however large or small the price differential might be." Fourth, as to the objection that it ignores economic reality, the Court emphasized that its decision means only that brand differences do not oust the statute and that

> transactions like those involved in this case may be examined by the Commission under §2(a). The Commission will determine, subject to judicial review, whether the differential under attack is discriminatory within the meaning of the Act, whether competition may be injured, and whether the differential is cost justified or is defensible as a good faith effort to meet the price of a competitor.

The dissent of Justices Stewart and Harlan included the following points:

> [1] Nothing in FTC v. Anheuser-Busch . . . requires an equation in all circumstances between a price differential and price discrimination. So long as Borden makes private label brands available to all customers of its premium milk, it is unlikely that price discrimination within the meaning of §2(a) can be made out. [2] [I]t is unlikely that economic differences between premium and private label brands can realistically be taken into account. . . . Even if relevant cost data can be agreed upon, the cost ratio between Borden's premium and private label products is hardly the most significant factor in Borden's pricing decision. . . . Moreover, even if price discrimination is found here, its effect on competition may prove even more difficult to determine than in more conventional cases of price discrimination. . . .

On remand, the court of appeals decided for Borden.[10] Rivals had increased their absolute sales. And although Borden managed to increase its market share from 9.9 percent in 1955 to 10.7 percent in 1957, there was insufficient causal connection between the price differential and the alleged competitive injury. Competitors'

10. Borden Co. v. FTC, 381 F.2d 175 (5th Cir. 1967).

evidence related to the price differential among rival private labels and not to any difference between Borden's branded and private label products. Nor was there any evidence that Borden sold private label milk below cost or at an unprofitable price. Furthermore, the examiner had found that 86 percent of its private label sales resulted from f.o.b. pricing at its favorable plant locations relative to more remote rivals who used delivered prices.

With respect to the claim of secondary-line injury, the court of appeals noted the absence of proof that anyone desiring private label milk was refused equal private label terms by Borden. Nor was there any proof that the price differential exceeded the degree of consumer preference for the branded product. Such a differential conferred no competitive advantage on the recipient of the cheaper private brand product. The differential seemed to the court to approximate the benefit of advertising and promotion received by the purchaser of the branded product.[11]

613. Delta Corporation sells a highly successful automatic dishwasher bearing its name. It sells the machine for $300 directly to retailers who usually resell it at prices in the range of $400 to $450. Delta sells the identical machine without any identifying name plates for $225 to large retail houses — such as Sears, Montgomery Ward, and Macy's — which resell the machines under their own names at prices in the range of $300 to $350.

(a) Has Delta discriminated in price with respect to "commodities of like grade and quality"?

(b) Would your ¶a answer differ if Delta had regularly and emphatically offered to sell the unbranded machines to all retailers for $225? What answer is suggested in *Borden?* In *Morton Salt?* In *American Oil?* What is your conclusion?

(c) Suppose that Delta has discriminated within the meaning of §2(a) and that it cannot show cost savings of $75 per unbranded machine. Has it violated §2(a)? Does *Morton Salt* give the answer?

---

11. See also Kroger Co. v. FTC, 438 F.2d 1372 (6th Cir.), cert. denied, 404 U.S. 871 (1971) (secondary-line injury found where there were lower price sales for goods distributed under buyer's private label, discriminations were as high as 41 percent for cottage cheese and averaged more than 12 percent in the most important market, competition is keen and profit margins low in the retail food business, and dairy products are often used as loss leaders); Standard Oil Co. (Cal.) v. Perkins, 396 F.2d 809 (9th Cir. 1968), rev'd on other grounds, 395 U.S. 642 (1969) (discriminatory not to give private label purchasers of gasoline the same privileges as distributors of supplier's branded gasoline: price assistance during price wars, credit card privileges, and allowances for painting, advertising, and maintaining stations); J. von Kalinowski, Availability as a Defense to Private Label Marketing, 39 Antitr. L.J. 835 (1970).

Could one argue that this pricing scheme amounts to a functional discount? If so, does that help Delta?

(d) As counsel for Delta, you are preparing to disprove competitive injury. A staff of lawyers, economists, accountants, and statisticians is at your disposal. They await your instructions. Tell them what you want and how to get it.

(e) Would your answers differ if the unbranded machines were economy models without built-in heaters that raise the temperature of ordinary tap water? To include a heater adds about $10 to manufacturing cost.

6C.   AFFIRMATIVE DEFENSES UNDER §2(a) AND §2(b)[1]

Cost Justification

614.   Introduction. (a) *Scope of defense; burden of proof.* Clayton Act §2 does not condemn all price discrimination affecting competition among sellers or buyers; it does not prohibit differences in price that reflect differences in the cost of supplying different purchasers.[2] Regardless of the effect on other sellers or upon disfavored buyers, a seller may lawfully grant price preferences not exceeding its savings in the cost of serving favored buyers as compared with the cost of serving other buyers.

Cost savings have justified very few price differentials. Although it offers a complete and absolute defense to price discrimination, the structure of §2(a) and the language of §2(b) make plain that cost justification is an affirmative defense that the seller must prove. And the Supreme Court has remarked on "the intricacies inherent in

---

1. The final two provisos in §2(a) are not explored here. One indicates that "nothing herein contained shall prevent persons ... from selecting their own customers in bona fide transactions and not in restraint of trade," suggesting that an outright refusal to deal, for example, with specified wholesalers would not constitute price discrimination, although such a refusal would remain subject to any other applicable antitrust law. The other expressly exempts price changes occasioned by changing market conditions. The "changing conditions" proviso was relied on in Peter Satori v. Studebaker-Packard Corp., 1964 Trade Cas. ¶71309 (S.D. Cal.); Valley Plymouth v. Studebaker-Packard Corp., 219 F. Supp. 608 (S.D. Cal. 1963).

2. Note, however, that the second proviso to §2(a) authorizes the Federal Trade Commission to "fix and establish quantity limits" in certain cases. Where such limits are fixed, discriminatory discounts on larger quantities are prohibited even though fully cost-justified. The Commission attempted unsuccessfully to impose such a limit with respect to rubber tires. B.F. Goodrich Co. v. FTC, 242 F.2d 31 (D.C. Cir. 1957).

the attempt to show costs" under §2 and has observed that "[p]roof of a cost justification being what it is, too often no one can ascertain whether a price is cost-justified."[3] Nor has the Commission been generous in accepting imperfect or partial cost justifications, although it has said that de minimis deficiencies will be overlooked.[4]

(b) *Difficulties in proving cost differences.* Several obvious difficulties confront any effort to relate costs to prices. First, how close a connection is to be expected? Even in highly competitive markets, price adjustments do not occur instantly in response to changes in cost conditions, so at any given time one might observe some discrepancies.

Second, which costs are relevant? In principle, prospective marginal costs are the ones most relevant to price determination, but the courts have insisted on using historical accounting costs, which may not reflect current conditions.

Third, the allocation of such costs among various products made by the firm and among the various customers it serves tends to be arbitrary. Some groupings of products and customers for some time period are necessary, and expenses must be allocated somehow among them. For these reasons and because accurate information is often simply not available or too costly to collect and analyze, most business decisions, including prices, are based on rough estimates. In practice, cost justification data are usually collected after the event in the hope of justifying a challenged price differential. As *Borden* illustrates, neither judges nor commissioners have been very receptive to the inevitable approximations.

The policy problem is thus apparent. Requiring too precise a justification for every differential eviscerates the defense and thereby interferes with efficient pricing. But accepting unduly casual proof would save virtually all price differentials, contrary to the statutory purpose. The tendency has been to err in the direction of strictness, as it is often said that "the cost defense has proved largely illusory in practice."[5]

(c) *The relevant costs.*[6] Section 2(a) counts only savings "in the cost of [1] manufacture, sale, or delivery [2] resulting from the

---

3. Automatic Canteen Co. of Am. v. FTC, 346 U.S. 61, 68, 79 (1953).

4. See F. Rowe, Price Discrimination Under the Robinson-Patman Act §10.9 (1962, Supp. 1964); he believes that the Commission was becoming more tolerant of "substantial" although imperfect cost justification. Cost justifications were established in Morton v. National Dairy Prods. Corp., 414 F.2d 403 (3d Cir. 1969), cert. denied, 396 U.S. 1006 (1970) (lower price charged buyer taking delivery at seller's plant); American Motors Corp. v. FTC, 384 F.2d 247 (6th Cir. 1967), cert. denied, 390 U.S. 1012 (1968).

5. Report of the Attorney General's National Committee to Study the Antitrust Laws 171 (1955), quoted in *Texaco.*

6. See generally Rowe, note 4, §10.7.

differing methods or quantities in which such commodities are . . . sold or delivered." Consider manufacturing and distribution costs.

Manufacturing costs. The proviso accepts differences in manufacturing costs "resulting from the differing methods or quantities" of sale. Savings might flow from early ordering, which permits smoother scheduling, avoidance of overtime, and more efficient production during the slack season. Where production for particular customers requires special equipment, tooling, or plant arrangements, the cost of such special arrangements should be allocated to the relevant order, and this means lower unit production costs for large orders than for small ones. Such savings in manufacturing costs fit within the statutory language and its purpose but have seldom been asserted in the litigated cases.

Distribution costs. The language of the proviso emphasizes differences in sales or delivery costs. This is understood to include the relevant costs of promotion. A manufacturer selling an advertised brand through one distribution channel and also selling unbranded goods through another channel may allocate advertising expenditures to the branded commodity. A manufacturer certainly may consider differences in the costs of taking, processing, and billing orders or in packing and shipping. Thus, if the manufacturer maintains a warehouse for servicing some customers while others take delivery in large quantities at the seller's plant, the warehouse expenses may be allocated to the former customers. In such cases, however, the Commission has rejected an allowance for a return on the capital invested in the warehouse operation on the ground that such a return is profit and not a paid-out cost. But providing and stocking a warehouse is not free. The market value of capital is evident when the manufacturer builds the warehouse or finances inventories with borrowed funds. The economic cost should not be ignored because the funds were not borrowed or because measurement is difficult.

Compensation of salespeople and brokers. To count savings in brokerage might appear to give the favored buyer an allowance in lieu of brokerage in violation of §2(c).[7] In addition, when brokers or salespeople are paid a differing percentage of the sale price, the seller may seem to be manipulating costs. Suppose, for example, that a manufacturer pays its salespeople an 11 percent commission on sales made at price 100 and 10 percent on sales made at 99. The different payments to salespeople fully account for the price difference. But if the manufacturer and its sales force are seen as a single economic entity, they are simply taking a lower return on sales to the favored buyer. On that view, the transaction may not satisfy the

---

7. See ¶625.

purpose of the proviso. But query: Should the manufacturer and its sales force be regarded as a single economic entity — always, sometimes, when? There would seem to be less ground for objecting to the inclusion in cost savings of commissions or other expenses, such as patent royalties, which are expressed as a constant percentage of sales price.

UNITED STATES v. BORDEN CO.
370 U.S. 460 (1962)

Justice CLARK. [Borden and Bowman sold milk products at prices that discriminated between independently owned grocery stores and large grocery store chains. The question was whether the defendants' cost studies were sufficient to demonstrate that their pricing policies were cost justified.]

The Government candidly recognizes in its briefs filed in the instant case that "[a]s a matter of practical necessity ... when a seller deals with a very large number of customers, he cannot be required to establish different cost-reflecting prices for each customer." In this same vein, the practice of grouping customers for pricing purposes has long had the approval of the Federal Trade Commission. We ourselves have noted the "elusiveness of cost data" in ... *Automatic Canteen.* In short, to completely renounce class pricing as justified by class accounting would be to eliminate in practical effect the cost justification proviso as to sellers having a large number of purchasers, thereby preventing such sellers from passing on economies to their customers. It seems hardly necessary to say that such a result is at war with Congress' language and purpose.

But this is not to say that price differentials can be justified on the basis of arbitrary classifications or even classifications which are representative of a numerical majority of the individual members. At some point practical considerations shade into a circumvention of the proviso. A balance is struck by the use of classes for cost justification which are composed of members of such selfsameness as to make the averaging of the cost of dealing with the group a valid and reasonable indicium of the cost of dealing with any specific group member. High on the list of "musts" in the use of the average cost of customer groupings under the proviso of §2(a) is a close resemblance of the individual members of each group on the essential point or points which determine the costs considered.

In this regard we do not find the classifications submitted by the appellees to have been shown to be of sufficient homogeneity. Certainly, the cost factors considered were not necessarily encompassed within the manner in which a customer is owned. Turning first to Borden's justification, we note that it not only failed to show that the economies relied upon were isolated within the favored class but affirmatively revealed that members of the classes utilized were substantially unlike in the cost saving aspects considered. For instance, the favorable cost comparisons between the chains and the larger independents were for the greater part controlled by the higher average volume of the chain stores in comparison to the average volume of the 80-member class to which these independents were relegated. The District Court allowed this manner of justification because "most chain stores do purchase larger volumes of milk than do most independent stores." However, such a grouping for cost justification purposes, composed as it is of some independents having volumes comparable to, and in some cases larger than, that of the chain stores, created artificial disparities between the larger independents and the chain stores. It is like averaging one horse and one rabbit. . . . This volume gap between the larger independents and the chain stores was further widened by grouping together the two chains, thereby raising the average volume of the stores of the smaller of the two chains in relation to the larger independents. Nor is the vice in the Borden class justification solely in the paper volumes relied upon, for it attributed to many independents cost factors which were not true indicia of the cost of dealing with those particular consumers. To illustrate, each independent was assigned a portion of the total expenses involved in daily cash collections, although it was not shown that all independents paid cash and in fact Borden admitted only that a "large majority" did so.

Likewise the details of Bowman's cost study show a failure in classification. Only one additional point need be made. Its justification emphasized its costs for "optional customer service" and daily cash collection with the resulting "delay to collect." As shown by its study these elements were crucial to Bowman's cost justification. In the study the experts charged all independents and no chain store with these costs. Yet, it was not shown that all independents received these services daily or even on some lesser basis. Bowman's studies indicated only that a large majority of independents took these services on a daily basis. Under such circumstances the use of these cost factors across the board in calculating independent store costs is not a permissible justification, for it possibly allocates costs to some independents whose mode of purchasing does not give rise to them. The burden was upon the profferer of the classification to negate this possibility, and this burden has not been met here. If these factors control the cost of dealing, then their presence or absence might with more justification be the password for admission into the various price categories.[13] ...

In sum, the record here shows that price discriminations have been permitted on the basis of cost differences between broad customer groupings, apparently based on the nature of ownership but in any event not shown to be so homogeneous as to permit the joining together of these purchasers for cost allocations purposes. If this is the only justification for appellees' pricing schemes, they are illegal. We do not believe that an appropriate decree would require the trial court continuously to "pass judgment on the pricing practices of these defendants." ...

Reversed. ...

Justice DOUGLAS, concurring. ... Where centralized purchasing for many stores takes place, the costs of dealing with the group as a class become relevant to the problem under §2(a). But where, as here, no centralized purchasing is involved, the store-by-store costs are the only criteria relevant to the §2(a) problem. Otherwise those with the most prestige get the largest discounts and the independent merchants are more and more forced to the wall.

The case was argued as if the grant of discounts was a natural right and that the Act should be construed so as to make the granting of them easy. The Act reflects, however, a purpose to control practices that lead to monopoly and an impoverishment of our middle class. I would therefore read it in a way that preserves as much of our traditional free enterprise as possible. Free enterprise is not free when monopoly power is used to breed more monopoly. That is the case here unless store-by-store costs are used as the criteria for discounts. ...

[Justice Harlan, dissenting, would affirm the district court's judgment that (1) the cost studies, although imperfect, were conscientiously prepared and generally justified the price differentials and (2) an injunction should be denied in this old litigation that could, if the government wished, be pursued further in the Federal Trade Commission.][8]

---

13. Another suspect feature is that classifications based on services received by independents were apparently frozen — making it impossible for them to obtain larger discounts by electing not to receive the cost-determinative services — with no justifiable business reason offered in support of the practice.

8. Frankfurter, J., did not participate.

615. (a) Do you agree with the *Borden* Court?

(b) How could Borden and Bowman structure their discounts so as to be acceptable to the Court? Must they precisely measure the costs of each delivery, or would some intermediate solution be acceptable? How can they find out?

(c) Suppose they could prove that more precise discounting systems (such as charging for special services store-by-store, at each delivery) would be more costly to administer than the amount of the price differentials involved. Would that fact exonerate them, or would they be forced to charge identical prices to all, ignoring any cost differences?

(d) Why would Borden and Bowman have used this pricing scheme if it was not cost justified?

(e) Could you persuasively support the proposition that the cost justification defense ought to be repealed because it is a mere illusion that entraps the unwary and obscures from Congress and the courts the real impact of §2(a)?

(f) Would you favor amending the cost justification proviso to read as follows: "That nothing shall prevent price differentials which make only due allowance for savings in any of the seller's costs, determined by any sound accounting principles, which may reasonably flow from differences in the categories of transactions involved"?

Meeting Competition in Good Faith

616. Introduction. Section 2(b) allows a seller to rebut a prima facie case "by showing that his lower price . . . was made in good faith to meet an equally low price of a competitor."[9] The defense has been held to be absolute; that is, a seller will be exonerated even if adverse competitive effects result.[10] It should also be noted that the language refers to the "equally low price" charged by a competitor, making the defense applicable when one meets competition but not when one beats (undercuts) the competition. Consider the purposes and effects of this defense.

(a) It has been argued that (1) price discrimination is unlawful only when it causes primary- or secondary-line injury, (2) a discrimination cannot cause such injury when the favored buyer can readily

---

9. The provision also allows the defense where the seller is "furnishing . . . services or facilities to any purchaser . . . in good faith to meet . . . the services or facilities furnished by a competitor." Thus, the defense is applicable to challenges under §2(e) (and under §2(d); see ¶626b).

10. Standard Oil Co. v. FTC, 340 U.S. 231 (1951).

obtain the lower price from other suppliers, and (3) therefore, the "meeting competition" defense merely makes explicit what is implicit in the statutory requirement of competitive injury. Do you agree?

(b) "The meeting competition defense resembles provisions found in earlier cartel agreements. Such agreements usually provided that no seller may undercut the cartel price by offering selective price concessions to individual buyers in an attempt to gain their business at the expense of rival sellers but that a cartel member may match a lower price so that no discounter gains from its devious act, although no one should undercut the discounted price, lest matters be made worse." How close is the resemblance? Does this suggest that the Robinson-Patman Act with its meeting competition defense may reinforce anticompetitive oligopoly pricing? If so, would you recommend repealing the Act or just the defense?

617. Good faith and knowledge of rivals' prices. (a) *Federal Trade Commission v. A.E. Staley Manufacturing Co.*, 324 U.S. 746, 759-760 (1945). Staley granted beneficial discriminatory terms to certain buyers after receiving verbal information from its sales force, brokers, and potential buyers indicating that its competitors had been offering favorable prices.

> The Commission commented on the tendency of buyers to seek to secure the most advantageous terms of sales possible, and upon the entire lack of a showing of diligence on the part of respondents to verify the reports which they received, or to learn of the existence of facts which would lead a reasonable and prudent person to believe that the granting of a lower price would in fact be meeting the equally low price of a competitor. The Commission thought that respondents' allowance of discretionary prices, in circumstances which strongly suggested that the buyers' claims were without merit, as well as respondents' readiness to grant discriminatory prices without taking any steps to verify the existence of a lower price of competitors, and the entire absence of any showing that respondents had taken any precaution to conduct their business in such manner as to prevent unwarranted discriminations in price, all taken together, required the conclusion that respondents had not sustained the burden of showing that their price discriminations were made in good faith to meet the lower prices of competitors.
>
> Section 2(b) does not require the seller to justify price discriminations by showing that in fact they met a competitive price. But it does place on the seller the burden of showing that the price was made in good faith to meet a competitor's. . . . We agree with the Commission that the statute at least requires the seller, who has knowingly discriminated in price, to show the existence of facts which would lead a

reasonable and prudent person to believe that the granting of a lower price would in fact meet the equally low price of a competitor.

(b) *United States v. United States Gypsum Co.*, 438 U.S. 422, 452-459 & n.32 (1978). The defendants were competing producers who exchanged presale price quotations, in apparent violation of the Sherman Act under the *Container* case, reproduced in Chapter 2D. They sought to defend their behavior on the ground that they were merely verifying rivals' prices in order to determine whether a preferential price to a particular buyer would qualify for the meeting competition defense under Robinson-Patman Act §2(b). The Court nonetheless found a Sherman Act violation.

> *Staley*'s "investigate or verify" language coupled with the *Corn Products*'[11] focus on "personal knowledge of the transactions" have apparently suggested to a number of courts that, at least in certain circumstances, direct verification of discounts between competitors may be necessary to meet the burden of proof requirements of the §2(b) defense....
>
> A good-faith belief, rather than absolute certainty, that a price concession is being offered to meet an equally low price offered by a competitor is sufficient to satisfy the §2(b) defense. While casual reliance on uncorroborated reports of buyers or sales representatives without further investigation may not ... be sufficient to make the requisite showing of good faith, nothing in the language of §2(b) or the gloss on that language in *Staley* and *Corn Products* indicates that direct discussions of price between competitors are required....
>
> On the contrary, the §2(b) defense has been successfully invoked in the absence of interseller verification on numerous occasions.... And in Kroger Co. v. FTC, 438 F.2d 1372, 1376-1377 (CA6 1971), aff'g Beatrice Foods Co., 76 F.T.C. 719 (1969), the defense was recognized despite the fact that the price concession was ultimately found to have undercut that of the competition and thus technically to have fallen outside the "meet not beat" strictures of the defense. As these cases indicate, and as the Federal Trade Commission observed, it is the concept of good faith which lies at the core of the meeting-competition defense, and good faith "is a flexible and pragmatic, not technical or doctrinaire, concept.... Rigid rules and inflexible absolutes are especially inappropriate in dealing with the §2(b) defense; the facts and circumstances of the particular case, not abstract theories or remote conjectures, should govern its interpretation and application." ...
>
> The so-called problem of the untruthful buyer which concerned the Court of Appeals does not in our view call for a different approach to the §2(b) defense. The good-faith standard remains the benchmark against which the seller's conduct is to be evaluated, and we agree with the government and the FTC that this standard can be

11. Corn Prods. Ref. Co. v. FTC, 324 U.S. 726, 741 (1945).

satisfied by efforts falling short of interseller verification in most circumstances where the seller has only vague, generalized doubts about the reliability of its commercial adversary — the buyer. [Good faith would be indicated by] evidence that a seller had received reports of similar discounts from other customers ... or was threatened with a termination of purchases if the discount were not met.... Efforts to corroborate the reported discount by seeking documentary evidence or by appraising its reasonableness in terms of available market data would also be probative as would the seller's past experience with the particular buyer in question....

As an abstract proposition, resort to interseller verification as a means of checking the buyer's reliability seems a possible solution to the seller's plight, but ... interseller verification — if undertaken on an isolated and infrequent basis with no provision for reciprocity or cooperation — will not serve its putative function of corroborating the representations of unreliable buyers regarding the existence of competing offers. Price concessions by oligopolists generally yield competitive advantages only if secrecy can be maintained; when the terms of the concession are made publicly known, other competitors are likely to follow and any advantage to the initiator is lost in the process.... See also *Container.* Thus, if one seller offers a price concession for the purpose of winning over one of his competitor's customers, it is unlikely that the same seller will freely inform its competitor of the details of the concession so that it can be promptly matched and diffused. Instead, such a seller would appear to have at least as great an incentive to misrepresent the existence or size of the discount as would the buyer who received it. Thus verification, if undertaken on a one-shot basis for the sole purpose of complying with the §2(b) defense, does not hold out much promise as a means of shoring up buyers' representations.

The other variety of interseller verification is, like the conduct charged in the instant case, undertaken pursuant to an agreement, either tacit or express, providing for reciprocity among competitors in the exchange of price information. Such an agreement would make little economic sense, in our view, if its sole purpose were to guarantee all participants the opportunity to match the secret price concessions of other participants under §2(b). For in such circumstances, each seller would know that his price concession could not be kept from his competitors and no seller participating in the information-exchange arrangement would, therefore, have any incentive for deviating from the prevailing price level in the industry. See *Container.* Regardless of its putative purpose, the most likely consequence of any such agreement to exchange price information would be the stabilization of industry prices....

We are left, therefore, on the one hand, with doubts about both the need for and the efficacy of interseller verification as a means of facilitating compliance with §2(b), and, on the other, with recognition of the tendency for price discussions between competitors to contribute to the stability of oligopolistic prices and open the way for the growth of prohibited anticompetitive activity. To recognize even a limited . . . exception for interseller verification in such circumstances would be to remove from scrutiny under the Sherman Act conduct falling near its core with no assurance, and indeed with serious doubts, that competing antitrust policies would be served thereby. In *Automatic Canteen,* the Court suggested that as a general rule the Robinson-Patman Act should be construed so as to insure its coherence with "the broader antitrust policies that have been laid down by Congress"; that observation buttresses our conclusion that exchanges of price information — even when putatively for purposes of Robinson-Patman Act compliance — must remain subject to close scrutiny under the Sherman Act.

The Court concluded by observing:

That the §2(b) defense may not be available in every situation where a competing offer has in fact been made is not, in our view, a meaningful objection to our holding. The good-faith requirement of the §2(b) defense implicitly suggests a somewhat imperfect matching between competing offers actually made and those allowed to be met. Unless this requirement is to be abandoned, it seems clear that inadequate information will, in a limited number of cases, deny the defense to some who, if all the facts had been known, would have been entitled to invoke it. For reasons already discussed, interseller verification does not provide a satisfactory solution to this seemingly inevitable problem of inadequate information. Moreover, §2(b) affords only a defense to liability and not an affirmative right under the Act. While sellers are, of course, entitled to take advantage of the defense when they can satisfy its requirements, efforts to increase its availability at the expense of broader, affirmative antitrust policies must be rejected.

(c) *Great Atlantic & Pacific Tea Co. v. Federal Trade Commission,* 440 U.S. 69, 83-85 & n.17 (1979).[12] The buyer, A&P, asked Borden to bid a price at which it would supply private label milk.

[A&P,] despite its longstanding relationship with Borden, was dissatisfied with Borden's first bid and solicited offers from other dairies. . . . "Thereafter, . . . A&P received an offer from Bowman Dairy that was lower than Borden's [first] offer. [A&P then telephoned Borden] and stated, 'I have a bid in my pocket. You [Borden] people are so far out of line it is not even funny. You are not even in the ball park.' [Although Borden asked A&P for some details, A&P said it could not tell Borden] anything except that a $50,000 improvement in Borden's bid 'would not be a drop in the bucket.' Contrary to its

---

12. In a portion of the opinion reproduced in Ch. 6D, the Court held that a buyer inducing a discrimination was not liable under Robinson-Patman Act §2(f) unless the seller violated §2(a). There was no specific finding in the Commission or the Court of Appeals whether the seller Borden had a "meeting competition" defense in selling at a preferential price to A&P.

usual practice, A&P then offered Borden the opportunity to submit another bid." [From this, the Court said that] Borden could justifiably conclude that A&P's statements were reliable and that it was necessary to make another bid offering substantial concessions to avoid losing its account with the petitioner.

Borden was unable to ascertain the details of the Bowman bid. It requested more information about the bid from the petitioner, but this request was refused. It could not then attempt to verify the existence and terms of the competing offer from Bowman without risking Sherman Act liability. *Gypsum*. Faced with a substantial loss of business and unable to find out the precise details of the competing bid, Borden made another offer stating that it was doing so in order to meet competition. Under these circumstances, the conclusion is virtually inescapable that in making that offer Borden acted in a reasonable and good-faith effort to meet its competition, and therefore was entitled to a meeting-competition defense.

Staley and *Corn Products* were distinguished because, in the present case

> the source of the information was a person whose reliability was not questioned and who had personal knowledge of the competing bid. Moreover, Borden attempted to investigate by asking A&P for more information about the competing bid. Finally, Borden was faced with a credible threat of a termination of purchases by A&P if it did not make a second offer.

618. Seller Sigma supplies competing retailers at price 95. One of its most important customers is large retailer Rho, whose purchasing officials were recently observed in earnest conversation with the chief sales representative of Sigma's rival. Thereafter, Rho began to insist on lower prices, to speak of competition among suppliers, and to reduce the volume of purchases from Sigma, who is greatly troubled. Sigma is prepared to sell to Rho at 90 but is concerned about Clayton Act §2. Sigma consults you. What advice would you give in each of the following situations?

(a) Sigma says: "I am willing to gamble that, in the event of litigation under §2, evidence will turn up that my rival is now actually selling to Rho at 90 or less. On that assumption, will §2(b) protect me if I now reduce my price to Rho?"[13]

(b) Sigma says: "I asked Rho whether it was buying from my rival and at what price but Rho said that it was its common practice never

---

13. Double H Plastics v. Sonoco Prods. Co., 575 F. Supp. 389 (E.D. Pa. 1983), aff'd in part and rev'd in part on other grounds, 732 F.2d 351 (3d Cir.), cert. denied, 469 U.S. 900 (1984) (defense fails because no evidence that any employee of defendant attempted to verify).

to disclose to sellers the specific offers made by their competitors. Will §2(b) protect me if I reduce my price to Rho?"

(c) Sigma says: "Rho's buyer told my sales representative that my rival was selling to them at price 90. I cross-examined my representative very carefully and sent another to Rho's purchasing chief in order to verify and confirm the first report. (1) Will §2(b) protect me if I reduce my price to Rho? (2) Could I improve my legal position by asking my rival whether it gives Rho a special discount? (3) What further steps should I take to assure §2(b) protection?"

(d) Rho seeks preferential prices from all of its suppliers. It approaches those supplying each item it sells and asks their best price. It also asks questions along the following lines: "You have just indicated that 95 per case is your best price. But what if I told you that Cutter will sell to me at 90? Will you match that price?" Through such exchanges, Rho receives some vaguely affirmative responses, at which point it calls back a current supplier, Sigma, who has responded favorably to the prior questioning, and says: "Two of your rivals have indicated a willingness to sell to me at 90. Will you now meet their price, or must I send all my orders elsewhere?" Sigma presses for specifics, but Rho will not budge, beyond promising that there are in fact other offers, with various unspecified contingencies, at a price of 90. May Sigma sell to Rho at 90? If so, is there anything left of the secondary-line prohibition?[14]

(e) Sigma says: "Two months ago, I wrote the Federal Trade Commission and stated the belief that my rival is selling to Rho at price 90 while charging competing buyers 95. I told the Commission I had been selling to Rho for years and that my costs in dealing with Rho were certainly not 5 points below my cost of serving other buyers. I urged the Commission to investigate but can't wait any longer for them to move against my rival. I will sell to Rho at 90. While I am not absolutely certain, assume the clear reasonableness of my conclusion that it is selling to Rho at 90. Will §2(b) protect me?"[15]

619. Good faith and pricing systems. (a) *Federal Trade Commission v. A.E. Staley Manufacturing Co.*, 324 U.S. 746, 753-754, 757 (1945). *Staley* involved a seller that asserted the meeting competition defense to justify its pricing in accordance with a basing point pricing scheme practiced by the rest of the industry. Because

14. Consider Rho's liability in these circumstances after examining Ch. 6D.

15. The White House Task Report on Antitrust Policy (1968) recommended amending §2(b) to provide that "the meeting competition defense shall be allowed even though the price met is unlawful except in a suit seeking prospective relief against substantially all the competitors practicing the discrimination." Could you properly reach the same result under the existing statute?

Staley's plant was not located at the Chicago basing point, it could not claim the cost justification defense. The Supreme Court rejected Staley's claim.

But §2(b) does not concern itself with pricing systems or even with all the seller's discriminatory prices to buyers. It speaks only of the seller's lower price and of that only to the extent that it is made "in good faith to meet an equally low price of a competitor." The Act thus places emphasis on individual competitive situations, rather than upon a general system of competition. Respondents are here seeking to justify delivered prices which discriminate in favor of buyers in Chicago and at points nearer, freightwise, to Chicago than to Decatur, by a pricing system involving phantom freight and freight absorption. We think the conclusion is inadmissible, in view of the clear Congressional purpose not to sanction by §2(b) the excuse that the person charged with a violation of the law was merely adopting a similarly unlawful practice of another.... Even though respondents, at many delivery points, enjoyed freight advantages over their competitors, they did not avail of the opportunity to charge lower delivered prices. Instead they maintained their own prices at the level of their competitors' high prices, based upon the competitors' higher costs of delivery, by including phantom freight in their own delivered prices.... We cannot say that a seller acts in good faith when it chooses to adopt such a clearly discriminatory pricing system, at least where it has never attempted to set up a non-discriminatory system, giving to purchasers, who have the natural advantage of proximity to its plant, the price advantages which they are entitled to expect over purchasers at a distance.

(b) *Falls City Industries v. Vanco Beverage*, 460 U.S. 428, 434-435, 441, 443-444, 446, 449-451 (1983). The defendant brewer sold beer to wholesalers in Indiana and Kentucky. It raised prices in Indiana by more than it raised prices in Kentucky, where the prices of rival brewers allegedly prevented it from equalizing Kentucky-Indiana prices. The defendant was thus charging more to the plaintiff wholesaler in Evansville, Indiana, than it was charging its wholesalers in Henderson, Kentucky. These two cities, separated by a 10-mile four-lane highway, are regarded as a single metropolitan area. The retailers purchasing from plaintiff, an Indiana wholesaler, therefore paid more and charged more than the Kentucky retailers, lost consumer business to Kentucky retailers, and therefore purchased less from the plaintiff wholesaler.[16]

The defendant resisted the plaintiff's claim of unlawful price discrimination by asserting that its lower Kentucky price was within the §2(b) immunity for the good faith meeting of competition. The

16. State law required the defendant to sell to all Indiana wholesalers at a single price and prevented Indiana retailers from buying from Kentucky wholesalers.

lower court rejected this defense as inapplicable because the discrimination resulted not from lowering the Kentucky price but from raising the Indiana price and because the lower Kentucky price was not a response to an "individual situation" but a general pricing system. The Supreme Court unanimously reversed.

The Court briefly stated the liability rule. "In keeping with the Robinson-Patman Act's prophylactic purpose," a showing of a "reasonable possibility that a price difference may harm competition" creates a prima facie case that is sufficient, unless rebutted by an affirmative defense, "to support injunctive relief and to authorize further inquiry" into whether plaintiff has been damaged. Under *Morton Salt*, "injury to competition is established prima facie by proof of a substantial price discrimination between competing purchasers over time."

On the §2(b) defense, the Court seemed to confine *Staley* to its facts: "Staley had not priced in response to competitors' discrete pricing decisions, but from the outset had followed an industrywide [basing point pricing] practice of setting its prices according to a single, arbitrary scheme that by its nature *precluded* independent pricing in response to normal competitive forces." Here, by contrast, the sustained price discrimination between Evansville and Henderson "might well have evolved in the two States without collusion, notwithstanding the existence of a common retail market along the border."

The defense is not limited to situations in which a price "difference resulted from subtraction rather than addition." Nor does §2(b) "distinguish between one who meets a competitor's lower price to retain an old customer and one who meets a competitor's lower price in an attempt to gain new customers." Finally, in *Staley*,

> as in each of the later cases in which this Court has contrasted "general systems of competition" with "individual competitive situations" ... the seller's lower price was quoted not "*because* of lower prices by a competitor," but "*because* of a preconceived pricing scale which [was] operative regardless of variations in competitors' prices." ... In those cases, the contested lower prices were not truly "*responsive* to rivals' competitive prices," ... and therefore were not genuinely made to meet competitors' lower prices. Territorial pricing, however, can be a perfectly reasonable method — sometimes the most reasonable method — of responding to rivals' low prices. We choose not to read into §2(b) a restriction that would deny the meeting-competition defense to one whose area wide price is a well tailored response to competitors' low prices.

The case was remanded on the question whether "a reasonable and prudent businessman would believe that the lower price he charged was generally available from his competitors throughout the territory and throughout the period in which he made the lower price available."

(c) If sellers are not permitted to match competitors' prices in situations like those in *Staley* or *Falls City*, what (legal) alternatives would be available? What would be their effect on competition?

620. Return to the situation of Sigma and Rho from ¶618 and advise as to the legality of Sigma's proposed actions.

(a) Sigma says: "I have a copy of my rival's published price list. It shows that it gives a 5-point discount below its regular price of 95 on all sales to a buyer purchasing more than 20,000 units within a calendar year. Rho's annual purchases exceed that volume. I have just revised my price list to incorporate the same provision and have every hope of regaining Rho's business. Will §2(b) protect me?"

(b) Sigma says: "Assuming that §2(b) permits me to sell to Rho at 90 may I continue selling to it at that price next month? Next year?"

621. What is the function of the meeting competition defense? What purpose is served by the good faith requirement? Does the defense equally serve the Robinson-Patman Act's purposes with respect to primary- and secondary-line injury?

6D. SUPPLEMENTARY PROVISIONS

Buyer Liability

622. Congressional concern with buyers. The Robinson-Patman amendment was mainly concerned with the impact of price discrimination upon less-favored buyers. The principal evil perceived by the 1936 Congress was the grant of "unfair" preferences to large buyers to the detriment of their smaller competitors. And although §2 appears to be addressed mainly to sellers, it was well understood that the discriminating seller was often the "innocent victim" of the buyer's power. In light of this understanding, it is somewhat surprising that only as an afterthought[1] was §2(f) added to the legislation to make it unlawful for a buyer "knowingly to induce or receive a discrimination in price which is prohibited by this section." Buyer

---

1. See ABA Antitrust Section, The Robinson-Patman Act, Monograph No. 4, Volume II, at 70-71 (1983).

liability with respect to an unlawful "discrimination in price" is thus an approximate corollary to §2(a).[2]

Section 2(f) has not been the focus of enforcement activities over the Act's history,[3] perhaps because of the difficulties of proving a violation, as described below. We begin by summarizing *Automatic Canteen* and continue with the Supreme Court's more recent statement in *A&P*, both of which focus on the connection between seller liability under §2(a) and buyer liability under §2(f).

623. *Automatic Canteen Co. of America v. Federal Trade Commission*, 346 U.S. 61, 62, 66-67, 73-74, 80 (1953). Canteen, a large buyer of candy and confectionery products for resale through vending machines, "received, and in some instances solicited, prices it knew were as much as 33% lower than prices quoted other purchasers, but the Commission [had] not attempted to show that the price differentials exceeded any cost savings that sellers may have enjoyed in sales to petitioner." The dispute centered on how much the Commission had to prove to make out a prima facie case under §2(f). "The Commission made no finding negativing the existence of cost savings or stating that whatever cost savings there were did not at least equal price differentials petitioner may have received. It did not make any findings as to petitioner's knowledge of actual cost savings. . . ." The Commission offered to prove only that Canteen never inquired as to whether the price differentials it knowingly received were in excess of cost savings. The Commission's argument emphasized that §2(b) explicitly gave defendants (sellers) the burden of proof as to defenses; hence, it had made out a prima facie case of a §2(a) violation *by sellers*, and thereby a prima facie case against *buyers*, assuming it could make the additional showing that the buyers had knowledge of the facts constituting the §2(a) violation by sellers.

The Court rejected this approach, holding that the §2(f) requirement that the buyer "knowingly" receive the illegal discrimination demanded more proof. Placing the burden of cost justification on sellers charged under §2(a) could be justified by their access to the relevant information, whereas buyers in the ordinary course of business could not be expected to have any such access. Section 2(f) predicates the buyer's liability upon a seller's violation, which must be proved more expressly. Although the section was designed to

2. Buyer liability with respect to other Robinson-Patman Act prohibitions is discussed in ¶625e and ¶626f.

3. See, e.g., ABA Monograph, note 1, at 71 n.50 (only 2.1 percent of FTC Robinson-Patman Act orders between 1936 and 1969, and only two complaints between 1970 and June 1977).

enable sellers to resist unlawful pressures by informing the buyer that a proposed discount was unlawful, accepting the Commission's light burden would put "the buyer at his peril whenever he engages in price bargaining. Such a reading must be rejected in view of the effect it might have on that sturdy bargaining between buyer and seller for which scope was presumably left in the areas of our economy not otherwise regulated."

The Commission might have met its burden of proof in a number of ways. For example,

> a buyer who knows that he buys in the same quantities as his competitor and is serviced by the seller in the same manner or with the same amount of exertion as the other buyer can fairly be charged with notice that a substantial price differential cannot be justified. . . . If the methods or quantities differ, the Commission must only show that such differences could not give rise to sufficient savings in the cost of manufacture, sale or delivery to justify the price differential, and that the buyer, knowing these were the only differences, should have known that they could not give rise to sufficient cost savings.[4]

Automatic Canteen clearly settled that §2(a) defenses potentially available to sellers served as an obstacle to §2(f) enforcement against buyers. Yet, after some time, the question arose whether the possible availability to the seller of the meeting competition defense excused all buyers. This issue was resolved, although not entirely, in *A&P*.

GREAT ATLANTIC & PACIFIC TEA COMPANY v. FEDERAL TRADE COMMISSION
440 U.S. 69 (1979)

Justice STEWART. . . . A&P asked Borden, its longtime supplier, to submit an offer to supply under private label certain of A&P's milk and other dairy product requirements. After prolonged negotia-

---

4. In American Motors Specialties Co. v. FTC, 278 F.2d 225, 228 (2d Cir.), cert. denied, 364 U.S. 884 (1960), some buyers formed buying cooperatives to take advantage of quantity discounts offered by sellers — these discounts were made available to the cooperatives despite the fact that the cooperative members received their shipments directly from the sellers. The court affirmed the Commission's finding of a §2(f) violation.

> Petitioners of course knew that they, as individual firms, were receiving goods in the same quantities and were served by sellers in the same manner as their competitors, and hence organized themselves into a buying group in order to obtain lower prices than their unorganized competitors. Hence, by the very fact of having combined into a group and having obtained thereby a favorable price differential, they each, under *Automatic Canteen*, were charged with notice that this price differential they each enjoyed could not be justified.

tions, Borden offered to grant A&P a discount for switching to private-label milk provided A&P would accept limited delivery service. . . . A&P, however, was not satisfied with this offer and solicited offers from other dairies. A competitor of Borden, Bowman Dairy, then submitted an offer which was lower than Borden's.

At this point, A&P's Chicago buyer contacted Borden's chain store sales manager and stated, "I have a bid in my pocket. You [Borden] people are so far out of line it is not even funny. You are not even in the ball park." When the Borden representative asked for more details, he was told nothing except that a $50,000 improvement in Borden's bid "would not be a drop in the bucket." . . . Borden decided to submit a new bid which doubled the estimated annual savings to A&P, from $410,000 to $820,000. In presenting its offer, Borden emphasized to A&P that it needed to keep A&P's business and was making the new offer in order to meet Bowman's bid. A&P then accepted Borden's bid after concluding that it was substantially better than Bowman's. . . .

I . . .

[T]he Court of Appeals for the Second Circuit . . . held that . . . as a matter of law A&P could not successfully assert a meeting competition defense because it, unlike Borden, had known that Borden's offer was better than Bowman's.

II . . .

Liability under §2(f) . . . is limited to situations where the price discrimination is one "which is prohibited by this section." While the phrase "this section" refers to the entire §2 of the Act, only subsections (a) and (b) dealing with seller liability involve discriminations in price. Under the plain meaning of §2(f), therefore, a buyer cannot be liable if a prima facie case could not be established against a seller or if the seller has an affirmative defense. In either situation, there is no price discrimination "prohibited by this section." The legislative history of §2(f) fully confirms the conclusion that buyer liability under §2(f) is dependent on seller liability under §2(a). . . .

III

The petitioner, relying on this plain meaning of §2(f) and the teaching of the *Automatic Canteen* case, argues that it cannot be liable under §2(f) if Borden had a valid meeting competition defense. The respondent, on the other hand, argues that the petitioner may be liable even assuming that Borden had such a defense.

The meeting-competition defense, the respondent contends, must in these circumstances be judged from the point of view of the buyer. Since A&P knew for a fact that the final Borden bid beat the Bowman bid, it was not entitled to assert the meeting competition defense even though Borden may have honestly believed that it was simply meeting competition. Recognition of a meeting-competition defense for the buyer in this situation, the respondent argues, would be contrary to the basic purpose of the Robinson-Patman Act to curtail abuses by large buyers.

A

The short answer to these contentions of the respondent is that Congress did not provide in §2(f) that a buyer can be liable even if the seller has a valid defense. The clear language of §2(f) states that a buyer can be liable only if he receives a price discrimination "prohibited by this section." If a seller has a valid meeting competition defense, there is simply no prohibited price discrimination. . . .

B

In the *Automatic Canteen* case, the Court warned against interpretations of the Robinson-Patman Act which "extend beyond the prohibitions of the Act and, in so doing, help give rise to a price uniformity and rigidity in open conflict with the purposes of other antitrust legislation." Imposition of §2(f) liability on the petitioner in this case would lead to just such price uniformity and rigidity.

In a competitive market, uncertainty among sellers will cause them to compete for business by offering buyers lower prices. Because of the evils of collusive action, the Court has held that the exchange of price information by competitors violates the Sherman Act. *Container.* Under the view advanced by the respondent, however, a buyer, to avoid liability, must either refuse a seller's bid or at least inform him that his bid had beaten competition. Such a duty of affirmative disclosure would almost inevitably frustrate competitive bidding and, by reducing uncertainty, lead to price matching and anticompetitive cooperation among sellers.[14]

Ironically, the Commission itself, in dismissing the charge under §5 of the Federal Trade Commission Act in this case, recognized the dangers inherent in a duty of affirmative disclosure:

> The imposition of a duty of affirmative disclosure, applicable to a
> buyer whenever a seller states that his offer is intended to meet

14. A duty of affirmative disclosure might also be difficult to enforce. In cases where a seller offers differing quantities or a different quality product, or offers to serve the buyer in a different manner, it might be difficult for the buyer to determine when disclosure is required.

competition, is contrary to normal business practice and, we think, contrary to the public interest. . . .
We fear a scenario where the seller automatically attaches a meeting competition caveat to every bid. The buyer would then state whether such bid meets, beats, or loses to another bid. The seller would submit a second, a third, and perhaps a fourth bid until finally he is able to ascertain his competitor's bid.

The effect of the finding that the same conduct of the petitioner violated §2(f), however, is to impose the same duty of affirmative disclosure which the Commission condemned as anticompetitive, "contrary to the public interest," and "contrary to normal business practice," in dismissing the charge under §5 of the Federal Trade Commission Act. Neither the Commission nor the Court of Appeals offered any explanation for this apparent anomaly.

As in the *Automatic Canteen* case, we decline to adopt a construction of §2(f) that is contrary to its plain meaning and would lead to anticompetitive results. Accordingly, we hold that a buyer who has done no more than accept the lower of two prices competitively offered does not violate §2(f) provided the seller has a meeting competition defense.[15] . . .[5]

---

15. In Kroger Co. v. FTC, 438 F.2d 1372, the Court of Appeals for the Sixth Circuit held that a buyer who induced price concessions by a seller by making deliberate misrepresentations could be liable under §2(f) even if the seller has a meeting competition defense.

This case does not involve a "lying buyer" situation. The complaint issued by the FTC alleged that "A&P accepted the said offer of Borden with knowledge that Borden had granted a substantially lower price than that offered by the only other competitive bidder without notifying Borden of this fact." The complaint did not allege that Borden's second bid was induced by any misrepresentation. The Court of Appeals recognized that the *Kroger* case involved a "lying buyer," but stated that there was no meaningful distinction between the situation where "the buyer lies or merely keeps quiet about the nature of the competing bid."

Despite this background, the respondent argues that A&P did engage in misrepresentations and therefore can be found liable as a "lying buyer" under the rationale of the *Kroger* case. The misrepresentation relied upon by the respondent is a statement allegedly made by a representative of A&P to Borden after Borden made its second bid which would have resulted in annual savings to A&P of $820,000. The A&P representative allegedly told Borden to "sharpen your pencil a little bit because you are not quite there." But the Commission itself referred to this comment only to note its irrelevance, and neither the Commission nor the Court of Appeals mentioned it in considering the §2(f) charge against A&P. This is quite understandable, since the comment was allegedly made *after* Borden made its second bid and therefore cannot be said to have induced the bid as in the *Kroger* case.

Because A&P was not a "lying buyer," we need not decide whether such a buyer could be liable under §2(f) even if the seller has a meeting competition defense.

5. The Court then held, in the portion of the opinion abstracted in ¶617c, that Borden satisfied the meeting competition defense and therefore that A&P had not violated the Act.

[Justice Marshall dissented. He believed that buyer and seller liability are largely independent and that each has different defenses to prima facie unlawful price discriminations. In his view, once a prima facie violation by the seller was induced by the buyer, the buyer's good faith belief (or its absence) about the seller's defenses determined whether §2(f) was violated.]

624. Buyer Beta buys from seller Sigma at price 95, which Beta knows to be discriminatory. Beta also knows that Sigma cannot justify the discrimination under the cost-saving proviso to §2(a). These facts are shown in a §2(f) proceeding against Beta.

(a) Suppose that Beta introduces evidence that Sigma began selling at 95 only after Beta reported the true fact that one of Sigma's rivals offered to sell to Beta at 95. Will Beta prevail in the §2(f) proceedings? What result if Beta had lied? Can the suggestion in the Court's footnote 15 that a different result is possible for the "lying buyer" be reconciled with the rest of its opinion?

(b) Suppose that Sigma and its rivals distribute the same product in about the same way, selling to about the same range of customers. Beta approached several of them and informed each that it was talking to the others. One of the sellers offered to sell to Beta at 95. It was only after Sigma learned of this that it began selling to Beta at 95. Will Beta prevail in the §2(f) proceedings?

(c) State more explicitly the concern the *Automatic Canteen* Court had in mind when it referred to "putting the buyer at his peril," with a resulting adverse effect on "sturdy bargaining between buyer and seller." How would the Commission's approach have threatened such bargaining? How does this threat differ from that imposed by the burden of proving the cost justification defense now placed on sellers?

(d) How does the Court's opinion in *Container* bear on the issues discussed in ¶¶a-c?

Brokerage

ROBINSON-PATMAN ACT §2(c)

It shall be unlawful for any person engaged in commerce, in the course of such commerce, to pay or grant, or to receive or accept, anything of value as a commission, brokerage, or other compensation, or any allowance or discount in lieu thereof, except for services rendered in connection with the sale or purchase of goods, wares, or merchandise, either to the other party to such transaction or to an agent, representative, or other intermediary therein where such intermediary is acting in fact for or in behalf, or is subject to the direct or indirect control, of any party to such transaction other than the person by whom such compensation is so granted or paid.

625.   The brokerage prohibition. (a) *Statutory purpose as stated by the Supreme Court.*[6]

The Robinson-Patman Act was enacted in 1936 to curb and prohibit all devices by which large buyers gained discriminatory preferences over smaller ones by virtue of their greater purchasing power. A lengthy investigation revealed that large chain buyers were obtaining competitive advantages in several ways other than direct price concessions and were thus avoiding the impact of the Clayton Act. One of the favorite means of obtaining an indirect price concession was by setting up "dummy" brokers who were employed by the buyer and who, in many cases, rendered no services. The large buyers demanded that the seller pay "brokerage" to these fictitious brokers who then turned it over to their employer. This practice was one of the chief targets of §2(c) of the Act. But it was not the only means by which the brokerage function was abused and Congress in its wisdom phrased §2(c) broadly, not only to cover the other methods then in existence but all other means by which brokerage could be used to effect price discrimination.

Obviously, if sellers forbidden from charging discriminatory prices were allowed to charge buyers the same price while providing "brokerage" or other allowances as rebates, the prohibition of §2(a) could be entirely circumvented. But §2(c) does more than merely catch such indirect or disguised price discrimination. It operates as an independent prohibition that in many respects is more strict than the prohibitions in §2(a). It is to these differences we now turn.

(b) *Requirements for violation and availability of defenses.* One should first note that §2(c) has no "effects" clause, either like the broad effects clause of §2(a) or the narrower provisions of other sections of the Clayton Act. The payment or receipt of brokerage, except for services rendered, is itself a violation. Nor is discrimination explicitly required, so that §2(c) appears to be violated even when the same compensation is offered to all buyers, although more recent decisions have increasingly brought this into question.[7] Moreover, it has gener-

---

6. FTC v. Henry Broch & Co., 363 U.S. 166, 168-169 (1960).

7. *Broch*, discussed in ¶¶c-d, emphasized the Robinson-Patman Act's focus on preventing "unfair preferences" wherein "the buyer [receives] a discriminatory price," suggesting that nondiscriminatory brokerage might not constitute a violation. Id. at 174. Although note 10 suggests that prohibiting equally available compensation might be justified by the statute's policy of forcing pricing into the open, some subsequent cases have required discrimination. Thomasville Chair Co. v.

ally been held that the defenses of meeting competition and cost justification are unavailable.[8] Furthermore, brokers themselves are covered by §2(c)'s "any person" language. Thus, as suggested by the *Broch* case in ¶d, brokers may not reduce their commissions to selected buyers in order to compete for sales; nor may they induce sellers to offer lower prices to buyers using their brokerage firm in return for charging the seller reduced commissions. That no adverse effects of the allowance need be shown and defenses are not permitted makes the potential deterrence greater and has centered controversy on the "except for services rendered" proviso of §2(c).

(c) *When brokerage is "for services rendered."* The statute permits payments "for services rendered." One reading of this language makes it analogous to the cost justification defense. Thus, if a seller ordinarily paid its brokers $5 per unit sold, a similar payment (or a price discount in lieu thereof) would be permitted to those buying directly in cases where the buyer performed the services otherwise carried out by the seller's brokers. This interpretation, however, was rejected in one case on the ground that the statute requires that the services be rendered "to the other party ... or to [its] agent";[9] the services provided by the buyer (or its agent or broker) were deemed provided to itself rather than to the seller, even though the seller benefited by avoiding service it otherwise would have had to provide. Such a reading renders the proviso for services inapplicable except where the payments are to intermediaries working directly on behalf of the seller. This interpretation, in combination with the minimal requirements noted in ¶b, makes the statute a broad, per se prohibition.

If buyers had been allowed to receive the brokerage amount themselves, they would perform the broker's functions internally whenever they could do so for less. Forbidding the payments protects independent brokers from such competition, although at some social cost and, as we shall see, without necessarily protecting smaller buyers. The justification commonly offered for this harsh result is that the intense prohibition forces differential pricing into the open.[10] For example, the seller might simply offer lower prices to those who do not need the services of the seller's brokers. Yet

---

FTC, 306 F.2d 541, 545 (5th Cir. 1962), while others have not. Gibson, 95 F.T.C. 553, 739-741 (1980), aff'd, 682 F.2d 554 (5th Cir. 1982), cert. denied, 460 U.S. 1068 (1983).

8. *Broch*, note 6, at 170-171 & n.8.

9. See, e.g., Southgate Brokerage Co. v. FTC, 150 F.2d 607 (4th Cir.), cert. denied, 326 U.S. 774 (1945).

10. For example, ¶b noted that §2(c) may be violated when identical compensation is offered to all buyers. The rationale would be that such indirect payments are difficult to observe and may not always remain equal. Moreover, the seller always has the lawful option of reducing prices.

even this "open" price discrimination has sometimes been held illegal under §2(c), without regard to cost justification, as a payment "in lieu of brokerage," as described in ¶d.

Strictly limiting brokerage allowances available to buyers and their agents does not necessarily limit the advantage of large, powerful buyers. Such buyers may purchase the entire output of some suppliers without regard to any brokerage; the price would fully reflect the buyer's bargaining advantage; nor would there be any other buyer at a higher price from that seller. Similarly, sellers may limit their sales to large buyers, who can all be treated equally as to price, without any brokerage, to the same effect. Unfortunately, smaller buyers — even buying jointly as cooperatives — may be too small to take such routes, and therefore remain limited by §2(c), which prevents them from receiving rebates reflecting the costs they save sellers. More generally, buyers have little incentive to engage in activity that reduces purchasing-related cost since the seller must charge all its customers for the costs it incurs in serving some.

The current status of the "services rendered" proviso is somewhat uncertain. *Broch*,[11] the only Supreme Court decision interpreting §2(c), indicated that the case involved

> no evidence that the buyer rendered any services to the seller or to the respondent nor that anything in its method of dealing justified its getting a discriminatory price by means of a reduced brokerage charge. We would have quite a different case if there were such evidence and we need not explore the applicability of §2(c) to such circumstances.

The Court's initial phrasing as whether "the buyer rendered any services *to the seller*" combined with its citation without disapproval of earlier cases interpreting that language narrowly suggests that *Broch* does not alter the law in this respect, although the remainder of the quoted language might be seen as receptive to somewhat broader justifications. Subsequent cases have been more willing to approve rebates where services provided by buyers (or their agents) provide cost savings to the seller in an equivalent amount.[12]

11. Note 6, at 173.
12. *Thomasville Chair*, note 7, at 545: Although §2(c) is recognized to be independent of §2(a) in the *Broch* decision,

> as we read it, the Court's opinion says that a reduction in price, giving effect to reduced commissions paid by the seller, are violations of §2(c) only if such reduction in price is "discriminatory." We read that to mean "without justification based on actual bona fide differences in the costs of sales resulting from the differing methods or quantities in which such commodities are sold or delivered."

The Commission subsequently dismissed the complaint, stating that it understood the court to require proof of "a causal relationship between the reduced brokerage and the reduced sales price," and made clear that it did not acquiesce in the

(d) *Identifying "a commission, brokerage, or other compensation, or any allowance or discount in lieu thereof."* A discriminatorily lower price under §2(a) and §2(b) or a promotional allowance under §2(d) might be seen as a rebate, "discount," or "other compensation" and thus fall within §2(c), but so broad a reading would make those other sections surplusage. Payments or discounts not styled "commission" or "brokerage" are covered by §2(c) only if "in lieu" of brokerage. *Broch* involved a buyer who insisted on a lower price as a condition to placing a large order. The seller indicated to its broker that the lower price would be offered, and the sale would thus proceed, if the broker would be willing to absorb a portion of the lower price by accepting less than its usual commission. The Court held that this discount was in lieu of brokerage and therefore illegal. The transaction went to the core of the statute, as the discount was granted "to meet the demands of a favored buyer."[13] "We conclude that the statute clearly applies to payments or allowances by a seller's broker to the buyer, whether made directly to the buyer, or indirectly, through the seller."[14] The problem, as the Court viewed it, was that "the reduction in brokerage was made to obtain this particular order" rather than the broker simply lowering its commission with respect to sales to all buyers.[15] Thus, where a price differential was financed in part by concessions from the seller's broker, §2(c) was held to apply.[16] One commentator has

---

court's opinion as such. 63 F.T.C. 1048, 1049 (1963). See also Central Retailer-Owned Grocers v. FTC, 319 F.2d 410, 412-415 (7th Cir. 1963) (discount apparently based on savings in sales expense viewed as functional, rather than in lieu of brokerage); Allen Pen Co. v. Springfield Photo Mount Co., 653 F.2d 17, 25 (1st Cir. 1981) (price differences based on use of broker insufficient; "must show that the sales agent . . . was interposed as a device or sham").

13. 363 U.S. at 170.

14. Id. at 175.

15. Id. at 176.

16. Earlier in the opinion, the Court stated that

[b]efore the Act was passed the large buyers, who maintained their own elaborate purchasing departments and therefore did not need the services of a seller's broker because they bought their merchandise directly from the seller, demanded and received allowances reflecting these savings in the cost of distribution. In many cases they required that "brokerage" be paid to their own purchasing agents. After the Act was passed they discarded the facade of "brokerage" and merely received a price reduction equivalent to the seller's ordinary brokerage expenses in sales to other customers. When haled before the Commission, they protested that the transaction was not covered by §2(c) but, since it was a price reduction, was governed by §2(a). They also argued that because no brokerage services were needed or used in sales to them, they were entitled to a price differential reflecting this cost saving. Congress had anticipated such a contention by the "in lieu thereof" provision. Accordingly, the Commission and the courts early rejected the contention that such a price reduction was lawful because the buyer's purchasing organization had saved the seller the amount of his ordinary brokerage expense. [Id. at 171-172.]

described this result as "totally perverse once it is accepted that the purpose of that statute is to force price discriminations disguised as brokerage payments into the open. There was no element of concealment in the *Broch* case."[17]

Related problems arise in connection with functional discounts. As discussed in Chapter 6B, sellers may offer lower prices to wholesalers than to retailers without violating §2(a), because the effects requirement would not generally be satisfied. The applicability of §2(c) raises additional questions. Consider a seller that distributes to wholesalers at $95 per unit, who in turn resell to retailers at $100. If the seller instead employed brokers, at a commission of $5 per unit, to market its goods to retailers at a price of $100, much the same would be accomplished. The wholesaling scheme could be viewed as involving a $5 "discount in lieu" of brokerage. Since, as described in ¶c, the wholesalers' services may not be viewed as rendered to the seller, the proviso would be inapplicable and liability would result. Nonetheless, traditional functional discounts have been permitted.[18] Discounts to wholesalers are not viewed as in lieu of brokerage because wholesalers purchase the goods and establish their own resale prices, assuming the risks involved.[19]

Students can judge for themselves the implications of the Supreme Court's decision in *Broch*. The Commission and the courts are working out those implications. Some cases resist change while others deny that saved brokerage has anything to do with discounts granted to those buyers purchasing without the aid of brokers used by other buyers. Perhaps there is a movement toward the relative clarity of this formulation:

> [T]he purpose of attaching per se illegality to the §2(c), (d), and (e) prohibitions was precisely to force unearned commissions out in the open. False brokerage qua brokerage is absolutely forbidden. False brokerage qua "a naked quotation in price" does not fall into the "masquerade" category; rather it falls into the trap deliberately set for it by the law. Discriminatory concessions which cannot disguise themselves as brokerage or "allowances" are thus forced to

17. R. Posner, The Robinson-Patman Act 45 (1976).

18. See, e.g., Empire Rayon Yarn Co. v. American Viscose Corp., 364 F.2d 491, 493 (2d Cir. 1966), cert. denied, 385 U.S. 1002 (1967); *Gibson*, note 7, at 743 ("Arguably, the 'services rendered' exception is broad enough to encompass any justification which might be offered under the functional discount rubric. . . .").

19. Of course, this distinction generates some disputes concerning what constitutes a true wholesaler. In addition, some courts have responded to the situation where a firm is engaged in wholesaling and retailing by permitting a discount on that portion of its purchases that are sold to other retailers, but not on that portion it sells directly.

show their true character, and to be measured by the sections of the law dealing with discrimination.[20]

(e) *Buyer liability.* Section 2(c) explicitly indicates that the prohibition is applicable to any person who pays or receives brokerage. In *Broch*, the Court suggested that the buyer's not being "aware that its favored price was based on a discriminatory reduction in respondent's brokerage commission is immaterial" to the broker's liability, although "[t]he buyer's intent might be relevant were he charged with receiving an allowance in violation of §2(c)."[21]

Discriminatory Allowances or Services

ROBINSON-PATMAN ACT §2(d) AND §2(e)

(d) It shall be unlawful for any person engaged in commerce to pay or contract for the payment of anything of value to or for the benefit of a customer of such person in the course of such commerce as compensation or in consideration for any services or facilities furnished by or through such customer in connection with the processing, handling, sale, or offering for sale of any products or commodities manufactured, sold, or offered for sale by such person, unless such payment or consideration is available on proportionally equal terms to all other customers competing in the distribution of such products or commodities.

(e) It shall be unlawful for any person to discriminate in favor of one purchaser against another purchaser or purchasers of a commodity bought for resale, with or without processing, by contracting to furnish or furnishing, or by contributing to the furnishing of, any services or facilities connected with the processing, handling, sale, or offering for sale of such commodity so purchased upon terms not accorded to all purchasers on proportionally equal terms.

626. The prohibition on discriminatory allowances or services.
(a) *The statutory concern.* A seller forbidden by §2(a) from reducing

---

20. H.R. Rep. No. 2966, 84th Cong., 2d Sess. 97-98 (1956). In Lupia v. Stella D'Oro Biscuit Co., 586 F.2d 1163, 1170 (7th Cir. 1978), cert. denied, 440 U.S. 982 (1979), the court refused to characterize an indirect price discrimination as unlawful brokerage because "[t]he discount is straightforward and not disguised in any manner. Thus a per se rule, eliminating examination of competitive effects, used in brokerage cases ... where anticompetitive practices and effects are hard to identify, is neither necessary nor proper here." See K. Bernard, Handling Modern Buyers: A New Look at Payment for Services Under the Robinson-Patman Act, 44 Albany L. Rev. 89 (1979).

21. 363 U.S. at 174.

its price to a favored buyer might instead offer a payment toward that buyer's advertising or provide the buyer's advertising in an amount equivalent to the discount it would otherwise have given. Sections 2(d) and 2(e) control such discriminatory allowances or services in order to prevent circumvention of the rules limiting price discrimination. Although the two sections do not employ parallel language, the differences are largely attributed to sloppy drafting, and courts have generally interpreted them in a parallel fashion.[22]

(b) *Requirements for violation and availability of defenses.* No injury to competition need be shown, although both sections are understood to require a discrimination among competing customers. The cost justification defense is not available, although a defense for good faith meeting of competition is.[23] As a result, an allowance or provision of services, when provided on a discriminatory basis to competing sellers, will be illegal, even if direct price discrimination in such circumstances would not. As with §2(c), one of the primary rationalizations for the relative strictness of these supplementary prohibitions is to force preferences into the form of openly discriminatory prices.

(c) *When is an allowance or service "available on proportionally equal terms"?*[24] Although only §2(e) explicitly mentions discrimination, both sections require it[25] because neither is offended unless the seller treats buyers disproportionally in reasonably contemporaneous transactions involving goods of like grade and quality.[26]

Initially, it is required that the allowance or service be effectively "available." This has been interpreted to require appropriate notice and functional availability. The notice requirement has been interpreted somewhat strictly. Although a plan concealed from

22. See, e.g., notes 23, 24.

23. The Supreme Court addressed defenses in FTC v. Simplicity Pattern Co., 360 U.S. 55 (1959). Because the cost justification proviso is part of §2(a), which only addresses price discrimination, it was deemed inapplicable to "[s]ubsections (c), (d), and (e) ... [which] unqualifiedly make unlawful certain business practices other than price discriminations." Id. at 65. Congress had, however, provided some escape in the §2(b) proviso, which refers to "services or facilities" in addition to price. In Exquisite Form Brassiere v. FTC, 301 F.2d 499 (D.C. Cir. 1961), cert. denied, 369 U.S. 888 (1962), the court rejected the Commission's claim that the meeting competition defense was unavailable under §2(d) since the literal language of §2(b) refers to "services or facilities" rather than allowances used to pay for them, finding no basis in statutory policy for differential treatment. The Commission now accepts this view. 16 C.F.R. §240.14.

24. §2(e) uses "accorded" rather than "available," although the Commission and courts consider both words to express a single idea. See, e.g., Vanity Fair Paper Mills v. FTC, 311 F.2d 480 (2d Cir. 1962); Lever Brothers Co., 50 F.T.C. 494 (1953).

25. *Exquisite Form*, note 23, at 502.

26. Atalanta Trade Corp. v. FTC, 258 F.2d 365 (2d Cir. 1958).

some dealers and a plan refused to some dealers is clearly not available to all, the courts have also required appropriate efforts to inform all dealers. It is not generally necessary that an actual offer be made to each, leaving some uncertainty as to the precise actions required.[27] The Commission has promulgated regulations to clarify its enforcement policy.[28]

The allowance or service must not only be available in that sense; it must be functionally available. An offer formally open to all dealers violates this requirement when it cannot realistically be accepted by smaller purchasers.[29] For example, if a manufacturer provided an advertising allowance limited to use on television, smaller dealers may not make enough sales to finance any useful amount of television time. Such a manufacturer must offer an allowance that can be used for advertising through such alternatives as newspapers or handbills.[30]

To be permitted, an allowance or service must also be available on a "proportionally equal" basis. Under the FTC guidelines, proportional equality may be measured by the customer's cost or the seller's cost.[31] The guidelines note that the easiest way of treating competing customers on proportionally equal terms is by basing the payments made on the dollar volume or amount of the product purchased during a specific period. But problems may arise when the sellers provide services — for example, the services of a person to model clothes or to demonstrate an appliance for varying periods of time may depend upon the volume of purchases. But such a model or demonstrator is not practicable at all for the 10 minutes to which a smaller dealer would be entitled. Relatedly, from the manufacturer's point of view, "equivalent payments" for different promotional services are not of equivalent value. For small dealers, less effective promotional devices (although supported by "equivalent payments") will, by definition, not attract customers to the same degree as more effective devices used by their larger rivals.

These requirements prevent sellers from concentrating their promotional allowances or services on the particular dealers or particular activities that are most cost-effective in increasing sales. Of course, sellers might lawfully discontinue relationships with those dealers who are thus made too costly by §2(d) and §2(e). In addition, some sellers can promote their products directly through, for

27. See *Vanity Fair*, note 24, at 485.
28. FTC *Fred Meyer* Guides, 16 C.F.R. §240.1-§240.15.
29. Compare the analysis of functional discounts in *Morton Salt*, Ch. 6B.
30. E.g., *Lever Brothers*, note 24, at 510 ("Nor does the law require that a comprehensive plan must be so tailored that every feature of it will be usable or suitable for every customer. In many cases that would be an impossibility.").
31. 16 C.F.R. §240.9.

example, national advertising, while others have no choice but to rely on their retailers and thus be constrained by these provisions.

(d) *The competing customer requirement.* These sections — §2(d) explicitly and §2(e) through interpretation[32] — parallel the secondary-line provision of §2(a) in requiring discrimination between competing customers. For example, a seller may freely offer promotional allowances for local advertising in Kansas City but not in Atlanta.

An important variation arose in *Fred Meyer,*[33] where suppliers granted an allowance to a direct-purchasing retailer where no equivalent was granted to wholesalers or to retailers purchasing through such wholesalers and reselling in competition with the direct-purchasing retailer.[34] The Supreme Court found a violation, "holding that 'customers' in §2(d) includes retailers who buy through wholesalers and compete with a direct buyer in the resale of the supplier's product."[35] Some problem was presented in forming a remedy. The Court did not require the supplier directly to reach indirect purchasing retailers in order to offer equivalent allowances. The supplier may utilize "wholesalers to distribute payments or administer a promotional program, so long as the supplier takes responsibility, under rules and guides promulgated by the Commission for the regulation of such practices, for seeing that the allowances are made available to all who compete in the resale of his product."[36]

(e) *Distinguishing price discrimination from promotional allowances.*[37] Sellers hoping to avoid the stricter prohibition of §2(d), preferring to be judged under §2(a), might provide price discounts rather than separate promotional allowances, thus raising a problem of characterization. If the seller's payment is directly tied to or in

32. Zwicker v. J.I. Case Co., 596 F.2d 305 (8th Cir. 1979).

33. FTC v. Fred Meyer, 390 U.S. 341 (1968).

34. Standard functional discounts of the sort addressed in Ch. 6B are not covered by §2(d) and §2(e) because wholesalers and retailers are not in competition. Id. at 348-349 ("we agree ... that, on the facts of this case, §2(d) reaches only discrimination between customers competing for resales at the same functional level and, therefore, does not mandate proportional equality between [the direct buyer] and the two wholesalers").

35. Id. at 354.

36. Id. at 358. See 16 C.F.R. §240.11. Justice Harlan's dissent suggested that accomplishing the task of making "promotional allowances available to retailers with whom [suppliers] do not deal is no simple matter," 390 U.S. at 361, and one commentator referred to this result as "an administrative nightmare for the seller." R. Posner, note 17, at 48. See also Morris Elec. v. Mattel, 595 F. Supp. 56 (N.D.N.Y. 1984) (wholesaler has standing where manufacturer has furnished promotional allowances favoring direct purchasing retailers over indirect purchasing retailers supplied by plaintiff wholesaler).

37. This issue is explored further in ABA Monograph, note 1, at 53-59.

anticipation of the buyer providing services funded by such payments, §2(d) would apply.[38] In cases of ambiguity, courts have asked whether the discount is to facilitate the original sale (from supplier to retailer) rather than the subsequent resale (from retailer to ultimate consumer).[39] The former category is judged under §2(a) and has generally been deemed to include credit terms, freight allowances, and supply preferences.[40]

Harsher scrutiny for allowances made in return for genuine services than for discriminatory discounts to powerful buyers may seem contrary to the statutory purpose.[41] After all, a promotional allowance must be spent in a manner that benefits the seller, and perhaps indirectly competing retailers as well, whereas a simple price cut can be used to lower prices or in any other manner that aids the favored buyer in competition with others. Although the presumed rationale for stricter treatment of promotional allowances is to force preferential treatment into the open, even open promotional allowances not made proportionally available are judged more harshly than pure price discrimination, open or concealed.

(f) *Buyer liability.* Section 2(d) and §2(e) do not speak of the customers' liability. Yet Commission policy is to reach customers who induce or knowingly receive illegal allowances or services under §5 of the Federal Trade Commission Act,[42] an approach that has received court endorsement.[43]

38. See American News Co. v. FTC, 300 F.2d 104, 108 (2d Cir.), cert. denied, 371 U.S. 824 (1962). For a listing of covered services, see 16 C.F.R. §240.7.
39. E.g., Tri-Valley Packing Assn. v. FTC, 329 F.2d 694, 707-710 (9th Cir. 1964).
40. ABA Monograph, note 1, at 55-56.
41. R. Posner, note 17, at 47-48.
42. 16 C.F.R. §240.13.
43. See, e.g., Grand Union Co. v. FTC, 300 F.2d 92 (2d Cir. 1962).

Appendix

Selected Statutes[1]

SHERMAN ACT[2]

§1. Every contract, combination in the form of trust or otherwise, or conspiracy, in restraint of trade or commerce among the
several States, or with foreign nations, is declared to be illegal.[3]
Every person who shall make any contract or engage in any combination or conspiracy hereby declared to be illegal shall be deemed
guilty of a felony, and, on conviction thereof, shall be punished by
fine not exceeding $10,000,000 if a corporation, or, if any other
person, $350,000, or by imprisonment not exceeding three years, or
by both said punishments, in the discretion of the court.[4]

1. Minor modifications have been made from the United States Code. Most
notably, for ease of reference, section numbers and cross-references refer to names
of and numbers in various Acts, rather than the codifications thereof.
2. 26 Stat. 209 (1890), codified as amended, 15 U.S.C. §§1-7.
3. Amendments in 1975, 89 Stat. 801, repealed the 1937 amendments, 50 Stat.
673, 693, which had immunized from federal antitrust law those resale price
maintenance arrangements permitted by state law. The 1937 legislation had attached two provisos to the first sentence of §1:

> *Provided,* That nothing herein contained shall render illegal, contracts or agreements
> prescribing minimum prices for the resale of a commodity which bears or the label or
> container of which bears, the trademark, brand, or name of the producer or distribu-
> tor of such commodity and which is in free and open competition with commodities
> of the same general class produced or distributed by others, when contracts or agree-
> ments of that description are lawful as applied to intrastate transactions, under any
> statute, law, or public policy now or hereafter in effect in any State, Territory, or the
> District of Columbia in which such resale is to be made, or to which the commodity is
> to be transported for such resale, and the making of such contracts or agreements
> shall not be an unfair method of competition under section 5, as amended and
> supplemented, of the Act entitled "An Act to create a Federal Trade Commission, to
> define its powers and duties, and for other purposes," approved September 26, 1914:
> *Provided further,* That the preceding proviso shall not make lawful any contract or
> agreement, providing for the establishment or maintenance of minimum resale prices
> on any commodity herein involved, between manufacturers, or between producers, or
> between wholesalers, or between brokers, or between factors, or between retailers, or
> between persons, firms, or corporations in competition with each other.

4. The penalty provisions in §1-3 were substantially changed in 1974, 88 Stat.
1706, 1708. Until then, violations were misdemeanors, without distinction between
individuals and corporations, and with a maximum fine of $50,000 (increased
from $5000 in 1955, 69 Stat. 282) and maximum imprisonment of one year.

§2.   Every person who shall monopolize, or attempt to monopolize, or combine or conspire with any other person or persons, to monopolize any part of the trade or commerce among the several States, or with foreign nations, shall be deemed guilty of a felony, and, on conviction thereof, shall be punished by fine not exceeding $10,000,000 if a corporation, or, if any other person, $350,000, or by imprisonment not exceeding three years, or by both said punishments, in the discretion of the court.

§3.   Every contract, combination in form of trust or otherwise, or conspiracy, in restraint of trade or commerce in any Territory of the United States or of the District of Columbia, or in restraint of trade or commerce between any such Territory and another, or between any such Territory and Territories and any State or States or the District of Columbia, or with foreign nations, or between the District of Columbia and any State or States or foreign nations, is declared illegal. Every person who shall make any such contract or engage in any such combination or conspiracy, shall be deemed guilty of a felony, and, on conviction thereof, shall be punished by fine not exceeding $10,000,000 if a corporation, or, if any other person, $350,000, or by imprisonment not exceeding three years, or by both said punishments, in the discretion of the court.

§4.   The several district courts of the United States are invested with jurisdiction to prevent and restrain violations of this act; and it shall be the duty of the several United States attorneys, in their respective districts, under the direction of the Attorney General, to institute proceedings in equity to prevent and restrain such violations. Such proceedings may be by way of petition setting forth the case and praying that such violation shall be enjoined or otherwise prohibited. When the parties complained of shall have been duly notified of such petition the court shall proceed, as soon as may be, to the hearing and determination of the case; and pending such petition and before final decree, the court may at any time make such temporary restraining order or prohibition as shall be deemed just in the premises.

§5.   Whenever it shall appear to the court before which any proceeding under section 4 of this act may be pending, that the ends of justice require that other parties should be brought before the court, the court may cause them to be summoned, whether they reside in the district in which the court is held or not; and subpoenas to that end may be served in any district by the marshal thereof.

§6. Any property owned under any contract or by any combination, or pursuant to any conspiracy (and being the subject thereof) mentioned in section 1 of this act, and being in the course of transportation from one State to another, or to a foreign country, shall be forfeited to the United States, and may be seized and condemned by like proceedings as those provided by law for the forfeiture, seizure, and condemnation of property imported into the United States contrary to law.

§7. This act shall not apply to conduct involving trade or commerce (other than import trade or import commerce) with foreign nations unless —

(1) such conduct has a direct, substantial, and reasonably foreseeable effect —

(A) on trade or commerce which is not trade or commerce with foreign nations, or on import trade or import commerce with foreign nations; or

(B) on export trade or export commerce with foreign nations, of a person engaged in such trade or commerce in the United States; and

(2) such effect gives rise to a claim under the provisions of this act, other than this section.

If this act applies to such conduct only because of the operation of paragraph (1)(B), then this act shall apply to such conduct only for injury to export business in the United States.[5]

§8. The word "person," or "persons," wherever used in this act shall be deemed to include corporations and associations existing under or authorized by the laws of either the United States, the laws of any of the Territories, the laws of any State, or the laws of any foreign country.

CLAYTON ACT[1]

§1. (a) "Antitrust laws," as used herein, includes the Act entitled "An Act to protect trade and commerce against unlawful restraints and monopolies," approved July second, eighteen hundred

---

5. Original §7, providing for private treble damage actions, was superceded by Clayton Act §4.

1. 38 Stat. 730 (1914), codified as amended, 15 U.S.C. §§12-27. As originally enacted, each Clayton Act section began with the word "that," which is omitted here. Modern amendments abandoned that practice.

and ninety;[2] sections seventy-three to seventy-seven, inclusive, of an Act entitled "An Act to reduce taxation, to provide revenue for the Government, and for other purposes," of August twenty-seventh, eighteen hundred and ninety-four;[3] an Act entitled "An Act to amend sections seventy-three and seventy-six of the Act of August twenty-seventh, eighteen hundred and ninety-four, entitled 'An Act to reduce taxation, to provide revenue for the Government, and for other purposes,'" approved February twelfth, nineteen hundred and thirteen;[4] and also this Act.

"Commerce," as used herein, means trade or commerce among the several States and with foreign nations, or between the District of Columbia or any Territory of the United States and any State, Territory, or foreign nation, or between any insular possessions or other places under the jurisdiction of the United States, or between any such possession or place and any State or Territory of the United States or the District of Columbia or any foreign nation, or within the District of Columbia or any Territory or any insular possession or other place under the jurisdiction of the United States: *Provided,* That nothing in this Act contained shall apply to the Philippine Islands.

The word "person" or "persons" wherever used in this Act shall be deemed to include corporations and associations existing under or authorized by the laws of either the United States, the laws of any of the Territories, the laws of any State, or the laws of any foreign country.

(b) This Act may be cited as the "Clayton Act."

§2. (a) It shall be unlawful for any person engaged in commerce, in the course of such commerce, either directly or indirectly, to discriminate in price between different purchasers of commodities of like grade and quality, where either or any of the purchases involved in such discrimination are in commerce, where such commodities are sold for use, consumption, or resale within the United States or any Territory thereof or the District of Columbia or any insular possession or other place under the jurisdiction of the United States, and where the effect of such discrimination may be substantially to lessen competition or tend to create a monopoly in any line of commerce, or to injure, destroy, or prevent competition with any person who either grants or knowingly re-

2. The Sherman Act.
3. These were the Wilson Tariff Act's antitrust amendments. 28 Stat. 509, 570 (1894), codified as amended, 15 U.S.C. §§8-11. These provisions forbid combinations or contracts in restraint of import trade.
4. 37 Stat. 667 (1913), 15 U.S.C. §§8, 11.

ceives the benefit of such discrimination, or with customers of either of them: *Provided,* That nothing herein contained shall prevent differentials which make only due allowance for differences in the cost of manufacture, sale, or delivery resulting from the differing methods or quantities in which such commodities are to such purchasers sold or delivered: *Provided, however,* That the Federal Trade Commission may, after due investigation and hearing to all interested parties, fix and establish quantity limits, and revise the same as it finds necessary, as to particular commodities or classes of commodities, where it finds that available purchasers in greater quantities are so few as to render differentials on account thereof unjustly discriminatory or promotive of monopoly in any line of commerce; and the foregoing shall then not be construed to permit differentials based on differences in quantities greater than those so fixed and established: *And provided further,* That nothing herein contained shall prevent persons engaged in selling goods, wares, or merchandise in commerce from selecting their own customers in bona fide transactions and not in restraint of trade: *And provided further,* That nothing herein contained shall prevent price changes from time to time where in response to changing conditions affecting the market for or the marketability of the goods concerned, such as but not limited to actual or imminent deterioration of perishable goods, obsolescence of seasonal goods, distress sales under court process, or sales in good faith in discontinuance of business in the goods concerned.

(b) Upon proof being made, at any hearing on a complaint under this section, that there has been discrimination in price or services or facilities furnished, the burden of rebutting the prima-facie case thus made by showing justification shall be upon the person charged with a violation of this section, and unless justification shall be affirmatively shown, the Commission is authorized to issue an order terminating the discrimination: *Provided, however,* That nothing herein contained shall prevent a seller rebutting the prima-facie case thus made by showing that his lower price or the furnishing of services or facilities to any purchaser or purchasers was made in good faith to meet an equally low price of a competitor, or the services or facilities furnished by a competitor.

(c) It shall be unlawful for any person engaged in commerce, in the course of such commerce, to pay or grant, or to receive or accept, anything of value as a commission, brokerage, or other compensation, or any allowance or discount in lieu thereof, except for services rendered in connection with the sale or purchase of goods, wares, or merchandise, either to the other party to such transaction or to an agent, representative, or other intermediary therein where such intermediary is acting in fact for or in behalf, or is subject to the direct or indirect control, of any party to such transaction other than the person by whom such compensation is so granted or paid.

(d) It shall be unlawful for any person engaged in commerce to pay or contract for the payment of anything of value to or for the benefit of a customer of such person in the course of such commerce as compensation or in consideration for any services or facilities furnished by or through such customer in connection with the processing, handling, sale, or offering for sale of any products or commodities manufactured, sold, or offered for sale by such person, unless such payment or consideration is available on proportionally equal terms to all other customers competing in the distribution of such products or commodities.

(e) It shall be unlawful for any person to discriminate in favor of one purchaser against another purchaser or purchasers of a commodity bought for resale, with or without processing, by contracting to furnish or furnishing, or by contributing to the furnishing of, any services or facilities connected with the processing, handling, sale, or offering for sale of such commodity so purchased upon terms not accorded to all purchasers on proportionally equal terms.

(f) It shall be unlawful for any person engaged in commerce, in the course of such commerce, knowingly to induce or receive a discrimination in price which is prohibited by this section.[5]

5. Before its amendment by the Robinson-Patman Act of 1936, 49 Stat. 1526, 15 U.S.C. §13, this section read as follows:

> That it shall be unlawful for any person engaged in commerce, in the course of such commerce, either directly or indirectly, to discriminate in price between different purchasers of commodities, which commodities are sold for use, consumption, or resale within the United States or any Territory thereof or the District of Columbia or any insular possession or other place under the jurisdiction of the United States, where the effect of such discrimination may be to substantially lessen competition or tend to create a monopoly in any line of commerce: *Provided*, That nothing herein contained shall prevent discrimination in price between purchasers of commodities on account of differences in the grade, quality, or quantity of the commodity sold, or that makes only due allowance for difference in the cost of selling or transportation, or discrimination in price in the same or different communities made in good faith to meet competition: *And provided further*, That nothing herein contained shall prevent persons engaged in selling goods, wares, or merchandise in commerce from selecting their own customers in bona fide transactions and not in restraint of trade.

Robinson-Patman Act §3, 15 U.S.C. §13a, reads:

> It shall be unlawful for any person engaged in commerce, in the course of such commerce, to be a party to, or assist in, any transaction of sale, or contract to sell, which discriminates to his knowledge against competitors of the purchaser, in that, any discount, rebate, allowance, or advertising service charge is granted to the purchaser over and above any discount, rebate, allowance, or advertising service charge available at the time of such transaction to said competitors in respect of a sale of goods of like grade, quality, and quantity; to sell, or contract to sell, goods in any part of the United States at prices lower than those exacted by said person elsewhere in the United States for the purpose of destroying competition, or eliminating a competitor

§3. It shall be unlawful for any person engaged in commerce, in the course of such commerce, to lease or make a sale or contract for sale of goods, wares, merchandise, machinery, supplies, or other commodities, whether patented or unpatented, for use, consumption, or resale within the United States or any Territory thereof or the District of Columbia or any insular possession or other place under the jurisdiction of the United States, or fix a price charged therefor, or discount from, or rebate upon, such price, on the condition, agreement, or understanding that the lessee or purchaser thereof shall not use or deal in the goods, wares, merchandise, machinery, supplies, or other commodities of a competitor or competitors of the lessor or seller, where the effect of such lease, sale, or contract for sale or such condition, agreement, or understanding may be to substantially lessen competition or tend to create a monopoly in any line of commerce.

§4.[6] (a) Except as provided in subsection (b), any person who shall be injured in his business or property by reason of anything forbidden in the antitrust laws may sue therefor in any district court of the United States in the district in which the defendant resides or is found or has an agent, without respect to the amount in controversy, and shall recover threefold the damages by him sustained, and the cost of suit, including a reasonable attorney's fee. . . .

(b) Except as provided in paragraph (2), any person who is a foreign state may not recover under subsection (a) an amount in excess of the actual damages sustained by it and the cost of suit, including a reasonable attorney's fee. . . .

---

in such part of the United States; or, to sell, or contract to sell, goods at unreasonably low prices for the purpose of destroying competition or eliminating a competitor.

Any person violating any of the provisions of this section shall, upon conviction thereof, be fined not more than $5,000 or imprisoned not more than one year, or both.

Purchases by cooperative associations and by nonprofit institutions are the subject of Robinson-Patman Act §4 and of 52 Stat. 446 (1938), 15 U.S.C. §§13b, 13c.

6. Sections 4A and 4B were added by 69 Stat. 282 (1955), which also made conforming amendments to §5 and added the proviso to current §5(i). Sections 4C-4H were added by 90 Stat. 1394-1396 (1976). 94 Stat. 1154, 1156-1157 (1980) added to §§4, 4A, and 4C(a)(2) permission for the court to award interest on its judgment for all or any part of the period between the filing of the complaint and the date of the judgment if "just in the circumstances." To make that determination, the court is to consider only whether either party (1) offered motions claims, or defenses "so lacking in merit" as to show an intentional delay or bad faith, (2) violated any rule or order concerning expeditious proceedings, or (3) acted "primarily for the purpose of delaying the litigation or increasing" its cost. A fourth element is to be considered under §4A: whether prejudgment interest is necessary to compensate the United States for its injury.

§4A.   Whenever the United States is hereafter injured in its business or property by reason of anything forbidden in the antitrust laws it may sue therefor in the United States district court for the district in which the defendant resides or is found or has an agent, without respect to the amount in controversy, and shall recover threefold the damages[7] by it sustained and the cost of suit. . . .

§4B.   Any action to enforce any cause of action under sections 4, 4A or 4C shall be forever barred unless commenced within four years after the cause of action accrued. . . .

§4C.   (a)(1) Any attorney general of a State may bring a civil action in the name of such State, as parens patriae on behalf of natural persons residing in such State, in any district court of the United States having jurisdiction of the defendant, to secure monetary relief as provided in this section for injury sustained by such natural persons to their property by reason of any violation of the Sherman Act. The court shall exclude from the amount of monetary relief awarded in such action any amount of monetary relief (A) which duplicates amounts which have been awarded for the same injury, or (B) which is properly allocable to (i) natural persons who have excluded their claims pursuant to subsection (b)(2) of this section, and (ii) any business entity.

(2) The court shall award the State as monetary relief threefold the total damage sustained as described in paragraph (1) of this subsection, and the cost of suit, including a reasonable attorney's fee. . . .

(b)(1) In any action brought under subsection (a)(1) of this section, the State attorney general shall, at such times, in such manner, and with such content as the court may direct, cause notice thereof to be given by publication. If the court finds that notice given solely by publication would deny due process of law to any person or persons, the court may direct further notice to such person or persons according to the circumstances of the case.

(2) Any person on whose behalf an action is brought under subsection (a)(1) may elect to exclude from adjudication the portion of the State claim for monetary relief attributable to him by filing notice of such election with the court within such time as specified in the notice given pursuant to paragraph (1) of this subsection.

(3) The final judgment in an action under subsection (a)(1) shall be res judicata as to any claim under section 4 of this Act by

7. This section previously restricted the government to actual damages.

any person on behalf of whom such action was brought and who fails to give such notice within the period specified in the notice given pursuant to paragraph (1) of this subsection.

(c) An action under subsection (a)(1) shall not be dismissed or compromised without the approval of the court, and notice of any proposed dismissal or compromise shall be given in such manner as the court directs.

(d) In any action under subsection (a) —

(1) the amount of the plaintiffs' attorney's fee, if any, shall be determined by the court; and

(2) the court may, in its discretion, award a reasonable attorney's fee to a prevailing defendant upon a finding that the State attorney general has acted in bad faith, vexatiously, wantonly, or for oppressive reasons.

§4D.   In any action under section 4C(a)(1), in which there has been a determination that a defendant agreed to fix prices in violation of the Sherman Act, damages may be proved and assessed in the aggregate by statistical or sampling methods, by the computation of illegal overcharges, or by such other reasonable system of estimating aggregate damages as the court in its discretion may permit without the necessity of separately proving the individual claim of, or amount of damage to, persons on whose behalf the suit was brought.

§4E.   Monetary relief recovered in an action under section 4C(a)(1) shall

(1) be distributed in such manner as the district court in its discretion may authorize; or

(2) be deemed a civil penalty by the court and deposited with the State as general revenues;

subject in either case to the requirement that any distribution procedure adopted afford each person a reasonable opportunity to secure his appropriate portion of the net monetary relief.

§4F.   (a) Whenever the Attorney General of the United States has brought an action under the antitrust laws, and he has reason to believe that any State attorney general would be entitled to bring an action under this Act based substantially on the same alleged violation of the antitrust laws, he shall promptly give written notification thereof to such State attorney general.

(b) To assist a State attorney general in evaluating the notice or in bringing any action under this Act, the Attorney General of the United States shall, upon request by such State attorney general, make available to him, to the extent permitted by law, any investigative files or other materials which are or may be relevant or material to the actual or potential cause of action under this Act.

§4G. For the purposes of sections 4C, 4D, 4E, and 4F of this Act:

(1) The term "State attorney general" means the chief legal officer of a State, or any other person authorized by State law to bring actions under section 4C of this Act, and includes the Corporation Counsel of the District of Columbia, except that such term does not include any person employed or retained on

(A) a contingency fee based on a percentage of the monetary relief awarded under this section; or

(B) any other contingency fee basis, unless the amount of the award of a reasonable attorney's fee to a prevailing plaintiff is determined by the court under section 4C(d)(1).

(2) The term "State" means a State, the District of Columbia, the Commonwealth of Puerto Rico, and any other territory or possession of the United States.

(3) The term "natural persons" does not include proprietorships or partnerships.

§4H. Sections 4C, 4D, 4E, 4F, and 4G shall apply in any State, unless such State provides by law for its nonapplicability in such State.

§5. (a) A final judgment or decree heretofore or hereafter rendered in any civil or criminal proceeding brought by or on behalf of the United States under the antitrust laws to the effect that a defendant has violated said laws shall be prima facie evidence against such defendant in any action or proceeding brought by any other party against such defendant under said laws as to all matters respecting which said judgment or decree would be an estoppel as between the parties thereto: *Provided,* That this section shall not apply to consent judgments or decrees entered before any testimony has been taken. Nothing contained in this section shall be construed to impose any limitation on the application of collateral estoppel, except that, in any action or proceeding brought under the antitrust laws, collateral estoppel effect shall not be given to any finding made by the Federal Trade Commission under the antitrust laws or under section 5 of the Federal Trade Commission Act which could give rise to a claim for relief under the antitrust laws.

(b) Any proposal for a consent judgment submitted by the United States for entry in any civil proceeding brought by or on behalf of the United States under the antitrust laws shall be filed with the district court before which such proceeding is pending and published by the United States in the Federal Register at least 60 days prior to the effective date of such judgment. Any written comments relating to such proposal and any responses by the United States thereto, shall also be filed with such district court and published by the United States in the Federal Register within such sixty-day period. Copies of such proposal and any other materials and documents which the United States considered determinative in formulating such proposal, shall also be made available to the public at the district court and in such other districts as the court may subsequently direct. Simultaneously with the filing of such proposal, unless otherwise instructed by the court, the United States shall file with the district court, publish in the Federal Register, and thereafter furnish to any person upon request, a competitive impact statement which shall recite —

(1) the nature and purpose of the proceeding;

(2) a description of the practices or events giving rise to the alleged violation of the antitrust laws;

(3) an explanation of the proposal for a consent judgment, including an explanation of any unusual circumstances giving rise to such proposal or any provision contained therein, relief to be obtained thereby, and the anticipated effects on competition of such relief;

(4) the remedies available to potential private plaintiffs damaged by the alleged violation in the event that such proposal for the consent judgment is entered in such proceeding;

(5) a description of the procedures available for modification of such proposal; and

(6) a description and evaluation of alternatives to such proposal actually considered by the United States.

(c) The United States shall also cause to be published, commencing at least 60 days prior to the effective date of the judgment described in subsection (b) of this section, for 7 days over a period of 2 weeks in newspapers of general circulation of the district in which the case has been filed, in the District of Columbia, and in such other districts as the court may direct —

(i) a summary of the terms of the proposal for the consent judgment,

(ii) a summary of the competitive impact statement filed under subsection (b) of this section,

(iii) and a list of the materials and documents under subsection (b) of this section which the United States shall make available for purposes of meaningful public comment, and the place where such materials and documents are available for public inspection.

(d) During the 60-day period as specified in subsection (b) of this section, and such additional time as the United States may request and the court may grant, the United States shall receive and consider any written comments relating to the proposal for the consent judgment submitted under subsection (b) of this section. The Attorney General or his designee shall establish procedures to carry out the provisions of this subsection, but such 60-day time period shall not be shortened except by order of the district court upon a showing that (1) extraordinary circumstances require such shortening and (2) such shortening is not adverse to the public interest. At the close of the period during which such comments may be received, the United States shall file with the district court and cause to be published in the Federal Register a response to such comments.

(e) Before entering any consent judgment proposed by the United States under this section, the court shall determine that the entry of such judgment is in the public interest. For the purpose of such determination, the court may consider —

(1) the competitive impact of such judgment, including termination of alleged violations, provisions for enforcement and modification, duration or relief sought, anticipated effects of alternative remedies actually considered, and any other considerations bearing upon the adequacy of such judgment;

(2) the impact of entry of such judgment upon the public generally and individuals alleging specific injury from the violations set forth in the complaint including consideration of the public benefit, if any, to be derived from a determination of the issues at trial.

(f) In making its determination under subsection (e) of this section, the court may

(1) take testimony of Government officials or experts or such other expert witnesses, upon motion of any party or participant or upon its own motion, as the court may deem appropriate;

(2) appoint a special master and such outside consultants or expert witnesses as the court may deem appropriate; and request and obtain the views, evaluations, or advice of any individual, group or agency of government with respect to any aspects of the proposed judgment or the effect of such judgment, in such manner as the court deems appropriate;

(3) authorize full or limited participation in proceedings before the court by interested persons or agencies, including appearance amicus curiae, intervention as a party pursuant to the Federal Rules of Civil Procedure, examination of witnesses or documentary materials, or participation in any other manner and extent which serves the public interest as the court may deem appropriate;

(4) review any comments including any objections filed with the United States under subsection (d) of this section concerning the proposed judgment and the responses of the United States to such comments and objections; and

(5) take such other action in the public interest as the court may deem appropriate.

(g) Not later than 10 days following the date of the filing of any proposal for a consent judgment under subsection (b) of this section, each defendant shall file with the district court a description of any and all written or oral communications by or on behalf of such defendant, including any and all written or oral communications on behalf of such defendant, or other person, with any officer or employee of the United States concerning or relevant to such proposal, except that any such communications made by counsel of record alone with the Attorney General or the employees of the Department of Justice alone shall be excluded from the requirements of this subsection. Prior to the entry of any consent judgment pursuant to the antitrust laws, each defendant shall certify to the district court that the requirements of this subsection have been complied with and that such filing is a true and complete description of such communications known to the defendant or which the defendant reasonably should have known.

(h) Proceedings before the district court under subsections (e) and (f) of this section, and the competitive impact statement filed under subsection (b) of this section, shall not be admissible against any defendant in any action or proceeding brought by any other party against such defendant under the antitrust laws or by the United States under section 4A of this Act nor constitute a basis for the introduction of the consent judgment as prima facie evidence against such defendant in any such action or proceeding.

(i) Whenever any civil or criminal proceeding is instituted by the United States to prevent, restrain, or punish violations of any of the antitrust laws, but not including an action under section 4A of this Act, the running of the statute of limitations in respect of every private or State right of action arising under said laws and based in whole or in part on any matter complained of in said proceeding shall be suspended during the pendency thereof and for one year thereafter: *Provided, however,* That whenever the running of the statute of limitations in respect of a cause of action arising under section 4 or 4C is suspended hereunder, any action to enforce such cause of action shall be forever barred unless commenced either within the period of suspension or within four years after the cause of action accrued.[8]

---

8. Section 5 originally included only paragraphs (a) and (i). Current paragraphs (b)-(h) were added by 88 Stat. 1706-1708 (1974). Paragraph (i) was amended in 1976 to apply to state actions under §4C, also added at that time, 90 Stat. 1383, 1394-1396 (1976). The final sentence of §5(a) was added by 94 Stat. 1154-1157 (1980).

§6. The labor of a human being is not a commodity or article of commerce. Nothing contained in the antitrust laws shall be construed to forbid the existence and operation of labor, agricultural, or horticultural organizations, instituted for the purposes of mutual help, and not having capital stock or conducted for profit, or to forbid or restrain individual members of such organizations from lawfully carrying out the legitimate objects thereof; nor shall such organizations, or the members thereof, be held or construed to be illegal combinations or conspiracies in restraint of trade, under the antitrust laws.

§7. No person engaged in commerce or in any activity affecting commerce shall acquire, directly or indirectly, the whole or any part of the stock or other share capital and no person subject to the jurisdiction of the Federal Trade Commission shall acquire the whole or any part of the assets of another person engaged also in commerce or in any activity affecting commerce, where in any line of commerce or in any activity affecting commerce in any section of the country, the effect of such acquisition may be substantially to lessen competition or to tend to create a monopoly.[9]

No person shall acquire, directly or indirectly, the whole or any part of the stock or other share capital and no person subject to the jurisdiction of the Federal Trade Commission shall acquire the whole or any part of the assets of one or more persons engaged in commerce or in any activity affecting commerce, where in any line of commerce in any activity affecting commerce in any section of the country, the effect of such acquisition, of such stocks or assets, or of the use of such stock by the voting or granting of proxies or otherwise, may be substantially to lessen competition, or to tend to create a monopoly.

This section shall not apply to persons purchasing such stock solely for investment and not using the same by voting or otherwise to bring about, or in attempting to bring about, the substantial lessening of competition. Nor shall anything contained in this section prevent a corporation engaged in commerce or in any activity

9. Before its amendments by the Celler-Kefauver Act of 1950, 64 Stat. 1125, 15 U.S.C. §18, the first paragraph provided:

> That no corporation engaged in commerce shall acquire directly or indirectly, the whole or any part of the stock or other share capital of another corporation engaged also in commerce, where the effect of such acquisition may be to substantially lessen competition between the corporation whose stock is so acquired and the corporation making the acquisition, or to restrain such commerce in any section or community, or tend to create a monopoly of any line of commerce.

94 Stat. 1154, 1158 (1980) expanded the coverage of §7 by embracing entities other than corporations and those engaged "in any activity affecting commerce."

affecting commerce from causing the formation of subsidiary corporations for the actual carrying on of their immediate lawful business, or the natural and legitimate branches or extensions thereof, or from owning and holding all or a part of the stock of such subsidiary corporations, when the effect of such formation is not to substantially lessen competition.

Nor shall anything herein contained be construed to prohibit any common carrier subject to the laws to regulate commerce from aiding in the construction of branches or short lines so located as to become feeders to the main line of the company so aiding in such construction or from acquiring or owning all or any part of the stock of such branch lines, nor to prevent any such common carrier from acquiring and owning all or any part of the stock of a branch or short line constructed by an independent company where there is no substantial competition between the company owning the branch line so constructed and the company owning the main line acquiring the property or an interest therein, nor to prevent such common carrier from extending any of its lines through the medium of the acquisition of stock or otherwise of any other common carrier where there is no substantial competition between the company extending its lines and the company whose stock, property, or an interest therein is so acquired.

Nothing contained in this section shall be held to affect or impair any right heretofore legally acquired: *Provided,* That nothing in this section shall be held or construed to authorize or make lawful anything heretofore prohibited or made illegal by the antitrust laws, nor to exempt any person from the penal provisions thereof or the civil remedies therein provided.

Nothing contained in this section shall apply to transactions duly consummated pursuant to authority given by the Secretary of Transportation, Federal Communications Commission, Federal Power Commission, Interstate Commerce Commission, the Securities and Exchange Commission in the exercise of its jurisdiction under section 10 of the Public Utility Holding Company Act of 1935, the United States Maritime Commission, or the Secretary of Agriculture under any statutory provision vesting such power in such Commission, Board, or Secretary.

§7A. (a) Except as exempted pursuant to subsection (c), no person shall acquire, directly or indirectly, any voting securities or assets of any other person, unless both persons (or in the case of a tender offer, the acquiring person) file notification pursuant to rules under subsection (d)(1) and the waiting period described in subsection (b)(1) has expired, if—

(1) the acquiring person, or the person whose voting securities or assets are being acquired, is engaged in commerce or in any activity affecting commerce;

(2)(A) any voting securities or assets of a person engaged in manufacturing which has annual net sales or total assets of $10,000,000 or more are being acquired by any person which has total assets or annual net sales of $100,000,000 or more;

(B) any voting securities or assets of a person not engaged in manufacturing which has total assets of $10,000,000 or more are being acquired by any person which has total assets or annual net sales of $100,000,000 or more; or

(C) any voting securities or assets of a person with annual net sales or total assets of $100,000,000 or more are being acquired by any person with total assets or annual net sales of $10,000,000 or more; and

(3) as a result of such acquisition, the acquiring person would hold —

(A) 15 per centum or more of the voting securities or assets of the acquired person, or

(B) an aggregate total amount of the voting securities and assets of the acquired person in excess of $15,000,000.

In the case of a tender offer, the person whose voting securities are sought to be acquired by a person required to file notification under this subsection shall file notification pursuant to rules under subsection (d).

(b)(1) The waiting period required under subsection (a) shall

(A) begin on the date of the receipt by the Federal Trade Commission and the Assistant Attorney General in charge of the Antitrust Division of the Department of Justice (hereinafter referred to in this section as the "Assistant Attorney General") of —

(i) the completed notification required under subsection (a), or

(ii) if such notification is not completed, the notification to the extent completed and a statement of the reasons for such noncompliance,

from both persons, or, in the case of a tender offer, the acquiring person; and

(B) end on the thirtieth day after the date of such receipt (or in the case of a cash tender offer, the fifteenth day), or on such later date as may be set under subsection (e)(2) or (g)(2).

(2) The Federal Trade Commission and the Assistant Attorney General may, in individual cases, terminate the waiting period specified in paragraph (1) and allow any person to proceed with any acquisition subject to this section, and promptly shall cause to be published in the Federal Register a notice that neither

intends to take any action within such period with respect to such acquisition.

(3) As used in this section

(A) The term "voting securities" means any securities which at present or upon conversion entitle the owner or holder thereof to vote for the election of directors of the issuer or, with respect to unincorporated issuers, persons exercising similar functions.

(B) The amount or percentage of voting securities or assets of a person which are acquired or held by another person shall be determined by aggregating the amount or percentage of such voting securities or assets held or acquired by such other person and each affiliate thereof.

(c) The following classes of transactions are exempt from the requirements of this section —

(1) acquisitions of goods or realty transferred in the ordinary course of business;

(2) acquisitions of bonds, mortgages, deeds of trust, or other obligations which are not voting securities;

(3) acquisitions of voting securities of an issuer at least 50 per centum of the voting securities of which are owned by the acquiring person prior to such acquisition;

(4) transfer to or from a Federal agency or a State or political subdivision thereof;

(5) transactions specifically exempted from the antitrust laws by Federal statute;

(6) transactions specifically exempted from the antitrust laws by Federal statute if approved by a Federal agency, if copies of all information and documentary material filed with such agency are contemporaneously filed with the Federal Trade Commission and the Assistant Attorney General;

(7) transactions which require agency approval under section 404(a) of the Competitive Equality Banking Act of 1987, section 18(c) of the Federal Deposit Insurance Act (12 U.S.C. §1828(c)), or section 3 of the Bank Holding Company Act of 1956 (12 U.S.C. §1842);

(8) transactions which require agency approval under section 4 of the Bank Holding Company Act of 1956 (12 U.S.C. §1843), or section 5 of the Home Owners' Loan Act of 1933 (12 U.S.C. §1464), if copies of all information and documentary material filed with any such agency are contemporaneously filed with the Federal Trade Commission and the Assistant Attorney General at least 30 days prior to consummation of the proposed transaction;

(9) acquisitions, solely for the purpose of investment, of voting securities, if, as a result of such acquisition, the securities ac-

quired or held do not exceed 10 per centum of the outstanding voting securities of the issuer;

(10) acquisitions of voting securities, if, as a result of such acquisition, the voting securities acquired do not increase, directly or indirectly, the acquiring person's per centum share of outstanding voting securities of the issuer;

(11) acquisitions, solely for the purpose of investment, by any bank, banking association, trust company, investment company, or insurance company, of (A) voting securities pursuant to a plan of reorganization or dissolution; or (B) assets in the ordinary course of its business; and

(12) such other acquisitions, transfers, or transactions, as may be exempted under subsection (d)(2)(B).

(d) The Federal Trade Commission, with the concurrence of the Assistant Attorney General and by rule in accordance with section 553 of title 5, consistent with the purposes of this section

(1) shall require that the notification required under subsection (a) be in such form and contain such documentary material and information relevant to a proposed acquisition as is necessary and appropriate to enable the Federal Trade Commission and the Assistant Attorney General to determine whether such acquisition may, if consummated, violate the antitrust laws; and

(2) may—

(A) define the terms used in this section;

(B) exempt, from the requirements of this section, classes of persons, acquisitions, transfers, or transactions which are not likely to violate the antitrust laws; and

(C) prescribe such other rules as may be necessary and appropriate to carry out the purposes of this section.

(e)(1) The Federal Trade Commission or the Assistant Attorney General may, prior to the expiration of the 30-day waiting period (or in the case of a cash tender offer, the 15-day waiting period) specified in subsection (b)(1) of this section, require the submission of additional information or documentary material relevant to the proposed acquisition, from a person required to file notification with respect to such acquisition under subsection (a) of this section prior to the expiration of the waiting period specified in subsection (b)(1) of this section, or from any officer, director, partner, agent, or employee of such person.

(2) The Federal Trade Commission or the Assistant Attorney General, in its or his discretion, may extend the 30-day waiting period (or in the case of a cash tender offer, the 15-day waiting period) specified in subsection (b)(1) of this section for an additional period of not more than 20 days (or in the case of a cash tender offer, 10 days) after the date on which the Federal Trade

Commission or the Assistant Attorney General, as the case may be, receives from any person to whom a request is made under paragraph (1), or in the case of tender offers, the acquiring person, (A) all the information and documentary material required to be submitted pursuant to such a request, or (B) if such request is not fully complied with, the information and documentary material submitted and a statement of the reasons for such non-compliance. Such additional period may be further extended only by the United States district court, upon an application by the Federal Trade Commission or the Assistant Attorney General pursuant to subsection (g)(2).

(f) If a proceeding is instituted or an action is filed by the Federal Trade Commission, alleging that a proposed acquisition violates section 7 of this Act, or section 5 of the Federal Trade Commission Act, or an action is filed by the United States, alleging that a proposed acquisition violates such section 7 or section 1 or 2 of the Sherman Act, and the Federal Trade Commission or the Assistant Attorney General (1) files a motion for a preliminary injunction against consummation of such acquisition pendente lite, and (2) certifies the United States district court for the judicial district within which the respondent resides or carries on business, or in which the action is brought, that it or he believes that the public interest requires relief pendente lite pursuant to this subsection, then upon the filing of such motion and certification, the chief judge of such district court shall immediately notify the chief judge of the United States court of appeals for the circuit in which such district court is located, who shall designate a United States district judge to whom such action shall be assigned for all purposes.

(g)(1) Any person, or any officer, director, or partner thereof, who fails to comply with any provision of this section shall be liable to the United States for a civil penalty of not more than $10,000 for each day during which such person is in violation of this section. Such penalty may be recovered in a civil action brought by the United States.

(2) If any person, or any officer, director, partner, agent, or employee thereof, fails substantially to comply with the notification requirement under subsection (a) or any request for the submission of additional information or documentary material under subsection (e)(1) of this section within the waiting period specified in subsection (b)(1) and as may be extended under subsection (e)(2), the United States district court

(A) may order compliance;

(B) shall extend the waiting period specified in subsection (b)(1) and as may have been extended under subsection (e)(2) until there has been substantial compliance, except that, in the case of a tender offer, the court may not extend such waiting period on the basis of a failure, by the person whose stock is sought to be acquired, to comply substantially with such notification requirement or any such request; and

(C) may grant such other equitable relief as the court in its discretion determines necessary or appropriate,

upon application of the Federal Trade Commission or the Assistant Attorney General.

(h) Any information or documentary material filed with the Assistant Attorney General or the Federal Trade Commission pursuant to this section shall be exempt from disclosure under section 552 of Title 5, and no such information or documentary material may be made public, except as may be relevant to any administrative or judicial action or proceeding. Nothing in this section is intended to prevent disclosure to either body of Congress or to any duly authorized committee or subcommittee of the Congress.

(i)(1) Any action taken by the Federal Trade Commission or the Assistant Attorney General or any failure of the Federal Trade Commission or the Assistant Attorney General to take any action under this section shall not bar any proceeding or any action with respect to such acquisition at any time under any other section of this Act or any other provision of law.

(2) Nothing contained in this section shall limit the authority of the Assistant Attorney General or the Federal Trade Commission to secure at any time from any person documentary material, oral testimony, or other information under the Antitrust Civil Process Act, the Federal Trade Commission Act, or any other provision of law.

(j) Beginning not later than January 1, 1978, the Federal Trade Commission, with the concurrence of the Assistant Attorney General, shall annually report to the Congress on the operation of this section. Such report shall include an assessment of the effects of this section, of the effects, purpose, and need for any rules promulgated pursuant thereto, and any recommendations for revisions of this section.

§8. (a)(1) No person shall, at the same time, serve as a director or officer in any two corporations (other than banks, banking associations, and trust companies) that are —

(A) engaged in whole or in part in commerce; and

(B) by virtue of their business and location of operation, competitors, so that the elimination of competition by agreement between them would constitute a violation of any of the antitrust laws;

if each of the corporations has capital, surplus, and undivided profits aggregating more than $10,000,000 as adjusted pursuant to paragraph (5) of this subsection.

(2) Notwithstanding the provisions of paragraph (1), simultaneous service as a director or officer in any two corporations shall not be prohibited by this section if—

(A) the competitive sales of either corporation are less than $1,000,000, as adjusted pursuant to paragraph (5) of this subsection;

(B) the competitive sales of either corporation are less than 2 per centum of that corporation's total sales; or

(C) the competitive sales of each corporation are less than 4 per centum of that corporation's total sales.

For purposes of this paragraph, "competitive sales" means the gross revenues for all products and services sold by one corporation in competition with the other, determined on the basis of annual gross revenues for such products and services in that corporation's last completed fiscal year. For the purposes of this paragraph, "total sales" means the gross revenues for all products and services sold by one corporation over that corporation's last completed fiscal year.

(3) The eligibility of a director or officer under the provisions of paragraph (1) shall be determined by the capital, surplus and undivided profits, exclusive of dividends declared but not paid to stockholders, of each corporation at the end of that corporation's last completed fiscal year.

(4) For purposes of this section, the term "officer" means an officer elected or chosen by the Board of Directors.

(5) For each fiscal year commencing after September 30, 1990, the $10,000,000 and $1,000,000 thresholds in this subsection shall be increased (or decreased) as of October 1 each year by an amount equal to the percentage increase (or decrease) in the gross national product, as determined by the Department of Commerce or its successor, for the year then ended over the level so established for the year ending September 30, 1989. As soon as practicable, but not later than January 31 of each year, the Federal Trade Commission shall publish the adjusted amounts required by this paragraph.

(b) When any person elected or chosen as a director or officer of any corporation subject to the provisions hereof is eligible at the time of his election or selection to act for such corporation in such capacity, his eligibility to act in such capacity shall not be affected by any of the provisions hereof by reason of any change in the capital, surplus and undivided profits, or affairs of such corporation from whatever cause, until the expiration of one year from the date on which the event causing ineligibility occurred.

§11. (a) Authority to enforce compliance with sections 2, 3, 7, and 8 of this Act by the persons respectively subject thereto is hereby vested in the Interstate Commerce Commission where applicable to common carriers subject to the Interstate Commerce Act, as amended; in the Federal Communications Commission where applicable to common carriers engaged in wire or radio communication or radio transmission of energy; in the Secretary of Transportation where applicable to air carriers and foreign air carriers subject to the Federal Aviation Act of 1958; in the Board of Governors of the Federal Reserve System where applicable to banks, banking associations, and trust companies; and in the Federal Trade Commission where applicable to all other character of commerce to be exercised as follows:

(b) Whenever the Commission, Board, or Secretary vested with jurisdiction thereof shall have reason to believe that any person is violating or has violated any of the provisions of sections 2, 3, 7, and 8 of this Act, it shall issue and serve upon such person and the Attorney General a complaint stating its charges in that respect, and containing a notice of a hearing upon a day and at a place therein fixed at least thirty days after the service of said complaint. The person so complained of shall have the right to appear at the place and time so fixed and show cause why an order should not be entered by the Commission, Board, or Secretary requiring such person to cease and desist from the violation of the law so charged in said complaint. The Attorney General shall have the right to intervene and appear in said proceeding and any person may make application, and upon good cause shown may be allowed by the Commission, Board, or Secretary to intervene and appear in said proceeding by counsel or in person. . . .

(*l*) Any person who violates any order issued by the commission, board, or Secretary under subsection (b) after such order has become final, and while such order is in effect, shall forfeit and pay to the United States a civil penalty of not more than $5,000 for each violation, which shall accrue to the United States and may be recovered in a civil action brought by the United States. Each separate violation of any such order shall be a separate offense, except that in the case of a violation through continuing failure or neglect to obey a final order of the commission, board, or Secretary each day of continuance of such failure or neglect shall be deemed a separate offense.

§12. Any suit, action, or proceeding under the antitrust laws against a corporation may be brought not only in the judicial district whereof it is an inhabitant, but also in any district wherein it may be found or transacts business; and all process in such cases may be served in the district of which it is an inhabitant, or wherever it may be found.

§13. In any suit, action, or proceeding brought by or on behalf of the United States subpoenas for witnesses who are required to attend a court of the United States in any judicial district in any case, civil or criminal, arising under the antitrust laws may run into any other district: *Provided,* That in civil cases no writ of subpoena shall issue for witnesses living out of the district in which the court is held at a greater distance than one hundred miles from the place of holding the same without the permission of the trial court being first had upon proper application and cause shown.

§14. Whenever a corporation shall violate any of the penal provisions of the antitrust laws, such violation shall be deemed to be also that of the individual directors, officers, or agents of such corporation who shall have authorized, ordered, or done any of the acts constituting in whole or in part such violation, and such violation shall be deemed a misdemeanor, and upon conviction therefor of any such director, officer, or agent he shall be punished by a fine of not exceeding $5,000 or by imprisonment for not exceeding one year, or by both, in the discretion of the court.

§15. The several district courts of the United States are invested with jurisdiction to prevent and restrain violations of this Act, and it shall be the duty of the several United States attorneys, in their respective districts, under the direction of the Attorney General, to institute proceedings in equity to prevent and restrain such violations. Such proceedings may be by way of petition setting forth the case and praying that such violation shall be enjoined or otherwise prohibited. When the parties complained of shall have been duly notified of such petition, the court shall proceed, as soon as may be, to the hearing and determination of the case; and pending such petition, and before final decree, the court may at any time make such temporary restraining order or prohibition as shall be deemed just in the premises. Whenever it shall appear to the court before which any such proceeding may be pending that the ends of justice require that other parties should be brought before the court, the court may cause them to be summoned whether they reside in the district in which the court is held or not, and subpoenas to that end may be served in any district by the marshal thereof.

§16. Any person, firm, corporation, or association shall be entitled to sue for and have injunctive relief, in any court of the United States having jurisdiction over the parties, against threatened loss or damage by a violation of the antitrust laws, including sections two, three, seven, and eight of this Act, when and under the same conditions and principles as injunctive relief against threatened

994 Clayton Act §16

conduct that will cause loss or damage is granted by courts of equity, under the rules governing such proceedings, and upon the execution of proper bond against damages for an injunction improvidently granted and a showing that the danger of irreparable loss or damage is immediate, a preliminary injunction may issue: *Provided,* That nothing herein contained shall be construed to entitle any person, firm, corporation, or association, except the United States, to bring suit for injunctive relief against any common carrier subject to the jurisdiction of the Surface Transportation Board under the ICC Termination Act, codified under Subtitle IV of Title 49. In any action under this section in which the plaintiff substantially prevails, the court shall award the cost of suit, including a reasonable attorney's fee, to such plaintiff. . . .

§20.[10] No restraining order or injunction shall be granted by any court of the United States, or a judge or the judges thereof, in any case between an employer and employees, or between employers and employees, or between employees, or between persons employed and persons seeking employment, involving, or growing out of, a dispute concerning terms or conditions of employment, unless necessary to prevent irreparable injury to property, or to a property right, of the party making the application, for which injury there is no adequate remedy at law, and such property or property right must be described with particularity in the application, which must be in writing and sworn to by the applicant or by his agent or attorney.

And no such restraining order or injunction shall prohibit any person or persons, whether singly or in concert, from terminating any relation of employment, or from ceasing to perform any work or labor, or from recommending, advising, or persuading others by peaceful means so to do; or from attending at any place where any such person or persons may lawfully be, for the purpose of peacefully obtaining or communicating information, or from peacefully persuading any person to work or to abstain from working; or from ceasing to patronize or to employ any party to such dispute, or from recommending, advising, or persuading others by peaceful and lawful means so to do; or from paying or giving to, or withholding from, any person engaged in such dispute, any strike benefits or other moneys or things of value; or from peaceably assembling in a lawful manner, and for lawful purposes; or from doing any act or thing which might lawfully be done in the absence of such dispute by any party thereto; nor shall any of the acts specified in this

10. Codified at 29 U.S.C. §52.

paragraph be considered or held to be violations of any law of the United States.[11]

FEDERAL TRADE COMMISSION ACT[1]

§1. A commission is created and established, to be known as the Federal Trade Commission (hereinafter referred to as the Commission), which shall be composed of five Commissioners, who shall be appointed by the President, by and with the advice and consent of the Senate. . . .

§4. The words defined in this section shall have the following meaning when found in this Act, to wit:

"Commerce" means commerce among the several States or with foreign nations, or in any Territory of the United States or in the District of Columbia, or between any such Territory and another, or between any such Territory and any State or foreign nation, or

---

11. The contempt provisions, §§21-25, were repealed, 62 Stat. 683, 864, when the general criminal code, Title 18, was revised and enacted in 1948. Section 26 provides that the invalidity of a portion of the act shall not affect the remainder of it.

1. 38 Stat. 717 (1914) codified as amended, 15 U.S.C. §§41-58. The Wheeler-Lea Act, 52 Stat. 111 (1958) added the second clause to §5(a)(1), elaborated the procedural provisions of §5, and added the false advertising provisions. Additional procedural amendments were made by 87 Stat. 576, 591-592 (1973). That statute also substituted the General Accounting Office for the Office of Management and Budget as the supervisor of independent agency surveys and questionnaires. See 82 Stat. 1302 (1968), as amended, 44 U.S.C. §§3501-3511. This change eliminated the OMB veto, which had prevented the FTC from requiring conglomerate firms to report financial data, such as profits, for each "line of business" within the firm. 87 Stat. 592 improved the enforcement powers of the Commission by adding the proviso to §6(h) and by adding a new §13(b) enabling the Commission to seek preliminary injunctions. Further expansions of enforcement provisions were enacted in the Magnuson-Moss — Federal Trade Commission Improvement Act, 88 Stat. 2183 (1975), which added new §§18-20, expanded FTC investigatory powers in §6, made Commission access to the courts relatively independent of the Justice Department in §16, and provided new civil penalties for knowing violations of FTC rules in §5(m). Additional legislation, 94 Stat. 374 (1980), amended §§5(b), 6, 10, and 18; added new §20 on civil investigative demands, §21 on confidentiality of certain materials, §22 on notice and published "regulatory analysis" of rules issued under §§6 or 18, and §23 on rules related to Federal Reserve Board rulings; and redesignated former §§20-21 as §§24-25. The 1980 legislation also restricted FTC authority with respect to children's advertising, cancellation of any trademark, regulation of the funeral industry, and agricultural cooperatives. It also provided that an FTC rule becomes effective 90 days after being presented to Congress unless the House and Senate disapprove it by concurrent resolution.

between the District of Columbia and any State or Territory or foreign nation.

"Corporation" shall be deemed to include any company, trust, so-called Massachusetts trust, or association, incorporated or unincorporated, which is organized to carry on business for its own profit or that of its members, and has shares of capital or capital stock or certificates of interest, and any company, trust, so-called Massachusetts trust, or association, incorporated or unincorporated, without shares of capital or capital stock or certificates of interest, except partnerships, which is organized to carry on business for its own profit or that of its members.

"Documentary evidence" includes all documents, papers, correspondence, books of account, and financial and corporate records.

"Acts to regulate commerce" means the Act entitled "An Act to regulate commerce," approved February 14, 1887, and all Acts amendatory thereof and supplementary thereto and the Communications Act of 1934 and all Acts amendatory thereof and supplementary thereto.

"Banks" means the types of banks and other financial institutions referred to in the Wheeler-Lea Trade Commission Act (codified as 15 U.S.C. §57a(f)(2)).

"Antitrust Acts" means the Act entitled "An Act to protect trade and commerce against unlawful restraints and monopolies," approved July 2, 1890;[2] also sections 73 to 77, of an Act entitled "An Act to reduce taxation, to provide revenue for the Government, and for other purposes," approved August 27, 1894;[3] also the Act entitled 'An Act to amend sections 73 and 76 of the Act of August 27, 1894, entitled "An Act to reduce taxation, to provide revenue for the Government, and for other purposes,'" approved February 12, 1913; and also the Act entitled "An Act to supplement existing laws against unlawful restraints and monopolies, and for other purposes," approved October 15, 1914.[4]

§5.   (a)(1) Unfair methods of competition in or affecting commerce, and unfair or deceptive acts or practices in or affecting commerce, are declared unlawful.

(2) The Commission is empowered and directed to prevent persons, partnerships, or corporations, except banks, savings and loan institutions described in §18(f)(3), Federal credit unions described in §18(f)(4), common carriers subject to the Acts to regulate commerce, air carriers and foreign air carriers subject to

2. The Sherman Act.
3. The Wilson Tariff Act.
4. The Clayton Act.

the Federal Aviation Act of 1958, and persons, partnerships, or corporations insofar as they are subject to the Packers and Stockyards Act, 1921, as amended, except as provided in section 406(b) of said Act, from using unfair methods of competition in or affecting commerce and unfair or deceptive acts or practices in or affecting commerce.[5]

(3) This subsection shall not apply to unfair methods of competition involving commerce with foreign nations (other than import commerce) unless —

(A) such methods of competition have a direct, substantial, and reasonably foreseeable effect —

(i) on commerce which is not commerce with foreign nations, or on import commerce with foreign nations; or

(ii) on export commerce with foreign nations, of a person engaged in such commerce in the United States; and

(B) such effect gives rise to a claim under the provisions of this subsection, other than this paragraph.

If this subsection applies to such methods of competition only because of the operation of subparagraph (A)(ii), this subsection

---

5. The phrase "in or affecting commerce" was substituted for "in commerce" in §§5, 6, and 12 by 88 Stat. 2193 (1975). Additional amendments, 89 Stat. 801 (1975), deleted the following provisions regarding fair trade pricing:

(2) Nothing contained in this section or in any of the Antitrust Acts shall render unlawful any contracts or agreements prescribing minimum or stipulated prices or requiring a vendee to enter into contracts or agreements prescribing minimum or stipulated prices for the resale of a commodity which bears, or the label or container of which bears, the trade-mark, brand, or name of the producer or distributor of such commodity and which is in free and open competition with commodities of the same general class produced or distributed by others, when contracts or agreements of that description are lawful as applied to intrastate transactions under any statute, law, or public policy now or hereafter in effect in any State, Territory, or the District of Columbia in which such resale is to be made, or to which the commodity is to be transported for such resale.

(3) Nothing contained in this section or in any of the Antitrust Acts shall render unlawful the exercise or the enforcement of any right or right of action created by any statute, law, or public policy now or hereafter in effect in any State, Territory, or the District of Columbia, which in substance provides that willfully and knowingly advertising, offering for sale, or selling any commodity at less than the price or prices prescribed in such contracts or agreements whether the person so advertising, offering for sale, or selling is or is not a party to such a contract or agreement, is unfair competition and is actionable at the suit of any person damaged thereby.

(4) Neither the making of contracts or agreements as described in paragraph (2) of this subsection, nor the exercise or enforcement of any right or right of action as described in paragraph (3) of this subsection shall constitute an unlawful burden or restraint upon, or interference with, commerce.

(5) Nothing contained in paragraph (2) of this subsection shall make lawful contracts or agreements providing for the establishment or maintenance of minimum or stipulated resale prices on any commodity referred to in paragraph (2) of this subsection, between manufacturers, or between producers, or between wholesalers, or between brokers, or between factors, or between retailers, or between persons, firms, or corporations in competition with each other.

shall apply to such conduct only for injury to export business in the United States.

(b) Whenever the Commission shall have reason to believe that any such person, partnership, or corporation has been or is using any unfair method of competition or unfair or deceptive act or practice in or affecting commerce, and if it shall appear to the Commission that a proceeding by it in respect thereof would be to the interest of the public, it shall issue and serve upon such person, partnership, or corporation a complaint stating its charges in that respect and containing a notice of a hearing upon a day and at a place therein fixed at least thirty days after the service of said complaint. The person, partnership, or corporation so complained of shall have the right to appear at the place and time so fixed and show cause why an order should not be entered by the Commission requiring such person, partnership, or corporation to cease and desist from the violation of the law so charged in said complaint. Any person, partnership, or corporation may make application, and upon good cause shown may be allowed by the Commission to intervene and appear in said proceeding by counsel or in person. . . .

(c) Any person, partnership, or corporation required by an order of the Commission to cease and desist from using any method of competition or act or practice may obtain a review of such order in the court of appeals of the United States, within any circuit where the method of competition or the act or practice in question was used or where such person, partnership, or corporation resides or carries on business, by filing in the court, within sixty days from the date of the service of such order, a written petition praying that the order of the Commission be set aside. . . .

(g) An order of the Commission to cease and desist shall become final —

(1) Upon the expiration of the time allowed for filing a petition for review, if no such petition has been duly filed within such time; but the Commission may thereafter modify or set aside its order to the extent provided in the last sentence of subsection (b) of this section.

(2) Except as to any order provision subject to paragraph (4), upon the sixtieth day after such order is served, if a petition for review has been duly filed; except that any such order may be stayed, in whole or in part and subject to such conditions as may be appropriate, by —

(A) the Commission;

(B) an appropriate court of appeals of the United States, if (i) a petition for review of such order is pending in such court, and (ii) an application for such a stay was previously submitted to the Commission and the Commission, within the 30-day period beginning on the date the application was received by the Commission, either denied the application or did not grant or deny the application; or

(C) the Supreme Court, if an applicable petition for certiorari is pending.

(3) For purposes of subsection (m)(1)(B) of this section and of section 57b(a)(2) of this title, if a petition for review of the order of the Commission has been filed —

(A) upon the expiration of the time allowed for filing a petition for certiorari, if the order of the Commission has been affirmed or the petition for review has been dismissed by the court of appeals and no petition for certiorari has been duly filed;

(B) upon the denial of a petition for certiorari, if the order of the Commission has been affirmed or the petition for review has been dismissed by the court of appeals; or

(C) upon the expiration of 30 days from the date of issuance of a mandate of the Supreme Court directing that the order of the Commission be affirmed or the petition for review be dismissed.

(4) In the case of an order provision requiring a person, partnership, or corporation to divest itself of stock, other share capital, or assets, if a petition for review of such order of the Commission has been filed —

(A) upon the expiration of the time allowed for filing a petition for certiorari if the order of the Commission has been affirmed or the petition for review has been dismissed by the court of appeals and no petition for certiorari has been duly filed;

(B) upon the denial of a petition for certiorari, if the order of the Commission has been affirmed or the petition for review has been dismissed by the court of appeals; or

(C) upon the expiration of 30 days from the date of issuance of a mandate of the Supreme Court directing that the order of the Commission be affirmed or the petition for review be dismissed. . . .

(*l*) Any person, partnership, or corporation who violates an order of the Commission after it has become final, and while such order is in effect, shall forfeit and pay to the United States a civil penalty of not more than $10,000 for each violation, which shall accrue to the United States and may be recovered in a civil action brought by the Attorney General of the United States. Each separate violation of such an order shall be a separate offense, except that in the case of a violation through continuing failure to obey or neglect to obey a final order of the Commission, each day of continuance of such failure or neglect shall be deemed a separate offense. In such actions, the United States district courts are empowered to grant mandatory injunctions and such other and further equitable relief as they deem appropriate in the enforcement of such final orders of the Commission.

(m)(1)(A) The Commission may commence a civil action to recover a civil penalty in a district court of the United States against any person, partnership, or corporation which violates any rule under this chapter respecting unfair or deceptive acts or practices (other than an interpretive rule or a rule violation of which the Commission has provided is not an unfair or deceptive act or practice in violation of subsection (a)(1) of this section) with actual knowledge or knowledge fairly implied on the basis of objective circumstances that such act is unfair or deceptive and is prohibited by such rule. In such action, such person, partnership, or corporation shall be liable for a civil penalty of not more than $10,000 for each violation.

(B) If the Commission determines in a proceeding under subsection (b) of this section that any act or practice is unfair or deceptive, and issues a final cease and desist order other than a consent order with respect to such act or practice, then the Commission may commence a civil action to obtain a civil penalty in a district court of the United States against any person, partnership, or corporation which engages in such act or practice —

(1) after such cease and desist order becomes final (whether or not such person, partnership, or corporation was subject to such cease and desist order), and

(2) with actual knowledge that such act or practice is unfair or deceptive and is unlawful under subsection (a)(1) of this section.

In such action, such person, partnership, or corporation shall be liable for a civil penalty of not more than $10,000 for each violation.

(C) In the case of a violation through continuing failure to comply with a rule or with subsection (a)(1) of this section, each day of continuance of such failure shall be treated as a separate violation, for purposes of subparagraphs (A) and (B). In determining the amount of such a civil penalty, the court shall take into account the degree of culpability, and history of prior such conduct, ability to pay, effect on ability to continue to do business, and such other matters as justice may require.

(2) If the cease and desist order establishing that the act or practice is unfair or deceptive was not issued against the defend-

ant in a civil penalty action under paragraph (1)(B) the issues of fact in such action against such defendant shall be tried de novo. Upon request of any party to such an action against such defendant, the court shall also review the determination of law made by the Commission in the proceeding under subsection (b) of this section that the act or practice which was the subject of such proceeding constituted an unfair or deceptive act or practice in violation of subsection (a) of this section.

(3) The Commission may compromise or settle any action for a civil penalty if such compromise or settlement is accompanied by a public statement of its reasons and is approved by the court.[6]

(n) The Commission shall have no authority under this section or section 57a of this title to declare unlawful an act or practice on the grounds that such act or practice is unfair unless the act or practice causes or is likely to cause substantial injury to consumers which is not reasonably avoidable by consumers themselves and not outweighed by countervailing benefits to consumers or to competition. In determining whether an act or practice is unfair, the Commission may consider established public policies as evidence to be considered with all other evidence. Such public policy considerations may not serve as a primary basis for such determination.

§6. The Commission shall also have power —

(a) To gather and compile information concerning, and to investigate from time to time the organization, business, conduct, practices, and management of any person, partnership, or corporation engaged in or whose business affects commerce, excepting banks, savings and loan institutions described in §18(f)(3), Federal credit unions described in §18(f)(4), and common carriers subject to the Act to regulate commerce, and its relation to other persons, partnerships, and corporations.[7]

(b) To require, by general or special orders, persons, partnerships, and corporations, engaged in or whose business affects commerce, excepting banks, savings and loan institutions described in §18(f)(3), Federal credit unions described in §18(f)(4), and common carriers subject to the Act to regulate commerce, or any class of them, or any of them, respectively, to file with the Commission in such form as the Commission may prescribe annual or special, or both annual and special, reports or answers in writing to specific

6. Former subparagraph (m), 87 Stat. 576, 592 (1973), is now covered by §16 as amended by 88 Stat. 2198-2199.

7. 88 Stat. 2183, 2198-2199 (1975) extended the investigatory power of the FTC to include any "person, partnership or corporation," rather than simply any "corporation." Conforming changes were made in §§9 and 10.

questions, furnishing to the Commission such information as it may require as to the organization, business, conduct, practices, management, and relation to other corporations, partnerships, and individuals of the respective persons, partnerships, and corporations filing such reports or answers in writing. Such reports and answers shall be made under oath, or otherwise, as the Commission may prescribe, and shall be filed with the Commission within such reasonable period as the Commission may prescribe, unless additional time be granted in any case by the Commission.

(c) Whenever a final decree has been entered against any defendant corporation in any suit brought by the United States to prevent and restrain any violation of the antitrust Acts, to make investigation, upon its own initiative, of the manner in which the decree has been or is being carried out, and upon the application of the Attorney General it shall be its duty to make such investigation. It shall transmit to the Attorney General a report embodying its findings and recommendations as a result of any such investigation, and the report shall be made public in the discretion of the Commission.

(d) Upon the direction of the President or either House of Congress to investigate and report the facts relating to any alleged violations of the antitrust Acts, by any corporation.[8]

(e) Upon the application of the Attorney General to investigate and make recommendations for the readjustment of the business of any corporation alleged to be violating the antitrust Acts in order that the corporation may thereafter maintain its organization, management, and conduct of business in accordance with law.

(f) To make public from time to time such portions of the information obtained by it hereunder as are in the public interest; and to make annual and special reports to the Congress and to submit therewith recommendations for additional legislation; and to provide for the publication of its reports and decisions in such form and manner as may be best adapted for public information and use: *Provided,* That the Commission shall not have any authority to make public any trade secret or any commercial or financial information which is obtained from any person and which is privileged or confidential, except that the Commission may disclose such information to officers and employees of appropriate Federal law enforcement agencies or to any officer or employee of any State law enforcement agency upon the prior certification of an officer of any such Federal or State law enforcement agency that such infor-

---

8. 48 Stat. 283, 291 (1933), 15 U.S.C. §46a: "... no new investigations shall be initiated by the Commission as the result of a legislative resolution, except the same be a concurrent resolution of the two Houses of Congress."

mation will be maintained in confidence and will be used only for official law enforcement purposes.

(g) From time to time to classify corporations and (except as provided in section 18(a)(2) of this Act) to make rules and regulations for the purpose of carrying out the provisions of this Act.

(h) To investigate, from time to time, trade conditions in and with foreign countries where associations, combinations, or practices of manufacturers, merchants, or traders, or other conditions, may affect the foreign trade of the United States, and to report to Congress thereon, with such recommendations as it deems advisable.

(i) With respect to the International Antitrust Enforcement Assistance Act of 1994 [15 U.S.C. §6201 et seq.], to conduct investigations of possible violations of foreign antitrust laws (as defined in Section 12 of such Act [15 U.S.C. §6211]).

Provided, That the exception of "banks, savings and loan institutions described in §18(f)(3), Federal credit unions described in §18(f)(4), and common carriers subject to the Act to regulate commerce" from the Commission's powers defined in clauses (a) and (b) of this section, shall not be construed to limit the Commission's authority to gather and compile information, to investigate, or to require reports or answers from, any person, partnership, or corporation to the extent that such action is necessary to the investigation of any person, partnership, or corporation, group of persons, partnerships, or corporations, or industry which is not engaged or is engaged only incidentally in banking, in business as a savings and loan institution, in business as a Federal credit union, or in business as a common carrier subject to the Act to regulate commerce.

The Commission shall establish a plan designed to substantially reduce burdens imposed upon small businesses as a result of requirements established by the Commission under clause (b) relating to the filing of quarterly financial reports. . . .

No officer or employee of the Commission or any Commissioner may publish or disclose information to the public, or to any Federal agency, whereby any line-of-business data furnished by a particular establishment or individual can be identified. . . .

Nothing in this section (other than the provisions of clause (c) and clause (d)) shall apply to the business of insurance, except that the Commission shall have authority to conduct studies and prepare reports relating to the business of insurance. . . .

§7.   In any suit in equity brought by or under the direction of the Attorney General as provided in the antitrust Acts, the court may, upon the conclusion of the testimony therein, if it shall be then of opinion that the complainant is entitled to relief, refer said suit to the Commission, as a master in chancery, to ascertain and report an appropriate form of decree therein. The Commission shall proceed upon such notice to the parties and under such rules of procedure as the court may prescribe, and upon the coming in of such report such exceptions may be filed and such proceedings had in relation thereto as upon the report of a master in other equity causes, but the court may adopt or reject such report, in whole or in part, and enter such decree as the nature of the case may in its judgment require. . . .

§11. Nothing contained in this Act shall be construed to prevent or interfere with the enforcement of the provisions of the antitrust Acts or the Acts to regulate commerce, nor shall anything contained in said sections be construed to alter, modify, or repeal the said antitrust Acts or the Acts to regulate commerce or any part or parts thereof.

§13. . . .
(b) Whenever the Commission has reason to believe —
(1) that any person, partnership, or corporation is violating, or is about to violate, any provision of law enforced by the Federal Trade Commission, and
(2) that the enjoining thereof pending the issuance of a complaint by the Commission and until such complaint is dismissed by the Commission or set aside by the court on review, or until the order of the Commission made thereon has become final, would be in the interest of the public —
the Commission by any of its attorneys designated by it for such purpose may bring suit in a district court of the United States to enjoin any such act or practice. Upon a proper showing that, weighing the equities and considering the Commission's likelihood of ultimate success, such action would be in the public interest, and after notice to the defendant, a temporary restraining order or a preliminary injunction may be granted without bond: *Provided, however,* That if a complaint is not filed within such period (not exceeding 20 days) as may be specified by the court after issuance of the temporary restraining order or preliminary injunction, the order or injunction shall be dissolved by the court and be of no further force and effect: *Provided further,* That in proper cases the Commission may seek, and after proper proof, the court may issue, a permanent injunction. Any suit may be brought where such person, partnership, or corporation resides or transacts business, or wherever venue is proper under section 1391 of Title 28. In addition, the court may, if the court determines that the interests of justice require that any other person, partnership, or corporation should be

a party in such suit, cause such other person, partnership, or corporation to be added as a party without regard to whether venue is otherwise proper in the district in which the suit is brought. In any suit under this section, process may be served on any person, partnership, or corporation wherever it may be found. . . .

§16.   (a)(1) Except as otherwise provided in paragraph (2) or (3), if—

(A) before commencing, defending, or intervening in, any civil action involving this chapter (including an action to collect a civil penalty) which the Commission, or the Attorney General on behalf of the Commission, is authorized to commence, defend, or intervene in, the Commission gives written notification and undertakes to consult with the Attorney General with respect to such action; and

(B) the Attorney General fails within 45 days after receipt of such notification to commence, defend, or intervene in, such action;

the Commission may commence, defend, or intervene in, and supervise the litigation of, such action and any appeal of such action in its own name by any of its attorneys designated by it for such purpose.

(2) Except as otherwise provided in paragraph (3), in any civil action—

(A) under section 13 of this Act (relating to injunctive relief);

(B) under section 17b of this Act (relating to consumer redress);

(C) to obtain judicial review of a rule prescribed by the Commission, or a cease and desist order issued under section 5 of this Act; or

(D) under the second paragraph of section 9 of this Act (relating to enforcement of a subpoena) and under the fourth paragraph of such section (relating to compliance with section 6 of this Act);

the Commission shall have exclusive authority to commence or defend, and supervise the litigation of such action and any appeal of such action in its own name by any of its attorneys designated by it for such purpose, unless the Commission authorizes the Attorney General to do so. The Commission shall inform the Attorney General of the exercise of such authority and such exercise shall not preclude the Attorney General from intervening on behalf of the United States in such action and any appeal of such action as may be otherwise provided by law.

(3)(A) If the Commission makes a written request to the Attorney General, within the 10-day period which begins on the date of the entry of the judgment in any civil action in which the Commission represented itself pursuant to paragraph (1) or (2), to represent itself through any of its attorneys designated by it for such purpose before the Supreme Court in such action, it may do so, if—

(i) the Attorney General concurs with such request; or

(ii) the Attorney General, within the 60-day period which begins on the date of the entry of such judgment—

(a) refuses to appeal or file a petition for writ of certiorari with respect to such civil action, in which case he shall give written notification to the Commission of the reasons for such refusal within such 60-day period; or

(b) the Attorney General fails to take any action with respect to the Commission's request.

(B) In any case where the Attorney General represents the Commission before the Supreme Court in any civil action in which the Commission represented itself pursuant to paragraph (1) or (2), the Attorney General may not agree to any settlement, compromise, or dismissal of such action, or confess error in the Supreme Court with respect to such action, unless the Commission concurs.

(C) For purposes of this paragraph (with respect to representation before the Supreme Court), the term "Attorney General" includes the Solicitor General.

(4) If, prior to the expiration of the 45-day period specified in paragraph (1) of this section or a 60-day period specified in paragraph (3), any right of the Commission to commence, defend, or intervene in, any such action or appeal may be extinguished due to any procedural requirement of any court with respect to the time in which any pleadings, notice of appeal, or other acts pertaining to such action or appeal may be taken, the Attorney General shall have one-half of the time required to comply with any such procedural requirement of the court (including any extension of such time granted by the court) for the purpose of commencing, defending, or intervening in the civil action pursuant to paragraph (1) or for the purpose of refusing to appeal or file a petition for writ of certiorari and the written notification or failing to take any action pursuant to paragraph 3(A)(ii).

(5) The provisions of this subsection shall apply notwithstanding chapter 31 of Title 28, or any other provision of law.

(b) Whenever the Commission has reason to believe that any person, partnership, or corporation is liable for a criminal penalty under this chapter, the Commission shall certify the facts to the Attorney General, whose duty it shall be to cause appropriate criminal proceedings to be brought....

§18. (a)(1) Except as provided in subsection (h), the Commission may prescribe —

(A) interpretive rules and general statements of policy with respect to unfair or deceptive acts or practices in or affecting commerce (within the meaning of section 5(a)(1) of this Act), and

(B) rules which define with specificity acts or practices which are unfair or deceptive acts or practices in or affecting commerce (within the meaning of section 5(a)(1) of this Act) except that the Commission shall not develop or promulgate any trade rule or regulation with regard to the regulation of the development and utilization of the standards and certification activities pursuant to this section. Rules under this subparagraph may include requirements prescribed for the purpose of preventing such acts or practices.

(2) The Commission shall have no authority under this Act, other than its authority under this section, to prescribe any rule with respect to unfair or deceptive acts or practices in or affecting commerce (within the meaning of section 5(a)(1) of this Act.) The preceding sentence shall not affect any authority of the Commission to prescribe rules (including interpretive rules), and general statements of policy, with respect to unfair methods of competition in or affecting commerce. . . .

(h) The Commission shall not have any authority to promulgate any rule in the children's advertising proceeding pending on May 28, 1980 or in any substantially similar proceeding on the basis of a determination by the Commission that such advertising constitutes an unfair act or practice in or affecting commerce.

(i) . . . (2) . . . the Commission shall promulgate a final rule, which shall authorize the Commission or any Commissioner to meet with any outside party concerning any rulemaking proceeding of the Commission. Such rule shall provide that —

(A) notice of any such meeting shall be included in any weekly calendar prepared by the Commission; and

(B) a verbatim record or a summary of any such meeting, or of any communication relating to any such meeting, shall be kept, made available to the public, and included in the rulemaking record.

(j) . . . the Commission shall promulgate a final rule, which shall prohibit any officer, employee, or agent of the Commission with any investigative responsibility or other responsibility relating to any rulemaking proceeding within any operating bureau of the Commission, from communicating or causing to be communicated to any Commissioner or to the personal staff of any Commissioner any fact which is relevant to the merits of such proceeding and which is not on the rulemaking record of such proceeding, unless such communication is made available to the public and is included in the rulemaking record. The provisions of this subsection shall not apply to any communication to the extent such communication is required for the disposition of ex parte matters as authorized by law.

§19. (a)(1) If any person, partnership, or corporation violates any rule under this Act respecting unfair or deceptive acts or practices (other than an interpretive rule, or a rule violation of which the Commission has provided is not an unfair or deceptive act or practice in violation of section 5(a)), then the Commission may commence a civil action against such person, partnership, or corporation for relief under subsection (b) in a United States district court or in any court of competent jurisdiction of a State.

(2) If any person, partnership, or corporation engages in any unfair or deceptive act or practice (within the meaning of section 5(a)(1)) with respect to which the Commission has issued a final cease and desist order which is applicable to such person, partnership, or corporation, then the Commission may commence a civil action against such person, partnership, or corporation in a United States district court or in any court of competent jurisdiction of a State. If the Commission satisfies the court that the act or practice to which the cease and desist order relates is one which a reasonable man would have known under the circumstances was dishonest or fraudulent, the court may grant relief under subsection (b).

(b) The court in an action under subsection (a) shall have jurisdiction to grant such relief as the court finds necessary to redress injury to consumers or other persons, partnerships, and corporations resulting from the rule violation or the unfair or deceptive act or practice, as the case may be. Such relief may include, but shall not be limited to, rescission or reformation of contracts, the refund of money or return of property, the payment of damages, and public notification respecting the rule violation or the unfair or deceptive act or practice, as the case may be; except that nothing in this subsection is intended to authorize the imposition of any exemplary or punitive damages.

(c)(1) If (A) a cease and desist order issued under section 5(b) has become final under section 5(g) of this Act with respect to any person's, partnership's, or corporation's rule violation or unfair or deceptive act or practice, and (B) an action under this section is brought with respect to such person's, partnership's, or corporation's rule violation or act or practice, then the findings of the Commission as to the material facts in the proceeding under section 5(b) with respect to such person's, partnership's, or corporation's rule violation or act or practice, shall be conclusive unless (i) the terms of such cease and desist order expressly provide that the Commission's findings shall not be conclusive, or (ii) the order became final by reason of section 5(g)(1), in which case such finding shall be conclusive if supported by evidence. . . .

(d) No action may be brought by the Commission under this section more than 3 years after the rule violation to which an action under subsection (a)(1) relates, or the unfair or deceptive act or practice to which an action under subsection (a)(2) relates; except that if a cease and desist order with respect to any person's, partnership's, or corporation's rule violation or unfair or deceptive act or practice has become final and such order was issued in a proceeding under section 5(b) which was commenced not later than 3 years after the rule violation or act or practice occurred, a civil action may be commenced under this section against such person, partnership, or corporation at any time before the expiration of one year after such order becomes final.

(e) Remedies provided in this section are in addition to, and not in lieu of, any other remedy or right of action provided by State or Federal law. Nothing in this section shall be construed to affect any authority of the Commission under any other provision of law.

Table of Cases

Index

**DISCRIMINATION IN PRICE OR SER-
VICES.** *See* Monopolization; Pat-
ents; Robinson-Patman Act;
Tying; Vertical integration
DISSOLUTION. *See* Enforcement
DISTRIBUTION RESTRAINTS (limiting
competition among dealers in a
single manufacturer's product).
See also Conspiracy; Oligopoly
Agency, 414-415
Ancillary justification, 128c, 404b
Attempted monopolization, 355, 409,
Packard
Bibliography, 402, 405, 408
Competition among manufacturers, 403o
Consignment. *See* agency
Customer limitation, 410
  authorities, 410a
  controlling reseller, 410a
  limiting competition among dealers,
    410b
  limiting competition with manufac-
    turer, 410c
  territorial limitations compared, 410
Dealer termination, 416-421, *Colgate,
  Monsanto*
Defined, 400-401
Dual distribution, 412
Effects, 402-403, 408, 410
Exclusive outlet. *See* sole outlet
Fair trade laws, 405
Horizontal combination among re-
  strained dealers compared,
    404d, 421, *Dr. Miles*
Justifications, 403, 408b, 410-411
McGuire Act, 405
Manufacturer interest in competition
  among subsequent distributors
  in limiting competition, 403, 404c,
    408b, 410-411
  in maximizing competition, 402, 412
Miller-Tydings Act, 405
Refusal to deal and vertical agreement,
    416-421, *Colgate, Monsanto, Busi-
    ness Electronics*
Resale price maintenance, 402-405, *Dr.
  Miles*
  ancillary justification, 128c, 404b
  customer limitations, 410
  effects, 403, 404e, 413a
  fair trade laws, 405
  horizontal price fixing by dealers com-
    pared, 404d, *Dr. Miles*
  justifications, 403, 404c
  manufacturer interests, 402-403, 404c,
    408, 411-412
  maximum prices, 406, 413c

refusal to deal, 416-421, *Colgate, Monsanto, Business Electronics*
suggested resale price, 416-421,
  *Business Electronics, Colgate, Mon-
  santo*
Sylvania implications, 413
territorial limitation compared, 413a
Restraint on alienation, 404a, *Dr. Miles,
  Sylvania*
Sole outlet, 355, 409, *Packard*
Standing, 407
Territorial limitation, 408, 410-413,
  Sylvania
  customer limitation compared, 410
  horizontal market division compared,
    413d
  justifications, 408, 411, *Sylvania*
  less restrictive alternatives, 403b
  proofs, 412
  resale price maintenance compared,
    413, *Sylvania*
  sole outlet compared, 408
DIVESTITURE. *See* Enforcement
DIVIDING MARKETS. *See* Distribution restraints; Territorial division by
  competitors

ECONOMICS, BASIC, Ch. 1A
EFFICIENCY. *See* Concentration
ENFORCEMENT. *See also* Foreign com-
  merce; Robinson-Patman Act
Advisory opinions, 156
Appeals, 155
Bibliography. *See* particular topics
Big case, 154
Cease and desist order, 142
Class actions, 147
Clearances, 156
Collateral estoppel, 158b
Consent decree, 141
Criminal provisions
  appropriateness, 137
  burden of proof, 138
  effect on statutory development, 138
  fairness, 137
  frequency of use, 136
  good faith, relevance of, 137-138
  government practice, 136
  offenses, 135
  penalties, 135
  statutes relevant, 135, 138
Damages. *See* private actions
Defense to nonantitrust suit, 149, 186
Discovery, 151
Dissolution, divestiture, 139-140, 142c,
    314-316. *See also* equitable relief

1028   *Index*

References are to paragraph numbers and to names listed in the Table of Cases

EXEMPTIONS (*cont.*)
Political action, Ch. 2F
Primary jurisdiction, 160, 162e, 174
Rationale, 110, 118, 162a
Regulated industries, generally, 162
State law, relation to federal antitrust
law. *See also* Interstate com-
merce
coexistence, 163-165
conferring exemption, 165
precedence for state law, 163
preempted by federal law, 164
Stock exchanges, 162g
Transportation, 162c, e
EXPORT ASSOCIATIONS, 174

FACILITATING PRACTICES. *See* Basing
point pricing; Collaboration
among competitors; Data dissemination
FAIR TRADE. *See* Distribution restraints
**FEDERAL TRADE COMMISSION, GEN-
ERALLY**
Advisory opinions, 156
Composition, 142b
Consent procedures, 142b
Enforcement guides
advertising allowances, 626
basing point pricing, 250d
mergers, 344, 527
Federal Trade Commission Act, generally
historical background, 132
relation to other antitrust laws. *See* ju-
risdiction
text, *Appendix*
Harmonization with Antitrust Division,
142f
Harmonization with original judicial ju-
risdiction, 524, 526
Judicial review, 142d, 446-448
Jurisdiction, 142a, 174, 446-448, *Cement
Inst., FOGA*
Remedial powers, 142c, 253, 429
Rule-making, 142e
FISHERY ASSOCIATIONS, 160
FOREIGN COMMERCE
Act of state, 176a
Agent of foreign government, 176
Basic issues, 168
Bibliography, 168
Comity, 171-176
Conflicting national interests, 172
Domestic effects
appraising significance, 175
as test of statutory coverage, 171
generally, 170-175

Exports
export associations, 174
restraints affecting, 174
Webb-Pomerene Act, 168, 174
Foreign conduct, 170-175
Foreign governmental action causes the
restraint, 171-176
coercion or compulsion, 176
sovereign immunity, 176b
In rem jurisdiction, 170
Jurisdiction. *See* in rem jurisdiction, per-
sonal jurisdiction, statutory
reach
Per se offenses, 175
Personal jurisdiction, 169
Remedial problems, 173
Significance of restraints, 175
Sovereign immunity, 176b
Statutory reach
American Banana test, 171
contemporary test, 171, 175
Substantiality of effects, 175
Summary, 177
Wilson Tariff Act, 135, 170
FRANCHISE AGREEMENT. *See* Distribu-
tion restraints; Exclusive deal-
ing; Tying

**GOVERNMENT, DEALING WITH, AS
SHERMAN ACT VIOLATION**
As an immunity for otherwise illegal con-
duct, 275
Litigation, 271, 310-311, 322, *Calif. Mo-
tor, Professional Real Estate*
Lobbying, 270, 275-276, *Noerr, OMNI,
SCTLA*
influencing standard-setting organiza-
tions, *Indian Head*

HISTORICAL INTRODUCTION. *See* Sherman Act, generally

**INFLUENCING GOVERNMENT AC-
TION.** *See* Government, dealing
with, as Sherman Act violation
INJUNCTION. *See* Enforcement
IN PARI DELICTO, 148
**INTERLOCKING DIRECTORS AND OF-
FICERS,** 530
INTERSTATE COMMERCE, 166-167
INTRABRAND COMPETITION. *See* Distri-
bution restraints
INTRAENTERPRISE CONSPIRACY. *See*
Conspiracy

PREDATORY PRICING, 328-330, 403c, 533, 605-606, *Barry Wright, Brooke Group*

PRICE DISCRIMINATION. *See* Monopolization; Patents; Robinson-Patman Act; Tying; Vertical Integration

PRICE FIXING. *See also* Basing point pricing; Collaboration among competitors; Conspiracy; Data dissemination; Distribution restraints; Foreign commerce; Oligopoly; Patents; Per se rule

Alleged justification, 201
countervailing power, 117c, 201h
financing desirable activities, 201g
living with excess capacity, 201d, *Socony*
preserving needed capacity, 201e
preventing cutthroat competition, 201d
protecting quality from debasement, *Engineers*
reasonableness of price set, 202, *Socony, Trenton*
reducing uncertainty, 201f
Bibliography, 201
Breakdowns, 201, 230
Compensation to losers of competitive bidding, 243c
Early cases, 202-205, *Addyston*
Effects, relevance of, 209, *Socony*
Maximum prices, 210, 218, 406, *Maricopa*
Per se idea. *See* Per se rule
Power, relevance of, 209, *Socony*
Reasonableness of price, relevance of, 202, *Socony, Trenton*
Relation to common law restraint of trade. *See* early cases
Various forms, 214
Vertical. *See* Distribution restraints

PRICE LEADERSHIP. *See* Oligopoly
PRICE REPORTING. *See* Data dissemination

PRIMARY JURISDICTION, 160, 162
PRIVATE ACTION. *See* Enforcement; Robinson-Patman Act

PUBLIC POLICIES, GENERALLY, 104-105, 114, 117, 129-130, 132, 180-181, 212, 305, 321, 501-502, 505, 507, 525, 531, 536, 543b, *Engineers*

REASONABLE RESTRAINTS. *See* Restraint of trade
RECIPROCITY, 540-541, 543a, *Consolidated Foods*

REFUSAL TO DEAL. *See* Attempt to monopolize; Concerted refusal to deal; Conspiracy; Distribution restraints; Exclusive dealing; Price discrimination; Tying

REGULATED INDUSTRIES, 162. *See also* Exemptions

REMEDIES. *See* Enforcement; Foreign commerce

REQUIREMENTS CONTRACTS. *See* Exclusive dealing

RESALE PRICE MAINTENANCE. *See* Distribution restraints

RES JUDICATA, 158

RESTRAINT OF TRADE. *See* Basing point pricing; Collaboration among competitors; Common law; Concerted refusal to deal; Conspiracy; Data dissemination; Distribution restraints; Exclusive dealing; Foreign commerce; Merger; Oligopoly; Patents; Per se rule; Price fixing; Reciprocity; Territorial division by competitors; Tying

RESTRICTED DISTRIBUTION. *See* Distribution restraints

ROBINSON-PATMAN ACT
Bibliography, 600
Brokerage
buyer liability, 625e
defenses, 625b
elements, 625b
"for services rendered," 625c
identifying violative terms, 625d
legislative intent, 625a
Buyer liability
brokerage, 625e
burden of proof, 623
commerce requirement, 622
discriminatory allowances or services, 626f
legislative background, 622-623
meeting-competition defense, 624, *A&P*
Cost justification defense
burden of proof, 614a
classification of customers, 615, *Borden*
difficulties in proving cost differences, 614b
relevant costs savings, 614c
scope of the defense, 614a
significance of the defense, 614-615
Discounts. *See* price discrimination
Discriminatory allowances or services
buyer liability, 626f
competing customer requirement, 626d

Index

References are to paragraph numbers and to names listed in the Table of Cases